EUROPEAN WRITERS

EUROPEAN WRITERS

GEORGE STADE

EDITOR IN CHIEF

Volume 14

INDEX

Charles Scribner's Sons
NEW YORK

Collier Macmillan Canada
TORONTO

Maxwell Macmillan International
NEW YORK   OXFORD   SINGAPORE   SYDNEY

Library of Congress Cataloging-in-Publication Data
(Revised for vol. 14)

European writers.

Vols. 5– . Jacques Barzun, editor, George Stade,
editor in chief.
   Includes bibliographies.
   Contents: v. 1–2. The Middle Ages and the
Renaissance: Prudentius to medieval drama.
Petrarch to Renaissance short fiction—[etc.]
—v. 5–7. The Romantic century: Goethe to Pushkin.
Hugo to Fontane. Baudelaire to the well made play.
—   —v. 14. Index.
   1. European literature—History and criticism—
Addresses, essays, lectures. I. Jackson, W. T. H.
(William Thomas Hobdell), 1915–1983.
II. Stade, George.   III. Barzun, Jacques
PN501.E9   1983   809'.894   83–16333

ISBN 0–684–16594–5 (v. 1–2)   ISBN 0–684–17916–4 (v. 10)
ISBN 0–684–17914–8 (v. 3–4)   ISBN 0–684–18798–1 (v. 11)
ISBN 0–684–17915–6 (v. 5–7)   ISBN 0–684–19158–X (v. 12)
ISBN 0–684–18923–2 (v. 8)   ISBN 0–684–19159–8 (v. 13)
ISBN 0–684–18924–0 (v. 9)   ISBN 0–684–19221–7 (v. 14)

Charles Scribner's Sons   Collier Macmillan Canada, Inc.
Macmillan Publishing Company   1200 Eglinton Avenue East
866 Third Avenue   Suite 200
New York, New York 10022   Don Mills, Ontario M3C 3N1

1 3 5 7 9 11 13 15 17 19   B/C   20 18 16 14 12 10 8 6 4 2

PRINTED IN THE UNITED STATES OF AMERICA

The paper in this book meets the guidelines for permanence and durability of
the Committee on Production Guidelines for Book Longevity of the
Council on Library Resources.

EDITORIAL STAFF
(1981–1990)

CONTENTS

ALPHABETICAL LIST OF SUBJECTS 1

CHRONOLOGICAL LIST OF SUBJECTS 11

SUBJECTS BY LANGUAGE 21

GENERAL BIBLIOGRAPHY 25

INDEX 33

LIST OF CONTRIBUTORS 693

ACKNOWLEDGMENTS 701

EUROPEAN WRITERS

ALPHABETICAL LIST OF SUBJECTS

European Writers comprises 261 essays on continental authors and their works, arranged chronologically from Prudentius to Milan Kundera. Of these, 252 directly concern individual authors or anonymous works. In a few cases related writers are addressed in the same essay: for example, the Goncourts, the Poetic Realists (Storm, Keller, and Meyer), or the French novelists of the eighteenth century (Prévost, Laclos, and Constant). All writers and works receiving such discrete treatment are indexed below for the sake of alphabetic access. An additional 9 essays focusing on genres or themes (belonging primarily to the Middle Ages and the Renaissance) are listed in a following section on page 10.

Part One: Writers and Works

vol.: page

ADY, ENDRE (1877–1919)	9:859
AKHMATOVA, ANNA (1899–1966)	10:1521
ALFIERI, VITTORIO (1749–1803)	4:661
ANDERSEN, HANS CHRISTIAN (1805–1875)	6:863
ANDRÍC, IVO (1892–1975)	11:1751
ANOUILH, JEAN (1910–1987)	13:2843
APOLLINAIRE, GUILLAUME (1880–1918)	9:881
AQUINAS, THOMAS, SAINT (*ca.* 1224–1274), AND SCHOLASTICISM	1:405
ARAGON, LOUIS (1897–1982)	11:2061
ARIOSTO, LODOVICO (1474–1533)	2:619
ARP, JEAN (1886–1966)	10:1365
ARTAUD, ANTONIN (1895–1948)	11:1961
AUGUSTINE, SAINT (354–430)	1:23
AYMÉ, MARCEL (1902–1967)	12:2433
AZORÍN (1873–1967)	9:639
BABEL, ISAAC (1894–1941)	11:1885
BALZAC, HONORÉ DE (1799–1850)	5:635

ALPHABETICAL LIST OF SUBJECTS

BAROJA, PÍO (1872–1956)   9:589

BARTHES, ROLAND (1915–1980)   13:3079

BAUDELAIRE, CHARLES (1821–1867)   7:1323

BEAUMARCHAIS, PIERRE-AUGUSTIN CARON DE (1732–1799)   4:563

BEAUVOIR, SIMONE DE (1908–1986)   12:2701

BELY, ANDREY (1880–1934)   9:905

BENJAMIN, WALTER (1892–1940)   11:1703

BEOWULF   1:51

BERGSON, HENRI (1859–1941)   8:45

BERLIOZ, HECTOR (1803–1869)   6:771

BEYLE, HENRI. *See* STENDHAL

BLASCO IBÁÑEZ, VICENTE (1867–1928)   8:355

BLOK, ALEXANDER (1880–1921)   9:959

BOCCACCIO, GIOVANNI (1313–1375)   2:509

BOILEAU-DESPRÉAUX, NICOLAS (1636–1711)   3:177

BÖLL, HEINRICH (1917–1985)   13:3165

BOSSUET, JACQUES BÉNIGNE (1627–1704)   3:151

BRECHT, BERTOLT (1898–1956)   11:2089

BRETON, ANDRÉ (1896–1966)   11:1939

BROCH, HERMANN (1886–1951)   10:1385

BÜCHNER, GEORG (1813–1837)   6:1169

BURCKHARDT, JACOB (1818–1897)   6:1225

BUTOR, MICHAEL (*b.* 1926)   13:3287

CALDERÓN DE LA BARCA, PEDRO (1600–1681)   2:871

CALVINO, ITALO (1923–1985)   13:3259

CAMOËNS, LUÍS VAZ DE (1524?–1580)   1:747

CAMUS, ALBERT (1913–1960)   13:3049

CANETTI, ELIAS (*b.* 1905)   12:2615

ČAPEK, KAREL (1890–1938)   10:1565

CARDUCCI, GIOSUE (1835–1907)   7:1495

CASTIGLIONE, BALDESAR (1478–1529)   2:645

CAVAFY, CONSTANTIN (1863–1933)   8:205

CELA, CAMILO JOSÉ (*b.* 1916)   13:3105

ALPHABETICAL LIST OF SUBJECTS

CÉLINE, LOUIS FERDINAND (1894–1961)	11:1859
CERVANTES, MIGUEL DE (1547–1613)	2:819
CHANSON DE ROLAND AND THE *CHANSONS DE GESTE*	1:89
CHATEAUBRIAND, FRANÇOIS RENÉ DE (1768–1848)	5:113
CHEKHOV, ANTON (1860–1904)	7:1855
CHÉNIER, ANDRÉ (1762–1794)	4:691
CHRÉTIEN DE TROYES (12th Century)	1:185
CLAUDEL, PAUL (1868–1955)	8:471
COCTEAU, JEAN (1889–1963)	10:1543
COLETTE (1873–1954)	9:617
CONSTANT, BENJAMIN (1767–1830)	4:405
CORNEILLE, PIERRE (1606–1684)	3:23
CROCE, BENEDETTO (1866–1952)	8:311
D'ANNUNZIO, GABRIELE (1863–1938)	8:175
DANTE ALIGHIERI (1265–1321)	1:431
DELACROIX, EUGÈNE (1798–1863)	5:513
DESCARTES, RENÉ (1596–1650)	3:1
DIDEROT, DENIS (1713–1784)	4:475
DINESEN, ISAK (1885–1962)	10:1281
DOSTOEVSKY, FEODOR (1821–1881)	7:1349
DUMAS PÈRE ALEXANDRE (1802–1870)	6:719
DUPIN, AMANTINE-AURORE-LUCILE. *See* SAND, GEORGE	
DÜRRENMATT, FRIEDRICH (*b.* 1921)	13:3215
EÇA DE QUEIROZ, JOSÉ MARIA (1845–1900)	7:1683
EKELÖF, GUNNAR (1907–1968)	12:2635
ELYTIS, ODYSSEUS (*b.* 1911)	13:2955
ERASMUS (*ca.* 1466–1536)	2:571
FÉNELON, FRANÇOIS DE SALIGNAC DE LA MOTHE- (1651–1715)	3:261
FERREIRA DE CASTRO, JOSÉ MARIA (1898–1974)	11:2143
FLAUBERT, GUSTAVE (1821–1880)	7:1373
FONTANE, THEODOR (1819–1898)	6:1299

ALPHABETICAL LIST OF SUBJECTS

FOSCOLO, UGO (1778–1827)	5:313
FOUCAULT, MICHEL (1926–1984)	13:3323
FREUD, SIGMUND (1856–1939)	8:1
FRISCH, MAX (*b.* 1911)	13:2895
GARCÍA LORCA, FEDERICO (1898–1936)	11:2167
GAUTIER, THÉOPHILE (1811–1872)	6:1033
GENET, JEAN (1910–1986)	13:2865
GEORGE, STEFAN (1868–1933)	8:447
GHELDERODE, MICHEL DE (1898–1962)	11:2113
GIDE, ANDRÉ (1869–1951)	8:495
GINZBURG, NATALIA (*b.* 1916)	13:3131
GIRAUDOUX, JEAN (1882–1944)	9:1041
GOETHE, JOHANN WOLFGANG VON (1749–1832)	5:1
GOGOL, NIKOLAY VASILIEVICH (1809–1852)	6:971
GOLDONI, CARLO (1707–1793)	4:421
GOMBROWICZ, WITOLD (1904–1969)	12:2563
GONCHAROV, IVAN (1812–1891)	6:1061
GONCOURT, EDMOND LOUIS ANTOINE DE (1822–1896), AND JULES ALFRED HUOT DE (1830–1870)	7:1395
GORKY, MAXIM (1868–1936)	8:417
GOTTFRIED VON STRASSBURG (*fl.* 12th century)	1:237
GRASS, GÜNTER (*b.* 1927)	13:3365
GRILLPARZER, FRANZ (1791–1872)	5:417
GUNNARSSON, GUNNAR (1889–1975)	10:1497
HAMSUN, KNUT (1859–1952)	8:21
HARDENBERG, GEORG FRIEDRICH PHILIP. *See* NOVALIS	
HAŠEK, JAROSLAV (1883–1923)	9:1091
HAUPTMANN, GERHART (1862–1946)	8:147
HEBBEL, FRIEDRICH (1813–1863)	6:1089
HEINE, HEINRICH (1797–1856)	5:489
HERDER, JOHANN GOTTFRIED VON (1744–1803)	4:639
HESSE, HERMANN (1877–1962)	9:833

ALPHABETICAL LIST OF SUBJECTS

HOFFMANN, E. T. A. (1776–1822)   5:261

HOFMANNSTHAL, HUGO VON (1874–1929)   9:689

HÖLDERLIN, FRIEDRICH (1770–1843)   5:143

HUGO, VICTOR (1802–1885)   6:693

HUYSMANS, JORIS KARL (1847–1907)   7:1709

IBSEN, HENRIK (1828–1906)   7:1421

IONESCO, EUGÈNE (b. 1912)   13:2989

JARRY, ALFRED (1873–1907)   9:665

JIMÉNEZ, JUAN RAMÓN (1881–1958)   9:991

JOHNSON, EYVIND (1900–1976)   12:2361

KAFKA, FRANZ (1883–1924)   9:1151

KAZANTZAKIS, NIKOS (1883–1957)   9:1067

KELLER, GOTTFRIED (1819–1890)   6:922

KHLEBNIKOV, VELIMIR (1885–1922)   10:1331

KIERKEGAARD, SØREN (1813–1855)   6:123

KLEIST, HEINRICH VON (1777–1811)   5:291

KLOPSTOCK, FRIEDRICH GOTTLIEB (1724–1803)   4:511

KOSZTOLÁNYI, DEZSŐ (1885–1936)   10:1231

KRLEŽA, MIROSLAV (1893–1981)   11:1807

KUNDERA, MILAN (b. 1929)   13:3389

LA ROCHEFOUCAULD, FRANÇOIS VI, DUC DE (1613–1680)   3:51

LA BRUYÈRE, JEAN DE (1645–1696)   3:229

LACLOS, PIERRE-AMBROISE-FRANÇOIS CHODERLOS DE (1741–1803)   4:400

LA FONTAINE, JEAN DE (1621–1695)   3:73

LAFORGUE, JULES (1860–1887)   7:1883

LAGERKVIST, PÄR (1891–1974)   10:1677

LAMPEDUSA, GIUSEPPE TOMASI DI (1896–1957)   11:2009

LAXNESS, HALLDÓR (b. 1902)   12:2457

LECONTE DE LISLE, CHARLES MARIE (1818–1894)   6:1245

LEOPARDI, GIACOMO (1798–1837)   5:541

ALPHABETICAL LIST OF SUBJECTS

LERMONTOV, MIKHAIL YURIEVICH (1814–1841)   6:1195

LESAGE, ALAIN-RENÉ (1668–1747)   3:317

LESSING, GOTTHOLD EPHRAIM (1729–1781)   4:537

LUKÁCS, GYÖRGY (1885–1971)   10:1251

LUTHER, MARTIN (1483–1546)   2:669

MACHADO, ANTONIO (1875–1939)   9:743

MACHIAVELLI, NICCOLÒ (1469–1527)   2:595

MAETERLINCK, MAURICE (1862–1949)   8:119

MALLARMÉ, STÉPHANE (1842–1898)   7:1567

MALRAUX, ANDRÉ (1901–1976)   12:2413

MANDELSHTAM, OSIP (1891–1938)   10:1619

MANN, HEINRICH (1871–1950)   8:519

MANN, THOMAS (1875–1955)   9:715

MANZONI, ALESSANDRO (1785–1873)   5:367

MARINETTI, FILIPPO TOMMASO (1876–1944)   9:797

MAUPASSANT, GUY DE (1850–1893)   7:1759

MAURIAC, FRANÇOIS (1885–1970)   10:1307

MAYAKOVSKY, VLADIMIR (1893–1930)   11:1835

MÉRIMÉE, PROSPER (1803–1870)   6:745

MEYER, CONRAD FERDINAND (1825–1898)   6:930

MICHELET, JULES (1798–1874)   5:571

MICKIEWICZ, ADAM (1798–1855)   5:607

MILOSZ, CZESLAW (b. 1911)   13:2929

MOBERG, VILHELM (1893–1973)   11:2203

MOLIÈRE (1622–1673)   3:101

MONTAIGNE, MICHEL DE (1533–1592)   2:769

MONTALE, EUGENIO (1896–1981)   11:1987

MONTESQUIEU (1689–1755)   3:345

MONTHERLANT, HENRY DE (1895–1972)   11:1915

MORAVIA, ALBERTO (1907–1990)   12:2673

MUSIL, ROBERT (1880–1942)   9:931

MUSSET, ALFRED DE (1810–1857)   6:999

ALPHABETICAL LIST OF SUBJECTS

NERVAL, GÉRARD DE (1808–1855)   6:943

NIBELUNGENLIED, THE (13th century)   1.211

NIETZSCHE, FRIEDRICH (1844–1900)   7:1645

NOVALIS (1772–1801)   5:205

OLESHA, YURI (1899–1960)   11:2233

ORTEGA Y GASSET, JOSÉ (1883–1955)   9:1119

PASCAL, BLAISE (1623–1662)   3:125

PASCOLI, GIOVANNI (1855–1912)   7:1825

PASTERNAK, BORIS (1890–1960)   10:1591

PAVESE, CESARE (1908–1950)   12:2759

PÉREZ GALDÓS, BENITO (1843–1920)   7:1597

PERSE, SAINT JOHN (1887–1975)   10:1429

PESSOA, FERNANDO (1885–1935)   10:1475

PETRARCH (1304–1374)   2:475

PIRANDELLO, LUIGI (1867–1936)   8:389

PRÉVOST, ANTOINE-FRANÇOIS (1697–1763)   4:393

PROUST, MARCEL (1871–1922)   8:545

PRUDENTIUS (348–*ca.* 410)   1:1

PUSHKIN, ALEXANDER (1799–1837)   5:659

QUASIMODO, SALVATORE (1901–1968)   12:2387

QUENEAU, RAYMOND (1903–1976)   12:2511

RABELAIS, FRANÇOIS (*ca.* 1494–1553)   2:693

RACINE, JEAN (1639–1699)   3:207

RICHTER, JEAN PAUL (1763–1825)   5:53

RILKE, RAINER MARIA (1875–1926)   9:767

RIMBAUD, ARTHUR (1854–1891)   7:1785

RITSOS, YANNIS (1909–1990)   12:2815

ROBBE-GRILLET, ALAIN (*b.* 1922)   13:3237

ROMANCE OF THE ROSE, THE, AND MEDIEVAL ALLEGORY   1:309

ALPHABETICAL LIST OF SUBJECTS

RONSARD, PIERRE DE, AND THE PLÉIADE (1524–1585)	2:721
ROUSSEAU, JEAN JACQUES (1712–1778)	4:449
SADE, DONATIEN ALPHONSE FRANÇOIS, MARQUIS DE (1740–1814), AND THE FRENCH LIBERTINE TRADITION	4:615
SAINT-EXUPÉRY, ANTOINE DE (1900–1944)	12:2307
SAINTE-BEUVE, CHARLES-AUGUSTIN (1804–1869)	6:837
SAND, GEORGE (1804–1876)	6:813
SARRAUTE, NATHALIE (b. 1900)	12:2333
SARTRE, JEAN-PAUL (1905–1980)	12:2589
SCHILLER, FRIEDRICH VON (1759–1805)	5:27
SCHLEGEL, FRIEDRICH VON (1772–1829)	5:177
SCHNITZLER, ARTHUR (1862–1931)	8:89
SCHOPENHAUER, ARTHUR (1788–1860)	5:395
SEFERIS, GEORGE (1900–1971)	12:2255
SILONE, IGNAZIO (1900–1978)	12:2273
SIMENON, GEORGES (1903–1989)	12:2479
SIMON, CLAUDE (b. 1913)	13:3021
SÖDERGRAN, EDITH (1892–1923)	11:1781
SOLZHENITSYN, ALEXANDER (b. 1918)	12:3187
STAËL, MADAME DE (1766–1817)	5:89
STENDHAL (1783–1842)	5:343
STORM, THEODOR (1817–1888)	6:915
STRINDBERG, AUGUST (1849–1912)	7:1731
SVEVO, ITALO (1861–1928)	8:67
TAINE, HIPPOLYTE (1828–1893)	7:1449
TASSO, TORQUATO (1544–1595)	2:791
TIECK, LUDWIG (1773–1853)	5:233
TOCQUEVILLE, ALEXIS DE (1805–1859)	6:893
TOLSTOY, LEO (1828–1910)	7:1471
TRAKL, GEORG (1887–1914)	10:1409

ALPHABETICAL LIST OF SUBJECTS

TSVETAEVA, MARINA (1892–1941)	11:1731
TURGENEV, IVAN (1818–1883)	6:1275
TYCHYNA, PAVEL (1891–1967)	10:1651
UNAMUNO, MIGUEL DE (1864–1936)	8:283
UNDSET, SIGRID (1882–1949)	9:1017
UNGARETTI, GIUSEPPE (1888–1970)	10:1453
VALÉRY, PAUL (1871–1945)	8:569
VALLE-INCLÁN, RAMÓN DEL (1866–1936)	8:331
VEGA, LOPE DE (1562–1635)	2:845
VERGA, GIOVANNI (1840–1922)	7:1543
VERLAINE, PAUL (1844–1896)	7:1619
VESAAS, TARJEI (1897–1970)	11:2035
VICO, GIOVANNI BATTISTA (1668–1744)	3:293
VIGNY, ALFRED VICTOR DE (1797–1863)	5:447
VILLON, FRANÇOIS (1431–ca. 1465)	2:535
VITTORINI, ELIO (1908–1966)	12:2733
VOLTAIRE (1694–1778)	4:367
WAGNER, RICHARD (1813–1883)	6:1147
WALTHER VON DER VOGELWEIDE (ca. 1170–ca. 1228)	1:287
WEDEKIND, FRANK (1864–1918)	8:229
WEIL, SIMONE (1909–1943)	12:2787
WIELAND, CHRISTOPH MARTIN (1753–1813)	4:587
WITKIEWICZ, STANISŁAW IGNACY (1885–1939)	10:1205
WOLFRAM VON ESCHENBACH (ca. 1170–ca. 1220)	1:263
YOURCENAR, MARGUERITE (1903–1987)	12:2535
ZAMYATIN, YEVGENY IVANOVICH (1884–1937)	10:1181
ZOLA, ÉMILE (1840–1902)	7:1517

ALPHABETICAL LIST OF SUBJECTS

Part Two: Themes and Genres

CHRONOLOGICAL LIST OF SUBJECTS

The Middle Ages and the Renaissance

Volume 1

PRUDENTIUS (348–*ca.* 410)	1
SAINT AUGUSTINE (354–430)	23
BEOWULF AND ANGLO-SAXON POETRY (*ca.* 600–1066)	51
THE *CHANSON DE ROLAND* AND THE *CHANSONS DE GESTE* (*ca.* 1100–*ca.* 1450)	89
THE CID IN EPIC AND BALLAD (*ca.* 1100–*ca.* 1600)	113
ARTHURIAN LEGEND (*ca.* 1135–*ca.* 1250)	137
TROUBADOURS AND TROUVÈRES (*ca.* 1100–*ca.* 1300)	161
CHRÉTIEN DE TROYES (*d. ca.* 1190)	185
THE *NIBELUNGENLIED* (*ca.* 1200)	211
GOTTFRIED VON STRASSBURG (*d.* after 1210)	237
WOLFRAM VON ESCHENBACH (*ca.* 1170–*ca.* 1220)	263
WALTHER VON DER VOGELWEIDE (*ca.* 1170–*ca.* 1228)	287
THE *ROMANCE OF THE ROSE* AND MEDIEVAL ALLEGORY (*ca.* 1225–*ca.* 1285)	309
MEDIEVAL SATIRE (*ca.* 1300–*ca.* 1450)	337
NORSE SAGAS (*ca.* 1100–*ca.* 1350)	377
SAINT THOMAS AQUINAS AND SCHOLASTICISM (*ca.* 1224–*ca.* 1274)	405
DANTE ALIGHIERI (1265–1321)	431
MEDIEVAL DRAMA (*ca.* 1900–*ca.* 1550)	451

Volume 2

PETRARCH (1304–1374)	475
GIOVANNI BOCCACCIO (1313–1375)	509

11

CHRONOLOGICAL LIST OF SUBJECTS

FRANÇOIS VILLON (1431–ca. 1465) — 535

ERASMUS (ca. 1466–1536) — 571

NICCOLÒ MACHIAVELLI (1469–1527) — 595

LODOVICO ARIOSTO (1474–1533) — 619

BALDESAR CASTIGLIONE (1478–1529) — 645

MARTIN LUTHER (1483–1546) — 669

FRANÇOIS RABELAIS (ca. 1494–1553) — 693

PIERRE DE RONSARD AND THE PLÉIADE (1524–1585) — 721

LUÍS VAZ DE CAMOËNS (1524?–1580) — 747

MICHEL DE MONTAIGNE (1533–1592) — 769

TORQUATO TASSO (1544–1595) — 791

MIGUEL DE CERVANTES (1547–1616) — 819

LOPE DE VEGA (1562–1635) — 845

PEDRO CALDERÓN DE LA BARCA (1600–1681) — 871

RENAISSANCE PASTORAL POETRY — 899

RENAISSANCE SHORT FICTION — 927

The Age of Reason and the Enlightenment

Volume 3

RENÉ DESCARTES (1596–1650) — 1

PIERRE CORNEILLE (1606–1684) — 23

FRANÇOIS VI, DUC DE LA ROCHEFOUCAULD (1613–1680) — 51

JEAN DE LA FONTAINE (1621–1695) — 73

MOLIÈRE (1622–1673) — 101

BLAISE PASCAL (1623–1662) — 125

JACQUES BÉNIGNE BOSSUET (1627–1704) — 151

NICOLAS BOILEAU-DESPRÉAUX (1636–1711) — 177

JEAN RACINE (1639–1699) — 207

JEAN DE LA BRUYÈRE (1645–1696) — 229

FRANÇOIS DE SALIGNAC DE LA MOTHE-FÉNELON (1651–1715) — 261

GIOVANNI BATTISTA VICO (1668–1744) — 293

CHRONOLOGICAL LIST OF SUBJECTS

ALAIN-RENÉ LESAGE (1668–1747) — 317

MONTESQUIEU (1689–1755) — 345

Volume 4

VOLTAIRE (1694–1778) — 367

THREE FRENCH NOVELISTS: ANTOINE-FRANÇOIS PRÉVOST (1697–1763),
 CHODERLOS DE LACLOS (1741–1803), BENJAMIN CONSTANT (1767–1830) — 393

CARLO GOLDONI (1707–1793) — 421

JEAN JACQUES ROUSSEAU (1712–1778) — 449

DENIS DIDEROT (1713–1784) — 475

FRIEDRICH GOTTLIEB KLOPSTOCK (1724–1803) — 511

GOTTHOLD EPHRAIM LESSING (1729–1781) — 537

PIERRE-AUGUSTIN CARON DE BEAUMARCHAIS (1732–1799) — 563

CHRISTOPH MARTIN WIELAND (1733–1813) — 587

THE MARQUIS DE SADE (1740–1814) AND THE FRENCH
 LIBERTINE TRADITION — 615

JOHANN GOTTFRIED VON HERDER (1744–1803) — 639

VITTORIO ALFIERI (1749–1803) — 661

ANDRÉ CHÉNIER (1762–1794) — 691

The Romantic Century

Volume 5

JOHANN WOLFGANG VON GOETHE (1749–1832) — 1

FRIEDRICH VON SCHILLER (1759–1805) — 27

JEAN PAUL RICHTER (1763–1825) — 53

MADAME DE STAËL (1766–1817) — 89

FRANÇOIS RENÉ DE CHATEAUBRIAND (1768–1848) — 113

FRIEDRICH HÖLDERLIN (1770–1843) — 143

FRIEDRICH VON SCHLEGEL (1772–1829) — 177

NOVALIS (1772–1801) — 205

LUDWIG TIECK (1773–1853) — 233

E. T. A. HOFFMANN (1776–1822) — 261

CHRONOLOGICAL LIST OF SUBJECTS

HEINRICH VON KLEIST (1777–1811)   291

UGO FOSCOLO (1778–1827)   313

STENDHAL (1783–1842)   343

ALESSANDRO MANZONI (1785–1873)   367

ARTHUR SCHOPENHAUER (1788–1860)   395

FRANZ GRILLPARZER (1791–1872)   417

ALFRED VICTOR DE VIGNY (1797–1863)   447

HEINRICH HEINE (1797–1856)   489

EUGÈNE DELACROIX (1798–1863)   513

GIACOMO LEOPARDI (1798–1837)   541

JULES MICHELET (1798–1874) AND ROMANTIC HISTORIOGRAPHY   571

ADAM MICKIEWICZ (1798–1855)   607

HONORÉ DE BALZAC (1799–1850)   635

ALEXANDER PUSHKIN (1799–1837)   659

Volume 6

VICTOR HUGO (1802–1885)   693

ALEXANDRE DUMAS père (1802–1870)   719

PROSPER MÉRIMÉE (1803–1870)   745

HECTOR BERLIOZ (1803–1869)   771

GEORGE SAND (1804–1876)   813

CHARLES-AUGUSTIN SAINTE-BEUVE (1804–1869)   837

HANS CHRISTIAN ANDERSEN (1805–1875)   863

ALEXIS DE TOCQUEVILLE (1805–1859)   893

POETIC REALISM: THEODOR STORM (1817–1888), GOTTFRIED KELLER (1819–1890), CONRAD FERDINAND MEYER (1825–1898)   913

GÉRARD DE NERVAL (1808–1855)   943

NIKOLAY VASILIEVICH GOGOL (1809–1852)   971

ALFRED DE MUSSET (1810–1857)   999

THÉOPHILE GAUTIER (1811–1872)   1033

IVAN GONCHAROV (1812–1891)   1061

FRIEDRICH HEBBEL (1813–1863)   1089

SØREN KIERKEGAARD (1813–1855)   1123

CHRONOLOGICAL LIST OF SUBJECTS

RICHARD WAGNER (1813–1883)   1147

GEORG BÜCHNER (1813–1837)   1169

MIKHAIL YURIEVICH LERMONTOV (1814–1841)   1195

JACOB BURCKHARDT (1818–1897)   1225

CHARLES MARIE LECONTE DE LISLE (1818–1894)   1245

IVAN TURGENEV (1818–1883)   1275

THEODOR FONTANE (1819–1898)   1299

Volume 7

CHARLES BAUDELAIRE (1821–1867)   1323

FEODOR DOSTOEVSKY (1821–1881)   1349

GUSTAVE FLAUBERT (1821–1880)   1373

EDMOND LOUIS ANTOINE DE GONCOURT (1822–1896)
    AND JULES ALFRED HUOT DE GONCOURT (1830–1870)   1395

HENRIK IBSEN (1828–1906)   1421

HIPPOLYTE TAINE (1828–1893)   1449

LEO TOLSTOY (1828–1910)   1471

GIOSUE CARDUCCI (1835–1907)   1495

ÉMILE ZOLA (1840–1902)   1517

GIOVANNI VERGA (1840–1922)   1543

STÉPHANE MALLARMÉ (1842–1898)   1567

BENITO PÉREZ GALDÓS (1843–1920)   1597

PAUL VERLAINE (1844–1896)   1619

FRIEDRICH NIETZSCHE (1844–1900)   1645

JOSÉ MARIA EÇA DE QUEIROZ (1845–1900)   1683

JORIS KARL HUYSMANS (1847–1907)   1709

AUGUST STRINDBERG (1849–1912)   1731

GUY DE MAUPASSANT (1850–1893)   1759

ARTHUR RIMBAUD (1854–1891)   1785

GIOVANNI PASCOLI (1855–1912)   1825

ANTON CHEKHOV (1860–1904)   1855

JULES LAFORGUE (1860–1887)   1883

THE WELL-MADE PLAY   1909

CHRONOLOGICAL LIST OF SUBJECTS
The Twentieth Century

Volume 8

SIGMUND FREUD (1856–1939)	1
KNUT HAMSUN (1859–1952)	21
HENRI BERGSON (1859–1941)	45
ITALO SVEVO (1861–1928)	67
ARTHUR SCHNITZLER (1862–1931)	89
MAURICE MAETERLINCK (1862–1949)	119
GERHART HAUPTMANN (1862–1946)	147
GABRIELE D'ANNUNZIO (1863–1938)	175
CONSTANTINE CAVAFY (1863–1933)	205
FRANK WEDEKIND (1864–1918)	229
MIGUEL DE UNAMUNO (1864–1936)	283
BENEDETTO CROCE (1866–1952)	311
RAMÓN DEL VALLE-INCLÁN (1866–1936)	331
VICENTE BLASCO IBÁÑEZ (1867–1928)	355
LUIGI PIRANDELLO (1867–1936)	389
MAXIM GORKY (1868–1936)	417
STEFAN GEORGE (1868–1933)	447
PAUL CLAUDEL (1868–1955)	471
ANDRÉ GIDE (1869–1951)	495
HEINRICH MANN (1871–1950)	519
MARCEL PROUST (1871–1922)	545
PAUL VALÉRY (1871–1945)	569

Volume 9

PÍO BAROJA (1872–1956)	589
COLETTE (1873–1954)	617
AZORÍN (1873–1967)	639
ALFRED JARRY (1873–1907)	665
HUGO VON HOFMANNSTHAL (1874–1929)	689
THOMAS MANN (1875–1955)	715
ANTONIO MACHADO (1875–1939)	743

CHRONOLOGICAL LIST OF SUBJECTS

RAINER MARIA RILKE (1875–1926)   767

FILIPPO TOMMASO MARINETTI (1876–1944)   797

HERMANN HESSE (1877–1962)   833

ENDRE ADY (1877–1919)   859

GUILLAUME APOLLINAIRE (1880–1918)   881

ANDREY BELY (1880–1934)   905

ROBERT MUSIL (1880–1942)   931

ALEXANDER BLOK (1880–1921)   959

JUAN RAMÓN JIMÉNEZ (1881–1958)   991

SIGRID UNDSET (1882–1949)   1017

JEAN GIRAUDOUX (1882–1944)   1041

NIKOS KAZANTZAKIS (1883–1957)   1067

JAROSLAV HAŠEK (1883–1923)   1091

JOSÉ ORTEGA Y GASSET (1883–1955)   1119

FRANZ KAFKA (1883–1924)   1151

Volume 10

YEVGENY IVANOVICH ZAMYATIN (1884–1937)   1181

STANISŁAW IGNACY WITKIEWICZ (1885–1939)   1205

DEZSŐ KOSZTOLÁNYI (1885–1936)   1231

GYÖRGY LUKÁCS (1885–1971)   1251

ISAK DINESEN (1885–1962)   1281

FRANÇOIS MAURIAC (1885–1970)   1307

VELIMIR KHLEBNIKOV (1885–1922)   1331

JEAN ARP (1886–1966)   1365

HERMANN BROCH (1886–1951)   1385

GEORG TRAKL (1887–1914)   1409

SAINT-JOHN PERSE (1887–1975)   1429

GIUSEPPE UNGARETTI (1888–1970)   1453

FERNANDO PESSOA (1888–1935)   1475

GUNNAR GUNNARSSON (1889–1975)   1497

ANNA AKHMATOVA (1889–1966)   1521

JEAN COCTEAU (1889–1963)   1543

KAREL ČAPEK (1890–1938)   1565

CHRONOLOGICAL LIST OF SUBJECTS

BORIS PASTERNAK (1890–1960)   1591

OSIP MANDELSHTAM (1891–1938)   1619

PAVLO TYCHYNA (1891–1967)   1651

PÄR LAGERKVIST (1891–1974)   1677

Volume 11

WALTER BENJAMIN (1892–1940)   1703

MARINA TSVETAEVA (1892–1941)   1731

IVO ANDRIĆ (1892–1975)   1751

EDITH SÖDERGRAN (1892–1923)   1781

MIROSLAV KRLEŽA (1893–1981)   1807

VLADIMIR MAYAKOVSKY (1893–1930)   1835

LOUIS FERDINAND CÉLINE (1894–1961)   1859

ISAAC BABEL (1894–1941)   1885

HENRY DE MONTHERLANT (1895–1972)   1915

ANDRÉ BRETON (1896–1966)   1939

ANTONIN ARTAUD (1895–1948)   1961

EUGENIO MONTALE (1896–1981)   1987

GIUSEPPE TOMASI DI LAMPEDUSA (1896–1957)   2009

TARJEI VESAAS (1897–1970)   2035

LOUIS ARAGON (1897–1982)   2061

BERTOLT BRECHT (1898–1956)   2089

MICHEL DE GHELDERODE (1898–1962)   2113

JOSÉ MARIA FERREIRA DE CASTRO (1898–1974)   2143

FEDERICO GARCÍA LORCA (1898–1936)   2167

VILHELM MOBERG (1898–1973)   2203

YURI OLESHA (1899–1960)   2233

Volume 12

GEORGE SEFERIS (1900–1971)   2255

IGNAZIO SILONE (1900–1978)   2273

ANTOINE DE SAINT-EXUPÉRY (1900–1944)   2307

NATHALIE SARRAUTE (*b.* 1900)   2333

EYVIND JOHNSON (1900–1976)   2361

CHRONOLOGICAL LIST OF SUBJECTS

SALVATORE QUASIMODO (1901–1968)   2387

ANDRÉ MALRAUX (1901–1976)   2413

MARCEL AYMÉ (1902–1967)   2433

HALLDÓR LAXNESS (*b.* 1902)   2457

GEORGES SIMENON (1903–1989)   2479

RAYMOND QUENEAU (1903–1976)   2511

MARGUERITE YOURCENAR (1903–1987)   2535

WITOLD GOMBROWICZ (1904–1969)   2563

JEAN-PAUL SARTRE (1905–1980)   2589

ELIAS CANETTI (*b.* 1905)   2615

GUNNAR EKELÖF (1907–1968)   2635

ALBERTO MORAVIA (1907–1990)   2673

SIMONE DE BEAUVOIR (1908–1986)   2701

ELIO VITTORINI (1908–1966)   2733

CESARE PAVESE (1908–1950)   2759

SIMONE WEIL (1909–1943)   2787

YANNIS RITSOS (1909–1990)   2815

Volume 13

JEAN ANOUILH (1910–1987)   2843

JEAN GENET (1910–1986)   2865

MAX FRISCH (*b.* 1911)   2895

CZESLAW MILOSZ (*b.* 1911)   2929

ODYSSEUS ELYTIS (*b.* 1911)   2955

EUGÈNE IONESCO (*b.* 1912)   2989

CLAUDE SIMON (*b.* 1913)   3021

ALBERT CAMUS (1913–1960)   3049

ROLAND BARTHES (1915–1980)   3079

CAMILO JOSÉ CELA (*b.* 1916)   3105

NATALIA GINZBURG (*b.* 1916)   3131

HEINRICH BÖLL (1917–1985)   3165

ALEXANDER SOLZHENITSYN (*b.* 1918)   3187

FRIEDRICH DÜRRENMATT (*b.* 1921)   3215

ALAIN ROBBE-GRILLET (*b.* 1922)   3237

CHRONOLOGICAL LIST OF SUBJECTS

SUBJECTS BY LANGUAGE

ANGLO-SAXON
  See ENGLISH

CZECH
  Čapek, Karel, 10:1565
  Hašek, Jaroslav, 9:1091
  Kundera, Milan, 13:3389

DANISH
  Andersen, Hans Christian, 6:863
  Dinesen, Isak, 10:1281
  Gunnarsson, Gunnar, 10:1497
  Kierkegaard, Søren, 6:1123

ENGLISH
  Beowulf, 1:51
  Dinesen, Isak, 10:1281
  Pessoa, Fernando, 10:1475

FRENCH
  Anouilh, Jean, 13:2843
  Apollinaire, Guillaume, 9:881
  Aragon, Louis, 11:2061
  Arp, Jean, 10:1365
  Artaud, Antonin, 11:1961
  Aymé, Marcel, 12:2433
  Balzac, Honoré de, 5:635
  Barthes, Roland, 13:3079
  Baudelaire, Charles, 7:1323
  Beaumarchais, Pierre-Augustin
    Caron de, 4:563
  Beauvoir, Simone de, 12:2701
  Bergson, Henri, 8:45
  Berlioz, Hector, 6:771
  Boileau-Despréaux, Nicolas, 3:177
  Bossuet, Jacques Bénigne, 3:151
  Breton, André, 11:1939
  Butor, Michael, 13:3287
  Camus, Albert, 13:3049

Céline, Louis Ferdinand, 11:1859
Chanson de Roland, 1:89
Chateaubriand, François Rene de, 5:113
Chénier, André, 4:691
Chrétien de Troyes, 1:185
Claudel, Paul, 8:471
Cocteau, Jean, 10:1543
Colette, 9:617
Constant, Benjamin, 4:405
Corneille, Pierre, 3:23
Delacroix, Eugène, 5:513
Descartes, René, 3:1
Diderot, Denis, 4:475
Dumas père, Alexandre, 6:719
Fénelon, François de Salignac de la
    Mothe-, 3:261
Flaubert, Gustave, 7:1373
Foucault, Michel, 13:3323
Gautier, Théophile, 6:1033
Genet, Jean, 13:2865
Ghelderode, Michel de, 11:2113
Gide, André, 8:495
Giraudoux, Jean, 9:1041
Goncourt, Edmond Louis Antoine de,
    7:1395
Goncourt, Jules Alfred Huot de, 7:1395
Hugo, Victor, 6:693
Huysmans, Joris Karl, 7:1709
Ionesco, Eugène, 13:2989
Jarry, Alfred, 9:665
Kundera, Milan, 13:3389
La Bruyère, Jean de, 3:229
La Fontaine, Jean de, 3:73
Laclos, Choderlos de, 4:400
Laforgue, Jules, 7:1883
La Rochefoucauld, François VI,
    Duc de, 3:51
Leconte de Lisle, Charles Marie, 6:1245
Lesage, Alain-René, 3:317

Maeterlinck, Maurice, 8:119
Mallarmé, Stéphane, 7:1567
Malraux, André, 12:2413
Maupassant, Guy de, 7:1759
Mauriac, François, 10:1307
Mérimée, Prosper, 6:745
Michelet, Jules, 5:571
Mickiewicz, Adam, 5:607
Milosz, Czeslaw, 13:2929
Molière, 3:101
Montaigne, Michel de, 2:769
Montesquieu, Charles-Louis de
   Secondat, Baron de, 3:345
Montherlant, Henry de, 11:1915
Mothe-Fénelon, François de Salignac
   de la. *See* Fénelon.
Musset, Alfred de, 6:999
Nerval, Gérard de, 6:943
Pascal, Blaise, 3:125
Perse, Saint-John, 10:1429
Prévost, Antoine-François, 4:393
Proust, Marcel, 8:545
Queneau, Raymond, 12:2511
Rabelais, François, 2:693
Racine, Jean, 3:207
Rimbaud, Arthur, 7:1785
Robbe-Grillet, Alain, 13:3237
Romance of the Rose, 1:309
Ronsard, Pierre de, 2:721
Rousseau, Jean Jacques, 4:449
Sade, Donatien Alphonse François,
   Marquis de, 4:615
Saint-Exupéry, Antoine de, 12:2307
Sainte-Beuve, Charles-Augustin, 6:837
Sand, George, 6:813
Sarraute, Nathalie, 12:2333
Sartre, Jean-Paul, 12:2589
Simenon, Georges, 12:2479
Simon, Claude, 13:3021
Staël, Madame de, 5:89
Stendhal, 5:343
Taine, Hippolyte, 7:1449
Tocqueville, Alexis de, 6:893
Ungaretti, Giuseppe, 10:1453
Valéry, Paul, 8:569
Verlaine, Paul, 7:1619
Vigny, Alfred Victor de, 5:447
Villon, François, 2:535
Voltaire, 4:367
Weil, Simone, 12:2787

Yourcenar, Marguerite, 12:2535
Zola, Émile, 7:1517

GERMAN
Arp, Jean, 10:1365
Benjamin, Walter, 11:1703
Böll, Heinrich, 13:3165
Brecht, Bertolt, 11:2089
Broch, Hermann, 10:1385
Büchner, Georg, 6:1169
Burckhardt, Jacob, 6:1225
Canetti, Elias, 12:2615
Dürrenmatt, Friedrich, 13:3215
Fontane, Theodor, 6:1299
Freud, Sigmund, 8:1
Frisch, Max, 13:2895
George, Stefan, 8:447
Goethe, Johann Wolfgang von, 5:1
Gottfried von Strassburg, 1:237
Grass, Günter, 13:3365
Grillparzer, Franz, 5:417
Hauptmann, Gerhart, 8:147
Hebbel, Friedrich, 6:1089
Heine, Heinrich, 5:489
Herder, Johann Gottfried von, 4:639
Hesse, Hermann, 9:833
Hoffmann, E. T. A., 5:261
Hofmannsthal, Hugo von, 9:689
Hölderlin, Friedrich, 5:143
Kafka, Franz, 9:1151
Keller, Gottfried, 6:922
Kleist, Heinrich von, 5:291
Klopstock, Friedrich Gottlieb, 4:511
Lessing, Gotthold Ephraim, 4:537
Lukács, György, 10:1251
Luther, Martin, 2:669
Mann, Heinrich, 8:519
Mann, Thomas, 9:715
Meyer, Conrad Ferdinand, 6:930
Musil, Robert, 9:931
Nibelungenlied, 1:211
Nietzsche, Friedrich, 7:1645
Novalis, 5:205
Richter, Jean Paul, 5:53
Rilke, Rainer Maria, 9:767
Schiller, Friedrich von, 5:27
Schlegel, Friedrich von, 5:177
Schnitzler, Arthur, 8:89
Schopenhauer, Arthur, 5:395
Södergran, Edith, 11:1781

Storm, Theodor, 6:915
Tieck, Ludwig, 5:233
Trakl, Georg, 10:1409
Wagner, Richard, 6:1147
Walther von der Vogelweide, 1:287
Wedekind, Frank, 8:229
Wieland, Christoph Martin, 4:587
Wolfram von Eschenbach, 1:263

GREEK
Cavafy, Constantin, 8:205
Elytis, Odysseus, 13:2955
Kazantzakis, Nikos, 9:1067
Ritsos, Yannis, 12:2815
Seferis, George, 12:2255

HUNGARIAN
Ady, Endre, 9:859
Kosztolányi, Dezső, 10:1231
Lukács, György, 10:1251

ICELANDIC
Gunnarsson, Gunnar, 10:1497
Laxness, Halldór, 12:2457
see also OLD NORSE

ITALIAN
Alfieri, Vittorio, 4:661
Ariosto, Lodovico, 2:619
Boccaccio, Giovanni, 2:509
Calvino, Italo, 13:3259
Carducci, Giosue, 7:1495
Castiglione, Baldesar, 2:645
Croce, Benedetto, 8:311
D'Annunzio, Gabriele, 8:175
Dante Alighieri, 1:431
Foscolo, Ugo, 5:313
Ginzburg, Natalia, 13:3131
Goldoni, Carlo, 4:421
Lampedusa, Giuseppe Tomasi de,
    11:2009
Leopardi, Giacomo, 5:541
Machiavelli, Niccolò, 2:595
Manzoni, Alessandro, 5:367
Marinetti, Filippo Tommaso, 9:797
Montale, Eugenio, 11:1987
Moravia, Alberto, 12:2673
Pascoli, Giovanni, 7:1825
Pavese, Cesare, 12:2759
Petrarch, 2:475
Pirandello, Luigi, 8:389

Quasimodo, Salvatore, 12:2387
Silone, Ignazio, 12:2273
Svevo, Italo, 8:67
Tasso, Torquato, 2:791
Ungaretti, Giuseppe, 10:1453
Verga, Giovanni, 7:1543
Vico, Giovanni Battista, 3:293
Vittorini, Elio, 12:2733

LATIN
Aquinas, Thomas, Saint, 1:405
Ariosto, Lodovico, 2:619
Augustine, Saint, 1:23
Boccaccio, Giovanni, 2:509
Castiglione, Baldesar, 2:645
Dante Alighieri, 1:431
Descartes, René, 3:1
Erasmus, 2:571
Luther, Martin, 2:669
Petrarch, 2:475
Prudentius (Aulus Prudentius
    Clemens), 1:1
Vico, Giovanni Battista, 3:293

NORWEGIAN
Hamsun, Knut, 8:21
Ibsen, Henrik, 7:1421
Undset, Sigrid, 9:1017
Vesaas, Tarjei, 11:2035
see also OLD NORSE

OLD NORSE
Norse Sagas, 1:377

POLISH
Gombrowicz, Witold, 12:2563
Mickiewicz, Adam, 5:607
Milosz, Czeslaw, 13:2929
Witkiewicz, Stanisław Ignacy, 10:1205

PORTUGUESE
Camoëns, Luís Vaz de, 2:747
Eça de Queiroz, José Maria, 7:1683
Ferreira de Castro, José Maria, 11:2143
Pessoa, Fernando, 10:1475

PROVENÇAL
Troubadours, 1:161

RUSSIAN
Akhmatova, Anna, 10:1521

SUBJECTS BY LANGUAGE

Babel, Isaac, 11:1885
Bely, Andrey, 9:905
Blok, Alexander, 9:959
Chekhov, Anton, 7:1855
Dostoevsky, Feodor, 7:1349
Gogol, Nikolay Vasilievich, 6:971
Goncharov, Ivan, 6:1061
Gorky, Maxim, 8:417
Khlebnikov, Velimir, 10:1331
Lermontov, Mikhail Yurievich, 6:1195
Mandelshtam, Osip, 10:1619
Mayakovsky, Vladimir, 11:1835
Olesha, Yuri, 11:2233
Pasternak, Boris, 10:1591
Pushkin, Alexander, 5:659
Solzhenitsyn, Alexander, 13:3187
Tolstoy, Leo, 7:1471
Tsvetaeva, Marina, 11:1731
Turgenev, Ivan, 6:1275
Zamyatin, Yevgeny Ivanovich, 10:1181

SERBO-CROATIAN
Andrič, Ivo, 11:1751
Krleža, Miroslav, 11:1807

SPANISH
Azorín, 9:639
Baroja, Pío, 9:589
Blasco Ibáñez, Vicente, 8:355
Calderón de la Barca, Pedro, 2:871
Cela, Camilo José, 13:3105
Cervantes, Miguel de, 2:819
García Lorca, Federico, 11:2167
Jiménez, Juan Ramón, 9:991
Machado, Antonio, 9:743
Ortega y Gasset, José, 9:1119
Pérez Galdós, Benito, 7:1597
Unamuno, Miguel de, 8:283
Valle-Inclán, Ramón del, 8:331
Vega, Lope de, 2:845

SWEDISH
Ekelöf, Gunnar, 12:2635
Johnson, Eyvind, 12:2361
Lagerkvist, Pär, 10:1677
Moberg, Vilhelm, 11:2203
Södergran, Edith, 11:1781
Strindberg, August, 7:1731

UKRAINIAN
Tychyna, Pavel, 10:1651

GENERAL BIBLIOGRAPHY

THE MIDDLE AGES

Since most medieval literature is anonymous, many literary works, genres, and themes are treated collectively in *European Writers.* The reader is directed to the appropriate essays in volume 1 for general bibliography on the following:

Allegory. *See* "The *Romance of the Rose* and Medieval Allegory."

Arthurian Literature. *See* "Arthurian Literature."

Courtly Love. *See* "Dante," "Gottfried von Strassburg," "The *Romance of the Rose* and Medieval Allegory," and "Troubadours and Trouvères."

Drama. *See* "Medieval Drama."

The Epic. *See* articles on individual epic poems by title.

The Grail. *See* "Arthurian Literature," "Chrétien de Troyes," and "Wolfram von Eschenbach."

Philosophy. *See* "Saint Thomas Aquinas."

Satire. *See* "Medieval Satire."

LATIN AND GENERAL LITERATURE

Auerbach, Erich. *Mimesis: The Representation of Reality in European Literature.* Translated by Willard R. Trask. Princeton, 1953.

———. *Scenes from the Drama of European Literature.* Translated by Willard R. Trask. New York, 1959.

Curtius, Ernst R. *European Literature and the Latin Middle Ages.* Translated by Willard R. Trask. Princeton, 1953.

de Rougemont, Denis. *Love in the Western World.* Translated by Montgomery Belgion, New York, 1940.

Dictionary of the Middle Ages. Edited by Joseph R. Strayer. 13 vols. New York, 1982–1989.

Dronke, Peter. *Medieval Latin and the Rise of the European Love-Lyric.* 2 vols. 2d ed. Oxford, 1968.

———. *The Medieval Lyric.* London, 1968.

Huizinga, Johan. *The Waning of the Middle Ages.* Translated by F. Hopman. London, 1924.

Jackson, W. T. H. *The Literature of the Middle Ages.* New York, 1960.

Ker, W. P. *Epic and Romance.* London, 1897; repr. 1957.

Lewis, C. S. *The Discarded Image.* Cambridge, 1964.

Raby, F. J. E. *A History of Christian-Latin Poetry from the Beginnings to the Close of the Middle Ages.* 2 vols. 2d ed. Oxford 1953.

———. *A History of Secular Latin Poetry in the Middle Ages.* 2 vols. 2d ed. Oxford, 1957.

Robertson, D. W., Jr. *A Preface to Chaucer.* Princeton, 1962.

Vinaver, Eugene. *The Rise of Romance.* Oxford, 1971.

LITERARY HISTORY

FRANCE

Bec, Pierre. *La lyrique française au moyen âge (XIIe–XIIIe siècles): Contribution à une typologie des genres.* 2 vols. Paris, 1977–1978.

Dictionnaire des lettres françaises: Le moyen âge. Edited by Robert Bossuat, Louis Pichard, and Guy Raynaud de Lage. Paris, 1964.

Fox, John. *The Middle Ages.* (Vol. 1 of *A Literary History of France,* P. Charvet, ed.) London, 1974.

GERMANY

Bostock, John Knight. *A Handbook on Old High German Literature.* Oxford, 1976.

de Boor, Helmut, and Richard Newald, eds. *Geschichte der deutschen Literatur.* 5th ed. Vols. 2 and 3. Munich, 1962–1963.

Die deutsche Literatur des Mittelalters: Verfasserlexikon. Edited by Kurt Ruh et al. 2d ed. Berlin, 1978–.

Salmon, Paul. *Literature in Medieval Germany.* New York, 1967.

Sayce, Olive. *The Medieval German Lyric, 1150–1300.* Oxford, 1982.

ITALY

Emilio Cecchi and Natalino Sapegno, eds. *Storia della letteratura italiana.* 2 vols. (Rome, 1965).

SPAIN

Deyermond, A. D. *A Literary History of Spain: The Middle Ages.* New York, 1971.

THE RENAISSANCE

GENERAL HISTORIES

Aston, Margaret. *The Fifteenth Century: The Prospect of Europe.* London, 1968.

Braudel, Fernand. *The Mediterranean and the Mediterranean World in the Age of Philip II.* Translated by Sian Reynolds. 2 vols. London, 1973.

Burckhardt, Jakob. *The Civilization of the Renaissance in Italy.* Translated by S. G. C. Middlemore. Introduction by Benjamin Nelson and Charles Trinkhaus. New York, 1975.

Chadwick, Owen. *The Reformation.* London, 1964.

Dickens, A. G. *The Counter Reformation.* London, 1968.

———. *Reformation and Society in the Sixteenth Century.* London, 1966.

Ferguson, Wallace K. *The Renaissance.* New York, 1940.

Grimm, H. J. *The Reformation Era.* New York, 1965.

Hale, J. R. *Renaissance Europe, 1480–1520.* London, 1971.

Rice, Eugene. *The Foundations of Early Modern Europe, 1460–1559.* New York, 1971.

Rupp, E. G. *Patterns of Reformation.* London, 1969.

CULTURAL HISTORY

Ariès, Philippe. *The Hour of Our Death.* Translated by Helen Weaver. New York, 1981.

Bolgar, R. R. *The Classical Inheritance.* Cambridge, 1952.

Chartier, Roger. *History of Private Life.* Edited by Philippe Ariès and Georges Duby. Cambridge, Mass., 1989.

Chartier, Roger, ed. *The Passions of the Renaissance.* Translated by Arthur Goldhammer. (Vol. 3 of *A History of Private Life,* edited by Philippe Ariès and Georges Duby.) Cambridge, Mass., 1989.

Cohn, Norman. *The Pursuit of the Millennium.* London, 1970.

Eisenstein, Elizabeth L. *The Printing Press as an Agent of Change: Communications and Cultural Transformations in Early Modern Europe.* Cambridge, 1979.

Evenett, Henry Outram. *The Spirit of the Counter Reformation.* Cambridge, 1968.

Febvre, Lucien, and Henri-Jean Martin. *The Coming of the Book: The Impact of Printing.* Translated by David Gerard; edited by Geoffrey Nowell-Smith and David Wootton. London, 1976.

Kristeller, Paul O. *Renaissance Thought: The Classic, Scholastic, and Humanist Strains.* New York, 1961.

Panofsky, Erwin. *Renaissance and Renascences in Western Thought.* Stockholm, 1960.

Scaglione, Aldo D. *Nature and Love in the Late Middle Ages.* Berkeley, Calif., 1963.

Tayler, Edward W. *Nature and Art in Renaissance Literature.* New York and London, 1964.

Trinkaus, Charles. *In Our Image and Likeness: Humanity and Divinity in Italian Humanist Thought.* 2 vols. Chicago, 1970.

Weiss, Roberto. *The Renaissance Discovery of Classical Antiquity.* Oxford, 1969.

GENRES

Bowra, C. M. *From Virgil to Milton.* London and New York, 1945.

Grant, William Leonard. *Neo-Latin Literature and the Pastoral.* Chapel Hill, N.C., 1965.

Marinelli, Peter V. *Pastoral.* London, 1971.

Poggioli, Renato. *The Oaten Flute: Essays on Pastoral Poetry and the Pastoral Ideal.* Cambridge, Mass., 1975.

Radcliff-Umstead, Douglas. *The Birth of Modern Comedy in Renaissance Italy.* Chicago, 1969.

Romance: Generic Transformation from Chré-

tien de Troyes to Cervantes. Edited by Kevin Brownlee and Marina Scordilis Brownlee. Hanover, N.H., and London, 1985.

Toliver, Harold. *Pastoral Forms and Attitudes.* Berkeley, Calif., 1971.

NATIONAL LITERARY HISTORIES

FRANCE

Gundersheimer, Werner L., ed. *French Humanism, 1470–1600.* London, 1969.

MacFarlane, I. D. *Renaissance France, 1470–1589.* (Vol. 1, pt. 2, of *A Literary History of France,* edited by P. E. Charvet.) London and New York, 1974.

Sebatier, Robert. *Histoire de la poésie française.* 2 vols. Paris, 1975.

GERMANY

Salmon, Paul B. *Literature in Medieval Germany.* New York, 1967.

ITALY

Jannaco, Carmine, and Martino Capucci, *Il seicento,* 2d ed. (Vol. 7 of *Storia letteraria d'Italia.*) Milan, 1973.

Rossi, Vittorio. *Il quattrocento,* revised edition. (Vol. 6 of *Storia letteraria d'Italia.*) Milan, 1973.

Toffanin, Giuseppe. *Il cinquecento,* 7th ed., new printing. (Vol. 6 of *Storia letteraria d'Italia.*) Milan, 1973.

THE AGE OF REASON AND THE ENLIGHTMENT

GENERAL HISTORIES

Ashley, Maurice. *The Golden Century: Europe, 1598–1715.* New York and Washington, 1969.

Aston, Trevor, ed. *Crisis in Europe, 1560–1600.* London, 1965.

Braudel, Fernand. *Civilization and Capitalism, 15th–18th Centuries.* 3 vols. Translated by Sian Reynolds. New York, 1981–1984.

Clark, George. *The Seventeenth Century.* 2d ed. Oxford, 1947.

Ogg, David. *Europe in the Seventeenth Century.* London, 1960.

INTELLECTUAL HISTORY

Cassirer, Ernst. *The Philosophy of the Enlightenment.* Translated by Fritz C. A. Koelln and James P. Pettegrove. Princeton, 1951.

Febvre, Lucien. *Le problème de l'incroyance au 16e siècle.* Paris, 1942.

Gay, Peter. *The Enlightenment: An Interpretation.* 2 vols. New York, 1967–1969.

Havens, George R. *The Age of Ideas: From Reaction to Revolution in Eighteenth-Century France.* New York, 1955.

Hazard, Paul. *The European Mind, 1680–1715.* Translated by J. Lewis May. Cleveland and New York, 1963.

———. *European Thought in the Eighteenth Century.* Translated by J. Lewis May. Cleveland and New York, 1963.

Willey, Basil. *The Seventeenth-Century Background.* London, 1934.

———. *The Eighteenth-Century Background.* London, 1940.

CULTURAL HISTORY

Bazin, Germain. *The Baroque: Principles, Styles, Modes, Themes.* London, 1968.

Lough, John. *Writer and Public in France from the Middle Ages to the Present Day.* Oxford, 1978.

Martin, Henri-Jean. *Livre, pouvoirs et société à Paris au XVIIe siècle.* Paris and Geneva, 1969.

Martin, Henri-Jean, and Roger Chartier, eds. *Histoire de l'édition française,* vol. 1, *Le livre conquérant: Du moyen âge au milieu du XVIIe siècle.* Paris, 1982.

Skrine, Peter N. *The Baroque: Literature and Culture in Seventeenth-Century Europe.* New York, 1978.

Weinstein, Arnold, *Fictions of the Self, 1550–1800.* Princeton, 1981.

NATIONAL HISTORIES

FRANCE

Adam, Antoine. *Histoire de la littérature française au 18e siècle.* 5 vols. Paris, 1948–1956.

Brémond, Henri. *A Literary History of Religious Thought in France from the Wars of Religion down to Our Own Times.* Translated by K. L. Montgomery. 3 vols. New York, 1928–1936.

Lancaster, Henry Carrington. *A History of French Dramatic Literature in the Seventeenth Century.* 4 vols. Baltimore, 1929–1940.

———. *French Tragedy in the Time of Louis XV and Voltaire.* 2 vols. Baltimore, 1950.

Lough, John. *An Introduction to Seventeenth-Century France.* London, 1954.

Niklaus, Robert. *The Eighteenth Century, 1715–1789.* (Vol. 3 of *A Literary History of France,* edited by P. E. Charvet.) London and New York, 1970.

Sabatier, Robert. *Histoire de la poésie française.* Vols. 2–4. Paris, 1975.

Tapié, Victor-L. *France in the Age of Louis XIII and Richelieu.* Translated and edited by D. McN. Lockie. London, 1974.

Treasure, G. R. R. *Seventeenth-Century France.* Garden City, N.Y., 1967.

Yarrrow, P. J. *The Seventeenth Century, 1600–1715.* (Vol. 2 of *A Literary History of France,* edited by P. E. Charvet.) London and New York, 1967.

GERMANY

Hoffmeister, Gerhart, ed. *German Baroque Literature: The European Perspective.* New York, 1983.

Pascal, Roy. *German Literature in the Sixteenth and Seventeenth Centuries: Renaissance—Reformation—Baroque.* (Vol. 2 of *Introductions to German Literature,* edited by August Gross.) London and New York, 1968.

Stahl, Ernst L. *German Literature of the Eighteenth and Nineteenth Centuries.* (Vol. 3 of *Introductions to German Literature,* edited by August Gross.) London and New York, 1968.

ITALY

Jannaco, Carmine, and Martino Capucci. *Il seicento.* 2d ed. (Vol. 7 of *Storia letteraria d'Italia.*) Milan, 1973.

Mazzoni, Guido. *L'ottocento,* 2d ed. 2 vols. (Vol. 9 of *Storia letteraria d'Italia.*) Milan, 1973.

Natali, Giulio. *Il settecento,* 6th ed. 2 vols. (Vol. 8 of *Storia letteraria d'Italia.*) Milan, 1973.

SPAIN

Cook, John A. *Neo-Classic Drama in Spain: Theory and Practice.* Dallas, 1959.

THE ROMANTIC CENTURY

REFERENCE

Columbia Dictionary of Modern European Literature. Edited by J.-A. Bédé and W. B. Edgerton. Enlarged edition. New York, 1980.

Princeton Encyclopedia of Poetry and Poetics. Edited by Alex Preminger. Enlarged edition. Princeton, 1974.

ANTHOLOGIES

Anderson, Eugene Newton, ed. *Europe in the Nineteenth Century: A Documentary Analysis of Change and Conflict.* Indianapolis, 1961.

Hugo, Howard E., ed., *The Romantic Reader.* New York, 1957.

Wagner, Donald O. *Social Reformers: Adam Smith to John Dewey.* New York, 1939.

Weber, Eugen. *Paths to the Present: Aspects of European Thought From Romanticism to Existentialism.* New York, 1960.

Wilshire, Bruce, ed. *Romanticism and Evolution in the Nineteenth Century.* New York, 1968.

PERIODS

Abrams, M. H. *The Mirror and the Lamp.* New York, 1953.

Barzun, Jacques. *Classic, Romantic, and Modern.* Rev. ed. Chicago, 1975.

Bentley, Eric. *The Playwright as Thinker.* New ed. New York, 1980.

Bowle, John. *Politics and Opinion in the Nineteenth Century.* London, 1954.

Cassirer, Ernst. *Rousseau, Kant, Goethe.* Princeton, 1945.

Droz, Jacques. *Europe Between Revolutions: 1815–1848.* New York, 1967.

Ewen, Frederic. *Heroic Imagination: The Creative Genius of Europe from Waterloo to 1848.* New York, 1984.

Friedell, Egon. *A Cultural History of the Modern Age,* vol. 3. New York, 1953.

Frye, Northrop, ed. *Romanticism Reconsidered.* New York, 1963.

Garraty, John A., and Peter Gay, eds. *Columbia History of the World,* vol. 3. New York, 1972.

Geyl, Peter. *Napoleon: For and Against.* New Haven, Conn., 1949.

GENERAL BIBLIOGRAPHY

Gooch, G. P. *History and Historians in the Nineteenth Century.* New York, 1913.

Hayes, C. J. H. *Historical Evolution of Modern Nationalism.* New York, 1939.

Mackintosh, Hugh Ross. *Types of Modern Theology.* New Haven, Conn., 1937.

Merz, John Theodore. *A History of European Thought in the Nineteenth Century.* 4 vols. Edinburgh, 1907.

Neff, Emery E. *A Revolution in European Poetry: 1660–1900.* New York, 1940.

Royce, Josiah. *The Spirit of Modern Philosophy.* New ed. New York, 1955.

Troeltsch, Ernst. *Protestantism and Progress.* Translated by W. Montgomery. New York, 1958.

Wellek, René. *A History of Modern Criticism: 1750–1950,* vol. 2, *The Romantic Age.* New Haven, Conn., 1955.

Wright, Ernest Hunter. *The Meaning of Rousseau.* New York, 1929. Repr. 1963.

LITERARY HISTORIES

FRANCE

Dansette, Adrien. *A Religious History of Modern France.* New York, 1961.

Dickinson, G. Lowes. *Revolution and Reaction in Modern France.* London, 1892.

Finch, M. B., and E. A. Peers, *The Origins of French Romanticism.* London, 1920.

Robinson, Christopher. *French Literature in the Nineteenth Century.* New York, 1978. 1975.

Saintsbury, George. *A Short History of French Literature.* Oxford 1917.

GERMANY

Behler, Ernst. *The Philosophy of German Idealism.* New York, 1987.

Silz, Walter. *Early German Romanticism.* Cambridge, Mass., 1929.

Crosby, D. H., and G. C. Schoolfield, eds. *Studies in the German Drama.* Chapel Hill, N.C., 1974.

Waerner, Robert M. *Romanticism and the Romantic School in Germany.* New York, 1910.

Willoughby, L. A. *The Romantic Movement in Germany.* Oxford, 1930.

ITALY

Whitfield, John H. *A Short History of Italian Literature.* Rev. ed. New York, 1980.

POLAND

Krzyzanowski, Julian. *Polish Romantic Literature.* London, 1930.

RUSSIA

Lavrin, Janko. *Russian Writers: Their Lives and Literature.* New York, 1954.

Miliukov, Paul. *Outlines of Russian Culture,* part 2, *Literature.* Edited by Mikhail Karpovich. Philadelphia, 1942.

SPAIN

Peers, E. A. *The Romantic Movement in Spain: A Short History.* Liverpool, 1949. Repr. 1968.

GENRES AND ATTITUDES

Bate, Water Jackson. *From Classic to Romantic.* Cambridge, 1946.

Bishop, Lloyd. *Romantic Irony in French Literature from Diderot to Beckett.* Nashville, Tenn., 1989.

Praz, Mario. *The Romantic Agony.* 2nd ed. New York, 1954.

Snow, C. P. *The Realists.* New York, 1980.

Williams, Roger L. *The Horror of Life.* Chicago, 1980.

Stowe, William W. *Balzac, James, and the Realistic Novel.* New York, 1987.

Symons, Arthur. *The Symbolist Movement in Literature.* Rev. ed. New York, 1958.

THE OTHER ARTS

Barzun, Jacques. *Berlioz and the Romantic Century.* 3rd ed. 2 vols. New York, 1969.

Calvocoressi, Michael D. *Masters of Russian Music.* New York, 1936.

Gautier, Théophile. *The Romantic Ballet.* Translated by Cyril W. Beaumont. New York, 1932.

Gray, Cecil. *A History of Music.* New York 1935. Chapters 12–17.

Robinson, Paul. *Opera and Ideas: From Mozart to Strauss.* New York, 1985.

Schmidgall, Gary. *Literature as Opera.* New York, 1977.

Bernard, Bruce. *The Impressionist Revolution.* New York, 1986.

Myers, Bernard S. *Modern Art in the Making.* New York, 1950.

Holden, Angus. *Elegant Modes of the Nineteenth-Century Costume.* London, 1935.

THE TWENTIETH CENTURY

MODES AND THEMES

Booth, Wayne C. *A Rhetoric of Irony.* Chicago, 1974.

Poggioli, Renato. *The Theory of the Avant-Garde.* Translated by Gerald Fitzgerald. Cambridge, Mass., 1968.

Rosmarin, Adena. *The Power of Genre.* Minneapolis, Minn., 1985.

Szondi, Peter. *Theory of the Modern Drama.* Translated by Michael Hays. Minneapolis, Minn., 1987.

Williams, Raymond. *Marxism and Literature.* Oxford, 1977.

LITERARY STUDIES

GENERAL

Bradbury, Malcolm, and James McFarlane, eds. *Modernism: A Guide to European Literature, 1890–1930.* Harmondsworth, England, 1976.

Ellman, Richard, and Charles Feidelson, eds. *The Modern Tradition: Backgrounds of Modern Literature.* New York, 1965.

Esslin, Martin. *The Theatre of the Absurd.* Garden City, N. Y., 1961. Repr. 1987.

Encyclopedia of World Literature in the Twentieth Century. Edited by Leonard S. Klein. 4 vols. New York, 1981–1984.

Karl, Frederick H. *Modern and Modernism: The Sovereignty of the Artist, 1885–1925.* New York, 1988.

Rühle, Jürgen. *Literature and Revolution: A Critical Study of the Writer and Communism in the Twentieth Century.* Translated by Jean Steinberg. New York, 1969.

Russell, Charles. *Poets, Prophets, and Revolutionaries: The Literary Avant-Garde from Rimbaud Through Postmodernism.* New York, 1985.

Wellwarth, George E. *The Theater of Protest and Paradox: Developments in the Avant-Garde Drama.* New York, 1964. Repr. 1971.

Wilson, Edmund. *Axel's Castle: A Study in the Imaginative Literature of 1870 to 1930.* New York, 1931.

MOVEMENTS

Becker, G. J., ed. *Documents of Modern Literary Realism.* Princeton, 1963.

Bronner, Stephen E., and Douglas Kellner. *Passion and Rebellion: The Expressionist Heritage.* New York, 1988.

Culler, Jonathan. *Structuralist Poetics: Structuralism, Linguistics, and the Study of Literature.* Ithaca, N.Y., 1975.

Golding, John. *Cubism: A History and an Analysis, 1907–1914.* 3d rev. ed. Boston, 1988.

Hughes, Robert. *The Shock of the New.* New York, 1980.

Kurzweil, Edith. *The Age of Structuralism: Levi-Strauss to Foucault.* New York, 1980.

Lunn, Eugene. *Marxism and Modernism: An Historical Study of Lukács, Brecht, Benjamin, and Adorno.* Berkeley and Los Angeles, 1982.

Marcus, Steven. *Freud and the Culture of Psychoanalysis.* Boston, 1984.

Martin, Marianne. *Futurist Art and Theory.* Oxford, 1968.

Matthews, J. H. *Surrealism and the Novel.* University Park, Penn., 1966.

Motherwell, Robert, ed. *The Dada Painters and Poets.* New York, 1951. Repr. 1981.

Nadeau, Maurice. *The History of Surrealism.* Translated by Richard Howard. New York, 1965. Repr. 1989.

Perloff, Marjorie. *The Futurist Moment: Avant-Garde, Avant Guerre, and the Language of Rupture.* Chicago, 1986.

Richter, Hans. *Dada: Art and Anti-Art.* New York, 1966.

Wright, Elizabeth. *Psychoanalytic Criticism: Theory in Practice.* London, 1984.

INTELLECTUAL AND SOCIAL BACKGROUND

Anderson, Perry. *Considerations on Western Marxism.* London, 1976. Repr. 1987.

Carsten, F. L. *The Rise of Fascism.* Berkeley and Los Angeles, 1967. Repr. 1982.

Eksteins, Modris. *Rites of Spring: The Great War of the Twentieth Century.* New York, 1989.

Gay, Peter. *Weimar Culture: The Outsider as Insider.* New York, 1968.

Gay, Peter. *Freud, Jews, and Other Germans: Masters and Victims in Modernist Culture.* New York, 1978.

Hobsbawm, Eric. *The Age of Empire, 1875–1914.* New York, 1987.

Krauss, Rosalind E. *The Originality of the Avant-Garde and Other Modernist Myths.* Cambridge, Mass., 1985.

Lottman, Herbert. *The Left Bank: Writers, Art-*

ists, and Politics from the Popular Front to the Cold War. Boston, 1982.

Poster Mark. *Existential Marxism in Postwar France: Sartre to Althusser.* Princeton, 1975.

Schorske, Carl. *Fin-de-Siècle Vienna.* New York, 1980.

NATIONAL LITERARY HISTORIES

EASTERN EUROPE

Gerould, Daniel, ed. *Twentieth Century Polish Avant-Garde Drama.* Ithaca, N.Y., 1977.

Klaniczay, Tibor, ed. *History of Hungarian Literature.* Budapest, 1983.

Milosz, Czeslaw. *A History of Polish Literature.* Berkeley and Los Angeles, 1969. Reprinted 1983.

FRANCE

Auster, Paul, ed. *The Random House Book of Twentieth-Century French Poetry.* New York, 1982.

Brée, Germaine. *Twentieth-Century French Literature.* Translated by Louise Guiney. Chicago, 1983.

Brée, Germaine. *Women Writers in France.* New Brunswick, N.J., 1973.

Guicharnaud, Jacques. *Modern French Theater from Giraudoux to Beckett.* New Haven, Conn., 1961.

Raymond, Marcel. *From Baudelaire to Surrealism.* Rev. ed. New York, 1949.

Roudiez, Leon S. *French Fiction Today: A New Direction.* New Brunswick, N.J., 1972.

GERMANY

Bullivant, Keith, ed. *The Modern German Novel.* Leamington Spa, 1987.

Gray, Ronald. *The German Tradition in Literature, 1871–1945.* Cambridge, 1965.

Heller, Erich. *The Disinherited Mind: Essays in Modern German Literature and Thought.* New York, 1975.

Sokel, Walter H. *The Writer in Extremis: Expressionism in Twentieth-Century Literature.* Stanford, Calif., 1959.

ITALY

Gatt-Rutter, J. A. *Writers and Politics in Modern Italy.* London, 1978.

Pacifici, Sergio. *The Modern Italian Novel from Pea to Moravia.* Carbondale, Ill., 1979.

RUSSIA

Bowlt, John E. *Russian Art of the Avant-Garde: Theory and Criticism, 1902–1934.* New York, 1976.

Brown, Deming. *Soviet Russian Literature Since Stalin.* Cambridge, 1978.

Markov, Vladimir. *Russian Futurism: A History.* Berkeley and Los Angeles, 1968.

Maslennikov, Oleg. *Lyrics from the Russian: Symbolists and Others.* Berkeley and Los Angeles, 1968.

Poggioli, Renato. *The Poets of Russia, 1890–1930.* Cambridge, Mass., 1960.

SCANDINAVIA

Gustafson, Alrik. *Six Scandinavian Novelists.* New York, 1940.

Rossel, Sven H. *A History of Scandinavian Literature, 1870–1980.* Translated by Anne C. Ulmer. Minneapolis, Minn., 1982.

SPAIN

Butt, John. *Writers and Politics in Modern Spain.* New York, 1978.

Ilie, Paul. *The Surrealist Mode in Spanish Literature.* Ann Arbor, Mich., 1968.

Morris, C. B. *A Generation of Spanish Poets, 1920–1936.* Cambridge, 1971.

INDEX

USING THE INDEX

The index is chiefly designed to offer access to discussions of specific literary works and themes. Each title is listed beneath the name of its author in the linguistic form by which it is most commonly known today, whether this be the original (*Vita nuova, Die Meistersinger*) or a translation (*The Prince, Crime and Punishment*). In most cases, cross-references are provided for both the native and the translated form of the title: *New Life. See* Dante Alighieri, *Vita nuova.* Access is thereby made possible even when the author is not known. Where the European work has never actually appeared in English (as is the case with much modern literature), a translation is still provided for cross-referencing: Communication Vessels. See Cela, Camilo José, *Los vasos comunicantes.* Such "courtesy" translations, which are not italicized, facilitate access to critical discussions that are often unique in English.

Alphabetization is word by word: "À la fenêtre" precedes "Abendlied." In familiar tongues (the Romance languages, German, and Greek), definite and indefinite aritcles, as well as conjunctions and most prepositions, are ignored in the alphabetization and, where appropriate, inverted to the end: *Vasos comunicantes, Los.* However, in subentries the normal order is retained. Therefore the main Cela entry lists the preceding work under "L," as shown in the paragraph above. In other languages, the sort is according to the very first word, even when it is an article like the Russian "V" or the Hungarian "A." All major works are indexed by title; short stories and individual lyrics are indexed when there is a significant discussion in the text.

No attempt has been made to "analyze" or outline the thematic contents of the individual essays of *European Writers.* It is assumed that the reader interested primarily in Boccaccio or Tolstoy will simply turn to the appropriate article, guided either by the alphabetical listing herein, the chronological plan of the series itself, or the other outlines provided in the present volume. Themes, genres, and selected nonliterary persons and topics have been indexed, however, enabling the student of comparative literature to track sources and influences and to explore what different writers have said about love or death, God or the class structure—to the extent that such topics happen to be addressed in the individual essays.

A

"A. Blok." *See* Mandelshtam, Osip

"À Albert Dürer." *See* Hugo, Victor

À bas le progrès. *See* Goncourt, Edmond Louis Antoine de

"A békés eltávozás." *See* Ady, Endre

A bús férfi panaszai. *See* Kosztolányi, Dezső

"A chy ne iest' tse sami nakhvalky abo zh zapomorochennia vid uspikhov." *See* Tychyna, Pavlo, *Chernihiv*

A concilio dentro en Roma, the Cid epic and, 1:133a

A Dačice Tale. *See* Hašek, Jaroslav, "Historie dačicka"

"A Duna vallomása." *See* Ady, Endre

"A fekete zongora." *See* Ady, Endre

"À Gare de l'Est-en." *See* Ady, Endre

"A Halál rokona." *See* Ady, Endre

"A Halál-tó fölött." *See* Ady, Endre

A halottak élén. *See* Ady, Endre

"A harcunkat megharcoltuk." *See* Ady, Endre

"A Hortobágy poétája." *See* Ady, Endre

"A José María Palacio." *See* Machado, Antonio, *Campos de Castilla*

"A könnyek asszonya." *See* Ady, Endre

"A krisztusok martirja." *See* Ady, Endre

"À la fenêtre, pendant la nuit." *See* Hugo, Victor

"À la Feuille de Rose, Maison Turque" ("At the Rose Leaf, Turkish Brothel"). *See* Maupassant, Guy de

"À la grande nuit, ou le bluff surréaliste." *See* Artaud, Antonin

"À la musique." *See* Rimbaud, Arthur

À la recherche du temps perdu. *See* Proust, Marcel, *Remembrance of Things Past*

"À l'automobile." *See* Marinetti, Filippo Tommaso

A lélek és s formák. *See* Lukács, György

"A lelki szegénységről." *See* Lukács, György

"À l'Italie." *See* Apollinaire, Guillaume

À l'ombre des jeunes filles en fleurs. *See* Proust, Marcel, *Remembrance of Things Past (À la recherche du temps perdu)*, *Within a Budding Grove*

"A Luigia Pallavicini." *See* Foscolo, Ugo

"A magunk szerelme." *See* Ady, Endre

"A magyar Messiások." *See* Ady, Endre

"A magyar ugaron." *See* Ady, Endre

"A megszépitő fátuma." *See* Ady, Endre

A modern dráma fejlődésének története. *See* Lukács, György

A Mölna Elegy. *See* Ekelöf, Gunnar

"À mon Pegase." *See* Marinetti, Filippo Tommaso, "À l'automobile"

"A nagy cethalhoz." *See* Ady, Endre

"A nagy pénztárnok." *See* Ady, Endre

"À propos de Beckett." *See* Ionesco, Eugène, *Antidotes*

A quale tribù appartieni? *See* Moravia, Alberto, *Which Tribe Do You Belong To?*

"A qualunque animale alberga in terra." *See* Petrarch, *Canzoniere*

À quoi rêvent les jeunes filles. *See* Musset, Alfred de

À rebours. *See* Huysmans, Joris Karl

A rossz orvos. *See* Kosztolányi, Dezső

"À sa maîtresse." *See* Ronsard, Pierre de

"A sárga láng." *See* Ady, Endre

"A Satana" ("To Satan"). *See* Carducci, Giosue

"A se stesso." *See* Leopardi, Giacomo, "To Himself"

A secreto agravio secreta venganza. *See* Calderón de la Barca, Pedro, *For a Secret Offense, a Secret Revenge*

A Sibilla. *See* Quasimodo, Salvatore

"A Silvia." *See* Leopardi, Giacomo, "To Sylvia"

"A Szajna partján." *See* Ady, Endre

A szegény kisgyermek panaszai. *See* Kosztolányi, Dezső

"A Tisza-parton." *See* Ady, Endre

A tíz legszebb. *See* Kosztolányi, Dezső

A Toll (The Pen) (journal), Ady's poetry and, 10:1244b

À travers chants. *See* Berlioz, Hector

"À travers l'Europe." *See* Apollinaire, Guillaume, *Calligrammes*

"À très bientôt." *See* Sarraute, Nathalie, *L'Usage de la parole*

"A vár fehér asszonya." *See* Ady, Endre

A varászlo halála. *See* Csáth, Géza

À vau-l'eau

À vau-l'eau. See Huysmans, Joris Karl
"A vén csavargó." *See* Ady, Endre
"A vén faun üzenete." *See* Ady, Endre
A véres költő. See Kosztolányi, Dezső
"À Zurbarán." *See* Gautier, Théophile
"Ab la dolchor." *See* William IX of Aquitaine, duke
Abandoned Pirate Ships. *See* Ady, Endre, "Az elhagyott kalóz-hajók"
Abba, Marta, Pirandello and, 8:394b, 395a
Abbatucci, Marie, Edmond Goncourt and, 7:1413b
"Abbé Aubain, L'" ("Abbot Aubain"). *See* Mérimée, Prosper
"Abbot and the Learned Lady, The." *See* Erasmus
Abel. See Alfieri, Vittorio
Abel (O.T. character), Nerval and, 6:951b, 953b
Abel Sanchez. See Unamuno, Miguel de
Abélard, Peter, 1:406a
   in Gottfried's *Tristan,* 1:253a
   Sic et non (*Yes and No*), 1:406b–407a
"Abelard und Heloise." *See* Richter, Jean Paul
Abencerraje. See Montemayor, Jorge de, *Los siete libros de la Diana*
"Abendland." *See* Trakl, Georg, "The Occident"
"Abendlied." *See* Keller, Gottfried
Abendstunde im Spätherbst. See Dürrenmatt, Friedrich, *Incident at Twilight*
Abenteuer des Don Sylvio von Rosalva, Die. See Wieland, Christoph Martin
Abenteurer und die Sängerin, Der. See Hofmannsthal, Hugo von
"Abhandlung Eden." *See* Wedekind, Frank
Ability to Mourn, The. *See* Böll, Heinrich, *Die Fähigkeit zu trauern*
Abindarraez y Jarifa, Montemayor's *Diana* and, 2:923a
Aboard the Aquitaine. See Simenon, Georges, *45° à l'ombre*
"About an Interlocutor." *See* Mandelshtam, Osip, "Osobesednike"
"About Holy Church." *See* Rutebeuf, "De Sainte Église"
"About Love." *See* Chekhov, Anton, "O lyubvi"

About Myself. *See* Böll, Heinrich, "Über mich selbst"
Above the Barriers. See Pasternak, Boris
Above Death Lake. *See* Ady, Endre, "A Halál-tó fölött"
"Above God's Best Creation." *See* Blok, Alexander, "Nad luchshim sozdaniem bozh'im"
Abraham, Karl, Freud and, 8:4a
Abraham (O.T. patriarch)
   in Kierkegaard's *Fear and Trembling,* 6:1137b–1138a
   in Mann's *Joseph and His Brothers,* 9:731b
   in Prudentius' *Psychomachia,* 1:5a
Abraxas (Gnostic deity), in *Demian,* 9:840b, 843b, 844b
Abrégé de l'art poétique françois. See Ronsard, Pierre de
Abruzzi, in D'Annunzio's writings, 8:177a, 179b–180a, 189b, 196b
"Absage." *See* Hesse, Hermann
Absence, An. *See* Ginzburg, Natalia, "Un'assenza"
Absence, image of, Mallarmé, 7:1570a–1571a
"Absentia animi." *See* Ekelöf, Gunnar
"Absolon boldog szégyene" (Absolom's Happy Disgrace). *See* Ady, Endre
Absolute at Large, The. See Čapek, Karel, *Továrna na absolutno*
Absolute Love. *See* Jarry, Alfred, *L'Amour absolu*
Absolutism
   doctrine of, attacked in La Bruyère's *Caractères,* 3:248a-b
   Kleist and, 5:293a
Abstemius, La Fontaine and, 3:92b–93a
Absurd
   Hamsun's use of, 8:28a
   in Schnitzler's works, 8:107a
Absurd, theater of the
   Artaud and, 11:2067b
   Ghelderode and, 11:2113b
   Gombrowicz and, 12:2584b–2586a
   Ionesco and, 13:3016b–3017a, 3017b
   Marinetti and, 9:822a
   see also Witkiewicz, Stanisław Ignacy
Absurdism

Aymé and, 12:2438b
Baroja's *Paradox, King* and, 9:600b–601a
Camus and, 13:3058a–3067a
Grass and, 13:3366a–3367a
Sartre and, 12:2590b
"Abyss, The." *See* Baudelaire, Charles
Abyss, The. See Yourcenar, Marguerite,
    L'Oeuvre au noir
Académie Française
    Augier and, 7:1917b
    Boileau and, 3:180a
    Claudel and, 8:487b, 488b
    Corneille and, 3:27a, 27b
      indictment of *Le Cid*, 3:178b
    Fénelon and, 3:269a
    founded, 3:26a
    Hugo's election to, 6:704b
    La Bruyère and, 3:230b–231a, 232b
    La Fontaine and, 3:77b
    La Rochefoucauld and, 3:68a
    Musset and, 6:1000b, 1031a
    Valéry and, 8:584a
    Vigny's admission to, 5:479b
    Yourcenar and, 12:2535a–2536a
Academy of Fine Arts (France). *See* Institut
"Academy of Pataphysics," 13:3004a
Academy, Platonic. *See* Platonic Academy
"Acathist Hymn," 13:2971b
Accademia d'Italia, Marinetti and, 9:826b
Accession, The. *See* Pascoli, Giovanni,
    "L'Avvento"
Acción Popular, Lorca's death and, 11:2200b
According to Dürer. *See* Yourcenar,
    Marguerite, *La mort conduit l'attelage*
According to Greco. *See* Yourcenar,
    Marguerite, *La mort conduit l'attelage*
According to Rembrandt. *See* Yourcenar,
    Marguerite, *Comme l'eau qui coule*
Account of a Journey from Paris to Limousin.
    See La Fontaine, Jean de, *Relation d'un
    voyage de Paris en Limousin*
Account of Quietism. See Bossuet, Jacques
    Bénigne, *Relation sur le quiétism*
Acero de Madrid, El. See Lope de Vega, *Steel
    in Madrid*
Achard, Marcel, 7:1923a
Achilles, in Kleist, 5:300a-b

Acmeism
    Akhmatova and, 10:1522b, 1523a
    Gumilyov's definition of, 10:1522b, 1632b
    Mandelshtam and, 10:1624b, 1632a–1635a
    moral position of, 10:1539b
    nature of, 10:1524b, 1633b–1634a
    political persecution against, 10:1639b
    symbolists and, 10:1522b–1523a, 1539b
Acquainted with the Night. See Böll, Heinrich,
    And Never Said a Word
Acque e terre. See Quasimodo, Salvatore,
    Waters and Lands
"Across Europe." *See* Apollinaire, Guillaume,
    Calligrammes, "À travers l'Europe"
Across the Fields of Song. *See* Berlioz, Hector,
    À travers chants
Acrostic, Gottfried's use of, 1:247a-b
Act of Passion. See Simenon, Georges, *Lettre à
    mon juge*
Act Without Words I. See Beckett, Samuel
Acta Augustana. See Luther, Martin
Acting
    Diderot on, 4:494a-b
    Lessing on, 4:547b
    profession of
      in France and England, 4:372b
      Maeterlinck on, 8:130b–131b
Action
    futurist art as, 9:809b, 811b
    Nietzsche on, 9:813a
    Robbe-Grillet and, 13:3238a-b
    thought and, in Valéry's *Dance and the
    Soul*, 8:586b
Action Française
    Céline's involvement in, 11:1862a
    Roman Catholic Church and, 13:3238a
"Actor, The." *See* Gautier, Théophile, "Deux
    acteurs pour un rôle"
"Actor and the Workman, The." *See*
    Mandelshtam, Osip, "Akter i Rabochii"
Actor's Exit, The. *See* Ghelderode, Michel de,
    Sortie de l'acteur
Acts of the Apostles, The. See Gréban, Simon
Actuelles: Chroniques. See Camus, Albert
"Ad fontem Arculi." *See* Dorat, Jean

Ad Henricum Angliae regem epistola de vita et gestis Guidubaldi Urbini Ducis. *See* Castiglione, Baldesar

Ad Nepotianum. See Jerome, Saint

"Ad se ipsum." *See* Petrarch

Adages. See Erasmus

Adagiorum chiliades. See Erasmus, *Adages*

Adagiorum collectanea. See Erasmus, *Adages*

Aðalhending, in *dróttkvæt* stanzas, 1:378b

Adam. See Böll, Heinrich, *Wo warst du, Adam*

Adam, Adolphe, *Giselle*, Heine's influence on, 5:506a

Adam of Bremen, *History*, 1:381b

Adam the Creator. See Čapek, Karel, *Adam stvořitel*

Adam de la Halle, 1:458b–461a

   Jeu de la feuillée, 1:457a, 459b–460a, 460b

   Jeu de Robin et Marion (Play of Robin and Marion), 1:457a, 459a, 460b–461a

   parody of *Chanson d'Audigier* in, 1:89b

"Ádám hol vagy?" *See* Ady, Endre

Adam, Juliette, *Mes souvenirs*, 8:572b

Adam (O.T. character)

   in Kleist, 5:297b–298a

   in Klopstock's verse, 4:520b–522a

   in poetry of Laforgue, 7:1903b

   see also Old Testament, Eden myth

Adam, One Afternoon, and Other Stories. See Calvino, Italo

Adam in Paradise. See Ortega y Gasset, José, "Adán en el paraíso"

Adam, Paul

   Machado and, 9:750a

   Marinetti and, 9:805b

Adam stvořitel. See Čapek, Karel

Adamov, Arthur

   Anouilh and, 13:2844b

   Artaud aided by, 11:1978b–1979a

   Strindberg and, 7:1732a, 1754a

Adams, John Quincy, and Wieland, 4:605a

"Adán en el paraíso." *See* Ortega y Gasset, José

"Add nekem a szemeidet." *See* Ady, Endre

Addison, Joseph, 9:711a

   on Boileau, 3:180a-b

   Klopstock and, 4:533a-b

   Richter and, 5:58b

"Adebar." *See* Grass, Günter, *Gleisdreieck*

Adelard of Bath, 1:408a

Adenet le Roi, *chansons de geste* of, 1:109b–110a

"¡Adentro!" *See* Unamuno, Miguel de

Aderfofádes, I. See Kazantzakis, Nikos

Adieu. See Balzac, Honoré de

"Adieu." *See* Rimbaud, Arthur

"Adieu du cavalier, L'." *See* Apollinaire, Guillaume

"Adieu ma terre ronde." *See* Queneau, Raymond, *L'Instant fatal*

Adler, A. P., Kierkegaard and, 6:1125b

Adler, Alfred, Freud and, 8:4a, 13a

"Admonition to the Italian Powers." *See* Alfieri, Vittorio

Admonitions for Peace on the Twelve Articles. See Luther, Martin

Adolescence

   in Kundera, 13:3402a–3403a

   Mauriac and, 10:1308a–1310a

   in Moravia's works, 12:2680b–2681b

   sexuality and, in Colette's *The Ripening Seed*, 9:631a–633a

   in Wedekind's *Spring's Awakening*, 8:237a–239b

Adolescent d'autrefois, Un. See Mauriac, François, *Maltaverne*

Adolphe. Anecdote trouvée dans les papiers d'un inconnu et publiée par M. B. C. (*Adolphe: An Anecdote Found Amoung the Papers of an Unknown Person and Published by M. Benjamin de Constant*). *See* Constant, Benjamin, *Adolphe*

Adonis. See La Fontaine, Jean de

Adorable Clio. See Giraudoux, Jean

Adornment of Spiritual Marriage, The. See Ruysbroeck, Jan van

Adorno, Theodor

   Ästhetische Theorie (*Aesthetic Theory*), 10:1422a

   on Benjamin's works, 11:1725b–1726a

   on "homeland," 8:522a

   on Trakl, 10:1422a-b

"Über den Fetischcharakter in der Musik und die Regression des Hörers" ("On the Fetish-Character in Music and the Regression of Listening"), 11:1726a-b

Adrienne Lecouvreur. See Scribe, Eugène

Adultera, L'. See Fontane, Theodor

"Adulterous Woman, The." See Vigny, Alfred Victor de, Poèmes antiques et modernes

Adultery
in Chrétien's poems, 1:146b
in D'Annunzio's The Intruder, 8:182a–183b
Dumas fils and, 7:1917b
in Feydeau's plays, 7:1924b
Gottfried and, 1:240b–241b
in Maupassant's works, 7:1769b–1770a, 1772a, 1777a
Pérez Galdós on, 7:1611b–1613a
in Schnitzler's works, 8:92b, 93b–94a, 95a-b, 97a, 103b–104a
see also Flaubert, Gustave, Madame Bovary; Tolstoy, Leo, Anna Karenina

Advancement of Learning. See Bacon, Francis

Advantages of Windfowl, The. See Grass, Günter, Die Vorzüge der Windhühner

Advent. See Gunnarsson, Gunnar; Strindberg, August

Adventure, in Lermontov's works, 6:1218b

"Adventure of a Nearsighted Man, The." See Calvino, Italo

Adventure story technique, in Baroja, 9:594a, 604b–605a

Adventurer and the Singer, The. See Hofmannsthal, Hugo von, Der Abenteurer und die Sängerin

Adventurer's Beginnings, An. See Mérimée, Prosper, Débuts d'un aventurier

Adventures. See Goldoni, Carlo

Adventures of Cornelius Nightly, The. See Kosztolányi, Dezső, Esti Kornél kalandjai

Adventures of Don Sylvio of Rosalva, The. See Wieland, Christoph Martin, Die Abenteuer des Don Sylvio von Rosalva

Adventures, Inventions, and Mystifications of Silvestre Paradox. See Baroja, Pío, Aventuras, inventos, y mixtificaciones de Silvestre Paradox

Adventures of Jérôme Bardini. See Giraudoux, Jean, Aventures de Jérôme Bardini

Adventures of M. Robert Chevalier, Call'd De Beauchêne, Captain of Privateers in New-France, The. See Lesage, Alain-René, Les aventures de M. Robert Chevalier, dit de Beauchêne, capitaine de flibustiers

Adventures, Pranks, Tricks, Visions and Dreams of the Great Combat Pilot, Traveler, Showman and Magician Till Eulenspiegel, The. See Hauptmann, Gerhart, Des grossen Kampffliegers . . .

Adventures of Telemachus, Son of Ulysses, The. See Fénelon, François de Salignac de la Mothe-, Les aventures de Télémaque, fils d'Ulysse

Advertisement, The. See Ginzburg, Natalia

"Advice to a Young Author." See Wieland, Christoph Martin, "Briefe an einen jungen Dichter"

Ady, Endre, 9:859a–880b
"A békés eltávozás" (Peaceful Departure), 9:879a
"A Duna vallomása" (The Confession of the River Danube), 9:873a
"A fekete zongora" (The Black Piano), 9:862b–863a
"À Gare de l'Est-en" (At the Gare de L'Est), 9:872a
"A Halál rokona" (The Kinsman of Death), 9:861b–862a, 876b
"A Halál-tó fölött" (Above Death Lake), 9:865a
A halottak élén (Leading the Dead), 9:871b, 879b
"A harcunkat megharcoltuk" (We Fought Our Fight), 9:865b–866a
"A Hortobágy poétája" (The Poet of the Hortobágy), 9:865a-b
"A könnyek asszonya" (The Lady of Tears), 9:867b, 868b
"A krisztusok martirja" (Martyr of Many Christs), 9:868a
"A magunk szerelme" (Love of Ourselves), 9:870b

Ady, Endre

Ady, Endre (cont.)

"A magyar Messiások" (The Hungarian Messiahs), 9:863b, 876a

"A magyar ugaron" (The Hungarian Fallow), 9:865a, 865b

"A megszépitő fátuma" (The Fate of the Embellisher), 9:874a

"A nagy cethalhoz" (To the Giant Whale), 9:860b

"A nagy pénztárnok" (The Grand Cashier), 9:861b, 862b

"A sárga láng" (The Yellow Flame), 9:874b

"A Szajna partján" (Along the Seine), 9:872a

"A Tisza-parton" (On the Tisza River), 9:863a-b, 878a

"A vár fehér asszonya" (The White Woman of the Fort), 9:867a

"A vén csavargó" (The Old Tramp), 9:877a

"A vén faun üzenete" (Message of an Aged Faun), 9:867b–868a, 870a

"Absolon boldog szégyene" (Absolom's Happy Disgrace), 9:868a

"Add nekem a szemeidet" (Give Me Your Eyes), 9:868b–869a

"Akiknek dajkája vagyok" (Those Whose Wet Nurse I Am), 9:878b

"Akit ën csókolok" (Those Whom I Kiss), 9:876a

"Álmom: Az Isten" (My Dream-God), 9:861a

"Az anyám és én" (My Mother and I), 9:862b

"Az elhagyott kalóz-hajók" (Abandoned Pirate Ships), 9:875b

"Az eltévedt lovas" (The Lost Horseman), 9:877a

"Az én két asszonyom" (My Two Women), 9:869a

"Az én koporsó paripám" (My Coffin-Stallion), 9:875b–876a

"Az értől az oceanig" (From the Brook Ér to the Ocean), 9:878b

Az Illés szekerén (In Elijah's Chariot), 9:877a, 877b

"Az Ös Kaján" (The Ancient Demon), 9:876b

"Az utolsó hajók" (The Last Ships), 9:875b

"Az utolsó mosoly" (The Last Smile), 9:876a

"Bihar vezér földjén" (On the Land of the Tribal Leader Bihar), 9:868b

"Borz báró esete" (The Case of Baron Borz), 9:863b–864a

"Bugnak a tárnák" (The Caves Are Roaring), 9:878a

"Csónak a Holt Tengeren" (Boat on the Dead Sea), 9:868b

"Csukott szemű csókok" (Kisses Kissed with Closed Eyes), 9:869a-b

"Egy ismerös kisfiú" (A Little Boy I Know), 9:868a

"Egy ócska konflisban" (In an Old Hansom), 9:867b

"Egy párisi hajnalon" (A Parisian Dawn), 9:871b, 877b

"Éjszakai Isten" (The Night-God), 9:861a

"El a faluból" (Away from the Village), 9:878a

"Elbocsátó szép üzenet" (A Kind Message of Dismissal), 9:870b

"Elfogyni az ölelésben" (To Be Consumed by Embraces), 9:861b, 869b

"Elillant évek szőlőhegyén" (In the Vineyard of Bygone Years), 9:878a

"Elindult egy leány" (A Girl Set Out), 9:869b

"Este a Bois-ban" (An Evening in the Bois), 9:871b

"Fekete hold éjszakája" (The Night of the Black Moon), 9:869a

"Futás a Gond elöl" (Flight from Worries), 9:862b

"Góg és Magóg" (Son of Gog and Magog), 9:876b–877a

"Ha fejem lehajtom" (When My Head I Rest), 9:878b

"Ha holtan találkozunk" (When Dead, We Meet), 9:867a

"Hare a Nagyúrral" (Battle with the Swine-Headed Lord), 9:861a, 861b

"Heine úr lovagol" (Master Heinrich Goes for a Ride), 9:862a

"Hiába hideq a hold" (In Vain Is the Moon Cold), 9:866b–867a

"Hiába kisértesz hófehéren" (In Vain You Haunt Me Whitely, Like Snow), 9:867b

"Hunyhat a máglya" (Let the Fires Die out), 9:867a

"Ifjú karok kikötőjében" (In the Harbor of Young Arms), 9:875b

"Ima Baál Istenhez" (Praying to God Baal), 9:877b

"Isten a vigasztalan" (The Cheerless God), 9:861a

"Jöjj, Léda, megölellek" (Come, Leda, Let Me Embrace You), 9:868b, 870a

"Judás és Jézus" (Judas and Jesus), 9:877a

"Költözés Átok-városból" (Moving Away from Curse-City), 9:876a

"Korán jöttem ide" (I Arrived Too Early), 9:877a

Kosztolányi and, 10:1233b–1234a, 1237a, 1244b

Krleža and, 11:1811a

"Lázár a palota elött" (Lazarus in Front of the Palace), 9:876a

"Léda ajkai között" (Between Leda's Lips), 9:868b

"Léda a kertben" (Leda in the Garden), 9:868b

"Léda Párisba készül" (Leda Is Leaving for Paris), 9:871b

"Lédával a Tavaszban" (With Leda in the Spring), 9:868b

"Lelkek a pányván" (Tethered Souls), 9:878a

"Lótusz" (Lotus), 9:863a

"Magyar jakobinus dala" (Song of a Hungarian Jacobine), 9:860a-b

"Mammom szerzetes zsoltára" (The Psalm of the Monk of Mammon), 9:862b

"Maradhatsz és szerethetsz" (You May Remain and Love Me), 9:869a

"Margita élni akar" (Margita Wants to Live), 9:872b, 873a-b

"Mária és Veronika" (Mary and Veronica), 9:869a

"Mátyás bolond diákja" (Matthias' Demented Scholar), 9:863b

"Megcsókolom Csók-kisasszonyt" (I Shall Kiss the Girl of Kisses), 9:869b

"Megöltem egy pillangot" (I Killed a Butterfly), 9:876a

"Mert engem szeretsz" (Because You Love Me), 9:867a

"Midász király sarja" (The Descendant of King Midas), 9:878a

"Miért is tettem?" (Why Have I Done It?), 9:873a

"Mihályi Rozália csókja" (The Kiss of Rosalie Mihalyi), 9:875a

"Ne lássatok meg!" (Do Not See Me!), 9:878a

"Nekünk Mohács kell" (We Need Mohács), 9:865a

"O fajtám vére" (Blood of My Race), 9:871a

"Örök harc és nász" (Eternal War and Nuptial), 9:868a

"Páris az én Bakonyom" (Paris Is My Bakony Mountain), 9:876b

"Párisba beszökött az ősz" (Autumn Slipped into Paris), 9:872a

"Pénz és karnevál" (Money and Carnival), 9:862b

"Régi énekek ekhója" (Echoes of Old Songs), 9:865a

"Rózsaliget a pusztán" (Rose Garden in the Desert), 9:877a

"Sirni, sirni, sirni" (To Weep, to Weep, to Weep), 9:875a

"Szent Junius hivása" (Saint June Is Calling), 9:868b

"Szeretném, ha szeretnének" (I Desire to Feel Loved), 9:866b

"Tüzes seb vagyok" (I Am a Burning Wound), 9:867b

"Üdvözlet a győzőnek" (Hail to the Conqueror), 9:879a

Új versek (New Poems), 9:859b, 10:1233b
   Lukács and, 10:1254b

"Új vizeken járok" (Departing for New Waters), 9:877b, 878b

"Ülök az asztal-trónon" (I Sit on the Tabletop Throne), 9:878a

"Uram, ostorozz meg" (God, Flog Me), 9:860b

"Vajjon milyennek láttál" (How Did You See Me?), 9:871a

"Valamikor lyányom voltál" (Long Ago, You Were My Daughter), 9:868a-b

"Várom a másikat" (I Am Waiting For the Other), 9:869a

Ady, Endre (*cont.*)
  Vér és arany (Blood and Gold), 9:862a, 862b
  "Vizió a lápon" (Vision on the Marsh),
    9:878a
  "Vörös szekér a tengeren" (Red Chariot on
    the Sea), 9:864a
  "Zúg-Zeng a jégcimbalom" (The
    Ice-Cimbalon Rings and Clangs),
    9:873a
Adynaton, in Prudentius' *Cathemerinon*, 1:19b
Aegean Sea, Elytis and, 13:2957a, 2985a
Aeneid. *Sec* Vergil (Publius Vergilius Maro)
Aereopoesia, 9:827a, 827b
"Aerial Ways." *See* Pasternak, Boris, *Rasskazy*
    (*Stories*)
Aero-Poem on the Gulf of La Spezia, The. See
    Marinetti, Filippo Tommaso,
    L'Aereopoema del golfo dell Spezia
Aeschylus
  Oresteia, 9:1053b–1054a, 12:2549b
    Iphigenia in Tauris and, 5:12a, 12b
  Prometheus Bound, 9:684a
    Giraudoux and, 9:1060b
  translated by Claudel, 8:476a, 489a
Aesop
  fables. *See* Fables, Aesopian
  La Fontaine's *Fables* and, 3:76b, 80b
  Vigny compared to, 5:455b
Aesthetic autonomy
  of Rilke, 9:768b, 769a
  see also Art-for-art's-sake principle
Aesthetic Culture. *See* Lukács, György,
    Esztétikai kultúra
Aesthetic idealism. *See* Idealism, aesthetic
Aesthetic Letters. *See* Schiller, Friedrich von
*Aesthetic as Science of Expression and
    General Linguistic. See* Croce,
    Benedetto, *Estetica come scienza
    dell'espressione e linguistica generale*
Aesthetic Theory. See Adorno, Theodor,
    Ästhetische Theorie
Aestheticism
  Baroja and, 9:592b, 593b–594b
  in Olesha's works, 11:2249b–2250a
  of Robbe-Grillet, 13:3085b–3086a
Aesthetics
  of Benjamin, 11:1708b–1709a, 1728b–1729a

Böll's "aesthetic of the humane," 13:3173a
Brecht's left-wing, 11:2090a
Butor's, 13:3289a–3290a
Croce on, 8:318a–319b, 325a-b
Diderot and, 4:487a–489a
futurist, of Khlebnikov, 10:1335b
Genet and, 13:2866a, 2868b–2869a, 2870a-b,
    2871a-b, 2888a, 2889a, 2891b
Kierkegaard and, 6:1134b–1137a, 1141a-b
of *La lámpara maravillosa*, 8:333a-b
Lessing's influence on, 4:545b–546b
of Mallarmé, 7:1574b–1575b, 1576a–1578a,
    1591a–1592a
Marxist, 11:2104b, 2105a
of music, Schopenhauer's contribution to,
    5:412a–414a
pessimism and, 13:3026a-b
of Pessoa, 10:1475b–1476a
in Richter's *Walt and Vult*, 5:75b
Sartre and, 12:2597a–2599b
of Schiller, 5:38a–39b
Schopenhauer's denial of will and,
    5:411b–412a
sexuality as, in fiction of Simon, 13:3026b
Stalinist, 11:2090a
symbolist, George and, 8:450b
Vico and, 8:325a-b
see also Art, philosophy of; Beauty;
    Boileau-Despréaux, Nicolas, *Art
    poétique*; Poetics
Aeterni patri. See Leo XIII, Pope
Af Uggi Greipssons Optegnelser. See
    Gunnarsson, Gunnar, *Kirken paa
    Bjerget*
Afanismos tis Milos, O. See Ritsos, Yannis
Affetti di un disperato. See Vico, Giovanni
    Battista
Afham, William. *See* Kierkegaard, Søren
Africa
  in Céline, 11:1869b–1870a
  Dinesen and, 10:1286a-b, 1288a–1289b,
    1292b–1293a
  Marinetti and, 9:805a
Africa. See Petrarch
African Guest, The. See Zamyatin, Yevgeny
    Ivanovich, *Afrikanskii gost'*
African Love. See Mérimée, Prosper

African Walks. *See* Moravia, Alberto, *Passeggiate africane*

"Afrika" (Africa). *See* Zamyatin, Yevgeny Ivanovich

Afrikanskii gost'. See Zamyatin, Yevgeny Ivanovich

"After Death." *See* Turgenev, Ivan, "Klara Milich"

"After the Deluge." *See* Rimbaud, Arthur

"After a Flight." *See* Montale, Eugenio, *Satura*

After the Play. See Gogol, Nikolay Vasilievich

"After a Reading of Dante." *See* Hugo, Victor, "Après une lecture de Dante"

After Russia. *See* Tsvetaeva, Marina, *Posle Rossii*

"After Twelve Years." *See* Blok, Alexander, "Cherez dvenadtsat' let"

Afterlife. *See* Immortality

Afternoon. *See* Machado, Antonio, *Soledades* (Solitudes), "Tarde"

Afternoon of a Faun. See Mallarmé, Stéphane, *L'Après-midi d'un faune*

"Afterward." *See* Montale, Eugenio, *The Storm and Other Things* (*La bufera e altro*), "Dopo"

"Afterword." *See* Akhmatova, Anna, *Poem Without a Hero*

Aftonland. See Lagerkvist, Pär

"Aftonvandring." *See* Södergran, Edith

"Aftopsia, I." *See* Elytis, Odysseus, *Exi kai mia tipsis yia ton ourano*

Afuera, afuera, Rodrigo, Sancho II y cerco de Zamora as source of, 1:132b

"Against *Amore* and Parliamentarism." *See* Marinetti, Filippo Tommaso, "Contro l'amore e il parlamentarismo"

Against the Assailants of God. See Aquinas, Thomas, St., *Contra impugnantes Dei cultum et religionem*

Against the Doctrine of Defection from the Religious Life. See Aquinas, Thomas, St., *Contra doctrinam retrahentium a religione*

Against the Errors of the Greeks. See Aquinas, Thomas, St., *Contra errores Graecorum*

Against the Grain. See Huysmans, Joris Karl, *À rebours*

Against the Heavenly Prophets. See Luther, Martin

Against Latomus. See Luther, Martin

Against Lying. See Augustine, St., *Contra mendacium*

Against the Papacy at Rome, Founded by the Devil. See Luther, Martin

"Against Past-Loving Venice." *See* "Contro Venezia passatista"

Against the Thieving and Murderous Gangs of Peasants. See Luther, Martin

Agamemnon, in Kierkegaard, 6:1138a

Agamemnon. See Alfieri, Vittorio

Agamemnon. *See* Ritsos, Yannis, *Tetarti dhiastasi* (*The Fourth Dimension*), *Aghamemnon*

Agathodämon. See Wieland, Christoph Martin

Age of Constantine the Great, The. See Burckhardt, Jacob

Âge de raison, L'. See Sartre, Jean-Paul, *The Age of Reason*

Age Is Surveyed, An. *See* Mann, Heinrich, *Ein Zeitalter wird besichtigt*

Age of Louis XIV, The. *See* Voltaire, *Le siècle de Louis XIV*

Age of Reason, the
Foucault and, 13:3351b–3355b
as partial misnomer, 4:639b
see also Enlightenment

Age of Reason, The. See Sartre, Jean-Paul

Age of Suspicion, The. See Sarraute, Nathalie, *L'Ère du soupçon*

Aggression, Freud's concept of, 8:14a-b

Aghamemnon. See Ritsos, Yannis, *Tetarti dhiastasi*

Aghrypnia. See Ritsos, Yannis

"Agianapa I." *See* Seferis, George

"Agianapa II." *See* Seferis, George

Aging
in La Bruyère's *Caractères*, 3:249b
in Walther, 1:297b–298a

Aglavaine and Sélysette (*Aglavaine et Sélysette*). *See* Maeterlinck, Maurice

Agneau, L'. See Mauriac, François, *The Lamb*

Agnes Bernauer. See Hebbel, Friedrich

Agnete and the Merman. See Andersen, Hans Christian

Agonías de nuestro tiempo, Las. See Baroja,
Pío

Agonies of Our Time, The. *See* Baroja, Pío,
Las agonías de nuestro tiempo

Agostino. See Moravia, Alberto

Agrafena, St., in Akhmatova's "So dnia
Kupal'nitsy-Agrafeny," 10:1527b–1528a

Agricola, John, Luther and, 2:686a

Agricola, Rudolph, Erasmus and, 2:572a

Agrigento, in Pirandello's *I vecchi ei giovani*,
8:389b–390a

Ágrip af Noregs konunga sögum
(*Compendium of Sagas about Kings of
Norway*), 1:380b

Agrippina, in Kosztolányi's *Bloody Poet*,
10:1236a

Agrippine, in Racine's *Britannicus*,
3:212b–213b

Aguila de blasón. See Valle-Inclán, Ramón
del, *Las comedias bárbaras*

Ägyptische Helena, Die. See Hofmannsthal,
Hugo von

"Ah." *See* Montale, Eugenio, *Altri versi e
poesie disperse*

Ahasuerus (the Wandering Jew)
in Lagerkvist's writings, 10:1698b–1700b
in weltschmerz literature, 5:420a-b

Ahasverus död. See Lagerkvist, Pär

"Ahî wie kristenlîche nû der bâbest lachet."
See Walther von der Vogelweide

Ahnfrau, Die. See Grillparzer, Franz, *The
Ancestress*

"Ahriman." *See* Azorín

Aias. See Ritsos, Yannis, *Tetarti dhiastasi*

Aicard, Jean, Rimbaud and, 7:1806b

Aigle à deux têtes, L'. See Cocteau, Jean

Aimée. See Sand, George

Aimeric of Veire, 1:413a

Aîné des Ferchaux, L'. See Simenon, Georges

"Aiolia." *See* Seferis, George

Air of the Continent, The. See Pirandello,
Luigi, *L'Aria del continente*

Air de l'eau, L'. See Breton, André

"Airone morto." *See* Quasimodo, Salvatore

Airplane, Marinetti and, 9:814b, 827a

Ajace. See Foscolo, Ugo

Ajalbert, Jean, adaptation of *La fille Elisa*,
7:1415b

Ajax. *See* Foscolo, Ugo, *Ajace*; Ritsos, Yannis,
Tetarti dhiastasi (*The Fourth
Dimension*), *Aias*

Akhmatova, Anna, **10:1521a–1542b**
Babel and, 11:1905b
Blok and, 9:959b, 985b–986a
Chetki (*Rosary*), success of acmeism and,
10:1523a
"Folk Song" ("Pesenka"), 10:1527b, 1528a
"I Both Wept and Repented" ("Ia i plakala i
kaialas"), 10:1525b–1526a, 1528a
"In Praise of Peace," 10:1530b
"Iva" ("The Willow"), 10:1533b
Iz shesti knig (*From Six Books*), destruction
of, 10:1530a
Mandelshtam and, 10:1629a, 1632a
"To Cassandra," 10:1638a
"Muzhestvo" ("Courage"), siege of Leningrad
and, 10:1529b
"On prav—opiat' fonar', apteka" (He's
right—once again the lamp, the
drugstore), 9:959b
Pasternak and, 10:1598a, 1604b
Poem Without a Hero (*Poema bez geroia*),
9:985b–986a, 10:1533b–1540b
"Afterword," 10:1538b
"Dedication," 10:1535a
"Guest from the Future," 10:1537b
as her masterwork, 10:1521b
"In Place of a Preface," 10:1535a
moral argument of, 10:1541b
"Nineteen Thirteen," 10:1535b
"Petersburg Tale," 10:1531a-b, 1534a,
1535b–1538b
"Reshka," 10:1538b–1539a
"Second Dedication," 10:1535a
"Third and Last Dedication," 10:1535a-b
poetic personae of, 10:1528a-b
"Posledniaia roza" ("The Last Rose"),
10:1530b–1531a
"Pridu tuda, i otletit tomlen'e," 10:1528a
"Proterty si kovrik pod ikonoi," 10:1526a-b
Requiem (*Rekviem*), 10:1531a–1533b
"Net, eto ne ia" ("No, That Is Not I"),
10:1532b–1533a

Stalinist Terror and, 10:1521b

"The Sentence" ("Prigovor"),
10:1531b–1532a, 1533a

"Uvodili tebia na rassvete" (They Led You
Away at Dawn), 10:1532a-b

"Scheli v Sadu vyryty," Stalinist denigration
of, 10:1530a

"So dnia Kupal 'nitsy-Agrafeny,"
10:1527b–1528a

"Song of the Last Meeting" ("Pesnia
poslednei vstrechi"), 10:1523a-b
persona in, 10:1528a

"Trostnik" ("The Reed"), 10:1533b

Tsvetaeva and, 11:1736a, 1748a

Vecher (*Evening*), as exemplary of acmeism,
10:1523a

"Voronezh," Mandelshtam in, 10:1646b

"Zharko veet veter dushnyi" (The Oppressive
Wind Blows Hot), 10:1528a

Akhmatova, Lev (son), persecution of,
10:1529b, 1530b

"Akiknek dajkája vagyok." *See* Ady, Endre

"Akit én csókolok." *See* Ady, Endre

Akragas. *See* Agrigento

Aksakov, Konstantin, Goncharov and, 6:1064a

"Akter i Rabochii." *See* Mandelshtam, Osip

Al di là del comunismo. See Marinetti, Filippo
Tommaso

"Al padre." *See* Quasimodo, Salvatore

Al servicio de algo. See Cela, Camilo José

Aladdin motif, Andersen and, 6:872a

Aladdin's Lamp. See Cocteau, Jean, *La lampe
d'Aladin*

Alain-Fournier
Laforgue and, 7:1883a
Le Grand Meaulnes (*The Wanderer*)
Nerval and, 6:969
Saint-Exupéry's "L'Évasion de Jacques
Bernis" and, 12:2311b

Alanus de Insulis, Gottfried and, 1:238a,
245a-b

Alarcos. See Schlegel, Friedrich von

Alaric (Visigoth), in Augustine's *City of God*,
1:35a

"Alas, courtly singing." *See* Walther von der
Vogelweide, "Owe, hovelichez singen"

Alas, Leopoldo. *See* Clarín

"Alas the lovely face." *See* Petrarch,
Canzoniere, "Oimè il bel viso"

"Alas, where have all my years vanished?" *See*
Walther von der Vogelweide, "Owê war
sint verswunden alliu miniu jâr?"

Alatyr'. See Zamyatin, Yevgeny Ivanovich

Alba (city), in Corneille's *Horace*, 3:34b, 35a

Albaniad. See Elytis, Odysseus

Albatros, L' (*The Albatross*). *See* Baudelaire,
Charles

Albee, Edward, Ibsen's influence on, 7:1444a

Alberti, Rafael
Jiménez and, 9:992a
Machado and, 9:746b, 760b

Albertus. See Gautier, Théophile

Albertus Magnus
Aquinas and, 1:411a–412a, 415a
Dante and, 1:433b
Summa, 1:411b

Albrecht von Halberstadt, 1:242b

Albrizzi, Isabella Teotochi, *Portraits*, on Ovid
and Alfieri, 4:686a

Album de vers anciens, 1890–1920 (*Album of
Old Verses, 1890–1920*). *See* Valéry,
Paul

Album zutique, 7:1807a

Alcaic forms of poetry, Hölderlin and, 5:155a

Alcalde de Zalamea, El. See Calderón de la
Barca, Pedro, *The Mayor of Zalamea*

Alceste. See Wieland, Christoph Martin

Alchemy
in Goethe's *Faust*, 5:22b
in Richter's *The Comet*, 5:82b
Rimbaud and, 7:1804b
Strindberg's interest in, 7:1738a
in Yourcenar's *The Abyss*, 12:2554b,
2557a-b

Alchimiste. See Dumas père, Alexandre

Alcibiades, Montaigne and, 2:782a

Alcoholism, in Simenon's novels, 12:2492b,
2499a

Alcon. See Castiglione, Baldesar

Alcova d'acciaio, L'. See Marinetti, Filippo
Tommaso

Alcuin, letter to the Lindisfarne monks,
1:64a-b

Alcyone. See D'Annunzio, Gabriele

"Al'debaran." *See* Olesha, Yuri
Aldhelm of Sherborne, bishop, 1:65a
Aldine Press
  Castiglione and, 2:649a
  Erasmus and, 2:577b–578a
Aleixandre, Vicente, 9:760b
Aleksandrovna, Mariia, 11:1732a–1733a
Alemán, Mateo
  Guzmán de Alfarache, 2:829b, 837b, 841b
    influence on short fiction, 2:950b
    Lesage's *Gil Blas* and, 3:329a
    Masuccio's *Novellino* as source for, 2:940a
    point of view in, 2:950b–951a
Alémán, Mateo, *Guzmán de Alfarache*,
    translations of, 3:340b–341a
Alembert, Jean Le Rond d', on Pascal, 3:147b
Alepoudhelis, Odysseus. *See* Elytis, Odysseus
Aleramo, Sibilla, Quasimodo and, 12:2388b
Alexander the Great, and the pirate Diomede,
    in Villon's *Testament*, 2:564a
Alexander the Great. *See* Racine, Jean,
    Alexandre le grand
Alexander of Hales, 1:409b
Alexander I, czar of Russia, 5:607b, 612b
  Pushkin and, 5:660b, 661a
Alexander IV, pope, on Dominicans, 1:414a
Alexander VI, pope, Baroja's interest in,
    9:603a
Alexandre le grand. See Racine, Jean
Alexandria: A History and a Guide. See
    Forster, E. M.
Alexandria
  history
    in Cavafy's poetry, 8:206b–207b, 209a,
      209b–210a, 210b–211a, 216b–217b,
      219b–220b
    Christian/Pagan conflict, 8:216b–218a
    decline of Hellenism, 8:209a, 210b–211a,
      219b
    Ptolemaic dynasty's end, 8:212a–213a
  Ungaretti's youth in, 10:1453a–1455a
Alexandria Quartet. See Durrell, Lawrence
"Alexandrian Kings." *See* Cavafy, Constantine,
    "Alexandrinoi vasileis"
Alexandrine (meter)
  Baudelaire and, 6:1043a, 7:1327a-b
  in Berlioz' works, 6:792b
  definition of, 7:1636a
  in Gautier's *España*, 6:1042a
  in La Fontaine's *Fables*, 3:81b–82b, 83b
  in Laforgue's "The Coming of Winter,"
    7:1898b–1899a
  in Musset's "October Night," 6:1024b–1025a
  in Racine's plays, 3:221a, 6:1033b
  in Verlaine's poetry, 7:1636a, 1637b
"Alexandrinoi vasileis." *See* Cavafy,
    Constantine
Alexandrov, G., conspiracy charges, 11:1912a
Alexis ou le traité du vain combat (Alexis).
    See Yourcenar, Marguerite
Alexis, Paul, Maupassant and, 7:1763b
Alexis, Willibald, Scott's influence on, 5:431b
Alfieri, Giulia (sister), Alfieri's first letter to,
    4:668b
Alfieri, Vittorio, **4:661a–689b**
  Abel, as *tramelogedia*, 4:678b
  "Admonition to the Italian Powers," 4:667a
  Agamemnon, 4:683b
  Antigone
    defense of, 4:678a
    inflexibility of, 4:683a-b
  Chénier and, 4:699a-b
  Cleopatra, 4:664b, 678b
  Don Garcia, 4:683b
  "Etruria Avenged," 4:674b
  Foscolo and, 5:321a–322a
  Free America, 4:675b
  Gallophobe, 4:667a, 675a-b
  Journals, 4:667b–668a
  letters of, 4:668a–670a
  lyric poetry of, 4:670a–671b
  Machiavelli and, 2:615b
  Mary Stuart, his unhappiness with, 4:683b
  Memoirs, 4:662a–668a
    commentary on his theatre in,
      4:677b–678b, 685a-b
    conception of *Saul* in, 4:682b
    posthumous influence of, 4:687b
  Myrrha, 4:685a–687a
  Octavia, 4:683b
  Of Tyranny, 4:671b–673a
    banned in Tuscany, 4:674b
    conception of, 4:665b
  Orestes, 4:683b

Panegyric to Trajan by Pliny, 4:675b
  "Paris Rid of the Bastille," 4:666b, 675b
Philip, 4:678b–680b
  compared to *Virginia*, 4:681b–682a
  inflexibility of, 4:683a-b
  sources of, 4:678b
  translation from French into Italian,
    4:664b, 665a
Political Tetralogy, 4:676b
  The Antidote, 4:676a, 676b
  The Few, 4:676b
  The One, 4:676b
  Too Many, 4:676b
Polynices
  inflexibility of, 4:683a-b
  translation from French into Italian,
    4:664b
Rosmunda, 4:683b
Satires, 4:674b–675a
Saul, 4:682b–685b
  compared to *Myrrha*, 4:686a, 687a
  production of, 4:666a-b
Sketch of the Universal Judgment (*Esquisse
    du jugement universel*), 4:667b, 676a
The Divorce, 4:677a-b
The Little Window, 4:676b–677a
The Pazzi Conspiracy
  conception of, 4:665b
  humanizing of antagonism in, 4:683b
The Poets, 4:664b, 676a
The Prince and Letters (*Du prince et des
    lettres*), 4:673a–674b
  Chénier and, 4:709a
  conception of, 4:671b
  Croce's review of, 4:688a-b
  "Exhortation to Liberate Italy from the
    Barbarians," 4:674a
Timoleon, humanizing of antagonism in,
    4:683b
  translations from Greek by, 4:667a
Virginia, 4:680b–682b
  humanizing of antagonism in, 4:683b
  "Virtue Unkown," 4:675b–676a
Alfonso XII of Spain, king
  Blasco Ibáñez and, 8:356a
  reign of, 9:743a
Alfonso XIII of Spain, king

attempts on life, 9:598a, 601a
  Baroja's themes using, 9:603a
Alfred of Wessex, king, Danish invasions and,
    1:64a
Alger of Liège, 1:406a
Alger Républicain (newspaper), Camus and,
    13:3056b
Algeria, Camus and, 13:3074b–3075a
Ali Pasha. *See* Andrić, Ivo, "Alipaša"
Alienation
  of Ady, 9:863a-b, 865b, 877b
  in Apollinaire's "The Traveler," 9:893a
  in Beauvoir's *Memoirs of a Dutiful
    Daughter*, 12:2709b
  in Broch, 10:1392b
  Canetti and, 12:2629a
  in Goncharov's works, 6:1063a-b
  Hebbel on, 6:1100b–1101a
  in Lermontov's works, 6:1198a
  in Lukács, 10:1253a-b, 1274a
  in Richter's *The Invisible Lodge*, 5:62a
  in Simenon's works, 12:2490b–2491a,
    2492a-b, 2504a
  Trakl and, 10:1426a
  see also Isolation; Loneliness
Aline et Valcour. *See* Sade, Donatien
    Alphonse François, marquis de
"Alipaša." *See* Andrić, Ivo
"Alkandis Lied" (Alkandi's Song). *See*
    Schnitzler, Arthur
Alkonost, Bely and, 9:924a
All for the Best. *See* Pirandello, Luigi, *Tutto
    per bene*
"All the day I weep." *See* Petrarch, *Canzoniere*,
    "Tutto 'l dì piango"
All as It Should Be. *See* Pirandello, Luigi,
    Tutto per bene
All for Love. *See* Dryden, John
All Men Are Mortal. *See* Beauvoir, Simone de
All My Sons. *See* Miller, Arthur
All Said and Done. *See* Beauvoir, Simone de
All Souls Day. *See* Ritsos, Yannis, *Ydhria*;
    Trakl, Georg, *Totentag*
All That Fall. *See* Beckett, Samuel
All-Russian Union of Writers. *See*
    Vserossiiskii soiuz pisatelei

"Alla luna." *See* Leopardi, Giacomo, "To the Moon"

"Alla noia." *See* Ungaretti, Giuseppe, "To Ennui"

"Alla nuova luna." *See* Quasimodo, Salvatore

"Alla primavera." *See* Leopardi, Giacomo, "To Spring"

"Alla sera." *See* Foscolo, Ugo

"Alla stazione in una mattina d'autunno." *See* Carducci, Giosue

"Alla sua donna." *See* Leopardi, Giacomo, "To His Lady"

Alladine and Palomides (*Alladine et Palomides*). *See* Maeterlinck, Maurice

"All'amica risanata." *See* Foscolo, Ugo

Allan-Despréaux, Madame, Musset and, 6:1030b

Allegory
  in Andrić's works, 11:1770b–1771a
  in Ariosto, 2:630a-b
  in Augustine's *Confessions*, 1:32a
  Baudelaire's use of, 7:1328b–1329a
  Bely's *The Silver Dove* as, 9:916b–917a
  in Benjamin's works, 9:812a, 11:1715a-b, 1718a–1720a
  in Calderón's works, 2:893b–894a
  Camus and, 13:3074a
  in Chekhov's "The Steppe," 7:1861b
  in Chrétien's *Yvain*, 1:202a-b
  in Christian interpretation of classical literature, 1:3a-b, 7b, 10a, 465a
  in Dante's *Divine Comedy*, Pascoli on, 7:1848b–1849a
  in Delacroix's works, 5:535b
  Diderot and, 4:484a
  Gogol's style and, 6:983b
  Gottfried and, 1:245a-b, 247b–248b
  in Hamsun's works, 8:33a
  in Hebbel's works, 6:1118b–1119a
  in Hölderlin's works, 5:161a-b, 165b–166a
  in Hugo's works, 6:703a
  in Laforgue's "Lament of the Poor Knight Errant," 7:1894a, 1894b
  in Leopardi's works, 5:560b
  Marinetti and, 9:806a, 812b
  Mauriac and, 10:1326a-b
  medieval, **1:309a–335b**
  in Musil's *The Man Without Qualities*, 9:955a
  in names of characters, 4:404b, 405b–406a
  natural history as, in Walther's poems, 1:291b
  in Novalis' works, 5:221a
  in Prudentius' works, 1:3a–6b, 20a
    Cathemerinon, 1:7a-b
    Hamartigenia, 1:9a-b
    Peristephanon, 1:12b
    Symmachus, 1:10a-b
  in Rabelais's works, 2:714a, 714b
  Richter's *Titan* and, 5:72a-b
  in Tasso's works, 2:809b–810a
  Trakl and, 10:1417b

"Allegory of poets" (Dante), 1:440a

"Allegory of theologians" (Dante), 1:440a

Allegri, Antonio. *See* Correggio

Allegria di naufragi. *See* Ungaretti, Giuseppe

Allegria, L'. *See* Ungaretti, Giuseppe

Allemann, Beda, on Rilke and Mallarmé, 9:779b, 782b

Allen, Hope Emily, Undset and, 9:1018a

Allen, Woody, *The Purple Rose of Cairo*, and Queneau's *Flight of Icarus*, 12:2519b

Aller retour. *See* Aymé, Marcel

"Allerêrst lebe ich mir werde." *See* Walther von der Vogelweide

Allesch, Johannes von, Musil and, 9:932a

Allgemeines Brouillon. *See* Novalis

Alliance, theme of. *See* Contract, theme of

"All'Italia." *See* Leopardi, Giacomo

Alliteration
  in Anglo-Saxon poetry, 1:66b
  in *Fljótsdæla saga*, 1:398b–399a
  in Quasimodo's works, 12:2393a
  in "Tarde," 9:748b–749a
  in Ungaretti's poetry, 10:1462b
  in Verlaine's poetry, 7:1635a

All'uscita. *See* Pirandello, Luigi

Allusion
  in Ekelöf's works, 12:2647b, 2659a–2669a
  in Jiménez's works, 9:1000a
  in Malraux's works, 12:2428a-b

Allusions. *See* Ritsos, Yannis, *Piimata IV*

Alma castellana (1600–1800), El. *See* Azorín

"Alma minha gentil." *See* Camoëns, Luís Vaz de, *Rimas*

Almanach illustré du Père Ubu. See Jarry, Alfred

Almansor. See Heine, Heinrich

Almas de violeta. See Jiménez, Juan Ramón

Almeh, The. See Vigny, Alfred Victor de, *Scenes from the Desert: The Almeh*

Almogaver, Juan Boscán, Petrarchan influence, 2:504b

"Álmom: Az Isten." *See* Ady, Endre

"Almond Tree in Pannonia, An." *See* Pannonius, Janus, "De amygdalo in Pannonia nata"

Alms of Alcippe, The. See Yourcenar, Marguerite, *Les Charités d'Alcippe et autres poèmes*

Alone. See Strindberg, August, *Ensame*

Alone. *See* Zamyatin, Yevgeny Ivanovich, "Odin"

"Alone and filled with care." *See* Petrarch, *Canzoniere*, "Solo et pensoso i più deserti campi"

Along the Seine. *See* Ady, Endre, "A Szajna partján"

Alonso, Dámaso, *Nota Emilianense* discovered by, 1:102b

Alonso, Ruiz, Lorca's death and, 11:2200b–2201a

"Alos Noe, O." *See* Elytis, Odysseus, *Exi kai mia tipsis yia ton ourano*

Alouette, L'. See Anouilh, Jean, *The Lark*

Alphabet, Claudel on, 8:489a

Als der Krieg zu Ende war. See Frisch, Max, *When the War Was Over*

Alsfelder *Passion*, 1:466b

Also sprach Zarathustra. See Nietzsche, Friedrich, *Thus Spoke Zarathustra*

"Altars of Fear, The." *See* Chénier, André, "Les autels de la peur"

Alte und der neue Glaube, Der. See Strauss, David

Altercazione. See Medici, Lorenzo de'

Altersstil, of Hesse, 9:855a

Altertumswissenschaft, romantic historiography and, 5:579b

Althusser, Louis

Foucault and, 13:3329b

on Montesquieu's *The Spirit of the Laws*, 3:353a–354a

Al'tman, Moisei, portrait of Khlebnikov by, 10:1340a-b

Alton, Aimée d', 6:1002a, 1027a, 1027b

Altra vita, Un'. See Moravia, Alberto

Altri versi e poesie disperse. See Montale, Eugenio

Alturas de Macchu Picchu, Las. See Neruda, Pablo

Alvarez Quintero brothers, Valle-Inclán and, 8:341a

"Alvdrottningens spira." *See* Södergran, Edith

Alzire. See Voltaire

"Am Quell der Donau." *See* Hölderlin, Friedrich

Amadas and Ydoine, 1:324a

Amadeus. *See* Hoffmann, E. T. A.

Amadigi. See Tasso, Bernardo

Amalasunta. See Goldoni, Carlo

Amante infelice, L'. See Moravia, Alberto

"Amante liberal, El" ("The Generous Lover"), 2:832a-b

Amants d'Avignon, Les. See Triolet, Elsa

Amants de Venise, Les. See Maurras, Charles

Amaranta. See Casalio

Amateur theater. *See* Theater, amateur

Amateurism, Burckhardt on, 6:1242a-b

Amatory Disillusions. *See* Zayas y Sotomayor, Maria de, *Desengaños amorosos*

Amatory and Exemplary Tales. *See* Zayas y Sotomayor, Maria de, *Novelas amorosas y exemplares*

Amatory Happenings and Wonders in Eight Exemplary Novellas. *See* Montalbán, Juan Pérez de, *Sucesos y prodigios de amor en ocho novelas ejemplares*

Amatory Improvisations. *See* Medici, Lorenzo de', *Selve d'amore*

Amazons, in Kleist, 5:300a-b

Ambiguity
   in Butor, 13:3290a
   Camus and, 13:3076a
   Cela and, 13:3122a
   in Gottfried, 1:245b–246a, 253b
   in Hoffmann, 5:271b

Ambiguity (*cont.*)
    in Johnson's works, 12:2363b, 2364a, 2364b, 2378a
    in Kleist, 5:302b, 306a
    linguistic, in Musil's *The Man Without Qualities*, 9:936a
    in Meyer, 6:935a–937a
    in Moravia's works, 12:2694a, 2695b
    in Walther, 1:295b
Ambition's Criminal. *See* Ferreira de Castro, José Maria, *Criminoso por ambição*
Ambizione sbagliate, Le. See Moravia, Alberto, *Mistaken Ambitions*
Ambra. See Medici, Lorenzo de'
Ambrose, St.
    Augustine and, 1:28a, 28b, 30a
    Hexameron, Boccaccio's use of, 2:519a
    Prudentius' *Cathemerinon* and, 1:7a
    vs. Symmachus, 1:10a
Ambrosio; or, The Monk. See Lewis, Gregory
"Âme du vin, L'." *See* Baudelaire, Charles, "The Soul of the Wine"
Âme et la danse, L'. See Valéry, Paul
Amédée. See Ionesco, Eugène
Amelius, 3:19b
Amen Corner. See Baldwin, James
America
    Chateaubriand's travels in, 5:114b–116a
    Hamsun and, 8:22b–24b, 25a
    Jiménez in, 9:992b
    Mayakovsky's poems about, 1849a-b
    Moberg on, 11:2220b, 2222b, 2223a-b
    see also United States
American colonies, Herder's prophecy concerning, 4:653b
American Humor: A Study of the National Character. See Rourke, Constance M.
American Indians, in Butor, 13:3314a–3315a
"American Letter." *See* MacLeish, Archibald
American literature
    nineteenth century, Maeterlinck and, 8:123a-b
    Pavese and, 12:2673a, 2770b
    Simon and, 13:3043b
    twentieth century, Kafka and, 9:1156b
"American Renaissance," Herder's influence on, 4:654a

American Revolution
    Alfieri's *Free America* and, 4:675b
    and Beaumarchais, 4:577b–578a
Amerika. See Kafka, Franz
Amers. See Perse, Saint-John, *Seamarks*
"Âmes du purgatoire, Les." *See* Mérimée, Prosper, "Souls in Purgatory"
Amica America. See Giraudoux, Jean
Amica delle mogli, L'. See Pirandello, Luigi
Amici Pedanti, 7:1496b
Amies, Les. See Verlaine, Paul
Amigo Manso, El. See Pérez Galdós, Benito
Aminta. See Tasso, Torquato
Amis de Marcel Aymé (society), 12:2454b
Amis et Amile, 1:464a
"Amité du Prince." *See* Perse, Saint-John, "Friendship of the Prince"
Amitiés particulières, Les. See Peyrefitte, Roger
"Among the admirers of Carmen." *See* Blok, Alexander, "Sredi poklonnikov Karmen"
"Among the Intelligentsia." *See* Gorky, Maxim, *My Universities*
Among the Orange Trees. See Blasco Ibáñez, Vicente, *Entre naranjos*
Among Women Only. See Pavese, Cesare
"Amor che ne la mente mi ragiona." *See* Dante Alighieri, *Convivio*
Amor de Don Perlimplín con Belisa en su jardín, El. See García Lorca, Federico
Amor de Perdição. See Castelo Branco, Camilo
"Amor é fogo que arde sem se ver." *See* Camoëns, Luís Vaz de, *Rimas*
Amor fati, Nietzsche's view of, 7:1657b, 1671a
"Amor pastorius." *See* Petrarch
Amor y pedagogia. See Unamuno, Miguel de
Amore coniugale, L'. See Moravia, Alberto, *Conjugal Love*
Amores tardíos, Los. See Baroja, Pío
Amori difficili, Gli. See Calvino, Italo, *Difficult Loves*
Amori senza amore. See Pirandello, Luigi
"Amorous Shepherd, The." *See* Petrarch, "Amor pastorius"
Amour. See Verlaine, Paul
Amour absolu, L'. See Jarry, Alfred

Amour africain, L'. See Mérimée, Prosper,
    African Love
Amour fou, L'. See Breton, André
Amours. See Jodelle, Étienne
"Amours de Cassandre." *See* Ronsard, Pierre
    de
"Amours de Marie." *See* Ronsard, Pierre de
Amours de Psyché et de Cupidon, Les. See La
    Fontaine, Jean de
Amours et nouveaux eschanges des pierres
    precieuses, vertus et proprietez d'icelles,
    Les. See Belleau, Remy
Amours jaunes, Les. See Corbière, Tristan
"Amours, Les." *See* Ronsard, Pierre de
Amours tragiques de Pyrame et Thisbé. See
    Viau, Théophile de
Amphion. See Proust, Marcel
Amphitrite, in Lampedusa's *The Leopard,*
    11:2012b–2013a
Amphitryon 38. See Giraudoux, Jean
Amphitryon. See Kleist, Heinrich von; Molière;
    Plautus
Amulett, Das (*The Amulet*). *See* Meyer,
    Conrad Ferdinand
Amy, Pierre, 2:695b
"An das Vaterland." *See* Keller, Gottfried
"An den Knaben Elis." *See* Trakl, Georg
"An den Tragiker." *See* Hebbel, Friedrich
"An der Angel." *See* Böll, Heinrich
"An die Deutschen." *See* Hölderlin, Friedrich
"An die Musik." *See* Rilke, Rainer Maria
"An die Natur." *See* Hölderlin, Friedrich
"An Stella." *See* Hölderlin, Friedrich
Anabaptists
    Bossuet on, 3:171b
    Luther and, 2:682a-b
Anabasis. See Perse, Saint-John; Xenophon
Anacreon, influence on Renaissance pastoral
    poetry, 2:910b
Anaforá ston Gréko. See Kazantzakis, Nikos
Anagnostopoulos, Athan, 13:2977a
Anagogy, Cassian on, 1:4b
Analogy
    argument from, Aquinas on, 1:421b
    in Augustine's *On the Trinity,* 1:40a
    in Chrétien's *Lancelot,* 1:198a
    Marinetti and, 9:816a, 816b–817a

"Analyse der Phobie eines fünfjährigen
    Knaben." *See* Freud, Sigmund
Analyse raisonnée de l'histoire de France. See
    Chateaubriand, François René de
"Analyse und Synthese" ("Analysis and
    Synthesis"). *See* Musil, Robert
"Analysis of a Phobia of a Five-Year-Old Boy."
    See Freud, Sigmund, "Analyse der
    Phobie eines fünfjährigen Knaben"
Analytical Studies. *See* Balzac, Honoré de,
    Études analytiques
"Ànapo." *See* Quasimodo, Salvatore
Anarchism
    Baroja and, 9:590b–591a, 594a, 597a,
        600b–601a
    in decadent literature, 9:1097a-b
    Hašek's acceptance of, 9:1093a-b
    Jarry and, 9:667a-b
    of Khlebnikov, 10:1339a
    modernism and, 9:864b
    Pascoli and, 7:1827b
    surrealism and, 11:2067a
    of Valle-Inclán, 8:336b
Anathemata, The. See Jones, David
Anatol. See Schnitzler, Arthur
Anatomy of the Novella. See Clements, Robert;
    Gibaldi, Joseph
Ancelot, Madame, salon of, Vigny's
    participation in, 5:451a
Ancestress, The. See Grillparzer, Franz
Ancien régime, 3:280b–281a
    Büchner and, 6:1186b–1189b
    as depicted in La Bruyère's *Caractères,*
        3:229b
    Lesage's *Crispin* and, 3:321a
    lettres de cachet during, 4:616a, 626b
    Sade and, 4:620a-b
    Voltaire's opposition to, 4:384b–386a
Ancien régime et la révolution, L'. See
    Tocqueville, Alexis de, *The Old Régime*
    and the French Revolution
Ancien Régime, L' (*The Ancient Regime*). *See*
    Taine, Hippolyte
Ancient Demon, The. *See* Ady, Endre, "Az Ös
    Kaján"

Ancient Gyrfalcons, The. *See* Valle-Inclán, Ramón del, *La guerra carlista* (The Carlist War), *Gerifaltes de antaño*

Ancient Kingdom, The. *See* Moberg, Vilhelm, *Det Gamla riket*

"Ancient Lament, An." *See* Carducci, Giosue, "Pianto antico"

And Bely and Blok and Esenin and Kluiev. *See* Tychyna, Pavlo, *Pluh* (*The Plow*), "I Bileyi i Blok i Iesenin i Kliuiev"

And He Did Himself. See Silone, Ignazio, *Ed egli si nascose*

And He Shook off the Dust from His Feet. *See* Hašek, Jaroslav, "I vyklepal prach z obuvi své"

"And I Leaned and Lay on Their Beds." *See* Cavafy, Constantine, "Ki akoumpisa kai plagiasa stes klines ton"

And Never Said a Word. See Böll, Heinrich

And Pippa Dances! See Hauptmann, Gerhart, *Und Pippa tanzt!*

And So Ad Infinitum. See Čapek, Karel, *R.U.R.*

And Where Were You, Adam? See Böll, Heinrich, *Wo warst du, Adam?*

Andalucia trágica, La. See Azorín

Andalusia
   in Lorca's poetry, 11:2193a–2194b
   in Machado works, 9:752b–753a, 758b, 759a, 764a
   poets from, 9:993a

"Andenken." *See* George, Stefan, *Algabal*; Hölderlin, Friedrich

"Andere, Der." *See* Schnitzler, Arthur

"Andere Zustand, Der" (Musil). *See* "Other Condition, The" (Musil)

Andersen, Hans Christian, **6:863a–891b**
   "A Drop of Water," 6:886b
   A Poet's Bazaar, 6:877b
   A Visit to Portugal, 6:877b
   Agnete and the Merman, 6:874a
   "Auntie," 6:887a
   Digte, 6:877a
   Dinesen and, 10:1299a
   "Everything in Its Right Place," 6:886b
   Fairy Tales Told for Children (*Eventyr fortalte for Børn*), 6:878b
   Fantasies and Sketches (*Phantasier og Skizzer*), 6:877a
   H. C. Andersens Levnedsbog 1805–1831, 6:864a
   "In the Duckyard," 6:886b–887a
   In Spain, 6:877b
   In Sweden, 6:877b
   Journey on Foot from Holmens Canal to the East Point of Amager, 6:877a-b
   "Little Ida's Flowers," 6:882a-b
   Love on St. Nicholas Tower, 6:873b
   Lovely, 6:886b
   Lucky Peter, 6:876b–877a
   New Fairy Tales (*Nye Eventyr*), 6:878b
   O. T., 6:869a-b, 876a
   On the Last Day, 6:886b
   Only a Fiddler (*Kun en Spillemand*), 6:870a, 876a
   Pearls and Gold, 6:875a
   The Blossom of Happiness, 6:874b–875a
   "The Cripple," 6:887a
   "The Dung Beetle," 6:886b
   "The Emperor's New Clothes," 6:882b
   The Fairy Tale of My Life (*Mit Livs Eventyr*), 6:864a
   "The Gardener and His Master," 6:888b–889b
   "The Ice Maiden," 6:887b–888b
   The Improvisatore, 6:870a, 875a-b
   "The Little Mermaid," 6:882b–883b
      Yourcenar's dramatic adaptation, 12:2546a
   The Mulatto, 6:874b
   "The Muse of the Twentieth Century," 6:887a
   "The Nightingale," 6:883b–884a
   "The Pixy at the Grocer's," 6:886b
   "The Princess and the Pea," 6:882a
   "The Puppeteer," 6:886b
   "The Rags," 6:887a
   "The Red Shoes," 6:885a
   "The Shadow," 6:885b–886a
   "The Snail and the Rosebush," 6:887a
   "The Story of a Mother," 6:886b
   "The Tinderbox," 6:880b–882a
   "The Traveling Companion," 6:882a-b

The True Story of My Life (*Märchen meines Lebens ohne Dichtung*), 6:864a

The Two Baronesses (*De to Baronesser*), 6:876b

The Two Maidens, 6:886b

"The Ugly Duckling," 6:884a–885a

"There Is a Difference," 6:886b

"Thumbelina," 6:882a-b

To Be or Not to Be?, 6:876b

Youthful Attempts, 6:866a-b

Anderson, Mariang, Mandelshtam and, 10:1646b–1647a

Anderson, Sherwood, Pavese and, 12:2763a

Andorra: A Play in Twelve Scenes (*Andorra: Stück in zwölf Bildern*). *See* Frisch, Max

André Chénier. See Giordano, Umberto

André del Sarto. See Musset, Alfred de

Andreas-Salomé, Lou
Nietzsche and, 7:1667b, 1679a
Rilke and, 9:769b

Andreev, Leonid Nikolaevich
Gorky and, 8:418a, 419b, 422a, 443b–444a
in the Crimea, 8:442b
Zamyatin and, 10:1182a

Andreeva, Maria Fedorovna, 8:420b

Andreevna, Alexandra, 9:964a-b, 965a-b

"Andrey Kolosov." *See* Turgenev, Ivan

Andrian, Leopold von, 9:690b

Andrić, Ivo, **11:1751a–1779b**
"A Summer in the South" ("Letovanje na jugu"), 11:1768a, 1768b–1769a
"Alipaša" (Ali Pasha), 11:1772b
"Bar Titanic" ("Bife Titanik"), 11:1767a–1768a
Bosnian Chronicle (*Travnićka hronika*), 11:1751a, 1753a, 1758b, 1761b–1763b
Brother Petar stories, 11:1754a-b, 1756b
"Čelebi Hafiz" ("Fiery Hafiz"), 11:1756b
"Ćorkan i Švabica" ("Ćorkan and the German Girl"), 11:1755b–1756a
Devil's Yard (*Prokleta avlija*), 11:1751a, 1769b, 1776a–1777a
Ex Ponto, 11:1752b
"In the Camp" ("Za logorovanja"), 11:1755a, 1755b, 1756a, 1757a
Književni jug (The Literary South), 11:1752b, 1753a

Kuća na osami (The House on Its Own), 11:1771b–1772a, 1776a, 1777a-b

"Legenda o pobuni" (The Legend About the Rebellion), 11:1770b

Lica (Faces), 11:1769a-b, 1772a

"Most na Žepi" ("The Bridge on the Žepa"), 11:1758a-b

"Mustapha Magyar" ("Mustafa Madžar"), 11:1755a-b, 1756a

Nemiri (Anxieties), 11:1752b

Nove pripovetke (New Stories), 11:1766b

Omerpaša Latas (Omerpasha Latas), 11:1753a, 1753b, 1769b, 1771b–1772a, 1773a–1774a

"Panorama," 11:1768a, 1768b

"Pismo is 1920 godine," 11:1764a–1765b, 1766a

"Proba" (The Rehearsal), 11:1775b

"Razgovor s Gojom" (Conversation with Goya), 11:1774b

"Robinja" (The Slave), 11:1772b

"Slepac" (The Blind Man), 11:1770b–1771a

"Smrt u Sinanovoj tekjii" (Death in the Sinan Tekke), 11:1757a-b

Šta sanjam i šta mi se dogadja (What I Dream and What Happens to Me), 11:1771a

The Bridge on the Drina (*Na Drini ćuprija*), 11:1751a, 1753a, 1753b, 1758b, 1759a–1761b, 1775a, 1776a

"The Vizier's Elephant," 11:1765b–1766b, 1775a-b

The Woman from Sarajevo (*Gospodjica*), 11:1751a, 1753b, 1758b, 1763b

"Thirst" ("Žej"), 11:1756a, 1757b–1758a

"Trup" (The Torso), 11:1756b

"U musafirhani" (At the Monastery), 11:1754a

"Woman on the Rock" ("Žena na kamenu"), 11:1768a-b

"Zeko," 11:1766b–1767a

Znakovi pored puta (Signs by the Roadside), 11:1753b, 1771b

Andrieu, Pierre, Delacroix's letter to, 5:534b–535a

Androgyny, in Sarraute's works, 12:2352b

Andromache
- in Baudelaire's "The Swan," 7:1340b–1342b
- in Chateaubriand's works, 5:123a

Andromaque. See Racine, Jean

Andromeda, in Lampedusa's *The Leopard,* 11:2012a

Andromède. See Corneille, Pierre

Andronic. See Cambistron, Jean Galbert de

Andronnikova, Salomeya, Princess, Mandelshtam's poems dedicated to, 10:1637a

Âne rouge, L'. See Simenon, Georges

Anecdotes, in Renaissance short fiction, 2:930a-b, 937b–939a, 952b

Anecdotes of Destiny. See Dinesen, Isak

Anfimov, Vladimir, subjects suggested to Khlebnikov by, 10:1340a, 1354a

Ange Heurtebise, L'. See Cocteau, Jean

Ange Pitou. See Dumas père, Alexandre

"Angel." *See* Olesha, Yuri

"Angel, An." *See* Lermontov, Mikhail Yurievich, "Angel"

Angel and beast imagery, Montherlant's use of, 11:1922b–1923a, 1924a

Angel Comes to Babylon, An. See Dürrenmatt, Friedrich

Angel Guerra. See Pérez Galdós, Benito

Angel Heurtebise, The. See Cocteau, Jean, *L'Ange Heurtebise*

Angel of Information and Other Plays, The. See Moravia, Alberto, *L'Angelo dell'informazione e altri testi teatrali*

Angela Borgia. See Meyer, Conrad Ferdinand

Angèle. See Dumas père, Alexandre

"Angeli eletti et l'anime beate, Li." *See* Petrarch, *Canzoniere*

Angelic Avengers, The. See Dinesen, Isak

Angelico, Fra, Taine on, 7:1463b

Angélique ou L'Enchantement (Angélique; or, Being Enchanted). *See* Robbe-Grillet, Alain

Angelism, in Balzac's works, 5:643b

Angelita. See Azorín

Angélo, tyran de Padoue (Angelo, the Tyrant of Padua). *See* Hugo, Victor

Angelo. See Pushkin, Alexander

Angelo dell'informazione e altri testi teatrali, L'. See Moravia, Alberto

"Angelo nero, L'." *See* Montale, Eugenio, *Satura*

Angels of Sin, The. See Giraudoux, Jean, *Les anges du péché*

Angelus, in Claudel's *The Tidings Brought to Mary,* 8:483a-b

Angélus, L'. See Maupassant, Guy de

"Angelus Novus" (journal), 11:1713a-b

Anger. See Ionesco, Eugène, *La colère*

Anges du péché, Les. See Giraudoux, Jean

Anges noir, Les. See Mauriac, François, *The Dark Angels*

Ångest. See Lagerkvist, Pär

Angestellten, Die. See Kracauer, Siegfried

Angiola Maria. See Carcano, Giulio

Angioletti, Annamaria, 12:2408a-b

Anglické listy. See Čapek, Karel

Anglo-Saxon Chronicle
- poems in, 1:64b
- on the slaying of King Cyneheard, 1:64a

Anglo-Saxon poetry, **1:51a–87b**
- surviving codices, 1:64b
- techniques, 1:66a–69a
- *see also Beowulf*

Anglophilia, Fontane and, 6:1301b–1303b

"Angoisse" ("Anguish"). *See* Mallarmé, Stéphane

Angola, 11:2145b

"Angry gaze of your colorless eyes, The." *See* Blok, Alexander, "Serdityi vzor bestsvetnykh glaz"

Anguish and Joy of the Christian Life. See Mauriac, François, *Souffrances et bonheur du chrétien*

Anhang: Vermischte Meinungen und Sprüche. See Nietzsche, Friedrich

Anicet ou le panorama, roman (Anicet; or, The Panorama, Novel). *See* Aragon, Louis

Anihta hartia. See Elytis, Odysseus

Anima, in Hugo's works, 6:702a

"Anima che diverse cose tante." *See* Petrarch, *Canzoniere*

Animal de fondo (Animal of the Depths). *See* Jiménez, Juan Ramón

Animal with a Halo, The. *See* Gunnarsson, Gunnar, *Dyret med Glorien*
Animal imagery
   in Balzac's works, 5:643a
   in Blasco Ibáñez' novels
      Reeds and Mud, 8:381a
      The Cabin, 8:373b
      The Mayflower, 8:363a-b, 365b
   in Claudel's *Joan of Arc at the Stake*, 8:488a-b
   in Colette's works, 9:626a-b
   in Musset's works, 6:1019b
   of Pirandello, 8:397b, 400b
   in Sarraute's works, 12:2338b
Animal instinct, in Mauriac, 10:1321a-b
Animal physiology, in Montesquieu's *Observations on Natural History*, 3:348a-b
Animal poems, Leconte de Lisle, 6:1266a–1267b
Animals
   in Aymé's works, 12:2434a–2435a, 2449b
   as characters in La Fontaine's *Fables*, 3:86b–95a
   see also Beastliness
"Animaux malades de la peste, Les" ("The Animals Sick with the Plague"). *See* La Fontaine, Jean de, *Fables*
Anipotahti politia. See Ritsos, Yannis
Änkeman Jarl. See Moberg, Vilhelm
Anker, Nini Roll, 9:1018a
"Ankomst i Hades." *See* Södergran, Edith, "Arrival in Hades"
Anna Karenina. See Tolstoy, Leo
Anna Meunier. *See* Huysmans, Joris Karl
"Anna, soror" ("Anna, Sister"). *See* Yourcenar, Marguerite, *Comme l'eau qui coule*
Annales school of historians, Unamuno's anticipation of, 8:288a
Annar heimur. See Laxness, Halldór, *Salka Valka*
Annat, Père, Pascal and, 3:136b, 137b
"Anne Akhmatovoi." *See* Blok, Alexander
Anne de Gonzague, funeral oration by Bossuet on, 3:165b–166a
Anne, Queen of France, 3:55a, 55b, 56a, 58b, 59b

La Rochefoucauld and, 3:56b, 57a-b, 58a, 60a, 61a
Anneaux de Bicêtre, Les. See Simenon, Georges
Année dernière à Marienbad, L'. See Robbe-Grillet, Alain, *Last Year at Marienbad*
Année, L'. See Brazais, marquis de
Annenskii, Innokentii
   acmeists' departure from, 10:1523a
   Akhmatova and, 10:1522a
   on downfall of Petrine Russia, 10:1619b–1620a
   Mandelshtam and, 10:1627a, 1629a
Annihilation of Milos, The. *See* Ritsos, Yannis, *O afanismos tis Milos*
Annihilation, theme of
   in Ionesco's works, 13:2989b
      The Bald Soprano, 13:2992b–2993a
"Anniversary." *See* Elytis, Odysseus, *Prosanatolizmi (Orientations)*, "Epetios"
"Anniversary" ("Anniversario"). *See* Montale, Eugenio, *The Storm and Other Things*
"Anno Domini MCMXLVII." *See* Quasimodo, Salvatore
Annominatio, in Rutebeuf's "Des Jacobins," 1:346b
Annonce faite à Marie, L'. See Claudel, Paul
Annunciation, travesty of in Pushkin's *The Gabrieliad*, 5:665a-b
Annunzio, Gabriele de. *See* D'Annunzio, Gabriele
"Another Fan/of Mademoiselle Mallarmé's." *See* Mallarmé, Stéphane, "Autre éventail/de Mademoiselle Mallarmé"
"Another Lament of Lord Pierrot." *See* Laforgue, Jules, *Les complaintes (Street Ballads)*, "Autre complainte de Lord Pierrot"
"Another Turning of the Worm." *See* Zamyatin, Yevgeny Ivanovich, "Mucheniki nauki"
Another World. *See* Laxness, Halldór, *Salka Valka*
Anouilh, Jean, **13:2843a–2864b**
   Antigone, 13:2844b, 2848b, 2849b, 2850a–2853a
      prologue, 13:2850a-b

Anouilh, Jean (*cont.*)
Antigone (*cont.*)
style, 13:2853b
antitheater, 13:2843b, 2844b
Ardèle, 13:2857b–2858a, 2862a
Becket; or, The Honor of God (*Becket ou l'honneur de Dieu*), 13:2844b, 2860a–2861a
Cécile ou l'école des pères (*Cécile; or, The School for Fathers*), 13:2855b, 2856a
characters, source for, 13:2846b
Dear Antoine (*Cher Antoine*), 13:2843a, 2843b, 2845a, 2853a, 2860a, 2861a, 2863a
dialogue, 13:2853a, 2862b
Épuration (*The Purge*), 13:2859a
Eurydice (*Legends of Lovers; Point of Departure*), 13:2845a, 2846a, 2850a
false dramas, 13:2845a
Giraudoux and, 9:1041b
Jézabel, 13:2848b, 2849b–2850a
origin of fate, 13:2849a
Joan of Arc and, 8:488a
La foire d'empoigne (*Catch as Catch Can*), 13:2860a
La grotte (*The Cavern*), 13:2850b, 2861a
La répétition ou l'amour puni (*The Rehearsal*), 13:2855b–2856a
Le boulanger, la boulangère et le petit mitron (*The Baker, His Wife, and His Little Apprentice*), 13:2844b, 2861b, 2862a–2863a
Le rendez-vous de Senlis (*The Rendezvous at Senlis; Dinner with the Family*), 13:2845a
Les poissons rouges ou mon père ce héros (*The Goldfish; or, My Father, That Hero*), 13:2845a, 2859b–2860a, 2861a, 2862a, 2863a-b
L'Hurluberlu (*The Fighting Cock*), 13:2862a
L'Invitation au château (*Ring Round the Moon*), 13:844b, 2855b–2856a
L'Orchestre, 13:2844b, 2861b
Mandarine, 13:2845b
Médée (*Medea*), 13:2848b–2849a, 2850a, 2853b–2854a
origin of fate, 13:2849a
nouvelles pièces noires (new black plays), 13:2846b–2854a
and *pièces noires*, 13:2849a
Ornifle ou le courant d'air (Ornifle; or, The Draft), 13:2858a
pièces brilliantes, 13:2855b–2856a
pièces costumées, 13:2860a
pièces grinçantes, 13:2856a–2861a
pièces noires (black plays), 13:2846a–2848b
pièces roses, 13:2854a–2856a
Poor Bitos (*Pauvre Bitos*), 13:2851a, 2858b, 2859a, 2859b–2860a
Restless Heart (*La sauvage*), 13:2845a, 2846b–2847a, 2855a
origin of fate, 13:2849a
Romeo and Jeannette; Fading Mansions (*Roméo et Jeannette*), 13:2848b, 2853a-b
origin of fate, 13:2849a
satires, 13:2860a
The Ermine (*L'Hermine*), 13:2844, 2845a, 2845b, 2846a-b, 2848a, 2854a
origin of fate, 13:2849a
The Lark (*L'Alouette*), 13:2844b, 2860a–2861a
The Waltz of the Toreadors (*La valse des toréadors*), 13:2856a-b, 2857a–2858a
Thieves' Carnival (*Le bal des voleurs*), 13:2844b, 2854b–2855a
Time Remembered (*Léocadia*), 13:2853b, 2855a
Toto, 13:2862a–2863a
Traveler Without Luggage (*Le voyageur sans bagage*), 13:2846a, 2854b, 2861b
origin of fate, 13:2849a
Y'avait un prisonnier (*There Was a Prisoner*), film rights, 13:2845b
Anouilh, Jean, and Aurenche, Jean, *Humulus le muet* (*Humulus the Mute*), 13:2845b, 2854b, 2861b
Anouilh, Jean, and Barrault, Jean-Louis, *La petite Molière*, 13:2845a
Anselm of Canterbury, St., 1:406a-b, 420b
Anselm of Laon, 1:406b
Ansichten eines Clowns. See Böll, Heinrich, *The Clown*
Answer from the Silence. *See* Frisch, Max, *Antwort aus der Stille*

Answer to Future Gossip, An. *See*
      Mayakovsky, Vladimir, "Otvet na
      budushchie spletni"
"Answers to Nine Questions on the Novel."
      See Moravia, Alberto, "Risposta a nove
      domande sul romanzo"
"Ante Lucem." *See* Blok, Alexander
"Anté-Christ, Le." *See* Vigny, Alfred Victor de
Antero de Quental. *See* Quental, Antero de
Anthès-Heeckeren, George d', Pushkin and,
      5:663b–664a
Anthologie de l'humour noir. See Breton,
      André
Anthony, St., Flaubert and, 7:1374a
Anthropi kai topia. See Ritsos, Yannis, *Ta*
      Epikerika
Anthropocentrism
   Milosz and, 13:2937a
   Voltaire on, 4:385b, 389b–390a
Anthropos me to gharyfallo, O. See Ritsos,
      Yannis
Anthroposophical Society (Moscow), Bely and,
      9:924a, 924b
Anthroposophy
   Bely and, 9:919b
   Turgeneva and, 9:920a
Anti Machiavel. See Frederick II of Prussia,
      king
Anti-aesthetic poetry, Ekelöf and, 12:2644a
Anti-Christ, The. See Nietzsche, Friedrich
Anti-Christ, The. *See* Vigny, Alfred Victor de,
      "L'Anté-Christ"
Anti-Memoirs. See Malraux, André
Anti-Semite and Jew. See Sartre, Jean-Paul
Anti-Semitism
   Bergson and, 8:46a-b
   in Bourget's fiction, 8:520b
   in Céline's writing, 11:1862a-b, 1863a
   and the Dreyfus affair, 7:1517a-b,
      1537a–1539a
   in fascist Italy, 13:3134b–3136a
   Freud and, 8:5a
   in Ghelderode's plays, 11:2135b–2136a
   in the Goncourts' *Manette Salomon*, 7:1408a
   in Hašek's writings, 9:1107b
   and Heine, 5:492b
   of Heinrich Mann, 8:522a

Mandelshtam's experience of, 10:1631b
   Marinetti and, 9:825b
   Nietzsche and, 7:1665a, 1679a
   Pessoa and, 10:1480b–1481a, 1494a
   Schnitzler and, 8:98a-b, 103a-b, 105b–106a,
      114a
   in Svevo's background, 8:71a-b
   in twentieth century Russia, 11:1891a
   of Wagner, 7:1651a, 1665a
      admission of, 6:1162b
      German nationalism and, 6:1153a, 1159a
      in journals, 6:1164a
      Meyerbeer and, 6:1152a
      Wagnerism and, 6:1147b
   see also Holocaust
Antibarbari (The Antibarbarians). *See*
      Erasmus
Antibarbus. See Strindberg, August
Antichrist, Der. See Nietzsche, Friedrich, *The*
      Anti-Christ
Antichrist, Tegernsee. *See* Tegernsee
      Antichrist
Antici, Carlo, Leopardi and, 5:542b, 546a,
      562a
Anticlericalism
   French Third Republic and, 5:590b
   in Ghelderode's *Chronicles of Hell*,
      11:2121b
   Heine and, 5:497b
   Italian
      Carducci, 7:1497a, 1500a, 1501a, 1511b
      Verga's "Il reverendo," 7:1557b–1558a
   of Michelet, 5:582b
   Spanish, Pérez Galdós, 7:1609b, 1616b
   Voltaire and, 4:367a–368a, 378a–379b,
      383b–384a, 390b–391a
   see also Atheism
Anticlimax, in Chrétien's *Lancelot*, 1:197a-b
Antidote, The. See Alfieri, Vittorio, Political
      Tetralogy
Antidotes. See Ionesco, Eugène
Antigone
   Beauvoir and, 12:2716a
   in Laforgue's "Lament of Monotonous
      Autumn," 7:1888b
Antigone. See Alfieri, Vittorio; Anouilh, Jean;
      Cocteau, Jean; Sophocles

Antigone des Sophokles, Die (*The Antigone of Sophocles*). *See* Brecht, Bertolt
Antihero
  development of, Lessing's influence on, 4:551a
  in Svevo's novels, 8:81b
Antimémoires. See Malraux, André, *Anti-Memoirs*
Antinomianism, Milosz and, 13:2948a
"Antinomien des bürgerlichen Denkens, Die." *See* Lukács, György
"Antinomies of Bourgeois Thought, The." *See* Lukács, György, "Die Antinomien des bürgerlichen Denkens"
Antiquarianism, folk culture and, 4:641b, 643b, 658b
Antiquarian's Family, The. *See* Goldoni, Carlo, *La famiglia dell'antiquario*
"Antiquités de Rome, Les." *See* Bellay, Joachim du
Antiquity. *See* Classical literature; Classical world
Antithesis
  in Boileau's works, 3:193a, 203b
  in Camoëns' "Amor é fogo que arde sem se ver," 2:751a
  in *cancioneiros*, 2:753a
  Hegelian. *See* Dialectics, Hegelian
  in *Hrafnkels saga*, 1:394b
  in Olesha's works, 11:2242a
  typology and, 1:3b
Antitradition futuriste, L'. See Apollinaire, Guillaume
Antoine, André, 7:1930b–1931a
Antoine et Julie. See Simenon, Georges
Antokol'skii, Pavel, on Pasternak's *Early Trains*, 10:1608b–1609a
Antonin Artaud: Dessins et portraits. See Artaud, Antonin
Antonio Azorín. See Azorín
Antonio of Brescia, 1:414a
Antonovich, Maksim, on Turgenev, 6:1287b
Antony. See Dumas père, Alexandre
Antony and Cleopatra. See Shakespeare, William
Antwort aus der Stille. See Frisch, Max
Anxieties. *See* Andrić, Ivo, *Nemiri*

Anxiety
  Freud's concept of, 8:4b
  Kierkegaard and, 6:1139a–1140a
  Sartre and, 12:2595b–2596b
"Apellesova cherta" ("The Apelles Mark"). *See* Pasternak, Boris, *Rasskazy* (*Stories*)
"Aphigisi." *See* Seferis, George
Aphorismen und Betrachtungen. See Schnitzler, Arthur
Aphorisms
  in Boileau's writing, 3:188a
  in Valéry's *Tel quel*, 8:584a-b
  see also Maxims
Aphorisms and Observations. See Schnitzler, Arthur, *Aphorismen und Betrachtungen*
"Apo tin scholin tou perionymou philosophou." *See* Cavafy, Constantine
"Apo to imerologio tou '46." *See* Seferis, George
Apocalypse
  in Arp, 10:1367b–1368a
  images of, in Trakl, 10:1410a–1411a
  see also Bible
"Apocalypsis Goliae Episcopi" ("Revelation of Golias the Bishop"), 1:354a
Apocryphal Stories. See Čapek, Karel, *Apokryfy*
Apokryfy. See Čapek, Karel
Apollinaire on Art. See Apollinaire, Guillaume, *Chroniques d'art*
Apollinaire, Guillaume, 8:546b, **9:881a–903b**
  "À l'Italie" ("To Italy"), 10:1456a
  Alcools, 9:885b–886a
    "Automne malade" ("Sick Autumn"), 9:887a, 888b
    "collage" technique in, 9:889b
    "Cors de chasse" ("Hunting Horn"), 9:894a-b
    "La Loreley," 9:887a
    "La tzigane" ("The Gypsy"), 9:887b, 888b
    Laurencin and, 9:894a, 894b
    "Le larron" ("The Thief"), 9:885b, 886a
    "Le pont Mirabeau" ("The Mirabeau Bridge"), 9:885a, 894a, 894b
    "Le voyageur" ("The Traveler"), 9:893a-b, 895a, 896b, 901a
    "L'Ermite" ("The Hermit"), 9:885b, 886a

"Les colchiques" ("Crocuses"), 9:887a, 888a, 888b, 894a

"Mai" ("May"), 9:887b–888a, 895a

"Merlin et la vieille femme" ("Merlin and the Old Lady"), 9:885b

punctuation of, 9:882a-b

"Rhénanes" series, 9:887a-b

"Zone," 9:884b, 885a, 894b–895a, 895a–896b, 901a

"Arbre" ("Tree"), 9:897a

"Au prolétaire" ("To the Proletariat"), 9:886b, 887b

"Aubade," 9:889b–890a

Breton and, 11:1939a-b

Calligrammes, 9:882a, 897a-b, 900a

    "À travers l'Europe" ("Across Europe"), 9:896b

    "collage" technique in, 9:889b

    "Fête" ("Festival"), 9:898a

    "La petite auto" ("The Little Car"), 9:884b

    "Les fenêtres" ("The Windows"), 9:896b

    "Lettre-océan" ("Letter-Ocean"), 9:884b, 895a

"Chef de section," 9:898a

Chroniques d'art (Apollinaire on Art), 9:883b

"Clair de lune" ("Moonlight"), 9:886b

on Cocteau, 10:1546b

"Cortège," 9:882b–883a, 891a-b, 895a

diction of, 10:1456a

"Fiançailles" ("The Betrothal"), 9:891b–892b, 893b, 894a, 895a, 896b, 900a

    "The Hills" and, 9:900b

Ghelderode and, 11:2134b

Il y a (There Is/Are), 9:885b

influence on Yourcenar's poetry, 12:2553a

Jarry and, 9:666a

"La chanson du mal-aimé" ("The Song of the Unloved Lover"), 9:888b–891a, 893b, 895a, 896b

    "Les sept epées" ("The Seven Swords"), 9:890a-b

"La jolie rousse" ("The Pretty Redhead"), 9:885a, 899b, 900a, 900b–901a

"La victoire" ("The Victory"), 9:899a

"L'Adieu du cavalier" ("The Horseman's Good-bye"), 9:897b

L'Antitradition futuriste (The Futurist Antitradition), 9:898b

Le bestiaire, ou cortège d'Orphée (Bestiary; or, The Parade of Orpheus), 9:894a

    "L'Écrevisse" ("The Crayfish"), 9:883a

"Le Brasier" ("The Brazier"), 9:891b, 892b, 894a, 900b

Le flâneur des deux rives (The Left- and Right-Bank Stroller), 9:895a

    "Le passant de Prague" ("The Wanderer of Prague"), 9:895a

Le guetteur mélancolique (The Melancholy Watchman), 9:885b

Le poète assassiné (The Poet Assassinated), 9:883b, 901a, 901b

"L'Emigrant de Landor Road," 9:891a, 895a

L'Enchanteur pourrissant (The Rotting Magician), 9:885b

"Les collines" ("The Hills"), 9:900a, 900b, 901a, 901b, 902a

Les mamelles de Tirésias (The Breasts of Tiresias), 9:898b–899a, 899b–900a

"L'Esprit nouveau et les poètes" ("The New Spirit and the Poets"), 9:884a-b

L'Hérésiarque et cie (The Heresiarch and Co.), "Que vlo-ve" ("What Do You Want?"), 9:887a

"Liens" ("Bonds"), 9:897a

"Lundi rue Christine" ("Monday rue Christine"), 9:897a

Méditations esthétiques: Les peintres cubistes (The Cubist Painters: Aesthetic Meditations), 9:883b, 884a, 885b, 892b, 896b

Lagerkvist and, 10:1682b

"Merveille de la guerre" ("Marvels of War"), 9:885a-b

"Moi aussi je suis peintre" ("I Too Am a Painter"), 9:897a

"Mon cher Ludovic" ("My Dear Ludovic"), 9:901b

Oeuvres poétiques, 9:885b

Ombre de mon amour (Shadow of My Love), 9:898a

"Onirocritique" ("Dreamcritique"), 9:891b

Apollinaire, Guillaume (*cont.*)
　"Poème lu au mariage d'André Salmon"
　　　("Poem Read at the Marriage of André
　　　Salmon"), 9:892b
　"Poèmes retrouvés" ("Rediscovered Poems"),
　　　9:885b
　Sade praised by, 4:637a
　"Salomé," 9:888b
　Tendre comme le souvenir (*Tender as a
　　　Memory*), 9:898a
　　"La tranchée" ("The Trench"), 9:898a
　　"Tristesse d'une étoile" ("A Star's Sadness"),
　　　9:900a, 900b, 901a
　Ungaretti and, 10:1455b–1456a
　"Vendémiaire," 9:892b, 895a
　Vitam impendere amori, 9:885a, 900a
Apollinaris Sidonius, *Epistles*, 1:15a
Apollo
　in Ady's poetry, 9:867b–868a, 870a, 876b
　Daphne and, in Petrarch's *Canzoniere*,
　　　2:493a, 496a, 496b
　in Rilke's "Archaic Torso of Apollo," 9:785b
　sibyl of, in Lagerkvist's *Sibyl*,
　　　10:1698b–1699a
Apollon de Bellac, L' (*The Apollo of Bellac*).
　　　See Giraudoux, Jean
Apollon (journal)
　acmeist manifestos in, 10:1632b
　Mandelshtam published by, 10:1631b
Apologie. *See* La Rochefoucauld, François VI,
　　　duc de
Apologie pour Fénelon. *See* Brémond, Henri
Apologue, La Fontaine and, 3:77a, 80b–81a,
　　　95a
"Apology." *See* Chénier, André
"Apology for Raymond Sebond." *See*
　　　Montaigne, Michel de, *Essais*
Apomnimonevmata. *See* Makriyannis, Yannis
"Apophasi tis lysmonias, I." *See* Seferis,
　　　George
Apostasy, in Butor, 13:3296a-b
Apostle, The. *See* Petőfi, Sándor, *Az apostol*
Apothegms. *See* Maxims
"Apotheosis." *See* Ekelöf, Gunnar
Apotheosis. *See* Prudentius
Apparition, The. *See* Zamyatin, Yevgeny
　　　Ivanovich, "Videnie"

"Appeal by the Presidents of the Planet Earth,
　　　An." *See* Khlebnikov, Velimir,
　　　"Vozzvanie predsedatelei zemnogo
　　　shara"
"Appendice storica su la colonna infame." *See*
　　　Manzoni, Alessandro, *Fermo e Lucia*
Apprendre à marcher. *See* Ionesco, Eugène
*Apprenticeship and Travels of Wilhelm
　　　Meister, The*. *See* Goethe, Johann
　　　Wolfgang von
"Aprel'." *See* Zamyatin, Yevgeny Ivanovich
Aprel' semnadtsatogo. *See* Solzhenitsyn,
　　　Aleksandr, *The Red Wheel*
"Après le deluge." *See* Rimbaud, Arthur, "After
　　　the Deluge"
"Après une lecture de Dante." *See* Hugo,
　　　Victor
Après-midi d'un faune, L'. *See* Mallarmé,
　　　Stéphane
April 1917. *See* Solzhenitsyn, Aleksandr, *The
　　　Red Wheel*
April, in Elytis' *To imerologio enos atheatou
　　　Apriliou*, 13:2983a
"April." *See* Zamyatin, Yevgeny Ivanovich,
　　　"Aprel'"
April Tale. *See* Valle-Inclán, Ramón del,
　　　Cuento de abril
A. P. Rosell, bankdirektör (*A. P. Rosell, Bank
　　　Director*). *See* Moberg, Vilhelm
Apuleius, Lucius
　De deo Socratis, Ronsard's "Les Daimons"
　　　and, 2:733a
　Golden Ass
　　Flaubert and, 7:1380a
　　influence on Renaissance short fiction,
　　　2:931a
"Aquesta gens, cant son en lur gaieza." *See*
　　　Peire Cardenal
Aquinas, Thomas, St., **1:405a–429b**
　on Aristotle's *De fallaciis*, 1:410b–411a
　Augustine and, 1:23a
　Catena aurea (*The Golden Chain*), 1:415a,
　　　415b–416a, 416b
　Compedium theologiae (*Compendium of
　　　Theology*), 1:419a

Contra doctrinam retrahentium a religione (*Against the Doctrine of Defection from the Religious Life*), 1:417b

Contra errores Graecorum (*Against the Errors of the Greeks*), 1:415a

Contra impugnantes Dei cultum et religionem (*Against the Assailants of God*), 1:414a

Dante and, 1:433b

De aeternitate contra murmurantes (*On Eternity Against the Critics*), 1:422a

De angelis (*On Angels*), 1:419a

De anima (*On the Soul*), 1:418a

De divinis nominibus (*On the Divine Names*), 1:416a

De ente et essentia ad fratres et socios meos (*On Being and Essence*), 1:412b

De hebdomadibus (*On Axioms*), 1:414b

De ingressu puerorum in religione (*On Entry of Boys into Religious Life*), 1:417b

De malo (*On Evil*), 1:416b

De perfectione spiritualis vitae (*On the Perfection of the Spiritual Life*), 1:417b

De potentia Dei (*On the Power of God*), 1:416b

De principiis naturae ad Fratrem Sylvestrum (*On the Principles of Nature*), 1:412b

De propositionalibus modalibus (*On Modal Propositions*), 1:410b–411a

De rationibus fidei contra Saracenos Graecos et Armenos ad cantorem Antiochiae (*The Foundations of Faith Established Against the Saracens, Greeks, and Armenians*), 1:416a

De regno (*On the Rule of Princes*), 1:416a, 426a

De spiritualibus creaturis (*On the Spiritual Creatures*), 1:416b

De substantiis separatis (*On Separated Substances*), 1:419a

De unione verbi incarnati (*On Union with the Incarnate Word*), 1:418a

De unitate intellectus (*On the Unity of the Intellect*), 1:418b

De virtutibus (*On the Virtues*), 1:418a

Expositio, 1:415a

on justice, 7:1672b

Quaestiones disputate de veritate (*Disputed Questions of Truth*), 1:413a

Scriptum super Sententias (*Commentaries on the Sentences*), 1:412a-b

Summa contra Gentiles (*A Summary Against the Gentiles*), 1:414a-b, 415a, 421b

Summa theologica (*A Summary of Theology*), 1:416b–417a

Dante and, 1:448b

Scriptum super Sententias and, 1:412b

Summa contra Gentiles and, 1:414b

"Treatise on the Divine Government," Bossuet and, 3:157b

Aquis submersus. *See* Storm, Theodor

Arabeski (*Arabesques*). *See* Bely, Andrey

Arabesques. *See* Gogol, Nikolay Vasilievich

Arabian Nights' Entertainments, The
Flaubert and, 7:1379a

George and, 8:457a

Valle-Inclan's *Comedia de ensueño* and, 8:342a

Arabic art, Delacroix and, 5:530b

Arabic philosophy. *See* Islamic philosophy

Arabic poetry, Mickiewicz's *Crimean Sonnets* and, 5:615a, 616a

Arabs, Sicilian, in Pirandello's *I vecchi ei giovani*, 8:389b–390a

Arachne, in La Fontaine's "L'Araignée et l'hirondelle," 3:90a, 90b, 92b

Aragon, Louis, 9:901a, **11:2061a–2087b**

Anicet ou le panorama, roman (*Anicet; or, The Panorama, Novel*), 11:2065b

Aurélien, 11:2081a-b

Aux intellectuels révolutionnaires (*To Revolutionary Intellectuals*), 11:2073b

Blanche ou l'oubli (*Blanche; or, Forgetfulness*), 11:2083b–2084a, 2084b, 2085b

"Complainte des chômeurs" (*Lament of the Strikers*), 11:2074b

Elsa Triolet choisie par Aragon (*Elsa Triolet Chosen by Aragon*), 11:2084b

"Front rouge" ("Red Front"), 11:2073b–2074a

Henri Matisse, roman (*Henri Matisse, A Novel*), 11:2084a

Aragon, Louis (*cont.*)

Hourra l'Oural (Hurrah for the Urals), 11:2075b–2076a

Je n'ai jamais appris à écrire ou les incipits (I Have Never Learned to Write; or, The Opening Words), 11:2066a-b

La diane française (French Reveille), 11:2080b

La grande gaieté (Great Gaiety), 11:2069b

La mise à mort (Put to Death), 11:2083a-b

La semaine sainte (*Holy Week*), 11:2082a-b

Lampedusa's *The Leopard* praised by, 11:2011a

Le crève-coeur (Heartbreak), 11:2079b

Le crime contre l'esprit (*Les Martyrs*) (Crimes Against the Spirit [The Martyrs]), 11:2078b, 2079a

Le libertinage (*The Libertine*), 11:2061b

Le monde réel cycle (The Real World), 11:2076a–2078a, 2080b–2081b

Le mouvement perpétuel (Perpetual Motion), 11:2065b

Le museé Grévin (The Wax Museum), 11:2078b, 2080a

Le nouveau crève-coeur (New Heartbreak), 11:2081b

Le paysan de Paris (*Paris Peasant; Nightwalker*), 11:2065b–2066b
  Apollinaire and, 9:889b

Le peinture au défi (Painting as Challenge), 11:2069b–2070a

"Le prix de l'esprit" (The Price of Intellect), 11:2068a-b

Le traité du style (Essay on Style), 11:2065a-b, 2069b

Les beaux quartiers (*Residential Quarter*), 11:2077a-b, 2081a

Les cloches de Bâle (*The Bells of Basel*), 11:2076a–2077a, 2077b

Les oeuvres romanesques croisées d'Elsa Triolet et de Louis Aragon (The Crossed Works of Fiction of Elsa Triolet and Louis Aragon), 11:2084b

Les voyageurs de l'impériale (*The Century Was Young; Passengers of Destiny*), 11:2080b–2081a

Les yeux d'Elsa (Elsa's Eyes), 11:2080a

L'Homme communiste (Communist Man), 11:2081b–2082a

Littératures soviétiques (Soviet Literature), 11:2076a

Persécuté persécuteur (The Persecuted and the Persecutor), 11:2075b

Pour un réalisme socialiste (Toward Socialist Realism), 11:2064a-b, 2075b, 2076a

"Prélude au temps de cerises" (Prelude to Cherry Blossom Time), 11:2074b–2075a

Queneau and, 12:2511a

Servitude et grandeur des français (The Slavishness and Greatness of the French People), 11:2080a-b

Théâtre-roman (Theater-Novel), 11:2084a

"Araignée et l'hirondelle, L'." *See* La Fontaine, Jean de, *Fables*

Aranitsis, Eugenios, 13:2975b

"Arano." *See* Pascoli, Giovanni, *Myricae*

Arany, János, Ady and, 9:860a, 864b

Aranysárkány. See Kosztolányi, Dezső

Araspes und Panthea. See Wieland, Christoph Martin

Arbeitsjournal. See Brecht, Bertolt

Arbenin. See Lermontov, Mikhail Yurievich

Arbetet. See Johnson, Eyvind

Árbol de la ciencia, El. See Baroja, Pío

Arbouin, Gabriel, 9:897a

"Arbre." *See* Apollinaire, Guillaume

Arcades Project. *See* Benjamin, Walter

Arcadia
  in Renaissance pastoral poetry, 2:899b–900a
  Sannazaro's piscatorial transposition of, 2:909a
  in Vergil's poetry, 2:901a, 901b

Arcadia. See Lope de Vega; Sannazaro, Jacopo; Sydney, Philip

Arcadia in Brenta, L'. See Goldoni, Carlo

Arcana coelestia. See Swedenborg, Emanuel

Arcane 17. See Breton, André

Archaeology
  Foucault and, 13:3345a–3350b
  Mérimée and, 6:760b–761a, 763a

Archaeology of Knowledge, The (*L'Archéologie du savoir*). *See* Foucault, Michel

"Archaïscher Torso Apollos" ("Archaic Torso of Apollo"). *See* Rilke, Rainer Maria, *Neue Gedichte* (*New Poems*)

Archaisms, in Leopardi's works, 5:555b

Archenholz, Johann von, *On England and Italy*, Richter and, 5:59a

Archer, William
  Ibsen translations, 7:1429a, 1436b
  Play-making, 7:1927a

"Archetype." *See* Elytis, Odysseus, *To photodendro kai i dekati tetarti omorfia* (*The Light Tree*), "Arhetipon"

Archetypes, in *Romance of the Rose*, 1:315b–316a

"Archi ton, I." *See* Cavafy, Constantine

Archibald Douglas. *See* Fontane, Theodor

Archilochus, Chénier and, 4:704b, 714a-b

Archimedes, in Descartes's *Meditations on First Philosophy*, 3:11a

"Archipelagus, Der." *See* Hölderlin, Friedrich

Archipenko, Alexander, 9:896b

Architecture
  Akhmatova's symbology, 10:1525a, 1525b, 1528a
  in Musil's *The Man Without Qualities*, 9:945b–946a
  style of, in Gautier's works, 6:1044a–1045a
  Valéry on, 8:585a, 585b

"Architecture." *See* Leconte de Lisle, Charles Marie

Architecture of Trees, The. *See* Ritsos, Yannis, *I arhitektoniki ton dhentron*

Archives du nord (Archives of the North). *See* Yourcenar, Marguerite

Archpoet
  "Estuans instrinsicus ira vehementi" ("Raging inside with violent anger"), 1:357a–358b, 359a
  "Fama tuba dante sonum" ("Fame with its trumpet blowing"), 1:342b–343a
  parody and, 1:370b–371a
  "Salve mundi domine, Cesar noster ave" ("Greetings, master of the world, our Caesar, hail"), 1:371a

Archpoet's Confession. *See* Archpoet, "Estuans instrinsicus ira vehementi"

Ardor of Youth, The. *See* Mauriac, François, *Le jeune homme*

Arendt, Hannah, Heinrich Mann and, 8:529b–530a, 533b

Aretej ili Legenda o Svetoj Ancili, Rajskoj Ptici (Aretaeus; or, The Legend of St. Ancilla, the Bird of Paradise). *See* Krleža, Miroslav

Aretino, Pietro, Camoëns and, 2:758b–759a

"Argamak." *See* Babel, Isaac, *Red Cavalry*

Argent, L'. *See* Zola, Émile

Argenti, *Sfortunato* (The Unfortunate One), Renaissance pastoral drama and, 2:917a

Argentina, Gombrowicz and, 12:2564b

"Argentine Ant, The." *See* Calvino, Italo

Argonautas, Los (The Argonauts). *See* Blasco Ibáñez, Vicente

Argonauts. *See* Jason

Argot, Céline's use of, 11:1865b–1866a

Argumentation. *See* Debates

Arguments Against the Aristotelians. *See* Gassendi, Pierre

"Argus." *See* Petrarch

Argyriou, Alexandros, on Seferis' *Thrush*, 12:2268a

"Arhetipon." *See* Elytis, Odysseus, *To photodendro kai i dekati tetarti omorfia*

Arhitektoniki ton dhentron, I. *See* Ritsos, Yannis

Ari Thorgilsson the Learned, *Íslendingabók* (*Book of the Icelanders*), 1:379b–380a, 381b, 388a, 395b, 399a

Aria del continente, L'. *See* Pirandello, Luigi

Ariadne auf Naxos (Ariadne on Naxos). *See* Hofmannsthal, Hugo von

Ariane et Barbe-Bleue, ou la délivrance inutile. *See* Maeterlinck, Maurice

"Arias otoñales." *See* Jiménez, Juan Ramón

Arias tristes. *See* Jiménez, Juan Ramón

Ariès, Philippe
  death in Western society, 2:536a-b, 542a, 555b–556a
  literary testament, 2:538a
  two afterlives, 2:545b, 546a

"Ariettes oubliées." *See* Verlaine, Paul

Ariosto, Lodovico, **2:619a–644b**

Ariosto, Lodovico (*cont.*)
  I suppositi, 2:623b
  Il negromante, 2:623b
  La cassaria, 2:622a–623a
  La Lena, 2:623a-b
  Orlando furioso, 2:624b–643b, 791a, 798a-b
    Boiardo's *Orlando innamorato* and, 2:906b
    Calvino and, 13:3267b–3268b
    Camoëns and, 2:747a, 762b–763a, 765b, 766b
    Lampedusa's *The Leopard* and, 11:2013b
    Lope de Vega and, 2:849a
    novellas as sources for, 2:940a
    pastoral interlude in, 2:910a
    sources for, 2:514b
    Petrarchan influence, 2:504a
    Tasso and, 2:791a, 792a, 817a
Ariostos o prosehtikos afighite stighmes tou viou tou kai tou ipnou tou (Ariostos the Mindful Narrates Moments from His Life and Sleep). *See* Ritsos, Yannis
Aristaenetus, translated into French by Lesage, 3:320a
Aristides of Miletus, Milesian tales and, 2:930b
Aristipp und einige seiner Zeitgenossen (*Aristipp and Some of His Contemporaries*). *See* Wieland, Christoph Martin
"Aristocracia y democracia" (Aristocracy and Democracy). *See* Jiménez, Juan Ramón
Aristocracy
  Alfieri's antagonism toward, 4:663a, 664a
  in Andersen, 6:882a-b
  Aymé's satire of, 12:2440b–2441a
  in Beaumarchais' *Marriage of Figaro*, 4:579a-b
  in Camoëns' *The Lusiads*, 2:764b
  in Castiglione, 2:653b–654a
  Corneille and, 3:24a
    Cinna, 3:44a
    Horace, 3:35b
  in Dinesen, 10:1295b–1296b
  French
    in Italian wars, 2:693b–694a
    in Simon's *The Georgics*, 13:3043a
    see also Monarchy, French

  Goldoni and, 4:422b, 436a
  in Gombrowicz, 12:2584b–2585a
  Goncharov's view of, 6:1062b–1063b, 1072a, 1079b
  in La Bruyère's *Caractères*, 3:245b–247a, 253a-b
  in "Pois l'iverns d'ogan es anatz," 1:348a–349a
  in Proust's *Remembrance of Things Past*, 8:551a–555b
  in Rabelais's *Fifth Book*, 2:713b
  in Stendhal, 5:349b–350a
  in Vico's analysis, 3:302a
Aristophanes
  Céline and, 11:1873a
  Lysistrata, 9:1047a
    Ghelderode's *Le siège d'Ostende* and, 11:2133a
  Staël on, 5:109b
  The Clouds, Elytis' *Maria Nephele* and, 13:2977a
Aristotelian unities. *See* Unities, dramatic
Aristotelianism, Luther and, 2:675b–675a
Aristotle
  aisthesis, 9:1132b–1133a
  Aquinas and, 1:414b, 418b, 423b
  Brecht on, 11:2093b
  Claudel and, 8:472a
  Dante and, 1:432a, 442a, 443b
  De anima (*On the Soul*), William of Moerbeke and, 1:417a
  De fallaciis (*On Fallacies*), 1:410b–411a
  doctrine of the tragic flaw, 3:219b, 220a
  on dramatic plot, Scribe and, 7:1911a
  entelechy and, 5:188a
  Ethics, Petrarch on, 2:488a
  and Lessing, 4:545a
  Lope de Vega and, 2:851b
  Magic Mountain and, 9:723b
  Metaphysics, Dante and, 1:439a
  Nicomachean Ethics, 7:1677b
    translations of, 1:408b
  Physics, *De principiis naturae ad Fratrem Sylvestrum* and, 1:412b
  Poetics
    Boileau's discussion of tragedy and, 3:196b–197a

Lessing on, 4:547b–548a

medieval drama and, 1:452b

poetry and philosophy in, 5:186b–187a

Racine and, 3:220a

Renaissance poetic theory and, 2:750a

Politics, Aquinas and, 1:425a, 425b

Rhetoric, Lessing on, 4:537b–548a

Rilke and, 9:775b

Schiller and, 5:44b

Schlegel and, 5:186b–187a

scholastic dialectic and, 1:405a

Schopenhauer's critique of, 5:398b

translated, 1:408a-b

Valle-Inclán and, 8:331b, 345b

Western rediscovery of, 1:407b–409a

Arithmetic, Pascal's works on, 3:130a-b, 132a

Ark, The. *See* Tsvetaeva, Marina, *Kovcheg*

"Arkhierey." *See* Chekhov, Anton

Arkhipelag Gulag. *See* Solzhenitsyn,
    Aleksandr, *The Gulag Archipelago*

Arland, Marcel, Malraux and, 12:2416a

Arlequin colonel. *See* Lesage, Alain-René

Arma Christi, in Villon's *Testament*, 2:559a,
    559b

Armance. *See* Stendhal

Armchair Theater. *See* Musset, Alfred de

Arme Spielmann, Der. *See* Grillparzer, Franz

"Armeggiamenti." *See* Pirandello, Luigi

Armen, Die. *See* Mann, Heinrich, *Das
    Kaiserreich*

Army. *See* Military, the

Army Chaplain Schmelzle's Trip to Flätz. *See*
    Richter, Jean Paul, *Des Feldpredigers
    Schmelzle Reise nach Flätz*

Arnakis, George, on Seferis, 12:2263a

Arnauld, Antoine, Pascal and, 3:129a, 130a,
    132b, 134a

Arnaut Daniel, 1:439a, 441b

Bernart and, 1:177a

courtly love in works of, 1:175b

"En cest sonet coind'e leri" ("To this
    gracious and joyful tune"), 1:177a

"Lo ferm voler," 1:176b

Petrarch's *Canzoniere*, quotations in, 2:493b

rim estramp and, 1:176b–177a

as troubadour, 1:175a–177b

Arniches, Carlos, *La cara de Dios* (The Face
    of God), Valle-Inclán and, 8:333b

Arnim, Achim von, and Brentano, Clemens,
    Des Knaben Wunderhorn (*The Boy's
    Magic Horn*), Grillparzer and, 5:436b

Arnim, Bettina von, *The Notebooks of Malte
    Laurids Brigge* and, 9:791a

Arnold, Matthew

"Dover Beach," Leopardi and, 5:556b

Mann and, 9:715b

postclassical literature and, 5:182a

on Sainte-Beuve, 6:838a, 839b

Taine and, 7:1449a

Arnoldi, Lev, 6:994a

Aron, Raymond, Sartre and, 12:2592a-b, 2606a

Arouet, François-Marie. *See* Voltaire

Around the World. *See* Ferreira de Castro,
    José Maria, *A volta ao mundo*

Arp, Jean, **10:1365a–1384b**

"Concrétion humaine" ("Human
    Concretion"), 10:1374a-b

dadaism and, 11:2063a-b

"Davos Configuration II," 10:1376a-b

Der Pyramidenrock (The Pyramid Skirt),
    10:1370b

der vogel selbdritt (Bird with Two Others),
    10:1367a–1368a

"Die Ebene" ("The Plain"), 10:1379a

Die Flucht aus der Zeit (*The Flight out of
    Time*), 10:1370a

die wolkenpumpe (The Cloud-pump),
    10:1367b, 1370b–1371a

Dreams and Projects, 10:1381a

"Ein Stag fährt Gondel" (Gondola Travel),
    10:1381b–1382a

"Je suis un point" ("I Am a Point"),
    10:1377b–1378a

Jours effeuillés (Days with Leaves),
    10:1368a-b, 1376b–1377a

"La vie de pinceau" (Life of the Brush),
    10:1378b–1379a

Le siège de l'air (The Seat of Air), 10:1379b

Le soleil recerclé (The Recircled Sun),
    10:1381b

On My Way, 10:1379b

Poèmes sans prénoms (Poems Without First
    Names), 10:1377a

Arp, Jean (*cont.*)

    "Pousses" ("Sprouts"), 10:1379b–1381a

    "The Skeleton of the Day," 10:1375a–1376a

    "Träume vom Tod und Leben" (Dreams of Life and Death), 10:1375a

    Unsern täglichen Traum (Our Daily Dream), 10:1369b

    Vers le blanc infini (Toward White Infinity), 10:1381b

    "Vier Knöpfe zwei Löcher vier Besen" (Four Buttons Two Holes Four Brooms), 10:1373a-b

    weisst du schwarzt du (If You White, You Black), 10:1373b–1372a

    "Worte" (Words), 10:1382a-b

    worttraüme und schwarze sterne (Word-Dreams and Black Stars), 10:1379b

Arrabal, Fernando, Sarraute and, 12:2355a

Arras, 1:459a

Arrest (*Verhaftung*), Kafka and, 9:1162a

"Arria Marcella." *See* Gautier, Théophile

"Arrival in Hades." *See* Södergran, Edith

"Arrostia tou Keitou, I." *See* Cavafy, Constantine

Arroyo, Ciriaco Morón, on Ortega y Gasset, 9:1120a, 1130b–1131a

Arroz y tartana. See Blasco Ibáñez, Vicente

"Ars historica," Bossuet and, 3:160a

Ars poetica. See Horace

"Ars Victrix." *See* Dobson, Austin

"Arsène Guillot." *See* Mérimée, Prosper

"Arsenio." *See* Gozzano, Guido; Montale, Eugenio, *Cuttlefish Bones*

Art

    Arp and, 10:1365a–1366a, 1374a–1375a

    Bergson's view of, 8:56a–57b

    Berlioz' view of, 6:775b, 776b, 797b–798b

    Breton's criticism, 11:1948b–1951a

    Butor and, 13:3305a–3307a

    Calvino and, 13:3283a

    Camus' view of, 13:3050a, 3075b–3076b

    Castiglione's view of, 2:655a–656b

    Christian, Gogol on, 6:979a

    Claudel and, 8:487b

    "death of," Marinetti on, 9:801a

    decadent, Croce on, 8:319a

    Diderot's criticism of, 4:487b–489a

    European, Delacroix's comparative view of, 5:530b–531a

    in Gautier's works, 6:1040a–1041a

    Gide's view of, 8:516a

    Goncharov's view of, 6:1073b

    Hamsun's concept of, 8:23b, 39b

    history of, Burckhardt and, 6:1231a–1234b

    Leconte de Lisle's view of, 6:1271a-b

    life and, Baroja's debate with Ortega y Gasset, 9:608b–609b

    love and, *Romance of the Rose* and, 1:314b–317a

    Malraux and, 12:2415b, 2425b–2427a

    meaning of, in Hesse's *The Glass Bead Game*, 9:854a

    médiocrité and, 2:715b

    nature and, in Rousseau, 4:465a-b

    in Olesha's works

        "Liompa," 11:2244b

        "The Cherry Stone," 11:2243b

    philosophy of

        of Ady, 9:875a

        of Blasco Ibáñez, 8:357a

        in Croce's *Estetica come scienza dell'espressione e linguistica generale*, 8:312b, 318b–319b

        in Croce's *Il concetto della storia nelle sue relazione col concetto dell'arte*, 8:313b, 314a, 318a

        of Hegel, 8:320a-b, 324b

        of Marinetti, 9:797b–798a, 799a-b, 801a, 801b

        of Musil, 9:955b–956a

        of Proust, 8:566a-b

        of Rilke, 9:777a, 782b–783a, 789a-b

        of Thomas Mann, 9:724a-b

        in Valle-Inclan's *La lámpara maravillosa*, 8:333a-b

        in Vico's *Scienza nuova*, 8:320a

        see also Aesthetics; Art-for-art's-sake principle

    poetic modernism and, 9:768a

    reality and, Eyvind Johnson on, 12:2372b–2373a

    Rimbaud's view of, 7:1787a, 1799a, 1805a, 1811a, 1818a

state and, Staël on, 5:97a
"tactile," Apollinaire and, 9:899a
as theme, in Thomas Mann, 9:724a-b
Tieck's view of, 5:236a–239a
Tsvetaeva's view of, 11:1745a
universality of
    Butor on, 13:3299a–3300a
    Dürrenmatt on, 13:3217b–3218a
    in Wagner's political theories, 6:1149a,
        1158a–1159a, 1161a-b
Wilde's credo of, 9:592b
see also Iconography; Reality
Art of Being Bored, The. See Pailleron,
    Édouard, *Le monde où l'on s'ennuie*
Art criticism
    of Apollinaire, 9:883b, 896b
    of Baudelaire, 7:1630b
    of Gautier, 5:523b, 7:1630b
    of Goncourt brothers, 7:1396b–1398a
    of Huysmans, 7:1714a, 1720a
    in post-Napoleonic period, 5:523a-b
    Romantic, 6:786a
    of Taine, 7:1461b–1464a
Art and Death. See Artaud, Antonin, *L'Art et le
    mort*
Art du dix-huitième siècle, L' (*Art of the
    Eighteenth Century*). *See* Goncourt,
    Edmond Louis Antoine and Jules Alfred
    Huot de
Art et le mort, L'. See Artaud, Antonin
Art of French Fiction, The. See Turnell, Martin
Art of Gogol, The. *See* Bely, Andrey,
    Masterstvo Gogolia
Art in Greece. *See* Taine, Hippolyte,
    Philosophie de l'art en Grèce
Art in Italy. *See* Taine, Hippolyte, *Philosophie
    de l'art en Italie*
"Art, L'." *See* Gautier, Théophile, *Enamels and
    Cameos*
Art magique, L'. See Breton, André, and
    Legrand, Gérard
Art moderne, L'. See Huysmans, Joris Karl
Art moderne, L' (literary review), 8:121a-b
Art in the Netherlands. See Taine, Hippolyte,
    Philosophie de l'art dans les Pays-Bas
Art nouveau movement, Hauptmann and,
    8:155a

Art of the Novel, The. See Kundera, Milan,
    Uměni románu
Art poétique. See Boileau-Despréaux, Nicolas;
    Claudel, Paul
"Art poétique." *See* Verlaine, Paul
Art poétique français. See Sebillet, Thomas
Art of Poetry. See Boileau-Despréaux, Nicolas,
    Art poétique
"Art of Poetry, The." *See* Verlaine, Paul, "Art
    poétique"
Art and Revolution. See Wagner, Richard
Art romantique, L'. See Baudelaire, Charles
Art and Science. *See* Pirandello, Luigi, *Arte e
    scienza*
Art of this World and of the Other World. *See*
    Ortega y Gasset, José, "Arte de este
    mundo y del otro"
Art transpositions. *See* "Transpositions d'art"
Art world, Ungaretti and, 10:1455b
Art-for-art's-sake movement, in Belgium,
    8:121a
Art-for-art's-sake principle
    Benjamin and, 11:1705a
    "Futurist Manifesto" and, 9:809b
    George and, 8:448b, 453b, 460b
    Mallarmé and, 8:571b
    see also Aesthetic autonomy
Art-Work of the Future, The. *See* Wagner,
    Richard, *Das Kunstwerk der Zukunft*
Artamonov Business, The. See Gorky, Maxim
Artaud, Antonin, **11:1961a–1985b**
    "A la grande nuit, ou le bluff surréaliste"
        ("In Total Darkness; or, The Surrealist
        Bluff"), 11:1966b–1967a
    "À un ami" ("To a Friend"), on thought,
        11:1967b–1968a
    Antonin Artaud: Dessins et portraits,
        11:1976a
    Cahiers de Rodez (The Rodez Notebooks),
        11:1978b
    D'un voyage au pays des Tarahumaras
        (*Peyote Dance*), 11:1974a–1975a
        "The Mountain of Signs" ("La montagne
           des signes"), 11:1974a-b
        "The Peyote Dance" ("La danse du
           peyotl"), 11:1974a-b, 1975a, 1976a

Artaud, Antonin (*cont.*)
    D'un voyage au pays des Tarahumaras
      (*Peyote Dance*) (*cont.*)
      "The Rite of the Peyote Among the
        Tarahumara," 11:1976a-b
      "The Rite of the Peyote Among the
        Tarahumara," timing of, 11:1974a-b
    Ghelderode and, 11:2114a
    Heliogabalus; or, The Anarchist Crowned
      (*Héliogabale, ou l'anarchiste couronné*),
      11:1973a
    "Héloïse et Abélard," 11:1970b
    Ionesco and, 13:3018a-b
    and Jarry, 9:667b
    "La conquête du Mexique" (The Conquest of
      Mexico), misunderstanding underlying,
      11:1973b
    La coquille et le clergyman (*The Seashell
      and the Clergyman*), 11:1971a
    "La décomposition de Paris" (The
      Decomposition of Paris), adverse effects
      of, 11:1974b
    L'Art et le mort (*Art and Death*), on suicide,
      11:1967a
    "Le jet de sang" ("The Spurt of Blood"),
      failure of, 11:1971a
    "Le retour d'Artaud le mômo" ("The Return
      of Artaud, le Mômo"), 11:1979b
    "Le théâtre et la peste" ("The Theater and
      the Plague"), 11:1971b–1972a
    Le théâtre et son double (*The Theater and
      Its Double*), 11:1972a-b
      "Un athlétisme affectif" ("An Emotional
        Athleticism"), 11:1982b
      preface to, 11:1983b
    Les Cenci (*The Cenci*), 11:1971a-b
    Les nouvelles révélations de l'être (*The New
      Revelations of Being*), tarot and,
      11:1974b
    "Letter to the Head Psychiatrists of Nut
      Houses," *Van Gogh, the Man Suicided
      by Society* and, 11:1979b
    Lettres de Rodez, spirituality in, 11:1978b
    Lettres à Génica Athanasiou, 11:1969a
    "L'Évolution du décors" ("The Evolution of
      Décor"), on the theater, 11:1969b
    poetic turbulence, 11:1954b

    Point final, Marxism condemned in,
      11:1966b
    Révolution surréaliste, La (journal)
      contributions, 11:1966a-b
    Sarraute and, 12:2355a
    Suppôts et supplications
      insight into poets' predicament, 11:1977b
      spirituality in, 11:1978b
    The Nerve Meter (*Le pèsenerfs*)
      on his writings, 11:1963a
      on the reality of mind, 11:1968b
    The Umbilicus of Limbo (*L'Ombilic des
      limbes*), 11:1968b–1969a
      on his writings, 11:1963a
      "Paul les Oiseaux ou la place de l'amour"
        ("Paul the Birds; or, The Place of
        Love"), 11:1968a
    theater of the absurd and, 11:2067b
    To Have Done with the Judgment of God
      (*Pour en finir avec le jugement de dieu*),
      11:1981a–1982a
    "Tutuguri, The Rite of the Black Sun,"
      11:1981a
      timing of, 11:1974a-b
    "Uccello le poil" ("Uccello the Hair"),
      11:1969a-b
    "Une note sur le peyotl" ("A Note on
      Peyote"), 11:1981a
    Van Gogh, le suicidé de la societé (*Van
      Gogh, the Man Suicided by Society*),
      11:1979b–1981a
Artaud, Marie-Ange (sister), on Artaud's
    Catholicism, 11:1962b
Arte de este mundo y del otro. See Ortega y
    Gasset, José
Arte della guerra. See Machiavelli, Niccolò,
    The Art of War
Arte e scienza. See Pirandello, Luigi
"Arte nuevo de hacer comedias en este tiempo,
    El." *See* Lope de Vega, "The New Art of
    Writing Comedies at This Time"
"Artémis." *See* Nerval, Gérard de
Artful Widow, The. See Goldoni, Carlo, *La
    vedova scaltra*
Arthour and Merlin, 1:153b
Arthurian legend, **1:137a–159a**, 242b–243a
    Ariosto and, 2:625a-b

Celtic literature and, 1:141a–143b

Chrétien's *Lancelot* and, 1:198b

in England, 1:153b–154a

fallibility in, 1:227a

in France, 1:144a–152b

Gawain's role, 1:155a–158b

Geoffrey of Monmouth and, 1:138a–139a, 140b

Greban's *Passion* and, 1:470b

historical roots of, 1:137a-b

Nibelungenlied and, 1:227b

poems concerning, 1:150b–151a

Provençal literature and, 1:139a–140a

in Scandinavia, 1:152b–153a

Wolfram and, 1:268a–281a

women in, 1:228a

see also Chrétien de Troyes

Artifice, Barthes and, 13:3084b

Artificial Paradises. See Baudelaire, Charles

Artisan class, Diderot and, 4:476a–477a

Artist

in Andersen's works, 6:883b–884a

autonomy of, Vittorini on, 12:2749a

Aymé's satire of, 12:2445a

Cela on, 13:3125b–3126a

great, Dürrenmatt's view of, 13:3215b

as hero

in Hamsun's works, 8:26b–27a, 39b

in Schnitzler's works, 8:102b

nature of, Gide on, 8:497a-b

performing, Marinetti as, 9:820b

in Richter's works, 5:85a

Schopenhauer's appeal to, 5:397a-b, 401a, 414a, 415a

society and, Mann and, 9:723b–724b

Artist, The. See Goncharov, Ivan, *The Precipice*

"Artist, The." *See* Blok, Alexander, "Khudozhnik"

Artistic ethics. *See* Ethics

Artistic Wonders of the World. *See* Ferreira de Castro, José Maria, *As maravilhas artísticas do mundo*

"Artist's Profession of Faith, The." *See* Baudelaire, Charles

Artists, The. See Schiller, Friedrich von

"Artists of the World!" *See* Khlebnikov, Velimir, "Khudozhniki mira!"

Artsybashev, Mikhail, Zamyatin's early work published by, 10:1182a

"As frontizan." *See* Cavafy, Constantine

As a Man Grows Older. See Svevo, Italo

As maravilhas artísticas do mundo. See Ferreira de Castro, José Maria

As You Desire Me. See Pirandello, Luigi, *Come tu mi vuoi*

As You Like It. See Shakespeare, William

"Ascètes, Les." *See* Leconte de Lisle, Charles Marie

Asceticism, of Artaud, 11:1977a-b, 1982a-b

Ascham, Roger, Castiglione and, 2:664b

Aseev, Nikolai, Pasternak's early poetry praised by, 10:1598a

Ashes. See Bely, Andrey, *Pepel*

Ashes. See Valle-Inclán, Ramón del, *El yermo de las almas*

Así que pasen cinco años. See García Lorca, Federico

Asia Minor disaster (*katastrophi*), in Seferis' writing, 12:2257b, 2261a

Asís de Borbón, Francisco de, Don, in *El ruedo ibérico*, 8:339a-b

"Askese" ("Askesis"). *See* Grass, Günter, *Gleisdreieck*

Askisis. See Ritsos, Yannis, *Piimata III*

"Asma iroiko kai penthimo yia ton hameno anthipolohaghos tis Alvanias." *See* Elytis, Odysseus

Asmodée; or, The Intruder (Asmodée). See Mauriac, François

Asmodeus, in Lesage's *Le diable boiteux*, 3:324b, 325a-b

"Asparukh." *See* Khlebnikov, Velimir

Aspasia poems. *See* Leopardi, Giacomo

Assassin est mon maître, Un (An Assassin Is My Master). *See* Montherlant, Henry de

Assassin, L'. See Simenon, Georges

"Assenza, Un." *See* Ginzburg, Natalia

"Assiuolo, L'." *See* Pascoli, Giovanni, *Myricae*

Association, free. *See* Free association

Associationist psychology, Bergson's view of, 8:51a–52a

Assommoir, L'. See Zola, Émile

Assonance
  in *Poema de mio Cid*, 1:116a-b
  in Quasimodo's works, 12:2393a
  in Verlaine's poetry, 7:1635a
Ass's Shadow, The. *See* Wieland, Christoph
    Martin, "Der Schatten des Esels"
Assumption of Hannele, The. See Hauptmann,
    Gerhart, *Hanneles Himmelfahrt*
Ästhetische Theorie. See Adorno, Theodor
Astrée, La (*Astrea*). *See* D'Urfé, Honoré
Astronomy
  Dürrenmatt and, 13:3215b–3216a
  in Lampedusa's *The Leopard*, 11:2018a-b,
    2022a–2023a
  in Stendhal's *The Charterhouse of Parma*,
    11:2021b–2022a
"Asya." *See* Turgenev, Ivan
At the Arches Bridge. *See* Simenon, Georges,
    Au pont des Arches
At the Barber's. *See* Hašek, Jaroslav, "U holîe"
At the Base of Silence. *See* Ritsos, Yannis,
    "Stous propodhes tis siopis"
"At the Circus." *See* Olesha, Yuri, "V tsirke"
At the Drop of a Hat. See Sarraute, Nathalie,
    Pour un oui ou pour un non
At the Exit. See Pirandello, Luigi, *All'uscita*
"At the Fountain of Arcueil." *See* Dorat, Jean,
    "Ad fontem Arculi"
At the Gare de l'Est. *See* Ady, Endre, "A Gare
    de l'Est-en"
"At Grandmother's." *See* Babel, Isaac, "U
    babushki"
At the Monastery. *See* Andrić, Ivo, "U
    musafirhani"
At the Service of Something. *See* Cela, Camilo
    José, *Al servicio de algo*
"At the Source of the Danube." *See* Hölderlin,
    Friedrich, "Am Quell der Donau"
At the Spa. See Hesse, Hermann, *Kurgast*
At the Station on an Autumn Morning. *See*
    Carducci, Giosue, "Alla stazione in una
    mattina d'autunno"
At the Theater. *See* Ionesco, Eugène
At the Top of My Voice. *See* Mayakovsky,
    Vladimir, "Vo ves' golos"
"At the Window During the Night." *See* Hugo,
    Victor, "À la fenêtre, pendant la nuit"

Atala. See Chateaubriand, François René de
Atem, Der. See Mann, Heinrich
Athalie. See Racine, Jean
Athanasiou, Génica, Artaud's relationship
    with, 11:1963b, 1967a-b
Atheism
  in La Bruyère's *Caractères*, 3:256a
  and Lagerkvist, 10:1697b
  of Leopardi, 5:542a
  Montaigne's "Apology for Raymond Sebond"
    on, 2:783a
  in Richter's "The Speech of Christ," 5:59a
  in Sade's writings, 4:632a, 635b
  Voetius on, 3:19b–20a
Athena
  in Fénelon's *Télémaque*, 3:285a, 285b, 287a
  in *Oresteia*, 5:12a
Athena (goddess), in La Fontaine's
    "L'Araignée et l'hirondelle," 3:89b, 90a
Athenaeum. See "Angelus Novus"
Athenäum (journal), Richter and, 5:71b
Athens, as portrayed by La Bruyère, 3:232a-b
Athens in Arms. *See* Ritsos, Yannis, "Athina
    sta opla"
"Athina sta opla." *See* Ritsos, Yannis
"Athlétisme affectif, Un." *See* Artaud, Antonin,
    Le théâtre et son double (*The Theater
    and Its Double*)
Atilla. See Zamyatin, Yevgeny Ivanovich
Atlan, Liliane, Sarraute and, 12:2355a
Atlantis. See Hauptmann, Gerhart
Atom Station, The. See Laxness, Halldór,
    Atómstöðin
Atomic age, Frisch and, 13:2898b, 2901a-b
"Atomikistis." *See* Ritsos, Yannis
Atomism, 3:21b
Atómstöðin. See Laxness, Halldór
Atonement, The. See Broch, Hermann, *Die
    Entsühnung*
Atriden-Tetralogie (*Atridae Tetralogy*). *See*
    Hauptmann, Gerhart
Att övervaka överheten. See Moberg, Vilhelm
Atta Troll: Ein Sommernachtstraum (*Atta
    Troll: A Midsummer Night's Dream*).
    See Heine, Heinrich
Attack upon "Christendom." See Kierkegaard,
    Søren

Áttartala, 1:380a

Attempt at Self-Criticism. See Nietzsche, Friedrich, *Versuch einer Selbstkritik*

Attente de Dieu. See Weil, Simone, *Waiting for God*

Attenzione, L'. See Moravia, Alberto, *The Lie*

Attisches Museum (Attic Museum). See Wieland, Christoph Martin

"Au beau demi-jour de 1934." *See* Breton, André

"Au bord de l'eau." *See* Maupassant, Guy de

"Au grand jour." *See* Breton, André

"Au lecteur." *See* Baudelaire, Charles

Au pont des Arches. See Simenon, Georges

"Au prolétaire." *See* Apollinaire, Guillaume

"Au théâtre." *See* Ionesco, Eugène

"Aubade." *See* Apollinaire, Guillaume

Auber, Daniel François Esprit, *La muette de Portici*, 7:1428a

Aubigné, Théodore Agrippa d'
    Les tragiques, 12:2553a
    on Ronsard, 2:740b

Aubriot, Hugh, 1:345b–346a

Auden, W. H.
    on Berlioz, 6:772a
    on Claudel, 8:484a
    on Cocteau, 10:1543a
    Rilke and, 9:768b

Audience
    for medieval drama, 1:456b, 458b
    for miracle plays, 1:462a, 465a
    participation of
        in Butor, 13:3310a–3312a
        in Calvino, 13:3281a–3283a
        in medieval satire, 1:364b, 365b, 373a
        see also Reader participation
    for Redentin Easter play, 1:468a-b
    Sartre and, 12:2597b–2599b
    Walther and, 1:307a
    Wolfram and, 1:265b

Audience, The. See García Lorca, Federico, *El público*

Audigier, 1:459a

Auðunar þáttr, 1:384a

"Auf zwei Vettern." *See* Grillparzer, Franz

"Aufgabe des Übersetzers, Die." *See* Benjamin, Walter, "The Task of the Translator"

Aufruhr in den Cevennen, Der. See Tieck, Ludwig

Aufstieg und Fall der Stadt Mahagonny. See Brecht, Bertolt, *The Rise and Fall of the State of Mahagonny*

Aufzeichnungen des Malte Laurids Brigge, Die. See Rilke, Rainer Maria

Augier, Émile, 7:1917a, 1919b–1920b
    Gabrielle, 7:1917b–1918a
    Le fils de Giboyer (Giboyer's Son), 7:1920a
    Le gendre de M. Poirier (M. Poirier's Son-in-Law), 7:1918a, 1919b–1920a
    Le mariage d'Olympe (Olympe's Marriage), 7:1918a, 1919a
    Les effrontés (The Shameless Ones), 7:1918a, 1920a
    Mme. Caverlet, 7:1919a
    verse drama, 7:1426b

Augsburg *General Gazette*, and Heine, 5:503b

Augury. See George, Stefan, *Algabal*, "Vogelschau"

August 1914. See Solzhenitsyn, Aleksandr

August. See Hamsun, Knut

"August Night." *See* Musset, Alfred de, *Nights*

Augusta, Queen of Prussia, Laforgue and, 7:1884a

Augustine, St., **1:23a–50b**
    Anselm of Canterbury and, 1:406b
    Aquinas and, 1:425a
    Benediktbeuern Christmas play and, 1:454a, 454b
    Bossuet and, 3:152b–153a
    City of God (De civitate dei), 1:33a–37a
        Artaud's "Le théâtre et la peste" and, 11:1972a
        Bossuet and, 3:157b, 169b
        on Greek language, 1:26b–27a
        influence of, 1:36b–37a
        on passion, 1:44b
        Prudentius and, 1:2b–3a, 11b
        structure of, 1:34a
        on Vergil, 1:27a
    Claudel and, 8:492a
    Confessions (Confessionum), 1:25a–33a
        Aeneid and, 1:27a-b

Augustine, St. (*cont.*)
  Confessions (*Confessionum*) (*cont.*)
    autobiographical elements, 2:542b
    City of God and, 1:34b
    goal of, 1:25b
    Ionesco's *La quête intermittente* and,
      13:3018a
    On Christian Doctrine and, 1:41b, 42a
    On the Trinity and, 1:37b, 38b–39a, 40a
    pear theft episode, 1:28a-b, 29a
    Petrarch's use of, 2:477a, 482b–483a, 494a
  Contra mendacium (*Against Lying*), 1:48a,
    49a
  Cornelis Jansen and, 3:127a
  Dante and, 1:433b
  De doctrina christiana (*On Christian
    Doctrine*), 1:27b, 41b–44a, 45b, 3:159b,
    164a
    scholastic dialectic and, 1:405b
  De libero arbitrio (*On Free Will*), 1:24b, 26b,
    44a–45b
  De magistro (*On the Christian Teacher*),
    1:45b–46a
  De mendacio (*On Lying*), 1:48a, 48b–49a
  De musica (*On Music*), 1:46b–47b
  De ordine (*On Order*), 1:44a, 47a
  De praedestinatione sanctorum (*On the
    Predestination of Saints*), 1:405b
  De trinitate (*On the Trinity*), 1:24a-b,
    37a–41b, 47a
    goal of, 1:37b, 38b
  De vera religione (*Of True Religion*), 1:47b
  Ekelöf and, 12:2656a
  Erasmus and, 2:573a, 590a
  Erigena and, 1:405b–406a
  Jansenists and, 3:133b
  Luther and, 2:671b–672b
  Pascal's *Lettres provinciales* and, 3:136b
  power of words, 2:553b
  Retractationes (*Retractations*), 1:23b–24a,
    41b
  Sententiae in IV libris distinctae and,
    1:407a
  see also Monica (mother of Augustine)
Augustinian order
  Aquinas and, 1:423b–424a
  Aristotelianism and, 1:409a-b

  Erasmus and, 2:572a-b
  Luther and, 2:671a
Augustus, Roman Emperor, in Corneille's
  Cinna, 3:37a-b, 38a–39b, 40a–42a,
  43a–44a
Aul Bastundzhi. See Lermontov, Mikhail
  Yurievich
"Auntie." *See* Andersen, Hans Christian
"Auprès d'un mort" ("Beside a Dead Man").
  See Maupassant, Guy de
"Aura celeste che 'n quel verde lauro, L'." *See*
  Petrarch, *Canzoniere*
Aurélia. See Nerval, Gérard de
Aurélien. See Aragon, Louis
Aurenche, Jean (joint author). *See* Anouilh,
  Jean, and Aurenche, Jean
Aurevilly, Barbey d', on the Goncourts,
  7:1411b
Aurora roja. See Baroja, Pío, *Red Dawn*
Aus dem Tagebuch einer Schnecke. See Grass,
  Günter, *From the Diary of a Snail*
*Aus den Memoiren des Herren von
  Schnabelewopski. See* Heine, Heinrich
"Aus der Geschichte einer infantilen Neurose."
  See Freud, Sigmund
Aus Indien. See Hesse, Hermann
Ausgefragt. See Grass, Günter
"Ausgesetzt auf den Bergen des Herzens." *See*
  Rilke, Rainer Maria
Ausnahme und die Rëgel, Die. See Brecht,
  Bertolt
Ausonius
  "De rosis nascentibus" (The Budding
    Roses), 2:728a-b
  Idylls, Descartes and, 3:4b
Auspicious Song for the Chosen Nation. *See*
  D'Annunzio, Gabriele, "Canto augurale
  per la nazione eletta"
Austen, Jane, Ginzburg and, 13:3161a
Austin, J. L., Valéry and, 8:575a
Australia, Butor's visit to, 13:3315a–3316a
Austria
  imperial court, response to Schnitzler's
    works, 8:97a
  importance of Krleža and, 11:1808a-b
  Schnitzler's popularity in, 8:89b, 103b, 105b,
    106a

Strindberg's career in, 7:1737a

Trakl and, 10:1409a–1410a

Austro-Hungarian Empire, Krleža and, 11:1808a

Auswahl aus des Teufels Papieren. See Richter, Jean Paul

"Autels de la peur, Les." *See* Chénier, André

Auteuil, Boileau's stay at, 3:180a

Authaltsame Aufstieg des Arturo Ui, Der. See Brecht, Bertolt, *The Resistible Rise of Arturo Ui*

Authenticity
in Canetti, 12:2624b–2625b
human, society and, in Rousseau, 4:463a–467a

Author
Claudel on, 8:491a
as profession, *see also* Wieland, Christoph Martin

Author in His Time, An. *See* Johnson, Eyvind, "En författare i sin tid"

"Author of *The Crimes of Love* to Villeterque, Hack Writer, The." *See* Sade, Donatien Alphonse François, marquis de

Author-figures, in Hoffmann, 5:285b, 287a-b

Author-function, Foucault and, 13:3346b–3347a

Authorial intervention
in Blasco Ibáñez' novels, *The Mayflower*, 8:360a-b
in Calvino, 13:3268b
in Dante's *De monarchia*, 1:442b–443a
in Kafka, 9:1159b–1160a
Marinetti and, 9:801b, 803a-b, 804a

Authorial viewpoint
in Blasco Ibáñez' novels
El ruedo ibérico, 8:339a
Reeds and Mud, 8:378b–379a, 379b
The Cabin, 8:374b
in Camus, 13:3059a–3060a
in Chekhov's "The Steppe," 7:1861b
in Lermontov's works, 6:1212a-b
in Pascoli's poetry, 7:1831a
in Proust's *Remembrance of Things Past*, 8:548b–549a
of Queneau, 12:2515a

see also Narrative convention; Narrative viewpoint

Authoritarianism, of Valle-Inclán, 8:337a

Authority
Foucault and, 13:3323b–3327b, 3339a–3341b
Luther's view of, 2:682b

Author's Confession. See Gogol, Nikolay Vasilievich

"Autism," in Musil's fiction, 9:934a

Auto da Índia. See Vicente, Gil

Auto de Filodemo. See Camoëns, Luís Vaz de

Auto de los reyes magos (Play of the Magi), 1:457a

Auto sacramentale, 1:471a

Auto-da-Fé. See Canetti, Elias, *Die Blendung*

Autobiografia. See Vico, Giambattista

Autobiographical novel
of Milosz, 13:2934a-b
Strindberg's use of form, 7:1732a–1733a, 1734b–1735a, 1736a-b, 1738a, 1738b–1739a

Autobiography
Andersen's multiple versions, 6:863b, 864a-b
Augustine's *Confessions* as, 1:25a-b, 26a
in Babel's fiction, 11:1892b–1893a, 1908a-b
in Baroja's writings, 9:608a, 611b
Barthes and, 13:3097a–3099a
Beauvoir and, 12:2703b–2704a, 2706b
Bely's autobiographical novels, 9:905a-b
of Berlioz, 6:772b, 793b–795a
in Butor's writings, 13:3309a
Canetti and, 12:2631a–2632a
Cela and, 13:3118b–3119a
of Chateaubriand, 5:113b
Dinesen and, 10:1282b–1293b
of Dumas père, 6:739b–740b
Ferreira de Castro's fiction as, 11:2156a, 2159b, 2160b
fictional, Pérez Galdós' *El amigo Manso*, 7:1609a-b
in Foscolo's *Ultima lettere di Jacopo Ortis*, 5:319b–324a
in Frisch's sketches, 13:2895a, 2896a-b, 2897a
Genet and, 13:2889a

Autobiography (*cont.*)
of Goethe, 6:1090a
in Grass's writings, 13:3384a-b
of Gunnarsson, 10:1498a, 1502a
in Gunnarsson's works, 10:1502a, 1510b
of Hebbel, 6:1090a
Hesse's *The Journey to the East* as, 9:851b
of Huysmans, 7:1720a
Kafka and, 9:1156b
of Kazantzakis, 9:1086b–1087a
in Keller's *Green Henry*, 6:924a–926b
in Kierkegaard's *Stages on Life's Way*,
6:1133a–1134a
in Leopardi's verse, 5:562b
Mauriac and, 10:1317b–1321b
of Musset, 6:1012b
of Pasternak, 10:1602a–1604a, 1613a–1615a
of Richter, 5:54b–55a
Rilke's *Notebooks of Malte Laurids Brigge*
and, 9:790a
Rimbaud's *Season in Hell* as, 7:1818a
in Ritsos' works, 12:2833b–2834b
of Robbe-Grillet, 13:3238b
Rousseau and, 4:460b–461a
Saint-Exupéry and, 12:2328b–2329a
of Sand, 6:830b–831a
in Sarraute's writings, 12:2342a-b
Simon's fiction as, 13:3021b–3022a
of Tsvetaeva, 11:1746a, 1747a
in Undset's works, 9:1018b–1019a
of Wagner, 6:1165a-b
in Witkiewicz's novel *622 Downfalls of
Bungo*, 10:1210a-b
Autobiography. See Grillparzer, Franz,
Selbstbiographie; Richter, Jean Paul,
Selberlebensbeschreibung; Yeats,
William Butler
"Autobiography." *See* Zamyatin, Yevgeny
Ivanovich, "Avtobiografiia"
Autobiography, An. See Croce, Benedetto,
Contributo alla critica di me stesso
Autodidact literature, Eyvind Johnson and,
12:2364b
Automa, L'. See Moravia, Alberto
Automatic writing, 13:2958a, 2973b
Arp and, 10:1369b

Automatism, of Breton, 11:1949b, 1951a-b,
1954a, 1957a-b
Automism
in dada, 11:2064b, 2065a
psychic, 11:2069b
"Automne malade." *See* Apollinaire,
Guillaume, *Alcools*
Automobile, Marinetti and, 9:804a-b, 806b,
810a, 814b
Autonomy, artistic. *See* Artist, autonomy of
"Autopsy, The." *See* Elytis, Odysseus, *Exi kai
mia tipsis yia ton ourano* (*Six and One
Remorses for the Sky*), "I aftopsia"
Autos sacramentales, Calderón and, 2:883b,
893b–894b
"Autre complainte de Lord Pierrot." *See*
Laforgue, Jules, *Les complaintes*
"Autre éventail/de Mademoiselle Mallarmé."
See Mallarmé, Stéphane
Autre Tartuffe ou la mère coupable, L'. See
Beaumarchais, Pierre-Augustin Caron
de
Autres textes sur l'art. See Claudel, Paul
"Autrier jost' una sebissa, L'." *See* Marcabru
Autumn. *See* Machado, Antonio, *Soledades*
(Solitudes), "Otoño"
"Autumn." *See* Quasimodo, Salvatore,
"Autunno"; Strindberg, August
Autumn Airs. *See* Jiménez, Juan Ramón,
"Arias otoñales"
Autumn Leaves. See Hugo, Victor, *Les feuilles
d'automne*
Autumn Night. *See* Krleža, Miroslav, "Jesenja
noć"
Autumn Slipped into Paris. *See* Ady, Endre,
"Párisba beszökött az ősz"
Autumn Sonata. *See* Valle-Inclán, Ramón del,
*Sonatas: Memorias del Marqués de
Bradomín* (*The Pleasant Memoirs of the
Marquis de Bradomín*), *Sonata de otoño*
Autumn Song. *See* Verlaine, Paul, "Chanson
d'automne"
"Autunno." *See* Quasimodo, Salvatore
Aux intellectuels révolutionnaires. See Aragon,
Louis
"Avangardisti a Mentone, Gli." *See* Calvino,
Italo

Avanguardia, L' (Roman Socialist periodical), Silone's editorship of, 12:2277b

Avant-garde
  Apollinaire and, 9:884a, 898b, 899a, 899b
  Azorín and, 9:651b–652a
  Bakunin and, 9:667a-b
  in Czechoslovakia, 10:1567a
    Čapek and, 10:1566a
  in Hungary, Lukács and, 10:1254a
  Ionesco and, 13:2989b, 3017b–3018a
  Jarry and, 9:665a–669a
  literary establishment and, 9:667b
  Marinetti and, 9:803a, 820b, 823a, 823b
  in Poland. *See* Witkiewicz, Stanisław Ignacy
  see also Dada; Krleža, Miroslav; Surrealism
Avant-Scène, L' (French journal), Anouilh's writings in, 13:2861b
Avanti! (Italian Socialist daily)
  Marinetti and, 9:825b
  Silone's articles in, 12:2295a
Avare, L'. See Molière
Avarice. *See* Greed
Avariés, Les. See Brieux, Eugène
Avatar. See Gautier, Théophile
Avellaneda, Alonso F. de, Cervantes' *Don Quixote* and, 2:838a-b, 3:323a-b
Avenarius, Ferdinand, Kafka and, 9:1152a
"Avenger, The." *See* Chekhov, Anton, "Mstitel"
Avenir est dans les oeufs, L'. See Ionesco, Eugène
Avenir, L' (journal), Vigny's column in, 5:464a
Aventuras, inventos, y mixtificaciones de Silvestre Paradox. See Baroja, Pío
Aventures de Jérôme Bardini. See Giraudoux, Jean
Aventures de M. Robert Chevalier, dit de Beauchêne, capitaine de flibustiers, Les. See Lesage, Alain-René
Aventures de Télémaque, fils d'Ulysse, Les. See Fénelon, François de Salignac de la Mothe-
Averroës
  Aristotelianism and, 1:407b–408a, 408b
  Dante and, 1:442b
Averroism
  Latin, 1:409b–410a, 418a-b, 424b
  Petrarch on, 2:479a

Aveugle, L'. See Chénier, André, "The Blind Man"
Aveugles, Les. See Maeterlinck, Maurice
Avezzano earthquake of 1915, in Silone's novels, 12:2276a-b, 2277a-b, 2291b–2293a
Avgust chetyrnadtsatogo. See Solzhenitsyn, Aleksandr, *August 1914*
"Aviateur, L'" ("The Aviator"). *See* Saint-Exupéry, Antoine de
Avicenna
  Aristotelianism and, 1:407b, 408a
  Summa contra Gentiles and, 1:414b
  William of Auvergne and, 1:409a
Avignon papacy, Petrarch and, 2:477a-b, 484b–485a, 490a
Aviraneta, Eugenio de, as protagonist of Baroja novel, 9:610b–611a
Avrenos's Clients. *See* Simenon, Georges, *Les clients d'Avrenos*
"Avril." *See* Belleau, Remy, *Bergeries*
Avsked till Hamlet. See Johnson, Eyvind
Avtobiograficheskii ocherk. See Pasternak, Boris, *I Remember: Sketch for an Autobiography*
"Avtobiografiia." *See* Zamyatin, Yevgeny Ivanovich
"Avvento, L'." *See* Pascoli, Giovanni
"Avventura di un miope, L'." *See* Calvino, Italo, "The Adventure of a Nearsighted Man"
Avventura d'un povero cristiano, L'. See Silone, Ignazio
Avvocato veneziano, L'. See Goldoni, Carlo
"Awakening, The." *See* Babel, Isaac, "Probuzhdenie"
Away from the Village. *See* Ady, Endre, "El a faluból"
Axel. See Villiers de l'Isle Adam
Axion Esti, To. See Elytis, Odysseus
Ayghi (Greek newspaper), Ritsos' articles in, 12:2818a
Aymar, Zenobia Camprubi, Jiménez and, 9:992a, 997b, 998b
Ayme, Albert, Butor and, 13:3312a-b
Aymé, Marcel, **12:2433a–2456b**
  Aller retour (Round Trip), 12:2435b–2436a

Aymé, Marcel (*cont.*)
Bouvard et Pécuchet, 12:2434b
Brûlebois, 12:2434a, 2447b
Clérambard, 12:2440a, 2440b–2441a, 2454a
Derrière chez Martin, 12:2452b
En arrière (Backward), 12:2437b
Gustalin, 12:2435a-b, 2441a, 2444a-b
La convention Belzébir (The Belzébir Decree), 12:2437a, 2449a, 2453b
"La grâce," 12:2453b
La mouche bleue (The Blue Fly), 12:2448a
La tête des autres (Other People's Heads), 12:2443a-b, 2449a
Le boeuf clandestin (The Clandestine Steak), 12:2441b, 2450b
Le confort intellectuel (Intellectual Comfort), 12:2440b, 2443a
"Le faux policier" (The False Policeman), 12:2442a
"Le paon" (The Peacock), 12:2438a
Le vaurien (The Good-for-Nothing), 2:2445a, 12:2444b, 2447a
Le vin de Paris (Paris Wine), 12:2442b
Les maxibules, 12:2441a, 2450a
Les oiseaux de lune (Moonbirds), 12:2436b–2437a
Les quatre vérités (The Four Truths), 12:2445a
"L'Huissier" (The Bailiff), 12:2440b
Louisiane, 12:2442b–2443a, 2448b–2449a
Lucienne et le boucher (Lucienne and the Butcher), 12:2449b–2450a
"Oscar et Erick," 12:2437b
"Propos de la jument" (The Mare's Comments), 12:2453a-b
Side Effects, 12:2438a
Silhouette du scandale, 12:2442b, 2451b
The Barkeep of Blémont (Uranus), 12:2434a, 2440a, 2442b, 2445a-b, 2450b–2451a, 2451b
The Conscience of Love (Les tiroirs de l'inconnu), 12:2445a, 2445b, 2449a, 2450a-b, 2452a
The Fable and the Flesh (La vouivre), 12:2437b, 2438b, 2439a
The Green Mare (La jument verte), 12:2434a, 2438a, 2438b, 2452b, 2454a
The Hollow Field (La table-aux-crevés), 12:2434a, 2439a
The House of Men (Maison basse), 12:2440a, 2444a
The Miraculous Barber (Travelingue), 12:2438b, 2440a-b, 2441a, 2444b, 2447b
The Second Face (La belle image), 12:2436a, 2438b
The Secret Stream (Le moulin de la sourdine), 12:2439b–2440a, 2443a
The Transient Hour (Le chemin des écoliers), 12:2440a, 2445b, 2451a-b
The Wonderful Farm (Contes du chat perché), 12:2434a-b, 2446a-b, 2449b, 2454a
The Wonderful Farm (Contes du chat perché)
"Le nain" (The Dwarf), 12:2435a, 2442b
"Le petit coq noir" (The Little Black Cock), 12:2435a
"Les boeufs" (The Oxen), 12:2434b–2435a
Vogue la galère, 12:2436a-b
"Az anyám és én." See Ady, Endre
Az apostol. See Petőfi, Sándor
"Az elhagyott kalóz-hajók." See Ady, Endre
"Az eltévedt lovas." See Ady, Endre
"Az én két asszonyom." See Ady, Endre
"Az én koporsó paripám." See Ady, Endre
"Az értől az oceanig." See Ady, Endre
Az Illés szekerén. See Ady, Endre
Az irástudatlanok árulása. See Kosztolányi, Dezső
"Az Ös Kaján." See Ady, Endre
"Az utolsó hajók." See Ady, Endre
"Az utolsó mosoly." See Ady, Endre
Azaña, Manuel, Valle-Inclán and, 8:336b
Azeglio, Masimo d', on Alfieri's achievement, 4:688a
"Azione parlata, L'." See Pirandello, Luigi
Azorín, **9:639a–661b**
Al margen de los clásicos (Marginalia on the Classics), 9:644b
Angelita, 9:642a
Antonio Azorín, 9:643a-b, 648a
Buscapiés, 9:644b
Capricho (Caprice), 9:656a–657a
Castilla (Castile), 9:649a

Cervantes, o la casa encantada (Cervantes; or, The Haunted House), 9:642a-b
Clásicos y modernos (Classics and Moderns), 9:644b
Diario de un enfermo (The Diary of a Sick Man)
  Azorín as protagonist in, 9:643a-b
  critical attention to, 9:640a
  novel form of, 9:645b–646a
Don Juan, 9:641b, 649b, 650a-b
Doña Inés, 9:641b, 648a, 650b–651b
El alma castellana (1600–1800) (The Soul of Castile 1600–1800), 9:640a, 745a
El caballero inactual (The Timeless Gentleman), 9:652b–653a
El enfermo (The Sick Man), 9:654b–655b
El escritor (The Writer), 9:654a-b, 655b
El libro de Levante (The Book of the Levant), 9:653a-b
El licenciado Vidriera. See Azorín, *Tomás Rueda*
"El problema" (The Problem), 9:656a
Españoles en Paris (Spaniards in Paris), 9:642b
"Fragmentos de un diario" ("Fragments of a Diary"), 9:640a
friendship with Baroja, 9:592b–593a
La Andalucia trágica (Tragic Andalusia), 9:640b
La evolución de la crítica (*The Evolution of Criticism*), 9:644a
La isla sin aurora (The Island Without Dawn), 9:656a, 657a–659b
La ruta de don Quijote (Don Quixote's Way), 9:643b
La sociologia criminal (Criminal Sociology), 9:643a
La voluntad, 9:640b, 643a-b, 648a
Las confesiones de un pequeño filósofo (Confessions of a Little Philosopher), 9:639b–640a
  Azorín as protagonist in, 9:643a-b
  impressionism in, 9:648a–649a
"Las nubes" (The Clouds), 9:649a
Lecturas españolas (Spanish Readings), 9:644b
"Lo Fatal" (The Fatality), 9:649a
Lo invisible (Trilogia) (The Invisible: Trilogy), 9:641b
longevity of, 9:613a
Los dos Luises y otros ensayos (The Two Luises and Other Essays), 9:641b
Los pueblos, La Andalucia trágica, y otros artículos, 9:640b, 643b
Los valores literarios (Literary Values), 9:644b–645a
Machado and, 9:745b
María Fontán, 9:659b
Moratín, 9:644b
Obras completas, 9:642b
Pensando en España (Thinking of Spain), 9:642b
Pueblo (The People), 9:653b–654a
Rivas y Larra, 9:641b
Salvadora de Olbena, 9:645b, 659b–660b
skepticism of, 9:597a
Tomás Rueda, 9:649b–650a
Un pueblecito, 9:641a
"Una ciudad y un balcón" (A City and a Balcony), 9:649a
"Una flauta en la noche" (A Flute in the Night), 9:649a
Una hora de España entre 1560 y 1590 (An Hour of Spain Between 1560 and 1590), 9:641b
Valle-Inclán and, 8:331a, 333b
"Azorín, o los primores de lo vulgar." *See* Ortega y Gasset, José
"Azy iz uzy." *See* Khlebnikov, Velimir

B

Baader, Franz, Novalis and, 5:210a

Baader-Meinhof Group, Böll on, 13:3170b

Baal. *See* Brecht, Bertolt

"Bab-El': Moi listki" ("Bab-El: My Notes"). *See* Babel, Isaac

"Babámovy archeologické snahy" (Babám's Endeavors as an Archaeologist). *See* Hašek, Jaroslav

Babbage, Charles, Mandelshtam's "Verses On the Unknown Soldier" and, 10:1646b

"Babe tsarstvo." *See* Chekhov, Anton

"Babel en creux." *See* Butor, Michel

Babel, Isaac, **11:1885a–1914b**

   "Avtobiografiia" ("Autobiography"), 11:1895a, 1903a

     "apprenticeship among the people," 11:1904b

   "Bab-El': Moi listki" ("Bab-El: My Notes"), 11:1904a

   Benia Krik, 11:1886a, 1901a

   Detstvo (Childhood), 11:1896a

   "Dezertir" ("The Deserter"), 11:1905b–1906a, 1906b

   "Di Grasso," 11:1892b, 1910b–1911a

   "Dnevnik" (*Diary*), 11:1904a

   Etchings, 11:1887b

   Evreika (The Jewess), 11:1887b–1888a, 1899a

   excess in writing, 11:1897a

   family in writing, 11:1898a–1899a

   fictional background, 11:1895b

   "Gapa Guzhva," 11:1887b

   "Gedali," 11:1909b

   on Gorky, 11:1904b

   "Guy de Maupassant," 11:1901b, 1905a, 1906b

   "Iisusov grekh" ("The Sign of Jesus"), 11:1905a

   "Ilia Isaakovich i Margareta Prokofievna" ("Ilia Isaakovich and Margarita Prokofievna"), 11:1903a-b

   "Khodia: Iz knigi *Petersburg 1918*" ("The Chinaman: From the Book *Petersburg 1918*"), 11:1904b

   "Kolia Topuz," 11:1887a

   "Kolyvushka," 11:1887b

   "Kostel v Novograde" ("Novograde Cathedral"), 11:1909b–1910a

   "Liniia i tsvet" ("Line and Color"), 11:1909b

   "Mama, Rimma, i Alla" ("Mother, Rimma, and Alla"), 11:1903a

   Mandelshtam's *Egipetskaia marka* and, 10:1643a-b

   Mariia (*Maria*), 11:1887a, 1887b, 1888a-b, 1898b

   Maupassant and, 11:2250b

   mimetic construct, 11:1907b

   "Moi listki: Odessa" ("My Notes: Odessa"), 11:1891b–1892a, 1900b

   "Moi pervyi gus" ("My First Goose"), 11:1901a

   "Odessa," 11:1895b

   Odessa Tales (*Odesskie rasskazy*), 11:1885b–1886a, 1892a, 1896b, 1900b

   film script, 11:1886a

   "Kak eto delalos' v Odesse" ("The Way It Used to Be Done in Odessa"), 11:1885b, 1901a

   "Korol" ("The King"), 11:1885b, 1897a

   "Liubka Kozak" ("Liubka the Cossack"), 11:1885b

   narrator, 11:1888a-b

   "Otets" ("The Father"), 11:1885b

   voices, 11:1906a-b, 1907a

   "Perekhod cherez Zbruch" ("Crossing the Zbruch," 11:1909b

   "Pervaia liubov" ("First Love"), 11:1896a, 1896b, 1898a, 1898b

   post-Stalinist literature and, 11:2251b

   posthumous rehabilitation, 11:1888b–1889a

   "Potselui" ("The Kiss"), 11:1893b, 1910a-b

   "Probuzhdenie" ("The Awakening"), 11:1912b

   Red Cavalry (*Konarmiia*), 11:1885a-b, 1892b–1893a, 1896b, 1900b, 1911b

   "Argamak," 11:1893b

   controversy over, 11:1909a

   Liutov, 11:1906b, 1909b–1910a

   narrator, 11:1888a-b

   voices, 11:1906a, 1906b–1907a

"Smert' Dolgusheva" ("The Death of Dolgushev"), 11:1906b

"Staryi Shloime" ("Old Shloime"), 11:1902a-b

"Sud" ("The Trial"), 11:1910a

"Sulak," 11:1910b

The Story of My Dovecote (Istoriia moei golubiatni), 11:1886b, 1893a-b, 1894b, 1897a-b, 1899b
 narrator, 11:1888a-b

"Through the Crack" ("V shchelochku"), 11:1887b

"U babushki" ("At Grandmother's"), 11:1896a–1897a, 1902b

"V podvale" ("In the Basement"), 11:1895b, 1898a

Velikaia Krinitsa, 11:1887b

Velikaia Staritsa, 11:1887b

Vidal adaptations, 11:1905b, 1907a

voice of the other, 11:1906a-b

Zakat (Sunset), 11:1886a-b

Babel, Nathalie, The Lonely Years, 11:1887b, 1902a

"Babette's Feast." See Dinesen, Isak

Babits, Mihály, 10:1234a
 Kosztolányi and, 10:1233a-b, 1245a, 1247b

"Baby." See Chekhov, Anton

Babylas. See Ghelderode, Michel de

Bacchus
 in Ady's "In the Vineyard of Bygone Years," 9:878a
 in Camoëns' The Lusiads, 2:761b, 763a

Bacchus. See Cocteau, Jean

Bacchus and His Companions. See Velázquez, Diego Rodríguez de Silva, Los borrachos

"Bacchusfest, Das." See Schnitzler, Arthur

Bachelard, Gaston
 Butor and, 13:3287b–3288a
 The Poetics of Space, 5:60a, 84a

Bachelier de Salamanque, Le (The Bachelor of Salamanca). See Lesage, Alain-René

Bachelors, The. See Montherlant, Henry de

Bachmann, Ingeborg, Frisch and, 13:2906b

Bachofen, Johann Jakob
 Das Mutterrecht (Matriliny), Klages and, 8:462b
 Hesse's Demian and, 9:840b

Backbone Flute, The. See Mayakovsky, Vladimir, Fleita-pozvonochnik

Backbone Piece. See Eirík Oddsson, Hryggjarstykki

"Backstage." See Zamyatin, Yevgeny Ivanovich, "Zakulisy"

Backward. See Aymé, Marcel, En arrière

Backward Glance O'er Travel'd Roads, A. See Whitman, Walt

Bacon, Francis
 Advancement of Learning, 3:296a-b
 Diderot and, 4:489b–490a
 Machiavelli and, 2:615b
 New Organon, 3:294a
 The Wisdom of the Ancients, 3:297a
 Vico and, 3:294a, 296a-b, 297a, 298a, 8:325b

"Bad Blood." See Rimbaud, Arthur, "Mauvais Sang"

Bad faith, in Butor's Change of Heart, 13:3295b–3296a

Bad Physician, The. See Kosztolányi, Dezső, A rossz orvos

Bad Thoughts and Others. See Valéry, Paul, Mauvaises pensées et autres

Bad-Humor Poem. See Walther von der Vogelweide, Unmutston

Badener Lehrstücke vom Einverständnis, Das. See Brecht, Bertolt

Bäder von Lucca, Die. See Heine, Heinrich

"Badger's Den, The." See Mandelshtam, Osip, "Barsuch'ia nora"

Bagatelles pour un massacre. See Céline, Louis-Ferdinand

Baggensen, Jens Immanuel, Parthenais, Manzoni's involvement with, 5:371b

Bagritsky, Eduard, Babel and, 11:1892a

Bahnwärter Thiel: Novellistische Studie aus dem märkischen Kiefernforst. See Hauptmann, Gerhart

Bahr, Hermann
 Hofmannsthal and, 9:689a, 690b
 Schnitzler and, 8:92a

Baigne, Monsieur de, 3:5a

Bailiff Joshua Freudel's Complaint Against His Accursed Demon. *See* Richter, Jean Paul, *Des Amts-Vogts Josuah Freudel Klaglibell gegen seinen verfluchten Dämon*

Bailiff, The. *See* Aymé, Marcel, "L'Huissier"

Baillet, Adrien, 3:4a, 4b

"Bain d'une dame romain, Le." *See* Vigny, Alfred Victor de, *Poèmes antiques et modernes*

Baiser au lépreux, Le. See Mauriac, François, *A Kiss for the Leper*

"Bait, The." *See* Donne, John

Bajazet. See Racine, Jean

Bajky a podpovídky. See Čapek, Karel

Bajza, József, Ady and, 9:865a

Bakakaj. See Gombrowicz, Witold, *Pamiętnik z okresu dojrzewania*

Baker, His Wife, and His Little Apprentice, The. *See* Anouilh, Jean, *Le boulanger, la boulangère et le petit mitron*

Bakhtin, Mikhail
  carnivalesque theory, 11:1865a
  polyphonic construction, 13:3200b
  Rabelais and His World, 2:701a

Bakunin, Mikhail
  Jarry and, 9:667a-b
  Turgenev and, 6:1276b

Bal des voleurs, Le. See Anouilh, Jean, *Thieves' Carnival*

Bal du Comte Orgel, Le. See Radiguet, Raymond

"Bal, Le." *See* Vigny, Alfred Victor de, *Poèmes antiques et modernes*

"Balada o Juraji Čupovi." *See* Čapek, Karel

Baladas de primavera. See Jiménez, Juan Ramón

Balade du Grand Macabre, La. See Ghelderode, Michel de

Balade Petrice Kerempuha. See Krleža, Miroslav

Balaganchik. See Blok, Alexander, *The Puppet Show*

Balance, principle of, in Montesquieu's thought, 3:357a

Balance, The. See Vesy

Balázs, Béla, Lukács and, 10:1254a, 1254b, 1263b–1264b

Balázs Béla és akiknek nem kell. See Lukács, György

Balbo, Felice
  Ginzburg and, 13:3152b
  Marinetti and, 9:827a

Balcon, Le, See Genet, Jean, *The Balcony*

Balcony, The, See Genet, Jean

Bald Soprano, The. See Ionesco, Eugène, *La cantatrice chauve*

Baldus. See Folengo, Teofilo

Baldwin, James, *Amen Corner*, Yourcenar's translation, 12:2543a

"Balia, La." *See* Pirandello, Luigi

Baliński, Staś, Gombrowicz and, 12:2564a-b

Baliverneries d'Eutrapel. See Du Fail, Noël

Ball, Hugo
  Arp and, 10:1369a–1370a
  Hesse and, 9:845b

"Ball, The." *See* Vigny, Alfred Victor de, *Poèmes antiques et modernes*, "Le bal"

Ballad
  Fontane and, 6:1304a, 1305b–1306b
  German, of Hebbel, 6:1117b
  Hugo's use of form, 6:694b, 698b–699a
  Lermontov's use of, 6:1204b
  literary, use of folk sources, 4:647b, 656b
  Mérimée's imitations of, 6:747b, 750b–751a, 754a, 756b
  in Polish literature, 5:609a–610a
  in Spain, 1:131b–132a
    the Cid in, 1:132a–134a
  Trakl and, 10:1417b

"Ballad of the Fried Tongues, The." *See* Villon, François

"Ballad of the Hanged Men." *See* Villon, François, "Villon's Epitaph"

"Ballad of the King of Thule, The." *See* Laforgue, Jules, *Les complaintes (Street Ballads)*, "Complainte du roi de Thulé"

Ballad meter
  Spanish, 1:131b
  in Calderón's works, 2:874a

"Ballad to the Moon." *See* Musset, Alfred de, "Ballade à la lune"

"Ballad of the Women of Olden Times." *See* Villon, François, *The Testament*

"Ballad of the Women of Paris." *See* Villon, François

"Ballade à la lune." *See* Musset, Alfred de

Ballads of Petrica Kerempuh, The. *See* Krleža, Miroslav, *Balade Petrice Kerempuha*

Ballet
  and Cocteau, 10:1545b, 1546b
  Heine's influence on, 5:506a-b

Ballo in maschera, Un. See Verdi, Giuseppe

Balmes, Jaime, Unamuno's reading of, 8:285a

Balmont, Constantine, *Under the Northern Sky*, Bely on, 9:912a

Baltrušaijtis, Jurgis, Mandelshtam aided by, 10:1646a

Balzac and French Realism. *See* Lukács, György, *Balzac und der französische Realismus*

Balzac, Honoré de, **5:635a–655b**
  Adieu, 5:643a, 655a
  Anouilh and, 13:2844a
  Baudelaire and, 7:1340b
  Beauvoir and, 12:2708b
  Berlioz and, 6:772a, 774b
  Böll and, 13:3166a
  and Colette's single name, 9:619b
  David Séchard ou les souffrances d'un inventeur (David Séchard; or, The Sufferings of an Inventor), 5:648b
  Dostoevsky and, 7:1351a
  Dumas and, 6:726a
  Études analytiques (Analytical Studies), 5:641a, 641b
  Études de moeurs au XIXme siècle (Studies of Manners in the Nineteenth Century), 5:641a, 6:641b
  Études philosophiques (Philosophical Studies), 5:641a, 641b–543b
  Eugénie Grandet, Pérez Galdós and, 7:1605b, 1606b
  Flaubert and, 7:1378b
  Gautier and, 6:1034b
  Giraudoux and, 9:1059b
  Goncharov and, 6:1066a
  Goncourts and, 7:1399a
  Hamsun and, 8:23a
  "Histoire des parents pauvres" ("Story of Poor Relations"), 5:654a
  Illusions perdues (Lost Illusions), 5:648b, 649a–651a, 6:1066a
  influence of, on Colette, 9:636b
  La comédie humaine (The Human Comedy), 5:635b, 636b, 637a–642b, 12:2503b
    Chekhov and, 7:1868a
    and Colette's works, 9:636b
    Goncourts and, 7:1398b
    Lesage's *Gil Blas* and, 3:330b
    Lukács, 10:1261b–1262a
    Pérez Galdós and, 7:1600a-b, 1615a
  La cousine Bette (Cousin Bette), 5:654a-b
  La fille aux yeux d'or (The Girl with the Golden Eyes), 5:642a, 650b–651a
  La maison Nucingen (The Firm of Nucingen), 5:642a
  La muse du département (The Muse of the District), 5:649a
  La peau de chagrin (The Wild Ass's Skin), 5:637a–642b, 655b
    Sand and, 6:820a
    Unamuno and, 8:306a
  La physiologie du mariage, 5:635b
  La recherche de l'absolu (The Quest of the Absolute), 5:644a
  Le cabinet des antiques (The Cabinet of Antiquities), 5:649a
  Le chef d'oeuvre inconnu (The Unknown Masterpiece), 5:643b–644a
  Le Colonel Chabert, 5:643a, 644a–645a, 645b
  Le cousin Pons (Cousin Pons), 5:654b–655a, 665a
  Le curé de Tours (The Vicar of Tours), 5:644a, 645a-b
  Le curé de village (The Village Parson), 5:653a
  Le lys dans la vallée (The Lily of the Valley), 5:649a, 652b–653b
  Le médecin de campagne, 5:651b–652a
  Le père Goriot (Old Goriot), 5:646a–648a, 650a-b, 655b
    Dostoevsky and, 7:1360b
    Proust's *Remembrance of Things Past* and, 8:550b

Balzac, Honoré de (*cont.*)
  Lermontov and, 6:1205b
  Les Chouans, 5:635b, 637a, 6:1205b
  Les deux poètes (*The Two Poets*), 5:648b
  Les paysans (*The Peasants*), 5:652a-b,
    7:1532a-b
  L'Histoire des treize (*The Thirteen*),
    12:2485b
  Louis Lambert, 5:643b
  Lukács on, 10:1271a-b
  Maupassant and, 7:1782b
  Mauriac and, 10:1312a-b
  naturalism and, 7:1711b
  Ortega y Gasset and, 9:1122b
  Pasternak and, 10:1594a
  Proust and, 8:545b, 551b, 554a
  Sainte-Beuve and, 6:841a-b
  Sarrasine, 5:642b
    Barthes on, 13:3092b–3094a
  Sarraute and, 12:2333b, 2334a, 2337b
  Scènes de la vie privée (*Scenes from Private
    Life*), 5:641a
  Simenon and, 12:2503a, 2503b
  Simon on, 13:3044a
  Splendeurs et misères des courtisanes
    (*Splendors and Miseries of Courtesans*),
    5:648b, 650a, 655a-b
    Pérez Galdós and, 7:1600b
  Strindberg and, 7:1753b
  Taine on, 7:1449a, 1454a
  Un grand homme de province à Paris (*A
    Provincial Celebrity in Paris*, 5:648b
  Une fille d'Eve (*A Daughter of Eve*), 5:649a
  Une passion dans le désert (*A Passion in
    the Desert*), 5:642b–543a
  Verga compared to, 7:1562a-b
Balzac, Jean-Louis Guez de, Bossuet and,
  3:161b
*Balzac und der französische Realismus. See
  Lukács, György
Bamberg, Felix, Hebbel and, 6:1095b, 1096a,
  1098b
Ban on Love, The. See* Wagner, Richard, *Das
  Liebesverbot*
Banana Tourist. See Simenon, Georges,
  Touriste de bananes
Bance, Alan, on Böll, 13:3178b

Bancroft, George, 4:653b
Bandamanna saga (*The Story of the
  Confederates*), 1:395a
Bandello, Matteo
  novellas of, 2:942a–943b
  oral tradition and, 2:928a
Bandet. See Strindberg, August
Banket u Blitvi. See Krleža, Miroslav
Bankrupt Merchant, The. *See* Goldoni, Carlo,
  Il mecante fallito
Banner of the Upright Seven, The. See Keller,
  Gottfried
Banners. *See* Krleža, Miroslav, *Zastave*
Bánóczy, László, Lukács and, 10:1254a
Banquet. See Dante Alighieri, *Convivio*
Banquet in Blithuania. *See* Krleža, Miroslav,
  Banket u Blitvi
Banquet, The. See Plato
Banville, Théodore de
  poetry of, 7:1621a
  Verlaine and, 7:1620b, 1627b
Banya. See Mayakovsky, Vladimir
Baptism, Luther and, 2:677a-b
Baptized Chinaman, The. *See* Bely, Andrey,
  Kreshchenyi Kitaets
"Bar Titanic." *See* Andrić, Ivo
Barabbas. See Ghelderode, Michel de;
  Lagerkvist, Pär
Barante, Prosper de, 5:93a, 572a, 572b, 581a
Barbarian Odes. See Carducci, Giosue, *Odi
  barbare*
Barbarians. See Gorky, Maxim, *Varvary*
Barbaric Plays. *See* Valle-Inclán, Ramón del,
  Las comedias bárbaras
Barbarous Prose. *See* Eça de Queiroz, José
  Maria, *Prosas bárbaras*
Barber of Seville, The. See Beaumarchais,
  Pierre-Augustin Caron de, *Le barbier de
  Séville*
Barbèra publishing house, Carducci and,
  7:1496b, 1498a
Barberine's Distaff. See Musset, Alfred de, *La
  quenouille de Barberine*
Barbey d'Aurevilly, Jules
  Baudelaire and, 7:1326b
  Flaubert and, 7:1382b
  Huysmans and, 7:1625a

Barbier, Auguste, Lermontov and, 6:1199a
Barbier de Séville, Le. See Beaumarchais, Pierre-Augustin Caron de
Barbudo, Antonio Sánchez, Jiménez and, 9:1002a, 1010a
Barbusse, Henri
  Böll and, 13:3167a
  Céline and, 11:1873a
  editorship of *Le Monde*, 11:2071b
"Barche sulla Marna." *See* Montale, Eugenio, *The Occasions*
Barclay, Alexander, first English eclogues by, 2:914b
Bardi, Bice de'. *See* Beatrice
Bardiet (patriotic drama), Klopstock and, 4:523b–524b
Bards
  tradition of, Herder and, 4:648b–649a
  Welsh, 1:141a
Barillon's Marriage. See Feydeau, Georges, *Le mariage de Barillon*
Barja, César, on Ortega y Gasset, 9:1135b, 1143a-b
Bark Tree, The. See Queneau, Raymond, *Le chiendent*
Barkeep of Blémont, The. See Aymé, Marcel
Barn náttúrunnar. See Laxness, Halldór
Barnes, Peter, Strindberg and, 7:1754a
Baroja, Carmen. *See* Raggio, Carmen Baroja y
Baroja, Pío, **9:589a–616b**
  Aventuras, inventos, y mixtificaciones de Silvestre Paradox (Adventures, Inventions, and Mystifications of Silvestre Paradox)
    aesthetic concerns, 9:593b–594b
    eccentric nature, 9:592a-b
    hybridization in, 9:602a
    modeled on Dickens, 9:594a
    picaresque tone, 9:599b
    social analysis in, 9:596b
  Azorín's approval of, 9:644b, 645b
  Blasco Ináñez and, 8:357b
  Camino de perfección (Way to Perfection)
    environmental influences in, 9:597a
    intent and tone, 9:594b–596a
    shifting narrative in, 9:601b

Canciones del suburbio (Songs of the Suburb), 9:613a
Cela and, 13:3110a
César o nada (Caesar or Nothing)
  contemporary Spain in, 9:605a
  individualism in, 9:604a
  life vs. abstraction in, 9:606b
  protagonists in, 9:603a
Desde la última vuelta del camino (From the Last Bend in the Road), 9:609b
El calios de las tormentas (The Cape of Storms), 9:612b
El dolor (estudio de psico-física) (Pain Psycho-Physical Study), medical ideas in, 9:592a
El gran corbellino del mundo (The Great Whirlwind of Life), 9:611b–612a
El mayorazgo de Labraz (*The Lord of Labraz*)
  balance in, 9:599a
  environmental influences in, 9:597a
  protagonist in, 9:596a
  spiritual journey in, 9:601b
El mundo es ansí (The Way of the World)
  integration of art and life, 9:608b–609a
  significance of, 9:593b, 609a
Historias lejanas (Distant Tales), 9:593a
Idilios vascos (Basque Idylls), 9:593a
Idilios y fantasías (Idylls and Fantasies), 9:593a
Juventud, egolatria (*Youth and Egolatry*), 9:611b
La busca (*The Quest*), composition of, 9:596b–597a
La casa de Aizgorri (The House of Aizgorri), 9:593b
La ciudad de la niebla (The City of Fog)
  genetic inheritance in, 9:603b
  historical themes of, 9:601a
  misogyny in, 9:601b–602a
  racial influences in, 9:605b
  shift in view, 9:601a
La dama errante (The Wandering Lady)
  anarchist plot of, 9:598a
  hybridization in, 9:602a
  misogyny in, 9:601b–602a

Baroja, Pío (*cont.*)
  La familia de Errotuco (The Family of
    Errotuco), 9:612b
  La feria de los discretos (*The City of the
    Discreet*)
    farcical elements, 9:599b
    milieu, 9:599a
  La lucha por la vida (The Struggle for Life)
    balance in, 9:599a
    Blasco Ináñez's *The Mob* and, 8:385a
    contemporary Spain in, 9:605a
    individual and society, 9:598b–599a
    opportunism in, 9:599a
    picaresque format of, 9:596b
    political ideas in, 9:591a
    Santos draws upon, 9:596b
  La nave de los locos (The Ship of Fools),
    Baroja answers Ortega in, 9:608b
  La ruta del aventurero (*The Route of the
    Adventurer*), 9:611a
  La selva oscura (The Dark Forest), 9:612b
  La sensualidad pervertida (Perverted
    Sexuality), 9:611b
  Las agonías de nuestro tiempo (The
    Agonies of Our Time), 9:611b–612a
  Las horas solitarias (The Solitary Hours),
    9:611a
  Las inquietudes de Shanti Andía (*The
    Restlessness of Shanti Andía*),
    9:604b–605a
  Las tragedias grotescas (The Grotesque
    Tragedies), farcical elements, 9:601a
  Las veleidades de la fortuna (The Caprices
    of Fortune), 9:611b–612a
  Los amores tardíos (Late Loves), 9:612a
  Los últimos románticos (The Last
    Romantics)
    farcical elements, 9:601a
    nostalgia in, 9:605a
    optimism of, 9:607b
    time period of, 9:604b
  Los visionarios (The Visionaries), 9:612b
  Machado and, 9:745b
  Memorias de un hombre de acción
    (Memoires of a Man of Action), Galdós
    and, 9:610a
  Ortega y Gasset on, 9:1137a

Paradox, King (*Paradox, rey*)
    farcical elements, 9:599b–601a
    hybridization in, 9:599a, 602a
  Red Dawn (*Aurora roja*)
    bourgeois life in, 9:599a
    composition, 9:596b–597a
    political solutions in, 9:597b–598a
  social criticism, 9:1121b
  The Tree of Knowledge (*El árbol de la
    ciencia*)
    autobiographical flavor, 9:608a
    medical influence, 9:590b
    narrative structure, 9:605b–608a
    philosophical problems in, 9:605b–608a
    questions science, 9:594b, 606b–608a
  Valle-Inclán and, 8:331a, 338a-b
  Vidas sombrías (Somber Lives), 9:592a-b
  Weeds (*Mala hierba*), 9:596b–597a
  Zalacaín el aventurero (Zalacaín the
    Adventurer) conservative forces in,
    9:604a-b
    historical setting of, 9:602a–603a
    hybrid nature of, 9:612a
Baroja, Ricardo, 9:590b
Baroja, Serafín, 9:589b, 590b
Baron fantôme, Le. See Cocteau, Jean
Baron in the Trees, The. See Calvino, Italo, *I
    nostri antenati*
Baroncelli, Jacques de, Giraudoux and,
    9:1059b
Barone rampante, Il. See Calvino, Italo, *I
    nostri antenati* (Our Ancestors), *The
    Baron in the Trees*
Baroque period
  Baudelaire and, 7:1330b–1331a
  Benjamin and, 11:1715b, 1716b
    see also Trauerspiel
  Gombrowicz and, 12:2566b–2567b
  Grass and, 13:3382a–3383b
  Grillparzer and, 5:421b–422b, 437b
  Spanish, Cela and, 13:3116a
  tension of opposites in, 5:421b, 422a-b
Baróti, Dezsö, on Ady, 9:861b, 875a
Barque of Dante, The. See Delacroix, Eugène
Barraca, La. See Blasco Ibáñez, Vicente, *The
    Cabin*

Barraca, La (Lorca's theater troupe),
    11:2199a–2200b
Barrault, Jean-Louis, 13:3001b
    Camus and, 13:3069b
    Giraudoux and, 9:1058b
    Rabelais, 2:700b
Barrault, Jean-Louis (joint author). *See*
        Anouilh, Jean, and Barrault, Jean-Louis
Barrenness of Souls, The. *See* Valle-Inclán,
        Ramón del, *El yermo de las almas*
Barrès, Maurice
    Gide and, 8:495b
    Mauriac and, 10:1312a, 1315b–1316a
    on Verlaine, 7:1639a
Barreto, Francisco, 2:754b–755a
Barrière, Théodore, 7:1920b
Barros, João de, *Decades Concerning Asia*,
        2:760b, 763b, 764b
Barsacq, André, Anouilh and, 13:2844b
"Barsuch'ia nora." *See* Mandelshtam
Barthes, Roland, **13:3079a–3104b**
    A Lover's Discourse: Fragments (*Fragments
        d'un discours amoureux*), 13:3080a,
        3096a, 3099a–3101b
    on Butor, 13:3302a
    Camera Lucida: Reflections on Photography
        (*La chambre clair: Note sur la
        photographie*), 13:3096a, 3101b–3102b
    Critical Essays (*Essais critiques*), 13:3084b
    Elements of Semiology (*Éléments de
        sémiologie*), 13:3091a-b
    concept of character in fiction, 8:304a
    Empire of Signs (*L'Empire des signes*),
        13:3094a–3095a
    Ionesco and, 13:2999a
    "Literal Literature" ("Littérature littérale"),
        13:3085a
    Michelet (*Michelet par lui-même*),
        13:3083b–3084a
    "Mother Courage Blind" ("Mère Courage
        aveugle"), 13:3086b
    Mythologies, 13:3084a
    New Novel and, 13:3240a
    "Objective Literature" ("Littérature objectif"),
        13:3084b–3085a
    "On Gide and His Journal," 13:3081b–3082a
    On Racine (*Sur Racine*), 13:3090a–3091a

    on Queneau, 12:2522a, 2526a
    on Robbe-Grillet, 13:3084b–3085a, 3240a
    Roland Barthes by Roland Barthes (*Roland
        Barthes par Roland Barthes*), 13:3096a,
        3097b–3099a
    S/Z, 13:3092b–3094a
    Sade, Fourier, Loyola, 13:3095a-b
    "The Eiffel Tower," 13:3088a–3089a
    The Fashion System (*Le système de la
        mode*), 13:3087a–3088a
    The Grain of the Voice (*Le grain de la voix*),
        13:3087a-b
    "The Last Word on Robbe-Grillet?" ("Le
        point sur Robbe-Grillet?"), 13:3085b
    The Pleasure of the Text (*Le plaisir du
        texte*), 13:3096a–3097b
    "The Two Criticisms" ("Les deux critiques"),
        13:3089a
    "What Is Criticism?" ("Qu'est-ce que la
        critique?"), 13:3089a–3090a
    Writing Degree Zero (*Le degré zéro de
        l'écriture*), 13:3082a–3083b
"Barynya." *See* Chekhov, Anton
Barzun, Jacques, *Race: A Study in Modern
        Superstition*, 7:1454b
Basile, Giambattista, *Lo cunto de li cunti* (*The
        Tale of Tales*), 2:944b–945b
Basque culture, Unamuno influenced by,
        8:283b
Basque Idylls. *See* Baroja, Pío, *Idilios vascos*
Bassani, Giorgio
    Il giardino dei Finzi-Contini (*The Garden of
        the Finzi-Continis*), 13:3145a
    Lampedusa described by, 11:2010b
Bastille, the, Sade's imprisonment at,
        4:618b–619b
Bataille de Pharsale, La. *See* Simon, Claude
Bataille des dames. *See* Scribe, Eugène
"Bataille des vices contre les vertus." *See*
        Rutebeuf
Batalha de Caia, A. *See* Eça de Queiroz, José
        Maria
Batalha Reis, Jaime, Eça and, 7:1686a, 1686b
"Batalla del Rio Jarama." *See* Neruda, Pablo
"Bateau ivre, Le." *See* Rimbaud, Arthur
Båten om kvelden. *See* Vesaas, Tarjei, *The
        Boat in the Evening*

Bath of a Roman Lady, The. *See* Vigny, Alfred Victor de, *Poèmes antiques et modernes,* "Le bain d'une dame romaine"

Bathers, The. See Courbet, Gustave

Bathhouse, The. See Mayakovsky, Vladimir, *Banya*

Bathing, in Gottfried, 1:253b–254a

Bathos, in Chrétien's *Lancelot,* 1:197b

Baths of Caracalla (Rome), Carducci on, 7:1509b–1510b

Baths of Lucca, The. See Heine, Heinrich, *Die Bäder von Lucca*

Bâtons, chiffres et lettres. See Queneau, Raymond

"Battaglia peso + odore." *See* Marinetti, Filippo Tommaso

Battifolle, countess of, Dante and, 1:444b

Battle at Hemmingstedt, The. See Hebbel, Friedrich, *Die Schlacht bei Hemmingstedt*

Battle of Brunanburh (Anglo-Saxon poem), 1:66a

Battle of Caia, The. See Eça de Queiroz, José Maria, *A batalha de Caia*

Battle of the Cats, The. See Lope de Vega, *La gatomaquia*

Battle of Hermann, The. See Klopstock, Friedrich Gottlieb

"Battle of *Hernani.*" *See* Gautier, Théophile

Battle of Maldon (Anglo-Saxon poem), 1:64b–65a, 66a

Battle for Man's Soul, The. See Prudentius, *Psychomachia*

Battle of Nancy, The. See Delacroix, Eugène

Battle of Pharsalus, The. See Simon, Claude, *La bataille de Pharsale*

Battle of Poitiers, The. See Delacroix, Eugène

Battle of Roncevaux
  in *Chanson de Roland,* 1:92a–94a
  variant versions, 1:91a

Battle with the Swine-Headed Lord. *See* Ady, Endre, "Hare a Nagyúrral"

"Battle of the Vices Against the Virtues." *See* Rutebeuf, "Bataille des vices contre les vertus"

"Battle Weight + Smell." *See* Marinetti, Filippo Tommaso, "Battaglia peso + odore"

Battles 1915–1917: A New Teaching About War. See Khlebnikov, Velimir, *Bitvy 1915–1917: Novoe uchenie o voine*

Battles. *See* Warfare

Baudelaire. See Sartre, Jean-Paul

Baudelaire, Charles, **7:1323a–1348b**
  "A Voyage to Cythera," 7:1327a–1330b
  Ady and, 9:859b, 860a, 861b
  "Albatross," "The Lord of the Island" and, 8:455b
  art criticism of, 7:1630b
  Artificial Paradises, 7:1326a
  "Au lecteur," 11:1877a
  Beauvoir and, 12:2710a
  Benjamin and, 11:1724a, 1725a–1726a
  Blok and, 9:969b
  "Carrion," 7:1330b–1331a, 1331b
  Chateaubriand and, 5:139b–140a
  "Correspondences," 7:1333a–1334a
    Nerval style and, 6:951b
  on the creative process, 12:2348a
  Curiosités esthétiques (*Aesthetic Curiosities*), 9:883b
  on Delacroix and Hugo, 5:517a
  Eça and, 7:1685b
  "Elevation," 7:1334b–1335a
  Eliot's *The Waste Land* and, 7:1340a
  "Evening Harmony," 7:1338b–1339a
  fascination with "damned women," 5:121a
  Gautier and, 6:1035a, 1050b
  George and, 8:450a, 451a
  "Hunting Horn" and, 9:894b
  insolite expressions of, 9:886b
  Intimate Journals, 7:1333b
  "Jewels," 7:1331a-b
  Jiménez and, 9:993b
  L'Albatros (*The Albatross*), translated into Hungarian, 9:863a
  L'Art romantique, on Laclos's *Les liaisons dangereuses,* 4:401a
  Le voyage, 7:1797b–1800a
    Ekelöf and, 12:2650b–2651a
  on Leconte de Lisle, 6:1261b

Les fleurs du mal (*The Flowers of Evil*),
    7:1325b–1342b, 1409b, 1621a,
    1640b–1641a
    Musset and, 6:1000b, 1022a
    Pascoli and, 7:1829b, 1838b
    Rubens and, 6:1043a
    Sainte-Beuve on, 6:842a
    "The Kinsman of Death" and, 9:862a
    translated by George, 8:447a, 451a-b,
      455b
"Les phares" (The Lighthouses), 6:1043a,
    7:1630b
Marinetti and, 9:805b
on Michelet's *L'Amour*, 5:596b
Montale's defense of, 11:2003a-b
noia and, 5:552b
"Obsession," 7:1333b–1334a
"Paris Dream," 7:1334a-b
Paris Spleen, 7:1326a-b
"Parisian Scenes," 7:1340b
"Pays de Cocagne" ("Country of
    Abundance"), *Algabal* and, 8:453b
Pessanha and, 10:1483b, 1485a
and the *poète-maudit* (accursed poet) cult,
    7:1572a-b
portrayal of French culture, 7:1400a-b
Proust and, 8:545b, 562b
Queneau's *Saint Glinglin* and,
    12:2514b–2515a
Rimbaud and, 7:1786a, 1791a, 1797b–1800a,
    1808b
Sade praised by, 4:637a
Sainte-Beuve and, 6:841b–842b
Salon of 1846, 7:1325b, 1329b, 1342a–1344b
"Salon of 1859," 7:1325b, 1331a
Sand and, 6:813a
Simenon and, 12:2503b
"Spleen," 7:1335b–1337b
Tableaux Parisiens (Parisian Scenes),
    Benjamin's translation of, 11:1704b,
    1707b
"The Abyss," 7:1334a-b
"The Artist's Profession of Faith," 7:1331a
"The Beautiful Ship," 7:1338a-b
"The Cracked Bell," 7:1336a, 1337b
"The Essence of Laughter," 7:1325b
"The Invitation to the Voyage," 7:1338a

"The Irreparable," 7:1339a-b
"The Longing for Nothingness,"
    7:1334b–1335a
"The Painter of Modern Life," 7:1325b,
    1342b, 1344b
"The Soul of the Wine," 7:1331b
"The Swan," 7:1339b–1342b
"To the Reader," *Tête d'or* and, 8:474a
translated by Ady, 9:862a
"transpositions d'art" in works of, 6:1043a
"Un voyage à Cythère" ("A Voyage to
    Cythera"), in Lampedusa's *The Leopard*,
    11:2015b–2016a
"Unluck," 7:1329b
Verde and, 10:1483b, 1485a
Verlaine and, 7:1621a
Baudrillart, Monsignor, Claudel and, 8:484b
Bauer, Felice, 9:1153a, 1153b–1154a, 1154b,
    1169a
Bauernfeld, Eduard von
    Bürgerlich und Romantisch (*Bourgeois and
      Romantic*), 7:1925b
    Grillparzer's friendship with, 5:418a-b
Baum, Oskar, Kafka and, 9:1152b
Bayard, Jean, 7:1911a
Bayreuth, Wagner's project in, 6:1162b,
    1163a-b
Bayreuth Festival, 6:1163b, 1165a
    Nietzsche and, 7:1664b–1665a
Bayreuther Blätter (*Bayreuth Leaves*), 6:1163b,
    1164a, 1166b
Baza de espadas. *See* Valle-Inclán, Ramón del,
    El ruedo ibérico
Bazán, Emilia de Pardo. *See* Pardo Bazán,
    Emilia de
Bazard, Armand, Vigny and, 5:463b
Bazlen, Roberto, Svevo and, 8:70b
Beach, The. *See* Pavese, Cesare
Bear and the Moon, The. *See* Claudel, Paul,
    L'Ours et la lune
Beast fables, medieval satire and, 1:369b,
    372b–373a
"Beast in the Jungle, The." *See* James, Henry
Beatrice
    biography of, 1:432b–433a
    Dante and
      Convivio and, 1:441a

Beatrice (*cont.*)
  Dante and (*cont.*)
    in *Divine Comedy*, 1:446b, 448a
    in *Vita nuova*, 1:437a-b, 438a, 439a
Beatrice. See Schnitzler, Arthur, *Frau Beate und ihr Sohn*
Beatrice Cenci. See Moravia, Alberto
Béatrice et Benedict (Beatrice and Benedict). See Berlioz, Hector
"Beau navire, Le." *See* Baudelaire, Charles, "The Beautiful Ship"
Beauchêne. See Lesage, Alain-René, *Les aventures de M. Robert Chevalier, dit de Beauchêne, capitaine de flibustiers*
Beaulieu, Fauré, translator of Unamuno's *Tragic Sense of Life*, 8:299a
Beaumarchais, Pierre-Augustin Caron de, **4:563a–585b**
  on classicism, 4:549b
  Essai sur le genre dramatique sérieux (Essay on Serious Drama), 4:565a
  Eugénie, 4:565a–566a, 580b
  Figaro compared with Lesage's Crispin, 3:320b
  Ibsen and, 7:1436b
  La folle journée ou le mariage de Figaro (The Follies of a Day; or, The Marriage of Figaro), 4:578b–582b
  L'Autre Tartuffe ou la mère coupable (The Other Tartuffe; or, The Guilty Mother), 4:582b–583a, 584a
  Le barbier de Séville (The Barber of Seville), 4:568b, 573a–577b
  Les deux amis ou le négociant de Lyon (The Two Friends; or, The Merchant of Lyon), 4:566a–567b
  Lettres de jeunesse, 4:563b
  Mémoires (Memorials), 4:568a–572b
  Tarare, 4:583a-b
  The Marriage of Figaro (Le mariage de Figaro), 7:1428a
  Scribe and, 7:1912a
Beaumont, Francis, and Fletcher, John, *The Triumph of Death*, Bandello as source for, 2:943b
Beaumont, Pauline de, Chateaubriand and, 5:123b

Beaurain, Karol, Witkiewicz and, 10:1211b
Beautiful Captive, The. *See* Robbe-Grillet, Alain, *La belle captive*
"Beautiful Ship, The." *See* Baudelaire, Charles
Beautiful Summer, The. See Pavese, Cesare
Beauty
  in Andrić's works, 11:1758a-b, 1773b–1774a
  in Castiglione, 2:662a-b
  in Chrétien, 1:189a-b
  Delacroix's views on, 5:529b–531a, 538b–539a
  Foscolo's treatment of, 5:335b–338a
  in Hölderlin's works, 5:146a, 147a
  in Leopardi's works, 5:563a-b
  in Richter's *The School for Aesthetics*, 5:77b–78a
  Schiller on, 5:38a
  in Walther, 1:296b
Beauty. See Jiménez, Juan Ramón, *Belleza*
Beauty of Angelica, The. See Lope de Vega, *La hermosura de Angélica*
Beauty and the Beast. See Cocteau, Jean, *La belle et la bête*
Beauty of Dying in the Prime of Youth, The. *See* Richter, Jean Paul, "Die Schönheit des Sterbens in der Blüte des Lebens"
Beauty of the Skies, The. *See* Laxness, Halldór, *Fegurð himinsins*
Beauvoir, Simone de, **12:2701a–2731b**
  A Very Easy Death (Une mort très douce), 12:2714a
  All Men Are Mortal (Tous les hommes sont mortels), 12:2714a, 2714b, 2720a
  All Said and Done (Toute compte fait), 12:2702a, 2703a, 2704a, 2704b, 2721a, 2729b
  Force of Circumstance (La force des choses), 12:2701b, 2702a, 2703a, 2704a, 2714b, 2718b, 2720a, 2721a, 2727a, 2727b, 13:3069b
  Giraudoux and, 9:1041b
  Les belles images, 12:2713b, 2727b
  Les bouches inutiles (Useless Mouths), 12:2716a, 2720a

Memoirs of a Dutiful Daughter (*Mémoires d'une jeune fille rangée*), 12:2701a, 2704b, 2705a, 2706a, 2707b, 2715a, 2789a
  act of reading and, 12:2706b–2707a
  alienation in, 12:2709b
  on her femininity, 12:2708a
  purpose of, 12:2712b
Must We Burn Sade? (*Faut-il brûler Sade?*), 12:2715a
Old Age (*La vieillesse*), 12:2701b, 2714a
Sarraute and, 12:2335a
Sartre and, 12:2603a, 2702a, 2711b, 2717b, 2720a
She Came to Stay (*L'Invitée*), 12:2702b, 2703a, 2714a, 2715a, 2716b
The Blood of Others (*Le sang des autres*), 12:2712a, 2714a, 2715a, 2718b, 2720a, 2723b
The Ethics of Ambiguity (*Pour une morale de l'ambiguité*), 12:2719b, 2720a
The Mandarins (*Les Mandarins*), 12:2703b, 2720b, 2726b, 2727a, 2728a–2728b
The Prime of Life (*La force de l'âge*), 12:2702b, 2705a, 2709a, 2711b, 2712a, 2724b
The Second Sex (*Le deuxième sexe*), 11:1933b, 12:2703b, 2720a, 2721a–2726b, 2729a
  on children, 12:2705a
  her memoirs and, 12:2708a
  on Laforgue, 7:1892a
  reception of, 12:2701b–2702a
  She Came to Stay and, 12:2717a
The Woman Destroyed (*La femme rompue*), 12:2713b
Weil and, 12:2789a
When Things of the Spirit Come First (*Quand prime le spirituel*), 12:2713b
Beaux draps, Les. See Céline, Louis-Ferdinand
Beaux quartiers, Les. See Aragon, Louis
Beaver Coat: A Comedy of Thieves, The. See Hauptmann, Gerhart
Bebel, Heinrich, influence on Renaissance short fiction, 2:952a-b
Bebo's Girl. See Cassola, Carlo, *La ragazza di Bube*

Becarria, Cesare, *Dei delitti e delle pene* (*On Crimes and Punishments*), 5:368a
Because You Love Me. *See* Ady, Endre, "Mert engem szeretsz"
Beccari, *Il Sacrificio*, as first pastoral drama, 2:917a
Becker, Paula, 9:770a
Becket; or, The Honor of God (*Becket ou l'honneur de Dieu*). *See* Anouilh, Jean
Becket, Thomas à, in Meyer, 6:935b
Beckett, Samuel
  Act Without Words I, 13:3026a
  All That Fall, 13:3034b
  Anouilh and, 13:2844b
  antecedents to, in Maeterlinck, 8:127b, 131b
  Butor and, 13:3289a
  Céline and, 11:1883b
  Chekhov and, 7:1858a
  Giraudoux and, 9:1041b
  Ibsen and, 7:1754a
  insolite expressions of, 9:886b
  Ionesco and, 13:3015b–3016a, 3016b–3017a, 3018b
  Rilke's *The Notebooks of Malte Laurids Brigge* and, 9:792a
  Sarraute and, 12:2337b
  Simenon and, 12:2504a-b
  Unnamable, 11:1879b
  Valle-Inclán and, 8:351b
  Waiting for Godot, 13:3026a, 3035b
    Anouilh on, 13:2844b
  Yourcenar and, 12:2541a
Becoming. *See* Ritsos, Yannis, *Ghignesthe*
Becque, Henry, Ibsen and, 7:1443b
Bécquer, Gustavo
  Jiménez and, 9:991a-b, 994b, 1008a
  Rimas, 9:994b, 999a
Bedbug, The. See Mayakovsky, Vladimir, *Klop*
Bede
  Historia ecclesiastica gentis Anglorum (*Ecclesiastical History of the English Nation*)
    on Caedmon, 1:65a-b
    on the conversion of England, 1:62b–64a
Bedier, Joseph
  Machado and, 9:746a
  Poema de mio Cid scholarship and, 1:126b

Beelzebub Sonata, The; or, What Really Happened in Mordovar. *See* Witkiewicz, Stanisław Ignacy, *Sonata Belzebuba, czyli Prawdziwe zdarzenie w Mordowarze*

Beer-Hofmann, Richard
  Hofmannsthal and, 9:690b
  Schnitzler and, 8:92a

Beethoven. See Wagner, Richard

Beethoven, Ludwig van
  Berlioz and, 6:777b, 779a–780a, 782b, 786a-b, 807a, 810a
  Butor and, 13:3312b
  Carnap's view of, 5:413b
  Doctor Faustus and, 9:733b, 734a
  Grillparzer and, 5:433a-b
  Hoffmann on, 5:273a–274a
  Marinetti and, 9:801b, 822a
  Ninth Symphony, 5:36a
  Ortega y Gasset on, 9:1135b
  Strindberg and, 7:1748a
  Wagner and, 6:1154b–1155a

"Beethovens Instrumental-Musik." *See* Hoffmann, E. T. A.

Beffe della vita e della morte. See Pirandello, Luigi

Before the Cock Crows. *See* Pavese, Cesare, *Prima che il gallo canti*

Before Daybreak. *See* Hauptmann, Gerhart, *Vor Sonnenaufgang, Soziales Drama*

"Before the Light." *See* Blok, Alexander, "Ante Lucem"

"Before San Guido." *See* Carducci, Giosue, "Davanti San Guido"

Before the Start. *See* Tsatsos, Constantine, "Prin apo to xekinama"

Before the Storm. *See* Fontane, Theodor, *Vor dem Sturm*

"Before such a renowned man." *See* Walter of Châtillon, "Tanto viro locuturi"

Befristeten, Die. See Canetti, Elias, *The Numbered*

Beggar imagery, in Olesha's "In the World," 11:2241b

Beginning of the Century, The. *See* Bely, Andrey, *Nachalo veka*

Beginnings. *See* Mauriac, François, *Commencements d'une vie*

Begriff der Kunstkritik in der deutschen Romantik, Der. See Benjamin, Walter

"Beguiling of Gylfi, The." *See* Snorri Sturluson, *Edda*

Béguin, Albert, Nerval style and, 6:944b

Behan, Brendan, Böll's translations, 13:3167b

Behn, Aphra, *Miscellany, Being a Collection of Poems by Several Hands*, 3:52b

Behrens, Peter, *Feste des Lebens und der Kunst (Festival of Life and of Art)*, 11:1796a

Being
  Aquinas on, 1:424a
  Sartre and, 12:2594b–2595b

Being and Nothingness: An Essay on Phenomenological Ontology. See Sartre, Jean-Paul

"Being one day alone at the window." *See* Petrarch, *Canzoniere*, "Standomi un giorno solo a la fenestra"

Being and Time. See Heidegger, Martin, *Sein und Zeit*

Beiträge zur Analyze der Empfindungen. See Mach, Ernst

Beiträge zur Historie und Aufnahme des Theaters. See Lessing, Gotthold Ephraim

Béjart, Armande, Molière and, 3:103b–104a, 105a

Béjart, Madeleine, Molière and, 3:102b

Bekenntnis zum Übernationalen, Das. See Mann, Heinrich

Bekenntnisse des Hochstaplers Felix Krull. See Mann, Thomas

Bekhterev, V. M., 8:441b

Bel Inconnu, Le. See Renaut de Beaujeu

Bel indifférent, Le. See Cocteau, Jean

Bel-ami. See Maupassant, Guy de

"Bela." *See* Lermontov, Mikhail Yurievich

Béla Balázs and Those Who Have No Use for Him. *See* Lukács, György, *Balázs Béla és akiknek nem kell*

Belardo el furioso (Belardo the Madman). See Lope de Vega

Belfry. *See* Ritsos, Yannis, *Kodhonostasio*

Belgian literature

La jeune Belgique (literary review) and, 8:121a-b, 122b, 124a

La pléiade: Revue littéraire, artistique, musicale et dramatique (literary review), 8:122a, 124a

La Wallonie (literary review) and, 8:121a-b, 124a

L'Art moderne (literary review) and, 8:121a-b

Belgium, history, in plays of Ghelderode, 11:2129b, 2134a

Belief. *See* Doubt and belief; Faith; Religious belief; Scepticism

Belinsky, Vissarion

Dostoevsky and, 7:1351a–1353b

Goncharov and, 6:1061a, 1064a, 1085b

"Letter to Gogol," 6:974a

On Gogol's Stories, 6:996a

Turgenev and, 6:1276a–1277a

Bell in the Knoll, The. See Vesaas, Tarjei

Bella. See Giraudoux, Jean

Bella estate, La. See Pavese, Cesare, *The Beautiful Summer*

Bella vita, La. See Moravia, Alberto

Bellay, Guillaume du, 2:696b, 697a

Bellay, Jean du, Rabelais and, 2:696b, 697a, 697b

Bellay, Joachim du, 2:724a–726a

Défense et illustration de la langue française (*Defense and Illustration of the French Language*), 2:723b, 725a–726a, 739b, 743a-b

on epic poetry, 2:734a

Les quatre premiers livres des odes and, 2:726a

on philosophy, 2:732a

Pléiade and, 2:724a

on French language, 6:1033b

"Les Antiquités de Rome," 2:724a

"Les Regrets," 2:724a-b

Petrarchan influence, 2:504b

Belle. See Simenon, Georges, *La mort de Belle*

Belle captive, La. See Robbe-Grillet, Alain

Belle époque, la

Machado and, 9:744b

Proust and, 8:546b

see also Paris

Belle et la bête, Le. See Cocteau, Jean

Belle image, La. See Aymé, Marcel, *The Second Face*

"Belle matinée, Une." *See* Yourcenar, Marguerite, *Comme l'eau qui coule*

Belleau, Remy

Bergeries

"Avril," 2:912a

pastoral poetry in, 2:912a

Les Amours et nouveaux eschanges des pierres precieuses, vertus et proprietez d'icelles, 2:742b

Ronsard and, 2:723b

Belles images, Les. See Beauvoir, Simone de

Belleza. See Jiménez, Juan Ramón

Bellini, Giovanni, Marinetti and, 9:812a

Bellini, Vincenzo

Goncharov and, 6:1078a

Wagner and, 6:1151a

Bells of Basel, The. See Aragon, Louis, *Les cloches de Bâle*

Bells of Bicêtre, The. See Simenon, Georges, *Les anneaux de Bicêtre*

Belomorsko-Baltyskii Kanal imeni Stalina (*The White Sea-Baltic Canal in the Name of Stalin*), Gorky and, 8:422b

Beloved Returns, The. See Mann, Thomas, *Lotte in Weimar*

Belt, The. *See* Moravia, Alberto, *La cintura*

Bely, Andrey, **9:905a–929b**, 11:1839a

Arabeski (Arabesques), 9:913b

Blok and, 9:967b, 973a-b

downfall of Petrine Russia and, 10:1620a-b

"Emblematika smysla" ("Emblematics of Meaning"), 9:914a

"Formy iskusta" (The Forms of Art), 9:915a

Kotik Letaev, 9:905b–910b, 924a, 11:1886b

Kreshchenyi Kitaets (The Baptized Chinaman), 9:908a–910b

Krizis kul'tury (The Crisis of Culture), 9:924a

Krizis mysli (The Crisis of Thought), 9:924a

Krizis zhizni (The Crisis of Life), 9:924a

Lug zelenyi (The Green Meadow), 9:913b

Mandelshtam criticized by, 10:1645b

Maski (Masks), 9:925a-b, 927a

Bely, Andrey (*cont.*)
  Masterstvo Gogolia (The Art of Gogol),
    9:925a, 925b–926b
  Mezhdu dvukh revoliutsii (Between Two
    Revolutions), 9:916a-b
  Moskva (*Moscow*), 9:925a
  Na rubezhe dvukh stoletii (On the Border of
    Two Centuries), 9:910a, 910b–912a,
    918a
  Nachalo veka (The Beginning of the
    Century), 9:915b
  in Pasternak's *Sketch for an Autobiography*,
    10:1614a
  Pepel (Ashes), 9:916b
  Pervoe svidanie (*The First Encounter*),
    9:924a
  Peterburg (*Petersburg*), 9:920b–923b, 925b,
    927a, 983a
  Pochemu ia stal simvolistom (Why I Became
    a Symbolist), 9:926b
  Putevye zametki (Travel Notes), 9:920a
  Russian symbolism and, 9:963b
  Serebrianyi golub' (*The Silver Dove*),
    9:914b, 916b–919a, 984a
    Petersburg and, 9:920b, 921b, 925b
  Simvolizm (Symbolism), 9:913b
  Symphonies, 9:913a-b, 916a, 917a, 919b,
    921b
  Tsvetaeva and, 11:1739b, 1745b–1746a
  Vospominaniia o A. A. Bloke
    (Reminiscences of A. A. Blok), 9:912a,
    915b, 924b
  Vospominaniia o Shteinere (Reminiscences
    of Steiner), 9:923b
  Vozvrashchenie na rodinu (Returning
    Home), 9:924b
  Zapiski chudaka (Notes of an Eccentric),
    9:905a, 921b, 923b, 924b
Belyjs "Peterburg." See Ivanov-Razumnik, V. R.
Belzébir Decree, The. *See* Aymé, Marcel, *La
  convention Belzébir*
Bem, A., on Pasternak's *Second Birth*,
  10:1604b
Bembo, Pietro
  in Castiglione, 2:661b–662b
  lusus pastorales of, 2:909a
  Petrarchan influence, 2:504a–505a

"Bemerkungen uber einen Fall von
  Zwangsneurose." *See* Freud, Sigmund
"Ben vuelh." *See* William IX of Aquitaine,
  duke
Benavente y Martínez, Jacinto, 11:2188b
  Valle-Inclán and, 8:331a
Benda, Julien, Ortega y Gasset on, 9:1143a
Beneath the Shadow of the Mountain. See
  Ritsos, Yannis, *Kato ap ton iskio tou
  vounou*
Beneath the Wheel. See Hesse, Hermann,
  Unterm Rad
"Benedetto sia 'l giorno." *See* Petrarch,
  Canzoniere
Benedictines
  in early 17th-century France, 3:264b
  Rabelais and, 2:695b
Benediktbeuern Christmas play, 1:454a–455a,
  458b
Benelli, Sem, Marinetti and, 9:806a
Benet of Canfield, Fénelon and, 3:265a, 275a,
  279b
Benia Krik. See Babel, Isaac
Benjamin Constant de Rebecque. *See*
  Constant, Benjamin
Benjamin, Walter, **11:1703a–1730a**
  on allegory, 9:812b
  Arcades Project ("Passagenarbeit"),
    11:1724a, 1725b
  on art, 9:812a
  *Der Begriff der Kunstkritik in der deutschen
    Romantik* (The Concept of Art
    Criticism), 11:1704a-b
  "Der Erzähler" ("The Storyteller"), 8:392a
  on Döblin's works, 11:1727a
  *Ein Lyriker im Zeitalter des
    Hochkapitalismus* (*Charles Baudelaire,
    A Lyric Poet in the Era of High
    Capitalism*), 11:1724a
  on Marinetti, 9:824b
  "Moscow," 11:1721b
  "On Language as Such and on the Human
    Language" ("Über Sprache über-haupt
    and über die Sprache des Menschen"),
    11:1704b, 1706b–1707b
  One-Way Street (*Einbahnstrasse*), 11:1703a

"Reise durch die deutsche Inflation" ("A Tour Through the German Inflation"), 11:1720b–1721a

Rilke and, 9:777a-b

Schriften (Writings), 11:1703a-b

The Origin of German Tragic Drama (*Ursprung des deutschen Trauerspiels*), 5:65b, 11:1703a, 1704b, 1713b–1721a

"The Task of the Translator" ("Die Aufgabe des Übersetzers"), 11:1074b, 1707b–1709b

Trauerspiel, 11:1714a–1720a, 1724a

Benn, Gottfried, Heinrich Mann's *Die Göttinnen* and, 8:525a

Benni, Ia., on Babel, 11:1908a-b

Benoît de Sainte-Maure, *Roman de Troie* (*Romance of Troy*), Boccaccio's use of, 2:512a

Benoni. See Hamsun, Knut

Bens, Jacques, on Queneau, 12:2517b–2518a

Bentley, Eric, on farce, 7:1924a

Benvenuto Cellini. See Berlioz, Hector

Beowulf, **1:51a–87b**

critical approaches, 1:71b–74b

Grettis saga and, 1:392b

Hrólfs saga kraka and, 1:401a

manuscript of, 1:69a–71a

relationship to oral tradition, 1:55b–58a

traditional story and, 1:58a–60a

Ynglinga saga and, 1:388a

Berättelser ur min levnad. See Moberg, Vilhelm

Béranger, Pierre de, Michelet and, 5:596a

Berceo, Gonzalo de, Jiménez and, 9:1008a

Berend, Eduard, 5:74b

Berendsohn, Walter, on Ekelöf's works, 12:2657b–2658a

Berengarius Turonensis. See Lessing, Gotthold Ephraim

Bérenger de Tours, and Lessing, 4:541a

Berenguer Error, The. See Ortega y Gasset, José, "El error Berenguer"

Bérénice. See Racine, Jean

Beresford, William, 11:2144b–2145a

Berg, Alban, *Wozzeck*, 9:734b

Bergens, Andrée, on Queneau, 12:2524a

Berger extravagant, Le. See Sorel, Charles

"Bergerie." *See* Ronsard, Pierre de

Bergerie (poetic genre), *Jeu de Robin et Marion* and, 1:460b, 461a

Bergeries. See Belleau, Remy; Desportes, Philippe; Racan, Honorat de

Bergin, Thomas, 1:440b

Bergmann, Hugo, Kafka and, 9:1152a

Bergson, Henri, **8:45a–66b**

An Introduction to Metaphysics ("Introduction à la métaphysique"), 8:57b–59a

Beauvoir and, 12:2711a

Čapek and, 10:1566a

Creative Evolution (*L'Évolution créatrice*), 8:46a, 58a, 59a–61a, 62a, 63b, 64b, 9:1073a

Creative Evolution (*L'Évolution creatrice*), 11:2244a

Czech literature and, 10:1568b

Durée et simultanéité (*Duration and Simultaneity*), 8:46a

Ekelöf and, 12:2665b

élan vital, 9:1073a, 1075a, 1077b

Envy and, 11:2236a

influence of, 9:591a

and Jarry, 9:670b

Kazantzakis and, 9:1071b–1072a, 1072b–1074b, 1080a

Laughter (*Le rire*), 7:1922a-b, 8:55a–56a

L'Énergie spirituelle (*Mind-Energy*), 8:55a

Machado and, 9:746a, 761b, 762b–763a

Matter and Memory (*Matière et mémoire*), 8:45b, 48a-b, 50b, 52b–55a, 55b, 59a, 61a, 61b

monism, 9:1073a-b

Montaigne and, 2:787b

Olesha and, 11:2242a, 2244a

on Ortega y Gasset, 9:1121b

Siebenkäs and, 5:70a

The Creative Mind (*La pensée et le mouvant*), 8:57b

The Two Sources of Morality and Religion (*Les deux sources de la morale et de la religion*), 8:46a, 61b–63b

Bergson, Henri (*cont.*)
  *Time and Free Will: An Essay on the
    Immediate Data of Consciousness
    (Essai sur les données immédiates de la
    conscience*), 8:45b, 48a–52b, 54b, 55a,
    55b, 56a-b, 58b, 59a, 61a, 61b
  Valéry and, 8:584a
  Valle-Inclán and, 8:350b
Bergwerke zu Falun, Die. See Hoffmann,
  E. T. A.
"Bericht an Seine Majestät der König Ludwig
  II von Bayern Über eine in München zu
  erichtende deutsche Musikschule." *See*
  Wagner, Richard
*Beritten hin und zurück: Ein Vorspiel auf dem
  Theater. See* Grass, Günter, *Rocking
  Back and Forth*
Berlepsch, Emilie von, 5:71a
Berlin
  bombing of, World War I, in Céline's *Nord*,
    11:1882a
  Heine in, 5:492a-b
  in Heinrich Mann's *Im Schlaraffenland*,
    8:523a–524a
  literary society, 8:235b
  Strindberg's career in, 7:1735a-b
  Wedekind in, 8:235b
Berlin. See Mann, Heinrich, *Im
  Schlaraffenland*
Berlin Alexanderplatz. See Döblin, Alfred
Berlin, Isaiah
  Akhmatova and, 10:1535a-b, 1537b
  on Herder
    conception of individualism, 4:652a-b
    Russian successors of, 4:652b–653a
    theory of language creation, 4:648b
    use of *Humanität*, 4:646a
  The Hedgehog and the Fox, Schopenhauer
    and, 5:398a
Berlin Privileged Journal. *See Berlinische
  priviligierte Zeitung*
Berlin, University of, founding of, 5:50a
Berliner Abendblätter (newspaper), Kleist and,
  5:307a
Berliner Ensemble, Brecht and, 11:2089b
Berliner Schnauze, 8:523a, 528b

Berlinische priviligierte Zeitung (Berlin
  Privileged Journal), and Lessing,
  4:538b, 542a-b
Berlioz, Hector, **6:771a–812b**
  À travers chants (Across the Fields of
    Song), 6:806a–807b
  Béatrice et Benedict (*Beatrice and Benedict*),
    6:807b–809a
  Benvenuto Cellini, 6:783b, 784a, 791a, 799a
    Vigny's work on, 5:470b
  Choeur des ombres (Chorus of Shades),
    6:783a
  Elégie (Elegy), 6:792a-b
  Episode de la vie d'un artiste (*Episode in
    the Life of an Artist*), 6:782
  "Euphonia," 6:796a
  Evenings with the Orchestra (*Les soirées de
    l'orchestre*), 6:779a, 784b, 785b, 796a,
    796b–798a
  Francs-Juges (The Fehmic Court),
    6:774b–775a, 775b
  Gautier's poetry and, 6:1056b, 1057a
  Harold en Italie (*Harold in Italy*), 6:783b,
    784a
  Huit scènes de Faust (*Eight Scenes from
    Faust*), 6:779a, 790b, 791a
  La damnation de Faust (*Damnation of
    Faust*), 6:780b, 790b–793b, 796a, 799b,
    808b, 809a
    Nerval and, 6:948
  Le retour à la vie (*The Return to Life*). *See*
    Berlioz, Hector, *Lelio*
  Lelio, 6:781b–782b, 783a, 799b
  L'Enfance du Christ (*The Childhood of
    Christ*), 6:791a-b, 793a, 799b–800a
  Les grotesques de la musique (Musical
    Grotesques), 6:803b–805b, 806b
  Les Troyens (*The Trojans*), 6:722a,
    800b–803b, 805b, 809a
  Mémoires (*Memoirs*), 6:772a, 793b–795a
    early life, 6:772b–773b
    first exposure to opera, 6:774a
    on Shakespeare, 6:778a-b
  "On the Notions of 'Classic' and 'Romantic'
    in Music," 6:779a-b
  Requiem, 6:783b, 784b, 791b, 796b, 810b

Roméo et Juliet (*Romeo and Juliet*), 6:778b,
    783b, 784a, 790b, 791b, 796b, 799b,
    800b
"Suicide from Enthusiasm," 6:797b
Symphonie fantastique (*Fantastic
    Symphony*), 6:773b, 777a-b, 778b, 779a,
    781b, 782a
Symphonie funèbre et triomphale (*Funeral
    and Triumphal Symphony*), 6:783b
Te Deum, 6:795a-b, 796a, 800a
*Traité d'instrumentation et d'orchestration
    moderne* (*Treatise on Instrumentation
    and Orchestration*), 6:772a
Tristia, 6:795a
Vigny's friendship with, 5:470b
"Voyage en Dauphiné" (Trip to Dauphiné),
    6:794b
Voyage musical en Allemagne et en Italie
    (*Musical Travels in Germany and Italy*),
    6:789a–790a
Bernanos, Georges
    Böll and, 13:3167a
    conversion in work of, 7:1625b
Bernard, Charles de
    Gerfaut, 6:1220b
    Lermontov and, 6:1220b
Bernard of Clairvaux, St., 1:406a
    Dante and, 1:433b
Bernard, Claude
    *Introduction à l'étude de la médecine
        expérimentale* (*Introduction to the Study
        of Experimental Medicine*), 7:1528a,
        1865a
    influence on Baroja, 9:592a
Bernard, Tristan, Queneau and, 12:2528a
Bernardo, Aldo, hermeticism and, 12:2390a
Bernardus Silvestris, Gottfried and, 1:238a,
    245a-b
Bernart de Ventadorn, 1:439a
    Arnaut and, 1:177a
    "Can lo boschatges" ("When the woods"),
        1:173a-b
    courtly love in works of, 1:172b, 173b–174a
    naturalness in works of, 1:173b–174a
    as troubadour, 1:172a–175a
Bernhardt, Sarah, 7:1916b
    Marinetti and, 9:805b

Maupassant and, 7:1763a
    in Musset's *Lorenzaccio*, 6:1010a
Bernheim, Ernst, Croce and, 8:313b
Bernheim, Hippolyte, Freud and, 8:7a
Berni, Francesco, Petrarchan influence, 2:504b
Bernoulli, Marie, 9:836b
Béroul
    Gottfried and, 1:240a
    Tristan story and, 1:148b
Berretto a sonagli, Il. See Pirandello, Luigi
Bertaux, Pierre, Hölderlin and, 5:143a
Bertha Garlen. See Schnitzler, Arthur, *Frau
    Berta Garlan*
Berthelot, Marcellin, 8:474a
    Mathilde Bonaparte and, 7:1416a
Berthelot, Philippe, Claudel and, 8:474a, 479b
Bertold ("Berthold"). *See* Hesse, Hermann
Bertran de Born, 1:441b
    "Un sirventes on motz no falh" (A *sirventes*
        in which not a word fails of its mark),
        1:343b–344a
Bertrand, Aloysius, Rimbaud and, 7:1808b
Bertrand de Bar-sur-Aube, *Girart de Vienne*,
    cycles of *chansons de geste* delineated
    in, 1:106b–109b
Bertrand et Raton (Bertrand and Raton). *See*
    Scribe, Eugène
"Beruf des Dichters, Der." *See* Canetti, Elias,
    "The Writer's Profession"
Bérulle, Pierre de, 3:5a, 5b
    Bossuet and, 3:163b–164a
    Fénelon and, 3:264b, 265a, 275a, 279b
Besant, Annie
    The Secret Doctrine, Bely and, 9:916b
    Thought-Forms, 8:396b
"Beschreibung eines Kampfes." *See* Kafka,
    Franz
"Beslut." *See* Södergran, Edith
Besonnenheit, Hoffmann and, 5:274a
Besse, Dom Jean-Martial, Huysmans and,
    7:1728a-b
Best Magistrate, the King, The. See Lope de
    Vega
Bestiaire, ou cortège d'Orphée, L' (*Bestiary; or,
    The Parade of Orpheus*). *See*
    Apollinaire, Guillaume

Bestiaires, Les. *See* Montherlant, Henry de, *The Matador*

Bestuzhev-Marlinsky, Alexander, Lermontov and, 6:1206a-b

Besuch der alten Dames, Der. *See* Dürrenmatt, Friedrich, *The Visit*

Besy. *See* Dostoevsky, Feodor, *The Possessed*

Bête humaine, La. *See* Zola, Émile

Bethel. *See* Wedekind, Frank

Betoret-Paris, Eduardo, on *The Cabin*, 8:371a

Betrachtung. *See* Kafka, Franz

Betrachtungen eines Unpolitischen. *See* Mann, Thomas, *Reflections of a Nonpolitical Man*

Betrayal, theme of, in Lermontov's works, 6:1198a

"Betrothal in Santo Domingo, The." *See* Kleist, Heinrich von

"Betrothal, The." *See* Apollinaire, Guillaume, "Fiançailles"

Betrothed, The: A Milanese Story of the Seventeenth Century Discovered and Retold by Alessandro Manzoni. *See* Manzoni, Alessandro

"Betrothed, The." *See* Chekhov, Anton, "Nevesta"

Betty. *See* Simenon, Georges

Between Leda's Lips. *See* Ady, Endre, "Léda ajkai között"

Between Life and Death. *See* Sarraute, Nathalie, *Entre la vie et la mort*

Between the Races. *See* Mann, Heinrich, *Zwischen den Rassen*

Between Two Revolutions. *See* Bely, Andrey, *Mezhdu dvukh revoliutsii*

"Between Yes and No." *See* Camus, Albert

Bewitchment, The. *See* Broch, Hermann, *Die Verzauberung*

Beyen, Roland, 11:2119b

Beyle, Marie-Henri. *See* Stendhal

Beyond Communism. *See* Marinetti, Filippo Tommaso, *Al di là del comunismo*

Beyond the Don. *See* Sofoniia of Riazan, "Zadonshchina"

Beyond Good and Evil. *See* Nietzsche, Friedrich

Beyond Painting. *See* Ernst, Max

Beyond the Pleasure Principle. *See* Freud, Sigmund

Beyond the Shadow of the Cypress Trees. *See* Ritsos, Yannis, *Pera ap ton iskio ton kyparission*

Beyond the Stars. *See* Leconte de Lisle, Charles Marie, "Ultra coelos"

"Bez belukh flagov." *See* Mayakovsky, Vladimir

"Bezhin Meadow." *See* Turgenev, Ivan

"Bezliub'e." *See* Pasternak, Boris

Bianchi, Mario, Alfieri's letters concerning, 4:668b–669b

Biard, Jean Dominique, *The Style of La Fontaine's "Fables"*, 3:85b, 86a

Bibbiena, Bernardo Dovizi da, in Castiglione, 2:657b–658b

Biberpelz, Die. *See* Hauptmann, Gerhart, *The Beaver Coat: A Comedy of Thieves*

Bible
  in Ady's poetry, 9:860b, 873b
  Apocalypse, translated into modern Greek, 13:2981b
  Augustine and
    City of God, 1:34a-b, 35b
    Confessions, 1:25b, 27b
    On Christian Doctrine, 1:41b–42a, 43b
  Book of Judges, as source for Vigny's "La fille de Jephté," 5:455a
  in Claudel's plays, 8:488b–489a
  commentaries, of Aquinas, 1:412b–413a
  Creation myth, in Mallarmé's *Igitur*, 7:1587b–1589b
  in Dante's *Convivio*, 1:440a-b
  Eden myth
    Tieck's version of in *Blond Eckbert*, 5:247a–248a
    in Zamyatin's *We*, 10:1189a, 1190a
  Genesis
    Augustine on, 1:32a-b
    "Lament of the Poor Knight Errant" and, 7:1894a
  Gospel of John, as source for Vigny's "La femme adultère," 5:456a
  Gospel of Matthew
    in Dante's *De monarchia*, 1:443b
    in Hauptmann, 8:150a

Gospels, Aquinas' *Catena aurea* on, 1:415b
Hamsun and, 8:32a
Herder's view of, 4:649b
in Klopstock, 4:521a–523a
New Testament
  commentaries, of Aquinas, 1:418a
  Dostoevsky and, 7:1354b–1355a
  Erasmus and, 2:581a–582b
  Luther and, 2:680a-b
  Prudentius and, 1:16b
Old Testament
  English cycle plays and, 1:469a
  interpretation of, Church Fathers on,
    1:3b–4a
parodied, in medieval satire, 1:369b–370a
Prudentius and, 1:20a
Revelation of St. John
  Blasco Ináñez' *The Four Horsemen of the
    Apocalypse* and, 8:385b
  parodied, in "Apocalypsis Goliae
    Episcopi," 1:354a
Romans, Luther and, 2:672a
Septuagint, *City of God* and, 1:36a-b
in Södergran's works, 11:1803a
Song of Solomon
  Hamsun and, 8:32a
  influence on pastoral literature, 2:903b
  "Lament of the Poor Knight Errant" and,
    7:1894b
  in Lampedusa's *The Leopard*, 11:2015a-b
  Perse's poetry and, 10:1446b
  as source of Vigny's "La femme adultére,"
    5:456a
  "The Lament of the Pianos You Hear in
    Rich Neighborhoods" and, 7:1887a
  themes from, Giraudoux's *Judith*,
    9:1050b–1051a
see also Typology, biblical
Biblical poetry, Anglo-Saxon, 1:65b
Biblical symbolism. *See* Symbolism
Bibliophilia, in Canetti's *Die Blendung*,
  12:2621b–2623b
Bibliothek der Weltliteratur, Eine. See Hesse,
  Hermann
Bibliothèque bleue, *chansons de geste* in,
  1:110a
Bibliothèque Mazarine, Proust and, 8:547a

Bich Bozhii. See Zamyatin, Yevgeny Ivanovich
Biedermann und die Brandstifter. See Frisch,
  Max, *The Firebugs*
Biedermeier period
  Grillparzer and, 5:434a-b, 438a, 443b
  Hebbel and, 6:1100a, 1101a
  Keller and, 6:925b
  Storm and, 6:916b–917a
Bierbaum, O. J., *Deutsche Chansons* (*German
  Songs*), 8:260a
Bièvre de Saint-Séverin, La. See Huysmans,
  Joris Karl
"Bife Titanik." *See* Andrić, Ivo, "Bar Titanic"
Big Bob. See Simenon, Georges, *Le grand Bob*
Big Wurstel Puppet Theater, The. *See*
  Schnitzler, Arthur, "Zum grossen
  Wurstel"
"Bihar vezér földjén." *See* Ady, Endre
"Bijoux, Les." *See* Maupassant, Guy de
Bijoux indiscrets, Les. See Diderot, Denis
"Bijoux, Les." *See* Baudelaire, Charles,
  "Jewels"
Bílá nemoc. See Čapek, Karel
Bilbao, Unamuno's youth in, 8:284a-b
Bild, Das. See Houwald, Ernst
Bild-Zeitung (German newspaper), Böll's
  criticism of, 13:3170a-b
Bildnis. See Graven images
Bildungsroman
  Goethe and, 5:16a-b
  Grass and, 13:3368b
  Hesse's *The Glass Bead Game* as, 9:853a
  Keller and, 6:924a–926b
  Kundera and, 13:3402a–3403a
  Mann's *Magic Mountain* as, 9:720b–721a
  Musil's *Young Törless* as, 9:933a-b
  Richter and, 5:73b, 83a
  and Wieland, 4:594b
"Bill of Duties." *See* Broch, Hermann
Billiards at Half-Past Nine (*Billard um
  halbzehn*). *See* Böll, Heinrich
Bin; oder, Die Reise nach Peking (*Bin; or, The
  Trip to Peking*). *See* Frisch, Max
Binni, Walter, on Leopardi, 5:566a
Biografie: Ein spiel. See Frisch, Max,
  Biography: A Game

Biographical criticism, Sainte-Beuve and, 6:842a–843a, 845b–848b
Biography: A Game. See Frisch, Max
Biography
    Icelandic, 1:383a-b
    Kafka and, 9:1156b
    Sartre and, 12:2597a, 2606a–2611a
    Scandinavian, 1:382a–383b
Biological determinism
    in Wedekind's plays, 8:248b
    Spring's Awakening, 8:239a
Biomorphic art, Arp and, 10:1370a-b
Bion
    influence on Renaissance pastoral poetry, 2:900b–901a
    Lament for Adonis, influence on Renaissance pastoral elegy, 2:900b–901a
Biran, Maine de, Bergson and, 8:46b
Birba, La. See Goldoni, Carlo
Bird, The. See Michelet, Jules
Bird on the Beach, The. *See* Laxness, Halldór, *Salka Valka*
Bird imagery
    in George's "Der Herr der Insel," 8:455a-b
    in Jiménez's poetry, 9:1009b
Bird with Two Others. *See* Arp, Jean, *der vogel selbdritt*
Birds. See Perse, Saint-John
Birds Are Still . . ., The. *See* Tychyna, Pavlo, *Soniachni klarnety*, "Ishche ptashky . . ."
Birds on High, The. *See* Pirandello, Luigi, "Gli uccelli dell'alto"
Birds, The. See Vesaas, Tarjei
Birn, Randi, *Orion Blinded*, 13:3042b
Birsch-Pfeiffer, Charlotte, 7:1926a
Birth of the Clinic, The. See Foucault, Michel
Birth of Tragedy, The. See Nietzsche, Friedrich
Bisexuality, Mann brothers and, 8:521a
Bishop, Morris, *A Renaissance Storybook*, Sermini's novellas in, 2:936b
"Bishop, The." *See* Chekhov, Anton, "Arkhierey"
Bismarck. See Wedekind, Frank
Bismarck, Otto von
    Fontane's *Effi Briest* and, 6:1317a–1318a

Wagner and, 6:1162b, 1163a
"Bit of Theology, A." *See* Hesse, Hermann, "Ein Stückchen Theologie"
Bitterness, in Walther, 1:299a–300a
Bitvy 1915–1917: Novoe uchenie o voine. See Khlebnikov, Velimir
Bizarre Kingdom, The. *See* Malraux, André, *Le royaume farfelu*
Bizarrías de Belisa, Las. See Lope de Vega
Bizet, Georges
    Berlioz and, 6:809a
    Carmen, 7:1920b
    Mérimée and, 6:763b–764b
Bjarnar saga Hítdœlakappa (The Story of Björn the Hítadal Champion), 1:384b–385a, 398a
Björger. See Hamsun, Knut
Bjørnson, Bjørnstjerne
    Hamsun and, 8:22b, 23a, 24a, 33b
    Ibsen and, 7:1422a
    Norwegian realism and, 9:1037a
"Black Angel, The." *See* Montale, Eugenio, *Satura*, "L'Angelo nero"
Black Cliffs, The. See Gunnarsson, Gunnar, *Svartfugl*
Black Death
    in Boccaccio's *Decameron*, 2:494a, 521a-b
    Petrarch on, 2:478b, 485a
Black Horses, The. *See* Vesaas, Tarjei, *Dei Svarte hestane*
Black humor
    of Artaud, 11:1967b, 1978a
    in Aymé's works, 12:2438b
    in poetry of Apollinaire, 9:886b, 897b
Black Hundreds movement, Khlebnikov's involvement with, 10:1337a
Black Masses of the Good Inn. See Ionesco, Eugène, *La soif et la faim (Hunger and Thirst)*, *Les messes noires de La Bonne Auberge*
"Black Monk, The." *See* Chekhov, Anton, "Chorny monakh"
Black Piano, The. *See* Ady, Endre, "A fekete zongora"
Black Saint, The. *See* Ritsos, Yannis, *O mavros Aghios*

"Black Sheep." *See* Böll, Heinrich, "Die schwarzen Schafe"

Black Tulip, The. See Dumas père, Alexandre, *La tulip noire*

Black Woman and the Rose, The. *See* Jiménez, Juan Ramón, "La negra y la rosa"

Blackamoor of Peter the Great, The. See Pushkin, Alexander

Blackball, The. *See* Simenon, Georges, *La boule noire*

Blacks, in Lorca's poetry, 11:2183b–2185b

Blacks, The, See Genet, Jean

Blacks and Whites (political factions in medieval Florence), 1:434a, 434b

"Blacksmith, The." *See* Rimbaud, Arthur

Blake, William
    Jiménez and, 9:997a, 1004a
    Marriage of Heaven and Hell, 5:59a
    Sade compared to, 4:636a
    Songs of Innocence, 5:67b

Blanc, Charles, *Les peintres des fêtes galantes: Watteau, Lancret, Pater, Boucher* (The Painters of the *Fêtes galantes*), 7:1628a

Blanc et le noir, Le. See Voltaire

Blanc, Louis
    concept of historian, 5:581b
    on the French Revolution, 5:591b
    Histoire de la Révolution de 1848, 5:585b–586a
    Michelet and, 5:591a-b

Blanca von Kastilien (Blanche of Castile). *See* Grillparzer, Franz

Blanche ou l'oubli (Blanche; or, Forgetfulness). *See* Aragon, Louis

Blanchot, Maurice, on Musil's *The Man Without Qualities*, 9:937a

Blanco, Josefina, Valle-Inclán and, 8:341a

Blancs et les bleus, Les. See Dumas père, Alexandre

Blandade kort. See Ekelöf, Gunnar

Blank verse
    in Claudel's plays, 8:472b
    in German theater, Lessing's influence on, 4:558a

Blasco del Cacho, María, 8:356a

Blasco Ibáñez, Vicente, **8:355a–388b**

Arroz y tartana (*The Three Roses*), 8:357a, 368a, 373b, 375b

Cuentos valencianos (Valencian Tales), 8:357a, 358b

"Dimoni" ("Demon"), 8:358b

El intruso (*The Intruder*), 8:357a, 358a

El préstamo de la difunta (The Dead Woman's Loan), 8:358b

Entre naranjos (*The Torrent*), 8:358a

Historia de la guerra europea de 1914 (History of the European War, 1914–1919), 8:356b

La bodega (*The Fruit of the Vine*), 8:357a, 357b, 358a

La catedral (*The Shadow of the Cathedral*), 8:357a

La condenada (The Condemned Woman), 8:357a

La horda (*The Mob*), 8:357a, 357b, 385a

La maja desnuda (*Woman Triumphant*), 8:357a, 358a

La reina Calafia (*Queen Calafia*), 8:357b

La tierra de todos (*The Temptress*), 8:357b

La voluntad de vivir (The Will to Live), 8:357a

Los argonautas (The Argonauts), 8:357b

Los cuatro jinetes del Apocalipsis (*The Four Horsemen of the Apocalypse*), 8:356b, 357b, 358a, 385b–386a

Los enemigos de la mujer (*The Enemies of Women*), 8:357b

Los muertos mandan (*The Dead Command*), 8:357b, 385a-b

Luna Benamor, 8:357b

Mare nostrum (*Our Sea*), 8:357b, 358a

Reeds and Mud (*Cañas y barro*), 8:357a, 358a, 378a–385a
    characterization, 8:381b–382b
    descriptive passages, 8:379b–381a
    plot, 8:378a-b, 383a-b
    setting, 8:378a
    style, 8:381a
    The Cabin and, 8:373b, 375a, 375b, 376a
    The Mayflower and, 8:359a, 359b, 361b, 364a, 365b–366a, 366b, 368a, 368b
    themes, 8:382b–383a, 384a
    unity, 8:383b–385a

Blasco Ibáñez, Vicente (*cont.*)
  Sangre y arena (*Blood and Sand*), 8:357a,
    358a
  The Cabin (*La barraca*), 8:357a, 358a, 358b,
    370a–378a
    bibliographical history, 8:370a
    characterization, 8:374b–375b
    French translation of, 8:356a, 370a
    plot, 8:370b, 376b–377b
    Reeds and Mud and, 8:382a, 383a
    The Mayflower and, 8:359a, 359b, 361b,
      364a, 366b, 368a, 368b
    themes, 8:371b, 372b, 375a, 375b
    unity, 8:377b
  The Condemned Woman (*La condenada*),
    8:357a, 358b
  The Mayflower (*Flor de Mayo*), 8:357a, 358a,
    358b–370a
    characterization, 8:362a-b, 364a–366b
    plot, 8:359a-b, 367b–369a
    Reeds and Mud and, 8:382a
    setting, 8:359a
    style, 8:361a–364b
    The Cabin and, 8:373b, 375a, 375b
    themes, 8:366b–367a
    unity, 8:369a-b
  "Venganza moruna" ("Moorish Vengeance"),
    8:370a
Blasphemy, Augustine on, 1:49a
Blasting and Bombardiering. See Lewis,
  Wyndham
Blätter aus dem Brotsack. See Frisch, Max
Blätter für die Kunst (*Pages for Art*), George
  and, 8:450a-b, 461a
Blaubart: Eine Erzählung. See Frisch, Max,
  Bluebeard: A Tale
Blavatsky, Helena, *The Secret Doctrine*, 9:916b
Blé en herbe, Le. See Colette
Bleaching Yard, The. See Vesaas, Tarjei
"Blechmusik." *See* Grass, Günter, *Die Vorzüge
  der Windhühner*
Blechtrommel, Die. See Grass, Günter, *The
  Tin Drum*
Blei, Franz, Musil and, 9:932b
Bleikeplassen. See Vesaas, Tarjei, *The
  Bleaching Yard*
Blendung, Die. See Canetti, Elias

"Blessed be the day." *See* Petrarch,
  Canzoniere, "Benedetto sia 'l giorno"
Blicker von Steinach, Gottfried and, 1:244a
Blind Geronimo and His Brother. *See*
  Schnitzler, Arthur, "Der Blinde
  Geronimo und sein Bruder"
"Blind Kittens, The." *See* Lampedusa,
  Giuseppe Tomasi di, *Two Stories and a
  Memory* (*Racconti*), "Il mattino di un
  mezzadro"
Blind Man, The. *See* Andrić, Ivo, "Slepac"
"Blind Man, The." *See* Chénier, André
Blind Orion Searching for the Dawn, The. See
  Poussin, Nicolas
Blind Orion, The. *See* Simon, Claude, *Orion
  aveugle*
Blind, The. See Maeterlinck, Maurice, *Les
  aveugles*
"Blinde Geronimo und sein Bruder, Der." *See*
  Schnitzler, Arthur
Blindes Hus, De. See Gunnarsson, Gunnar
Blindness
  Barthes on, 13:3088b
  Canetti on, 12:2622a-b
  Diderot and, 4:485a–486a
Bliss, Barthes on, 13:3096a–3097b
Blixen, Karen. *See* Dinesen, Isak
"Blixtens trångtan." *See* Södergran, Edith
Bliznets v tuchakh. See Pasternak, Boris
Bloch, Ernst
  association with Lukács, 10:1258a-b
  Das Prinzip Hoffnung (*The Principle of
    Hope*), 10:1258a
  Geist der Utopie (*Spirit of Utopia*), 11:1705b
  Geist des Utopie, 10:1258a-b
Bloch, Grete, 9:1153b
Blockheads. See Ghelderode, Michel de
Blok, Alexander, **9:959a–986b**, 11:1839a
  Ady and, 9:859b
  "Anne Akhmatovoi" ("To Anna
    Akhmatova"), 9:985b
  "Ante Lucem" ("Before the Light"), 9:970a
  Balaganchik (*The Puppet Show*),
    Khlebnikov's "Chertik" and, 10:1356b
  Bely and, 9:914b–915b, 916a, 917b, 924a
  "Carmen" cycle, 9:970a, 970b–972b, 982a

"Cherez dvenadtsat' let" ("After Twelve Years"), 9:965b

"Chernaia krov'" ("Black Blood") cycle, 9:970a, 971a

"Da, tak diktuet vdokhnovenie" ("Yes, thus does inspiration dictate"), 9:978a-b

"Devushka iz Spoleto" ("The Girl from Spoleto"), 9:968a-b

Dnevniki (Diaries), 9:980b

"Dvoinik" ("The Double"), 9:977b

"Dvoiniku" ("To My Double"), 9:966b–967a

"Faina," 9:970a, 973b

"Golos iz khora" ("A Voice from the Chorus"), 9:959b–960a

"Gorod" ("The City"), 9:973b

"Greshit' besstydno, neprobudno" ("Shamelessly, endlessly sinning"), 9:979b–980a

"I nam ne dolgo liubovat'sia" ("We are not long given to admire"), 9:960b

"Ia ee pobedil, nakonets" ("I have conquered her at last"), 9:971a-b

"Intelligentsiia i revoliutsiia" ("The Intelligentsia and the Revolution"), 9:980b, 981a

"Ishchu spaseniia" ("I seek salvation"), 9:963a-b

"Ital'ianskie stikhi" ("Italian Poems"), 9:977a

"K muze" ("To My Muse"), 9:970a-b

Katilina, 9:982a, 983b

Khlebnikov's *Death's Mistake* and, 10:1357a

"Khranila ia sredi mladkh sozvuchii" ("I have preserved among the young harmonies"), 9:969b

"Khudozhnik" ("The Artist"), 9:972a-b

Korol' na ploshchadi (*The King in the Square*), 9:973b

literary celebrity, 11:1893b, 1894b

on Mandelshtam, 10:1639a-b

"Milyi drug, i v etom tikhom dome" ("Dearest friend, even in this quiet house"), 9:961a

"Na pole kulekovom" ("On the Battlefield of Kulekovo"), 9:974b

"Na smert' mladentsa" ("On the Death of a Child"), 9:977a

"Na voinu" ("To War"), 9:979b

"Nad luchshim sozdaniem bozh'im" ("Above God's best creation"), 9:971b

"Narod i intelligentsiia" ("The People and the Intelligentsia"), 9:974b, 980b

"Net, nikogda moei i ty nich' ei ne budesh" ("No, never mine, nor anyone's will you ever be"), 9:972a

"Neznakomka" ("The Stranger"), 9:973b

Neznakomka (*The Unknown Lady*), 9:973b, 979b

   Khlebnikov's "Chertik" and, 10:1356b

"O, kak smeialis' vy nad nami" ("O, how you laughed at us"), 9:975b–976a

"O da, liubov' vol'na, kak ptitsa" ("O yes, love is free like a bird"), 9:971b–972a

"O naznachenii poeta" (On the Calling of the Poet), 9:985a-b

"O, net! Ia ne khochu, chtob pali my s toboi" ("O, no! I do not wish for us to fall"), 9:969a-b

"O sovremennom sostoianii russkogo simvolizma" ("On the Present State of Russian Symbolism"), 9:919a, 972b, 974a, 976a-b

"Osenni vecher byl. Pod zvuk dozhdia stekliannvi" ("It was an autumn night. Beneath the vitreous sound of the rain"), 9:979a

Pasternak and, 10:1592b–1593a, 1611b

Sketch for an Autobiography, 10:1614a

"Pesn' Ada" ("The Song of Hell"), 9:977a-b

Pesnia sud'by (*The Song of Fate*), 9:973b

"Pliaski smerti" ("The Dances of Death"), 9:979a

Poslednie dni imperatorskoi vlasti (The Last Days of the Imperial Regime), 9:980a-b

power and beauty, seductiveness of, 11:1901a

"Predchuvstvuiu Tebia" ("I sense Your coming"), 9:960b–961a

Retribution (*Vozmezdie*)

   Akhmatova on, 10:1531b

   on contemporary life, 9:960a-b

   on downfall of Petrine Russia, 10:1620a

   family in, 9:977b

   first draft of, 9:976b

Blok, Alexander (*cont.*)
  Retribution (Vozmezdie) (*cont.*)
    poet's task in, 9:976a
    on Warsaw, 10:1620b
    work on, 9:978b, 985a
  Ritsos' translations, 12:2819a
  Roza i krest (*The Rose and the Cross*),
    9:978b
  "Sbylos' prorochostvo moe" ("My prophecy
    has come to pass"), 9:969a
  "Serdityi vzor bestsvetnykh glaz" ("The
    angry gaze of your colorless eyes"),
    9:971b
  Skify (*The Scythians*), 9:983a
    on the new barbarism, 10:1620a
  Snezhnaia maska (The Snow Mask), 9:970a,
    970b, 973b, 982a
  Sobranie stikhotvorenii v trekh knigakh
    (Collected Verses in Three Volumes),
    9:978b
  "Sredi poklonnikov Karmen" ("Among the
    admirers of Carmen"), 9:971b
  Stikhi o Prekrasnoi Dame (Poems About the
    Most Beautiful Lady), 9:962a-b, 966b,
    970a, 975a
  "Stikhi o Rossii" (Poems About Russia),
    9:980a
  "Stikhiia i kul'tura" ("Nature and Culture"),
    9:974b, 982b, 984a
  The Puppet Show, 9:968a, 970b, 973b, 979b
  The Twelve (*Dvenadtsat'*), 9:981a–982b
    destructive forces in, 9:983b
    Khlebnikov's "The Night Search" and,
      10:1354b
    meter in, 9:962a, 981b
    Ritsos' translation of, 12:2837b
  Tsvetaeva and, 11:1736a, 1736b
  "Unizhenie" ("Humiliation"), 9:978a
  "Vkhozhu ia v temnye khramy" ("I enter
    dark churches"), 9:968b
  "Vnov' u sebia . . . Unizhen, zol i rad"
    ("Once again I am in my room"),
    9:969b–970a
  voice of the other, 11:1906a
  "Vol'nye mysli" ("Free Thoughts"), 9:973b
  in *Vospominaniia o A. A. Bloke*, 9:912a
  "Zhenshchina" ("A Woman"), 9:978b

Blok, Alexander L'vovich, 9:964a-b
Blok, Alexandra Andreevna, 9:914b, 964a-b,
  965a, 965b
Blok, Georgii (cousin), Mandelshtam's *The
  Noise of Time* published by, 10:1643a
Blokha. See Zamyatin, Yevgeny Ivanovich
Blomberg, Erik, Ekelöf and, 12:2648a
Blomstermålningar. See Strindberg, August
Blonde Eckbert, Der (*Blond Eckbert*). *See*
  Tieck, Ludwig
Blonde, The. *See* Cela, Camilo José, *La catira*
Blondel, Enrichetta, Manzoni's marriage to,
  5:369b
Blood in the Arena. See Blasco Ibáñez,
  Vicente, *Sangre y arena*
Blood and Gold. *See* Ady, Endre, *Vér és arany*
Blood imagery, in Ady's "Blood and Gold,"
  9:862a
Blood of My Race. *See* Ady, Endre, "O fajtám
  vére"
Blood of Others, The, See Beauvoir, Simone de
Blood Pact. *See* Valle-Inclán, Ramón del,
  Ligazón
Blood of a Poet, The. See Cocteau, Jean, *Le
  sang d'un poète*
Blood of the Poor, The. See Böll, Heinrich, *Le
  sang du pauvre*
Blood and Sand. See Blasco Ibáñez, Vicente,
  Sangre y arena
Blood vengeance. *See* Vengeance
Blood Wedding. See García Lorca, Federico
"Bloody Mystery Play of January Ninth." *See*
  Mandelshtam, Osip
Bloody Poet, The. See Kosztolányi, Dezső, *A
  véres költő*
"Bloody Sunday" (9 January 1905), 9:916a
Blossom of Happiness, The. See Andersen,
  Hans Christian
Blossom in My Heart, A. *See* Tychyna, Pavlo,
  Soniachni klarnety, "Tstvit v moemu
  sertsi"
Bloy, Léon
  Böll and, 13:3167a, 3167b
  Catholic revival and, 7:1709b
"Bludnyi syn." *See* Gumilev, Nikolai
Blue Angel, The (*Der blaue Engel*) (motion
  picture), 8:527a, 528b, 536b

Blue Bird, The. See Maeterlinck, Maurice
Blue Book, The. See Strindberg, August
Blue Bubbles. See Maeterlinck, Maurice,
    Bulles bleues
Blue (color), Trakl and, 10:1418b
Blue flower, as symbol of German
    romanticism, 5:225a-b
Blue Flowers. See Queneau, Raymond, *Les
    fleurs bleues*
Blue Fly, The. *See* Aymé, Marcel, *La mouche
    bleue*
Blue God, The. *See* Cocteau, Jean, *Le dieu
    bleu*
Blue Lantern, The. See Colette, *Le fanal bleu*
"Blue Room, The." *See* Mérimée, Prosper, "La
    chambre bleue"
Blue Train, The. Cocteau, Jean, *Le train bleu*
Bluebeard: A Tale. See Frisch, Max
Bluebeard story, Maeterlinck's adaptation of,
    8:136a-b
Blues et gospels. See Yourcenar, Marguerite
Bluette, in Musset's *Fantasio*, 6:1006b
Blumen des Bösen, Die. See George, Stefan
Blumen-, Frucht- und Dornenstücke. See
    Richter, Jean Paul
Blüthenstaub. See Novalis, *Pollen*
Blyumkin, Yakov, Mandelshtam's
    denouncement of, 10:1645b
"Bo-be-o-bee sang the mouth." *See*
    Khlebnikov, Velimir, "Bobeobi
    pelis'guby"
Boards of Fate, The. See Khlebnikov, Velimir,
    Doski sud'by
Boat on the Dead Sea. *See* Ady, Endre,
    "Csónak a Holt Tengeren"
Boat in the Evening, The. See Vesaas, Tarjei
"Boats on the Marne." *See* Montale, Eugenio,
    The Occasions (Le occasioni), "Barche
    sulla Marna"
Bobel, Isaac Manievich. *See* Babel, Isaac
"Bobeobi pelis'guby." *See* Khlebnikov, Velimir
Bobinack. See Johnson, Eyvind
"Bobok." *See* Dostoevsky, Feodor
"Bobo's Metamorphosis." *See* Milosz, Czeslaw,
    "Gucio zaczarowany"
Boccaccio. See Hesse, Hermann
Boccaccio, Giovanni, **2:509a–534b**

Amorosa visione (Amorous Vision), 2:514b,
    515a-b, 518a
on Beatrice, 1:432b
Berlioz and, 6:808a
Bucolicum carmen (Bucolic Song), 2:904b
Caccia di Diana (Diana's Hunt),
    2:511b–512a
Castiglione and, 2:658a-b
Corbaccio, 2:530a-b
on Dante's *De vulgari eloquentia,* 1:441b
*De casibus virorum illustrium (On the Fates
    of Illustrious Men),* 2:529b
De mulieribus claris (On Famous Women),
    2:519a-b, 529b
Decameron, 2:494a, 510a, 511b–512a,
    517a-b, 518a–527a, 530a, 6:808a
    acceptance of, 2:527a-b
    brigata, 2:520b–521a, 522a–523b, 524b,
        526a
    Calvino and, 13:3279a-b
    Cento novelle antiche's influence on,
        2:933b–934b
    as collection of novellas, 2:927a
    compassione, 2:520b–521a, 521b–522a,
        524b
    Fortuna, Amore, and *Ingegno,*
        2:519b–520a, 523b
    frame characters, 2:522b–523a
    French culture and, 2:694a
    Griselda story, 2:526b–527a
    image of women in, 2:518b–519a, 523a-b
    narrator's proem, 2:518b–519b
    popularity of, 2:934b
    reaction to plague, 2:521a-b
    reality principle, 2:518b, 522a-b, 524a-b
    Renaissance short fiction and, 2:933a,
        933b–934b
    Valle delle donne, 2:524a
    wheel, 2:524a–525b
Dioneo
    in the *Comedio ninfe,* 2:523a
    in the *Decameron,* 2:522a, 523a-b
*Elegia di madonna Fiammetta (Elegy of
    Madonna Fiammetta),* 2:515b–517a,
    518a, 530b
*Esposizioni sopra il Dante (Discourses on
    Dante),* 2:531a

Boccaccio, Giovanni (*cont.*)
Fiammetta myth, 2:510b, 512b, 513a-b, 515a–517a
Filocolo, 2:512b–513a, 518a, 526b
Filostrato, 2:518a
poetic form, 2:512a
sources for, 2:512a-b
Genealogia deorum gentilium (Genealogy of the Gentile Gods), 2:509a-b, 529a
Hellenic influence, 2:529a-b
La Fontaine and, 3:76a
lectura Dantis, 2:531a-b
Lucius Apuleius' influence on, 2:931a
Ninfale d'Ameto (*The Nymph of Admetus*), influence on Renaissance pastoral poetry, 2:904b, 905a-b
Ninfale fiesolano (*Nymphs of Fiesole*), 2:516b–518a, 518a
influence on Renaissance pastoral poetry, 2:904b–905a
novella form, 510a, 2:518a-b, 527a
ottava rima, 2:512a, 516b–517a
"Pantheon," Christian theme of, 2:904b
Petrarch and, 2:478b–479a, 509a-b–510a, 527b–528b
pronta risposta, 2:520a
religious conversion, 2:530a
Renaissance pastoral poetry and, 2:904b–905a
Teseida (*Book of Theseus*), 2:513b–514a
"Teseida delle nozze d'Emilia" (Theseid of the Nuptials of Emilia), 2:514a
themes, 2:511b
Trattatello in laude di Dante (*Treatise in Praise of Dante*), 2:531a
use of Latin, 2:528a-b
see also Decameron tradition
Boccace. See Hauvette, Henri
Boccioni, Umberto, Marinetti and, 9:815a, 825a
Bocher, Edouard, Musset and, 6:1018a
Böcklin, Arnold, 9:836a
Hamsun and, 8:31b
Self-Portrait, Södergran and, 11:1804a
The Isle of the Dead, Södergran and, 11:1804a

Boda de sangre. See García Lorca, Federico, *Blood Wedding*
Bodalsia telenok s dubom. See Solzhenitsyn, Aleksandr
Bodega, La. See Blasco Ibáñez, Vicente
Bodel, Jean
congé and, 1:460a
Jeu de Saint Nicolas, 1:459a-b, 463a-b
Bödeln. See Lagerkvist, Pär
Bodenhausen, Eberhard von, Hofmannsthal and, 9:691a
Bodmer, Johann Jakob
Klopstock and, 4:513a–514a
Wieland and, 4:588a, 592a-b
Body. *See* Human body
Body and Blood. *See* Ritsos, Yannis, *To soma kai to ema*
Body and mind. *See* Mind and body
"Body politic," Montesquieu's thought and, 3:357a
"Body of Summer." *See* Elytis, Odysseus, *Ilios o protos* (*Sun the First*), "Soma tou kalokeriou"
Boehme, Jacob. *See* Böhme, Jakob
Boehringer, Robert
Ewiger Augenblick (*Eternal Moment*), 8:448b
George and, 8:465b
Boethius, Anicius Manlius Severinus
Commentaries, 1:405a
Dante and, 1:432a
De trinitate (*On the Trinity*), Aquinas on, 1:414b
Opuscula sacra (*Sacred Studies*), 1:405b
The Consolation of Philosophy
"Doces lembranças de passada glória" and, 2:752b
Petrarch and, 2:486b
"Sôbolos rios" and, 2:754b
Boethius of Dacia, 1:410a
Boeuf clandestin, Le. See Aymé, Marcel
Boeuf sur le toit, Le. See Cocteau, Jean
"Boeufs, Les." *See* Aymé, Marcel, *The Wonderful Farm*
Bogatyr, as character type, in Pushkin's fairy tales, 5:683a, 683b, 684a
Bogdanov, Aleksandr, Gorky and, 8:421a

"Bogi." *See* Khlebnikov, Velimir

Boh. See Moravia, Alberto

Bohemians, in satire of Deschamps, 1:344b–345b, 350a

Bohemians of the Latin Quarter. See Murger, Henri, *Scènes de la vie de bohème*

Böhme, Jakob
Arp and, 10:1377b, 1379b–1381a
Hauptmann influenced by, 8:163b, 166a, 170a
Novalis and, 5:210a

Boiardo, Matteo Maria
Ariosto and, 2:624b–625b, 627a-b
Latin eclogues of, 2:906b
Orlando innamorato, sources for, 2:514b

Boileau-Despréaux, Nicolas, **3:177a–205b**
Académie Française and, 3:77b
anesthetic slumber, criticism and, 3:197b
Anouilh and, 13:2845b–2846a
Art poétique (*Art of Poetry*), 3:179b, 183b, 188b, 189b, 191a, 191b, 199a-b
on the elegy, 3:195a–196b
La Fontaine and, 3:77a
on the nature of aesthetic experience, 3:193b–194a, 196b–197b
perfectionism of, 3:188b
reputation of, 3:181a, 181a-b
on Ronsard, 2:741a, 741b
Épîtres, 3:178b, 179a, 182b, 184b, 191b, 193a, 201a, 201b–202a, 202b
épître 12, 3:180a-b
épître 9, 3:201a
La Bruyère and, 3:230b
Le dialogue des héros de roman, 3:193b
Le lutrin, 3:179b, 198a-b
Lesage's *Le diable boiteux* and, 3:324b
Lettres à Brossette, 3:183a-b, 191b
Lettres à Racine, 3:187b, 190a-b, 197b–198a, 199a
Ode on the Taking of Namur, 3:182a-b
Oeuvres diverses, 3:179a-b
Réflexions critiques sur Longin, 3:180b, 184a
Satires, 3:178a-b, 179a, 181a, 186b, 193a, 202b
satire 9, 3:185b–186a, 189b–190a, 194b, 197b, 198a–199a, 201b

Traité du sublime, 3:199a

Boisdeffre, Pierre de, on Simenon, 12:2497b

Bok um finn. See Vesaas, Tarjei

Boland, Suzanne, 9:1043b

Bölcsőtől a koporsóig. See Kosztolányi, Dezső

Boldino, Pushkin's stay at, 5:662b–663a

Böll, Heinrich, **13:3165a–3186b**
"An der Angel" ("On the Hook"), 13:3174a–3175a
And Never Said a Word (*Und sagte kein einziges Wort*), 13:3169a, 3179a–3180a, 3181b, 3183a
on *Bild-Zeitung*, 13:3170a–3171a
Billiards at Half-Past Nine (*Billard um halbzehn*), 13:3180a, 3180b, 3181b
"Brief an einen jungen Katholiken" (Letter to a Young Catholic), 13:3170a, 3172a
Das Vermächtnis (*A Soldier's Legacy*), 13:3177b, 3178a
"Der Zeitgenosse und die Wirklichkeit" (The Contemporary and Reality), 13:3172a-b
dialogue, 13:3170a, 3172a
Die Fähigkeit zu trauern (The Ability to Mourn), 13:3169b
"Die Moskauer Schuhputzer" ("Missing Person"), 13:3171a
"Die schwarzen Schafe" ("Black Sheep"), 13:3168b
"Die Sprache als Hort der Freiheit" (Language as the Bulwark of Freedom), 13:3173a-b
Die verlorene Ehre der Katharina Blum (*The Lost Honor of Katharina Blum*), 13:3181a
Die Verwundung und andere frühe Erzählungen (*The Casualty and Other Early Stories*), 13:3173b
Du fährst zu oft nach Heidelberg und andere Erzählungen (You Go to Heidelberg Too Often and Other Stories), 13:3169a, 3173b
"Du fährst zu oft nach Heidelberg" ("Too Many Trips to Heidelberg"), 13:3177b
Ein- und Zusprüche (Objections and Exhortations), 13:3169b, 3170a

Böll, Heinrich (*cont.*)

Essayistische Schriften und Reden (Essayistic Writings and Speeches), 13:3169a, 3169b

"Frankfurter Vorlesungen" (Frankfurt Lectures), 13:3172b–3173a, 3174a

Group Portrait with Lady (*Gruppenbild mit Dame*), 13:3167a-b, 3182a–3183a

"Hierzulande" (In This Country), 13:3170a, 3171a–3172a

historic chronicles, 13:3166a, 3169b, 3171b, 3179b–3180a

"Ich han dem Mädche nix jedonn" (I Didn't Do Anything to the Girl), 13:3169b–3170a

"Interview mit mir selbst" ("Interview with Myself"), 13:3165b

Interviews, 13:3169b

Irisches Tagebuch (*Irish Journal*), 13:3173b–3174a

"Jahrgang 1922" (Class of 1922), 13:3174a

language, 13:3174a, 3174b

Le sang du pauvre (*The Blood of the Poor*), 13:3167a

Missing Persons and Other Essays, 13:3169b

"Murke's Collected Silences" ("Doktor Murkes gesammeltes Schweigen"), 13:3175b, 3176b–3177a

narrative form, 13:3171a, 3180a, 3182b

"Nicht nur zur Weihnachtszeit" (Christmas Not Just Once a Year), 13:3175b–3176a

"Raderberg, Raderthal," 13:3166a-b, 3170a

Romane und Erzählungen (Novels and Stories), 13:3169a, 3174b, 3175a

"Stichworte" (Catchwords), 13:3168a

style, 13:3171a

"Suchanzeigen" ("Missing Person"), 13:3171a

The Clown (*Ansichten eines Clowns*), 13:3180b, 3181b

The Safety Net (*Fürsorgliche Belagerung*), 13:3169a, 3180a, 3180b, 3181b

The Stories of Heinrich Böll, 13:3168b, 3174a

"The Thrower-Away" ("Der Wegwerfer"), 13:3175b, 3177a-b

The Train Was on Time (*Der Zug war pünktlich*), 13:3168b, 3177b, 3178a

The Unguarded House (*Haus ohne Hüter*), 13:3180a, 3181b

time frame of novels, 13:3180a-b

translations, 13:3167b

"Über mich selbst" (About Myself), 13:3170a

Vermintes Gelände (Mined Terrain), 13:3169b

Wanderer kommst du nach Spa . . . (*Traveller, If You Come to Spa . . .*), 13:3168b, 3174a-b, 3175b

Was soll aus dem Jungen bloss werden? (*What's to Become of the Boy?*), 13:3166b–3167a

"Will Ulrike Meinhof Gnade oder freies Geleit?" (Does Ulrike Meinhof Want Mercy or Free Passage?), 13:3170a–3171a

Wo warst du, Adam? (*And Where Were You, Adam?*), 13:3168a, 3168b, 3178a–3179a

epigraphs, 13:3178b, 3179a

Women in a River Landscape (*Frauen vor Flusslandschaft*), 13:3169a, 3180a, 3180b, 3181b

"Zundhölzer" (Matches), 13:3177b

Bölöni, György, Ady and, 9:861b

Bolsheviks

Blok and, 9:980b

George and, 8:455b

Gorky and, 8:421a, 444a

in *Dostigaev*, 8:439a

Heinrich Mann and, 8:535a

Social Democratic Party and, 8:420a

Zamyatin and, 10:1182a, 1187a-b, 1190b

see also Communism; Marxism; Russian Revolution (1917)

Bol'shim detiam skazki. See Zamyatin, Yevgeny Ivanovich

Bonaparate, Napoleon, Svevo and, 8:73b

Bonaparte liberatore (Bonaparte the Liberator). *See* Foscolo, Ugo

Bonaparte, Louis Napoleon. *See* Napoleon III (Louis Napoleon Bonaparte)

Bonaparte, Napoleon

Apollinaire and, 9:881a, 883b

in Balzac's works, 5:643a

on Beaumarchais' *The Marriage of Figaro*,
4:579a
Berlioz and, 6:775b, 781a
Büchner and, 6:1169b
in Chateabriand's autobiography,
5:135b–136b
De la littérature on, 5:95a-b
Dumas and, 6:721a
in Fontane, 6:1312b
Foscolo and, 5:314a–315a
Goethe and, 5:8b, 10a
Grillparzer's *König Ottokars Glück und Ende*
and, 5:431a
Heine and, 5:491a
Hoffmann and, 5:264a, 268b–269a
Hundred Days of
Chateaubriand during, 5:128b
Vigny's part in, 5:449b
Manzoni's ode to, 5:369a
Nietzsche on, 7:1675b
in Pushkin's poetry, 5:675b
Richter and, 5:80a, 82a
Staël and, 5:92a-b, 93b, 94a, 97a
Stendhal and, 5:350a-b
The Maid of Orleans and, 5:47b
in Vigny's *The Military Condition*, 5:475a-b
Bonaparte, Princess Mathilde
intellectual circle, 7:1416a-b
Taine and, 7:1467a
Bonaventura, St.
Aquinas and, 1:418b
Commentary on the "Sentences," 1:409b
Dante and, 1:433b
Boncza, Berta, 9:870a–871b, 875b
Bond, The. See Strindberg, August, *Bandet*
"Bonds." See Apollinaire, Guillaume, "Liens"
Bonfire of the Vanities, The. See Wolfe, Tom
Bonheur des dames, Au. See Zola, Émile
Boniface VIII, pope, Dante and, 1:434a, 442a
Bonington, Richard, Delacroix and, 5:519a,
519b
Bonjour, Adrian, on *Beowulf*, 1:72a
Bonnard, Pierre, and Jarry, 9:665a
Bonne chanson, La. See Verlaine, Paul
Bonnefoy, Claude, 13:2990a, 2994a, 3008a
Bonnefoy, Yves
on French language, 6:1033b

on surrealism, 9:901a
Valéry and, 8:570a
Bonnes, Les. See Genet, Jean, *The Maids*
Bonneuil, Michele (Camille) de, Chénier's
affair with, 4:698b–699a, 700b
Book, The. See Mallarmé, Stéphane
Book About Finn, The. *See* Vesaas, Tarjei, *Bok
um finn*
Book of Christopher Columbus, The. See
Claudel, Paul, *Livre de Christophe
Colomb*
Book Considered as an Object, The. *See* Butor,
Michel
Book of Count Lucanor and Patronio, The. See
Manuel, Don Juan, *El conde Lucanor*
Book of the Courtier, The. See Castiglione,
Baldesar
Book of Creation, The. See Sefer Yetsirah
Book of the Crowns of Martyrdom, The. See
Prudentius, *Liber Peristephanon*
Book of Daily Hymns, The. See Prudentius,
Liber Cathemerinon
Book of Disquiet. *See* Pessoa, Fernando, *Livro
do desassossego*
Book of Exercises. See Seferis, George,
Tetradio gymnasmaton
Book of Hours, The. See Rilke, Rainer Maria,
Das Stundenbuch
Book of the Icelanders. See Ari Thorgilsson
the Learned, *Íslendingabók*
Book of Jokes. See Poggio Bracciolini, Gian
Francesco, *Liber facetiarum*
Book of the Judge. See Kierkegaard, Søren
Book of Judges. *See* Old Testament
*Book of Kriemhild, The. See Nibelungenlied,
The*
Book of Laughter and Forgetting, The. See
Kundera, Milan
Book of the Levant, The. *See* Azorín, *El libro
de Levante*
Book of Love. See Sainte-Beuve,
Charles-Augustin, *Livre d'amour*
Book of Missions, The. *See* Ortega y Gasset,
José, *El libro de las misiones*
Book of Monastic Life, The. See Rilke, Rainer
Maria, *Das Stundenbuch*

Book of Pictures, The. See Rilke, Rainer Maria, *Das Buch der Bilder*

Book of Poems. *See* García Lorca, Federico, *Libro de poemas*

Book of Settlements. See Landnámabók

Book of Signs, The. See Elytis, Odysseus, *Simatologon*

Book of Songs. See Heine, Heinrich, *Buch der Lieder*

Book of Theseus. See Boccaccio, Giovanni, *Teseida*

Book of Three Hundred Novellas. *See* Sacchetti, Franco, *Libro delle trecentonovelle*

Bookbinder, Hilarius. *See* Kierkegaard, Søren

Books Abroad. See Milosz, Czeslaw

Books of Eclogues and Eulogies, The. See George, Stefan, *Die Bücher der Hirten- und Preisgedichte . . .*

Books on Matters to Be Remembered. *See* Petrarch, *Rerum memorandarum libri*

Books on Personal Matters. *See* Petrarch, *Rerum familiarium libri*

Books of the Polish Nation and Polish Pilgrimage. See Mickiewicz, Adam

Boomerang, as a metaphor, in Butor, 13:3315a–3316a

Boomerang. See Butor, Michel

Boon, Jan, Ghelderode and, 11:2115b

Boors, The. See Goldoni, Carlo

Bopp, Franz, philology and, founding of, 7:1649a

Borchardt, Rudolf, Hofmannsthal and, 9:691a

Borck, Caspar Wilhelm von, translation of Shakespeare's *Julius Caesar*, 4:543a

Bordeaux
    Montaigne and, 2:778b–779a
    Parlement of, 2:770b, 772a

Bordeaux, Academy of, Montesquieu and, 3:345a, 348a

"Bordeaux ou l'adolescence" (Bordeaux; or, Adolescence). *See* Mauriac, François

Borders, in Kundera, 13:3404b

Boredom
    in Büchner, 6:1187a–1188b
    Schopenhauer's view of, 5:407a-b
    see also Noia

Borel, Jacques, *Tata*, Sarraute's *C'est beau* and, 12:2356b

Borges, Jorge Luis
    Caeiro and, 10:1489b
    Calvino and, 13:3278a
    Cervantes and, 8:297a

Borghesia. See Ginzburg, Natalia

Borgia, Cesare
    as character in Baroja novel, 9:603a-b
    Machiavelli and, 2:596a-b, 601b–602a

Borgslægtens Historie. See Gunnarsson, Gunnar

Boris Godunov. See Moussorgsky, Modest; Pushkin, Alexander

Børn av tiden. See Hamsun, Knut

Born, Jürgen, 9:1156a

Börne, Ludwig, and Heine, 5:503b–504a

Bornecque, Jacques-Henry, on Verlaine, 7:1621b, 1630a

"Borodino." *See* Lermontov, Mikhail Yurievich

Borrachos, Los. See Velázquez, Diego Rodríguez de Silva

Bortstieber, Gertrúd, marriage to Lukács, 10:1265a

"Borz báró esete." *See* Ady, Endre

Boscán, Juan, pastoral poetry of, 2:912b–913a

Bosch, Hieronymus, Céline and, 11:1865a, 1867a, 1875b

Böse Geist Lumpazivagabundus, Der. See Nestroy, Johann

Bösen Köche, Die. See Grass, Günter, *The Wicked Cooks*

Bosnia, Andrić in, 11:1751b, 1752a-b, 1753a–1755a, 1764a

Bosnian Chronicle. See Andrić, Ivo

Bosnian Story. See Andrić, Ivo, *Bosnian Chronicle*

"Boss, The." *See* Gorky, Maxim, "Khoziain"

Bosseur, Dominique, Butor and, 13:3312a

Bosseur, Jean-Yves, Butor and, 13:3312a-b

Bossuet, Jacques Bénigne, **3:151a–175b**
    against quietism, 3:258b
    Claudel and, 8:472a
    Discours sur l'histoire universelle (*Discourse on Universal History*), 3:168b–170b, 4:383b
    organization of, 3:169a-b

"Existence and Attributes of God and the Immortality of the Soul," 3:152a

Exposition de la foi catholic (*Exposition of the Catholic Doctrine*), 3:172a

Fénelon and, 3:262a, 265a, 265b, 271a–272a, 277b, 278a-b

funeral orations, 3:163a–167a

  on Anne de Gonzague, 3:165b–166a

  on Henri de Gornay, 3:163b

  on Henrietta Maria of France, 3:163b, 164b–165a, 166b, 171a-b

  on Joseph François Bourgoing, 3:163a, 163b–164a, 168a

  on Louis de Bourbon, prince de Condé, 3:166a, 166b

  on Maria Theresa, 3:165b

  on Michel Le Tellier, 3:166a, 166b

  on Nicholas Cornet, 3:164a

  on the queen-mother, 3:164a-b

  on Yolande de Monterby, 3:163a-b

Histoire des variations des églises protestantes (*History of the Variations in the Protestant Churches*), 3:166a, 170b–171b

Instruction sur les états d'oraison (*Instruction on the States of Prayer*), 3:172b, 271a

Justification of the "Moral Reflections," 3:172b

La Bruyère and, 3:230b

La tradition des nouveaux mystiques (*The Tradition of the New Mystics*), 3:271a

La traité de la connaissance de Dieu et de soi-même (*Treatise on the Knowledge of God and of Oneself*), 3:160a-b, 173b

"Le sermon pour la préparation à la mort" ("Sermon Concerning Preparation for Death"), 3:161a-b

"Le sermon sur la loi de Dieu" ("Sermon Concerning God's Law"), 3:160b–161a

Madame Guyon and, 3:270a-b

Maximes et réflections sur la comédie (*Maxims and Reflections on the Theater*), 3:173a-b

Oeuvres complètes

  Lachat ed., 3:157a

  Lebarq ed., 3:157b

Oraisons funèbres et panégyriques, 3:153a-b, 157b–158a

"Panégyrique de Saint-Bernard" (Panegyric on St. Bernard), 3:153a-b

Politique tirée des propres paroles de l'écriture sainte (Politics Derived from the Very Words of Holy Scripture), 3:157a

Refutation of the Catechism of Paul Ferry, 3:155a

Relation sur le quiétism (*Aspects of Quietism*), 3:173a, 271b

"Sermon Concerning the Good Will and Severity of the Lord," 3:170a

"Sermon sur la mort" ("Sermon on Death"), 3:161b–162b

theory of kingship and, 3:281a

Treatise on Concupiscence, 3:173b

Weil and, 12:2803a

Boston, in Claudel's *Connaissance de l'Est*, 8:476a

"Botta e risposta." *See* Montale, Eugenio, *Satura*

Bottega del caffè, La. See Goldoni, Carlo

"Bottle in the Sea, The." *See* Vigny, Alfred Victor de, *Les destinées*

Bottom of the Bottle, The. See Simenon, Georges, *Le fond de la bouteille*

Boucher, Alfred, 8:471b

Boucher, François

  Delacroix and, 5:531a-b

  in Goncourts' *L'Art du dix-huitième siècle*, 7:1397a

Bouches inutiles, Les, See Beauvoir, Simone de

Bought and Sold. See Moravia, Alberto, *Il paradiso*

Bouilhet, Louis, Maupassant and, 7:1760b

Boulanger, la boulangère et le petit mitron, Le. See Anouilh, Jean

"Boule de Suif." *See* Maupassant, Guy de

Boule noire, La. See Simenon, Georges

Boullain, Joseph-Antoine, Huysmans and, 7:1721b–1722a, 1724a-b

Bourbon Restoration, Chateaubriand and, 5:113a

Bourbon-Condé, Anne-Geneviève de, 3:59a-b,
  60a, 61a, 61b–62a
Bourdalou, Louis, 3:163a
Bourgemestre de Furnes, Le. See Simenon,
  Georges
Bourgeois drama
  French
    and Beaumarchais, 4:565a–567b, 573b,
      582b–583a
    and Diderot, 4:565a, 565b
*Bourgeois gentilhomme, Le (The Bourgeois
  Gentleman). See* Apollinaire,
  Guillaume; Molière
Bourgeois and Romantic. See Bauernfeld,
  Eduard von, *Bürgerlich und Romantisch*
Bourgeoisie
  Baudelaire and, 7:1323a-b
  in Büchner's works, 6:1191a–1192a
  in Diderot, 4:493a-b
  in fiction of Simon, 13:3029a-b, 3039a-b
  French
    in Louis Blanc's view, 5:591b
    medieval drama and, 1:458b–459a
    in Michelet's view, 5:591a-b
  Freytag's *The Journalists* and, 7:1926a
  German
    Heinrich Mann and, 8:521b, 522a
    in Redentin Easter play, 1:468a-b
  in Ginzburg's novels, 13:3138b, 3143b
  in Goethe's *Wilhelm Meister*, 5:15b, 16b
  Gogol on, 6:985a
  Goldoni and, 4:436a-b, 440b–444b
  Goncourts on, 7:1403a
  in La Bruyère's *Caractères*, 3:244a-b
  in Laforgue's works, 7:1891a-b
  Mallarmé and, 7:1572a-b
  in Maupassant's works, 7:1765b,
    1768b–1769b
  mentality of, Baroja's view of, 9:589b, 598a,
    599a
  in Moravia's works, 12:2676a-b
  Pinero and, 7:1928a
  Portugal, Ferreira de Castro and, 11:2149a-b
  Richter and, 5:80b
  Russian
    in Chekhov's "Three Years," 7:1868b

  Gorky and, 8:428b, 429a-b, 430b, 432a-b,
    435a, 437b, 439a
  Spanish, Pérez Galdós on, 7:1611a-b
  Stendhal and, 5:350b
  theater and, 7:1909a-b, 1917a
  in Verga's *Maestro-don Gesualdo*,
    7:1559a–1562b
  Walther and, 1:304b
Bourgeoisie. See Ginzburg, Natalia, *Borghesia*
Bourges, Michel de, Sand and, 6:823b–824a
Bourget, Paul
  Cosmopolis, 8:520b
  Le disciple (The Disciple), 7:1625a
  Maupassant and, 7:1782a
  on Taine, 7:1461b
  on Verlaine, 7:1639a
Bourgoing, Joseph François, funeral oration on
  by Bossuet, 3:163a, 163b–164a, 168a
Bourret, Étienne de, 1:426b
Bourru bienfaisant, Le. See Goldoni, Carlo
"Bouteille à la mer, La." *See* Vigny, Alfred
  Victor de, *Les destinées*
Boutroux, Émile, Bergson and, 8:46b
Bouvard, Augusta Froustey, Vigny's affair
  with, 5:480a
Bouvard et Pécuchet. See Aymé, Marcel;
  Flaubert, Gustave; Queneau, Raymond
Bovary Method, The. *See* Johnson, Eyvind,
  "Metoden Bovary"
Bowra, C. M.
  on Cavafy, 8:220b, 222b
  on Pasternak's conception of history,
    10:1599a
  on the Ptolemaic dynasty, 8:213a
  Seferis and, 12:2255a
Boxed tales
  influence on Renaissance short fiction,
    2:931a
  see also Frame story
Boy Suffers, A. See Meyer, Conrad Ferdinand,
  Das Leiden eines Knaben
Boy, The. *See* Gunnarsson, Gunnar, *Drengen*
"Boyarin Orsha" ("Boyar Orsha"). *See*
  Lermontov, Mikhail Yurievich
Boy's Magic Horn, The. See Arnim, Achim
  von, and Brentano, Clemens, *Des
  Knaben Wunderhorn*

Boys, The. See Montherlant, Henry de

Boží muka. See Čapek, Karel

Bracco, Roberto, Ibsen's influence on, 7:1443b

Bracquemond, Félix, Japanese influence, 7:1398a

Braga, Teófilo, Eça and, 7:1684b–1685a

Brahm, Otto
  Hofmannsthal and, 9:693a
  Schnitzler and, 8:95a, 96b, 97a, 97b, 106a

Brahms, Johannes
  Nietzsche-Wagner conflict and, 7:1665a-b
  Triumphlied, 7:1665a-b
  Wagner and, 6:1148a

Brain, Bergson's view of, 8:52a–54a

Branca, Vittore, Boccaccio biography, 2:511a

Brand. See Ibsen, Henrik

Brända tomten. See Strindberg, August

Brandeis, Irma, Montale and, 11:1991a-b, 1998b

Brandes, Georg, 7:1753b
  Hamsun and, 8:24a, 24b, 25a
  on Ibsen, 7:1433a
  Schnitzler and, 8:111b

Brandt, Susanna Margaretha, 5:18a

Brandt, Willy, Grass and, 13:3379a–3380a

Brandur paa Bjarg (Brandur on the Bjarg Farm). See Gunnarsson, Gunnar

Brannen. See Vesaas, Tarjei

Brant, Sebastian, Das Narrenschiff (The Ship of Fools), Richter and, 5:57b, 83b

"Branzilla, Die." See Mann, Heinrich

Braque, Georges, 9:889b

"Brasier, Le." See Apollinaire, Guillaume

Brat'ia Karamozovy. See Dostoevsky, Feodor, The Brothers Karamazov

Braun, Yakov, on Zamyatin's We, 10:1189b

Brave New World. See Huxley, Aldous

Brazais, marquis de
  L'Année, 4:697b
  Chénier's friendship with, 4:697b

"Brazier, The." See Apollinaire, Guillaume, "Le Brasier"

Brazil
  Ferreira de Castro and, 11:2150a–2151a, 2154b–2155a
  Portuguese prosperity and, 11:2144a-b

Bread and Wine. See Kosztolányi, Dezső, Kenyér és bor

Bread and Wine. See Silone, Ignazio, Pane e vino

Break of Day. See Colette, La naissance du jour

Break of Noon. See Claudel, Paul, Le partage de midi

"Break, The." See Pasternak, Boris, Themes and Variations

Breasts. See Gómez de la Serna, Ramón, Senos

Breasts of Tiresias, The. See Apollinaire, Guillaume, Les mamelles de Tirésias

Breath, A. See Pirandello, Luigi, "Soffio"

Breath, The. See Mann, Heinrich, Der Atem

Brecht, Bertolt, **11:2089a–2111a**
  A Man's a Man (Mann ist Mann), 9:1049b, 11:2090b, 2096b, 2102a
  Arbeitsjournal (Working Diary), 11:2103b, 2108a
  Baal, 11:2090b, 2095b
  Barthes on, 13:3086a–3087a
  Benjamin and, 11:1703a, 1704a, 1722b–1723a
  Čapek and, 10:1584a-b
  concept of realism, 13:3172b
  Coriolanus (Coriolan), 11:2091b
  Das Badener Lehrstücke vom Einverständnis (The Didactic Play of Baden: On Consent), 11:2091a
  Der Flug der Lindberghs (The Flight of the Lindberghs), 11:2091a
  Dialoge aus dem Messingkauf (The Messingkauf Dialogues), 11:2104a
  Die Antigone des Sophokles (The Antigone of Sophocles), 11:2091b, 2104a
  Die Ausnahme und die Rëgel (The Exception and the Rule), 11:2091a
  Die Geschäftedes Herrn Julius Caesar (Business Deals of Mr. Julius Caesar), 11:2102b
  Die Heilige Johanna der Schlachthöfe (Saint Joan of the Stockyards), 11:2091a
  Die Horatier und die Kuriatier (The Horatians and the Curiatians), 11:2091a

Brecht, Bertolt (*cont.*)

Die Rundköpfe und die Spitzköpfe (*The Roundheads and the Peakheads*), 11:2091a

Die sieben Todsünden Kleinbürger (*The Seven Deadly Sins*), 11:2092b

Die Tage der Kommune (*The Days of the Commune*), 11:2091b

Don Juan, 11:2091b

Drums in the Night (*Trommeln in der Nacht*), 11:2090b, 2096a, 2097b, 2107b

in East Germany, 9:718b

"estrangement" acting, 8:260a

Flüchtlingsgespräche (*Refugee Conversations*), 11:2102b

Frisch and, 13:2902a-b

Furcht und Elend des Dritten Reiches (*The Private Life of the Master Race; Fear and Misery in the Third Reich*), 11:2091a, 2097b

Galileo (*Leben des Galilei*), 11:2091b, 2097a, 2104a, 2106a

Grass and, 13:3376b–3377b

Grillparzer's presage of, 5:427a

Hašek's *Good Soldier Švejk*, continuation of, 9:1116a

He Who Says Yes/He Who Says No (*Der Jasager/Der Neinsager*), 11:2091a, 2097b

Heinrich Mann and, 8:519a-b, 523a, 541b

Ibsen and, 7:1444a, 1754a

In the Jungle of Cities (*Im Dickicht der Städte*), 11:2090b, 2096a

Ionesco and, 13:2998b, 2999a, 2999b, 3004b, 3011b

Kleines Organon das Theater (*Organon for the Theater*), 11:2104b

Leben Eduards des Zweiten von England (*Edward II*), 11:2090b

Lehrstücke of, 11:2091a, 2098a

Life of Galileo, and Lagerkvist, 10:1693b

lyric grotesques, 8:257b

Mann and, 9:728a

Manual of Piety (*Hauspostille*), 11:2090b, 2091a, 2100b

Me-ti, Buch der Wendungen (Me-ti, the Book of Twists and Turns), 11:2101, 2103b

Mother Courage and Her Children (*Mutter Courage und ihre Kinder*), 11:2091b, 2094a, 2097a, 2098b, 2104a, 2106a

parables in works of, 13:2916a

on poetry, 9:768b

Puntila and Matti, His Hired Man (*Herr Puntila und sein Knecht Matti*), 11:2091b, 2098a, 2106a

Rilke and, 9:789b

Rojas's *Celestina* and, 13:2905b

Sarraute and, 12:2355b

Schulopern of, 11:2091a

Schweyk in the Second World War (*Schweyk im zweiten Weltkrieg*), 11:2098b

Señora Carrar's Rifles (*Die Gewehre der Frau Carrar*), 11:2091a, 2097b, 2104a

Strindberg and, 7:1732a

Tales from the Calendar (*Kalendergeschichten*), 11:2102b–2103a

The Caucasian Chalk Circle (*Der Kaukasische Kreidekreis*), 11:2091b, 2097b

The Good Woman of Setzuan (*Der gute Mensch von Sezuan*), 11:2091b, 2092b, 2098a

Dürrenmatt and, 13:3221b

The Measures Taken (*Die Massnahme*), 11:2091a, 2093a, 2096b

The Mother (*Die Mutter*), 11:2091a

The Resistible Rise of Arturo Ui (*Der authaltsame Aufstieg des Arturo Ui*), 11:2091b

The Rise and Fall of the State of Mahagonny (*Aufstieg und Fall der Stadt Mahagonny*), 11:2090b, 2102a

The Threepenny Opera (*Die Dreigroschenoper*), 11:2090b, 2091a, 2102a, 2106b

The Trial of Joan of Arc at Rouen (*Der Prozess der Jeanne d'Arc zu Rouen*), 11:2091b

The Tutor (*Der Hofmeister*), 11:2091b

The Visions of Simone Machard (*Die Gesichte der Simone Machard*), 11:2091b

Trumpets and Drums (*Pauken und Trompeten*), 11:2091b

Tui-Novel, 11:2103b
Turandot; or, The Congress of Whitewashers (*Turandot oder Der Kongress der Weisswäscher*), 11:2091b, 2103b
Valle-Inclán and, 8:351b
on Wedekind, 8:229a-b
well-made play and, 7:1931a
Werke, Grosse kommentierte Berliner und Frankfurter Ausgabe (Great Berlin and Frankfurt Edition with Commentary), 11:2108a
Breitinger, Johann Jakob, Klopstock and, 4:513a–514a
Brekkukotsannáll. See Laxness, Halldór
Brémond, Henri, *Apologie pour Fénelon*, 3:261a, 262a
Brenner, Der (journal)
Broch and, 10:1386b
Trakl and, 10:1414a
Brenner, József, Kosztolányi and, 10:1232b
Brennu-Njáls saga (*The Story of Njál of the Burning*). See *Njál's Saga*
Brentano, Clemens
Des Knaben Wunderhorn (*The Boy's Magic Horn*) (with Arnim), Grillparzer and, 5:436b
Die Gründung Prags (*The Founding of Prague*), as source for Grillparzer's *Libussa*, 5:440b
Geschichte vom Braven Kasperl und dem schönen Annerl (*The Story of the Honorable Caspar and Fair Annie*), romanticism in, 5:426a
Godwi, Richter's *The Invisible Lodge* and, 5:63a
in Hesse's *The Journey to the East*, 9:852a
"La Loreley" and, 9:887a
Bresson, Robert, Giraudoux and, 9:1059b
Bretagne, Charles, Rimbaud and, 7:1789a
Breteuil, Gabrielle Émilie Le Tonnelier de. See Châtelet, Madame du
Breton, André, **11:1939a–1960b**
ambivalence toward madness, 11:1979b–1980a
Anthologie de l'humour noir, 11:1946b
on Apollinaire, 9:897b–898a
Aragon and, 11:2061b, 2062a, 2074b

Arcane 17, 11:1941a, 1946b–1947a
liberty principle, 11:1947a
lyrical theme, 11:1947b
themes, 11:1941b
Artaud and, 11:1966a, 1966b, 1968a
attitude to women, 11:2070b
"Au beau demi-jour de 1934," 11:1956a-b
"Au grand jour" (In the Open), condemnation of Artaud in, 11:1966b
Clair de terre, 11:1953a
and Cocteau, 10:1546b–1547a
Communicating Vessels (*Les vases communicants*), 11:1941a, 1943b, 1949a, 1953b
Fata Morgana, 11:1946b, 1956b
"First Surrealist Manifesto," 13:2958a
"Forêt de noire," 11:1951a
Introduction au discours sur le peu de réalité, 11:1941a, 1946a
language, 11:1952b, 1954a
"La force d'attendre" (The Strength to Wait), 11:2067b–2068a
La lampe dans l'horloge, 11:1947a
L'Air de l'eau, 11:1953b, 1956a-b
L'Amour fou (*Mad Love*), 11:1941a, 1945a, 1946a-b, 1947a-b, 1952b–1953a
element of surprise, 11:1954a-b
Le revolver à cheveux blancs (The White-Haired Revolver), 11:1953b
imagination, 11:1955a-b
Le surréalisme et la peinture (*Surrealism and Painting*), 11:1941a, 1948b, 1949b–1950b
Légitime défense, 11:1941a
Les pas perdus, 11:1941b
"Les mots sans rides" (Words Without Wrinkles), 11:1953a
liberty principle, 11:1948a, 1957b
L'Immaculée conception
language, 11:1943a, 1958a-b
"Les possessions," 11:1943a
"L'Union libre," 11:1953a–1954a
Manifeste du surréalisme (*Surrealist Manifesto*), 9:899b–900a, 11:1940a-b, 2064b, 2170b
automatism, 11:1951a-b
definition of surrealism, 11:1951a-b

Breton, André (*cont.*)
  Manifeste du surréalisme (*Surrealist
    Manifesto*) (*cont.*)
    in Spain, 9:760b
  Monts de piété, 11:1951a
  Nadja, 11:1941a, 1941b–1943a, 1944a
    Apollinaire and, 9:889b
    photographs, 11:1942b, 1943a
  Ode à Charles Fourier, 11:1948b, 1957a-b
  Poèmes, 11:1948b
  Point du jour, 11:1944b
  Position politique du surréalisme, 11:1944b,
    1945a
    art and politics, 11:1948b–1949a
  "Prolégomènes à un troisième manifeste du
    surréalisme ou non" (*Prolegomena to a
    Third Manifesto of Surrealism or Else*),
    11:1946b
  Queneau and, 12:2511a, 2517b
  Qu'est-ce que le surréalisme? (*What Is
    Surrealism?*), 10:1546b–1547a, 11:1944b
  Ralentir travaux, 11:1953a
  "Second manifest du surréalisme" ("The
    Second Manifesto of Surrealism"),
    11:2072a
  "Situation du surréalisme entre les deux
    guerres," 11:1946b
  "Sur la route de San Romano," 11:1958b
  "Tournesol," 11:1945b
  "Vigilance," 11:1949a
Breton, André, and Éluard, Paul
  Dictionaire abrégé du surréalisme, 11:1944b
  Notes sur la poésie, 11:1944b
Breton, André, and Legrand, Gérard, *L'Art
  magique*, 11:1948b
Breton, André, and Soupault, Philippe, *Les
  champs magnétiques* (*The Magnetic
  Fields*), 11:1940a, 1951a
Breton, André, and Trotsky, Leon, *Pour un art
  révolutionnaire indépendant*, 11:1949a
Breuer, Josef, Freud and, 8:3a-b, 6b, 14a-b
Breughel, Pieter
  Céline and, 11:1865a, 1875b
  Festival of Folly, 11:1865a
  Maeterlinck influenced by, 8:120a, 122a
Breva, Juan, in Lorca's poetry, 11:2172a-b
Breysig, Kurt, George and, 8:448b, 465b

Briand, Aristide, Perse and, 10:1437b–1438a,
  1439b, 1440a
Briand-Kellogg Pact, Perse and, 10:1439b
Bridal Crown, The. See Strindberg, August,
  Kronbruden
Bride of Abydos, The. See Byron, George
  Gordon, Lord
Bride of Messina, The. See Schiller, Friedrich
  von
Bride's Spring, The. See Moberg, Vilhelm,
  Brudarnas källa
Bridge on the Drina, The. See Andrić, Ivo
Bridge, The. See Ritsos, Yannis, *I ghefira*
"Bridge on the Žepa, The." *See* Andrić, Ivo,
  "Most na Žepi"
Bridges, The. See Vesaas, Tarjei
"Brief an einen jungen Katholiken." *See* Böll,
  Heinrich
"Brief, Ein." *See* Hofmannsthal, Hugo von,
  "The Letter of Lord Chandos"
Brief Novels of the Country. *See* Verga,
  Giovanni, *Novelle rusticane*
"Briefe an einen jungen Dichter." *See* Wieland,
  Christoph Martin
Briefe an Wilhelm Fliess. See Freud, Sigmund
Briefe aus Berlin. See Heine, Heinrich
Briefe, die neueste Literatur betreffend. See
  Lessing, Gotthold Ephraim
Briefe über Spinoza. See Jacobi, Friedrich
Briefe und bevorstehender Lebenslauf. See
  Richter, Jean Paul
Brieux, Eugène
  La robe rouge (*The Red Robe*), 7:1921a
  Les avariés (*Damaged Goods*), 7:1430b,
    1921a
Brigade, the. See Pléiade, the
Brighton Rock. See Greene, Graham
Brik, Lilya, Mayakovsky and, 11:1836a, 1836b,
  1839a
Brimheiði. See Gunnarsson, Gunnar
Bringas Woman, The. See Pérez Galdós,
  Benito, *La de Bringas*
Bringing Up Children. *See* Ritsos, Yannis,
  Dhiaplasi ton pedhon
Brinvillier, Marie Madeleine, 12:2664b
Brion, Friederike, 5:4a, 4b, 18b

Britannicus, in Kosztolányi's *Bloody Poet*, 10:1236a-b

Britannicus. See Racine, Jean

Britanny, writers and thinkers of, 3:317b–318b

Brocéliande. See Montherlant, Henry de

Broch, Hermann, 8:533a, 539a, **10:1385a–1408b**
  "Bill of Duties," 10:1403a, 1405b
  Canetti and, 12:2615b
  Die Entsühnung (The Atonement), 10:1395a
  Die Schlafwandler (*The Sleepwalkers*), Musil's *The Man Without Qualities* and, 9:941a
  Die Verzauberung (The Bewitchment), 10:1395b–1398a
  Esch oder die Anarchie (*Esch; or, Anarchism*), 10:1389b–1393b
  Hesse and, 9:855b
  Hugo von Hofmannsthal and His Time, 10:1386a, 1403b
  Huguenau oder die Sachlichkeit (*Huguenau; or, Objectivism*), 10:1389b–1393b
  Klein und Wagner and, 9:842a
  Massenwahntheorie (Theory of Mass Psychology), 10:1396a-b
  Musil and, 9:933a
  Pasenow oder die Romantik (*Pasenow; or, Romanticism*), 10:1389b–1393b
  The Death of Vergil, 10:1399a–1402b
    Hesse's *The Glass Bead Game* and, 9:853a
  The Guiltless (*Die Schuldlosen*), 10:1386a, 1404a–1405b
  The Sleepwalkers (*Die Schlafwandler*), 10:1385a, 1389b–1393b
  The Unknown Quantity (*Die unbekannte Grösse*), 10:1395a-b
  "Trotzdem: Humane Politik" (Nevertheless: A Humane Politics), 10:1387b–1388a

Brod, Max, Kafka and, 9:1152a-b, 1156a, 1158b, 1166b, 1167a, 1174b

Brodersen, Arvid, *Stefan George*, 8:447b

Brødrene. See Gunnarsson, Gunnar

Brodsky, Joseph
  Akhmatova's aid for, 10:1541a
  Khlebnikov criticized by, 10:1331a
  Tsvetaeva and, 11:1748b–1749a

"Broken are the high column and the green laurel." *See* Petrarch, *Canzoniere*, "Rotta è l'alta colonna e'l verde lauro"

Broken Jug, The. See Kleist, Heinrich von

Broken Souls. See Kazantzakis, Nikos, *Spasmènes psihés*

Brokiga iakttagelser. See Södergran, Edith

"Bröllopsfesten." *See* Lagerkvist, Pär

Brontë, Emily, *Wuthering Heights*, Baroja's work compared to, 9:596a-b

Bronze Horseman, The. See Bely, Andrey; Pushkin, Alexander; Pushkin, Alexander, *Mednyi Vsadnik*

Brooks, Peter, on French melodrama, 5:30b

"Broom Flower, The." *See* Leopardi, Giacomo

Brossette, Claude, Boileau and, 3:180b, 183a-b, 191b

"Brother and Sister, The." *See* Goethe, Johann Wolfgang von

"Brothers." *See* Ungaretti, Giuseppe, *Allegria di naufragi* (Mirth of Shipwrecks), "Fratelli"

Brothers Karamazov, The. See Dostoevsky, Feodor

"Brothers Karamazov, The." *See* Hesse, Hermann, *Blick ins Chaos* (*In Sight of Chaos*), "Die Brüder Karamasoff"

Brothers Rico, The. See Simenon, Georges, *Les frères Rico*

Brothers, The. *See* Gunnarsson, Gunnar, *Brødrene*

Brott och brott. See Strindberg, August, *Crimes and Crimes*

Brown, Charles Brockden, *Wieland; or, The Transformation*, 4:608b

Brown, John, Novalis on, 5:210b

Brown, Marshall, on Novalis, 5:209b

Browning, Robert
  Hofmannsthal and, 9:689b
  Unamuno and, 8:297a
  verse drama, 7:1426b

Brozas, Francisco Sánchez de las. *See* Sánchez de las Brozas, Francisco

"Bruchstück einer Hysterie-Analyse." *See* Freud, Sigmund

Brücke, Ernst, Freud and, 8:2b

Bruckner, Ferdinand, *Die Rassen* (*Races*),
Frisch and, 13:2912a
Brudarnas källa. See Moberg, Vilhelm
"Brüder Karamasoff, Die." *See* Hesse,
Hermann, *Blick ins Chaos* (*In Sight of
Chaos*)
Bruderzwist in Habsburg, Eine. See
Grillparzer, Franz, *Family Strife in
Hapsburg*
Bruene. See Vesaas, Tarjei, *The Bridges*
Brulard, Henry. See Stendhal, *Vie de Henry
Brulard*
Brûlebois. See Aymé, Marcel
Bruler, Jean. *See* Vercors
Brunetière, Ferdinand, on Edmond Goncourt,
7:1413b
Brunhild, the *Nibelungenlied* and,
1:211b–212a, 213a, 222a–223a
"Bruto minore." *See* Leopardi, Giacomo,
"Brutus the Younger"
"Brutus the Younger." *See* Leopardi, Giacomo
Bruyère, Jean de la, Yourcenar and, 12:2538b
Bryusov, Valery, 6:996b
downfall of Petrine Russia and, 10:1620a-b
"Invasion of the Huns," 11:1839b
"Kon' bled" ("Pale Horse"), Khlebnikov's
"The Crane" and, 10:1352b–1353a
Mandelshtam and, 10:1631b
Russian symbolism and, 9:962b
Buber, Martin
Broch and, 10:1404a
Die Kreatur, Benjamin's article for, 11:1721b
Kafka and, 9:1153b
Buch der Bilder, Das. See Rilke, Rainer Maria
Buch der hängenden Gärten. See George,
Stefan, *Die Bücher der Hirten- und
Preisgedichte . . .*
Buch der Lieder. See Heine, Heinrich
Buch vom mönchischen Leben, Das. See Rilke,
Rainer Maria, *Das Stundenbuch*
*Bücher der Hirten- und Preisgedichte . . ., Die.
See* George, Stefan
Buchez, Philippe
"Chant d'ouvrier" ("Workers' Song"),
5:463b–464a
Vigny and, 5:463b–464a, 469b
Büchner, Georg, **6:1169a–1194b**

Brecht and, 11:2095a–2095b
Chénier compared to, 4:715b
Danton's Death, 11:2095b
Danton's Death (*Dantons Tod*), 6:1173b,
1174b–1182b
the hero and, 5:434b
Grillparzer compared to, 5:443a, 444a
Hauptmann and, 8:152a
"Lenz," 6:1182b–1186b
Leonce and Lena, 6:1186b–1189b
Frisch and, 13:2923b
"On Cranial Nerves," 6:1186a
romanticism and, 13:2923b
"The Hessian Courier," 6:1173b–1174b
weltschmerz of, 5:419b–420b
Woyzeck, 6:1189b–1192a
morality and economics in, 13:3232a
Büchse der Pandora, Die. See Wedekind,
Frank, *Pandora's Box*
Buckle, Henry, Bergson and, 8:47a
Bucolic poetry
in Boileau's view, 3:195a
etymology of term, 2:902a
see also Pastoral poetry
Bucolicum carmen (Bucolic Song). *See*
Boccaccio, Giovanni; Petrarch
Budapest, Ady and, 9:872b–873a, 876a
Budapesti napló (journal), 9:875a
Kosztolányi and, 10:1233a, 1233b
Budberg, Vera, Khlebnikov's romantic
involvement with, 10:1336b
Buddenbrooks. See Mann, Thomas
Buddha. See Kazantzakis, Nikos
Buddhism
Bely and, 9:912a
Flaubert and, 7:1378a
Hauptmann and, 8:166a-b, 168a
in Hesse's *Siddhartha*, 9:845a
Kazantzakis and, 9:1076b–1077a
Leconte de Lisle and, 6:1265a–1266a
Weil and, 12:2793b
Budding Roses, The. *See* Ausonius, "De rosis
nascentibus"
Bueil de Racan, Honorat de, in "Epître à
Huet," 3:79a
Bueno, Manuel, Valle-Inclán and, 8:332b

Bufera e altro, La. See Montale, Eugenio, *The Storm and Other Things*
Buff, Charlotte, 5:6a
Buffon, Georges-Louis Leclerc de
    Discourse on Style (Discours sur le style), Chénier and, 4:709a
    Marya Volkonsky and, 7:1474b
Bug-Jargal. See Hugo, Victor
Bugaev, Alexandra Dmitrievna, 9:907a
Bugaev, Boris. *See* Bely, Andrey
Bugaev, Nikolay Vasilevich, 9:906b–907a, 910a, 911b, 914b
Bugiardo, Il. See Goldoni, Carlo
"Bugnak a tárnák." *See* Ady, Endre
Building Speculation. *See* Calvino, Italo, *La speculazione edilizia*
Bukharin, Nikolai, Mandelshtam aided by, 10:1643a, 1644a, 1646a
Bulgarin, Faddei, "Natural School" of, 6:996a
Bull on the Last Banquet of Our Most Holy Lord the Pope. See Luther, Martin
"Bull, The." *See* Södergran, Edith, "Tjuren"
Bulles bleues. See Maeterlinck, Maurice
Bullfighting, in Montherlant's novels, 11:1915b–1916a, 1917b, 1928a–1929a
Bülow, Cosima von, 7:1652b, 1655b, 1656a
    Wagner and, 6:1162b
        autobiography of Wagner completed by, 6:1165a-b
Bülow, Hans, 7:1652b
Bunbury, Lydia
    death of, 5:480a-b
    Vigny's marriage to, 5:454a-b, 458a, 478b, 479a
Bunin, Ivan
    Chekhov and, 7:1857b
    translation of Tennyson's "Godiva," 10:1644b
Buñuel, Luis
    films based on Galdós' novels, 7:1617a
    Lorca and, 11:2169a-b, 2177b
Buon padre, Il. See Goldoni, Carlo
Buona figliuola, La. See Goldoni, Carlo
Buona moglie, La. See Goldoni, Carlo
Burckhardt, Carl J., Hofmannsthal and, 9:691a, 700b
Burckhardt, Jacob, **6:1225a–1244b**

Cicerone, 6:1229a, 1231b–1233a
Hesse and, 9:836a, 853a
History of Architecture and Decoration of the Italian Renaissance, 6:1236b
History of Greek Culture (Der Griechische Kulturgeschichte), 6:1229b, 1236b–1237a
Judgments on History and Historians (Historische Fragmente, 6:1230a-b
    as historical philosophy, 6:1237b–1241a
Meyer and, 6:932b
Notes on Renaissance Sculpture, 6:1236b
Recollections of Rubens (Erinnerungen aus Rubens), 6:1229b, 1233a–1234a
Reflections on History (Weltgeschichtliche Betrachtungen), 6:1225a-b, 1229b–1230b
    as historical philosophy, 6:1237b–1241a
Schlegel and, 5:197a
The Age of Constantine the Great (Die Zeit Konstantins ds Grossen), 6:1229a
    as art history, 6:1231b
    as cultural history, 6:1234b–1235a
The Civilization of the Renaissance in Italy (Die Kultur der Renaissance in Italien), 6:1229a, 1235a–1236b
Bureaucracy
    Aymé's satire of, 12:2441b–2442a
    in Calvino, 13:3268a
    Tocqueville on, 6:898b–899b
Bürger, Gottfried August, 5:48b
Bürger und seine Stimme, Der. See Grass, Günter, *The Citizen and His Voice*
Bürgerlich und Romantisch. See Bauernfeld, Eduard von
"Bürgerliche Trauerspiel." *See* Tragedy, middle-class
Burgess, Anthony, Zamyatin's influence on, 10:1181a
Burglar Šejba's Expedition. *See* Hašek, Jaroslav, "Výprava zloděje Šejby"
Burgomaster of Furnes, The. See Simenon, Georges, *Le bourgemestre de Furnes*
Burgraves, Les. See Hugo, Victor
Burgtheater (Vienna), 7:1925a
    Hofmannsthal and, 9:692b, 693a

Burgtheater (Vienna) (*cont.*)
  Schnitzler's work performed at, 8:95a, 97b,
    98a, 104b
Burgundians
  the *Nibelungenlied* and, 1:213a-b
  in satire of Sidonius, 1:350a-b
Burial at Ornans. *See* Courbet, Gustave
Burial of the Count of Orgaz. *See* Greco, El
Burial of Monsieur Bouvet, The. *See* Simenon,
    Georges, *L'Enterrement de Monsieur*
    Bouvet
Burial Mound, The. *See* Ibsen, Henrik
Burian, E. F., dramatization of Hašek's *Good*
    Soldier Švejk, 9:1112b
Buridan, Jean, in Wedekind's *Zensur*, 8:269a
Burke, Edmund, *Reflections on the French*
    Revolution, Chénier's attack on,
    4:702b–703a
Burlesque
  in Chrétien's works, 1:150a
  in Pirandello's *Tonight We Improvise*,
    8:411b
Burlyuk, David
  Hylaea group and, 10:1335b, 1344b
  Khlebnikov and, 10:1334a-b, 1336a
  Mayakovsky and, 11:1835a-b
Burne-Jones, Edward, Bely and, 9:912a
Burned House, The. *See* Strindberg, August,
    Brända tomten
Burning Brand: Diaries 1935–1950. *See*
    Pavese, Cesare
Burning Bush, The. *See* Undset, Sigrid, *Den*
    Brændende busk
"Burnt Norton." *See* Eliot, T. S., *Four Quartets*
Burroughs, William, Céline and, 11:1859a,
    1874a
Burton, Robert, *Anatomy of Melancholy*,
    encyclopaedic features of, 5:551a
Busca, La. *See* Baroja, Pío
Buscapiés. *See* Azorín
Buscón, El. *See* Quevedo, Francisco de
Business. *See* Commerce
Business Deals of Mr. Julius Caesar, The. *See*
    Brecht, Bertolt, *Die Geschäftedes Herrn*
    Julius Caesar
Buster Keaton's Promenade. *See* García Lorca,
    Federico, *El paseo de Buster Keaton*

But . . . *See* Ferreira de Castro, José Maria,
    Mas . . .
Butler, Alban, *Lives of the Saints*, 8:472a
Butor, Michel, **13:3287a–3321b**
  A Change of Heart (*La modification*),
    13:3295a–3297a
  "Babel en creux," 13:3294b
  Boomerang, 13:3315a–3316a
  Chantier (Construction Site), 13:3289b
  Degrés (Degrees), 13:3289b, 3297b–3300a
  Description de San Marco, 13:3303a-b
  Dialogue avec 33 variations de Ludwig van
    Beethoven sur une valse de Diabelli,
    13:3312b
  Dialogue des règnes (Dialogue of the
    Kingdoms), 13:3305b–3306a
  Elseneur, 13:3312b
  Histoire extraordinaire (Extraordinary Tale),
    13:3307b
  Illustrations, 13:3306a–3307a
  Imprécations contre la fourmi d'Argentine
    (Curses Against the Argentine Ant)
    (with Ania Staritsky), 13:3306a
  Improvisations sur Flaubert, 13:3289a
  "Le livre considéré comme objet" (The Book
    Considered as an Object), 13:3300b
  "Le rêve de l'huitre" (Dream of an Oyster),
    13:3313b
  L'Emploi du temps (Passing Time),
    13:3292a–3295a
  Litanie d'eau (Ocean Litany),
    13:3305b–3306a
  "Mathematics and the Idea of Necessity,"
    13:3287b
  Matière de rêves (The Stuff of Dreams),
    13:3308a–3309a, 3312b–3313a
  Mille et un plis (A Thousand and One
    Folds), 13:3308b
  Mobile: Study for a Representation of the
    United States, 13:3300b–3303a
  Niagara (*6 810 000 litres d'eau par*
    scconde), 13:3303b–3305b
  Où, 13:3314a–3315a
    "J'ai fui Paris" (I Fled Paris),
      13:3314b–3315a
    "Je hais Paris" (I Hate Paris), 13:3315a
  Passage de Milan, 13:3290a–3292a

Paysage de répons (Landscape of Responses), 13:3309b

Portrait de l'artiste en jeune singe (Portrait of the Artist as a Young Monkey), 13:3307b–3308a

Quadruple fond (Fourfold False Bottom), 13:3308b

Rencontre (Meeting), 13:3305b

Répertoire, 13:3289a

Sarraute and, 12:2333a

Second sous-sol (Second Basement), 13:3308b, 3313a

Seize et une variations (Sixteen and One Variations), 13:3312a-b

Signaux de fumée (with Alex Cassel), 13:3306a

The Spirit of Mediterranean Places, 13:3297a-b

Travaux d'approche (Maneuverings), 13:3289b

Troisième dessous (Third Floor Below Ground), 13:3308b

"Un possibilité," 13:3293b

Une chanson pour Don Juan, 13:3312a-b

Votre Faust: Fantaisie variable genre opéra (Your Faust: Variable Fantasy in the Operatic Mode), 13:3309b–3312a

Butt, Der. See Grass, Günter, *The Flounder*

Butterfly of Dinard, The. See Montale, Eugenio

Butterfly's Evil Spell, The. See García Lorca, Federico, *El maleficio de la mariposa*

Buy the Blind Man's Song. *See* Ekelöf, Gunnar, *Köp den blindes sång*

"By the Edge of the Stream." *See* Maupassant, Guy de, "Au bord de l'eau"

By the Holy Mountain. *See* Laxness, Halldór, *Undir helgahnúuk*

By Letter. *See* Zamyatin, Yevgeny Ivanovich, "Pis'menno"

By the Open Sea. See Strindberg, August, *I havsbandet*

"By the Rivers of Babylon." *See* Camoëns, Luís Vaz de, *Rimas* (*Lyrics*), "Sôbolos rios"

Byron, George Gordon, Lord
Ady and, 9:860a
Cain, Vigny and, 5:453a-b
Chateaubriand on, 5:137a

Childe Harold's Pilgrimage, Mickiewicz and, 5:615a, 616a

Dinesen and, 10:1294b

Don Juan, Pushkin's *Eugene Onegin* and, 5:671a

on *Don Quixote*, 8:296b

Dostoevsky and, 7:1350b

Goethe and, 5:10a, 23a-b

Grillparzer's *Sappho* praised by, 5:426b

Heaven and Earth, Vigny's "Le déluge" and, 5:457a

Hofmannsthal and, 9:689b

Leconte de Lisle and, 6:1267b

Lermontov and, 6:1198a-b, 1199a, 1200a, 1202a, 1202b–1203a, 1206a, 1211b

on Mandelshtam's poems, 10:1642b

Mérimée and, 6:749a, 760a

Pushkin and, 5:667b–668a

Schlegel and, 5:184a

Siege of Corinth, Vigny's "Helena" and, 5:451b

Taine on, 7:1458b

The Bride of Abydos, 6:1202b

Vigny and, 5:450b, 451a, 451b, 453a-b, 454b, 457a

weltschmerz of, 5:419b–420b

Byways. See Hesse, Hermann, *Umwege*

Byzantine hymnology. *See* Hymns, Byzantine

Byzantine romance, Lope de Vega and, 2:849a

Byzantium, Ekelöf and, 12:2646a–2647a

C

Ça Ira (literary journal), Ghelderode and, 11:2134b
Cabalga Diego Laínez, Rodrigo-Jimena relationship in, 1:133a
Cabalistic writings, Benjamin and, 11:1706a-b
Caballero de Olmedo, El. See Lope de Vega, *The Knight from Olmedo*
Caballero encantado, El. See Pérez Galdós, Benito
Caballero inactual, El. See Azorín
Cabanis, Pierre Jean Georges, Manzoni and, 5:368b
Cabaret
  German, 8:260a–262a
  Hašek's involvement with, 9:1093a, 1093b, 1095b
Cabaret Voltaire, Arp and, 10:1369a-b
Cabaret Voltaire, Le (journal), 9:897a
Cabellera. See Machado, Antonio
Cabin, The. See Blasco Ibáñez, Vicente
Cabinet of Antiquities, The. See Balzac, Honoré de, *Le cabinet des antiques*
Cabinet des antiques, Le. See Balzac, Honoré de
Caccia di Diana. See Boccaccio, Giovanni
Cadavers. *See* Corpses
Cadavre, Un. See Ribemont-Dessaignes, Georges
Cadre (framework), in Maupassant's works, 7:1771b, 1772a-b
Caedmon, *Hymn*, 1:55a, 65b
Caeiro, Alberto, 10:1488a, 1489b–1490b
Caesar, Gaius Julius
  in Corneille's *Pompey's Death*, 3:46a-b
  Gallic War, Cervantes and, 2:827b
  in Mérimée's works, 6:765a
  Petrarch's biography of, 2:480a
  Strindberg and, 7:1737b
Caesar or Nothing. See Baroja, Pío, *César o nada*
Caesarion, in Cavafy's poetry, 8:213b–214a
"Caesarion." *See* Cavafy, Constantine, "Kaisarion"
"Cafetière, La." *See* Gautier, Théophile

Caffein d'Europa, 9:828a
Cage of Rooks and Pallid Swifts. *See* Cela, Camilo José, "Gayola de grajos y vencejos"
Cages, in Kafka's fiction, 9:1172b, 1173b
Cagliostro, Allesandro de, in Dumas's works, 6:737a
Cagnotte, La. See Labiche, Eugène
Cahier rouge, Le. See Constant, Benjamin
Cahier vert. See Sainte-Beuve, Charles-Augustin
Cahiers. See Valéry, Paul
Cahiers d'André Walter, Les. See Gide, André, *The White Notebook*
Cahiers de Rodez. See Artaud, Antonin
Cahiers, Les (literary review), Mauriac and, 10:1307b
Cahiers pour une morale. See Sartre, Jean-Paul
Cahors, curriculum at (17th century), 3:263a-b
Cailleaux, Ludovic de, Leconte de Lisle and, 6:1267b
Caillois, Roger, Yourcenar and, 12:2559a
Cain. See Byron, George Gordon, Lord
Cain. *See* Kosztolányi, Dezső, *Káin*
Cain (O.T. character)
  in Klopstock, 4:521b, 523a
  in Leconte de Lisle's "Qaïn," 6:1267b–1268b
  Nerval and, 6:951b, 953b
  in Richter's *The Comet*, 5:81b, 82b
  in weltschmerz literature, 5:420a-b
"Čáka pěšáka Trunce." *See* Hašek, Jaroslav
Calas affair, the, Voltaire and, 4:379b–380a
Calculus of probabilities, invented by Pascal, 3:128b
Calderón de la Barca, Pedro, **2:871a–895a**
  A House with Two Doors Is Hard to Guard (*Casa con dos puertas mala es de guardar*), 2:874b–875a, 879a–880a, 882b
  adapted by Lesage, 3:320b
  Azorín's literary criticism of, 9:645a
  Devotion to the Cross (*La devoción de la Cruz*), 2:891a-b
  Grillparzer's *The Ancestress* and, 5:425a
  El gran teatro del mundo (*The Great Theatre of the World*), *theatrum mundi* metaphor in, 5:422a

For a Secret Offense, a Secret Revenge (*A secreto agravio secreta venganza*), 2:884a

Grillparzer and, 5:421b, 425a

Hofmannsthal and, 9:693b, 702b, 703a

Life Is a Dream (*La vida es sueño*), 2:875a–877a, 888a–890b, 9:1007a

  Grillparzer and, 5:422b, 424b

Lorca and, 11:2183a, 2199b

Machado on, 9:762a

Primera parte (*First Part*), 2:873a

The Constant Prince (*El príncipe constante*), 2:872a, 875a, 890b–891a

The Great Theater of the World (*El gran teatro del mundo*), 2:894a-b

The Mayor of Zalamea (*El alcalde de Zalamea*), 2:887b–888a

The Painter of His Dishonor (*El pintor de su deshonra*), 2:884a

The Phantom Lady (*La dama duende*), 2:880b

The Physician of His Honor (*El médico de su honra*), 2:877a-b, 884a–887a

The Prodigious Magician (*El mágico prodigioso*), 2:874b, 876b, 891b–892b

There's Nothing Like Keeping Silent (*No hay cosa como callar*), 2:880b–881a

Unamuno on, 8:288b–289a

Caleb Williams. *See* Godwin, William

Caligula. *See* Camus, Albert

Caligula, Roman emperor, in La Fontaine's "The Lion's Court," 3:87b

Calios de las tormentas, El. *See* Baroja, Pío

Calitri, Charles, *The Goliath Head*, 13:3043b

Call of Life, The. *See* Schnitzler, Arthur, *Der Ruf des Lebens*

Calligramme. *See* Analogy

Callimachus, Ronsard and, 2:731b

Callot, Jacques, Hoffmann and, 5:280a–281a

Calomnie, La. *See* Scribe, Eugène

Calpurnius, influence on Renaissance pastoral poetry, 2:902a-b

Calven, Rae, on Cavafy, 8:225b

Calvin, John

  in Bossuet's *History of the Variations in the Protestant Churches*, 3:171a

  Pascal's *Lettres provinciales* and, 3:136b

Calvinism

  Luther and, 2:686a

  Ronsard on, 2:738a-b

Calvino, Italo, **13:3259a–3286b**

  Adam, One Afternoon, and Other Stories, 13:3263b

  Cosmicomics, 13:3276b–3278a

    "Quanto scommettiamo" ("How Much Shall We Bet?"), 13:3277b

    "Un segno nello spazio" ("A Sign in Space"), 13:3277b–3278a

  Difficult Loves (*Gli amori difficili*), 13:3260a

    "Mine Field" ("Campo di Mine"), 13:3260a–3261b

    "Gli avangardisti a Mentone (The Vanguardists in Menton), 13:3259a

  I nostri antenati (Our Ancestors), 13:3264b–3269a

    The Baron in the Trees (*Il barone rampante*), 13:3264b, 3266a–3267a

    The Cloven Viscount (*Il visconte dimezzato*), 13:3264b–3266a

    The Nonexistent Knight (*Il cavaliere inesistente*), 13:3264b, 3267a–3268b

  I racconti (Stories), 13:3272a

  If on a winter's night a traveler, 13:3281a–3283a

  "Il Midollo del leone" (The Lion's Medulla), 13:3273a

  Invisible Cities (*Le città invisibili*), 13:3279b–3280b

  Italian Folktales (*Fiabe italiane*), 13:3276a-b

  La speculazione edilizia (Building Speculation), 13:3271a-b

  L'Entrata in guerra (Entering the War), 13:3264a

  Marcovaldo; or, The Seasons in the City, 13:3271b–3272a

  Mr. Palomar, 13:3283b–3284b

  "Priscella," 13:3278b

  "Smog" ("La nuvola di smog"), 13:3264b, 3270a–3271a

  t zero, 13:3278a-b

    "The Chase" (L'Inseguimento"), 13:3278a

    "The Count of Monte Cristo," 13:3278a-b

    "The Night Driver" ("Il guidatore notturno"), 13:3278a

Calvino, Italo (*cont.*)
"The Adventure of a Nearsighted Man" ("L'Avventura di un miope"), 13:3272a–3273a
"The Argentine Ant" ("La formica argentina"), 13:3264b, 3269a–3270a
The Castle of Crossed Destinies, 13:3279a-b
"The Crow Comes Last" ("Ultimo viene il corvo"), 13:3261a-b
The Path to the Nest of Spiders (*Il sentiero dei nidi di ragno*), 13:3260b, 3262a–3263b
"The Soft Moon" ("La molle Luna"), 13:3278b
The Watcher (*La giornata d'uno scrutatore*), 13:3273a–3274b
Vittorini and, 12:2733a
Calzabigi, Ranieri de', criticism of Alfieri's works, 4:666b, 681a
Cambistron, Jean Galbert de, *Andronic*, as source of Alfieri's *Philip*, 4:678b
Cambrai, Fénelon's stay in, 3:272a-b
Caméléon du berger, Le. See Ionesco, Eugène, *L'Impromptu de l'Alma*
Camera Lucida: Reflections on Photography. See Barthes, Roland
Camille. See Dumas fils, Alexandre, *La dame aux camélias*
Camino de perfección. See Baroja, Pío
Camoëns, Luís Vaz de, **2:747a–767b**
Auto de Filodemo (*The Play of Filodemo*), 2:754b, 757a–758b
correspondence, 2:758b–760a
El-Rei Seleuco (*King Seleucus*), 2:754b, 756a–757a, 758b
importance of, 7:1683a
Rimas (*Lyrics*), 2:749a–754b
"Alma minha gentil" ("Gentle Spirit"), 2:749b
"Amor é fogo que arde sem se ver" ("Love is a fire that burns invisibly"), 2:750b–751a
"Doces lembranças da passada glória" ("Sweet memories of past glory"), 2:752b
letters with, 2:758b
"Sete anos de pastor Jacob servia" ("Seven years a shepherd Jacob served"), 2:752a-b
"Sôbolos rios" ("By the rivers of Babylon"), 2:753b–754b
"Um mover d'olhos brando e piadoso" ("A gentle, pitying glance"), 2:751b–752a, 753b
The Lusiads (*Os Lusíadas*), 2:760a–766b, 10:1476a-b
publication of, 2:748a
sources, 2:751a, 759b
Vergil and, 2:747a
The Two Amphitryons (*Os Enfatriões*), 2:754b, 2.755a–756a
Campagne, Une (*A Campaign*). *See* Zola, Émile
Campaigns and Intervals. See Giraudoux, Jean, *Lectures pour une ombre* (Readings for a Shadow)
Campan Thal, The. See Richter, Jean Paul, *Das Kampanerthal*
Campanha alegre, Uma. See Eça de Queiroz, José Maria
Campe, Julius, and Heine, 5:496a-b
"Campo dei Fiori." *See* Milosz, Czeslaw
"Campo di Mine." *See* Calvino, Italo, *Difficult Loves* (*Gli amori difficili*), "Mine Field"
Campos, Álvaro de, 10:1488a, 1490b–1491b
Campos de Castilla. See Machado, Antonio
Camus, Albert, **13:3049a–3078b**
A Happy Death, 13:3058b–3059a
Actuelles: Chroniques, 13:3071a–3072a
Beauvoir and, 12:2728a
"Between Yes and No," 13:3058a
Caligula, 13:3053a, 3054a, 3062a–3064b
Chekhov and, 7:1857b
Chénier compared to, 4:715b
"Création et liberté" (Creation and Liberty), 13:3050a
"Death in the Soul," 13:3058a
Elytis and, 13:2965a
Exile and the Kingdom (*L'Exil et le royaume*), 13:3049a, 3054a, 3074a–3075a
Fragments d'un combat (Fragments of a Combat), 13:3056b

Giraudoux and, 9:1041b
Hesse and, 9:844a
"Irony," 13:3058a
"Jonas; or, The Artist at Work," 13:3074b
Le premier homme (The First Man),
    13:3049b, 3075a-b
"Love of Life," 13:3058a
Notebooks, 13:3053a
Nuptials at Típasa (*Noces*), 13:3053a,
    3058a-b
Queneau and, 12:2511b, 2512b
Révolte dans les Asturies (Revolt in the
    Asturias), 13:3053a
Rimbaud and, 7:1808a
Sartre and, 12:2602a
Silone and, 12:2276b
Simenon and, 12:2504a
Simon's *The Palace* and, 13:3037b
State of Siege, 13:3054a, 3069b
Strindberg and, 7:1752b
Summer (*L'Été*), 13:3072a–3073a
The Fall (*La chute*, 13:3054a, 3073a–3074a
The Just Assassins (*Les justes*), 13:3054a,
    3070b–3071a
"The Manifesto of Integral Conformism,"
    13:3057a-b
The Misunderstanding (*Le malentendu*),
    13:3054a, 3063a–3065a
The Myth of Sisyphus (*Le mythe de
    Sisyphus*), 13:3025b–3026a, 3026b,
    3053b, 3065a–3067a
The Plague (*La peste*), 13:3054a,
    3068a–3069b
  Malraux and, 12:2413b
The Possessed (*Les possédés*), 13:3054a,
    3075a
The Rebel (*L'Homme révolté*), 13:3054a,
    3069b–3070b
  Dostoevsky and, 7:1350a
The Renegade, 13:3074a-b
"The Sea Close By," 13:3072a-b
The Stranger (*L'Étranger*), 13:3049a, 3053b,
    3058b–3062a
The Stranger (*L'Étranger*), Pavese and,
    12:2767b
The Wrong Side and the Right Side
    (*L'Envers et l'endroit*), 13:3053a, 3058a

Weil and, 12:2787b, 2794b, 2808b
  Yourcenar and, 12:2539a
"Can lo boschatges." *See* Bernart de
    Ventadorn
Canard enchainé, Le, Queneau's writings and,
    12:2523a
Cañas y barro. See Blasco Ibáñez, Vicente,
    Reeds and Mud
Cancer Ward. See Solzhenitsyn, Aleksandr
"Canción de jinete." *See* García Lorca,
    Federico
Cancioneiro geral. See Resende, Garcia de
Cancioneiro poetry, 2:753a
  Camoëns' poetry and, 2:754a, 755b
Cancionero. See Unamuno, Miguel de
Canciones. See García Lorca, Federico
"Canciones." *See* Machado, Antonio,
    Soledades (Solitudes)
Canciones del suburbio. See Baroja, Pío
"Canciones a Guiomar." *See* Machado,
    Antonio
"Canciones y coplas." *See* Machado, Antonio,
    Soledades, galerías, y otros poemas
    (Solitudes, Galleries, and Other Poems)
Candamo, Francisco Bances
  Lope de Vega's plays and, 2:856b–857a
  *Teatro de los teatros de los pasados y
    presentes siglos* (*Theater of the
    Theaters of Past and Present Centuries*),
    2:856b–857a
Candida. See Shaw, George Bernard
Candide. See Voltaire
"Cándido." *See* Azorín
Candle in the Wind, A. See Solzhenitsyn,
    Aleksandr, *Svecha na vetru*
Candle-Bearer, The. See Musset, Alfred de, *Le
    chandelier*
Canetti, Elias, **12:2615a–2633b**
  Crowds and Power (*Masse und Macht*),
    12:2615b, 2625b–2628a
  Die Blendung (*Auto-da-Fé*)), 12:2615a-b,
    2619a-b, 2620b–2625b
  on Musil, 9:933a
  "Power and Survival" ("Macht und
    Überleben"), 12:2626b
  The Comedy of Vanity (*Komödie der
    Eitelkeit*), 12:2628a-b

Canetti, Elias (*cont.*)
  The Numbered (*Die Befristeten*),
    12:2628a–2630b
  The Tongue Set Free (*Die gerettete Zunge*),
    12:2631a–2632a
  "The Writer's Profession" ("Der Beruf des
    Dichters"), 12:2617b, 2627a-b
  Wedding (*Hochzeit*), 12:2628a-b
Cangé manuscript, 1:461b, 464a
Canossa, Ludovico, in Castiglione,
    2:653b–656a
Canso
  as genre in troubadour poetry, 1:167a
  rhyme in, 1:176a-b
  see also Sirventes
Canson, Marcabru and, 1:372b
Cantar de mio Cid. See Menéndez Pidal,
    Ramón; *Poema de mio Cid*
Cantari (street songs), ottava rima in, 2:512a
Cantatrice chauve, La. See Ionesco, Eugène
Cantatrice, La. See Goldoni, Carlo
Canterbury Tales. See Chaucer, Geoffrey
Canti. See Leopardi, Giacomo
Canti di Castelvecchio. See Pascoli, Giovanni
Canticle. See John of the Cross, St.
Cántico espiritual. See Juan de la Cruz, San
"Canto augurale per la nazione eletta." *See*
    D'Annunzio, Gabriele
"Canto jondo, El." *See* García Lorca, Federico
"Canto notturno di un pastore errante
    dell'Asia." *See* Leopardi, Giacomo,
    "Night Song of a Wandering Shepherd
    of Asia"
Canto novo. See D'Annunzio, Gabriele
Cantos. See Pound, Ezra
Canular (French joke), 7:1906b
Canzone
  in Dante's *De vulgari eloquentia*, 1:441b
  Leopardi's variations on, 5:555b
"Canzone del bucato, La." *See* Pascoli,
    Giovanni, *Primi poemetti*
Canzone dell'amore, La (*Song of Love*)
    (motion picture), 8:395a
Canzoni of 1824. *See* Leopardi, Giacomo
Canzoniere. See Petrarch
Cap and Bells. See Pirandello, Luigi, *Il
    berretto a sonagli*

Cap de Bonne-Espérance, Le. See Cocteau,
    Jean
Capable, Vincent. *See* Camus, Albert
Cape of Good Hope, The. See Cocteau, Jean,
    Le Cap de Bonne-Espérance
Cape of Storms, The. *See* Baroja, Pío, *El calios
    de las tormentas*
Čapek generation, 10:1568b
Čapek, Josef, 10:1565a-b, 1568a, 1586a
  Země mnoha jmen (*The Land of Many
    Names*), 10:1577b
Čapek, Karel, **10:1565a–1589b**
  Absolute at Large, The, 10:1574a, 1575a-b
  Adam stvořitel (*Adam the Creator*),
    10:1577b–1578a
  An Ordinary Life, 10:1582b–1583b
  Anglické listy (*Letters from England*),
    10:1585b–1586a
  Apokryfy (*Apocryphal Stories*), 10:1586a,
    1586b
  Bajky a podpovídky (Fables and Would-be
    Tales), 10:1586b
  "Balada o Juraji Čupovi" ("The Epic Exploit
    of Juraj Čup"), 10:1580b, 1581b
  Bílá nemoc (*Power and Glory*), 10:1584a-b
  Boží muka (*Wayside Crosses*), 10:1566a,
    1569b, 1580a
  Dašenka čili Život štěněte (*Dashenka; or,
    The Life of a Puppy*), 10:1586a-b
  Devatero pohádek (*Fairy Tales*), 10:1586a
  Envy and, 11:2238a
  Francouzská poesie nové doby (French
    Poetry of the New Era), 10:1566a
  "Hora" (The Mountain), 10:1570a
  Hordubal, 10:1567b, 1581a–1582a
  Hovory s T. G. Masarykem (*President
    Masaryk Tells His Story*), 10:1567b
  Krakatit, 10:1577a-b
  Kritika slov (A Critique of Words), 10:1570b,
    1585b
  Letter from Holland, 10:1585b
  Loupežník (The Outlaw), 10:1566a,
    1570b–1571a
  Marsyas čili na okraj literatury (*In Praise of
    Newspapers*), 10:1586a
  Matka (*The Mother*), 10:1584b

Měl jsem psa a kočku (*I Had a Dog and a Cat*), 10:1586b

O nejbližších věcech (*Intimate Things*), 10:1579a

O věcech obedných čili Zóon politikon (On Political Matters, or Zoon Politikon), 10:1579a-b

Obrázky z Holandska (*Letters from Holland*), 10:1579b

Obyčejný život (*An Ordinary Life*), 10:1567b

"Pád rodu Votických" ("The Fall of the House of Votický"), 10:1580a

"Pomoc!" ("Help!"), 10:1570a

Povětroň (*Meteor*), 10:1567b, 1582a-b

Povídky z druhé kapsy (Tales from the Other Pocket), 10:1567b

Povídky z jedné kapsy (Tales from One Pocket), 10:1567b, 1579b–1580b

Pragmatismus čili Filosofie practického života (Pragmatism; or, The Philosophy of Practical Life), 10:1566a

President Masaryk Tells His Story, 10:1579b

"Proč nejsem kominista" ("Why I Am Not a Communist"), 10:1579a, 1587a

První parta (*The First Rescue Party*), 10:1583b, 1585a

R.U.R., 10:1566b, 1571b–1574a, 1572b–1573a

  comedy prologue, 10:1572b

  as a "comedy of truth," 10:1573a-b

  faults of, 10:1573b–1574a

"Šlépěj" (The Imprint), 10:1569b

"Soud pana Havleny" ("Mr. Havlena's Verdict"), 10:1580b–1581a

"Tajemstuí písma" ("The Secrets of Handwriting"), 10:1580a

Tales from Two Pockets, 10:1579b, 1587a, 1589b

Továrna na absolutno (*The Absolute at Large*), 10:1567a

Trapné povídky (*Money and Other Stories*), 10:1570a-b

Válka s mloky (*The War with the Newts*), 10:1567b–1268a, 1574a–1575a, 1587a, 1588a

Věc Makropulos (*The Macropulos Secret*), 10:1574a, 1576b–1577a, 1588a

Zahradníkův rok (*The Gardener's Year*), 10:1586a

"Závrat" ("Vertigo"), 10:1580b

Život a dílo skladatele Foltýna (*The Cheat*), 10:1568a, 1584b–1585b

"Ztracená cesta" (The Lost Way), 10:1569b–1270a

Čapek, Karel, and Josef Čapek

Krakonošova zahrada (The Garden of Krakonoš), 10:1568b–1569a

Lásky hra osudná (The Fateful Game of Love), 10:1569a-b, 1576a

The World We Live In, 10:1575b–1576b

Zářivé hlubiny (The Luminous Depths), 10:1565b, 1569a-b

Čapek-Chod, K. M.

Kašpar Lén, mstitel (Kašpar Lén, the Avenger), 9:1096b

Z vln života (From the Tide of Life), 9:1096b

Capitaine Fracasse, Le. *See* Gautier, Théophile, *Captain Fracasse*

Capital, A (The Capital City). *See* Eça de Queiroz, José Maria

Capitalism

  American, described by Mayakovsky, 11:1841a

  in Blok's works, 9:973b

  Christianity and, Böll on, 13:3182b–3183a

  in Heinrich Mann's *Berlin*, 8:523a-b

  Wedekind's critique of, 8:263b

Capitalization, in Gombrowicz, 12:2581a-b

Capitulation, A. *See* Wagner, Richard

Capponi, Gino, letter about Manzoni's *The Betrothed* to, 5:375b–376a

Capreolus, John, *Defensiones theologiae divi Thomae Aquinatis*, 1:427b

Caprice. *See* Azorín, *Capricho*

Caprice (*Un caprice*). *See* Musset, Alfred de

Caprices de Marianne, Les. *See* Musset, Alfred de, *The Whims of Marianne*

Caprices of Fortune, The. *See* Baroja, Pío, *Las veleidades de la fortuna*

Capricho. *See* Azorín

Caprichos, Los. *See* Gautier, Théophile

Captain Fracasse. *See* Gautier, Théophile

Captain's Daughter, The. *See* Pushkin, Alexander

Captain's Daughter, The. *See* Valle-Inclán, Ramón del, *Martes de Carnaval* (Shrove Tuesday), *La hija del capitán*

Captive Mind, The. See Milosz, Czeslaw

"Captive Spirit, A." *See* Tsvetaeva, Marina, "Plennyi dukh"

Captive, The. See Proust, Marcel, *Remembrance of Things Past* (À la recherche du temps perdu)

Capuana, Luigi, Pirandello and, 8:391b

Capucines, Les. See Ingres, Jean Auguste Dominique

Cara de Dios, La. See Arniches, Carlos

Cara de Plata. See Valle-Inclán, Ramón del, *Las comedias bárbaras*

Caractères ou les moeurs de ce siècle, Les. See La Bruyère, Jean de

Carcano, Giulio, *Angiola Maria*, in Lampedusa's *The Leopard*, 11:2015a

Carcere, Il. See Pavese, Cesare, *The Political Prisoner*

Cardinal d'Espagne, Le. See Montherlant, Henry de

"Cardinal's First Tale, The." *See* Dinesen, Isak

"Cardinal's Last Tale, The." *See* Dinesen, Isak

Carducci, Giosue, **7:1495a–1516b**
  "A Satana" ("To Satan"), 7:1497a, 1501a, 1511b
  Alfieri's works published by, 4:674b
  "Alla stazione in una mattina d'autunno" ("At the Station on an Autumn Morning"), 7:1512b–1513a
  antagonism to Giovanni Verga, 7:1546a, 1547a
  changing evaluations of, 7:1495a, 1513b–1514b
  D'Annunzio and, 8:176b, 177b, 189a, 191b
  "Davanti San Guido" ("Before San Guido"), 7:1507a-b
  "Dinanzi alle terme di Caracalla" (In Front of the Baths of Caracalla), 7:1509b–1510b
  early work of, 7:1499b–1501a
  Giambi ed epodi (Iambics and Epodes), 7:1501a–1503a
  and his contemporaries, 7:1495a–1496a, 1498a-b, 1504a
  historical themes in, 7:1502a, 1507b–1508a, 1509a–1510a
  "Il comune rustico" (The Rustic Commune), 7:1507a–1508a
  "Nella Piazza di San Petronio" (In San Petronio Square), 7:1512a-b
  Odi barbare (*Barbarian Odes*), 7:1497b, 1506a, 1508a–1509b
  Pascoli and, 7:1826a, 1827a, 1829a, 1829b, 1847a
  "Pianto antico" ("An Ancient Lament"), 7:1505b–1506a
  Rime e ritmi (Rhymes and Rhythms), 7:1513a-b
  Rime nuove (*New Lyrics*), 7:1503a–1508a
  "San Martino" (St. Martin's Day), 7:1504a-b
  Unamuno and, 8:297a
  Vittorini and, 12:2735b

Cardwell, Richard, on Blasco Ináñez's *The Cabin*, 8:370a, 374b, 376b, 377a

"Caretaker's Desk." *See* Ritsos, Yannis, *Thyrorio*

Caricatura, La (literary journal), Machado and, 9:744a

Carlism
  in Valle-Inclán's works
    La guerra carlista, 8:337a–338b
    Sonata de invierno, 8:335b, 337a
    Tragedia pastoril en tres actos, 8:344b–345a

Carlist War, The. *See* Valle-Inclán, Ramón del, *La guerra carlista*

Carlist Wars
  Baroja and, 9:589a-b, 602a-b
  beginning of, 9:610a
  First, in Valle-Inclán's *Sonata de invierno*, 8:335b
  Unamuno and, 8:284a-b

Carlos I of Portugal, king, 11:2146a

Carlyle, Thomas
  on Germany, 5:105b
  influence of, 9:591a
  on Mickiewicz's *Books*, 5:624b
  Richter and, 5:80b, 84a
  Sartor Resartus, 7:1736a
  Strindberg and, 7:1732a
  Taine and, 7:1449a, 1456b–1457a, 1464a

The Life of Friedrich Schiller, Alfieri's
  tyrants compared to Schiller's, 4:661b
  Unamuno and, 8:291b
"Carmen." *See* Gautier, Théophile
Carmen. See Mérimée, Prosper
Carmen Campidoctoris. See Ripoll
Carmen de Hastingae proelio. See Guy of
  Ponthieu
Carmen (opera). *See* Bizet, Georges
Carmina Burana, "Manus ferens munera,"
  1:364a-b
Carmosine. See Musset, Alfred de
Carnal love. *See* Sexual passion
Carnality
  Gombrowicz and, 12:2566a–2567b
  in Rabelais's works
    Fourth Book, 2:712a
    Pantagruel, 2:702b, 704a-b
Carnap, Rudolf, on musical expression of
  worldviews, 5:413b
"Carnet de notes de *Mémoires d'Hadrien." See*
  Yourcenar, Marguerite
Carnets. See Camus, Albert, *Notebooks;*
  Saint-Exupéry, Antoine de, *Citadelle*
*Carnets de la drôle de guerre: November
  1939–Mars 1940, Les. See* Sartre,
  Jean-Paul, *The War Diaries*
Carnevale dei morti, Il. See Pirandello, Luigi
"Carnevale di Gerti." *See* Montale, Eugenio,
  The Occasions (Le occasioni), "Gerti's
  Carnival"
"Carnival." *See* Dinesen, Isak
Caro Michele. See Ginzburg, Natalia
Carocci, Alberto, editorship of *Solaria,*
  12:2736a
Carolingian cycle, Ariosto and, 2:624b–643b
Carriage of the Holy Sacrament, The. See
  Mérimée, Prosper
"Carriage, The." *See* Gogol, Nikolay
  Vasilievich
Carrillo, Enrique Gómez, Machado and, 9:744b
"Carrion." *See* Baudelaire, Charles
Carroll, Lewis
  Elytis' *Maria Nephele* and, 13:2980a
  Through the Looking Glass
    Artaud's "translation" of, 11:1983a
    Robbe-Grillet and, 13:3252b

Carrosse du Saint-Sacrement, Le. See
  Mérimée, Prosper, *The Carriage of the
  Holy Sacrament*
Carsten Curator. See Storm, Theodor, *Curator
  Carsten*
"Carta a Georgina Hübner en el cielo de
  Lima." *See* Jiménez, Juan Ramón
*Carta Marina et Descriptio Septentrionalium.
  See* Magnus, Olaus
Cartas de Inglaterra. See Eça de Queiroz, José
  Maria
Cartas familiares e bilhetes de Paris. See Eça
  de Queiroz, José Maria
Carte de tendre. See Scudéry, Madeleine de
Cartesian Circle, 3:13a, 17a, 18b
Cartesianism
  rejected by Vico, 3:296a-b, 297b
  see also Descartes, René; Dualism,
    Cartesian
Carvajal Family, The. See Mérimée, Prosper,
  La famille de Carvajal
"Casa al mare." *See* Ginzburg, Natalia
Casa in collina, La. See Pavese, Cesare, *The
  House on the Hill*
Casa con dos puertas mala es de guardar. See
  Calderón de la Barca, Pedro, *A House
  with Two Doors Is Hard to Guard*
Casa de Aizgorri, La. See Baroja, Pío
Casa de Bernarda Alba, La. See García Lorca,
  Federico, *The House of Bernarda Alba*
"Casa del doganiere, La." *See* Montale,
  Eugenio
"Casa del Granella, La." *See* Pirandello, Luigi
"Casada infiel, La." *See* García Lorca,
  Federico
Casalio, *Amaranta,* Renaissance pastoral
  drama and, 2:916b–917a
Casanova, Giovanni
  memoirs of, Hofmannsthal and, 9:696b,
    705b
  Sade compared to, 4:616b–617a
*Casanovas Heimfahrt (Casanova's
  Homecoming). See* Schnitzler, Arthur
Case of the Bandleader, The. *See* Mayakovsky,
  Vladimir, "Koe-chto po povodu
  dirizhera"

Case of Baron Borz, The. *See* Ady, Endre, "Borz báró esete"

Casella (musician), Dante and, 1:432a

"Casino Lectures." *See* Quental, Antero de

Casona, Alejandro, plays of, 9:642a

Cassandra (Trojan prophetess)
  George and, 8:466a
  Heinrich Mann and, 8:531b
  La Fontaine's "The Swallow and the Little Birds" and, 3:88a-b

Cassaria, La. See Ariosto, Lodovico

Casse-pipe. See Céline, Louis-Ferdinand

Cassedy, Steven, on Bely, 9:914a

Cassel, Alex, Butor and, 13:3306b

Cassi, Geltrude, Leopardi and, 5:544b

Cassian
  Collationes, on Old Testament interpretation, 1:4a-b
  Institutiones, *Psychomachia* and, 1:15a

Cassiodorus, *Institutiones divinarum et humanarum litterarum* (*Instruction in Divine and Human Letters*), 1:405b

Cassius, Jaroslav Kolman, Hašek's satire on, 9:1109a

Cassola, Carlo, *La ragazza di Bube* (*Bebo's Girl*), Ginzburg's novels and, 13:3145a

Cassou, Jean, translation of Unamuno's *How to Make a Novel*, 8:305a

"Castanea." *See* Pascoli, Giovanni

Castanheda, Fernão Lopes de, *History of the Discovery and Conquest of India by the Portuguese*, 2:760b, 763b, 764b

Caste. See Robertson, Tom

Castellane, Cordélia de, Chateaubriand and, 5:130b

Castello dei destini incrociati. See Calvino, Italo, *The Castle of Crossed Destinies*

Castelo Branco, Camilo
  Amor de Perdição (*A Love of Perdition*, 7:1696b–1697a
  popularity of, 7:1696b

Castelvecchio, Pascoli and, 7:1828a, 1828b

Castets, Ferdinand, 1:444b

Casticismo, Unamuno on, 8:287b–288a

Castiglione, Baldesar, **2:645a–667b**

Ad Henricum Angliae regem epistola de vita et gestis Guidubaldi Urbini Ducis (*A Letter Concerning the Life and Deeds of Guidobaldo, Duke of Urbino, to Henry, King of England*), 2:647b
  Alcon, 2:647a, 650a, 908b
  Gottfried and, 1:257a–258b
  oral tradition and, 2:928a
  The Book of the Courtier (*Il cortegiano*), 2:650a–665a
    anecdotes in, 2:938b
    The Lusiads and, 2:762a
    as urban pastoral, 2:908b
  Tirsi (*Thyrsis*), 2:646b–647a, 650a, 908b

Castigo sin venganza, El. See Lope de Vega

Castile
  Azorín's works about, 9:643a, 649a
  in Machado's *Campos de Castilla*, 9:757a

Castilho, António Feliciano de, Antero de Quental and, 7:1685a-b

Castilian romance, Machado and, 9:763a

Castilian Soul, The. See Azorín, *El alma castellana*

Castilla (Castile). *See* Azorín

Castillo Solórzano, Alonso de, novellas of, 2:951a-b

Castle of Crossed Destinies. See Calvino, Italo

Castle, The. See Kafka, Franz

Castle to Castle. See Céline, Louis-Ferdinand, *D'un château l'autre*

Castle Wetterstein: Drama in Three Acts. See Wedekind, Frank

Castration, theme of, in Olesha's *Envy*, 11:2238b

Castris, A. Leone De, on Pirandello's *Shoot!*, 8:400b

Castro, Guillén de
  Las mocedades del Cid, 1:133b–134a
    Corneille and, 3:31b

Castro, João de, 2:761a

Castro, José Maria Ferreira de. *See* Ferreira de Castro, José Maria

Casualty and Other Early Stories, The. See Böll, Heinrich, *Die Verwundung und andere frühe Erzählungen*

Cat imagery, in Rabelais, 2:712b–714a

Cat and Mouse. See Grass, Günter

Cat, The. See Colette, *La chatte*; Simenon,
Georges, *Le chat*

Catachresis, Richter's *School for Aesthetics*
on, 5:78b

"Catacombpainting." *See* Ekelöf, Gunnar

Cataline. See Ibsen, Henrik

Cataline's Conspiracy. *See* Mérimée, Prosper,
Conjuration de Catalina

Catastrophism, Milosz and, 13:2930b, 2941a-b

Catch as Catch Can. See Anouilh, Jean, *La
foire d'empoigne*

Catchwords. *See* Böll, Heinrich, "Stichworte"

Catedral, La. See Blasco Ibáñez, Vicente

Categorical imperative, Kleist and, 5:294b

"Categories." *See* Ekelöf, Gunnar

Categorization
Canetti and, 12:2621a
Sartre and, 12:2590b

Catena aurea. See Aquinas, Thomas, St.

Caterina av Siena. See Undset, Sigrid

Cathar heresy, Gottfried and, 1:238a

Catharsis
Freud's use of, 8:3a, 6b–7a
Lessing on, 4:547b–548a

Cathedral schools
Gottfried and, 1:238a
scholasticism and, 1:406a

Cathédrale, La (The Cathedral). See
Huysmans, Joris Karl

Cathemerinon. See Prudentius, *Liber
Cathemerinon*

Catherine Blum. See Dumas père, Alexandre

Catherine II the Great, empress of Russia
Diderot and, 4:503a-b
fairy tale of, 10:1625b
in Pushkin's *Captain's Daughter,*
5:688a–689b

Catherine of Siena. See Undset, Sigrid,
Caterina av Siena

Catilina. See Ibsen

Catiline. See Ibsen, Henrik

Catira, La. See Cela, Camilo José

Catullus, Caius Valerius, Blok and,
9:983b–984a

Caucasian Chalk Circle, The. See Brecht,
Bertolt

"Caucasian Veteran, The." *See* Lermontov,
Mikhail Yurievich, "Kavkazetz"

Caucasus
Lermontov and, 6:1196b–1197a, 1199a-b,
1202b–1203b, 1213b–1214a, 1215a,
1218b–1219b
in Pushkin's poetry, 5:666a-b

"Caucasus, The." *See* Lermontov, Mikhail
Yurievich, "Kavkaz"

Causality
Aquinas' *Summa theologica* on, 1:421a
in Kleist, 5:305a-b

Cause du peuple, La (journal), Sand's
founding of, 6:831b

Causeries. See Dumas père, Alexandre

Causeries du lundi. See Sainte-Beuve,
Charles-Augustin

Cavafy, Constantine, **8:205a–228b**,
13:2955b–2956a, 2956b
"Alexandrinoi vasileis" ("Alexandrian
Kings"), 8:213b–214a
diction, 8:225b
"Apo tin scholin tou perionymou
philosophou" ("From the School of the
Renowned Philosopher"), 8:216a-b
"As frontizan" ("They Should Have Taken
Care"), 8:222b–223a
"Che fece . . . il gran rifiuto," 8:222b
"Eige etelefta" ("If Dead Indeed"),
8:218b–219b
"Endimo tis Mikras Asias" ("In a Township
in Asia Minor)," 8:213a
"Genealogia" ("Genealogy"), 8:209a-b, 223b
"I archi ton" ("Their Beginning"), 8:217b
"I arrostia tou Keitou" ("Kleitos' Illness"),
8:218a-b
"I doxa ton Ptolemaion" ("The Glory of the
Ptolemies"), 8:211b
"I dysareskeia tou Selefkidou" ("The
Displeasure of Selefkidis"), 8:212b
"I polis" ("The City"), 8:207a-b
"I psyches ton geronton" ("The Souls of Old
Men"), 8:208b
"Iasi tofos" ("Tomb of Iasis"), 8:223a
"Idoni" ("To Sensual Pleasure"),
8:223b–224a

Cavafy, Constantine (*cont.*)
"Ierefs tou Serapiou" ("Priest of the
Serapeum"), 8:217b
influence of Mouseion on, 8:211b–212a,
214a-b
"Irodis Attikos" ("Herodes Atticus"), 8:208a
"Ithaki" ("Ithaca"), 8:227a
"Kaisarion" ("Caesarion"), 8:214b–215a
Kazantzakis and, 9:1067a
"Ki akoumpisa kai plagiasa stes klines ton"
("And I Leaned and Lay on Their
Beds"), 8:217b–218a
"Meres tou 1896" ("Days of 1896"), 8:223a
"Na meinei" ("To Remain"), 8:224b–225a
"Noisis" ("Understanding"), 8:223b
"Omnyei" ("He Resolves"), 8:208b–209a,
223a
"Otan diegeirontai" ("When They Are
Roused"), 8:224a-b
"Perimenontas tous varvarous" ("Waiting for
the Barbarians"), 8:221b–222b
"Poly spanios" ("Very Seldom"),
8:205b–206a
"Presveis ap' tin Alexandreia" ("Envoys from
Alexandria"), 8:212b
Seferis and, 12:2255b, 2269b
"Ta epikindyna" ("Things That Are
Dangerous"), 8:218a
"Teleiomena" ("Finalities"), 8:221a
"The God Abandons Antony," 8:215a-b
"Theatron tis Sidonos" ("Theater of Sidon"),
8:210b, 217b
diction, 8:226a
"To 31 P.Ch. stin Alexandreia" ("31 B.C. in
Alexandria"), 8:213b
"Ton Evraion (50 M.Ch.)" ("Of the Jews A.D.
50"), 8:215b–216a
"Troes" ("Trojans"), 8:221a-b
Ungaretti and, 10:1453a
Yourcenar on, 12:2553a
Yourcenar's translations, 12:2543a-b
Cavalcanti, Guido
"Chi è questa che vèn, ch'ogn'om la mira?"
("Who is this lady who comes, and
every man looks at her?"), 2:752a
Dante and, 1:432a, 432b, 439a
Petrarch's *Canzoniere*, quotations in, 2:493b

Cavalier bizarre, Le. *See* Ghelderode, Michel
de
Cavalier poets. *See* Metaphysical poets
Cavaliere e la dama, Il. See Goldoni, Carlo
Cavaliere inesistente, Il. See Calvino, Italo,
The Nonexistent Knight
"Cavalleria rusticana." *See* Verga, Giovanni
Cavallo nella luna, Un. See Pirandello, Luigi
Cave of Salamanca, The. See Cervantes,
Miguel de, *La cueva de Salamanca*
Cave, The. *See* Zamyatin, Yevgeny Ivanovich,
Peshchera
Cavern, The. See Anouilh, Jean, *La grotte*
Caves Are Roaring, The. *See* Ady, Endre,
"Bugnak a tárnák"
Caves du Vatican, Les. See Gide, André, *The
Vatican Swindle*
Caxton, William, Poggio's influence on, 2:938a
Ce formidable bordel! See Ionesco, Eugène
"Ce que dit la bouche d'ombre." *See* Hugo,
Victor
Ce que je crois. See Mauriac, François
Ce que savait Maisie. See James, Henry, *What
Maisie Knew*
Ce qui était perdu. See Mauriac, François,
That Which Was Lost
"Ce qu'on dit au poète à propos de fleurs." *See*
Rimbaud, Arthur
Céard, Henry, Maupassant and, 7:1763b
Cecchi, Emilio, on Silone, 12:2294a-b
Cech, Annemarie, 13:3167b
Čechoslovan (Czech periodical), Hašek's
articles in, 9:1094a
Cécile. See Constant, Benjamin; Fontane,
Theodor
Cécile ou l'école des pères (Cecile; or, The
School for Fathers). *See* Anouilh, Jean
Cefalo. See Correggio
Cela, Camilo José, **13:3105a–3129b**
Al servicio de algo (At the Service of
Something), 13:3125b–3126a
Baroja influences, 9:613a
Christos versus Arizona (Christ Versus
Arizona), 13:3125a
Diccionario secreto (Secret Dictionary),
13:3125b

El Ciudadano Iscariote Reclús (Citizen Iscariote Reclús), 13:3119a

Enciclopedia del erotismo (Encyclopedia of Eroticism), 13:3125b

Gavilla de fábulas sin amor (Sheaf of Fables Without Love), 13:3119a

"Gayola de grajos y vencejos" (Cage of Rooks and Pallid Swifts), 13:3125a-b

"Himno a la Muerte" (Hymn to Death), 13:3116a

Journey to Alcarria (*Viaje a la Alcarria*), 13:3112a–3113a

La Catira (The Blonde), 13:3117b–3118a

La cucaña (The Greased Pole), 13:3118b–3119a

La rueda de los ocios (The Wheel of Idle Moments), 13:3117b

Los vasos comunicantes (Communicating Vessels), 13:3118a-b

María Sabina, 13:3123a-b

Mazurca para dos muertos (Mazurka for Two Dead Men), 13:3123b–3125a

Mis páginas preferidas (My Favorite Pages), 13:3126b

Mrs. Caldwell Speaks to Her Son (*Mrs. Caldwell habla con su hijo*), 13:3116a–3117b

Nuevas andanzas y desventuras de Lazarillo de Tormes (New Wanderings and Misadventures of Lazarillo of Tormes), 13:3111b–3112a

Oficio de tinieblas 5 (Tenebrae Service 5), 13:3121b–3123a

Pisando la dudosa luz del día (Walking on the Hesitant Light of Day), 13:3116a

Rest Home (*Pabellón de reposo*), 9:645b, 13:3110b–3111a

The Family of Pascual Duarte (*La familia de Pascual Duarte*), 13:3106a–3110a

The Hive (*La colmena*), 13:2106a-b, 3113a–3116a

Tobogán de hambientos (The Hungry People's Slide), 13:3126a

Vísperas, festividad y octava de San Camilo del año 1936 en Madrid (Eve, Festivity, and Octave of Saint Camillus in the Year 1936 in Madrid), 13:3119a–3121a

Celan, Paul, Rilke and, 9:789b

"Ćelebi Hafiz." *See* Andrić, Ivo

"Celebration of a Childhood." *See* Perse, Saint-John

"Celebration of Spring." *See* Klopstock, Friedrich Gottlieb

Celestina, La. *See* Rojas, Fernando de

Celestine V, pope, in Silone's *Story of a Humble Christian*, 12:2299a-b

Celibacy, clerical, in Galdos' *Tormento*, 7:1609b

Célibataires, Les. *See* Montherlant, Henry de, *The Bachelors*

Céline, Louis-Ferdinand, **11:1859a–1884b**

Bagatelles pour un massacre, 11:1862a

Bardamu-Destouches character, 11:1868b–1870a, 1871a-b, 1877b–1878b, 1881a-b

Casse-pipe, 11:1861a, 1863a, 1863b

character development, 11:1867b–1868a

critical acceptance of, 11:1863b–1864a

Death on the Installment Plan (*Mort à credit*), 11:1860a, 1861a, 1861b, 1864a, 1868b, 1872b–1876a

overture, 11:1874a

D'un château l'autre (Castle to Castle), 11:1863a, 1864b, 1881a-b

title symbolism, 11:1867a-b

Entretiens avec la Professeur Y (Conversations with Professsor Y), 11:1864b

Féerie pour une autre fois I (Masque for Some Tomorrow), 11:1863a, 1879b–1881a

literary style, 11:1864a, 1880b–1881a

prisoner's monologue, 11:1867a-b

title symbolism, 11:1867a-b

four novelistic sequences, 11:1864a

Guignol's Band, 11:1861a, 1862b, 1863a, 1867a, 1868b, 1876a-b, 1877a–1879a

literary style, 11:1864a

Journey to the End of the Night (*Voyage au bout de la nuit*), 7:1526b, 11:1859a, 1861a, 1861b–1862a, 1864a, 1865a, 1867b–1872b, 1875b–1876a

Musil's *The Man Without Qualities* and, 9:943b

Céline, Louis-Ferdinand (*cont.*)
  Journey to the End of the Night (*cont.*)
    trip to Africa, 11:1869b–1870a
  "La naissance d'une fée," 11:1862a
  La vie et l'oeuvre de Philippe-Ignace Semmelweis (*The Life and Work of Semmelweis*), 11:1861b
  Le Pont de Londres (London Bridge), 11:1878a
  L'École des cadavres, 11:1862a
  L'Église (The Church), 11:1861b
  Les beaux draps (A Nice Mess), 11:1863b, 1877b
  Lucette Almanzor and, 11:1862b–1863a
  Mea Culpa, 11:1862a
  Nord (*North*), 11:1863a, 1868b, 1881a, 1881b–1882b
  Normance: Féerie pour une autre fois II, 11:1863a, 1875b, 1876b–1877a, 1880a-b
    language, 11:1880b–1881a
  political pamphlets, 11:1862a
  Pont de Londres (London Bridge), 11:1863b
  Queneau and, 12:2516a, 2516b, 2523a
  Rigodon (*Rigadoon*), 11:1863a, 1864b, 1883a
  three points of suspension, 11:1865a, 1865b, 1867b, 1873a
  use of spoken language, 12:2523a
  "Van Bagaden," 11:1862a
  "Voyou Paul, brave Virginie," 11:1862a
Cell, The. *See* Pavese, Cesare, *The Political Prisoner*
Cellini, Benvenuto
  Alfieri's autobiography compared to, 4:662a
  Berlioz and, 6:783b, 784a, 791a, 799a
"Cellulairement" (Cellularly). *See* Verlaine, Paul
"Celoso extremeño, El." *See* Cervantes, Miguel de
Celtic mythology, Melusina, in Breton's novels, 11:1941b, 1947b–1948a
Cénacle
  Balzac and, 5:635b
  Musset and, 6:1001b, 1002b
  Sainte-Beuve and, 6:838a
Cénacle du Doyenné, Verlaine and, 7:1627b
Cenci, Les (The Cenci). *See* Artaud, Antonin
Cene, Le. See Grazzini, Antonfrancesco

"Cenit." *See* Jiménez, Juan Ramón; Machado, Antonio, *Soledades* (Solitudes)
Cenizas. See Valle-Inclán, Ramón del, *El yermo de las almas*
Cennacle
  Antero de Quental and, 7:1686a, 1688b
  Eça and, 7:1686a-b
  growth of, 7:1687a-b
Censorship: a Theodicy in One Act. See Wedekind, Frank, *Die Zensur: Eine Theodizee in einem Akt*
Censorship
  Alfieri and, 4:674a-b
  Beaumarchais and, 4:573a, 578b, 579b–580a, 583b
  Büchner and, 6:1174b
  Cela and, 13:3106a, 3110a-b
  and Cocteau, 10:1556a, 1557b, 1558a
  German, Elytis' *Sun the First* and, 13:2962a
  Goldoni and, 4:428b
  Gombrowicz and, 12:2565a
  Goncharov's career as censorship official, 6:1083a-b
  Greece, Elytis and, 13:2972a, 2972b
  of Grillparzer's *Ottokar*, 5:433b
  Hauptmann and, 8:152b, 165b
  Heine and, 5:491a-b, 496a, 501a, 502b–503a
  in Portugal, 11:2148b
    Ferreira de Castro and, 11:2143a, 2149b, 2153a
  Rabelais and, 697a-b
  Rousseau and, 4:458a–459a
  Staël and, 5:93a-b
  Turgenev and, 6:1279b–1280b
  of Wedekind, 8:239b–240a
  see also Index of Prohibited Books
Cent mille milliards de poèmes. See Queneau, Raymond
Cent nouvelles nouvelles, 2:945b–946a
  Boccaccio's influence on, 2:945b
Cent nouvelles nouvelles de Phillipe de Vigneulles, Les. See Vigneulles, Phillip de
Cent phrases pour éventails. See Claudel, Paul

120 journées de Sodom, ou l'école du libertinage, Les. See Sade, Donatien Alphonse François, marquis de

Cento e quattro accidenti in una notte, I. See Goldoni, Carlo

Cento novelle antich (Hundred Ancient Tales), influence on Renaissance short fiction, 2:933b–934b

Central Europe, Kundera and, 13:3389a-b, 3410a–3411a

Centre Universitaire Méditerranéen, Valéry and, 8:584a

Century Was Young, The. See Aragon, Louis, *Les voyageurs de l'impériale*

"Cep'." *See* Olesha, Yuri, "The Chain"

Cercle des Mahé, Le. See Simenon, Georges

Cerco de Numancia, El. See Cervantes, Miguel de

Certains (Certainties). See Huysmans, Joris Karl

"Certi obblighi." *See* Pirandello, Luigi

Cervantes, Miguel de, **2:819a–842a**

  Ariosto and, 2:642b

  Azorín's approval of, 9:644b

  Croce on, 8:319a

  Don Quixote, 8:77b

    Avellaneda's pirating of, 2:838a-b

    basis for, 2:828a

    books after, 2:821a-b

    Canetti and, 12:2621b–2622a

    Cervantes' other works mentioned in, 2:821b

    chivalry and, 2:835a

    comedy in, 2:836a

    complexity of, 2:839b

    composition of, 2:837a–838a

    Corneille and, 3:24a

    discussed by Lukács, 10:1261b–1262a

    Don Quixote as Christlike figure, 8:296b

    funding for, 2:821a

    Gogol and, 6:986a, 995b

    influence on short fiction, 2:950b

    inspiration for, 2:837a

    interpretation of, 2:839b–840a

    Jiménez and, 9:1005a

    Lesage and, 3:323a-b

    life and art in, 2:840a–841a

    marriage in, view of, 2:883b

    Milesian tales discounted in, 2:930b

    Montemayor's *Diana* in, 2:922b

    multiplication of narrators in, 2:836a–837a

    novel form and, 2:828a-b, 835–836a

    Ortega y Gasset on, 9:1128a, 1133b, 1137a-b

    parody of, 2:828b

    as parody of pastoral literature, 2:906b, 922b–923a

    Pirandello's *Henry IV* and, 8:405a

    publication of, 2:821b–822a

    Simon's *The Wind* and, 13:3033a, 3033b

    source of, 2:821a

    Stagg's study of, 2:837a-b

    structure of, 2:838b–839b

    success of, 2:821b, 822a

    Turgenev on, 6:1282b–1283a

    two versions of, 2:835a

    Unamuno on, 8:289a-b, 295a–297a, 9:1128a

    Wieland and, 4:593a

  Eight Plays and Eight Interludes (Ocho comedias y ocho entremeses), 2:821a-b, 832b

  "El celoso extremeño" ("The Jealous Hidalgo"), 2:821b, 831b

  El cerco de Numancia (The Siege of Numantia), 2:825a-b

  El juez de los divorcios (The Divorce Judge), 2:826a

  El rufián viudo (The Widowed Pimp), 2:826a

  El trato de Argel (The Commerce of Algiers), 2:825a-b

  El viejo celoso (The Old Jealous Husband), 2:826a

  Exemplary Tales (Novelas ejemplares), 2:821a, 822a, 831a–833a

    dominance of, 2:949b

    "El coloquio de los perros" ("Dialogue of the Dogs"), 2:759b, 923a

    innovation of, 2:950a

    Lope de Vega and, 2:849a

    structure of, 2:928b

Grillparzer and, 5:421b

Cervantes, Miguel de (*cont.*)
  Journey to Parnassus (*Viaje del Parnaso*),
    2:821a, 823a
  La cueva de Salamanca (*The Cave of
    Salamanca*), 2:826a-b
  La Galatea, 2:820b, 822a, 830a–831a, 833a
    influence of Montemayor's *Diana* on,
    2:922b
  "La gitanilla" ("The Gypsy Maid"), 2:834b,
    11:2180b
  "La ilustre fregona" ("The Illustrious
    Kitchen Maid"), 2:834b
  Lope de Vega and, 2:821b, 822b–823a,
    824b–825a, 845b
  "Master Glass" ("El licenciado"),
    2:833a–834a, 834b–835a
  Ortega y Gasset and, 9:1122b
  Pedro de Urdemalas, 2:825b, 826a
  Pérez Galdós and, 7:1607a-b
  "Rinconete and Cortadill," 2:832b
  Svevo and, 8:77b
  "The Deceitful Marriage," 2:834b–835a,
    834a-b
  The Trials of Persiles and Sigismunda (*Los
    trabajos de Persiles y Sigismunda*),
    2:821b, 822a, 828a, 832b, 835a,
    841a–842a
  The Wonder Show (*El retablo de las
    maravillas*), 2:826b–827a
  "To the Catafalque of Philip II in Seville,"
    2:824a
  Valle-Inclán and, 8:339a, 346a
  Vittorini and, 12:2734a
Cervantes, o la casa encantada (*Cervantes; or,
  The Haunted House*). *See* Azorín
Ces plaisirs. See Colette, *Le pur et l'impur*
Césaire, Aimé, "Zone" and, 9:896a
César o nada. See Baroja, Pío
César-Antéchrist. See Jarry, Alfred
Céspedes y Meneses, Gonzales, *Historias
    peregrinas y ejemplares* (Strange and
    Exemplary Histories), 2:951b
C'est beau. See Sarraute, Nathalie
Ceux de la soif. See Simenon, Georges
Cézanne, Paul
  poetic modernism and, 9:768a
  Rilke and, 9:771a

Zola and, 7:1518a-b, 1531a
Chaadaev, Pyotr Yakovlevich, Mandelshtam's
    essay on, 10:1639b
Chabrier, Emmanuel, Verlaine and, 7:1620b
Chadwick, H. M., on Germanic poetry, 1:54a
Chagall, Marc, 9:896b
  Hesse's *Klingsor's Last Summer* and, 9:843a
Chain and Ball. See Feydeau, Georges, *Un fil
    à la patte*
"Chain of Roses, The." *See* Klopstock,
    Friedrich Gottlieb
"Chain, The." *See* Olesha, Yuri
"Chair chaude des mots, La." *See* Queneau,
    Raymond, *Le chien à la mandoline*
Chair et le sang, La. See Mauriac, François,
    Flesh and Blood
Chaises, Les (*The Chairs*). *See* Ionesco,
    Eugène
Chalais, comte de, 3:55b, 56a
Chalais Conspiracy, 3:56a
Chaliapin, Fedor, Gorky and, 8:419b–420a
Chamberlain, Houston Stewart, *Foundation of
    the Nineteenth Century*, Wagner and,
    6:1166b
Chamberlin, Vernon, on Blasco Ináñez's *The
    Cabin*, 8:370a
Chambers, Whittaker, Heinrich Mann and,
    8:541b
"Chambre bleue, La." *See* Mérimée, Prosper
*Chambre claire, La: Note sur la photographie.
    See* Barthes, Roland, *Camera Lucida:
    Reflections on Photography*
Chamisso, Adelbert von
  Andersen and, 6:867b, 877b
  Peter Schlemihl, 9:1020b
"Champ d'oliviers, Le." *See* Maupassant, Guy
    de, "The Olive Grove"
Champfleury, Jules, documentary novel,
    9:1398a
Champignol malgré lui (*Champignol in Spite
    of Himself*). *See* Feydeau, Georges
Champs magnétiques, Les. See Breton, André,
    and Soupault, Philippe
Chance
  in Arp, 10:1374b–1375a
  in Dürrenmatt's works, 13:3219a,
    3224b–3227a

in Frisch's works, 13:2913a-b
Machiavelli on, 2:605a
Mallarmé's view of, 7:1589b–1591a
Strindberg's view of, 7:1731a-b,
    1736b–1737a, 1752b
Chandelier, Le. See Musset, Alfred de
"Chandos Letter." *See* Hofmannsthal, Hugo
    von
Chandoux, Sieur de, 3:5a, 5b
Change
    Rimbaud's view of, 7:1786b–1789a
    see also Constancy and change, theme of;
        New, Rimbaud's view of
Change of Heart, A. See Butor, Michel
Changing of the Guard, The. *See* Montherlant,
    Henry de, *La relève du matin*
Channel Islands, Hugo's exile to, 6:705b–706b
Chanson
    Ady and, 9:861b
    Chrétien de Troyes and, 1:179a, 185b
    Colin and, 1:181a
Chanson d'Audigier, musical line of, 489b
"Chanson d'automne." *See* Verlaine, Paul
Chanson de geste, Wolfram and, 1:282b
Chanson de Guillaume, 1:109a-b
Chanson de Roland, **1:89a–106a**
    aoi in, 1:98b
    authorship of, 1:98a-b
    character of the hero, 1:60b
    Charlemagne's ineptitude in, 1:145a
    Chrétien's *Cligés* and, 1:193b–194b
    circumstances of composition, 1:105a–106a
    compared with *Beowulf*, 1:75b
    functions of, 1:101a–105a
    meaning of, 1:98b–101a
    versions of, 1:89a, 90a–91b
    Vigny's "The Horn" and, 5:457b
Chanson de Roland y el neotradicionalismo.
    See Menéndez Pidal, Ramón
"Chanson des ingénues." *See* Verlaine, Paul
"Chanson du mal-aimé, La." *See* Apollinaire,
    Guillaume
Chanson pour Don Juan, Une. See Butor,
    Michel
Chansons de geste, **1:89a–111b**
    chansons not in the cycles, 1:109b
    Charlemagne cycle, 1:107a
decline of, 1:140a
Doon de Mayence cycle (cycle of rebellious
    barons), 1:107a–108b
function of, 1:139a
Garin de Monglane cycle (William cycle),
    1:108b–109b
    Chanson de Roland and, 1:104b
jongleurs and, 1:139a, 139b
overview of, 1:89a–90a, 106a-b, 109b–110b
Poema de mio Cid and, 1:115b, 125a
stability of genre, 1:154a
subjects of, 1:139a
see also Chanson de Roland
"Chant d'ouvrier." *See* Buchez, Philippe
"Chant par celle qui fut là." *See* Perse,
    Saint-John, *Chant pour un équinoxe*
Chant pour un équinoxe. See Perse, Saint-John
Chantier. See Butor, Michel
Chants de Maldoror. See Lautréamont, Comte
    de
Chants du crépuscule, Les. See Hugo, Victor
Chanut, Pierre, 3:22a
Chaos, Nietzsche on, 9:944a
Chaos and Night. See Montherlant, Henry de
Chapeau de paille d'Italie. See Labiche,
    Eugène
Chapelain, Jean
    attacked by Boileau, 3:178b–179a
    La pucelle (The Maiden), 3:178b–179a
        Boileau and, 3:193b
Chaplin, Charlie
    Céline and, 11:1870a, 1872a-b, 1875b
    Ghelderode's *Pantagleize* and, 11:2129a,
        2134b
    Modern Times, 11:1872a-b
    Olesha and, 11:2245b, 2246b
    Svevo and, 8:71a-b
    The Gold Rush, 8:71a
    The Great Dictator, 8:71b
    The Kid, 9:1046b
Chapter the Last. See Hamsun, Knut, *Siste
    kapitel*
Char, René, Elytis and, 13:2965a
"Character in Distress, A." *See* Pirandello,
    Luigi, "La tragedia di un personaggio"
Character, national, literature and, Unamuno's
    view of, 8:288b–289a

"Character without author," in Pirandello,
    8:395b, 396a-b, 405b–406a, 412a
Characteristic Nature of the Aesthetic, The.
    See Lukács, György, *Die Eigenart des*
    Ästhetischen
Characterization
  in Balzac's works, 5:638a-b
  in Canetti's works, 12:2618a–2619b
  in Cela, 13:3113b–3114a
  in Eça's works, 7:1691a, 1697b–1698a,
    1699a–1700a, 1705a
  in Giraudoux's works, 9:1061b–1062a
  in Gogol's works, 6:994b
  in Gombrowicz's works, 12:2577b
  Hašek's use of character types,
    9:1099a–1100a, 1109a
  in Laxness' works, 12:2461b, 2466a, 2472a-b
  in Lermontov's works, 6:1211a–1212a
  in Malraux's works, 12:2528a
  in Pavese's works, 12:2767a–2768a
  in Queneau's works, 12:2526a-b, 2527a-b,
    2528a–2530a, 2530a, 2531a, 2531a-b
  in Ritsos' poems, 12:2830a
  in Sarraute's works, 12:2334b
  in Sartre's works, 12:2594a
  in Simenon's "Maigret" novels,
    12:2485a–2488b
  in Stendhal's works, 5:361b–362a
  in Strindberg's works, 7:1748a–1752b
  in Vittorini's *In Sicily*, 12:2746
  in Yourcenar's works, 12:2541a-b
Characters. See La Bruyère, Jean de,
    Caractères
Charakteristiken, Schlegel and, 5:180a-b, 186b
Charcot, Jean-Martin
  Freud and, 8:3a
  Strindberg and, 7:1753b
Chardin, Jean Baptiste Siméon, in Goncourts'
    L'Art du dix-huitième siècle, 7:1397a
Charités d'Alcippe et autres poèmes, Les. See
    Yourcenar, Marguerite
Charity, Bossuet's sermons on, 3:154a-b
Charity. *See* Pérez Galdós, Benito,
    Misericordia
Charlemagne
  Augustine's *City of God* and, 1:36b–37a

in Eyvind Johnson's *The Days of His Grace,*
    12:2379a
  legend of, 1:137a
"Charleroi." *See* Verlaine, Paul
"Charles XI's Vision." *See* Mérimée, Prosper,
    "Vision de Charles XI"
Charles V, Holy Roman Emperor
  Castiglione and, 2:649a
  Erasmus and, 2:583a
  Francis I and, 2:694b
Charles VII of France, king, in *The Maid of*
    Orleans, 5:46b
Charles IX of France, king, *Franciade* and,
    2:734b, 735a
Charles I of Spain, king, Hugo and, 6:695b
Charles of Anjou
  Aquinas and, 1:419a
  Robin et Marion and, 1:461a
Charles Baudelaire, A Lyric Poet in the Era of
    High Capitalism. See Benjamin, Walter,
    Charles Baudelaire, Ein Lyricker im
    Zeitalter des Hochkapitalismus
Charles Demailly. See Goncourt, Edmond
    Louis Antoine and Jules Alfred Huot de
Charles IX. See Chénier, Marie-Joseph
    (brother)
Charles of Valois, Dante and, 1:434a
Charles XII. See Strindberg, August
Charles XII, king of Sweden, Voltaire's history
    of, 4:372b, 382a-b
"Charogne, Une." *See* Baudelaire, Charles,
    "Carrion"
Charolais, count de, Sade as scapegoat for,
    4:617b
Charpentier, Julie von, Novalis and, 5:208a
Charrière, Isabelle Agnès Élizabeth de
  Constant and, 4:409a-b
  Lettres écrites de Lausanne (Letters Written
    from Lausanne), 4:409a
  Lettres neuchâteloises (Neuchâtel Letters),
    4:409a
Charron, Pierre
  De la sagesse (Of Wisdom), 2:785a-b
  Trois Veritez (Three Truths), 2:785a
Charte de la Résistance, La, 11:2081b
Charterhouse of Parma, The (La Chartreuse de
    Parme). See Stendhal

"Chase, The." *See* Calvino, Italo, *t zero*

Chastushka, 9:962a

"Chasy." *See* Zamyatin, Yevgeny Ivanovich

Chat, Le. See Simenon, Georges

Chat noir, Le, Verlaine's works in, 7:1638b

Chateaubriand et son group littéraire (Chateaubriand and His Literary Group). *See* Sainte-Beuve, Charles-Augustin

Chateaubriand, François René de, 3:318a, **5:113a–140a**

  Analyse raisonnée de l'histoire de France (Descriptive Analysis of the History of France), 5:132b

  as apologist for Christianity, 5:372b

  Atala, 5:117a–119b

    Balzac and, 5:651a

    and *Génie du christianisme*, 5:117a-b, 118b–119a

    manuscript of, 5:116a

    publication of, 5:113a, 117a

  Berlioz and, 6:782a, 793b–794a

  Butor and, 13:3304a–3305a

  Congrès de Vérone (Congress of Verona), 5:130a, 138a-b

  De Buonaparte et des Bourbons (*On Bonaparte and the Bourbons*), 5:113a, 127b–128b

  De la monarchie selon la charte (*Monarchy According to the Charter*), 5:113a, 128b–129a

  Essai historique, politique et moral sur les révolutions anciennes et modernes . . . (Historical, Political, and Moral Essay on Ancient and Modern Revolutions . . .), 5:116a-b, 5:122a

  Essai sur la littérature anglaise (On English Literature), 5:113b, 132a, 137a-b

  Études historiques (Historical Studies), 5:132b

  Génie du christianisme (*The Genius of Christianity*), 5:117a, 121b–123b

    and *Atala*, 5:117a-b, 118b–119a

    Chénier and, 4:692b, 716b–717a

    political career of Chateaubriand after, 5:123b

    publication of, 5:113a

  Vigny's "Eloa" and, 5:453a

  Hugo and, 6:693b

  Lermontov and, 6:1199a

  Les martyrs (*Martyrs*), 5:113a, 124b–125a

    Vigny's "Eloa" and, 5:453a

  Les Natchez, 5:115b–116a, 125a

  Lettre à M. de Fontanes sur la Campagne romaine (Letter . . . on the Roman Campagna), 5:123b–124a

  L'Itineraire de Paris à Jérusalem, 5:125b–127b

    publication of, 5:113a

    "terre classique" in, 5:124b

  Mémoires d'outre-tombe (Memoirs from Beyond the Grave), 5:129a–132a, 6:793b–794a

    childhood in, 5:114a

    development as writer in, 5:133b–134a

    importance of, 5:113b

    influence of, 5:139b

    motifs of, 5:134b–135a

    Napoleon's story in, 5:135a–136b

    Proust and, 5:140a

    structure of, 5:113b, 133a-b

  Moïse, 5:132b

  Oeuvres complètes, 5:130b

    political writings in, 5:129a

    publication of, 5:113b, 132b

    youth poems in, 5:114a-b

  on Pascal, 3:148a

  polemical writings, 5:113a-b, 127b–129a

  Réflexions politiques sur quelques écrits du jour et sur les intérêts de tous les français (Political Reflections Concerning Several Writings of the Day and the Interests of All the French), 5:129a

  René, 5:119b–121b, 6:1015a

    and *Génie du christianisme*, 5:117a

    publication of, 5:113a

    youth poems in, 5:114a-b

  Sainte-Beuve on, 7:1411a

  Sand and, 6:817b

  Vie de Rancé (Life of Rancé), 5:113b, 132a, 138b–139b

  Vigny and, 5:450b, 453a

Chateaubriand, François René de (*cont.*)
  Voyage en Amérique (*Travels in America*),
    5:115a
Châtelet, Madame du, Voltaire and,
    4:373a–374a, 375a
Châtillon, duchesse de, 3:61b
Châtiments. See Hugo, Victor
Chatte, La. See Colette
Chatterton. See Vigny, Alfred Victor de
Chatterton, Thomas, in Vigny's works,
    5:467b–468b, 471a–472b
Chaucer, Geoffrey
  Arthurian legend and, 1:153b
  Canterbury Tales
    French fabliaux's influence on, 2:933b
    Juvenal and, 1:350a
    "Monk's Tale," 1:459b
    Sercambi's novellas compared to, 2:935b
  Romance of the Rose and, 1:333b–334b
  "The Knight's Tale," sources for, 2:514a
  "The Merchant's Tale," Wieland and, 4:605b
  Troilus and Criseyde, Petrarchan influence,
    2:504a
Chavalier de la Charrette, Le. See Chrétien de
    Troyes, *Lancelot*
Chavannes, Pierre Puvis de, Jiménez and,
    9:994a
Chayka. See Chekhov, Anton, *The Seagull*
"Che fece . . . il gran rifiuto." *See* Cavafy,
    Constantine
Cheat, The. See Čapek, Karel, *Život a dílo
    skladatele Foltýna*
Cheat, The. *See* Goldoni, Carlo, *Il frappatore*;
    Simon, Claude, *Le tricheur*
Cheerless God, The. *See* Ady, Endre, "Isten a
    vigasztalan"
Cheever, John, 13:3039a
"Chef de section." *See* Apollinaire, Guillaume
Chef d'oeuvre inconnu, Le. See Balzac, Honoré
    de
Cheka, in Babel's novels, 11:1887a
Chekhonte, Antosha. *See* Chekhov, Anton
Chekhov, Anton, **7:1855a–1881b**
  "Arkhierey" ("The Bishop"), 7:1874b–1875a
  "Babe tsarstvo" ("A Woman's Kingdom"),
    7:1868a
  "Baby" ("Peasant Wives"), 7:1864a-b

"Barynya" ("The Lady of the Manor"),
    7:1860a
Bely and, 9:927b
"Chelovek v futlyare" ("The Man in a
    Shell"), 7:1872a-b
"Chorny monakh" ("The Black Monk"),
    7:1867a-b
"Dama s sobachkoy" ("The Lady with a
    Dog"), 7:1874a-b
"Dom s mezoninom" ("The House with a
    Mezzanine"), 7:1868b
"Drama na okhote" ("The Shooting Party"),
    7:1859b–1860a
"Duel" ("The Duel"), 7:1865b–1866a, 1867a
"Dushechka" ("The Darling"),
    7:1873a–1874a, 1875a
"Eger" ("The Huntsman"), 7:1858b, 1860b
"Ekzamen na chin" ("Examination for
    Advancement"), 7:1859a-b
Ginzburg and, 13:3161a
Gorky and, 8:418a, 419b, 422a, 434b–435a
  Barbarians, 8:436b
  in the Crimea, 8:442b, 443a
"Gusev," 7:1865b
Ibsen and, 7:1435b, 1754a
"Ionich," 7:1873a
Ivanov, 7:1876a-b
"Khoroshie lyudi" ("Good People"), 7:1862a
"Knyaginya" ("The Princess"), 7:1863a
"Kryzhovnik" ("Gooseberries"), 7:1871b,
    1872a, 1872b
Lermontov and, 6:1224a
Mann on, 9:737b
Maupassant and, 7:1770b
"Moya zhizn" ("My Life"), 7:1868b
"Mstitel" ("The Avenger"), 7:1859a
"Muzhiki" ("The Peasants"), 7:1860a,
    1868b–1869a
in *Na rubezhe dvukh stoletii*, 9:911b
"Nevesta" ("The Betrothed"), 7:1874b–1875b
"O lyubvi" ("About Love"), 7:1872a,
    1872b–1873a
"Orden" ("The Decoration"), 7:1858b–1859a
Ostrov Sakhalin (*The Island: A Journey to
    Sakhalin*), 7:1856b
"Palata No. 6" ("Ward No. 6"), 7:1856b,
    1863a, 1866a–1867a

"Poprygunya" ("The Grasshopper"),
    7:1863a-b
"Pripadok" ("The Nervous Breakdown"),
    7:1861b–1862a
Queer People and, 8:437a
Skazki Mel'pomene (*Tales of Melpomene*),
    7:1856a
"Skripka Rotshilda" ("Rothschild's Fiddle"),
    7:1869b–1870b, 1871a
"Skuchnaya istoriya" ("A Dreary Story"),
    7:1865b
"Sluchay iz praktiki" ("A Doctor's Visit"),
    7:1868a-b
"Spat khochetsya" ("Sleepy"), 7:1860a-b
"Step" ("The Steppe"), 7:1856b,
    1860b–1861b, 1865b–1866a, 1870a
Strindberg and, 7:1731b, 1742a, 1749a
"Svedskaya spichka" ("The Swedish
    Match"), 7:1859b–1860a
The Cherry Orchard (*Vishnevy sad*),
    7:1877b–1879a, 9:1064b
  and Anouilh's *Cher Antoine*, 13:2843a
  "The Grasshopper" and, 7:1863b
The Seagull (*Chayka*), 7:1876a, 1876b,
    1877a, 1879a
  Dachniki and, 8:436a
The Three Sisters (*Tri sestry*), 7:1877a-b,
    1878b–1879b
  "In the Ravine" and, 7:1869b
"Tri goda" ("Three Years"), 7:1868b, 1869a
"Tsvety zapozdalye" ("Late-Blooming
    Flowers"), 7:1860a
"Uchitel slovesnosti" ("The Teacher of
    Literature"), 7:1871a-b
Uncle Vanya (*Dyadya Vanya*),
    7:1876b–1877a, 1879a, 9:1064b
  "In the Ravine" and, 7:1869b
  "The Grasshopper" and, 7:1863b
"V ovrage" ("In the Ravine"), 7:1869a-b
"V ssylke" ("In Exile"), 7:1864b
"Vory" ("Thieves"), 7:1864a
"Vragi" ("Enemies"), 7:1862a
"Zhena" ("The Wife"), 7:1864b
Chekhov, Pavel Egorovich, 7:1855b
"Chelkash." *See* Gorky, Maxim
"Chelovecheski material." *See* Olesha, Yuri
Chelovek. See Mayakovsky, Vladimir

"Chelovek v futlyare." *See* Chekhov, Anton
Chemin des écoliers, Le. See Aymé, Marcel,
    The Transient Hour
Chemins de la liberté, Les. See Sartre,
    Jean-Paul
Chemins de la mer, Les. See Mauriac,
    François, *The Unknown Sea*
Chemistry, Strindberg's interest in, 7:1738a
Chêne et chien. See Queneau, Raymond
"Chêne et le roseau, Le." *See* La Fontaine,
    Jean de, *Fables*
Chénier, André, **4:691a–718b**
  "A Warning to the People of France About
      Their True Enemies," 4:701b–702a, 703a
  "Apology," 4:698a
  Camille poems of, 4:698b
  *Essai sur les causes et les effets de la
      perfection et de la décadence des lettres
      et des arts* (Essay on the Causes and
      Effects of Perfection and Decadence in
      Arts and Letters), 4:708b–710a
    equality of action and writing in, 4:713b
    importance to Chénier's aesthetics, 4:705b
  "Hymn to Justice," 4:699b–700a
  Iambes, 4:714a–716b
    "Hymne aux Suisses de Châteauvieux"
        ("Hymn on the Triumphal Entry of the
        Swiss of Châteauvieux"), 4:704a-b
    modern value of, 4:694a
  "Invention," 4:706a–707b
    "Essay" and, 4:705b, 708b–709a
  "La malade," 4:698a
  "Les autels de la peur" ("The Altars of
      Fear"), 4:703a
  "Liberty," 4:699b
  Lycoris poems of, 4:696b–697b
  "Ode to Charlotte Corday," 4:713a-b
  "Ode to Versilles," 4:711a–712a
  "On the Causes of the Disorders Troubling
      France and Stopping the Establishment
      of Liberty," 4:703b–704a
  "Réflexions sur l'esprit de parti"
      ("Reflections on the Spirit of the Party"),
      4:702b–703a
  "The Blind Man" ("L'Aveugle"), 4:707b–708a
    incorporation into the "Essay," 4:705b

Chénier, André (*cont.*)
  "The Epistle on My Work" (*Épitre sur mes ouvrages*), 4:708a-b
    importance to Chénier's aesthetics, 4:705b
  "The Republic of Letters" (*La république des lettres*), 4:699a, 710a-b
    importance to Chénier's aesthetics, 4:705b
    satire in, 4:708a
  "The Tennis Court," 4:702a-b
  "The Young Captive" ("La jeune captive"), 4:692a-b, 714a
    posthumous publication of, 4:716b
  "The Young Tarentine," posthumous publication of, 4:716b
  Vigny and, 5:450b
    in *Stello*, 5:467b–468a, 468b–469a
Chénier, Elizabeth (mother), 4:694b, 695a, 696a
  essays of, 4:696a
  salon of, 4:694b, 695a, 696a
Chénier, Louis (father), 4:694a–695b
Chénier, Marie-Joseph (brother)
  Charles IX, 4:700b
  defense of Jacobins by, 4:704b
  early plays of, 4:699a
  on Goldoni, 4:433a-b
  split with André, 4:703b
Cher Antoine. See Anouilh, Jean, *Dear Antoine*
Cherdyn', Mandelshtam's exile to, 10:1646a
"Cherez dvenadtsat' let." *See* Blok, Alexander
Chéri. See Colette
Chérie. See Goncourt, Edmond Louis Antoine de
Cherkesy. See Lermontov, Mikhail Yurievich
Cherniak, Ia. *See* Benni, Ia.
Chernihiv. See Tychyna, Pavlo
Chernyshevsky, Nikolay
  Chto delat'? (*What Is to Be Done?*), family in, 11:2240a
  Dostoevsky and, 7:1357a
  on Tolstoy, 7:1479b
  Turgenev and, 6:1281a, 1287b
Cherry Orchard, The. See Chekhov, Anton
"Cherry Stone, The." *See* Olesha, Yuri
"Chert." *See* Tsvetaeva, Marina
"Chertik." *See* Khlebnikov, Velimir

Chertkov, Vladimir, Tolstoy's diaries and, 7:1477a
Cherubini, Luigi, Berlioz and, 6:775a
Chesterton, G. K.
  Böll and, 13:3167a
  Claudel and, 8:487a
  The Man Who Was Thursday, Čapek and, 10:1570a
"Chestnut, The." *See* Pascoli, Giovanni, "Castanea"
Chetki. See Akhmatova, Anna
Chetvertaia proza. See Mandelshtam, Osip, *Fourth Prose*
Cheval blanc, Le. See Triolet, Elsa
Chevalerie Vivien, La, 1:109a
Chevalier, Adèle, Huysmans and, 7:1721b
Chevalier au Lion, Le. See Chrétien de Troyes, *Yvain*
Chevalier de Maison-Rouge, Le. See Dumas père, Alexandre
Chevalier de Pas, 10:1481a, 1482b, 1488a
Chevalier d'Harmental, Le. See Dumas père, Alexandre
"Chevalier double, Le." *See* Gautier, Théophile
Chevalier du Papegau, Le, 1:154a
Chevalier à l'épée, Le
  Chrétien de Troyes and, 1:149b, 157a, 185b
  Gawain in, 1:157a
Chevaliers de la Table Ronde, 3:74a
Chevaliers de la table ronde, Les. See Cocteau, Jean, *The Knights of the Round Table*
Chevreuse, duchesse de. *See* Rohan-Montbazon, Marie de
"Chi è questa che vèn, ch'ogn'om la mira?" *See* Cavalcanti, Guido
"Chi vuol veder quantunque po Natura." *See* Petrarch, *Canzoniere*
"Chiare fresche et dolci acque." *See* Petrarch, *Canzoniere*
Chiarelli, Luigi, *La maschera e il volto* (The Mask and the Face), 8:393b
Chiari, Pietro, Goldoni and, 4:428b–430a
Chiaromonte, Nicola
  on Silone, 12:2275a
  Tempo presente and, 12:2302a
Chicago, in Mayakovsky's poetry, 11:1846a-b

Chichikov's Adventures; or, Dead Souls. See Gogol, Nikolay Vasilievich, *Dead Souls*

Chicot the Jester. See Dumas père, Alexandre, *La dame de Monsoreau*

Chief, The. See Mann, Heinrich, *Das Kaiserreich* (The Era of the Kaiser), *Der Kopf*

Chieftaincies, Icelandic, 1:377b–378a

Chien à la mandoline, Le. See Queneau, Raymond

Chiendent, Le. See Queneau, Raymond

"Child of Europe." *See* Milosz, Czeslaw

Child of Nature. *See* Laxness, Halldór, *Barn náttúrunnar*

Child of Pleasure, The. See D'Annunzio, Gabriele

Child Wife, The. See Ibsen, Henrik, *A Doll's House*

Child-murder dramas, Hauptmann's *Rose Bernd* and, 8:159b–160b

Childhood
    Anouilh's treatment of, 13:2861b–2863a
    in Elytis' works
      Sun the First, 13:2962a-b, 2974a-b
      "The Light Tree," 13:2974a-b
    Goncharov's view of, 6:1081a-b
    in Ionesco's works, 13:3018b
    in poetry of Pascoli, 7:1833b, 1834a-b, 1835a, 1837a
    in prose of Chekhov, 7:1860a-b
    Sartre's view of, 12:2608b–2609a
    in works of Olesha, 11:2249a, 2250a

Childhood. See Babel, Isaac, *Detstvo*

Childhood. See Gorky, Maxim; Sarraute, Nathalie, *Enfance*; Tolstoy, Leo

"Childhood." *See* Rimbaud, Arthur, "Enfance"

Childhood in Agram 1902–1903. *See* Krleža, Miroslav, *Djetinjstvo u Agramu godine 1902–3*

Childhood of Christ, The. See Berlioz, Hector, *L'Enfance du Christ*

Childhood of Luvers, The. See Pasternak, Boris

"Childhood of Lyuvers, The." *See* Pasternak, Boris, *Rasskazy* (Stories), "Zhenia's Childhood"

Childhood memoirs, Italian fashion for, D'Annunzio and, 8:201a

Children
    Augustine on, 1:26a-b, 45a
    language of, Valéry on, 8:575a
    Mauriac and, 10:1311b–1312a
    in Montherlant's novels, 11:1932a-b
    in religion, Aquinas on, 1:417b
    socialization of, Augustine on, 1:26b

Children of the Age. See Hamsun, Knut, *Børn av tiden*

Children of Man. *See* Vesaas, Tarjei, *Manneskebonn*

Children of the Slime. *See* Queneau, Raymond, *Les enfants du limon*

Children of the Sun. See Gorky, Maxim, *Deti solntsa*

Chimères, Les (Chimeras). *See* Nerval, Gérard de

China, Perse in, 10:1435a–1436b

"Chinaman: From the Book *Petersburg 1918*, The." *See* Babel, Isaac, "Khodia: Iz knigi *Petersburg 1918*"

Chinese poetry, translated by Claudel, 8:489a

Chinese Wall, The. See Frisch, Max

Chinesische Mauer, Die. See Frisch, Max, *The Chinese Wall*

"Chiodo, Il." *See* Pirandello, Luigi

Chioma di Berenice, La. See Foscolo, Ugo

Chirico, Giorgio de, 9:896b

Chivalry
    Ariosto and, 2:624b–643b
    Cervantes and, 2:828b, 835a
    Chrétien de Troyes and
      Conte du Graal, 1:147a-b, 207b
      Yvain, 1:202b–203a
    Gottfried and, 1:237a–260b
    in Grass's works, 13:3372a–3373b
    Greek romances and, 2:828b
    in Simon's fiction, 13:3028b, 3029a-b
    Staël's *De l'Allemagne* on, 5:107b
    Walther and, 1:289b
    Wolfram on, 1:268a–281a
      responsibilities of the knight, 1:280a-b, 284b–285a

Choderlos de Laclos. *See* Laclos, Pierre-Ambroise-François Choderlos de

Choeur des ombres. *See* Berlioz, Hector

Choice, Kundera and, 13:3392b, 3408b

Choice, moral
in Gombrowicz's works, 12:2572a–2573a
Sartre and, 12:2589a–2591a, 2594b–2595b

Choice of Poetry. *See* Verlaine, Paul, *Choix de poésies*

Choices of the Elite. *See* Giraudoux, Jean, *Choix des élues*

Choix de poésies. *See* Verlaine, Paul

Choix des élues. *See* Giraudoux, Jean

Chopin, Frédéric
Hesse and, 9:835b, 836a
Sand and, 6:827b–829a

"Chorny monakh." *See* Chekhov, Anton

Chorus of Shades. *See* Berlioz, Hector, *Choeur des ombres*

Chorus, the, Verga's use of, 7:1555a, 1558b, 1562b

Choses et gens de chez nous. *See* Ghelderode, Michel de

Chouans, Les. *See* Balzac, Honoré de

Chrétien de Troyes, **1:185a–208a**, 242b
Arthurian legend and, 1:140b, 144b–148a
chansons and, 1:179a, 185b
characterization in works of, 1:145b–146a
Cligés, 1:192a–195b
Angrés affair in, 1:193a–194a
Arthurian legend and, 1:144b, 145b
Chanson de Roland and, 1:193b–194b
courtly love in, 1:146b, 193a, 194b–195a
dating of, 1:185b
Gawain in, 1:155b
humor in, 1:150a
sources of, 1:140a, 192a-b
Tristan story and, 1:192b
Conte du Graal, 203b–207a
Arthurian legend and, 1:144b, 145a
chivalry in, 1:147a-b, 207b
continuations of, 1:149a
controversy concerning, 1:203b
courtly love in, 1:146b–147a, 204a-b
dating of, 1:185b
Fair Unknown and, 1:149b
"Gauvain" episode in, 1:203b, 206b–207b
Gawain in, 1:156a-b, 157a-b
grail legend and, 1:205b–206b
humor in, 1:150a
importance of, 1:203b
"Perceval" episode in, 1:203b, 204a–206b
sources of, 1:143b, 203b
supernatural in, 1:145a
Swedish translations of, 1:153a
Tristan story and, 1:207b–208a
courtoisie and, 1:147a-b, 154b
Erec et Enide, 1:188a–192a
courtly love in, 1:189b–190b
dating of, 1:185b
humor in, 1:150a
irony in, 1:191a
Joie de la cort episode in, 1:191b–192a
love in, 1:146a-b
sources of, 1:143b, 188b–189a
supernatural in, 1:145a
Swedish translations of, 1:153a
La Mule sans frein and, 1:149b, 157a
Lancelot, 1:195b–199a
ambiguity in, 1:196a-b, 198b–199a
analogy to Christian dramas, 1:198a
anticlimax in, 1:197a-b
Arthurian legend and, 1:198b
bathos in, 1:197b
courtly love in, 1:146b, 199a
dating of, 1:185b
Gawain in, 1:155b–156a, 158a
humor in, 1:150a, 197b–198a
incongruity in, 1:196b–197a
irony in, 1:197b
sexual innuendo in, 1:198a-b, 199a
sources of, 1:195b
supernatural in, 1:145a
Le Chevalier à l'épée and, 1:149b, 157a
Matter of Britain and, 1:141a–142a, 148b
paradise and, 1:324b–325a
Philomena, 1:185b–187b
art of Chrétien and, 1:187b–188a
dating of, 1:185b
descriptive passages in, 1:186b
emotions in, 1:187b–188a
Ovid and, 1:185b–186a
rape scene in, 1:186b–187b
quest theme and, 1:150a
Sir Gawain and the Green Knight and, 1:149b

Swedish translations of works of, 1:153a
Tristan story and, 1:148b
troubadour poetry and, 1:179a, 185b
Welsh legends and, 1:143b
Wolfram and, 1:268a–272a
Yvain, 1:199a–203b
  allegory in, 1:202a-b
  change in, from Welsh account, 1:201b
  chivalry in, 1:202b–203a
  courtly love in, 1:200a–201a, 203a
  dating of, 1:185b
  Gawain in, 1:156a
  interpretations of, 1:199a, 199b–200a, 203a-b
  sources of, 1:143b, 199a
  supernatural in, 1:145a
  Swedish translations of, 1:153a
"Chrevo." *See* Zamyatin, Yevgeny Ivanovich
Christ, Bergson's view of, 8:62b–63a
Christ. *See* Jesus Christ
"Christ." *See* Turgenev, Ivan
"Christ aux oliviers, Le." *See* Nerval, Gérard de
Christ figures, 8:296b
  by Hauptmann
    Der neue Christophorus, 8:161b, 162b, 163b, 167a, 169a, 170a–171a, 172a
    Emanuel Quint, 8:162b–163b
    Loth, 8:150a
  Don Quixote as, 8:296b
  Dostoevsky on, 13:3033a
  Pérez Galdós' *Nazarín*, 7:1614a-b, 1617a
  Strindberg's treatment of, 7:1739a, 1745b–1746a
Christ and the Priests. *See* Hašek, Jaroslav, "Khristos i popy"
Christ Recrucified. See Kazantzakis, Nikos, *O Hristós ksanastavronetai*
Christ Stopped at Eboli. See Levi, Carlo, *Cristo si e fermato a Eboli*
Christ in the Tomb. See Rubens, Peter Paul
Christ und Bürger heute und morgen (German periodical), Böll's "Brief an einen jungen Katholiken," 13:3172a
Christ of Velázquez, The. See Unamuno, Miguel de, *El Cristo de Velázquez*

Christendom or Europe (*Christenheit oder Europa, Die*). *See* Novalis
Christentum der Vernunft, Das. See Lessing, Gotthold Ephraim
Christian Discourses. See Kierkegaard, Søren
Christian poetry
  pagan rhetoric and, 1:19a
  of Prudentius, 1:2a-b, 13b–14a, 14b–15b
Christianity
  in Alexandria
    Cavafy's poetry and, 8:211a, 215b
    displacement of paganism by, 8:216b–217a
  in *Beowulf*, 1:72b–73a, 83b
  in Butor's fiction, 13:3293a
  Chateaubriand and
    in *Atala*, 5:117a-b
    in *Essai historique, politique et moral sur les révolutions*, 5:116b–117a
    in *Génie du christianisme*, 5:117a, 121b, 123a-b
  chivalry and, in Wolfram, 1:283a–285b
  as civilizing force, in Staël's works, 5:98a, 107b
  Dostoevsky and, 7:1354b–1355a, 1359b, 1368a–1369a
  Germanic poetry and, 1:54b–55a
  in Ghelderode's *Chronicles of Hell*, 11:2121b
  in Gorky's works
    Mother, 8:433b–434a
    The Confession, 8:434a-b
  Gottfried and, 1:251b
  hostility to, in Zamyatin's *We*, 10:1189b
  Huysmans and, 7:1719b
  in Iceland, 1:379a
  and Lagerkvist, 10:1679b, 1692a, 1699b
  Leconte de Lisle's hostility to, 6:1256b–1258a
  Moberg on, 11:2221a, 2225a
  moral virtues, Vesaas and, 11:2039a
  Neoplatonism and, Augustine and, 1:29a
  Nerval's view of, 6:958a–959a, 961a
  Nietzsche and, 7:1645a-b, 1648a-b, 1672b–1673b
  Novalis and, 5:219a–221a, 221b, 222b–223a

Christianity (*cont.*)

Rimbaud's view of, 7:1791a–1792b, 1818b–1819b

satire and, 1:337b–338a, 338b, 339a, 340a, 356a

Schiller's criticism of in *The Gods of Greece*, 5:39b

Schlegel and, 5:195b

Schopenhauer and, 5:398b, 7:1890a

in Silone's fiction, 12:2302a-b

Weil and, 12:2790a, 2792a, 2792b–2793b, 2800a, 2802a–2802b

see also Art, Christian; Conversion; Hell, Christian; Mythology, Christian; Religion; Roman Catholic Church; Russian Orthodox Church

Christianity at Glacier. See Laxness, Halldór, *Kristnihald undir Jökli*

Christianity of Reason, The. See Lessing, Gotthold Ephraim, *Das Christentum der Vernunft*

Christina of Sweden, queen

Descartes and, 3:22a

in Dumas's works, 6:721a

Strindberg's treatment of, 7:1739a, 1745b, 1750b

Christine. See Dumas père, Alexandre

Christmas Night 1914. *See* Claudel, Paul, *La nuit de Noël de 1914*

Christmas Night. *See* Pascoli, Giovanni, "La notte di Natale"

Christmas Not Just Once a Year. *See* Böll, Heinrich, "Nicht nur zur Weihnachtszeit"

Christmas plays, medieval, 1:454a, 455a, 456b

Christopher Columbus. *See* Krleža, Miroslav, *Kristofor Kolumbo*

Christos versus Arizona (Christ Versus Arizona). *See* Cela, Camilo José

Chronicle. See Villani, Giovanni

Chronicle of a Decade, The. *See* Elytis, Odysseus, "To chronico mias dekaetias"

Chronicle of the Kings of England. See William of Malmesbury

Chronicle of the Reign of Charles IX. See Mérimée, Prosper

Chronicles of Hell. See Ghelderode, Michel de, *Fastes d'enfer*

"Chronico mias dekaetias, To." *See* Elytis, Odysseus

Chronicon mundi. See Lucas, bishop of Tuy

Chronique. See Perse, Saint-John

Chronique du règne de Charles IX. See Mérimée, Prosper, *Chronicle of the Reign of Charles IX*

Chroniques d'art. See Apollinaire, Guillaume

"Chrysalis." *See* Montale, Eugenio, *Cuttlefish Bones*

Chrysothemis. *See* Ritsos, Yannis, *Hrysothemis*

"Chto budet c chekhoslovatskoy burzhuaznoy respublikoy." *See* Hašek, Jaroslav

Chto delat'? See Chernyshevski, Nikolay

Chudaki. See Gorky, Maxim

Church architecture, Elytis' *To Axion Esti* and, 13:2967b

Church fathers

Aquinas' *Catena aurea* and, 1:415b

Greek, Claudel and, 8:476a

on Old Testament interpretation, 1:3b–4a

Prudentius and, 1:20a

Church on the Hill, The. *See* Gunnarsson, Gunnar, *Kirken paa Bjerget*

Church Homilies. See Luther, Martin, *Kirchenpostillen*

Church and Monastic Life: Three Essays On the Norwegian Middle Ages. *See* Undset, Sigrid, *Kirke ag klosterliv: Tre essays fra norsk middelalder*

Church and state, in drama of Claudel, 8:471b

Church, The. *See* Céline, Louis-Ferdinand, *L'Église*

Churchill, Randolph (son of Winston), Akhmatova's persecution and, 10:1535b

Churchill, Winston

in Ekelöf's works, 12:2650a

Heinrich Mann and, 8:542a

"Churchyard Phantasy." *See* Södergran, Edith, "Kyrkogårdsfantasi"

Chute, La. See Camus, Albert, *The Fall*

Chuttia iedynnoi rodyny. See Tychyna, Pavlo

Chwistek, Leon, Witkiewicz and, 10:1209a-b, 1212a

Ciascuno a suo modo. See Pirandello, Luigi,
    Each in His Own Way
"Cicada and the Ant, The." *See* La Fontaine,
    Jean de, *Fables*, "Le cigale et la fourmi"
Cicero, Marcus Tullius
    Augustine and, 1:27b–28a, 38a-b, 42a, 43a-b
    Dante and, 1:432a
    De oratore (*On Oratory*), anecdotes in,
        2:930a
    German translation of, 4:610a
    as hero of Chénier's "Essay," 4:709b
    Hortensius, Augustine and, 1:28b
    letters, Petrarch's transcription of, 2:478b,
        488b
    Petrarch on, 2:488a
Cicerone. See Burckhardt, Jacob
Ciceronianus (*The Ciceronian*). *See* Erasmus
Cid, Le. See Corneille, Pierre
Cid, The, **1:113a–136b**
    in ballads, 1:131b–134a
    in chronicles, 1:114a-b, 130b–131b
    as historical person, 1:113a, 120b–121b
    Mocedades de Rodrigo, 1:129a–130b
    see also Poema de mio Cid
Cidade e as serras, A. See Eça de Queiroz,
    José Maria, *The City and the Mountains*
"Ciel est, par-dessus le toit, Le." *See* Verlaine,
    Paul
Ciel et l'enfer, Le. See Mérimée, Prosper,
    Heaven and Hell
"Cielo e terra." *See* Montale, Eugenio, *Satura*
"Ciencia y la religión como problemas
    políticos, La." *See* Ortega y Gasset, José
"Cigale et la fourmi, Le." *See* La Fontaine,
    Jean de, *Fables*
Cigarrales de Toledo. See Tirso de Molina
"Cikáni o 'hodech'." *See* Hašek, Jaroslav
"Cinci." *See* Pirandello, Luigi
Cinema. *See* Cocteau, Jean; Film
Cinna. See Corneille, Pierre
Cino da Pistoia
    Boccaccio and, 2:511a
    Dante and, 1:432a, 441b
    Petrarch's *Canzoniere*, quotations in, 2:493b
Cinq grandes odes. See Claudel, Paul
Cinq nô modernes. See Yourcenar, Marguerite

Cinq-Mars ou une conjuration sous Louis XIII
    (*Cinq-Mars; or, A Conspiracy Under
    Louis XIII*). *See* Vigny, Alfred Victor de
Cinque maggio, Il. See Manzoni, Alessandro
Cinquecento, Tasso and, 2:794b
Cinquième livre des odes. See Ronsard, Pierre
    de
Cinthio. *See* Giraldi, Giambattista
Cintura, La. See Moravia, Alberto
Cinzio. *See* Giraldi, Giambattista
*Ciò che è vivo e ciò che è morto nella filosofia
    di Hegel. See* Croce, Benedetto
Ciociara, La. See Moravia, Alberto, *Two
    Women*
Circassians, The. See Lermontov, Mikhail
    Yurievich, *Cherkesy*
Circe (mythological figure), in Camoëns' "Um
    mover d'olhos brando e piadoso,"
    2:751b, 752a
Circle et carré (journal), Arp and, 10:1372a
Circulatory systems, in Montesquieu's thought,
    349b–352b
Circumlocutions, in Wolfram, 1:265b–266a
Circus
    in Olesha's works, 11:2241b–2242a, 2250a,
        2252a-b
    symbolism of, in Laforgue's poetry, 7:1897a,
        1903b
    in Wedekind's plays, 8:234a, 240b–241a,
        245b, 247a–249a
    see also Clowns
Circus performers, in Olesha's *The Three Fat
    Men*, 11:2248a
Circus Thoughts. *See* Wedekind, Frank,
    Zirkusgedanken
Cirlot, Juan Eduardo, mysticism and, 9:1009a
Cistern, The. See Seferis, George, *I sterna*
Citadelle. See Saint-Exupéry, Antoine de
Cities of the Plain. See Proust, Marcel,
    Remembrance of Things Past (*À la
    recherche du temps perdu*
Citizen and His Voice, The. See Grass, Günter
Citizen Iscariote Reclús. *See* Cela, Camilo
    José, *Ciudadano Iscariote Reclús, El*
"Città del silenzio, La." *See* D'Annunzio,
    Gabriele
Città e la casa, La. See Ginzburg, Natalia

Cittá invisibili, Le. See Calvino, Italo,
 Invisible Cities
Cittá morta, La. See D'Annunzio, Gabriele
City
 Hamsun's use of, 8:26a, 34b, 39b
 vs. country
  in Ginzburg's works, 13:3135b,
   3139a–3141a
  in Pavese's works, 12:2778a
"City and a Balcony, A." *See* Azorín, "Una
 ciudad y un balcón"
City in Darkness. *See* Johnson, Eyvind, *Stad i*
 mörker
City of the Discreet, The. See Baroja, Pío, *La*
 feria de los discretos
City of Fog, The. *See* Baroja, Pío, *La ciudad de*
 la niebla
City of God, The. See Augustine, Saint
City and the House, The. See Ginzburg,
 Natalia, *La città e la casa*
City in Light. *See* Johnson, Eyvind, *Stad i ljus*
City of Lucca, The. See Heine, Heinrich, *Die*
 Stadt Lucca
"City of Man, The: A Declaration on World
 Democracy," Broch and, 10:1403a
City and the Mountains, The. See Eça de
 Queiroz, José Maria
"City of Silence, The." *See* D'Annunzio,
 Gabriele, "La città del silenzio"
"City That Never Sleeps, The." *See* García
 Lorca, Federico, "Ciudad sin sueño"
"City, The." *See* Blok, Alexander, "Gorod";
 Cavafy, Constantine, "I polis"
City, The. See Claudel, Paul
City Whose Prince Is a Child, The. *See*
 Montherlant, Henry de, *La ville dont le*
 prince est un enfant
"City Without a Name." *See* Milosz, Czeslaw,
 "Miasto bez imienia"
Ciudad de la niebla, La. See Baroja, Pío
"Ciudad sin sueño." *See* García Lorca,
 Federico
"Ciudad y un balcón, Una." *See* Azorín
Ciudadano Iscariote Reclús, El. See Cela,
 Camilo José
Civic poetry, Russian, Blok, 9:972b–976b

Civilian Shrapnel, A. *See* Mayakovsky,
 Vladimir, "Shtatskaya shrapnel"
"Civilización y cultura." *See* Unamuno, Miguel
 de
Civilization
 Maupassant's view of, 7:1775a-b
 Michelet's conception of, 5:576b–577a
 Prudentius on, 1:17b
 Western
  "Futurist Manifesto" on, 9:811a-b
  Rilke on, 9:776a-b, 778b–779a, 782a, 782b
Civilization and Its Discontents. See Freud,
 Sigmund
Civilization of the Renaissance in Italy, The.
 See Burckhardt, Jacob
"Clair de lune." *See* Apollinaire, Guillaume;
 Verlaine, Paul
Clair de terre. See Breton, André
Clair-obscur. See Cocteau, Jean
Clairon, Madame, 5:89b
Clan des Ostandais, Le. See Simenon, Georges
Clan theme, in Simenon's works,
 12:2489a–2490a
Clandestine Steak, The. *See* Aymé, Marcel, *Le*
 boeuf clandestin
Clarín
 Azorín and, 9:640a, 644b, 645a-b
 on Valle-Inclán, 8:333b
Clarinets of the Sun. *See* Tychyna, Pavel,
 Soniachni klarnety
Clarissa Harlowe. See Richardson, Samuel
Clarity, Camus and, 13:3076b
Clark, Robert T., Jr.
 on cultural prejudice during the
  Enlightenment, 4:640a
 on Herder
  contribution to folklore movement, 4:645a
  egalitarianism, 4:651a
  humane nationalism, 4:641a
  withheld sections of his works, 4:652b
Clarté, Aragon and, 11:2066b, 2067b, 2068a-b
Clásicos y modernos. See Azorín
Class of 1922, The. *See* Böll, Heinrich,
 "Jahrgang 1922"
Class, social
 in Arras, 1:459a
 in Augier's plays, 7:1918a

Büchner on rights of lower classes,
6:1189b–1192a
conflict between, in Michelet's conception,
5:595b, 596a
in Goethe's *Wilhelm Meister*, 5:15b
hereditary privilege, in La Bruyère's
Caractères, 3:245b–247a
inequality, Canetti and, 12:2629b–2630a
Lope de Vega and, 2:852a–853b
medieval satire on, 1:348a, 352b–356a
Michelet on, 5:575a-b, 592b–593a
mobility in, Andersen and, 6:876b
in Montherlant's novels, 11:1925b
in Schiller's works
Intrigue and Love, 5:34a-b
William Tell, 5:49b
Spanish, in Blasco Ibáñez' fiction,
8:342b–344b, 357b, 366a, 367a-b
upper class in Maupassant's works,
7:1773b, 1781b–1782a
see also Social injustice
Class structure
French
Goncourts' treatment of, 7:1407a
Zola on, 7:1525b–1526b
Herder's unconventional view of, 4:642a-b,
643b–644a
Italian
ca. 1900, 7:1545b–1546a
in Verga's works, 7:1559a–1562b,
1563b–1564a
in La Bruyère's *Caractères*, 3:243b–245b,
244a, 245b–247a
Tolstoy's treatment of, 7:1478a-b,
1488b–1489a
Class Struggle. *See* Ferreira de Castro, José
Maria, "Luta de classes"
Classic, literary, Sainte-Beuve's definition of,
6:855b–859b
Classical drama
Corneille and, 3:26a
medieval drama and, 1:473a
Molière and, 3:102a
Nietzsche's *Birth of Tragedy* on,
7:1656b–1657b, 1658a-b
tragedy, Ibsen's use of, 7:1421a-b, 1437a,
1438b

Classical literature
Alfieri's Greek translations, 4:667a
Ariosto and, 2:630b–631b
Christian allegory and, 1:7b, 319a, 465a
Du Bellay's *Défense et illustration* on,
2:725a, 725b
Erasmus and, 2:572a-b, 589b
Eyvind Johnson and, 12:2373b–2374b
Greek, Schlegel and, 5:179a–180b
Greek epigrammatists' influence on Cavafy,
8:211b–212a
Hölderlin's use of classic meters, 5:155a
Latin translations, by Delacroix, 5:514b
Machiavelli and, 2:612b–613a
Montaigne and, 2:773a
Petrarch's sources in *Canzoniere*, 2:493a
poetry
Augustine on, 1:27a, 47a
Carducci's use of forms and meters,
7:1497b, 1501a-b, 1508a–1509b
Renaissance pastoral poetry and,
2:900a–903b
Walther and, 1:290a-b
Prudentius and, 1:18b–19a, 20a
Quasimodo and, 12:2398a-b
in Ronsard's verse
"À sa maîtresse," 2:727b–728a
"Amours de Cassandre," 2:729b
Sánchez de las Brozas on, 2:751b
satire
personification in, 1:366b
purpose of, 1:340b–341a
Roman morality and, 1:350a
vernacular poetry and, 1:339b
Silver Age of Latin poetry, 7:1641a
Taine on, 7:1454b–1455a
Tasso and, 2:804a-b
Undset and, 9:1020b, 1025a
see also Epic, classical; Hellenism;
Mythology, Greco-Roman
Classical world
Baudelaire and, 7:1329b–1330b, 1340b
Delacroix's view of imitation of,
5:525b–526a
Ekelöf and, 12:2635a
Flaubert and, 7:1385a–1387a
Nietzsche and, 7:1648a, 1649a

Classical world (*cont.*)
    as standard of excellence, for Machiavelli,
        606b–607a
    see also Gods, pagan; Greece, ancient;
        Rome, ancient
Classicism
    Delacroix and, 5:517a, 530a
    French
        aims of, 3:80a-b
        Boileau's *Art poétique* and, 3:179b
        Ionesco and, 13:3018b
        La Fontaine and, 3:76b–77b, 80a
        Laforgue and, 7:1895a-b
        Yourcenar's *Alexis* and, 12:2538a
        general tenets of, La Bruyère and,
            3:235b–236a
        German, *see also* Wieland, Christoph Martin
        hermeticism and, 12:2390b
        Hugo's rebellion against, 6:695a-b
        Nerval and, 6:947a
        realism and, Milosz on, 13:2939a-b
        of Schlegel, 5:180b–181b
        see also La Bruyère, Jean de; Racine, Jean
Classicism/romanticism controversy, Carducci
        and the, 7:1500a, 1503b–1504a
Classics and Moderns. *See* Azorín, *Clásicos y*
        modernos
Classification
    Barthes on, 13:3095a-b
    in Calvino, 13:3274b–3275a
Claude Gueux. See Hugo, Victor
Claudel, Camille, 8:471b
Claudel, Paul, **8:471a–494b**
    Apollinaire and, 9:892b
    Art poétique (*Poetic Art*), 8:474a, 477b
    attacked by surrealists, 11:2066b
    Autres textes sur l'art (Other Writings on
        Art), 8:487b
    Catholic revival and, 7:1709b, 10:1431a-b
    Cent phrases pour éventails (A Hundred
        Sentences for Fans), 8:489a-b
        "Encre" ("Ink"), 8:489a-b, 491a
    Cinq grandes odes (*Five Great Odes*),
        8:479b, 489b
        "L'Esprit et l'eau" ("Water and the Spirit"),
        8:479b
        "Magnificat," 8:479b, 489b–490b

Connaissance de l'Est (*The East I Know*),
    8:476a
conversion in work of, 7:1625a-b
Corona benignitatis anni Dei (*Coronal*),
    8:484b, 485a, 491a-b
Dodoitzu, 8:489a
Giraudoux and, 9:1060a
Jeanne d'Arc au bûcher (Joan of Arc at the
    Stake), 8:488a-b
La femme et son ombre (Woman and Her
    Shadow), 8:488b
La jeune fille Violaine (The Damsel
    Violaine), 8:480a–483a
    first version, 8:480a-b
    second version, 8:480b–483a
La lune à la recherche d'elle-même (The
    Moon in Search of Herself), 8:488b
La messe là-bas (The Mass There),
    8:485a–487a
    "Le pain bénit" ("The Holy Bread"),
    8:486b–487a
La nuit de Noël de 1914 (Christmas Night
    1914), 8:484b–485a
La parabole du festin (The Parable of the
    Feast), 8:488a
La sagesse, ou la parabole du festin
    (Wisdom; or, The Parable of the Feast),
    8:488a
La ville (*The City*), 8:474a–475b, 481b
L'Annonce faite à Marie (*The Tidings*
    Brought to Mary), 8:480a, 483a–484b,
    488b
Le pain dur (*Crusts*), 8:471b, 488b
Le partage de midi (*Break of Noon*), 8:476b,
    477a–479b, 490b, 491b
Le père humilié (*The Humiliation of the*
    Father), 8:471b, 485b, 488b
Le ravissement de Scapin (The Kidnapping
    of Scapin), 8:486a, 488b
Le soulier de satin (*The Satin Slipper*),
    8:491b–492a
L'Échange (The Exchange), 8:476a-b, 477a,
    480b
L'Endormie (The Sleeping Woman), 8:472b
Les conversations dans le Loir-et-Cher
    (Conversations in the Department of
    Loir-and-Cher), 8:487a

L'Histoire de Tobie et de Sara (The Story of Tobit and Sara), 8:489a

L'Homme et son désir (Man and His Desire), 8:485a

Livre de Christophe Colomb (*The Book of Christopher Columbus*), 8:471a, 487b

L'Oeil écoute (*The Eye Listens*), 8:487b

L'Otage (*The Hostage*), 8:471b, 484b, 487b, 488b

L'Ours et la lune (The Bear and the Moon), 8:488b

on Montherlant's *La relève du matin*, 11:1917b

Morceau d'un drame (Fragment of a Play), 8:472b

Perse and, 10:433a, 1432a, 1434b–1435a

Pour encre, poète (For Ink, Poet), 8:491a

Processional pour saluer le siècle nouveau (Processional with Which to Greet the New Century), 8:479b

Protée (Proteus), 8:484b, 488b

Sartre on, 12:2707a

Sous le signe du dragon (Under the Sign of the Dragon), 8:477a

Tête d'Or (Golden Head), 8:472b–474a, 474b, 475b, 477b, 484a, 492a

The City, 12:2552b

The Satin Slipper, 12:2550b

Weil and, 12:2806a

Claude's Confession. See Zola, Émile, *La confession de Claude*

Claude's Wife. See Dumas fils, Alexandre, *La femme de Claude*

"Claudia." *See* Södergran, Edith

Claudian, garden motif in, 1:324a-b

Claudine en ménage (*Claudine Married*). *See* Colette

Claudine à l'école (*Claudine at School*). *See* Colette

Claudine à Paris (*Claudine in Paris*). *See* Colette

Claudine s'en va (*Claudine and Annie*). *See* Colette

"Claustrophobia." *See* Grass, Günter

Clavijo. See Goethe, Johann Wolfgang von

Clay and the Wheel, The. *See* Vesaas, Tarjei, *Leiret og hjulet*

Clé des champs, La (French journal), Breton's articles in, 11:1954b

"Clear, fresh, sweet waters." *See* Petrarch, *Canzoniere*, "Chiare fresche et dolci acque"

Cleland, John, *Fanny Hill*, French translation of, 6:1033a

Clemency and civilization, in Corneille's *Cinna*, 3:43b–44a

Clemens, Samuel. *See* Twain, Mark

Clement of Alexandria, St., in Fénelon's works, 3:270b–271a

Clement IV, pope, Aquinas and, 1:417a

Clement V, pope, Henry VII and, 1:434b

Clement VII, pope, Castiglione and, 2:648b–249a

Clementina von Porretta. See Wieland, Christoph Martin

Clements, Robert, *Anatomy of the Novella* (with Gibaldi), oral tradition emphasized by, 2:927b–928a

Clenched Hands, The. *See* Moberg, Vilhelm, *De Knutna händerna*

Cleopatra. See Alfieri, Vittorio

Clérambard. See Aymé, Marcel

Clergy

  Aymé's satire of, 12:2441a-b

  Gottfried and, 1:238a-b

  in Jerome's *Ad Nepotianum*, 1:349b

  Jeu de Saint Nicolas and, 1:463b

  in medieval satire, 1:352a, 355b–356a, 11:345b–348a

    of Philip of Paris, 1:360b–361a

  Miracle de St. Ignace and, 1:464a

  in "Whii werre and wrake," 1:349a-b

  see also Anticlericalism; Mendicant orders; Religious orders

Clermont, Jesuit College of, Molière's studies at, 3:102a

Clients d'Avrenos, Les. See Simenon, Georges

Cligés. See Chrétien de Troyes

Climacus, Johannes. *See* Kierkegaard, Søren

Climate

  effect of on politics, Montesquieu and, 3:348a

  in Simenon's novels, 12:2501a–2502a

Climate. *See* Ekelöf, Gunnar, "Klimat"

Clitandre. See Corneille, Pierre

Cloak-and-sword plays
  of Calderón, 2:873b, 879a, 880b, 883a
  of Lope de Vega, 2:857a, 867a-b

"Cloche fêlée, La." *See* Baudelaire, Charles, "The Cracked Bell"

Cloches de Bâle, Les. See Aragon, Louis

Cloister, The. See Strindberg, August, *Klostret*

Clothing, theme of
  in "Ego dixi," 1:347b–348a
  in "Mum and the Sothsegger," 1:354b–355a

Cloud imagery, in Elytis' *Maria Nephele*, 13:2977a

Cloud in Trousers, A. *See* Mayakovsky, Vladimir, *Oblako v shtanakh*

Cloud-pump, The. *See* Arp, Jean, *die wolkenpumpe*

Clouds over Metapontion, The. *See* Johnson, Eyvind, *Molnen över Metapontion*

Clouds, The. See Aristophanes

Clouds, The. *See* Azorín, "Las nubes"

Člověk zahrada šírá. See Kundera, Milan

Cloven Viscount, The. See Calvino, Italo

"Clown Chastised, The." *See* Mallarmé, Stéphane, "Le pitre châtié"

Clown, The. See Böll, Heinrich

Clowns
  in Ghelderode's *La transfiguration dans le cirque*, 11:2129a
  in Laforgue's *The Imitation of Our Lady of the Moon*, 7:1897a

"Club des hachichins, Le." *See* Gautier, Théophile

Coach-Traveler's Companion. *See* Wickram, Jörg, *Rollwagenbüchlein*

"Coast Guard's House, The." *See* Montale, Eugenio, "La casa del doganiere"

Cobla (rhyme scheme), 1:176a, 176b

Coblenz, Ida, 8:454b, 455b, 457b, 459b, 464b

Cocagne. See Flaubert, Gustave

Cochin, Charles-Nicolas, in Goncourts' *L'Art du dix-huitième siècle*, 7:1397a

Cochlaeus, Johannes, Luther and, 2:684a

Cock-and-Bull Stories of Eutrapel. *See* Du Fail, Noël, *Baliverneries d'Eutrapel*

Cockaigne. See Mann, Heinrich, *Im Schlaraffenland*

Cockroaches. See Witkiewicz, Stanisław Ignacy, *Karaluchy*

Cocteau, Jean, **10:1543a–1563b**
  Antigone, 10:1550b
  Bacchus, 10:1558a
  Clair-obscur, 10:1561a
  Discours du grand sommeil (*Discourse of the Great Sleep*), 10:1545a, 1546a, 1547b–1548a
  Genet and, 13:2866b
  Ghelderode and, 11:2134b
  Giraudoux and, 9:1041b
  Intimate Relations (*Les parents terribles*), 10:1556a-b, 1560a
  Journal d'un inconnu (*The Hand of a Stranger*), 10:1560a
  La belle et la bête (*Beauty and the Beast*), 10:1559a
  La crucifixion, 10:1561a
  La danse de Sophocle (*Sophocles' Dance*), 10:1544b–1545a
  La difficulté d'être (*The Difficulty of Being*), 10:1559b–1560a
  La lampe d'Aladin (*Aladdin's Lamp*), 10:1544b–1545a
  La machine à écrire (*The Typewriter*), 10:1557b
  La voix humaine (*The Human Voice*), 10:1554a
  L'Aigle à deux têtes (*The Eagle with Two Heads*), 10:1557b–1558a
  L'Ange Heurtebise (*The Angel Heurtebise*), 10:1546a, 1551a, 1552a
  Le baron fantôme (The Phantom Baron), 10:1558b
  Le bel indifférent (*The Indifferent Beau*), 10:1554a
  Le boeuf sur le toit (*The Do-Nothing Bar*), 10:1550b
  Le Cap de Bonne-Espérance (*The Cape of Good Hope*), 10:1544b, 1545a, 1546a
  Le cordon ombilical, 10:1560a
  Le dieu bleu (The Blue God), 10:1545b
  Le grand écart (*The Grand Écart*), 10:1544b, 1547b–1549a
  Le passé défini (*Past Tense*), 10:1560a
  Le Potomak, 10:1545b, 1546b

Le prince frivole (*The Frivolous Prince*), 10:1544b–1545a

Le requiem, 10:1561a

Le sang d'un poète (*The Blood of a Poet*), 10:1544b, 1558b

Le secret professionnel (*Professional Secrets*), 10:1547b

Le train bleu (*The Blue Train*), 10:1545b

Les enfants terribles (*The Holy Terrors*), 10:1544a, 1544b, 1548a, 1552b–1554a

Les enfants terribles (*The Holy Terrors*) (the film), 10:1560a

Les mariés de la Tour Eiffel (*The Eiffel Tower Wedding Party*), 10:1550b

Les monstres sacrés (*The Holy Terrors*), 10:1557a

L'Éternel retour (The Eternal Return), 10:1558b–1559a

modernization of myth, 13:2846b

Oedipe-roi (*Oedipus Rex*), 10:1554a-b

Opéra: Oeuvre poetique, 10:1546a, 1551a

Opium, 10:1547b

Orphée (*Orpheus*) (film and play), 10:1544a, 1551a–1552b, 1559a, 1560a

Parade and, 9:898b, 899b, 10:1545b, 1546b

Paraprosodies, 10:1561a

Plain-chant, 10:1547b

Portraits-souvenirs, 10:1555b

on Proust, 10:1559b

Renaud et Armide, 10:1557b

Roméo et Juliette, 10:1545b

Ruy Blas, 10:1558b

The Infernal Machine (*La machine infernale*), 10:1554a–1555b

The Knights of the Round Table (*Les chevaliers de la table ronde*), 10:1557a

The Testament of Orpheus (*Le testament d'Orphée*), 10:1560a-b

Thomas l'imposteur (*Thomas the Imposter*), 10:1547b–1548a, 1549b–1550a

Codex Puteanus, 1:1b

Codex Regius, 1:386b, 400a

Coe, Richard, 13:2997a

Coelho, Adolfo, at Democratic Conferences of 1871, 7:1689b

"Coeur de pitre." *See* Rimbaud, Arthur

"Coeur volé." *See* Rimbaud, Arthur

"Coffee Pot, The." *See* Gautier, Théophile, "La cafetière"

Coffee-House, The. *See* Goldoni, Carlo, *La bottega del caffè*

Coffin Shop, A. *See* Hašek, Jaroslav, "Obchod s rakvemi"

Cogitation. *See* Thought

Cognition, Bergson's view of, 8:49b

Cohen, Hermann
on the novel, 9:1137b
Ortega y Gasset and, 9:1124a-b
Pasternak and, 10:1593a

Cohen, Robert, *Giraudoux: Three Faces of Destiny*, 9:1056a-b

Coigny, Aimée de
subject of Chénier's "The Young Captive," 4:692a–693b, 714a
in Vigny's *Stello*, 5:468b

Coimbra School, 7:1685a-b

Coin des "Amen," Le. See Baldwin, James, *Amen Corner*

Coin in Nine Hands, A. See Yourcenar, Marguerite, *Denier du rêve*

Coincidence, role in Breton's poetry, 11:1956b

Coined words. *See* Neologisms

Cola di Rienzo, Petrarch on, 2:478a-b, 484a, 484b, 485a

Colbert, Jean Baptiste, 3:75a

"Colchiques, Les." *See* Apollinaire, Guillaume, *Alcools*

Cold Land. *See* Ferreira de Castro, José Maria, *Terra fria*

Colección de poesías castellanas anteriores al siglo XV. See Sánchez, Tomás Antonio

"Colère de Samson, La." *See* Vigny, Alfred Victor de, *Les destinées*

Colère, La. See Ionesco, Eugène

Coleridge, Samuel Taylor
allegory and, 1:320a-b
Baudelaire and, 7:1335b
Bergson and, 8:51a
classical forms and mythology discarded by, 5:372b
Dinesen and, 10:1296a
Ekelöf and, 12:2650a
Jarry and, 9:675b
Richter's *School for Aesthetics* and, 5:77b

Colet, John, Erasmus and, 2:574a-b
Colet, Louise, Vigny's affair with, 5:480a
Colette, 8:135a, **9:617a–638b**
  Chéri
    art form in, 9:630a-b
    liaison in, 9:622b
    plot of, 9:627b–629b
    stage version of, 9:623a
  Claudine en ménage (*Claudine Married*),
    9:618a
  Claudine à l'école (*Claudine at School*),
    9:618a, 620b, 624a, 624b
  Claudine à Paris (*Claudine in Paris*), 9:618a
  Claudine s'en va (*Claudine and Annie*),
    9:618a, 624a
  Dialogues de bêtes (*Creature
    Conversations*), 9:621a, 635a
  Duo, 9:629b, 636a
  Gigi, 9:623a
  Julie de Carneilhan, 9:624a
  La chatte (*The Cat*), 9:634a–635a, 636a
  "La dame du photographe" ("The
    Photographer's Missus"), 9:623b
  La femme cachée (*The Other Woman*),
    9:633b
  La fin de Chéri (*The Last of Chéri*), 9:619a,
    630b–631a, 636a
  "La lune de pluie" ("The Rainy Moon"),
    9:623b
  La maison de Claudine (*My Mother's
    House*), 9:619b, 620a
  La naissance du jour (*Break of Day*), 9:624a
  La retraite sentimentale (*The Retreat from
    Love*), 9:624a-b
  La seconde (*The Other One*), 9:633b
  La vagabonde (*The Vagabond*), 9:624b–627a
    autobiographical material in, 9:624a
    and female nature, 9:636a
    home in, 9:629b
    and writing, 9:621a
  Le blé en herbe (*The Ripening Seed*),
    9:621a, 622b, 631a–633a
    serialization of, 9:631a
  Le fanal bleu (*The Blue Lantern*),
    9:635b–636a
  "Le képi" ("The Kepi"), 9:623b, 633a

  Le Maison de Claudine (*My Mother's
    House*), 9:619b–620a
  Le pur et l'impur (*The Pure and the
    Impure*), 9:621b–622a, 621b, 634a
  Le toutounier, 9:629b
  L'Entrave (*The Shackle*), 9:622b, 627a-b
  L'Envers du music-hall (*Music-Hall
    Sidelights*), 9:625a–626a
  L'Étoile vesper (*The Evening Star*),
    9:635b–636a
  L'Ingénue libertine (*The Innocent Libertine*),
    9:637a
  Mes apprentissages (*My Apprenticeships*),
    9:618a, 620b, 634a
  Mitsou, ou comment l'esprit vient aux filles
    (*Mitsou, or How Girls Get Wise*),
    9:622b, 625a
  Sido, 9:619b
Coligny-Châtillon, Louise de, 9:882a
Colin Muset
  poetic genres used by, 1:181a
  "Qant je voi lou tans refroidier" ("When I
    see the weather grow cold"), 1:182a-b
  as trouvère, 1:181a–182b
Colin, tutor of Claudel, 8:471b
Collage, as defined by Max Ernst, 11:2065a
"Collage" aesthetics, Marinetti and, 9:815b,
  817a
"Collage" technique, of Apollinaire, 9:889b
Collationes. See Cassian
Collationes Catholicae et canonicae scripturae
  (*Collations of Catholic and Canonical
  Scripture*). *See* William of Saint Amour
Collected Poems, 1931–1987. See Milosz,
  Czeslaw
Collection, The. See Sammlung, Die
Collectivism
  in Olesha's works, 11:2239b, 2242a
  Sartre's view of, 12:2604a–2607b
Collège de France
  French romantic historiography and,
    5:580b–581a, 582a, 582b–583a
  Machado at, 9:746a
  Michelet and, 5:571a, 600a
  Mickiewicz and, 5:629b–630b
  Valéry and, 8:570a, 585a
College of 'Pataphysics, 9:685b–686a

Collège Stanislas, 13:3022b

Collett, Camilla, Norwegian realism and, 9:1037a

Collier de la reine, Le. See Dumas père, Alexandre

Collin, Jonas, Andersen and, 6:866b–867b

"Collines, Les." *See* Apollinaire, Guillaume

"Colloque sentimental." *See* Verlaine, Paul

Colloquialism, in Elytis' *Maria Nephele*, 13:2977a

Colloquialisms, in Tasso's works, 2:796a

Colloquies. See Erasmus

Colloquies of the Drugs and Simples of India. See Orta, Garcia da

"Colloquii coi personaggi." *See* Pirandello, Luigi

Colmena, La. See Cela, Camilo José, *The Hive]*

Cologne, archbishop of, Archpoet and, 1:357b

Colomba. See Mérimée, Prosper

Colon, Jenny, Nerval and, 6:945b, 948a, 958b, 960b, 967b

Colonel Arlequin. See Lesage, Alain-René, *Arlequin colonel*

Colonel Chabert, Le. See Balzac, Honoré de

Colonel's Photograph, The. See Ionesco, Eugène, *La photo du colonel*

Colonialism
  Italian, in Pascoli's "La grande proletaria se è mossa," 7:1849b–1850a
  in Montherlant's *La rose de sable*, 11:1926a-b
  Portuguese, 11:2143b, 2145b–2146a

"Coloquio de los perros, El." *See* Cervantes, Miguel de, *Exemplary Tales*

Color perception, Bergson's view of, 8:49a

Color symbolism
  in Elytis' "Variations on a Sunbeam," 13:2963a, 2963b
  Mallarmé's azure, 7:1571a-b
  Trakl and, 10:1418b–1419a
  in Zamyatin's writing, 10:1191b–1192a

Colorblindness imagery, in Olesha's "Liompa," 11:2242b–2243a

Colosso, Il. See Goldoni, Carlo

Columbus, Christopher, in Claudel's *The Mass There*, 8:487a

Column of Infamy, The. See Manzoni, Alessandro

Combat avec l'ange (Combat with the Angel). *See* Giraudoux, Jean

Combat (journal)
  Barthes and, 13:3082a
  Camus and, 13:3053b–3054a

"Come, il quando, ed il perché, Il." *See* Verga, Giovanni

Come, Leda, Let Me Embrace You. *See* Ady, Endre, "Jöjj, Léda, megölellek"

Come prima, meglio di prima. See Pirandello, Luigi

Come tu mi vuoi. See Pirandello, Luigi

Comedia, varieties of, 2:873b

Comedia de ensueño. See Valle-Inclán, Ramón del

Comédia de Rubena. See Vicente, Gil

Comedia famosa, of Calderón, 2:887a

Comédia sobre a divisa da cidade de Coimbra. See Vicente, Gil

Comedias bárbaras, Las. See Valle-Inclán, Ramón del

Comédie de la mort, La. See Gautier, Théophile

Comédie Française, 9:1055a
  Beaumarchais and, 4:566a, 573a, 577b
  Claudel's *L'Annonce faite à Marie* and, 8:483a, 488b
  Dumas's work performed at, 6:720a–722a
  fairground theatricals and, 3:326a-b
  Lesage and, 3:320b, 322b
  Musset's works at, 6:1000a
  production of Montherlant's *La reine morte*, 11:1919a
  Scribe and, 7:1910b, 1916a
  Voltaire and, 4:381b–382a

Comédie humaine. See Simenon, Georges

Comédie humaine, La. See Balzac, Honoré de

Comédie Italienne, Goldoni and, 4:431a–432a

Comédie larmoyante (sentimental comedy)
  Goldoni and, 4:428b
  Lessing and, 4:551a

Comédie-vaudevilles, of Scribe, 7:1910a-b, 1915a-b

Comedies of Words. See Schnitzler, Arthur, *Komödie der Worte*

Comedy
   antithetical pairing of forces in,
      3:105b–106a
   in Barthes' writings, 13:3103a-b
   Bergson on, 7:1922a-b
   Calderón's varieties of, 2:873b, 881b
   comic types in, 3:108a
   derivation of, 3:105b
   in Dinesen, 10:1281a-b
   French, seventeenth century, 3:25a
   German, and Lessing, 4:551b–554b
   Gogol and, 6:972a, 981b–982b
   Goldoni and, 4:421a
   Greek
      alazon (imposter) type, 3:108b, 111b
      eiron (victim) type, 3:108b, 109a, 111b
   Italian, of Alfieri, 4:676a–677b
   Lessing on, 4:548b
   of Lope de Vega, 2:851a, 852a–855a
   in Maupassant's works, 7:1767a-b, 1773b
   Molière and, 3:105a–109a
   Moravia's novels, 12:2691a-b
   in Musset's works, 6:1007a
   Schnitzler's use of, 8:101b–102a, 105b, 112b
   in Svevo's novels, 8:72a-b, 77b, 82a-b
   tragedy and, Lope de Vega and, 2:851b,
      865b
   of Wagner, 6:1157a-b
   see also Humor; Laughter
Comedy. See Kazantzakis, Nikos, *Komodía*
Comedy of the Florentine Nymphs. *See*
      Boccaccio, Giovanni, *Ninfale d'Ameto*
Comedy of Love, A. See Ibsen, Henrik
Comedy of manners
   French
      seventeenth century, 3:25a-b
      see also Beaumarchais, Pierre-Augustin
         Caron de, *Le barbier de Séville*
Comedy, Satire, Irony, and Deeper Meaning.
      See Grabbe, Christian Dietrich
Comedy of Seduction. *See* Schnitzler, Arthur,
      Komödie der Verführung
Comedy of Vanity, The. See Canetti, Elias
"Comércio e indústria no norte da Inglaterra,
      1874–1875." *See* Eça de Queiroz, José
      Maria

Comet, The; or, Nicholas Marggrave, A Comic
      Story. *See* Richter, Jean Paul, *Der
      Komet, oder Nikolaus Marggraf, eine
      komische Geschichte*
Comic Tales. See Wieland, Christoph Martin,
      Comische Erzählungen
Comic, the, humorism and, 8:395b
Comic Theater, The. *See* Goldoni, Carlo, *Il
      teatro comico*
Comic-strips, in Queneau's writing,
      12:2516a-b
Coming of Peace, The. See Hauptmann,
      Gerhart, *Das Friedensfest*
"Coming of Winter, The." *See* Laforgue, Jules,
      "L'Hiver qui vient"
Comische Erzählungen. See Wieland,
      Christoph Martin
Command and I Will Obey You. See Moravia,
      Alberto, *Una cosa è una cosa*
Commandant of Bugulma. *See* Hašek,
      Jaroslav, "Velitelem města Bugulmy"
Comme l'eau qui coule. See Yourcenar,
      Marguerite
Commedia. See Dante Alighieri, *Divine
      Comedy*
Commedia dell'arte
   Goldoni and, 4:427a-b, 433b–434b
   influence on French farce, 4:564b–565a,
      574a
   Pirandello's *Tonight We Improvise* and,
      8:410b
   Titan and, 5:72a
   Watteau and, 7:1628a-b
Commedia delle ninfe fiorentine. See
      Boccaccio, Giovanni, *Ninfale d'Ameto*
"Commedia Pastorale." *See* Tasso, Torquato,
      Aminta
Commemorative Masque. See Hauptmann,
      Gerhart, *Festspiel in deutschen Reimen*
Commencements d'une vie. See Mauriac,
      François
*Comment préparer un oeuf dur. See Pour
      préparer un oeuf dur*
"Comment Wang-Fô fut sauvé." *See*
      Yourcenar, Marguerite, *Nouvelles
      orientales*

Commentaries. See Boethius, Anicius Manlius Severinus

Commentaries on the Sentences. See Aquinas, Thomas, St., *Scriptum super Sententias;* Duns Scotus

Commentary, Foucault's theory of, 13:3342a–3345a, 3346a–3347a

Commentary on the Art of Acting, A. See Wedekind, Frank, *Schauspielkunst: Ein Glossarium*

Commentary on a Falling Star. See Johnson, Eyvind, *Kommentar till ett stjärnfall*

Commentary on the Magnificat. See Luther, Martin

Commentary on the "Sentences". See Bonaventura, Saint

Commerce, Aymé's satire of, 12:2445a-b

Commerce of Algiers, The. See Cervantes, Miguel de, *El trato de Argel*

Commerce and Industry in the North of England, 1874–1875. *See* Eça de Queiroz, José Maria, "Comércio e indústria no norte da Inglaterra, 1874–1875"

Commercialism, culture and, Sainte-Beuve on, 6:854a-b

Commission for the Protection of Monuments (Russia), Gorky and, 8:421b

Commitment in Spite of Myself. *See* Moravia, Alberto, *Impegno controvoglia*

Committee for a Free Germany (Mexico), Heinrich Mann and, 8:541b

Committee for the Improvement of Living Conditions for Scholars (Russia), Gorky and, 8:421b

Common Miracles. *See* Ritsos, Yannis, *Ghrafi tiflou*

Common people
  Hugo's view of, 6:712b
  Montaigne on, 2:782b–783a
  see also Working class

Common sense, in Molière's plays, 3:115a-b

Common Story, A. See Goncharov, Ivan

Communal House of Schaerbeek, 11:2115b

Communicating Vessels. See Breton, André

Communicating Vessels. *See* Cela, Camilo José, *Los vasos comunicantes*

Communication
  in Pavese's works, 12:2779a
  see also Conversation; Language

Communication to My Friends, A. See Wagner, Richard, *Eine Mitteilung an meine Freunde*

Communism
  Artaud and, 11:1966b
  Baroja's ambivalence about, 9:594a
  Benjamin and, 11:1721b
  Brecht and, 11:2090a, 2096b, 2098a, 2107a
  Camus and, 13:3052b–3053a
  Foucault and, 13:3333a-b
  in France, *see also* Aragon, Louis
  Hašek's involvement with, 9:1094a-b
  Heine's opinion of, 5:508b
  Heinrich Mann and, 8:523b–524a, 535a, 536b
  Icarian, Hauptmann and, 8:151b
  Ionesco and, 13:3018a
  Kazantzakis' view of "meta-Communism," 9:1068a, 1076b–1077a, 1078a
  Malraux and, 12:2416a-b, 2417b, 2424a
  Marinetti and, 9:824a, 826a
  Milosz and, 13:2931a-b, 2933b–2934a, 2935a-b
  Moberg on, 11:2228b
  Montale's antagonism toward, 11:2002b, 2003b
  Moravia and, 12:2682a
  Quasimodo and, 12:2389a
  Sartre and, 12:2600b–2603b
  Silone and, 12:2273a–2274a, 2285a, 2286a, 2295a–2296a
  Vittorini and, 12:2749a-b, 2751a
  Weil and, 12:2787a, 2790a-b
  in Yugoslavia, Krleža and, 11:1808b–1809b, 1813a-b
  see also Bolsheviks; Marxism; Socialism; Stalinism

Communist Man. *See* Aragon, Louis, *L'Homme communiste*

Communist Party
  Böll's criticism of, 13:3182b
  Calvino and, 13:3264a
  Greek, Ritsos and, 12:2816b–2818a
  Hungarian, Lukács and, 10:1252b

Communist Party (*cont.*)
  Italian
    Ginzburg and, 13:3133b
    Silone's involvement in, 12:2273b–2274a,
      2277b–2278a
  Kundera and, 13:3390a–3391b
Communist Revolution. *See* Russian
  Revolution (1917)
Communists and Peace, The (*Les
  communistes et la paix*). *See* Sartre,
  Jean-Paul
Como, Lake, Manzoni's description of, 5:377b
Cómo se hace una novela. See Unamuno,
  Miguel de
Compagnia del Porcospino, Moravia and,
  12:2690a
Compagno, Il. See Pavese, Cesare, *The
  Comrade*
Compagnon du tour de France, Le. See Sand,
  George
"Compagnons d'Ulysse, Les." *See* La Fontaine,
  Jean de, *Fables*
"Compaigno, no puosc mudar." *See* William
  IX of Aquitaine, duke
"Companho faray un vers." *See* William IX of
  Aquitaine, duke
"Companho" poems. *See* William IX of
  Aquitaine, duke
"Companho, taint ai agutz d'avols conres." *See*
  William IX of Aquitaine, duke
Comparative mythology. *See* Mythology,
  comparative
Compassion
  Schopenhauer's view of, 5:404b–405a
    critique of, 5:405b–406b
    denial of will and, 5:410b
  in Wolfram, 1:275b, 279b–280a
Compendium musicae. See Descartes, René
*Compendium of Sagas about Kings of Norway.
    See* Ágrip af Noregs konunga sögum
Compendium theologiae (*Compendium of
    Theology*). *See* Aquinas, Thomas, St.
Complaint (genre), as satire, 1:338b–339a
"Complaint of Holy Church." *See* Rutebeuf,
  "Complainte de sainte Eglise"
Complaint of Peace, The. See Erasmus,
  Querela pacis

"Complainte de l'automne monotone." *See*
  Laforgue, Jules, *Les complaintes*
"Complainte de l'orgue de Barbarie." *See*
  Laforgue, Jules, *Les complaintes*
"Complainte de sainte Eglise." *See* Rutebeuf
"Complainte des chômeurs." *See* Aragon,
  Louis
"Complainte des pianos qu'on entend dans les
  quartiers aisés." *See* Laforgue, Jules,
  Les complaintes
"Complainte du pauvre chevalier-errant." *See*
  Laforgue, Jules, *Les complaintes*
"Complainte du roi de Thulé." *See* Laforgue,
  Jules, *Les complaintes*
Complaintes, Les. See Laforgue, Jules
Complementarios, Los (The
  Complementaries). *See* Machado,
  Antonio
Composers
  Maeterlinck's influence on, 8:143a
  see also names of individual composers
Compte-rendu au roi. See Necker, Jacques
Comptes amoureux. See Flore, Jeanne
Comptes du monde adventureux, Les (*Tales
    from the Adventurous World*), sources
    for, 2:946b
"Comrade Churygin Has the Floor." *See*
  Zamyatin, Yevgeny Ivanovich, "Slovo
  predostavliaetsia tovarishchu
  Churyginu"
Comrade, The. See Pavese, Cesare
Comrades. See Strindberg, August,
  Kamraterna
Comte, Auguste
  Bergson and, 8:46b
  Eça and, 7:1685a
  Positive Philosophy, on Bossuet,
    3:168b–169a
  positivism, 7:1452a
  Strindberg and, 7:1753b
Comte de Monte-Cristo, Le. See Dumas père,
  Alexandre
Comtesse de Charny, La. See Dumas père,
  Alexandre
Comtesse de Rudolstadt, La. See Sand,
  George, *Countess Rudolstadt*
"Comune rustico, Il." *See* Carducci, Giosue

Comus. See Milton, John

Conceits, literary, in Tasso's works, 2:795b–796a

Concept of Anxiety, The. See Kierkegaard, Søren

Concept of Art Criticism, The. *See* Benjamin, Walter, *Der Begriff der Kunstkritik in der deutschen Romantik*

Concept of Irony, The: With Constant Reference to Socrates. See Kierkegaard, Søren

Concepts and Principles Implied by the Concept of Existence. *See* Witkiewicz, Stanisław Ignacy, *Pojęcia i twierdzenia implikowane przez pojęcie istnienia*

Conceptual knowledge, Bergson's view of, 8:58b–59a

Concerning the Procession of the Holy Spirit. See Nicholas of Durazzo, *Libellus de processione Spiritus Sancti*

"Concerning the Scientific Form of Historical Materialism." *See* Croce, Benedetto, *Materialismo storico ed economia marxistica*

Concerning Shakespeare's Handling of the Marvelous. *See* Tieck, Ludwig, *Über Shakespeares Behandlung des Wunderbaren*

Concerning the Writer. *See* Wedekind, Frank, *De scriptore*

"Concert at the Railroad Station." *See* Mandelshtam, Osip, "Kontsert na vokzale"

Concert in Autumn. *See* Kosztolányi, Dezső, *Őszi koncert*

Concile féerique, Le. See Laforgue, Jules

Conciliator, role of in Michelet's histories, 5:593a-b

Concluding Unscientific Postscript. See Kierkegaard, Søren

Concrete art, Arp and, 10:1368a-b

Concrete poetry
  Apollinaire and, 9:884b
  Marinetti and, 9:815a

"Concrétion humaine." *See* Arp, Jean

Condamné à mort, Le, See Genet, Jean

Condé. *See* Louis de Bourbon, prince de Condé

Conde de Abranhos, O. See Eça de Queiroz, José Maria

Condé family, 3:60a

Conde Lucanor, El. See Manuel, Don Juan

Condemned Man, The. See Genet, Jean, *Le condamné à mort*

Condemned Woman, The. See Blasco Ibáñez, Vicente

Condenada, La. See Blasco Ibáñez, Vicente, *The Condemned Woman*

Condillac, Étienne Bonnot de, Manzoni's thought and, 5:368b

Condition humaine, La. See Malraux, André

Conditions in France, 1833. See Heine, Heinrich, *Französische Zustände*

Condorcet. *See* Lycée Bonaparte (Condorcet)

Condorcet, Marquis de
  Essay on the Application of Analysis to the Probable Outcome of Decisions Taken by a Plurality of Votes, 5:97a
  Sketch of a Historic View of the Progress of the Human Mind, 5:96a

Conducting Bodies. See Simon, Claude, *Les corps conducteurs*

Confesiones de un pequeño filósofo, Las. See Azorín

Confession (the word), 1:25b

Confession, A. See Tolstoy, Leo

Confession Concerning the Lord's Supper. See Luther, Martin

Confession de Claude. See Zola, Émile

Confession d'un enfant du siècle (Confession of a Child of the Century). See Musset, Alfred de

Confession of the River Danube, The. *See* Ady, Endre, "A Duna vallomása"

Confession, The. See Gorky, Maxim, *Ispoved'*

Confessions. See Augustine, St.; Heine, Heinrich, *Geständnisse*; Rousseau, Jean Jacques

Confessions of an English Opium-Eater. See De Quincey, Thomas

Confessions du Comte ***, Les. See Duclos, Charles

Confessions of Felix Krull. See Mann, Thomas, *Bekenntnisse des Hochstaplers Felix Krull*

Confessions of a Little Philosopher. *See* Azorín, *Las confesiones de un pequeño filósofo*

Confessions of Zeno, The. See Svevo, Italo

"*Confiteor* de l'artiste, Le." *See* Baudelaire, Charles, "The Artist's Profession of Faith"

Conflagration imagery. *See* Fire imagery

Conflict
  in Giraudoux's works, 9:1060a–1061a
  in Strindberg's works, 7:1742b–1745a, 1752b

"Conflictatio" ("The Conflict"). *See* Petrarch

Confluence, in Montesquieu's thought, 3:347b–364a

Conformist, The. *See* Dürrenmatt, Friedrich, *The Sell-out*

Conformist, The (Il conformista). See Moravia, Alberto

Conformity, theme of, in Gombrowicz's works, 12:2568b, 2579a–2580b

Confort intellectuel, Le. See Aymé, Marcel

Confrontation, in Butor's works, 13:3302a–3303b

Confucianism, Flaubert and, 7:1378a

Congé (poetic genre), 1:460a

Congrès de Vérone. See Chateaubriand, François René de

Congress of Soviet Writers (First, 1934), Olesha at, 11:2234b, 2249b

Congress of Verona. *See* Chateaubriand, François René de, *Congrès de Vérone*

Congreve, William, Lessing and, 4:549b

Conjectures on Original Composition. See Young, Edward

Conjugal Love. See Moravia, Alberto

Conjuration de Catalina. See Mérimée, Prosper

Connaissance de l'Est. See Claudel, Paul

Connaissance, La (journal), on Valéry, 8:569a

Connaissance surnaturelle, La, See Weil, Simone

Conon de Béthune, as trouvère, 1:180a–181a

Conquérants, Les. See Malraux, André, *The Conquerors*

"Conqueror, The." *See* Schiller, Friedrich von

Conquerors, The. See Malraux, André

Conquest of the Stars, The. See Marinetti, Filippo Tommaso, *La conquête des étoiles*

Conquête des étoiles, La. See Marinetti, Filippo Tommaso

"Conquête du Mexique, La" (The Conquest of Mexico). *See* Artaud, Antonin

Conrad III, emperor, Cacciaguida and, 1:431a

Conrad, Joseph
  Apollinaire on, 9:881a
  Cavafy and, 8:206a
  Heart of Darkness
    Baroja's work compared to, 9:600a
    Céline's *Journey* and, 11:1870a, 1870b
  Lord Jim, Nerval and, 6:969a
  Perse and, 10:1434b, 1436b
  Simon and, 13:3034a, 3035a
  Spanish translations, 9:1119b
  Strindberg and, 7:1741a
  Witkiewicz and, 10:1212b, 1219b

Conrad, Michael Georg
  naturalist group, 8:235b, 236b
  Wedekind and, 8:232a

Conscience, in Rousseau, 4:466a-b

Conscience l'innocent (Conscience the Innocent). See Dumas père, Alexandre

Conscience of Love, The. See Aymé, Marcel

Consciousness
  in Bergson's thought, 8:50a–51a, 52a, 59b
  in Camus, 13:3061b, 3073b
  Freud's concept of, 8:5b
  in Johnson's works, 12:2362a, 2369a, 2380a-b
  in Ortega y Gasset, 9:604a
  in Pirandello's *Each in His Own Way*, 8:409b
  Proust on, 8:566a
  Sartre and, 12:2589b–2590a, 2591b–2593a
  see also Unconscious

Conservateur littéraire, Le (journal), 6:693b, 694a, 696b
  Chateaubriand and, 5:113a, 129a
  launching of, 5:450b
  Vigny's early contributions to, 5:451a

Conservatism

Ady on, 9:863b–864a, 865b–866a
Apollinaire and, 9:898b
of Azorín, 9:640b–641a
in Baroja's *Zalacaín el aventurero*, 9:604a-b
of Chateaubriand, 5:113a
of Delacroix, 5:536a-b
of Giraudoux, 9:1064b–1065a
of Leopardi, 5:547b
of Mann's *Reflections of a Nonpolitical Man*, 9:718a, 719b
see also Slavic nationalism
Considerations on the Causes of the Greatness of the Romans and Their Decline. See Montesquieu, Charles-Louis de Secondat, baron de
Considerations on the Government of Poland. See Rousseau, Jean Jacques
Considérations sur la Révolution française (Considerations on the Principal Events of the French Revolution). See Staël, Madame de
Consolation of Philosophy. See Boethius, Anicius Manlius Severinus
Consolations, Les (Consolations). See Sainte-Beuve, Charles-Augustin
"Consolatory Tale, A." *See* Dinesen, Isak
Conspiracies, The. *See* Moberg, Vilhelm, *Komplotterna*
"Conspiracy in 1537, A." *See* Sand, George, "Une conspiration en 1537"
Conspiracy of Feelings, The. See Olesha, Yuri, *Zagovor chuvstv*
Conspiracy of Fiesco at Genoa, The. See Schiller, Friedrich von
"Conspiration en 1537, Une." *See* Sand, George
Constancy and change, theme of, in Montaigne's *Essays*, 2:774a, 778a
"Constancy of Jurisprudence." *See* Vico, Giovanni Battista, *Diritto universale*
Constant, Benjamin, 4:393a–394a, **405a–416a**, 418b–419b
  Adolphe, 4:393b–394a, 405a–406a, 410b, 412a–416a, 5:92a, 6:1015a
    Proust's *Remembrance of Things Past* and, 8:550b, 556a
  Cécile, 4:393b, 410b–411a, 412a-b
De la religion considérée dans sa source, ses formes et ses développements, 4:411b
De la religion (On Religion), Vigny and, 5:465b
Journaux intimes (Intimate Journals), 4:393b, 410b–411a, 412a–413a
Le cahier rouge (The Red Notebook), 4:393b, 408a-b, 409b
and Madame de Charrière, 4:409a-b
in Vigny's "Paris," 5:464b
Constant Nymph, The. See Giraudoux, Jean
Constant Prince, The. See Calderón de la Barca, Pedro
Constantine the African, 1:408a
Constantine, Roman emperor, 1:443a-b
Constantius, Constantin. *See* Kierkegaard, Søren
Constellating, Arp and, 10:1374b–1376b
Construction Site. *See* Butor, Michel, *Chantier*
Constructivism
  Arp and, 10:1365b, 1371a-b
  influence of, 8:587a-b
  in Russia, 11:1845a
  Valéry and, 8:572a, 573a-b
Consuelo. See Sand, George
"Conte." *See* Rimbaud, Arthur
Conte di Carmagnola, Il. See Manzoni, Alessandro
"Conte di Montecristo, Il." *See* Calvino, Italo, *t zero*, "The Count of Monte Cristo"
Conte du Graal. See Chrétien de Troyes
Contemplatio in caligine divina, 9:941b–942a
Contemplation, Augustine on, 1:46a
Contemplation of Death. *See* D'Annunzio, Gabriele, *Contemplazione della morte*
Contemplations, Les (Contemplations). See Hugo, Victor
Contemplative life, active life vs., in Grillparzer's dramas, 5:422a-b, 428b, 439b, 441b
Contemplazione della morte. See D'Annunzio, Gabriele
Contemporary Literature (journal). *See Lettere d'Oggi*

Contemporary Portraits. *See* Sainte-Beuve, Charles-Augustin, *Portraits contemporains*

Contemporary Portugal. *See* Oliveira Martins, Joaquim Pedro de, *Portugal contemporáneo*

Contemporary and Reality, The. *See* Böll, Heinrich, "Der Zeitgenosse und die Wirklichkeit"

Contemporary, The (Russian periodical). *See Sovremennik*

Contes. See Musset, Alfred de

Contes cruels. See Villiers de l'Isle-Adam

Contes d'Espagne et d'Italie. See Musset, Alfred de, *Tales of Spain*

Contes d'Eutrapel. See Du Fail, Noël

Contes du chat perché. See Aymé, Marcel, *The Wonderful Farm*

Contes du lundi. See Daudet, Alphonse

Contes d'un matin, Les. See Giraudoux, Jean

Contes et fabliaux du dix-huitième siècle. See Sade, Donatien Alphonse François, marquis de

Contes et nouvelles. See La Fontaine, Jean de

Contes fantastiques. See Hoffmann, E. T. A.

Contes à Ninon. See Zola, Émile

Contes (tales), Diderot and, 4:501a–502a

Continents, The. *See* Milosz, Czeslaw, *Kontynenty*

Contini, Gianfranco, on Pascoli, 7:1826a, 1831b, 1850a

Continuation of the Conversation. See Diderot, Denis, *Suite de l'entretien*

Continuation des amours. See Ronsard, Pierre de, *Les Amours*

Contra doctrinam retrahentium a religione. See Aquinas, Thomas, St.

Contra errores Graecorum. See Aquinas, Thomas, St.

Contra impugnantes Dei cultum et religionem. See Aquinas, Thomas, St.

Contra mendacium. See Augustine, St.

Contract, theme of, in Claudel, 8:476b

Contradiction
   in Gombrowicz's works, 12:2572a–2573a
   in Rimbaud's works, 7:1793a-b, 1805b–1806a, 1818a

"Contradiction of Franc Gonthier, The." *See* Villon, François

Contre Sainte-Beuve. See Proust, Marcel

Contributions to the Analysis of the Sensations. See Mach, Ernst, *Beiträge zur Analyze der Empfindungen*

Contributions to the History and Improvement of the Theater. See Lessing, Gotthold Ephraim, *Beiträge zur Historie und Aufnahme des Theaters*

Contributo alla critica di me stesso. See Croce, Benedetto

"Contro l'amore e il parlamentarismo." *See* Marinetti, Filippo Tommaso

"Contro Venezia passatista" ("Against Past-Loving Venice"), 9:813b

Control, Camus and, 13:3076b

Convention Belzébir, La. See Aymé, Marcel

Conventional signs, Augustine on, 1:42b

Conversation
   in Castiglione, 2:657a-b
   in La Bruyère's *Caractères*, 3:240a-b

"Conversation." *See* Turgenev, Ivan

Conversation About Dante. See Mandelshtam, Osip, *Razgovor o Dante*

"Conversation between a Bookseller and a Poet." *See* Pushkin, Alexander

Conversation between d'Alembert and Diderot. See Diderot, Denis, *Entretien entre d'Alembert et Diderot*

Conversation between a Father and His Children. See Diderot, Denis, *Entretien d'un père avec ses enfants*

Conversation with the Censor, A. *See* Hašek, Jaroslav, "Rozmluvas cenzorem"

Conversation with Goya. *See* Andrić, Ivo, "Razgovor s Gojom"

Conversation with a Tax Collector, on Poetry. *See* Mayakovsky, Vladimir, "Razgovor s fininspektorom o poezii"

Conversations dans le Loir-et-Cher, Les (Conversations in the Department of Loir-et-Cher). *See* Claudel, Paul

Conversations with Goethe. See Eckermann, Johann Peter

Conversations of Madrid's Chimneys. See
     Lesage, Alain-René, *Entretiens des*
     cheminées de Madrid
Conversations with Professor Y. See Céline,
     Louis-Ferdinand, *Entretiens avec la*
     Professeur Y
Conversations on "The Illegitimate Son". See
     Diderot, Denis, *Entretiens sur le "Fils*
     naturel"
Conversazione in Sicilia. See Vittorini, Elio
"Converse at Night in Copenhagen." *See*
     Dinesen, Isak
Conversion
   of Augustine, 1:30b–31a
   of Claudel, 8:472a, 474a
   theme of
       in *Iconia* legend plays, 1:463a
       in *Jeu de Saint Nicolas*, 1:463b
       in miracle plays, 1:464b
Convito, Pascoli and, 7:1846b
Convivial Poems. See Pascoli, Giovanni,
     Poemi conviviali
Convivio. See Dante Alighieri
"Convivium religiosum." *See* Erasmus
Cooper, James Fenimore
   Balzac and, 5:642a
   Mickiewicz and, 5:618a
Copeau, Jacques
   Anouilh and, 13:2844b
   Claudel and, 8:480a, 487b
"Copernicus" ("Il Copernico"). *See* Leopardi,
     Giacomo
Coppée, François
   Maeterlinck and, 8:121a
   Verlaine and, 7:1620b
Coppet (Switzerland), 5:90b, 93a
Coquille et le clergyman, La. See Artaud,
     Antonin
Corbière, Tristan
   Les amours jaunes (Yellow Loves), 7:1639b
   Verlaine and, 7:1639b–1640a, 1639b
Corbin, Henri, *Spiritual Body and Celestial*
     Earth, 13:2972b–2973a
Corday, Charlotte
   Chénier's ode in honor of, 4:713a-b
   Richter on, 5:80a
Corde raide, La. See Simon, Claude

Cordeliers, in Rutebeuf's "Des Jacobins,"
     1:346b–347a
Cordon ombilical, Le. See Cocteau, Jean
"Corilla." *See* Nerval, Gérard de
Corinne. See Staël, Madame de
Corinto. See Medici, Lorenzo de'
Coriolanus (Coriolan). See Brecht, Bertolt
"Ćorkan and the German Girl." *See* Andrić,
     Ivo, "Ćorkan i Švabica"
"Ćorkan i Švabica" ("Ćorkan and the German
     Girl"). *See* Andrić, Ivo
Corneille, Pierre, **3:23a–49b**
   Andromède, 4:47b–48a
   Anouilh and, 13:2862b
   attacked by Bossuet, 3:173a
   Boileau and, 3:177a
   Cinna, 3:34a, 35a, 37a–44b
   Clitandre, 3:25b
   compared with Racine, 3:207a
   Discourses on Dramatic Poetry, 3:24b
   Dostoevsky and, 7:1350b
   Horace, 3:33b–37a, 37b
   La mort de Pompée (Pompey's Death),
       3:38a, 46a-b
   La place royale, 3:25b–26a, 30b–31a, 33b
   La suite du menteur (Liar II), 3:46a
   La toison d'or (The Golden Fleece), 3:47b
   Le Cid, 3:27a–34a, 45b
       indicted by the Académie française,
           3:178b
       sources of, 1:134b
   Le menteur (The Liar), 3:46a
   Lessing on, 4:544b, 547b–548a
   L'Illusion comique, 3:27a, 28b
   Médée (Medea), 3:26b–27a, 33b, 45b
   Mélite, 3:25a, 25b
   neoclassical tradition and, 9:1041a
   Nicomède, 3:46b–47b
       performed by Molière's troupe, 3:103b
   as one of French *classiques*, 3:273b
   Othon, 3:47b
   Pascal and, 3:126b
   Pertharite, roi des Lombards, 3:24b
   Polyeucte, 3:44b–45b
   Rodogune, 3:38a
   Sainte-Beuve on, 6:857b
   Staël on, 5:97a

Corneille, Pierre (*cont.*)
  Suréna, 3:33b, 48a
  Taine on, 7:1460a
  Tite et Bérénice, 3:47b, 213b
  views on Racine, 3:208a-b
Cornelisen, Ann, on Ginzburg, 13:3160a
Cornelius Nightly. *See* Kosztolányi, Dezső, *Esti Kornél*
Cornet, Nicolas, funeral oration on by Bossuet, 3:164a
Corona benignitatis anni Dei. See Claudel, Paul
Corona trágica, La. See Lope de Vega
Coronal. See Claudel, Paul, *Corona benignitatis anni Dei*
Corporeal universe. *See* Material universe
Corps conducteurs, Les. See Simon, Claude
Corpses
  in Ionesco's plays
    Amédée, 13:2997b–2998a
    The Killing Game, 13:3011a
Corpse's Regalia, The. *See* Valle-Inclán, Ramón del, *Martes de Carnaval* (Shrove Tuesday), *Las galas del difunto*
Corpus Christi cycle plays, 1:468b–469a
Corpus Christi festival, Aquinas and, 1:416a
Corpus Juris Civilis. See Digest
Corrales
  Calderón and, 2:872b
  Lope de Vega and, 2:850a-b
Correa, Luís Franco, 2:754b
Correggio, *Cefalo*, Renaissance pastoral drama and, 2:916b
Correspondence. *See* Letters
Correspondence littéraire (journal), Diderot and, 4:487b–488a
"Correspondences" ("Correspondances"). *See* Baudelaire, Charles
Correspondência de Fradique Mendes, A. See Eça de Queiroz, José Maria
Corridor and Stairs. See Ritsos, Yannis, *Dhiadhromos kai skala*
Corruption
  civic, Machiavelli's view of, 2:609b–612a
  human, in Dürrenmatt's works, 13:3231a
"Cors de chasse." *See* Apollinaire, Guillaume, *Alcools*

Corsair, The. See Lermontov, Mikhail Yurievich, *Korsar*
Corsica
  Mérimée's travels in, 6:761b
  Rousseau and, 4:459a
Corte de los milagros, La. See Valle-Inclán, Ramón del, *El ruedo ibérico*
"Cortège." *See* Verlaine, Paul
Cortegiano, Il. See Castiglione, Baldesar
Corydon: Traité d'un vain désir. See Gide, André
Cosa e altri racconti, La. See Moravia, Alberto, *Erotic Tales*
Cosa è una cosa, Una. See Moravia, Alberto
Coscienza di Zeno, La. See Svevo, Italo, *The Confessions of Zeno*
Così è (se vi pare). See Pirandello, Luigi
Cosmic elements, in Ungaretti's poetry, 10:1467b
Cosmic Round (organization). *See Kosmische Runde*
Cosmicomiche, Le. See Calvino, Italo, *Cosmicomics*
Cosmopolis. See Bourget, Paul
Cosmopolitanism
  Calvino and, 13:3259a
  of Staël's *De l'Allemagne*, 5:105b–106a
Cosmos. See Gombrowicz, Witold
Cossacks, The. See Tolstoy, Leo
Costa, Joaquín, Europeanization, 9:1121b
Costa Ramos, Maria Eugénia Haas da. *See* Liz, Diana de
Coste, Marguerite, Sade accused by, 4:616b
Costenoble, Philostène. *See* Ghelderode, Michel de
Costumbrismo
  of Blasco Ináñez, 8:357b
    in *Reeds and Mud*, 8:381a, 383b–384a
    in *The Cabin*, 8:373b–374a
    in *The Mayflower*, 8:362b–363a, 368b–369a
Costume. *See* Clothing
Cosway, Mary, Chénier's poems for, 4:699a
Côté de Guermantes, Le. See Proust, Marcel, *Remembrance of Things Past* (*À la recherche du temps perdu*), *The Guermantes Way*

Cotin, Charles, criticized by Boileau, 3:186a–187b

Cotton, Sir Robert, manuscript collection of, 1:69a

Cotton Vitellius A. XV (MS), preservation of, 1:69a-b

Coulanges, Fustel de, Burckhardt and, 6:1243b

Councils of the church. *See* Church councils

Count of Abranhos, The. *See* Eça de Queiroz, José Maria, *O conde Abranhos*

Count of Monte Cristo, The. See Dumas père, Alexandre, *Le comte de Monte-Cristo*

"Count of Monte Cristo, The." *See* Calvino, Italo, *t zero*

Count Öderland. *See* Frisch, Max, *Graf Öderland*

Count Orgel. *See* Radiguet, Raymond, *Le bal du Comte Orgel*

Counter-decadence. *See* "Esprit nouveau, l'"

Counter-Reformation
in France, 3:264a, 264b
Tasso's poetry and, 2:791b

Counterfeit Coin, The. *See* Gorky, Maxim, *Fal'shivaia moneta*

Counterfeiters, The. See Gide, André; Gide, André, *Les faux-monnayeurs*

Counterpoint, in Butor's fiction, 13:3313a-b

Counterpoint (music), Hesse and, 9:847a, 848a

Countertransference, Freud's concept of, 8:7b

Countess Cathleen, The. See Yeats

Countess Mizzi; or, The Family Reunion. See Schnitzler, Arthur, *Komtesse Mizzi oder der Familientag*

Countess Rudolstadt. See Sand, George

Country
Hamsun's use of, 8:34b, 36a-b, 37a-b
see also Nature, Hamsun's use of

"Country of Abundance." *See* Baudelaire, Charles, "Pays de Cocagne"

Country Doctor, The. See Kafka, Franz

Country-Houses of Toledo. *See* Tirso de Molina, *Cigarrales de Toledo*

Coup de Grâce. See Yourcenar, Marguerite, *Le coup de grâce*

Coup de lune, Le. See Simenon, Georges

Coupe et les lèvres, La. See Musset, Alfred de

"Cour du lion, La." *See* La Fontaine, Jean de, *Fables*

"Courage." *See* Akhmatova, Anna, "Muzhestvo"

Courbet, Gustave
Burial at Ornans, 5:532a
Delacroix on, 5:531b–532a
Eça and, 7:1689a
Goncourts on, 7:1409a-b
The Bathers, 5:532a
The Painter's Studio, 5:532a

Couronne et la lyre, La. See Yourcenar, Marguerite

Courrier sud. See Saint-Exupéry, Antoine de

Courrière, Berthe, Huysmans and, 7:1721a-b

Cours de philosophie: Introduction à l'histoire de la philosophie. See Cousin, Victor

Course of Lectures on Modern History, A. See Schlegel, Friedrich von

Course of Time, The. *See* Johnson, Eyvind, *Tidens gäng*

Court of Miracles, The. *See* Valle-Inclán, Ramón del, *El ruedo ibérico* (The Iberian Cycle), *La corte de los milagros*

Court, royal
Camoëns on, 2:759b–760a
in Gottfried, 1:255b–256b
in La Bruyère's *Caractères*, 3:244b–245b
La Rochefoucauld and, 3:52a
in Racine's plays, 3:225b–227a
in *Romance of the Rose*, 1:311a-b
Ronsard and, 2:727a
Walther and, 1:298b–299a
see also Monarchy

Courtier
Castiglione and, 2:650a–665a
Gottfried and, 1:237a-b, 257a–258b
in La Bruyère's *Caractères*, 3:244b–245b

Courtier, The. See Castiglione, Baldesar, *The Book of the Courtier*

Courtly love, 1:241b–243a
in Arnaut's works, 1:175b
in Bernart's works, 1:172b, 173b–174a
Chrétien de Troyes and
Cligés, 1:146b, 193a, 194b–195a
Conte du Graal, 1:146b–147a, 204a-b

Courtly love (*cont.*)
 Chrétien de Troyes and (*cont.*)
  Erec et Enide, 1:1.146a-b, 189b–190b
  Lancelot, 1:146b, 199a
  Philomena, 1:189b–190b, 193a, 194b–195a
  Yvain, 1:200a–201a, 203a
 definition of, 1:140a
 fin amor, *Romance of the Rose* and,
   1:315a–316a
 in Jaufre's works, 1:171b–172a
 in Marcabru's works, 1:166a, 169b–171b
 in Raimon de Miraval's works, 1:166a
 in William IX's works, 1:165a–166a
Courtly Love Songs from the Swabian Epoch.
   See Tieck, Ludwig, *Minnelieder aus
   dem schwäbischen Zeitalter*
Courtois d'Arras, 1:459b
Courtoisie
 Arthurian legend and, 1:154b
 Chrétien de Troyes and, 1:147a-b, 154b
 see also Chivalry
Courtship, in Tasso's works, 2:795b
Courtyards. *See* Corrales
Cousin Bazilio. See Eça de Queiroz, José Maria
Cousin Bette. See Balzac, Honoré de, *La
   cousine Bette*
Cousin Pons, Le (*Cousin Pons*). *See* Balzac,
   Honoré de
Cousin, Victor
 *Cours de philosophie: Introduction à
   l'histoire de la philosophie
   (Introduction to the History of
   Philosophy)*, Vigny and, 5:465a, 477a
 Michelet and, 5:578b
 on Taine, 7:1452a
 Vigny's response to, 5:464a
Cousine Bette, La. See Balzac, Honoré de
Covetous Knight, The. See Pushkin, Alexander
Cowley, Malcolm
 Jiménez and, 9:992b
 on Silone, 12:2294a
Coxcombs, The. See Lesage, Alain-René, *Les
   petits maîtres*
"Cozza et Borgia." *See* Leconte de Lisle,
   Charles Marie
"Cracked Bell, The." *See* Baudelaire, Charles
Craft. *See* Tsvetaeva, Marina, *Remeslo*

Craig, Edward Gordon, on Musco, 8:393a-b
Crane, Hart
 on Apollinaire, 9:894b
 Laforgue and, 7:1883b, 1897a
 Lorca and, 11:2182b
"Crane, The." *See* Khlebnikov, Velimir
Crayencour, Marguerite. *See* Yourcenar,
   Marguerite
"Crayfish, The." *See* Apollinaire, Guillaume,
   Le bestiaire, ou cortège d'Orphée
   (*Bestiary; or, The Parade of Orpheus*),
   "L'Ecrevisse"
"Crayonné au théâtre." *See* Mallarmé,
   Stéphane
Crazy Boy, The. *See* García Lorca, Federico,
   "El niño loco"
Crazy Jane Talks to the Bishop. See Yeats,
   William Butler
"Création et liberté" (Creation and Liberty).
   See Camus, Albert
Création et rédemption (*Creation and
   Redemption*). *See* Dumas père,
   Alexandre
Creation myth
 Aquinas on, 1:421b–422b
 in Augustine's *Confessions*, 1:32b
 Norse, in Laxness' novels, 12:2471b–2742a
 in Rabelais's *Pantagruel*, 2:702a-b
 in *Representacio Adae*, 1:457b
 in Valéry's *Eupalinos*, 8:586a
Creations 1906–1908. *See* Khlebnikov, Velimir,
   Tvoreniia 1906–1908
Creative Evolution. See Bergson, Henri
Creative Mind, The. See Bergson, Henri
Creative process, Simenon on, 12:2502a-b
Creativity
 in Bergson's thought, 8:59b–60b
 Camus's view of, 13:3066b–3067a
 in Musil's *The Man Without Qualities*,
   9:948b, 951a
 Sartre's view of, 12:2590a, 2608a–2609a
 Valéry on, 8:571b–572a
Creature Conversations. See Colette,
   Dialogues de bêtes
Crébillon. *See* Jolyot, Prosper
Creditors (*Fordringsägare*). *See* Strindberg,
   August

Credo, Claudel's *The City* and, 8:474b, 475a-b
Creed, Robert, on the oral-formulaic composition of *Beowulf*, 1:67b
Crepuscolari (literary school). *See* Twilight poets
"Crepúsculo." *See* Machado, Antonio, *Soledades*
Crescent Moon, The. See Tagore, Rabindranath
Creuzer, Friedrich, Richter and, 5:84a
Crève-coeur, Le. See Aragon, Louis
"Cricket Beneath the Waterfall, The." *See* Krleža, Miroslav, "Cvrčak pod vodopadom"
Crime contre l'esprit, Le (Les martyrs). See Aragon, Louis
Crime and punishment
  in Baroja's *La dama errante*, 9:598a-b
  in Kafka, 9:1166a-b
  of Sade, 4:621a, 622a, 626a-b, 630b–631b, 632b–633b
Crime and Punishment. See Dostoevsky, Feodor
Crime stories
  Chekhov and, 7:1859b–1860a
  see also Detective fiction
Crime Was in Granada, The. *See* Machado, Antonio, "El crimen fue en Granada"
Crimea, in Mickiewicz's poetry, 5:615a–616a
Crimean Sonnets. See Mickiewicz, Adam, *Sonety Krymskie*
Crimean War
  Mickiewicz and, 5:631b
  Tolstoy and, 7:1471a
"Crimen fue en Granada, El." *See* Machado, Antonio
Crimes Against the Spirit (The Martyrs). *See* Aragon, Louis, *Le crime contre l'esprit (Les martyrs)*
Crimes and Crimes (Brott och brott). See Strindberg, August
Crimes de l'amour, Les. See Sade, Donatien Alphonse François, marquis de
Crimes of Love, The. See Sade, Donatien Alphonse François, marquis de
Criminal Sociology. *See* Azorín, *La sociologia criminal*

Criminal symbolism, in Hesse's *Klein und Wagner*, 9:842a-b, 843b
Criminality, Genet and, 13:2868b, 2871a, 2874a-b, 2889b
Criminoso por ambição. See Ferreira de Castro, José Maria
Crimson Saber, The. *See* Khlebnikov, Velimir, "Malinovaia shashka"
Crinagoras, 13:2981b–2982a
"Cripple, The." *See* Andersen, Hans Christian
"Crisalide." *See* Montale, Eugenio, *Cuttlefish Bones (Ossi di seppia)*, "Chrysalis"
"Crise de vers." *See* Mallarmé, Stéphane
Crisis. See Hesse, Hermann, *Krisis*
Crisis of Culture, The. *See* Bely, Andrey, *Krizis kul'tury*
Crisis of Life, The. *See* Bely, Andrey, *Krizis zhizni*
"Crisis of the new," Rimbaud and, 7:1785b–1786a
Crisis of Thought, The. *See* Bely, Andrey, *Krizis mysli*
"Crisis of Verse." *See* Mallarmé, Stéphane, "Crise de vers"
Crispin, rival de son maître (Crispin, His Master's Rival). See Lesage, Alain-René
Cristinas Heimreise (Cristina's Journey Home). See Hofmannsthal, Hugo von
Cristo de Velázquez, El. See Unamuno, Miguel de
Cristo si e fermato a Eboli. See Levi, Carlo
Critica, La (journal), Croce and, 8:316b, 327b
Critical Essays. See Barthes, Roland
Critical Letters. See Lessing, Gotthold Ephraim, *Kritische Briefe*
Critical and Literary Portraits. *See* Sainte-Beuve, Charles-Augustin, *Critiques et portraits littéraires*
"Critico fantastico, Un." *See* Pirandello, Luigi
Critique of Aesthetic Judgment, The. See Kant, Immanuel
Critique de la raison dialectique. See Sartre, Jean-Paul, *Critique of Dialectical Reason*
Critique of Dialectical Reason. See Sartre, Jean-Paul
Critique of Judgment. See Kant, Immanuel

Critique of Political Economy, The. See Marx,
	Karl, *Zur Kritik der Politische Ökonomie*
Critique of Practical Reason, The. See Kant,
	Immanuel
Critique of Pure Reason, The. See Kant,
	Immanuel
Critique of Words, A. *See* Čapek, Karel, *Kritika
	slov*
Critiques et portraits littéraires. See
	Sainte-Beuve, Charles-Augustin
Croatian God Mars, The. *See* Krleža, Miroslav,
	Hrvatski bog Mars
Croatian writers. *See* Krleža, Miroslav
Croce, Benedetto, **8:311a–329b**
	on Alfieri, 4:688a-b
	on Carducci, 7:1514a-b
	*Ciò che è vivo e ciò che è morto nella
		filosofia di Hegel (What Is Living and
		What Is Dead of the Philosophy of
		Hegel)*, 8:323a
	*Contributo alla critica di me stesso (An
		Autobiography)*, 8:311a, 314b–315a,
		326b–327a, 328a
	*Estetica come scienza dell'espressione e
		linguistica generale (Aesthetic as
		Science of Expression and General
		Linguistic)*, 8:312b, 318a, 318b–319a,
		320b, 326b
		Machado and, 9:762a
	*Filosofia della pratica: Economica ed etica
		(Philosophy of the Practical: Economic
		and Ethic)*, 8:321b–322b
	*Filosofia, poesia, storia (Philosophy, Poetry,
		History)*, 8:313a-b, 327a-b
	on futurism, 9:813b
	*Il concetto della storia nelle sue relazione
		col concetto dell'arte* (The Idea of
		History and Its Relationship with the
		Idea of Art), 8:313b–314b, 318a, 321a
	Il manifesto degli intellettuali antifascisti
		(Manifesto of the Anti-Fascist
		Intellectuals), 8:327a
	*La filosofia di Giambattista Vico (The
		Philosophy of Giambattista Vico)*,
		3:312b, 8:325a–326a
	"La storia ridotta sotto il concetto generale
		dell'arte," 8:313a-b

	on Leopardi, 5:551a
	*Logica come scienza del concetto puro
		(Logic as the Science of the Pure
		Concept)*, 8:317b, 318a
	*Materialismo storico ed economia
		marxistica (Historical Materialism and
		the Economics of Karl Marx)*,
		8:315a–316a
	Montale and, 11:1989a–1990a
	Pascoli and, 7:1825a, 1825b, 1826a, 1831b,
		1833b
	Saggio sullo Hegel (Essay on Hegel),
		8:323a–325a
	*Storia d'Europa nel secolo XIX (History of
		Europe in the Nineteenth Century)*,
		8:327b
	on technical progress, 11:1999a
	Storia d'Italia (A History of Italy), twilight
		poets and, 11:1997a
	*Storia d'Italia dal 1871 al 1915 (History of
		Italy, 1871–1915)*, 8:327b
	*Teoria e storia della storiografia (History:
		Its Theory and Practice)*, 8:320b–321b
	Vittorini and, 12:2735b
Crocodile Song; or, A Talk about Truth. *See*
	Krleža, Miroslav, *Krokodilina ili
	razgovor o istini*
"Crocuses." *See* Apollinaire, Guillaume,
	Alcools, "Les colchiques"
Cromwell. See Hugo, Victor; Mérimée, Prosper
Cronaca bizantina (literary journal), 7:1497b
Crónica de Castilla
	Crónica particular del Cid and, 1:131a
	Gesta de las mocedades de Rodrigo in,
		1:129a-b
	sources of, 1:131a
Crónica de veinte reyes, Poema de mio Cid in,
	1:114a-b, 131a
Crónica general, Lope de Vega and, 2:858a
Crónica particular del Cid, Crónica de Castilla
	and, 1:131a
Crónica rimada. See Mocedades de Rodrigo
Crónicas de Londres. See Eça de Queiroz, José
	Maria
Croquis parisiens. See Huysmans, Joris Karl
Cros, Charles, Rimbaud and, 7:1808b

Cross-examined. *See* Grass, Günter, *Ausgefragt*

Crossed Works of Fiction of Elsa Triolet and Louis Aragon, The. *See* Aragon, Louis, *Les oeuvres romanesques croisées d'Elsa Triolet et de Louis Aragon*

"Crossing the Zbruch." *See* Babel, Isaac, "Perekhod cherez Zbruch"

Crossman, Richard H. S., *The God That Failed*, Silone's essay in, 12:2273b

Crothers, Rachel, Ibsen's influence on, 7:1443b

"Crow Comes Last, The." *See* Calvino, Italo

Crowd symbolism, in Queneau's *The Bark Tree*, 12:2526b

Crowds of Lourdes, The. See Huysmans, Joris Karl, *Les foules de Lourdes*

Crowds and Power. See Canetti, Elias

Crowley, Aleister, Pessoa and, 10:1494a

Crown and the Lyre, The. *See* Yourcenar, Marguerite, *La couronne et la lyre*

Crucible, The. See Miller, Arthur

Crucifixion, La. See Cocteau, Jean

Cruel Tales. See Villiers de l'Isle-Adam, *Contes cruels*

Cruelty, theater of. *See* Theater of cruelty

Cruelty, theme of, in Gombrowicz's works, 12:2574a–2577a

Cruickshank, John, on Montherlant, 11:1933a-b, 1935b

Crusaders of the Cause, The. *See* Valle-Inclán, Ramón del, *La guerra carlista* (The Carlist War), *Los cruzados de la causa*

Crusades, First, *chansons de geste* regarding, 1:109b

Crusading, Walther and, 1:303b

Crusading epic, Wolfram and, 1:282b–285b

Crusts. See Claudel, Paul, *Le pain dur*

Cruzados de la causa, Los. See Valle-Inclán, Ramón del, *La guerra carlista*

Cry and Landscapes, A. *See* Ungaretti, Giuseppe, *Un grido e paesaggi*

Csáth, Géza, 10:1235a
   A varászlo halála ("The Magician Dies"), "The Night of the Black Moon" and, 9:869a
   Ady and, 9:869b

Csinszka. *See* Boncza, Berta

"Csóonak a Holt Tengeren." *See* Ady, Endre

"Csukott szemű csókok." *See* Ady, Endre

Cuarta crónica general, as literary source, 1:131b

Cuatro jinetes del Apocalipsis, Los. See Blasco Ibáñez, Vicente

Cuba, Eça in, 7:1690a–1691b

Cubism, 8:546b
   Apollinaire and, 9:884a, 891b, 892a, 897a, 901b
   Khlebnikov's *Slovo kak takovoe* and, 10:1345a
   Lagerkvist and, 10:1683a–1684a
   Lorca and, 11:2170a
   Pessoa and, 10:1486a
   Russian futurists and, 11:1839b–1840b
   "Zone" and, 9:896a-b
   see also Witkiewicz, Stanisław Ignacy

Cubist Painters: Aesthetic Meditations, The. See Apollinaire, Guillaume, *Méditations esthétiques: Les peintres cubistes*

Cubo-futurists. *See* Futurists

Cucaña, La (The Greased Pole). *See* Cela, Camilo José

Cuento de abril. See Valle-Inclán, Ramón del

Cuentos valencianos. See Blasco Ibáñez, Vicente

Cuernos de Don Friolera, Los. See Valle-Inclán, Ramón del, *Martes de Carnaval*

Cueva de Salamanca, La. See Cervantes, Miguel de

"Cujus regio, ejus religio" (The crown decides the religion of the state) principle, 3:158b

Culhwch and Olwen
   Arthurian legend and, 1:138a, 142b
   hero in, 1:155a-b
   Irish legends and, 1:141a

Cultural Life of Modern America. See Hamsun, Knut, *Fra det moderne Amerikas Aaandsliv*

Cultural relativism, in Herder's idea of *Humanität*, 4:646a-b, 649a-b, 652a-b

Culture
   Cela on, 13:3125a-b

Culture (*cont.*)
    European, Kundera and, 13:3396a–3397b
    Foucault and, 13:3328a
      knowledge and, 13:3351b–3355b
    history of, Burckhardt on, 6:1234b–1237a
    institutions of, Sainte-Beuve on, 6:850a-b
    Malraux on, 12:2426a
    Nietzsche and, 7:1659b–1660a
    primitive, in Mérimée's works, 6:762a
    Rimbaud's view of, 7:1786b–1787a
    Sainte-Beuve on, 6:848b–855b
    Western
      in Butor, 13:3299a-b, 3306b
      Ekelöf and, 12:2645a-b
"Culture as an Alibi." *See* Frisch, Max, "Kultur
    als Alibi"
Cumani, Maria, 12:2388b, 2402b, 2404b
Cunard, Nancy, Aragon and, 11:2069b, 2070b
Cunto de li cunti, Lo. See Basile, Giambattista
Cup and the Lip, The. See Musset, Alfred de,
    La coupe et les lèvres
Curator Carsten. See Storm, Theodor
Curchod, Suzanne, 5:89a-b
Curé de Tours, Le. See Balzac, Honoré de
Curé de village, Le. See Balzac, Honoré de
"Curé et le mort, Le." *See* La Fontaine, Jean
    de, *Fables*
Curée, La. See Zola, Émile
Curia, papal. *See* Papal curia
Curiosités esthétiques. See Apollinaire,
    Guillaume
Curses Against the Argentine Ant. *See* Butor,
    Michel, *Imprécations contre la fourmi
    d'Argentine*
Curtain, The. *See* Pavese, Cesare, *The
    Beautiful Summer*
Curtius, Ernst Robert
    George and, 8:448b, 449a, 449b
    on Ortega y Gasset, 9:119a-b, 1126b–1127a
Curva da estrada, A. See Ferreira de Castro,
    José Maria
Curve in the Road, The. *See* Ferreira de
    Castro, José Maria, *A curva da estrada*
Custine, Delphine de, Chateaubriand and,
    5:127b
"Custom of the Island of Cea, A." *See*
    Montaigne, Michel de, *Essays*

"Customs Men, The." *See* Rimbaud, Arthur,
    "Les reparties de Nina"
Cuttlefish Bones. See Montale, Eugenio
*Cuttlefish, The; or, The Hyrcanian World
    View. See* Witkiewicz, Stanisław Ignacy
"Cvrčak pod vodopadom." *See* Krleža, Miroslav
*Cybernetics; or, Control and Communication
    in the Animal and the Machine. See*
    Wiener, Norbert
Cycle plays, English. *See* Corpus Christi cycle
    plays
Cyclops. See Euripides
"Cygne, Le." *See* Baudelaire, Charles, "The
    Swan"
Cynewulf, 1:65b
Cynthius. *See* Giraldi, Giambattista
Cyrus. See Wieland, Christoph Martin
Cysat, Renward, 1:466a
Czartoryski, Prince Adam, Mickiewicz and,
    5:612b, 632a
Czech literature
    anticlericalism, 9:1096a
    Hašek's contributions to, 9:1096b
    satire, 9:1096a
Czech Novel, A. *See* Scheinpflugová, Olga,
    Čský román
Czechoslovakia, Hussite revolutionary
    ideology, 9:1092b

D

"Da, tak diktuet vdokhnovenie." *See* Blok, Alexander

"Da un lago svizzero." *See* Montale, Eugenio, *The Storm and Other Things* (*La bufera e altro*), "From a Swiss Lake"

DaCal, Ernesto Guerra, on Eça, 7:1702a

Dachniki. See Gorky, Maxim

Dačice Tale, A. *See* Hašek, Jaroslav, "Historie dačická"

Dactyl meter, in Blok's works, 9:961b

Dada (French journal)
Breton's articles in, 11:1939b
Zurich writers, 11:1940a

Dadaism
Apollinaire's "Arbre" and, 9:897a
Aragon and, 11:2061a, 2062a-b
Arp and, 10:1365b, 1368b, 1369a–1371a
beginnings of, 11:2062b–2064a
Breton's contribution to, 11:1939b–1940a
Ghelderode and, 11:2113b, 2134b, 2135a
Lorca and, 11:2169b
opposition to literary form, 11:1953a
as response to its times, 11:1965b
Tzara in Paris, 11:1965a
Valéry's *Charmes* and, 8:583b

Daemonic force, Goethe's concept of, in *Egmont*, 5:10a

Daffinger, Moritz, Grillparzer betrayed by, 5:435b

Dag tilovers og andre Historier, En. See Gunnarsson, Gunnar

"Dagen svalnar." *See* Södergran, Edith

Dahon, Renée, Maeterlinck and, 8:139b, 141a-b

Daily Express (London), Solzhenitsyn's writings in, 13:3195b

"Daimons, Les." *See* Ronsard, Pierre de

Dal, Vladimir, compilation of proverbs, 13:3209a

Dalberg, Wolfgang Heribert von, 5:33a, 34b

"D'alberi sofferte forme." *See* Quasimodo, Salvatore

D'Alembert. *See* Alembert, Jean Le Rond d'

D'Alembert's Dream. See Diderot, Denis, *Rêve de d'Alembert*

Dali, Salvador
Lorca and, 11:2169b, 2181b
"Rèverie" (Dream), 11:2074b

Dama duende, La. See Calderón de la Barca, Pedro, *The Phantom Lady*

Dama errante, La. See Baroja, Pío

"Dama s sobachkoy." *See* Chekhov, Anton

Damaged Goods. See Brieux, Eugène, *Les avariés*

Dame aux camélias, La. See Dumas fils, Alexandre

Dame de Monsoreau, La. See Dumas père, Alexandre

Dame de pique, La. See Pushkin, Alexander, *The Queen of Spades*

"Dame du photographe, La." *See* Colette

"Damnation." *See* Ungaretti, Giuseppe

Damnation de Faust, La. See Berlioz, Hector

Damnation of Faust. See Berlioz, Hector, *La damnation de Faust*

Damned (or Maligned) Poets, The. *See* Verlaine, Paul, *Les poètes maudits*

Damsel Violaine, The. *See* Claudel, Paul, *La jeune fille Violaine*

Danas (Today), Krleža and, 11:1818a-b

Dance
Mallarmé and, 7:1575b, 1586a
in Rilke's *Sonnets to Orpheus*, 9:787b–788a, 789a
in Valéry's *Dance and the Soul*, 8:586a-b, 587a

Dance of Death, The. See Strindberg, August

"Dance of Death." *See* García Lorca, Federico, "Danza de la muerte"

Dance of Death. See Wedekind, Frank, *Death and the Devil*

"Dance of Life." *See* Munch, Edvard

Dance and the Soul. See Valéry, Paul, *L'Âme et la danse*

"Dances of Death, The." *See* Blok, Alexander, "Pliaski smerti"

Danchet, Antoine, friendship with Lesage, 3:319a

Danger and Destiny. *See* Kosztolányi, Dezső, *Végzet és veszély*

Dangerous Acquaintances. See Laclos,
Pierre-Ambroise-François Choderlos de,
Les liaisons dangereuses
Danischmend. See Wieland, Christoph Martin
Danish language, Gunnarsson and,
10:1497a-b
Danish Mistress of Hof, The. *See* Gunnarsson,
Gunnar, *Borgslægtens Historie* (The
History of the Family at Borg), *Den
danske Frue paa Hof*
"*Dannazione.*" *See* Ungaretti, Giuseppe,
"Damnation"
D'Annunzio, Gabriele, **8:175a–203b**
aestheticism of, 9:592b
Alcyone, 8:190b, 192a–194b
autobiographical prose of, 8:199a–201b
"Canto augurale per la nazione eletta"
(Auspicious Song for the Chosen
Nation), 8:191b–192a
Canto novo (New Song), 8:177a-b, 188b
changing evaluations of, 8:175a–176a,
201b–202a
Contemplazione della morte (Contemplation
of Death), 8:199b
Elegie romane (Roman Elegies),
8:188b–189b
Elettra, 8:190b, 191b–192a
Episcopo & Company (*Giovanni Episcopo*),
8:181b–183a
Forse che sì forse che no (Maybe Yes,
Maybe No), 8:187b–188b, 199b
Francesca da Rimini, 8:196a-b
French plays by, 8:197b
"Furit aestus" (Summer Rages),
8:193b–194a
Hofmannsthal's *Die Frau im Fenster* based
on story by, 9:695b
"Il peccato di maggio" (May Sin), 8:178a-b
Intermezzo di rime (Intermezzo of Rhyme),
8:177b–178b, 188b
Isaotta Guttadàuro e altre poesie (Isaotta
Guttadàuro and Other Poems),
8:178b–179a, 180b
Italian national theater project, 8:186b, 200b
"La città del silenzio" (The City of Silence),
8:191b–192a
La città morta (*The Dead City*), 8:195a-b

La fiaccola sotto il moggio (The Light Under
the Bushel), 8:197a
La Gioconda (*Gioconda*), 8:195b–196a
La gloria (Glory), 8:195b–196a
La Leda senz cigno (Leda Without the
Swan), 8:199b–200a
La nave (The Ship), 8:197a-b
"La sera fiesolana" (Fiesole Evening),
8:193a-b
*Laudi del cielo del mare della terra e degli
eroi* (Praises of the Sky, of the Sea, of
the Earth, and of the Heroes),
8:190b–194b
Le faville del maglio (Sparks from the
Forge), 8:201a
Le novelle dellla Pescara (*Tales of My
Native Town*), 8:179b–180b
Le vergini delle rocce (*Maidens of the
Rocks*), 8:184b–186a
Libro segreto (Secret Book), 8:201a-b
L'Isottèo—La Chimera (Isottèo—The
Chimera), 8:178b–179a, 180b, 188b
Maia, 8:190b–191b
Marinetti and, 9:812a
Montale's opposition to, 11:1988a–1989a,
1993b, 1994a
Notturno (Nocturne), 8:200a–201a
Odi navali (Naval Odes), 8:190b
Pascoli and, 7:1826a, 1828a, 1831b
Più che l'amore (More than Love), 8:197a
Poema paradisiaco (Paradisiacal Poem),
8:188b, 189b–190b
political activities of, 8:187a-b, 194b–195a,
198a–199a
Primo vere (First Spring), 8:176b–177a,
189b
Quasimodo's essay on, 12:2408a
short stories by, 8:179b–180b
Solus ad solam, 8:199a-b
Svevo and, 8:68b–69a, 70b–71a, 72a, 76b,
85b
The Child of Pleasure (*Il piacere*), 8:68b
8:179b, 8:180b–181b
The Daughter of Jorio (*La figlia di Iorio*),
8:196b–197a
Pirandello and, 8:395a

The Flame of Life (*Il fuoco*), 8:69a, 186a–187b

The Intruder (*L'Innocente*), 8:181b, 182b–183b

The Triumph of Death (*Il trionfo della morte*), 8:68b, 183b–184b

theater writing of, 8:194b–195a, 197b–198a

"veristic" or realistic works of, 8:177b

Vittorini and, 12:2735b

Dans le labyrinthe. See Robbe-Grillet, Alain, *In the Labyrinth*

Danse de Sophocle, La. See Cocteau, Jean

"Danse du peyotl, La." *See* Artaud, Antonin, *D'un voyage au pays des Tarahumaras* (*Pcyote Dance*), "The Peyote Dance"

Dante Alighieri, **1:431a–450b**

Alfieri and, 4:671b, 688a

Augustine and, 1:35b, 48a

Blok and, 9:969a

Boccaccio and, 2:511a, 531a-b

Canzoniere (*Rime*), 1:444b

Claudel and, 8:472a

Convivio (*Banquet*), 1:435a, 439a–441a

"Amor che ne la mente mi ragiona," 1:440b

incompleteness of, 1:440b–441a

"Le dolci rime d'amor ch'i'solìa," 1:440b

"Voi che 'ntendendo," 1:440a

Croce on, 8:318a

D'Annunzio and, 8:191b, 196a

De monarchia (*On Monarchy*), 1:442a–444a

De vulgari eloquentia (*On Eloquence in the Vernacular*), 1:435a, 441a–442a

vernacular poetry, categories of, 2:514a

Delacroix and, 5:518b

Dinesen and, 10:1294b

Divine Comedy (*Commedia*), 1:445a–448b

allegory and, 1:319b

Aquinas and, 1:419b

Augustine's *Confessions* and, 1:28a, 31a

Boccaccio's adaptation, 2:515a-b

cyclical nature of, 5:651b

Gogol and, 6:973a, 995a

Huysmans and, 7:1709a

Inferno, 5:650b, 8:167b–168a, 169b, 405a, 11:2016a, 13:3199a

Kosztolányi's *Esti Kornél* and, 10:1243b

Nerval's style and, 6:945b

Pascoli on, 7:1834a, 1848a–1849a

Petrarch and, 2:491a, 528a

Psychomachia and, 1:20b

Purgatorio, 11:2015b

translated by George, 8:447a

and Vittorini's *In Sicily*, 12:2743b

George and, 8:462a, 462b, 463b

Hofmannsthal and, 9:689b

Hugo and, 6:704a-b

Inferno, 2:752b

influence on Renaissance pastoral poetry, 2:903b–904a

Machado and, 9:760a

Machiavelli and, 2:597b–598a

Mandelshtam on, 10:1622a

in Meyer's *Marriage of the Monk*, 6:936a

Montale and, 11:1994b

Nerval and, 6:966b

Pascoli on, 7:1828b

on Pier Celestine, 12:2299b

Quasimodo and, 12:2390b, 2407b–2408a

rhyme in troubadour poetry and, 1:176a-b

rime petrose, Petrarch's use of, 2:493b

Romance of the Rose and, 1:332b–333b

Sacrilegio and, 8:349a

Unamuno and, 8:297a

Vita nuova (*New Life*), 1:435b–439b

allegory and, 1:320b–321a

Convivio and, 1:440a

"Donne ch'avete intelletto d'amore," 1:436a-b

Nerval's style and, 6:945b

as a source for Mickiewicz, 5:614b

"Tanto gentile e tanto honesta pare" ("So gentle and so full of dignity my lady appears"), 2:752a

see also Beatrice

Dantons Tod (*Danton's Death*). *See* Büchner, Georg

"Danza de la muerte." *See* García Lorca, Federico

Danzig Trilogy. See Grass, Günter

Daphné. See Vigny, Alfred Victor de

Daphne (mythological figure), 6:952b

"D'après Dürer." *See* Yourcenar, Marguerite, *La mort conduit l'attelage*

"D'après Greco." *See* Yourcenar, Marguerite,
    La mort conduit l'attelage
"D'après Rembrandt." *See* Yourcenar,
    Marguerite, *Comme l'eau qui coule*
Darboux, Jean-Gaston, in *Kotik Letaev*, 9:907b
Dare e avere. See Quasimodo, Salvatore
Dares and Dictys, version of Homer, 1:447a
Darío, Rubén, 8:297a
    Jiménez and, 9:993b
    Machado and, 9:745b, 762b
    modernismo and, 9:993b–994a
    Ortega y Gasset on, 9:1135b
    Valle-Inclán and, 8:332b, 336a
Dark Angels, The. See Mauriac, François
Dark Brain of Piranesi and Other Essays, The.
    See Yourcenar, Marguerite, *Sous*
    bénéfice d'inventaire
Dark Forest, The. *See* Baroja, Pío, *La selva*
    oscura
Dark poetry, Russian, Blok, 9:976b–979a
Dark Visage, The. See Rozanov, Vasilii,
    Temnyilik
"Darling, The." *See* Chekhov, Anton,
    "Dushechka"
Dart, The. *See* Machado, Antonio, *Soledades*
    (Solitudes), "La saeta"
Darts. See Eça de Queiroz, José Maria
Darwin, Charles
    Bergson and, 8:47a, 60b
    Descent of Man, 6:1164b
    Huysmans and, 7:1711b
    Kazantzakis and, 9:1075a
    Lagerkvist and, 10:1681b
    Nietzsche and, 7:1660a
    Ortega y Gasset and, 9:11212b
    Strindberg and, 7:1753b
    Svevo and, 8:75b
    The Origin of Species, 8:47a
    theory of evolution
        Ibsen on, 7:1442a
        Taine's borrowings from, 7:1453b, 1456b
Darwinism
    Bergson and, 8:60b
    in Chekhov's "The Duel," 7:1866a
    in Leconte de Lisle, 6:1266b–1267b
    Maupassant and, 7:1775a
    Milosz and, 13:2939a
    poetic realism and, 6:914a
    Portuguese literature and, 10:1484b
    social, in D'Annunzio's works, 8:68b
    Svevo's view of, 8:85a-b
    in Verga's works, 7:1552b, 1554a, 1561b
Dašenka čili Život štěněte (Dashenka; or; The
    Life of a Puppy). See Čapek, Karel
Dassel, Reinald von. *See* Reinald von Dassel
Daudet, Alphonse
    attack on Zola and, 7:1533a
    Contes du lundi (Monday's Tales), 7:1762b
    Maupassant and, 7:1762b, 1763a
    Turgenev and, 6:1291a
Daughter of Eve, A. See Balzac, Honoré de,
    Une fille d'Eve
Daughter of Jorio, The. See D'Annunzio,
    Gabriele
Daughters of Fire. See Nerval, Gérard de
Daumier, Honoré
    Baudelaire and, 7:1329b
    Goncourts on, 7:1397a
Daunou, Pierre-Claude-François, Sainte-Beuve
    and, 6:857b
D'Autres et moi. See Mauriac, François
"Davanti San Guido." *See* Carducci, Giosue
David. See Klopstock, Friedrich Gottlieb
David, Jacques-Louis
    Chénier's friendship with, 4:699b, 702a-b
    Delacroix and, 5:517a, 531b
    neoclassism and, 5:523b
    The Death of Marat, 7:1410a
David Séchard ou les souffrances d'un
    inventeur (David Séchard). See Balzac,
    Honoré de
David Strauss, der Bekenner und der
    Schriftsteller (David Strauss, the
    Confessor and Writer). See Nietzsche,
    Friedrich
Davies, John, translator of La Rochefoucauld,
    3:52b
Davni dani. See Krleža, Miroslav
Davor. See Grass, Günter, *Max*
"Davos Configuration II." *See* Arp, Jean
Dawn. See Nietzsche, Friedrich, *Morgenröte*
Dawn songs
    Walther and, 1:293b–295b
    Wolfram and, 1:267a–268a

"Dawn, The." *See* Södergran, Edith, "Gryningen"

"Dawn, The

Day After Day. See Quasimodo, Salvatore

"Day and the Age, The." *See* Zamyatin, Yevgeny Ivanovich, "O segodniashnem i o sovremennom"

Day of the Dead, The. *See* Pascoli, Giovanni, *Myricae* (Tamarisks), "Il giorno dei morti"

Day of the Dupes, 3:56a

"Day Goes By, A." *See* Pirandello, Luigi, "Una giornata"

Day Is Breaking. *See* Kazantzakis, Nikos, *Ksimerónei*

"Day Is Cooling, The." *See* Södergran, Edith, "Dagen svalnar"

Daybreak. See Schnitzler, Arthur, *Spiel im Morgengrauen*

Daybreak Drunkenness. *See* Kosztolányi, Dezső, "Hajnali részegség"

"Days of 1896." *See* Cavafy, Constantine, "Meres tou 1896"

Days. *See* George, Stefan, *Algabal*, "Tage"

Days of the Commune, The. See Brecht, Bertolt, *Die Tage der Kommune*

Days of His Grace, The. See Johnson, Eyvind

"Days of Korolenko, The." *See* Gorky, Maxim, "Vremia Korolenko"

Days with Leaves. *See* Arp, Jean, *Jours effeuillés*

Days and Nights. *See* Jarry, Alfred, *Les jours et les nuits*

Day's Work of the Fates, A. See Lesage, Alain-René, *Une journée des parques*

Days of Wrath. See Malraux, André

De aeternitate contra murmurantes. See Aquinas, Thomas, St.

"De amygdalo in Pannonia nata." *See* Pannonius, Janus

De angelis. See Aquinas, Thomas, St.

De anima. See Aquinas, Thomas, St.; Aristotle

De antiquissima Italorum sapientia ex linguae latinae originibus eruenda. See Vico, Giovanni Battista

De Bosis, Adolfo, Pascoli and, 7:1828a

De Buonaparte et des Bourbons. See Chateaubriand, François René de

De civitate dei. See Augustine, St., *City of God*

De coelo et ejus mirabilibus et de inferno. See Swedenborg, Emanuel

De concierto están los condes, the Cid epic and, 1:133a

De conscribendis epistolis. See Erasmus

De constantia jurisprudentia liber alter. See Vico, Giovanni Battista, *Diritto universale*

De contemptu mundi. See Erasmus

De copia verborum ac rerum. See Erasmus

De deo Socratis. See Apuleius

De divinis nominibus. See Aquinas, Thomas, St.

De doctrina christiana. See Augustine, St.

De ente et essentia ad fratres et socios meos. See Aquinas, Thomas, St.

De fallaciis. See Aristotle

De gestis Caesaris. See Petrarch

De hebdomadibus. See Aquinas, Thomas, St.

De ingressu puerorum in religione. See Aquinas, Thomas, St.

De investigatione Antichristi. See Gerhoh of Reichersberg

De la démocratie en Amérique. See Tocqueville, Alexis de, *Democracy in America*

De la littérature considérée dans ses rapports avec les institutions sociales. See Staël, Madame de

De la monarchie selon la charte. See Chateaubriand, François René de

"De la nature." *See* Lebrun, "Pindare"

De la religion. See Constant, Benjamin

De la sagesse. See Charron, Pierre

"De la tragédie." *See* Musset, Alfred de

De l'Allemagne. See Heine, Heinrich; Staël, Madame de

De l'amour. See Stendhal, *On Love*

De l'autorité de Cassien. See Fénelon, François de Salignac de la Mothe-

De l'esprit des lois. See Montesquieu, Charles-Louis de Secondat, baron de

De l'esprit géométrique. See Pascal, Blaise

"De l'estat du monde." *See* Rutebeuf

De libero arbitrio. See Augustine, St.; Erasmus

"De l'influence des passions." *See* Staël, Madame de

De l'intelligence (On Intelligence). See Taine, Hippolyte

De magistro. See Augustine, St.

De malo. See Aquinas, Thomas, St.

De mendacio. See Augustine, St.

De mente heroica. See Vico, Giovanni Battista

De mi país. See Unamuno, Miguel de

De monarchia. See Dante Alighieri

De mulieribus claris. See Boccaccio, Giovanni

De musica. See Augustine, St.

De natura rerum. See Lucretius

De nostri temporis studiorum ratione. See Vico, Giovanni Battista, *On the Study Methods of Our Time*

De oratore. See Cicero, Marcus Tullius

De ordine. See Augustine, St.

De otio religioso. See Petrarch

De perfectione spiritualis vitae. See Aquinas, Thomas, St.

De periculis novissimorum temporum. See William of Saint Amour

De potentia Dei. See Aquinas, Thomas, St.

De praedestinatione sanctorum. See Augustine, St.

De principiis naturae ad Fratrem Sylvestrum. See Aquinas, Thomas, St.

De propositionalibus modalibus. See Aquinas, Thomas, St.

De Quincey, Thomas

  Confessions of an English Opium-Eater, 9:894a

    Baudelaire and, 7:1326a

    in Edmond Goncourt's *La Faustin,* 7:1417a

    Musset's translation of, 6:1002b

De ratione studii. See Erasmus

De rationibus fidei contra Saracenos Graecos et Armenos ad cantorem Antiochiae. See Aquinas, Thomas, St.

De re militari. See Vegetius

De rebus Hispaniae. See Jiménez de Rada, Rodrigo

De regimine principum. See Aquinas, Thomas, St., *De regno*

De remediis utriusque fortunae. See Petrarch

"De Rosis Nascentibus." *See* Ausonius

"De Sainte Eglise." *See* Rutebeuf

De Sanctis, Francesco, on veneration of Alfieri, 4:688a

De sarcienda ecclesiae concordia. See Erasmus

De scriptore. See Wedekind, Frank

De sermone. See Pontano, Giovanni

De servo arbitrio. See Luther, Martin

De Sinner, Louis, Leopardi and, 5:548b

De Spectaculis. See Tertullian

De substantiis separatis. See Aquinas, Thomas, St.

De sui ipsius et multorum ignorantia. See Petrarch

De to Baronesser. See Andersen, Hans Christian, *The Two Baronesses*

De trinitate. See Boethius

De trinitatis. See Augustine, St.

De un cancionero apócrifo. See Machado, Antonio

De unione verbi incarnati. See Aquinas, Thomas, St.

De unitate intellectus. See Aquinas, Thomas, St.

De universi juris uno principio et fine uno liber unum. See Vico, Giovanni Battista, *Diritto universale*

De vera religione. See Augustine, St.

De viris illustribus. See Petrarch

De virtutibus. See Aquinas, Thomas, St.

De vita solitaria. See Petrarch

De vulgari eloquentia. See Dante Alighieri

De-historicization, in works of Ionesco, 13:3011b–3012a

"Dead, The." *See* Joyce, James

"Dead of '92." *See* Rimbaud, Arthur, "Morts de quatre-vingts-douze"

Dead City, The. See D'Annunzio, Gabriele, *La città morta*

Dead Command, The. See Blasco Ibáñez, Vicente, *Los muertos mandan*

"Dead Hand, The" ("La main d'écorché"). *See* Maupassant, Guy de

"Dead Heron." *See* Quasimodo, Salvatore, "Airone morto"

Dead House, The. See Ritsos, Yannis, *To nekro spiti*

Dead Men's Carnival. *See* Pirandello, Luigi, *Il carnevale dei morti*

Dead Queen, The. *See* Montherlant, Henry de, *La reine morte*

Dead Souls. See Gogol, Nikolay Vasilievich

Dead Woman in Love, The. *See* Gautier, Théophile, "La morte amoureuse"

Dead Woman's Loan, The. *See* Blasco Ibáñez, Vicente, *El préstamo de la difunta*

Deafness, Diderot and, 4:486b–487a

Dealing with Inspiration. *See* Frisch, Max, "Vom Umgang mit dem Einfall"

Dear Antoine. See Anouilh, Jean

Dear Michael. See Ginzburg, Natalia, *Caro Michele*

"Dearest friend, even in this quiet house." *See* Blok, Alexander, "Milyi drug, i v etom tikhom dome"

Death
   in Ady's poetry, 9:875a, 875b–876b, 876b
   in Andrić's works, 11:1770a-b
   in Apollinaire's poetry, 9:898a
   in Arp's works, 10:1374a–1375b, 1378b–1379b
   in Azorín's works, 9:641b–642a
   Barthes on, 13:3101a–3102a
   in Baudelaire's poems, 7:1336b–1337b
   Beauvoir and, 12:2714a-b, 2715b, 2716a
   in Berlioz' works, 6:778a-b
   Broch and, 10:1399a–1402b
   in Calvino's works, 13:3284b
   in Camus's works, 13:3058a-b, 3059a–3062a, 3062a–3063a
   Canetti and, 12:2626b–2627b, 2628b–2631b
   in Carducci's works, 7:1505b–1506a
   in Cela's works, 13:3109a-b, 3123b–3125a
   in Céline's works, 11:1868a, 1873b–1877a
   in Chekhov
      "Rothschild's Fiddle," 7:1869b–1870a
      "The Steppe," 7:1861a-b
   in D'Annunzio's works, 8:183b–184b, 200a–201b
   "Death of God," in Nietzsche, 7:1666b, 1670a
   Delacroix's views on, 5:518b

   in Dinesen's works, 10:1298b–1299a
   in Elytis' verse, 13:2982a, 2982b
      "Light Tree," 13:2973a
      To imerologio enos atheatou Apriliou, 13:2983a, 2983b
   fear of, in Gautier's poetry, 6:1057a-b
   of Foucault, 13:3323a-b
   Foucault and, 13:3326a-b
   Freud's view of Eros and Thanatos, 8:5b, 14a, 15b
   Genet and, 13:2869a, 2870a, 2875b
   in Ghelderode's plays, 11:2115a
      Chronicles of Hell, 11:2120a–2121b
   in Gottfried, 1:252a-b
   in Gunnarsson's works, 10:1504b
   Hamsun's use of, 8:31b–32a
   Hauptmann dramas on, 8:158b–160b
   heroic, in Alfieri's works, 4:668a
   in Hugo's works, 6:703b, 709a
   in Ionesco's works, 13:2989b, 3007b
      A Stroll in the Air, 13:3004b
      Exit the King, 13:3007a
      The Flight, 13:3008b
      The Killing Game, 13:3011a, 3011b
   Jiménez' views on, 9:995b, 1002b–1003a
   Kleist and, 5:309b–310a
   in Lampedusa's *The Leopard,* 11:2017b–2018a, 2018b–2019a
   in Leconte de Lisle, 6:1263a-b, 1269b
   in Leopardi's works, 5:543b
   in Machado's poetry, 9:757b
   Mandelshtam on, 10:1621b, 1637b
   in Mann's *Magic Mountain,* 9:722b
   in Maupassant's works, 7:1773a-b, 1774a, 1775b
   Moberg on, 11:2224b
   in Montaigne's *Essays,* 2:773b, 775a, 782a
   Nerval on, 6:961a, 966b
   in Pascoli
      Canti di Castelvecchio, 7:1843b
      Myricae, 7:1836b
      "The Purple Foxglove," 7:1842b–1843a
   in Pirandello, 8:413a
   in Proust's *Remembrance of Things Past,* 8:559a–561a, 565a
   in Quasimodo's works, 12:2408b
   in Queneau's works, 12:2532b–2533a, 2532b

Death (*cont.*)

in Rabelais's *Pantagruel*, 2:703b–704a

and rebirth

in Arp, 10:1374a–1377a

in Klopstock, 4:521b–522a

in Richter's works, 5:58a-b

Hesperus, 5:65b, 66a

Siebenkäs, 5:68b, 69a

The Invisible Lodge, 5:62a-b

in Rilke's poetry, 9:774a

of Rimbaud, 7:1821b

in Robbe-Grillet's works, 13:3241b, 3255a–3256a

in Ronsard's poetry

Les Derniers vers de Pierre Ronsard, 2:740a

"Sur la Mort de Marie," 2:730b

in Schnitzler's works, 8:92b, 93a-b, 100a, 100b, 101b, 105b–106a, 112b

Schopenhauer's view of, 5:408a–409a

in Simon's *The Grass*, 13:3034a-b

in Tolstoy's novels, 7:1485b–1487a

in Turgenev, 6:1295a-b

Unamuno's view of, 8:287b, 299b–300a

in Valéry's *Graveyard by the Sea*, 8:578b–579a

Vesaas and, 11:2042a, 2049a–2049b

Weil and, 12:2796b–2798b, 2808a

Witkiewicz and, 10:1211b–1212a, 1221a-b

in Yourcenar's works, 12:2556a–2557a, 2558a–2559a

of Zola, 7:1539a

see also Corpses; Graveyard meditations; Mortality; Murder; Reincarnation; Suicide

Death. See Maeterlinck, Maurice, *La mort*

Death of Adam, The. See Klopstock, Friedrich Gottlieb

Death of Ahasuerus, The. See Lagerkvist, Pär, *Ahasverus död*

"Death of art." *See* Art, "death of"

"Death of a Bachelor, The." *See* Schnitzler, Arthur, "Der Tod des Junggesellen"

Death and the Devil. See Wedekind, Frank

Death of Doctor Faust, The. See Ghelderode, Michel de, *La mort du Docteur Faust*

"Death of Dolgushev, The." *See* Babel, Isaac, "Smert' Dolgusheva"

Death of Dr. Faust, The. See Ghelderode, Michel de, *La mort du docteur Faust*

Death drive, Freud's concept of, 8:14b–15b

Death Drives the Team. *See* Yourcenar, Marguerite, *La mort conduit l'attelage*

Death of Empedocles, The. See Hölderlin, Friedrich, *Der Tod des Empedokles*

Death and the Fool. See Hofmannsthal, Hugo von

Death of Hermann, The. See Klopstock, Friedrich Gottlieb

Death on the Installment Plan. See Céline, Louis-Ferdinand

Death of Ivan Ilich, The. See Tolstoy, Leo

Death Looks in the Window. See Ghelderode, Michel de, *La mort regarde à la fenêtre*

Death of Marat, The. See David, Jacques-Louis

Death of the Minister Plenipotentiary. See Tynianov, Yurii, *Smert' Vazir-Mukhtara*

"Death of a Poet." *See* Pasternak, Boris, *Second Birth*

"Death of the Poet, The." *See* Lermontov, Mikhail Yurievich, "Smert poeta"

Death of the Rich Man, The. *See* Pascoli, Giovanni, "La morte del ricco"

Death of Sardanapalus. See Delacroix, Eugène

Death of Seneca, The. See L'Hermite, Tristan, *La mort de Sénèque*

Death in the Sinan Tekke. *See* Andrić, Ivo, "Smrt u Sinanovoj tekjii"

Death of Socrates, The. *See* Lamartine, Alphonse de, "La mort de Socrate"

"Death in the Soul." *See* Camus, Albert

Death of Tintagiles, The. See Maeterlinck, Maurice, *La mort de Tintagiles*

Death in Venice. See Mann, Thomas

Death of Vergil, The. See Broch, Hermann

Death Who Walks the Streets. *See* Montherlant, Henry de, *Don Juan*

Death wish, in Foscolo, 5:327b

Death of the Wolf, The. *See* Vigny, Alfred Victor de, *Les destinées*

"Death of Zand, The." *See* Olesha, Yuri

Death's Comedy. *See* Gautier, Théophile

Death's Mistake. *See* Khlebnikov, Velimir

Deathwatch, *See* Genet, Jean
Débâcle, Le. See Zola, Émile
"Debate Between the Poet and His Heart." *See*
    Villon, François
Debates
    in Giraudoux's works, 9:1062a-b
    in medieval drama, 1:466b, 473b
Debenedetti, Giacomo, Svevo and, 8:86a
Debit and Credit. See Quasimodo, Salvatore,
    Dare e avere
Debit och Kredit (Debit and Credit). See
    Strindberg, August
Debs, Benedikt, 1:466b, 469a, 470a
Debt, theme of, in Rabelais's *Third Book*,
    2:708b–709b, 711a
Debucourt, Philibert-Louis, in Goncourts' *L'Art*
    du dix-huitième siècle, 7:1397a
Debussy, Claude, 7:1586a
    Maeterlinck and, 8:136b–137a, 143a
    Ortega y Gasset on, 9:1135b
    Proust and, 8:546b
Débuts d'un aventurier. See Mérimée, Prosper
Decadence
    Dinesen and, 10:1298a-b
    in fin-de siècle Vienna, Schnitzler and,
        8:113b
    theme of, in writing of Heinrich Mann,
        8:521b
Decadent art. *See* Art, decadent
Decadent movement, 7:1416b–1417a
    Flaubert and, 7:1641a
    Hašek's parody of, 9:1097a
    Huysmans and, 7:1709a, 1716b
    Laforgue and, 7:1895b–1896b
    Mallarmé and, 7:1641a
    in nineteenth century, 7:1641a
    parody of, 7:1641a
    Verlaine and, 7:1641a-b
Decades Concerning Asia. See Barros, João de
Decameron. See Boccaccio, Giovanni
Decameron tradition
    definitional problems, 2:927a–928b
    in France, 2:945b–949b
    in Italy, 2:933b–945b
    in northern Europe, 2:952a–953a
    novella and, 2:927a–928b
    in Spain, 2:949b–952a

Decamps, A. G., Goncourts on, 7:1397a
Decavalles, Andonis, 13:2977a
    on Seferis' *The Cistern*, 12:2263b
"Deceitful Marriage, The." *See* Cervantes,
    Miguel de
"December Night." *See* Musset, Alfred de,
    Nights
Decembrists
    Goncharov and, 6:1062b
    uprising of, Lermontov and, 6:1195a,
        1216b–1217a
Decennale primo. See Machiavelli, Niccolò
Decennale secondo. See Machiavelli, Niccolò
Deception
    in Ariosto, 2:621b–624a, 629b–630a
    in Chrétien's *Cligés*, 1:195a
    in Gottfried, 1:254a–257a
    in the *Nibelungenlied*, 1:228b–229b
"Decision." *See* Södergran, Edith, "Beslut"
Decision (journal), Heinrich Mann and,
    8:541a
"Decision to Forget, The." *See* Seferis, George,
    "I apophasi tis lysmonias"
"Déclaration des amis de la Constitution
    ci-devant réunis aux Feuillants"
    ("Declaration of the Friends of the
    French Constitution Formerly Reunited
    as the Feuillants"). *See* Feuillant club
Déclaration des quatre articles (1682), 3:272a
Declension, internal. *See* Internal declension
Decline of the West. See Spengler, Oswald,
    Der Untergang des Abendlandes
"Décomposition de Paris, La" (The
    Decomposition of Paris). *See* Artaud,
    Antonin
Deconstructive linguistic operations, of
    Marinetti, 9:814b, 816a-b
"Decoration, The." *See* Chekhov, Anton,
    "Orden"
Découvertes. See Ionesco, Eugène
Dédale, Le. See Hervieu, Paul
"Dedication." *See* Akhmatova, Anna, *Poem*
    Without a Hero
Dedikation. See Ekelöf, Gunnar
Deeds of the Romans. See Gesta Romanorum

Deeds That Have Now Become Words. *See* Pirandello, Luigi, "Fatti che or son parole"

Deep, Dark, Troubled River. *See* Yourcenar, Marguerite, *Fleuve profond, sombre rivière*

Deep Song. *See* García Lorca, Federico

Defamiliarization, concept of, Olesha and, 11:2251a-b

DeFelice, Renzo, on Marinetti, 9:810b, 824a, 824b

Defence, The. *See* Nabokov, Vladimir, *Zashchita Luzhina*

Défense et illustration de la langue française (Defense and Illustration of the French Language). *See* Bellay, Joachim du

Defensiones theologiae divi Thomae Aquinatis. *See* Capreolus, John

"Defica." *See* Nerval, Gérard de

Defoe, Daniel
    Journal of the Plague Year, 13:3010a, 3011b
    Moll Flanders, Moravia and, 12:2682b
    Robinson Crusoe
        Baroja compared to, 9:600a
        Vittorini and, 12:2736a-b

Deformity, in Lagerkvist's writings, 10:1685b

"Defteros dialogos i monologos pano stin poiesi." *See* Seferis, George

Degas danse dessin (Degas, Dance, Drawing). *See* Valéry, Paul

Degas, Edgar
    Delacroix and, 5:536b
    Goncourts on, 7:1397a-b
    Huysmans and, 7:1714a
    Ingres and, 5:536b
    social realism and, 7:1631a

Degeneration. *See* Nordau, Max

Degeneration, familial. *See* Family disintegration

Degré zéro de l'écriture, Le. *See* Barthes, Roland, *Writing Degree Zero*

Degrés. *See* Butor, Michel

Deguileville, Guillaume, *Romance of the Rose* and, 1:332b

Dehmel, Richard, George and, 8:459b

Dehumanization
    in Dürrenmatt's works, 13:3229b–3231a

in Giraudoux's works, 13:3229b

in Kafka's works, 13:3229b

Dehumanization of Art, The. *See* Ortega y Gasset, José, *Deshumanización del arte, La*

Dei delitti e delle pene. *See* Becarria, Cesare

"Dei sepolcri." *See* Foscolo, Ugo

Deism
    Diderot and, 4:483a–484a
    see also Religion

Deities, pagan. *See* Gods, pagan

"Del camino." *See* Machado, Antonio, *Soledades*

Del modo di trattare i popoli della Valdichiana ribellati. *See* Machiavelli, Niccolò

"Del realismo en pintura." *See* Ortega y Gasset, José

Del sentimiento trágico de la vida en los hombres y los pueblos. *See* Unamuno, Miguel de

Delacroix, Charles, 5:514a

Delacroix, Eugène, **5:513a–539b**
    Berlioz and, 6:771a, 779a
    color theory, 7:1408b
    Death of Sardanapalus, 5:515b, 526b
    Dictionary of the Fine Arts and of Painting, 5:537a–538a
    Faust lithographs, 5:519b
    Flaubert on, 7:1389b
    Greece Expiring on the Ruins of Missolonghi, 5:523b
    Journal, 5:513a-b, 514a, 532a–536b
    Liberty Leading the People, 5:526b, 535b
    Massacre at Chios, 5:515a, 523b, 526b, 527a
    "On Art Criticism," 5:524a
    "Questions on Beauty," 5:529b–530a
    The Barque of Dante, 5:515a
    The Battle of Nancy, 5:515b
    The Battle of Poitiers, 5:535b
    The Emperor Justinian Composing the Institutes, 5:515b
    "Variations of Beauty," 5:529b, 530a-b

Delacroix, Ferdinand, Goncourts on, 7:1397a

Delaunay, Robert, 9:884a, 884b, 896b

Delécluze, Étienne Jean, on Delacroix, 5:523b

Deleitar aprovechando. *See* Tirso de Molina

Deleuze, Gilles, Bergson and, 8:64a

Delgado, Humberto, 11:2154b

Delibes, Miguel, Baroja influences, 9:613a

Délices, Les, Voltaire's activities at, 4:377a

Délire à deux. See Ionesco, Eugène

"Délires I: Vierge folle/L'Époux infernal" ("Delirium I: The Foolish Virgin/The Infernal Bridegroom"). See Rimbaud, Arthur

Dell'origine e dell'ufficio della letteratura. See Foscolo, Ugo

Del'mas, Lyubov' Alexandrovna Andreeva-, 9:970b–971a, 983a

Delo Artamonovykh. See Gorky, Maxim, The Artamonov Business

Deloney, Thomas, translation of Des Périers nouvelles by, 2:949a

Delphine. See Staël, Madame de

Delprat, Edouard, Vigny's friendship with, 5:452a

"Delta." See Montale, Eugenio, Cuttlefish Bones

"Deluge at Norderney, The." See Dinesen, Isak

"Déluge, Le." See Vigny, Alfred Victor de, Poèmes antiques et modernes

Delvaux, Paul, Butor and, 13:3313a

Delzant, Alidor, on the Goncourts, 7:1401a

Demagoguery, Mann's Mario and the Magician as metaphor of, 9:726a–727a

Demain il fera jour. See Montherlant, Henry de

DeMaria, Luciano, on Marinetti, 9:827a

Dembowski, Mathilde Viscontini, Stendhal and, 5:347a-b

Demesne of the Swans, The. See Tsvetaeva, Marina, Lebedinyi stan

Demeter, in Machado's "Olivo del camino," 9:759a

Demetrius. See Hebbel, Friedrich; Schiller, Friedrich von

Demi-monde, Le. See Dumas fils, Alexandre

Demian. See Hesse, Hermann

Demigod, in Hölderlin's works, 5:158b, 160a-b

"Democracia morbosa." See Ortega y Gasset, José

Democracy

  Baroja's ambivalence about, 9:594a

  despotism and, Tocqueville on, 6:898b–899b

  Foscolo and, 5:325b

  Hamsun's attitude to, 8:23b

  Ortega y Gasset on, 9:1142b–1143a

  Portugal, 11:2145b, 2154a-b

  Tocqueville on historical evolution toward, 6:894a

Democracy in America. See Tocqueville, Alexis de

Democratic Conferences of 1871, 7:1688b–1689b

"Demon." See Blasco Ibáñez, Vicente, Cuentos valencianos (Valencian Tales), "Dimoni"

Démon du bien, Le (The Demon of Good). See Montherlant, Henry de

"Demon" ("The Demon"). See Lermontov, Mikhail Yurievich

Demonism, Witkiewicz and, 10:1209b–1210a

Demonizm Zakopanego. See Witkiewicz, Stanisław Ignacy

Demons

  in Alsfelder Passion, 1:466b

  in Descartes's Meditations on First Philosophy, 3:10b–11a, 12a, 14a

  in Greban's Passion, 1:470a

  in Ronsard's "Les Daimons," 2:733a

Demos. See Camus, Albert

Demou, Nikos, 13:2979a

Demoustier, Charles-Albert

  Dumas père and, 6:728a

  Lettres a Émile sur la mythologie, 6:728a

Den befriade människan. See Lagerkvist, Pär

Den Brændende busk. See Undset, Sigrid

Den Danske Frue paa Hof. See Gunnarsson, Gunnar, Borgslægtens Historie

Den Fredlöse. See Strindberg, August

Den Gaadefulde. See Hamsun, Knut

Den knutna näven. See Lagerkvist, Pär

Den langa resan. See Lagerkvist, Pär

Den lyckliges väg. See Lagerkvist, Pär

Den osynlige. See Lagerkvist, Pär

Den siste glede. See Hamsun, Knut

Den starkare. See Strindberg, August

Den Uerfarne Reisende. See Gunnarsson, Gunnar, Kirken paa Bjerget

Denmark, Hamsun in, 8:23b

Denouement, in plays of Scribe,
7:1911b–1912a
"Dentelle s'abolit . . ., Une." *See* Mallarmé,
Stéphane
Deor (Anglo-Saxon poem), 1:66a
Departing for New Waters. *See* Ady, Endre,
"Uj vizeken járok"
Dépêche de Toulouse (newspaper), Heinrich
Mann and, 8:537a, 540a
Dependence, principles of, in Montesquieu's
thought, 3:347b–364a
Depersonalization technique, in Sarraute's
works, 12:2343b–2344a, 2344b
Dépit amoureux, Le. See Molière
Depression, Kierkegaard and, 6:1125a,
1126b–1128b
Derenkov, Andrei, 8:441b
Dermit, Edouard, and Cocteau, 10:1559a
"Dernier amour du Prince Genghi, Le." *See*
Yourcenar, Marguerite, *Nouvelles
orientales*
Dernier amour, Le. See Sand, George
Dernier jour d'un condamné, Le. See Hugo,
Victor
Dernière Aldini, La. See Sand, George
Derniers jours de H. Heine, Les. See Selden,
Camille
Derniers jours, Les. See Queneau, Raymond
Derniers poèmes. See Leconte de Lisle,
Charles Marie
Derniers vers de Pierre Ronsard, Les. See
Ronsard, Pierre de
Derrida, Jacques, Gombrowicz and, 12:2568a
Derrière chez Martin. See Aymé, Marcel
Derzhavin, Gavriil
Pushkin and, 5:660b–661a
"Reka vremen" ("The River of Time"),
Mandelshtam's "The Slate Ode" and,
10:1641b–1642a
sequel to Catherine the Great's fairy tale,
10:1625b
*Des Amts-Vogts Josuah Freudel Klaglibell
gegen seinen verfluchten Dämon. See*
Richter, Jean Paul
*Des arts nouveaux, ou Le hasard dans la
production artistique. See* Strindberg,
August

*Des Feldpredigers Schmelzle Reise nach Flätz.
See* Richter, Jean Paul
Des fleurs de bonne volonté. See Laforgue,
Jules
"Des Jacobins." *See* Rutebeuf
Des Knaben Wunderhorn. See Arnim, Achim
von, and Brentano, Clemens
Des Lebens Überfluss. See Tieck, Ludwig
"Des' nadkhodyla vesna." *See* Tychyna, Pavlo,
Soniachni klarnety
Des Périers, Bonaventure
Marguerite of Navarre as patron of, 2:948b
*Nouvelles récréations et joyeux devis (Novel
Pastimes and Merry Tales),*
2:948b–949a
*Des Rektors Florian Fälbels und seiner
Primaner Reise nach dem Fichtelberg.
See* Richter, Jean Paul
"Des toten Shakespear's Klage unter den toten
Zuhörern in der Kirche, dass kein Gott
sei." *See* Richter, Jean Paul
Des vers. See Maupassant, Guy de
Desbordes-Valmore, Marceline, Verlaine on,
7:1640a-b
Descartes, René, **3:1a–22b**
Beaumarchais on, 4:572b
Beauvoir and, 12:2711a, 2716a
Boileau and, 3:177a
Claudel and, 8:473a, 486a
Compendium musicae, 3:3a
*Discours de la méthode (Discourse on
Method)*
Meditations and, 3:9b
organization of, 3:7a-b
publication of, 3:6b
three dreams in, 3:4a-b
on unity of knowledge, 3:3b–4a
discussed in La Bruyère's *Caractères,*
3:256b–257a
Gombrowicz and, 12:2567b–1268a, 2570a
Le monde, 3:6b
Meditations on First Philosophy, 3:7b–8a,
9b–11a, 11b, 11a–12b, 13a–14a,
14a–15b, 15b–17a, 20b, 21a, 22a
Corneille and, 3:24a
Montaigne and, 2:785b, 786a

Ortega y Gasset and, 9:1122b, 1130b–1131a,
    1131b–1132a
*Passions de l'âme (The Passions of the
    Soul)*, 3:21b
*Principia philosophiae (The Principles of
    Philosophy)*, 3:13a, 20b–21b
reason as abstraction, 9:1129b
Schlegel and, 5:199a
Schopenhauer contrasted with, 5:400a
Valéry and, 8:573b, 574a-b
Vico and, 3:295a, 297a-b
in Vigny's *Cinq-Mars*, 5:460b
Descendant of King Midas, The. *See* Ady,
    Endre, "Midász király sarja"
Descent from the Cross, The. See Rubens,
    Peter Paul
"Descent into Reverie." *See* Hugo, Victor, "La
    pente de la rêverie"
Descent of Man. See Darwin, Charles
Deschamps, Émile
    translated Shakespeare's *Romeo and Juliet*
        (with Vigny), 5:462a
    Vigny's friendship with, 5:450b, 454b
Deschamps, Eustache
    on Bohemians, 1:344b–345b, 350a
    on financial experts, 1:353a–354a
    on Hundred Years' War, 1:362b–364a
    strophic poetry and, 1:372b
    wordplay of, 1:371b
Description, Barthes on, 13:3084b–3085a
Description de San Marco. See Butor, Michel
*Description of the Method Used by Duke
        Valentino in Killing Vitellozzo Vitelli,
        Oliverotto da Fermo, and Others. See*
        Machiavelli, Niccolò, *Descrizione del
        modo tenuto dal duca Valentino . . .*
"Description of a Struggle." *See* Kafka, Franz,
    "Beschreibung eines Kampfes"
Descriptive Analysis of the History of France.
    See Chateaubriand, François René de,
    *Analyse raisonnée de l'histoire de
    France*
*Descrizione del modo tenuto del duca
        Valentino nello ammazzare Vitellozzo
        Vitelli, Oliverotto da Fermo, il Signor
        Pagolo e il duca di Gravina Orsini. See*
        Machiavelli, Niccolò

Desde la última vuelta del camino. See Baroja,
    Pío
"Desdichado, El." *See* Nerval, Gérard de
Desengano
    Camoëns and, 2:759a, 759b
    in "Sôbolos rios," 2:754a
Desengaños amorosos. See Zayas y
    Sotomayor, Maria de
Desert and After, The. *See* Ungaretti,
    Giuseppe, *Il deserto e dopo*
Desert of Love, The (Le désert d'amour). See
    Mauriac, François
Desert Rose, The. *See* Montherlant, Henry de,
    La rose de sable
"Deserter, The." *See* Babel, Isaac, "Dezertir"
Deserto e dopo, Il. See Ungaretti, Giuseppe
Desheredada, La. See Pérez Galdós, Benito
*Deshumanización del arte, La (The
        Dehumanization of Art). See* Ortega y
        Gasset, José
"Desiatiminutnaia drama." *See* Zamyatin,
    Yevgeny Ivanovich
Desire
    Leconte de Lisle's theory of, 6:1265b–1266a
    paradox of, in Rimbaud's works,
        7:1792a–1793b, 1816a-b
    Schopenhauer on, 5:402b–403a
    see also Love; Sexual passion
"Desire spurs me." *See* Petrarch, *Canzoniere*,
    "Voglia mi sprona"
Desmoulins, Camille, Chénier denounced by,
    4:702a
Desnos, Robert, 11:1953a
    Artaud and, 11:1975b
    Ekelöf and, 12:2661b–2662a
Despair
    in Goncharov's works, 6:1065b
    Hamsun's use of, 8:28a
    in Schnitzler's works, 8:101a-b
"Despedida." *See* García Lorca, Federico
"Desperate Character, A." *See* Turgenev, Ivan
Desportes, Philippe
    Bergeries, 2:912a
    Petrarchan influence, 2:504a
    Ronsard and, 2:731b
Despotism
    democratic, Tocqueville on, 6:898b–899b

Despotism (*cont.*)
    enlightened, in Richter's *The Comet*, 5:82a
    in Montesquieu's conception, 3:357b–358b
    Staël's *De la littérature* on, 5:97b
    see also Montesquieu, Charles-Louis de
        Secondat, baron de, *The Persian Letters*;
        Tyranny
Desprès, Louis, on Verlaine, 7:1639a
Destin des Malou, Le. See Simenon, Georges
Destinées, Les. See Vigny, Alfred Victor de
Destins. See Mauriac, François, *Lines of Life*
Destiny. *See* Fate
Destiny from the 30's, A. *See* Ekelöf, Gunnar,
    "Ett 30-talsöde"
Destouches, Louis-Ferdinand. *See* Céline,
    Louis-Ferdinand
Destruction. See Marinetti, Filippo Tommaso
Destruction of Reason, The. See Lukács,
    György, *Die Zerstörung der Vernunft*
"Destruction of Syntax." *See* Marinetti, Filippo
    Tommaso, "Distruzione della sintassi"
Destutt de Tracy, influence on Manzoni,
    5:368b
"Dêswar Reimar, dû rinwest mich." *See*
    Walther von der Vogelweide
Det besegrade livet. See Lagerkvist, Pär
Det eviga leendet. See Lagerkvist, Pär
"Det fasansfulla tåget." *See* Södergran, Edith
"Det finns någonting." *See* Ekelöf, Gunnar
Det heliga landet. See Lagerkvist, Pär
"Det lilla fälttåget." *See* Lagerkvist, Pär
"Det märkvädiga landet." *See* Lagerkvist, Pär
"Detachment." *See* Ungaretti, Giuseppe,
    Allegria di naufragi (Mirth of
    Shipwrecks), *Distacco*
"Details on Cyprus." *See* Seferis, George,
    "Leptomereies stin Kypro"
Detective fiction
    of Čapek, 10:1579b–1581a
    Dürrenmatt's, 13:3222a–3224a
    evolution of, 12:2485b–2486a
    Frisch and, 13:2921b
    Hamsun's use of, 8:29a-b
    Ionesco and, 13:2992a
        Victims of Duty, 13:2996b, 2997a, 3017b
    of Robbe-Grillet, 13:3242a–3245b
    Schnitzler's use of, 8:104a

Silone and, 12:2296b
see also Mystery fiction
Determinism
    in Balzac's works, 5:639b–640a
    in literary criticism, 10:1484b
    Portuguese literature and, 10:1484b
    Taine and, 10:1484b
    Voltaire on, 4:387a-b
    see also Fatalism
Deti solntsa. See Gorky, Maxim
"Deti Vydry." *See* Khlebnikov, Velimir
Detstvo. See Babel, Isaac; Gorky, Maxim,
    Childhood
"Detstvo Liuvers." *See* Pasternak, Boris,
    Rasskazy (*Stories*)
Deutsche Chansons. See Wedekind, Frank
Deutsche Dichtung (anthology of verse),
    8:460b, 467a
Deutsche Erzähler. See Hofmannsthal, Hugo
    von
Deutsche Messe, Die. See Luther, Martin
Deutsche Realisten des 19. Jahrhunderts. See
    Lukács, György
Deutschland: Ein Wintermärchen. See Heine,
    Heinrich
"Deux acteurs pour un rôle." *See* Gautier,
    Théophile
"Deux amis." *See* Maupassant, Guy de
Deux amis ou le négociant de Lyon, Les. See
    Beaumarchais, Pierre-Augustin Caron
    de
"Deux archers, Les." *See* Hugo, Victor
"Deux critiques, Les." *See* Barthes, Roland,
    "The Two Criticisms"
Deux héritages, Les. See Mérimée, Prosper
"Deux maîtresses, Les." *See* Musset, Alfred de
Deux poètes, Les. See Balzac, Honoré de
Deux sources de la morale et de la religion,
    Les. See Bergson, Henri
"Deux tableaux de Valdès Léal." *See* Gautier,
    Théophile
Deuxième sexe, Le. See Beauvoir, Simone de,
    The Second Sex
Devastation, in Kundera, 13:3401a-b
Devatero pohádek. See Čapek, Karel
Devenir social, Le, Labriola and, 8:314b
Deviat'sot piatyi god. See Pasternak, Boris

"Devii bog." *See* Khlebnikov, Velimir
Devil
  in Goethe's works
    Faust, 5:21a-b
    Urfaust, 5:19b
  Lucifer, in Dante's *Divine Comedy*, 1:447a
  as narrator, in Butor, 13:3311b
  in "Pange lingua, necem Petri qui turbavit
    Angliam," 1:370a
  in Prudentius' works, 1:15b–16a
    Hamartigenia, 1:8b–9a
  in Redentin Easter play, 1:468a
  in Richter's *Selection of the Devil's Papers*,
    5:57b–58a
  see also Demons; Satan
Devil in the Flesh. See Radiguet, Raymond, *Le
  diable au corps*
Devil and the Good Lord, The. See Sartre,
  Jean-Paul
Devil in the Hills, The. See Pavese, Cesare
"Devil, The." *See* Tsvetaeva, Marina, "Chert"
Devil upon Two Sticks, The. See Lesage,
  Alain-René, *Le diable boiteux*
Devil's Due, The. *See* Musset, Alfred de, *La
  quittance du diable*
Devil's General, The. See Zuckmayer, Carl,
  Des Teufels General
Devils of Loudon, The. See Huxley, Aldous
Devil's Pool, The. See Sand, George
"Devil's Sermon, The." *See* Ekelöf, Gunnar
Devil's Yard. See Andrić, Ivo
Devin du village, Le. See Rousseau, Jean
  Jacques
Devoción de la Cruz, La. See Calderón de la
  Barca, Pedro, *Devotion to the Cross*
Devotio moderna (modern devotion), Erasmus
  and, 2:571b–572a
Devotion to the Cross. See Calderón de la
  Barca, Pedro
Devotional literature, Kierkegaard and,
  6:1143a
"Devushka." *See* Zamyatin, Yevgeny Ivanovich
"Devushka iz Spoleto." *See* Blok, Alexander
"Dezertir." *See* Babel, Isaac
*Dhekaohto lianotraghoudha tis pikris
  patridhas. See* Ritsos, Yannis

Dhentro tis fylakis kai i ghinekes, To. See
  Ritsos, Yannis
Dhiadhromos kai skala. See Ritsos, Yannis
Dhiaplasi ton pedhon. See Ritsos, Yannis
"Dhihty, To." *See* Ritsos, Yannis
"Dhikos mas hellos, O." *See* Seferis, George
Dhokimasia. See Ritsos, Yannis
"Di Grasso." *See* Babel, Isaac
"Di pensier in pensier, di monte in monte."
  See Petrarch
"Di sera, un geranio." *See* Pirandello, Luigi
*Día era de los reyes. See En Burgos está el
  buen rey*
Diable au corps, Le. See Radiguet, Raymond
Diable boiteux, le. See Lesage, Alain-René
Diable et le bon Dieu, Le. See Sartre,
  Jean-Paul, *The Devil and the Good Lord*
Diaghilev, Sergey
  Cocteau and, 10:1545b
  Mallarmé's influence on, 7:1575b
  Mir iskusstva (World of Art), 9:962b
  Russian symbolism and, 9:962b
Dial, The, Hofmannsthal's "Vienna Letters" in,
  9:692b, 694b
Dialect, Hamsun's use of, 8:34a
Dialectic
  Abelard's *Sic et Non* on, 1:407a
  in Augustinianism, 1:409b
  Brecht and, 11:2096b, 2108b
  Ibsen and, 7:1445a
  in scholasticism, 1:405a–406b
  in universities, 1:409a
  see also Marxism
Dialectical materialism
  Calvino and, 13:3274a-b
  Heinrich Mann and, 8:536a
  literature and, 11:2072b, 2073b
Dialectical method, Hamsun's use of, 8:37b
Dialectical theology. *See* Scholasticism
Dialectics, Hegelian
  Croce and
    in *Filosofia della pratica*, 8:321b
    in *Saggio sullo Hegel*, 8:323b–324b
Dialectics of Nature. See Engels, Friedrich,
  Dialektik der Natur
Dialoge aus dem Messingkauf. See Brecht,
  Bertolt

183

Dialoghi con Leucò. See Pavese, Cesare,
    Dialogues with Leucò
Dialogo. See Ginzburg, Natalia
"Dialogo della Natura e di un islandese." *See*
    Leopardi, Giacomo, "Dialogue of Nature
    and an Icelander"
"Dialogo della Natura e di un'anima." *See*
    Leopardi, Giacomo, "Dialogue Between
    Nature and a Soul"
"Dialogo di Cristoforo Columbo e di Pietro
    Gutiérrez." *See* Leopardi, Giacomo,
    "Dialogue of Christopher Columbus and
    Pedro Gutiérrez"
"Dialogo di Plotino e di Porfirio." *See*
    Leopardi, Giacomo, "Dialogue of
    Plotinus and Porphyry"
"Dialogo di Torquato Tasso e del suo genio
    familiare." *See* Leopardi, Giacomo,
    "Dialogue Between Torquato Tasso and
    His Familiar Spirit"
"Dialogo" (Dialogue). *See* Montale, Eugenio,
    Satura
Dialogo (Dialogue). *See* Ungaretti, Giuseppe
*Dialogo difficile: Sono liberi gli scrittori
    russi?, Un. See* Silone, Ignazio
"Dialogos pano stin poiesi." *See* Seferis,
    George
Dialogue
    Castiglione and, 2:652b–653a
    internal, allegory and, 1:323b–324a
    in medieval secular drama, 1:471a-b
    in Sarraute's works, 12:2344a, 2354b
    in Schiller's plays
        Intrigue and Love, 5:33b
        The Maid of Orleans, 5:47a-b
    Scribe and, 7:1915b
    in Walther, 1:294a
*Dialogue avec 33 variations de Ludwig van
    Beethoven sur une valse de Diabelli.
    See* Butor, Michel
"Dialogue Between Nature and a Soul." *See*
    Leopardi, Giacomo
"Dialogue Between Torquato Tasso and His
    Familiar Spirit." *See* Leopardi, Giacomo
"Dialogue of Christopher Columbus and Pedro
    Gutiérrez." *See* Leopardi, Giacomo

*Dialogue Concerning the Two Chief World
    Systems. See* Galilei, Galileo
Dialogue dans le marécage, Le. See Yourcenar,
    Marguerite
Dialogue des héros de roman, Le. See
    Boileau-Despréaux, Nicolas
Dialogue des règnes. See Butor, Michel
"Dialogue of the Dogs, The." *See* Cervantes,
    Miguel de, *Exemplary Tales (Novelas
    ejemplares),* "El coloquio de los perros"
Dialogue on Dramatic Poetry. See Eliot, T. S.
Dialogue form novels
    by Galdós, 7:1612b–1613a, 1615b–1616a
    Fernando de Rojas' *La Celestina,* 7:1613a
Dialogue on Language, A. See Machiavelli,
    Niccolò, *Discorso o dialogo intorno alla
    nostra lingua*
Dialogue in the Marsh, The. *See* Yourcenar,
    Marguerite, *Le dialogue dans le
    marécage*
"Dialogue of Nature and an Icelander." *See*
    Leopardi, Giacomo
"Dialogue of Plotinus and Porphyry." *See*
    Leopardi, Giacomo
Dialogue on Poetry. See Schlegel, Friedrich
    von
"Dialogue on Poetry." *See* Seferis, George,
    "Dialogos pano stin poiesi"
*Dialogues: Rousseau juge de Jean-Jacques.
    See* Rousseau, Jean Jacques
Dialogues. See Tasso, Torquato
Dialogues with the Characters. *See* Pirandello,
    Luigi, "Colloquii coi personaggi"
Dialogues de bêtes. See Colette
*Dialogues des morts (Dialogues of the Dead).
    See* Fénelon, François de Salignac de la
    Mothe-
Dialogues of Diogenes of Sinope, The. See
    Wieland, Christoph Martin
"Dialogues familiers sur la poésie des
    prolétaires." *See* Sand, George
Dialogues with Leucò. See Pavese, Cesare
*Dialogues sur le quiétisme (Dialogues on
    Quietism). See* La Bruyère, Jean de
Diamant, Der. See Hebbel, Friedrich
Diamant des Geisterkönigs, Der. See
    Raimund, Ferdinand

Diamant, Dora, 9:1155b

Diamond of the King of Spirits, The. *See* Raimund, Ferdinand, *Der Diamant des Geisterkönigs*

Diana. *See* Gil Polo, Gaspar, *Diana enamorada*; Mann, Heinrich, *Die Göttinnen*; Montemayor, Jorge de, *Los siete libros de la Diana*; Pérez, Alonso, *Segunda parte de la Diana*

Diana e la Tuda (*Diana and Tuda*). *See* Pirandello, Luigi

Diana enamorada (*Diana in Love*). *See* Gil Polo, Gaspar

Diana, La. *See* Montemayor, Jorge de

Diana's Hunt. *See* Boccaccio, Giovanni, *Caccia di Diana*

Diane française, La. *See* Aragon, Louis

Diaphanea, 13:2965a-b, 2972b, 2973a, 2975a, 2975b

"Diapsalmata." *See* Kierkegaard, Søren

Diaries. *See* Blok, Alexander, *Dnevniki*

Diario d'amore. *See* Leopardi, Giacomo

Diario de poeta y mar. *See* Jiménez, Juan Ramón

Diario de un enfermo. *See* Azorín

Diario de un poeta recién casado. *See* Jiménez, Juan Ramón, *Diario de poeta y mar*

Diario íntimo. *See* Unamuno, Miguel de

Diario in pubblico. *See* Vittorini, Elio

Diary. *See* Gombrowicz, Witold

Diary. *See* Krleža, Miroslav, *Dnevnik*

Diary of an Invisible April, The. *See* Elytis, Odysseus, *To imerologio enos atheatou Apriliou*

Diary form
of Azorín, 9:645b
D'Annunzio's use of, 8:199a-b
Frisch and, 13:2903a

Diary of Love. *See* Leopardi, Giacomo, *Diario d'amore*

Diary of a Newlywed Poet. *See* Jiménez, Juan Ramón, *Diario de poeta y mar* (Diary of Poet and Sea)

Diary of Poet and Sea. *See* Jiménez, Juan Ramón, *Diario de poeta y mar*

"Diary of a Seducer." *See* Kierkegaard, Søren

Diary of a Sick Man, The. *See* Azorín, *Diario de un enfermo*

"Diary of a Superfluous Man." *See* Turgenev, Ivan

"Diary of a Writer." *See* Dostoevsky, Feodor

Diatribe du docteur Akakia, Le (Diatribe of Doctor Akakia). *See* Voltaire

Diavolo sulle colline, Il. *See* Pavese, Cesare, *The Devil in the Hills*

Diccionario secreto (Secret Dictionary). *See* Cela, Camilo José

"Dichter in Zeiten der Wirren, Der." *See* George, Stefan, *Das neue Reich*

"Dichterberuf." *See* Hölderlin, Friedrich

Dichterbund (poets' brotherhood), Hölderlin in, 5:145a

Dichterleben. *See* Tieck, Ludwig

Dichtung und Wahrheit. *See* Goethe, Johann Wolfgang von

Dicionário de milagres. *See* Eça de Queiroz, José Maria

Diciotto liriche. *See* Pincherle, Alberto

Dickens, Charles
Baroja reads, 9:590b, 598a-b
Böll and, 13:3166a
Caste and, 7:1926b
David Copperfield, Kafka's *Amerika* and, 9:1156a
Dostoevsky and, 7:1351b
Eça and, 7:1691a
Hard Times, 9:598b
Nerval and, 6:961b
Oliver Twist, 9:598b
Pérez Galdós compared with, 7:1609b, 1612a
Pessoa and, 10:1481b–1482b
philanthropism of, 6:995b
Pickwick Papers, 6:986a
Baroja imitates, 9:594a
Pessoa and, 10:1482a
Richter and, 5:68a, 80b
Strindberg and, 7:1753b

Dickinson, Emily
Ginzburg on, 13:3160a
Jiménez and, 9:1000a
Ungaretti and, 10:1464a

185

Dictionary of the Fine Arts and of Painting.
    See Delacroix, Eugène
Dictionary of Heresies, Flaubert and, 7:1378a
Dictionary of Miracles. *See* Eça de Queiroz,
    José Maria, *Dicionário de milagres*
Dictionnaire abrégé du surréalisme. See
    Breton, André, and Éluard, Paul
Dictionnaire philosophique. See Voltaire
Dictionnaire universel. See Furetière, Antoine
Dictys. *See* Dares
Didactic Play of Baden, The: On Consent. See
    Brecht, Bertolt, *Das Badener Lehrstück
    vom Einverständnis*
Didactic satire. *See* Satire
Didascalia. See Hugh of St. Victor
Diderot, Denis, **4:475a–509b**
    Beaumarchais and, 4:565a
    Delacroix and, 5:531b
    *Discours sur la poésie dramatique
        (Discourse on Dramatic Poetry),* 4:493b
    *Éléments de physiologie (Elements of
        Physiology),* 4:491b–492a
    Éloge de Richardson (Eulogy of Richardson),
        4:495a-b
    *Entretien d'un père avec ses enfants (A
        Conversation Between a Father and His
        Children),* 4:476b
    *Entretien entre d'Alembert et Diderot
        (Conversation Between d'Alembert and
        Diderot),* 4:490a–491b
    *Entretiens sur le "Fils naturel"
        (Conversations on "The Illegitimate
        Son"),* 4:493b
    *Essai sur les règnes de Claude et de Néron
        (Essay on the Reigns of Claudius and
        Nero),* 4:504a-b
    Essai sur Sénèque (Essay on Seneca),
        4:504a-b
    Essais sur la peinture (Essays on Painting),
        4:476b, 488b
    *Est-il bon? Est-il méchant? (Is He Good? Is
        He Bad?),* 4:494b–495a
    Goldoni and, 4:431b–432a
    Greuze and, 5:531b
    on Greuze's paintings, 11:2028a-b
    Jacques le fataliste, 4:499b–501a
    Kundera and, 13:3397b, 3409a–3410a

*La promenade du sceptique (The Skeptic's
    Walk),* 4:484a
La religieuse (The Nun), 4:477a, 495b–497b
Le fils naturel (The Illegitimate Son), 4:493b
Le neveu de Rameau (Rameau's Nephew),
    4:497b–499b, 7:1787a
Le père de famille (Father of a Family),
    4:493b
*Les bijoux indiscrets (The Indiscreet
    Jewels),* 4:484b
on Lesage's *Gil Blas,* 3:339b
Lessing and, 4:548a-b, 561b
Lettre sur les aveugles (Letter on the Blind),
    4:481a, 485a–486a
*Lettre sur les sourds et muets (Letter on the
    Deaf and Mute),* 4:486b–487a
*Mémoires sur différents sujets de
    mathématiques (Notes on Various
    Mathematical Subjects),* 4:480a
on Montaigne, 2:786b
Observations sur le Nakaz, 4:503b
On Dramatic Poetry, 4:548b
*Paradoxe sur le comédien (Paradox on
    Acting),* 4:494a-b
*Pensées philosophiques (Philosophic
    Thoughts),* 4:483a–484a
*Pensées sur l'interprétation de la nature
    (Thoughts on the Interpretation of
    Nature),* 4:489b–490a
*Plan d'une université pour le gouvernement
    de Russie,* 4:503b
*Réfutation de l'ouvrage d'Helvétius intitulé
    "L'Homme" (Refutation of Hevetius'
    Work Entitled "Man"),* 4:502a-b
Rêve de d'Alembert (D'Alembert's Dream),
    4:490a–491b
Rimbaud and, 7:1787a
Rousseau and, 4:451b–452b
Salons, 4:487a–489a
*Suite de l'entretien (Continuation of the
    Conversation),* 4:490a–491b
Supplément au voyage de Bougainville,
    4:502b
on unity of time, 12:2558b
Voltaire and, 4:369a
Diego, Gerardo, *Poesía española* and, 9:763b

Diehards, The. *See* Zamyatin, Yevgeny Ivanovich, "Kriazhi"

Dienstbüchlein. See Frisch, Max

Dieresis (*diesis*), in troubadour verse, 1:176a

Diesseits. See Hesse, Hermann

Diet of Worms, Luther and, 2:678b–679b

Dietrich, Christian, *Don Juan und Faust*, Frisch and, 13:2906a

Dietrich von Bern, in Norse sagas, 1:401b

Dietrichstein, Count, Grillparzer commissioned by, 5:433a, 433b

Dieu. See Hugo, Victor

Dieu bleu, Le. See Cocteau, Jean

Dieux ne sont pas morts, Les. See Yourcenar, Marguerite

Díez-Canedo, Enrique, Jiménez and, 9:997b, 1010a

Difficult Loves. See Calvino, Italo

Difficult Man, The. See Hofmannsthal, Hugo von

Difficulté d'être, La. See Cocteau, Jean

"Difficulties of a Statesman." *See* Eliot, T. S.

Difficulty of Being, The. See Cocteau, Jean, *La difficulté d'être*

Digest, Vico and, 3:298b, 299b, 301a, 303a

"Digitale purpurea." *See* Pascoli, Giovanni, *Poemetti*

"Digression." *See* Mickiewicz, Adam

Digte. See Andersen, Hans Christian; Gunnarsson, Gunnar

Dikter. See Södergran, Edith

Dikter På vers och prosa. See Strindberg, August

Dilemme, Un (A Dilemma). See Huysmans, Joris Karl

Dilettante-artist, Montale's affinity for, 11:1987a-b, 1993a

Dilthey, Wilhelm
  Bergson and, 8:47a, 52a
  Das Erlebnis und die Dichtung, 5:173b
  Hölderlin and, 5:173b
  Lukács and, 10:1253b
  Ortega y Gasset and, 9:1139b

Dimanche. See Simenon, Georges

Dimanche de la vie, Le. See Queneau, Raymond

"Dimanches." *See* Laforgue, Jules

Dimanches d'un bourgeois de Paris, Les. See Maupassant, Guy de

Dimaras, Constantin, 12:2543a-b

"Dimoni." *See* Blasco Ibáñez, Vicente, *Cuentos valencianos*

Dinable, Robert le, Strindberg and, 7:1737b

"Dinanzi alle terme di Caracalla." *See* Carducci, Giosue

Dinesen, Isak, **10:1281a–1305b**
  "A Consolatory Tale," 10:1293a-b
  Anecdotes of Destiny (Skaebne Anekdoter), 10:1292a
  "Babette's Feast," 10:1299b–1300b
  "Barua a soldani," 10:1283b
  "Carnival," 10:1295a, 1300b
  "Converse at Night in Copenhagen," 10:1294b
  "Echoes," 10:1303a
  Ehrengard, 10:1295a-b, 1303b
  Last Tales (Sidste Fortaellinger), 10:1292a
  Out of Africa, 10:1291b
    as autobiography, 10:1282b–1283a, 1288a–1289b
    as European pastoral, 10:1297b
  "Peter and Rosa," 10:1298b–1299a
  "Second Meeting," 10:1296b–1297a
  Seven Gothic Tales, 10:1291b
  Shadows on the Grass, 10:1292b
    as autobiography, 10:1282b–1283b
  "Sorrow-Acre," 10:1299a
  "Tempests," 10:1293b
  The Angelic Avengers (Gengaeldelsens Veje), 10:1292a
  "The Cardinal's First Tale," 10:1301b–1302a
  "The Cardinal's Last Tale," 10:1293a
  "The Deluge at Norderney," 10:1295a
  "The Dreamers," 10:1293b
  "The Immortal Story," 10:1300b, 1303b–1304a
  "The Invincible Slave-Owners," 10:1298a
  "The Monkey," 10:1296a
  "The Pearls," 10:1294b
  "The Poet," 10:1294b, 1303a-b
  "The Roads Round Pisa," 10:1299b
    characters in, 10:1300b
    Dante and, 10:1294b
    plot in, 10:1302b

Dinesen, Isak (*cont.*)
 "The Sailor-boy's Tale," 10:1296a
 "The Young Man with the Carnation,"
  10:1293a
 Winter's Tales, 10:1291b
Dinesen, Vilhelm
 Hamsun and, 8:29b
 Jagtbreve (Hunting Letters), 8:29b
Dinggedichte (thing-poems), 9:785a
 Meyer and, 6:931b–932a
Dingsymbollen. See Object-symbols
Dinis, Júlio
 As Pupilas do Senhor Reitor (The Priest's
  Wards), 7:1697a
 Os Fidalgos da Casa Mourisca (*The
  Fidalgos of Casa Mourisca*), 7:1697a
Dio Kurt, Il. See Moravia, Alberto
"Dio tou kosmou, Ta." *See* Elytis, Odysseus,
 *To photodendro kai i dekati tetarti
 omorfia*
Dionigi of Borgo San Sepolcro, Petrarch and,
 2:511a-b
Dionysian tradition, Fénelon and, 3:275a
Dionysius the Areopagite. *See*
 Pseudo-Dionysius
Dionysus
 in Hölderlin's works, 5:159b, 160a–161a,
  161b
 Ibsen and, 7:1437a, 1439a
 Vesaas and, 11:2052b
"Dionysus." *See* Elytis, Odysseus,
 Prosanatolismi
Diósi, Adél, 9:859b, 866b–870b, 871a-b
Diplomacy, in La Bruyère's *Caractères*, 3:248a
Diporti, I. See Parabosco, Girolamo
Directly Beyond the Village. *See* Tychyna,
 Pavlo, *Pluh* (*The Plow*), "Zrazuzh za
 selom"
Disciple, Le (The Disciple). *See* Bourget, Paul
Disciples à Saïs, Les. See Novalis, *The
 Novices of Saïs*
Disciplina clericalis. See Petrus Alfonsi
Discipline and Punish. See Foucault, Michel
Discontinuity, principle of, Foucault and,
 13:3349a–3350b
Discorsi del poema eroico. See Tasso,
 Torquato

Discorsi dell'arte poetica. See Tasso, Torquato
*Discorsi sopra la prima deca di Tito Livio, I.
 See* Machiavelli, Niccolò, *The
 Discourses on the First Decade of Titus
 Livius*
*Discorso di un italiano intorno alla poesia
 romantica. See* Leopardi, Giacomo,
 *Discourse of an Italian on Romantic
 Poetry*
*Discorso o dialogo intorno alla nostra lingua.
 See* Machiavelli, Niccolò
*Discorso su alcuni punti della storia
 longobardica in Italia. See* Manzoni,
 Alessandro
Discours. See Ronsard, Pierre de
Discours de la méthode. See Descartes, René
Discours de la servitude volontaire. See La
 Boétie, Etienne de
*Discours de reception à l'Académie Française.
 See* La Bruyère, Jean de
Discours du grand sommeil. See Cocteau, Jean
Discours en vers sur l'homme. See Voltaire
*Discours pour le sacre de l'électeur de
 Cologne. See* Fénelon, François de
 Salignac de la Mothe-
Discours sur la poésie dramatique. See
 Diderot, Denis
Discours sur le style. See Buffon,
 Georges-Louis Leclerc de, *Discourse on
 Style*
Discours sur les sciences et les arts. See
 Rousseau, Jean Jacques
Discours sur l'histoire universelle. See
 Bossuet, Jacques Bénigne
*Discours sur l'origine de l'inégalité parmi les
 hommes. See* Rousseau, Jean Jacques
Discourse
 Foucault and, 13:3325b–3327b
 order of, 13:3345a–3348b
*Discourse of an Italian on Romantic Poetry.
 See* Leopardi, Giacomo
*Discourse Concerning the Mechanical
 Operation of the Spirit. See* Swift,
 Jonathan
Discourse on Dramatic Poetry. See Diderot,
 Denis, *Discours sur la poésie
 dramatique*

Discourse on the Function of the Kidneys. See Montesquieu, Charles-Louis de Secondat, baron de

Discourse of the Great Sleep. See Cocteau, Jean, *Discours du grand sommeil*

Discourse on Language, The. See Foucault, Michel

Discourse on Method. See Descartes, René, *Discours de la méthode*

Discourse on the Origin of Inequality. See Rousseau, Jean Jacques, *Discours sur l'origine de l'inégalité parmi les hommes*

"Discourse on Poetry." *See* Quasimodo, Salvatore

Discourse on Remodeling the Government of Florence, A. See Machiavelli, Niccolò, *Discursus florentinarum rerum post mortem iunioris Laurentii Medices*

Discourse on the Sciences and the Arts. See Rousseau, Jean Jacques, *Discours sur les sciences et les arts*

Discourse on Style. See Buffon, Georges-Louis Leclerc de

Discourse on Universal History. See Bossuet, Jacques Bénigne, *Discours sur l'histoire universelle*

Discourse in Verse on Man. See Voltaire, *Discours en vers sur l'homme*

Discourse on Voluntary Servitude. See La Boétie, Étienne de, *Discours de la servitude volontaire*

Discourses. See Machiavelli, Nicolò

Discourses on Dante. See Boccaccio, Giovanni, *Esposizioni sopra il Dante*

Discourses on Dramatic Poetry. See Corneille, Pierre

Discourses on the Heroic Poem. See Tasso, Torquato, *Discorsi del poema eroico*

Discoveries. *See* Ionesco, Eugène, *Découvertes*

"Discovertà del vero Dante." *See* Vico, Giovanni Battista

"Discovery." *See* Södergran, Edith, "Upptäckt"

"Discovery of the True Dante." *See* Vico, Giovanni Battista, "Discovertà del vero Dante"

Discretion, as a courtly virtue, Castiglione on, 2:656b–657a

Discursus florentinarum rerum post mortem iunioris Laurentii Medices. See Machiavelli, Niccolò

Discussions. See Firenzuola, Angelo, *Ragionamenti*

"*disent les imbéciles.*" *See* Sarraute, Nathalie

Disguise, Kierkegaard and, 6:1128b–1129a

Disillusionment
  in Musset's works, 6:1002b, 1011b
  in Schnitzler's works, 8:101a-b

Disinherited Lady, The. See Pérez Galdós, Benito, *La desheredada*

Disobedience. *See* Moravia, Alberto

Displacement ("translation"), in Butor's works, Barthes on, 13:3302a–3303a

"Displeasure of Selefkidis, The." *See* Cavafy, Constantine, "I dysareskeia tou Selefkidou"

Disprezzo, Il. See Moravia, Alberto

Disputà. See Raphael

Disputed Questions of Truth. See Aquinas, Thomas, St., *Quaestiones disputate de veritate*

Dissertation on Modern Music. See Rousseau, Jean Jacques

"Distacco." *See* Ungaretti, Giuseppe, *Allegria di naufragi*

Distant Days. *See* Krleža, Miroslav, *Davni dani*

Distant Tales. *See* Baroja, Pío, *Historias lejanas*

"District Behind the Lines, A." *See* Pasternak, Boris, "Uezd v tylu"

Districto de Evora. See Eça de Queiroz, José Maria

"Distruzione della sintassi." *See* Marinetti, Filippo Tommaso

Disubbidienza, La. See Moravia, Alberto, *Disobedience*

Dithmarschen, Hebbel and, 6:1089b

Dittochaeon. See Prudentius

Diu Krône. See Heinrich von dem Türlin

Diván del Tamarit (Divan). See García Lorca, Federico

Divers jeux rustiques (Diverse Rustic Diversions). See Du Bellay, Joachim

Diversions, The. See Parabosco, Girolamo, *I diporti*

Diversity, theme of, in Montaigne's *Essays*, 2:777a-b

"Dives eram et dilectus." *See* Hugh Primas

Divinas palabras. See Valle-Inclán, Ramón del

Divine
    Bergson's view of, 8:62b–63a
    in Dinesen, 10:1281a
    Leconte de Lisle's view of, 6:1252b–1259a
    see also God

Divine Comedy. See Dante Alighieri

Divine grace, in Mauriac, 10:1324a

Divine intervention
    in Kleist, 5:296a-b
    in Rousseau, 4:465b–466a

Divine Words. See Valle-Inclán, Ramón del, *Divinas palabras*

Divinity of Christ, The. See Prudentius, *Apotheosis*

Divorce, in Staël's *Delphine*, 5:92b

Divorce Judge, The. See Cervantes, Miguel de, *El juez de los divorcios*

Divorce, The. See Alfieri, Vittorio

"Divortium." *See* Petrarch

Dīwān över Fursten av Emgión (Dīwān over the Prince of Emgión). *See* Ekelöf, Gunnar

Dix années d'exil. See Staël, Madame de

"Dix ans après en littérature." *See* Sainte-Beuve, Charles-Augustin

Dix ans de la vie d'une femme. See Scribe, Eugène

Djetinjstvo u Agramu godine 1902–3. See Krleža, Miroslav

"Djinns, Les." *See* Hugo, Victor

"Djoumâne." *See* Mérimée, Prosper

"Dlia pol'zy dela." *See* Solzhenitsyn, Aleksandr

"Dnevnik." *See* Babel, Isaac

Dnevnik. See Krleža, Miroslav

Dnevniki. See Blok, Alexander

"Do matki Polki." *See* Mickiewicz, Adam

"Do Not Ask Us for the Word Which Can Give a Shape." *See* Montale, Eugenio, *Cuttlefish Bones* (*Ossi di seppia*), "Non chiederci la parola che squadri da ogni lato"

"Do not attempt foreign tongues . . ." *See* Mandelshtam, Osip, "Ne iskushai chuzhikh narechii"

Do Not See Me!. *See* Ady, Endre, "Ne lássatok meg!"

Do You Hear Them? See Sarraute, Nathalie, *Vous les entendez?*

Do-Nothing Bar, The. See Cocteau, Jean, *Le boeuf sur le toit*

Döblin, Alfred
    Berlin Alexanderplatz, 11:1727a
    Berlin and, 8:523a
    Grass and, 13:3387a
    Mann brothers and, 8:541b

Dobrolyubov, Nikolay
    Dostoevsky and, 7:1357a
    Turgenev and, 6:1281a, 1285b

Dobrý voják Švejk a jiné podivné historky. See Hašek, Jaroslav

Dobrý voják Švejk v zajetí. See Hašek, Jaroslav

Dobson, Austin, "Ars Victrix," 6:1058a

"Doces lembranças da passada glória." *See* Camoëns, Luís Vaz de, *Rimas*

Docteur amoureux, Le. See Molière

"Docteur Héraclius Gloss, Le" ("Doctor Heraclius Gloss"). *See* Maupassant, Guy de

Docteur Pascal, Le (*Dr. Pascal*). *See* Zola, Émile

Doctor Faust. See Heine, Heinrich

Doctor Faustus. See Mann, Thomas

Doctor Zhivago. See Pasternak, Boris

Doctorow, E. L., Kleist's influence on, 5:311a-b

Doctor's Duty, The. See Pirandello, Luigi, *Il dovere del medico*

Doctors, medical. *See* Physicians

"Doctor's Visit, A." *See* Chekhov, Anton, "Sluchay iz praktiki"

Doctrinaires (French political thinkers), Tocqueville and, 6:897a

Documentary novels
    by Galdós, 7:1611a–1612b

Zola's Rougon-Macquarts series, 7:1522a-b, 1523b–1536a, 1607a

Dodoitzu. See Claudel, Paul

Dödsdansen. See Strindberg, August, *The Dance of Death*

Does Ulrike Meinhof Want Mercy or Free Passage? *See* Böll, Heinrich, "Will Ulrike Meinhof Gnade oder freies Geleit?"

Dog with Mandolin. *See* Queneau, Raymond, *Le chien à la mandoline*

Dog in the Manger, The. See Lope de Vega, *El perro de hortelano*

"Dog, The." *See* Turgenev, Ivan

Dog Years. See Grass, Günter

Dogmatism and Criticism. See Schelling, Friedrich Wilhelm von

Dogmatism, theme of, in Ionesco's *Hunger and Thirst*, 13:3009b, 3010a

Dogs in literature, Alfieri's Achilles, 4:671a

Dohnanyi, Ernst von, Schnitzler and, 8:98a

"Dokastikon, Ta." *See* Elytis, Odysseus, *To Axion Esti*

Dokimes. See Seferis, George

Doktor Faustus. See Mann, Thomas, *Doctor Faustus*

Doktor Gräsler, Badearzt. See Schnitzler, Arthur

Doktor Katzenbergers Badereise. See Richter, Jean Paul

"Doktor Murkes gesammeltes Schweigen." *See* Böll, Heinrich, "Murke's Collected Silences"

"Dolce collina." *See* Quasimodo, Salvatore, "The Gentle Hill"

"Dolci rime d'amor ch'i'solìa, Le." *See* Dante Alighieri, *Convivio*

Dolina Issy. See Milosz, Czeslaw, *The Issa Valley*

"Doll House, A." *See* Strindberg, August

Doll's House, A. See Ibsen, Henrik

Dolor (estudio de psico-física), El. See Baroja, Pío

"Dolore di cose che ignoro." *See* Quasimodo, Salvatore

Dolore, Il. See Ungaretti, Giuseppe

"Dolorida." *See* Vigny, Alfred Victor de, *Poèmes antiques et modernes*

Dom iskusstv (House of Arts) (journal), Zamyatin's involvement with, 10:1192b

Dom literatorov (House of Writers) (organization), Zamyatin's involvement with, 10:1192b

"Dom s mezoninom." *See* Chekhov, Anton

"Dom u Starogo Pimena." *See* Tsvetaeva, Marina

Domaren. See Moberg, Vilhelm

Dombrowski, Robert, on Marinetti, 9:824b

Domenichi, Ludovico, *Facetie, motti et burle (Jokes, Witticisms, and Pranks)*, anecdotes in, 2:938b

"Dominant Thought, The." *See* Leopardi, Giacomo

Dominicans
   Aquinas and, 1:410b, 411a, 414b, 417b, 418b, 426b
   Luther and, 2:674b–675a
   in Rutebeuf's "Des Jacobins," 1:346a–347a
   University of Paris and, 1:413b–414a

"Domoi." *See* Mayakovsky, Vladimir

Don Carlos. See Schiller, Friedrich von; Vischard, César, abbot of Saint-Réal

Don César Ursin. See Lesage, Alain-René

Don Friolera's Horns. *See* Valle-Inclán, Ramón del, *Martes de Carnaval* (Shrove Tuesday), *Los cuernos de Don Friolera*

Don Garcia. See Alfieri, Vittorio

Don Giovanni. See Mozart, Wolfgang Amadeus

Don Juan
   Bradomín and, 8:334a
   Butor and, 13:3312a-b
   in Frisch's works, 13:2905b–2906b, 2923b
   in Hofmannsthal's plays
      Cristinas Heimreise, 9:700a-b
      Der Abenteurer und die Sängerin, 9:696b–694a
   in Mérimée's works, 6:748a, 760a-b
   in Pushkin's *Stone Guest*, 5:681b–682a

Don Juan. See Azorín; Brecht, Bertolt; Ghelderode, Michel de; Molière

Don Juan; oder, Die Liebe zur Geometrie. See Frisch, Max

Don Juan Tenorio. See Zorilla, José

Don Juan und Faust. See Dietrich, Christian

"Don Paez." *See* Musset, Alfred de

Don Quixote. See Cervantes, Miguel de

Don Quixote's Way. *See* Azorín, *La ruta de don Quijote*

Doña Inés. See Azorín

Doña Perfecta. See Pérez Galdós, Benito

Doña Rosita la soltera (*Dona Rosita, the Spinster*). *See* García Lorca, Federico

Donadieu's Will. *See* Simenon, Georges, *Le testament Donadieu*

Donati, Forese, 1:432a

Donation of Constantine, 1:443a-b

Donaueschingen *Passions*, 1:466a-b

Donetti, Bice, 12:2388a, 2402b

Doni, Antonfrancesco
   I marmi (*The Marbles*), novellas as sources for, 2:940a
   Panchatantra translated by, 2:940b

Donleavy, J. P., Céline's influence on, 11:1859a

Donna di garbo, La. See Goldoni, Carlo

"Donne ch'avete intelletto d'amore." *See* Dante Alighieri, *Vita nuova*

Donne curiose, Le. See Goldoni, Carlo

Donne di Messina, Le. See Vittorini, Elio

Donne, John
   influence on pastoral lyric, 2:915b
   tension of opposites in, 5:421b
   "The Bait," pastoral argument in, 2:915a-b
   "Twickenham Garden," Arcadia in, 2:899b–900a
   wit of, 2:874b

"Don't fret, don't cry, don't pine . . ." *See* Pasternak, Boris, *Second Birth* (*Vtoroe rozhdenie*), "Ne volnuisia, ne plach', ne trudi . . ."

Don't Look Back! *See* Johnson, Eyvind, *Romanen om Olof*

Doorbell. *See* Ritsos, Yannis, *To roptro*

"Dopo." *See* Montale, Eugenio, *The Storm and Other Things*

"Dopo una fuga." *See* Montale, Eugenio, *Satura*, "After a Flight"

Doppelgänger
   Andersen and, 6:886a

   in Pirandello's *The Late Mattia Pascal*, 8:398a
   Richter and, 5:54a, 68a
    in *Siebenkäs*, 5:68b
   Storm and, 6:920b

Doppelgänger, Ein. See Storm, Theodor

Doppelroman, Hesse's *Narcissus and Goldmund* as, 9:849b

"Dora Markus." *See* Montale, Eugenio, *The Occasions*

Dorat, Jean
   "Ad fontem Arculi" ("At the Fountain of Arcueil"), 2:723a-b
   Ronsard and, 2:722b–723a, 733a

Dorfliteratur. See Peasant literature

"Dormeur du val, Le." *See* Rimbaud, Arthur

"Doro asimenio poiema." *See* Elytis, Odysseus, *To photodendro kai i dekati tetarti omorfia*

Dorotea, La. See Lope de Vega

"Dorozhenka." *See* Solzhenitsyn, Aleksandr

Dorp, Martin, Erasmus and, 2:582b

Dorst, Tankred
   Eiszeit (*Ice Age*), 8:41a
   Hamsun and, 8:41a

Dort, Bernard, 13:2999a

Dorval, Marie
   Mélingue's affair with, 5:470b
   Sand and, 6:820b
   Vigny and, 5:470a, 472b, 483b
    affair with, 5:466a-b, 467a, 478b–479a

"Dos grandes metáforas, Las." *See* Ortega y Gasset, José

Dos Luises y otros ensayos, Los. See Azorín

Dos Passos, John
   Broch and, 10:1392b
   visits Baroja, 9:613a

Doski sud'by. See Khlebnikov, Velimir

Dostigaev i drugie (Dostigaev and Others). *See* Gorky, Maxim

Dostoevsky, Feodor, **7:1349a–1371b**
   "A Faint Heart," 7:1353a
   "A Gentle Creature," 7:1362b, 1366a
   A Raw Youth, 7:1366b–1367b
   Belinsky and, 7:1351a–1353b
   "Bobok," 7:1366a
   Camus and, 13:3055b, 3075a

Chekhov and, 7:1869a
Crime and Punishment (Prestuplenie i nakazanie), 7:1360a–1361b
  Petersburg and, 9:922b
  The Three of Them and, 8:432a
  Zamyatin's "The Flood" and, 10:1196b–1197a
D'Annunzio and, 8:182a, 197a
"Diary of a Writer," 7:1366a-b
Doctor Faustus and, 9:733a
Epoch magazine, 7:1358b–1359a
Gogol and, 6:974a, 986b
Gombrowicz and, 12:2574b
Goncharov and, 6:1083b
Hamsun and, 8:28a
Hesse on, 9:843b–844a
idea of guilt, 12:2490a
interpretation of Pushkin's *The Gypsies*, 5:667b
Kafka and, 9:1156a
Lermontov and, 6:1224a
literary celebrity, 11:1893b
Lukács on, 10:1259a, 1259b–1260a, 1263b, 1272a
Mauriac and, 10:1312b
"Mr. Prokharchin," 7:1353a
Netochka Nezvanova, 7:1353a-b
Notes from Underground (Zapiski iz podpol'ia), 7:1359a–1360a
  Rilke and, 9:781a
  Zamyatin's *We* and, 10:1189b–1190a
Ortega y Gasset on, 9:1138a
Poor Folk, 7:1351a–1352a
Pushkin's *Covetous Knight* and, 5:680a
Sarraute and, 12:2333a
Simon and, 13:3031a-b, 3032b–3033a, 3033b
Solzhenitsyn and, 13:3196b
Svevo and, 8:68b
The Brothers Karamazov (Brat'ia Karamozovy), 7:1367b–1369b, 10:1189b
  Doctor Faustus and, 9:733b
  Don Carlos and, 5:35b
  Leconte de Lisle and, 6:1257b
The Double, 7:1352a-b
"The Dream of a Ridiculous Man," 7:1366a
The Eternal Husband, 7:1363b–1364a
The Friend of the Family, 7:1356a-b

The Gambler, 7:1361b
"The Heavenly Christmas Tree," 7:1366a
"The Honest Thief," 7:1353a
The House of the Dead, 7:1357a-b
The Idiot (Idiot), 7:1362a–1363b
  Benjamin's essay on, 11:1707b
  Myshkin as Christlike figure, 8:296b
  Olesha and, 11:2235b, 2244b
The Insulted and the Injured, 7:1357b–1358b
"The Landlady," 7:1353a
"The Life of a Great Sinner," 7:1364a–1365a
"The Peasant Marei," 7:1366a
The Possessed (Besy), 6:1083b, 7:1354a-b, 1364b–1366a, 10:1189b–1190a, 11:1901a
Thomas Mann on, 9:737b
Time (magazine), 7:1356b–1357a, 1358b
Trakl and, 10:1413a
Turgenev and, 6:1289a
"Uncle's Dream," 7:1355b–1356a
"Vlas," 7:1366a
Western values and, 7:1666a
"Winter Notes on Summer Impressions," 7:1358b
Zamyatin's *We* and, 10:1189a–1190a
Double, A. *See* Storm, Theodor, *Ein Doppelgänger*
"Double Entry." *See* Ekelöf, Gunnar
Double jardin, Le (The Double Garden). See Maeterlinck, Maurice
Double Misunderstanding, The (La double méprise). See Mérimée, Prosper
"Double, The." *See* Blok, Alexander, "Dvoinik"
Double, The. See Dostoevsky, Feodor
Double Wedding. *See* Kundera, Milan, *Ptákovina, čili Dvoje uši—dvoje svadba*
Doubles, Stendhal and, 5:343b
Doubrovsky, Serge, 13:3024a, 3043b
Doubt
  Dürrenmatt and, 13:3216a-b
  hyperbolic, in Descartes's *Meditations on First Philosophy*, 3:10a-b, 11b–12a, 18b
  Nerval and, 6:958b, 960a, 968a
  in Rabelais, 2:710a-b
  see also Skepticism
"Dover Beach." *See* Arnold, Matthew

Dovere del medico, Il. See Pirandello, Luigi

Down with Progress. See Goncourt, Edmond
Louis Antoine de, *À bas le progrès*

Down There. See Huysmans, Joris Karl, *Là-bas*

Downstream. See Huysmans, Joris Karl, *À
vau-l'eau*

Dowry legend, 1:462a-b

Dowson, Ernest, Verlaine and, 7:1642a

"Doxa ton Ptolemaion, I." *See* Cavafy,
Constantine

Doyle, Arthur Conan, contribution to mystery
genre, 12:2485b–2486a

Dózsa, György, Ady on, 9:864b

Dr. Graesler, Resort Physician. See Schnitzler,
Arthur, *Doktor Gräsler, Badearzt*

Dr. Katzenberger's Trip to a Spa. *See* Richter,
Jean Paul, *Doktor Katzenbergers
Badereise*

Drageoir à épices, Le. See Huysmans, Joris
Karl

Dragon, The. See Jarry, Alfred, *La dragonne*

"Dragon, The." *See* Zamyatin, Yevgeny
Ivanovich, "Drakon"

Dragonne, La. See Jarry, Alfred

Dragontea, La. See Lope de Vega

Dragoumis, Ion, Kazantzakis and, 9:1076b

"Drakon." *See* Zamyatin, Yevgeny Ivanovich

Drama

    Aristotelian conception of, 11:2105a

    Brecht's theory of, 11:2089b, 2093b,
        2099a–2099b

    conventions, theory of the three unities. *See*
        Unities, dramatic

    didactic, Brecht's *Schulopern*, 11:2091a

    Diderot as playwright, 4:492a–495a

    English, well-made play and, 7:1926a–1928a

    forms, Schnitzler's use of, 8:93b–98b,
        100b–102a, 104b–108a

    French
        antitheater, 13:2844b
        Lessing and, 4:538b, 547b–548b
        Schiller's *Mary Stuart* and, 5:45b
        well-made play and, 7:1909a–1924b

    Frisch's theories of, 13:2916b

    German
        chronicle, 8:268a
        comedies, 8:153b–154b

        epic, 8:229b, 268a
        "estrangement" acting, 8:260a
        Lessing and, 4:540b, 547a, 558a
        literary cabaret, 8:260a-b
        middle-class tragedies, 8:159b–160b
        pantomime, 8:242b–246b
        Wedekind's influence, 8:229a
        well-made play and, 7:1925a–1926a
        see also Naturalism; *Trauerspiel*

    gestus in, 11:2099a–2100b

    Goethe and, 11:2105a

    of Gombrowicz, 12:2584b–2586a

    Greek
        and Cocteau, 10:1550b–1552a,
          1554a–1555b
        Wagner on, 6:1153b

    historical. *See* Historical drama

    Hugo's work in, 6:695a-b, 704b

    Ibsen's use of verse in, 7:1426b

    Ionesco on, 13:2992a-b

    Lermontov's work in, 6:1201a–1202b

    Lope de Vega and, 2:851a–855a, 852a,
        858b–859a

    Marinetti and, 9:820b–823a

    Marxist, 11:2098b, 2103b–2104a, 2104b

    Maupassant's work in, 7:1763a-b

    medieval, **1:451a–474b**, 2:850a
        Claudel's *Joan of Arc at the Stake* as,
          8:488a-b
        English, 1:452a, 468b–469a
        French, 1:457a, 469a–470b
        German, 1:466a–468b
        Italian, 1:471a
        late, 1:465b–473b
        Latin, 1:453b–456b
        secular, 1:471a–473a
        sources, 1:452a-b
        Spanish, 1:471a
        terminology, 1:452b–453a
        vernacular, 1:457a–461a

    Mérimée's work in, 6:747a, 747b–750b, 754a

    Moberg's, 11:2210a, 2226b–2227b

    one-act play, Schnitzler's use of, 8:96b–97a,
        97a-b, 100b–101a, 102a, 106b

    pastoral, 2:916a–920a
        of Castiglione, 2:646b–647a
        Tasso and, 2:794b

Pirandello on, 8:392a-b

Polish. *See* Mickiewicz, Adam, *Dziady*

problematic plays of Calderón, 2:873b

realism in German, 11:2098a

religious

of Calderón, 2:872a-b, 890b–892b

of Hebbel, *Agnes Bernauer*,
6:1108a–1109b

of Hebbel, *Herod and Mariamne*,
6:1105b–1108a

Kierkegaard and, 6:1137a–1139a, 1141a-b

Renaissance, 1:470b–471a, 473a

Russian, Blok, 9:970b, 973b, 979b

of Sarraute, 12:2354a–2357b

Schiller and, 11:2105a

Sicilian, Pirandello and, 8:393b

spectacular, of Sardou, 7:1916b

Strindberg's work in, 7:1732b, 1735a,
1735b–1736a, 1739a, 1741b–1753a,
1741a-b

twentieth-century, Scribe and,
7:1931b–1932a

Vesaas and, 11:2053a–2053b

of Voltaire, 4:381b–382a

see also Absurd, theater of;
Cloak-and-sword plays; Epic drama;
Folk drama; Historical drama; Miracle
plays; Mystery plays; "Panic theater";
Theater of cruelty; "Theater of the
grotesque"; Thesis plays; *Trauerspiel*
(dramatic genre); Well-made play

"Drama na okhote." *See* Chekhov, Anton

Dramatic irony. *See* Irony, dramatic

Dramatic monologue, Milosz's use of,
13:2943a

Dramatic unities. *See* Unities, dramatic

"Drame de Venise." *See* Musset, Alfred de,
Sand's affair with; Sand, George

Drápa (Norse poetic form), 1:378b

Drawing, Valéry on, 8:575b

Drayman Henschel. See Hauptmann, Gerhart,
Fuhrmann Henschel

Dream. *See* Dali, Salvador, "Rèverie"

"Dream, A." *See* Lermontov, Mikhail Yurievich,
"Son"

Dream of an Oyster. *See* Butor, Michel, "Le
rêve de l'huitre"

Dream of a Battlefield, A. *See* Richter, Jean
Paul, "Ein Traum von einem
Schlachtfeld"

Dream Comedy. See Valle-Inclán, Ramón del,
Comedia de ensueño

Dream Is Life, A. See Grillparzer, Franz

"Dream and Madness." *See* Trakl, Georg

Dream Play. See Strindberg, August

Dream Play, A. See Strindberg, August

Dream Play, The. See Ionesco, Eugène

"Dream of a Ridiculous Man, The." *See*
Dostoevsky, Feodor

Dream of the Rood (Anglo-Saxon poem), 1:65b

Dream, The. See Montherlant, Henry de; Zola,
Émile, *Le réve*

Dream Tragedy. *See* Valle-Inclán, Ramón del,
Tragedia de ensueño

Dream of Vaux, The. *See* La Fontaine, Jean de,
Le songe de Vaux

Dream vision, in *Romance of the Rose*,
1:310a–311a, 325b–326b

"Dreamcritique." *See* Apollinaire, Guillaume,
"Onirocritique"

Dreamers. See Hamsun, Knut, *Svaermere*

"Dreamers, The." *See* Dinesen, Isak

Dreams

allegory and, 1:324b

in Breton's thought, 11:1943b–1944a

Butor and, 13:3307b–3309a, 3312b–3313a

in Descartes's *Meditations on First
Philosophy*, 3:9b–10a

Diderot and, 4:491a

Freud's concept of, 8:3a–4a, 9a–12a

in Goncharov's works, 6:1076a–1077b,
1082a

in Hugo's works, 6:697a-b

in Ionesco's plays, 13:2997a, 2999b,
3015b–3016a, 3016b

Le piéton de l'air, 13:2998a

Kafka and, 9:1156b–1157a, 1160b

Maeterlinck and, 8.123a-b

Nerval and, 6:966a–968a

reality and, in Andrić's works, 11:1758a

in Richter's fiction, 5:58b, 65a-b

in Svevo's novels, 8:72b

in Tieck, 5:240a-b

Vesaas and, 11:2047a, 2056b

Dreams (*cont.*)
in Yourcenar's fiction, 12:2540b,
2545b–2546a
Dreams and Destinies. *See* Yourcenar,
Marguerite, *Les songes et les sorts*
Dreams Drowning. See Ghelderode, Michel de
Dreams of Life and Death. *See* Arp, Jean,
"Träume vom Tod und Leben"
Dreams and Projects. See Arp, Jean
Dreams of Roses and Fire. See Johnson,
Eyvind
"Dreary Story, A." *See* Chekhov, Anton,
"Skuchnaya istoriya"
Drei Abhandlungen zur Sexualtheorie. See
Freud, Sigmund
"Drei Elixire, Die." *See* Schnitzler, Arthur
Drei Frauen. See Musil, Robert
Drei gerechten Kammacher, Die. See Keller,
Gottfried, *The Three Righteous
Combmakers*
Drei Gesänge. See George, Stefan
"Drei Minuten Roman." *See* Mann, Heinrich
Drei und dreissig Gedichte. See Heine,
Heinrich
Dreigroschenoper, Die. See Brecht, Bertolt,
The Threepenny Opera
Drengen. See Gunnarsson, Gunnar
Dresden
civil war in, Wagner and, 6:1153a
Mickiewicz's stay in, 5:619a
Dress. *See* Clothing
Dreyfus Affair, 7:1517a-b, 1537a–1539a
Apollinaire and, 9:886b
Chekhov and, 7:1856a
Eça's position on, 7:1695b
Huysmans and, 7:1728b
Proust and, 8:546b–547a
Zola and, 7:1517a-b, 1537a–1539a
Drini ćuprija, Na. See Andrić, Ivo, *The Bridge
on the Drina*
Drives, Freud's concept of, 8:4b, 5b, 11a,
14a-b
Drömmar om rosor och eld. See Johnson,
Eyvind, *Dreams of Roses and Fire*
Drömspelet. See Strindberg, August, *A Dream
Play*

"Drop of Water, A." *See* Andersen, Hans
Christian
Droplaugarsona saga (*The Story of Droplaug's
Sons*), 1:385b–386a, 396a, 398b
Dróttkvætt stanza, 1:378a-b
"Drought." *See* Perse, Saint-John, "Sécheresse"
Droysen, Gustav, Croce and, 8:313b
Drugs
Cocteau and, 10:1547b
Gautier's opium dream narratives, 6:1050b
in Hesse's *Steppenwolf,* 9:848b
Montale's experimentation with, 11:2003a
Trakl and, 10:1411a-b
Witkiewicz and, 10:1226b
see also Laudanum
Druhý sešit směšných lásek. See Kundera,
Milan, *The Second Book of Laughable
Loves*
Drums in the Night. See Brecht, Bertolt
Drunkard. See Zola, Émile, *L'Assommoir*
"Drunken Boat, The." *See* Rimbaud, Arthur,
"Le bateau ivre"
Dry Heart, The. See Ginzburg, Natalia, *È stato
così*
"Dryade, La" (The Dryad). *See* Vigny, Alfred
Victor de, *Poèmes antiques et modernes*
Dryden, John
All for Love, Lessing and, 4:550a
Essay of Dramatick Poesie, and Lessing,
4:543b
Dschinnistan. See Wieland, Christoph Martin
Du Bartas, *La Sepmaine où création du
monde* (*The Week; or, The Creation of
the World*), 2:816a-b
Du Bellay, Joachim
*Défense et illustration de la langue
française* (The Defense and Making
Illustrious of the French Language),
Pléiade poets and, 2:911b
Divers jeux rustiques (*Diverse Rustic
Diversions*), "D'un vanneur de blé aux
vents" ("From a Winnower of Corn to
the Winds"), 2:911b
pastoral lyrics of, 2:911b

Du côté de chez Swann. See Proust, Marcel, *Remembrance of Things Past* (*À la recherche du temps perdu*), *Swann's Way*

Du fährst zu oft nach Heidelberg und andere Erzählungen. See Böll, Heinrich

Du Fail, Noël
  Baliverneries d'Eutrapel (Cock-and-Bull Stories of Eutrapel), 2:947a
  Contes d'Eutrapel, 2:947a
  Propos rustiques (*Rustic Talk*), 2:947a

Du Plessis, Alexandrine, vicomtesse, Vigny's letters to, 5:480a

Du prêtre, de la femme et de la famille. See Michelet, Jules

Du prince et des lettres. See Alfieri, Vittorio, *The Prince and Letters*

"Du skriker till livet." *See* Ekelöf, Gunnar

"Du store Eros." *See* Södergran, Edith

"Du thésauriseur et du singe." *See* La Fontaine, Jean de, *Fables*

Dual Monarchy. *See* Habsburg Empire

Dualism
  in Augustine's *City of God*, 1:36b
  in Bergson's works, 8:54b–55a
  in Böll's war stories, 13:3178b
  in Calvino, 13:3265a–3266a
  Cartesian, discussed in La Bruyère's *Caractères*, 3:256b–257a
  in Dostoevsky
    Notes from the Underground, 7:1359b
    The Brothers Karamazov, 7:1368b
    The Double, 7:1352a-b
    The Friend of the Family, 7:1356a
    The Insulted and the Injured, 7:1358a
  Gogol and, 6:978a
  in Hebbel's works, 6:1098b, 1118a
  in Hesse's *Narcissus and Goldmund*, 9:849b
  in Hoffmann's works, "Duplizität des Seins," 5:280b
  in Laforgue's poetry, 7:1905a, 1905b
  Prudentius on, 1:16a-b, 17a, 18a-b

Dubois, Cardinal, Lesage's *Gil Blas* and, 3:337a

Dubois, Paul, Sainte-Beuve and, 6:837a

"Duce aviatore, Il." *See* Marinetti, Filippo Tommaso

Duchamp, Marcel
  dadaism and, 11:2063b
  poetic language, 11:1953a
  "readymade" paintings of, 11:1965b

Duchesse de Langeais, La (*The Duchess of Langeais*). *See* Giraudoux, Jean

"Duchoux." *See* Maupassant, Guy de

Duclos, Charles, *Les confessions du Comte ****, 3:322a-b

Dudevant, Amantine-Aurore-Lucile. *See* Sand, George

Due cortigiane. See Moravia, Alberto

Due gemelli veneziani, I. See Goldoni, Carlo

Duel
  in Corneille's *Le Cid*, 3:27b
  Lermontov's death in, 6:1223a
  Pushkin's death in, 5:664a
  Schnitzler's view of, 8:98b–99a, 105a

"Duel." *See* Chekhov, Anton

Duel of Angels. See Giraudoux, Jean, *Pour Lucrèce*

Duel sous Richelieu, Un (*A Duel Under Richelieu*). *See* Hugo, Victor, *Marion de Lorme*

"Duel, The." *See* Kleist, Heinrich von

Duel, The. See Kuprin, Aleksandr, *Poedinok*

Dufy, Raoul, 9:894a

Duineser Elegien (*Duino Elegies*). *See* Rilke, Rainer Maria

Dujardin, Édouard, *Les lauriers sont coupés* (*We'll to the Woods No More*), 7:1906a

Dukas, Paul, Maeterlinck and, 8:136b, 143a

Duke Theodor of Gothland. See Grabbe, Christian Dietrich, *Herzog Theodor von Gothland*

Dulac, Germaine, direction of Artaud's *La coquille et le clergyman* by, 11:1971a

Dulce bellum inexpertis. See Erasmus

Dullin, Charles, Anouilh and, 13:2844b

"Duma." *See* Lermontov, Mikhail Yurievich

Dumas fils, Alexandre, 7:1917a-b, 1919a-b, 1920a, 1920b
  Dumas père and, 6:723b
  farceurs and, 7:1922a
  Françillon, 7:1919b

Dumas fils, Alexandre (*cont.*)

La dame aux camélias (*The Lady of the Camelias; Camille*), 6:723b, 7:1917a-b, 1918a, 1918b, 1919b

La femme de Claude (*Claude's Wife*), 7:1917b, 1918b

Le demi-monde (*The Demi-Monde*), 7:1917b, 1918b

Le fils naturel (*The Natural Son*), 7:1917b, 1918b–1919a

Les idées de Madame Aubray (The Ideas of Madame Aubray), 7:1919a

L'Étrangère (The Foreign Woman), 7:1917a, 1919a

Un père prodigue (A Prodigal Father), 7:1917b

verse drama, 7:1426b

Dumas père, Alexandre, **6:719a–743b**

Alchimiste (with Gérard de Nerval), 6:947b

Ange Pitou, 6:724a, 726b, 731b, 733b, 735b, 737b–738a

Angèle, 6:722b, 723a

Antony, 6:721b–722b

Catherine Blum, 6:740b

Causeries, 6:725a

Christine, 6:720a, 720b

Conscience l'innocent (*Conscience the Innocent*), 6:740b

Création et rédemption (*Creation and Redemption*), 6:741a

Gaule et France, 6:725a

Henri III et sa cour (*Henry III and His Court*), 6:719a, 721b, 735b

Histoire de mes bêtes (*The Story of My Pet Animals*), 6:741a

Impressions de voyage en Suisse (*Travels in Switzerland*), 6:739b

Isabelle de Bavière, 6:725a

Joseph Balsamo, 6:724a, 725b, 726b, 727a–728b, 734a, 737a-b

La comtesse de Charny, 6:726b, 739b

La dame de Monsoreau (*Chicot the Jester*), 6:720b, 726b, 729a

La reine Margot (*Marguerite de Valois*), 6:724a, 725b, 728a-b, 735b

La tour de Nesle, 6:723a-b

La tulip noire (*The Black Tulip*), 6:731a, 734a, 736b–737a

Le chevalier de Maison-Rouge, 6:726b, 729a-b, 733a-b

Le chevalier d'Harmental, 6:724b, 731a

Le collier de la reine (*The Queen's Necklace*), 6:726a, 726b, 729a, 733b, 736b

Le comte de Monte Cristo (*The Count of Monte Cristo*), Calvino and, 13:3278a

Le comte de Monte-Cristo (*The Count of Monte Cristo*), 6:724a, 731b 732b, 738a–739a

Le meneur de loups (*The Wolf Man*), 6:740a, 740b–741a

Le mousquetaire (newspaper), 6:741a

Le vicomte de Bragelonne (*The Man in the Iron Mask*), 6:724a, 727a, 730a, 733a

Les blancs et les bleus (*The Whites and the Blues*), 6:741a

Les quarante-cinq (*The Forty-Five*), 6:725a, 734a

Les Stuarts, 6:725a

Les trois mousquetaires (*The Three Musketeers*), 6:724a, 729b–730a, 733a, 734b

Mademoiselle de Belle-Isle, 6:723a

Mes mémoires (*My Memoirs*), 6:739b–740a

Nerval and, 6:947b, 949b, 959a

Ortega y Gasset reads, 9:1122b

Richard Darlington, 6:722b, 723a

Souvenirs dramatiques, 6:721b, 741a

The Mohicans of Paris, in Proust's *Remembrance of Things Past*, 8:554a

Vingt ans après (*Twenty Years After*), 6:725b, 726a, 727a, 730a–731b, 732b–733a, 734b–735a, 741b

Dumas père, Alexandre, and Nerval, Gérard de, *Piquillo*, 6:947b

Dumb Boy, The. *See* García Lorca, Federico, "El niño mudo"

Dumesnil, Alfred, Michelet and, 5:576b, 598a

D'un diable qui prêcha merveilles. See Ghelderode, Michel de

D'un nouveau complot contre les industriels. See Stendhal

"D'un vanneur de blé aux vents." *See* Du Bellay, Joachim, *Divers jeux rustiques*

D'un voyage au pays des Tarahumaras. See Artaud, Antonin

Dunciad, The. See Pope, Alexander

"Dung Beetle, The." *See* Andersen, Hans Christian

Dunn, Olav, Norwegian realism and, 9:1037a

Duns Scotus
    Aquinas and, 1:426b–427a
    Commentaries on the Sentences, 1:426b
    Quodlibeta, 1:426b

Duo. See Colette

Duplessis-Mornay. *See* Mornay, Philippe de

Durandus of Saint-Pourçain, 1:426b

Duranty, Edmond, on Flaubert, 7:1382a-b

Duration and Simultaneity. See Bergson, Henri, *Durée et simultanéité*

Durch (Through) (literary organization), 8:148a

Durchschnittsmensch, 9:936b

Durée et simultanéité. See Bergson, Henri

Durée réelle, in Bergson's thought. *See* Real duration

Dürer, Albrecht
    Grass and, 13:3379b
    Hugo and, 6:704a
    Taine on, 7:1463b

D'Urfé, Honoré
    L'Astrée (*Astrea*), 2:924a-b
        Montemayor's *Diana* and, 2:923b–924a
    Sireine, Montemayor's *Diana* and, 2:924a

Durkheim, Émile, Bergson and, 8:45b, 61b

Durrell, Lawrence, 12:2260b
    Alexandria Quartet, Cavafy in, 8:205a-b
    on Cavafy, 8:205a, 207b, 225a
    on Elytis, 13:2985a-b
    Justine, 8:225a

Dürrenmatt, Friedrich, **13:3215a–3235b**
    An Angel Comes to Babylon (*Ein Engel kommt nach Babylon*), 13:3220b–3222a
    Das Unternehmen der Wega (Operation Vega), 13:3232a-b
    Der Meteor, 13:3220a-b
    "Der Tunnel," 13:3216b–3217b
    Frank V, 13:3230a-b

Incident at Twilight (*Abendstunde im Spätherbst*), 13:3232b–3233b
    Romulus the Great (*Romulus der Grosse*), 13:3226a-b
        historical drama vs., 5:431b
    The Judge and His Hangman (*Der Richter und sein Henker*), 13:3222a, 3222b–3223a
    The Marriage of Mr. Mississippi (*Die Ehe des Herrn Mississippi*), 13:3226a, 3226b–3227b
    The Physicists (*Die Physiker*), 13:3226a, 3227b–3230a, 3231a
    The Pledge (*Das Versprechen*), 13:3222a, 3224b–3225b
    The Quarry (*Der Verdacht*), 13:3222a, 3222b, 3223a–3224a
    The Sell-out (*Der Mitmacher*), 13:3230b–3231a
    The Visit (*Der Besuch der alten Dames*), 13:3229b, 3231a–3232a

Durry, Marie-Jeanne, 9:894b

Duse, Eleonora, 7:1548b
    D'Annunzio's relationship with, 8:186a-b, 194a, 195a

"Dushechka." *See* Chekhov, Anton

Dushyanta, in Apollinaire's "The Song of the Unloved Lover," 9:889b, 890b

Duty, theme of
    in Corneille's plays, 3:23b
        Horace, 3:35b, 36b
        Le Cid, 3:29a
        Polyeucte, 3:44b

Duval, Jeanne, Baudelaire and, 7:1324b–1325b

Dva brata. See Lermontov, Mikhail Yurievich

"Dvadtsat' shest' i odna." *See* Gorky, Maxim

Dvärgen. See Lagerkvist, Pär

Dvenadtsat'. See Blok, Alexander, *The Twelve*

"Dvoinik." *See* Blok, Alexander

"Dvoiniku." *See* Blok, Alexander

Dwarf, The. *See* Aymé, Marcel, *The Wonderful Farm* (*Contes du chat perché*), "Le nain"

Dwarf, The. *See* Lagerkvist, Pär, *Dvärgen*

Dwelling Places of God, The. *See* Vesaas, Tarjei

Dyadya Vanya. See Chekhov, Anton, *Uncle Vanya*

Dying. See Schnitzler, Arthur, *Sterben*

Dying Hercules. See Rotrou, Jean de, *Hercule mourant*

Dyk, Viktor, Hašek and, 9:1096a

Dym, dym, dym. See Tsvetaeva, Anastasiia

"Dynamics of Transference, The." *See* Freud, Sigmund, "Zur Dynamik der Übertragung"

Dynamism
    in *Beowulf,* 1:57a-b
    in oral cultures, 1:56a

Dyret med Glorien. See Gunnarsson, Gunnar

"Dysareskeia tou Selefkidou, I." *See* Cavafy, Constantine

Dystopia
    Canetti and, 12:2628b–2630b
    in Čapek's novels, 10:1574b–1575b, 1577a–1578a

Džadžić, Petar, *Hrastova greda u kamenoj kapiji* (The Oak Beam in the Stone Bridge), 11:1760b

Dziady. See Mickiewicz, Adam

"Dziecie Europy." *See* Milosz, Czeslaw, "Child of Europe"

Dziennik. See Gombrowicz, Witold, *Diary*

E

È stato così. See Ginzburg, Natalia

Each in His Own Way. See Pirandello, Luigi

Eagle with Two Heads, The. See Cocteau, Jean, *L'Aigle à deux têtes*

Earini symfonia. See Ritsos, Yannis

"Early Graves, The." *See* Klopstock, Friedrich Gottlieb

Early Trains. See Pasternak, Boris

"Earrings, The." *See* Montale, Eugenio, *The Storm and Other Things* (*La bufera e altro*), "Gli orecchini"

Earth. *See* Gunnarsson, Gunnar, *Jord*

"Earth." *See* Quasimodo, Salvatore, "Terra"

Earth. See Zola, Émile, *La terre*

Earth Is Ours, The. See Moberg, Vilhelm

Earth, Mother, Vesaas and, 11:2042a–2042b

Earth Spirit. See Wedekind, Frank

Earthbound Omens. *See* Tsvetaeva, Marina, *Zemnye primety*

"Earthen Pot and the Iron Pot, The." *See* La Fontaine, Jean de, *Fables,* "Le pot de terre et le pot de fer"

Earthquake, Lisbon, Portugal (1755), Voltaire on, 4:377a-b

"Earthquake in Chile, The." *See* Kleist, Heinrich von

"Earth's Sob, The." *See* Laforgue, Jules, "Le sanglot de la terre"

East I Know, The. See Claudel, Paul, *Connaissance de l'Est*

"Eastbourne." *See* Montale, Eugenio, *The Occasions*

Easter, Elytis' *To imerologio enos atheatou Apriliou* and, 13:2983a

Easter. *See* Storm, Theodor, "Ostern"

Easter Day. *See* Khlebnikov, Velimir, "Velik-Den"

Easter (*Påsk*). *See* Strindberg, August

Eastern philosophy and religions
    Hauptmann's amalgamations of, 8:165b–166a, 168a, 169b–170a
    influence on Schopenhauer, 5:403a, 405b, 410a
    Khlebnikov's "Esir" and, 10:1359a

Weil and, 12:2793b

Easter plays, medieval, 1:454a, 455a, 456b, 467a–468b

"Easter Procession, The." *See* Solzhenitsyn, Aleksandr, "Paskhal'nyi krestnyi khod"

Eastern literature, in medieval European tale collections, 2:932a-b

"Ebauche d'un serpent." *See* Valéry, Paul, *Charmes*

"Ebene, Die." *See* Arp, Jean

Ebionites, Prudentius' *Apotheosis* on, 1:8a

Ebreo, Leone, Castiglione and, 2:662a-b

Eça de Queiroz, José Maria, **7:1683a–1707a**, 11:2147b

   A batalha de Caia (The Battle of Caia), 7:1692a

   A capital (The Capital City), 7:1692a

   A correspondência de Fradique Mendes, 7:1686b

   A emigração como força civilizadora (Emigration as a Civilizing Force), 7:1690b

   A tragédia da Rua das Flores (The Tragedy of Flores Street), 7:1696a

   Cartas de Inglaterra (*Letters from England*), 7:1692a

   Cartas familiares e bilhetes de Paris (Family Letters and Parisian Notes), 7:1695a

   "Comércio e indústria no norte da Inglaterra, 1874–1875" (Commerce and Industry in the North of England, 1874–1875), 7:1691a-b

   Cousin Bazilio (*O primo Basílio*), 7:1699a–1700a

     observations for planning, 7:1687b

     sexual degradation of middle class in, 7:1691b

   Crónicas de Londres (Tales from London), 7:1692a

   Darts (*Farpas*), 7:1688a-b

   Dicionário de milagres (Dictionary of Miracles), 7:1693b

   Districto de Evora, 7:1686a

   Ecos de Paris (Echoes from Paris), 7:1695a

   "Idealismo e realismo" (Idealism and Realism), 7:1692a, 1701a

   Lendas de Santos (Legends of Saints), 7:1693b

   O conde Abranhos (The Count of Abranhos), 7:1692a

   O Egipto (Egypt), 7:1686b–1687a

   "O francesismo" (Francophilia), 7:1695b

   "O realismo como nova expressão da arte" (Realism as a New Expression of Art), 7:1689a

   Prosas bárbaras (Barbarous Prose), 7:1685b

   Revista de Portugal, 7:1693b

   "Scenes of Portuguese Life," 7:1692a

   "Singularidades duma rapariega loura" ("Peculiarities of a Fair-Haired Girl"), 7:1690b–1691a

   Teoria da vontade (Theory of the Will), 7:1693a

   The City and the Mountains, 7:1695a, 1705b–1706a

   The Illustrious House of Ramires (*A ilustre casa de Ramires*), 7:1695a, 1704a–1705b

   The Maias (*Os Maias*), 7:1692b–1693a, 1693b–1694a, 1703a–1705b

     Pinheiro Chagas and, 7:1694a, 1703a

   The Mandarin (*O mandarim*), 7:1692b, 1701a–1702a

   The Relic (*A relíquia*), 7:1693b, 1701b, 1702a–1703a

   The Sin of Father Amaro (*O crime do Padre Amaro*), 7:1687b, 1697a–1699a

     Antero de Quental's editing of, 7:1691b

     comparison of versions of, 7:1697b

     criticism of, 7:1700a

     versions of, 7:1691a, 1691b–1692a

   Uma campanha alegre (A Happy Campaign), 7:1688a-b

Eça de Queiroz, José Maria, and Ramalho Ortigão, *O mistério de estrada de Sintra* (The Mystery of Sintra Road), 7:1687b

Ecatommiti, Gli. See Giraldi, Giambattista

Ecce Homo. See Nietzsche, Friedrich

Eccentric Old Man, The. *See* Goldoni, Carlo, *Il vecchio bizzaro*

Ecclesiastes. See Erasmus

Ecclesiastical History of the English Nation.
    See Bede, *Historia ecclesiastica gentis Anglorum*
Échange, L'. See Claudel, Paul
Échec de Pavese, L'. See Fernandez, Dominique
Echegaray, José, Valle-Inclán and, 8:341a, 350b
"Echoes." *See* Dinesen, Isak
Echoes from Paris. *See* Eça de Queiroz, José Maria, *Ecos de Paris*
Echoes of Old Songs. *See* Ady, Endre, "Régi énekek ekhója"
Eck, John, Luther and, 2:684a
Eckermann, Johann Peter, *Conversations with Goethe*, 5:8b, 17b
Eckhart, Meister, Jiménez and, 9:1013b
Éclair, L' (French periodical), Goncourts' articles in, 7:1396a
Eclogues
    of Boccaccio, 2:904b
    of Boiardo, 2:906b
    classical, 2:901a, 902a-b
    of Dante, 2:904a
    English, 2:914b–915a
    High Renaissance, 2:908a, 908b–909b
    of Mantovano, 2:907a-b
    of Petrarch, 2:904a-b
    of Pléiade poets, 2:912a
    see also Lusus pastorales; Pastoral poetry
Eclogues. See Vergil
École des bouffons, L'. See Ghelderode, Michel de, *The School for Buffoons*
École des cadavres, L'. See Céline, Louis-Ferdinand
École des femmes, L'. See Molière
École des indifférents, L'. See Giraudoux, Jean
École des maris, L'. See Molière
"École du bon sens," 7:1918a
École frénétique, Lermontov and, 6:1201b, 1205b
"Ecologa." *See* Tasso, Torquato, *Aminta*
Economics, Croce and, 8:314b
Ecos de Paris. See Eça de Queiroz, José Maria
"Écrevisse, L." *See* Apollinaire, Guillaume, *Le bestiaire, ou cortège d'Orphée*

Écrits de Londres et dernières lettres. See Weil, Simone, *Writings from London and Last Letters*
Écrits historiques et politiques. See Weil, Simone, *Historical and Political Writings*
Écrits pour l'art (magazine), 8:450b
Écriture artiste (artist writing). *See* Style Goncourt
Écriture (writing), Barthes and, 13:3082a–3083b
Ecstatic pessimism, of Milosz, 13:2936a, 2946a
Ed è subito sera. See Quasimodo, Salvatore, *Suddenly It's Evening*
Ed egli si nascose. See Silone, Ignazio
Edbrødrene. See Gunnarsson, Gunnar, *The Sworn Brothers*
Edda. See Snorri Sturluson
Eddic poetry, 1:378a, 383a
Eden and Afterward. *See* Robbe-Grillet, Alain, *L'Eden et après*
Eden et après, L'. See Robbe-Grillet, Alain
Eden myth. *See* Bible
Édes Anna. See Kosztolányi, Dezső
Edfelt, Johannes, Ekelöf and, 12:2636b
"Edification Implied in the Thought That as Against God We Are Always Wrong, The." *See* Kierkegaard, Søren
Edith Södergran's dikter 1907–1909 (Edith Sodergran's Poems). *See* Södergran, Edith
"Eduard a Bůh." *See* Kundera, Milan, "Edward and God"
Education
    Augustine on, 1:45b
    Aymé's satire of, 12:2443b–2444b, 2446b
    in Butor, 13:3299a-b
    in eighteenth-century Italy, Alfieri's satire of, 4:674b–675a
    Foucault and, 13:3330a
    in France, after the 1830 revolution, 5:589b
    in Gottfried, 1:257a-b
    in La Bruyère's *Caractères*, 3:251a
    Luther and, 2:683b
    medieval, satire and, 1:366a-b, 369b–370a, 371a

Prussian, Heinrich Mann and, 8:520a, 528a
in Richter's *The Invisible Lodge*, 5:62a
role of, in Michelet's thinking, 5:594b–595a
Rousseau and, 4:449b, 457a
Schiller on, 5:36a
in Walther, 1:300a-b
in Wolfram, 1:274a
Education of an Orator, The. *See* Quintilian,
    Institutio oratoria
Education of a Christian Prince, The. *See*
    Erasmus, *Institutio principis Christiani*
Education of the Human Race. *See* Lessing,
    Gotthold Ephraim, *Die Erziehung des*
    Menschengeschlechts
Éducation sentimentale, L'. *See* Flaubert,
    Gustave, *Sentimental Education*
"Edward and God." *See* Kundera, Milan
Edward II. *See* Brecht, Bertolt
Effi Briest. *See* Fontane, Theodor
Effrontés, Les. *See* Augier, Émile
Efron, Sergei, 11:1734a, 1739a, 1739b–1740a,
    1747a-b
Egalitarianism
    of Herder, 4:650b–653a, 655a
    see also Cultural relativism
"Eger." *See* Chekhov, Anton
Egg symbolism, in Hesse's *Demian*, 9:840b
Egil Skallagrímsson, "Sonatorrek" ("The Loss
    of Sons"), 1:387b
Egils saga. *See* Snorri Sturluson
Egipetskaia marka. *See* Mandelshtam, Osip
Eglantine. *See* Giraudoux, Jean
Egle. *See* Giraldi, Giambattista
Église, L'. *See* Céline, Louis-Ferdinand
Egmont. *See* Goethe, Johann Wolfgang von
Ego
    Freud's concept of, 8:4b, 6a
    see also Self
"Ego dixi, dii estis" ("Song upon the Tailors"),
    1:347a–348a
Ego and the Id, The. *See* Freud, Sigmund, *Das*
    Ich und das Es
Egoism
    Büchner's view of, 6:1180a–1182a
    in Ibsen's plays, 7:1441a-b
        Peer Gynt, 7:1425a
    in plays of Corneille, 3:31a

Schopenhauer's view of, 5:404b–405a
    critique of, 5:405b–406b
"Egoisten, Die" (The Egoists). *See* Schnitzler,
    Arthur
Egor Bulychov i drugie. *See* Gorky, Maxim
Egy asszony beszál. *See* Kosztolányi, Dezső
"Egy ismerös kisfiú." *See* Ady, Endre
"Egy ócska konflisban." *See* Ady, Endre
"Egy párisi hajnalon." *See* Ady, Endre
Egypt
    Greek community in, Cavafy's family and,
        8:209a–210a
    Marinetti and, 9:804b–805a
Egypt. *See* Eça de Queiroz, José Maria, *O*
    Egipto
Egyptian art, Delacroix and, 5:530b
Egyptian Helen, The. *See* Hofmannsthal, Hugo
    von, *Die ägyptische Helena*
Egyptian Stamp, The. *See* Mandelshtam, Osip,
    Egipetskaia marka
Ehe des Herrn Mississippi, Die. *See*
    Dürrenmatt, Friedrich, *The Marriage of*
    Mr. Mississippi
Ehrenburg, Ilya
    Babel and, 11:1911b
    on Dadaism, 11:2062b
    on Pasternak's *Zhenia's Childhood*,
        10:1601a
    People and Life, Olesha and, 11:2250b
    Ritsos on, 12:2829a
    Ritsos' translations of, 12:2819a, 2837b,
        2838a
Ehrengard. *See* Dinesen, Isak
Eichendorff, Joseph von
    Leben eines Taugenichts (*Memoirs of a*
        Good-for-Nothing), Richter's *Walt and*
        Vult and, 5:77a
    "Mondnacht" ("Moonlit Night"), 9:778a
    Schiller and, 5:27b
    Storm and, 6:915b
Eiffel Tower, Apollinaire and, 9:884b, 885a
"Eiffel Tower, The." *See* Barthes, Roland
Eiffel Tower Wedding Party, The. *See* Cocteau,
    Jean, *Les mariés de la Tour Eiffel*
"Eige etelefta." *See* Cavafy, Constantine
Eigenart des Ästhetischen, Die. *See* Lukács,
    György

Eigenschaften (the word), 9:945a

"Eigensinn." *See* Hesse, Hermann

Eigensinn und Laune. See Tieck, Ludwig

8 Souls in a Bomb. See Marinetti, Filippo
    Tommaso, *8 anime in una bomba*

Eight Plays and Eight Interludes. See
    Cervantes, Miguel de

Eight Scenes from Faust. See Berlioz, Hector,
    Huit scènes de Faust

Eighteen Lyrics. *See* Pincherle, Alberto,
    Diciotto liriche

Eighteen Short Songs of the Bitter Motherland.
    See Ritsos, Yannis, *Dhekaohto*
    lianotraghoudha tis pikris patridhas

Eighteenth-Century Woman, The. See
    Goncourt, Edmond Louis Antoine and
    Jules Alfred Huot de, *La femme au*
    dix-huitième siècle

Eikhenbaum, Boris
    on Blok, 9:985b
    on Blok and Tolstoy, 11:1894a

Eilhart von Oberge, Tristan story and, 1:148b

Ein- und Zusprüche. See Böll, Heinrich

Einaudi, Giulio (publisher)
    Calvino and, 13:3263b–3264a
    Ginzburg and, 13:3152b
    Pavese and, 12:2760a-b

Einbahnstrasse. See Benjamin, Walter,
    One-Way Street

"Einem jungen Führer im ersten Weltkrieg."
    See George, Stefan, *Drei Gesänge*

"Eingang." *See* Rilke, Rainer Maria, *Das Buch*
    der Bilder (*The Book of Pictures*)

Einhard, *Life of Charlemagne*, historical
    evidence for Roland in, 1:102a

Einsame Menschen. See Hauptmann, Gerhart

Einsame Weg, Der. See Schnitzler, Arthur

"Einsamkeit." *See* Lenau, Nikolaus

Einstein, Albert, 8:528a
    Bergson and, 8:46a
    Freud and, 8:2a
    Mann's *Magic Mountain* and, 9:722b
    Spanish translations, 9:1119b

"Einzige, Der." *See* Hölderlin, Friedrich

Eirík Oddsson, *Hryggjarstykki* (*Backbone*
    Piece), 1:380a

Eisen, Charles-Dominique-Joseph, in
    Goncourts' *L'Art du dix-huitième siècle*,
    7:1397a

Eisenstein, Sergei, conspiracy charges,
    11:1912a

Eisler, Hanns, Heinrich Mann and, 8:541b

Eiszeit. See Dorst, Tankred

Either/Or. See Kierkegaard, Søren

Ekelöf, Gerhard, 12:2637b–2638a

Ekelöf, Gunnar, **12:2635a–2671b**
    A Mölna Elegy (*En Mölna-elegi*), 12:2640a,
        2646a, 2647b, 2659a–2669a
    "Absentia animi," 12:2647b, 2654a–2658a
    "Apotheosis," 12:2639b
    Blandade kort (Shuffled Cards), 12:2639b,
        2647b
    "Catacombpainting," 12:2639a-b
    "Categories," 12:2642b–2643a
    Dedikation, 12:2639b
    "Den enskilde är död" (The Private Self Is
        Dead), 12:2643a
    "Det finns någonting" (There Is Something),
        12:2642b
    Dīwān över Fursten av Emgión (Dīwān over
        the Prince of Emgión), 12:2646a-b
    "Double Entry," 12:2640b
    "Du skriker till livet" ("You Scream to Life"),
        12:2643a
    En natti i Otočac (A Night in Otočac),
        12:2640b
    "En outsiders väg" (An Outsider's Way),
        12:2638b, 2662b, 2668a
    "En verklighet (drömd)" (A Reality
        [Dreamed]), 12:2643b–2644a
    "Ett 30-talsöde" (A Destiny from the 30's),
        12:2649a-b, 2650a
    "Fabel," 12:2644b–2645a
    Frjesång (Ferry Song), 12:2640a,
        2642b–2643a
    Guide to the Underworld (*Vgvisare till*
        underjorden), 12:2642b, 2646a, 2647a
    Hundra år modern fransk dikt (One
        Hundred Years of Modern French
        Poetry), 12:2650b–2651a
    "Jarrama," 12:2647b, 2648a–2650a
    "Klimat" (Climate), 12:2645b

Köp den blindes sång (Buy the Blind Man's Song), 12:2639b

Lägga patience (Play at Patience), 12:2647b

"Lord of Something Else," 12:2655b–2656a, 2656b–2657a

"Modus vivendi," 12:266a-b

Non serviam (I Shall Not Serve), 12:2643b

Om hösten (In Autumn), 12:2643b

Promenader (Promenades), 12:2647a-b

Sagan om Fatumeh (The Tale of Fatumeh), 12:2646a, 2646b

"Samothrace," 12:2640b, 2647b, 2650a–2654a

Sent på jorden (Late on Earth), 12:2638b–2639a, 2640a

Södergran and, 11:1781a-b

"Sonataform, Methylated Prose," 12:2639a

Sorgen och stjrnan (The Sorrow and the Star), 12:2639b–2640a

Strountes (Tryflings), 12:2644a-b

"Tag och skriv" ("Take and Write"), 12:2640b–2642a, 2640a-b, 2643a-b, 2660b

"The Devil's Sermon," 12:2647a

"The Gymnosophist," 12:2655b–2656a

"The Land-of-the-Freeze," 12:2645a

Utflykter (Excursions), 12:2647b

Valfrnsdkaper (Elective Affinities), 12:2647a, 2662a-b

Verklighetsflykt (Escape from Reality), 12:2647b

"When They Slip Out," 12:2645a

Ekelund, Vilhelm, and Lagerkvist, 10:1679a, 1679b

Ekloyi. See Elytis, Odysseus

"Ekzamen na chin." *See* Chekhov, Anton

"El a faluból." *See* Ady, Endre

"Ela." *See* Zamyatin, Yevgeny Ivanovich

Élan vital, in Bergson's thought, 8:59b–60b, 62a-b

"Elbocsátó szép üzenet." *See* Ady, Endre

Elder of the Ferchaux, The. *See* Simenon, Georges, *L'Aîné des Ferchaux*

Elder, The. *See* Zamyatin, Yevgeny Ivanovich, "Starshina"

Eldur í Kaupinhafn. See Laxness, Halldór

"Elect angels and blessed souls, The." *See* Petrarch, *Canzoniere*, "Li angeli eletti et l'anime beate"

Election, divine, in Mann's *Joseph and His Brothers*, 9:729a-b, 730b, 731b

Elective Affinities. See Ekelöf, Gunnar, *Valfrndskaper*

Elective Affinities. See Goethe, Johann Wolfgang von, *Die Wahlverwandschaften*

Electra; or, the Fall of the Masks. *See* Yourcenar, Marguerite, *Electre ou la chute des masques*

Electra, in Ritsos' poetry, 12:2834a-b

Electra. See Hofmannsthal, Hugo von; Pérez Galdós, Benito

Electre (Electra). See Giraudoux, Jean

Electre ou la chute des masques. See Yourcenar, Marguerite

Electronic culture, Marinetti and, 9:820a

Electroshock therapy, Artaud's experience with, 11:1975b–1976a

Elegia di madonna Fiammetta. See Boccaccio, Giovanni

"Elegia di Pico Farnese" ("Elegy of Pico Farnese"). *See* Montale, Eugenio, *The Occasions*

Elegias intermedias. See Jiménez, Juan Ramón

Elegias lamentables. See Jiménez, Juan Ramón

Elegias puras. See Jiménez, Juan Ramón

Elégie. See Berlioz, Hector

"Elegie an Marina Zwetajewa-Efron." *See* Rilke, Rainer Maria

Elegie renane. See Pirandello, Luigi

Elegie romane. See D'Annunzio, Gabriele

"Elégie XVII." *See* Ronsard, Pierre de

Elegies

by Hölderlin, 5:159b, 160a–161a, 163b–164a

as discussed by Boileau, 3:195b–196b

of Jiménez, 9:996b

Renaissance pastoral, influence of classical sources on, 2:900b–901a

Elégies, mascarades et bergeries. See Ronsard, Pierre de

Elegy. See Berlioz, Hector, *Elégie*

Elegy of Madonna Fiammetta. See Boccaccio, Giovanni, *Elegia di madonna Fiammetta*

Elek, Artur, 9:872b
Elektra. *See* Hofmannsthal, Hugo von, *Electra*
Elementargeister (*Elemental Spirits*). *See*
    Heine, Heinrich
Elementary Ethics. *See* Queneau, Raymond,
    Morale élémentaire
Elements and Culture, The. *See* Blok,
    Alexander, "Stikhiia i kul'tura"
Éléments de physiologie (*Elements of
    Physiology*). *See* Diderot, Denis
Elements of Semiology (*Éléments de
    sémiologie*). *See* Barthes, Roland
Elements of Theology. *See* Proclus
"Eleni." *See* Seferis, George, *Imerologio
    katastromatos C*
Elettra. *See* D'Annunzio, Gabriele
"Elevation" ("Élévation"). *See* Baudelaire,
    Charles
Elf Scharfrichter, Die (*The Eleven
    Executioners*), Wedekind's acting role,
    8:260a-b
"Elf-Queen's Wand, The." *See* Södergran,
    Edith, "Alvdrottningens spira"
"Elfogyni az ölelésben." *See* Ady, Endre
Elga. *See* Hauptmann, Gerhart
"Elillant évek szőlőhegyén." *See* Ady, Endre
"Elindult az Ajgó Márton . . ." *See* Hašek,
    Jaroslav
"Elindult egy leány." *See* Ady, Endre
Elins Erweckung (*Elin's Awakening*). *See*
    Wedekind, Frank
Eliot, George
    "German Wit: Heinrich Heine," 5:509b
    The Mill on the Floss, 5:104a
    Unamuno and, 8:291b
Eliot, T. S.
    acmeism and, 10:1522b
    Apollinaire and, 9:882b
    Baudelaire and, 7:1340a
    Catholicism and, 5:195a
    Cavafy and, 8:206a
    Christianity's decline, 5:195b
    Dialogue on Dramatic Poetry, 7:1445b
    "Difficulties of a Statesman," Seferis'
        translation, 12:2259a
    Elytis and, 13:2968a, 2977a, 2977b
    Gautier and, 6:1058a-b

"Hamlet and His Problems," 7:1831a
on Henry James, 9:715b
Herder's influence on, 4:647b–648a
Hesse and, 9:855b
"Hippopotamus," 6:1058a
on Ibsen, 7:1445b
Jiménez and, 9:1004a
Kazantzakis and, 9:1069a
Laforgue and, 7:1883a-b, 1896a, 1896b,
    1899a
on Mallarmé, 7:1576a
Marina, Seferis and, 12:2259b
on Montaigne, 2:787b
Montale and, 11:2006b
Montale's "Arsenio" published by, 11:1991a
Murder in the Cathedral, Seferis' translation,
    12:2261a
on Ortega y Gasset, 9:1123b
"Portrait of a Lady," Laforgue and, 7:1891a
postclassical literature and, 5:182a
Rilke and, 9:768a, 780a, 788a, 789a
romanticism and, 10:1455a
Seferis and, 12:2255a, 2261a, 2269b,
    13:2956b
Simon and, 13:3025b
Sweeney Agonistes, Laforgue and, 7:1890a
The Four Quartets
    "Burnt Norton," 9:779b–780a
    Jiménez and, 9:1011b
"The Love Song of J. Alfred Prufrock,"
    Laforgue and, 7:1888a, 1889a, 1893a
The Use of Poetry and the Use of Criticism,
    9:893a-b
The Waste Land, 7:1340a, 1902b, 1906a
    Hesse and, 9:843b
    Milosz's translation of, 13:2931a
    Nerval's style and, 6:955a, 957a
    Quasimodo and, 12:2407b
    Seferis' translation, 12:2261a
    Simon and, 13:3024a, 3024b, 3025a,
        3037a
    Trakl and, 10:1410b–1411a
Valéry and, 8:587a
Elisa. *See* Goncourt, Edmond Louis Antoine
    and Jules Alfred Huot de, *La fille Elisa*
Elixiere des Teufels, Die. *See* Hoffmann,
    E. T. A.

Elizabeth I of England, queen, in Schiller's
Mary Stuart, 5:45a, 45b

Elizabeth of the Hague, princess, Descartes
and, 3:20b, 21b

Elle est là. See Sarraute, Nathalie

Elle et lui. See Sand, George

Ellernklipp. See Fontane, Theodor

Elleve aar. See Undset, Sigrid, *The Longest
Years*

Ellipsis, in poetry of Apollinaire, 9:887b–888a

Ellis. *See* Kobylinskii, Lev

"Eloa ou la soeur des anges" (Eloa; or, The
Sister of Angels). *See* Vigny, Alfred de

Éloge de Richardson. See Diderot, Denis

Éloges (*Eloges and Other Poems*). *See* Perse,
Saint-John

Eloquence, theme of, in Staël's *De la
littérature*, 5:98b

Elpénor. See Giraudoux, Jean

Elpenor. See Goethe, Johann Wolfgang von

Elsa Triolet choisie par Aragon (Elsa Triolet
Chosen by Aragon). *See* Aragon, Louis

Elsa's Eyes. *See* Aragon, Louis, *Les yeux
d'Elsa*

Elseneur. See Butor, Michel

Éluard, Paul
Breton and, 11:1954b
Elytis and, 13:2957a, 2957b, 2958a
Exemples, 11:1953a
Ritsos' translations, 12:2838a
"Sans âge" ("Without Age"), Seferis'
translation, 12:2259b

Éluard, Paul, and André Breton
Dictionnaire abrégé du surréalisme,
11:1944b
Notes sur la poésie, 11:1944b

Elysian Fields, in Fénelon's *Télémaque*,
3:287b

Elytis, Odysseus, **13:2955a–2988b**
Albaniad, 11:2964a
Anihta hartia (*Open Book*), 13:2961a-b,
2964b, 2966a, 2972b
"Prota-Prota" (First of All), 13:2974a

"Asma iroiko kai penthimo yia ton hameno
anthipolohaghos tis Alvanias" ("The
Heroic and Elegiac Song for the Lost
Second Lieutenant of the Albanian
Campaign"), 11:2966b, 13:2963b–2964a
Ekloyi (Selections), 13:2972b
"Equivalences chez Picasso" (Equivalences
in Picasso), 13:2965b–2966a
Exi kai mia tipsis yia ton ourano (*Six and
One Remorses for the Sky*),
13:2966a–2967b
"I aftopsia" ("The Autopsy"), 13:2966b
"Lakonikon" ("Laconic"), 13:2967a, 2983a
"O alos Noe" ("The Other Noah"),
13:2967a-b
"O ipnos ton yeneon" ("The Sleep of the
Brave"), 13:2966b
"I kalossini stis likopories" (Kindness in the
Wolfpasses), 13:2962a
Ilios o protos (*Sun the First*), 1:2985a,
13:2961a–2963b, 2974a-b
"Paralayes pano se mian ahtida"
("Variations on a Sunbeam"), 13:2961b,
2963a-b
"Soma tou kalokeriou" ("Body of
Summer"), 13:2962b–2963a
Maria Nephele, 13:2972a, 2976b–2981a
"I Parusia" ("The Presence"), 13:2979a-b
"Imnos sti Maria Nephele" ("A Hymn to
Maria Nephele"), 13:2980a
"Patmos," 13:2979b–2980a
"Stalin," 13:2980b
structure, 13:2977b–2978b
The Axion Esti and, 13:2968a, 2979a,
2981a
"The Eternal Wager," 13:2979b, 2981a
"The Hungarian Uprising," 13:2980b,
2981a
"Through the Mirror," 13:2980a
"To Stigma" ("The Stigma"), 13:2979b
Nobel Prize and, 12:2255b
O mikros naftilos (*The Little Mariner*),
13:2983b–2985a
"Kai me phos kai me thanaton,"
13:2984b–2985a
Prosanatolismi (*Orientations*),
13:2958b–2961a

Elytis, Odysseus (*cont.*)
  Prosanatolismi (*cont.*)
    "Dionysus," 13:2959b, 2960a-b
    "Epetios" ("Anniversary"), 13:2959a-b,
      2980a
    "I thitia tou kalokeriou" ("In the Service of
      Summer"), 13:2960a-b, 2961b
    "I treli rodia," 13:2960b
    "Orion," 13:2959b–2960a
    "Prota Roiemata" ("First Poems"),
      13:2959a
  Simatologon (The Book of Signs), 13:2979a
  surrealist experimentation, 12:2815b
  Ta eterothale (*The Siblings*)
    "The Leaf-Diviner," 13:2976b
    "Villa Natacha," 13:2972a
  Ta Ro tou Erota (The R's of Eros), 13:2972b
  To Axion Esti (*The Axion Esti*), 13:2964a,
    2966a, 2967b–2971b
    "I Genesis" ("The Genesis"),
      13:2968b–2969a
    Maria Nephele and, 13:2979a, 2981a
    "Ta Pathi" ("The Passion"),
      13:2969a–2971b
    "To Doxastikon" ("The Gloria"), 13:2967b
  "To chronico mias dekaetias" (The
    Chronicle of a Decade), 13:2957b
  To imerologio enos atheatou Apriliou (The
    Diary of an Invisible April), 13:2982b,
    2983a-b
  To monogramma (*The Monogram*),
    13:2975a–2976b
  To photodendro kai i dekati tetarti omorfia
    (*The Light Tree and the Fourteenth
    Being*), 13:2972a–2975a
    "Arhetipon" ("Archetype"), 13:2974a
    "Doro asimenio poiema" ("Silver Gift
      Poem"), 13:2974b–2975a
    "I kori pou ferne o vorias" ("The Girl the
      North Wind Brought"), 13:2973b–2974a
    Maria Nephele and, 13:2979b, 2980a
    "Peri Politas" ("On the Republic"),
      13:2974a
    "Ta dio tou kosmou" ("The Two Aspects
      of the World"), 13:2972b, 2973a, 2973b
    "Ton Vaion" ("Palm Sunday"), 13:2973b,
      2974a-b

Tria poiemata me simea efkerias (Three
  Poems Under a Flag of Convenience),
  13:2981b, 2982a–2983a, 2983b
Elzta saga, 1:382a, 384a
Emanationism, Prudentius' *Apotheosis* on,
  1:8a
Emaux et camées. See Gautier, Théophile,
  Enamels and Cameos
Embarquement pour l'île de Cythère, L' (*The
  Embarkation for Cythera*). See Watteau,
  Jean Antoine
Embirikos, Andreas, 13:2958a
Emblazoned Eagle, The. See Valle-Inclán,
  Ramón del, *Las comedias bárbaras*
  (Barbaric Plays), *Aguila de blasón*
"Emblematika smysla" ("Emblematics of
  Meaning"). See Bely, Andrey
Emergency Exit. See Silone, Ignazio, *Uscita di
  sicurezza*
Emerson, Ralph Waldo
  Elytis and, 13:2965a, 2965b
  Hamsun and, 8:24a
  Henri and, 4:657b–658a
  Herder's influence on, 4:654a–655a, 657b
  Journals, on folk tradition, 4:654b
  Maeterlinck and, 8:123a, 132b, 134a
  Mickiewicz and, 5:631a
  on Montaigne, 2:773a, 787a
  Nature, extension of Herder's thought by,
    4:655a
  supernatural in works of, 5:551a-b
Emigração como força civilizadora, A. See Eça
  de Queiroz, José Maria
"Emigrant de Landor Road, L'." See
  Apollinaire, Guillaume
Emigrants (*Emigrantes*). See Ferreira de
  Castro, José Maria
Emigrants, The. See Moberg, Vilhelm
Emigration
  Eça on, 7:1690b
  Ferreira de Castro on, 11:2155a-b
  Hamsun's use of, 8:38a
  Italian, Pascoli on, 7:1841b–1842a, 1849b
  Moberg on, 11:2205, 2219a–2226b
Emigration as a Civilizing Force. See Eça de
  Queiroz, José Maria, *A emigração como
  força civilizadora*

Emigrés
  Central European, Kafka and, 9:1156b
  German
    Hesse and, 9:852a-b
    Thomas Mann and, 9:727b
Émile. See Rousseau, Jean Jacques
Emilia Galotti. See Lessing, Gotthold Ephraim
"Emotional Athleticism, An." *See* Artaud,
    Antonin, *Le théâtre et son double (The
    Theater and Its Double)*
Emotionalism, Kundera and, 13:3395a-b
Emotions, The: Outline of a Theory. See
    Sartre, Jean-Paul
Empedocles, Hölderlin's play about,
    5:155b–158a
Emperor and Galilean. See Ibsen, Henrik
*Emperor Justinian Composing the Institutes,
    The. See* Delacroix, Eugène
Emperor Octavian. *See* Tieck, Ludwig, *Kaiser
    Octavianus*
Emperor and the Witch, The. See
    Hofmannsthal, Hugo von, *Der Kaiser
    und die Hexe*
"Emperor's New Clothes, The." *See* Andersen,
    Hans Christian
Empfang bei der Welt. See Mann, Heinrich
Empfindungen eines Christen. See Wieland,
    Christoph Martin
Empire, cultural, Sainte-Beuve on,
    6:851b–853b
Empire des signes, L'. See Barthes, Roland,
    Empire of Signs
Empiricists, Schopenhauer contrasted with,
    5:400a
Emploi du temps, L'. See Butor, Michel
Empress of Newfoundland, The. *See*
    Wedekind, Frank, *Die Kaiserin von
    Neufundland*
Empty Canvas, The. See Moravia, Alberto
Emvaritio tou ikeanou, To. See Ritsos, Yannis
En arrière. See Aymé, Marcel
En Burgos está el buen rey, Rodrigo-Jimena
    relationship in, 1:133a
"En cest sonet coind'e leri." *See* Arnaut Daniel
En 18 . . .. See Goncourt, Edmond Louis
    Antoine and Jules Alfred Huot de

"En el centenario de una universidad." *See*
    Ortega y Gasset, José
"En famille." *See* Maupassant, Guy de
"En författare i sin tid. *See* Johnson, Eyvind
En häxa (A Witch). See Strindberg, August
En ménage. See Huysmans, Joris Karl
En Mölna-elegi. See Ekelöf, Gunnar, *A Mölna
    Elegy*
En Natti i Otočac. See Ekelöf, Gunnar
En passant. See Queneau, Raymond
"En patinant." *See* Verlaine, Paul
En rade. See Huysmans, Joris Karl
En route. See Huysmans, Joris Karl
*En Santa Gadea de Burgos, Sancho II y cerco
    de Zamora* as source of, 1:132b
En torno al casticismo. See Unamuno, Miguel
    de
En torno a Galileo. See Ortega y Gasset, José
En vakker dag. See Vesaas, Tarjei, *One Fine
    Day*
En vandrer spiller med sordin. See Hamsun,
    Knut
Enamels and Cameos. See Gautier, Théophile
"Enas gerontas stin akropotamia." *See* Seferis,
    George, *Imerologio katastromatos B*
"Enas logos gia to kalokairi." *See* Seferis,
    George
Enchanted Knight, The. *See* Pérez Galdós,
    Benito, *El caballero encantado*
Enchanteur pourrissant, L'. See Apollinaire,
    Guillaume
Enchiridion militis Christiani. See Erasmus
Enciclopedia del erotismo. See Cela, Camilo
    José
Encina, Juan del, 1:471a
    pastoral poetry of, 2:912b
Encomiastic poetry, Ariosto and, 2:628b–629a
"Encounter." *See* Montale, Eugenio, *Cuttlefish
    Bones (Ossi di seppia),* "Incontro"
Encounter, The. *See* Zamyatin, Yevgeny
    Ivanovich, "Vstrecha"
Encounters of an Adventurous Snail. *See*
    García Lorca, Federico, "Los encuentros
    de un caracol aventurero"
"Encre." *See* Claudel, Paul, *Cent phrases pour
    éventails*

"Encuentros de un caracol aventurero, Los."
  See García Lorca, Federico
Encyclopaedisierungscalcul. See Novalis
Encyclopedia of Eroticism. *See* Cela, Camilo
  José, *Enciclopedia del erotismo*
Encyclopédie
  Diderot and, 4:482a–483a
  Rousseau and, 4:454a–455b
Encyclopedists, Voltaire's defense of,
  4:378a–379b
End of the Affair, The. See Greene, Graham
"End of Cronos." *See* Ungaretti, Giuseppe,
  "Fine di Crono"
End of a Dialogue. *See* Tsatsos, Constantine,
  "To telos enos dialogou"
End of the Night, The. See Mauriac, François
"End of the Novel, The." *See* Mandelshtam,
  Osip, "Konets romana"
"End in Paris, An." *See* Wagner, Richard
End of Satan, The. See Hugo, Victor, *La fin de
  Satan*
"Endimo tis Mikras Asias." *See* Cavafy,
  Constantine
Endormie, L'. See Claudel, Paul
Eneas, allegory and, 1:323b
"Enemies." *See* Chekhov, Anton, "Vragi"
Enemies. See Gorky, Maxim, *Vragi*
Enemies of Women, The. See Blasco Ibáñez,
  Vicente, *Los enemigos de la mujer*
Enemigos de la mujer, Los. See Blasco Ibáñez,
  Vicente
Enemy of the People, An. See Ibsen, Henrik
Enemy, The. See Mauriac, François
Énergie spirituelle, L'. See Bergson, Henri
Energy, Stendhal's theory of, 5:349a-b, 356a-b
Enfance. See Sarraute, Nathalie
Enfance du Christ, L'. See Berlioz, Hector
Enfant chargé de chaînes, L'. See Mauriac,
  François, *Young Man in Chains*
Enfantin, Prosper, Vigny and, 5:463b
Enfants du limon, Les. See Queneau, Raymond
Enfants terribles, Les. See Cocteau, Jean
Enfermo, El. See Azorín
Engel kommt nach Babylon, Ein. See
  Dürrenmatt, Friedrich, *An Angel Comes
  to Babylon*
Engels, Friedrich

Communist Manifesto. See Marx, Karl
Dialektik der Natur (Dialectics of Nature),
  Lukács and, 10:1266b
  Labriola and, 8:314b
*Ludwig Feuerbach und der Ausgang der
  klassischen deutschen Philosophie
  (Ludwig Feuerbach and the Demise of
  Classical German Philosophy)*, Lukács
  and, 10:1266a–1267a
  property rights and, 4:651b
  on women, 11:2240a
Enghaus, Christine, Hebbel and, 6:1097a,
  1098a
England
  art, Delacroix's interest in, 5:519a-b
  Benjamin Constant's reaction to, 4:409b
  Berlioz in, 6:793b
  Cavafy's education in, 8:210a
  Chénier in, 4:700a-b
  culture, Aymé's satire of, 12:2447a-b
  Eça in, 7:1691a–1692a
  Freud in, 8:4b–5a
  hostility to in Hamsun's works, 8:36b
  Michelet on, 5:594b, 603a
  Staël's view of in *Corinne*, 5:102a
  Voltaire's reaction to, 4:371b–372a,
    384b–386a
England, Anglo-Saxon
  Christianization of, and cultural change,
    1:62b–64b
  monastic culture in, 1:63b, 64a
England's Helicon
  Montemayor's *Diana* in, 2:923a
  pastoral elements of, 2:915a-b
Englische Fragmente (English Fragments). See
  Heine, Heinrich
Englishs0047language
  Pessoa and, 10:1481b, 1483a-b
  phrasebooks, 13:2991a-b
English literature
  Anglo-Saxon poetry, 1:51a–87b
  Delacroix's attraction to, 5:519a-b
  French classicism and, 7:1895b–1896a
  Montaigne and, 2:785a
  poetry, Ronsard and, 2:741a
  Romantic period, 7:1452b
  Taine on, 7:1449b, 1452a–1461a

Enigma, in Augustine's *On the Trinity*, 1:38b

Enigmatic Man, The. *See* Hamsun, Knut, *Den Gaadefulde*

Enjambment, in Rilke's "Archaic Torso of Apollo," 9:786a, 787b

Enjoyable Work. *See* Jiménez, Juan Ramón, "El trabajo gustoso"

"Enlèvement de la redoute, L'." *See* Mérimée, Prosper

Enlightened despotism. *See* Despotism, enlightened

Enlightened, The. See Nerval, Gérard de, *Les illuminés*

Enlightenment
  Alfieri and, 4:662a, 669b
  Bergson and, 8:46b
  Diderot and, 4:475a–505b
  in fiction of Simon, 13:3027b
  in Goethe's *Faust*, 5:20b, 21a
  Herder's antagonism to, 4:640a, 647a, 650a
  Manzoni as heir to, 5:368a
  Nerval and, 6:946a
  in Novalis' works, 5:219b–220a
  pastoral poetry and, 2:899a
  in Portugal, 11:2144b
  Rabelais and, 2:700b
  Rimbaud's view of, 7:1791b
  Sade and, 4:630a
  Staël and, 5:96a, 105b
  Stendhal and, 5:346a, 351a–352a
  Voltaire and, 4:384a
  see also Age of Reason

Enneads. See Plotinus

Ennui, in Stendhal, 5:356b–357a, 362a

"Ennui." *See Noia*; Ungaretti, Giuseppe, "Noia"

"Enough." *See* Turgenev, Ivan

Enracinement, L', See Weil, Simone, *The Need for Roots*

Enrico IV. See Pirandello, Luigi, *Henry IV*

Ensame. See Strindberg, August

"Ensayo de estética a manera de prólogo." *See* Ortega y Gasset, José

Ensimismamiento y alteración. See Ortega y Gasset, José

"Enskilde är död, Den." *See* Ekelöf, Gunnar

Ensor, James, Ghelderode and, 11:2123a, 2130a, 2132b–2133a

Entangled in Stories: On the Existence of Man and Thing. *See* Schapp, Wilhelm, *Geschichten verstrickt: Zum Sein von Mensch und Ding*

Entelecheia. See Entelechy

Entelechy, Aristotle and, 5:188a

"Entering." *See* Rilke, Rainer Maria, *Das Buch der Bilder* (*The Book of Pictures*), "Eingang"

Entering the War. *See* Calvino, Italo, *L'Entrata in guerra*

Enterrement de Monsieur Bouvet, L'. See Simenon, Georges

Entertaining Mixture of Witticisms and the Most Extraordinary Happenings, An. *See* Lesage, Alain-René, *Mélange amusant de saillies d'esprit et de traits historiques des plus frappants*

Enthusiasm, Staël on, 5:109a–110a

"Entrance of Romance, The." *See* Tieck, Ludwig

Entrata in guerra, L'. See Calvino, Italo

Entrave, L'. See Colette

Entre la vie et la mort. See Sarraute, Nathalie

Entre naranjos. See Blasco Ibáñez, Vicente

Entremés de los romances, 2:837a

Entretien d'un père avec ses enfants. See Diderot, Denis

Entretien entre d'Alembert et Diderot. See Diderot, Denis

Entretiens avec la Professeur Y. See Céline, Louis-Ferdinand

Entretiens des cheminées de Madrid. See Lesage, Alain-René

Entretiens sur le "Fils naturel". See Diderot, Denis

Entropy, Zamyatin's treatment of, 10:1197b–1198a

Entstehung des "Doktor Faustus," Die. See Mann, Thomas

Entsühnung, Die. See Broch, Hermann

"Enumeration of Meters." *See* Snorri Sturluson, *Edda*

"Enumeration of the Ynglings." *See* Thjódólf of Hvin, "Ynglingatal"

Envers du music-hall, L'. *See* Colette

Envers et l'endroit, L'. *See* Camus, Albert, *The Wrong Side and the Right Side*

Environmental influences, in Baroja's novels, 9:594a, 605b

Environmentalism, Giraudoux and, 9:1064b

"Envoys from Alexandria." *See* Cavafy, Constantine, "Presveis ap' tin Alexandreia"

Envy. *See* Olesha, Yuri

Enzensberger, Hans Magnus, Rilke and, 9:789b

Eoff, Sherman, on Blasco Ibáñez' *The Cabin*, 8:376b

Epanalepsis, in poetry of Ady, 9:874b–875a

Epanalipsis. *See* Ritsos, Yannis

"Epanastates." *See* Ritsos, Yannis

"Epetios." *See* Elytis, Odysseus, *Prosanatolismi*

Epic
  Ariosto and, 2:630b–632b
  Beowulf as, 1:51a
  Berlioz' use of, 6:800b–803b
  Boileau on, 3:196b
  of Camoëns, 10:1476a-b
  Camoëns on, 2:764a
  classical, Camoëns' *The Lusiads* and, 2:761a, 765b
  courtly, the *Nibelungenlied* and, 1:227a–228a, 233a-b
  crusading, Wolfram and, 1:282b–285b
  drama, 11:2093b–2094b, 2104b
  Greek, Pascoli's *Poemi conviviali* and, 7:1846b
  of Hebbel, 6:1097b
    Mutter und Kind (*Mother and Child*), 6:1115b–1116a
    The Lay of the Nibelungs, 6:1112a–1115b
  Homeric, Tasso and, 2:804b
  in Klopstock, 4:516b–521a
  Lope de Vega and, 2:848a, 849a
  Lukács on, 10:1260a-b
  prose, of Chateaubriand, 5:115b–116a, 124b–125a
  Prudentius' *Psychomachia* and, 1:6a, 20b–21a
  Ronsard and, 2:734a-b

short poem as, 5:455a

Staël's *De la littérature* on, 5:96a

of Tasso, 2:799b–800b

Vergilian, Tasso and, 2:804b

see also Historical song (literary genre)

"Epic Exploit of Juraj Čup, The." *See* Čapek, Karel

Epic poetry, anonymity of, 1:215b

Epic Poetry. *See* Pascoli, Giovanni, *Epos*

Epic Voices. *See* Valle-Inclán, Ramón del, *Voces de gesta*

Epicureanism
  in Molière's *Don Juan*, 3:114a-b
  in Pascal's view, 3:140b

Epicurus, Gassendi and, 3:18b, 21b

Epidemia, L' (*The Epidemic*). *See* Moravia, Alberto

Epigrams
  of Hebbel, 6:1117a-b
  in Italian literature, of Alfieri, 4:671b
  see also Maxims

Epigraphs, in Ekelöf's works, 12:2652b

"Epikaleo toi ten theon." *See* Seferis, George

"Epikindyna, Ta." *See* Cavafy, Constantine

Epilogo, L' (*The Epilogue*). *See* Pirandello, Luigi, *La morsa*

Epiphany, in Camus, 13:3061a-b

"Épis, Les." *See* Leconte de Lisle, Charles Marie

Episcopo & Company. *See* D'Annunzio, Gabriele

Episode de la vie d'un artiste (*Episode in the Life of an Artist*). *See* Berlioz, Hector

Episodes. *See* Galdós, Benito Pérez, *Episodios nacionales*

Episodios nacionales. *See* Peréz Galdós, Benito

Episteme, Foucault and, 13:3345b, 3351a–3355b

Epistemological writings, of Mallarmé, 7:1584a-b, 1590a–1591b, 1592b

Epistemology
  Sartre and, 12:2591a–2593b
  see also Knowledge

"Epistle on My Work, The" ("The Epistle to Lebrun"). *See* Chénier, André

Epistles. *See* Apollinaris Sidonius; Horace

Epistolae metricae. See Petrarch

Epistolae obscurorum virorum (Epistles of Obscure Men), influence on short fiction, 2:952b

Epistolae seniles. See Petrarch

Epistolae variae. See Petrarch

Epistolario familiare giovanile. See Pirandello, Luigi

Epistolary literature, Petrarch and, 2:490b

Epistolary novel
  18th century, by Laclos, 4:393a–394a, 400b–405a, 416a
  eighteenth-century, 4:401a–403a
  Goethe's *The Sorrows of Young Werther* and, 5:5b
  Grass and, 13:3374b

Epistrofi tis Ifighenias, I. See Ritsos, Yannis

"Epitaffio per Bice Donetti." *See* Quasimodo, Salvatore

Epitafios. See Ritsos, Yannis

Epitalamio. See Valle-Inclán, Ramón del

"Epitaph for Bice Donetti." *See* Quasimodo, Salvatore, "Epitaffio per Bice Donetti"

"Epitaphe de Marie." *See* Ronsard, Pierre de

Epitaphium Damonis. See Milton, John

"Epître à Huet." *See* La Fontaine, Jean de

Épître sur mes ouvrages. See Chénier, André, "The Epistle on My Work"

Epoch (magazine). *See* Dostoevsky, Feodor

Epos. See Pascoli, Giovanni

Épuration. See Anouilh, Jean

"Equilibrium Between the Aesthetical and the Ethical in the Composition of Personality." *See* Kierkegaard, Søren

Equinoxe de septembre, L'. See Montherlant, Henry de

"Equivalences chez Picasso" (Equivalences in Picasso). *See* Elytis, Odysseus

"Er wartet auf den vazierenden Gott." *See* Schnitzler, Arthur

Era of the Kaiser, The. *See* Mann, Heinrich, *Das Kaiserreich*

Eramo, Luce d', on Silone, 12:2294b

"Erano i capei d'oro a l'aura sparsi." *See* Petrarch, *Canzoniere*

Erasers, The. See Robbe-Grillet, Alain

Erasmus, **2:571a–593b**

Adages (*Adagiorum collectanea*, rev. ed. *Adagiorum chiliades*), 2:575a, 577b–578a

Antibarbari (The Antibarbarians), 2:572b

Cervantes and, 2:819b–820a

Ciceronianus (*The Ciceronian*), 2:589a-b

Colloquies, 2:573b, 587b–589a

"Convivium religiosum" (Godly Feast), 2:588a

De conscribendis epistolis (On Writing Letters), 2:573b

De contemptu mundi (On Contempt of the World), 2:572b

De copia verborum ac rerum (On Abundance of Words and Ideas), 2:573b, 579b

De libero arbitrio (*On Free Will*), 2:587a-b, 685b

De ratione studii (On the Method of Study), 2:573b, 579b

De sarcienda ecclesiae concordia (*On Restoring Concord in the Church*), 2:591a-b

Dulce bellum inexpertis, 2:581a

Ecclesiastes, 2:591b

Enchiridion militis Christiani (Handbook of the Christian soldier), 2:575b–576b

influence on Renaissance short fiction, 2:952a-b

"Inquisitio de fide" (Inquiry Concerning Faith), 2:588b

Institutio principis Christiani (*The Education of a Christian Prince*), 2:583a

Julius exclusus (Julius Excluded), 2:579b–580a

Luther and, 2:685b–686a

Mantovano compared to Vergil by, 2:907a

Paraclesis, 2:581b–582a

Querela pacis (*The Complaint of Peace*), 2:583a

Ratio verae theologiae (*The Method of True Theology*), 2:582a, 584b–585a

Sileni Alcibiadis (The Sileni of Alcibiades), 2:581a

"The Abbot and the Learned Lady," 2:588b–589a

Erasmus (*cont.*)
  The Praise of Folly, 2:577a, 578b–579b,
    819b
    "Hymne de l'or" and, 2:733a
    Richter's *The Praise of Stupidity* and,
      5:57a
    "The Shipwreck," 2:588a-b
Erato and Apollyon (*Erato e Apòllion*). *See*
    Quasimodo, Salvatore
"Erdbeben in Chile, Das." *See* Kleist, Heinrich
    von, "The Earthquake in Chile"
Erdgeist. *See* Wedckind, Frank, *Earth Spirit*
Ère du soupçon, L'. *See* Sarraute, Nathalie
Erec et Enide. *See* Chrétien de Troyes
Eremita, Victor. *See* Kierkegaard, Søren
Erfahrung
  Frisch and, 13:2914a-b
  vs. *Erlebnis*, 9:721a-b
Erfolglosigkeit. *See* Köpke, Wulf
Erica e i suoi fratelli (Erica and Her Siblings).
    See Vittorini, Elio
Erigena. *See* Eriugena
Erik XIV. *See* Strindberg, August
Erikson, Erik, Freud and, 8:8a
Erinnerungen aus Rubens. *See* Burckhardt,
    Jacob, *Recollections of Rubens*
Eriugena, John Scottus, 1:405b–406a
  power of words, 2:553b
Erizzo, Sebastiano, novellas of, 2:944b
Erlebnis, 9:721a
  Frisch and, 13:2914a-b
  vs. *Erfahrung*, 9:721a-b
Erlebnis und die Dichtung, Das. *See* Dilthey,
    Wilhelm
Erlebnisdichtung (poetry of personal
    experience), Meyer and, 6:932a
Erlebnislyrik (experiential poetry), Klopstock
    and, 4:512b
Ermine, The. *See* Anouilh, Jean
"Ermitas de Córdoba, Las." *See* Ortega y
    Gasset, José
"Ermite, L'." *See* Apollinaire, Guillaume,
    Alcools
Ernst, Max
  Arp and, 10:1371a, 1372b
  Beyond Painting, 11:2065a
  Breton on, 11:1950a, 1950b

  convulsive love, 11:1845a-b
  dadaism and, 11:2063a-b
  disparate realities, 11:1956b
  La femme 100 têtes, Breton's preface,
    11:1941a
Ernst, Paul, Czech literature and, 10:1568b,
    1569a
Ernst und Falk. *See* Lessing, Gotthold
    Ephraim
Ernstes Leben, Ein. *See* Mann, Heinrich
"Eroismo, L'." *See* Montale, Eugenio
Eros
  Chekhov's "The Darling" and,
    7:1873b–1874a
  Freud on, 8:5b, 14a, 15b
  Hauptmann on, 8:167a-b
  see also Courtly love; Love
Erotic tales
  as antecedents to Renaissance short fiction,
    2:930b–933a
  Milesian tale, 2:930b–931a
Erotic Tales. *See* Moravia, Alberto
Eroticism
  in Apollinaire's poetry, 9:898a
  in Čapek's works, 10:1568b–1569a
  Diderot and, 4:484b
  in Flaubert, 7:1374b–1375b, 1389a-b
  in Laforgue's poetry, 7:1893b–1894b, 1899b,
    1901b, 1902a
  in Maupassant, 7:1763a-b
  of Michelet, 13:3083b
  in Perse's poetry, 10:1432b, 1446b
  in Robbe-Grillet's works, 13:3253b–3254a
  in Södergran's works, 11:1799b–1800a
  in Tasso's works, 2:805b
  in Ungaretti's poetry, 10:1464a
  see also Libertinism; Love affairs
"Erotikos logos." *See* Seferis, George, *Strophe*
Erotokrotis, Seferis and, 12:2260a
Erreurs amoureuses. *See* Tyard, Pontus de
"Error Berenguer, El." *See* Ortega y Gasset,
    José
Error, mental, in Descartes's *Meditations on
    First Philosophy*, 3:14b–15b
"Erste lange Eisenbahnfahrt, Die." *See* Kafka,
    Franz
"Erzähler, Der." *See* Benjamin, Walter

Erziehung des Menschengeschlechts, Die. See Lessing, Gotthold Ephraim

Erziehungsroman, Kosztolányi and, 10:1239b

Es kommt der Tag. See Mann, Heinrich

"Es winkt zu Fühlung." *See* Rilke, Rainer Maria

Escalante, Miguel Ángel, on Blasco Ibáñez's *Reeds and Mud,* 8:380b

Escalier de fer, L'. See Simenon, Georges

Escape. *See* Imprisonment and escape

Escape from Reality. *See* Ekelöf, Gunnar, *Verklighetsflykt*

Escape of Jacques Bernis, The. *See* Saint-Exupéry, Antoine de, "L'évasion de Jacques Bernis"

Esch oder die Anarchie (Esch; or, Anarchism). See Broch, Hermann

Escobar, Juan de, *Historia y romancero del Cid,* 1:133a-b

Escritor, El. See Azorín

Escurial. See Ghelderode, Michel de

Esenin, Sergei
    downfall of Petrine Russia and, 10:1620a-b
    Mayakovsky and, 11:1849b–1850a
    Piimata (Poems), Ritsos' translation of, 12:2837b
    in Solzhenitsyn's "Krokhotki," 13:3203a
    voice of the other, 11:1906a

Esfinge, La. See Unamuno, Miguel de

"Esir." *See* Khlebnikov, Velimir

"Esiste un decadentismo in Italia?" *See* Montale, Eugenio, *The Storm and Other Things*

"Espacio." *See* Jiménez, Juan Ramón

Espagnols en Danemarck, Les. See Mérimée, Prosper

España. See Gautier, Théophile

España invertebrada. See Ortega y Gasset, José

Espana Moderna, La (Modern Spain) (journal), Unamuno and, 8:287b

España (Spanish periodical), Ortega y Gasset's articles in, 9:111b

Españoles de tres mundos (caricatura lírica). See Jiménez, Juan Ramón

Españoles en Paris. See Azorín

Esperanto, theme of, in Ferreira de Castro's *A lã e a neve,* 11:2161b

Esperpento drama, 8:346a, 347a, 347b, 350a–351b

Espoir, L'. See Malraux, André, *Man's Hope*

Esposizioni sopra il Dante. See Boccaccio, Giovanni

"Esprit et l'eau, L'." *See* Claudel, Paul, *Cinq grandes odes*

"Esprit nouveau et les poètes, L'." *See* Apollinaire, Guillaume

"Esprit nouveau, L'," Apollinaire's theory of, 9:884a, 896a, 899a

"Esprit pur, Le." *See* Vigny, Alfred Victor de, *Les destinées*

Esquisse du jugement universel. See Alfieri, Vittorio, *Sketch of the Universal Judgment*

Esquisse d'une théorie des émotions. See Sartre, Jean-Paul, *The Emotions: Outline of a Theory*

Essai historique, politique et moral sur les révolutions anciennes et modernes considérées dans leurs rapports avec la révolution français. See Chateaubriand, François René de

Essai sur la guerre sociale. See Mérimée, Prosper

Essai sur la littérature anglaise. See Chateaubriand, François René de

Essai sur le genre dramatique sérieux. See Beaumarchais, Pierre-Augustin Caron de

Essai sur les causes et les effets de la perfection et de la décadence des lettres et des arts. See Chénier, André

Essai sur les données immédiates de la conscience. See Bergson, Henri, *Time and Free Will: An Essay on the Immediate Data of Consciousness*

Essai sur les fictions. See Staël, Madame de

Essai sur les moeurs et l'esprit des nations. See Voltaire

Essai sur les règnes de Claude et de Néron. See Diderot, Denis

Essai sur Sénèque. See Diderot, Denis

Essais. See Montaigne, Michel de

Essais critiques. See Barthes, Roland, *Critical Essays*

Essais sur la peinture. See Diderot, Denis

Essay in Aesthetics by Way of a Preface. *See* Ortega y Gasset, José, "Ensayo de estética a manera de prólogo"

Essay on Causes Affecting Minds and Characters. See Montesquieu, Charles-Louis de Secondat, baron de

Essay on the Causes and Effects of Perfection and Decadence in Arts and Letters. *See* Chénier, André, *Essai sur les causes et les effets de la perfection et de la décadence des lettres et des arts*

Essay on Conic Sections. *See* Pascal, Blaise, *Essay pour les coniques*

Essay of Dramatick Poesie. See Dryden, John

Essay on Epic Poetry. See Voltaire

Essay on Fictions. See Staël, Madame de, *Essai sur les fictions*

Essay on Hegel. *See* Croce, Benedetto, *Saggio sullo Hegel*

Essay on the Inequalities of Races. See Gobineau, Arthur de

"Essay on Man." *See* Pope, Alexander

Essay on the Manners and Spirit of Nations, An. *See* Voltaire, *Essai sur les moeurs et l'esprit des nations*

"Essay on the Novel." *See* Maupassant, Guy de; Sade, Donatien Alphonse François, marquis de, *The Crimes of Love*

Essay on the Passive State. See Fénelon, François de Salignac de la Mothe-, *Mémoire sur l'état passif*

Essay pour les coniques. See Pascal, Blaise

Essay on the Reigns of Claudius and Nero. See Diderot, Denis, *Essai sur les règnes de Claude et de Néron*

Essay on Seneca. See Diderot, Denis, *Essai sur Sénèque*

Essay on Serious Drama. See Beaumarchais, Pierre-Augustin Caron de, *Essai sur le genre dramatique sérieux*

Essay on the Social Marsic War. *See* Mérimée, Prosper, *Essai sur la guerre sociale*

"Essay on the Spanish Lullaby." *See* García Lorca, Federico

Essay on Style. *See* Aragon, Louis, *Le traité du style*

Essayistische Schriften und Reden (Essayistic Writings and Speeches). *See* Böll, Heinrich

Essays. See Montaigne, Michel de; White, E. B.

Essays on Painting. See Diderot, Denis, *Essais sur la peinture*

Essays on Thomas Mann. See Lukács, György

"ESSD." *See* Ritsos, Yannis

"Essence of Laughter, The." *See* Baudelaire, Charles

Essence, philosophical, in Descartes's *Meditations on First Philosophy*, 3:12a, 12b, 16b, 17b

Esslin, Martin, 13:3016b, 3018a

Est-il bon? Est-il méchant? See Diderot, Denis

Estación total con las canciones de la nueva luz, La. See Jiménez, Juan Ramón

Estates, medieval
  in *Representacio Adae*, 1:458a
  satire of. *See* Satire, medieval

"Este a Bois-ban." *See* Ady, Endre

Este family, Ariosto and, 2:619a–620a

Esté, Le. See Poissenot, Bénigne

Estelle et Némorin. See Florian, Jean-Pierre de

Estensi, Tasso and, 2:792b–793a

Estetica come scienza dell'espressione e linguistica generale. See Croce, Benedetto

"Estética de 'Elenano Gregoriio el Botero', La." *See* Ortega y Gasset, José

Estevanille Gonzales, surnommé le garçon de bonne humeur. See Lesage, Alain-René

Esther. See Grillparzer, Franz; Racine, Jean

Esthetics. *See* Aesthetics

Esthetics of Negligence, The. See Lapp, John C.

Esti Kornél. See Kosztolányi, Dezső

Esti Kornél kalandjai. See Kosztolányi, Dezső

Estío. See Jiménez, Juan Ramón

Estissac, Geoffroy d', 2:695b, 697a

Estoria de España
  epics of the Cid in, 1:131a
  Poema de mio Cid in, 1:114b, 131a
  see also *Primera crónica general*

Estoria del Cid (*Layenda de Cardeña*), *Poema de mio Cid* in, 1:114b

Estoria del Cid (*Leyenda de Cardeña*), factual basis of, 1:121b–122a

"Estuans instrinsicus ira vehementi." *See* Archpoet

Et Håndslag. See Johnson, Eyvind

État de siège, L'. See Camus, Albert, *State of Siege*

Etchings. See Babel, Isaac

Été, L'. See Camus, Albert, *Summer*

Eternal, temporal vs., in Mandelshtam's poetry, 10:1627a-b

Eternal Husband, The. See Dostoevsky, Feodor

Eternal Moment. See Boehringer, Robert, *Ewiger Augenblick*

Eternal recurrence, Nietzsche's theory of, 7:1677b–1678a

Eternal return, Kundera and, 13:3407a-b

Eternal Return, The. See Cocteau, Jean, *L'Éternel retour*

Eternal Smile, The. See Lagerkvist, Pär, *Det eviga leendet*

"Eternal Wager, The." *See* Elytis, Odysseus, *Maria Nephele*

Eternal War and Nuptial. *See* Ady, Endre, "Örök harc és nász"

Éternel retour, L'. See Cocteau, Jean

Eternidade. See Ferreira de Castro, José Maria

Eternidades (Eternities). *See* Jiménez, Juan Ramón

"Éternité, L'." *See* Rimbaud, Arthur

Eternity, *see also* Ferreira de Castro, José Maria, *Eternidade*; Immortality; Serpent, self-devouring

Eterothale, Ta. See Elytis, Odysseus

Ethelwold of Winchester, bishop, *Regularis concordia*, 1:453b–454a, 456b

Etherealization, in Kierkegaard's *Either/Or*, 6:1131b–1132a

Ethics
artistic, in Simon's *Conducting Bodies*, 13:3041a, 3041b–3042a
Broch and, 10:1386b–1391b, 1399a–1402b
Camus and, 13:3055a
Canetti and, 12:2617b
in Croce's *Filosofia della pratica*, 8:321b–322b
of "Futurist Manifesto," 9:809b
Genet and, 13:2869a, 2871a
Hesse on, 9:844b
of Hume, similarity to Schopenhauer's, 5:405a
of Kant, Schopenhauer's critique of, 5:404a-b
Kierkegaard on the ethical life, 6:1136a–1138a, 1141a-b
in Machiavelli, 2:604a–608b
medieval satire and, 1:350a-b, 355b
Milosz's views on, 13:2942a-b, 2945a
in Musil's *The Man Without Qualities*, 9:936a, 939b–940a
of Plato, fundamental question in, 5:405a-b
in plays of Corneille, 3:33b
of Schopenhauer, 5:403a–406b, 410a–412a
in Silone's fiction, 12:2302a-b
Staël's *De la littérature* on, 5:95a, 96a, 97b–98a
Tolstoy's ideals, 7:1472b–1473a
see also Choice, moral; Morality; Virtue

Ethics of Ambiguity, The. See Beauvoir, Simone de

Ethiopia
Mussolini's campaign in
Montherlant on, 11:1918b
in Silone's novels, 12:2285b, 2287b

Ethiopian History. See Heliodorus, *Historia Aethiopica*

Ethnicity, in Gombrowicz, 12:2573a–2574a

Ethnikon Apeleftherotikon Metopon, Ritsos' involvement with, 12:2817a

Ethnology, Bergson's view of, 8:61b–63a

Ethnomusicology, Herder's insights supported by, 4:644b

Étoile vesper, L'. See Colette

Étourdi, L'. See Molière

Étranger, L'. See Camus, Albert

Étrangère, L'. See Dumas fils, Alexandre

Être et le néant, L': Essai d'ontologie phénoménologique. See Sartre, Jean-Paul, *Being and Nothingness*

"Étrennes des orphelins, Les." *See* Rimbaud, Arthur

"Étroits sont les vaisseaux." *See* Perse, Saint-John, "Narrow Are the Vessels"
"Etruria Avenged." *See* Alfieri, Vittorio
"Etruscan Vase, The." *See* Mérimée, Prosper
Etsi animarum. See Innocent IV, pope
"Ett 30-talsöde." *See* Ekelöf, Gunnar
"Etuda." *See* Hašek, Jaroslav
Étude sur Virgile. See Sainte-Beuve, Charles-Augustin
Études analytiques. See Balzac, Honoré de
"Études de mains." *See* Gautier, Théophile, *Enamels and Cameos*
Études de moeurs au XIXme siècle. See Balzac, Honoré de
Études funèbres. See Strindberg, August
Études historiques. See Chateaubriand, François René de
Études philosophiques. See Balzac, Honoré de
Études sur l'histoire romaine. See Mérimée, Prosper
Étudiant, L'. See Michelet, Jules; Valles, Jules
"Etwas über den Menschen." *See* Richter, Jean Paul
Eucharist
  in Gottfried, 1:245b
  Luther and, 2:677a-b
  symbolism of, in *Gargantua*, 2:706a
Euclidean geometry, Bergson and, 8:47b
Eugene Onegin. See Pushkin, Alexander
Eugénie. See Beaumarchais, Pierre-Augustin Caron de
Eugénie, empress of the French, Mérimée and, 6:755b–756a, 766a-b, 767a
Eugénie Grandet. See Balzac, Honoré de
Eugénie, oder Die Bürgerzeit. See Mann, Heinrich
"Eugenio Montale poeta fisico e metafisico" (Eugenio Montale as Physical and Metaphysical Poet). *See* Pancrazi, Pietro
Eulalia, St., in Prudentius' *Peristephanon*, 1:12a, 14b, 16b–17a, 19b
Eulogy
  Caedmon's *Hymn* and, 1:65b
  in Germanic poetry, 1:53b, 54b
Eunuch, The. See La Fontaine, Jean de, *L'Eunuque*
Eunuchs

in Montesquieu's thought, 3:351b–352a
  Persian Letters, 3:358a–363b
Eunuque, L'. See La Fontaine, Jean de
Eupalinos. See Valéry, Paul
"Euphonia." *See* Berlioz, Hector
Euphuism, Giraudoux's style related to, 9:1064a
Euripides
  Cyclops
    influence on Renaissance pastoral drama, 2:916a
    Pirandello and, 8:394a
  Electra, 12:2549b
  Hippolytus, as model for Racine's *Phèdre*, 3:215a
  Iphigenia in Tauris, Goethe and, 5:11b
  Kleist and, 5:300b–301a
  Medea
    Anouilh's adaptation, 13:2853b
    Ibsen's *Hedda Gabler* and, 7:1421a-b, 1438b
Europa Socialista (Roman Socialist journal). *See* Silone, Ignazio
Europe
  culture, in Johnson's *Krilon* trilogy, 12:2372a
  Goncharov's view of, 6:1073a
Europe in Nineteen-Hundred Forty-Two. *See* Krleža, Miroslav, "Evropa godine tisuću devet stotina četrdeset i druge"
Européen (journal), 5:469b
Eurydice, Nerval and, 6:959a
Eurydice. See Anouilh, Jean
Eustace, St., legend of, Hašek's adaptation, 9:1098a-b
Evan of Tréguier, 1:420a
Evangelicals
  French, 2:694b
  see also Huguenots
"Évasion de Jacques Bernis, L'." *See* Saint-Exupéry, Antoine de
Eve, Festivity, and Octave of Saint Camillus in the Year 1936 in Madrid. *See* Cela, Camilo José, *Vísperas, festividad y octava de San Camilo del año 1936 en Madrid*

Eve, Frank C., "In the Beginning; an Interpretation of Sunlight Energy," Zamyatin and, 10:1197b–1198a

Eve future, L'. *See* Villiers de l'Isle-Adam

Eve (O.T. character)
Adam and. *See* Bible, Eden myth
in Kleist, 5:297b–298a
in Klopstock, 4:520b–521a
in poetry of Laforgue, 7:1903b
in "Sketch of a Serpent," 8:582a-b

Evening. *See* Akhmatova, Anna, *Vecher*

Evening Album. *See* Tsvetaeva, Marina, *Vechernii al'bom*

Evening at Grinde; or, The Good Angel. *See* Vesaas, Tarjei, *Grindekveld eller den gode engelen*

Evening in the Bois, An. *See* Ady, Endre, "Este a Bois-ban"

"Evening of the Feast Day, The." *See* Leopardi, Giacomo

"Evening Harmony." *See* Baudelaire, Charles

Evening Land. *See* Lagerkvist, Pär, *Aftonland*

"Evening with Mr. Teste, An." *See* Valéry, Paul, "Une soirée avec Monsieur Teste"

"Evening Promenade." *See* Södergran, Edith, "Aftonvandring"

Evening Star, The. *See* Colette, *L'Étoile vesper*

Evenings at Médan. *See* *Soirées de Médan, Les*

Evenings on a Farm near Dikanka. *See* Gogol, Nikolay Vasilievich

Evenings with the Orchestra. *See* Berlioz, Hector

Eventyr fortalte for Børn. *See* Andersen, Hans Christian, *Fairy Tales Told for Children*

Everyman, 1:471b, 472a, 473a
see also Hofmannsthal, Hugo von, *The Salzburg Everyman*

"Everything in Its Right Place." *See* Andersen, Hans Christian

Evil
in Dürrenmatt's works, 13:3223b–3224a, 3230a-b
Hugo's view of, 6:712a, 713a-b
in Kundera, 13:3401b
in Mauriac's works, 1322b–1324a
in Milosz's works, 13:2946a-b
nonresistance to. *See* Nonresistance to evil

Schopenhauer's view of, 5:401a, 402b, 403b
Voltaire on, 4:386a–388a
see also Good and evil

Evil demon. *See* Demon, evil

Evil Spirit Lumpazivagabundus, The. *See* Nestroy, Johann, *Der böse Geist Lumpazivagabundus*

Evolución de la crítica, La. *See* Azorín

Evolution
Bergson's view of, 8:59a
in Calvino, 13:3276b–3278a
Canetti and, 12:2626a-b
in Hebbel's works, 6:1098b
see also Darwinism

Évolution créatrice, L'. *See* Bergson, Henri, *Creative Evolution*

Evolution of Criticism, The. *See* Azorín, *La evolución de la crítica*

"Évolution du décors, Le" ("The Evolution of Décor"). *See* Artaud, Antonin

"Evraion (50 M.Ch.)." *See* Cavafy, Constantine

Evreika. *See* Babel, Isaac

"Evropa godine tisuću devet stotina četrdeset i druge." *See* Krleža, Miroslav

Ewald, Johannes, Dinesen and, 10:1294b

Ewiger Augenblick. *See* Boehringer, Robert

Ex Ponto. *See* Andrić, Ivo

Examen de conscience. *See* Fénelon, François de Salignac de la Mothe-

"Examination for Advancement." *See* Chekhov, Anton, "Ekzamen na chin"

Examples, use of, in Castiglione, 2:654b

Exception and the Rule, The. *See* Brecht, Bertolt, *Die Ausnahme und die Regel*

Excerpts from Diaries. *See* Tychyna, Pavlo, *Iz shchodennykovykh zapysiv*

Exchange, The. *See* Claudel, Paul, *L'Échange*

Exclusion, rules of, Foucault and, 13:3347b

Excommunication, Luther and, 2:678b

Excursion to Russia, An. *See* Krleža, Miroslav, *Izlet u Rusiju*

"Excursion to the Woodlands." *See* Turgenev, Ivan

Excursions. *See* Ekelöf, Gunnar, *Utflykter*

Exegesis
allegorical, among Greek Church Fathers, 1:5a

Exegesis (*cont.*)
  Augustine on, 1:42a–43a, 49a
Exemplary Tales. See Cervantes, Miguel de
Exercices de style, Les. See Queneau,
    Raymond
Exercises. See Ritsos, Yannis, *Piimata III*
Exercises in Style. See Queneau, Raymond,
    Les exercices de style
Exercises in Thinking. *See* Richter, Jean Paul,
    "Übungen im Denken"
Exeter Book, 1:64b, 66a
"Exhortation au camp du Roy Henry II." *See*
    Ronsard, Pierre de
"Exhortation pour la paix." *See* Ronsard, Pierre
    de
"Exhortation to Liberate Italy from the
    Barbarians." *See* Alfieri, Vittorio, *The
    Prince and Letters*; Machiavelli, Nicolò,
    The Prince
Exhumations littéraires. See Gautier,
    Théophile
Exi kai mia tipsis yia ton ourano. See Elytis,
    Odysseus
Exil. See Perse, Saint-John, *Exile*
Exil et le royaume, L'. See Camus, Albert,
    Exile and the Kingdom
Exil, L'. See Montherlant, Henry de
Exile
  of Azorín, 9:642b
  of Baroja, 9:612b–613a
  of Broch, 10:1399a-b
  of Dante, 1:434b–435a
  Ekelöf and, 12:2645a–2646a
  Foscolo in, 5:316a-b
  of Freud, 8:4b–5a
  of Ginzburg, 13:3135b, 3141a-b
  Gombrowicz and, 12:2563a
  of Heine, 6:499b
  of Jiménez, 9:992b
  of Kundera, 13:3394b
  of Machado, 9:747a-b
  of Machiavelli, 2:598a
  of Maeterlinck, 8:142a–143b
  of Mandelshtam, 10:1646a-b
  of Mann, 9:727b–728a
  of Milosz, 13:2931b–2932a, 2933a
  of Ortega y Gasset, 9:1146b

  of Perse, 10:1441b–1447a
  of Silone, 12:2275b, 2294a
  of Solzhenitsyn, 13:3194a–3195a
  of Staël, 5:92a, 93b
  of Unamuno, 8:304b–305a
  of Undset, 9:1024a–1025b
  of Zamyatin, 10:1199a-b
Exile. See Perse, Saint-John
Exiles. See Joyce, James
Exiles, Antoine-François Prévost de. *See*
    Prévost, Antoine-François
Existence
  Augustine on, 1:44b
  in Milosz's works, 13:2945a–2947a
Existentialism
  Beauvoir and, 12:2705b, 2714b, 2717b,
    2718a, 2719a-b, 2722a-b, 2723b
  Bergson and, 8:52a-b, 64a
  in Böll's writing, 13:3174b–3175b
  Breton association with, 11:1948a
  Butor and, 13:3288a
  Cela and, 13:3116a
  Foucault and, 13:3331a-b
  French, Kafka and, 9:1156b
  Frisch and, 13:2915b
  Ghelderode and, 11:2113b
  Hesse and, 9:844a
  Kierkegaard and, 6:1142a
  Machado and, 9:761b
  Marxism and, 12:2718a
  Ortega y Gasset's intractable reality, 9:1126b
  Pascal and, 3:148a-b
  pessimism and, 13:3025b
  of Pirandello, 8:397b
  Sartre and, 12:2589a–2612a, 2718a, 2719a-b
  Simenon and, 12:2504a
  theater of the absurd and, 13:3016b
  Unamuno as precursor of, 8:292b–293a,
    298b–299a, 299b
  view of suffering, 13:3174b–3175a
  see also Krleža, Miroslav
Existentialism and Humanism. See Sartre,
    Jean-Paul
Exit the King. See Ionesco, Eugène, *Le roi se
    meurt*
Exodus (Anglo-Saxon poem), 1:65b

"Expanding the Boundaries of Russian
Literature." *See* Khlebnikov, Velimir, "O
rasshirenii predelov russkoi
slovesnosti"

Experience
Benjamin and, 11:1727b–1728b
Bergson's theory of "lived experience," 8:52a
in Malraux's fiction, 12:2427b–2428a
Proust and, 11:1727b

Expérience poetique, L'. See Reneville, Roland
de

Expériences nouvelles touchant le vide. See
Pascal, Blaise

Experimental Novel, The. See Zola, Émile, *Le
roman expérimental*

Experimentation, in Butor, 13:3308b–3309a

"Expiation, L'." *See* Hugo, Victor

Explain, Mr. Offering Box. *See* Walther von der
Vogelweide

Explanation of the Articles of Issy. See
Fénelon, François de Salignac de la
Mothe-, *Explication des articles d'Issy*

*Explanations of the Apothegms of the Saints.
See* Fénelon, François de Salignac de la
Mothe-, *Explication des maximes des
saints*

Explication des articles d'Issy. See Fénelon,
François de Salignac de la Mothe-

Explication des maximes des saints. See
Fénelon, François de Salignac de la
Mothe-

Exploitation
in Blasco Ibáñez's fiction
The Cabin, 8:375b
The Mayflower, 8:367a-b
in Gorky's fiction, 8:427a

Exploits and Opinions of Doctor Faustroll
'Pataphysician, The: A Neo-Scientific
Novel. *See* Jarry, Alfred, *Gestes et
opinions du docteur Faustroll,
'pataphysicien: Roman neo-scientifique*

"Exposed on the Mountains of the Heart." *See*
Rilke, Rainer Maria, "Ausgesetzt auf den
Bergen des Herzens"

Expositio. See Aquinas, Thomas, St.

Exposition de la foi catholic. See Bossuet,
Jacques Bénigne

Exposition Universelle of 1855, 5:536b

Express, L' (journal), Mauriac and, 10:1307b

Expressionism
Arp and, 10:1365b
in Azorín's works, 9:639b
in Čapek's works, 10:1571b
German
Hesse's *Demian* and, 9:839b
well-made play and, 7:1931a
Lagerkvist and, 10:1683a, 1684b
in Strindberg's works, 7:1742a
Witkiewicz and, 10:1222a-b

Expressivism, in Tolstoy's writing, 7:1487a-b

"Extemporary Sonnet." *See* Lope de Vega

Exteriority, principle of, Foucault and,
13:3349b–3350b

External world. *See* Material universe

Extra Day and Other Stories, An. *See*
Gunnarsson, Gunnar, *En Dag tilovers
og andre Historier*

Extraordinary Adventure, Which Happened to
Vladimir Mayakovsky in the Summer,
While on Vacation. *See* Mayakovsky,
Vladimir, "Neobychainoe priklyuchenie,
byvshee s Vladimirom Mayakovskim
letom na dache"

Extraordinary Tale. *See* Butor, Michel, *Histoire
extraordinaire*

Extravagances of Belisa, The. See Lope de
Vega, *Las bizarrías de Belisa*

Eye imagery, in poetry of Ady, 9:867a

Eye Listens, The. See Claudel, Paul, *L'Oeil
écoute*

Eye symbolism, in "Lament of Monotonous
Autumn," 7:1888b

Eyeglasses imagery, in Queneau's works,
12:2515a

Eyes. *See* Zamyatin, Yevgeny Ivanovich,
"Glaza"

Eyrbyggja saga, 1:389a-b, 396b

Ez ist nu tac. See Wolfram von Eschenbach

Ezekiel, Book of
in Villon's *Testament,* 2:563b
denunciation of "The Shepherds of
Israel," 2:566b

F

"Fabel." *See* Ekelöf, Gunnar

Fabeln. See Lessing, Gotthold Ephraim

Faber, Frederick William, Unamuno's reading of, 8:290b

Fable, A: Belfagor, the Devil Who Took a Wife. See Machiavelli, Niccolò, *Favola: Belfagor arcidiavolo che prese moglie*

Fable about Mr. Good and a Sweet Girl, A. *See* Zamyatin, Yevgeny Ivanovich, "Skazka o Gospodine Khoroshem i o miloi baryshne"

Fable and the Flesh, The. See Aymé, Marcel

Fable of Polyphemus and Galatea, The. See Góngora, Luis de, *Fábula de Polifemo y Galatea*

Fables

Aesopian, influence on Renaissance short fiction, 2:930a

Aymé and, 12:2434a–2437a

of Ekelöf, 12:2644b–2645a

La Fontaine on, 3:80a, 80b

of Moravia, 12:2696a

Vigny's use of, 5:455b

see also Fairy tale

Fables. See Fénelon, François de Salignac de la Mothe-; La Fontaine, Jean de; Lessing, Gotthold Ephraim, *Fabeln*

Fables choisies. See La Fontaine, Jean de

Fables and Would-be Tales. *See* Čapek, Karel, *Bajky a podpovídky*

Fabliaux

Diderot and, 4:484b

influence on Renaissance short fiction, 2:933a-b, 945b

Rabelais and, 2:699a

Fábula de Polifemo y Galatea. See Góngora, Luis de

Face of God, The. *See* Arniches, Carlos, *La cara de Dios*

Faces. *See* Andrić, Ivo, *Lica*

Facetia (joke), in Renaissance short fiction, 2:937b–939a

Facetie, motti et burle. See Domenichi, Ludovico

Fâcheux, Les. See Molière

Facial imagery, in Rilke, 9:775a-b, 776a

Fact and fiction, in Dinesen's tales, 10:1282b–1283b

Fact and Fiction. See Goethe, Johann Wolfgang, *Dichtung und Wahrheit*

Facta et dicta memorabilia. See Valerius Maximus

Fadren. See Strindberg, August, *The Father*

Faerie Queene, The. See Spenser, Edmund

Fáfnismál, 1:398a

Fähigkeit zu trauern, Die. See Böll, Heinrich

Fähnlein der sieben Aufrechten, Das. See Keller, Gottfried, *The Banner of the Upright Seven*

Fail, Noël du, 3:91a-b

"Faina." *See* Blok, Alexander

"Faint Heart, A." *See* Dostoevsky, Feodor

Fair Maiden, The. *See* Laxness, Halldór, *Hið ljósa man*

Fair Unknown

Chrétien de Troyes and, 1:149b

earliest version of, 1:149a-b

Fairies, The. See Wagner, Richard, *Die Feen*

Fairy Council, The. See Laforgue, Jules, *Le concile féerique*

Fairy tale

in America, 6:880a

of Hoffmann, Hesse's *Steppenwolf* and, 9:847b

Hoffmann and, 5:281b–286a

Keller's *Mirror, the Cat* as, 6:928a

Olesha's *The Three Fat Men* as, 11:2247a-b, 2248a

Tieck and, 5:245b

see also Andersen, Hans Christian; Folklore; Pushkin, Alexander

Fairy Tale of My Life, The. See Andersen, Hans Christian

Fairy Tale, The. *See* Schnitzler, Arthur, *Das Märchen*

Fairy Tales. See Čapek, Karel, *Devatero pohádek*

Fairy Tales Told for Children. See Andersen, Hans Christian

Fairytale Prince, The. *See* Moberg, Vilhelm, *Sagoprinsen*

"Faith." *See* Pascoli, Giovanni, *Myricae* (Tamarisks), "L'Orfano"

Faith. *See* Unamuno, Miguel de, "La fe"

Faith and Love. See Novalis

Faith, religious
  in Hesse's "Ein Stückchen Theologie," 9:849a
  in Ionesco's plays, 13:3009a, 3009b, 3017a
  Kierkegaard and, 6:1133b, 1137b–1138a, 1142b–1144a
  Leopardi's loss of, 5:544b–545a, 545b
  reason and, Aquinas on, 1:424b
  of Unamuno, 8:292a, 293a-b, 298b–299a
    early piety, 8:284b
    loss of, 8:285b
    reason and, 8:290b–291a
    as symbolized in *Don Quixote*, 8:296a
  in Valle-Inclán's *Sacrilegio*, 8:349b
  see also Conversion

Faithful Blackbird, The. *See* Jiménez, Juan Ramón, "El mirlo fiel"

Faithful Servant of His Master, A. See Grillparzer, Franz

Faithful Shepherd. See Guarini, Giambattista, *Pastor fido*

Faithful Shepherdess, The. See Fletcher, John

Faithful Wife, The. See Undset, Sigrid, *Den trofaste hustru*

Fajardo, Diego de Saavedra, Azorín's approval of, 9:644b

Falconet, Étienne, monument of Czar Peter, 5:622a-b

"Falešný autostop." *See* Kundera, Milan, "The Hitchhiking Game"

Falkberget, Johan, Norwegian realism and, 9:1037a

"Fall of Atlantis, The." *See* Khlebnikov, Velimir, "Gibel' Atlantidy"

Fall from grace, in Trakl, 10:1421a

"Fall of the House of Usher, The." *See* Poe, Edgar Allan

"Fall of the House of Votický, The." *See* Čapek, Karel, "Pád rodu Votických"

Fall, The. See Camus, Albert

Fall Wagner, Der (*The Fall of Wagner*). *See* Nietzsche, Friedrich

"Fallen Laurel, The." *See* Petrarch, "Laurea Occidens"

False Policeman, The. *See* Aymé, Marcel, "Le faux policier"

"False and True Green, The." *See* Quasimodo, Salvatore

Fal'shivaia moneta. See Gorky, Maxim

Falso e vero verde, Il. See Quasimodo, Salvatore, *The False and the True Green*

Fama póstuma. See Lope de Vega

"Fama tuba dante sonum." *See* Archpoet

"Fame with its trumpet blowing." *See* Archpoet, "Fama tuba dante sonum"

Fame, theme of, in Staël's *Corinne*, 5:101a, 102a

Famiglia. See Ginzburg, Natalia

Famiglia dell'antiquario, La. See Goldoni, Carlo

Famiglia Manzoni, La. See Ginzburg, Natalia

Familia de Errotuco, La. See Baroja, Pío

Familia de Pascual Duarte, La. See Cela, Camilo José, *The Family of Pascual Duarte*

"Familiar Dialogues on the Poetry of the Proletarians." *See* Sand, George, "Dialogues familiers sur la poésie des prolétaires"

Familiaries. See Petrarch, *Rerum familiarium libri*

Familie Schroffenstein, Die. See Kleist, Heinrich von

Famille de Carvajal, La. See Mérimée, Prosper

Family
  Augustinian trinitarianism and, 1:38b–39a
  Aymé's satire of, 12:2445b–2446b
  disintegration of
    in Gorky's fiction, 8:429a-b, 430b–431a, 440b
    in Mann's *Buddenbrooks*, 9:716a–717b
  familial conflicts, in Storm's works, 6:919b–921b
  filial obligation, in Cela, 13:3122b
  La Rochefoucauld and, 3:51b, 60b
  myth of, Cela and, 13:3109b–3110a
  in Olesha's *Envy*, 11:2239b–2240b
  parent-child conflict, in Strindberg's works, 7:1743b–1744a

Family (*cont.*)
    sanctity of family relations, in Schiller's
      William Tell, 5:49a
    in Simenon's novels, 12:2482a
    in Vico's conception, 3:309b
    see also Kinship
Family. See Ginzburg, Natalia, *Famiglia*
"Family Affair, A." *See* Maupassant, Guy de,
    "En famille"
Family of Errotuco. *See* Baroja, Pío, *La familia*
    de Errotuco
Family Happiness. See Tolstoy, Leo
Family Idiot, The. See Sartre, Jean-Paul
Family Letters and Parisian Notes. *See* Eça de
    Queiroz, José Maria, *Cartas familiares e*
    bilhetes de Paris
Family Lie, The. See Simenon, Georges,
    Malempin
Family Reconciliation, A. See Hauptmann,
    Gerhart, *Das Friedensfest*
Family romance, Freud's concept of, 8:2b
Family saga
    of Galsworthy, 10:1500a-b
    of Gunnarsson, 10:1500b
    of Mann, 10:1500a
    Mauriac and, 10:1325b–1326a
    Zola's Rougon-Macquarts series, 7:1522a-b,
      1523b–1536a, 1607a
Family Sayings. See Ginzburg, Natalia
Family Strife in Hapsburg. See Grillparzer,
    Franz
Family Tragedy, A. *See* Hašek, Jaroslav,
    "Rodinná tragédie"
Famine
    in Chekhov's "The Wife," 7:1864b
    in Manzoni's *The Betrothed*, 5:385b–387a,
      392a-b
Famous comedy. *See Comedia famosa*
Fanal bleu, Le. See Colette
"Fanciullino, Il." *See* Pascoli, Giovanni
Fancy Dress Party, The. See Moravia, Alberto
Fangen, Ronald, Hamsun and, 8:40a
Fanny Hill. See Cleland, John
Fanshawe, Richard, 2:765b, 766a, 766b
"Fantaisie." *See* Nerval, Gérard de
Fantasia of the Unconscious. See Lawrence,
    D. H.

Fantasies on Art for Friends of Art. *See* Tieck,
    Ludwig, *Phantasien über die Kunst für*
    Freunde der Kunst
Fantasies and Sketches. See Andersen, Hans
    Christian
Fantasiestücke in Callots Manier. See
    Hoffmann, E. T. A.
Fantasio. See Musset, Alfred de
Fantastic Symphony. See Berlioz, Hector,
    Symphonie fantastique
Fantasy
    in Berlioz' works, 6:782a–783a
    Eça and, 7:1701a-b
    in Gautier's works, 6:1049a-b
    Genet and, 13:2877a-b
    in Giraudoux's works, 9:1062b–1063a
    historical, Calvino and, 13:3264b–3272a
    in Mérimée's works, 6:746b, 760b–761b,
      766b–767a
    Pérez Galdós, *El caballero encantado*,
      7:1615b
    see also Reality
"Fantasy." *See* Nerval, Gérard de, "Fantaisie"
Fantasy Pieces in the Manner of Callot. *See*
    Hoffmann, E. T. A., *Fantasiestücke in*
    Callots Manier
"Fantôme de Staline, Le." *See* Sartre,
    Jean-Paul, *The Ghost of Stalin*
"Fanum vacunae." *See* Pascoli, Giovanni
Far East. *See* Orient
Far from the Highway. *See* Moberg, Vilhelm,
    Långt frå landsvägen
"Far och jag." *See* Lagerkvist, Pär
"Farai un vers de dreyt nien." *See* William IX
    of Aquitaine, duke
Faraway Gardens. *See* Jammes, Francis,
    Jardines lejanos
Farce
    in Chrétien's *Lancelot*, 1:198a
    French, 7:1921b–1924b
      and Beaumarchais, 4:564b–565a, 574a
      seventeenth century, 3:25a
    of Frisch, 13:2905a
    German, of Wagner, 6:1163a
    Hávarðar saga Ísfirðings as, 1:396b
    historical evolution of, 3:102b–103a
    in Jarry's works, 9:681a, 683b–684a

medieval, 1:471a, 472a
Moravia and, 12:2679a-b
typical characters and plots, 3:103a
Farce des ténébreux, La. See Ghelderode,
Michel de
Farce of the Girl Who Loved the King, The.
See Valle-Inclán, Ramón del, *Farsa de
la enamorada del rey*
Farce of the Noble Queen, The. *See*
Valle-Inclán, Ramón del, *Farsa y
licencia de la reina castiza*
Farce of the Shadow Cult, The. *See*
Ghelderode, Michel de, *La farce des
ténébreux*
Farewell Party, The. See Kundera, Milan
Farewell to Hamlet. *See* Johnson, Eyvind,
Avsked till Hamlet
Færeyinga saga, 1:381a
Farfalla di Dinard, La. See Montale, Eugenio,
The Butterfly of Dinard
Faria e Sousa, Manuel de, 2:749b, 751a, 754b
Farm at Grinde, The. The Morning. *See*
Vesaas, Tarjei, *Grindegard, Morgonen*
Farpas. See Eça de Queiroz, José Maria, *Darts*
Fars reise. See Vesaas, Tarjei
Farsa de la enamorada del rey. See
Valle-Inclán, Ramón del
Farsa y licencia de la reina castiza. See
Valle-Inclán, Ramón del
"Farys. Kasyda." *See* Mickiewicz, Adam
Fasching: Eine Studie (Fasching: A Study).
See Hauptmann, Gerhart
Fasci di Combattimento, 9:799b, 825b
Fascism
Croce and, 8:316a, 326b–327a,
11:1989b–1990a
D'Annunzio and, 8:175a–176a, 185b, 191b,
199a, 201b, 11:1988b, 1989a
Ferreira de Castro and, 11:2153a
futurism and, 9:799b–800a, 813b
German, 7:1678b
Ginzburg and, 13:3133b–3134a, 3135a,
3146b, 3160b
Heinrich Mann and, 8:527a, 537a, 539b
in *Man of Straw*, 8:533a
in Italy, Carducci's poetry and,
7:1510b–1511a

leftist vs. liberal opposition to,
13:3151b–3152a
Mann's *Mario and the Magician* and, 9:727a
Marinetti and, 9:823b, 824b, 825b–826a,
827a
Montale and, 11:1988b, 1990a, 1991a,
1995a–1996a
Moravia and, 12:2677b, 2678b, 2684b, 2691b
Pirandello and, 8:394b
postsymbolist poets and, 7:1579b
Quasimodo and, 12:2388b–2389a
Rhinocéros and, 13:3001a
Sade as precursor of, 4:636a
Silone and, 12:2293a-b, 2294b–2295a,
2297b, 2303a-b
Svevo's view of, 8:71a-b
in *The Lesson*, 13:2994a
Unamuno and, 8:307b
Vittorini and, 12:2740a, 2747a-b
Yourcenar and, 12:2540a
see also National Socialism; Totalitarianism
"Fascismo e la letteratura, Il" ("Fascism and
Literature"). *See* Montale, Eugenio, *The
Storm and Other Things*
Fashion
in La Bruyère's *Caractères*, 3:251b–253a
women's, Mallarmé's journal on, 7:1576a-b,
1578a
Fashion System, The. See Barthes, Roland
Fastes d'enfer. See Ghelderode, Michel de
Fastnachtspiele, 1:471a
Fastoul, Baude, 1:460a
Fata Morgana. See Breton, André; Trakl, Georg
"Fatal, Lo." *See* Azorín
Fatal Skin, The. See Balzac, Honoré de, *La
peau de chagrin*
Fatalism
in Baroja's *Zalacaín el aventurero*,
9:602b–603a
in Blasco Ibáñez's fiction
Reeds and Mud, 8:382b
The Cabin, 8:372b, 376a, 377a
The Mayflower, 8:360b, 366b
Büchner and, 6:1172b–1173a
in Diderot, 4:499b–501a
"Fatalist, The." *See* Lermontov, Mikhail
Yurievich

Fatality, The. *See* Azorín, "Lo fatal"
Fate
  Anouilh's view on origin of, 13:2849a
  in Corneille's *Cinna*, 3:43b
  in Dinesen, 10:1290a–1291b
  in Dumas's works, 6:733b–739a
  in *Gísla saga Súrssonar*, 1:396a
  Grillparzer's view of, 5:425a–426b
  in Hugo's works, 6:701a, 713a-b
  in Jiménez' "Espacio," 9:1011b
  in Kleist's works, 5:295b
  in Leconte de Lisle, 6:1267b–1268b
  in Lermontov's works, 6:1220b
  in Malraux's works, 12:2419a-b
  Rilke on, 9:775b–776a, 776b
  tragedies of, influence on Grillparzer,
    5:425a–426b
  in Vigny's *Les destinées*, 5:480b
Fate of the Embellisher, The. *See* Ady, Endre,
  "A megszépítő fátuma"
Fate of the Malous, The. See Simenon,
  Georges, *Le destin des Malou*
Fateful Fork, The. *See* Platen, August von, *Die
  verhängnisvolle Gabel*
Fateful Game of Love, The. *See* Čapek, Karel,
  and Josef Čapek, *Lásky hra osudná*
Fates, the, in Vigny's *Les destinées*, 5:481a
Fates, The. See Vigny, Alfred Victor de, *Les
  destinées*
Father
  image of, in Michelet's writing, 5:594a-b
  in Kafka's works, 9:1162a, 1163b–1165a,
    1166a
  in Nerval's poetry, 6:944b–945a
  in Proust's *Remembrance of Things Past*,
    8:558b, 559a
  in Schiller's works
    The Robbers, 5:32a
    William Tell, 5:49a
  in Staël's *Sophie*, 5:90b
Father, The. See Strindberg, August
Father, *see also* Salvation, paternal
Father of a Family. See Diderot, Denis, *Le
  père de famille*
Father of the Family. See Tasso, Torquato,
  Padre di famiglia

"Father of Heaven, after the lost days." *See*
  Petrarch, *Canzoniere*, "Padre del Ciel,
  dopo i perduti giorni"
Father Mouret's Sin. See Zola, Émile, *La faute
  de l'abbé Mouret*
Father Sergius. See Tolstoy, Leo
"Father, The." *See* Babel, Isaac, *Odessa Tales*,
  "Otets"; Maupassant, Guy de, "Le père"
Fatherland in Danger, The. See Goncourt,
  Edmond Louis Antoine and Jules Alfred
  Huot de, *La patrie en danger*
Fathers of the church. *See* Church fathers
Father's Journey. See Vesaas, Tarjei, *Fars reise*
Fathers and Sons. See Turgenev, Ivan
"Fatti che or son parole." *See* Pirandello, Luigi
Faubourg. See Simenon, Georges
Faulkner, William
  Anouilh and, 13:2844a
  Bergson and, 8:64b
  Camus and, 13:3055b
  Céline and, 11:1860a
  Queneau and, 12:2516a
  Simon and, 13:3024b, 3025b, 3029b, 3037a
  Spanish translations, 9:1119b
  The Sound and the Fury, 7:1906a
Faure, Elie
  Delacroix and, 5:528a
  Oeuvres littéraires, 5:528a
Faure, François, bishop of Amiens, funeral
  oration on the queen-mother, 3:164a-b
Fauré, Gabriel, Maeterlinck and, 8:130b, 136b
Fauriel, Claude
  on Goethe's *Hermann und Dorothea*,
    5:371b–372a
  letter from Manzoni to, 5:376b–377a
  Manzoni and, 5:368a, 368b, 369a, 371b
Faust. See Goethe, Johann Wolfgang von;
  Lessing, Gotthold Ephraim
"Faust." *See* Turgenev, Ivan
Faust legend
  Butor and, 13:3309b–3312a
  in Gombrowicz, 12:2572a-b
  Lagerkvist and, 10:1693a-b
  in Rutebeuf's *Miracle of Théophile*, 1:464a

see also Berlioz, Hector, *La damnation de Faust*; Goethe, Johann Wolfgang von, *Faust*; Heine, Heinrich, *Doctor Faust*; Mann, Thomas, *Doctor Faustus*

Faust (opera). *See* Gounod, Charles

Faustbuch. See Spies, Johann

Faustin, La. See Goncourt, Edmond Louis Antoine de

Faustus (Manichaean teacher), 1:28b

Faut-il brûler Sade? See Beauvoir, Simone de, *Must We Burn Sade?*

Faute de l'abbé Mouret, La. See Zola, Émile

Fauves, Les (painters), 8:546b

"Faux policier, Le." *See* Aymé, Marcel

Faux-monnayeurs, Les. See Gide, André; Gide, André, *The Counterfeiters*

Favel ensam (Favel Alone). *See* Johnson, Eyvind

Faville del maglio, Le. See D'Annunzio, Gabriele

Favola: Belfagor arcidiavolo che prese moglie. See Machiavelli, Niccolò

"Favola Boschereccia." *See* Tasso, Torquato, *Aminta*

Favola del figlio cambiato, La. See Pirandello, Luigi

Fayette, Marie-Madeleine de La. *See* La Fayette, Marie-Madeleine de

FBI (U.S.). *See* Federal Bureau of Investigation

"Fe, La." *See* Unamuno, Miguel de

Fear
   in Andrić's works, 11:1767b
   in Calvino, 13:3260b–3261b

Fear and Misery in the Third Reich. See Brecht, Bertolt, *Furcht und Elend des Dritten Reiches*

Fear and Trembling. See Kierkegaard, Søren

"Feast During the Plague, A." *See* Pushkin, Alexander, "Pir vo vremia chumy"

Feast in Time of Plague. See Pushkin, Alexander

Federal Bureau of Investigation (U.S.), Heinrich Mann and, 8:519a, 541b

"Fédérigo." *See* Mérimée, Prosper

Fedhra. See Ritsos, Yannis, *Tetarti dhiastasi*

Feeling of One Family, A. *See* Tychyna, Pavlo, *Chuttia iedynnoi rodyny*

"Feelings of a Desperate Man." *See* Vico, Giovanni Battista, *Affetti di un disperato*

Feen, Die. See Wagner, Richard

Fegurð himinsins. See Laxness, Halldór

Fehmic Court, The. *See* Berlioz, Hector, *Francs-Juges*

Feijóo y Montenegro, Benito, Ortega y Gasset and, 9:1120b

"Fekete hold éjszakája." *See* Ady, Endre

Felix und Galathea. See Wedekind, Frank

Félix Vargas. See Azorín, *El caballero inactual*

Fellow travelers, in Olesha's "The Death of Zand," 11:2248b

Feltrinelli, Giangiacomo, Pasternak published by, 10:1611b–1612a, 1613b

Femeninas. See Valle-Inclán, Ramón del

Feminine principle, in Hugo's works, 6:702a–703b, 711a, 713b, 715b

Feminism
   in Ariosto, 2:638a
   Beauvoir and, 12:2701b, 2705a, 2705b, 2723a, 2729a
   Grass and, 13:3380a–3382a
   Sand and, 6:833a-b
   Wedekind and, 8:236b, 267a
   see also Sexes, relations between; Women

Femme 100 têtes, La. See Ernst, Max

"Femme adultère, La." *See* Vigny, Alfred Victor de, *Poèmes antiques et modernes*

Femme au dix-huitième siècle, La. See Goncourt, Edmond Louis Antoine and Jules Alfred Huot de

Femme cachée, La. See Colette

Femme de Claude, La. See Dumas fils, Alexandre

"Femme de Paul, La." *See* Maupassant, Guy de

Femme est un diable, ou la tentation de Saint Antoine, Une. See Mérimée, Prosper

Femme et son ombre, La. See Claudel, Paul

Femme galante, in La Bruyère's *Caractères*, 3:238a

Femme rompue, La, See Beauvoir, Simone de

Femmes. See Verlaine, Paul

Femmes savantes, Les. See Molière

Fénelon, François de Salignac de la Mothe-,
3:261a–291b
Bossuet and, 3:172a, 172b–173a, 174b
Correspondance, 3:266a, 267a-b, 278b–279a
De la nature de l'homme, 3:275a
De l'autorité de Cassien (*Regarding the
Authority of Cassianus*), 3:270b
Dialogues des morts (*Dialogues of the
Dead*), 3:269a-b, 288b
*Discours pour le sacre de l'électeur de
Cologne* (*Sermon on the Occasion of the
Coronation of the Elector of Cologne*),
3:281a
Examen de conscience (Scrutiny of a
Conscience), 3:282a
*Explanation of the Maxims of the Saints on
the Inner Life*, Bossuet and,
3:172b–173a
Explication des articles d'Issy (*Explanation
of the Articles of Issy*), 3:271b
Explication des maximes des saints
(*Explanations of the Apothegms of the
Saints*), 3:271a-b, 276a-b, 277a, 277b
Fables, 3:269b
Gnostique de Saint Clément d'Alexandrie
(*The Gnosticism of Saint Clement of
Alexandria*), 3:270b
La Bruyère's *Dialogues sur le quiétisme* and,
3:258b
Les aventures de Télémaque, fils d'Ulysse
(*The Adventures of Telemachus, Son of
Ulysses*), 3:269b, 272b, 273a, 278b,
281b, 282a, 282b, 284a–289a
editions of, 3:284a
Homer's *Odyssey* and, 3:284b, 285a,
286a-b
reception of, 3:284b
style of, 3:287b–288a
Wieland and, 4:596b
Lettre à l'Académie, 3:269b
Lettre à Louis XIV, 3:272b, 281a-b
*Lettres au P. Lami, Bénédictine, sur la grâce
et la prédestination* (*Letters to Father
Lamy, of the Order of St. Benedict,
Regarding Grace and Predestination*),
3:275b, 284a

Mémoire sur l'état passif (*Essay on the
Passive State*), 3:270b
religious writings of, 3:273b–280a
Tables de Chaulnes, 3:273a, 282b–283b
Traité de l'éducation des filles (*Treatise on
the Education of Girls*), 3:266b
Traité de l'existence de Dieu (*Treatise on
the Existence of God*), 3:275a-b
Fénéon, Félix, and Jarry, 9:670b
"Fenêtres, Les." *See* Apollinaire, Guillaume,
Calligrammes
Ferdière, Gaston
Artaud's electroshock therapy and,
11:1975b–1976a
on Artaud's insanity, 11:1962b
Ferdinand VII of Spain, king, restoration of,
9:610a-b
Ferdydurke. See Gombrowicz, Witold
Ferenczi, Sándor
Freud and, 8:4a
Kosztolányi and, 10:1237b
Fergus. See Guillaume le Clerc
Ferguson, Francis, on Pirandello's *Six
Characters*, 8:408b
Feria de los discretos, La. See Baroja, Pío
Fermentation, in Montesquieu's thought,
3:348b–349a
Fermo e Lucia. See Manzoni, Alessandro
Fernández de Cordova, Gonzalo, in Manzoni's
The Betrothed, 5:387a
Fernandez, Dominique, *L'Échec de Pavese*,
12:2764a
Fernández y González, Manuel, Blasco Ibáñez
and, 8:355b
Ferny, France (Ferny-Voltaire), Voltaire in,
4:378a, 380a-b
Féron, Élie, Goldoni and, 4:431b–432a
Ferrara, Ariosto and, 2:619a-b
Ferreira, António, Camoëns and, 2:755a
Ferreira de Castro, José Maria,
11:2143a–2165b
A curva da estrada (The Curve in the Road),
11:2154a, 2161b–2162b
A lã e a neve (Wool and Snow), 11:2154a,
2161a-b
A tempestade (The Storm), 11:2153a-b,
2160b–2161a

A volta ao mundo (Around the World), 11:2153b

As maravilhas artísticas do mundo (Artistic Wonders of the World), 11:2154a

Criminoso por ambição (Ambition's Criminal), 11:2150b, 2151a, 2155b

Emigrants (*Emigrantes*), 11:2151b, 2155b–2157b

Eternidade (Eternity), 11:2152a, 2159b–2160b, 2161b, 2164a

Jungle (*A selva*), 11:2143a, 2151b–2152a, 2154b, 2157b–2159b, 2160b

"Luta de classes" (Class Struggle), 11:2153a

Mas . . . (But . . .), 11:2151b, 2155b

O instinto supremo (The Supreme Instinct), 11:2154b–2155a, 2163b–2164a

O intervalo (Intermission), 11:2152b–2153a

Os fragmentos, "Origem de *O intervalo*," 11:2152b–2153a

Pequenos mundos e velhas civilizações (Little Worlds and Ancient Civilizations), 11:2153b

Terra fria (Cold Land), 11:2152a, 2160b, 2161b

The Mission, 11:2154a, 2162b–2163b, 2164a

Ferry, Paul, Bossuet and, 3:155a, 159a

Ferry Song. See Ekelöf, Gunnar, *Frjesång*

"Ferry, The." *See* Quasimodo, Salvatore

Feste des Lebens und der Kunst. See Behrens, Peter

"Festival." *See* Apollinaire, Guillaume, *Calligrammes*, "Fête"

Festival of Bacchus, The. *See* Schnitzler, Arthur, "Das Bacchusfest"

Festival of Life and of Art. See Behrens, Peter, *Feste des Lebens und der Kunst*

Festival of Our Lord of the Ship, The. See Pirandello, Luigi, *Sagra del Signore della nave*

"Festivals of Patience." *See* Rimbaud, Arthur, "Fêtes de la patience"

Festspiel in deutschen Reimen. See Hauptmann, Gerhart

Fet, Afanasy
  Bely and, 9:915a
  on the Tolstoys, 7:1475b

"Fête." *See* Apollinaire, Guillaume, *Calligrammes*

"Fête chez Thérèse, La." *See* Hugo, Victor

"Fêtes de la patience." *See* Rimbaud, Arthur

Fêtes galantes. See Verlaine, Paul

Fetish, The. See Moravia, Alberto, *L'Automa*

Fetishism, in Canetti, 12:2621b

Fettered by Film. *See* Mayakovsky, Vladimir, *Zakovannyi fil'moi*

Feuchtersleben, Karoline von, 5:71a

Feudalism
  in Vico's conception, 3:302a, 303a, 308a
  Walther and, 1:289b
  in Wolfram, 1:271a-b

Feuerbach, Ludwig, Keller and, 6:924a-b

Feuillant club
  Chénier's membership in, 4:703b
  "Déclaration des amis de la Constitution ci-devant réunis aux Feuillants" ("Declaration of the Friends of the French Constitution Formerly Reunited as the Feuillants"), 4:703b

Feuilles d'automne, Les. See Hugo, Victor

Feuilleton
  Berlioz' use of form, 6:785a-b, 796b
  in Czech literature, 10:1567a, 1578b
  Dumas's use of form, 6:724b–725a
  Gautier's use of form, 6:1047a-b

Feuquières, marquis de, Bossuet and, 3:151a

Feux. See Yourcenar, Marguerite

Few Stories, A. See Laxness, Halldór, *Nikkrar sögur*

Few, The. See Alfieri, Vittorio, Political Tetralogy

Few Words on Language Reform, A. *See* Kosztolányi, Dezső, *Pár szó a nyelvújíráshoz*

Feydeau, Georges, 7:1921b–1922a, 1923a–1924b
  Anouilh and, 13:2854a-b
  Champignol malgré lui (*Champignol in Spite of Himself*), 7:1924a
  Le mariage de Barillon (*Barillon's Marriage*), 7:1923b
  Un fil à la patte (*Chain and Ball*), 7:1923b

Fiabe italiane. See Calvino, Italo, *Italian Folktales*

Fiaccola sotto il moggio, La. See D'Annunzio, Gabriele

"Fialový hrom." *See* Hašek, Jaroslav

"Fiançailles." *See* Apollinaire, Guillaume

Fiançailles de M. Hire, Les. See Simenon, Georges

Fibel. See Richter, Jean Paul, *Das Leben Fibels, des*

Fibel, Die. See George, Stefan

Fichte, Johann Gottlieb
    Benjamin's essay on, 11:1709a-b
    elaboration of Kant's views by, 5:395b–396a
    free self and, 5:211b
    Herder's individualism contrasted with, 4:652a
    Hölderlin and, 5:148a–149a
    Novalis and, 5:206a, 208a, 210a
    in Richter's *Titan*, 5:74a
    Schlegel and, 5:183a-b
    Staël and, 5:92b
    Wissenschaftslehre (*Science of Knowledge*), 5:210a

Ficino, Marsilio, Ronsard's "Les Daimons" and, 2:733a

Ficker, Ludwig von, Trakl and, 10:1414a

Fiction
    autonomy of the fictional character, 5:376a-b
    categories of, in Richter's *School for Aesthetics*, 5:59b
    Hoffmann's poetics of, 5:279b–281b
    lying and, 1:49a-b
    Moravia's concept of, 12:2686b–2687b
    Staël on, 5:99b–100a
    see also Novel

Fidalgos of Casa Mourisca, The. See Dinis, Júlio, *Os Fidalgos da Casa Mourisca*

Fideism, of Montaigne, 2:785a, 785b, 786a

"Fides." *See* Pascoli, Giovanni, *Myricae* (Tamarisks), "L'Orfano"

Fielding, Henry
    Richter and, 5:68b, 78a
    Sade's admiration for, 4:627a-b
    Staël and, 5:99b
    Tom Jones, 4:595b
    Wieland influenced by, 4:593a. 4.595b

Fielding, Thales, Delacroix and, 5:519a, 519b

Fields of Castile. *See* Machado, Antonio, *Campos de Castilla*

"Fiery Hafiz." *See* Andrić, Ivo, "Čelebi Hafiz"

Fiesco. See Schiller, Friedrich von, *The Conspiracy of Fiesco at Genoa*

Fiesole Evening. *See* D'Annunzio, Gabriele, "La sera fiesolana"

"Fiesta del trabajo, La." *See* Ortega y Gasset, José

"Fifteen Minutes of Poetry on the X Mas." *See* Marinetti, Filippo Tommaso, "Quarto d'ora di poesia della X Mas"

Fifth Book of the Odes, The. *See* Ronsard, Pierre de, *Cinquiéme livre des odes*

Fifth and Last Book of the Heroic Deeds and Sayings of the Good Pantagruel. See Rabelais, François, *Le Cinquiesme et dernier livre des faicts et dicts héroïques du bon Pantagruel*

Fifth of May, The. *See* Manzoni, Alessandro, *Il cinque maggio*

Figaro, Le (journal)
  and Cocteau, 10:1555b
  Mauriac and, 10:1307b
  Sand and, 6:819b
  "The Futurist Manifesto" and, 9:800b, 801a

Fighting Cock, The. See Anouilh, Jean, *L'Hurluberlu*

Fighting for Souls. *See* Hašek, Jaroslav, "Zápas o duše"

Figlia di Iorio, La. See D'Annunzio, Gabriele, *The Daughter of Iorio*

Figlio d'Arlecchino perduto e ritrovato, Il. See Goldoni, Carlo

Figurative language, Richter's *The School for Aesthetics* on, 5:78b

Figurative representation, in medieval satire, 1:347a, 367a–369b

"Figures of Creation." *See* Södergran, Edith, "Skaparegestalter"

Figures et anecdotes de la grand guerre. See Vidal, Gaston

Figyelő (journal), 9:875a

Fil à la patte, Un. See Feydeau, Georges

Filid, 1:141a

Fille aux yeux d'or, La. See Balzac, Honoré de

"Fille de Jephté, La." *See* Vigny, Alfred Victor de, *Poèmes antiques et modernes*

Fille de l'air, La. See Gozzi, Carlo

Fille d'Eve, Une. See Balzac, Honoré de

Fille Elisa, La. See Goncourt, Edmond Louis Antoine and Jules Alfred Huot de

Filles du feu, Les. See Nerval, Gérard de, *Daughters of Fire*

"Fillo tis lefkas, To." *See* Seferis, George

Film
    Aymé and, 12:2434a
    Broch and, 10:1395a-b
    Cocteau and, 10:1544a, 1556a, 1560a, 1588b–1589a
    Malraux and, 12:2423b
    Moravia and, 12:2683b, 2684b, 2690a-b
    Robbe-Grillet and, 13:3240b

Film scripts, D'Annunzio and *Cabiria*, 8:197b–198a

Films based on literature
    Buñuel's versions of Galdós novels, 7:1617a
    Cela's *Pascal Duarte*, 13:3110a
    Cela's *The Hive*, 13:3115b
    Dinesen's *Out of Africa*, 10:1288a
    Ibsen plays filmed, 7:1444a
    Ibsen's *Doll's House*, 7:1444a
    Kosztolányi's novels, 10:1238a
    Kundera's *The Joke*, 13:3399b
    Moberg's novels, 11:2226b
    Moravia's *The Conformist*, 12:2684b
    Nazarín, 7:1617a
    Pirandello
        As You Desire Me, 8:395a
        La canzone dell'amore, 8:395a
    Queneau's *Zazie*, 12:2517b
    The Blue Angel (Heinrich Mann), 8:527a, 528b, 536b
    of Vesaas' novels, 11:2053b
    Visconti's *La terra trema* based on Verga's *I Malavoglia*, 7:1556b–1557a
    Yourcenar's *Coup de grâce*, 12:2544a
    Zamyatin's "The Cave," 10:1194a

Filocolo. See Boccaccio, Giovanni

Filodemo. See Camoëns, Luís Vaz de, *Auto de Filodemo*

Filoktitis. See Ritsos, Yannis

"Filomila." *See* Ritsos, Yannis, *Epanalipsis*

Filosofia della pratica: Economica ed etica. See Croce, Benedetto

"Filosofia dello spirito, La." *See* Philosophy, of Croce

Filosofia di Giambattista Vico, La. See Croce, Benedetto

Filostrato. See Boccaccio, Giovanni

Fils de Giboyer, Le. See Augier, Émile

Fils de personne. See Montherlant, Henry de

Fils, Le. See Simenon, Georges

Fils naturel, Le. See Diderot, Denis; Dumas fils, Alexandre

"Fils, Un." *See* Maupassant, Guy de

Filth imagery, in Queneau's works, 12:2514a-b

Fin amor. See Courtly love

Fin de Chéri, La. See Colette

Fin de la nuit, La. See Mauriac, François, *The End of the Night*

Fin de Satan, La. See Hugo, Victor

Finale in Youth. *See* Johnson, Eyvind, *Romanen om Olof*

"Finalities." *See* Cavafy, Constantine, "Teleiomena"

Financiers, in Deschamps' satire, 1:353a–354a

"Fine di Crono." *See* Ungaretti, Giuseppe

Fine of Two Hundred Francs, A. See Triolet, Elsa, *Le premier accroc coûte deux cents francs*

Finiteness, Foucault and, 13:3324b–3361b

Fink und Fliederbusch (Fink and Fliederbusch). *See* Schnitzler, Arthur

Finland, Russian October Revolution and, 11:1790b–1791a

Finnboga saga ramma, 1:397b, 398a

Finnegans Wake. See Joyce, James

Fiore, Il (*The Flower*), Dante and, 1:444b

Fiorenza. See Mann, Thomas

Fire, The. *See* Vesaas, Tarjei, *Brannen*

Fire in Copenhagen. *See* Laxness, Halldór, *Eldur í Kaupinhafn*

Fire Games. *See* Robbe-Grillet, Alain, *Le jeu avec le feu*

Fire imagery
    in Apollinaire's poetry, 9:892b, 900a
    in Canetti, 12:2622b–2623b
    in Hesse's prose, 9:834a, 844b

Fire imagery (*cont.*)
  in Ionesco's *The Bald Soprano*,
    13:2992b–2993a
  in works of Prudentius, 1:16a
Fire That Consumes, The. See Montherlant,
    Henry de, *La ville dont le prince est un
    enfant*
Firebugs, The. See Frisch, Max
Firenzuola, Angelo
  novellas of, 2:940b–941a
  Ragionamenti (Discussions), 2:941a
"Fireplace, The." *See* Klopstock, Friedrich
    Gottlieb
Fires. See Yourcenar, Marguerite, *Feux*
Fires of St. Dominic, The. *See* Zamyatin,
    Yevgeny Ivanovich, *Ogni sviatogo
    Dominika*
Firm of Nucingen, The. See Balzac, Honoré de,
    La maison Nucingen
First of All. *See* Elytis, Odysseus, *Anihta
    hartia (Open Book)*, "Prota-Prota"
First Circle, The. See Solzhenitsyn, Aleksandr
First Decade. See Machiavelli, Niccolò,
    Decennale primo
First Encounter, The. See Bely, Andrey, *Pervoe
    svidanie*
"First Evening." *See* Rimbaud, Arthur,
    "Première soirée"
First Four Books of the Odes, The. *See*
    Ronsard, Pierre de, *Les quatre premiers
    livres des odes*
First Grammatical Treatise, The, 1:380a
"First and Last Declaration, A." *See*
    Kierkegaard, Søren
First and Last Notebooks, See Weil, Simone
"First Long Railroad Ride, The." *See* Kafka,
    Franz, "Die ferste lange Eisenbahnfahrt"
"First Love." *See* Babel, Isaac, "Pervaia
    liubov"; Gorky, Maxim, "O pervoi
    liubvi"; Turgenev, Ivan
First Man, The. *See* Camus, Albert, *Le premier
    homme*
First Part. See Calderón de la Barca, Pedro,
    Primera parte
"First Poems." *See* Elytis, Odysseus,
    Prosanatolismi (Orientations), "Prota
    poiemata"

First Rescue Party, The. See Čapek, Karel,
    První parta
First Short Narrative Poems. *See* Pascoli,
    Giovanni, *Primi poemetti*
First Spring. *See* D'Annunzio, Gabriele, *Primo
    vere*
"First Surrealist Manifesto." *See* Breton, André
First Warning, The. See Strindberg, August,
    Första varningen
Fischer, S. (German publisher), Hesse and,
    9:836a
Fischer-Dieskau, Dietrich, on Nietzsche and
    Wagner, 7:1653a
Fish Can Sing, The. See Laxness, Halldór,
    Brekkukotsannáll
"Fisher of Men, The." *See* Zamyatin, Yevgeny
    Ivanovich
Fisocofollia, Marinetti's theory of, 9:822a-b
Fitch, Clyde, Ibsen's influence on, 7:1443b
Fitzgerald, F. Scott, Babel and, 11:1888b
Fiume (Yugoslavia), D'Annunzio's seizure of,
    8:198b–199a
Five Great Odes. See Claudel, Paul, *Cinq
    grandes odes*
Five Modern Nō. *See* Yourcenar, Marguerite,
    Cinq nô modernes
"Five Songs." *See* Rilke, Rainer Maria, "Fünf
    Gesänge"
Five Women. See Musil, Robert
Five Year Plan (First), Olesha and, 11:2245a,
    2251a
Flachsland, Caroline, marriage to Herder,
    4:639b
Flagman Thiel. See Hauptmann, Gerhart,
    *Bahnwärter Thiel: Novellistische Studie
    aus dem märkischen Kiefernforst*
Flame of Life, The. See D'Annunzio, Gabriele
Flaminio, Marcantonio, *Iusis pastorales* of,
    2:909a-b
Flammarion, Camille, *Lumen*, Mandelshtam's
    "Verses On the Unknown Soldier" and,
    10:1646b
Flanders Road, The. See Simon, Claude, *La
    route des Flandres*
Flandre littéraire, La, Ghelderode and,
    11:2134b

Flâneur des deux rives, Le. See Apollinaire,
    Guillaume
Flashback technique
    Anouilh's use of, 13:2861a
    in Camoëns' *The Lusiads*, 2:761a
    in Undset's works, 9:1037b
Flaubert, Gustave, **7:1373a–1394b**
    "A Simple Heart," 7:1392a
        influence on Lampedusa's *The Leopard*,
            11:2020a
    Azorín's literary criticism of, 9:645a
    Berlioz and, 6:772a, 808b
    Bouvard and Pécuchet, 7:1390b–1392a
    Chateaubriand and, 5:139b–140a
    Cocagne, 11:1900b
    decadent movement, 7:1416b, 1641a
    Eça and, 7:1685b, 1689a
    epigraph to D'Annunzio's *La Chimera*,
        8:179a
    Eugénie and, 8:536b
    Goncourts and, 7:1398b–1399a, 1412a
    Hamsun and, 8:23a
    Heinrich Mann and, 8:520b
    "Hérodias," 7:1385a, 1392b
    Kafka and, 9:1152b, 1156a
    Laforgue's "The Lament of the Pianos You
        Hear in Rich Neighborhoods" and,
        7:1887b
    *L'Éducation sentimentale (Sentimental
        Education)*, 7:1373a, 1374a,
        1375b–1377b, 1387a–1390b, 1763a
        discussed by Lukács, 10:1261b, 1262a
        Paris in, 5:650b
    Madame Bovary, 6:760a, 7:1374a,
        1381b–1385a, 1763b, 1768b
        Eca's use of, 7:1689a
        Musset and, 6:1000b, 1022a-b
        Proust's *Remembrance of Things Past*
        and, 8:550b
        Sainte-Beuve on, 6:841b
        Sarraute on, 12:2334a
    Maupassant and, 7:1759b, 1760a–1762b,
        1763a-b, 1764a–1765a, 1766a, 1768b,
        1782b
    Memoirs of a Madman, 7:1374a
    Mérimée and, 6:760a
    on Montaigne, 2:787a
    on Musset, 6:1031a
    naturalism and, 7:1711b
    November, 7:1374a–1375b
    portrayal of French culture, 7:1400a-b
    Proust and, 8:545b, 554a
    Queneau and, 12:2512a, 2516a, 2528a
    Richter's *Siebenkäs* and, 5:68a
    "Saint Julian the Hospitaller," 7:1385a,
        1392b
    Sainte-Beuve on, 6:858a-b
    Salammbô, 6:808b, 7:1385a–1387a,
        11:1900b
        Marinetti and, 9:805a
    Sand and, 6:832b–833a
    Sarraute and, 12:2233b
    Sartre and, 12:2606b–2611a
    Strindberg and, 7:1753b
    Taine and, 7:1449a, 1452a
    The Temptation of Saint Anthony,
        7:1377b–1378b, 1385a
    Turgenev and, 6:1291a
    Un coeur simple, La Bruyère and, 3:256a
"Flauta en la noche, Una." *See* Azorín
Flea, The. *See* Zamyatin, Yevgeny Ivanovich,
    Blokha
Fleas; or, The Dance of Pain, The. *See*
    Wedekind, Frank, *Die Flöhe, oder der
    Schmerzenstanz*
Fléchier, Valentin, 3:163a
Fleeting Return. *See* Jiménez, Juan Ramón,
    "Retorno fugaz"
Flegeljahre. See Richter, Jean Paul
Fleita-pozvonochnik. See Mayakovsky,
    Vladimir
Flemish Peoples' Theater, Ghelderode and,
    11:2115a, 2116a, 2119b
Flesh and Blood. See Mauriac, François
Fletcher, John, *The Faithful Shepherdess*,
    Guarini's influence on, 2:920a
Fletcher, John, and Beaumont, Francis, *The
    Triumph of Death*, Bandello as source
    for, 2:943b
Fleurs bleues, Les. See Queneau, Raymond
Fleurs du mal, Les. See Baudelaire, Charles
Fleurville, Mathilde Mauté de, 7:1622a–1623a,
    1623b–1624a, 1638b
Fleury, Cardinal de, Voltaire and, 4:372b–373a

Fleury Play Book, 1:462a, 462b

Fleuve de feu, Le. See Mauriac, François, *The River of Fire*

Fleuve profond, sombre rivière. See Yourcenar, Marguerite

Fliegende Holländer, Der. See Wagner, Richard, *The Flying Dutchman*

Flies, as literary symbol, Machado and Sartre used, 9:753a-b

"Flies, The." *See* Machado, Antonio, *Soledades* (Solitudes), "Humorismos, fantasías, y apuntos"

Flies, The. See Sartre, Jean-Paul

Fliess, Wilhelm, Freud and, 8:3b, 9a, 10a-b, 15a

Flight from Worries. See Ady, Endre, "Futás a Gond elöl"

Flight of Icarus, The. See Queneau, Raymond, *Le vol d'Icare*

Flight into Darkness. See Schnitzler, Arthur, *Flucht in die Finsternis*

Flight of the Lindberghs, The. See Brecht, Bertolt, *Der Flug der Lindberghs*

Flight out of Time, The. See Arp, Jean, *Die Flucht aus der Zeit*

Flight, The. See Ionesco, Eugène, *La soif et la faim* (Hunger and Thirst), *La fuite*

Flight theme
in Ionesco's *A Stroll in the Air*, 13:3005a, 3005b
in Simenon's works, 12:2481b–2482a, 2495a–2496a

Flight to Arras. See Saint-Exupéry, Antoine de, *Pilote de guerre*

Fljótsdæla saga, 1:398b–399a

Flodoard, *Annales*, historical veracity of *Raoul de Cambrai* and, 1:108b

Flöhe, oder der Schmerzenstanz, Die. See Wedekind, Frank

Flokkr, 1:378b

Flood. See Grass, Günter

"Flood, The." *See* Zamyatin, Yevgeny Ivanovich

Flor de Mayo. See Blasco Ibáñez, Vicente, *The Mayflower*

Flor de santidad. See Valle-Inclán, Ramón del

Florbelle's Days; or, Nature Unveiled. See Sade, Donatien Alphonse François, marquis de

Flore, Jeanne, *Comptes amoureux*, 2:946b–947a

Florence
Alfieri's life in, 4:667a-b
politics and government
Dante and, 1:433b
Machiavelli and, 2:595a–596a

Florenskii, Pavel, *Stolp i utverzhdenie istiny* (Pillar and Ground of Truth), Mandelshtam and, 10:1630b, 1633a

Florentine History. See Machiavelli, Nicolò, *The History of Florence*

Florentinische Nächte (Florentine Nights). *See* Heine, Heinrich

Florian Geyer. See Hauptmann, Gerhart

Florian, Jean-Pierre de
Berlioz and, 6:773b, 775a
Estelle et Némorin, 6:773b, 775a

Florian's Wife. See Pirandello, Luigi, *Come prima, meglio di prima*

"Florville and Courval." *See* Sade, Donatien Alphonse François, marquis de, *The Crimes of Love*

Flounder, The. See Grass, Günter

Flower, Fruit, and Thorn Pieces. See Richter, Jean Paul, *Blumen-, Frucht- und Dornenstücke*

Flower imagery
in George's *Algabal*, 8:453a-b
in Valéry's "Narcisse parle," 8:571a
see also Lilacs

Flower Paintings. See Strindberg, August, *Blomstermålningar*

Flower of Sanctity. See Valle-Inclán, Ramón del, *Flor de santidad*

Flowers of Evil, The. See Baudelaire, Charles, *Les fleurs du mal*

Flowers of Good Will. See Laforgue, Jules, *Des fleurs de bonne volonté*

Flüchtlingsgespräche. See Brecht, Bertolt

Flucht aus der Zeit, Die. See Arp, Jean

Flucht in die Finsternis. See Schnitzler, Arthur

Flug der Lindberghs, Der. See Brecht, Bertolt

Fluids, motion of, in Montesquieu's thought, 3:348b–364a

"Flûte, La" (The Flute). *See* Vigny, Alfred Victor de, *Les destinées*

"Flute in the Night, A." *See* Azorín, "Una flauta en la noche"

Flying and airplane themes, of D'Annunzio, 8:187b–188a

Flying Dutchman, the, Heine and, 5:501a

Flying Dutchman, The. See Wagner, Richard

Flytings, 1:383a

Förrädarland. See Moberg, Vilhelm

"Fog." *See* Pascoli, Giovanni, "Nebbia"; Seferis, George

Fog imagery, in poetry of Pascoli, 7:1829b–1830b, 1840a

Foire d'empoigne, La. See Anouilh, Jean

Folengo, Teofilo, *Baldus,* Rabelais and, 2:698b

Folie amoureuse, in Chrétien's *Yvain,* 1:202b

Folie et déraison: Histoire de la folie à l'âge classique. See Foucault, Michel, *Madness and Civilization: A History of Insanity in the Age of Reason*

Folk drama, Schiller's *William Tell* as, 5:48b

"Folk Song." *See* Akhmatova, Anna

Folk song and folklore

Akhmatova's use of, 10:1527b–1528a

Andersen and, 6:878b–881a

antiquarianism and, 4:641b, 643b

in Basile's *Lo cunto de li cunti,* 2:945a

Belorussian, in Mickiewicz's *Dziady,* 5:611a-b

definitional issues, 4:642b–643a, 644b–645a

"folk song" ("Volkslied") coined by Herder, 4:641a

Frost on the folk sources of art, 4:648a

German, George and, 8:467a

Grillparzer's *Hero and Leander* and, 5:436b

Herder's study of, 4:641b–645a

American cultural pluralism and, 4:647a

idioms as the wellsprings of national language, 4:642b, 643b–644a

international implications of, 4:645a, 650a-b

opposition to, 4:644b

seminal powers of the peasantry, 4:642a-b, 643a, 643b

Hungarian, Ady and, 9:874a

Icelandic, in Laxness' novels, 12:2470b–2471b

Lermontov's use of, 6:1203a-b, 1204b

in Pushkin's works, 5:682b–685a

in Straparola's *Piacevoli notti,* 2:941b

Whitman's valuation of, 4:656a-b

see also Fairy tale

Folk Song U.S.A.. See Lomax, John and Alan

Folk superstition. *See* Superstition

Folktales

Calvino and, 13:3276a-b

Grass and, 13:3371a, 3380a–3382a

plot functions in, 1:58b

Folle de Chaillot, La. See Giraudoux, Jean

Folle journée ou le mariage de Figaro, La. See Beaumarchais, Pierre-Augustin Caron de

Follies of a Day or The Marriage of Figaro, The. See Beaumarchais, Pierre-Augustin Caron de, *La folle journée ou le mariage de Figaro*

Fonction fabulatrice, La (myth-making faculty), in Bergson's thought, 8:62b

Fond de la bouteille, Le. See Simenon, Georges

Fondat, Abel de Malartic de, Chénier's friendship with, 4:695a-b

"Fondazione e manifesto del futurism." *See* Marinetti, Filippo Tommaso, "The Futurist Manifesto"

Fontamara. See Silone, Ignazio

Fontane Prize, Hesse's *Demian* and, 9:841a

Fontane, Theodor, **6:1299a–1322b**

Archibald Douglas, 6:1305b–1306b

Buddenbrooks and, 9:716b, 717b

Cécile, 6:1311b

Der Stechlin (Lake Stechlin), 6:1319b

Die Likedeeler (The Sharers), 6:1319b

Die Poggenpuhls (*The Poggenpuhl Family*), 6:1319a

Effi Briest, 6:1316b–1319a

Ellernklipp, 6:1311b

Frau Jenny Treibel (*Jenny Treibel*), 6:1319a

Graf Petöfy (Count Petöfy), 6:1311b

Grete Minde, 6:1311b

Heinrich Mann's *Berlin* and, 8:523b

Fontane, Theodor (*cont.*)
Irrungen, Wirrungen (*A Suitable Match*),
6:1312b–1314a
L'Adultera (*The Woman Taken in Adultery*),
6:1311b
Mathilde Möhring, 6:1319a
on politics, 9:719b
Quitt, 6:1319a
Schach von Wuthenow (*A Man of Honor*),
6:1311b–1312b
Stine, 6:1319a
Unterm Birnbaum (Under the Pear Tree),
6:1311b
Unwiederbringlich (*Beyond Recall*),
6:1314a–1316b
Vor dem Sturm (Before the Storm),
6:1310b–1311b
Wanderungen durch die Mark Brandenburg
(Travels Through the March of
Brandenburg), 6:1308b–1309b
Fontane, Theodore, on Hauptmann, 8:149a,
153a
Fonte, Maria de, 11:2145b
Food imagery
Grass and, 13:3380a–3382a
in Queneau's works, 12:2514b–2515a
in Rabelais's works, 2:711b–713a
Fool in Christ, The: Emanuel Quint. *See*
Hauptmann, Gerhart, *Der Narr in
Christo Emanuel Quint*
Fool, the, in Grillparzer's *Der arme Speilmann*
(*The Poor Musician*), 5:440a
"fools say." *See* Sarraute, Nathalie, "disent les
imbéciles"
Footnotes, Richter's use of in fiction, 5:81a
"For an 'Homage to Rimbaud'." *See* Montale,
Eugenio, *The Storm and Other Things*
For a Butterfly. *See* Sartre, Jean-Paul, "Pour un
papillon"
For the first time I live worthily. *See* Walther
von der Vogelweide, "Allerêrst lebe ich
mir werde"
"For the Good of the Cause." *See* Solzhenitsyn,
Aleksandr, "Dlia pol'zy dela"
For Ink, Poet. *See* Claudel, Paul, *Pour encre,
poète*

For a New Novel. *See* Robbe-Grillet, Alain,
Pour un nouveau roman
For One Hour. *See* Schnitzler, Arthur, "Um
eine Stund"
"For the resonant valor." *See* Mandelshtam,
Osip, "Za gremuchuiu doblest . . ."
For a Secret Offense, a Secret Revenge. *See*
Calderón de la Barca, Pedro
For Self-Examination. *See* Kierkegaard, Søren
"For whatever animals dwell on earth." *See*
Petrarch, *Canzoniere*, "A qualunque
animale alberga in terra"
For Whom the Bell Tolls. *See* Hemingway,
Ernest
Force of Circumstance. *See* Beauvoir, Simone
de
Force de l'âge, La. *See* Beauvoir, Simone de,
The Prime of Life
Force des choses, La, *See* Beauvoir, Simone
de, *Force of Circumstance*
Ford, Onslow, automatism, 11:1949b
Fordringsägare. *See* Strindberg, August,
Creditors
Forefathers. *See* Mickiewicz, Adam, *Dziady*
Forefathers' Eve. *See* Mickiewicz, Adam
Foreign language study, advocated in La
Bruyère's *Caractères*, 3:254a
Foreign Woman, The. *See* Dumas fils,
Alexandre, *L'Étrangere*
Foreigners, theme of
in medieval satire, 1:344b, 350a-b
in satire of Juvenal, 1:350b
Foreshadowing (rhetorical device)
in Gottfried, 1:252a-b
in Norse sagas, 1:402a
Forest Maiden, The. *See* Khlebnikov, Velimir,
"Lesnaia deva"
Forest Solitude. *See* Tieck, Ludwig,
Waldeinsamkeit
"Forêt de noire." *See* Breton, André
"Forgeron, Le." *See* Rimbaud, Arthur, "The
Blacksmith"
Forget, Joséphine de, Delacroix and, 5:521a-b,
534a
Forgetfulness, theme of, in Machado's
"Parergon," 9:760a

Forgetting, theme of, Kundera and, 13:3396b, 3404b–3407a

"Förhoppning." *See* Södergran, Edith

Form
in Arp, 10:1382b–1383a
Gombrowicz and, 12:2568a–2569a, 2579a–2580b
reality and, Musil and, 9:955b

Form, poetic. *See* Poetic form

"Formica argentina, La." *See* Calvino, Italo, "The Argentine Ant"

Formist Theater, Witkiewicz and, 10:1227b–1228a

Formists, Polish, Witkiewicz and, 10:1214a

Forms of Art, The. *See* Bely, Andrey, "Formy iskusta"

Formula Missae et Communionis. See Luther, Martin

Formulaic diction
in *Beowulf*, 1:74b
in oral cultures, 1:56b, 67a

"Formy iskusta." *See* Bely, Andrey

Fornaldar saga, 1:397a, 397b, 398a, 400a, 400b

Forsber, Dea, 9:1018a

Forse che sì forse che no. See D'Annunzio, Gabriele

"Forse un mattino, andando in un'aria di vetro." *See* Montale, Eugenio, *Cuttlefish Bones*

Första varningen. See Strindberg, August

Forster, E. M., 13:3043a
Alexandria: A History and a Guide, 8:205a
Mouseion, 8:211b–212a
on Alexandrian Christianity, 8:216b
on Alexandrian philosophy, 8:215b
on Cavafy, 8:205a, 207b–208a
Jiménez and, 9:1007b
on Lampedusa's "The Blind Kittens," 11:2032b
on Nikos Kazantzakis, 9:1068a
Pharos and Pharillon, 8:205a, 207b–208a
Two Cheers for Democracy, 9:1007b

Forsyte Saga. See Galsworthy, John

Fort comme la mort. See Maupassant, Guy de

Fortællingen om Viga-Ljot og Vigdis. See Undset, Sigrid

Fortællinger om Kong Artur og ridderne av det runde bord. See Undset, Sigrid

Fortini, Pietro, *Novelle*, 2:944b

Fortunat (Fortunatus). *See* Tieck, Ludwig

Fortune
in Camoëns' *The Lusiads*, 2:764b
in Corneille's *Cinna*, 3:38a-b, 39b, 40b, 42b
false, in the *Nibelungenlied*, 1:227b

Fortune des Rougon, La (The Fortune of the Rougons). See Zola, Émile

Fortunes of the Bear from Hamagbúh, The. *See* Hašek, Jaroslav, "Osudy medvěda od Hamagbúha"

Fortunio. See Gautier, Théophile

45° in the Shade. *See* Simenon, Georges, *45° à l'ombre*

Forty-Five, The. See Dumas père, Alexandre, *Les quarante-cinq*

Forum, Krleža and, 11:1828b

Forza del destino, La. See Verdi, Giuseppe

Foscolo, Ugo, **5:313a–341b**
"A Luigia Pallavicini," 5:328b–329a
Ajace (Ajax), 5:315b
"Alla sera," 5:327b–328a
"All'amica risanata," 5:329b–330b
Bonaparte liberatore (Bonaparte the Liberator), 5:314a-b
"Dei sepolcri," 5:331a–335b
Dell'origine e dell'ufficio della letteratura (On the Origin and Function of Literature), 5:315b
"In morte del fratello Giovanni," 5:327a-b
La chioma di Berenice (The Lock of Berenice), 5:315a
"Laura, lettere" ("Laura, Letters"), 5:319b–320a
"Le Grazie," 5:335b–338a
Notizia intorno a Didimo chierico (Note on Didymus the Cleric), 5:324b–325a
Poesie, 5:326a
Ricciarda, 5:315b
Tieste (Thyestes), 5:313b–314a
Ultime lettere di Jacopo Ortis (Last Letters of Jacopo Ortis), 5:314a-b, 318b–324a
veneration of Alfieri by, 4:687b

Fóstbrœðra saga, 1:385a-b

Foucault, Michel, 12:2715b, **13:3323a–3364b**

Foucault, Michel (*cont.*)
  on "author-function," 9:803a
  biographical criticism and, 6:842b
  Discipline and Punish (*Surveiller et punir*),
    13:3356b–3359a
  Gombrowicz and, 12:2570a
  *Madness and Civilization: A History of
    Insanity in the Age of Reason* (*Folie et
    déraison: Histoire de la folie à l'âge
    classique*, 13:3330b, 3335a–3338b
  Mental Illness and Psychology (*Maladie
    mentale et personnalité*), 13:3330b
  "Nietzsche, Marx, Freud," 13:3342b
  The Archaeology of Knowledge
    (*L'Archaeologie du savoir*),
    13:3345b–3346a
  The Birth of the Clinic (*La naissance de la
    clinique*), 13:3338b–3340a
  The Discourse on Language (*L'Ordre du
    discours*), 13:3341b–3342a
  The History of Sexuality (*Histoire de la
    sexualité*), 13:3359a–3361a
  The Order of Things (*Les mots et les
    choses*), 13:3350b–3355b
  "What Is an Author?" ("Qu'est-ce qu'un
    auteur"), 13:3327a
Foucher, Paul, Musset and, 6:1002b
Foules de Lourdes, Les. See Huysmans, Joris
  Karl
Foundation of the Nineteenth Century. See
  Chamberlain, Houston Stewart
*Foundations of Faith Established Against the
  Saracens, Greeks, and Armenians, The.
  See* Aquinas, Thomas, St., *De rationibus
  fidei contra Saracenos Graecos et
  Armenos ad cantorem Antiochiae*
"Founding and Manifesto of Futurism, The."
  See Marinetti, Filippo Tommaso, "The
  Futurist Manifesto"
Founding of Prague, The. See Brentano,
  Clemens, *Die Gründung Prags*
Fountain of Bakhchisaray, The. See Pushkin,
  Alexander
Fountain of Gold, The. See Pérez Galdós,
  Benito, *La fontana de oro*
Fountain symbolism
  allegory and, 1:324b–326a

  in poetry of Laforgue, 7:1903b
Fountain, The. *See* Machado, Antonio,
  Soledades (Solitudes), "La fuente"
Fouqué, Friedrich, Richter's *Walt and Vult*
  and, 5:77a
Fouquet, Nicolas, 3:75a, 75b, 76a
Four Books of the Sentences, The. See Peter
  Lombard, *Sententiae in IV libris
  distinctae*
Four Buttons Two Holes Four Brooms. *See*
  Arp, Jean, "Vier Knöpfe zwei Löcher vier
  Besen"
Four Dialogues for Scholars. See Petrarch, *De
  remediis utriusque fortunae*
Four Epochs of Growth. See Tolstoy, Leo
"Four Horsemen." *See* Jouve, Pierre Jean, "Les
  quatre cavaliers"
Four Horsemen of the Apocalypse, The. See
  Blasco Ibáñez, Vicente, *Los cuatro
  jinetes del Apocalipsis*
Four Quartets, The. See Eliot, T. S.
Four Strangers, The. *See* Johnson, Eyvind, *De
  fyra främlingarna*
Four Truths, The. *See* Aymé, Marcel, *Les
  quatre vérités*
Fourfold False Bottom. *See* Butor, Michel,
  Quadruple fond
Fourier, Charles
  Breton and, 11:1947b
  Leconte de Lisle and, 6:1249a–1250b
  Rimbaud and, 7:1811a
"Foursome." *See* Montale, Eugenio, *Altri versi
  e poesie disperse*, "Quartetto"
Fourteen Consolations. See Luther, Martin
Fourteen (numeral), Elytis and, 13:2972b,
  2973b
Fourth Book. See Rabelais, François
Fourth Dimension, The. See Ritsos, Yannis,
  Tetarti dhiastasi
Fourth Prose. See Mandelshtam, Osip
Fourth Writers Congress (Czechoslovakia),
  Kundera and, 13:3393b
Fox and the Camellias, The. See Silone,
  Ignazio, *La volpe e le camelie*
Fra det moderne Amerikas Aandsliv. See
  Hamsun, Knut

"Fra det ubevidste sjæleliv." *See* Hamsun, Knut

Fra Norges ældre jernalder. See Undset, Ingvald

Fradique Mendes, Carlos, 7:1686b, 1693a

"Fragment." *See* Södergran, Edith

"Fragment of an Analysis of a Case of Hysteria." *See* Freud, Sigmund, "Bruchstück einer Hysterie-Analyse"

"Fragment of Autobiography: About My Novels, A." *See* Moravia, Alberto

"Fragment de l'Essai sur les causes et les effets de la perfection et de la décadence des lettres et des arts, Un." *See* Chénier, André, *Essay on the Causes and Effects of Perfection and Decadence in Arts and Letters*

Fragment of a Play. *See* Claudel, Paul, *Morceau d'un drame*

Fragmenti. See Krleža, Miroslav

"Fragmentos de un diario" ("Fragments of a Diary"). *See* Azorín

Fragmentos, Os. See Ferreira de Castro, José Maria

Fragments. See Oskolki (magazine)

"Fragments du Narcisse" ("Fragments of Narcissus"). *See* Valéry, Paul

Fragments d'un Combat (Fragments of a Combat). *See* Camus, Albert

Fragments d'un discours amoureux. See Barthes, Roland, *A Lover's Discourse: Fragments*

Fragments of a Journal. See Ionesco, Eugène, *Journal en miettes*

Fragments in the Vernacular. *See* Petrarch, *Canzoniere*

Fragola e panna. See Ginzburg, Natalia

Fragonard, Jean Honoré, in Goncourts' *L'Art du dix-huitième siècle*, 7:1397a

Frame analysis. See Goffman, Erving

Frame story
of Chekhov, 7:1871b–1872a
influence of Eastern literature on, 2:932a
Renaissance short fiction, 2:928b, 929a
see also Boxed tales

Framtidens skugga. See Södergran, Edith

France
art
David and, 5:531b
Delacroix on, 5:531a–532a
neoclassicists vs. colorists, 7:1408b
Prix de Rome, 7:1409a
Bergson in, 8:45b–46b
Brecht's influence in, 11:2089b
civil war (1562), 2:737b
culture
Babel and, 11:1900a
Portugal and, 11:2147b
culture of, Flaubert and, 7:1373a, 1387b–1388a
drama
langue littéraire parlée, 7:1415b
naturalist theater, 7:1443b
"well-made play," Ibsen's use of, 7:1430a
in Dumas's historical novels, 6:726a–728a
Heine's attitude toward, 5:499b–500b
Hugo's political career in, 6:704b–705b
literature, du Bellay's *Défense et illustration* on, 2:725a-b
in Michelet's view, 5:574b, 577a, 584b–585b, 590a, 594a-b
destiny of, 5:590a
Introduction to Universal History, 5:584b–584a
as *mère patrie*, 5:597a
nineteenth-century, 7:1568b–1569a, 1785b–1786a, 1909a
Baudelaire and, 7:1342b–1346b
politics
Sand and, 6:831b
Tocqueville and, 6:899b–900b
as portrayed by La Bruyère, 3:232a-b
provincial life, Mauriac on, 10:1315a–1316a
regency under Philippe d'Orléans, 3:334a-b, 335a-b, 337a
religious thought in, Bergson and, 8:64a-b
Revolution of 1848
Heine and, 5:507a
Michelet and, 5:595a, 598a, 600a, 601a
Revolution of July 1830
Büchner and, 6:1171a-b
Dumas and, 6:721b
French romantic historiography and, 5:572b

France (*cont.*)
  Revolution of July 1830 (*cont.*)
    and Heine, 5:498a-b
    Louis Blanc and, 5:585b–586a
    Michelet and, 5:585a-b, 586a, 587a
    Sand and, 6:818b
    Vigny's response to, 5:463a-b, 469b
  Second Empire, 7:1415b, 1568b, 1917a
    French historiography and, 5:573a
    Michelet and, 5:600b
    Zola's *Les Rougon-Macquart* series,
      7:1522a-b, 1523b–1536a, 1607a
  under Francis I, 2:736a
  under Louis XIII, La Rochefoucauld and,
    3:54a–58a
  Vichy government, in Anouilh's plays,
    13:2850b–2851a
  Wagner on, 7:1656b
  Weil and, 12:2800a-b, 2806b, 2807a-b
  see also Franco-Prussian War of 1870;
      French language; French Resistance;
      French Revolution of 1789; July
      Monarchy; Politics, French
France, Anatole
  beginnings of surrealism and, 11:2066b
  Joan of Arc and, 8:488a
  Machado and, 9:744b
  Proust and, 8:546b
  on Sainte-Beuve, 6:839b
  Thaïs, Montale's "Nubi color magenta" and,
    11:2002b
  Valéry and, 8:584a
  Verlaine and, 7:1620b
France sentimentale, La. See Giraudoux, Jean
Frances, Esteban, automatism, 11:1949b
Francesca da Rimini, in Dante's *Inferno*,
    1:435b
Francesca da Rimini. See D'Annunzio,
    Gabriele
"Francesismo, O." *See* Eça de Queiroz, José
    Maria
Franciade. See Ronsard, Pierre de
Françillon. See Dumas fils, Alexandre
Francis of Assisi, St., Pasternak's *My Sister,
    Life* and, 10:1599a
Francis, Eve, 8:487b
Francis I of France, king

art patronage, 2:539a
poetry, Petrarchan influence, 2:504a
reign of, 2:694a-b
religious dissent and, 2:697a
Revolution of 1550 and, 2:721a
Valois-Hapsburg rivalry and, 2:736a
Franciscans
  in Paris, 1:409b
  Rabelais and, 2:695b
  Spiritual, Ockham and, 1:427a
Franco, Francisco, 9:595b, 747a
  Claudel and, 8:488b
  Ortega y Gasset and, 9:1148a-b
Franco-Prussian War of 1870, 7:1465a
  Bismarck during, 7:1655a
  Dumas fils on, 7:1917a
  French politics and the, 7:1568b–1569a
  Huysmans during, 7:1711a
  in literature, 7:1535a–1536a
  Mallarmé during, 7:1568b–1569a
  Maupassant and, 7:1760b, 1763b, 1770a-b,
    1773b–1774a
  Meyer and, 6:932a–933a
  Nietzsche during, 7:1655a-b
  Rimbaud and, 7:1785a, 1788b
  Verlaine during, 7:1622b
  Zola and, 7:1523b
    La débâcle, 7:1534a, 1535a–1535a
Franco-Russian Pact (1935), Perse and,
    10:1441a
François the Waif (François le champi). See
    Sand, George
Francophilia. *See* Eça de Queiroz, José Maria,
    "O francesismo"
Francouzská poesie nové doby. See Čapek,
    Karel
Francs-Juges. See Berlioz, Hector
"Frangia dei capelli . . . , La." *See* Montale,
    Eugenio, *The Storm and Other Things*
Frank, Joseph, *The Widening Gyre*, and
    Lessing, 4:545b
Frank V. See Dürrenmatt, Friedrich
"Franken." *See* George, Stefan
Frankfurt *Dirigierrolle* (theater prompt copy),
    1:452a
Frankfurt Lectures. *See* Böll, Heinrich,
    "Frankfurter Vorlesungen"

Frankfurt Passion plays, 1:466b

"Frankfurt Plan." *See* Hölderlin, Friedrich, "Der Tod des Empedokles"

"Frankfurter Vorlesungen." *See* Böll, Heinrich

Frankish Lands. *See* George, Stefan, "Franken"

Franz Sternbalds Wanderungen (Franz Sternbald's Travels). *See* Tieck, Ludwig

Franziska: Ein Modernes Mysterium in fünf Akten (Franziska: A Modern Mystery Play in Five Acts). *See* Wedekind, Frank

Französische Maler. See Heine, Heinrich

Französische Zustände. See Heine, Heinrich

Frappatore, Il. See Goldoni, Carlo

"Fratelli." *See* Ungaretti, Giuseppe, *Allegria di naufragi*

Fratricides, The. See Kazantzakis, Nikos, *I aderfofádes*

Frau Beate und ihr Sohn. See Schnitzler, Arthur

Frau Berta Garlan. See Schnitzler, Arthur

Frau im Fenster, Die. See Hofmannsthal, Hugo von

Frau Jenny Treibel. See Fontane, Theodor

"Frau mit dem Dolche, Die." *See* Schnitzler, Arthur

Frau ohne Schatten, Die. See Hofmannsthal, Hugo von

Frau Regel Amrain und ihr Jüngster. See Keller, Gottfried, *Regula Amrain and Her Youngest Son*

Fraud in literature
   of Kafka, 9:1173b–1174a
   "Ossianic" poetry of Macpherson, 4:648b

Frauen vor Flusslandschaft. See Böll, Heinrich, *Women in a River Landscape*

"Frauenlob." *See* George, Stefan, *Die Bücher der Hirten- und Preisgedichte . . . (The Books of Eclogues and Eulogies), Sagen und Sänge*

Fräulein Else. See Schnitzler, Arthur

Frazer, James, *The Golden Bough*, Nerval's anticipation of, 6:961a

Frederick V of Denmark, king, Klopstock and, 4:514a-b

Frederick VII of Denmark, king, in Fontane's *Beyond Recall*, 6:1316a-b

Frederick II of Prussia, king
   Alfieri's antagonism toward, 4:664a
   Anti Machiavel, 4:374a
   Lessing and, 4:537a, 538b
   Voltaire and, 4:373b–374a, 375a–376b, 377b, 390b

Frederick Barbarossa, in "Salve mundi domine, Cesar noster ave," 1:371a

Frederick of Thuringia, as playgoer, 1:462a

Frederick William III of Prussia, king, Richter and, 5:79a

Free America. See Alfieri, Vittorio

Free association
   in Apollinaire's poetry, 9:888a-b
   Freud's use of, 8:4a, 7a-b
   in Musil's *The Man Without Qualities*, 9:946b

Free Game. See Schnitzler, Arthur

Free indirect speech, in Musil's *The Man Without Qualities*, 9:940b

Free Institution of Teaching (Madrid), 9:743b–744a

Free Philosophical Association (Moscow), Bely and, 9:924a

Free Stage Society (Germany), 8:149a-b

Free thought, discussed in La Bruyère's *Caractères*, 3:255b–256a

"Free Thoughts." *See* Blok, Alexander, "Vol'nye mysli"

Free verse
   Berlioz' use of, 6:792b
   George on, 8:450b
   of Jiménez, 9:999a
   in La Fontaine's *Fables*, 3:81b
   Laforgue and, 7:1897b–1899a
   Maeterlinck and, 8:123b
   Marinetti and, 9:798b, 805b–806a, 815b
   Rimbaud's use of, 7:1787a, 1808b, 1897b
   Trakl and, 10:1417a–1418b

Free will
   Aquinas' *Summa theologica* on, 1:422b
   Augustine on, 1:26b
   Bergson's view of, 8:51b–52a, 55a
   in Croce's *Filosofia della pratica*, 8:322a-b
   Erasmus on, 2:587a-b
   Luther on, 2:685b
   Machiavelli on, 2:605a
   in Prudentius, 1:16a

Free-word style, 9:814b–820b
   aereopoesia and, 9:827a, 827b
   Apollinaire and, 9:897a, 898b
   of Marinetti, 9:798b–799a, 803a
Freedman, Ralph, on Hesse, 9:843a
Freedom
   Broch and, 10:1387b
   in Butor, 13:3311a
   in Camus, 13:3073b
   Cela and, 13:3112a-b
   in Dinesen, 10:1296b–1297a
   Genet and, 13:2889b, 2891b
   Kierkegaard and, 6:1139b
   Moberg and, 11:2204b, 2223a, 2224b,
      2227b–2229b
   Sade's libertinism and, 4:625b, 635b
   Sartre and, 12:2589a–2691a, 2595a–2596a,
      2606a–2609a
   in Vigny's "Les destinées," 5:481a
Freedom Booklet. *See* Richter, Jean Paul,
   Freiheitsbüchlein
Freedom of a Christian Man. See Luther,
   Martin
Freedom or Death. See Kazantzakis, Nikos, *O
   Kapetán Mihális*
Freedom of the press
   Tocqueville on, 6:896a
   see also Censorship
Freemasonry
   acmeist Guild of Poets and, 10:1635a
   Ady and, 9:859b
Freethinker, The. See Strindberg, August, *Den
   Fredlöse*
Freethinkers
   Bossuet and, 3:172a
   in La Bruyère's *Caractères*, 3:254b–257b
Fregat "Pallada". See Goncharov, Ivan, *The
   Frigate Pallas*
Fregoso, Ottaviano, in Castiglione,
   2:656b–657b, 660b–661b
Freiheitsbüchlein. See Richter, Jean Paul
Freiwild. See Schnitzler, Arthur, *Free Game*
"Fremde, Die." *See* Schnitzler, Arthur
French language
   Bellay on, 6:1033b
   Bonnefoy on, 6:1033b
   dialects of trouvères, 1:178b

   du Bellay's *Défense et illustration* on,
      2:725a, 732a
   early vernacular poetry, 2:538b
   in fiction of Heinrich Mann, 8:540a
   Gautier and
      "Anglo-Saxonizing" of, 6:1036a
      continuity of, 6:1046a
      criticism of, 6:1033a
      impact on, 6:1059a
      syntax, 6:1035b, 1046b
      vocabulary, 6:1035b
   Hugo and, 6:1033b, 1035a-b
   Musset and, 6:999a
   Queneau's research on, 12:2516b–2517a
   Racine and, 6:1033b
   Ungaretti and, 10:1455a-b
French Painters. See Heine, Heinrich,
   Französische Maler
French Painting of the Eighteenth Century. See
   Goncourt, Edmond Louis Antoine and
   Jules Alfred Huot de, *L'Art du
   dix-huitième siècle*
French Poetry of the New Era. See Čapek,
   Karel, *Francouzská poesie nové doby*
*French Realism: The Critical Reaction
   1830–1870. See* Weinberg, Bernard
French Resistance
   Aragon and, 11:2078a–2081a
   Mauriac and, 10:1307b–1308a
   Perse and, 10:1443b
French Reveille. See Aragon, Louis, *La diane
   française*
French Revolution of 1789, 7:1373a, 1465a
   Alfieri's reaction to, 4:666b–667a, 675a-b
   Beaumarchais and, 4:583b–584a
   Büchner and, 6:1169a–1171a
   Chateaubriand and, 5:116a-b, 122a
   Chénier's role during, 4:694a, 700b–705a
   Dumas and, 6:720a
   historiography and, 5:571b–572a
   Hölderlin and, 5:145a, 145b
   Laclos and, 4:401a
   in Michelet's and Louis Blanc's histories,
      5:591a-b
   Nerval on, 6:968b
   Novalis and, 5:215a
   Rimbaud and, 7:1790b

Rousseau and, 4:471a

Schiller and, 5:37a-b

Schnitzler's treatment of, 8:97a

Staël and, 5:91b–92a, 98a-b

in Taine's *Les origines de la France contemporaine*, 7:1465b–1467a

Tocqueville on, 6:905b–909a

Vigny's *Chatterton* on, 5:470b–471a

Wieland and, 4:610b

see also Reign of Terror

Frenzy for Two. See Ionesco, Eugène, *Délire à deux*

Frères Rico, Les. See Simenon, Georges

Frères Zemganno, Les. See Goncourt, Edmond Louis Antoine de

Freud, Anna, Freud and, 8:15b

Freud, Sigmund, **8:1a–20b**

A General Introduction to Psychoanalysis, in Montherlant's *Un assassin est mon maître*, 11:1929b–1930a

Ady and, 9:859b

"Analyse der Phobie eines fünfjährigen Knaben" ("Analysis of a Phobia of a Five-Year-Old Boy"), 8:16a

Andreas-Salomé and, 9:769b

anticipated by Sade, 4:621b

Apollinaire and, 9:884b

Augustine and, 1:41a

"Aus der Geschichte einer infantilen Neurose" ("From the History of an Infantile Neurosis"), 8:17b–18b

"Bemerkungen uber einen Fall von Zwangsneurose" ("Notes upon a Case of Obsessional Neurosis"), 8:16b–17b

Beyond the Pleasure Principle (*Jenseits des Lustprinzips*), 8:14a–16a

Briefe an Wilhelm Fliess, 8:10a

"Bruchstück einer Hysterie-Analyse" ("Fragment of an Analysis of a Case of Hysteria"), 8:4a, 16a

Butor and, 13:3289a

Čapek and, 10:1583a

Civilization and Its Discontents, 8:84b, 11:2206a

Das Ich und das Es (*The Ego and the Id*), 8:4b

"Das Motiv der Kästchenwahl" ("The Theme of Three Caskets"), 8:15b

Der Witz und seine Beziehung zum Unbewussten (*Jokes and Their Relation to the Unconscious*), 8:4a

"Die Widerstände gegen die Psychoanalyse" ("Resistances to Psychoanalysis"), 8:2a

"Die zukünftigen Chancen der psychoanalytischen Therapie" ("The Future Prospects of Psychoanalytic Therapy"), 8:7b

Drei Abhandlungen zur Sexualtheorie (*Three Essays on the Theory of Sexuality*), 8:4a

Gesammelte Werke, 8:9b, 12b–13a, 15b, 17b

Gombrowicz and, 12:2567b

Hemmung, Symptom und Angst (*Inhibitions, Symptoms and Anxiety*), 8:4b

Hesse and, 9:839a

on Ibsen's *Rosmersholm*, 7:1435a

Mann and, 9:721b, 728b, 737b

Marinetti and, 9:798b

Moberg and, 11:2206a, 2214a

Neue Folge der Vorlesungen zur Einführung in die Psychoanalyse (*New Introductory Lectures on Psycho-Analysis*), 8:4b

Nietzsche and, 7:1678a

"Our Attitude Towards Death," 13:3255b–3256a

Proust and, 8:558a

relevance of, 8:1a-b, 18b

Rilke and, 9:772a

Sartre and, 12:2595a-b

Schnitzler and, 8:89a, 112a

Spanish translations, 9:1119b

surrealism and, 11:2064b, 13:2958a

Svevo and, 8:72a, 79b–80a, 84b

Symposium and, 8:14a

The Interpretation of Dreams (*Die Traumdeutung*), 8:3b–4a, 9a–12a

Kafka and, 9:1157a

theory of infantile sexuality, Sade and, 4:624a

Totem and Taboo (*Totem und Tabu*), 8:12a–13a, 84b

Weil and, 12:2806a

Freud, Sigmund (*cont.*)
  "Weitere Bemerkungen über die
    Abwehrneuropsychosen" ("Further
    Remarks on the Neuropsychoses of
    Defence"), 8:6a
  Witkiewicz and, 10:1211b
  "Zur Dynamik der Übertragung" ("The
    Dynamics of Transference"), 8:7b–8a
  Zur Psychopathologie des Alltagslebens
    (*The Psychopathology of Everyday Life*),
    8:4a
Freud, Sigmund, and Breuer, Joseph, *Studien
    über Hysterie* (*Studies in Hysteria*), 8:3a
Frey Lope Félix de Vega Carpio. *See* Lope de
    Vega
Freytag, Gustav, 7:1927a
  Die Journalisten (*The Journalists*), 7:1926a
  Die Technik des Dramas (*The Technique of
    the Drama*), 7:1926a
Friar, Kimon, 13:2968a, 2973b, 2975a
  on Cavafy's *Waiting for the Barbarians*,
    8:222a-b
  on Seferis, 12:2255a, 2262a
"Frida." See Hamsun, Knut
Friday Circle, 10:1567a-b
Friðþjófs saga, 1:398a, 401a-b
Fried, Erich, Rilke and, 9:789b
Friedemann, Käte, on the novel, 9:1138a
"Friedensfeier." *See* Hölderlin, Friedrich
Friedensfest, Das. See Hauptmann, Gerhart
Friedman, Albert, racism attributed to Herder
    by, 4:641a
Friedrich, Caspar David, 5:76b
*Friedrich Hölderlins Leben, Dichtung und
    Wahnsinn. See* Waiblinger, Wilhelm
Friedrichshagen Circle, principles, 8:235b
Friend of the Family, The. See Dostoevsky,
    Feodor
Friend Manso, My. See Pérez Galdós, Benito,
    El amigo Manso
Friendly America. *See* Giraudoux, Jean, *Amica
    America*
Friends. *See* Verlaine, Paul, *Les amies*
Friend's Funeral, A. *See* Tychyna, Pavlo,
    Pokhoron druha

"Friends, I cannot change." *See* William IX of
    Aquitaine, duke, "Compaigno, no puosc
    mudar"
Friendship
  Augustine on, 1:29b–30a
  in Dumas's works, 6:728a–731a
  Gogol and, 6:977a
  in Ionesco's *Rhinocéros*, 13:3002b
  in Klopstock, 4:519b, 527b–528a
  in La Bruyère's *Caractères*, 3:238b–239b
  in Michelet's works, 5:578a
  in Rousseau, 4:467b
"Friendship of the Prince." *See* Perse,
    Saint-John
Frigate Pallas, The. See Goncharov, Ivan
Frisch, Max, **13:2895a–2924b**
  Andorra: A Play in Twelve Scenes (*Andorra:
    Stück in zwölf Bildern*), 13:2906b,
    2910a–2912a, 2912b
  Antwort aus der Stille (Answer from the
    Silence), 13:2898a
  Bin; oder, Die Reise nach Peking (Bin; or,
    The Trip to Peking), 13:2899b
  Biography: A Game (*Biografie: Ein Spiel*),
    13:2907a, 2912b, 2916b–2918a, 2919a-b
  Blätter aus dem Brotsack (Leaves from the
    Knapsack), 13:2899a
  Bluebeard: A Tale (*Blaubart: Eine
    Erzählung*), 13:2921a–2922a
  Die grosse Wut des Philipp Hotz (The Great
    Rage of Philipp Hotz), 13:2905a, 2923b
  Dienstbüchlein (Service Booklet), 13:2899a,
    2918a, 2919b
  Don Juan; oder, Die Liebe zur Geometrie
    (Don Juan; or, The Love of Geometry),
    13:2905b–2906a, 2912a, 2923b
  on *Erlebnis* and *Erfahrung*, 13:2914a-b
  Graf Öderland (Count Öderland),
    13:2903a–2904a, 2912a, 2922a
  Homo faber: A Report (*Homo faber: Ein
    Bericht*), 13:2906b, 2909a–2910a, 2918a,
    2920a, 2922a
  "Ich schreibe für Leser: Antworten auf
    vorgestellte Fragen" (I Write for
    Readers: Answers to Imagined
    Questions), 13:2914b–2915a

J'adore ce qui me brûle; oder, Die Schwierigen (I Adore Whatever Sets Me Afire: or, The Difficult Ones), 13:2899b

Jürg Reinhart: Eine sommerliche Schicksalsfahrt (*Jürg Reinhart: A Fateful Trip in the Summer*), 13:2896b–2897a, 2898a

"Kultur als Alibi" ("Culture as an Alibi"), 13:2898b

Man in the Holocene (*Der Mensch erscheint im Holozän*), 13:2919b–2921a, 2922a

Mein Name sei Gantenbein (translated as *A Wilderness of Mirrors* and *Gantenbein*), 13:2907a, 2912a-b, 2914a–2916b, 2917b–2918a, 2922a, 2923b

"Mimische Partitur?" (Mimic Score?), 13:2897b

Montauk, 13:2895a-b, 2897a, 2918a-b, 2919b, 2924b

Now They Sing Again: Attempt at a Requiem (*Nun singen sie wieder: Versuch eines Requiems*), 13:2900b–2901a, 2918b

Santa Cruz: Eine Romanze (Santa Cruz: A Romance), 13:2900a-b

"Schillerpreis-Rede" (Talk on Receiving the Schiller-Prize), 13:2916a

Sketchbook 1946–1949 (*Tagebuch 1946–1949*), 13:2911a

Sketchbook 1966–1971 (*Tagebuch 1966–1971*), 13:2895b, 2900a, 2901b–2902a, 2918a

Stiller (*I'm Not Stiller*), 13:2902a, 2906b–2907a, 2910a, 2913b, 2922a, 2923b

Tagebuch mit Marion, 13:2901b–2902a, 2911a

The Chinese Wall (*Die chinesische Mauer*), 13:2901a-b, 2902b, 2918a

The Firebugs (*Biedermann und die Brandstifter*), 13:2904a–2905b, 2906b, 2910b, 2911a, 2911b

Triptych: Three Scenic Panels (*Triptychon: Drei szenische Bilder*), 13:2918b–2919b

"Unsere Gier nach Geschichten" (Our Greed for Stories), 13:2913a–2914a

"Vom Umgang mit dem Einfall" (Dealing with Inspiration), 13:2913a

When the War Was Over (*Als der Krieg zu Ende war*), 13:2902a–2903a, 2908a, 2912b

Wilhelm Tell: A School Text (*Wilhelm Tell für die Schule*), 13:2905b, 2918a

Zürich-Transit: Skizze eines Films, 13:2912b, 2916b

Fritz Schwigerling. See Wedekind, Frank, *Der Liebestrank*

Frivolous Prince, The. See Cocteau, Jean, *Le prince frivole*

Frjesång. See Ekelöf, Gunnar

"Frô Welt." *See* Walther von der Vogelweide

Froben, Johann, Erasmus and, 2:580a-b

"Frog and the Rat, The." *See* La Fontaine, Jean de, *Fables*, "La grenouille et le rat"

"Frog Who Wants to Make Herself as Big as the Ox, The." *See* La Fontaine, Jean de, *Fables*, "La grenouille qui se veut faire aussi grosse que le boeuf"

"Frogs, The." *See* Pascoli, Giovanni, "Il ritorno a San Mauro," "Le rane"

"Frogs Who Ask for a King, The." *See* La Fontaine, Jean de, *Fables*, "Les grenouilles qui demandent un roi"

Fröhlich, Katharina, Grillparzer and, 5:419a, 421a

"Fröhlich Leben, Das." *See* Hölderlin, Friedrich

Fröhliche Wissenschaft, Die. See Nietzsche, Friedrich, *The Gay Science*; Södergran, Edith

Fröken Julie. See Strindberg, August, *Miss Julie*

From an Apocryphal Songbook. *See* Machado, Antonio, *De un cancionero apócrifo*

From the Brook Ér to the Ocean. *See* Ady, Endre, "Az értől az oceanig"

From a Catholic Point of View. *See* Laxness, Halldór, *Kaþólsk viðhorf*

From the Cradle to the Grave. *See* Kosztolányi, Dezső, *Bölcsőtől a koporsóig*

From the Diary of a Snail. See Grass, Günter

"From Dostoevsky to Kafka." *See* Sarraute, Nathalie, *L'Ère du soupçon*

"From the History of an Infantile Neurosis."
See Freud, Sigmund, "Aus der
Geschichte einer infantilen Neurose"

From the Last Bend in the Road. See Baroja,
Pío, Desde la última vuelta del camino

From Makronisos. See Ritsos, Yannis,
Makronisiotika

From Morn to Midnight. See Kaiser, Georg

From the Papers of One Still Living. See
Kierkegaard, Søren

From Provincial Places. See Giraudoux, Jean,
Provinciales

"From the School of the Renowned
Philosopher." See Cavafy, Constantine,
"Apo tin scholin tou perionymou
philosophou"

"From the Secret Notebook of Fellow Traveler
Zand." See Olesha, Yuri, "Koe-chto iz
sekretnykh zapisey poputchika Zanda"

From Six Books. See Akhmatova, Anna, Iz
shesti knig

From Street to Street. See Mayakovsky,
Vladimir, "Iz ulitsy v ulitsu"

"From a Swiss Lake." See Montale, Eugenio,
The Storm and Other Things

"From thought to thought, from mountain to
mountain." See Petrarch, "Di pensier in
pensier, di monte in monte"

From Two Books. See Tsvetaeva, Marina, Iz
dvukh knig

From the Unconscious Life of the Mind. See
Hamsun, Knut, "Fra det ubevidste
sjæleliv"

"From a Winnower of Corn to the Winds." See
Du Bellay, Joachim, Divers jeux
rustiques

Fronde of the Princes, 3:154b

Fronde, War of the, First (1649), 3:59b, 60a,
156a

Front Page, The. See Hecht, Ben; MacArthur,
Charles

"Front rouge." See Aragon, Louis

Frost, Robert
on folk sources of art, 4:648a
Jiménez and, 9:1004a

"Frouwe Mâze." See Walther von der
Vogelweide

Fru Inger til Østraat. See Ibsen, Henrik

Fruit symbolism, in Olesha's "Liompa,"
11:2243a

Fruit of the Vine, The. See Blasco Ibáñez,
Vicente, La bodega

Fruits d'or, Les. See Sarraute, Nathalie

Fruits of the Earth, The. See Gide, André

"Frülingswind, Ein." See Rilke, Rainer Maria

Fry, Christopher, A Phoenix Too Frequent,
3:95b

Frye, Northrop, on "Futurist Manifesto,"
9:809a

FSM expression, of Schlegel, 5:183b–184b

Ftohúlis tu Theú, O. See Kazantzakis, Nikos

Fu Mattia Pascal, Il. See Pirandello, Luigi,
The Late Mattia Pascal

"Fuente, La." See Machado, Antonio,
Soledades (Solitudes)

Fuente Ovejuna. See Lope de Vega

Fugitive, The (La Fugitive). See Proust,
Marcel, Remembrance of Things Past

Fuglane. See Vesaas, Tarjei, The Birds

Fuglinn í fjörunni. See Laxness, Halldór,
Salka Valka

Fuhrmann Henschel. See Hauptmann, Gerhart

Fuite de Monsieur Monde, La. See Simenon,
Georges

Fuite, La. See Ionesco, Eugène, La soif et la
faim

Fülep, Lukács and, 10:1264a

Fulfillment. See Moberg, Vilhelm

Fulton Theater (New York), Pirandello and,
8:394b

"Fumes" ("Il fumo"). See Pirandello, Luigi

Fundamentals of Language, The. See
Jakobson, Roman

Funeral orations
discussed in La Bruyère's Caractères, 3:254b
see also Bossuet, Jacques Bénigne

Funeral and Triumphal Symphony. See
Berlioz, Hector, Symphonie funèbre et
triomphale

Funerals, in Ekelöf's works, 12:2651b–2652a

"Fünf Gesänge." See Rilke, Rainer Maria

Fuoco, Il. See D'Annunzio, Gabriele, The
Flame of Life

"Für die Mouche." See Heine, Heinrich

Furcht und Elend des Dritten Reiches. See Brecht, Bertolt

Furetière, Antoine, 3:74a, 77b, 98b
  Dictionnaire universel, 3:97a
  Queneau and, 12:2528a

"Furit aestus." *See* D'Annunzio, Gabriele

Fürsorgliche Belagerung. See Böll, Heinrich, *The Safety Net*

Fürstin Russalka. See Wedekind, Frank

"Further Remarks on the Neuropsychoses of Defence." *See* Freud, Sigmund, "Weitere Bemerkungen über die Abwehrneuropsychosen"

"Füsse im Feuer, Die." *See* Meyer, Conrad Ferdinand

"Futás a Gond elöl." *See* Ady, Endre

"Future Beloved, The." *See* Klopstock, Friedrich Gottlieb

Future Is in Eggs, The. *See* Ionesco, Eugène, *L'Avenir est dans les oeufs*

"Future Prospects of Psychoanalytic Therapy, The." *See* Freud, Sigmund, "Die Zukünftigen Chancen der psychoanalytischen Therapie"

"Future, The." *See* Södergran, Edith, "Die Zukunft"

Futurism
  acmeism and, 10:1522b
  advocates of, 10:1486b
  Apollinaire and, 9:898b
  downfall of Petrine Russia and, 10:1620a-b
  Hylaean group and, 10:1334b–1335a, 1335b, 1337a
  Italian, three stages of, 9:799b–800a
  Khlebnikov's participation in, 10:1331a, 1334b–1335b, 1336a, 1344a–1345b, 1348a-b
  Khlebnikov's vision of history and, 10:1341b
  Mandelshtam's acmeism and, 10:1633a
  Marinetti and, 9:797a-b
  Montale and, 11:1987b–1988a
  Pasternak and, 10:1593a-b, 1603a
  Pessoa and, 10:1486a-b
  in the Soviet Union, 11:2070b, 2251a
  visual arts and, 10:1344b
  Witkiewicz and, 10:1222a-b
  see also Hylaea group; Liren' group; Mayakovsky, Vladimir

Futurismo e fascismo (Futurism and Fascism). See Marinetti, Filippo Tommaso

Futurist Antitradition, The. See Apollinaire, Guillaume, *L'Antitradition futuriste*

Futurist Manifesto of 1909, Pessoa and, 10:1486a

"Futurist Manifesto of Lust." *See* Saint-Point, Valentine de

"Futurist Manifesto, The." *See* Marinetti, Filippo Tommaso

Futurist Moment, The. See Perloff, Marjorie

"Futurist Synthetic Theater, The." *See* Marinetti, Filippo Tommaso, "Il teatro futurista sintetico"

Futuristi (literary school), 12:2389b

Fyra främlingarna, De. See Johnson, Eyvind

G

Gabinetto Vieusseux
    founding of, 5:547a
    Montale's employment at, 11:1990b–1991a
Gabrieliad, The. See Pushkin, Alexander
Gabrielle. See Augier, Émile
Gabrielle d'Estrée, in fiction of Heinrich
    Mann, 8:539a
Gace Brulé, as trouvère, 1:181a
Gadda, Carlo E., Vittorini and, 12:2755a
Gaea's Easter. See Pirandello, Luigi, *Pasqua di
    Gea*
Gaffney, James, on Silone's *Story of a Humble
    Christian*, 12:2300b
Gaguin, Robert, Erasmus and, 2:574a
"Galantuomini, I." *See* Verga, Giovanni
Galas del difunto, Las. See Valle-Inclán,
    Ramón del, *Martes de Carnaval*
"Galatea." *See* Petrarch
Galatea, La. See Cervantes, Miguel de
"Galerías." *See* Machado, Antonio, *Nuevas
    canciones* (New Songs) and *Soledades,
    galerías, y otros poemas* (Solitudes,
    Galleries, and Other Poems)
Galicia, in Valle-Inclán's drama, 8:347b–350a
Galicija (Galicia). *See* Krleža, Miroslav
Galigaï. See Mauriac, François, *The Loved and
    the Unloved*
Galilei, Galileo
    Descartes and, 3:1b–2a, 6a-b
    *Dialogue Concerning the Two Chief World
        Systems*, 3:6a
Galileo. See Brecht, Bertolt
Gallant Cassian. *See* Schnitzler, Arthur, "Der
    Tapfere Cassian"
Gallant Festival. *See* Verlaine, Paul, *Fêtes
    galantes*
Gallant Muses, The. *See* Rousseau, Jean
    Jacques, *Les muses galantes*
Gallergrinden. See Gripenberg
Galleries. *See* Machado, Antonio, *Nuevas
    canciones* (New Songs), "Galerías," and
    Soledades, galerías, y otros poemas
    (Solitudes, Galleries, and Other Poems),
    "Galerías"

Galliambic meter, in Blok's poetry, 9:984a
Gallic War. See Caesar, Gaius Julius
Gallican church, Bossuet and, 3:163b–164a,
    167b–168a
Gallimard, Gaston (publisher)
    Album de vers anciens, 1890-1920 and,
        8:576a
    Camus and, 13:3053b
    Sartre and, 12:2600b–2601a
Gallophobe. See Alfieri, Vittorio
Galsworthy, John
    Forsyte Saga, history of family in novel and,
        10:1500a-b
    Justice, 7:1443b
    Strife, 7:1443b
Gama, Vasco da, in Camoëns' *The Lusiads*,
    2:760a–761a, 762a-b, 764a
Gambler, The. See Dostoevsky, Feodor
Gambling, in Schnitzler's works, 8:110a-b
"Game of Backgammon, The." *See* Mérimée,
    Prosper
Gamla riket, Det. See Moberg, Vilhelm
Gand zum Weiher, Der. See Schnitzler, Arthur
Gandalin. See Wieland, Christoph Martin
Gandellini, Francesco Gori
    eulogized in Alfieri's "Virtue Unknown,"
        4:675b–676a
    friendship with Alfieri, 4:665b, 669a
Gandhi, Mahatma, Montale's appreciation of,
    11:1992b
Ganivet, Ángel, regenerationism, 9:1121b
Gantenbein. See Frisch, Max, *Mein Name sei
    Gantenbein*
"Gapa Guzhva." *See* Babel, Isaac
Gapon, Father, Gorky and, 8:420a
Garaudy, Roger, on Aragon, 11:2073a, 2073b,
    2075a
Garbo, Greta, in *As You Desire Me*, 8:394b
Garboli, Cesare, on Ginzburg, 13:3152b
García, José Soriano, 9:639b
García Lorca, Federico, **11:2167a–2202b**
    Así que pasen cinco años (*If Five Years
        Pass*), 11:2198a
    Blood Wedding (*Boda de sangre*), 9:1004a,
        11:2193a–2195a
    "Canción de jinete" ("Song of the
        Horseman"), 11:2176b–2177a

Canciones (*Songs*), 11:2168a, 2174b–2177a

"Ciudad sin sueño" ("The City That Never Sleeps"), 11:2183a

"Danza de la muerte" ("Dance of Death"), 11:2184a-b

"Deep Song" ("El canto jondo"), 11:2172a

Deep Song (*Poema del cante jondo*), 11:2168a, 2171b–2174a

"Despedida" (Good-bye), 11:2176b

Diván del Tamarit (*Divan*), 11:2187b–2188a

Doña Rosita la soltera (*Doña Rosita, the Spinster*), 11:2196b–2198a

El amor de Don Perlimplín con Belisa en su jardín (*The Love of Don Perlimplín for Belisa in His Garden*), 11:2190b–2193a

"El lagarto viejo" (The Old Lizard), 11:2170a-b

El maleficio de la mariposa (*The Butterfly's Evil Spell*), 11:2188b–2190b

"El niño loco" (The Crazy Boy), 11:2175a

"El niño mudo" (The Dumb Boy), 11:2175a

El paseo de Buster Keaton (*Buster Keaton's Promenade*), 11:2198a-b

El público (*The Audience*), 11:2198b–2199a

Elytis and, 13:2964b

"Essay on the Spanish Lullaby," 11:2176a

on Galdós, 7:1616b

Gypsy Ballads (*Romancero gitano*), 9:999a, 11:2168a, 2177a–2181b

Ibsen's influence on, 7:1444a

Impresiones y paisajes (*Impressions and Landscapes*), 11:2168b

Institución Libre de Enseñanza and, 9:1121a

Jiménez and, 9:999a, 1004a, 1008a

"Juan Breva," 11:2172b–2173a

"La casada infiel" (The Unfaithful Wife), 11:2178a

"La imágen poética de don Luis de Góngora" (The Poetic Image of Luis de Góngora), 11:2177a

Libro de poemas (*Book of Poems*), 11:2170a–2171a

Llanto por Ignacio Sánches Mejías (*Lament for the Death of a Bullfighter*), 11:2186b–2187a

"Los encuentros de un caracol aventurero" (Encounters of an Adventurous Snail), 11:2170b

Machado and, 9:746b, 760b

"Malagueña," 11:2171b, 2182b

"Martirio de Santa Olalla," Prudentius' *Peristephanon* and, 1:12a

"New York, Oficina y denuncia" ("New York, Office and Denunciation"), 11:2183a-b

"Oda al rey de Harlem" (The King of Harlem), 11:2184b–2185b

"Oda al Santísimo Sacramento del Altar" (Ode to the Most Holy Sacrament), 11:2181b–2182a

Ortega y Gasset and, 9:1119b

Poeta en Nueva York (*Poet in New York*), 11:2167a, 2182a–2186a

"Preciosa y el aire" (Preciosa and the Wind), 11:2180b–2181b

"Remansos" (Puddles), 11:2174b

Retablillo de don Cristóbal (*In the Flame of Don Cristóbal*), 11:2198b

"Reyerta" (Rumble), 11:2177b

Rilke and, 9:768a

"Romance de la Guardia Civil española" (Ballad of the Spanish Civil Guard), 11:2179b–2180b

"Romance sonámbulo" (Somnambulist Ballad), 11:2177b, 2178b

"Sorpresa" (Surprise), 11:2171b–2172a

Strindberg and, 7:1748a

The House of Bernarda Alba (*La casa de Bernarda Alba*), 11:2193a, 2195a–2196a

Valle-Inclán and, 8:332b

García Márquez, Gabriel, *One Hundred Years of Solitude*, precursors of, 7:1615b

"Garçon, un bock!" *See* Maupassant, Guy de

Garçons, Les. *See* Montherlant, Henry de, *The Boys*

Garden of the Chimeras, The. *See* Yourcenar, Marguerite, *Le jardin des chimères*

Garden of the Finzi-Continis, The. See Bassani, Giorgio, *Il giardino dei Finzi-Contini*

Garden of Krakonoš, The. *See* Čapek, Karel, and Josef Čapek, *Krakonošova zahrada*

Garden of Learning, The. *See* Milosz, Czeslaw, *Ogród nauk*

Garden motif, allegory and, 1:324a–326b

Garden of Priapus Messaline. See Jarry, Alfred, *Messaline: Roman de l'ancienne Rome*

"Garden, The." *See* Marvell, Andrew

Garden of Torments, The. See Mirbeau, Octave, *Le jardin des supplices*

"Gardener and His Master, The." *See* Andersen, Hans Christian

Gardener's Year, The. See Čapek, Karel

Gardens Are Closing, The. *See* George, Stefan, *Hymnen* (Odes), "Die Gärten schliessen"

Gargantua et Pantagruel. See Rabelais, François

Garibaldi, Giuseppe, 8:390a

Garibaldina, La. See Vittorini, Elio

Garnier (publisher), Machado and, 9:744b

Garnier, Robert, Corneille and, 3:35b

Garofano rosso, Il. See Vittorini, Elio

Garrett, Almeida
historical novel and, 7:1696b
Scott and, 7:1696b
Viagens na minha terra (Travels Through My Land), 7:1684b, 1696b

"Gärten schliessen, Die." *See* George, Stefan, *Hymnen*

Gas trilogy. *See* Kaiser, Georg

Gascó Contell, Emilio, on Blasco Ibáñez's *The Mayflower*, 8:358b–359a

Gassendi, Pierre
Arguments Against the Aristotelians, 3:18b
Descartes and, 3:18b–19b, 21b
Molière and, 3:102a

Gasset, Eduardo, founding of *El imparcial*, 9:1122b

Gæst den Enøjede. See Gunnarsson, Gunnar, *Borgslægtens Historie*

Gäst hos verkligheten. See Lagerkvist, Pär

Gastinel, Pierre, *Le romantisme d'Alfred de Musset*, 6:1006a-b

Gatomaquia, La. See Lope de Vega

Gattopardo, Il. See Lampedusa, Giuseppe Tomasi di, *The Leopard*

Gauguin, Paul, Huysmans and, 7:1714a

Gaujac, Pierre de, 2:770a

Gaule et France. See Dumas père, Alexandre

Gaulle, Charles de, Heinrich Mann and, 8:542a

Gaulmier, Jean
Breton's letter to, 11:1952a, 1957b
on Breton's *Ode à Charles Fourier*, 11:1957a-b

Gauthier-Villars, Henry, 9:617a–618b

Gautier, Jean-Jacques, 13:2999a

Gautier, Théophile, **6:1033a–1059b**
"À Zurbarán," 6:1042a
Albertus, 6:1034b, 1056a
"Arria Marcella," 6:1051b
art criticism by, 5:523b, 7:1630b
Avatar, 6:1051b–1052a
"Battle of *Hernani*," 6:1034a
Captain Fracasse (*Le Capitaine Fracasse*)
architectural style in, 6:1044b
literary allusions in, 6:1039a-b
on theater and performing arts, 6:1055b–1056a
"transposition d'art" in, 6:1043b
"Carmen," 6:1058b
decadent movement, 7:1416b
"Deux acteurs pour un rôle" ("The Actor"), 6:1050b, 7:1051a
"Deux tableaux de valdèdes Léal," 6:1042a-b
Eça and, 7:1687a
Enamels and Cameos (*Emaux et camées*), 6:1056a
on architectural style, 6:1044a-b
"Études de mains" in, 6:1051b
form of, 6:1056a
"L'Art," 6:1043a, 1058a, 1058b
as last work of, 6:1035a
Parnassian lines in, 6:1046b
preface of, 6:1034b
España, 6:1040a, 1042a-b, 1044a, 1056a
"Études de mains," 7:1796b
Exhumations littéraires (*Literary Exhumations*), 6:1047a
Fortunio, 6:1035b, 1053a-b
Giselle, 6:1035a, 1056a
Goncourts and, 7:1410a
Histoire du romantisme (*A History of Romanticism*), 6:695a, 1034a, 1047b

Hugo and, 6:695a

Jettatura, 6:1052a-b

Jiménez and, 9:993b

"King Candaulus," 6:1052b

"La cafetière" ("The Coffee Pot"),
6:1049b–1050a

La comédie de la mort (Death's Comedy),
6:1041b–1042a, 1042b, 1056b, 1058a

"La morte amoureuse" (The Dead Woman in
Love), 6:1050a-b

"La pipe d'opium" ("The Opium Smoker"),
6:1050b

"L'Art" (Art), 7:1630b

"Le chevalier double" ("The Twin Knight"),
6:1050b–1051a

"Le club des hachichins" ("The Hashish
Club"), 6:1050b

"Le pied de momie" (The Mummy's Foot),
6:1051a-b

"Le spectre de la rose," 6:1056b–1057a

Les Jeunes-France, 6:1034b, 1038a, 1050a

"L'Hippopotame," 6:1058a

L'Histoire de l'art dramatique,
7:1913b–1914a, 1924b

Los caprichos, 6:1042b

Mademoiselle de Maupin
androgyny in, 6:1041a
architectural style in, 6:1044b
characters in, 6:1055a-b
descriptive writing in, 6:1037a
literary allusions in, 6:1039b
preface of, 6:1034b. 6.1038a
publication of, 6:1034b
Shakespeare's text in, 6:1054a–1055b
"transpositions d'art" in, 6:1042b–1043a,
1043b–1044a

Mathilde Bonaparte and, 7:1416a

on Musset's *Lorenzaccio*, 6:1012a

"Omphale," 6:1043b, 1050a-b

"Onuphrius," 6:1050a

Partie carrée, 6:1040a, 1053b–1054a

Poésies, 6:1034a

poetry of, 7:1621a

preface by, for Baudelaire's *Les fleurs du
mal*, 7:1640b

on premiere of Hugo's *Hernani*, 6:1001b

Récits fantastiques (Tales of the Fantastic),
6:1040b, 1045b, 1049b

"Ribeira," 6:1042a

Rimbaud and, 7:1796b

Sainte-Beuve on, 7:1411a

on Scribe, 7:1913b–1914a, 1915a-b, 1924b

Spirite (*Stronger than Death; or Spirite*),
6:1038b, 1054a-b

"Symphonie en blanc majeur," 6:1056b

Taine and, 7:1452a

The Romance of a Mummy (*Le roman de la
momie*), 6:1045a, 1053a

Travels in Italy (*Italia*), 6:1045b,
1048a–1049a

Travels in Spain (*Voyage en Espagne*),
6:1039b, 1042b, 1045a-b, 1048a

Travels to Russia (*Voyage en Russie*),
6:1036a, 1048a, 1049a

"Une nuit de Cléopâtre" ("One of Cleopatra's
Nights"), 6:1033a, 1052b

Verlaine and, 7:1627b

Gavarni
Goncourts on, 7:1397a, 1408b
Mathilde Bonaparte and, 7:1416a

Gavilla de fábulas sin amor. See Cela, Camilo
José

Gavrilovna, Akulina, Pasternak and, 10:1591b

Gawain
Arthurian legend and, 1:155a–158b
Chrétien de Troyes and
Cligés, 1:155b
Conte du Graal, 1:156a-b, 157a-b,
206b–207a
Lancelot, 1:155b–156a, 158a
Yvain, 1:156a
in Geoffrey of Monmouth's *Historia*, 1:155a
in *La Mule sans frein*, 1:157a
in *Le Chevalier à l'épée*, 1:157a
in *Les Merveilles de Rigomer*, 1:157b–158a
in *Sir Gawain and the Green Knight*, 1:158b

Gawęda (narrative genre), Gombrowicz and,
12:2581a-b

Gay, Delphine, love for Vigny of, 5:451a-b

Gay Science, The. See Nietzsche, Friedrich

Gay, Sophie, Vigny and, 5:451b, 452a

"Gayola de grajos y vencejos." *See* Cela,
Camilo José

Gazeta futuristov (Futurist Gazette), 11:1844b

"Gebet." *See* Hebbel, Friedrich

Geburt der Tragödie, Die. See Nietzsche, Friedrich, *The Birth of Tragedy*

"Gedali." *See* Babel, Isaac

"Gedanken über die Ideale der Alten." *See* Wieland, Christoph Martin

"Gedanken zu Dostojewskys *Idiot.*" *See* Hesse, Hermann, *Blick ins Chaos* (*In Sight of Chaos*)

Gedankenexperiment. See Thought process, theme of

Gedichte 1853 und 1854. See Heine, Heinrich

Gedichte. See Heine, Heinrich; Trakl, Georg

"Gefährtin, Die." *See* Schnitzler, Arthur

Geheime Geschichte des Philosophen Peregrinus Proteus, Die. See Wieland, Christoph Martin

"Geheimes Deutschland." *See* George, Stefan, *Das neue Reich*

Gehörnte Siegfried, Der. See Hebbel, Friedrich, *Die Nibelungen* (*The Lay of the Nibelungs*), *The Invulnerable Siegfried*

Geist der Utopie. See Bloch, Ernst

Geist (the word), Heinrich Mann and, 8:521b

Geist und Tat. See Mann, Heinrich

Geistige Zeugung, 8:464b

Geistliche Lieder. See Luther, Martin; Novalis, *Sacred Songs*

Gelais, St., Petrarchan influence, 2:504a

"Gelsomino notturno, Il." *See* Pascoli, Giovanni, *Canti di Castelvecchio*

Gemälde, Die. See Tieck, Ludwig

Gendre de M. Poirier, Le. See Augier, Émile

Genealogia deorum gentilium (Genealogy of the Gentile Gods). *See* Boccaccio, Giovanni

"Genealogia" ("Genealogy"). *See* Cavafy, Constantine

Genealogy, Pérez Galdós on the Spanish obsession with, 7:1611a-b

Genealogy of Morals. See Nietzsche, Friedrich

General Assembly (Iceland), 1:377b, 378a, 379a, 383b

General Chronicle. See Crónica general

General Gazette (Augsburg), and Heine, 5:503b

General Introduction to Psychoanalysis. See Freud, Sigmund

General Outline. *See* Novalis, *Allgemeines Brouillon*

General System Theory. *See* Zalai, Béla, *Allgemeine Theorie der System*

Generation of 1830, Sainte-Beuve on, 6:852a-b

Generation of 1905, Marinetti and, 9:800a

Generation of 1914 and Modernism, The. See Wohl, Robert

Generation of 1927, Machado and, 9:746b

Generation of '98, 8:331a-b, 11:2169a-b
　Baroja and, 9:613a
　Blasco Ibáñez and, 8:355a, 357b
　ideas of, 9:589b, 591a-b, 593a
　Machado and, 9:744b, 745b
　Middle Ages and, 9:753a

Generational conflict. *See* Family

Generativity, as theme in Rabelais's *Pantagruel,* 2:703a-b, 704b

Género chico, Cervantes and, 2:826a

"Genesis, I." *See* Elytis, Odysseus, *To Axion Esti*

"Genesis, The." *See* Elytis, Odysseus, *To Axion Esti* (*The Axion Esti*), "I Genesis"

Genet, Jean, **13:2865a–2892b**
　Deathwatch (*Haute surveillance*), 13:2867a–2871b, 2875a, 2876b, 2885a
　Ghelderode and, 11:2118a
　Giraudoux and, 9:1041b
　Le condamné à mort (*The Condemned Man*), 13:2866b
　mythical works, 12:2355a
　Our Lady of the Flowers (*Notre-Dame-des-Fleurs*), 13:2866b
　Sartre on, 12:2606a–2608b
　The Balcony (*Le Balcon*), 13:2876b–2882a, 2884a, 2885a
　The Blacks (*Les Nègres*), 13:2882a, 2886a, 2886b
　　Ghelderode and, 11:2137a
　The Maids (*Les Bonnes*), 13:2871b–2876b, 2877a, 2879b, 2885a
　The Screens (*Les paravents*), 13:2884b, 2885a, 2886b

The Thief's Journal (*Journal du voleur*), 13:2865a, 2865b, 2889a, 2890a

Geneviève de Brabant, in Proust's *Remembrance of Things Past*, 8:552b

Gengaeldelsens Veje. See Dinesen, Isak, *The Angelic Avengers*

Genghi-Monogotari. See Shikibu, Murasaki

Génie du christianisme. See Chateaubriand, François René de

Génie du lieu, in Butor's writings, 13:3313b–3316a

"Génie" ("Genius"). *See* Rimbaud, Arthur

"Genies, The." *See* Hugo, Victor, "Les djinns"

Génitrix. See Mauriac, François

Genius
Andersen's view of, 6:883b–885a
female, in Staël's *Corinne*, 5:100a, 100b, 102a, 104b, 105a
in Musil's *The Man Without Qualities*, 9:952a
in *Romance of the Rose*, 1:330a–331b

Genius. See Lagerkvist, Pär

Genius of Christianity, The. See Chateaubriand, François René de, *Génie du christianisme*

Genoveva. See Hebbel, Friedrich

Gentile, Giovanni, Croce and, 8:316b

"Gentle Creature, A." *See* Dostoevsky, Feodor

"Gentle Hill, The." *See* Quasimodo, Salvatore

"Gentle, pitying glance, A." *See* Camoëns, Luís Vaz de, *Rimas* (*Lyrics*), "Um mover d'olhos brando e piadoso"

"Gentle Spirit." *See* Camoëns, Luís Vaz de, *Rimas* (*Lyrics*), "Alma minha gentil"

Gentleman and the Lady, The. See Goldoni, Carlo, *Il cavaliere e la dama*

"Gentry, The." *See* Verga, Giovanni, "I galantuomini"

Geocentrism, in sixteenth century, 3:8a

Geoffrey of Monmouth
Arthurian legend and, 1:138a–139a
Historia Regum Britanniae (*The History of the Kings of Britain*), Arthurian legend and, 1:138a, 138b, 140a, 155a

Geography
Ariosto's knowledge of, 2:636b–637a

phenomena of, in Montesquieu's works, 3:349b–350a

"Geometric and Mechanical Splendor and the Numerical Sensibility." *See* Marinetti, Filippo Tommaso, "Lo splendore geometrico e meccanico e la sensibilità numerica"

Geometry
as a model of demonstrative procedure, 3:130b–131a
Pascal's works, 3:130a–132a

Geopolitics, in Montesquieu's conception, 3:355a-b

George Dandin. See Molière

George, Stefan, **8:447a–470b**
Algabal, 8:452b–454a, 454b, 457b, 459a
"Andenken" (Memories), 8:454a
"Im Unterreich" (In the Subterranean Realm), 8:453b–454a
"Tage" (Days), 8:454a
"Vogelschau" (Augury), 8:454a
Das Jahr der Seele (The Year of the Soul), 8:454b, 459b–460a
"Sieg des Sommers" (Summer's Victory), 8:460a
"Traurige Tänze" (Sad Dances), 8:460a
"Überschriften und Widmungen" (Inscriptions and Dedications), 8:460a
"Waller im Schnee" (Pilgrims in the Snow), 8:460a
Das neue Reich (The Kingdom Come), 8:466a-b
"Das Lied" (The Song), 8:466b, 467a
"Der Dichter in Zeiten der Wirren" (The Poet in Times of Confusion), 8:466a-b
"Geheimes Deutschland," 8:468a
Der siebente Ring (The Seventh Ring), 8:463b–464a
"Lieder," 8:464a, 466b–467a
"Zeitgedichte" (Poems Addressed to Our Age), 8:463b
Der Stern des Bundes (The Star of the Covenant), 8:464a–466a, 468a

George, Stefan (*cont.*)
  Der Teppich des Lebens und die Lieder von Traum und Tod, mit einem Vorspiel (The Tapestry of Life and the Songs of Dream and Death, with a Prelude), 8:461a–462a, 466b, 468a
  Deutsche Dichtung and, 8:460b, 467a
  Die Blumen des Bösen (Flowers of Evil), translation of Baudelaire, 8:451a-b
  Die Bücher der Hirten- und Preisgedichte . . . (The Books of Eclogues and Eulogies . . .), 8:454a–459b
    Hängende Gärten poems, 8:457a–459b, 465a
    Hirtengedichte poems, 8:454b–455a
    Preisgedichte poems, 8:455b
    Sagen und Sänge poems, 8:455b–457a, 458a
  Die Fibel (The Primer), 8:449b
  Drei Gesänge (Three Cantos), 8:466a
    "Einem jungen Führer im ersten Weltkrieg" (To a Young Leader in the First World War), 8:466a
  "Franken" (Frankish Lands), 8:449b
  Hofmannsthal and, 9:689a, 690b, 691a
  Hölderlin and, 5:143a, 173b
  Hymnen (Odes), 8:448a, 454b
    "Die Gärten schliessen" (The Gardens are Closing), 8:451b
    "Weihe" (Initiation), 8:448b
  Pilgerfahrten (Pilgrimages), 8:451b–452b, 454b
    "Die Spange" (The Link), 8:452b
    "Mühle lass die arme still" (Windmill Cease to Move Your Arms), 8:451b–452b
  Richter's *The Invisible Lodge* and, 5:63a
  Richter's *Titan* and, 5:74b
  Rilke and, 9:790a
  "Ursprünge" (Origins), 8:449a-b
George, St., legend of, Ekelöf and, 12:2640b
George-Kreis, 8:447a, 451b, 457b
Georgian poetry, Pasternak's translations of, 10:1606b
Georgics. *See* Vergil
Georgics, The. *See* Simon, Claude, *Les Géorgiques*; Vergil

Géorgiques, Les. *See* Simon, Claude
Gérard of Abbeville, 1:417b
Gerard de Borgo San Donnino, *Introductorius in evangelium aeternum* (*Introduction to the Everlasting Gospel*), 1:413b
Gérard, François, Delacroix and, 5:514b
Gérardy, Paul, George and, 8:455b
Géraud, Edmond, Vigny and, 5:452a
Gerbert of Auxerre. *See* Sylvester II, Pope
Gereint Son of Erbin, Chrétien's *Erec et Enide* and, 1:188b
Gerettete Venedig, Das. *See* Hofmannsthal, Hugo von
Gerettete Zunge, Die. *See* Canetti, Elias, *The Tongue Set Free*
Gerfaut. *See* Bernard, Charles de
Gerhoh of Reichersberg, *De investigatione Antichristi*, 1:452a
Géricault, Théodore
  Delacroix and, 5:514b
  The Raft of the Medusa, Aragon and, 11:2082a-b
Gerifaltes de antaño. *See* Valle-Inclán, Ramón del, *La guerra carlista*
"German Art and German Politics." *See* Wagner, Richard
"German Bible, The." *See* Klopstock, Friedrich Gottlieb
"German Catechism." *See* Kleist, Heinrich von
German chauvinism, Herder's nationalism vs., 4:640b–641a, 644a, 646b
German drama. *See* Drama, German
German language
  Canetti and, 12:2616a-b
  Wieland's influence on, 4:589b–590a
  Wolfram's innovations, 1:264b–266b
German literature
  framework stories, 8:242b
  genres, 8:267a-b
  Giraudoux and, 9:1042a
  lyric grotesques, 8:257b
  Munich naturalist school, 8:232a
  post–World War II, 13:3174a-b
  twentieth-century poetry, George and, 8:450b
German Mass, The. *See* Luther, Martin, *Die Deutsche Messe*

German Mercury, The. See Wieland, Christoph
Martin, *Der Teutsche Merkur*
German Poetry. *See Deutsche Dichtung*
German Poets' Academy, 8:449a
"German question," in Mann's *Reflections of a
Nonpolitical Man*, 9:718a, 719a
German Realists of the Nineteenth Century.
See Lukács, György, *Deutsche Realisten
des 19. Jahrhunderts*
German Republic of Intellectuals, The. See
Klopstock, Friedrich Gottlieb
German Storytellers. *See* Hofmannsthal, Hugo
von, *Deutsche Erzähler*
"German Wit: Heinrich Heine." *See* Eliot,
George
Germania. See Staël, Madame de
Germania, De. See Tacitus
Germania (Nietzsche group), 7:1648a
Germanic society
in *Beowulf*, 1:53b–55b
Christianity and, *see also* England,
Anglo-Saxon
function of poetry in, 1:53a–54b
literature, Taine on, 7:1455a
"Germanien." *See* Hölderlin, Friedrich
Germany: A Winter's Tale. See Heine,
Heinrich, *Deutschland: Ein
Wintermärchen*
Germany
Andrić as ambassador to (1941), 11:1758b
Apollinaire's visit to, 9:887a, 888b
Berlioz in, 6:788b–789a, 798b–799a, 807b
Burckhardt and, 6:1227a-b
culture
Staël's *De l'Allemagne* on, 5:105a–109a
Wagner on, 6:1152a–1153b, 1158b–1159a
Giraudoux in, 9:1042a-b
Hamsun and, 8:21a-b, 36b, 40a–41a
history (1917 to 1960)
in Böll's chronicles, 13:3166a, 3169b,
3171b, 3179a-b
Grass and, 13:3365a–3387a
in Mann's *Doctor Faustus*, 9:735a-b
in Michelet's view, 5:603a
nationhood of, 11:2094b
patriotism in, Hauptmann and, 8:165b

peasant revolt of 1525, Hauptmann's play
about, 8:156a–157a
Robbe-Grillet's wartime service in,
13:3239a-b
Schnitzler's popularity in, 8:106a
Second Republic, in Böll's chronicles,
13:3179b
Silesian weavers revolt of 1844, Hauptmann
play about, 8:152b–153b
Socialism in, 8:147b–148a, 154a
Third Reich, in Céline's *Nord*,
11:1881b–1882a
unification of, poetic realism and, 6:913a-b
Weil and, 12:2790b
see also Nazis; Politics, German
Germany. See Heine, Heinrich, *De l'Allemagne*
Germany, East, Thomas Mann and, 9:728a
Germinal. See Zola, Émile
Germinie Lacerteux. See Goncourt, Edmond
Louis Antoine and Jules Alfred Huot de
Geroy nashego vremeni. See Lermontov,
Mikhail Yurievich, *A Hero of Our Times*
Gerpla. See Laxness, Halldór
"Gerti's Carnival." *See* Montale, Eugenio, *The
Occasions*
Gertrud (Gertrude). See Hesse, Hermann
Gerusalemme conquistada. See Tasso,
Torquato
Gerusalemme liberata. See Tasso, Torquato
Gesamtkunstwerk (Wagnerian term)
Apollinaire and, 9:899b
reciprocal relationships in, 6:1161a
Tieck and, 5:239a
Wagner and, 6:1150a, 1154a-b, 1159b,
1162a, 1164b
see also Wagner, Richard
Geschäftedes Herrn Julius Caesar, Die. See
Brecht, Bertolt
Geschichte der Abderiten, Die. See Wieland,
Christoph Martin
*Geschichte des Abfalls der vereinigten
Niederlande. See* Schiller, Friedrich von
Geschichte des Agathon, Die. See Wieland,
Christoph Martin
Geschichte des dreissigjährigen Krieges. See
Schiller, Friedrich von

Geschichte des Herrn William Lovell. See Tieck, Ludwig

Geschichte des Materialismus. See Lange, Friedrich

Geschichte und Klassenbewusstsein. See Lukács, György

Geschichte vom Braven Kasperl und dem schönen Annerl. See Brentano, Clemens

Geschichten verstrickt: Zum Sein von Mensch und Ding. See Schapp, Wilhelm

Gesellschaft auf dem Lande, Die. See Tieck, Ludwig

Gesellschaft für Modernes Leben (Society for Modern Life), Wedekind and, 8:236a

Gesichte der Simone Machard, Die. See Brecht, Bertolt, *The Visions of Simone Machard*

Gessler, Albert, Burckhardt and, 6:1229b

Gesta Danorum. See Saxo Grammaticus

Gesta de las mocedades de Rodrigo
    ballads derived from, 1:132b–133a
    literary qualities of, 1:130a-b
    Poema de mio Cid and, 1:114b
    as source of *Mocedades de Rodrigo*, 1:129a

Gesta Romanorum (Deeds of the Romans)
    Boccaccio and, 2:933a
    Renaissance short fiction and, 2:932b–933a

Geständnisse. See Heine, Heinrich

Gestern. See Hofmannsthal, Hugo von

Gestes et opinions du docteur Faustroll, 'pataphysicien: Roman neo-scientifique. See Jarry, Alfred

Gestiefelte Kater, Der. See Tieck, Ludwig

Gesture as language, in Kleist, 5:302b–303a

Gestures. See Ritsos, Yannis, *Hironomies*

Getting Married. See Strindberg, August

Getting Off with a Fright. See Vigny, Alfred Victor de, *Quitte pour la peur*

Getto, Giovanni, *Manzoni europeo*, on Manzoni's *The Betrothed* and Goethe's *Hermann und Dorothea*, 5:371a

Gewehre der Frau Carrar, Die. See Brecht, Bertolt, *Señora Carrar's Rifles*

"Gewitter, Das." *See* Trakl, Georg, "The Thunderstorm"

Geyer, Florian. *See* Hauptmann, Gerhart, *Florian Geyer*

Ghefira, I. See Ritsos, Yannis

Ghelderode, Michel de, **11:2113a–2141b**
    Blockheads (*Têtes de bois*), 11:2122a–2123b, 2129b
    Choses et gens de chez nous (Our Own Things and People), 11:2116a
    Don Juan, 11:2115a, 2115b, 2123b–2126b, 2129b, 2132b–2133a
    codas of, 11:2137a-b
    Dreams Drowning (*Noyade des songes*), 11:2135a-b
    D'un diable qui prêcha merveilles (Of a Devil Who Preached Wonders), 11:2133b–2134a
    Escurial, 11:2115b, 2117a–2118a
    Fastes d'enfer (*Chronicles of Hell*), 11:2116a, 2116b, 2120a–2122a, 2136a
    Hop Signor!, 11:2116a, 2116b, 2126a
    La balade du Grand Macabre, 11:2118a, 2134a
    La farce des ténébreux (The Farce of the Shadow Cult), 11:2126a
    La mort du docteur Faust (*The Death of Dr. Faust*), 1:2115b, 11:2115a, 2116a
    Butor's *Votre Faust* and, 13:3310b
    La mort regarde à la fenêtre (*Death Looks in the Window*), 11:2114b, 2122a
    La pie sur le gibet (*The Magpie on the Gallows*), 11:2121a, 2122a
    La transfiguration dans le cirque (Transfiguration in the Circus), 11:2129a
    La vie publique de Pantagleize, 11:2134b–2135a
    Le cavalier bizarre (*The Strange Rider*), 11:2115a
    Le siège d'Ostende (The Siege of Ostend), 11:2126a, 2126b, 2129b–2132b, 2133a-b
    Le soleil se couche (The Sun Sets), 11:2122a
    Lord Halewyn, 11:2136b
    Masques ostendais (Ostend Masks), 11:2132b
    Miss Jairus (*Mademoiselle Jaïre*), 11:2122a
    Pantagleize, 11:2115b, 2116b, 2126b–2129b, 2134b, 2137b
    Red Magic (*Magie rouge*), 11:2126a

Sortie de l'acteur (The Actor's Exit), 1:2122a, 11:2118a–2120a, 2126b

Strindberg and, 7:1754a

The School for Buffoons (*L'École des bouffons*), 11:2137a

Vénus (Venus), 11:2126b, 2135a

Ghibellines. *See* Guelfs and Ghibellines

Ghignesthe. See Ritsos, Yannis

Ghitonies tou kosmou, I. See Ritsos, Yannis

Ghost at Noon, A. See Moravia, Alberto

Ghost Sonata, The. See Strindberg, August

Ghost of Stalin, The. See Sartre, Jean-Paul

Ghosts

in Grillparzer's *The Ancestress*, 5:426a

in Mickiewicz's *Dziady*, 5:611b–612b

see also Supernatural

Ghosts. See Ibsen, Henrik

Ghosts in the Mirror. See Robbe-Grillet, Alain

Ghrafi tiflou. See Ritsos, Yannis

"Ghramma sto Zolio Kioyri." *See* Ritsos, Yannis, *Pimata III*

"Già la pioggia è con noi." *See* Quasimodo, Salvatore

Giambi ed epodi. See Carducci, Giosue

Gianni, Lapo, Dante and, 1:432a

Giara, La. See Pirandello, Luigi

Giardino dei Finzi-Contini, Il. See Bassani, Giorgio

Gibaldi, Joseph, *Anatomy of the Novella* (with Clements), oral tradition emphasized by, 2:927b–928a

Gibault, François, on Céline, 11:1860b, 1862a

Gibbon, Edward

History of the Decline and Fall of the Roman Empire, as source for Vigny's *Daphné*, 5:477a-b

Suzanne Curchod and, 5:89a, 89b

"Gibel' Atlantidy." *See* Khlebnikov, Velimir

Giboyer's Son. See Augier, Émile, *Le fils de Giboyer*

Gide, André, 8:135a, **495a–518b**

Album de vers anciens, 1890–1920 and, 8:576a

Barthes on, 13:3081b–3082a

Beauvoir and, 12:2710b, 2711a

Broch and, 10:1393a

Cavafy and, 8:206a

Claudel and, 8:480a, 487b

Corydon: Traité d'un vain désir, 12:2538a

on the creative process, 12:2348a

on Diderot, 4:501a

Ekelöf and, 12:2659a

Heinrich Mann and, 8:539a

Hesse and, 9:842a, 847a, 855b

on Hesse's *The Journey to the East*, 9:850b

Incidences, 8:516a

Jarry and, 9:666b

Journal, 8:496b–497a, 512a, 512b

La porte étroite (Strait Is the Gate), 8:504b–506a

La tentative amoureuse (The Lover's Attempt), 8:496a-b

on Lagerkvist, 10:1697b

Le traité du Narcisse (Narcissus), 8:495b

Le voyage d'Urien (Urien's Voyage), 8:495b

Mann and, 9:715b

Marshlands (Paludes)

humor in, 8:497b–498a

protagonist of, 8:498b–499b

Mauriac and, 10:1312b, 1322b–1323a

patrons of, 9:670b

Perse and, 10:1433b–1434a

Prometheus Misbound (*Le Prométhée mal enchaîné*), 8:499b–501b

Proust and, 8:545b

Retour de l'U.R.S.S. (Return from the U.S.S.R.), Pasternak's refusal to condemn, 10:1595b

on Saint-Exupéry, 12:2316a

Sarraute and, 12:2335a

Sartre on, 12:2707a

Seferis and, 12:2260a, 2269b

sexual liaisons of, 9:671a

Simenon and, 12:2480a

The Counterfeiters (*Les faux-monnayeurs*), 8:508a–511b, 9:666b–667a

Ekelöf and, 12:2659a

Hesse's *Steppenwolf* and, 9:847b

Johnson and, 12:2364b

The Fruits of the Earth (*Les nourritures terrestres*), 8:512a–514a

The Immoralist (*L'Immoraliste*), 8:501b, 503b–504b

Gide, André (*cont.*)
   The Pastoral Symphony (*La symphonie pastorale*), 8:506a–508a
   The Vatican Swindle (*Les caves du Vatican*), 8:501b–503b
      Apollinaire and, 9:883a
      Professor Unrat and, 8:529a
   The White Notebook (*Les cahiers d'André Walter*), 8:495a-b
   Theseus, 8:514a–515b
   Weil and, 12:2808b
   Yourcenar, 12:2537b
Gifford, Henry, on Pasternak's translations, 10:1607b
Giftas. *See* Strindberg, August, *Getting Married*
Giganti della montagna, I. *See* Pirandello, Luigi, *The Mountain Giants*
Gigi. *See* Colette
Gil Blas. *See* Lesage, Alain-René
Gil Polo, Gaspar, *Diana enamorada* (Diana in Love), influence on pastoral romance, 2:922a, 922b–923b
Gilbert, Joseph, in Vigny's *Stello*, 5:467b–468a
Gilgamesh (Sumerian epic), Canetti and, 12:2627a-b
Giner de los Ríos, Francisco
   Institución Libre de Enseñanza, 9:1121a
   Machado and, 9:744a, 758b
   regenerationism, 9:1121b
"Ginestra, La." *See* Leopardi, Giacomo, "The Broom Flower"
Ginzburg, Natalia, **13:3131a–3163b**
   A Light for Fools (*Tutti i nostri ieri*), 13:3131a, 3136b, 3144a, 3145a, 3146a, 3147a-b, 3148a-b
      northern vs. southern Italy, 13:3147b, 3148a
   alienation from Italian society, 13:3134a-b, 3137b
   autobiographical element, 13:3137b, 3150a
   Borghesia (*Bourgeoisie*), 13:3137a, 3156b
   Calvino and, 13:3160b–3161a, 3262a
   Caro Michele (*Dear Michael*), 13:3155a–3156b, 3159a
   "Casa al mare" (House by the Sea), 13:3138b–3139a, 3140b

confino in writing, 13:3141a
Cristo si e fermato a Eboli (*Christ Stopped at Eboli*) and, 13:3141b
Dialogo, 13:3154a
È stato così (*The Dry Heart*), 13:3136b, 3141b–3142a
epistolary novels, 13:3155a–3160a
Famiglia (*Family*), 13:3137a, 3156b–3158a
Family Sayings (*Lessico famigliare*), 13:3131a, 3133b, 3134a, 3136b, 3144a, 3150a–3153a
female voice, 13:3137b, 3138a, 3143b–3144a
Fragola e panna (Strawberry Ice Cream Cone), 13:3154a
I Married You for Fun (*Ti ho sposato per allegria*), 13:3136b, 3153a, 3154a-b
La città e la casa (*The City and the House*), 13:3137a, 3159a–3160a
La famiglia Manzoni (*The Manzoni Family*), 13:3137a, 3158a-b
"La madre" (Mother), 13:3136b, 3142a–3143a
La parrucca (The Wig), 13:3153b, 3154a
La segretaria (The Secretary), 13:3153b, 3154b–3155a
Le piccole virtù (*The Little Virtues*), 13:3136b, 3144a
Leone Ginzburg's death, 13:3135b–3136a
Mai devi domandarmi (*Never Must You Ask Me*), 13:3137a
"Mio marito" (My Husband), 13:3139a–3140a, 3140b, 3141a, 3142a
Opere, 13:3131a, 3132b, 3136a, 3137b, 3138a, 3138b, 3145a
Paese di mare (Seaside Resort), 13:3136b, 3153a, 3154a-b
Pavese and, 12:2761b–2762a, 2763b
plays, 13:3136b–3137a, 3153a–3155a
"Ritratto di un amico" ("Portrait of a Friend"), 12:2762a
Sagittario (*Sagittarius*), 13:3144a, 3149a
The Advertisement (*L'Inserzione*), 13:3153b–3154a
The Road to the City (*La strada che va in città*), 13:3136b, 3140a–3141a
"Un'assenza" (An Absence), 13:3138a-b
use of first person, 13:3138b–3139a, 3142a

Valentino, 13:3136b, 3143a-b

"Vecchiaia" (Old Age), 13:3145a

Vita immaginaria (Imaginary Life), 13:3137a

Voices in the Evening (*Le voci della sera*), 13:3131a, 3136b, 3149a–3150a, 3152b, 3153a

Gioberti, Vincenzo, veneration of Alfieri by, 4:688a

Gioconda, La. See D'Annunzio, Gabriele

"Gioia e la legge, La." *See* Lampedusa, Giuseppe Tomasi di, *Two Stories and a Memory*

Gioia, Melchiorre, as source for Manzoni's *The Betrothed*, 5:383a

Giolitti, Giovanni
  Croce and, 8:326b
  Marinetti and, 9:799a

Giono, Jean, Camus and, 13:3055b

Giordani, Pietro, Leopardi's correspondence with, 5:545b, 548a, 552a-b, 558b, 561b

Giordano, Umberto, *André Chénier*, Chénier's affair with de Coigny in, 4:693a

Giornata d'uno scrutatore, La. See Calvino, Italo, *The Watcher*

"Giornata, Una." *See* Pirandello, Luigi

"Giorno dei morti, Il." *See* Pascoli, Giovanni, *Myricae*

Giorno dopo giorno. See Quasimodo, Salvatore, *Day After Day*

Giotto, Dante and, 1:432a

"Giovane donna sotto un verde lauro." *See* Petrarch, *Canzoniere*

Giovanni del Virgilio, Dante's epistolary eclogues to, 2:903b–904a

Giovanni Episcopo. See D'Annunzio, Gabriele, *Episcopo & Company*

Gippius, Vladimir, Mandelshtam's letter to, 10:1628b

Gippius, Zinaida, Russian symbolism and, 9:967b

Giraldi, Giambattista
  Egle, as tragicomedy, 2:917a
  Gli ecatommiti (*The Hundred Stories*), 2:943b–944b
  Orbecche, Senecan tragedy and, 2:944b
  tragicomedy and, 2:917a

Giraldi, Giovanni Battista. *See* Giraldi, Giambattista

Girart de Roussillon, 1:107a–108a

Girart de Vienne. See Bertrand de Bar-sur-Aube

Giraudoux: Three Faces of Destiny. See Cohen, Robert

Giraudoux, Jean, **9:1041a–1065a**
  Adorable Clio, 9:1043b
  Amica America (Friendly America), 9:1043b
  Amphitryon 38, 9:1041a, 1049b–1050b
    conflict in, 9:1060a
    fantasy in, 9:1062b
    revival of, 9:1052a
  Aventures de Jérôme Bardini (Adventures of Jérôme Bardini), 9:1046a-b
  Bella, 9:1045b–1046a
  Cantique des cantiques (*Song of Songs*), 9:1055a-b
  Choix des élues (Choices of the Elite), 9:1047b
  Combat avec l'ange (Combat with the Angel), 9:1047a
  dehumanization in works of, 13:3229b
  Eglantine, 9:1046a
  Electre (Electra), 9:1041a, 1053b–1054b, 12:2549a
    characters in, 9:1062b
    comedy with serious elements in, 9:1053b
    contests in, 9:1060b
    theatricalism in, 9:1063b
  Elpénor, 9:1043b
  Intermezzo (*Intermezzo* or *The Enchanted*), 9:1041a, 1051b–1052a
    conflict in, 9:1060a
    fantasy in, 9:1062b
  Judith, 9:1041a, 1050b–1051a, 1062b
    conflict in, 9:1060a-b
    public reception of, 9:1051a
  Juliette, 9:1045b
  La Duchesse de Langeais (*The Duchess of Langeais*), 9:1059b
  La folle de Chaillot (*The Madwoman of Chaillot*), 9:1057b–1058a, 13:3229b
    conflict in, 9:1060b
    genre of, 9:1061a

Giraudoux, Jean (*cont.*)
　La France sentimentale (Sentimental
　　France), 9:1046b, 1051b, 1061b
　La menteuse (*Lying Woman*),
　　9:1047b–1048b, 1062b
　L'Apollon de Bellac (*The Apollo of Bellac*),
　　9:1056b, 1062b
　L'École des indifférents (The School for
　　Indifference), 9:1043a
　　Olesha's *Envy* and, 11:2236a
　Lectures pour une ombre (*Campaigns and
　　Intervals*), 9:1043b
　Les anges du péché (*The Angels of Sin*),
　　9:1059b
　Les contes d'un matin (Morning Stories),
　　9:1043a
　Les Gracques (The Gracchi), 9:1059a
　modernization of myth, 13:2848b
　Ondine, 9:1041a, 1055b–1056b, 1062a-b
　　contests in, 9:1060b
　　theatricalism in, 9:1063a-b
　　trial sequence in, 9:1061a
　Paris Impromptu, 9:1041a, 1054b–1055a
　Pour Lucrèce (*Duel of Angels*),
　　9:1058b–1059a, 1060b
　Provinciales (From Provincial Places),
　　9:1042b, 1043a, 1048b
　Queneau and, 12:2511a
　Siegfried, 9:1041a, 1044a, 1048b–1049b
　　Anouilh and, 13:2845b
　　characters in, 9:1062a
　　conflict in, 9:1060a
　Siegfried et le Limousin (*My Friend from
　　Limousin*), 9:1045a, 1048b
　Simon le pathétique (Simon the
　　Susceptible), 9:1043b
　Sodome et Gemorrha (*Sodom and
　　Gomorrah*), 9:1056b–1057b
　　characters in, 9:1062a
　　destiny in, 9:1060b
　　Strindberg and, 7:1751b
　Supplément au voyage de Cook (*The
　　Virtuous Island*), 9:1052b
　Suzanne et le Pacifique (*Suzanne and the
　　Pacific*), 9:657b–658a, 1043b,
　　1044b–1045a, 1052b
　Tessa, 9:1052a-b

　The Constant Nymph, 9:1052a
　Tiger at the Gates (*La guerre de Troie
　　n'aura pas lieu*), 9:1041a, 1052b–1053b
　　and classical literature, 9:1063a
　　conflict in, 9:1060b
　　dating of, 9:1053a
　　fantasy in, 9:1063a
　　love in, 9:1050a-b
　　Moral Tales and, 7:1907a
　　peace personification in, 9:1047a
Girgenti. *See* Agrigento
Girl, The. *See* Zamyatin, Yevgeny Ivanovich,
　　"Devushka"
"Girl at Sea." *See* Heine, Heinrich
"Girl from Spoleto, The." *See* Blok, Alexander,
　　"Devushka iz Spoleto"
Girl with the Golden Eyes, The. *See* Balzac,
　　Honoré de, *La fille aux yeux d'or*
Girl in His Past, The. *See* Simenon, Georges,
　　Le temps d'Anaïs
"Girl the North Wind Brought, The." *See*
　　Elytis, Odysseus, *To photodendro dai i
　　dekati tetarti omorfia* (*The Light Tree
　　and the Fourteenth Being*), "I kori pou
　　ferne o vorias"
Girl Set Out, A. *See* Ady, Endre, "Elindult egy
　　leány"
"Girl's Confession, A." *See* Proust, Marcel, *Les
　　plaisirs et les jours*
Girls, The. *See* Montherlant, Henry de
Girondins, in Michelet's view, 5:590a, 593b
"Girovage." *See* Ungaretti, Giuseppe
Giselle. *See* Adam, Adolphe; Gautier,
　　Théophile
Gísla saga Súrssonar, 1:396a-b, 397a
"Gitanilla, La." *See* Cervantes, Miguel de
Gitanjali. *See* Tagore, Rabindranath
Giudizio sulla G.C. *See* Tasso, Torquato
Giuoco delle parti, Il. *See* Pirandello, Luigi
Giv oss jorden! *See* Moberg, Vilhelm, *The
　　Earth Is Ours!*
Give Me Your Eyes. *See* Ady, Endre, "Add
　　nekem a szemeidet"
Gizur (Icelandic bishop), 1:379b
Gkragkanta. *See* Ritsos, Yannis
Glade Gaard og andre Historier, Den. *See*
　　Gunnarsson, Gunnar

"Gladiator." *See* Valéry, Paul, *Cahiers*

Gladiators, The. *See* Montherlant, Henry de, *The Matador*

Gladkov, Aleksandr, Pasternak's conversation with, 10:1608b

"Glahns Dód" (Glahn's Death). *See* Hamsun, Knut

"Glance at a Contemporary Effort in Danish Literature, A." *See* Kierkegaard, Søren

Glasperlenspiel, Das (The Glass Bead Game). See Hesse, Hermann

Glass of Water, The. See Scribe, Eugène, *Le verre d'eau*

Glatigny, Albert, Verlaine and, 7:1627b

Glauben und Liebe. See Novalis, *Faith and Love*

"Glaza." *See* Zamyatin, Yevgeny Ivanovich

Glebova-Sudeikina, Ol'ga Afanas'evna, Akhmatova's "Second Dedication" to, 10:1535a

Gleim, Ludwig, 5:70b

Gleisdreieck. See Grass, Günter

Gleoman, in Germanic society, 1:65a

Glissements progressifs du plaisir. See Robbe-Grillet, Alain, *Slow Slide into Pleasure*

Gloire des rois, La. See Perse, Saint-John

Gloria. See Pérez Galdós, Benito

Gloria, La. See D'Annunzio, Gabriele

"Gloria, The." *See* Elytis, Odysseus, *To Axion Esti (The Axion Esti)*, "To Dokaxtikon"

Glory. *See* D'Annunzio, Gabriele, *La gloria*

Glory of Kings. *See* Perse, Saint-John, *La gloire des rois*

"Glory of the Ptolemies, The." *See* Cavafy, Constantine, "I doxa ton Ptolemaion"

"Glosando a Ronsard y otras rimas." *See* Machado, Antonio, *Nuevas canciones*

"Glosas" (Glosses). *See* Ortega y Gasset, José

Glosses on Ronsard and Other Rhymes. *See* Machado, Antonio, *Nuevas canciones* (New Songs), "Glosando a Ronsard y otras rimas"

Glossolalia, of Artaud, 11:1983a-b

Gluck, Christoph Willibald
  Berlioz and, 6:774a-b, 775a-b, 776a-b, 779b, 786a, 787a-b, 805b, 806a, 807a

Iphigénie en Aulide, and Beaumarchais, 4:583a

Valéry's *The Young Fate* and, 8:577a

Gluttony, in Rabelais's *Fourth Book*, 2:712a-b

"Glyazhu na budushchnost s boyaznyu." *See* Lermontov, Mikhail Yurievich

Gnoli, Domenico, on *Poemetti*, 7:1825b

Gnosticism, Steiner and, 9:919b

Gnostique de Saint Clément d'Alexandrie (The Gnosticism of Saint Clement of Alexandria). See Fénelon, François de Salignac de la Mothe-

Gobetti, Piero, Montale and, 11:1989b, 1990a-b

Gobineau, Arthur de
  Essay on the Inequalities of Races, 6:1164a
  Tocqueville and, 6:910a-b

"Goblet of Blizzards, The." *See* Bely, Andrey, *Symphonies*

God
  in Ady's poetry, 9:860b–861a, 862b, 863a, 879a
  Bergson's view of, 8:62b–63a
  in Claudel's *Break of Noon*, 8:477b, 479a
  "death of"
    Foucault and, 13:3324b–3325a
    Nerval and, 6:954a-b
    in Nietzsche, 7:1666b, 1670a
  as deceiver, in Descartes's *Meditations on First Philosophy*, 3:10b, 14a-b, 15a
  Dumas's view of, 6:734a, 739a
  existence of
    Aquinas on, 1:420a–421a
    Augustine on, 1:44b
    in Descartes's *Meditations on First Philosophy*, 3:13a–14a, 16a–17a
    discussed in La Bruyère's *Caractères*, 3:256b–257a
    Lessing on, 4:561a
    in Pascal's *Pensées*, 3:141a–142a
  in Hölderlin's works, 5:158b
  Hugo's view of, 6:709b–712a–713b, 715b–716a
  knowability of, in Augustine's *Confessions*, 1:32a
  as last end of man, Aquinas on, 1:425a

God (*cont.*)
 in Mann's *Joseph and His Brothers*, 9:731b,
  732a
 Maupassant's view of, 7:1775a
 nature of
  Aquinas on, 1:420a, 421a-b
  Prudentius on, 1:8a-b
  Scriptum super Sententias on, 1:412a-b
 Rimbaud's view of, 7:1791b, 1821b
 Strindberg's view of, 7:1738a-b
 Unamuno's concept of, 8:298a, 300a
 Walther and, 1:302a–304b
 in Wolfram, 1:277a–278b
 see also Gods, pagan; Incarnation
God. See Hugo, Victor, *Dieu*
"God Abandons Antony, The." *See* Cavafy,
  Constantine
God, Flog Me! *See* Ady, Endre, "Uram,
  ostorozz meg"
God and Mammon. See Mauriac, François
God That Failed, The. See Crossman, Richard
  H. S.
God-Forsaken Hole, A. See Zamyatin, Yevgeny
  Ivanovich
Godard, Jean-Luc, *Pierrot le fou*, 11:1867b
Goddesses, The; or, Three Novels of the
  Duchess of Assy. *See* Mann, Heinrich,
  *Die Göttinnen, oder die drei Romane
  der Herzogin von Assy*
"Godiva." *See* Tennyson, Alfred Lord
Godly Feast. *See* Erasmus, "Convivium
  religiosum"
Godmanhood, Milosz and, 13:2937a-b
Gods Are Not Dead, The. *See* Yourcenar,
  Marguerite, *Les dieux ne sont pas morts*
Gods of Greece, The. See Schiller, Friedrich
  von
Gods, pagan
 Augustine's *City of God* on, 1:35a-b
 in Camoëns' *The Lusiads*, 2:762b–763a
 Prudentius' *Symmachus* on, 1:10a
 see also names of individual deities
"Gods, The." *See* Khlebnikov, Velimir, "Bogi"
Godwi. See Brentano, Clemens
Godwin, William, *Caleb Williams*, Pessoa
  and, 10:1493a

Goethe és kora (*Goethe and His Age*). *See*
  Lukács, György
Goethe, Johann Wolfgang von, **5:1a–26b**
 allegory and, 1:320a-b
 Altersstil of, 9:855a
 Andersen and, 6:877a-b
 Beaumarchais and, 4:569b–570a
 Berlioz and, 6:778b–779a, 782b, 790b, 791a,
  791b–792b
 Blok and, 9:979a
 Brecht and, 11:2093b–2095b, 2101a, 2105a
 in Claudel's *La nuit de Noël de 1914*,
  8:484b
 Clavigo, 5:4a-b
  Beaumarchais's influence on,
   4:569b–570b
 on the creative process, 12:2348a
 Das Jahr der Seele and, 8:459b
 "Der Zauberlehrling" ("The Sorcerer's
  Apprentice"), apprenticeship theme of,
  5:216b
 Dichtung und Wahrheit (*Poetry and Truth*),
  5:2b, 6a, 6:1090a
 Die Leiden des jungen Werthers (*The
  Sorrows of Young Werther*), 5:5a–8a,
  11b, 13a, 15a, 20b, 6:782b, 1015a
  "Abelard und Heloise" and, 5:56a
  Barthes on, 13:3099b
  Foscolo and, 5:319a–320b
  Klopstock and, 4:511a–512a
  Lukács and, 10:1255a, 1270a-b
  Staël's *De l'Allemagne* on, 5:108a
 Die natürliche Tochter (*The Natural
  Daughter*), 5:14b
 Die Wahlverwandtschaften (*Elective
  Affinities*), 5:15b, 16b–17a, 68a
  Benjamin's essay on, 11:1704b,
   1710a–1713b
 Dinesen and, 10:1294b
 Dostoevsky and, 7:1350b
 Egmont, 5:9a–10b, 36b
 Elpenor, 5:41b
 Faust, 5:2a-b, 5a, 14b, 17a, 17b–24a, 6:778b,
  782b, 790b, 791b–792b, 11:2095a
  Delacroix's lithographs inspired by,
   5:519b
  Der Stern des Bundes and, 8:464a

Egmont and, 5:9b, 10b
Herder as model for, 4:646a
Ibsen and, 7:1423a
Iphigenia in Tauris and, 5:12b
Khlebnikov's "Chertik" and, 10:1356b
Mann's *Doctor Faustus* and, 9:733b, 734a
Nerval's borrowing from, 6:945b, 946b,
    958b
Pasternak's *Doctor Zhivago* and, 10:1610b
personal experience and, 5:3a
Schiller and, 5:40b, 44b
Wedekind's plays influenced by, 8:269a,
    274b, 276a–277b
Faust II, George and, 8:447a
George on, 8:460b, 467a
Gide and, 8:496a
Götz von Berlichingen, 5:4a–5a, 9b, 10b
    historical drama and, 5:431b
Grillparzer and, 5:417a-b, 418b, 423a-b,
    443b
Heine and, 5:495a-b, 497a
"Helena," 5:14b
Herder's influence on, 4:639a-b, 645b–646a,
    647b, 656b
    Whitman's account, 4:655b
Hermann und Dorothea, 6:1115b–1116a
    Baggensen's *Parthenais* and, 5:371b
    Fauriel on, 5:371a–372b
    Manzoni's *The Betrothed* and,
        5:371a–372a, 380a
Hesse and, 9:835b
in Hesse's *Steppenwolf*, 9:848a, 848b
Hofmannsthal and, 9:689b, 690a, 710b
Hölderlin and, 5:143a, 148a, 155a
Hungarian romantics and, 9:863a
Iphigenia in Tauris (*Iphigenie auf Tauris*),
    5:10b–11a, 12a-b, 14a, 14b, 180b
    Grillparzer's critique of, 5:423a-b
    Grillparzer's *Sappho* and, 5:426b
    Hebbel and, 6:1109b
    human communication as potent in,
        5:420a
Italienische Reise (*Italian Journey*), 5:13b
Jiménez and, 9:1001b
on Kleist, 5:301a-b
Klopstock and, 4:514b–515a
Laforgue and, 7:1889b

Laune des Verliebten (The Lover's Whim),
    6:1149b
on Lesage's *Gil Blas*, 3:339b
Lessing and, 4:558a, 561b
Lukács on, 10:1256a, 1272b
Mandelshtam and, 10:1640a
in Mann's *Lotte in Weimar*, 9:738a
Manzoni and, 5:368b–369a, 392a
Maximen und Reflexionen (*Maxims and
    Reflections*), 5:15b, 17a
"May Song," 5:4a
Mérimée and, 6:750b
Mickiewicz and, 5:618a
Nerval and, 6:952b
Nietzsche and, 7:1647b, 1663a
Novalis and, 5:209a
on the novella, 9:725b
On Epic and Dramatic Poetry, 11:2093b
Ortega y Gasset on, 9:1135b
Richter and, 5:54a, 71a, 72a
    on *Hesperus*, 5:70b
    on *Titan*, 5:72b
Rilke and, 9:767b
Roman Elegies, 5:13a, 14a
    Pirandello and, 8:391a
Sainte-Beuve and, 6:855b
Schiller and, 5:38b–39a, 40a–42a, 50a
on Schiller's *The Maid of Orleans*, 5:47a
Schopenhauer's cultivation of, 5:395a-b
Staël and, 5:92b, 96a, 106a
Stella, 5:9a
Stirb und werde and, 11:1801a
Storm and, 6:915b
"The Brother and Sister," 5:12a
Theory of Color, 5:17a, 40b
Torquato Tasso, 5:12b–13a, 14a, 14b, 180b
    discussed by Lukács, György, 10:1270b
    Grillparzer's critique of, 5:423a-b
translation of Manzoni's writings by, 5:369a
Turgenev and, 6:1281a-b
"Über allen Gipfeln," analyzed by
    Kosztolányi, 10:1242a
Über Kunst und Altertum (*On Art and
    Antiquity*), Manzoni mentioned in,
    5:369a
Urfaust, 5:5a, 17b, 18a-b, 19a
    Devil in, 5:19b

Goethe, Johann Wolfgang von (*cont.*)
  "Urworte. Orpheus" ("Primal Words. Orphic"), 5:17a
  in Valéry's *My Faust*, 8:584b
  Venetian Epigrams, 5:14a
  Wagner and, 6:1149a-b, 1156b
  West-östlicher Divan (*The West-Eastern Divan*), 5:15a
    Ekelöf and, 12:2647a
    George and, 8:457a
    Ungaretti and, 10:1471a-b
  on Wieland, 4:602a, 605a, 610a
  Wilhelm Meister's Lehr- und Wanderjahre (*The Apprenticeship and Travels of Wilhelm Meister*)
    Schlegel's essay on, 11:1710a
    Wieland and, 4:594b
  Wilhelm Meisters Lehrjahre (*Wilhelm Meister's Apprenticeship*), 5:14b–15a, 16b, 40b, 41a, 72a, 6:924a–926b
    apprenticeship theme of, 5:216b
    Lukács on, 10:1261b, 1262a, 1269b–1270a
    Schlegel's review of, 5:190a
    two versions of, 10:1270a
  Wilhelm Meisters Wanderjahre (*Wilhelm Meister's Travels*), 5:15b–16b, 17a, 23b, 72a, 6:924a–926b
  Xenia, 5:41b–42a
  "Young Germany" movement and, 5:430b
Goethe, Ottilie von, Grillparzer's relations with, 5:418a
Goethe Prize, 8:449a
Goeze, Melchior, and Lessing, 4:559b–560a, 561a
Goëzman, Louis-Valentin, and Beaumarchais, 4:568a–572a, 573a, 576b
Goffman, Erving, *Frame Analysis*, 9:822a
"Gog e Magog" ("Gog and Magog"). *See* Pascoli, Giovanni, *Poemi conviviali*
"Gog e Magog" ("Gog and Magog")
"Góg és Magóg." *See* Ady, Endre
Gogol, Nikolay Vasilievich, **6:971a–996b**
  After the Play, 6:983b
  Arabesques, 6:973a, 979a
  Author's Confession, 6:983b
  Babel and, 11:1900b
  Bely on, 9:926a-b
    Bely's *The Silver Dove* and, 9:918b–919a
  Dead Souls, 6:973a, 973b, 974b, 985b–988b, 990b, 994a, 1066a
    Belinsky on, 6:996a
    Bely's *Petersburg* and, 9:922b
    symbolism of, 6:992a
  Dostoevsky and, 7:1350b
  Evenings on a Farm near Dikanka, 6:972a-b
  Goncharov and, 6:1065a, 1066a
  Government Inspector Unraveled, 6:983b
  Hans Küchelgarten, 6:971b
  "Ivan Shponka and His Aunt," 6:976a
  Khlebnikov and, 10:1357b–1358a
  Lermontov and, 6:1205a, 1221a, 1222b
  Mandelshtam's *Egipetskaia marka* and, 10:1643a-b
  Mann's *Doctor Faustus* and, 9:733b
  Marriage: A Completely Improbable Event in Two Acts, 6:984b–985b
  Mérimée and, 6:765b
  Mirgorod, 6:972b, 976b
  "Nevsky Avenue," 6:979a
  Nevsky Prospect, Bely's *Petersburg* and, 9:922b, 923b
  "Noch' pered Rozhdestvom" ("The Night Before Christmas"), Khlebnikov's "Vnuchka Malushi" and, 10:1350b
  "Notes of a Madman," 6:980a
    Bely's *Zapiski chudaka* and, 9:924b
  "Old World Landowners," 6:976b
  Selected Passages from Correspondence with Friends, 6:973b, 974a
  "Sorochinsky Fair," 6:975a
  "Strashnaia mest'" ("A Terrible Vengeance"), Khlebnikov's "Smert' Palivody" and, 10:1358a
  "Taras Bulba," 6:977b, 1205a
    Khlebnikov and, 10:1358a
  "The Carriage," 6:980b, 981a-b
  The Government Inspector, 6:973a, 973b, 983b–984b
    Mérimée's translation of, 6:765b
  "The Nose," 6:980b, 981a-b
  "The Overcoat" ("Shinel'"), 6:981b–982b
    Zamyatin's "Ela" and, 10:1196a
  "The Portrait," 6:979b

"The Story of the Quarrel of Ivan Ivanovich with Ivan Nikivorovich," 6:977a

"The Viy," 6:977b

Gogol's Stories, On. See Belinsky, Vissarion

"Gold Bug, The." *See* Poe, Edgar Allan

Gold (color), in Tieck, 5:240b–242b

Gold, as metaphor
in Ady's poetry, 9:861b, 862a
in Gottfried, 1:244b–245a
in Ronsard's "Hymne de l'or," 2:733a–734a

Gold Rush, The. See Chaplin, Charlie

Golden Age, in *Romance of the Rose,* 1:328a–329b

"Golden Apple of Desire, The." *See* Kundera, Milan

Golden Ass. See Apuleius, Lucius

Golden Bough, The. See Frazer, James

Golden Bowl. See James, Henry

Golden Chain, The. See Aquinas, Thomas, St., *Catena aurea*

Golden Fleece, The. See Corneille, Pierre, *La toison d'or*; Grillparzer, Franz

Golden Fruits, The. See Sarraute, Nathalie, *Les fruits d'or*

Golden Head. See Claudel, Paul, *Tête d'or*

Golden Kite, The. See Kosztolányi, Dezső, *Aranysárkány*

Golden mean
Castiglione and, 2:655b, 657b–658a
Machiavelli and, 2:612a
see also Moderation, theme of

Golden Mirror, The. See Wieland, Christoph Martin, *Der goldene Spiegel*

"Golden Pot, The." *See* Hoffmann, E. T. A.

Golden Resonance, The. *See* Tychyna, Pavlo, *Soniachni klarnety,* "Zolotyi homin"

"Golden Verses." *See* Nerval, Gérard de

Goldene Spiegel, Der. See Wieland, Christoph Martin

"Goldene Topf, Der." *See* Hoffmann, E. T. A., "The Golden Pot"

Goldene Vliess, Das. See Grillparzer, Franz, *The Golden Fleece*

Goldfish, The; or, My Father, That Hero. *See* Anouilh, Jean, *Les poissons rouges ou mon père ce héros*

Golding, John

on Marinetti's *Marfaka le futuriste,* 9:806b–807a

on words-in-freedom, 9:820a

Goldoni, Carlo, **4:421a–448b**

Adventures, 4:444a-b

Amalasunta, 4:424b

I cento e quattro accidenti in una notte (One-Hundred-and-Four Misfortunes in a Night), 4:425b

I due gemelli veneziani (*The Venetian Twins*), 4:426b

Il bugiardo (*The Liar*), 4:429a

Il buon padre (The Good Father), 4:424a

Il cavaliere e la dama (The Gentleman and the Lady), 4:428b

Il colosso, 4:423b–424a

Il figlio d'Arlecchino perduto e ritrovato (Harlequin's Son Lost and Found), 4:426b

Il frappatore (The Cheat), 4:426b

Il mecante fallito (The Bankrupt Merchant), 4:425b

Il teatro comico (The Comic Theater), 4:429a

Il vecchio bizzaro (The Eccentric Old Man), 4:430a

I pettegolezzi delle donne (Women's Gossip), 4:429a

La birba (The Scamp), 4:425a

La bottega del caffè (The Coffee-House), 4:429a

La buona figliuola (The Good Daughter), 4:430a

La buona moglie (The Good Wife), 4:429a, 439a

La cantatrice (The Singer), 4:424a

La donna de garbo (A Woman of Charm), 4:428a

La famiglia dell'antiquario (The Antiquarian's Family), 4:429a

La locandiera (The Mistress of the Inn), 4:429b, 439b–441a

La Pamela, 4:429a, 439a-b

La pupilla (The Ward), 4:425a

La putta onoratta (The Good Girl), 4:428a-b, 437b–439a

Goldoni, Carlo (*cont.*)

La sposa persiana (The Persian Bride),
4:430a

La trilogia della villeggiatura (Return),
4:443a–444b

La vedova scaltra (The Artful Widow),
4:428a-b

L'Arcadia in Brenta, 4:428b

L'Avvocato veneziano (The Venetian
Lawyer), 4:429a

Le bourru bienfaisant (The Well-meaning
Grouch), 4:432b

Le donne curiose (The Inquisitive Women),
4:429b

Mania, 4:443a–444a

Mémoires, 4:433a, 446a-b

Molière, 4:429a

Momolo cortesan (A Man of the World),
4:425b, 428a

Momolo sulla brenta (The Prodigal), 4:425b

Rosmonda, 4:425a

The Boors (I rusteghi), 4:431a, 441a–442b

The Servant of Two Masters (Il servitore di
due patrone), 4:426b, 436b–437b

The Squabbles of Chioggia (Le barrufe
Chiozzotte), 4:445a, 446a

Goldsmith, Oliver, The Vicar of Wakefield,
Balzac and, 5:651a

Golgota. See Krleža, Miroslav

Goliath Head, The. See Calitri, Charles

"Golos iz khora." See Blok, Alexander

Gombrowicz, Witold, **12:2563a–2588b**

Cosmos (Kosmos), 12:2565b, 2568a,
2569b–2570a, 2574b

Diary (Dziennik), 12:2565a-b, 2576a-b,
2586a–2587a

Ferdydurke, 12:2565b, 2578b–2580b
poses in, 12:2568b, 2570b
sadomasochism in, 12:2574b
sexuality in, 12:2568a

on "infantilization" of individuals, 10:1675a

Ivona, Princess of Burgundia (Iwona,
księżniczka Burgunda), 12:2577a,
2584b–2586a

Operetta (Operetka), 12:2577a, 2584b–2585b

Pamiętnik z okresu dojrzewania (Memoir
from the Time of Immaturity),
12:2577b–2578b

Pornografia, 12:2565b, 2568a, 2575a–2576a,
2583a–2584b

Possessed; or, The Secrets of Myslotch
(Opętani), 12:2577a

"Tancerz mecanasa Kraykowskiego" (Lawyer
Kraykowski's Dancer), 12:2578a-b

The Marriage (Ślub), 12:2577a,
2584b–2586a

Trans-Atlantyk, 12:2565b, 2573a–2574a,
2580b–2583a

Gomes Coelho, Joaquim Guilherme. See Dinis,
Júlio

Gómez de la Serna, Ramón, 9:609a

Senos (Breasts), 11:2169b–2170a

Gommes, Les. See Robbe-Grillet, Alain, The
Erasers

Goñi, Doña Carmen Nessi y. See Nessi y Goñi,
Doña Carmen

Goncharov, Ivan, **6:1061a–1087b**

A Common Story (Obyknovennaya istoriya),
6:1061a, 1065b–1069b, 1075a

An Uncommon Story, 6:1082b

Oblomov, 6:1061a-b, 1070a, 1073b–1082b,
1084b, 1085a

"Oblomov's Dream," 6:1073a, 1076–1077b,
1078a

Raysky, the Artist. See Goncharov, Ivan, The
Precipice

"Slugi starogo veka," 6:1085b

The Artist. See Goncharov, Ivan, The
Precipice

The Frigate Pallas (Fregat "Pallada"),
6:1061a, 1070a–1073a, 1076b

The Precipice (Obryv), 6:1061a, 1082b,
1083b–1085b

Goncharova, Natalya
Pushkin and, 5:662b, 663a
Tsvetaeva and, 11:1744b

Goncourt, Edmond Louis Antoine de
À bas le progrès (Down with Progress),
7:1398b, 1414b

Chérie, 7:1398b, 1404a, 1413b–1414b

Huysmans and, 7:1709a-b

La Faustin, 7:1398b, 1402b, 1413b, 1416b–1417a

Les frères Zemganno, 7:1398b, 1402b, 1413a-b

dramatic adaptation, 7:1415a

Maupassant and, 7:1763a-b

Goncourt, Edmond Louis Antoine and Jules Alfred Huot de, **7:1395a–1419b**

Académie Goncourt, 7:1395a-b

Azorín's literary criticism of, 9:645a

biographies of French women, 7:1396b

Charles Demailly, 7:1398a, 1403a, 1405a, 1410b

critical reception, 7:1403b–1404b

dramatic adaptation, 7:1415a

color imagery, 7:1401b, 1402a

écriture artiste, 7:1397b, 1399a-b, 1400b–1401a, 1409b

En 18 . . ., 7:1395a, 1396a

Gautier and, 7:1410a

Germinie Lacerteux, 7:1398a, 1399a, 1399b, 1401a-b, 1403a, 1406b–1407b, 1410b, 1413a-b, 1414b, 1416b

dramatic adaptation, 7:1415a

Henriette Maréchal, 7:1398a-b, 1414b–1415a, 1415b

Histoire de la société française pendant la Révolution (History of French Society During the Revolution), 7:1396b

Histoire de la société française pendant le Directoire (History of French Society During the Directory), 7:1396b

Huysmans and, 7:1709a-b

Idées et sensations (Ideas and Sensations), 7:1398b

importance of, 7:1627b

impressionism and, 7:1630b–1631a

Journal, 7:1395a, 1403a, 1403b, 1409b, 1416b, 1627b

La femme au dix-huitième siècle (Woman in the Eighteenth Century), 7:1396b, 1627b

La fille Elisa (Elisa), 7:1396a, 1398b, 1402a, 1406a, 1411b–1413a, 1712a

dramatic adaptation, 7:1415a, 1415b

La patrie en danger (The Fatherland in Danger), 7:1398b, 1414b

L'Art du dix-huitième siècle (Art of the Eighteenth Century), 7:1396b–1397a, 1627b, 1628b

on Greuze, 11:2028b–2029a

literary collaboration, 7:1400b–1401a

Madame Gervaisais, 7:1403a, 1410b–1411b, 1412a

Manette Salomon, 7:1403a, 1404b, 1406a, 1408a-b, 1630b, 9:1398a

dramatic adaptation, 7:1415a

themes, 7:1410a-b

narrative method, 7:1406a

political harassment, 7:1415a-b

Préfaces et manifestes littèraires (Prefaces and Literary Manifestos), 7:1398b

Prix Goncourt, 7:1395b, 1417b

Renée Mauperin, 7:1398a, 1403a

critical reception, 7:1405b–1406a

dramatic adaptation, 7:1415a

Soeur Philomène, 7:1398a, 1403a, 1405a-b, 1410b

dramatic adaptation, 7:1415a

stylistic devices, 7:1401a–1402b, 1402b–1403a

Taine and, 7:1452a

use of language, 7:1415b

Zola and, 7:1533a, 1712a

Goncourt, Jules Alfred Huot de. *See* Goncourt, Edmond Louis Antoine and Jules Alfred Huot de

Gondi, Jean François Paul de, on La Rochefoucauld's *Maximes,* 3:52a-b

Gondola Travel. *See* Arp, Jean, "Ein Stag fährt Gondel"

Góngora, Luis de

Azorín's approval of, 9:644b

Cela and, 13:3116a

Fábula de Polifemo y Galatea (The Fable of Polyphemus and Galatea), pastoral elements of, 2:914a

Jiménez and, 9:1008a

Lorca and, 11:2177a

Machado and, 9:753a

pastoral poetry of, 2:913a–914a

Soledades (Solitudes), pastoral elements of, 2:914a

Gontard, Susette
  Hölderlin and
    death of Susette, 5:155a, 159b, 167a
    relationship between, 5:149b–150a
Gonzaga family, Castiglione and, 2:645a–648a
Gonzenbach family, Hölderlin and, 5:163a
Good! A Poem of October. *See* Mayakovsky,
  Vladimir, *Khorosho! Oktyabr'skaya*
  poema
Good Daughter, The. *See* Goldoni, Carlo, *La*
  buona figliuola
Good and evil
  Augustine's *City of God* on, 1:33b, 36b
  Augustine's *On Free Will* on, 1:44a, 45a
  in Calvino's works, 13:3265b–3266a
  in Croce's *Filosofia della pratica*, 8:322a
  in Dürrenmatt's works, 13:3223b–3224a,
    3232b
  Goethe's view of
    in *Faust*, 5:21a
    in *Urfaust*, 5:20a
  in Ionesco's works, 13:3223b
  Milosz and, 13:2936a–2938a
  see also Virtues and vices
Good Father, The. *See* Goldoni, Carlo, *Il buon*
  padre
Good Girl, The. *See* Goldoni, Carlo, *La putta*
  onoratta
Good Life, The. *See* Moravia, Alberto, *La bella*
  vita
Good Morning, America. See Sandburg, Carl
"Good People." *See* Chekhov, Anton,
  "Khoroshie lyudi"
Good Samaritan, Weil and, 12:2810b
Good Soldier Švejk in Captivity, The. See
  Hašek, Jaroslav, *Dobrý voják Švejk v*
  zajetí
Good Soldier Švejk and His Fortunes in the
  World War, The. See Hašek, Jaroslav,
  Osudy dobrého vojáka Švejka za světové
  války
Good Soldier Švejk and Other Strange Tales,
  The. See Hašek, Jaroslav, *Dobrý voják*
  Švejk a jiné podivné historky
Good Song, The. *See* Verlaine, Paul, *La bonne*
  chanson

Good Wife, The. *See* Goldoni, Carlo, *La buona*
  moglie
Good Woman of Setzuan, The. See Brecht,
  Bertolt
Good-bye. *See* García Lorca, Federico,
  "Despedida"
Good-bye, My Round Earth. *See* Queneau,
  Raymond, *L'Instant fatal*
Good-for-Nothing, The. *See* Aymé, Marcel, *Le*
  vaurien
Goodbye, Unwashed Russia. *See* Lermontov,
  Mikhail Yurievich, "Proshchay,
  nemytaya Rossiya"
Goodness, in Rousseau, 4:464a
"Goodworld." *See* Khlebnikov, Velimir,
  "Ladomir"
"Gooseberries." *See* Chekhov, Anton,
  "Kryzhovnik"
Gorbachev, Georgii, on Babel, 11:1908b
Gore ot uma. See Griboedov, Alexander
Goremyka Pavel. See Gorky, Maxim
Gorenko, Anna Andreevna. *See* Akhmatova,
  Anna
Goriely, Benjamin, on Pasternak's "Deviat'sot
  piatyi god," 10:1601b
Gorky, Arshile, Breton on, 11:149a
Gorky, Maxim, **8:417a–446b**
  "An Incident from the Life of Makar," 8:440a
  attacked by Mayakovsky, 11:1847b–1848a
  autobiographical fiction, 11:1892b
  Babel and, 11:1886b, 1887a, 1903b, 1904a-b,
    1909a-b
  Belomorsko-Baltyskii Kanal imeni Stalina
    and, 8:422b–423a
  Blok and, 9:974a
  Breton on, 11:1955b
  Chekhov and, 7:1856a, 1857b, 1869a
  "Chelkash," 8:418a, 419a, 425a-b
  Childhood (Detstvo), 8:418a, 440a–441a
  Chudaki (Queer People), 8:435a
  Dachniki (Summer Folk), 8:417b, 436a-b
  Deti solntsa (Children of the Sun), 8:417b,
    420a, 436b, 437a
  Dostigaev i drugie (Dostigaev and Others),
    8:422b, 438b, 439a-b
  on Dostoevsky, 7:1349a

"Dvadtsat' shest' i odna" ("Twenty-Six Men and a Girl"), 8:417b–418a, 420b, 426a-b, 441b

Egor Bulychov i drugie (*Yegor Bulychov and Others*), 8:417b, 422b, 435a, 438b–439a, 439b

Fal'shivaia moneta (The Counterfeit Coin), 8:435a, 437b

Foma Gordeev, 8:418a, 419b, 427b, 428b, 429a–430a

  The Artamonov Business and, 8:430b

  The Three of Them and, 8:432a

Goremyka Pavel (*Orphan Paul*), 8:426b, 427a-b

Gorodok Okurov (The Little Town of Okurov), 8:420b

Ispoved' (*The Confession*), 8:421a, 427b, 433a, 434a-b

"Khoziain" ("The Boss"), 8:440a

"Konovalov," 8:425a, 425b–426a, 441b

Letopis' (The Chronicle), editorship of, 11:1903a

literary celebrity, 11:1893b

"Makar Chudra," 8:418a, 419a, 423b–424a, 425a

Moberg and, 11:2208a

"Moi interv'iu" (My Interviews), 8:420b

"Moi sputnik" ("My Travelling Companion"), 8:424b–425a

Mother (*Mat'*), 8:418a, 420b, 427b, 433a–434a

  Vassa Zheleznova and, 8:421a, 437a

My Apprenticeship (*V liudiakh*), 8:418a, 440a, 441a-b

My Universities (*Moi universitety*), 8:418a, 422a, 440a, 441b–442b

Na dne (*The Lower Depths*), 8:417b, 419b, 434b, 435b–436a, 437b

  premiere, 8:420a

Novaia zhizn' (New Life), 11:1904a, 1904b

"O pervoi liubvi" ("First Love"), 8:440a

"O vrede filosofii" ("On the Harm of Philosophy"), 8:440a

Ocherki i rasskazy (Stories and Sketches), 8:419a-b, 420a

on Pasternak's *Zhenia's Childhood*, 10:1601a

Poslednye (The Last Ones), 8:435a, 437a

power and beauty, seductiveness of, 11:1901a

Russian intellectuals aided by, 10:1192a

Somov i drugie (Somov and Others), 8:422b, 438a-b

Starik (The Old Man), 8:435a, 437b, 438a

"Starukha Izergil'" ("Old Izergil"), 8:424a-b, 425a

"Stepan Razin," 8:422a

"Storozh" ("The Watchman"), 8:440a

The Artamonov Business (*Delo Artamonovykh*), 8:427b, 428b, 429a, 432a, 439b

  analysis, 8:430a–431b

  characterization, 8:431a-b

  Childhood and, 8:440b

The Life of Klim Samgin (*Zhizn' Klima Samgina*), 8:422a, 427b, 428a-b

The Life of Matvei Kozhemyakin (*Zhizn' Matveia Kozhemiakina*), 8:421a, 427b, 428b, 432a, 432b–433a

The Petty Bourgeois (*Meshchane*), 8:417b, 419b, 435a-b

on Tolstoy, 7:1473a

Troe (*The Three of Them*), 8:427b, 432a-b

"V. G. Korolenko," 8:440a

"V Amerike" (In America), 8:420b

Varvary (*Barbarians*), 8:435a, 436b

Vassa Zheleznova, 8:421a, 435a, 437a-b, 438a

  "Soviet" version, 8:439b

Vragi (*Enemies*), 8:417b, 420b, 436b–437a

"Vremia Korolenko" ("The Days of Korolenko"), 8:440a

Zamyatin praised by, 10:1192b

Zykovy (*The Zykovs*), 8:435a, 437b

Gorla, Thérèse, 3:24b

"Gorod." *See* Blok, Alexander

Gorodok Okurov. See Gorky, Maxim

Gospel of John. *See* Bible

Gospel music, Yourcenar's translations, 12:2543a

Gospel of Nicodemus, Chrétien's *Lancelot* and, 1:198a

"Gospel of the Silver Mark," 1:362a-b

Gospel of Suffering, The. See Kierkegaard,
    Søren
Gospoda Glembajevi. See Krleža, Miroslav
Gospodjica. See Andrić, Ivo, *The Woman from
    Sarajevo*
"Gospozha Lenin." *See* Khlebnikov, Velimir
Gosse, Edmund
    Ibsen and, 7:1426b, 1436b
    Verlaine and, 7:1642a
"Got, dîner trinitâte." *See* Walther von der
    Vogelweide
Gothic tale
    Chekhov and, 7:1859b
    Dostoevsky and, 7:1350b
    Gogol and, 6:975a, 979b
    Hesse's *The Journey to the East* as, 9:851b
Gothic, the
    Dinesen and, 10:1295b–1297a
    Kierkegaard and, 6:1125b–1127a
Götterdämmerung. See Wagner, Richard
Götterdämmerung, Die. See Nietzsche,
    Friedrich, *The Twilight of the Idols*
Gottfried von Strassburg, **1:237a–262b**
    Thomas of Brittany's *Tristan* and, 1:148b,
        399b
    Tristan und Isold (*Tristan and Isolde*),
        1:239a–260b
        characterization, 1:257a–260b
        language in, 1:243b–250a
        major themes, 1:250a–257a
        manuscripts of, number of, 1:218b
        sources for, 1:239a–241a
    Walther and, 1:287a-b
    Wolfram and, 1:264b
Gotthein, Percy, 8.468aGreat
Gotthelf, Jeremias, Hofmannsthal and, 9:690a
*Göttinen, Die, oder die Drei Romane der
    Herzogin von Assy. See* Mann, Heinrich
Göttinger Hain (group of poets), Klopstock
    and, 4:512b
Gottsched, Johann Christoph
    and German neoclassicism, 4:542b–543a,
        544a-b
    and Lessing, 4:543a-b, 544a-b, 548a
Götz von Berlichingen. See Goethe, Johann
    Wolfgang von
Goudeket, Maurice, 9:618b, 622b, 623a

"Goujat" ("bumpkin"), in La Fontaine's verse,
    3:98b–99a
Gounod, Charles
    Faust, 5:18b
    Laforgue and, 7:1889b
Gourmont, Rémy de, and Jarry, 9:671a
Gournay, Marie de, 2:772b, 784b
Gourville, Jean de, 3:62a, 68b
"Goût du néant, Le." *See* Baudelaire, Charles,
    "The Longing for Nothingness"
"Goutte et l'araignée, La" ("The Gout and the
    Spider"). *See* La Fontaine, Jean de,
    Fables
"Gouttre, Le." *See* Baudelaire, Charles, "The
    Abyss"
Government
    Aymé's satire of, 12:2446b–2447a
    in La Bruyère's *Caractères*, 3:247a–248b
    Montesquieu's conception of, 3:353a, 356a-b
    universal, in Dante's *De monarchia*, 1:442b
Government Inspector, The. See Gogol,
    Nikolay Vasilievich
Government Inspector Unraveled. See Gogol,
    Nikolay Vasilievich
Govostis, Constantine, Ritsos and, 12:2816b
Gower, John, *Mirour de l'omme* (*Mirror of
    Man*), 1:355b–356a
Goya. See Ortega y Gasset, José
Goya, Francisco
    Gautier and, 6:1042b
    Hugo and, 6:698a
    Ortega y Gasset on, 9:1148a
    Valle-Inclán and, 8:346a
Goytisolo, Juan, Baroja's influence on, 9:613a
Gozzano, Guido
    "Arsenio," 8:71b
    "Invernale" (Winter Scene), 8:77a
    Montale and, 11:1989b
    Svevo and, 8:70b, 71b, 77a
Gozzi, Carlo
    Goldoni and, 4:430b–431a
    La fille de l'air, 5:103b
Graamand. See Gunnarsson, Gunnar
Grabbe, Christian Dietrich
    Comedy, Satire, Irony, and Deeper Meaning,
        fate tragedies satirized in, 5:425a
    Grillparzer's realism compared to, 5:444a

Herzog Theodor von Gothland (*Duke Theodor of Gothland*), Frisch and, 13:2923a-b
romanticism and, 13:2923b
weltschmerz of, 5:419b–420b
Grabenko, Yelena Andreevna, Lukács and, 10:1259a-b, 1260a, 1263b
"Gräber an der Küste." *See* Storm, Theodor
Gracchi (Roman politicians), Giraudoux's play about, 9:1059a
Gracchi, The. *See* Giraudoux, Jean, *Les Gracques*
Grace
in Castiglione, 2:654a–655b
"efficacious" and "sufficient," 3:133a-b, 134a
"Grâce, La." *See* Aymé, Marcel
Graces, in Foscolo's *Le grazie*, 5:335b–338a
"Graces that generous Heaven allots to few." *See* Petrarch, "Grazie ch'a pochi il Ciel largo destina"
Gracián, Baltasar, Azorín's literary criticism of, 9:645a
Gracq, Julien, *Poisson soluble*, 11:1952a
Gracques, Les. See Giraudoux, Jean
Graf Öderland. See Frisch, Max
Graf Petöfy. See Fontane, Theodor
Grail legend
Chrétien de Troyes and, *Conte du Graal*, 1:205b, 205b–206b
Gawain and, 1:158a-b
Rabelais and, 2:699a
theories of development, 1:151a–152b
in Wolfram, 1:269b–270a, 273a–281a
Grain de la voix, Le. See Barthes, Roland, *The Grain of the Voice*
Graindor de Douai, *chansons de geste* of, 1:109b
"Gramma tou Mathiou Paskali." *See* Seferis, George
Grammaire du vieil irlandais. See Vendryès, Joseph
Gramsci, Antonio
on futurism, 9:823b–824a
Italian Communist Party and, 12:2273b
L'Ordine Nuovo, 13:3133a-b

Quaderni dal carcere (*Prison Notebooks*), 8:85a
Svevo and, 8:70a-b, 85a
"Gran cero, El." *See* Machado, Antonio, *De un cancionero apócrifo*
Gran corbellino del munda, El. See Baroja, Pío
Gran teatro del mundo, El. See Calderòn de la Barca, Pedro
Granada, García Lorca and, 11:2168a, 2169a, 2200b–2201a
Grand Bob, Le. See Simenon, Georges
Grand Cashier, The. *See* Ady, Endre, "A nagy pénztárnok"
Grand chant courtois, *Romance of the Rose* and, 1:315a-b
Grand Condé. *See* Louis II de Bourbon, prince de Condé
Grand écart, Le (*The Grand Écart*). *See* Cocteau, Jean
Grand homme de province à Paris, Un. See Balzac, Honoré de
Grand Meaulnes, Le. See Alain-Fournier
Grand parangon des nouvelles nouvelles. See Nicolas de Troyes
Grande gaieté, La. *See* Aragon, Louis
Grande Milano tradizionale e futurista, La. See Marinetti, Filippo Tommaso
Grande proletaria si è mossa, La. See Pascoli, Giovanni
Grandet, Paul, on Verlaine, 7:1639a
Grandmother, The. See Simenon, Georges, *La vieille*
Grandsagne, Stéphane de, Sand and, 6:818a
Granite and Rainbow. See Woolf, Virginia
Grant, Richard
on the Goncourts, 7:1406a, 1407b
Charles Demailly, 7:1404a-b
Granville-Barker, Harley, *The Voysey Inheritance*, 7:1443b
Grapes of Wrath, The. See Steinbeck, John
Grass, Günter, **13:3365a–3388b**
Ausgefragt (Cross-examined), 13:3377b–3378a
Cat and Mouse (*Katz und Maus*), 13:3371b–3373b
"Claustrophobia" ("Platzangst"), 13:3378a

Grass, Günter (*cont.*)

   Die Vorzüge der Windhühner (The Advantages of Windfowl), 13:3365b–3366b

    "Blechmusik" ("Music for Brass"), 13:3366a

    "Polnische Fahne" (Polish Flag), 13:3366a

   Dog Years (*Hundejahre*), 13:3373b–3376b

   Flood (*Hochwasser*), 13:3366b

   From the Diary of a Snail (*Aus dem Tagebuch einer Schnecke*), 13:3379a–3380a

   Gleisdreieck (Triangle Junction), 13:3371a-b

    "Adebar," 13:3371a

    "Askese" ("Askesis"), 13:3371a-b

    "Trümmerfrau" (Rubble Woman), 13:3371a

   Headbirths; or, The Germans Are Dying Out (*Kopfgeburten; oder, Die Deutschen sterben aus*), 13:3383b–3384b

   Local Anaesthetic (*örtlich betäubt*), 13:3378a–3379a

   Max, 13:3377b

   Mister, Mister (*Onkel, Onkel*), 13:3366b

   "On My Teacher Döblin" ("Über meinen Lehrer Döblin"), 13:3373b

   Only Ten Minutes to Buffalo (*Noch zehn Minuten bis Buffalo*), 13:3366a-b

   Rocking Back and Forth (*Beritten hin und zurück*), 13:3366a-b

   The Citizen and His Voice (*Der Bürger und seine Stimme*), 13:3376b

   The Flounder (*Der Butt*), 13:3380a–3382a

   The Meeting at Telgte (*Das Treffen in Telgte*), 13:3382a–3383b

   The Plebeians Rehearse the Uprising (*Die Plebeier proben den Aufstand*), 13:3376b–3377b

   The Rat (*Die Rättin*), 13:3385a–3386a

   The Tin Drum (*Die Blechtrommel*), 13:3365a, 3367a–3371a

    Richter's *The Invisible Lodge* and, 5:63a

   The Wicked Cooks (*Die bösen Köche*), 13:3366b–3367a

   Über das Selbstverständliche (*Speak Out!*), 13:3376a-b

Grass, The. *See* Simon, Claude, *L'Herbe*

Grasset, Bernard, 9:1048b

"Grasshopper, The." *See* Chekhov, Anton, "Poprygunya"

Grasso, Domenico, on Silone's *Story of a Humble Christian*, 12:2300b

Gravelot, Hubert-François, in Goncourts' *L'Art du dix-huitième siècle*, 7:1397a

Graven images, in Frisch's works, 13:2902b–2903a, 2910b, 2911b, 2912a, 2913b, 2922a

Graves on the Coast. *See* Storm, Theodor, "Gräber an der Küste"

Graves, Robert, *The White Goddess*, Nerval's anticipation of, 6:961a

Graveyard meditations, Foscolo and, 5:331a–335b

Graveyard Reveries. See Strindberg, August, *Études funèbres*

Graveyard School, Klopstock and, 4:528b–529a

Gravitation, theme of, in Olesha's "Liompa," 11:2243a

Gravity and Grace. See Weil, Simone

Gray Man. *See* Gunnarsson, Gunnar, *Graamand*

Gray, Thomas

   Baudelaire and, 7:1329b

   Chénier's aesthetics compared to, 4:707a-b

"Grazie ch'a pochi il Ciel largo destina." *See* Petrarch

"Grazie, Le." *See* Foscolo, Ugo

Grażyna. See Mickiewicz, Adam

Grazzini, Antonfrancesco

   Le cene (*The Suppers*), 2:942a

   influence of Straparola's *Piacevoli notti* on, 2:941b–942a

Greased Pole, The. *See* Cela, Camilo José, *La cucaña*

Great Catechism, The. See Luther, Martin

Great Cycle, The. See Vesaas, Tarjei

Great Dictator, The. See Chaplin, Charlie

Great Dream, The. *See* Hauptmann, Gerhart, *Der grosse Traum*

Great Gaiety. *See* Aragon, Louis, *La grande gaieté*

"Great Garden, The." *See* Södergran, Edith, "Den stora trädgården"

Great Highway, The. See Strindberg, August, *Stora landsvägen*

Great Hour. *See* Ritsos, Yannis, *Trakter*

Great and Inestimable Chronicles of the Great and Enormous Giant Gargantua, The, 2:701b

Great Proletariat Has Stirred, The. *See* Pascoli, Giovanni, "La grande proletaria si è mossa"

Great Purge, the. *See* Stalinism, Terror

Great Rage of Philipp Hotz, The. *See* Frisch, Max, *Die grosse Wut des Philipp Hotz*

"Great Sally, The." *See* Elytis, Odysseus, *To Axion Esti (The Axion Esti)*, "Ta Pathi"

Great Scene, The. *See* Schnitzler, Arthur, "Grosse Szene"

Great Theatre of the World, The. See Calderón de la Barca, Pedro, *El gran teatro del mundo*

Great Traditional and Futurist Milan, The. See Marinetti, Filippo Tommaso, *La grande Milano tradizionale e futurista*

Great Weaver from Kashmir, The. *See* Laxness, Halldór, *Vefarinn mikli frákasmir*

Great Whirlwind of Life, The. *See* Baroja, Pío, *El gran corbellino del mundo*

"Great Zero, The." *See* Machado, Antonio, *De un cancionero apócrifo (From an Apocryphal Songbook)*, "El gran cero"

Greatness, human, Delacroix's views on, 5:535a

Greban, Arnoul, *Passion*, 1:469a, 469b–470b

Gréban, Simon, *The Acts of the Apostles*, 2:702a

Greco, El, *Burial of the Count of Orgaz*, 9:595a

Greece
civil war (1945–1947), Ritsos in, 12:2817a-b
D'Annunzio's trip to, 8:191a, 192a
Hauptmann's visit to, 8:162a-b
history
    Elytis' *The Little Mariner* and, 13:2984b
    twentieth century, 13:2956a-b, 2969b
landscape, Elytis and, 13:2958b, 2960a, 2968b
military junta (1967), 13:2972a, 2976b, 2980b, 2981a

Papadopoulos government, in Ritsos' writings, 12:821a, 2818b, 2824a, 2830b
politics, Kazantzakis' involvement in, 9:1068a-b

Greece, ancient
art
    Hölderlin and, 5:164a–165a
    Lessing on, 4:545b–546b
    Schlegel and, 5:179b–180a
    Burckhardt on, 6:1236b–1237a
    Chénier on, 4:710a
    Leconte de Lisle's attachment to, 6:1249b–1250a
    Schiller on, 5:38a, 38b, 39b, 40a
    as seen by Lukács, 10:1260b–1261a
    see also Classical world; Greek drama; Greek literature; Hellensim

Greece Expiring on the Ruins of Missolonghi. See Delacroix

Greed, theme of
in *Egils saga*, 1:387a
in medieval satire, 1:371a-b
Prudentius' *Psychomachia* on, 1:18a

Greek Anthology, influence on Renaissance pastoral poetry, 2:902b

Greek drama
Alfieri's translations of, 4:667a
Lessing on, 4:547b–548a
see also Classical literature, drama; Unities, dramatic

Greek language
Aquinas and, 1:415a-b
Augustine on, 1:26b–27a
demotic, Elytis' "Heroic and Elegiac Song" and, 13:2964a
Elytis on, 13:2965a, 2970a-b
modern, 13:2955b
    Cavafy's use of, 8:225b–226a
Unamuno on the study of, 8:286b

Greek literature
Delacroix's translations, 5:514b
Generation of 1930, 12:2255a
Hölderlin and, 5:164a–165a
Johnson and, 12:2373b–2374b
modern, schools, 12:2815a
New School of Athens, 12:2815a
poetry

Greek literature (*cont.*)
  poetry (*cont.*)
    decapentasyllabic verse, 12:2263b
    European influence, 12:2258b
    in George's *Der Teppich*, 8:462a
    historical periods, 12:2815a
    laic, 12:2838a
    metrical characteristics, 1:68a
    modern, 13:2955a-b, 2956b
    Yourcenar's translations, 12:2543a
    Quasimodo's translations, 12:2387b–2388a
Greek Lyric Poets. *See* Quasimodo, Salvatore,
  Lirici greci
Greek mythology. *See* Mythology, Greek
Greek National Theater
  Elytis and, 13:2972a
  Lyrical Stage, 12:2817a
Greek Orthodox liturgy. *See* Liturgy, Greek
  Orthodox
Greek Passion, The. See Kazantzakis, Nikos, *O
  Hristós ksanastavroñetai*
Greek romances
  Cervantes and, 2:828a, 828b, 841a-b
  chivalry and, 2:828b
  Renaissance intellectuals and, 2:841a
Greek Source, The. See Weil, Simone
"Green Cockatoo, The." *See* Schnitzler, Arthur
Green Greenfinch. *See* Jiménez, Juan Ramón,
  "Verde verderol"
Green Henry. See Keller, Gottfried
Green, Julien, Sarraute and, 12:2335a
"Green Lamp, The" (literary group), Olesha
  and, 11:2233b
Green Leaves. *See* Jiménez, Juan Ramón, *Las
  hojas verdes*
Green Mare, The. See Aymé, Marcel
Green Meadow, The. *See* Bely, Andrey, *Lug
  zelenyi*
Green Notebook. *See* Sainte-Beuve,
  Charles-Augustin, *Cahier vert*
Green Shutters, The. *See* Simenon, Georges,
  Les volets verts
Greene, Graham
  Brighton Rock, Robbe-Grillet and, 13:3244a
  on his characters, 12:2541a
  on Silone's *Fontamara*, 12:2293b
  The End of the Affair, 12:2550b

The Heart of the Matter, Robbe-Grillet and,
  13:3249b
Greene, Peter, 13:2968a-b
Greenland Lawsuits, The. See Richter, Jean
  Paul, *Grönländische Prozesse*
"Greetings, master of the world, our Caesar,
  hail." *See* Archpoet, "Salve mundi
  domine, Cesar noster ave"
Gregorio el Botero the Dwarf. *See* Ortega y
  Gasset, José, "La estética de 'Elenano
  Gregorio el Botero'"
Gregory IX, pope, Aristotelianism and,
  1:408b–409a
Gregory X, pope, Aquinas and, 1:415b
Gregory XIII, pope, Montaigne and, 2:778a-b
Gregory of Tours, *Historia Francorum* (History
  of the Franks), as source for
  Grillparzer's *Thou Shalt Not Lie*, 5:438a
"Grenouille et le rat, La." *See* La Fontaine,
  Jean de, *Fables*
"Grenouille qui se veut faire aussi grosse que
  le boeux, La." *See* La Fontaine, Jean de,
  Fables
"Grenouilles qui demandent un roi, Les." *See*
  La Fontaine, Jean de, *Fables*
Grenzsituationen (border situations), Broch
  and, 10:1389a
"Greshit' besstydno, neprobudno." *See* Blok,
  Alexander
Grete Minde. See Fontane, Theodor
Grétor, Willy, in Wedekind's plays, 8:270a
Grettis saga, 1:392a–393a, 397a
  plot compared with *Beowulf*, 1:59a-b
Greuze, Jean Baptiste
  Delacroix and, 5:531b
  Diderot and, 5:531b
  the Goncourts on, 7:1397a, 11:2028b–2029a
  The Paralytic, Diderot's admiration for,
  11:2028a
  The Punished Son, in Lampedusa's *The
  Leopard*, 11:2026b–2032a
Grey Eminence. See Huxley, Aldous
Grey, Thomas, Chateaubriand on, 5:137a
Griboedov, Alexander
  Gore ot uma (*Woe from Wit*), 6:1202a
  Khlebnikov's "Markiza Dezes" and,
  10:1356b

Lermontov and, 6:1202a

Griboedov Prize, 8:421a

Grido e paesaggi, Un. See Ungaretti, Giuseppe

Griechische Kulturgeschichte, Der. See
    Burckhardt, Jacob, *History of Greek*
    Culture

Grief. *See* Ungaretti, Giuseppe, *Il dolore*

Grieg, Edvard
    in *Na rubezhe dvukh stoletii,* 9:911b
    Peer Gynt music, 7:1422b

Griensteidl Society, Schnitzler and, 8:92a

"Grifel'naia oda." *See* Mandelshtam, Osip,
    "The Slate Ode"

Griffith, D. W., *Judith of Bethulia* (motion
    picture), 9:1050b

"Grigia." *See* Musil, Robert, *Drei Frauen*

Grigoriev, Apollon, 6:996b
    Dostoevsky and, 7:1357a
    on errors of fact in art, 10:1628a
    Mandelshtam's personal myth and, 10:1622a

Grigorovich, Dmitry V., Chekhov and, 7:1858b

Grillparzer, Anna Franziska (mother),
    influence on Franz, 5:419a

Grillparzer, Franz, **5:417a–445b**
    A Dream Is Life (*Der Traum ein Leben*),
        5:437a–438a
        theatrum mundi metaphor in, 5:422b
    A Faithful Servant of His Master (*Ein treuer*
        Diener seines Herrn), 5:433b–435a
        Blanca von Kastilien compared to, 5:424a
        Das Kloster bei Sendomir compared to,
            5:436a
        Hero and Leander compared to, 5:437a
        The Jewess of Toledo compared to, 5:442b
        "Young Germany" movement and, 5:430b
    "Auf zwei Vettern" ("To Two Cousins"), as
        early creative expression, 5:423b–424a
    Blanca von Kastilien (Blanche of Castile),
        5:424a-b
    Das Kloster bei Sendomir (The Monastery in
        Sendomir), 5:435a–436a
    Der arme Spielmann (*The Poor Musician*),
        5:439b–440a
        Family Strife in Hapsburg compared to,
            5:441b–442a
        publication of, 5:418a
    diaries of, 5:417a

Die unglücklichen Liebhaber (The Unhappy
    Lovers), 5:417b

Esther, his concealment of, 5:418a

Family Strife in Hapsburg (*Eine Bruderzwist*
    in Habsburg), 5:441a–442a
    his concealment of, 5:418a
    time as theme in, 5:422a

Hero and Leander (*Des Meeres und der*
    Liebe Wellen), 5:436a–437a
    A Dream Is Life compared to, 5:437b
    The Jewess of Toledo compared to, 5:442b

Hofmannsthal and, 9:689b, 690a

Kafka and, 9:1156a

König Ottokars Glück und Ende (*King*
    Ottokar, His Rise and Fall),
    5:430b–433a
    A Dream Is Life compared to, 5:438a
    censorship of, 5:433b

Libussa, 5:440a–441a
    Family Strife in Hapsburg compared to,
        5:441a-b
    his concealment of, 5:418a
    his desire for the destruction of, 5:441a

"Meine Erinnerungen an Beethoven"
    ("Memories of Beethoven"), 5:433a-b

Melusina, 5:433a

Sappho, 5:426b–428b
    Family Strife in Hapsburg compared to,
        5:441b
    Hero and Leander compared to,
        5:436b–437a
    The Golden Fleece compared to,
        5:429b–430a
    The Jewess of Toledo compared to, 5:442b
    time as theme in, 5:432b

Selbstbiographie (*Autobiography*)
    on *A Faithful Servant of His Master,*
        5:434a
    on historical tragedy, 5:432a-b
    on *Medea,* 5:430a
    on *Ottokar,* 5:431a
    on Schiller's influence, 5:424a

The Ancestress (*Die Ahnfrau*), 5:424b–426b
    A Dream Is Life compared to, 5:437b
    as beginning of his commitment to the
        stage, 5:417b
    Blanca von Kastilien and, 5:424a

Grillparzer, Franz (*cont.*)
　The Ancestress (*Die Ahnfrau*) (*cont.*)
　　rational vs. irrational in, 5:423b
　The Golden Fleece (*Das goldene Vliess*),
　　5:428b–430a
　　A Dream Is Life compared to, 5:438a
　　Libussa compared to, 5:440b–441a
　　Medea's comparative success, 5:430a
　　The Jewess of Toledo compared to, 5:442b
　　time as theme in, 5:422a
　The Jewess of Toledo (*Die Jüdin von
　　Toledo*), 5:442a–443a
　　Blanca von Kastilien and, 5:424a
　　his concealment of, 5:418a
　Thou Shalt Not Lie (*Weh dem, der lügt!*),
　　5:438a–439a
　　Grillparzer's withdrawal after, 5:428a,
　　　429a-b
　　rejection of, 5:418a, 438b
　　status of, 5:443b
Grillparzer Prize, Schnitzler and, 8:98a, 102a
Grillparzer, Wenzel (father), influence on
　Franz, 5:418b–419a
Grillwork Gate, The. *See* Gripenberg,
　Gallergrinden
Grimm Brothers
　Herder misinterpreted by, 4:658b
　Jungfrau Maleen (*Maid Maleen*),
　　8:124b–125a
　Maeterlinck and, 8:124b–125a, 139a
Grimm, Frédéric-Melchior, Sainte-Beuve on,
　6:851b
Grimmelshausen, J. J. (Hans) von
　Richter's *Flegeljahre* and, 5:74b
　Simplicissimus, Spanish picaresque and,
　　2:953a
Grinde-kveld eller den gode engelen. *See*
　Vesaas, Tarjei
Grindegard. Morgonen. *See* Vesaas, Tarjei
Gripenberg, *Gallergrinden* (The Grillwork
　Gate), 11:1785b
Grisi, Carlotta, Gautier and, 6:1035a
"Grodek." *See* Trakl, Georg
Gronfein, Evgeniia, marriage to Babel,
　11:1901b, 1905a
Grönländische Prozesse. *See* Richter, Jean
　Paul

Grænlendinga saga (*History of the
　Greenlanders*), 1:381a-b
Gros, Baron Jean-Antoine, Delacroix and,
　5:515a, 527b, 528b
Grossbuch. *See* Khlebnikov, Velimir
"Grosse Szene." *See* Schnitzler, Arthur
Grosse Traum, Der. *See* Hauptmann, Gerhart
Grosse Wut des Philipp Hotz, Die. *See* Frisch,
　Max
Grossen Kampffliegers, Landfahrers, Gauklers
　und Magiers Till Eulenspiegel
　Abenteuer, Streiche, Gaukeleien,
　Gesichte un Träume, Des. *See*
　Hauptmann, Gerhart
Grosseteste, Robert, 1:408b, 409a-b
Grosz, George, Heinrich Mann's *Kobes* and,
　8:535b
Grotenfelt, Södergran and, 11:1791b–1792a
Grotesque, the
　in Dürrenmatt's works, 13:3229a-b
　in Ghelderode's plays, 11:2113a, 2115a,
　　2135b
　in Grass's works, 13:3367b–3370b
　in *Hávarðar saga Ísfirðings*, 1:396b
　in Prudentius' works, 1:16b–17a
"Grotesque, Theater of the." *See* "Theater of
　the Grotesque"
Grotesque Tragedies, The. *See* Baroja, Pío, *Las
　tragedias grotescas*
Grotesques de la musique, Les. *See* Berlioz,
　Hector
Grotesques, Les. *See* Gautier, Théophile,
　Exhumations littéraires (*Literary
　Exhumations*)
Grotius, Hugo
　Law of War, Vico and, 3:298a, 299a
　Vico and, 3:300b, 307a
Grotte, La. *See* Anouilh, Jean
Grotteschi. *See* "Theater of the Grotesque"
Group Portrait with Lady. *See* Böll, Heinrich
Growth of the Soil. *See* Hamsun, Knut
Groza. *See* Ostrovsky, Alexander
Gründung Prags, Die. *See* Brentano, Clemens
Grüne Heinrich, Der. *See* Keller, Gottfried,
　Green Henry
"Grüne Kakadu, Der." *See* Schnitzler, Arthur,
　"The Green Cockatoo"

Grüne Kakadu, Der. See Schnitzler, Arthur, "The Green Cockatoo"

Grupp Krilon. See Johnson, Eyvind, Krilon trilogy

Gruppe 47
Böll and, 13:3168b
Grass and, 13:3365b

Gruppenbild mit Dame. See Böll, Heinrich, *Group Portrait with Lady*

"Gryningen." *See* Södergran, Edith

Gryphius, Andreas
in Grass's *Meeting at Telgte*, 13:3382a–3383b
Petrarchan influence, 2:504b

"Guardia de amor." *See* Jiménez, Juan Ramón

Guardo, Juana de, Lope de Vega and, 2:847a, 847b

Guarini, Giambattista
Pastor fido (*Faithful Shepherd*), 2:918a–920a
as tragicomedy, 2:917a
on tragicomedy, 2:917a-b

Guarini, Giovanni Battista. *See* Guarini, Giambattista

"Gucio zaczarowany." *See* Milosz, Czeslaw

Gudens hustru. See Moberg, Vilhelm

Guðjóusson, Halldór. *See* Laxness, Halldór

Gudok (journal), Olesha and, 11:2233b–2234a

Guds bustader. See Vesaas, Tarjei, *The Dwelling Places of God*

Guðsgjafaþula. See Laxness, Halldór

Guelfs and Ghibellines, 1:431a-b, 433b–434a
see also Blacks and Whites (political factions)

Guéric of Saint-Quentin, 1:411a

Guérin, Pierre-Narcisse, Delacroix and, 5:514b

Guermantes Way, The. See Proust, Marcel, *Remembrance of Things Past*

Guerra, La. See Machado, Antonio

Guerre de Troie n'aura pas lieu, La. See Giraudoux, Jean, *Tiger at the Gates*

"Guerre, La." *See* Ungaretti, Giuseppe

Guest the One-Eyed. See Gunnarsson, Gunnar, *Borgslægtens Historie* (The History of the Family at Borg), *Gæst den enøjede*

Guest of Reality. See Lagerkvist, Pär, *Gäst hos verkligheten*

Guetteur mélancolique, Le. See Apollinaire, Guillaume

Gueule de pierre. See Queneau, Raymond

Guevara, Antonio de, Azorín's approval of, 9:644b

Guevara, Luis Vélez de
El diablo cojuelo, Lesage's *Le diable boiteux* and, 3:324a
Reinar después de morir (To Reign After Death), 11:1919a

Gui, Bernard, 1:412a, 419b, 420a

Gui de Coucy, as trouvère, 1:179a–180a

Guicciardini, Ludovico, *L'hore di ricreatione* (*Hours of Recreation*), anecdotes in, 2:938b

"Guidatore notturno, Il." *See* Calvino, Italo, *t zero*, "The Night Driver"

Guide to the Underworld. See Ekelöf, Gunnar

"Guignol." *See* Jarry, Alfred

Guignol's Band. See Céline, Louis-Ferdinand

Guild of Poets. *See* Acmeism

Guild system, in Goethe's *Wilhelm Meister*, 5:16a

Guilhem de Montanhagol, 1:178a

Guillaume de Lorris, 1:310a
see also Romance of the Rose

Guillaume le Clerc, *Fergus*, 1:149b

Guillaume, Paul, 9:899a

Guillemardet, Félix, Delacroix's letters to, 5:518a-b, 520a

Guillén, Jorge, 9:760b
in Azorín's works, 9:652b
Jiménez and, 9:992a, 1005b
Ortega y Gasset and, 9:1119b

Guillén, Nicolas, Ritsos' translations of, 12:2819a, 2837b

Guillermo Dilthey y la idea de la vida. See Ortega y Gasset, José

Guilt
Canetti and, 12:2631a
Hebbel's concept of, 6:1100b
in Hugo's works, 6:696a–697b, 713a-b
in Ibsen's plays, 7:1425b
in Simenon's works, 12:2490a-b
in Undset's works, 9:1031a-b
in Wolfram, 1:270b–271a

Guiltless, The. See Broch, Hermann

Guilty protagonists, of Kafka, 9:1165a-b, 1166a-b, 1174a-b

"'Guilty'/'Not Guilty'? A Passion Narrative." *See* Kierkegaard, Søren, *Stages on Life's Way*

Guinizzelli, Guido, Dante and, 1:432b, 439a

Guiomar. *See* Valderrama, Pilar de

Guiraut de Bornelh, 1:441b

Guiraut Riquier, 1:178a-b

Guiton, Margaret, 3:90a-b

Guitry, Sacha, *If I Remember Right*, 9:736b

Guizot, François, Taine and, 7:1452a

"Gul-mullah's Trumpet." *See* Khlebnikov, Velimir, "Truba Gul'-Mully"

Gulag Archipelago, The. See Solzhenitsyn, Aleksandr

Gull-þóris saga, 1:397b–398a

Gulliver. See Simon, Claude

Gumilev, Nikolai
acmeist manifesto of, 10:1632b
Akhmatova and, 10:1522a-b, 1529a-b
"Bludnyi syn" ("The Prodigal Son"), Ivanov's attack on, 10:1632a
execution of, 10:1521a, 1639b
Mandelshtam and, 10:1626b, 1632a
Minsky's influence on, 10:1629a
power and beauty, seductiveness of, 11:1901a
Put' konkvistadorov (*The Path of the Conquistadors*), "romantic" school of poetry and, 10:1626b
on "the sublime tongue-tie," 10:1624a

Gundert, Hermann, 9:837a-b

Gundolf, Friedrich
on Burckhardt, 6:1225a
George and, 8:464b

Gunn, Nikola, 9:965b

Gunnar's Daughter. See Undset, Sigrid, *Fortællingen om Viga-Ljot og Vigdis*

Gunnarsson, Gunnar, **10:1497a–1518b**
Advent, 10:1516a
Borgslægtens Historie (The History of the Family at Borg), 10:1497a-b, 1498b–1500b, 1501b
Den danske Frue paa Hof (The Danish Mistress of Hof), 10:1499a-b

Gæst den Enøjede (*Guest the One-Eyed*), 10:1499b–1500a
Ormarr Ørlygsson, 10:1498b
Brandur paa Bjarg (Brandur on the Bjarg Farm), 10:1516a–1517a
Brimheiði (Surf Heath), 10:1517a
Brødrene (The Brothers), 10:1505b–1506a
"Da Lykken gik J. J. Snóksdal forbi" ("Fortune Passes By"), 10:1504b
De Blindes Hus (The House of the Blind), 10:1515b–1516a
Den glade Gaard og andre Historier (The Happy Farm and Other Stories), 10:1505a-b
Den unge Ørn (The Young Eagle), 10:1500a-b
Det nordiske Rige (The Nordic Realm), 10:1517b
Digte (Poems), 10:1498a
Drengen (The Boy), 10:1502a-b
Dyret med Glorien (The Animal with a Halo), 10:1506a
En Dag tilovers og andre Historier (An Extra Day and Other Stories), 10:1505b
Graamand (Gray Man), 10:1515a
Hvide-Krist (White Christ), 10:1514a–1515a
Jón Arason, 10:1497b, 1505b, 1512b–1514a
Jord (Earth), 10:1514a-b
Kirken paa Bjerget (The Church on the Hill), 10:1497b, 1506a–1512b
Den uerfarne Reisende (The Inexperienced Traveler), 10:1498a, 1509b–1511a
Hugleik den Haardtsejlende (Hugleik the Fearless Seafarer), 10:1511a–1512b
Leg med Straa (Playing with Straw), 10:1506a–1507a
Natten og Drømmen (*The Night and the Dream*, 10:1508a–1509b
Ships in the Sky (*Skibe paa Himlen*), 10:1502a, 1507a–1508a
"Kongesøn" (A King's Son), 10:1505a
Livets Strand (The Shore of Life), 10:1500b–1501b
Moðurminning (Remembering Mother), 10:1498a
Ramt (Struck), 10:1506a
Rævepelsene (The Sly Foxes), 10:1512a-b

Ringen (The Ring), 10:1505a

Salige er de Enfoldige (*Seven Days' Darkness*), 10:1503b–1504b

Sálumessa (Requiem), 10:1517a

Sjælemesse, 10:1517a

Smaa Historier, Ny Samling (Short Stories, New Collections), 10:1504b

Smaa Historier (Short Stories), 10:1504b–1505a

Smaa Skuespil (Short Plays), 10:1505b

Sonate-ved Havet (Sonata by the Sea), 10:1517a

Svartfugl (*The Black Cliffs*), 10:1512a, 1512b

The Sworn Brothers (*Edbrødrene*), 10:1502b–1503b

Varg i veum (Wolf in Sacred Places), 10:1501b–1502a

Vikivaki, 10:1515a-b

Vorljóð (Spring Poems), 10:1498a

Gunnlaug (monk), 1:382b

   Jóns saga helga, 1:383b

   Óláfs saga, 1:399a

Gunnlaugs saga ormstungu (*The Story of Gunnlaug Serpent-Tongue*), 1:398a-b

Gunther, the *Nibelungenlied* and, 1:211b–213a, 222a–224a

Gunther-Brunhild stories, the *Nibelungenlied* and, 1:213a, 213b

Gurlitt, Louis, Hebbel and, 6:1096a

"Gusev." *See* Chekhov, Anton

Guslar, 1:67a

Gustalin. See Aymé, Marcel

Gustav Adolfs Page. See Meyer, Conrad Ferdinand

Gustav Vasa. See Strindberg, August

Gute Mensch von Sezuan, Der. See Brecht, Bertolt, *The Good Woman of Setzuan*

Gutman, R. W., on Nietzsche and Wagner, 7:1653a

Gutzkow, Karl, 7:1925b–1926a

   Nero, Grillparzer's critique of, 5:430b

   "Young Germany" movement and, 5:430b

"Guy de Maupassant." *See* Babel, Isaac

Guy of Ponthieu, *Carmen de Hastingae proelio*, function of jongleur in, 1:102b–103a

Guyau, Marie-Jean, Azorín and, 9:644a, 645a

Guyon, Madame Jeanne Marie Bouvière de la Mothe-, 3:269b–270b

   Bossuet and, 3:172a-b

   Cantique des cantiques, 3:270b

   Fénelon and, 3:265b, 267a-b, 275b–276a

   inquiry at Issy and, 3:270b–271a

   Moyen court (*Short Method*), 3:268a, 270b, 277a

   quietism and, 3:268a-b

Guzla, La. See Mérimée, Prosper

Guzmán de Alfarache. See Alemán, Mateo

Gyges and His Ring. See Hebbel, Friedrich

"Gylfaginning." *See* Snorri Sturluson, *Edda*

Gymnadenia. See Undset, Sigrid

Gymnastics, language and, Valéry on, 8:575b

Gymnopaidia. See Seferis, George

"Gymnosophist, The." *See* Ekelöf, Gunnar

Gypsies

   in Hašek's writing, 9:1093a, 1102a

   in Lorca's poetry, 11:2169a-b, 2172a–2173b, 2177a–2181b, 2194b

   in Mérimée's works, 6:763a, 764b

"Gypsies." *See* Pushkin, Alexander, "Tsygany"

"Gypsies at the Fete." *See* Hašek, Jaroslav, "Cikáni o 'hodech'"

Gypsies, The. See Pushkin, Alexander

Gypsy Ballads. See García Lorca, Federico

"Gypsy Maid, The." *See* Cervantes, Miguel de, "La gitanilla"

"Gypsy, The." *See* Apollinaire, Guillaume, *Alcools*, "La tzigane"

"Gypsy Woman, The." *See* Södergran, Edith

Gyubal Wahazar, czyli Na przełęczach bezsensu (Gyubal Wahazar; or, Along the Cliffs of the Absurd). *See* Witkiewicz, Stanisław Ignacy

H

H. C. Andersens Levnedsbog 1805–1831. See Andersen, Hans Christian
"Ha fejem lehajtom." See Ady, Endre
"Ha holtan találkozunk." See Ady, Endre
Haas da Costa Ramos, Maria Eugénia. See Liz, Diana de
Habermas, Jürgen
  on Foucault, 13:3324b
  Zwischen den Rassen and, 8:530a
Habsburg Empire, in Krleža's Zastave, 11:1828b–1830a
"Hacia la tierra baja." See Machado, Antonio, Nuevas canciones (New Songs)
Hadji Abrek. See Lermontov, Mikhail Yurievich
Hadji-Murad. See Tolstoy, Leo
Hadlaub. See Keller, Gottfried
Haecke, Louis Van, Huysmans and, 7:1721b
Haecker, Theodor, writings in Böll's Wo warst du, Adam?, 13:3179a
"Hagia Sophia." See Mandelshtam, Osip
Hagiography, Eça and, 7:1693b
Hahn, Reynaldo, Proust and, 8:546b
Haiku
  Claudel and, 8:489a
  Kosztolányi and, 10:1245a-b
  Ungaretti and, 10:1464b
Hail to the Conqueror. See Ady, Endre, "Üdvözlet a győzőnek"
Hájek-Domažlický, Ladislav, Májové výkřiky (Shrieks of May) (with Jaroslav Hašek), 9:1096b–1097a
Hajimihail, Theophilos G., Seferis and, 12:2259a
"Hajnali részegség." See Kosztolányi, Dezső
Håkanson, Björn, Ekelöf and, 12:2636a
Hákon the Old of Iceland, king, 1:399a-b
Hákonar saga gamla. See Sturla Thórdarson
Haley, Alex, "roots phenomenon" and Herder's philosophy, 4:646b–647a
"Half Awake." See Ungaretti, Giuseppe, Allegria di naufragi (Mirth of Shipwrecks), "In dormiveglia"

"Half of Life." See Hölderlin, Friedrich, "Hälfte des Lebens"
Half-alexandrines, in Verlaine's poetry, 7:1637b
Half-line, in Anglo-Saxon poetry, 1:66b–67a
"Hälfte des Lebens." See Hölderlin, Friedrich
Hallberg, Peter, on Laxness, 12:2470a
Halldórs þáttr Snorrasonar, 1:384a
Halle, Adam de la. See Adam de la Halle
Hallfreðar saga, 1:384a-b
Hallucination, voluntary, in Breton's thought, 11:1958a
Halma. See Pérez Galdós, Benito
Hamann, Johann Georg
  Herder and, 4:639a
  on poetry, 5:3b
Hamartigenia. See Prudentius
Hamburg Dramaturgy, The. See Lessing, Gotthold Ephraim, Die Hamburgische Dramaturgie
Hamburger, Käte, on Rilke, 9:784a
Hamburgische Dramaturgie, Die. See Lessing, Gotthold Ephraim
Hamelin, Fortunée, Chateaubriand and, 5:130b
Hamilton, Nigel, on Heinrich Mann, 8:522a-b
Hamlet. See Shakespeare, William
"Hamlet." See Södergran, Edith
"Hamlet complex" of Schlegel, 5:178a-b
"Hamlet and Don Quixote." See Turgenev, Ivan
Hamlet figures, in Johnson's works, 12:2365a, 2366a-b
"Hamlet and His Problems." See Eliot, T. S.
Hampton, Christopher, Tales from Hollywood, 9:728a
Hamsun, Knut, **8:21a–43b**
  August, 8:37a–38a
  Benoni, 8:34a
  Bjørger, 8:22a
  Børn av tiden (Children of the Age), 8:35a
  Den Gaadefulde (The Enigmatic Man), 8:22a, 28b
  Den siste glede (Look Back on Happiness), 8:34a
  En vandrer spiller med sordin (With Muted Strings), 8:34a

Fra det moderne Amerikas Aandsliv (The Cultural Life of Modern America), 8:23b–24b

"Fra det ubevidste sjæleliv" (From the Unconscious Life of the Mind), 8:25b

"Frida" (unpublished), 8:22a

"Glahns Død" (Glahn's Death), 8:30a-b

Growth of the Soil (Markens grøde), 8:21a, 35a–36b, 39b, 11:2208b

Hunger (Sult), 8:23a, 23b–28a, 41a
  Gunnarsson's work and, 10:1511a

Konerne ved vandposten (The Women at the Pump), 8:35a, 36b

Landstrykere (Wayfarers), 8:37a

Moberg and, 11:2208b

Mysteries (Mysterier), 8:28a–29b, 31b, 34b

Norwegian realism and, 9:1037a

On Overgrown Paths (På gjenrodde stier), 8:25b, 41a-b

Pan, 8:29b–32b, 11:2208b

Ringen sluttet (The Ring Is Closed), 8:38b–39b

Rosa, 8:34a

Segelfoss by (Segelfoss Town), 8:35a, 11:2208b

Siste kapitel (Chapter the Last), 8:36b

"Skjærgaardsø" (Island Off the Coast), 8:31b

"Smaabyliv" (Small-Town Life), 8:28a

Sværmere (Dreamers), 8:34a

The Road Leads On (Men livet lever), 8:37a-b

Under høststjernen (Under the Autumn Star), 8:34a

Vesaas and, 11:2037a

Victoria, 8:32b–33a

Wanderer, The, 8:34a

Zamyatin and, 10:1188b

Han som fick leva om sitt liv. See Lagerkvist, Pär

Hand of a Stranger, The. See Cocteau, Jean, *Journal d'un inconnu*

Handbook of the Christian soldier. *See* Erasmus, *Enchiridion militis Christiani*

Handclasp, A. *See* Johnson, Eyvind, *Et Håndslag*

Handful of Blackberries, A. See Silone, Ignazio, *Una manciata di more*

Handke, Peter
  Die Stunde der wahren Empfindung (A Moment of True Feeling), 9:957a-b
  Ibsen and, 7:1754a

Hands Around. See Schnitzler, Arthur

"Hands of Jeanne Marie, The." *See* Rimbaud, Arthur, "Les mains de Jeanne Marie"

Hanging theme, in Queneau's works, 12:2520a

Hangman, The, See Lagerkvist, Pär, *Bödeln*

Hanneles Himmelfahrt. See Hauptmann, Gerhart

Hans Küchelgarten. See Gogol, Nikolay Vasilievich

Hans nådes tid. See Johnson, Eyvind, *The Days of His Grace*

Hans und Heinz Kirch (Hans and Heinz Kirch). See Storm, Theodor

Hænsa-þóris saga, 1:395b

Hańska, Madame, Balzac and, 5:613a, 635b–636a

Hanslick, Eduard, Wagnerism and, 6:1148b

Happiness
  in Camus, 13:3061a, 3064b–3065a
  in La Bruyère's *Caractères*, 3:242a
  sources of, in Valéry's *Graveyard by the Sea*, 8:579b

Happy Campaign, A. See Eça de Queiroz, José Maria, *Uma campanha alegre*

Happy Death, A. See Camus, Albert

Happy Farm and Other Stories, The. *See* Gunnarsson, Gunnar, *Den glade Gaard og andre Historier*

"Happy Life, The." *See* Hölderlin, Friedrich, "Das fröhliche Leben"

Happy Times in Norway. See Undset, Sigrid

Happy Warriors, The. See Laxness, Halldór, *Gerpla*

Hapsburgs, decline of, 10:1409a

Här har du ditt liv! See Johnson, Eyvind, *Romanen om Olof*

Harald Fairhair
  in sagas of Snorri Sturluson, 1:388a
  skaldic poetry and, 1:378b
  in *Vatnsdœla saga*, 1:390a

Hard Labor: Poems. See Pavese, Cesare, *Lavorare stanca*

Hard Times. See Dickens, Charles

Hard Winter, A. See Queneau, Raymond, *Un rude hiver*

Harðar saga, 1:397a

Hardenberg, Charlotte von, Benjamin Constant and, 4:410a-b, 412a-b

Hardenberg family, Novalis and, 5:206a

Hardenberg, Georg Friedrich Philip von. *See* Novalis

Harding, Gunnar, Ekelöf and, 12:2636a

Hardy, Alexandre
   Corneille and, 3:35b–36a, 36b
   dramatic unities and, 3:26b
   Guarini's influence on, 2:919b

Hardy, Thomas
   Jude the Obscure, reception of, 5:541a
   Proust and, 8:549b

"Hare a Nagyúrral." *See* Ady, Endre

Häring, George Wilhelm. *See* Alexis, Willibald

Harlem, in Lorca's poetry, 11:2183b–2185b

Harlequin's Son Lost and Found. *See* Goldoni, Carlo, *Il figlio d'Arlecchino perduto e ritrovato*

Harmadnapon. See Pilinszky, János

"Harmonie du soir." *See* Baudelaire, Charles, "Evening Harmony"

Harmony
   in Ariosto, 2:642b–643a
   in Montesquieu's thought, 3:347b–364a

Harold en Italie (*Harold in Italy*). *See* Berlioz, Hector

Harrington, Michael, on the revolt of the masses, 9:1145a

"Harry the Steppenwolf." *See* Hesse, Hermann, "Vom Steppenwolf"

Hart (Ukrainian union of proletarian writers), 10:1654b, 1655b

Hartina. See Ritsos, Yannis

Hartmann, Eduard von
   Philosophy of the Unconscious, Laforgue and, 7:1889a, 1890b, 1905b
   Strindberg and, 7:1753a

Hartmann, Nicolai, *aletheia*, 9:1128

Hartmann von Aue
   Chrétien's *Erec et Enide* and, 1:152b
   Gottfried and, 1:243a–244b
   Iwein, manuscripts of, number of, 1:218b
   Wolfram and, 1:264a-b, 285a-b

Harvesters, The. See Pavese, Cesare

Harzreise, Die (*The Harz Journey*). *See* Heine, Heinrich

Hašek, Jaroslav, **9:1091a–1118b**
   adaptation of popular tales, 9:1098a-b
   anti-German satire, 9:1108a-b
   "Babámovy archeologické snahy" (Babám's Endeavors as an Archaeologist), 9:1098b
   Bugulma cycle, 9:1109a–1110a
   "Čáka pěšáka Trunce" (Infantryman Trunec's Cap), 9:1102b
   Čapek and, 10:1580b, 1588a
   "Chto budet s chekhoslovatskoy burzhuaznoy respublikoy" (What Will Become of the Czechoslovak Bourgeois Republic?), 9:1108b
   "Cikáni o 'hodech'" (Gypsies at the Fete), 9:1093a
   Dobrý voják Švejk a jiné podivné historky (*The Good Soldier Švejk and Other Strange Tales*), 9:1104b–1106a
      Švejk's smile, 9:1105a-b
   Dobrý voják Švejk v zajetí (*The Good Soldier Švejk in Captivity*), 9:1106a–1107b
   "Elindult az Ajgó Márton . . ." (Márton Ajgó Set Off . . .), 9:1113b–1114a
   "Etuda" (A Study), 9:1097a-b
   "Fialový hrom" (Purple Thunderclap), 9:1099b
   "Historie dačická" (A Dačice Tale), 9:1100b
   "Historky z ražické bašty" (Tales from the Ražice Water-Bailiff's Cottage), 9:1098a
   "I vyklepal prach z obuvi své" (And He Shook Off the Dust from His Feet), 9:1109a
   "Jak jsem se setkal s autorem svého nekrologu" (How I Met the Author of My Obituary), 9:1109a
   "Jak Tövöl vrátil zlatník" (How Tövöl Returned a Guilder), 9:1102a
   "Jak vypadají ženy" (What Women Are Like), 9:1114a
   "Jste dcerou z lepší rodiny" (You Are a Young Lady from a Better-Class Family), 9:1113b

"Khristos i popy" (Christ and the Priests), 9:1108b

"Loupežný vrah před soudem" (A Murderer and Robber in Court), 9:1101a–1102a

Májové výkřiky (Shrieks of May) (with Ladislav Hájek-Domažlický), 9:1096b–1097a

"Malé nedorozuměni" (A Slight Misunderstanding), 9:1110a

Mann's Confessions of Felix Krull and, 9:737a

"Mladočeské volby na Malé straně" (The Young Czech Party's Election in the Lesser Town), 9:1100b

"Na opuštěné latríně" (On an Abandoned Latrine), 9:1103b

Nash put' (Our Way), 9:1095a

"Nešťastná historie s kocourem" (An Unfortunate Business with a Tomcat), 9:1101a

"Novoroční nadělení" (New Year Gift), 9:1100b–1101a

"Obchod s rakvemi" (A Coffin Shop), 9:1099a-b

"Obecní býk v Jablečnu" (The Jablečno Parish Bull), 9:1100b

"Oběť antimilitarismu" (A Victim of Antimilitarism), 9:1102b

Osudy dobrého vojáka Švejka za světové války (The Good Soldier Švejk and His Fortunes in the World War), 9:1091a, 1095b–1096a, 1110b–1116b
  Čapek and, 10:1578a
  characterization of Švejk, 9:1112a–1116a
  early versions, 9:1104b–1107b
  literary criticism, 9:1116a-b
  parody of decadent literature in, 9:1097a
  plot, 9:1111a–1112a
  sources for, 9:1096a-b
  Švejk's smile, 9:1114b
  treatment of women, 9:1113b–1114a

"Osudy medvěda od Hamagbúha" (The Fortunes of the Bear from Hamagbúh), 9:1100b

"Pan Florentin kontra Chocholka" (Mr. Florentin Versus Chocholka), 9:1103b

political prose, 9:1100b–1102b

Politické a sociální dějiny Strany mírného pokroku v mezích zákona (The Political and Social History of the Party of Moderate Progress Within the Limits of the Law), 9:1103b–1104b

"Psychiatrická záhada" (A Psychiatric Enigma), 9:1099b–1100a

"Rodinná tragédie" (A Family Tragedy), 9:1103a

"Rozmluva s cenzorem" (A Conversation with the Censor), 9:1091a-b

"Smutný osud nádražní misie" (The Sad Fate of the Railway Mission), 9:1103b

"Spartaks Helden" (The Heroes of Spartak), 9:1108b

"Sportovní fejeton" (Sports Column), 9:1100a-b

"Šťavnická Idyla" (Štiavnica Idyll), 9:1099a

"Svętci a zvířata" (Saints and Animals), 9:1098a-b

"U holiče" (At the Barber's), 9:109b–1099a

"Úřední horlivost pana Štěpána Brycha, výběrčího na pražském mostę" (The Professional Zeal of Mr. Štěpán Brych, Tollman on a Prague Bridge), 9:1100a

"Velitelem męsta Bugulmy" (Commandant of Bugulma), 9:1109b–1110a

"Vítězství, '" (Victory), 9:1096b

"Výprava zloděje Šejby" (Burglar Šejba's Expedition), 9:1099a

"Zápas o duše" (Fighting for Souls), 9:1098b

Hašek, Roman, in Pallas's Slovníček literární, 9:1116b

"Hashish Club, The." See Gautier, Théophile, "Le club des hachichins"

Hasidism, Kafka and, 9:1153a

Hass, Der: Deutsche Zeitgeschichte. See Mann, Heinrich

Hasus, J. P. F. See Richter, Jean Paul

Hatred: Essays in Modern German History. See Mann, Heinrich, Der Hass: Deutsche Zeitgeschichte

"Háttatal." See Snorri Sturluson, Edda

Hattingberg, Magda von, 9:771b

Hauff, Hermann, Hebbel and, 6:1094a

Hauff, Wilhelm, Scott's influence on, 5:431b

Haufniensis, Vigilius. See Kierkegaard, Søren

"Haunted House, The." *See* Pirandello, Luigi,
   "La casa del Granella"
Hauptmann, Carl, Wedekind and, 8:235
Hauptmann, Gerhart, **8:147a-174b**
   as an artist-sculptor, 8:151a–152a
   Atlantis (*Atlantis*), 8:156a
   Atriden-Tetralogie (Atridae Tetralogy),
      8:171a-b
   *Bahnwärter Thiel: Novellistische Studie aus
      dem märkischen Kiefernforst* (*Flagman
      Thiel*), 8:148a–149a
   in Bely's *Na rubezhe dvukh stoletii*, 9:911b
   Das Friedensfest (*A Family Reconciliation*),
      8:150a-b
      Wedekind's life in, 8:236b
   Der grosse Traum (The Great Dream),
      8:169a–170a
   Der Ketzer von Soana (*The Heretic of
      Soana*), 8:167a-b
   Der Narr in Christo Emanuel Quint (*The
      Fool in Christ: Emanuel Quint*),
      8:162b–163b
   Der neue Christophorus (*The New
      Christopher*), 8:161b, 162b, 163b, 167a,
      169a, 170a–171a, 172a
   Der rote Hahn (*The Red Hen*), 8:154b–155a
   *Des grossen Kampffliegers, Landfahrers,
      Gauklers und Magiers Till Eulenspiegel
      Abenteuer, Streiche, Gaukeleien,
      Gesichte und Traüme* (Adventures,
      Pranks, Dreams, . . . of Till
      Eulenspiegel), 8:162b, 168a–169a
   Die Ratten: Berliner Tragikomödie (*The
      Rats*), 8:164a–165a
   Die Weber (*The Weavers*), 8:152b–153b
      in Heinrich Mann's *Berlin*, 8:524a
   Einsame Menschen (*Lonely Lives*),
      8:150a–151a
   Elga, Grillparzer's *Das Kloster bei Sendomir*
      and, 5:435b–436a
   Fasching: Eine Studie (Fasching: A Study),
      8:152a
   Festspiel in deutschen Reimen
      (*Commemorative Masque*), 8:165a-b
   Florian Geyer, 8:156a–157a
      Fontane and, 6:1299a–1300a

   Fuhrmann Henschel (*Drayman Henschel*),
      8:157b–158b
   Grillparzer's influence on, 5:444a
   Hanneles Himmelfahrt (*The Assumption of
      Hannele*), 8:152a, 155a-b
   Ibsen's influence on, 7:1443b
   Indipohdi, 8:166a–167a
   "Jesus-Studien" (Jesus Studies), 8:150a
   Michael Kramer, 8:158b–159b
   religious and philosophical sources of,
      8:165b–166a, 168a, 169b–170a
   Rose Bernd, 8:159b–160b, 267a
   The Beaver Coat: A Comedy of Thieves (*Die
      Biberpelz*), 8:153b–154b
   The Island of the Great Mother (*Die Insel
      der grossen Mutter*), 8:162b, 167a–168a
   The Sunken Bell (*Die versunkene Glocke*),
      8:156a, 157a-b
   Und Pippa tanzt! (*And Pippa Dances!*),
      8:160b–162a
   Vor Sonnenaufgang, Soziales Drama (*Before
      Daybreak*), 8:149a–150a
   Wedekind and, 8:235a-b, 257b
      parodies of, 8:236b–237a, 244b
Haus ohne Hüter. See Böll, Heinrich, *The
   Unguarded House*
Hauser, Arnold, 7:1910a
Hauspostille. See Brecht, Bertolt, *Manual of
   Piety*
Haute surveillance, See Genet, Jean,
   Deathwatch
Hautefort, Marie de, 3:54b, 61a, 66b
Hauvette, Henri, *Boccace*, 2:510a
Hávarðar saga Ísfirðings (*Saga of Howard the
   Halt*), 1:396b–397a
   Undset and, 9:1019b
Hawthorne, Nathaniel, Maeterlinck and,
   8:123a
Haydn, Franz Joseph, Strindberg and, 7:1748a
Hayman, Ronald, on Nietzsche, 7:1679b
He Is Waiting for the Itinerant God. *See*
   Schnitzler, Arthur, "Er wartet auf den
   vazierenden Gott"
"He Resolves." *See* Cavafy, Constantine,
   "Omnyei"
He and She. See Musset, Paul de, *Lui et elle*

"He Who Finds a Horseshoe." *See* Mandelshtam, Osip, "Nashedshii podkovu"

He Who Says Yes/He Who Says No. See Brecht, Bertolt

"He?" *See* Maupassant, Guy de, "Lui?"

Headbirths; or, The Germans Are Dying Out. See Grass, Günter

Healing of the Novice Erasmus, The. *See* Zamyatin, Yevgeny Ivanovich, *O tom, kak istselen byl inok Erazm*

Hearing, sense of, in Elytis' "I Genesis," 13:2968b

"Heart of a Clown." *See* Rimbaud, Arthur, "Coeur de pitre"

Heart of Darkness. See Conrad, Joseph

Heart Hears Its Native Music, The. *See* Vesaas, Tarjei, *Hjarte høyrer sine heimlandstonar*

Heart of a Man, The. See Simenon, Georges, *Les volets verts*

Heart of the Matter, The. See Greene, Graham

Heartbreak. *See* Aragon, Louis, *Le crève-coeur*

Heaven, Augustine on, 1:33a

Heaven and Earth. See Byron, George Gordon, Lord

"Heaven and Earth." *See* Montale, Eugenio, *Satura*, "Cielo e terra"

Heaven and Hell. See Mérimée, Prosper

"Heavenly breeze that breathes in that green laurel, The." *See* Petrarch, *Canzoniere*, "L'Aura celeste che 'n quel verde lauro"

"Heavenly Christmas Tree, The." *See* Dostoevsky, Feodor

Hebbel, Friedrich, **6:1089a–1120a**

Agnes Bernauer, 6:1108a–1109b, 10:1256b

"An den Tragiker" (To the Tragedian), 6:1117a

Demetrius, 6:1089a

Der Diamant, 6:1099a, 1099b

Die Nibelungen (The Lay of the Nibelungs), 6:1112b–1115b

   Kriemhild's Revenge (*Kriemhilds Rache*), 6:1114a-b

   performance of, 6:1098a

   success of, 6:1089a, 1112a

The Invulnerable Siegfried (Der gehörnte Siegfried), 6:1113a-b

Die Schlacht bei Hemmingstedt (The Battle at Hemmingstedt), 7:1092b

Ein Trauerspiel in Sizilien (Sicilian Tragedy), 6:1096a, 1105b

"Gebet" (Prayer), 6:1118b–1119a

Genoveva, 6:1095a, 10:1256b

Grillparzer's dislike of, 5:418a-b

Gyges and His Ring, 6:1109b–1112a

Herod and Mariamne (Herodes und Mariamne), 6:1106a–1108a, 7:1428a

"Höchstes Gebot" (Ultimate Commandment), 6:1119a–1120a

on Ibsen, 7:1425a-b

"Ich und Du" (I and Thou), 6:1118a-b

Judith, 6:1094b–1095a, 1101a–1102a, 10:1256b

   Lukács and, 10:1263b

Julia, 6:1105b

   Lukács and, 10:1253a, 1253b, 1255b–1256b, 1256a-b

Maria Magdalena, 6:1102b–1103b, 1104b–1105a, 7:1428a, 8:267a, 10:1256b

   preface to, 6:1095a, 1100a, 1105a-b

Mutter und Kind (Mother and Child), 6:1097b, 1115b–1116a

My View on the Drama: A Reply to Professor Heilberg in Copenhagen, 6:1096b, 1100a

Neue Gedichte (New Poems), 6:1116b

   "Welt und Ich (The World and I), 6:1117b–1118a

Hebel, Johann Peter, *Unverhofftes Wiedersehen* (The Unanticipated Reencounter), 6:887b

Hébert, Jacques René, Büchner and, 6:1174a

Hecht, Ben (joint author). *See* MacArthur, Charles

Hecquet, Philippe, *Les vertus médicinales de l'eau commune* (The Medicinal Virtues of Ordinary Water), 3:333a

Hedda Gabler. See Ibsen, Henrik

Hedgehog and the Fox, The. See Berlin, Isaiah

Hedonism, in Gide's *Fruits of the Earth*, 8:512b–513a

Hegel, Georg Wilhelm Friedrich
  Apollinaire and, 9:901a
  art and, 5:412a
  Croce and, 8:313b, 314a, 315a-b, 316b,
    318b, 320a-b, 323a–325a
  dialectic, 7:1445a, 10:1266b–1267a,
    1267b–1268a
  education of, 9:835a
  Foucault and, 13:3331a–3333b
  Goncharov and, 6:1064a
  Hebbel and, 6:1100a, 1192a
  Heine and, 5:492a
  Herder's individualism contrasted with,
    4:652a
  Herder's stages of *Humanität* and, 4:648a-b
  Hölderlin and, 5:145a
  Ibsen and, 7:1425a, 1426a, 1445a
  influence of, 9:591a
  Kierkegaard and, 6:1141b–1142a
  Lukács and, 10:1256b, 1260a
  Mann's *Magic Mountain* and, 9:723a
  master-servant notion, Andersen and, 6:886a
  on the novel, 9:1137b
  on philosophy's development, 7:1660b
  on Schiller's *Wallenstein*, 5:44b
  Schlegel and, 5:177a
  Schopenhauer's competition with, 5:396a
  Taine and, 7:1453a
  The Phenomenology of Spirit
    discussed by Lukács, 10:1273b–1274a
    Richter and, 5:83b–84a
  Unamuno influenced by, 8:285a-b
  Vico and, 8:325a, 325b
  Zamyatin and, 10:1185b, 1196a, 1198a
Hegius, Alexander, Erasmus and, 2:572a
Heiberg, Johan Ludvig
  Andersen and, 6:872b–873a
  Kierkegaard and, 6:1128b
Heiðaharmur. See Gunnarsson, Gunnar,
  Brandur paa Bjarg
Heiðarvíga saga (*The Story of the
  Moor-killings*), 1:385b
Heidegger, Martin, 8:312b
  Being and existence, 9:1132b
  "Being-in-the-world," 9:1126b
  Bergson and, 8:52b, 65a
  Butor and, 13:3288a

  cogito, 9:1130b
  Grass and, 13:3375a–3376a
  Hölderlin and, 5:143a
  Kierkegaard and, 6:1140a
  Kosztolányi's *Golden Kite* and, 10:1239b
  Machado and, 9:763a
  Ortega y Gasset and, 9:1130b–1131b
  on poetry, 9:762b
  Sein und Zeit (*Being and Time*), Machado
    and, 9:761b
  theological arguments of, 11:1705b
Heidelberg, Lukács's stay in, 10:1257b–1263a
Heidelberger Ästhetik. See Lukács, György
Heidelberger Jahrbücher, Richter and, 5:79a
Heidelberger Philosophie der Kunst. See
  Lukács, György
Heights of Macchu Picchu, The. See Neruda,
  Pablo, *Las alturas de Macchu Picchu*
Heilagra manna sögur. See Unger, C. R.
Heilige, Der. See Meyer, Conrad Ferdinand
Heilige Johanna der Schlachthöfe, Die. See
  Brecht, Bertolt
Heimkehr, Die. See Heine, Heinrich
"Heimkunft." See Hölderlin, Friedrich
Heimskringla. See Snorri Sturluson
Heimsljós. See Laxness, Halldór
Heine, Heinrich, **5:489a–511b**
  Ady and, 9:862a
  Almansor, 5:493b
  on Andersen, 6:870b
  Apollinaire's "La Loreley" and, 9:887a
  Atta Troll: Ein Sommernachtstraum (*Atta
    Troll: A Midsummer Night's Dream*),
    5:504b–505a
  *Aus den Memoiren des Herren von
    Schnabelewopski* (*The Memoirs of Herr
    von Schnabelewopski*), 5:501a
  Berlioz and, 6:789b, 790a
  Briefe aus Berlin (*Letters from Berlin, 1822*),
    5:495a
  Buch der Lieder (*Book of Songs*),
    5:493a–494b, 496b, 497b
  De l'Allemagne, 5:501a-b
    counter to Staël's *De l'Allemagne*,
    5:106b–107a
  Der Salon (*The Salon*), 5:501a

Deutschland: Ein Wintermärchen (*Germany: A Winter's Tale*), 5:505a-b

Die Bäder von Lucca (*The Baths of Lucca*), 5:497b

Die Harzreise (*The Harz Journey*), 5:495a–496b

Die Harzreise (*The Journey to the Harz*), 9:1020b

Die Heimkehr (*Homecoming*), 5:493b

Die Nordsee (*The North Sea*), 5:493b

Die Romantische Schule (*The Romantic School*), 5:501b, 502a

"Die Schlesischen Weber" ("The Silesian Weavers"), 5:504b

Die Stadt Lucca (*The City of Lucca*), 5:497b

Doctor Faust, 5:506b

Drei und dreissig Gedichte (*Thirty-three Poems*), 5:493b

Elementargeister (*Elemental Spirits*), 5:503a, 506a

Englische Fragmente (*English Fragments*), 5:497a

Florentinische Nächte (*Florentine Nights*), 5:503a

Französische Maler (*French Painters*), 5:501a

Französische Zustände (*Conditions in France, 1833*), 5:501a

French romanticism and, 7:1685b

"Für die Mouche" ("To the Fly"), 5:509a-b

Gedichte 1853 und 1854 (*Poems, 1853 and 1854*), 5:508a

Gedichte (*Poems*), 5:493a

George's *Das Jahr der Seele* and, 8:459b

Geständnisse (*Confessions*), 5:508b–509a

"Girl at Sea," 5:419b

Hebbel and, 6:1095b–1096a

Heinrich Heine über Ludwig Börne (*Heinrich Heine on Ludwig Börne*), 5:503b–504a

in Heinrich Mann's *Professor Unrat*, 8:528a

Hölderlin and, 5:143a

Ideen, Das Buch Le Grand (*Ideas: The Book of Le Grand*), 5:496b–497a

"Im Anfang war die Nachtigall" ("In the Beginning Was the Nightingale"), Mandelshtam's "Knemetskoi rechi" and, 10:1645a

Knittelvers, Mandelshtam and, 10:1635b

Lermontov and, 6:1199a

Letters from Helgoland, 5:498a-b

Lutetia, 5:508a-b

on Musset, 6:1030b–1031a

Neue Gedichte (*New Poems*), 5:505a

Neuer Frühling (*New Spring*), 5:497b, 505a

Pirandello's "L'Azione parlata" and, 8:392a-b

Reise von München nach Genua (*Journey from Munich to Genoa*), 5:497b

Reisebilder (*Travel Pictures*), 5:493b, 496a–497b, 6:789b, 1150a

Romanzero, 5:507b–508a

Salon II, 5:501b–502a

Salon III, 5:503a

Salon IV, 5:503b

Sand and, 6:826b

Schiller and, 5:50a

Shakespeares Mädchen und Frauen (*Shakespeare's Maidens and Ladies*), 5:503a

Storm and, 6:915b

"Tannhäuser," 5:505a

The Gods of Greece, 5:39b

Tragödien, nebst einem lyrischen Intermezzo (*Tragedies with a Lyrical Intermezzo*), 5:493a-b

Über die französische Bühne (*On the French Stage*), 5:503b

Über Polen (*On Poland*), 5:495a

Variae, 5:502b, 505a

Vermischte Schriften (*Miscellaneous Writings*), 5:508a-b

Wagner and, 6:1150a-b

weltschmerz of, 5:419b–420b

William Ratcliff, 5:493b

Zur Geschichte der Religion und Philosophie in Deutschland (*On the History of Religion and Philosophy in Germany*). See Heine, Heinrich, *Salon II*

"Heine úr lovagol." See Ady, Endre

Heinrich Heine über Ludwig Börne (*Heinrich Heine on Ludwig Börne*). *See* Heine, Heinrich

Heinrich von dem Türlin, *Diu Krône*, 1:158b

Heinrich von Meissen, in George's *Sagen und Sänge*, 8:456b

Heinrich von Ofterdingen. *See* Novalis

Heinrich von Veldeke, 1:242b
  Gottfried and, 1:244a

"Heizer, Der." *See* Kafka, Franz, *Amerika*

Helden minne ir klage, Der. *See* Wolfram von Eschenbach

Helen. *See* Ritsos, Yannis, *I Eleni*

"Helen." *See* Seferis, George, *Imerologio katastromatos C* (*Logbook III*), "Eleni"

Helen of Troy
  in Goethe's *Faust*, 5:22a, 22b, 23a
  in Ritsos' poetry, 12:2831b–2832a

"Helena." *See* Goethe, Johann Wolfgang von; Vigny, Alfred Victor de, *Poèmes* (*Poems*)

"Hélène." *See* Leconte de Lisle, Charles Marie

"Helian." *See* Trakl, Georg

Heliocentrism, in sixteenth century, 3:8a

Heliodorus
  Cervantes and, 2:828a, 841a
  Historia Aethiopica (*Ethiopian History*), 2:828a

Heliogabalus; or, The Anarchist Crowned (*Héliogabale, ou l'anarchiste couronné*). *See* Artaud, Antonin

Heliogabalus, emperor of Rome
  Algabal and, 8:453a
  Artaud compared to, 11:1961b

Hell, Christian, 6:992b
  images of, in Rabelais's *Fifth Book*, 2:713a–714a

Hell of a Mess!, A. *See* Ionesco, Eugène, *Ce formidable bordel!*

Hellenism
  Seferis and, 12:2264a, 2265a, 2268b, 2269b
  see also Classical literature; Greece

Heller, Erich
  on Mann's *Doctor Faustus*, 9:735b
  on Nietzsche and Rilke, 9:776b
  on Schopenhauer's aesthetics, 5:414a

Heller, Joseph
  Catch-22, Confessions of Felix Krull and, 9:737a

Hašek and, 9:1099b

Hellingrath, Norbert von
  George and, 8:460b
  Hölderlin and, 9:771b

Helming, 1:378b

Hélo, hélo, por do viene, Poema de mio Cid as source for, 1:132a

Héloïse, in Gottfried, 1:253a

"Héloïse et Abélard." *See* Artaud, Antonin

"Help!" *See* Čapek, Karel, "Pomoc!"

Helvetian Republic, Voltaire in, 4:377a–378a

Hemingway, Ernest
  Babel and, 11:1888b
  Baroja and, 9:613a
  Camus and, 13:3055b
  For Whom the Bell Tolls, 13:3037a
    Vittorini's *Men and Not Men* and, 12:2746b
  Marinetti and, 9:805a

Hémistiches. *See* Half-alexandrines

Hemmet och stjärnan. *See* Lagerkvist, Pär

Hemmung, Symptom und Angst. *See* Freud, Sigmund

Hemsöborna. *See* Strindberg, August

Hemsterhuis, Franz, Novalis and, 5:208a

Hendecasyllabic line (poetry), 1:445b
  of Jiménez, 9:998a

Hennique, Léon, Maupassant and, 7:1763b

Henri II of France, king
  Rabelais and, 2:697b
  religious dissent and, 2:697a

Henri III of France, king
  in Dumas's works, 6:720b–721b, 726b, 729a
  Montaigne and, 2:779a

Henri IV of France, king, 3:264a
  in fiction of Heinrich Mann, 8:537b–540b
  La Flèche and, 3:1b
  Montaigne and, 2:779a
  Voltaire's *La henriade* on, 4:371a–372a
  see also Mann, Heinrich, *Die Vollendung des Königs Henri Quatre*

Henri de Gornay, funeral oration on by Bossuet, 3:163b

Henri III et sa cour. *See* Dumas père, Alexandre

Henri Matisse, roman (*Henri Matisse, A Novel*). *See* Aragon, Louis

Henri, Robert, influence of Emerson and Whitman on, 4:657b–658a

Henriade, La. See Voltaire

Henrietta Maria of England
  elegy for by Bossuet, 3:164b–165a
  funeral oration on by Bossuet, 3:163b, 166b, 167a, 171a-b

Henriette Maréchal. See Goncourt, Edmond Louis Antoine and Jules Alfred Huot de

Henry IV. See Shakespeare, William

Henry VI. See Shakespeare, William

Henry VII of Luxembourg, Holy Roman Emperor, Dante and, 1:434b–435a, 441a

Henry of Bergen, Erasmus and, 2:572b–573a

Henry Brulard. See Stendhal, *Vie de Henry Brulard*

Henry III and His Court. See Dumas père, Alexandre, *Henri III et sa cour*

Henry IV. See Pirandello, Luigi

Henry, King of France. See Mann, Heinrich, *Die Vollendung des Königs Henri Quatre*

Henry of Navarre. *See* Henri IV of France, king

Henry, O., Zamyatin and, 10:1200a

Heptaméron. See Marguerite of Navarre

Heptasyllabic verse
  in La Fontaine's *Fables*, 3:83b
  in Musset's *Nights*, 6:1024b

"Her golden hair was loosed to the breeze." *See* Petrarch, *Canzoniere*, "Erano i capei d'oro a l'aura sparsi"

Her Husband. See Pirandello, Luigi, *Suo marito*

Herakles. See Wedekind, Frank

Herbe, L'. See Simon, Claude

Herbois, Collot d', speech against Chénier, 4:704a

Herbort von Fritzlar, 1:242b

Herculano, Alexandre
  historical novel and, 7:1696b
  "O Pároco da Aldeia" (The Village Priest), 7:1695b

"Hercule chrestien." *See* Ronsard, Pierre de

Hercule mourant. See Rotrou, Jean de

Hercules
  in Camoëns' *The Two Amphitryons*, 2:756a
  in French literature, 2:743b
  in Ronsard's poetry, 2:743b–744b

Hercules, Rimbaud and, 7:1796a

Herder, Caroline, 5:13a

Herder, Johann Gottfried von, **4:639a–660b**, 8:314a
  Goethe and, 5:1b, 3b, 4a, 18b
  Ideen zur Philosophie der Geschichte der Menschheit (*Outlines of a Philosophy of the History of Man*)
    historical relativism in, 4:644a
    translated by Edgar Quinet, 5:583b
    translated by T. Churchill, 4:653b
    withheld sections of, 4:652b
  relation of self to external reality, 7:1477b–1478a
  Richter and, 5:58b, 71a, 71b
  The School for Aesthetics, 5:77b
  Titan and, 5:72b
  Schlegel and, 5:179b
  Stimmen der Völker in Liedern (*Voices of the People in Song*), 4:645a
  The Spirit of Hebrew Poetry (*Vom Geist der ebräischen Poesie*), 4:649a–650a
  translation by Marsh, 4:649b, 653b
  Wagner and, 7:1651b

"Here he is—look—exhausted from foreign lands." *See* Tsvetaeva, Marina, "Vot on—gliadi—ustavshii ot chuzhbin"

Here Is Your Life! See Johnson, Eyvind, *Romanen om Olof*

Heredia, José Maria de
  Gide and, 8:495b
  Jiménez and, 9:993b
  poetry of, 7:1621a
  Verlaine and, 7:1620b

Heredity
  in Storm, 6:919b–920a
  Zola on, 7:1522a–1523b

Hérésiarque et cie, L' (*The Heresiarch and Co.*). *See* Apollinaire, Guillaume

Heresy
  Augustine on, 1:24a
  and Bossuet's *History of the Variations in the Protestant Churches*, 3:170b–171a

Heresy (*cont.*)
　Prudentius on
　　Apotheosis, 1:7b–8b
　　Hamartigenia, 1:8b, 18a-b
　Romance of the Rose and, 1:332a-b
Heretic of Soana, The. See Hauptmann,
　　Gerhart, *Der Ketzer von Soana*
Hermann the German, 1:408b
Hermann, Johann Berhard, 5:56a
Hermann and the Princes. See Klopstock,
　　Friedrich Gottlieb
Hermann of Thuringia
　Walther and, 1:298b–299a
　Wolfram and, 1:263a-b
Hermann und Dorothea. See Goethe, Johann
　　Wolfgang von
Hermannsschlacht, Die. See Kleist, Heinrich
　　von
Hermano Juan, El. See Unamuno, Miguel de
Hermetic themes, in Arp, 10:1377a-b
Hermeticism
　Bernardo and, 12:2390a
　brevity and, 12:2394b
　classicism and, 12:2390b
　concept of, 12:2390a
　decline of, 12:2400b
　Quasimodo and, 12:2390b–2391a, 2395a,
　　2399a, 2407a, 2409a-b
　Romanticism and, 12:2390a-b
Hermine, L'. See Anouilh, Jean, *The Ermine*
"Hermit, The." *See* Apollinaire, Guillaume,
　　Alcools, "L'Ermite"
Hermit, The. See Ionesco, Eugène, *Le solitaire*
Hermitages of Córdoba, The. *See* Ortega y
　　Gasset, José, "Las ermitas de Córdoba"
Hermits, The. *See* Leconte de Lisle, Charles
　　Marie, "Les ascètes"
Hermosura de Angélica, La. See Lope de Vega
Hernández, Valentín, 8:287a
Hernani. See Hugo, Victor
Hero
　in Akhmatova's *Poem Without a Hero*,
　　10:1535a, 1538b, 1539b
　in Austrian literature, Grillparzer's *A*
　　Faithful Servant of His Master, 5:434a-b
　of *chanson de geste*, as exemplar,
　　1:102b–103a

in *Chanson de Roland*, 1:60b
in French literature, Sadean hero,
　　4:623a–624b, 628b–629a
in Germanic literature, *Beowulf*, 1:60a–62a
Gide's concept of in *Theseus*, 8:514b–515a
in Gottfried, 1:257a–258b
in Greek literature, Achilles in the *Iliad*,
　　1:60b
in Indo-European society, 1:60b–61a, 74a
in Italian literature, of Alfieri, 4:661a-b
Lermontov's concept of, 6:1220a
Roland as exemplar, 1:103a–104a
romantic, in Hoffmann, 5:284a-b
weltschmerz characters and, 5:434a-b
see also Biedermeier period; Heroism
Hero and Leander, Grillparzer's treatment of,
　　5:436a–437a
Hero and Leander. See Grillparzer, Franz
Hero of Our Times, A. See Lermontov, Mikhail
　　Yurievich
Herod, king
　Hebbel's play about, 6:1106a–1108a
　in Lagerkvist's *Herod and Mariamne*,
　　10:1701a-b
Herod and Mariamne. See Hebbel, Friedrich;
　　Lagerkvist, Pär, *Mariamne*
"Herodes Atticus." *See* Cavafy, Constantine,
　　"Irodis Attikos"
Herodes und Mariamne. See Hebbel,
　　Friedrich, *Herod and Mariamne*
Hérodiade. See Mallarmé, Stéphane
"Hérodias." *See* Flaubert, Gustave
Herodotus
　History, as source for Khlebnikov's
　　"Asparukh," 10:1356a-b
　"Life of Homer," Chénier and, 4:707b
Heroes of Spartak, The. See Hašek, Jaroslav,
　　"Spartaks Helden"
"Heroic and Elegiac Song for the Lost Second
　　Lieutenant of the Albanian Campaign,
　　The." *See* Elytis, Odysseus, "Asma
　　iroiko kai penthimo yia ton hameno
　　anthipolohaghos tis Alvanias"
Heroism
　in fiction of Olesha, 11:2252a
　in Goncharov's works, 6:1075a
　as a theme in *Beowulf*, 1:80b–81a, 82b–84a

see also Hero

"Heroism." See Montale, Eugenio, "L'Eroismo"

Hérold, Jacques, Butor and, 13:3305b–3306a, 3307a

Herr Bengts Husfru (Herr Bengt's Wife). See Strindberg, August

Herr Biedermann und die Brandstifter. See Frisch, Max, The Firebugs

"Herr der Insel, Der." See George, Stefan, Die Bücher der Hirten- und Preisgedichte . . . (The Books of Eclogues and Eulogies), Hirtengedichte poems

Herr Eugen Dühring's Revolution in Science. See Marx, Karl, and Friedrich Engels, Herrn Eugen Dührings Umwältung der Wissenschaft

Herr Puntila und sein Knecht Matti. See Brecht, Bertolt, Puntila and Matti, His Hired Man

Herrenhof (Viennese café), 9:1155a

Herrick, Robert, 2:728b

Herrmann, Ignát, Hašek and, 9:1096a

Hervarar saga ok Heiðreks konungs, 1:400b–401a

Hervart family, 3:77b

Hervieu, Paul, Le dédale (The Maze), 7:1921a

"Herzeliebez frowelîn." See Walther von der Vogelweide

Herzen, Alexander, Goncharov and, 6:1064a

Herzensergiessungen eines kunstliebenden Klosterbruders. See Tieck, Ludwig

Herzog Theodor von Gothland. See Grabbe, Christian Dietrich

He's right—once again the lamp, the drugstore. See Akhmatova, Anna, "On prav—opiat' fonar', apteka"

Hesiod
    Ronsard and, 2:732b
    Work and Days, Proust's Les plaisirs et les jours and, 8:547a

Hesperus: Oder 45 Hundesposttagen (Hesperus; or, 45 Dog-Post-Days). See Richter, Jean Paul

Hesse, Hermann, **9:833a–858b**
    "Absage" ("Letter of Decline"), 9:852a
    Aus Indien (Out of India), 9:837b

Bertold (Tales of Student Life, "Berthold"), 9:849b

Blick ins Chaos (In Sight of Chaos), 9:843b–844a, 846a, 852a
    "Die Brüder Karamasoff" ("The Brothers Karamazov"), 9:843b
    "Gedanken zu Dostojewsky's Idiot," 9:844a

Boccaccio, 9:837a

Das Glasperlenspiel (The Glass Bead Game), 9:833b, 852b–854a, 855b

Demian, 9:833a, 834a, 835a, 841a, 846a
    "Die Brüder Karamasoff" and, 9:843b
    Narcissus and Goldmund and, 9:849b, 850a, 850b
    Siddhartha and, 9:845a, 847a
    The Journey to the East and, 9:851b
    themes, 9:839a–840a, 840b–841a
    unity, 9:840b

Der Steppenwolf, 9:833a, 834a, 847b–849b, 855b
    Narcissus and Goldmund and, 9:849b, 850b
    setting, 9:846b–847a

Die Morgenlandfahrt (The Journey to the East), 9:834a, 850b–852a, 852b, 855b

Die Nürnberger Reise (The Journey to Nuremberg), 9:846a, 847a

Diesseits (In This World), 9:836b

"Eigensinn" ("Self-Reliance"), 9:841a

"Ein Stückchen Theologie" ("A Bit of Theology"), 9:849a

Eine Bibliothek der Weltliteratur (A Little Library of World Literature), 9:835b

Eine Stunde hinter Mitternacht (An Hour Beyond Midnight), 9:835b–836a

Franz von Assissi, 9:837a

Gertrud (Gertrude), 9:836b–837a

Hinterlassene Schriften und Gedichte von Hermann Lauscher (The Posthumous Writings and Poems of Hermann Lauscher), 9:836a

Klein and Wagner (Klein und Wagner), 9:842a–843a, 843b, 844b

Klingsor's Last Summer (Klingsors letzter Sommer), 9:834a, 842a, 843a, 844b
    Siddhartha and, 9:845a

Hesse, Hermann (*cont.*)
Knulp, 9:838a
Krieg und Frieden (*If the War Goes On*),
9:838b
Krisis (*Crisis*), 9:847b
Kurgast (*At the Spa*), 9:846a-b, 847a, 848a
"Kurzgefasster Lebenslauf" ("Life Story
Briefly Told"), 9:838b
Magister Ludi, *Doctor Faustus* and, 9:732b
Märchen, 9:844b
"Piktors Verwandlungen" ("Piktor's
Metamorphoses"), 9:844b
"Mein Glaube" ("My Belief"), 9:837b, 845a
Nachbarn (*Neighbors*), 9:836b
Narziss und Goldmund (*Narcissus and
Goldmund*), 9:833a-b, 849b–850b
setting, 9:835a
Peter Camenzind, 9:833a, 836a-b
on Richter's *Flegeljahre*, 5:74b
Romantische Lieder (*Romantic Songs*),
9:835b
Rosshalde, 9:837b–838a
Siddhartha, 9:833b, 837b, 844b–845b, 845b,
846a
Demian and, 9:847a
Narcissus and Goldmund and, 9:849b
Steppenwolf and, 9:849a
Stunden im Garten (*Hours in the Garden*),
9:834a, 852b
Umwege (*Byways*), 9:836a
Unterm Rad (*Beneath the Wheel*),
9:834b–835a, 836b
"Vom Steppenwolf" ("Harry the
Steppenwolf"), 9:849b
"Vorrede eines Dichters zu seinen
ausgewählten Werken" (A Writer's
Preface to His Selected Works), 9:838b,
839a
"Zarathustras Wiederkehr" ("Zarathustra's
Return"), 9:841a-b
Hesse, Johannes, 9:837b
Hessein, Marguerite, 3:76a-b
"Hessische Landbote, Der." *See* Büchner,
Georg, "The Hessian Courier"
Heteronyms
of Pessoa
Alberto Caeiro, 10:1488a, 1489b–1490b
Alexander Search, 10:1482b, 1488a
Álvaro de Campos, 10:1488a,
1490b–1491b
Bernardo Soares, 10:1492b–1493b
Chevalier de Pas, 10:1481a, 1482b, 1488a
Ricardo Reis, 10:1487b–1488a,
1491b–1492a
of Whitman, 10:1487b, 1491b
Hexameron von Rosenhain, Das. *See* Wieland,
Christoph Martin
Heyduk, Adolf, Hašek and, 9:1093a
Heym, Georg, on Rilke, 9:768b
"Hiába hideq a hold." *See* Ady, Endre
"Hiába kisértesz hófehéren." *See* Ady, Endre
Hið ljósa man. *See* Laxness, Halldór
Hidalgos, Lope de Vega and, 2:852a–853a,
857a, 865a
Hidalla, oder Sein und Haben (*Hidalla; or,
Debit and Credit*). *See* Wedekind,
Frank, *Karl Hetmann, der Zwergriese*
"Hierzulande." *See* Böll, Heinrich
High society. *See* Social classes, upper
Hija del capitán, La. *See* Valle-Inclán, Ramón
del, *Martes de Carnaval*
Hikmet, Nazim, Ritsos' translations of,
12:2819a, 2837b, 2838a
Hilarius, 1:462b
Hilary, St., Erasmus and, 2:590a-b
Hill of Lies, The. *See* Mann, Heinrich, *Ein
ernstes Leben*
Hiller, Kurt, Heinrich Mann and, 8:519a
"Hills, The." *See* Apollinaire, Guillaume, "Les
collines"
Himlens hemlighet. *See* Lagerkvist, Pär
"Himno a la Muerte." *See* Cela, Camilo José
Hindenburg, Carl Friedrich, Novalis and,
5:216a
Hindenburg, Paul von, Hitler and, 9:727b
Hinduism
Flaubert and, 7:1378a
in Leconte de Lisle, 6:1264a–1265a
Hingley, Ronald, 7:1876a
*Hinterlassene Schriften und Gedichte von
Hermann Lauscher*. *See* Hesse,
Hermann
Hipogriff, The. *See* Montherlant, Henry de, *Le
démon du bien]*

Hippolytus-Phaedra story, in Ritsos' dramatic monologues, 12:2823a, 2823b, 2825b
"Hippopotame, L'." *See* Gautier, Théophile
"Hippopotamus." *See* Eliot, T. S.
"Hirondelle et les petits oiseaux, L'." *See* La Fontaine, Jean de, *Fables*
Hironomies. See Ritsos, Yannis
"Hirtenflöte, Die." *See* Schnitzler, Arthur
Hirtengedichte. See George, Stefan, *Die Bücher der Hirten- und Preisge-dichte . . .*
His Helpmate. *See* Schnitzler, Arthur, "Die Gefährtin"
"His Reverence." *See* Verga, Giovanni, "Il reverendo"
Hiss, Alger, Heinrich Mann and, 8:541b
Histoire. See Simon, Claude
Histoire de Charles XII, roi de Suède. See Voltaire
Histoire de Don Pèdre Ier, roi de Castille. See Mérimée, Prosper
Histoire de Gil Blas de Santillane. See Lesage, Alain-René
Histoire de Hüon de Bordeaux, Wieland and, 4:605b
Histoire de Jenni. See Voltaire
Histoire de la littérature anglaise. See Taine, Hippolyte
Histoire de la peinture en Italie. See Stendhal
Histoire de la sexualité. See Foucault, Michel, *The History of Sexuality*
Histoire de la société française pendant la Révolution (*History of French Society During the Revolution*). *See* Goncourt, Edmond Louis Antoine and Jules Alfred Huot de
Histoire de la société française pendant le Directoire (*History of French Society During the Directory*). *See* Goncourt, Edmond Louis Antoine and Jules Alfred Huot de
Histoire de l'art dramatique, L'. See Gautier, Théophile
Histoire de M. Cleveland, fils naturel de Cromwell, écrite par lui-même, et traduite de l'anglais. See Prévost, Antoine-François

Histoire de ma vie. See Sand, George, *The Story of My Life*
Histoire de mes bêtes. See Dumas père, Alexandre
"Histoire de rats ou La Vertu c'est ce qui mène au crime." *See* Robbe-Grillet, Alain
Histoire de Tobie et de Sara, L'. See Claudel, Paul
"Histoire des parents pauvres." *See* Balzac, Honoré de
Histoire des républiques italiennes du Moyen Âge. See Sismondi, Simonde de
Histoire des treize, L'. See Balzac, Honoré de
Histoire des variations des églises protestantes. See Bossuet, Jacques Bénigne
Histoire du chevalier Des Grieux et de Manon Lescaut. See Prévost, Antoine-François
Histoire du romantisme. See Gautier, Théophile
"Histoire du vieux temps." *See* Maupassant, Guy de
"Histoire d'un merle blanc." *See* Musset, Alfred de
"Histoire d'une fille de ferme." *See* Maupassant, Guy de
Histoire extraordinaire. See Butor, Michel
Histoire modèle, Une. See Queneau, Raymond
Histoire secrète d'Isabelle de Bavière, reine de France. See Sade, Donatien Alphonse François, marquis de
Historia Aethiopica. See Heliodorus
Historia Baetica. See Verardi
Historia como sistema. See Ortega y Gasset, José
Historia de antiquitate regum Norwagiensium. See Theodoricus (Norwegian cleric)
Historia de duobus amantibus. See Piccolomini, Enea Silvio
Historia de la guerra europea de 1914. See Blasco Ibáñez, Vicente
Historia de la vida del buscón. See Quevedo, Francisco de, *El buscón*
Historia ecclesiastica gentis Anglorum. See Bede
Historia Francorum. See Gregory of Tours

*Historia Karoli Magni et Rotholandi
    (Pseudo-Turpin Chronicle)*, 1:90b–91a
Historia Regum Britanniae. See Geoffrey of
    Monmouth
Historia Roderici, Poema de mio Cid and,
    1:122b–123a
Historia y romancero del Cid. See Escobar,
    Juan de
Historian, Michelet on role of, 5:593b
Historias lejanas. See Baroja, Pío
Historias peregrinas y ejemplares. See
    Céspedes y Mcneses, Gonzales
Historic Tableau of French Poetry and the
    French Theater in the Sixteenth Century.
    See Sainte-Beuve, Charles-Augustin,
    *Tableau historique et critique de la
    poésie française et du théâtre français
    au XVIème siècle*
Historical consciousness, in nineteenth
    century, 7:1602b–1603b
Historical drama
    French, of Musset, 6:1005b–1006a, 1027a-b
    Grillparzer's view of, 5:431b–432b
    Hauptmann's *Florian Geyer*, 8:156a–157a
    of Sardou, 7:1916b
    Strindberg's use of form, 7:1745b
    see also Schiller, Friedrich von
*Historical Materialism and the Economics of
    Karl Marx. See* Croce, Benedetto,
    *Materialismo storico ed economia
    marxistica*
Historical moment, Flaubert and,
    7:1378b–1379a
Historical novel
    Azorín's *Doña Inés* as, 9:650b
    Diderot and, 4:501b
    of Dumas, 6:724a–728a, 741a
    of Garrett, 7:1696b
    of Gunnarsson, 10:1502b–1503b,
        1512a–1515a
    of Herculano, 7:1696b
    of Hugo, 6:700a-b, 715a-b, 724a-b
    influence of, 7:1696b
    of Johnson, 12:2376b
    Kosztolányi's *The Bloody Poet*,
        10:1235b–1237a
    of Lermontov, 6:1205a–1206b
    of Manzoni, 5:367a, 371a-b
    Meyer's novellas, 6:932a–934b, 935a–936a
    in nineteenth century, 7:1602b–1603b
    parodies of, 7:1705a
    Pérez Galdós' Spanish *episodios nacionales*,
        7:1602a–1604a, 1604a–1605a, 1613a,
        1615b
    in Portuguese literature, 7:1696b
    in post–World War II Italy, 13:3145a
    Pushkin's *Captain's Daughter*, 5:688a–589a
    Solzhenitsyn's movement toward dramatized
        history, 13:3208a-b
    Unamuno's *Paz en la guerra* as, 8:289b
    Vigny's treatise on, 5:458b–459b
Historical, Political, and Moral Essay on
    Ancient and Modern Revolutions in
    Their Relationships with the French
    Revolution. *See* Chateaubriand,
    François René de, *Essai historique,
    politique et moral sur les
    révolutions . . .*
Historical and Political Writings. See Weil,
    Simone
Historical relativism
    Herder's development of, 4:644a
    Sainte-Beuve and, 6:843a-b
Historical song (literary genre), Lermontov's
    use of form, 6:1214a–1215a
Historical Studies. *See* Chateaubriand,
    François René de, *Études historiques*
Historicism, Vico's axioms, 3:306a-b
"Historie dačická." *See* Hašek, Jaroslav
Histories. See Livy
Historiography
    of Canetti, 12:2626b–2627a
    in Croce's *Teoria e storia della storiografia*,
        8:321a
    Foucault and, 13:3327b, 3333a-b
    French
        after 1848, 5:583a
        Michelet and, 5:571a–606b
    Herder on, 5:3b
    positivist, Michelet and, 5:599a-b
    Romantic
        collapse of, 5:599a-b
        concept of historian's role, 5:581a-b
        French historians, 5:572a-b

Michelet and, 5:571a–573a, 5:593a-b
natural history and, 5:601b, 602a
other disciplines and, 5:578b–579a
social role in early 19th-century France,
    5:572a
of Sartre, 12:2603b–2611a
Scandinavian, 1:380a–381b, 383a
of Schiller, 5:36a-b
of Staël, 5:96a-b, 97a, 99b
Historische Fragmente. See Burckhardt, Jacob,
    Judgments on History and Historians
"Historky z ražické bašty." *See* Hašek, Jaroslav
History: Its Theory and Practice. See Croce,
    Benedetto, *Teoria e storia della
    storiografia*
History
    Augustine's use of, in *City of God*, 1:33a,
        33b, 34b
    Baroja's vision of, 9:602b–603a
        in early writings, 9:593b
        in novels, 9:598b, 601b, 610b–611a,
            610a-b
    Broch's philosophy of, 10:1386b–1387a
    Büchner on, 6:1172a–1173a, 1175a–1176a
    Burckhardt's philosophical perspective,
        6:1230a-b, 1237a–1241a
    in Dinesen, 10:1295a–1297a
    Foucault's view of power in, 13:3338a,
        3340b
    Hebbel's view of, 6:1100a
    Kazantzakis' doctrine of the transitional age,
        9:1070a–1071a, 1072a-b, 1075b
    Khlebnikov's theory of, 10:1341b–1344a
    Kundera and, 13:3401a–3402a, 3410a–3411a
    Machiavelli's view of, 2:606a–607a
    in Mérimée's works, 6:745a, 751a–754a,
        764b–765a
    in Michelet's conception, 5:579a–580a,
        581b–582a
    in Musil's *The Man Without Qualities*,
        9:945b, 946a, 953b
    Nietzsche on, 7:1660a–1661b
    in Novalis' works, 5:227b–228a
    personal, Sartre's view of, 12:2609b–2610a
    philosophy of
        in Claudel's *The City*, 8:474b
    Croce on, 8:312a, 312b, 313b–314a,
        320b–321b, 326a
    of Hegel, 8:324b
    of Vico, 3:304a-b, 8:325b
    poetry and
        Camoëns' *The Lusiads*, 2:763b,
            764b–765a
        Ronsard on, 2:735a
    Rilke on, 9:781b–782a
    Rimbaud's view of, 7:1809a
    themes
        Vico on, 3:313a-b
        Voltaire on, 4:371a–372b, 375b,
            382a–384a
    Tocqueville on, 6:894a, 898a-b, 905a
    truth and, Tsvetaeva and, 11:1745a
    Unamuno's view of, 8:288a
    see also Intrahistoria; Repetition, historical
History. See Adam of Bremen; Herodotus
History of the Abderites, The. See Wieland,
    Christoph Martin, *Die Geschichte der
    Abderiten*
History of Agathon, The. See Wieland,
    Christoph Martin, *Die Geschichte des
    Agathon*
*History of Architecture and Decoration of the
    Italian Renaissance. See* Burckhardt,
    Jacob
History of the Art of Antiquity. See
    Winckelmann, Johann J.
History of Bourgeois Perception. See Lowe,
    Donald
History of Charles XII. *See* Voltaire, *Histoire
    de Charles XII, roi de Suède*
History and Class Consciousness. See Lukács,
    György, *Geschichte und
    Klassenbewusstsein*
History of the Danes. See Saxo Grammaticus,
    Gesta Danorum
*History of the Decline and Fall of the Roman
    Empire. See* Gibbon, Edward
"History of a Dedication, A." *See* Tsvetaeva,
    Marina, *Istoriia odnogo posviashcheniia*
History of the Development of the Modern
    Drama. *See* Lukács, György, *A modern
    dráma fejlődésének története*

History of the Discovery and Conquest of India by the Portuguese. See Castanheda, Fernão Lopes de

History of the 1848 Revolution. See Blanc, Louis

History of English Literature. See Taine, Hippolyte, *Histoire de la littérature anglaise*

History of Europe in the Nineteenth Century. See Croce, Benedetto, *Storia d'Europa nel secolo XIX*

History of the European War, 1914–1919. See Blasco Ibáñez, Vicente, *Historia de la guerra europea de 1914*

History of the Family at Borg, The. See Gunnarsson, Gunnar, *Borgslægtens Historie*

History of France. See Michelet, Jules

History of the Franks. See Gregory of Tours, *Historia Francorum*

History of the French Revolution, 1847–1853. See Michelet, Jules

History of Greek Culture. See Burckhardt, Jacob

History of the Greenlanders. See Grœnlendinga saga

History of the Icelanders. See Sturla Thórdarson, *Íslendinga saga*

History of Italy, 1871–1915. See Croce, Benedetto, *Storia d'Italia dal 1871 al 1914*

History of Italy, A. See Croce, Benedetto, *Storia d'Italia*

History of the Jewish People and Its Capital Jerusalem. See Josephus, Flavius

History of the Kings of Britain, The. See Geoffrey of Monmouth, *Historia Regum Britanniae*

History of Materialism. See Lange, Friedrich, *Geschichte des Materialismus*

History of the Nineteenth Century. See Michelet, Jules

History of the Norwegian Kings. See Snorri Sturluson, *Heimskringla*

History of Norwegian Kings from Ancient Times. See Theodoricus (Norwegian cleric), *Historia de antiquitate regum Norwagiensium*

History of Painting in Italy, A. *See* Stendhal, *Histoire de la peinture en Italie*

History of the Poetry of the Greeks and Romans. See Schlegel, Friedrich von

History of Pugachev, The. See Pushkin, Alexander

History of the Revolt of the United Netherlands from the Spanish Government. See Schiller, Friedrich von, *Geschichte des Abfalls der vereinigten Niederlande*

History of Romanticism, A. See Gautier, Théophile, *Histoire du romantisme*

History of Sillytown, The. *See* Zamyatin, Yevgeny Ivanovich, *Istoriia goroda Glupova*

History of the Swedish People, A. See Moberg, Vilhelm, *Min svenska historia. Berättad för folket*

History as a System. See Ortega y Gasset, José, *Historia como sistema*

History of the Thirty Years War. See Schiller, Friedrich von, *Geschichte des dreissigjährigen Krieges*

History of a Town, The. See Shchedrin, N., *Istoriia odnogo goroda*

History of Two Lovers. See Piccolomini, Enea Silvio, *Historia de duobus amantibus*

History of Vanillo Gonzalez, Surnamed the Merry Bachelor, The. See Lesage, Alain-René, *Estevanille Gonzales, surnommé le garçon de bonne humeur*

History of Western Philosophy. See Russell, Bertrand

History of the World. See Veraldar saga

"Hitchhiking Game, The." *See* Kundera, Milan

Hitler, Adolf
in Frisch's works, 13:2903b, 2904b–2905a
Hamsun and, 8:40a
Heinrich Mann and, 8:519a, 536b, 537b, 539b
Wagner and, 6:1166b
Weil and, 12:2799b

"Hitler Spring." *See* Montale, Eugenio, *The Storm and Other Things*

Hitzig, Julius Eduard, Hoffmann and, 5:268b

Hive, The. See Cela, Camilo José

"Hiver qui vient, L'." *See* Laforgue, Jules

Hjalta þáttr, 1:384a

Hjarta høyrer sine heimlandstonar. See Vesaas, Tarjei

Hjärtats sånger. See Lagerkvist, Pär

Hjörungavág, battle of, 1:381a

Ho, ho, in how Christian a manner the Pope is now laughing. *See* Walther von der Vogelweide, "Ahî wie kristenlîche nû der bâbest lachet"

"Ho tanta fede in te." *See* Montale, Eugenio, *Altri versi e poesie disperse*

Hobbes, Thomas
Canetti and, 12:2626a
ideas of, in Baroja's *Tree of Knowledge*, 9:606a-b
Pirandello's *Six Characters* and, 8:407a
Staël's *De l'Allemagne* on, 5:108b

Hobbies, discussed in La Bruyère's *Caractères*, 3:252b

Hobsbawm, Eric, on Rimbaud and modernity, 7:1786a

"Höchstes Gebot." *See* Hebbel, Friedrich

Hochwasser. See Grass, Günter, *Flood*

Hochzeit. See Canetti, Elias, *Wedding*

Hochzeit der Sobeide, Die. See Hofmannsthal, Hugo von, *The Marriage of Zobeide*

Hochzeit des Mönchs, Die. See Meyer, Conrad Ferdinand

"Hochzeitsvorbereitungen auf dem Lande." *See* Kafka, Franz

Hoeufft medal, 7:1828a

Hoffmann, E. T. A., **5:261a–289b**
Andersen and, 6:877a
"Beethovens Instrumental-Musik," 5:273a-b
Berlioz and, 6:781b, 786b
Contes fantastiques (*Tales of the Fantastic*), 6:781b
"Das Majorat" ("The Deed of Entail"), 6:266b
Die Bergwerke zu Falun (*The Mines of Falun*), 6:887b
Die Elixiere des Teufels (*The Devil's Elixirs*), 5:262a
Die Maske (The Mask), 5:267a
Dostoevsky and, 7:1350b
Fantasiestücke in Callots Manier (Fantasy Pieces in the Manner of Callot), 5:262b, 6:1150b
Gautier and, 6:1049b–1050a
Gogol and, 6:975a, 979b
Hesse and
Hinterlassene Schriften und Gedichte von Hermann Lauscher, 9:836a
Narcissus and Goldmund, 9:849b
Steppenwolf, 9:847b
Lebens-Ansichten des Katers Murr . . . (*Life and Opinions of Kater Murr . . .*), 5:286a–287b
Lermontov and, 6:1222b
Master Flea, 5:278b
Maupassant and, 7:1762b, 1763a
"My Cousin's Corner Window," 5:281a-b
Nachtstücke (Night Pieces), 5:277a-b
Nutcracker and the Mouse King, 5:261a-b
Olesha's *The Three Fat Men* and, 11:2247b, 2248a
Richter's *The Invisible Lodge* and, 5:63a
"Ritter Gluck," 5:270b–272b
"Schreiben eines Klostergeistlichen an seinen Freund in der Hauptstadt" (Letters from a Friar to his Friend in the Capital), 5:268a
"The Golden Pot," 5:281b–286a, 6:875b
The Serapion Brethren, 5:277a–278a
Undine, 5:269b, 276b
Wagner and, 6:1150b, 1151a

Hoffmann, Ernst Theodor Wilhelm. *See* Hoffmann, E. T. A.

Hoffmann, Heinrich, *Struwwelpeter*, 6:885a

Hofmannsthal, Hugo von, **9:689a–714b**
"Ad me ipsum" (About Myself), 9:691a
Andreas; or, The United (*Andreas, oder die Vereinigten*), 9:710b–711a
Arabella, 9:708b–709a
Ariadne auf Naxos (*Ariadne on Naxos*), 9:694b, 706b–707a
"Chandos Letter," 9:767b

Hofmannsthal, Hugo von (*cont.*)

Cristinas Heimreise (Cristina's Journey Home), 9:693b, 699b, 700a, 705b

Das gerettete Venedig (Venice Preserved), 9:697a, 698a–698b

Das kleine Welttheater oder die Glücklichen (The Little Theater of the World), 9:695b

Das Märchen der 672. Nacht (The Tale of the Merchant's Son and His Four Servants), 9:709a–709b

"Das Schrifttum als geistiger Raum der Nation," (Literature as the Spiritual Realm of the Nation), 9:690b

Death and the Fool (Der Tor und der Tod), 9:689b, 695a

Der Abenteurer und die Sängerin (The Adventurer and the Singer), 9:696a, 696b, 700a

Der Kaiser und die Hexe (The Emperor and the Witch), 9:695b

Der Rosenkavalier, 9:694b, 705b–706a, 708a

Der Tod des Tizian (Titian's Death), 9:695a

Deutsche Erzähler (German Storytellers), 9:690a

Die ägyptische Helena (The Egyptian Helen), 9:692a, 708a

Die Frau im Fenster (Madonna Dianora), 9:695b

Die Frau ohne Schatten (The Woman Without a Shadow), 9:696a, 709a

Electra (Elektra), 9:697a–698b, 698a, 705b

Electra myth, 12:2549a

George and, 8:449b, 460b, 461a, 467a

Gestern (Yesterday), 9:694b–695a

on Grillparzer's Hero and Leander, 5:436a

Grillparzer's influence on, 5:444a

König Ödipus (Oedipus Rex), translation of Sophocles, 9:697a

Ödipus und die Sphinx (Oedipus and the Sphinx), 9:697a, 699a

Rilke and, 9:771b

Schnitzler and, 8:90b, 92a, 94a, 102b, 106a, 111b, 112b–113a

The Difficult Man (Der Schwierige), 9:693a, 693b, 694b, 700b, 701a

"The Letter of Lord Chandos" ("Ein Brief"), 9:691b, 697b

The Marriage of Zobeide (Die Hochzeit der Sobeide), 9:696a

The Salzburg Everyman (Jedermann), 9:693b, 701b–702b

The Salzburg Great Theater of the World (Das Salzburger grosse Welttheater), 9:693a, 693b, 694a, 700b–702b

The Tower (Der Turm), 9:694b, 703a–704b

The White Fan (Der weisse Fächer), 9:695b

"Vienna Letters," 9:692b

Hofmannsthal und seine Zeit. See Broch, Hermann, Hugo von Hofmannsthal and His Time

Hofmeister, Der. See Brecht, Bertolt, The Tutor

Hohe Karlsschule, 5:28a–29b, 31a

Hohenheim, Countess Franziska von, 5:29a

Hojas verdes, Las. See Jiménez, Juan Ramón

Holbach, Paul-Henri d', Sade and, 4:635b

Holbein, Hans, Erasmus and, 2:584a-b

Hölderlin, Friedrich, **5:143a–173b**

"Am Quell der Donau" ("At the Source of the Danube"), 5:164b–165a

"An die Deutschen" ("To the Germans"), 5:161b

"An die Natur," 5:148b–149a

"An Stella," 5:144a-b

"An Zimmern," 5:173a

"Andenken" ("Remembrance"), 5:170b–171a

"Brot und Wein," 5:160a–161a
divine presence in, 5:164b
original title of, 5:159b

"Das fröhliche Leben" ("The Happy Life"), 5:173a

"Der Archipelagus," 5:162b–163a

"Der Einzige" ("The Only One"), 5:167b, 168b–169a

"Der Ister," 5:170b, 171a

"Der Rhein," 5:161a-b, 165b–166a

Der Tod des Empedokles (The Death of Empedocles), 5:155b–158a

"Dichterberuf," 5:161b–162b

"Die Wanderung," 5:165a

education of, 9:835a

"Friedensfeier," 5:167b–168a

George's Maximin experience and, 8:462b

"Germanien," 5:165a-b

"Hälfte des Lebens" ("Half of Life"), 5:171b

Hegel and, 10:1273b

"Heimkunft" ("Homecoming"), 5:163b–164a, 164b

Hellingrath and, 8:460b–461a

Hesse and, 9:845b

"Hymne an die Freiheit," 5:147b

"Hymne an die Göttin der Harmonie," 5:147a-b

"Hymne an die Schönheit," 5:147a-b

Hymns to the Ideals of Mankind, 5:146b–147b

Hyperion, 5:148a, 150a–155a, 7:1648a
  beauty in, 5:146a
  discussed by Lukács, 10:1270b
  fragmentary metrical version of, 5:149a
  Musil's *The Man Without Qualities* and, 9:939a
  publication of, 5:150b
  reception of, 5:173a

"Mein Vorsatz" ("My Purpose"), 5:144b

"Mnemosyne," 5:170b, 171a-b

Nietzsche on, 7:1648a

"night songs" of, 5:171b–172a

"Patmos," 5:167b, 169a–170b

Rilke and, 9:768a, 771a-b

"Rousseau," 5:161b

Schiller and, 5:42a

Trakl and, 10:1422b–1423b

"Wie wenn am Feiertage," 5:158b–159b

Holeček, Josef, *Obšit (Demob),* influence on Hašek's Švejk, 9:1096b

Höll sumarlandsins. See Laxness, Halldór

Höllerer, Walter, Frisch and, 13:2910b

Hollingdale, R. J., on Nietzsche, 7:1648a-b

Hollow Field, The. See Aymé, Marcel

Holocaust
  in Böll's writing, 13:3168a
  Robbe-Grillet and, 13:3239b
  see also Anti-Semitism

"Holy Bread, The." *See* Claudel, Paul, *La messe là-bas* (The Mass There), "Le pain bénit"

Holy Fool, in Grass, 13:3372b

Holy Land
  in Chateaubriand's works, 5:124a-b, 125a

Walther and, 1:303b

Holy Land, The. See Lagerkvist, Pär, *Det heliga landet*

Holy Roman Empire
  in Dante's *De monarchia,* 1:443a, 443b
  in Tegernsee *Antichrist,* 1:455b
  Walther and, 1:301b–302b, 305a-b

Holy Terrors, The. See Cocteau, Jean, *Les enfants terribles*

Holy Week. See Aragon, Louis, *La semaine sainte*

Homage to Bacchus. See Velázquez, Diego Rodríguez de Silva, *Los borrachos*

Homage to James Joyce; or, The Coup d'État. *See* Moravia, Alberto, *Omaggio a James Joyce; ovvero, Il colpo di stato*

Hombre y la gente, El. See Ortega y Gasset, José

Hombres. See Verlaine, Paul

Home, in Pavese's works, 12:2764b, 2777a, 2782a-b

Home. See Maeterlinck, Maurice, *Intérieur*

Home Town. See Simenon, Georges, *Faubourg*

Homecoming. See Heine, Heinrich, *Die Heimkehr*

"Homecoming." *See* Hölderlin, Friedrich, "Heimkunft"

"Homecomings." *See* Quasimodo, Salvatore

Homelessness
  in Ekelöf's works, 12:2645a
  figurative, of Heinrich Mann, 8:522a-b

Homer
  as Alfieri's model poet, 4:673b
  Augustine and, 1:27a
  Chénier's aesthetics and, 4:706a-b, 707b
  in Dante's *Inferno,* 1:446b, 447a
  Delacroix on, 5:530a
  Dostoevsky and, 7:1350b
  Foscolo and, 5:333b–334a
  Hofmannsthal and, 9:689b
  "Hymn to Apollo," Chénier and, 4:707b
  Iliad
    Achilles as hero, 1:60b
    Italian translation of, Tasso and, 2:799b
    Marinetti's "Zang Tumb Tumb" and, 9:819b
    the *Nibelungenlied* and, 1:219b

Homer (*cont.*)
  Iliad (*cont.*)
    oral elements in, 1:56b
    praised by Boileau, 3:199b–201a
    in Seferis' "King of Asine," 12:2266a
    structure of, 1:75a
    Weil and, 12:2787a
  Lukács on, 10:1260b–1261a, 1261b
  Machado and, 9:760a
  Odyssey
    Camoëns' *The Lusiads* and, 2:761a
    Fénelon's *Télémaque* and, 3:284b, 285a,
      286a-b
    influence on Lampedusa's *The Leopard*,
      11:2030a
    Italian translation of, Tasso and, 2:799b
    Johnson and, 12:2373b–2374a, 2375a-b
    in Seferis' writing, 12:2262a-b
  in Ronsard's "Hymne de l'or," 2:734a
  Valle-Inclán and, 8:339a
  Vico and, 3:305b, 310b
  in Vigny's *Stello*, 5:469a-b
  see also Bardic tradition
Homer's Apotheosis. See Ingres, Jean Auguste
  Dominique
Homesickness, spiritual, in Dante's
  Purgatorio, 1:448a
Homeward Bound. See Mayakovsky, Vladimir,
  "Domoi"
Homme au petit chien, L'. See Simenon,
  Georges
Homme aux valises, L'. See Ionesco, Eugène
Homme comme un autre, Un. See Simenon,
  Georges
Homme communiste, L'. See Aragon, Louis
Homme en question, Un. See Ionesco, Eugène
"*Homme et la couleuvre, L'.*" *See* La Fontaine,
  Jean de, *Fables*
Homme et son désir, L'. See Claudel, Paul
"*Homme obscur, Un.*" *See* Yourcenar,
  Marguerite, *Comme l'eau qui coule*
"*Homme qui a aimé les Néréides, L'.*" *See*
  Yourcenar, Marguerite, *Nouvelles*
  orientales
Homme qui ment, L'. See Robbe-Grillet, Alain
Homme qui rit, L'. See Hugo, Victor

Homme révolté, L'. See Camus, Albert, *The*
  Rebel
Hommes d'aujourd'hui. See Huysmans, Joris
  Karl
Hommes de lettres, Les. See Goncourt,
  Edmond Louis Antoine and Jules Alfred
  Huot de, *Charles Demailly*
Hommes fatales, and Cocteau, 10:1544a-b
Homo europaeus, in 19th-century literature,
  8:206a-b
Homo faber: A Report (*Homo faber: Ein*
  Bericht). *See* Frisch, Max
Homoeroticism, in Andersen, 6:869a-b
"Homogeneous medium," in Bergson's
  thought, 8:49b–50b
Homosexuality
  in Balzac's works, 5:650a-b
  Barthes and, 13:3081a
  Cavafy's expression of, 8:206a, 207a,
    214b–215a, 217b–218a
  and Cocteau, 10:1544a, 1558a
  in Ghelderode's *Le siège d'Ostende*,
    11:2131b
  in Gombrowicz's *Trans-Atlantyk*, 12:2582a
  in Hašek's *Good Soldier Švejk*, 9:1114a-b
  Heinrich Mann and, 8:521a, 539a, 539b
  in Proust's *Remembrance of Things Past*,
    8:548b–549a, 559a
  of Rimbaud, 7:1789a, 1806b–1807b
  Schopenhauer's view of, 5:409a
  of Verlaine, 7:1620a, 1623b–1624a, 1625b
  in Yourcenar's *Alexis*, 12:2537b–2538a,
    2538b–2539a
  see also Bisexuality; Lesbianism; Pederasty
Honegger, Arthur, music for Claudel's *Jeanne*
  d'Arc au bûcher, 8:488a
"Honest Thief, The." *See* Dostoevsky, Feodor
Honnête homme, Montaigne and, 2:784a,
  785b, 786a
Honnêteté, La Rochefoucauld and, 3:64a, 66b
Honor
  in Calderón's plays, 2:877b–888b,
    881b–883a
  in Corneille's plays, 3:23b
    Le Cid, 3:29a, 29b
    Polyeucte, 3:44b
  in Gottfried, 1:254b–256a

in Tasso's works, 2:797b
Vigny's elevation of, 5:476a
Honorius, Roman Emperor, Prudentius and, 1:14b
Hooft, Pieter, Petrarchan influence, 2:504b
Hop Signor! See Ghelderode, Michel de
Hope, in Milosz's works, 13:2938a, 2939b–2940a
Hope. *See* Moravia, Alberto, *La Speranza*
"Hope." *See* Södergran, Edith, "Förhoppning"
Hopkins, Gerard Manley, Claudel and, 8:477b
Hoppla. See Toller, Ernst
"Hora." *See* Čapek, Karel
Hora de España entre 1560 y 1590, Una. See Azorín
Horace, Croce and, 8:312a
Horace. See Sand, George
Horace (Quintus Horatius Flaccus)
    Ariosto and, 2:621a
    Ars poetica, 1:13a
        Dante and, 1:447a
        Marcabru and, 1:340a
        "Quam sit lata scelerum" and, 1:338b–339a
        Tasso and, 2:799b
    Augustine's *On Music* and, 1:47a
    Boileau on, 3:182b
    Cathemerinon and, 1:7a
    Chénier on satire of, 4:708a
    in Dante's *Inferno*, 1:446b
    Epistles, "Quam sit lata scelerum" and, 1:339a
    French classicism and, 3:80a
    German translation of, 4:610a
    Klopstock and, 4:513b
    medieval satire and, 1:337a, 338a, 339b, 372a-b
    Neidhart von Reuental and, 1:367b
    Odes
        Camoëns' *The Lusiads* and, 2:764a
        epitaph, 2:541b
        Petrarch's *Canzoniere*, influence on, 2:493b
        patronage and, 1:351a
        Renaissance pastoral poetry and, 2:901b
        Renaissance poetic theory and, 2:750a
        Roman morality and, 1:350a

Ronsard and, 2:726a
Satires
    estates satire and, 1:355a
    Marcabru and, 1:339b–340a
    purpose of, 1:340b–341a
    self-criticism of, 1:356a-b
    technique of, 1:366b
Horas solitarias, Las. See Baroja, Pío
Horatier und die Kuriatier, Die (The Horatians and the Curiatians). See Brecht, Bertolt
Horda, La. See Blasco Ibáñez, Vicente
Hordubal. See Čapek, Karel
Hore di ricreatione, L'. See Guicciardini, Ludovico
Horiko ton sfouggaradhon, To. See Ritsos, Yannis
"Horla, Le." *See* Maupassant, Guy de
Horloger d'Everton, L'. See Simenon, Georges
"Horn Owl, The." *See* Pascoli, Giovanni, *Myricae* (Tamarisks), "L'Assiuolo"
"Horn, The." *See* Vigny, Alfred Victor de, *Poèmes antiques et modernes*
Horror, in Maupassant's works, 7:1762b–1763a
Horror Tragedy. See Schauertragödie
Horse in the Moon. See Pirandello, Luigi, *Un cavallo nella luna*
"Horseman's Good-bye, The." *See* Apollinaire, Guillaume, "L'Adieu du cavalier"
Horses in literature, of Alfieri, 4:671a
Hortensius. See Cicero
"Horus." *See* Nerval, Gérard de
Hostage, The. See Claudel, Paul, *L'Otage*
Hot-Houses. See Maeterlinck, Maurice, *Serres chaudes*
Hôtel de Bourgogne (Paris), 3:25a, 26b
Hour Beyond Midnight, An. See Hesse, Hermann, *Eine Stunde hinter Mitternacht*
Hour imagery. *See* Time imagery
Hour of Recognition. *See* Schnitzler, Arthur, "Stunde des Erkennens"
Hour of Spain Between 1560 and 1590, An. *See* Azorín, *Una hora de España entre 1560 y 1590*
Hourra l'Oural. See Aragon, Louis

Hours in the Garden. *See* Hesse, Hermann, *Stunden im Garten*

Hours of Recreation. *See* Guicciardini, Ludovico, *L'hore di ricreatione*

House of Aizgorri, The. *See* Baroja, Pío, *La casa de Aizgorri*

House of Arts (journal). *See Dom iskusstv*

House of Assignation, The. See Robbe-Grillet, Alain, *La maison de rendez-vous*

"House at Old Pimen's, The." *See* Tsvetaeva, Marina, "Dom u starogo Pimena"

House of Bernarda Alba, The. See García Lorca, Federico

House of the Blind, The. *See* Gunnarsson, Gunnar, *De Blindes Hus*

House by the Medlar Tree, The. See Verga, Giovanni, *I malavoglia*

House by the Sea. *See* Ginzburg, Natalia, "Casa al mare"

House of Cards. See Kuzmin, Mikhail, *Kartonnyi domik*

House in the Dark, The. See Vesaas, Tarjei

House of the Dead, The. See Dostoevsky, Feodor

House on the Hill, The. See Pavese, Cesare

House on Its Own, The. *See* Andrić, Ivo, *Kuća na osami*

House of Men, The. See Aymé, Marcel

"House with a Mezzanine, The." *See* Chekhov, Anton, "Dom s mezaninom"

House with Two Doors Is Hard to Guard, A. See Calderón de la Barca, Pedro

Houston, John Porter, on the Goncourts, 7:1402b, 1417a

Houwald, Ernst, *Das Bild* (*The Picture*), success of, 5:425a

Hovory s T. G. Masarykem. See Čapek, Karel

How Did You See Me? *See* Ady, Endre, "Vajjon milyennek láttál"

How I Met the Author of My Obituary. *See* Hašek, Jaroslav, "Jak jsem se setkal s autorem svého nekrologu"

"How Much Land Does a Man Need?" *See* Tolstoy, Leo

"How Much Shall We Bet?" *See* Calvino, Italo, *Cosmicomics*, "Quanto scooettiamo?"

How to Cook a Hard-boiled Egg. *See* Ionesco, Eugène, *Pour préparer un oeuf dur*

How to Make a Novel. See Unamuno, Miguel de, *Cómo se hace una novela*

"How to Write Poetry." *See* Mayakovsky, Vladimir

How Tövöl Returned a Guilder. *See* Hašek, Jaroslav, "Jak Tövöl vrátil zlatník"

"How Wang-Fo Was Saved." *See* Yourcenar, Marguerite, *Nouvelles orientales*

"How, When, and Why." *See* Verga, Giovanni, "Il come, il quando, ed il perché"

Howe, Irving
    Babel and, 11:1889a
    on Silone, 12:2284b–2285a, 2289b, 2300b

Howells, William Dean
    Gorky and, 8:420b
    on Ibsen, 7:1443b

Hrafnkels saga, 1:394a-b, 396a, 398b

Hrastova gredfa u kamenoj kapiji. See Džadžić, Petar

Hreiðar þáttr, 1:384a

Hristós ksanastavrónetai, O. See Kazantzakis, Nikos

Hrólfs saga kraka, 1:401a

Hrosvitha, 1:451a-b

Hrvatski bog Mars. See Krleža, Miroslav

Hryggjarstykki. See Eirík Oddsson

Hrysothemis. See Ritsos, Yannis

Huber, Catherine, 5:89b

Huber, Theresa, 5:83b

Hübner, Georgina, in Jiménez's *Laberinto*, 9:996b–997a

Hubris, in Mann's *Doctor Faustus*, 9:734a, 735a

Hugh Primas
    on bishop of Sens, 1:339a
    "Dives eram et dilectus" (Once I was rich and beloved), 1:341b–342b, 356b–357a
    "Ego dixi" and, 1:347b
    "Quid luges, lirice?" ("Why the lament, poet?"), 1:338a-b
    sinner persona of, 1:361b–362a

Hugh Selwyn Mauberley. See Pound, Ezra

Hugh of St. Cher, 1:412a

Hugh of St. Victor
    Dante and, 1:433b

Didascalia, Dante and, 1:448b
Hugleik den Haardtsejlende (Hugleik the
      Fearless Seafarer). *See* Gunnarsson,
      Gunnar, *Kirken paa Bjerget* (The Church
      on the Hill)
Hugo, Adéle, Sainte-Beuve and, 6:838a
Hugo, Victor, **6:693a–718b**
   "À Albert Dürer," 6:704a
   "À la fenêtre, pendant la nuit" ("At the
      Window During the Night"), 6:709b
   Ady and, 9:860a
   Angélo, tyran de Padoue (Angelo, the Tyrnt
      of Padua), 6:703b
   Apollinaire and, 9:892b
   "Après une lecture de Dante" ("After a
      Reading of Dante"), 6:704a-b
   Baudelaire and, 7:1327b, 1339b
   Berlioz and, 6:771a, 781a, 781b, 783b, 789b
   Bug-Jargal, 6:696b, 1206a
   Butor and, 13:3294b
   "Ce que dit la bouche d'ombre" ("What the
      Mouth of Darkness Says"), 6:709b–710a
   Chateaubriand and, 5:140a
   Châtiments (Punishments), 6:706a
   Chénier seen as romantic by, 4:693a, 693b
   classical forms and mythology discarded by,
      5:372b
   Claude Gueux, 6:710a
   Claudel and, 8:472a, 490b
   Cromwell, 6:695a, 1010a
      definition of new romantic drama in,
         5:461b
   Delacroix and, 5:517a
   Dieu (God), 6:715b–716a
   Dostoevsky and, 7:1351a
   Dumas and, 6:721b, 723b, 724a
   Eça and, 7:1963a
   French language and, 6:1033b, 1035a-b
   French romanticism and, 7:1685b
   Giraudoux and, 9:1041b
   Hernani, 6:695a-b, 701a, 721b, 1033b,
      9:1060a
      conflict with Vigny over, 5:462a
      Gautier and, 7:1913b
      Marinetti and, 9:822a
      Vigny and, 5:466a-b
   influence of, 7:1640b

   Jiménez and, 9:993b
   "La fête chez Thérèse" ("The Party at
      Therese's"), 6:708a-b, 7:1627b
   La fin de Satan (Satan Redeemed), 6:696b,
      713a-b
      Laforgue on, 7:1884b, 1906b
   La légende des siècles (Legends and
      Chronicles of the Ages), 6:711b–712a
      as short epic, 5:455a
   La muse française
      demise of, 5:454b
      Vigny's "Eloa" praised in, 5:454a
   "La pente de la rêverie" ("Descent into
      Reverie"), 6:698a-b, 707b
   Laforgue's "Simple Death Throes" and,
      7:1901b
   Le dernier jour d'un condamné (The Last
      Day of a Condemned Man), 6:710a,
      781b
   Le Rhin (The Rhine), 6:789b
   Le roi s'amuse (The King at Play), 6:703b
   "Le satyre," 6:712a-b
   Lermontov and, 6:1199a, 1205b–1206a
   Les Burgraves, 6:704b, 1030a
   Les chants du crépuscule (Twilight Songs),
      6:703b
   Les contemplations (Contemplations),
      6:707b–710a, 711b, 7:1627b
   "Les deux archers" ("The Two Archers"),
      6:698b–699a
   "Les djinns" ("The Genies"), 6:699a-b
   Les feuilles d'automne (Autumn Leaves),
      6:703b
   Les jumeaux (The Twins), 6:696b
   Les misérables, 6:710a–711b, 712b, 713b
      on Goethe, 5:7b
      Paris in, 5:650b
   Les orientales (Poems of the Orient),
      6:694b–695a, 698a, 699a-b, 12:2544b
      Flaubert and, 7:1379a
      Leconte de Lisle and, 6:1247a
   "Les pauvres gens" ("Poor Folks"), 6:712b
   Les rayons et les ombres (Lights and
      Shadows), 6:703b, 7:1630a
   Les travailleurs de la mer (The Toilers of
      the Sea), 6:697a, 713b–715a
   Les voix intérieures (Inner Voices), 6:703b

Hugo, Victor (*cont.*)
"L'Expiation," 5:136a-b
L'Homme qui rit (*The Laughing Man*),
6:715a-b
Lucrèce Borgia, 6:703b
Marie Tudor, 6:703b
Marion de Lorme
originally titled *Un duel sous Richelieu* (*A
Duel Under Richelieu*), 5:462a
rejection of, 5:462a
Maupassant and, 7:1764b
Mérimée and, 6:750b
Moberg and, 11:2208a
Napoléon-le-Petit (*Napoleon the Little*),
6:706a
Notre-Dame de Paris (*The Hunchback of
Notre Dame*), 6:696b, 699b–703a, 712b,
713b, 724a, 781a, 1206a
Paris in, 5:650b
Odes et ballades, 6:694b, 698b–699a, 703a-b
Pascoli and, 7:1835a
"Passé" ("The Past"), 6:703b–704a
"Pasteurs et troupeaux" ("Shepherds and
Flocks"), 6:709a-b
philanthropism of, 6:995b
Promontorium somnii, 6:697a-b, 701b
in Proust's *Remembrance of Things Past*,
8:554a
Quatrevingt-treize (*Ninety-Three*), 6:715b
on Racine, 3:227a-b
Rimbaud and, 7:1790a, 1791a, 1797b, 1811a
Ruy Blas, 6:704b
Sainte-Beuve and, 6:837a–838a, 857a, 859a,
7:1411a
Scott's *Quentin Durward* reviewed by,
5:458b
"Soleils couchants" ("Sunsets"), 6:706a-b
Strindberg and, 7:1753b
"Tristesse d'Olympio" ("Olympio's Sorrow"),
6:703b–704a
Verlaine and, 7:1621a, 1627b
Vigny compared to, 5:447a
Vigny's "Eloa" reviewed by, 5:454a, 479a
Vigny's friendship with, 5:450b, 454b, 461a,
479a
Zola and, 7:1764b

Hugo von Hofmannsthal and His Time. See
Broch, Hermann
Huguenau oder die Sachlichkeit (*Huguenau;
or, Objectivism*). *See* Broch, Hermann
Huguenots, 2:694b–695a, 737b
and Bossuet's *History of the Variations in
the Protestant Churches*, 3:171b
Fénelon and, 3:266a-b
revocation of the Edict of Nantes and,
3:158b–159a
Huis clos. See Sartre, Jean-Paul, *No Exit*
"Huissier, L'." *See* Aymé, Marcel
Huit scènes de Faust. See Berlioz, Hector
Hulewicz, Witold, Rilke and, 9:773b
Hulme, T. E., Bergson and, 8:61a
Human, All Too-Human. See Nietzsche,
Friedrich
Human Beast, The. See Zola, Émile, *La bête
humaine*
Human body
Gombrowicz and, 12:2566a–2567b
in Rabelais's *Pantagruel*, 2:702b–703a
in Rimbaud's works, 7:1788a, 1790a-b,
1794b–1795a, 1816b
soul and, in works of Prudentius, 1:17a-b
Human Comedy. See Balzac, Honoré de, *La
comédie humaine*
Human Comedy, The. See Balzac, Honoré de,
La comédie humaine
"Human Material." *See* Olesha, Yuri,
"Chelovecheski material"
Human nature. *See* Man, nature of
Human Voice, The. See Cocteau, Jean, *La voix
humaine*
Humanism
Boccaccio's contribution to, 2:528b, 529a
in Boccaccio's *Decameron*, 2:519a
Christian, Rabelais and, 2:701a
Erasmus and, 2:571b–592b
French, 2:695a
Francis I and, 2:694b
Gottfried and, 1:238a
Hebbel and, 6:1100b–1101a, 1119a
Johnson and, 12:2362b
and Lagerkvist, 10:1688b, 1691a–1693a,
1698b
Petrarch's contribution to, 2:475b, 503a

poetry and, 1:48a

Saint-Exupéry and, 12:2321b, 2327b–2328a

Humanitarianism

Goncourts' belief in, 7:1400a

sentimental, misreading of Gogol's works and, 6:995b

Humanität

Herder's vision of, 4:646a–650b

first stage (identification and acceptance of folk tradition), 4:646b–647a

Lomax's family of humanity and, 4:659a

second stage (development of indigenous culture), 4:647a–648a, 649a–650a

third stage (achievement of *Humanität*), 4:648a-b, 650a-b

Whitman and, 4:657a-b

Humanité, L'

Aragon and, 11:2068b

on Mayakovsky's suicide, 11:2071b

Humboldt, Alexander von, Schiller and, 5:36b, 50a

Hume, David

A Treatise of Human Nature, reaction to reception of, 5:396a

ethics of, 5:405a

Herder's radicalism contrasted with, 4:652a-b

Rousseau and, 4:459b–460a

Schopenhauer's critique of, 5:398b

"Humiliation." *See* Blok, Alexander, "Unizhenie"

Humiliation of the Father, The. See Claudel, Paul, *Le père humilié*

Humility, theme of

in "Estuans instrinsicus ira vehementi," 1:358a, 358b

in Rutebeuf's "Bataille des vices contre les vertus," 1:365a-b

Humor

Blasco Ibáñez' use of, 8:360b–361a, 379a-b

in Canetti, 12:2630a-b

Castiglione's discussion of, 2:657a–658b

in Claudel's plays, 8:479a, 488b

Gide's use of, 8:497b

Hamsun's use of, 8:28a, 34a, 36b

in Hesse's prose, 9:846a, 846b

Kierkegaard and, 6:1141b

in Mann's *Magic Mountain*, 9:722a

in Queneau's works, 12:2511b–2512a

Richter's The School for Aesthetics on, 5:78a-b

in Silone's writings, 12:2280b, 2284a-b, 2298b

Voltaire's use of, 4:388a–389b

Wedekind's use of, 8:230a, 234b–235a

see also Black humor; Comedy; Comic, the

Humorism, 8:412a

defined, 8:389a, 395b–396a

Pirandello and

The Late Mattia Pascal, 8:398b

"Un preteso poeta umorista," 8:391a

"Humorismos, fantasías y apuntos." *See* Machado, Antonio, *Soledades* (Solitudes)

Humorisms, Fantasies, and Sketches. *See* Machado, Antonio, *Soledades* (Solitudes), "Humorismos, fantasías, y apuntos"

Humors, theory of, 2:750b

Humulus le muet (Humulus the Mute). See Anouilh, Jean, and Aurenche, Jean

Hunchback of Notre Dame, The. See Hugo, Victor, *Notre-Dame de Paris*

Hundejahre. See Grass, Günter, *Dog Years*

Hundra år modern fransk dikt. See Ekelöf, Gunnar

Hundred Ancient Tales. See Cento novelle antich

Hundred Days. *See* Bonaparte, Napoleon

Hundred and a Hundred and a Hundred and a Hundred Pages of the Secret Book of Gabriele D'Annunzio Tempted by Death, A. See D'Annunzio, Gabriele, *Libro segreto*

Hundred Sentences for Fans, A. *See* Claudel, Paul, *Cent phrases pour éventails*

Hundred Stories, The. See Giraldi, Giambattista, *Gli ecatommiti*

Hundred Years' War

Deschamps on, 1:362b–364a

medieval satire and, 1:344b

in Petrarch's poetry, 2:485b

Hungarian Commune (1919)

Kosztolányi and, 10:1235a, 1236a

Hungarian Commune (1919) (*cont.*)
 Kosztolányi and (*cont.*)
  Wonder Maid, 10:1240a
Hungarian Fallow, The. *See* Ady, Endre, "A
 magyar ugaron"
Hungarian language, archaic, in poetry of
 Ady, 9:873b–874a, 874b
Hungarian Messiahs, The. *See* Ady, Endre, "A
 magyar Messiások"
"Hungarian Uprising." *See* Elytis, Odysseus,
 Maria Nephele
Hungary
 Ady on, 9:860a-b, 864b–865a
 importance of Krleža and, 11:1808a-b
 revolt (1956), effect on Akhmatova, 10:1530a
 secession of, *see also* Kosztolányi, Dezső
 war of independence (1848–1849), Ady's
  "The Case of Baron Borz" and,
  9:863b–864a
Hunger. See Hamsun, Knut
"Hunger Artist, A" ("Ein Hungerkünstler"). *See*
 Kafka, Franz
Hunger Awakener. See Hungrvaka
Hunger and Thirst. See Ionesco, Eugène, *La
 soif et la faim*
Hungrvaka (*Hunger Awakener*), 1:383a-b,
 399a
Hungry People's Slide, The. *See* Cela, Camilo
 José, *Tobogán de hambientos*
Hunt for Love, The. *See* Mann, Heinrich, *Die
 Jagd nach Liebe*
Hunter's Notes, A. See Turgenev, Ivan
Hunting Letters. *See* Dinesen, Vilhelm,
 Jagtbreve
"Huntsman, The." *See* Chekhov, Anton, "Eger"
"Hunyhat a máglya." *See* Ady, Endre
Huon de Bordeaux, 1:109b
Hüppauf, Bernd-Rüdiger, 9:950a
Huret, Jules, interview with Zola, 7:1533b,
 1536a
Hurluberlu, L'. See Anouilh, Jean
Hurrah to the Hilt! *See* Valle-Inclán, Ramón
 del, *El ruedo ibérico* (The Iberian
 Cycle), *¡Viva mi dueño!*
Hurrah for the Urals. *See* Aragon, Louis,
 Hourra l'Oural

Huset i mørkret. See Vesaas, Tarjei, *The
 House in the Dark*
Huskuld the Herald. *See* Vesaas, Tarjei,
 Sendemann Huskuld
Husserl, Edmund
 Bergson and, 8:52b
 Butor and, 13:3288a
 Logische Untersuchungen (*Logical
  Investigations*), 9:932a
 Ortega y Gasset and, 9:1131a, 1133a
 phenomenology, 9:1127b
 Sartre and, 12:2592a-b
 Spanish translations, 9:1119b
Hustrun. See Moberg, Vilhelm
Huszadik Század (Twentieth Century), Lukács
 and, 10:1253b
Hutten, Ulrich von, Meyer and, 6:932b
Huttens letzte Tage (Hutten's Last Days). *See*
 Meyer, Conrad Ferdinand
Huxley, Aldous
 Brave New World
  anticipated by Zamyatin's *We*, 10:1188b
  and Lagerkvist, 10:1687b
  Silone and, 12:2303a
 Broch and, 10:1392b, 1399b–1400a
 Grey Eminence, 3:267b
  Fénelon and, 3:279b
 on Montaigne, 2:788a
 Point Counter Point, Hesse's *Rosshalde* and,
  9:838a
 The Devils of Loudon, 3:267b
  Johnson and, 12:2377a
 Zamyatin's influence on, 10:1181a
Huygens, Constantijn, Petrarchan influence,
 2:504b
Huysmans, Joris Karl, **7:1709a–1729a**
 À rebours (*Against the Grain*), 7:1417a,
  1586a, 1610a, 1639a, 1716a–1719b
 case history in, 7:141a
 despair in, 7:1625a
 Laforgue and, 7:1885a
 Musil's *The Man Without Qualities* and,
  9:947a
 naturalism and, 7:1709b
 popularity of, 7:1709b
 Verlaine in, 7:1639a
 À vau-l'eau (*Downstream*), 7:1715b–1716a

Breton and, 11:1939a

Certains (Certainties), 7:1720b

Croquis parisiens (*Parisian Sketches*), 7:1713b–1714a

En ménage (*Living Together*), 7:1710b, 1714a–1715b

   Laforgue and, 7:1885a, 1887b

En rade (*In Harbor*), 7:1719b–1720a

En route, 7:1417a, 1725b–1726a, 1727a

Gauguin and, 7:1714a

Goncourts' influence on, 7:1417a

J.-K. Huysmans, 7:1720b

Jiménez and, 9:993b

La Bièvre de Saint-Séverin, 7:1720a

La cathédrale (*The Cathedral*), 7:1709b, 1726b, 1727b–1728a

Là-bas (*Down There*), 7:1722a–1724b

Là-haut (*Up There*), 7:1725a

L'Art moderne (*Modern Art*), 7:1714a, 1720b

Le drageoir à épices (*The Spice Dish*), 7:1711a-b

Les foules de Lourdes (*The Crowds of Lourdes*), 7:1729a

Les hommes d'aujourd'hui (Men of Today), 7:1720b

Les soeurs Vatard (*The Vatard Sisters*), 7:1713a-b, 1714a

L'Oblat (*The Oblate*), 7:1727b, 1729a

Mallarmé and, 7:1586a–1587b, 1718b–1719a

Marthe, histoire d'une fille (*Marthe, Story of a Prostitute*), 7:1711b–1713a

Maupassant and, 7:1763b

Mauriac and, 10:1313a

Sac au dos (Sack on Back), 7:1711b

Sainte Lydwine de Schiedam, 7:1726b

Un dilemme (*A Dilemma*), 7:1719b

on Verlaine's poetry, 7:1639a

Hvide-Krist. See Gunnarsson, Gunnar

Hydrostatics, Pascal's experiments, 3:126b, 127b, 132a-b

Hylaea group, 10:1344a–1345a

   Khlebnikov's association with, 10:1334b–1335b, 1337a-b

   Poshchechina obshchestvennomu vkusu (A Slap in the Face of Public Taste)

      hostility to old order in, 10:1344b

      Khlebnikov's contributions to, 10:1334a

   primitivism of, 10:1353a

   publicity stunt of, 10:1335a

   Sadok sudei (*A Trap for Judges*), 11:1835b

   Sadok sudei (*A Trap for Judges*) (miscellany)

      Khlebnikov's participation in, 10:1334a

      poetics of, 10:1344b–1345a

   Sadok sudei, II (*A Trap for Judges, II*), Khlebnikov's works in, 10:1335a

   Trebnik troikh (The Missal of the Three), Khlebnikov's works in, 10:1335a

   Troe (*The Three*), Khlebnikov's works in, 10:1335a

"Hylas, L'." *See* Ronsard, Pierre de

Hylomorphism, 1:412b, 423b

Hymn and Lament for Cyprus, A. *See* Ritsos, Yannis, *Ymnos kai thrinos ghia tin Kypro*

Hymn (poetic genre), Klopstock and, 4:530b–531b

"Hymn to Apollo." *See* Homer

Hymn to Death. *See* Cela, Camilo José, "Himno a la Muerte"

"Hymn to Intellectual Beauty." *See* Shelley, Percy Bysshe

"Hymn to Justice." *See* Chénier, André

"Hymn to Liberty." *See* Solomos, Dionysios, "Imnos is tin Eleftheria"

"Hymn to Maria Nephele, A." *See* Elytis, Odysseus, *Maria Nephele*, "Imnos sti Maria Nephele"

"Hymne an die Freiheit." *See* Hölderlin, Friedrich

"Hymne an die Göttin der Harmonie." *See* Hölderlin, Friedrich

"Hymne an die Schönheit." *See* Hölderlin, Friedrich

"Hymne aux Suisses de Châteauvieux" ("Hymn on the Triumphal Entry of the Swiss of Châteauvieux"). *See* Chénier, André, *Iambes*

"Hymne de Henry Deuxiesme." *See* Ronsard, Pierre de

Hymne de l'univers. See Teilhard de Chardin, Pierre

Hymnen. See George, Stefan

Hymns
 of Aquinas, 1:416a
 Byzantine, Elytis' *To Axion Esti* and,
  13:2967b–2968a, 2969a
 of Luther, 2:680b–681a, 685a
 of Ronsard, 2:731b–734a
Hymns to the Ideals of Mankind. See
  Hölderlin, Friedrich
Hymns to the Night. See Novalis
Hypallage, in "Futurist Manifesto," 9:809a
"Hypatie et Cyrille." *See* Leconte de Lisle,
  Charles Marie
Hyperbole
 in Boileau's critical style, 3:202b
 Gogol's use of, 6:989a–989b, 995a, 996b
 Wolfram's use of, 1:265a-b
Hyperbolic doubt. *See* Doubt, hyperbolic
Hyperion. See Hölderlin, Friedrich
Hypnosis
 Freud's use of, 8:6b–7a
 in Mann's *Mario and the Magician*, 9:726a-b
Hypocrisy
 Aymé's satire of, 12:2450b–2451b
 in Chekhov's prose, 7:1863a-b
 in "Estuans instrinsicus ira vehementi,"
  1:358a-b
 in Gombrowicz, 12:2572a-b, 2579a–2580b
 in Hugh Primas' "Dives eram et dilectus,"
  1:342a, 356b
 in Molière's works, 3:109b–111a, 119b–120a
 in Rutebeuf's "Des Jacobins," 1:346b–347a
 in Stendhal, 5:356a
 in Walther's *Unmutston*, 1:365b
Hyppolite, Jean, Foucault and, 13:3329b
Hysteria
 Freud's concept of, 8:3a-b, 16a-b
 mass, Broch and, 10:1396a–1399a

I

"I Am Afraid." *See* Zamyatin, Yevgeny
  Ivanovich, "Ia boius'"
"I Am a Burning Wound." *See* Ady, Endre,
  "Tüzes seb vagyok"
"I Am Dying." *See* Sarraute, Nathalie, *L'Usage
  de la parole*
"I Am a Point." *See* Arp, Jean, "Je suis un
  point"
"I am so weary." *See* Petrarch, *Canzoniere*, "Io
  son sì stanco"
"I Am Waiting for the Other." *See* Ady, Endre,
  "Várom a másikat"
"I Am Writing to You." *See* Lermontov,
  Mikhail Yurievich, "Ya k vam pishu"
I Arrived Too Early. *See* Ady, Endre, "Korán
  jöttem ide"
"I Bileyi i Blok i Iesenin i Kliuiev." *See*
  Tychyna, Pavlo, *Pluh*
"I Both Wept and Repented." *See* Akhmatova,
  Anna
I cry everyone's pardon. *See* Villon, François,
  The Testament, "Je crie a toutes gens
  mercis"
I den tiden. See Lagerkvist, Pär
I Desire to Feel Loved. *See* Ady, Endre,
  "Szeretném, ha szeretnének"
I Dhodheka. See Blok, Alexander
I Didn't Do Anything to the Girl. *See* Böll,
  Heinrich, "Ich han dem Mädche nix
  jedonn"
I Do Not Like Brecht. *See* Ionesco, Eugène, "Je
  n'aime pas Brecht"
"I and E. A Tale of the Stone Age." *See*
  Khlebnikov, Velimir, "I i E. Povest'
  kamennogo veka"
"I enter dark churches." *See* Blok, Alexander,
  "Vkhozhu ia v temnye khramy"
I Fled Paris. *See* Butor, Michel, *Où*, "J'ai fui
  Paris"
"I go weeping for my past time." *See* Petrarch,
  Canzoniere, "I' vo piangendo i miei
  passati tempi"
I Had a Dog and a Cat. See Čapek, Karel, *Měl
  jsem psa a koçku*

I Hate Paris. *See* Butor, Michel, *Où*, "Je hais Paris"

"I have conquered her at last." *See* Blok, Alexander, "Ia ee pobedil, nakonets"

I Have Never Learned to Write; or, The Opening Words. *See* Aragon, Louis, *Je n'ai jamais appris à écrire ou les incipits*

"I have preserved among the young harmonies." *See* Blok, Alexander, "Khranila ia sredi mladkh sozvuchii"

"I Have Such Faith in You." *See* Montale, Eugenio, *Altri versi e poesie disperse*

I havsbandet (*By the Open Sea*). *See* Strindberg, August

"I i E. Povest' kamennogo veka." *See* Khlebnikov, Velimir

I Killed a Butterfly. *See* Ady, Endre, "Megöltem egy pillangot"

"I Know the Hour When the Most Impassive Face." *See* Montale, Eugenio, *Cuttlefish Bones*

"I Look into the Past." *See* Olesha, Yuri, "Ya smotryu v proshloe"

I Married You for Fun. See Ginzburg, Natalia

"I nam ne dolgo liubovat'sia." *See* Blok, Alexander

I Remember. *See* Simenon, Georges, *Je me souviens*

"I seek salvation." *See* Blok, Alexander, "Ischu spaseniia"

"I Sense Your Coming." *See* Blok, Alexander, "Predchuvstvuiu Tebia"

"I set out alone on the road." *See* Lermontov, Mikhail, "Vykhozhu odin ia na dorogu"

I Shall Kiss the Girl of Kisses. *See* Ady, Endre, "Megcsókolom Csók-kisasszonyt"

"I shall make a song." *See* William IX of Aquitaine, duke, "Companho faray un vers"

I Shall Not Serve. *See* Ekelöf, Gunnar, *Non serviam*

"I shall roam . . ." *See* Mandelshtam, Osip, "Ia budu skitat'sia . . ."

I Sit on the Tabletop Throne. *See* Ady, Endre, "Ülök az asztal-trónon"

"I Surely Call upon God." *See* Seferis, George, "Epikaleo toi ten theon"

I and Thou. *See* Hebbel, Friedrich, "Ich und Du"

"I Too Am a Painter." *See* Apollinaire, Guillaume, "Moi aussi je suis peintre"

I vapenrock och linnebyxor. See Moberg, Vilhelm

"I' vo piangendo i miei passati tempi." *See* Petrarch, *Canzoniere*

"I vyklepal prach z obuvi své." *See* Hašek, Jaroslav

I will use against vices rebellious song. *See* "Utar contra vitia carmine rebelli"

"I would like." *See* William IX of Aquitaine, duke, "Ben vuelh"

I Write for Readers: Answers to Imagined Questions. *See* Frisch, Max, "Ich schreibe für Leser: Antworten auf vorgestellte Fragen"

"I Write to You from a Distant Place." *See* Michaux, Henri, "Je vous écris d'un pays lointain"

"Ia boius'." *See* Zamyatin, Yevgeny Ivanovich

"Ia budu skitat'sia . . ." *See* Mandelshtam, Osip

"Ia dukh, dukh vichnosti." *See* Tychyna, Pavlo, *V kosmichnomu orkestri*

"Ia ee pobedil, nakonets." *See* Blok, Alexander

"Ia i plakala i kaialas." *See* Akhmatova, Anna, "I Both Wept and Repented"

Iagoda, Genrikh, Gorky and, 8:423a-b

Iambics and Epodes. *See* Carducci, Giosue, *Giambi ed epodi*

Iashvili, Paolo
    in Pasternak's *Sketch for an Autobiography*, 10:1614b
    Pasternak's support for, 10:1595b

"Iasi tofos." *See* Cavafy, Constantine

"Iazyk bulyzhnika." *See* Mandelshtam, Osip

Ibáñez, Vicente Blasco. *See* Blasco Ibáñez, Vicente

Iberian Cycle, The. *See* Valle-Inclán, Ramón del, *El ruedo ibérico*

Ibn al-'Arabī, *Tarjumān al-ashwāq*, 12:2668a

Ibsen, Henrik, **7:1421a–1448b**

Ibsen, Henrik (*cont.*)
  A Doll's House (*Ett Dukkehjem*), 7:1421b,
    1428a–1430a, 1753b
    film version, 7:1444a
    foreign adaptations, 7:1443a-b
    Ionesco's *Rhinocéros* and, 13:3003a
    Laforgue and, 7:1892a
    Nora, 7:1428a–1429b, 1437a
    as well-made play, 7:1929a-b
  An Enemy of the People, 7:1423b,
    1432a–1433a, 1435b
    Miller adaptation, 7:1444a
  on autonomy of his characters, 5:376b
  Beckett and, 7:1754a
  in Bely's *Na rubezhe dvukh stoletii*, 9:911b
  Blok and, 9:984a-b
  Brand, 7:1424a-b, 1425b–1426a, 1426b,
    1733b, 1753b
    Mandelshtam and, 10:1628b
  Brecht and, 7:1754a
  Catiline, 7:1422b, 1437a, 9:984a-b
  Chekhov and, 7:1754a
  Dinesen and, 10:1294b
  Emperor and Galilean, 7:1426b, 1431b,
    1439b
  Frisch and, 13:2897b, 2916a
  Gengangere, 10:1256b
  Ghosts, 7:1421b, 1422a, 1430a–1432a,
    1435a, 8:24a
    foreign adaptations, 7:1443a
  Hamsun and, 8:23a, 24a, 24b, 25a, 28b–29a,
    42a
  Handke and, 7:1754
  Hedda Gabler, 7:1421a-b, 1423b,
    1436b–1437a, 1437a–1439b,
    10:1256b–1257a
    film verson, 7:1444a
  John Gabriel Borkman, 7:1422a, 1423b,
    1441b–1442a
    foreign adaptations, 7:1443b
  Lady Inger of Østraat (*Fru Inger til Østraat*),
    7:1422b, 1928a
  Lagerkvist on, 10:1685a
  letter to Sophie Adlersparre, 7:1430a
  Little Eyolf, 7:1422a, 1440b–1441a
  Love's Comedy, 7:1435b–1436a
  Lukács and, 10:1253a, 1253b, 1255b–1257a

  O'Neill and, 7:1754a
  Peer Gynt, 7:1424a, 1424b–1426a, 1426b,
    1444b, 1746a
    Buttonmolder, 7:1425a, 1426a
    film version, 7:1444a
  Pillars of Society (*Samfundets støtter*),
    7:1421b, 1422a, 1427a–1428a,
    1928b–1929a, 1930a
    Miller adaptation, 7:1444a
  Pinter and, 7:1754
  Pirandello and, 7:1754a
  Poems, 7:1426b
  reconciliation plays, 7:1436a-b, 1440b
  Rosmersholm, 7:1421b, 1434a–1435a,
    8:28b–29a
    as well-made play, 7:1930a-b
  sets, 7:1444a-b
  Shaw and, 7:1754a, 13:3215b
  Strindberg and, 7:1731b, 1733b, 1742a,
    1746a, 1749a, 1753b–1754a, 8:29a
  The Burial Mound, 7:1422b
  The Lady from the Sea, 7:1421b, 1424a,
    1435a–1436b
  The League of Youth, 7:1427a
  The Master Builder, 7:1439b, 8:25a
  The Pretenders, 7:1422b–1423a
    Gunnarsson and, 10:1505a
    Hákonar saga gamla and, 1:399a
  The Vikings of Helgeland, 7:1422b
    Völsunga saga and, 1:400b
  The Wild Duck (*Vildanden*), 7:1422a,
    1433a–1434a, 1439b, 10:1257a
  translated by Krleža, 11:1810b–1811a
  Wedekind and, 8:236b
  well-made play and, 7:1928a–1930b
  When We Dead Awaken, 7:1424a,
    1442a–1443a, 1753b
  on women, 11:2039b
Icare (French aviation journal),
    Saint-Exupéry's articles in, 12:2317a
Icarus legend
  in Apollinaire's "The Betrothal," 9:892a
  in Yourcenar's *Jardin des chimères*,
    12:2537a-b
Ice Age. See Dorst, Tankred, *Eiszeit*
"Ice Maiden, The." *See* Andersen, Hans
    Christian

Ice Palace, The. See Vesaas, Tarjei

Ice-Cimbalon Rings and Clangs, The. *See* Ady, Endre, "Zúg-Zeng a jégcimbalom"

"Ice-Skating." *See* Klopstock, Friedrich Gottlieb

Iceland
Christianization of, 12:2470b
history, sagas and, 1:377b–378a, 381b
independence from Denmark, in Laxness' novels, 12:2465b, 2474b
Irish settlers, folklore, 12:2470b–2471a
under Danish monarchy, 12:2473b

Icelandic language, Gunnarsson and, 10:1497a

Icelandic literature
history, 12:2473b–2474a
rhymed ballad, 12:2467a-b, 2473b, 2474b
see also Íslendinga sögur

Iceland's Bell. *See* Laxness, Halldór, *Íslandsklukkan*

Iceman Cometh, The. See O'Neill, Eugene

"Ich han dem Mädche nix jedonn." *See* Böll, Heinrich

"Ich hân mî lehen al die werlt, ich hâ mîn lêhen." *See* Walther von der Vogelweide

"Ich horte ein wazzer diezen." *See* Walther von der Vogelweide

"Ich innoz verdienen swachen haz." *See* Walther von der Vogelweide

"Ich sach mit mînen ongen." *See* Walther von der Vogelweide

"Ich saz ûf eime steine." *See* Walther von der Vogelweide

"Ich schreibe für Leser: Antworten auf vorgestellte Fragen." *See* Frisch, Max

"Ich sterbe." *See* Sarraute, Nathalie, *L'Usage de la parole*

Ich und das Es, Das. See Freud, Sigmund

"Ich und Du." *See* Hebbel, Friedrich

Iconia legend, 1:462b–463a

Iconoclasm
in Mérimée's works, 6:748a
Rimbaud as exemplar of, 7:1787a

Iconography, Christian, Prudentius and, 1:13a-b

Id, Freud's concept of, 8:4b, 6a

Ida-Elisabeth. See Undset, Sigrid

Idea de principio en Leibniz y la evolución de la teoría deductiva, La. See Ortega y Gasset, José

Idea dell'India, Un'. See Moravia, Alberto

Idea of History and Its Relationship with the Idea of Art, The. *See* Croce, Benedetto, *Il concetto della storia nelle sue relazioni col concetto dell'arte*

Idea of India, An. *See* Moravia, Alberto, *Un'idea dell'India*

Idea of Principle in Leibniz and the Evolution of Deductive Theory, The. See Ortega y Gasset, José, *La idea de principio en Leibniz y la evolución de la teoría deductiva*

Idea of progress. *See* Progress, idea of

Ideal, in Rousseau, 4:461b–463a

Idealism
aesthetic, of Gogol, 6:979a
in Balzac's works, 5:644a
Bergson's view of, 8:54b
Büchner and, 6:1176a-b, 1188a–1189b
Croce on, 8:323a
German, Staël's *De l'Allemagne* on, 5:108a–109a
in Hebbel's works, 6:1098b
Leconte de Lisle and, 6:1253b–1254a
magic, Novalis and, 5:210b
Musset on conflict with political action, 6:1004b–1005a
in poetry, Schlegel and, 5:183b

Idealism, humanistic, in Dürrenmatt's works, 13:3228b

"Idealismo e realismo" ("Idealism and Realism"). *See* Eça de Queiroz, José Maria

Ideas: The Book of Le Grand. See Heine, Heinrich, *Ideen, Das Buch Le Grand*

Ideas. See Schlegel, Friedrich von

Ideas. *See* Thought

Ideas and Beliefs. *See* Ortega y Gasset, José, *Ideas y creencias*

Ideas of Madame Aubray, The. See Dumas fils, Alexandre, *Les idées de Madame Aubray*

Ideas of Madame Aubray, The. *See* Dumas
fils, Alexandre, *Les idées de Madame
Aubray*
Ideas and Sensations. See Goncourt, Edmond
Louis Antoine and Jules Alfred Huot de,
Idées et sensations
Ideas sobre la novela. See Ortega y Gasset,
José
Ideas y creencias. See Ortega y Gasset, José
Idee elementari sulla poesia romantica. See
Visconti, Ermes
"Idée sur les romans." *See* Sade, Donatien
Alphonse François, marquis de, *The
Crimes of Love*
Ideen. See Schlegel, Friedrich von
Ideen, Das Buch Le Grand. See Heine,
Heinrich
*Ideen zur Philosophie der Geschichte der
Menschheit. See* Herder, Johann
Gottfried von
Idées de Madame Aubray, Les. See Dumas
fils, Alexandre
Idées et sensations. See Goncourt, Edmond
Louis Antoine and Jules Alfred Huot de
Identity
in Calvino, 13:3283a
in Canetti's works, 12:2624b–2625b
crisis of, in Goncharov's works, 6:1065b
in Ekelöf's works, 12:2641b, 2665a-b
Frisch's views on, 13:2922b–2924b
in Galdós, 7:1615a-b
in Ghelderode's *Escurial*, 11:2118a
Mach on, 9:939b
Ideograms
Elytis and
Simatologon, 13:2979a
"The Monogram," 13:2975b
Ideographs, Claudel on, 8:489a
Ideologues (French philosophical school),
Sainte-Beuve and, 6:857b
"Ideology critique," as practiced by Frankfurt
Institute writers, 11:1726a
Idilios vascos. See Baroja, Pío
Idilios y fantasías. See Baroja, Pío
Idiomatic language
Emerson's valuation of, 4:654b
Herder's valuation of, 4:642b

Whitman's valuation of, 4:656a-b
*Idiot de la famille: Gustave Flaubert de 1821
à 1857, L'. See* Sartre, Jean-Paul, *The
Family Idiot*
Idiot, The (Idiot). See Dostoevsky, Feodor
"Idoni." *See* Cavafy, Constantine
Idris und Zenide. See Wieland, Christoph
Martin
Idyllic moment
in Rousseau, 4:461b–462a
subversion of
Keller and, 6:928a
Storm and, 6:917a
Idylls
classical, 2:900b–901a
of Leopardi, 5:555a-b
of Lorenzo de' Medici, 2:906a
see also Pastoral poetry
Idylls. See Ausonius; Theocritus
Idylls and Fantasies. *See* Baroja, Pío, *Idilios y
fantasías*
"Ierefs tou Serapiou." *See* Cavafy, Constantine
"If the care that torments me." *See* Petrarch,
Canzoniere, "Se 'l pensier che mi
strugge"
"If Dead Indeed." *See* Cavafy, Constantine,
"Eige etelefta"
If Five Years Pass. See García Lorca, Federico,
Así que pasen cinco años
If I Remember Right. See Guitry, Sacha
"If it is not love." *See* Petrarch, *Canzoniere*,
"S'amor non è"
If Not Thus. See Pirandello, Luigi, *Se non così*
"If only I have him." *See* Novalis, *Sacred
Songs (Geistliche Lieder)*, "Wenn ich
ihn nur habe"
If the War Goes On. See Hesse, Hermann,
Krieg und Frieden
If on a winter's night a traveler. See Calvino,
Italo
If You Imagine. *See* Queneau, Raymond,
L'Instant fatal
If You White, You Black. *See* Arp, Jean, *weisst
du schwarzt du*
Iffland, August Wilhelm, 5:33a
Andersen and, 6:877b
Kleist and, 5:307a

"Ifjú karok kikötőjében." See Ady, Endre

Ifjúság, 9:859a

Igitur, The Madness of Elbehnon (Igitur ou la folie d'Elbehnon). See Mallarmé, Stéphane

Ignatius of Loyola, St., Spiritual Exercises, Yourcenar's adaptation, 12:2547b

Ignorance. See Knowledge

Igor Tale, The, in Tychyna's poetry, 10:1671a

"Ihr Morgen ist die Finsternis." See Frisch, Max, When the War Was Over

"Iisusov grekh." See Babel, Isaac

"Iks." See Zamyatin, Yevgeny Ivanovich

Il faut qu'une porte soit ouverte ou fermée. See Musset, Alfred de

Il fuoco. See D'Annunzio, Gabriele

Il ne faut jurer de rien. See Musset, Alfred de

Il y a. See Apollinaire, Guillaume

Ile. See O'Neill, Eugene

Ilf, Illia, Babel and, 11:1892a

"Ilia Isaakovich i Margareta Prokofievna." See Babel, Isaac

Iliad. See Homer

'Iliad," The; or, The Poem of Force. See Weil, Simone

Ilios o protos. See Elytis, Odysseus

Illegitimacy, in Ibsen's dramas, 7:1422a-b

Illegitimate Son, The. See Diderot, Denis, Le fils naturel

'Illiade, ou Le poème de la force," L'. See Weil, Simone, The "Iliad"; or, The Poem of Force

"Illness." See Pasternak, Boris, Themes and Variations

Illuminations, Les (Illuminations). See Rimbaud, Arthur

Illuminés, Les. See Nerval, Gérard de

Illusion
    in Ariosto, 2:635a
    reality and, in Andrić's works, 11:1768b–1769a
    in Schnitzler's works, 8:96b–97a
    see also Optical distortion

Illusion comique, L'. See Corneille, Pierre

Illusions perdues, Les. See Balzac, Honoré de

Illustrations. See Butor, Michel

Illustrators, book, Maeterlinck and, 8:139a

Illustrious House of Ramires. See Eça de Queiroz, José Maria

"Illustrious Kitchen Maid, The." See Cervantes, Miguel de, "La ilustre fregona"

Ilustre casa de Ramires, A. See Eça de Queiroz, José Maria, The Illustrious House of Ramires

"Ilustre fregona, La." See Cervantes, Miguel de

"Im Anfang war die Nachtigall." See Heine, Heinrich

Im Dickicht der Städte. See Brecht, Bertolt, In the Jungle of Cities

I'm Dreaming, But Am I? See Pirandello, Luigi, Sogno (ma forse no)

I'm Not Stiller. See Frisch, Max, Stiller

"Im Osten." See Trakl, Georg

Im Saal. See Storm, Theodor

Im Schlaraffenland. See Mann, Heinrich

Im Sonnenschein. See Storm, Theodor

Im Spiel der Sommerlüfte. See Schnitzler, Arthur

"Im Unterreich." See George, Stefan, Algabal

"Ima Baál Istenhez." See Ady, Endre

Image, L'. See Robbe-Grillet, Catherine

Image Maker of Harlem, The. See Nerval, Gérard de, L'Imagier de Harlem

"Imágen poética de don Luis de Góngora, La." See García Lorca, Federico

Images
    Bergson's view of, 8:57b
    see also Symbolism

"Images à Crusoé." See Perse, Saint-John, "Pictures for Crusoe"

Imagier de Harlem, L'. See Nerval, Gérard de

Imaginaire, L'. See Sartre, Jean-Paul, The Psychology of the Imagination

Imaginary Invalid, The. See Molière, Le malade imaginaire

Imaginary Life. See Ginzburg, Natalia, Vita immaginaria

Imaginary Museum of World Sculpture. See Malraux, André, Le musée imaginaire de la sculpture mondiale

Imagination
    of Aymé, 12:252a, 2453b
    in Balzac's works, 5:643b

Imagination (*cont.*)
  Delacroix's views on, 5:535a-b, 538a
  Leopardi's views on, 5:554a, 554b–555a
  Malraux and, 12:2428a
  Milosz and, 13:2938a
  Novalis and, 5:209b
  in Richter's works, 5:84b
  in Rousseau, 4:464a-b
  Sartre on, 12:2593a-b, 2605b–2609a
  Schlegel and, 5:183a-b
Imagination, L'. *See* Sartre, Jean-Paul,
    Imagination: A Psychological Critique
Imbonati, Carlo, Manzoni's poem
  commemorating, 5:368a
Imbroglio, L'. *See* Moravia, Alberto
Imerologhio mias vdhomadhas. *See* Ritsos,
    Yannis, *Ghignesthe*
Imerologio enos atheatou Apriliou, To. *See*
    Elytis, Odysseus
Imerologio katastromatos. *See* Seferis, George
Imitation, in Portuguese literature, 10:1484a
Imitation of Christ, The (*Imitatio Christi*). *See*
    Thomas à Kempis, St.
*Imitation de Notre-Dame la Lune selon Jules
    Laforgue, L'* (*The Imitation of Our Lady
    of the Moon According to Jules
    Laforgue*). *See* Laforgue, Jules
"Imitelis kai ypotypodhis triloghia." *See*
    Ritsos, Yannis
Immaculée conception, L'. *See* Breton, André
"Immanent criticism," 11:1709b
Immaturity, theme of, Gombrowicz and,
  12:2571a–2574a
Immensee. *See* Storm, Theodor
Immoralist, The (*L'Immoraliste*). *See* Gide,
    André
Immortal One, The. *See* Robbe-Grillet, Alain
"Immortal Story, The." *See* Dinesen, Isak
Immortality
  Aquinas' *Summa theologica* on, 1:423a
  Canetti and, 12:2627a
  in Machado's *Campos de Castilla*, 9:757b
  Pléiade and, 2:743b
  Proust on, 8:560a–561a, 565a, 565b
  Sartre and, 12:2598a-b
  Unamuno on, 8:291b

  in Valéry's *Graveyard by the Sea*, 8:578b,
    579a-b
Immortelle, L'. *See* Robbe-Grillet, Alain, *The
    Immortal One*
"Imnos is tin Eleftheria." *See* Solomos,
    Dionysios
"Imnos sti Maria Nephele." *See* Elytis,
    Odysseus, *Maria Nephele*
Imparcial, El (Spanish periodical)
  foundation and editorship, 9:1122a
  Generation of '98, 9:1121b
  Ortega y Gasset's articles in, 9:1124b
Impegno controvoglia. *See* Moravia, Alberto
*Impossible Dialogue Between Ivan Anissimov
    and Silone, An*. *See* Silone, Ignazio, *Un
    dialogo difficile: Sono liberi gli scrittori
    russi?*
"Impossible, L'" ("The Impossible"). *See*
    Rimbaud, Arthur
Impossible, theater of the, Camus and,
  13:3064a-b
Impotence, theme of
  in Ghelderode's plays, 11:2126b
  in Rabelais's *Fifth Book*, 2:713b, 716b
Imprécations contre la fourmi d'Argentine. *See*
    Butor, Michel
Impresiones y paisajes. *See* García Lorca,
    Federico
Impression, Sunrise. *See* Monet, Claude
Impressionism
  in art
    Chekhov and, 7:1858a
    Laforgue and, 7:1885a
    landscapes in, 7:1630b–1631a, 1632a-b
    Verlaine and, 7:1631a–1633b
  in Azorín's works, 9:639b, 645b, 648b–649a
  Blasco Ibáñez, 8:362a, 380b
  Delacroix and, 5:538a-b
  Goncourts and, 7:1630b–1631a
  Khlebnikov and, 10:1334a
  in Lermontov's works, 6:1206b–1207a
  in Lukács's view, 10:1256a
  in Tychyna's poetry, 10:1661b–1662b
Impressionists' Studio. *See* *Studiiya
    impressionistov*
Impressions de voyage en Suisse. *See* Dumas
    père, Alexandre

Impressions and Landscapes. See García
   Lorca, Federico, *Impresiones y paisajes*
Imprint, The. *See* Čapek, Karel, "Šlépěj"
Imprisonment
   escape and
      in Dumas's works, 6:731a–733a
      as major Romantic theme, 6:731a-b
   in Pessoa's works, 10:1493a
   of Sade, 4:615b–616a, 617a–619b, 636b
   of Zamyatin, 10:1182a
Impromptu de l'Alma, L' (*The Impromptu of
   Alma*). *See* Ionesco, Eugène
Impromptu de Paris, L'. See Giraudoux, Jean,
   Paris Impromptu
Impromptu de Versailles, L'. See Molière
Improvisation
   Goldoni and, 4:427a–428a
   in oral cultures, 1:56b–57a
   as part of Russian literary life, Mickiewicz
      and, 5:613b
"Improvisationen aus dem Capreser Winter"
   ("Improvisations from Winter on
   Capri"). *See* Rilke, Rainer Maria
Improvisations sur Flaubert. See Butor, Michel
Improvisatore, The (*Improvisatoren*). *See*
   Andersen, Hans Christian
"In '38." *See* Montale, Eugenio, *Altri versi e
   poesie disperse*
In America. *See* Gorky, Maxim, "V Amerike"
In an Old Hansom. *See* Ady, Endre, "Egy
   ócska konflisban"
In Autumn. *See* Ekelöf, Gunnar, *Om hösten*
"In the Basement." *See* Babel, Isaac, "V
   podvale"
"In the Beginning; an Interpretation of
   Sunlight Energy." *See* Eve, Frank C.
"In the Beginning was the Nightingale." *See*
   Heine, Heinrich, "Im Anfang war die
   Nachtigall"
"In the Camp." *See* Andrić, Ivo
In the Cosmic Orchestra. *See* Tychyna, Pavlo,
   V kosmichnomu orkestri
"In der Strafkolonie." *See* Kafka, Franz, "The
   Penal Colony"
"In dormiveglia." *See* Ungaretti, Giuseppe,
   Allegria di naufragi

"In the Duckyard." *See* Andersen, Hans
   Christian
In einer Familie. See Mann, Heinrich
In Elijah's Chariot. *See* Ady, Endre, *Az Illés
   szekerén*
In the Evening, a Geranium. *See* Pirandello,
   Luigi, "Di sera, un geranio"
"In Exile." *See* Chekhov, Anton, "V ssylke"
In the Face of Death. See Strindberg, August,
   Inför Döden
In the Flame of Don Cristóbal. See García
   Lorca, Federico, *Retablillo de don
   Cristóbal*
In Front of the Baths of Caracalla. *See*
   Carducci, Giosue, "Dinanzi alle terme di
   Caracalla"
In the Great Hall. See Storm, Theodor, *Im
   Saal*
In Harbor. See Huysmans, Joris Karl, *En rade*
In the Harbor of Young Arms. *See* Ady, Endre,
   "Ifjú karok kikötőjében"
In the Jungle of Cities. See Brecht, Bertolt
In the Labyrinth. See Robbe-Grillet, Alain
In medias res, in Johnson's works, 12:2375a
"In memoria." *See* Ungaretti, Giuseppe
*In memoria del "Manifesto dei communisti".
   See* Labriola, Antonio
In Memoriam. See Tennyson, Alfred
In Memory of the *Communist Manifesto. See*
   Labriola, Antonio, *In memoria del
   "Manifesto dei communisti"*
"In morte del fratello Giovanni." *See* Foscolo,
   Ugo
In My Heart. *See* Tychyna, Pavlo, *V sertsi u
   moim*
"In Old Russia." *See* Zamyatin, Yevgeny
   Ivanovich, "Rus"
In the Open. *See* Breton, André, "Au grand
   jour"
In a Parallel Manner. *See* Verlaine, Paul,
   Parallèlement
"In Place of a Preface." *See* Akhmatova, Anna,
   Poem Without a Hero
In the Play of the Summer Breezes. *See*
   Schnitzler, Arthur, *Im Spiel der
   Sommerlüfte*

In Praise of Newspapers. See Čapek, Karel,
  Marsyas čili na okraj literatury

"In Praise of Peace." *See* Akhmatova, Anna

"In qual parte del Ciel." *See* Petrarch,
  Canzoniere

"In the Ravine." *See* Chekhov, Anton, "V
  ovrage"

In San Petronio Square. See Carducci, Giosue,
  "Nella Piazza di San Petronio"

In Search of the National Identity. See
  Unamuno, Miguel de, *En torno al
  casticismo*

"In the Service of Summer." *See* Elytis,
  Odysseus, *Prosanatolismi*
  (*Orientations*), "I thitia tou kalokeriou"

In Sicily. See Vittorini, Elio, *Conversazione in
  Sicilia*

In a Small Country House. See Witkiewicz,
  Stanisław Ignacy, *W małym dworku*

In Spain. See Andersen, Hans Christian

In the Subterranean Realm. See George,
  Stefan, *Algabal*, "Im Unterreich"

In the Sunlight. See Storm, Theodor, *Im
  Sonnenschein*

In Sweden. See Andersen, Hans Christian

"In the sweet time of my first age." *See*
  Petrarch, *Canzoniere*, "Nel dolce tempo
  de la prima etade"

In This Country. See Böll, Heinrich,
  "Hierzulande"

In This World. See Hesse, Hermann, *Diesseits*

"In Total Darkness; or, The Surrealist Bluff."
  See Artaud, Antonin, "A la grande nuit,
  ou le bluff surréaliste"

"In a Township in Asia Minor." *See* Cavafy,
  Constantine, "Endimo tis Mikras Asias"

In Tunic and Linen Trousers. See Moberg,
  Vilhelm, *I vapenrock och linnebyxor*

In Vain Is the Moon Cold. See Ady, Endre,
  "Hiába hideq a hold"

*In Vain You Haunt Me Whitely, Like Snow.
  See* Ady, Endre, "Hiába kisértesz
  hófehéren"

In the Vineyard of Bygone Years. See Ady,
  Endre, "Elillant évek szőlőhegyén"

"In vino veritas." *See* Kierkegaard, Søren

In the Void. See Ritsos, Yannis, *Dhiadhromos
  kai skala*

"In what part of Heaven." *See* Petrarch,
  Canzoniere, "In qual parte del Ciel"

"In the World." *See* Olesha, Yuri, "V mire"

"Incantation." *See* Milosz, Czeslaw, "Zaklęcie"

"Incantation by Laughter." *See* Khlebnikov,
  Velimir, "Zakliatie smekhom"

Incarnation
  in Claudel's works
    Break of Noon, 8:478a
    La jeune fille Violaine, 8:482a
    "Magnificat," 8:490a
    The Tidings Brought to Mary,
      8:483b–484a

Incest
  in Chateaubriand's *René*, 5:121a
  in Eça's works, 7:1703a-b, 1704a
  in Hugo's works, 6:711a
  in Lope de Vega's *El castigo sin venganza*,
    2:866b–867a
  in Moravia's works, 12:2695a
  in Sade's writings, 4:628b
  in Schnitzler's works, 8:100a, 109b, 110a-b
  Trakl and, 10:1412a-b
  in Valle-Inclán's *Sonata de invierno*, 8:335b
  in Yourcenar's "Anna, soror,"
    12:2557b–2558a

Incidences. See Gide, André

"Incident at Krechetovka Station." *See*
  Solzhenitsyn, Aleksandr, "Sluchai na
  stantsii Kochetovka"

Incident at Twilight. See Dürrenmatt,
  Friedrich

"Incident from the Life of Makar, An." *See*
  Gorky, Maxim

Incognita, La. See Pérez Galdós, Benito

Incomparable Earth, The. See Quasimodo,
  Salvatore

Incongruity
  humorism and, 8:395b–396a
  Ritsos, 12:2835a-b

Inconstancy of human opinion, in La Bruyère's
  Caractères, 3:250a-b

"Incontro." *See* Montale, Eugenio, *Cuttlefish
  Bones*

Independent People. See Laxness, Halldór,
    Sjálfstætt fólk
Index of Prohibited Books
    Alfieri's works on, 4:672b, 674a
    Bergson and, 8:61a, 64b
    Dante's *De monarchia* on, 1:443b
    Maeterlinck and, 8:140a-b
    Masuccio's *Novellino* on, 2:940a
    Montaigne and, 2:785a, 786a
    Sebond's *Theologia naturalis* on, 2:772a
    Unamuno's *Tragic Sense of Life* and, 8:300b
    in Zamyatin's *Ogni sviatogo Dominika*,
        10:1193b
    see also Roman Catholic Church
India
    Hesse and, 9:837a, 837b
    in *Siddhartha*, 9:844b
Indian Summer. See Strindberg, August,
    "Indiansommar"
Indiana. See Sand, George
"Indiansommar." *See* Strindberg, August
Indifference
    in Camus, 13:3059a–3062a
    in Milosz's works, 13:2942a-b
Indifferent Beau, The. See Cocteau, Jean, *Le
    bel indifférent*
Indifferenti, Gli. See Moravia, Alberto;
    Moravia, Alberto, *The Time of
    Indifference*
Indipohdi. See Hauptmann, Gerhart
Indirection, in Schlegel's critical theory,
    5:189b–190a
Indiscreet Jewels, The. See Diderot, Denis, *Les
    bijoux indiscrets*
Individual
    diversity of, in Richter's fiction, 5:57a
    Kierkegaard and, 6:1123b–1124a
    relationship to society, in Baroja,
        9:598b–599a
    society and, Fontane on, 6:1303a–1304b,
        1309b–1310b
    Unamuno's view of, 8:292a-b, 300a
Individualism
    in Baudelaire, 7:1342b–1346b
    Canetti on, 12:2620a
    Frisch's views on, 13:2922b–2924b
    in German literature, of Herder, 4:652a-b

Gide's critique in *L'Immoraliste*,
    8:503b–504a
Gombrowicz and, 12:2587b
Mach on, 9:939b
in Olesha's *Envy*, 11:2239b
Sartre on, 12:2604a–2607b
in Taine's writing, 7:1452b–1457a
Individualist, The. See Ritsos, Yannis,
    "Atomikistis"
Indochine, L'. See Malraux, André
Indomabili, Gli. See Marinetti, Filippo
    Tommaso
Industrialism
    Broch and, 10:1386a-b
    Dinesen's criticism of, 10:1297b–1298a
    Hamsun's use of, 8:37b
    in Portugal, Methuen Treaty and, 11:2144b
    see also Mass production methods;
        Technology
Inès Mendo, ou le préjugé vaincu. See
    Mérimée, Prosper
Inexperienced Traveler, The. *See* Gunnarsson,
    Gunnar, *Kirken paa Bjerget* (The Church
    on the Hill), *Den uerfarne Reisende*
Inez Mendo; or, Prejudice Overcome. See
    Mérimée, Prosper, *Inès Mendo, ou le
    préjugé vaincu*
Infallible personae, in medieval satire,
    1:359b–361a
Infant García, vengeance motif in, 1:125a
Infantryman Trunec's Cap. *See* Hašek,
    Jaroslav, "Čáka pěšáka Trunce"
Infernal Machine, The. See Cocteau, Jean
Inferno. See Dante Alighieri, *Divine Comedy*;
    Strindberg, August
Infidelity. *See* Adultery
"Infinite, The" (*L'infinito*). *See* Leopardi,
    Giacomo
*Influence de Ronsard sur la poésie française
    (1550–1585), L'. See* Raymond, Marcel
*Influence of the Passions on the Happiness of
    Individuals and Nations. See* Staël,
    Madame de, *De l'influence des passions*
Inför döden. See Strindberg, August
Information (Italian journal). *See* Silone,
    Ignazio
"Ingenting." *See* Södergran, Edith

Ingénu, L'. See Voltaire

Ingénue libertine, L'. See Colette

"Ingénus, Les." *See* Verlaine, Paul

"Ingólfs þáttr," 1:393a-b

Ingres, Jean Auguste Dominique
  at Exposition Universelle of 1855, 5:536b
  Degas and, 5:536b
  Delacroix and, 5:517a
  Homer's Apotheosis, in Vigny's *Stello,*
    5:469b
  Les capucines, 5:533a
  neoclassicism, 7:1408b

Inhibitions, Symptoms and Anxiety. See
  Freud, Sigmund, *Hemmung, Symptom
  und Angst*

Initiation. *See* George, Stefan, *Hymnen* (Odes),
  "Weihe"

Injustice, social. *See* Social injustice

"Ink." *See* Claudel, Paul, *Cent phrases pour
  éventails* (*A Hundred Sentences for
  Fans*), "Encre"

Inner Voices. See Hugo, Victor, *Les voix
  intérieures*

Inni sacri. See Manzoni, Alessandro, *The
  Sacred Hymns*

Innocent III, pope
  in *Unmutston,* 1:344a-b
  Walther and, 1:301b–302b

Innocent IV, pope
  Aristotelianism and, 1:409a
  Etsi animarum, 1:413b–414a

Innocent XI, pope, quietism and, 3:268b

Innocent XII, pope, condemnation of Fénelon
  and, 3:272a

Innocent Libertine, The. See Colette, *L'Ingénue
  libertine*

Innocente, L'. See D'Annunzio, Gabriele, *The
  Intruder*

Innsbruck Easter play, 1:467b

Inquietudes de Shanti Andía, Las. See Baroja,
  Pío

"Inquisitio de fide" (Inquiry Concerning
  Faith). *See* Erasmus

Inquisition, Camoëns' *The Play of Filodemo*
  and, 2:758a

Inquisitive Women, The. *See* Goldoni, Carlo,
  Le donne curiose

Insanity. *See* Mental illness; Syphilis

Insatiability. See Witkiewicz, Stanisław
  Ignacy, *Nienasycenie*

Inscriptions and Dedications. *See* George,
  Stefan, *Das Jahr der Seele* (The Year of
  the Soul), "Überschriften und
  Widmungen"

"Insect, The." *See* Turgenev, Ivan

Insect world, Maeterlinck's works on, 8:136a,
  138a, 142a-b

"Inseguimento, L'." *See* Calvino, Italo, *t zero,*
  "The Chase"

Insel der grossen Mutter, Die. See
  Hauptmann, Gerhart, *The Island of the
  Great Mother*

Inserzione, L'. See Ginzburg, Natalia, *The
  Advertisement*

Inside the Walls. *See* Kosztolányi, Dezső, *Négy
  fal között*

Insolite (the word), 9:886b

Inspector-General, The. See Gogol, Nikolay
  Vasilievich, *The Government Inspector*

Inspiration, poetic, in Valéry's "The Pythia,"
  8:580b–581b

Instant fatal, L'. See Queneau, Raymond

Instantanés. See Robbe-Grillet, Alain,
  Snapshots

Instead of Sonnets and Octaves. *See* Tychyna,
  Pavlo, *Zamist' sonetiv i oktav*

Instinct, Bergson's view of, 8:60a-b

Institución Libre de Enseñanza (Madrid),
  9:1121a

Institut (Academy of Fine Arts), Delacroix's
  election to, 5:516b–517a

Institute of National Broadcasting (Greece),
  13:2964b

Institute of World Literature (Russia), Gorky
  and, 8:421b

Institutio oratoria. See Quintilian

Institutio principis Christiani. See Erasmus

"Institution pour l'adolescence du roi Charles
  IX." *See* Ronsard, Pierre de

Institutiones. See Cassian

*Institutiones divinarum et humanarum
  litterarum. See* Cassiodorus

Institutions, Foucault and, 13:3330a-b

Instruction in Divine and Human Letters. See Cassiodorus, *Institutiones divinarum et humanarum litterarum*

Instruction for Living. *See* Petrus Alfonsi, *Disciplina clericalis*

Instruction sur les états d'oraison (Instructions Regarding the Levels of Prayer). See Bossuet, Jacques Bénigne

Insulted and the Injured, The. See Dostoevsky, Feodor

Integration, in Montesquieu's thought, 3:347b–364a

"Intelectual y el otro, El" (The Intellectual and the Other). *See* Ortega y Gasset, José

Intellect
    Aquinas on, 1:424a
    Bergson's view of, 8:58a–59a, 59b–60b

Intellectual Comfort. *See* Aymé, Marcel, *Le confort intellectuel*

Intellectual and the Other, The. *See* Ortega y Gasset, José, *El intelectual y el otro*

Intellectualism
    Canetti and, 12:2620a–2623b
    of Mann, 9:715a, 715b–716a, 738a, 738b
    in *Magic Mountain*, 9:720b

Intellectuals
    in Frisch's works, 13:2909a
    German
        George and, 8:460b
        Heinrich Mann and, 8:519a
        Nazi propaganda and, 9:736a
    in Mann's *Reflections of a Nonpolitical Man*, 9:718b
    in Milosz's works, 13:2943a
    Portuguese, 11:2146b–2148a

Intellectuals contre la guerre du Maroc, Les (Intellectuals against the War in Morocco), 11:2067b

Intelligence, in Balzac's works, 5:643b

Intelligence des fleurs, L' (Intelligence of the Flowers). See Maeterlinck, Maurice

Intelligentsia, Russian
    Gorky and, 8:427b, 428a-b, 436b, 437a
    Revolution of 1905 and, 8:434a

"Intelligentsiia i revoliutsiia" ("The Intelligentsia and the Revolution"). *See* Blok, Alexander

Intentionality, Sartre and, 12:2593a

"Intenzioni (Intervista immaginaria)" ("Intentions Imaginary Interview"). *See* Montale, Eugenio

Intérieur. See Maeterlinck, Maurice

"Interior duplication," in Azorín's works, 9:642a-b

Interior monologue. *See* Monologue, interior

Interior (or *Home*). *See* Maeterlinck, Maurice, *Intérieur*

Interlace, Arthurian legend and, 1:151a

Interlude of the Ballads (Anonymous), 2:837a

Interludes
    Cervantes and, 2:825b, 826a
    Lope de Rueda and, 2:825b–826a

"Intermezzo." *See* Montale, Eugenio, *The Storm and Other Things*

Intermezzo. See Schnitzler, Arthur, *Zwischenspiel*

Intermezzo di rime (Intermezzo of Rhyme). *See* D'Annunzio, Gabriele

Intermezzo (Intermezzo or *The Enchanted). See* Giraudoux, Jean

Intermission. *See* Ferreira de Castro, José Maria, *O intervalo*

Intermittent Quest, The. *See* Ionesco, Eugène, *La quête intermittente*

Internal declension, Khlebnikov's theory of, 10:1346b–1347a

International Conference of Art Critics (1st: 1950), 13:2964b

International Congress of Revolutionary Writers (1930), 11:2072b

International, First, Michelet and, 5:586b–587a

International Gathering of Modern Painters (2nd: 1948), 13:2964b

International Union of Art Critics, 13:2964b

International Union of Revolutionary Writers, 11:2072b, 2073a-b

Internationalism
    implications of Herder's works, 4:645a, 650a-b
    of Whitman, 4:657a

Interplanetary Intervals. *See* Tychyna, Pavlo, *Pluh (The Plow)*, "Mizhplanetni intervaly"

Interpretation of Dreams, The. See Freud,
Sigmund
Intervention of Swords. See Valle-Inclán,
Ramón del, *El ruedo ibérico* (The
Iberian Cycle), *Baza de espadas*
"Interview mit mir selbst" (Interview with
Myself). *See* Böll, Heinrich
Intervista, L' (The Interview). *See* Moravia,
Alberto
Intimate Journal. See Sand, George, *Journal
intime*
Intimate Journals. See Baudelaire, Charles;
Constant, Benjamin, *Journaux intimes*
Intimate Memoirs. See Simenon, Georges,
Mémoires intimes
Intimate Relations. See Cocteau, Jean
Intimate Things. See Čapek, Karel, *O
nejbližších věcech*
*Intimations of Christianity Among the Ancient
Greeks. See* Weil, Simone
"Intimations of Immortality." *See* Wordsworth,
William
Intimism, of Azorín, 9:660b–661a
Intolerance, Pérez Galdós' novels of,
7:1605a–1607a
Intrahistoria
Unamuno's view of, 8:288a, 290a
in *Saint Emmanuel the Good*, 8:306a
Intransigeant, L' (French journal),
Saint-Exupéry's articles in, 12:2317a
Intrigue and Love. See Schiller, Friedrich von,
Kabale und Liebe
*Introduction au discours sur le peu de réalité.
See* Breton, André
"Introduction à la métaphysique." *See*
Bergson, Henri, *An Introduction to
Metaphysics*
"Introduction à la méthode de Léonard de
Vinci." *See* Valéry, Paul
*Introduction à l'étude de la médecine
expérimentale* (Introduction to the Study
of Experimental Medicine). *See* Bernard,
Claude
Introduction to the Everlasting Gospel. See
Gerard de Borgo San Donnino,
Introductorius in evangelium aeternum

Introduction to the History of Philosophy. See
Cousin, Victor, *Cours de philosophie:
Introduction à l'histoire de la
philosophie*
Introduction to Metaphysics, An. See Bergson,
Henri
"Introduction to the Method of Leonardo da
Vinci, The." *See* Valéry, Paul,
"Introduction à la méthode de Léonard
de Vinci"
"Introduction to Pechorin's Journal." *See*
Lermontov, Mikhail Yurievich, "Zhurnal
Pechorina predlisovie"
Introduction to Universal History. See
Michelet, Jules
"Introduction to a Variation." *See* Kundera,
Milan
Introductorius in evangelium aeternum. See
Gerard de Borgo San Donnino
Intruder, The. See Blasco Ibáñez, Vicente, *El
intruso*; D'Annunzio, Gabriele;
Maeterlinck, Maurice
Intruse, L'. See Maeterlinck, Maurice, *The
Intruder*
Intruso, El. See Blasco Ibáñez, Vicente
Intuition
Bergson's view of, 8:58a–59b, 60b
Croce on, 8:319a, 320b, 323a
in Musil's *The Man Without Qualities*,
9:937a
in poetics, 9:762a-b
in poetics of Pascoli, 7:1834a, 1835a
Intuitions préchrétiennes. See Weil, Simone
"Inutile beauté, L'." *See* Maupassant, Guy de
Invandrarna. See Moberg, Vilhelm, *Unto a
Good Land*
Invasão dos judeus, A (The Invasion of the
Jews). *See* Pessoa, Fernando
Invectiva contra eum qui maledixit Italiae. See
Petrarch
Invectiva contra medicum. See Petrarch
*Invectiva contra quendam magni status
hominem sed nullius scientiae aut
virtutis. See* Petrarch

Invective Against a Certain Man of High Status But of No Knowledge or Excellence. *See* Petrarch, *Invectiva contra quendam magni status hominem sed nullius scientiae aut virtutis*

Invective Against a Doctor. *See* Petrarch, *Invectiva contra medicum*

Invective Against Him Who Slandered Italy. *See* Petrarch, *Invectiva contra eum qui maledixit Italiae*

"Invention." *See* Chénier, André

"Invernale." *See* Gozzano, Guido

Invertebrate Spain. See Ortega y Gasset, José, *España invertebrada*

Investiture Controversy, Walther and, 1:301b–302a

"Invincible Slave-Owners, The." *See* Dinesen, Isak

Invincible Song, The. *See* Milosz, Czeslaw, *Pieśń niepodległa*

Invisible Cities. See Calvino, Italo

Invisible Lodge, The. See Richter, Jean Paul, *Die unsichtbare Loge*

Invisible (Trilogía), Lo (The Invisible: Trilogy). *See* Azorín

Invitation au château, L'. See Anouilh, Jean

"Invitation to the Voyage, The" ("L'Invitation au voyage"). *See* Baudelaire, Charles

Invitée, L'. See Beauvoir, Simone de, *She Came to Stay*

Involuntary memory, in Proust's *Remembrance of Things Past*, 8:562b, 564a–565a

Invulnerable Siegfried, The. See Hebbel, Friedrich, *Die Nibelungen*

"Io." *See* Self

Io e lui. See Moravia, Alberto, *Two: A Phallic Novel*

"Io son sì stanco." *See* Petrarch, *Canzoniere*

Ionesco, Eugène, **13:2989a–3020b**

   Amédée, 13:2997b–2998a, 3000a, 3007b, 3011a

   Anouilh and, 13:2844b

   Antidotes, "À propos de Beckett," 13:3017a

   Apprendre à marcher (Learning to Walk), 13:3004a

   "Au théâtre" (At the Theater), 13:2989a-b, 3010a

   Ce formidable bordel! (*A Hell of a Mess!*), 13:3013a-b, 3014b, 3016b

   Découvertes (Discoveries), 13:3011b–3012a, 3014a

   Délire à deux (*Frenzy for Two*), 13:3005b

   Giraudoux and, 9:1041b

   insolite expressions of, 9:886b

   Jacques (*Jack*), 13:2994a–2995b, 3010a

   "Je n'aime pas Brecht" (I Do Not Like Brecht), 13:2999b

   Jeune fille à marier (*Maid to Marry*), 13:2997a, 3010a

   Jeux de massacre (*Killing Game*), 13:3010a–3012a

   Journal en miettes (*Fragments of a Journal*), 13:3007b, 3008a, 3013b, 3015b–3016a, 3016b

      La quête intermittente and, 13:3017b

   La cantatrice chauve (*The Bald Soprano*), 13:2991a–2993a, 2995a, 2995b, 2996a

      Exit the King and, 13:3006a

      Pour préparer un oeuf dur and, 13:3010b

      Tynan on, 13:2998b

   La colère (*Anger*), 13:3005b

   La leçon (*The Lesson*), 13:2993a–2994a, 2995a, 2995b

   La nièce-épouse (*The Niece-Wife*), 13:2997b

   La photo du colonel (*The Colonel's Photograph*), 13:3004a-b, 3007b–3008a, 3018b

      "Spring 1939," 13:3008a

      "Une victime de devoir" ("A Victim of Duty"), 13:2996a

   La quête intermittente (The Intermittent Quest), 13:3017b–3018a

   La rhume onirique (The Oneiric Cold), 13:2997a

   La soif et la faim (*Hunger and Thirst*), 13:3008a–3010a, 3010b, 3011a, 3013b, 3015b

      La fuite (*The Flight*), 13:3008b–3009a, 3011a

      Le rendez-vous, 13:3009a

      Les messes noires de La Bonne Auberge (*Black Masses of the Good Inn*), 13:3009a–3010a

      religion and, 13:3017a

Ionesco, Eugène (*cont.*)
"La vase" ("The Mire"), 13:2995a, 3008a, 3013b
L'Avenir est dans les oeufs (The Future Is in Eggs), 13:2995a, 2996b
Le maître (The Leader), 13:2997a
Le nouveau locataire (The New Tenant), 13:2998a-b, 3014b
Le piéton de l'air (A Stroll in the Air), 13:2998a, 3004a-b, 3005b–3006a, 3007a, 3008a
Le roi se meurt (Exit the King), 13:3004a, 3006a–3007b, 3007b, 3008a, 3012b
Le salon d'automobile (The Motor Show), 13:2997a, 3010a
Le solitaire (The Hermit), 13:3013a–3014b
Le tableau (The Painting), 13:3010a
Les chaises (The Chairs), 13:2844b, 2995a, 2995b–2996a, 2996b
L'Homme aux valises (Man with Bags), 13:3015a–3016b, 3017a
L'Impromptu de l'Alma (The Impromptu of Alma), 13:2999a-b, 3008a, 3011b
Macbett, 13:3012a–3013a
Mêlées et démêlées (Mixed-up Mix-ups), 13:3010a
Notes et contre-notes (Notes and Counter Notes), 13:3008a
"Oriflamme," 13:2997b
Pierrot the Dabbler and, 7:1891a
Pour préparer un oeuf dur (How to Cook a Hard-Boiled Egg), 13:3010a-b
"Pourquoi est-ce que j'écris?" (Why Do I Write?), 13:3018b
Présent passé, passé présent (Present Past, Past Present), 13:2990a, 3008a, 3013b, 3016b
Rhinocéros, 13:3001a–3004a, 3005b, 3006a, 3017a
Sept petit sketches (Seven Short Sketches), 13:2995b
Strindberg and, 7:1754a
Tueur sans gages (The Killer), 13:2999b–3001a, 3001b, 3006a, 3007a, 3015b
good and evil in, 13:3223b
Un homme en question, 13:3010b

Valle-Inclán and, 8:351b
Victimes du devoir (Victims of Duty), 13:2995a, 2996a–2997a, 3000a, 3009a, 3017b
history of drama in, 13:3222b
Voyages chez les morts (Journeys Among the Dead), 13:3015a, 3017a-b
Witkiewicz's Pure Form theory and, 10:1216b
"Ionich." *See* Chekhov, Anton
Iphigenie auf Tauris (Iphigenia in Taurus). *See* Goethe, Johann Wolfgang von
Iphigénie en Aulide. See Gluck, Christoph Willibald
"Ipnos ton Yeneon, O." *See* Elytis, Odysseus, *Exi kai mia tipsis yia ton ourano*
"Ir sult sprechen willekomen." *See* Walther von der Vogelweide
Iran, Khlebnikov's journey to, 10:1340b–1341a
I Remember: Sketch for an Autobiography. See Pasternak, Boris
Irenaeus. *See* Camus, Albert
"Iride." *See* Montale, Eugenio, *The Storm and Other Things* (La bufera e altro), "Rainbow"
"Irini." *See* Ritsos, Yannis, *Aghrypnia*
Irisches Tagebuch (Irish Journal). *See* Böll, Heinrich
Irish legends, Welsh legends and, 1:141a
"Irodis Attikos." *See* Cavafy, Constantine
Iron Staircase, The. See Simenon, Georges, *L'Escalier de fer*
"Irons from the Fire." *See* Musset, Alfred de, "Les marrons du feu"
Irony
in Ariosto, 2:642b–643a
in Baroja's novels, 9:593b
Berlioz' use of, 6:780a
Blasco Ibáñez' use of, 8:360b, 382b
in Canetti, 12:2619a
in Cela, 13:3113b
in Chateaubriand's works, 5:127a-b
Chrétien de Troyes and
Cligés, 1:195a
Erec et Enide, 1:191a
Lancelot, 1:197b
in Delacroix's art criticism, 5:524b

dramatic, in Schiller's *Wallenstein's Camp*,
5:43a
in Eça's works, 7:1700b
in Goethe's *Faust*, 5:19b–20a, 23b
in Goncharov's works, 6:1069a-b
in Hesse's works, 9:846b, 847a
The Journey to the East, 9:850b, 851b
in Ibsen's *A Doll's House*, 7:1929b
Kierkegaard and, 6:1141b
Kundera and, 13:3397a-b
in La Fontaine's "The Matron of Ephesus,"
3:97a, 97b, 98b
in Laforgue's poetry, 7:1890a, 1894a-b,
1907a
of Machado, 9:764a
in Mann's works
Joseph and His Brethren, 9:731b
Magic Mountain, 9:722a
in Maupassant's works, 7:1765b, 1767a-b,
1768a, 1769a, 1769b
in Mérimée's works, 6:747b, 749b, 758b
in Milosz's works, 13:2943a-b
in Musil's *The Man Without Qualities*,
9:934b, 935a, 939a, 941a, 950a–952b,
953a-b, 956b
"the other condition" and, 9:955a
Pirandello's use of, 8:400a
in Prudentius' *Peristephanon*, 1:12b
in Rabelais
Fourth Book, 2:712a, 712b
Gargantua, 2:707b
Third Book, 2:709b
in Richter's prose, 5:57a, 65b, 78a-b
Romantic
in Musset's *Fantasio*, 6:1008a
Tieck and, 5:244a-b
in Rutebeuf's "Des Jacobins," 1:346b
Schlegel's concept of, 5:178a, 186a
in Simon's *Conducting Bodies*, 13:3042a
Socratic, in Leopardi's works, 5:559a
Staël on, 5:109b
in Stendhal, 5:354b–355b
Verga's use of, 7:1554b–1556b
Voltaire's use of, 4:367b, 375b–376a
in Walther's *Unmutston*, 1:365b
"Irony." *See* Camus, Albert

Irrationalism, philosophic, in Lukács's
conception, 10:1274b
Irrationality, in Broch's works, 10:1390b,
1395b–1398a
Irredentism, of Marinetti, 9:810b, 824a
"Irreparable, The" ("L'Irréparable"). *See*
Baudelaire, Charles
Irrungen, Wirrungen. *See* Fontane, Theodor
Irving, Washington, as a source for Pushkin,
5:684b
Is He Good? Is He Bad? See Diderot, Denis,
Est-il bon? Est-il méchant?
"I's [Liberated] from Chains." *See* Khlebnikov,
Velimir, "Azy iz uzy"
"Is There an Italian Decadence?" *See* Montale,
Eugenio, *The Storm and Other Things*
(*La bufera e altro*), "Esiste un
decadentismo in Italia?"
Is-slotter. *See* Vesaas, Tarjei, *The Ice Palace*
Isabelle de Bavière. *See* Dumas père,
Alexandre
Isagoge. *See* Porphyry
Isaotta Guttadàuro e altre poesie (Isaotta
Guttadàuro and Other Poems). *See*
D'Annunzio, Gabriele
"Ishche ptashky . . ." *See* Tychyna, Pavlo,
Soniachni klarnety
"Ishchu spaseniia." *See* Blok, Alexander
Isis, Nerval and, 6:961a, 967b
"Isis." *See* Nerval, Gérard de
Isis-Lilith, in Hugo's works, 6:713a-b
"Iskushenie greshnika." *See* Khlebnikov,
Velimir
Isla sin aurora, La. See Azorín
Islam, Flaubert and, 7:1378a
Islamic philosophy
Aristotelianism and, 1:407b–408a
Augustinianism and, 1:409b
Island of the Great Mother, The. See
Hauptmann, Gerhart
Island Off the Coast. *See* Hamsun, Knut,
"Skjærgaardsö"
Island states, in Montesquieu's conception,
3:355b–356a
Island, The. See Chekhov, Anton, *Ostrov
Sakhalin*

Island Without Dawn, The. *See* Azorín, *La isla sin aurora*

Islanders, The. See Zamyatin, Yevgeny Ivanovich

Íslandsklukkan. See Laxness, Halldór

Isle of the Dead, The. See Böcklin, Arnold

Isle sonante, L'. See Rabelais, François

Ísleif, Icelandic bishop, 1:379b

Íslendinga saga. See Sturla Thórdarson

Íslendinga sögur, 1:377a, 378a, 384a–386a, 401b

   Egils saga and, 1:386b

   Heimskringla and, 1:388b

   Óláfs saga helga and, 1:388a

Íslendingabók. See Ari Thorgilsson the Learned

Isma. See Sarraute, Nathalie

Ismene. See Ritsos, Yannis, *Ismini*

Ismini. See Ritsos, Yannis

Isolation, theme of

   in Chekhov's prose, 7:1856b, 1868a, 1871b

   "The Steppe," 7:1861a

   in Ionesco's *The New Tenant,* 13:2998b

Isottèo, L'—La Chimera (Isottèo—The Chimera). *See* D'Annunzio, Gabriele

Ispantsy. See Lermontov, Mikhail Yurievich

Ispoved'. See Gorky, Maxim

Issa Valley, The. See Milosz, Czeslaw

"Isten a vigaszatalan." *See* Ady, Endre

"Ister, Der." *See* Hölderlin, Friedrich

Isteroghrafo tis dhoxas, To. See Ritsos, Yannis

Istorie fiorentine. See Machiavelli, Niccolò, *The History of Florence*

Istoriia goroda Glupova. See Zamyatin, Yevgeny Ivanovich

Istoriia moei golubiatni. See Babel, Isaac, *The Story of My Dovecote*

Istoriia odnogo goroda. See Shchedrin, N.

"Istoriia odnogo posviashcheniia." *See* Tsvetaeva, Marina

Istrati, Panaït, Kazantzakis and, 9:1067a

"It has turned into mourning." *See* Walter of Châtillon, "Versa est in luctum"

It Is There. See Sarraute, Nathalie, *Elle est là*

"It was an autumn night. Beneath the vitreous sound of the rain." *See* Blok, Alexander, "Osenni vecher byl. Pod zvuk dozhdia stekliannvi"

Italia. See Gautier, Théophile, *Travels in Italy*

Italia Irredenta. See Irredentism

Italia liberata dai goti. See Trissino, Gian Giorgio

"Italia mia." *See* Petrarch, *Canzoniere*

Italian art, Delacroix and, 5:531a

Italian Folktales. See Calvino, Italo

Italian Journey. See Goethe, Johann Wolfgang von, *Italienische Reise*

Italian language, in Dante's *De vulgari eloquentia,* 1:441a

Italian literature

   poetry

      categories of, 2:514a

      Marinetti and, 9:806a

      Neapolitan period, 2:512b

      pre-Renaissance, D'Annunzio and, 8:178b–179a

      written vs. spoken language, 12:2279b–2280a

"Italian Poems." *See* Blok, Alexander, "Ital'ianskie stikhi"

Italian Poems. *See* Pascoli, Giovanni, *Poemi italici*

Italian Sensibility Born in Egypt, An. See Marinetti, Filippo Tommaso, *Una sensibilità italiana nata in Egitto*

Italian Straw Hat, The. See Labiche, Eugène, *Un chapeau de paille d'Italie*

Italian Triptych. *See* Ritsos, Yannis, *Italiko triptyho*

"Ital'ianskie stikhi." *See* Blok, Alexander

Italienische Reise. See Goethe, Johann Wolfgang von

Italiko triptyho. See Ritsos, Yannis

Italy

   Berlioz in, 6:780a–781a

   Burckhardt and, 6:1228b–1229a

   Chateaubriand on Roman landscape, 5:124a-b

   disunity of, Foscolo and, 5:321b

   Fascist

in Ginzburg's *A Light for Fools*,
13:3145a–3149a
in Vittorini's novels, 12:2740a, 2743a
foreign domination of
Castiglione and, 2:645b–646a
Machiavelli and, 2:601a-b
French nobility and, 2:694a
German exiles, 13:3135a-b
Goethe and, 5:13b–14b
heroes, Carducci on, 7:1502a
history, Carducci's poetry and, 7:1502a,
1507b–1508a, 1509a–1510a
Irredentist movement, 13:3132a,
3132b–3133a
post-World War II, in Vittorini's novels,
12:2748b, 2750a
Risorgimento
in Manzoni's poetry, 5:370a-b
in Pirandello's *The Old and the Young*,
8:390b
Second Industrial Revolution,
13:3144b–3145a
in Staël's *Corinne*, 5:101a-b, 102a
Stendhal and, 5:345a-b
war against Ethiopia, in Silone's novels,
12:2285b, 2287b
wars (16th cent.), 2:694a
see also Fascism; Renaissance, Italian;
Risorgimento
"Italy." *See* Pascoli, Giovanni, *Primi poemetti*
Italy Freed from the Goths. *See* Trissino, Gian
Giorgio, *Italia liberata dai goti*
"Ithaki" ("Ithaca"). *See* Cavafy, Constantine
Itineraire de Paris à Jérusalem, L'. *See*
Chateaubriand, François René de
Itinerarium Syriacum. *See* Petrarch
Itinerary and List of Cities. *See* Nikulás
Bergthórsson, *Leiðarvísir ok
borgaskipan*
It's Beautiful. *See* Sarraute, Nathalie, *C'est
beau*
Its Faithful Site. *See* Jiménez, Juan Ramón,
"Su sitio fiel"
It's Only a Joke. *See* Pirandello, Luigi, *Ma non
è una cosa seria*
It's Raining. *See* Montale, Eugenio, *Satura*,
"Piove"

Iulianós o Paravatis. *See* Kazantzakis, Nikos
Iunosheskie stikhi. *See* Tsvetaeva, Marina
"Iva." *See* Akhmatova, Anna
"Ivan Shponka and His Aunt" *See* Gogol,
Nikolay Vasilievich
Ivanov. *See* Chekhov, Anton
Ivanov, Georgii, on Mandelshtam, 10:1631a
Ivanov, Vsevolod
Babel and, 11:1900b
conspiracy charges, 11:1912a
Ivanov, Vyacheslav
acmeism and, 10:1632a
Blok and, 9:976b
Khlebnikov and, 10:1333b–1334a
Mandelshtam's letter to, 10:1629a-b
on *Petersburg*, 9:921b
Russian symbolism and, 9:963b
Ivanov-Razumnik, V. R.
Belyjs "Peterburg", 9:920b
Zamyatin's acquaintance with, 10:1187a
Ivanovna, Raissa, 9:911a
Ívars þáttr, 1:384a
Ivinskaia, Ol'ga Vsevolodovna
arrest of, 10:1596b
Pasternak and, 10:1596a, 1611a-b
"Ivolga." *See* Olesha, Yuri
Ivona, Princess of Burgundia. *See*
Gombrowicz, Witold
Iwein. *See* Hartmann von Aue
Iwona, księżniczka Burgunda. *See*
Gombrowicz, Witold, *Ivona, Princess of
Burgundia*
Iz dvukh knig. *See* Tsvetaeva, Marina
Iz shchodennykovykh zapysiv. *See* Tychyna,
Pavlo
Iz shesti knig. *See* Akhmatova, Anna
"Iz ulitsy v ulitsu." *See* Mayakovsky, Vladimir
Izbornik stikhov. *See* Khlebnikov, Velimir
Izlet u Rusiju. *See* Krleža, Miroslav
Izmail-Bey. *See* Lermontov, Mikhail Yurievich
Izzum. *See* Sarraute, Nathalie, *Isma*

J

J.-K. Huysmans. See Huysmans, Joris Karl
Jablečno Parish Bull, The. *See* Hašek,
    Jaroslav, "Obecní býk v Jablečnu"
Jack. See Ionesco, Eugène, *Jacques*
Jack and the Beanstalk, "young slacker"
    folklore motif in, 1:60a
Jacob (O.T. patriarch)
  in Camoëns' "Sete anos de pastor Jacob
    servia," 2:752a-b
  in Mann's *Joseph and His Brothers*,
    9:729b–730a, 731a
  Strindberg and, 7:1737b
Jacobi, Friedrich
  Briefe über Spinoza, 5:146a-b
  Hölderlin and, 5:145a-b
  Richter and, 5:58a, 71b
Jacobins
  Chénier's opposition to, 4:691a-b, 701b,
    702a-b, 703b–704b
  in Michelet's view, 5:590a
Jacobsen, Jens Peter, Hamsun and, 8:24a
Jacoppsen, A., Leopardi's letter to, 5:552a
Jacques. See Ionesco, Eugène; Sand, George
Jacques et son maître. See Kundera, Milan,
    Jacques and His Master
Jacques le fataliste. See Diderot, Denis
Jacques Vingtras. See Valles, Jules, *L'Étudiant*
Jadis et naguère. See Verlaine, Paul
J'adore ce qui me brûle; oder, Die
    Schwierigen. See Frisch, Max
"Jag." *See* Södergran, Edith
Jagd nach Liebe, Die. See Mann, Heinrich
Jagtbreve. See Dinesen, Vilhelm
Jahier, Valerio, Svevo and, 8:69a
Jahr der Seele, Das. See George, Stefan
"Jahrgang 1922." *See* Böll, Heinrich
Jahrhundertwende (turn of the century), Trakl
    and, 10:1409a–1410a
"J'ai fui Paris." *See* Butor, Michel, *Où*
"Jak jsem se setkal s autorem svého
    nekrologu." *See* Hašek, Jaroslav
"Jak Tövöl vrátil zlatník." *See* Hašek, Jaroslav
"Jak vypadají ženy." *See* Hašek, Jaroslav
Jakobson, Roman, 9:948b, 956b

on Khlebnikov, 10:1331a, 1348b
Khlebnikov aided by, 10:1340a
on Mayakovsky, 11:1894a
Style in Language, "Linguistics and
    Poetics," 9:944b
The Fundamentals of Language, 9:944b
on words-in-freedom, 9:820a
Jalousie du barbouillé, La. See Molière
Jalousie, La. See Robbe-Grillet, Alain, *Jealousy*
James, Henry
  Baroja compared with, 9:601a
  Claudel and, 8:476a
  on Flaubert, 7:1382a, 1383a-b
  on Gautier, 6:1035b, 1036a
  Golden Bowl, Royal Highness and, 9:737b
  on the Goncourts, 7:1410b–1411a, 1416b
  on Ibsen, 7:1435a, 1436b
  Mallarmé compared to, 7:1591a
  Mann and, 9:715b
  Maupassant and, 7:1780b
  "On the Occasion of 'Hedda Gabler',"
    7:1436b
  on Taine, 7:1468a
  "The Beast in the Jungle," 7:1867b
  "The Madonna of the Future," 7:1867b
  on Turgenev, 6:1290b–1291a
  What Maisie Knew, Yourcenar's translation,
    12:2543a
James, William
  anhedonia, 7:1484b
  Bergson and, 8:47b, 52a, 64a
  Čapek and, 10:1566a
  "On Some Omissions of Introspective
    Psychology," 8:52a
  Principles of Psychology, Unamuno
    influenced by, 8:288b
  on Tolstoy, 7:1484b, 1485a
  Unamuno's reading of, 8:293b, 294a
  Varieties of Religious Experience, 7:1485a
Jammes, Francis
  Claudel and, 8:479b
  Gide influenced by, 8:496b
  Jardines lejanos (Faraway Gardens), 9:996a
  Jiménez and, 9:996a
  Mandelshtam on, 10:1628a
  Perse and, 10:1431a
Jan van Ruusbroec. *See* Ruysbroeck

Janáček, Leoš, operatic setting to Čapek's *The Macropulos Secret*, 10:1577a

Janczewska, Jadwiga, Witkiewicz and, 10:1211b–1212a, 1219a

Janin, Jules
Berlioz and, 6:785b, 805a-b
on Delacroix, 5:521a

Janouch, Gustav, 9:1169a

Janseits von Gut und Böse. See Nietzsche, Friedrich, *Beyond Good and Evil*

Jansen, Cornelis, *Augustinus*, 3:127a, 136a

Jansenism, 3:265a, 265
Boileau and, 3:180b
Bossuet on, 3:164a
controversy with Jesuits, 3:129a
court of Louis XIV and, 3:226b–227a
Gallican church and, 3:167b
La Bruyère and, 3:258b
La Rochefoucauld and, 3:61b–62a
of Manzoni, 5:375b
Mauriac and, 10:1313b–1314a
Molière's *Tartuffe* and, 3:109b, 111b
Pascal and, 3:127a
Pasquier Quesnel and, 3:172b
Port-Royal, 3:128a, 129a, 129b
Voltaire and, 4:369b–370a, 372b–373a

Janson, Kristofer, Hamsun and, 8:22b, 23a, 23b

"January 1, 1924." *See* Mandelshtam, Osip, "1 ianvarie 1924"

Japan, Barthes on, 13:3094a–3095a

Japanese art, in Goncourt novels, 7:1397b–1398a

Japanese Nō plays, Yourcenar's adaptation of, 12:2539b

Jaquerie, La. See Mérimée, Prosper

Jar, The. See Pirandello, Luigi, *La giara*

Jarama, El. See Sánchez Ferlosio, Rafael

Jardin des chimères, Le. See Yourcenar, Marguerite

Jardin des supplices, Le. See Mirbeau, Octave

Jardines lejanos. See Jammes

Järn och människor. See Lagerkvist, Pär

"Jarrama." *See* Ekelöf, Gunnar

Jarry, Alfred, 8:546b, **9:665a–687b**
Almanach illustré du Père Ubu (Pa Ubu's Illustrated Almanac), 9:673a
Apollinaire and, 9:881b, 897b
Céline and, 11:1860a
César-Antéchrist, 9:677a
Gestes et opinions du docteur Faustroll, 'pataphysicien: Roman neo-scientifique (The Exploits and Opinions of Doctor Faustroll 'Pataphysician: A Neo-Scientific Novel), 9:668b–669a, 672b, 676a–677a, 680a
Ghelderode and, 11:2113b, 2133a, 2134b
"Guignol," 9:670b–671a
Ionesco and, 13:3004a, 3012a
La dragonne (The Dragon), 9:673b
L'Amour absolu (Absolute Love), 9:671b, 677a-b
Le surmâle (The Supermale), 9:671b, 673a, 677b–679b
Les jours et les nuits (Days and Nights)
hallucinations in, 9:675a–676a
journey in, 9:680b
love in, 9:677a
satire in, 9:672b
Les minutes de sable mémorial (Minutes of Memorial Sand), 9:671a, 675a
Messaline: Roman de l'ancienne Rome (The Garden of Priapus [Messaline]), 9:672b, 677b
pataphysics and, 12:2532a-b
"Questions de théâtre" (Questions of the Theater), 9:672a
Ubu cocu (*Ubu Cuckolded*), 9:681a, 682b, 683b–684a
Ubu cycle
phases of, 9:681b
physical action of, 9:682a-b
plays in, 9:681a
plots of plays in, 9:682b–685a
political element in, 9:681a
staging of, 9:682a
and theater of absurd, 9:680b–681a
tragedy in, 9:682a
Ubu enchaîné (*Ubu Enchained*), 9:681a, 684a–685a
Ubu roi (*Ubu the King*)
Baroja's *Paradox, King* compared to, 9:600a-b

Jarry, Alfred (*cont.*)
  Ubu roi (*Ubu the King*) (*cont.*)
    Le roi bombance and, 9:806a
    Mallarmé's review of, 9:681b
    plot of, 9:682b–683b
    production of, 9:671b–672a
    reaction to, 9:665a–666a
    sets for, 9:665a
    ur-text for, 9:670b
  Ubu sur la butte (Ubu on the Mound),
    9:681a
  "Visions actuelles et futures" (Visions of
    Present and Future), 9:667b

Jasager/Der Neinsager, Der. *See* Brecht,
    Bertolt, *He Who Says Yes/He Who Says
    No*
Jason (mythological figure), in Grillparzer's
    The Golden Fleece, 5:429b–430a
Jaspers, Karl
  Lukács and, 10:1259b
  nihilism and, 7:1670b
Jaufré, 1:153a
Jaufré Rudel
  courtly love in works of, 1:171b–172a
  as troubadour, 1:171a–172a
Jaurès, Jean, Bergson and, 8:45b
"Je crie a toutes gen mercis." *See* Villon,
    François, *The Testament*
"Je hais Paris." *See* Butor, Michel, *Où*
Je me souviens. *See* Simenon, Georges
Je n'ai jamais appris à écrire ou les incipits.
    See Aragon, Louis
"Je n'aime pas Brecht." *See* Ionesco, Eugène
"Je suis un point." *See* Arp, Jean
"Je vous écris d'un pays lointain." *See*
    Michaux, Henri
"Jealous Hidalgo, The." *See* Cervantes, Miguel
    de, "El celoso extremeño"
Jealousy
  in Ariosto, 2:639b–640a
  in Mérimée's works, 6:748b, 755b
  in Pirandello's *Tonight We Improvise*,
    8:411a
  in Proust's *Remembrance of Things Past*,
    8:556b–557b, 563b–564a
Jealousy. *See* Robbe-Grillet, Alain

Jean de Meun, 1:310a-b
  see also Romance of the Rose
Jean Paul. *See* Richter, Jean Paul
"Jean Pauls biographische Belustigungen
    unter der Gehirnschale einer Riesin"
    (Jean Paul's Biographical Amusements
    Under the Cranium of a Giantess). *See*
    Richter, Jean Paul
Jean Paul's Letters and Conjectural Biography.
    See Richter, Jean Paul, *Briefe und
    bevorstehender Lebenslauf*
Jean Santeuil. *See* Proust, Marcel
Jeanne. *See* Sand, George
Jeanne d'Arc au bûcher. *See* Claudel, Paul
Jeanson, Francis, Camus and, 13:3070a
Jedermann. *See* Hofmannsthal, Hugo von, *The
    Salzburg Everyman*
Jedyne wyjście. *See* Witkiewicz, Stanisław
    Ignacy
Jefferson, Thomas, on "natural aristocracy,"
    4:652a
"Jeli il pastore" (Jeli the Shepherd). *See* Verga,
    Giovanni
Jenny. *See* Undset, Sigrid
Jenseits des Lustprinzips. *See* Freud,
    Sigmund, *Beyond the Pleasure Principle*
Jensen, Johannes V., Hamsun and, 8:34b
Jeremiah (O.T. prophet), George and, 8:466a
Jerome, St.
  Ad Nepotianum, 1:349b
  Augustine and, 1:48a
  Epistles, satire and, 1:337b–338a
  Erasmus and, 2:573a, 581a-b
  Juvenal and, 1:350b
Jerusalem Conquered. *See* Tasso, Torquato,
    Gerusalemme conquistada
Jerusalem Delivered. *See* Tasso, Torquato,
    Gerusalemme liberata
"Jesenja noć." *See* Krleža, Miroslav
Jesenská-Polak, Milena, Kafka and, 9:1154a,
    1155a, 1175b
Jessner, Leopold, Strindberg and, 7:1748a
Jesuits
  attacked by Michelet, 5:589b, 590b
  Boileau and, 3:180b
  Bossuet on, 3:164a
  Calderón and, 2:871b

controversy with Jansenists, 3:129a
criticized by Pascal, 3:134a–138a
educational principles, 8:120b–121a
Molière's *Tartuffe* and, 3:109b
Voltaire and, 4:369b–370a
Jesuits, The. See Michelet, Jules
Jesus Christ
    in Berlioz' works, 6:791a-b, 793a, 799b–800a
    Buddha and, 9:845a
    in Ghelderode's plays, 11:2123a
    in Gottfried, 1:255a-b
    Hesse's *Demian* and, 9:840b, 841a
    in Hölderlin's works, 5:168a, 169a, 170a-b
    in Klopstock, 4:516b–521a
    in Nerval's works, 6:945a, 950b
    in Novalis' works, 5:208a
    passion of, Erasmus and, 2:574b–575a
    as persona in satire of Philip of Paris,
        1:360b–361a
    in Richter's *Flower, Fruit, and Thorn Pieces,*
        5:68b
    Second Coming of. *See* Second Coming of
        Christ
    symbols of, in works of Prudentius, 1:17a
    in Vigny's "The Mount of Olives," 5:485a-b
    Weil and, 12:2792b, 2793a, 2793b, 2794a,
        2796a, 2796b, 2797b, 2798a, 2799b,
        2800b, 2805a
    see also Christ figures; Christianity
Jesús, Teresa de, Azorín's literary criticism of,
    9:645a
"Jesus-Studien" (Jesus Studies). *See*
    Hauptmann, Gerhart
"Jet de sang, Le." *See* Artaud, Antonin
Jettatura. See Gautier, Théophile
Jeu avec le feu, Le. See Robbe-Grillet, Alain
Jeu de la feuillée. See Adam de la Halle
Jeu de pelerin, 1:461a
Jeu de Robin et Marion. See Adam de la Halle
Jeu de Saint Nicolas. See Bodel, Jean
Jeu parti, 1:459a
Jeune Belgique, La (literary review), 8:121a-b,
    122b, 124a
Jeune Bourgeoisie, La. See Goncourt, Edmond
    Louis Antoine and Jules Alfred Huot de,
    Renée Mauperin

"Jeune captive, La." *See* Chénier, André, "The
    Young Captive"
Jeune fille à marier. See Ionesco, Eugène
Jeune fille Violaine, La. See Claudel, Paul
Jeune homme, Le. See Mauriac, François
Jeune parque, La. See Valéry, Paul
"Jeune veuve, La." *See* La Fontaine, Jean de,
    Fables
"Jeune-Annam" movement, Malraux and,
    12:2414b
Jeunes filles, Les. See Montherlant, Henry de,
    The Girls
Jeunes-France, Les. See Gautier, Théophile
"Jeunesse." *See* Rimbaud, Arthur
Jeux de massacre. See Ionesco, Eugène
Jew, wandering. *See* Ahasuerus (the
    Wandering Jew)
Jewels, as metaphor, in Gottfried, 1:244b–245a
"Jewels." *See* Baudelaire, Charles
Jewess, The. See Babel, Isaac, *Evreika*
Jewess of Toledo, The. See Grillparzer, Franz
Jewry in Music. See Wagner, Richard
Jews
    in Metz, converted by Bossuet, 3:155b
    Weil and, 12:2788b, 2800b–2801b
Jews, The. See Lessing, Gotthold Ephraim, *Die
    Juden*
Jézabel. See Anouilh, Jean
Jiménez de Rada, Rodrigo, *De rebus
    Hispaniae,* 1:130b, 131a
Jiménez, Juan Ramón, **9:991a–1014a**
    Almas de violeta (Violet Souls), 9:994a,
        1004a
    Animal de fondo (Animal of Depths),
        9:1001b, 1008b, 1012a–1013b
    "Arias otoñales" (Autumn Airs), 9:995a
    Arias tristes (Sad Songs), 9:994b–995a,
        995b, 1001b–1002a
    "Aristocracia y democracia" (Aristocracy
        and Democracy), 9:1007a-b
    Baladas de primavera (Spring Ballads),
        9:996a-b, 997b
    Belleza (Beauty), 9:1002b, 1003a
    on *Campos de Castilla,* 9:758b
    "Carta a Georgina Hübner en el cielo de
        Lima" (Letter to Georgina Hübner in
        Lima's Heaven), 9:996b–997a

Jiménez, Juan Ramón (*cont.*)
  "Cenit" (Zenith), 9:1003a
  Diario de poeta y mar (Diary of Poet and Sea), 9:999a–1000b, 1007b
  "El mirlo fiel" (The Faithful Blackbird), 9:1009b
  "El poema," 9:995b
  El trabajo gustoso (Enjoyable Work) (collected lectures), 9:1006b
  "El trabajo gustoso" (Enjoyable Work) (lecture), 9:1006b, 1007b
  Elegias intermedias, 9:996b
  Elegias lamentables, 9:996b
  Elegias puras, 9:996b
  "Espacio" (Space), 9:1000a, 1009b–1010a, 1011b–1012a
    mortality in, 9:1013b
  Españoles de tres mundos (caricatura lírica) (Spaniards of Three Worlds Lyrical Caricatures), 9:1005a–1006a
  Estío (Summer), 9:998a
  Eternidades (Eternities), 9:1000b–1001b
  on God, 8:300b
  "Guardia de amor" (Love's Guardian), 9:998a
  La estación total con las canciones de la nueva luz (The Total Season with the Songs of the New Light), 9:1008b, 1009a-b
  "La negra y la rosa" (The Black Woman and the Rose), 9:1000b
  La Obra, 9:1001b, 1004b
  La soledad sonora, 9:996b
  Laberinto, 9:996b
  Las hojas verdes (Green Leaves), 9:996a
  Melancolia, 9:996b
  Ninfeas (Water Lilies), 9:994a, 1004a
  "Nocturnos" (Nocturnes), 9:995b
  "Nostaljia del mar" (Sea Nostalgia), 9:1002a
  Pastorales, 9:995b–996a
  Piedra y cielo (Stone and Sky), 9:995b, 1002a
  Platero y yo: Elegia andaluza (Platero and I: An Andalusian Elegy), 9:997a, 1003b, 1005a
  Poemas mágicos y dolientes, 9:996b
  Poesía (Poetry), 9:1002b–1003a
  "Poesía y literatura" (Poetry and Literature), 9:1007b
  "Política poética" (Poetical Politics), 9:1006a-b
  "Retorno fugaz" (Fleeting Return), 9:998a
  rewriting of his own poetry, 8:305b
  Rimas (Rhymes), 9:994a-b
  Segunda antolojía poética (Second Poetic Anthology), 9:1004b
  Sonetos espirituales (Sonnets of the Spirit), 9:997b, 1010b
  "Su sitio fiel" (Its Faithful Site), 9:1008b–1009a
  Tercera antolojía poética (Third Poetic Anthology), 9:1004b
  "Verde verderol" (Green Greenfinch), 9:996b
Joachim of Flora (Fiore), 1:413b
Joan of Arc
  in Chapelain's *La pucelle*, 3:193b
  Claudel and, 8:479b
  as favorite heroine of Michelet, 5:577b
  in Schiller's *The Maid of Orleans*, 5:46b–47b
Joan of Arc at the Stake. *See* Claudel, Paul, *Jeanne d'Arc au bûcher*
João VI of Portugal, king, 11:2145a
Job (O.T. character)
  Mann's *Joseph and His Brothers* and, 9:731b
  Strindberg and, 7:1737b
Jodelle, Étienne, 2:742b–743a
  Amours, 2:743a
Joglars. See Jongleurs
"Johannesbau," of Rudolf Steiner, 9:908a, 923b
John XXI, pope, Aquinas and, 1:426a-b
John XXII, pope, Aquinas and, 1:419b
John Chrysostom, St., as source for Vigny's *Daphné*, 5:477a
John of the Cross, St.
  Canticle, 9:1013a
  Cántico espiritual (Spiritual Canticle)
    "El Pastorcico" ("The Little Shepherd"), 2:913a
    pastoral elements of, 2:913a
  Jiménez and, 9:1008a, 1013a
  pastoral poetry of, 2:913a
John, Eric, on *Beowulf*, 1:70a, 73a-b

John Gabriel Borkman. See Ibsen, Henrik

John, Gospel of. *See* New Testament

John of San Giuliano, 1:411a

John of Vercelli, 1:417a

John of Wildershausen, 1:410b

Johnson, Eyvind, **12:2361a–2383a**

  Arbetet (Work), 12:2366b, 2367a

  Avsked till Hamlet (Farewell to Hamlet), 12:2366b, 2367a

  Bobinack, 12:2367a–2368b

  De fyra främlingarna (The Four Strangers), 12:2365a

  Dreams of Roses and Fire (*Drömmar om rosor och eld*), 12:2376b–2378a

  "En författare i sin tid" (An Author in His Time), 12:2363a

  Et Håndslag (A Handclasp), 12:2371a-b

  Favel ensam (Favel Alone), 12:2382a-b

  Kommentar till ett stjärnfall (Commentary on a Falling Star), 12:2366a-b

  Krilon trilogy, 12:2371b–2373a

  Lägg undan solen (Put Away the Sun), 12:2374b, 2382a

  Livsdagen lång (Life's Long Day), 12:2376b–2377a, 2380b–2382a

  "Metoden Bovary" (The Bovary Method), 12:2363a

  Minnas (Remembering), 12:2365b–2366a

  Moberg and, 11:2228a

  Molnen över Metapontion (The Clouds over Metapontion), 12:2376b–2377a, 2378a–2379a

  "Något om material och symboler" ("Something on Material and Symbols"), 12:2362a

  Några steg mot tystnaden (Some Steps Toward Silence), 12:2382b

  Nattövning (Night Maneuvers), 12:2370b

  as "proletarian writer," 11:2207b

  Regn i gryningen (Rain at Dawn), 12:2368b, 2370b

  Return to Ithaca (*Strändernas svall*), 12:237a–2376b, 2362a

  Romanen om Olof (The Novel About Olof), 12:2368b–2370a, 2383a

  "Romanfunderingar" (Thoughts on the Novel), 12:2364a-b

  Romantisk berättelse (*Romantic Tale*), 12:2370a-b

  Soldatens återkomst (The Return of the Soldier), 12:2370b–2371a

  Stad i ljus (City in Light), 12:2365b

  Stad i mörker (City in Darkness), 12:2365b

  The Days of His Grace (*Hans nådes tid*), 12:2376b–2377a, 2379a–2380b

  Tidens gäng (The Course of Time), 12:2370a

  Timans och rättfärdigheten (Timans and Justice), 12:2365a-b

Johnson, Samuel

  on Castiglione, 2:665a

  on "hunger of imagination," 5:407b

  and Lessing, 4:561b

  Schopenhauer compared to, 5:397b

  Taine on, 7:1458b

Joie de vivre, La. See Zola, Émile

Joined Hands. *See* Mauriac, François, *Les mains jointes*

"Jöjj, Léda, megölellek." *See* Ady, Endre

Joke, The. See Kundera, Milan

Jokes and Their Relation to the Unconscious. See Freud, Sigmund, *Der Witz und seine Beziehung zum Unbewussten*

Jokes, Witticisms, and Pranks. See Domenichi, Ludovico, *Facetie, motti et burle*

"Jolie rousse, La." *See* Apollinaire, Guillaume

Joll, James

  on *Marfaka le futuriste,* 9:806b

  Three Intellectuals in Politics, 9:824b

Jolyot, Prosper (Crébillon)

  Electra myth and, 12:2549a

  Lettres de la marquise de M— au comte de R—, 4:401a

  Voltaire's rivalry with, 4:375a

Jómsvíkinga saga, 1:381a

Jón Arason. See Gunnarsson, Gunnar

Jón Loptsson, 1:379b

Jón Ögmundarson, 1:379b, 383b

Jonah (O.T. prophet)

  "Fama tuba dante sonum" and, 1:343a

  Vesaas and, 11:2044a

"Jonas; ou, L'Artiste au travail." *See* Camus, Albert, "Jonas, or, The Artist at Work"

Jones, David, *The Anathemata,* 13:2968a-b

Jones, Ernest, Freud and, 8:3b, 4a, 12a, 13b

Jones, Henry Arthur, 7:1926b–1927a
  Mrs. Dane's Defence, 7:1927a
Jones, Robert, on Frank Wedekind, 8:234a
Jongleurs
  chansons de geste and, 1:90a, 139a, 139b
  troubadours and, 1:161a
Jóns saga helga. See Gunnlaug (monk)
Jonson, Ben
  Castiglione and, 2:664b
  Céline and, 11:1873a
  influence on pastoral lyric, 2:915b
  The Sad Shepherd, Fletcher's The Faithful
    Shepherdess and, 2:920a
Jord. See Gunnarsson, Gunnar
José. See Valdés, Palacio
Joseph Balsamo. See Dumas père, Alexandre
Joseph and His Brothers. See Mann, Thomas
Joseph (O.T. patriarch), in Mann's Joseph and
    His Brothers, 9:728b–729a, 730a-b
Joseph of Paris, Father, methods of religious
    concentration, 3:268a
Joseph und seine Brüder. See Mann, Thomas
Josephus, Flavius, History of the Jewish
    People and Its Capital Jerusalem,
    Hebbel and, 6:1105b
Joubert, Joseph
  on Boileau, 3:184b
  Journal intime, 3:203a
Journal. See Delacroix, Eugène
Journal for All. See Zhurnal dlya vsekh
Journal des débats (French periodical),
    Taine's articles for, 7:1451b
Journal du voleur, See Genet, Jean, The Thief's
    Journal
Journal d'un inconnu. See Cocteau, Jean
Journal d'un poète. See Vigny, Alfred Victor de
Journal en miettes. See Ionesco, Eugène
Journal, fictional, Gide's Marshlands as,
    8:499a
Journal intime. See Sand, George
Journal of the Plague Year. See Defoe, Daniel
Journalisten, Die (The Journalists). See
    Freytag, Gustav
Journalists, Aymé's satire of, 12:2444b–2445a
Journals. See Alfieri, Vittorio; Emerson, Ralph
    Waldo

Journaux intimes. See Baudelaire, Charles,
    Intimate Journals; Constant, Benjamin
Journée des parques, Une. See Lesage,
    Alain-René
Journées de Florbelle, ou la nature dévoilée,
    Les. See Sade, Donatien Alphonse
    François, marquis de
Journey on Foot from Holmens Canal to the
    East Point of Amager. See Andersen,
    Hans Christian
Journey from Munich to Genoa. See Heine,
    Heinrich, Reise von München nach
    Genua
Journey of Headmaster Fälbel and His Seniors
    to Fichtelberg, The. See Richter, Jean
    Paul, Des Rektors Florian Fälbels und
    seiner Primaner Reise nach dem
    Fichtelberg
Journey to Alcarria. See Cela, Camilo José
Journey to Armenia, The. See Mandelshtam,
    Osip
Journey to the East, The. See Hesse, Hermann,
    Die Morgenlandfahrt
Journey to the End of Night. See Céline,
    Louis-Ferdinand
Journey to Erzurum, A. See Pushkin, Alexander
Journey to Hercueil, The. See Ronsard, Pierre
    de, "Le Voyage d'Hercueil"
Journey to Nuremberg, The. See Hesse,
    Hermann, Die Nürnberger Reise
Journey to the Orient. See Nerval, Gérard de,
    Voyage en Orient
Journey to Parnassus. See Cervantes, Miguel
    de
Journeyman Joiner. See Sand, George, Le
    compagnon du tour de France
Journeys. See Voyages and voyagers
Journeys Among the Dead. See Ionesco,
    Eugène, Voyages chez les morts
Jours effeuillés. See Arp, Jean
Jours et les nuits, Les. See Jarry, Alfred
Jouve, Pierre Jean, "Les quatre cavaliers"
    ("Four Horsemen"), Seferis' translation,
    12:2260a
Jouvenal, Henry de, 9:619a, 622a-b
Jouvet, Louis
  Anouilh and, 13:2844b

in Claudel's *The Tidings Brought to Mary*, 8:483a

Giraudoux and
   absence of, 9:1056b
   last play, 9:1058b
   in new theater, 9:1052a-b
   return of, 9:1057b
   Siegfried production, 9:1044a, 1049b

Jovine, Francesco, on Silone, 12:2294a

Joy and the Law. *See* Lampedusa, Giuseppe Tomasi di, *Two Stories and a Memory (Racconti)*, "La gioia e la legge"

Joy, The. *See* Ungaretti, Giuseppe, *L'Allegria*

Joyce, James
   A Portrait of the Artist as a Young Man, 7:1587b, 8:69b
   Bergson and, 8:64b
   Broch and, 10:1393a–1394a
   Céline and, 11:1859a, 1883b
   on the creative process, 12:2348a
   on Dujardin's *We'll to the Woods No More*, 7:1906a
   Exiles, 7:1443b
   Finnegans Wake, 8:70a, 71b
      Marinetti and, 9:807b
      Queneau's *Saint Glinglin* and, 12:2524b
   Ginzburg and, 13:3133a
   Hesse and, 9:855a
   on Ibsen, 7:1436b
   Johnson and, 12:2364b
   Laforgue and, 7:1887b
   Lessing's influence on, 4:545b
   Marinetti and, 9:800a
   Musil's *The Man Without Qualities* and, 9:947b, 950b, 957a
   Pirandello and, 8:413b
   Proust and, 8:545a
   Queneau and, 12:2512a, 2516a, 2516b, 2523b, 2524a-b
   Rabelais and, 2:700b
   Sarraute and, 12:2333a, 2334a-b, 2337b
   Schlegel and, 5:191b
   Simon and, 13:3024b, 3025b, 3031a, 3038b, 3042b
   Svevo and, 8:67a, 69a–70a, 71b, 72a, 76b, 79b
   "The Dead," 8:79b

"the Vico road," 3:294a
translations by, of Hauptmann, 8:158b
Ulysses, 8:69b–70a
   criticized by Kosztolányi, 10:1237b
   date of Molly Bloom's birthday in, 9:669a
   Ekelöf and, 12:2666a
   Elytis' *Maria Nephele* and, 13:2979a
   Hesse's *Steppenwolf* and, 9:847b
   Johnson and, 12:2373a-b
   Latin mass and, 8:485b
   Moravia and, 12:2675b
   Perse and, 10:1438b
   Robbe-Grillet and, 13:3242a, 3243b
   Simon and, 13:3021a, 3024a
   on Valéry's "Sketch of a Serpent," 8:582b
   Vico and, 3:312b, 313a

Joyful Wisdom, The. See Södergran, Edith, *Die fröhliche Wissenschaft*

József, Attila, Ritsos' translations, 12:2819a, 2837b

"Jste dcerou z lepší rodiny." *See* Hašek, Jaroslav

"Juan Breva." *See* García Lorca, Federico

Juan de la Cruz, San. *See* John of the Cross, St.

Juan de Mairena. See Machado, Antonio

Juan de Timoneda, *El patrañuelo (Trifling Tales)*, 2:951a

Jubelsenior, Der. See Richter, Jean Paul

Judaism
   Aristotelianism and, 1:407b, 408a
   Augustine's *City of God* and, 1:36a
   customs, Svevo as source for Joyce's use of, 8:69b
   Heine and, 5:492b–493a, 507b
   Kafka and, 9:1153a-b, 1154b, 1156b
   of Mandelshtam, 10:1623a-b, 1630b–1631a
   in Mandelshtam's *The Noise of Time*, 10:1623b
   in Schnitzler's works, 8:103a-b, 105b–106a
   see also Hasidism; Yiddish theater

Judaism in Music. *See* Mendelssohn, Felix, *Das Judentum in der Musik*

"Judás és Jézus" (Judas and Jesus). *See* Ady, Endre

Jude the Obscure. See Hardy, Thomas

Juden, Die. See Lessing, Gotthold Ephraim

Judentum in der Musik, Das. See
Mendelssohn, Felix; Wagner, Richard,
Jewry in Music

Judge and His Hangman, The. See
Dürrenmatt, Friedrich

Judge, The. See Meyer, Conrad Ferdinand, *Die
Richterin*

Judge, The. *See* Moberg, Vilhelm, *Domaren*

Judge for Yourselves! See Kierkegaard, Søren

Judge-penitent, in Camus, 13:3073a-b

Judges. *See* Judicial system

Judges, Book of. *See* Bible

Judgment
historical, Croce on, 8:321b
logical, Croce on, 8:317a

Judgment Day
in English cycle plays, 1:469a
in medieval drama, 1:455b

Judgment on the G.C. See Tasso, Torquato,
Giudizio sulla G.C.

"Judgment, The." *See* Kafka, Franz, "Das
Urteil"

Judgments on History and Historians. See
Burckhardt, Jacob

Judicial system
Aymé's satire of, 12:2443a-b
criticized in La Bruyère's *Caractères*,
3:253b–254a

Jüdin von Toledo, Die. See Grillparzer, Franz,
The Jewess of Toledo

"Judith." *See* Frisch, Max, *When the War Was
Over*

Judith. See Giraudoux, Jean; Hebbel, Friedrich

Judith (Anglo-Saxon poem), 1:64b, 69b

Judith of Bethulia (motion picture). *See*
Griffith, D. W.

Judith (O.T. character), Hebbel's play *Judith*,
6:1094b–1095a, 1101a–1102a

Juez de los divorcios, El. See Cervantes,
Miguel de

Jugend des Königs Henri Quatre, Die. See
Mann, Heinrich

Juin, Hubert, on Edmond Goncourt, 7:1413a

Julia. See Hebbel, Friedrich

Julian the Apostate, Vigny's sympathy for,
5:476b

Julian the Apostate. *See* Kazantzakis, Nikos,
Iulianós o Paravatis

Julie de Carneilhan. See Colette

Julie, ou la nouvelle Héloïse (*Julie; or, The
new Héloise*). *See* Rousseau, Jean
Jacques

Juliette. See Giraudoux, Jean

Julius Caesar. See Shakespeare, William

Julius exclusus (Julius Excluded). *See*
Erasmus

Julius II, pope, Erasmus and, 2:579a–580a

July Monarchy
Heine's opinion of, 5:500a-b
Stendhal and, 5:359b

July Revolution of 1830. *See* France,
Revolution of July 1830

Jumeaux, Les. See Hugo, Victor

Jument perdue, La. See Simenon, Georges

Jument verte, La. See Aymé, Marcel, *The
Green Mare*

Jung, Carl
Freud and, 8:4a, 13a–14a, 15a, 17a
Hesse and, 9:839a, 841a
Spanish translations, 9:1119b
Symbols of Transformation, 12:2667b
Wandlungen und Symbole des Libido
(*Psychology of the Unconscious*), 8:13b

Junge Gelehrte, Der. See Lessing, Gotthold
Ephraim

Junge Hegel, Der. See Lukács, György

Junge Medardus, Der. See Schnitzler, Arthur

Junge Tischlermeister, Der. See Tieck, Ludwig

Junge Welt, Die. See Wedekind, Frank

Jungfrau Maleen. See Grimm Brothers

Jungfrukammare. See Moberg, Vilhelm

Jungle, The. See Ferreira de Castro, José Maria

Jüngste Tag, Der (expressionist series by Kurt
Wolff), 9:1156a

Junius manuscript, 1:64b

Junta para Ampliación de Estudios e
Investigaciones Científicas, Machado
and, 9:746a

Jupiter (god)
in Camoëns
The Lusiads, 2:763a
The Two Amphitryons, 2:755b, 756a

in La Fontaine's "L'Araignée et l'hirondelle,"
3:89b, 90a, 92b, 93a

in Molière's *Amphitryon*, 3:109a

see also Zeus

Jürg Jenatsch. See Meyer, Conrad Ferdinand

*Jürg Reinhart: Eine sommerliche
Schicksalsfahrt (Jürg Reinhart: A
Fateful Trip in the Summer). See* Frisch,
Max

Jurisprudence. *See* Judicial system; Law; Vico,
Giovanni Battista

Just as They Are. *See* Valéry, Paul, *Tel quel*

Justes, Les. See Camus, Albert, *The Just
Assassins*

Justice

Aymé and, 12:2443a

Camus and, 13:3069b–3071a

Hugo's view of, 6:712a, 715b

Voltaire's championship of, 4:379a–380a

in Yourcenar's *Electra*, 12:2549b

Justice. See Galsworthy, John

Justice Without Revenge. See Lope de Vega, *El
castigo sin venganza*

Justine. See Durrell, Lawrence

*Justine, ou les malheurs de la vertu (Justine;
or, The Misfortunes of Virtue). See*
Sade, Donatien Alphonse François,
marquis de

Juvenal (Decimus Iunius Iuvenalis)

medieval satire and, 1:337a, 338a, 339a

patronage and, 1:351a

Renaissance pastoral poetry, 2:901b

Roman morality and, 1:350a

Satires

Marcabru and, 1:339b

purpose of, 1:340b–341a

"Quam sit lata scelerum" and, 1:339a

technique, 1:366a

technique of, 1:366b

Juventud, egolatria. See Baroja, Pío

Juxtaposition

in Butor, 13:3302a

in Calvino, 13:3274a

K

"K muze." *See* Blok, Alexander

"K nemetskoi rechi." *See* Mandelshtam, Osip

"K S." *See* Lermontov, Mikhail Yurievich

"Ka." *See* Khlebnikov, Velimir

Kabale und Liebe. See Schiller, Friedrich von

Kablukov, Sergey, Mandelshtam and,
10:1631a, 1636b, 1637b

Kaemos, 13:2967a

Kafka, Franz, **9:1151a–1179b**

"A Country Doctor" ("Ein Landarzt"),
metaphor in, 9:1157b–1158b

"A Hunger Artist" ("Ein Hungerkünstler"),
9:1172b–1173b

Ady and, 9:859b

Amerika

"Der Heizer," 9:1155b–1156a

first version, 9:1153a

second version, 9:1154a

Artaud compared to, 11:1967b

Benjamin and, 11:1728a

"Beschreibung eines Kampfes" ("Description
of a Struggle"), 9:1152b, 1175b

Betrachtung (Meditation), 9:1152b–1153a,
1155b

Broch and, 10:1394a-b

Camus and, 13:3055b

Canetti and, 12:2615b, 2617b

Céline and, 11:1883b

Chekhov and, 7:1857b

"Das Urteil" ("The Judgment"), 9:1154a,
1158a, 1162a-b, 1164a–1165a, 1165a-b

dehumanization in works of, 13:3229b

"Die erste lange Eisenbahnfahrt" ("The First
Long Railroad Ride"), 9:1152b

Dürrenmatt and, 13:3216b

Grillparzer's influence on, 5:444a

Hašek and, 9:1099b

Heinrich Mann and, 8:533a, 539a

Hesse's *Steppenwolf* and, 9:848a

"Hochzeitsvorbereitungen auf dem Lande"
("Wedding Preparations in the
Country"), 9:1152b

Jewish literary idiom, 11:1889b

Kleist and, 5:310b

Kafka, Franz (*cont.*)
  Marinetti and, 9:800a
  on miracles, 6:960b
  Pirandello and, 8:413b
  Rilke and, 9:771b
  in Sarraute's *Age of Suspicion*, 12:2337b
  Simenon and, 12:2504a
  Spanish translations, 9:1119b
  Strindberg and, 7:1732a
  The Castle (*Das Schloss*), 9:1172b,
    1173b–1176a
    Herrenhof and, 9:1155a
    Robbe-Grillet and, 13:3244b
  The Country Doctor (*Ein Landarzt*),
    9:1154a-b, 1156a
  The Metamorphosis (*Die Verwandlung*),
    9:1154a, 1162b–1163a, 1164a,
    1165b–1166a
    metaphor in, 9:1157b, 1159a
  "The Penal Colony" ("In der Strafkolonie"),
    9:1157a, 1166a-b, 1167a-b
  The Trial (*Der Prozess*), 9:1154a,
    1159b–1160a, 1162a, 1168a–1172a
    excised passages of, 9:1170a-b
Kahlo de Rivera, Frida, Breton on, 11:1949a
Kahn, Gustave
  Marinetti and, 9:805b
  Unamuno and, 9:745a
"Kai me phos kai me thanaton." *See* Elytis,
  Odysseus, *O mikros naftilos*
Káin. See Kosztolányi, Dezső
Kairos, das schöne Leben and, 8:461b
"Kaisarion." *See* Cavafy, Constantine
Kaiser, Ernst, translation of Musil, 9:936b
Kaiser, Georg
  From Morn to Midnight, 7:1748a
  Gas trilogy, 7:1748a
    Čapek's *R.U.R.* and, 10:1572a-b
  Strindberg and, 7:1748a
Kaiser Octavianus. See Tieck, Ludwig
Kaiser und die Hexe, Der. See Hofmannsthal,
  Hugo von
Kaiserin von Neufundland, Die. See
  Wedekind, Frank
Kaiserreich, Das. See Mann, Heinrich
"Kak eto delalos' v Odesse." *See* Babel, Isaac,
  Odessa Tales

Kalb, Charlotte von, 5:35b, 70b, 71a
Kalb family, Hölderlin and, 5:147b–148a
Kalendergeschichten. See Brecht, Bertolt,
  Tales from the Calendar
Kallias. See Schiller, Friedrich von
"Kalossini stis likopories, I." *See* Elytis,
  Odysseus
Kalvos, Andreas, 13:2984a
  Lyra, Seferis' edition, 12:2260a
  Seferis and, 12:2269b
Kamen'. See Mandelshtam, Osip, *Stone*
Kamensky, Vasily
  Khlebnikov promoted by, 10:1334a
  "O Khlebnikove: slavozhd'" ("On
    Khlebnikov: Gloryleader"), 10:1336a
Kaminskaia, Olga, 8:419a
Kämpande ande. See Lagerkvist, Pär
Kampanerthal, Das. See Richter, Jean Paul
Kamraterna. See Strindberg, August
Kandinsky, Wassily, Arp and,
  10:1367a–1369a, 1372a
Kanegisser, Leonid, Mandelshtam's comment
  on, 10:1626b
Kant, Immanuel
  Baroja and, 9:591a-b, 606a-b
  Bely and, 9:914b
  Bergson and, 8:50b
  in Claudel's *La nuit de Noël de 1914*, 8:485a
  "Copernican revolution" and, 5:210a
  Critique of Judgment (*Kritik der
    Urteilskraft*), 9:1134b
    Staël's *De l'Allemagne* on, 5:108b
  Croce and, 8:316b, 317a, 318b
  "Ding an sich" (the thing in itself), 5:148b
  Herder and, 4:639a, 652b
  Hölderlin and, 5:145a-b, 148a-b
  Kleist and, 5:294b–295b
  Lukács and, 10:1260a, 1267b–1268a
  Machado and, 9:761b
  neo-Kantian philosophy, 9:1124a-b
    in Ortega y Gasset's writings, 9:1127b
  Novalis and, 5:208a, 210a
  Richter's *The Life of Fibel* and, 5:81a
  the sage and the artist in, 5:412a
  Schiller and, 5:36a, 38a, 39a
  Schopenhauer and, 5:395b–396a, 399a-b,
    400a, 414a-b

critique of ethics of, 5:404a-b
The Critique of Aesthetic Judgment,
    Schopenhauer's approval of, 5:411b
The Critique of Practical Reason (Kritik der
    praktischen Vernunft), 6:1092a
    Schopenhauer's rejection of, 5:399b
The Critique of Pure Reason
    Richter and, 5:57a
    Schopenhauer's admiration for, 5:399a-b
Kaos. See Lagerkvist, Pär
Kapetán Mihális, O. See Kazantzakis, Nikos
Kapital, Das. See Marx, Karl
Kapitanskaya dochka. See Pushkin, Alexander
Kapitulation, Eine. See Wagner, Richard
Kaplan, Alice, *Reproductions of Banality,*
    9:807a
Kapodístrias, O. See Kazantzakis, Nikos
Karaluchy. See Witkiewicz, Stanisław Ignacy
Karamzin, Nikolay, 6:1064b
    Lermontov and, 6:1206a, 1217a
Karandonis, Andreas, 13:2975a
    O poietis Giorgos Seferis, 12:2259a
Karásek, Jiří, Hašek on, 9:1114a
Karl August of Weimar, duke
    Goethe and, 5:8a, 14b, 29b
    Schiller and, 5:29b, 34b
Karl Eugen of Württemberg, duke
    Hohe Karlsschule and, 5:28a-b
    Schiller and, 5:29b
Karl Hetmann, der Zwergreise (Karl Hetmann,
    the Pygmy-Giant). *See* Wedekind, Frank
Karl Jónsson, *Sverris saga,* 1:382b–383a, 396b
Karlamagnús Saga, 1:399b
    Chanson de Roland in, 1:90b
    Charlemagne's sin in, 1:99b–100a
    Ganelon's motivation in, 1:100b–101a
"Kärlek." *See* Södergran, Edith
Kartashov, Alexander
    Mandelshtam's poem dedicated to,
        10:1637b–1638a
    Mandelshtam's "Sumerlei svobody" and,
        10:1638b
Kartofla. See Mickiewicz, Adam
Kartonnyi domik. See Kuzmin, Mikhail
Karyotakis, Kostas, 13:2956b
Kashirin, Akulina, 8:440b–441a
Kashirin, Vasili, 8:440b, 441a

"Kasyan of Krasivaya Mecha." *See* Turgenev,
    Ivan
Kataev, Valentin
    Babel and, 11:1892a
    conspiracy charges, 11:1912a
    Olesha and, 11:2233a
Käthchen von Heilbronn, Das. See Kleist,
    Heinrich von
Kathimerini, Elytis and, 13:2964b
Kaþólsk viðhorf. See Laxness, Halldór
Katilina. See Blok, Alexander
Kato ap ton iskio tou vounou. See Ritsos,
    Yannis
Katsimbalis, Constantine, Seferis on, 12:2259b
Katsimbalis, George K., Seferis and, 12:2255b
Katz und Maus. See Grass, Günter, *Cat and*
    Mouse
Kaufmann, Walter, 9:944a
    on Nietzsche, 7:1652b–1653a, 1664b
Kaukasische Kreidekreis, Der. See Brecht,
    Bertolt, *The Caucasian Chalk Circle*
"Kavkaz." *See* Lermontov, Mikhail Yurievich
"Kavkazetz." *See* Lermontov, Mikhail Yurievich
Kavkazky plennik. See Lermontov, Mikhail
    Yurievich
Kayden, Eugene, Pasternak's letter on *Doctor*
    Zhivago to, 10:1612a
Kazantzakis, Nikos, **9:1067a–1089b**
    Anaforá ston Gréko (*Report to Greco*),
        9:1086b
    Buddha, 9:1083b–1084a
    on Cavafy, 8:226b
    I aderfofádes (*The Fratricides*), 9:1085a
    Iulianós o Paravatis (Julian the Apostate),
        9:1071a
    Komodía (*Comedy*), 9:1070a-b
    kravyí, 9:170b, 1071b
    Ksimerónei (Day Is Breaking), 9:1070b
    letter to Dimitrios Kafoyerópoulos, 9:1071b
    Mélissa, 9:1071a, 1083a-b
    Nikifóros Fokás, 9:1071a
    O ftohúlis tu Theú (*Saint Francis*), 9:1085a
    O Hristós ksanastavrónetai (*Christ*
        Recrucified), 9:1071a, 1084a, 1085a,
        1085b
    O Kapetán Mihális (*Freedom or Death*),
        9:1071a, 1085a

Kazantzakis, Nikos (*cont.*)
  O Kapodístrias, 9:1071a
  O protomástoras (The Master Builder),
    9:1070b–1071a
  O teleftaíos pirasmós (The Last Temptation
    of Christ), 9:1071a, 1076a, 1085a, 1085b
  Odíssia (The Odyssey: A Modern Sequel),
    9:1068a, 1071b, 1079a–1082a
    ascending and descending god,
      9:1073b–1074a
    language, 9:1081b–1082a
    Odysseas, 9:1080a-b, 1085a
  Ofis ke kríno (Snake and Lily), 9:1070a,
    1076b
  Salvatores Dei: Askitikí (The Saviors of
    God: Spiritual Exercises), 9:1072b,
    1073a–1074a, 1077b, 1078b
    liberating God, 9:1075a-b
  Seferis and, 12:2255a
  Spasmènes psihés (Broken Souls), 9:1070b
  worldview, 9:1074a, 1075b–1076a
  Zorba the Greek (Víos ke politía tu Aléksi
    Zorbá), 9:1068b, 1071b, 1084a–1085a
Keats, John
  Chénier compared to, 4:698a
  idea of "chameleon poet" and, 10:1487a-b
  "Ode on a Grecian Urn"
    Lampedusa's *The Leopard* and,
      11:2012b–2013a, 2014a
    mythologizing in, 8:221a
  "Ode to Psyche," Baudelaire and, 7:1330a
  Undset and, 9:1021b
  Yeats on, 13:2973b
Keeley, Edmund, on Seferis, 12:2262a
Keller, Gottfried, **6:922b–930a**
  A Village Romeo and Juliet (Romeo und
    Julia auf dem Dorfe), 6:928b–929a
  "Abendlied" ("Evening Song"), 6:924a
  "An das Vaterland" (To the Fatherland),
    6:923b–924a
  Frisch and, 13:2922b
  Gesammelte Gedichte (Collected Poems),
    6:924a
  Green Henry (Der grüne Heinrich), 6:923a,
    924a–926b
    Frisch and, 13:2898b–2899a
    Peter Camenzind and, 9:836b

  Wieland and, 4:594b
  Hadlaub, 6:930a
  Hofmannsthal and, 9:690a
  Martin Salander, 6:930a
  Mirror, the Cat (Spiegel, das Kätzchen),
    6:928a
  Novellas of Zurich (Züricher Novellen),
    6:929b–930a
  Pankraz, the Sulker (Pankraz, der
    Schmoller), 6:927a
  Regula Amrain and Her Youngest Son (Frau
    Regul Amrain und ihr Jüngster),
    6:927a-b
  Seven Legends, 6:929b
  The Banner of the Upright Seven (Das
    Fähnlein der sieben Aufrechten), 6:930a
  The Lost Smile (Das verlorne Lachen),
    6:929a-b
  The People of Seldwyla (Die Leute von
    Seldwyla), 6:926b–927a
  The Three Righteous Combmakers (Die drei
    gerechten Kammacher), 6:927b–928a
Keller, Rose, marquise de Sade's whipping of,
  4:616a
Kellogg-Briand Pact, Claudel and, 8:487b
Keniston, Hayward, on Blasco Ibáñez' *The*
  Cabin, 8:376a
Kennan, George, on Solzhenitsyn's *Gulag*
  Archipelago, 13:3207a
Kennings, 1:378b
Kenyér és bor. See Kosztolányi, Dezső
"Képi, Le" ("The Kepi"). *See* Colette
Kępiński, Ted, Gombrowicz and, 12:2564a-b
Kepler, Johannes, education of, 9:835a
Kerényi, Károly, Mann and, 9:728b
Kermess, The. *See* Krleža, Miroslav, *Kraljevo*
Kern, Stephen, on time and space, 9:800b
Kerouac, Jack, Céline's influence on, 11:1859a
Kerr, Alfred, on Hauptmann, 8:154b–155a
Kesten, Hermann, Heinrich Mann and, 8:537a,
  541b
Ketman, Milosz's metaphor of, 13:2935b
Ketzer von Soana, Der. See Hauptmann,
  Gerhart
"Khadzhi-Tarkhan." *See* Khlebnikov, Velimir
"Khanskii Polon." *See* Tsvetaeva, Marina

Khazina, Nadezhda, Mandelshtam's marriage to, 10:1639a, 1639b

"Khirôn." *See* Leconte de Lisle, Charles Marie

Khlebnikov, Velimir, **10:1331a–1364b**

"Asparukh," 10:1356a-b

"Azy iz uzy" ("I's Liberated from Chains"), 10:1361b

Bitvy 1915–1917: Novoe uchenie o voine (*Battles 1915–1917: A New Teaching About War*), 10:1338a

Bitvy 1915-1917: Novoe uchenie o voine (*Battles 1915-1917: A New Teaching About War*), vision of history in, 10:1342b

"Bobeobi pelis'guby" ("Bo-be-o-bee sang the mouth")
   neologisms in, 10:1350b
   publication of, 10:1334b

"Bogi" ("The Gods"), 10:1357b

"Chertik" (The Little Devil), 10:1356b

Death's Mistake (*Oshibka smerti*), 10:1357a-b

"Deti Vydry" ("The Otter's Children"), 10:1360a-b
   inclusion of "Smert' Palivody" in, 10:1358a

"Devii bog" (The Virgins' God), 10:1356a

Doski sud'by (The Boards of Fate), 10:1343a–1344a

"Esir" ("The Slave"), 10:1359a

"Gibel' Atlantidy" (The Fall of Atlantis)
   love vs. logic in, 10:1353b
   vision of history in, 10:1344a

"Gospozha Lenin" ("Mrs. Laneen"), 10:1357a

Grossbuch, 10:1340a

"I i E. Povest' kamennogo veka" ("I and E. A Tale of the Stone Age"), 10:1353a

"Iskushenie greshnika" (A Sinner's Temptation), 10:1357b
   publication of, 10:1334a

Izbornik stikhov (Selected Poems), publication of, 10:1335a-b

"Ka," 10:1358b–1359a
   publication of, 10:1338a

"Khadzhi-Tarkhan," 10:1353b–1354a

"Khudozhniki mira!" ("Artists of the World!"), on language, 10:1346b, 1347b

"Kurgan Sviatogora" (Sviatogor's Mound), poetics of, 10:1346a-b

"Ladomir" ("Goodworld"), 10:1355a-b

"Lebediia budushchego" ("Swanland in the Future"), 10:1359b

"Lesnaia deva" (The Forest Maiden), 10:1353a

"Malinovaia shashka" (The Crimson Saber), 10:1359a

"Markiza Dezes" (The Marquis Desaix), 10:1356b–1357a

Mayakovsky and, 11:1835b

"Mirskontsa" ("The World in Reverse"), 10:1357a

"Nasha osnova" ("Our Fundamentals"), on transrational language, 10:1347b–1348a

"Nikolai," 10:1358a-b

"Noch' v okope" (A Night in a Trench), 10:13545b
   sympathy for Reds in, 10:1339b
   textual problems with, 10:1349a

"O rasshirenii predelov russkoi slovesnosti" ("Expanding the Boundaries of Russian Literature")
   on continentalism, 10:1348a
   goals for futurists in, 10:1348b

"October on the Neva" ("Oktiabr' na Neve"), 10:1339b

"Okhotnik Usa-Gali" ("Usa-Gali"), 10:1358a-b

"Otkaz" ("Refusal"), 10:1350b

"Pamiatnik" (The Monument), 10:1336b

"Pesn' miriazia" (The Song of the Peaceful One), 10:1357b

"Poet" ("The Poet"), 10:1354a-b

"Pruzhina chakhotki" ("The Mainspring of Consumptive Disease"), 10:1357b

"Ptichka v kletke" (Little Bird in a Cage), 10:1349a-b

"Pust' na mogil'noi plite prochtut . . ." ("Let them read on my gravestone . . ."), 10:1341b

"Razgovor Olega i Kazimira" ("Oleg and Kazimir. A Conversation"), linguistics in, 10:1347a

Khlebnikov, Velimir (*cont.*)
Ryav, Perchatki: 1908–1914 (Roar, The Gauntlets: 1908–1914), publication of, 10:1335a-b
"Self-Statement" ("Svoiasi")
on "Devii bog," 10:1356a
poetics of, 10:1345b–1346b
"Sestry-molnii" (Sisters-Lightning Flashes), 10:1361a-b
"Shaman i Venera" (The Shaman and Venus), 10:1353b
Slovo kak takovoe (The Word as Such) (with Kruchenykh), 10:1345a-b
"Slovo o El'" (The Song of L), his language theory and, 10:1347b
"Smert' Palivody" (Palivoda's Death), 10:1358a
"Snezhimochka" (Snowchild Baby), 10:1355b–1356a
Teacher and Student (*Uchitel' i uchenik*)
linguistics in, 10:1346b–1347a
vision of history in, 10:1342a-b
"The Crane" ("Zhuravl'"), 10:1352b–1353a
"Markiza Dezes" and, 10:1357a
"The Night Search" ("Nochnoi obysk"), 10:1354b–1355a
vision of history in, 10:1344a
"trans-sense language" of, 10:1347b–1348a, 1524b
"Truba Gul'-Mully" ("Gul-mullah's Trumpet"), 10:1355a
Truba marsian (The Trumpet of the Martians), 10:1338b–1339a
"Tsarapina po nebu" (A Scratch Across the Sky), 10:1361b
Tvoreniia 1906–1908 (Creations 1906–1908), publication of, 10:1335a-b
"Velik-Den" (Easter Day), 10:1357b–1358a
"Vila i leshii" (The Vila and the Wood-Goblin), 10:1353a-b
"Vnuchka Malushi" (Malusha's Granddaughter), 10:1352a-b
"Vozzvanie predsedatelei zemnogo shara" ("An Appeal by the Presidents of the Planet Earth"), 10:1339a
Vremia mera mira (Time—The Measure of the World), 10:1342b–1343a
"War in a Mousetrap" ("Voina v myshelovke"), 10:1360b–1361a
"Azi iz uzy" and, 10:1361b
classification of, 10:1360a
"Zakalennoe serdtse. Ia chernogorskoi zhizni" (The Tempered Heart. From Montenegrin Life), 10:1358a
"Zakliatie smekhom" ("Incantation by Laughter"), neologisms in, 10:1334a, 1350b
Zangezi, 10:1361b–1362b
his vision of history in, 10:1344a
paranoia in, 10:1341a
supertale defined in, 10:1359b–1360a
"Zhili gor" (Mountain Folk), 10:1358a
"Zverinets" ("The Menagerie"), dedication to Ivanov, 10:1334a
Khlebnikov, Viktor Vladimirovich. *See* Khlebnikov, Velimir
Khodasevich, Vladislav, 9:925a
on the revolution, 10:1638b
"Khodia: Iz knigi *Petersburg 1918.*" *See* Babel, Isaac
"Khokhol." *See* Romas, Mikhail
"Khor and Kalinych." *See* Turgenev, Ivan
"Khoroshie lyudi." *See* Chekhov, Anton
Khorosho! Oktyabr'skaya poema. See Mayakovsky, Vladimir
"Khoziain." *See* Gorky, Maxim
"Khranila ia sredi mladkh sozvuchii." *See* Blok, Alexander
"Khristos i popy." *See* Hašek, Jaroslav
"Khudozhnik." *See* Blok, Alexander
"Khudozhniki mira!" *See* Khlebnikov, Velimir
Khvyl'ovyi, Mykola, 10:1657a
on Ukrainian literature, 10:1655b
"Ki akoumpisa kai plagiasa stes klines ton." *See* Cavafy, Constantine
Kichle. See Seferis, George
Kid, The. See Chaplin, Charlie
Kiddle, Lawrence, on Blasco Ibáñez' *The Cabin*, 8:376a
Kidnapping of Scapin, The. *See* Claudel, Paul, *Le ravissement de Scapin*
"Kids, get your sleds ready for the ice." *See* Neidhart von Reuental, "Kint, bereitet iuch der sliten ûf daz îs"

Kielland, Alexander M., Hamsun and, 8:23a, 24a

Kierkegaard, Søren, **6:1123a–1146b**
  "A First and Last Declaration," 6:1142a
  "A Glance at a Contemporary Effort in Danish Literature," 6:1142a
  Attack upon "Christendom," 6:1125b, 1143a–1144a
  Book of the Judge, Kafka and, 9:1166b
  Butor and, 13:3293b
  Chénier compared to, 4:715b
  Christian Discourses, 6:1124a
  Concluding Unscientific Postscript, 6:1123a-b, 1141b–1142a
  "Diapsalmata," 6:1130b–1131a
  "Diary of a Seducer," 6:1130b–1132b
  Dinesen and, 10:1299a
  Either/Or, 6:1123a, 1130a–1132b, 7:1736a
    Doctor Faustus and, 9:733b
    stages in, 6:1135a–1137a
  "Equilibrium Between the Aesthetical and the Ethical in the Composition of Personality," 6:1136a-b
  Fear and Trembling, 6:1123a
    stages in, 6:1137b–1138a
  For Self-Examination, 6:1124a
  From the Papers of One Still Living, 6:1125b, 1127a-b
  "In vino veritas," 6:1140a-b
  incomprehensible deity, 9:1126b
  Judge for Yourselves!, 6:1124a
  Kafka and, 9:1154b, 1156b
  Lukács and, 10:1257a-b, 1275a
  On Authority and Revelation, 6:1125b
  Philosophical Fragments, 6:1123a
  Purity of Heart Is to Will One Thing, 6:1124a
  Repetition, 6:1123a, 1132b–1133a
    stages in, 6:1138a-b
  "Shadowgraphs," 6:1131a
  Stages on Life's Way, 6:1123a, 1133a–1134a
    "'Guilty?'/'Not Guilty?' A Passion Narrative," 6:1133a–1134a
    love in, 6:1140a–1141b
  Strindberg and, 7:1736a, 1753a
  The Concept of Anxiety, 6:1123a
    stages in, 6:1139a–1140a
  The Concept of Irony: With Constant Reference to Socrates, 6:1125b, 1129a
  "The Edification Implied in the Thought That as Against God We Are Always Wrong," 6:1137a-b
  The Gospel of Suffering, 6:1124a
  The Point of View for My Work as an Author, 6:1142a
  The Sickness unto Death, 6:1124a, 1143a
  Training in Christianity, 6:1124a, 1143a
  Two Ages: The Age of Revolution and the Present Age, 6:1125b
  Unamuno and, 8:291b, 294a, 299b, 9:1127b
  Upbuilding Discourses in Various Spirits, 6:1124a
  "Various Observations About Marriage in Reply to Objections," 6:1140b–1141a
  Works of Love, 6:1124a

Kiernan, Kevin, on the composition of *Beowulf*, 1:70b–71a

Kievan Rus, in Pushkin's *Ruslan and Lyudmila*, 5:664b–665a

Kihlman, Erik, Södergran and, 11:1802b

Kill, The. See Zola, Émile, *La curée*

Killer, The. See Ionesco, Eugène

Killing Game. See Ionesco, Eugène, *Jeux de massacre*

Kilwardby, Robert, 1:426b

Kimen. See Vesaas, Tarjei, *The Seed*

"Kina thaymata." *See* Ritsos, Yannis, *Ghrafi tiflou*

Kinck, Hans, Norwegian realism and, 9:1037a

Kind Message of Dismissal, A. *See* Ady, Endre, "Elbocsátó szép üzenet"

Kinder und Narren. See Wedekind, Frank, *Die junge Welt*

"Kindliches Königtum." *See* George, Stefan, *Die Bücher der Hirten- und Preisgedichte . . .*

Kindness in the Wolfpasses. *See* Elytis, Odysseus, "I kalossini stis likopories"

King of Asine and Other Poems, The. See Spencer, Bernard

"King of Asine, The." *See* Seferis, George, *Imerologio katastromatos (Logbook I)*, "O vasilias tis asinis"

King at Play, The. See Hugo, Victor, *Le roi s'amuse*

"King Candaulus." *See* Gautier, Théophile

King of Harlem, The. *See* García Lorca, Federico, "Oda al rey de Harlem"

King John. See Shakespeare, William

King Lear. See Shakespeare, William

"King Lear of the Steppes, A." *See* Turgenev, Ivan

King Nicolo; or, Such Is Life. See Wedekind, Frank, *König Nicolo, oder So ist das Leben*

King Ottokar, His Rise and Fall. See Grillparzer, Franz, *König Ottokars Glück und Ende*

King Riot. See Marinetti, Filippo Tommaso, *Le roi bombance*

King Seleucus. See Camoëns, Luís Vaz de, *El-Rei Seleuco*

King in the Square, The. See Blok, Alexander, *Korol' na ploshchadi*

"King, The." *See* Babel, Isaac, *Odessa Tales*

Kingdom Come, The. *See* George, Stefan, *Das neue Reich*

King's Son, A. *See* Gunnarsson, Gunnar, "Kongesøn"

Kingship. *See* Monarchy

Kinship
  in *Völsunga saga*, 1:400b
  in Wolfram, 1:279a-b
  see also Family

Kinsman of Death, The. *See* Ady, Endre, "A Halál rokona"

"Kint, bereitet iuch der sliten ûf daz îs." *See* Neidhart von Reuental

Kipling, Rudyard, Vittorini and, 12:2735b

Kippenberg, Anton, Rilke and, 9:771b, 772a

Király, István
  on Ady, 9:860b, 862a, 863b, 864b
  on "cattle folk," 9:865b
  on Paris, 9:871b

Kirchenpostillen. See Luther, Martin

Kirchner, Ernst, Ghelderode and, 11:2123a

"Kirdzhali." *See* Pushkin, Alexander

Kirke ag klosterliv: Tre essays fra norsk middelalder. See Undset, Sigrid

Kirken paa Bjerget. See Gunnarsson, Gunnar

Kishinev, Pushkin's stay at, 5:661b

Kiss for the Leper, A. See Mauriac, François

Kiss of Rosalie Mihalyi, The. *See* Ady, Endre, "Mihályi Rozália csókja"

"Kiss, The." *See* Babel, Isaac, "Potselui"

Kisses Kissed with Closed Eyes. *See* Ady, Endre, "Csukott szemű csókok"

Kite, The. See Pirandello, Luigi, *Se non cosí*

Kitsch, Kundera and, 13:3407b–3408a

Kjalnesinga saga, 1:398a

Kjeldene. See Vesaas, Tarjei

Klaeber, Frederick, on *Beowulf*, 1:71b

Klages, Ludwig, George and, 8:455b, 462b

Klæng Thorsteinsson, 1:383b

"Klara Milich." *See* Turgenev, Ivan

"Klarisse." *See* Novalis

Klee, Paul, Arp and, 10:1367a

Klein, Carl August, George and, 8:450b

Klein and Wagner (*Klein und Wagner*). *See* Hesse, Hermann

Kleine Stadt, Die. See Mann, Heinrich

Kleine Welttheater oder Die Glücklichen, Das. See Hofmannsthal, Hugo von

Kleines Organon das Theater. See Brecht, Bertolt

Kleines Theater (Berlin), *Enemies* and, 8:420b

Kleist, Ewald Christian von
  and Lessing, 4:539a, 539b
  in Mandelshtam's "Knemetskoi rechi," 10:1645a

Kleist, Heinrich von, **5:291a–312b**
  Amphitryon, 5:295b–296a
  Das Käthchen von Heilbronn, 5:306b–307b
  Die Familie Schroffenstein, 5:295b
  Die Hermannsschlacht (*The Battle of Hermann*), 5:306b
  "German Catechism," 5:306a
  Hofmannsthal and, 9:689b
  Kafka and, 9:1156a
  Michael Kohlhaas, 5:303b–304b
  Penthesilea, 5:299b–301a
  Prinz Friedrich von Homburg, 5:307b–308b
  Robert Guiskard, 5:298b–299a
  "Saint Cecelia; or, The Power of Music," 5:296a
  "The Betrothal in Santo Domingo" ("Die Verlöbung in St. Domingo"), 5:302a-b

The Broken Jug (*Der zerbrochene Krug*), 5:297a–298a

The Comet and, 5:82a

"The Duel," 5:296a-b

"The Earthquake in Chile" ("Das Erdbeben in Chile"), 5:303a-b

The Marquise of O (*Die Marquise von O . . .*), 5:304b–305b

"Über das Marionettentheater" ("On the Marionette Theater"), 5:299b

"Kleitos' Illness." *See* Cavafy, Constantine, "I arrostia tou Kleitou"

"Klimat." *See* Ekelöf, Gunnar

Klinger, Friedrich Maximilian von, *Sturm und Drang* (Storm and Stress), title as rubric for German romantic movement, 4:645b

Klingsor's Last Summer (*Klingsors letzter Sommer*). *See* Hesse, Hermann

Klokka i haugen. *See* Vesaas, Tarjei, *The Bell in the Knoll*

Klop. *See* Mayakovsky, Vladimir, *The Bedbug*

Klopstock, Friedrich Gottlieb, **4:511a–536bt**

and Bodmer, 4:592a

"Celebration of Spring," 4:511a–512a

David, 4:522a–523a

form of, 5:144a-b

George's *Das Jahr der Seele* and, 8:459b

Hermann and the Princes, 4:523b–524b

Hölderlin and, 5:144a-b

"Ice-Skating," 4:530a-b

"Lake Zurich," 4:528a-b

Lessing on, 4:545a

"On My Friends," 4:527b–528a

"Our Language to Us," 4:532a

Solomon, 4:522a–523a

The Battle of Hermann, 4:523b–524b

"The Chain of Roses," 4:531b–532a

The Death of Adam, 4:521a–522a

The Death of Hermann, 4:523b–524b

"The Early Graves," 4:528b

"The Fireplace," 4:520a

"The Future Beloved," 4:527a

"The German Bible," 4:532a

The German Republic of Intellectuals, 4:514b–515a

The Messiah, 4:516b–521a

"The Mount and the Grove," 4:529a-b

"The Worlds," 4:531a-b

"Thuiskon," 4:529b

"To Ebert," 4:527a-b

"To Fanny," 4:527b

"To Friend and Foe," 4:532a

"To the Infinite One," 4:531b

"Wingolf" ("Temple of Friendship"), 4:527b–528a

Klopstock, Robert, Kafka and, 9:1155a, 1155b

Klossowska, Baladine, 9:772b

Kloster bei Sendomir, Das. *See* Grillparzer, Franz

Klostret. *See* Strindberg, August

Klotz, Christian Adolph, and Lessing, 4:561a

Klyuev, Nikolay

downfall of Petrine Russia and, 10:1620a-b

Mandelshtam compared to, 10:1644a

Kniazev, Vsevolod, in Akhmatova's *Poem Without a Hero*, 10:1538b, 1540a-b

Knight, Wolfram as, 1:263a–264a

Knight from Olmedo, The. *See* Lope de Vega

"Knight Who Lies Idly, The." *See* George, Stefan, *Die Bücher der Hirten- und Preisgedichte . . .* (The Books of Eclogues and Eulogies), *Sagen und Sänge* poems

Knights of the Round Table, The. *See* Cocteau, Jean

Kniha smíchu a zapomnění. *See* Kundera, Milan, *The Book of Laughter and Forgetting*

Knipper, Olga, 7:1857a

Knittelvers. *See* Heine, Heinrich

Književna republika (Literary Republic), Krleža and, 11:1814a, 1814b–1815a, 1816b

Književni jug. *See* Andrić, Ivo

"Knock . . . Knock . . . Knock." *See* Turgenev, Ivan

Knoop, Wera Ouckama, 9:788a

Knowledge

Aquinas on, 1:423b–424b

Augustine on, 1:40a, 40b, 46a

carnal. *See* Sexual passion

certainty of, in Descartes's *Meditations on First Philosophy*, 3:13a, 17a

in Dante's *Convivio*, 1:439b–440a

Foucault and, 13:3325a–3361b

Knowledge (*cont.*)
in George's *Der Stern des Bundes*, 8:465a-b
of God. *See* God, knowability of
language and, in Valéry's "Sketch of a
Serpent," 8:583a
Montaigne's "Apology of Raymond Sebond"
on, 2:776b–777a
Ockham on, 1:427b
unity of, in Descartes's *Discourse on the
Method*, 3:3b–4a
in Wolfram, 1:277b–278a
Knowledge, nature of, Croce on, 8:318b
Knowledge (organization). *See* Znanie
Knulp. See Hesse, Hermann
Knutna händerna, De. See Moberg, Vilhelm
"Knyaginya." *See* Chekhov, Anton
Knyaginya Ligovskaya. See Lermontov,
Mikhail Yurievich, *Princess Ligovskaya*
"Knyazhna Meri." *See* Lermontov, Mikhail
Yurievich, *Princess Mary*
Kobes. See Mann, Heinrich
Kobylinskii, Lev (Ellis), Tsvetaeva and,
11:1733b
Kodály, Zoltán, Lukács and, 10:1254a, 1254b,
1264a
Kodhonostasio. See Ritsos, Yannis
"Koe-chto iz sekretnykh zapisey poputchika
Zanda." *See* Olesha, Yuri
"Koe-chto po povodu dirizhera." *See*
Mayakovsky, Vladimir
Koering, René, Butor and, 13:3312b
Koestler, Arthur
Hamsun and, 8:21a, 32b
mysticism and, 9:1009a
Silone and, 12:2273a
Koffka, Kurt, Stumpf and, 9:932a
Kogda razguliaetsia. See Pasternak, Boris,
When the Skies Clear
Köhler, Wolfgang, Stumpf and, 9:932a
Kolb, Jacqueline, 9:882a
"Kolia Topuz." *See* Babel, Isaac
Kollwitz, Käthe, Heinrich Mann and, 8:536b
"Költözés Átok-városból." *See* Ady, Endre
"Kolyvushka." *See* Babel, Isaac
*Komet, Der, oder Nikolaus Marggraf, eine
komische Geschichte. See* Richter, Jean
Paul

Kommentar till ett stärnfall. See Johnson,
Eyvind
Komodía. See Kazantzakis, Nikos
Komödie der Eitelkeit. See Canetti, Elias, *The
Comedy of Vanity*
Komödie der Verführung. See Schnitzler,
Arthur
Komödie der Worte. See Schnitzler, Arthur
Komplotterna. See Moberg, Vilhelm
Komtesse Mizzi oder der Familientag. See
Schnitzler, Arthur
"Kon' bled." *See* Bryusov, Valery
Konarmiia. See Babel, Isaac, *Red Cavalry*
Konerne ved vandposten. See Hamsun, Knut
"Konets romana." *See* Mandelshtam, Osip
"Kongesøn." *See* Gunnarsson, Gunnar
König Nicolo, oder So ist das Leben. See
Wedekind, Frank
König Ödipus. See Hofmannsthal, Hugo von
König Ottokars Glück und Ende. See
Grillparzer, Franz
König Rother, 1:401b
Königliche Hoheit. See Mann, Thomas
"Konovalov." *See* Gorky, Maxim
Konrad Wallenrod. See Mickiewicz, Adam
"Kontsert na vokzale." *See* Mandelshtam, Osip
Kontynenty. See Milosz, Czeslaw
Konungaævi, 1:380a
Konungen. See Lagerkvist, Pär
Köp den blindes sång. See Ekelöf, Gunnar
Kopelev, Lev, on Solzhenitsyn, 13:3199b
Kopf, Der. See Mann, Heinrich, *Das
Kaiserreich*
*Kopfgeburten; oder, Die Deutschen sterben
aus. See* Grass, Günter, *Headbirths; or,
The Germans Are Dying Out*
Köpke, Wulf, *Erfolglosigkeit*, 5:61b, 62b
"Korán jöttem ide." *See* Ady, Endre
"Kori pou ferne o vorias, I." *See* Elytis,
Odysseus, *To photodendro kai i dekati
tetarti omorfia*
Kormáks saga, 1:384b
Körner, Gottfried, 5:35b–36a, 37a
"Korol." *See* Babel, Isaac, *Odessa Tales*
Korol' na ploshchadi. See Blok, Alexander
Korolenko, Vladimir, Gorky and, 8:419a
Korsar. See Lermontov, Mikhail Yurievich

Korzeniowska, Czesława, Witkiewicz and, 10:1227b, 1228a

Kosík, Karel, on Jaroslav Hašek, 9:1115a-b

Kosmische Runde (organization), George and, 8:462b

Kosmos. See Gombrowicz, Witold, *Cosmos*

Kossuth, Lajos, Kosztolányi and, 10:1231a, 1232a

"Kostel v Novograde." *See* Babel, Isaac

Kostomarov, Mykola, *Books of the Life of the Ukrainian Nation*, influenced by Mickiewicz's *Books*, 5:624b

Kostro. *See* Apollinaire, Guillaume

Kostrowitzky, Angelica de, 9:881a, 881b, 882a

Kostrowitzky, Guillelmus Apollinaris de. *See* Apollinaire, Guillaume

Kosztolányi, Ágoston, 10:1231a–1232a

Kosztolányi, Árpád, 10:1231a, 1232a, 1235a

Kosztolányi, Dezső, **10:1231a–1249b**

   A bús férfi panaszai (The Laments of a Man of Sorrow), 10:1235a-b, 1244a

   A rossz orvos (The Bad Physician), 10:1235b

   A szegény kisgyermek panaszai (The Laments of a Small Child), 10:1234b

   A tíz legszebb (The Ten Most Beautiful Words), 10:1241b–1242a

   A véres költő (*The Bloody Poet*), 10:1235b

   Aranysárkány (*The Golden Kite*), 10:1238a–1239b

      critique of positivism in, 10:1239b

      three kinds of time in, 10:1238b–1239a

   Az irástudatlanok árulása (The Treason of the Illiterate), 10:1244b, 1245a

   Bölcsőtől a koporsóig (From the Cradle to the Grave), 10:1231b, 1241b

   diaries, 10:1232a-b

   Édes Anna (*Wonder Maid*), 10:1240a-b

   Egy asszony beszál (A Woman Is Talking), 10:1247a

   "Egysir," 10:1233a

   "Ének a semmiről" (A Song upon Nothing), 10:1246b

   Esti Kornél (Cornelius Nightly), 10:1232b, 1240b, 1242b–1244a, 1244b–1245a

      impact of, 10:1248a

   Esti Kornél kalandjai (The Adventures of Cornelius Nightly), 10:1243a, 1247a

   "Hajnali részegség" (Daybreak Drunkenness), 10:1246a-b

   Káin (Cain), 10:1235a

   Kenyér és bor (Bread and Wine), 10:1235a

   Latin arcélek (Roman Profiles), 10:1245b–1246a, 1247a

   Meztelenül (Naked), 10:1244b

   Modern költők (Modern Poets), 10:1234a

   Mostoha (Stepmother), 10:1240b

   Négy fal között (Inside the Walls), 10:1233b–1234a

   Nyelv és lélek (Language and Soul), 10:1241a, 1242a

   "Októberi táj" (October Landscape), 10:1246a-b, 1247b–1248a

   Őszi koncert (Concert in Autumn), 10:1235a

   Pacsirta (Skylark), 10:1237a–1238a

   Pár szó a nyelvújításhoz (A Few Words on Language Reform), 10:1241a

   Számadás (A Summing Up), 10:1244b, 1245a-b, 1246a-b

   "Szeptemberi áhítat" (September Ecstasy), 10:1246b–1247a

   Tengerszem (Tarn), 10:1243a, 1245b, 1247a-b

   Tollrajzok (Sketches), 10:1247a

   Túlvilági sćták (Walls Taken in the New World), 10:1241a

   Végzet és veszély (Danger and Destiny), 10:1247a

   "Vörös hervadás" (Red Withering), 10:1245b

Kotik Letaev. See Bely, Andrey

Kotsiubynskii, Mykhailo, friendship with Tychyna, 10:1653b

Kott, Jan, *Shakespeare Our Contemporary*, 13:3012a

Kotzebue, August, Andersen and, 6:877b

Kovcheg. See Tsvetaeva, Marina

Kracauer, Siegfried, *Die Angestellten* (White-Collar Workers), Benjamin's review of, 11:1723b

Krafft-Ebing, Richard von

   Psychopathia sexualis, 12:2693a

      Ady and, 9:869b

      "sadism" coined in, 4:637a

      Sade's predating of, 4:621b

Krakatit. See Čapek, Karel

Krakonošova zahrada. See Čapek, Karel, and
  Josef Čapek
Kraljevo. See Krleža, Miroslav
Krane, Borghild, 9:1017b–1018a
Krasiński, Zygmunt, Gombrowicz and,
  12:2585a-b
Krasnaia nov' (*Red Virgin Soil*) (journal)
  Babel's stories in, 11:1909a
  Envy and, 11:2235b
  My Universities in, 8:440a
Krasnaya Evropa (*Red Europe*) (Soviet
    periodical), Hašek's articles in, 9:1095a
Krasnoe derevo. See Pil'niak, Boris
Krasnoe koleso. See Solzhenitsyn, Aleksandr,
    The Red Wheel
Krasnyi voin (Red Warrior) (newspaper),
    Khlebnikov's work for, 10:1340a
Kraus, Karl
  Canetti and, 12:2617a-b
  compared to Krleža, 11:1808a
  Rilke and, 9:771b
  Schnitzler and, 8:92a
Krause, Karl Christian Friedrich, 9:591b
  Generation of '98 and, 9:744b
Krausism
  in Spain, 9:591b
    socio-historical roots, 9:593a
Krauss, Rosalind, on "Futurist Manifesto,"
    9:804b
Kreatur, Die. See Buber, Martin
Kreis
  George and
    in *Der Stern des Bundes*, 8:464b
    in *Der Teppich*, 8:461b
    see also George-Kreis
Kreisau Circle, 8:468a
Kreshchenyi Kitaets. See Bely, Andrey
Kreutzer, Conradin, Grillparzer's *Melusina*
    and, 5:433b
Kreutzer, Rodolphe, Berlioz and, 6:781a
Kreutzer Sonata, The. See Tolstoy, Leo
"Kriazhi." *See* Zamyatin, Yevgeny Ivanovich
Krieg und Frieden. See Hesse, Hermann
Kriemhild
  the *Nibelungenlied* and
    interpretation of, 1:221b–226a
    story of, 1:211a–213a

structure and, 1:220b–221b
Kriemhild's Revenge. See Nibelungenlied, The
Kriemhild's Revenge (*Kriemhilds Rache*). *See*
    Hebbel, Friedrich, *Die Nibelungen*
Krilon själv (Krilon Himself). *See* Johnson,
    Eyvind, Krilon trilogy
Krilon trilogy. *See* Johnson, Eyvind
Krilons resa (Krilon's Journey). *See* Johnson,
    Eyvind, Krilon trilogy
Krisis. See Hesse, Hermann
Kristin Lavransdatter. See Undset, Sigrid
Kristina. See Strindberg, August, *Queen
    Christina*
Kristni saga. See Sturla Thórðarson
Kristnihald undir Jökli. See Laxness, Halldór
Kristofor Kolumbo. See Krleža, Miroslav
Kritik der praktischen Vernunft. See Kant,
    Immanuel, *The Critique of Practical
    Reason*
Kritik der Urteilskraft. See Kant, Immanuel,
    Critique of Judgment
Kritika slov. See Čapek, Karel
Kritische Briefe. See Lessing, Gotthold
    Ephraim
Krizis kul'tury. See Bely, Andrey
Krizis mysli. See Bely, Andrey
Krizis zhizni. See Bely, Andrey
Krleža, Miroslav, **11:1807a–1834b**
  *Aretej ili Legenda o Svetoj Ancili, Rajskoj
    Ptici* (Aretaeus; or, The Legend of St.
    Ancilla, the Bird of Paradise),
    11:1827b–1928a
  Balade Petrice Kerempuha (The Ballads of
    Petrica Kerempuh), 11:1819a–1820a
  Banket u Blitvi (Banquet in Blithuania),
    11:1820b, 1828b, 1832a
  "Cvrčak pod vodopadom" ("The Cricket
    Beneath the Waterfall"),
    11:1830b–1831a
  Davni dani (Distant Days), 11:1827a-b
  Deset krvavih godina (Ten Years of Blood),
    11:1814b, 1820b
  Djetinjstvo u Agramu godine 1902-3
    (Childhood in Agram 1902-1903),
    11:1824b
  Dnevnik (Diary), 11:1831b

"Evropa godine tisuću devet stotina četrdeset i druge" (Europe in Nineteen-Hundred Forty-Two), 11:1821b–1822a

Fragmenti, 11:1811a

Galicija (Galicia), 11:1813b, 1814b, 1820b

Golgota, 11:1814a, 1814b

Gospoda Glembajevi (The Noble Glembays), 11:1815a

Hrvatski bog Mars (The Croatian God Mars), 11:1812b, 1814a

Izlet u Rusiju (An Excursion to Russia), 11:1814a-b

"Jesenja noć" (Autumn Night), 11:1817a-b

Kraljevo (The Kermess), 11:1811b, 1826a-b

Kristofor Kolumbo (Christopher Columbus), 11:1812b, 1824b, 1825a–1826a

Krokodilina ili razgovor o istini (Crocodile Song; or, A Talk about Truth), 11:1823a

Legenda (A Legend), 11:1825a

Moj obračun s njima (Settling Accounts), 11:1815b

Na rubu pameti (On the Edge of Reason), 11:1820b

Pan, 11:1811b–1812a

Podnevna simfonija (Midday Symphony), 11:1812a

Povratak Filipa Latinovicza (The Return of Philip Latinovicz), 11:1815b, 1828a-b

Put u raj (The Path to Paradise), 11:1830b–1831b

Saloma (Salomé), 11:1811a, 1830a

Tri simfonije (Three Symphonies), 11:1812a, 1822a

U agoniji, 11:1827b

Vučjak (The Village of Vučjak), 11:1814a, 1814b

Zaratustra i mladić (Zarathustra and the Youth), 11:1811a

Zastave (Banners), 11:1828b–1830a

Kröger, Nellie. *See* Mann, Nellie Kröger

Króka-Refs saga, 1:397b

Krokodilina ili razgovor o istini. *See* Krleža, Miroslav

Krolow, Karl, Rilke and, 9:789b

Kronberger, Maximilian, George and, 8:462b–463b, 464b

Kronbruden. *See* Strindberg, August

Kropotkin, Pyotr Alekseyevich
in Azorín's work, 9:643a
Herder's individualism compared to, 4:652a

"Krovavaia misteriia 9-go ianvaria." *See* Mandelshtam, Osip, "Bloody Mystery Play of January Ninth"

Kruchenykh, Aleksei, 10:1334b
Khlebnikov's letter to, 10:1348a

Kruchenykh, Aleksei, and Velemir Khlebnikov, *Pobeda nad solntsem* (*Victory over the Sun*), 11:1835b–1836a, 1839b, 1840b–1841a

Kruchenykh, Aleksei, and Velimir Khlebnikov, *Slovo kak takovoe* (*The Word as Such*), 10:1345a-b

Krüdener, Julie von, 5:71a

Krylov, Ivan Andreyevich, *The Peasant and the Farm Laborer*, 7:1877b

Krysolov. *See* Tsvetaeva, Marina

"Kryzhovnik." *See* Chekhov, Anton

Księgi narodu polskiego i pielgrzymstwa polskiego. *See* Mickiewicz, Adam

Ksimerónei. *See* Kazantzakis, Nikos

Kublitsky-Piottukh, Franz Feliksovitch, 9:964b, 965a

Kubok metelei. *See* Bely, Andrey, *Symphonies*

Kubrick, Stanley, 13:3017a

Kuća na osami. *See* Andrić, Ivo

Kuh, Emil, Hebbel and, 6:1097b, 1098a-b

Kühn, Sophie von, Novalis and, 5:206a–208a

Kühne, Gustave, Hebbel and, 6:1106a

"Kukil." *See* Tychyna, Pavlo, *Zamist' sonetiv i oktav*

"Kultur als Alibi." *See* Frisch, Max

Kultur der Renaissance in Italien, Die. *See* Burckhardt, Jacob, *The Civilization of the Renaissance in Italy*

Kultura (journal), Gombrowicz and, 12:2564b

Kulturkampf (battle for civilization), Fontane and, 6:1309b–1310b

Kun, Béla, 10:1259b
in Kosztolányi's *Wonder Maid*, 10:1240a
Lukács and, 10:1265a, 1268b

Kun en Spillemand. *See* Andersen, Hans Christian, *Only a Fiddler*

Kundera, Milan, **13:3389a–3413b**

Kundera, Milan (*cont.*)
  Člověk zahrada širá (Man, the Vast Garden),
    13:3391b
  "Edward and God" ("Eduard a Bůh"),
    13:3398b–3399a
  "Introduction to a Variation," 13:3409b
  Jacques and His Master (*Jacques et son
    maître*), 13:3409a–3410a
  Laughable Loves (*Směšné lásky*),
    13:3398a–3399b
  Life Is Elsewhere (*Život je jinde*; also *La vie
    est ailleurs*), 13:3394a, 3402a–3403a
  Majitelé klíčů (The Owners of the Keys),
    13:3392a-b
  Monology (Monologues), 13:3392a
  "Nobody Will Laugh" ("Nikdo se nebude
    smát"), 13:3398b–3399a
  Poslední máj (The Last May), 13:3391b
  Ptákovina, čili Dvoje uši—dvoje svadba
    (Double Wedding), 13:3394a
  "Somewhere Beyond," 13:3411a
  "Symposion," 13:3398b–3399a
  The Book of Laughter and Forgetting (*Kniha
    smíchu a zapomnění*), 13:3404b–3407a
  The Farewell Party (*Valčík na rozloučenou*),
    13:3403a–3404b
  "The Golden Apple of Desire" ("Zlaté jablko
    věčné touhy"), 13:3398a, 3399b
  "The Hitchhiking Game" ("Falešný
    autostop"), 13:3399a
  The Joke (*Žert*), 13:3399b–3402a
  "The Novel and Europe," 13:3396a–3397b
  The Second Book of Laughable Loves
    (*Druhý sešit směšných lásek*), 13:3398a
  The Third Book of Laughable Loves (*Třetí
    sešit směšných lásek*), 13:3398a
  "The Tragedy of Central Europe,"
    13:3410a–3411a
  The Unbearable Lightness of Being
    (*Nesnesitelná lehkost bytí*),
    13:3407a–3409a
  Umění románu (The Art of the Novel),
    13:3392a
Kunst und die Revolution, Die. See Wagner,
    Richard, *Art and Revolution*
Künstlerroman
  Andersen and, 6:875b

  Richter's *Walt and Vult* as, 5:75b
Künstlerroman of Johnson, 12:2368b
Kunstmärchen (literary tales), Andersen and,
    6:878b
Kunstwart, Der (journal), 9:1152a
Kunstwerk der Zukunft, Das. See Wagner,
    Richard, *Artwork of the Future*
"Kuny." *See* Zamyatin, Yevgeny Ivanovich
Kuomintang, Malraux and, 12:2414b, 2416a-b
Kuprin, Aleksandr
  Chekhov and, 7:1857b
  Gorky and, 8:419b
  Poedinok (*The Duel*), Zamyatin's *A
    God-Forsaken Hole* compared to,
    10:1183a-b
"Kurgan Sviatogora." *See* Khlebnikov, Velimir
Kurgast. See Hesse, Hermann
Kurka wodna. See Witkiewicz, Stanisław
    Ignacy
Kurt, the God. *See* Moravia, Alberto, *Il dio
    Kurt*
"Kurzgefasster Lebenslauf." *See* Hesse,
    Hermann
Kuzmin, Mikhail
  in Akhmatova's *Poem Without a Hero*,
    10:1537a-b, 1540a-b
  Kartonnyi domik (*House of Cards*),
    amorality of, 10:1540b
  Mandelshtam and, 10:1627a, 1640a
  on Pasternak's *Zhenia's Childhood*,
    10:1600b–1601a
Kvinnan och nåden. See Olsson, Hagar
Kvinnas man. See Moberg, Vilhelm
Kvinnor ropar heim. See Vesaas, Tarjei
Kypron, ou m'ethespisen. See Seferis, George
"Kyrkogårdsfantasi." *See* Södergran, Edith

L

La Boétie, Étienne de
Discours de la servitude volontaire
  (*Discourse on Voluntary Servitude*),
  2:771a
  Montaigne and, 2:769b, 770a–771b, 772a,
    775a, 782a
La Bruyère, Jean de, **3:229a–260b**
  Caractères, 3:229a
    concluding chapter remarks, 3:233b
    editorial history of, 3:231a
    form of the entries, 3:231a-b
    internal patterns of individual chapters,
      3:234a
    Lesage's *Le diable boiteux* and, 3:324b
    on literature, 3:234b–236b
    "Of Certain Usages," 3:253a–254a
    "Of the Court," 3:242b, 244b–245b
    "Of Fashion," 3:251b–253a
    "Of Freethinkers," 3:254b–257b
    "Of the Gifts of Fortune," 3:240b–242b
    "Of the Great," 3:245b–247a
    "Of the Heart," 3:238b–239b
    "Of Judgment," 3:250a–251b
    "Of Man," 3:248b–250a
    "Of Personal Merit," 3:236a–237a
    "Of the Pulpit," 3:254a-b
    "Of Society and Conversation,"
      3:239b–240b
    "Of the Sovereign or of the State,"
      3:247a–248b
    "Of the Town," 3:242b–244b
    "Of Women," 3:237a–238b
    organization of, 3:232b–233b
    scope of, 3:229b
    sources of, 3:232a
    style of, 3:234b
  on Corneille and Racine, 3:34a
  "Des esprits forts." *See* La Bruyère, Jean de,
    Caractères, "Of Freethinkers"
  Dialogues sur le quiétisme (*Dialogues on
    Quietism*), 3:258a–259a
  *Discours de réception à l'Académie
    Française*, 3:232b, 254b–255a

Discours sur Théophraste, 3:231a,
  231b–232a
*Les caractères de Théophraste traduits du
  grec, avec les caractères ou les moeurs
  de ce siècle*, 3:231a
  Lesage and, 3:322a
La Chassaigne, Françoise de, 2:771b
La coscienza di Zeno. See Svevo, Italo,
  Confessions of Zeno, The
La de Bringas. See Pérez Galdós, Benito
Lã e a neve, A. See Ferreira de Castro, José
  Maria
La Fayette, Marie-Madeleine de
  La Princesse de Clèves, 3:77a, 263b, 273b,
    4:405b
    La Rochefoucauld and, 3:62b
  La Rochefoucauld and, 3:61a, 67a, 68a, 68b
La Flèche (school: Anjou), 3:1b–2a
La Fontaine: "Fables." See Mourgues, Odette
  de
La Fontaine, Jean de, **3:73a–100b**
  Adonis, 3:75a
  Berlioz and, 6:791b, 792b
  Contes et nouvelles, 3:75b–76a, 81a, 81b,
    95b
  Dissertation sur joconde, defended by
    Boileau, 3:179a
  "Epître à Huet," 3:78b–79a, 79b
  Fables, 3:76b, 81a–86b
    animal characters, 3:86b–95a
    on brevity, 3:78a-b
    "Du thésauriseur et du singe" ("Of the
      Hoarder and the Monkey"), 3:93b–94b
    French classicism and, 3:273b
    "La cour du lion" ("The Lion's Court"),
      3:87b
    "La goutte et l'araignée" ("The Gout and
      the Spider"), 3:91a
    "La grenouille et le rat" ("The Frog and
      the Rat"), 3:85b
    "La grenouille qui se veut faire aussi
      grosse que le boeuf" ("The Frog Who
      Wants to Make Herself as Big as the
      Ox"), 3:83a
    "La jeune veuve" ("The Young Widow"),
      3:95a-b

La Fontaine, Jean de (*cont.*)
  Fables (*cont.*)
    "La matrone d'Ephèse" ("The Matron of Ephesus"), 3:95b–99a
    "La montagne qui accouche" ("The Mountain That Gives Birth"), 3:85b–86a
    "La querelle des chiens et des chats, et celle des chats et des souris" ("The Quarrel of the Dogs and the Cats, and The One Between the Cats and the Mice"), 3:84b–85a
    "L'Araignée et l'hirondelle" ("The Spider and the Swallow"), 3:89b–93a
    "Le chêne et le roseau" ("The Oak and the Reed"), 3:83a
    "Le cigale et la fourmi" ("The Cicada and the Ant"), 3:85b
    "Le curé et le mort" ("The Parish Priest and the Dead Man"), 3:82b
    "Le loup et l'agneau" ("The Wolf and the Lamb"), 3:89a
    "Le loup et les bergers" ("The Wolf and the Shepherds"), 3:88b–89a
    "Le petit poisson et le pêcheur" ("The Little Fish and the Fisherman"), 3:84b
    "Le pot de terre et le pot de fer" ("The Earthen Pot and the Iron Pot"), 3:83b
    "Le rat et l'huître" ("The Rat and the Oyster"), 3:91b
    "Le satyre et le passant" ("The Satyr and the Passerby"), 3:84a-b
    "Le trésor et les deux hommes" ("The Treasure and the Two Men"), 3:86a
    "Les animaux malades de la peste" ("The Animals Sick with the Plague"), 3:86a
    "Les compagnons d'Ulysse" ("Ulysses' Companions"), 3:89a
    "Les grenouilles qui demandent un roi" ("The Frogs Who Ask for a King"), 3:83b
    "L'Hirondelle et les petits oiseaux" ("The Swallow and the Little Birds"), 3:88a
    "L'Homme et la couleuvre" ("The Man and the Snake"), 3:88b
    meter, 3:81b–83b
    rhyme, 3:83b–86a
    stanza forms in, 7:1637b
  Fables choisies, 3:80a, 80b
  Giraudoux and, 9:1060a
  Le songe de Vaux (The Dream of Vaux), 3:75a
  Les amours de Psyché et de Cupidon (The Passions of Psyche and Cupid), 3:78a, 80b
  L'Eunuque (The Eunuch), 3:74b–75a
  Nouvelles en vers tirées de Boccace et de l'Arioste (Tales in Verse Drawn from Boccaccio and Ariosto), 3:75b
  Poème du Quinquina, 3:95b
  Relation d'un voyage de Paris en Limousin (Account of a Journey from Paris to Limousin), 3:75b
  Taine's thesis on, 7:1449a
  Vigny compared to, 5:455b
La Mettrie, Julien Offroy de, Sade and, 4:635b
"La Rochefoucauld." *See* Sainte-Beuve, Charles-Augustin
La Rochefoucauld, Andrée, duchesse de, 3:53b, 54a
La Rochefoucauld, François VI, duc de, **3:51a–71b**
  Apologie, 3:57a, 58b, 64b, 67a
  Mémoires, 3:57a, 57b, 58a, 63a–64a
    on Anne-Geneviève, 3:59a
    on Condé-Châtillon affair, 3:61b
  Portrait de La Rochefoucauld par lui-même, 3:62b–63a, 64b
  Portrait du Cardinal de Retz, 3:63a
  Réflexions diverses, 3:67a–68a
  Réflexions ou sentences et maximes morales, 3:52a–53b, 64a–67a, 263b
    French classicism and, 3:273b
    imitations of, 3:52b–53a
    on moral judgments, 3:58b
    on rulers, 3:60a-b
  Yourcenar and, 12:2538b
La Sablière, Madame de. *See* Hessein, Marguerite
La Sale, Antoine de, *Cent nouvelles nouvelles* and, 2:945b
La Tour, Maurice Quentin de, in Goncourts' *L'Art du dix-huitième siècle*, 7:1397a
La Vergne, Marie-Madeleine Pioche de, on La Rochefoucauld's *Maximes*, 3:52b

Là-bas. See Huysmans, Joris Karl

Là-haut. See Huysmans, Joris Karl

Laberinto. See Jiménez, Juan Ramón

Labiche, Eugène, 7:1921b

    La cagnotte (The Money Pool), 7:1923a

    Le voyage de M. Perrichon (Perrichon's Journey), 7:1923a

    Un chapeau de paille d'Italie (An Italian Straw Hat), 7:1922b

Labor, manual, Aquinas on, 1:413a-b

Labor movement

    Iceland, in Laxness' novels, 12:2465a-b, 2466a, 2469b–2470a, 2472a-b

    Zola's *Germinal*, 7:1529a–1530b

Labriola, Antonio

    Croce and, 8:312b, 314b, 315a

    In memoria del "Manifesto dei communisti" (In Memory of the *Communist Manifesto*), 8:314b

Labyrinthe du monde, Le (The Labyrinth of the World). *See* Yourcenar, Marguerite

"*Lac, Le.*" *See* Lamartine, Alphonse de

Lacan, Jacques, Artaud's condemnation of, 11:1979b

"Lace self-abolishes . . ." *See* Mallarmé, Stéphane, "Une dentelle s'abolit . . ."

Lacerba

    Marinetti and, 9:806a

    Ungaretti's poetry in, 10:1456a

Lachaud, Louise Ancelot, Vigny's letters to, 5:480a

Lachelier, Jules, Bergson and, 8:46b

Lachmann, Eduard, Hölderlin and, 5:143a

Lacis, Asja, Benjamin and, 11:1721b

Laclos, Pierre-Ambroise-François Choderlos de, 4:393a–394a, **400a–405a**, 417a–418b

    Giraudoux and, 9:1060a

    Les liaisons dangereuses (Dangerous Acquaintances), 4:393a–394a, 400b–405a, 416a

    compared to Sade's *Philosophy in the Bedroom*, 4:634a

"*Laconic.*" *See* Elytis, Odysseus, *Exi kai mia tipsis yia ton ourano (Six and One Remorses for the Sky)*, "Lakonikon"

Ladies' Battle, The. See Scribe, Eugène, *Bataille des dames*

Ladies' Delight. See Zola, Émile, *u bonheur des dames*

"*Ladomir.*" *See* Khlebnikov, Velimir

Lady of the Camelias, The. See Dumas fils, Alexandre, *La dame aux camélias*

Lady with the Dagger, The. *See* Schnitzler, Arthur, "Die Frau mit dem Dolche"

"Lady with a Dog, The." *See* Chekhov, Anton, "Dama s sobachkoy"

Lady of the Fountain, The. See Mabinogion: Gereint and Owein

Lady from the Sea, The. See Ibsen, Henrik

Lady Godiva. See Moravia, Alberto, *Un'Altra vita*

Lady Inger of Østraat. See Ibsen, Henrik

Lady Johanna Gray. See Wieland, Christoph Martin

"Lady Macbeth of the Mtsensk District." *See* Leskov, Nikolai, "Ledi Makbet Mtsenskogo uezda"

"Lady of the Manor, The." *See* Chekhov, Anton, "Barynya"

Lady of Tears, The. *See* Ady, Endre, "A könnyek asszonya"

Laforet, Carmen, Baroja influences, 9:613a

Laforgue, Jules, **7:1883a–1908b**

    Derniers vers (Last Poems), 7:1896b, 1898a–1906a

    Des fleurs de bonne volonté (Flowers of Good Will), 7:1897a

    "Dimanches" ("Sundays"), 7:1899b–1901a, 1904a, 1904b, 1905b

    Gide influenced by, 8:496a

    "Hunting Horn" and, 9:894b

    Le concile féerique (The Fairy Council), 7:1897a

    "Le mystère des trois cors" ("The Mystery of Three Horns"), 7:1899b

    "Le sanglot de la terre" ("The Earth's Sob"), 7:1884b

    "Légende" ("Legend"), 7:1902b–1903a

    Les complaintes (Street Ballads), 7:1885a-b, 1895a, 1896b

        "Autre complainte de Lord Pierrot" ("Another Lament of Lord Pierrot"), 7:1890a–1891a

Laforgue, Jules (*cont.*)
   Les complaintes (Street Ballads) (*cont.*)
      "Complainte de l'automne monotone"
        ("Lament of Monotonous Autumn"),
        7:1888a–1889b, 1893a
      "Complainte de l'orgue de Barbarie"
        ("Lament of the Hurdy-Gurdy"), 7:1896a
      "Complainte des pianos qu'on entend
        dans les quartiers aisés" ("The Lament
        of the Pianos You Hear in Rich
        Neighborhoods"), 7:1885b–1888a,
        1889a-b, 1892b, 1900a, 1901a
      "Complainte du pauvre chevalier-errant"
        ("Lament of the Poor Knight Errant"),
        7:1893b–1895a
      "Complainte du roi de Thulé" ("The
        Ballad of the King of Thule"),
        7:1889b–1890a, 1892b, 1893a
      "Lament of Nostalgia for the Prehistoric,"
        7:1892b–1893a, 1896b
    "L'Hiver qui vient" ("The Coming of
      Winter"), 7:1898a–1899b, 1902b, 1903a,
      1904b, 1905b
   *L'Imitation de Notre-Dame la Lune selon
      Jules Laforgue* (*The Imitation of Our
      Lady the Moon According to Jules
      Laforgue*), 7:1896b, 1897a, 1897b
   Mélanges posthumes, 7:1891b, 1892a
   "Moon Solo," 7:1902a, 1904a, 1904b, 1905b
   Moralités légendaires (*Moral Tales*),
      7:1906b–1907a
   "Pétition" ("Petition"), 7:1901a-b, 1903b,
      1905b
   Pierrot fumiste (*Pierrot the Dabbler*),
      7:1891a-b
   Rimbaud and, 7:1787a
   Seferis and, 12:2258a
   "Simple agonie" ("Simple Death Throes"),
      7:1901b–1902a
Laforgue, Leah, 7:1896b, 1897a
"Lagarto viejo, El." *See* García Lorca, Federico
Lagercrantz, Olof, Ekelöf and, 12:2637a, 2637b
Lagerkvist, Pär, **10:1677a–1702b**, 11:2203
   Aftonland (*Evening Land*), 10:1681a,
      1697b–1698a
   Ahasverus död (*The Death of Ahasuerus*),
      10:1697b, 1699a–1700a

Ångest (Anguish), 10:1684b, 1688a, 1697b
Barabbas, 10:1688a, 1695b–1697b
Bödeln (*The Hangman*), 10:1680b, 1687b,
   1690a–1691a, 1699b
"Bröllopsfesten" (The Marriage Feast),
   10:1689a-b
De vises sten (The Philosopher's Stone),
   10:1693a-b
Den befriade människan (The Liberated
   Man), 10:1692b–1693a
Den knutna näven (The Clenched Fist),
   10:1691b–1692a, 16977a-b
Den langa resan (The Long Journey),
   10:1684b
Den lyckliges väg (*The Way of the Happy
   Man*), 10:1680b, 1686b
Den osynlige (The Invisible One),
   10:1686b–1687a, 1688a
Det besegrade livet (The Conquered Life),
   10:1688a-b, 1690a, 1693a
Det eviga leendet (*The Eternal Smile*),
   10:1686a-b, 1688a, 1699b
Det heliga landet (*The Holy Land*),
   10:1697b, 1700b–1701a
"Det lilla fälttåget" ("The Children's
   Campaign"), 10:1692b
"Det märkvädiga landet" ("The Strange
   Country"), 10:1692b
Dvärgen (*The Dwarf*), 10:1687b,
   1693b–1695b
"Far och jag" (Father and I), 10:1681a-b
Gäst hos verkligheten (*Guest of Reality*),
   10:1680a, 1680b, 1681b, 1687b
Genius (Genius), 10:1691a
Han som fick leva om sitt liv (*The Man Who
   Lived His Life Over*), 10:1680b, 1689a
Hemmet och stjärnan (The Home and the
   Star), 10:1691a
Himlens hemlighet (The Secret of Heaven),
   10:1685a-b
Hjärtats sånger (*Songs of the Heart*),
   10:1688a
I den tiden (In That Time), 10:1692b
Järn och människor (Iron and Men),
   10:1683b–1684a
Kämpande ande (Struggling Spirit),
   10:1689a-b

Kaos (Chaos), 10:1684b, 1685a

Konungen (The King), 10:1689b–1690a

Låt människan leva (*Let Man Live*), 10:1693a-b, 1699b

Mannen utan själ (*The Man Without a Soul*), 10:1691a-b

Människor (People), 10:1682b

Mariamne (*Herod and Mariamne*), 10:1697b–1698a, 1701a-b

Midsommardröm i fattighuset (*Midsummer Dream in the Workhouse*), 10:1693a

Modern teater (*Modern Theater*), 10:1684b–1685a

"Morgonen" (The Morning), 10:1680b–1681a

Motiv (Motives), 10:1683b

Onda sagor (*Evil Tales*), 10:1681a-b, 1687b

Ordkonst och bildkonst (Word Art and Pictorial Art), 10:1682b–1683b

Pilgrim på havet (*Pilgrim at Sea*), 10:1697b, 1700a-b

Sang och strid (Song and Battle), 10:1691a

Seger i mörker (Victory in the Dark), 10:1691a-b

Sibyllan (*The Sibyl*), 10:1677b, 1681a, 1688a, 1698b–1699a

Sista mänskan (The Last Man), 10:1685a

Teater. Den svåra stunden (The Difficult Hour), 10:1685a

Två sagor om livet (The Tales About Life), 10:1682b

Vid lägereld (Beside the Watch-Fire), 10:1689b

Lagerlöf, Selma
Nils Holgerssons underbara resa (*The Wonderful Adventures of Nils*), Milosz and, 13:2929a
Yourcenar on, 12:253a

Lägg undan solen. See Johnson, Eyvind

Lägga patience. See Ekelöf, Gunnar

Lagut, Irène, 9:896b

Lais, Matter of Britain and, 1:148b–149a

Lais, Le. See Villon, François, *The Legacy*

"Lait de la mort, Le." *See* Yourcenar, Marguerite, *Nouvelles orientales*

Laius complex, in D'Annunzio's *The Intruder*, 8:182b–183b

Lake Stechlin. *See* Fontane, Theodor, *Der Stechlin*

"Lake Zurich." *See* Klopstock, Friedrich Gottlieb

"Lakonikon." *See* Elytis, Odysseus, *Exi kai mia tipsis yia ton ourano*

Lamartine, Alphonse de
Chateaubriand and, 5:139b–140a
Dumas and, 6:725a
Giraudoux and, 9:1060a
Histoire des Girondins, 6:725a
Hugo and, 6:694b, 705a
"La mort de Socrate" (The Death of Socrates), Vigny's "La flûte" and, 5:484b
"Le lac," Apollinaire's "The Song of the Unloved Lover" and, 9:890b
Leconte de Lisle and, 6:1267b
Lermontov and, 6:1199a
Marya Volkonsky and, 7:1474b
Méditations poétiques, 6:694b
Musset and, 6:1002b–1003a, 1025b, 1031a
Vigny and, 5:447a, 461a, 479a

Lambert, Johann Heinrich, Novalis and, 5:216a

Lamennais, Félicité Robert de, 3:317b–318a
on Manzoni's Catholicism, 5:370b
Paroles d'un croyant (*Words of a Believer*), 6:824a
Mickiewicz's *Books* and, 5:624b
Sand and, 6:824a
Vigny and, 5:463b, 464a, 464b

Lament. See Complaint

Lament for Adonis. See Bion

Lament for Bion. See Moschus

Lament for Damon. See Milton, John, *Epitaphium Damonis*

Lament for Daphnis. See Theocritus

Lament of the Dead Shakespeare Among the Dead Congregation in Church Because There Is No God. See Richter, Jean Paul, "Des toten Shakespear's Klage unter den toten Zuhörern in der Kirche, das kein Gott sei"

Lament for the Death of a Bullfighter. See García Lorca, Federico, *Llanto por Ignacio Sánches Mejías*

"Lament of the Hurdy-Gurdy." *See* Laforgue, Jules, *Les complaintes* (*Street Ballads*), "Complainte de l'orgue de Barbarie"

"Lament of Monotonous Autumn." *See* Laforgue, Jules, *Les complaintes* (*Street Ballads*), "Complainte de l'automne monotone"

"Lament of Nostalgia for the Prehistoric." *See* Laforgue, Jules, *Les complaintes*

"Lament of the Pianos You Hear in Rich Neighborhoods, The." *See* Laforgue, Jules, *Les complaintes* (*Street Ballads*), "Complainte des pianos qu'on entend dans les quartiers aisés"

"Lament of the Poor Knight Errant." *See* Laforgue, Jules, *Les complaintes* (*Street Ballads*), "Complainte du pauvre chevalier-errant"

"Lament for the South." *See* Quasimodo, Salvatore, "Lamento per il Sud"

Lament of the Strikers. *See* Aragon, Louis, "Complainte des chômeurs"

"Lamentation." *See* Petrarch, "Querulus"

Lamentation poetry
  Carducci, 7:1505b–1506a
  Wolfram, 1:282a-b

"Lamento per il Sud." *See* Quasimodo, Salvatore

Laments of a Man of Sorrow, The. *See* Kosztolányi, Dezső, *A bús férfi panaszai*

Laments of a Small Child, The. *See* Kosztolányi, Dezső, *A szegény kisgyermek panaszai*

Lamp imagery, in poetry of Pascoli, 7:1835b–1836a

Lamp of Marvels, The. See Valle-Inclán, Ramón del, *La lámpara maravillosa*

Lampadaridou-Pothou, Maria, 13:2975a-b, 2976a

Lámpara maravillosa, La. See Valle-Inclán, Ramón del

Lampe d'Aladin, La. See Cocteau, Jean

Lampe dans l'horloge. See Breton, André

Lampedusa, Giulio Fabrizio di (great-grandfather), accomplishments of, 11:2009b

Lampedusa, Giuseppe Tomasi di, **11:2009a–2034b**
  "Lezioni su Stendhal," 11:2011b, 2020b–2021a
  The Leopard (*Il gattopardo*), 11:2011a-b, 13:3145a
    Concetta compared to Manzoni's Lucia, 5:382b
    Greuze's painting and, 11:2026b–2032a
    initial rejection of, 11:2010b
    publication of, 11:2010b–2011a
    Stendhal's influence on, 11:2020b–2026b
    symbolism of, 11:2011b–2020b
    time and, 11:2009a
    Vittorini's reaction to, 12:2733b
  Two Stories and a Memory (*Racconti*)
    "Il mattino di un mezzadro" ("The Blind Kittens"), 11:2032b
    "La gioia e la legge" ("Joy and the Law"), 11:2032a-b
    "Places of My Infancy" ("I luoghi della mia prima infanzia"), 11:2009b–2010a
    "The Professor and the Siren" ("Lighea"), 11:2010a-b, 2019b, 2032b–2033a

Lancelot. See Chrétien de Troyes

"Land of Exile." *See* Pavese, Cesare, *Notte di festa*, "Terra d'esilio"

Land, Friz, Schnitzler and, 8:93a

Land of Many Names, The. See Čapek, Josef, *Země mnoha jmen*

Land That Is Not, The. *See* Södergran, Edith, *Landet som icke är*

Land of Traitors. *See* Moberg, Vilhelm, *Förrädarland*

Land of Ulro, The. See Milosz, Czeslaw

Land of Upside Down, The. See Tieck, Ludwig, *Die verkehrte Welt*

"Land-of-the-Freeze, The." *See* Ekelöf, Gunnar

Landarzt, Ein. See Kafka, Franz, *The Country Doctor*

Landauer, Christian, Hölderlin and, 5:159b–160a

Landet som ickel är. See Södergran, Edith

"Landlady, The." *See* Dostoevsky, Feodor

Landnámabók (*Book of Settlements*), 1:380a, 384a, 389a
  Sturlubók and, 1:393a, 396b, 399a

Landscape of Responses. *See* Butor, Michel, *Paysage de répons*

"Landskap i solnedgång" ("Landscape in Sunset"). *See* Södergran, Edith

Landstrykere. See Hamsun, Knut

Lanfranc of Bec, 1:406a

Lang, Fritz, 8:528a
  M, 7:1748a
  Metropolis, 7:1748a
  Strindberg and, 7:1748a

Lang, Josef B., 9:838b–839a

Langage, Le. See Vendryès, Joseph

Lange, Friedrich
  Geschichte des Materialismus . . . (*History of Materialism*), 7:1654a
  Nietzsche and, 7:1654a-b

Lange, Samuel Gotthold
  Klopstock and, 4:532a
  Lessing and, 4:542b

Langen, Albert
  Wedekind and, 8:257b, 270a
  in *Karl Hetmann*, 8:263a

Langer, Jiří (Georg), Kafka and, 9:1153a

Långt frå landsvägen. See Moberg, Vilhelm

Language
  Arp and, 10:1365b–1366a, 1372a–1373b
  Artaud's theories of, 11:1982b–1983b
  Augustine on, 1:26a-b, 42b, 45b–46a
  Barthes and, 13:3082a–3083b
    systems of in fashion magazine, 13:3087a–3088a
  Benjamin and, 11:1705a, 1706b–1707a
  Bergson on, 8:56b–57b, 11:2244a
  Breton's theories of, 11:1952a–1953a, 1953a-b, 1954b–1955a, 1956b
  Canetti and, 12:2616a–2617a, 2617b–2618a
  Cela and, 13:3117b–3118a
  Céline's use of slang, 11:1865a–1866a
  as constructor, in Valéry's *Eupalinos*, 8:585b–586a
  creation of
    Herder's theory, 4:648b–649a
    Whitman on, 4:655b–656a
  Croce on, 8:317a-b, 318a
  in Dinesen, 10:1301a-b
  Elytis' insight into, 13:2964b–2965a
  Foucault and, 13:3353a–3354b
  Hofmannsthal's views on, 9:691b–692a
  Johnson and, 12:2363a, 2368a, 2375b, 2377b, 2378b
  Kosztolányi's theory of, 10:1240b–1241b
  metaphoric vs. metonymic, Jakobson on, 9:944b
  Milosz on, 13:2948a–2952a
  Moravia's concept of, 12:2688a–2689a
  national character and, Unamuno on, 8:289a
  Nietzsche's view of, 7:1678a
  Olesha on, 11:2243b–2244a
  in Pavese's works, 12:2765a, 2771b
  Pessoa's use of, 10:1481b–1482a
  poetry and, 10:1524b
  Queneau on, 12:2516b–2517a, 2523a–2524a, 2525b–2526a
  Rimbaud's view of, 7:1787b, 1796a–1797b, 1798b–1800b, 1803b–1805b, 1808a–1809a, 1809a-b, 1811b–1802a, 1813b–1815a, 1815b–1816a
  in Rousseau, 4:470a–471a
  Sarraute and, 12:2342b–2343a, 2347a-b, 2349b–2350a, 2350b, 2356b
  Schopenhauer on music as, 5:413a
  as seducer, in Valéry's "Sketch of a Serpent," 8:582b–583a
  speech patterns, Canetti and, 12:2616b–2617a
  spoken, Pérez Galdós' stylistic use of, 7:1598b, 1608b–1609a, 1612b–1613a
  symbolist, Maeterlinck and, 8:123b–124a, 134a-b
  transrational, Khlebnikov's idea of, 10:1346a–1348a
  Válery's theory of, 8:574b–575b, 581b–582a, 587a-b
  see also Idiomatic language; Syntax

Language about language. *See* Epistemological writings

Language as the Bulwark of Freedom. *See* Böll, Heinrich, "Die Sprache als Hort der Freiheit"

"Language of Poetry, The." *See* Snorri Sturluson, *Edda*

Language and Soul. *See* Kosztolányi, Dezső, *Nyelv és lélek*

Languages in Contemporary Europe. *See* Meillet, Antoine, *Les languages dans l'Europe nouvelle*

"Langueur." *See* Verlaine, Paul

Lanzelet. See Ulrich von Zatzikhoven

Lao-tzu, *Tao-te Ching*, Ekelöf and, 12:2641a, 2642a

Laokoon, oder über die Grenzen der Malerie und Poesie (*Laocoon; or, The Boundaries Between Painting and Poetry*). *See* Lessing, Gotthold Ephraim

Laporte, Pierre de, 3:57b

Lapp, John C., *The Esthetics of Negligence*, 3:75b–76a

Larbaud, Valery, Perse and, 10:1434a

Large Greek Encyclopedia, The. *See* Ritsos, Yannis, *Meghali elliniki egkyklopedhia*

Lark, The. See Anouilh, Jean

Larra, Mariano José de, Azorín's approval of, 9:644b

"Larron, Le." *See* Apollinaire, Guillaume, *Alcools*

Larsen, Finn Stein, Södergran and, 11:1804a

Lasaulx, Ernst von, Burckhardt and, 6:1243b

"Lasca, Il." *See* Grazzini, Antonfrancesco

Lásky hra osudná. See Čapek, Karel, and Josef Čapek

Last Aldini, The. See Sand, George, *La dernière Aldini*

Last of Chéri, The. See Colette, *La fin de Chéri*

Last Day of a Condemned Man, The. See Hugo, Victor, *Le dernier jour d'un condamné*

"Last Day, The." *See* Seferis, George, *Imerologio katastromatos* (*Logbook I*), "I teleftaia mera"

Last Days of the Imperial Regime, The. *See* Blok, Alexander, *Poslednie dni imperatorskoi vlasti*

Last Days, The. *See* Queneau, Raymond, *Les derniers jours*

Last Judgment. *See* Judgment Day

Last Judgment, The. See Michelangelo

Last Letter Home, The. See Moberg, Vilhelm

"Last Love of Prince Genji, The." *See* Yourcenar, Marguerite, *Nouvelles orientales*

Last Love, The. See Sand, George, *Le dernier amour*

Last Masks. *See* Schnitzler, Arthur, "Die Letzten Masken"

Last May, The. *See* Kundera, Milan, *Poslední máj*

Last One Hundred Years Before Man, The. *See* Ritsos, Yannis, *I teleftea pro Anthropou ekatontaetia*

Last Ones, The. *See* Gorky, Maxim, *Poslednye*

Last Ones, The. See Rilke, Rainer Maria, *Die Letzten*

Last Poems. See Laforgue, Jules, *Derniers vers*

Last Promenade, The. *See* Pascoli, Giovanni, *Myricae* (Tamarisks), "L'Ultima passeggiata"

Last Romantics, The. *See* Baroja, Pío, *Los últimos románticos*

"Last Rose, The." *See* Akhmatova, Anna, "Posledniaia roza"

Last Rose, The. See Akhmatova, Anna, *Posledniaia roza*

Last Ships, The. *See* Ady, Endre, "Az utolsó hajók"

Last Smile, The. *See* Ady, Endre, "Az utolsó mosoly"

Last Son of Freedom, The. See Lermontov, Mikhail Yurievich, *Posledny syn volnosti*

"Last Song of Sappho, The." *See* Leopardi, Giacomo

"Last Stop, The." *See* Seferis, George, *Imerologio katastromatos B*

Last Summer, The. See Pasternak, Boris

Last Tales. See Dinesen, Isak

Last Temptation of Christ, The. See Kazantzakis, Nikos, *O teleftaíos pirasmós*

"Last Voyage, The." *See* Pascoli, Giovanni, *Poemi conviviali* (*Convivial Poems*), "L'Ultimo viaggio"

"Last Word on Robbe-Grillet, The?" *See* Barthes, Roland

Last Year at Marienbad. See Robbe-Grillet, Alain

"Last Year, The." *See* Lozinsky, Mikhail, "To byl poslednii god"

Låt människan leva. See Lagerkvist, Pär
Late Loves. *See* Baroja, Pío, *Los amores
    tardíos*
Late Mattia Pascal, The. See Pirandello, Luigi
Late Roman Art Industry, The. *See* Riegl,
    Alois, *Spätrömische Kunstindustrie*
Late Roses. *See* Storm, Theodor, *Späte Rosen*
"Late-Blooming Flowers." *See* Chekhov, Anton,
    "Tsvety zapozdalye"
Latin arcélek. See Kosztolányi, Dezső
Latin Averroists. *See* Averroists
Latin drama. *See* Classical literature; Drama,
    medieval
Latin language
    Camoëns' *The Lusiads* and, 2:766a
    Claudel and, 8:491b
    grammar parodied
        in medieval satire, 1:371b
        in "Utar contra vitia carmine rebelli,"
            1:352a
    Montaigne and, 2:770a, 784a
Latin literature. *See* Classical literature
Latini, Brunetto, Dante and, 1:431b
Latomus, Jacob, Erasmus and, 2:585a
Latour (valet of Sade), scandalous behavior of,
    4:616a-b
Laube, Heinrich, 7:1925b
    Grillparzer championed by, 5:430b
Laud, 1:465b
Lauda Sion salvatorem (Laud, O Sion, O my
    salvation), 1:416a
Laudanum, Artaud's addiction to, 11:1962a,
    1974b, 1979a
Laude (hymns of praise), D'Annunzio and,
    8:193a
*Laudi del cielo del mare della terra e degli
    eroi. See* D'Annunzio, Gabriele
Laughable Loves. See Kundera, Milan
Laughing Man, The. See Hugo, Victor,
    L'Homme qui rit
Laughter
    Bergson's view of, 8:55a–56a
    Kundera and, 13:3406b–3407a, 3410a
    see also Comedy
Laughter. See Bergson, Henri, *Le rire*
Laune des Verliebten. See Goethe, Johann
    Wolfgang

"Laura, lettere" ("Laura, Letters"). *See* Foscolo,
    Ugo
Laura (Petrarchan character), 2:476b, 485b,
    493a, 495a–499b, 504b
"Laurea Occidens." *See* Petrarch
Laureled Septeria. *See* Ritsos, Yannis, *Septiria
    kai dhafniforia*
Laurencin, Marie, 9:882a, 894a, 894b
"Laurette; or, The Red Seal" ("Laurette ou le
    cachet rouge"). *See* Vigny, Alfred Victor
    de, *The Military Condition*
Lauriers sont coupés, Les. See Dujardin,
    Édouard
Lausanne, Treaty of (1923), 13:2956a-b
Lausavísur, 1:378b
Lautréamont, Comte de
    Aragon and, 11:2064b
    Arp and, 10:1372b
    Breton on, 11:1950b
    Céline and, 11:1859b
    Chants de Maldoror (*Songs of Maldoror*),
        influenced by Mickiewicz, 5:620a-b
    Ghelderode and, 11:2113b
    Poésies, 11:1939b
    "poetry must be made by all," 11:1954b
    Rimbaud and, 7:1811a
Lavater, Johann Kaspar, 5:66b–67a
    Physiognomy, Chénier and, 4:698b
Lavorare stanca. See Pavese, Cesare
Lavoratore, Il (Italian Communist daily),
        Silone's editorship of, 12:2277b
Law
    Aymé's satire of, 12:2442a
    Goldoni and, 4:423b–424b
    Heine's legal studies, 5:491b–492a,
        492b–493a
    Hoffmann's legal studies, 5:265b–267a
    in Kafka's works, 9:1171a
    Leconte de Lisle's legal studies, 6:1247a,
        1248a
    see also Police
Law of nations, Vico's analysis of,
    3:301b–302a
Lawrence, D. H.
    Céline and, 11:1883a
    compared with Schnitzler, 8:113a
    Fantasia of the Unconscious, 5:185b

Lawrence, D. H. (*cont.*)
  Hesse and, 9:847b
  Schlegel and, 5:191b
  "The Ship of Death," Seferis' translation,
    12:2260a
  Verga and, 7:1543b–1544b, 1549b, 1553a
    translation of *Little Novels of Sicily*,
      7:1557b
    writings on, 7:1556a, 1562a
  Vittorini's translations, 12:2736a
Lawrence, St., in Prudentius' *Peristephanon*,
  1:12a-b
Lawyer Kraykowski's Dancer. *See* Gombrowicz,
  Witold, "Tancerz mecanasa
  Kraykowskiego"
Lawyers. *See* Legal system
Laxdœla saga, 1:382b, 388b–389a, 389b, 395a
Laxness, Halldór, **12:2457a–2478b**
  Atómstöðin (*The Atom Station*),
    12:2474b–2475a
  Barn náttúrunnar (Child of Nature),
    12:2457a
  Brekkukotsannáll (*The Fish Can Sing*),
    12:2475a
  Eldur í Kaupinhafn (Fire in Copenhagen),
    12:2473b
  Fegurð himinsins (The Beauty of the Skies),
    12:2472b
  Gerpla (*The Happy Warriors*), 12:2475a
    Fóstbrœðra saga and, 1:385b
  Guðsgjafaþula (A List of God's Gifts),
    12:2475a
  Gunnarsson and, 10:1417a-b, 1497a
  Heimsljós (*World Light*), 12:2475b
    Kraftbirtíngarhljómur guðdómsins,
      12:2472b–2473a
  Hið ljósa man (The Fair Maiden), 12:2473b
  Höll sumarlandsins (The Palace of the
    Summerland), 12:2472b
  Hús skáldsins (The Poet's House), 12:2472b
  Íslandsklukkan (Iceland's Bell),
    12:2473b–2474b
    literary style, 12:2474a-b
  Kaþólsk viðhorf (From a Catholic Point of
    View), 12:2457b
  Kristnihald undir Jökli (*Christianity at
    Glacier*), 12:2475a

Ljós heimsins (The Light of the World),
  12:2472b
Nokkrar sögur (A Few Stories), 12:2457b
Paradísarheimt (*Paradise Reclaimed*),
  12:2475a
Rauða Kverið (The Red Booklet), 12:2457b
rhymed ballads, 12:2467a-b, 2473b
Salka Valka, 12:2462a–2466b
  Annar heimur (Another World), 12:2464a
  Fuglinn í fjörunni (The Bird on the
    Beach), 12:2462a, 2464b–2465b
  Gunnarsson and, 10:1516a
  seagull, 12:2464b, 2466b
  Þú vínviður hreini (O Thou Pure Vine),
    12:2462a
Sjálfstætt fólk (*Independent People*),
  12:2466b–2472b, 2475b
  "Dry Spell," 12:2468a-b
  exploitation theme, 12:2467b–2468a
  "The Sea Cow," 12:2471a–2472a
Undir Helgahnúk (By the Holy Mountain),
  12:2457b
Vefarinn mikli frákasmir (The Great Weaver
  from Kashmir), 12:2457b–2462a, 2466a
  quest element, 12:2459a-b
  Ylfing family, 12:2459b–2460a
*Lay of the Love and Death of the Cornet
  Christoph Rilke, The. See* Rilke, Rainer
  Maria, *Die Weise von Liebe und Tod
  des Cornets Christoph Rilke*
Lay of the Nibelungs, The. See Hebbel,
  Friedrich
"Lázár a palota elött." *See* Ady, Endre
Lazarillo de Tormes
  Cela and, 13:3111b–3112a
  Cervantes and, 2:829b
  as first picaresque novel, 2:950b
  Lesage's *Gil Blas* and, 3:329a
  point of view in, 2:950b–951a
Lazarus. See Pirandello, Luigi, *Lazzaro*
Lazarus and Dives, parable of, in Villon's
  Testament, 2:565b
Lazarus in Front of the Palace. *See* Ady,
  Endre, "Lázár a palota elött"
Lazerge, François. *See* Montherlant, Henry de
Lazy Man's Dreams. *See* Moravia, Alberto, *I
  sogni del pigro*

Lazzaro. See Pirandello, Luigi

Le Bon, Gustave, treatment of the masses, 7:1407a

Le Carré, John, *Tinker, Tailor, Soldier, Spy,* 13:3029a

Le Poittevin, Alfred, 7:1759b, 1761b

Le Roy, Édouard, Bergson and, 8:64b

Le Roy, Grégoire, Maeterlinck and, 8:121a–122b

Le Tellier, Michel, funeral oration on by Bossuet, 3:166a

Lea och Rakel. See Moberg, Vilhelm

Leadbeater, C. W., *Thought-Forms,* Pirandello and, 8:396b

Leader, The. See Ionesco, Eugène, *Le maître*

Leading the Dead. *See* Ady, Endre, *A halottak élén*

"Leaf of the Poplar." *See* Seferis, George, "To fillo tis lefkas"

"Leaf-Diviner, The." *See* Elytis, Odysseus, *Ta eterothale*

League of Nations
   Bergson and, 8:46a
   Céline on, 11:1861a, 1862b
   Commission for Intellectual Cooperation, Valéry and, 8:584a

League of Youth, The. See Ibsen, Henrik

Leah and Rachel. *See* Moberg, Vilhelm, *Lea och Rakel*

Leander. *See* Hero and Leander

Learned Ladies, The. See Molière, *Les femmes savantes*

Learning to Walk. See Ionesco, Eugène, *Apprendre à marcher*

Leaves from the Knapsack. *See* Frisch, Max, *Blätter aus dem Brotsack*

"Lebediia budushchego." *See* Khlebnikov, Velimir

Lebedinyi stan. See Tsvetaeva, Marina

Leben des Galilei. See Brecht, Bertolt, *Galileo*

Leben des Quintus Fixlein, aus fünfzehn Zettelkästen gezogen, Das. See Richter, Jean Paul

Leben des vergnügten Schulmeisterlein Maria Wutz in Auenthal, Das. See Richter, Jean Paul

Leben Eduards des Zweiten von England. See Brecht, Bertolt, *Edward II*

Leben eines Taugenichts. See Eichendorff, Joseph von

Leben Fibels, des Verfassers der Bienrodischen Fibel, Das. See Richter, Jean Paul

Leben Jesu kritisch bearbeitet, Das. See Strauss, David

Leben und Lieder. See Rilke, Rainer Maria

Leben und Tod der heiligen Genoveva. See Tieck, Ludwig

Lebendige Stunden. See Schnitzler, Arthur

Lebens-Ansichten des Katers Murr nebst fragmentarischer Biographie des Kapellmeisters Johannes Kreisler in zufälligen Makulaturblättern. See Hoffmann, E. T. A.

Lebensphilosophie, in Musil's *The Man Without Qualities,* 9:941a-b, 945a

Lebey, Édouard, Valéry and, 8:572b

Leblanc, Georgette
   Maeterlinck and, 8:132b–133b, 135a, 136a–137b, 139a-b, 140a–141a
   Souvenirs (1895–1918) (Souvenirs: My Life with Maeterlinck), 8:132b–133b, 136b–137a, 140a

Lebreton, Charles, Leopardi's letter to, 5:550a

Lebrun, "Pindare"
   Chénier's friendship with, 4:696a-b, 697b
   "De la nature" ("On Nature"), Chénier's advice on, 4:696a-b

Lecanda, Juan José de, Unamuno and, 8:290b, 292a

Leçon de choses. See Simon, Claude

Leçon, La. See Ionesco, Eugène

Leconte de Lisle, Charles Marie, **6:1245a–1273b**
   "Architecture," 6:1249b
   "Cozza et Borgia," 6:1257b–1258a
   Dernier poèmes, 6:1252a
   Electra myth and, 12:2549a
   "Hélène," 6:1249b
   "Hypatie," 6:1255b
   "Hypatie et Cyrille," 6:1255b–1256a
   influence of, 7:1640b
   "Khirôn," 6:1253b

Leconte de Lisle, Charles Marie (*cont.*)
  "La mort de Valmiki," 6:1253b
  "La mort du moine," 6:1253b, 1257b
  "La Nazaréen," 6:1258a
  "La recherche de Dieu" (The Search for
    God), 6:1250a
  "La vipère," 6:1261a
  "Le manchy," 6:1261b
  "Le voile d'Isis" (The Veil of Isis), 6:1250a
  "Les ascètes" (The Hermits), 6:1250b
  "Les épis," 6:1249b
  "Les sandales d'Empédocle" (The Sandals of
    Empedocles), 6:1250a
  Mallarmé and, 8:571b
  Mandelshtam's "The Word and Culture"
    and, 10:1641a-b
  "Niobé," 6:1255b
  Poèmes antiques, 6:1242a
  Poèmes barbares, 6:1242a
  Poèmes et poèsies, 6:1242a
  Poèmes tragiques, 6:1242a
  poetry of, 7:1621a
  "Qaïn," 6:1253b, 1267b–1268b
  soirees of, 7:1620b
  "Solvet seclum," 6:1263b, 1268b
  "Ultra coelos" (Beyond the Stars), 6:1266a
Lecoulteux, Fanny, Chénier's love for,
    4:711b–713a
Lecoulteux, Laurent (husband)
  Chénier's friendship with, 4:712a
  death by guillotine, 4:712b
Lecouvreur, Adrienne, Voltaire and, 4:371b,
    372b
Lecturas españolas. See Azorín
Lectures on Dramatic Art. See Schlegel,
    August Wilhelm
*Lectures on the History of Ancient and
    Modern Literature*. See Schlegel,
    Friedrich von
Lectures pour une ombre. See Giraudoux, Jean
Leda. See Diósi, Adél
"Léda ajkai között." See Ady, Endre
Leda in the Garden. See Ady, Endre, "Léda a
    kertben"
Leda Is Leaving for Paris. See Ady, Endre,
    "Léda Párisba készül"
"Léda a kertben." See Ady, Endre

"Léda Párisba készül." *See* Ady, Endre
Leda senz cigno, La (Leda Without the Swan).
    See D'Annunzio, Gabriele
"Lédával a Tavaszban." *See* Ady, Endre
Ledesma, Navarro, on Valle-Inclán, 8:333b
"Ledi Makbet Mtsenskogo uezda." *See* Leskov,
    Nikolai
Ledianoi, Leonid, *Zapiski chudaka* (Notes of
    an Eccentric), 9:905a
Lee, Leah. See Laforgue, Leah
LEF (Levyi Front Isskustva), 11:1837a-b,
    1838a
  Mayakovsky and, 11:1847b
  Pasternak's involvement with, 10:1594a-b
Lefèvre, Jacques, Erasmus and, 2:582b
Lefranc, Abel, 2:701a
  compilation of Chénier's "Essay" by, 4:709b
Left- and Right-Bank Stroller, The. See
    Apollinaire, Guillaume, *Le flâneur des
    deux rives*
"Left-handed Craftsman, The." See Leskov,
    Nikolai, "Levsha"
Leg med Straa. See Gunnarsson, Gunnar,
    Kirken paa Bjerget (The Church on the
    Hill)
Legacy, The. See Schnitzler, Arthur, *Das
    Vermächtnis*; Villon, François
Legend
  Andrić and, 11:1774b–1775b
  in Middle Ages, 1:137a
  Welsh bards and, 1:141a
  see also Arthurian legend; Grail legend;
    Irish legends; Welsh legends
Legend, A. See Krleža, Miroslav, *Legenda*
Legend about the Rebellion, The. See Andrić,
    Ivo, "Legenda o pobuni"
Legenda. See Krleža, Miroslav
Legenda aurea, influence on Renaissance
    short fiction, 2:923a
"Legenda o pobuni." See Andrić, Ivo
Légende des siècles, La (The Legend of the
    Ages). See Hugo, Victor
"Légende" ("Legend"). See Laforgue, Jules
Légendes (Legends). See Strindberg, August
Legends and Chronicles of the Ages. See
    Hugo, Victor, *La légende des siècles*

Legends of Lovers; Point of Departure. See Anouilh, Jean, *Eurydice*

Legends of Saints. *See* Eça de Queiroz, José Maria, *Lendas de Santos*

Leger, Alexis. *See* Perse, Saint-John

Légitime défense. See Breton, André

Legouvé, Ernest, 7:1911a, 1915a, 1916a

Legrand, Gérard (joint author). *See* Breton, André

"Leguigon." *See* Baudelaire, Charles, "Unluck"

Leguillou, Jenny, Delacroix and, 5:533b–534a

Lehár, Franz, *Die lustige Witwe* (*The Merry Widow*), 7:1920b

Leibniz, Gottfried Wilhelm
  correspondence with Bossuet, 3:173b–174a
  Hölderlin and, 5:145a-b
  Machado and, 9:761b
  Novalis and, 5:210a, 216a
  optimist philosophy of, Voltaire's reaction to, 4:386b, 389b
  perspectivism, 9:1129a
  Schopenhauer's parody of, 5:413a-b

Leich, Walther and, 1:303a

Leiðarvísir ok borgaskipan. See Nikulás Bergthórsson

Leiden des jungen Werthers, Die. See Goethe, Johann Wolfgang von, *The Sorrows of Young Werther*

Leiden eines Knaben, Das. See Meyer, Conrad Ferdinand

Leipzig Literary Society, production of Wedekind's *Earth Spirit*, 8:258a

Leiret og hjulet. See Vesaas, Tarjei

Leiris, Michel, Butor and, 13:3305a

Lélia. See Sand, George

Lélio. See Berlioz, Hector

"Lelkek a pányván." *See* Ady, Endre

Lemaître, Jules, "Paul Verlaine et les poètes symbolistes et decadents" (Paul Verlaine and the Symbolist and Decadent Poets), 7:1639a-b

"Lemon Trees, The." *See* Montale, Eugenio, *Cuttlefish Bones*

Lena, La. See Ariosto, Lodovico

Lenau, Nikolaus
  "Einsamkeit" ("Solitude"), desolation of nature in, 5:420b
  weltschmerz of, 5:419b–420b

Lendas de Santos. See Eça de Queiroz, José Maria

Lenga lemosina, of troubadours, 1:162a

Lengefeld, Charlotte von, 5:30b

Lenin, Vladimir Ilyich
  on Dostoevsky, 7:1349a
  Goncharov and, 6:1061b
  Gorky and, 8:421a-b, 444a
    Mother, 8:418a
    The Confession, 8:421a
  Social Democratic Party and, 8:420a
  Valle-Inclán and, 8:337a

Lensing, Elise
  Hebbel and, 6:1093b, 1095a, 1095b, 1096a-b, 1097a
  correspondence with, 6:1094a, 1119b

"Lenz." *See* Büchner, Georg

Lenz, J. M. R., Büchner and, 6:1182b–1186b

Léo Burckart. See Nerval, Gérard de

Leo XIII, pope, *Aeterni patris*, 1:427b

Léocadia. See Anouilh, Jean, *Time Remembered*

León, Fray Luis de
  Azorín's literary criticism of, 9:645a
  Jiménez and, 9:998a

Leonardo da Vinci
  anecdotes by, 2:938b
  in Gautier's works, 6:1040b–1041a
  in Valéry's "The Introduction to the Method of Leonardo da Vinci," 8:573a, 584b

Leonce and Lena (*Leonce und Lena*). *See* Büchner, Georg

Leone Leoni. See Sand, George

Leoni, Barbara, D'Annunzio and, 8:183b–184a, 189a

Leonov, Leonid, conspiracy charges, 11:1912a

Leontiev, Konstantin, Mandelshtam and, 10:1640a

Leopard, The. See Lampedusa, Giuseppe Tomasi di

Leopardi, Adelaide, 5:542b–543a

Leopardi, Giacomo, **5:541a–567b**
  "All'Italia" ("To Italy"), 5:545b
  "Aspasia," 5:564b–565a
  Aspasia poems, 5:549b, 564b–565a
  Azorín's literary criticism of, 9:645a

A Hero of Our Times (*Geroy nashego vremeni*), 6:986b, 1066a, 1207a, 1209a, 1213b, 1217a, 1218a–1221a, 1222a

"Angel" ("An Angel"), 6:1200b

Arbenin, 6:1208

Aul Bastundzhi, 6:1203a-b

"Bela," 6:1217a, 1218b–1219a, 1220b

Bely and, 9:915a

"Borodino," 6:1196b, 1224a

"Boyarin Orsha" ("Boyar Orsha"), 6:1215a-b

Cherkesy (*The Circassians*), 6:1202b

"Demon" ("The Demon"), 6:1215b–1216a

"Duma" ("Meditation"), 6:1216b–1217a, 1220b

Dva brata (*Two Brothers*), 6:1208b–1209a, 1209b, 1210a

"Glyazhu na budushchnost s boyaznyu" ("With Fear I Gaze upon the Future"), 6:1216b

Goncharov and, 6:1064a

Hadji Abrek, 6:1203a-b, 1207a

Hero of Our Time, Dostoevsky and, 7:1353a

Ispantsy (*The Spaniards*), 6:1201a-b

Izmail-Bey, 6:1203a

"K S." ("To S."), 6:1200a

"Kavkaz" ("The Caucasus"), 6:1199a-b

"Kavkazetz" ("The Caucasian Veteran"), 6:1219a-b

Kavkazky plennik (*The Prisoner of the Caucasus*), 6:1202b

Korsar (*The Corsair*), 6:1203a

"Maksim Maksimych," 6:1219b, 1220b

Maskerad (*The Masquerade*), 6:1208a-b

Menschen und Leidenschaften (Men and Passions), 6:1201b–1202a

"Molitva" ("A Prayer"), 6:1213a

"Mongo," 6:1207b, 1214a

"Mtsyri" ("The Novice"), 6:1215a-b, 1216a

"Net, ya ne Bayron, ya drugoy" ("No, I'm Not Byron, I'm Another"), 6:1200a-b

"Pamyati A. I. Odoevskogo" ("Memories of A. I. Odoevsky"), 6:1217a

"Parus" ("The Sail"), 6:1204b

"Pesnya pro tsarya Ivana Vasilevicha" ("The Song of Czar Ivan Vasilevich, the Young Oprichnik Bodyguard , and the Bold Merchant Kalashnikov"), 6:1214a–1215a

Posledny syn volnosti (*The Last Son of Freedom*), 6:1203a

"Predskazanie" ("A Prophecy"), 6:1199b–1200a

Princess Ligovskaya (*Knyaginya Ligovskaya*), 6:1209a–1212b, 1217b

"Princess Mary" ("Knyazhna Meri"), 6:1213b, 1220a, 1220b

"Proshchay, nemytaya Rossiya" (Goodbye, unwashed Russia), 6:1222b–1223a

Sashka, 6:1198b, 1207b, 1214a

"Shtoss," 6:1222a-b

"Smert poeta" ("The Death of the Poet"), 6:1212b–1213a, 1215a, 1217b

"Son" ("A Dream"), 6:1223b

Stranny chelovek (*Strange Fellow*), 6:1202a-b

"Taman," 6:1219b–1220a, 1224a

"Tambovskaya kaznacheysha" ("The Tambov Cashier's Wife"), 6:1207b, 1214a

"The Fatalist," 6:1220a-b

"1830. Maya, 16 chisla" ("1830. May 16"), 6:1199b

Vadim, 6:1205a–1207a, 1209a, 1222b

"Vykhozhu odin ia na dorogu" ("I set out alone on the road"), Mandelshtam's "The Slate Ode" and, 10:1642a

"Ya k vam pishu" ("I Am Writing to You"), 6:1221b

"Zhurnal Pechorina predlisovie" ("Introduction to Pechorin's Journal"), 6:1219b

Leroux, Pierre, Sand and, 6:824a-b

Lerroux, Alejandro, Valle-Inclán and, 8:337a

Lesage, Alain-René, **3:317a–344b**

Arlequin colonel (*Colonel Arlequin*), 3:327a

"Au siècle des lumières" ("To the Age of Enlightenment"), 3:323a

Crispin, rival de son maître (*Crispin, His Master's Rival*), 3:317a, 320b–321a, 340a

Don César Ursin (imitation of Calderón de la Barca), 3:320b

Entretiens des cheminées de Madrid (*Conversations of Madrid's Chimneys*), 3:338a

Lesage, Alain-René (*cont.*)

Estevanille Gonzales, surnommé le garçon de bonne humeur (*The History of Vanillo Gonzalez, Surnamed the Merry Bachelor*), 3:341a

Gil Blas, 3:317a, 322b–323a, 327b, 328a–340a
  charges of plagiarism, 3:328b–329a
  classification of the novel, 3:329a-b
  final revision of, 3:342a
  interpolated tales in, 3:332a
  organization of, 3:328b, 330b–331a
  popularity of, 3:339a-b

La tontine, 3:326b, 338a

La valise trouvé (A Rediscovered Satchel), 3:341b–342a

Le bachelier de Salamanque (*The Bachelor of Salamanca*), 3:341a

Le diable boiteux (translated as *The Devil upon Two Sticks* and *The Devil on Two Crutches*), 3:320b, 323b–326a, 340a
  Mauriac's *Asmodée* and, 10:1326a
  new edition of, 3:338a
  reception of, 3:324b
  royal censor's *Note of approbation*, 3:325b
  translations of, 3:327a

Le point d'honneur (adaptation of Rojas), 3:320b

Les aventures de M. Robert Chevalier, dit de Beauchêne, capitaine de flibustiers (*The Adventures of M. Robert Chevalier, Call'd De Beauchêne, Captain of Privateers in New-France*), 3:340a-b

Les petits maîtres (*The Coxcombs*), 3:327a

Lettres galantes de Aristénète, 3:342a

Mélange amusant de saillies d'esprit et de traits historiques des plus frappants (An Entertaining Mixture of Witticisms and the Most Extraordinary Happenings), 3:342a

Théâtre espagnol (*Spanish Theater*), 3:320a

translations
  Avellaneda's *Nouvelle aventures de Don Quichotte de la Manche* (*New Adventures of Don Quixote de La Mancha*), 3:323a-b
  Guzman d'Alfarache, 3:340b

Lettres galantes d'Aristenète, 3:320a

Turcaret, 3:317a, 321a–322b, 340a

Une journée des parques (*A Day's Work of the Fates*), 3:341b

Lesbianism
  Colette's writings about, 9:621b–622a
  in Proust's *Remembrance of Things Past*, 8:558b–559a
  of Tsvetaeva, 11:1735a-b
  in Verlaine's works, 7:1626b
  see also Homosexuality

Leskov, Nikolai
  "Ledi Makbet Mtsenskogo uezda" ("Lady Macbeth of the Mtsensk District"), Zamyatin's "Rus" and, 10:1194b
  "Levsha" ("The Left-handed Craftsman"), Zamyatin's stage adaptation of, 10:1194a

"Lesnaia deva." *See* Khlebnikov, Velimir

Lessico famigliare. *See* Ginzburg, Natalia, Family Sayings

Lessing, Gotthold Ephraim, **5:437a–562b**

A Vademecum for Mr. Sam Gotth. Lange, 4:542b

Beiträge zur Historie und Aufnahme des Theaters (*Contributions to the History and Improvement of the Theater*), 4:543a

Berengarius Turonensis, 4:541a

Briefe, die neueste Literatur betreffend (*Letters Concerning Contemporary Literature*), 4:539b, 543a–545b
  on Wieland, 4:590b

Das Christentum der Vernunft (*The Christianity of Reason*), 4:561a

Der junge Gelehrte (*The Young Scholar*), 4:538a

Die Erziehung des Menschengeschlechts (*The Education of the Human Race*), 4:542a, 561a-b
  Richter and, 5:57a

Die Hamburgische Dramaturgie (*The Hamburg Dramaturgy*), 4:540b, 545a, 547a–549a, 558a, 7:1436b–1437a
  on Wieland, 4:597b

Die Juden (*The Jews*), 4:557b–558a

Emilia Galotti, 4:541a, 554b–557b

Goethe's *The Sorrows of Young Werther* and, 5:7a

Ernst und Falk, 4:542a

Fabeln (*Fables*), 4:539b

Faust, 4:544b, 549a

Grillparzer and, 5:417b, 423b, 443b

Ibsen and, 7:1436b

Kritische Briefe (*Critical Letters*), 4:542b

Laokoon, oder über die Grenzen der Malerie und Poesie (*Laocoon; or, The Boundaries Between Painting and Poetry*), 4:540a, 545b–546b

Lukács on, 10:1256b

Minna von Barnhelm, oder das Soldatenglück (*Minna von Barnhelm; or, The Soldier's Fortune*), 4:539a, 539b, 540a, 551b–554b

Lukács on, 10:1270b

Miss Sara Sampson, 4:539a, 549a–551b

Schiller's *Intrigue and Love* and, 5:33b

Nathan der Weise (*Nathan the Wise*), 4:542a, 557b–560b, 561a

Philotas, 4:539b

Pope ein Metaphysiker! (*Pope a Metaphysician!*), 4:543b

Rettungen des Horaz (*Rescuing Horace*), 4:543b

Rilke's "Archaic Torso of Apollo" and, 9:785b

Samuel Henzi, 4:558a

Schriften (*Works*), 4:542b

Theatralische Bibliothek (*Theatrical Library*), 4:543b

Lesson, The. See Ionesco, Eugène, *La leçon*

Lesueur, Jean Francois, Berlioz and, 6:775a-b, 776a, 781b

Let the Fires Die Out. See Ady, Endre, "Hunyhat a máglya"

Let Man Live. See Lagerkvist, Pär, *Låt människan leva*

Let My Name Be Gantenbein. *See* Frisch, Max, *A Wilderness of Mirrors*

"Let them read on my gravestone . . ." *See* Khlebnikov, Velimir, "Pust' na mogil'noi plite prochtut . . ."

Letamendi, José de, Baroja and, 9:606a

Létinois, Lucien, 7:1625b–1626a, 1638b

Letopis' (Russian journal), Babel's stories in, 11:1903a

"Letovanje na jugu." *See* Andrić, Ivo, "A Summer in the South"

"Let's Murder the Moonshine!" *See* Marinetti, Filippo Tommaso, "Uccidiamo il chiaro di luna!"

"Letter of an Exile." *See* Rihaku

Letter on the Blind. See Diderot, Denis, *Lettre sur les aveugles*

Letter Concerning the Life and Deeds of Guidobaldo, Duke of Urbino, to Henry, King of England, A. See Castiglione, Baldesar, *Ad Henricum Angliae regem epistola de vita et gestis Guidubaldi Urbini Ducis*

Letter on the Deaf and Mute. See Diderot, Denis, *Lettre sur les sourds et muets*

"Letter of Decline." *See* Hesse, Hermann, "Absage"

Letter form novel. *See* Epistolary novel

"Letter of Lord Chandos, The." *See* Hofmannsthal, Hugo von

"Letter of Mathios Paskalis." *See* Seferis, George, "Gramma tou Mathiou Paskali"

Letter on Providence. See Rousseau, Jean Jacques

Letter on Romanticism. *See* Manzoni, Alessandro, *Lettera sul romanticismo*

Letter to the Archbishop of Paris. See Rousseau, Jean Jacques

Letter to Georgina Hübner in Lima's Heaven. *See* Jiménez, Juan Ramón, "Carta a Georgina Hübner en el cielo de Lima"

"Letter to the Head Psychiatrists of Nut Houses." *See* Artaud, Antonin

Letter to a Hostage. See Saint-Exupéry, Antoine de, *Lettre à un otage*

Letter to Joliot-Curie. *See* Ritsos, Yannis, *Pimata III*

"Letter to Lamartine." *See* Musset, Alfred de, "Lettre à Lamartine"

Letter to Lord ***. *See* Vigny, Alfred Victor de, *Le more de Venise* (Shakespeare's *Othello*), "Lettre à Lord ***"

Letter to M. Chauvet on the Unities of Time and Place in Tragedy. *See* Manzoni, Alessandro, "Lettre à M. Chauvet sur l'unité de temps et de lieu dans la tragédie"

Letter to M. d'Alembert on Theater. See Rousseau, Jean Jacques, *Lettre à M. d'Alembert sur les spectacles*

Letter to M. de Fontanes on the Roman Campagna. *See* Chateaubriand, François René de, *Lettre à M. de Fontanes sur la Campagne romaine*

Letter to My Judge. *See* Simenon, Georges, *Lettre à mon juge*

"Letter to My Mother." *See* Quasimodo, Salvatore, "Lettera alla madre"

Letter to Posterity. See Petrarch, *Posteritati*

Letter to a Young Catholic. *See* Böll, Heinrich, "Brief an einen jungen Katholiken"

"Letter-Ocean." *See* Apollinaire, Guillaume, *Calligrammes*, "Lettre-océan"

"Lettera alla madre." *See* Quasimodo, Salvatore

Lettera sul romanticismo. See Manzoni, Alessandro

Letteratura (Italian journal)
   Ginzburg's stories in, 13:3136b
   Vittorini's writings in, 12:2741a

Lettere dal Sahara. See Moravia, Alberto

Lettere d'Oggi (Contemporary Literature [journal]), Pavese's works in, 12:2774a

Letters
   of Berlioz, 6:774b, 775b–776a, 778a-b, 781a-b, 800b, 809b–810a
   of Delacroix, 5:516a, 517b–523a, 538b
   of Dinesen, 10:1289a–1290b
   of Undset, 9:1018a–1019a
   of Voltaire
      Lettres philosophiques, 4:372b–373b, 384b–386a
      personal, 4:370a, 391a-b
   of Wagner, 6:1165b–1166a

Letters Concerning Contemporary Literature. See Lessing, Gotthold Ephraim, *Briefe, die neueste Literatur betreffend*

Letters on Don Carlos. See Schiller, Friedrich von

"Letters of Dupuis and Cotonet." *See* Musset, Alfred de

Letters on England. See Voltaire

Letters from Berlin, 1822. See Heine, Heinrich, *Briefe aus Berlin*

Letters from England. See Čapek, Karel, *Anglické listy*; Eça de Queiroz, José Maria, *Cartas de Inglaterra*

Letters from a Friar to His Friend in the Capital. *See* Hoffmann, E. T. A., "Schreiben eines Klostergeistlichen an seinen Freund in der Hauptstadt"

Letters from Holland. See Čapek, Karel, *Obrázky z Holandska*

Letters from the Sahara. *See* Moravia, Alberto, *Lettere dal Sahara*

"Letters from Spain." *See* Mérimée, Prosper, "Lettres adressées d'Espagne"

"Letters from Tula." *See* Pasternak, Boris, *Rasskazy (Stories)*

Letters of His Youth. *See* Saint-Exupéry, Antoine de, *Lettres de jeunesse*

Letters of Old Age. *See* Petrarch, *Epistolae seniles*

Letters to an Unknown Woman. See Mérimée, Prosper, *Lettres à une inconnue*

Letters to Father Lamy, of the Order of St. Benedict, Regarding Grace and Predestination. See Fénelon, François de Salignac de la Mothe-, *Lettres au P. Lami, Bénédictine, sur la grâce et la prédestination*

Letters to His Invented Friend. *See* Saint-Exupéry, Antoine de, *Lettres à l'amie inventée*

Letters to His Mother. *See* Saint-Exupéry, Antoine de, *Lettres à sa mère*

Letters to His Son. *See* Witkiewicz, Stanisław Ignacy, *Listy do syna*

Letters to Marcy. *See* Sand, George, *Lettres à Marcie*

Letters to the Poet. *See* Tychyna, Pavlo, *Pluh (The Plow)*, "Lysty do poeta"

Letters of a Traveler. *See* Sand, George, *Lettres d'un voyageur*

Letters Written from Lausanne. See Charrière, Isabelle Agnès Élizabeth de, *Lettres écrites de Lausanne*

Letters Written from the Mountain. See Rousseau, Jean Jacques

"Lettre à Lamartine." *See* Musset, Alfred de

"Lettre à Lord ***." *See* Vigny, Alfred Victor de, *Le more de Venise* (Shakespeare's *Othello*)

Lettre à Louis XIV. See Fénelon, François de Salignac de la Mothe-

Lettre à M. Chauvet sur l'unité de temps et de lieu dans la tragédie. See Manzoni, Alessandro

Lettre à M. d'Alembert sur les spectacles. See Rousseau, Jean Jacques

Lettre à M. de Fontanes sur la Campagne romaine. See Chateaubriand, François René de

Lettre à mon juge. See Simenon, Georges

Lettre à un otage. See Saint-Exupéry, Antoine de

"Lettre au Général X." *See* Saint-Exupéry, Antoine de

Lettre sur la providence. See Rousseau, Jean Jacques, *Letter on Providence*

Lettre sur les aveugles. See Diderot, Denis

Lettre sur les sourds et muets. See Diderot, Denis

"Lettre-océan." *See* Apollinaire, Guillaume, *Calligrammes*

Lettres à Génica Athanasiou. See Artaud, Antonin

Lettres à l'amie inventée. See Saint-Exupéry, Antoine de

Lettres à Marcie. See Sand, George

Lettres à sa mère. See Saint-Exupéry, Antoine de

Lettres à une inconnue. See Mérimée, Prosper

"Lettres adressées d'Espagne." *See* Mérimée, Prosper

Lettres au P. Lami, Bénédictine, sur la grâce et la prédestination. See Fénelon, François de Salignac de la Mothe-

Lettres de jeunesse. See Beaumarchais, Pierre-Augustin Caron de; Saint-Exupéry, Antoine de

Lettres de la marquise de M— au comte de R—. See Jolyot, Prosper (Crébillon)

Lettres de Rodez. See Artaud, Antonin

Lettres du voyant. See Rimbaud, Arthur

Lettres d'un voyageur. See Sand, George

Lettres écrites de Lausanne. See Charrière, Isabelle Agnès Élizabeth de

Lettres françaises, Les (journal)
    Aragon and, 11:2078b–2079a
    Sartre and, 12:2600b

Lettres neuchâteloises. See Charrière, Isabelle Agnès Élizabeth de

Lettres persanes. See Montesquieu, Charles-Louis de Secondat, baron de

Lettres philosophiques. See Voltaire

Lettres provinciales. See Pascal, Blaise

Letzten, Die. See Rilke, Rainer Maria

"Letzten Masken, Die." *See* Schnitzler, Arthur

Leubald. See Wagner, Richard

Leute von Seldwyla, Die. See Keller, Gottfried, *The People of Seldwyla*

Leutnant Gustl. See Schnitzler, Arthur, *None But the Brave*

"Lev." *See* Zamyatin, Yevgeny Ivanovich

Levaillant, Maurice, Chateaubriand and, 5:129b

Levana. See Richter, Jean Paul

Levi, Carlo
    Ginzburg and, 13:3137a
    Pavese and, 12:2760b, 2768b

Levi, Natalia. *See* Ginzburg, Natalia

Lévi-Strauss, Claude
    Barthes and, 13:3092a-b
    foreshadowed by Herder, 4:652a-b

Levin, Iuri I., on Mandelshtam, 10:1622b

Levitan, Isaac, 7:1858a

"Levsha." *See* Leskov, Nikolai

Lévy-Bruhl, Lucien, Bergson and, 8:61b

Levyi Front Isskustva. See LEF (Levyi Front Isskustva)

Lewdness, literary
    tradition of, 13:3253a-b
    see also Pornography

Lewes, George Henry, *Life of Goethe*, 5:105b

Lewis, C. S.
    allegory and, 1:320b–321a
    on Milton, 2:765a, 765b

Lewis, Cecil Day. *See* Day Lewis, Cecil

Lewis, M. G.
    Ambrosio; or, The Monk, influence on
        Grillparzer's *The Ancestress*, 5:424b
    Dostoevsky and, 7:1350b

Lewis, R. W. B.
    on Silone, 12:2275a, 2284a-b, 2285a
    The Picaresque Saint, 12:2750a
    on Vittorini, 12:2743b

Lewis, Wyndham, *Blasting and
    Bombardiering*, 9:823a, 824b

Lezhnev, A. Z.
    on Babel, 11:1889b–1900a, 1907a-b
    on Pasternak's *Zhenia's Childhood*,
        10:1600b

"Lezioni su Stendhal." *See* Lampedusa,
    Giuseppe Tomasi di

L'Hermite, Tristan
    La mort de Sénèque (*The Death of Seneca*),
        3:36b, 41a
    Mariamne, 3:32b, 36b, 41a

Lhôte, André, 13:3022b, 3025a

Li Tai Pe, translated by Claudel, 8:491a

Liaisons dangereuses, Les. See Laclos,
    Pierre-Ambroise-François Choderlos de

Liar II. See Corneille, Pierre, *La suite du
    menteur*

Liar, The. See Corneille, Pierre, *Le menteur;*
    Goldoni, Carlo, *Il bugiardo*

Liar, The. See Robbe-Grillet, Alain, *L'Homme
    qui ment*

Libellus de processione Spiritus Sancti. See
    Nicholas of Durazzo

Liber Cathemerinon. See Prudentius

Liber de Antichristo et eius ministris. See
    William of Saint Amour

Liber facetiarum. See Poggio Bracciolini, Gian
    Francesco

Liber Peristephanon. See Prudentius

Liber sine nomine. See Petrarch

Liberal arts
    in medieval satire, 1:352b–354a
    Vico and, 3:296a-b

Liberal, El (journal), Baroja's articles in,
    9:591a

Liberalism
    Diderot and, 4:504a

    of Heinrich Mann, 8:531a-b
    of Mérimée, 6:747b–748a, 749a
    of Moravia, 12:2692a-b
    in Portugal during Pessoa's time, 10:1478a
    in Pushkin's poems, 5:675a–676a
    Stendhal and, 5:359b–360a
    see also Politics

"Libertà." *See* Verga, Giovanni

Libertinage, Le (*The Libertine*). *See* Aragon,
    Louis

Libertinism
    attacked by Bossuet, 3:162a, 166a
    Constant introduced to, 4:409a-b
    in Molière's *Don Juan*, 3:115b, 116b
    Sade's espousal of, 4:617b–618a,
        625a–626b, 630a–631a, 631b–632a,
        633a, 634a–635a
        in fiction, 4:618a-b, 623a–624b, 625a-b,
        630a
    see also Scandals, sexual

Liberty
    in Corneille's *Cinna*, 3:42a, 42b
    in Staël's *De la littérature*, 5:94b, 95b–96a

"Liberty." *See* Chénier, André; Verga,
    Giovanni, "Libertà"

Liberty Leading the People. See Delacroix,
    Eugène

Librettos
    of Berlioz, 6:777a, 791a–793a, 801a–803b,
        807b–808b
    music and, in Wagner, 6:1149b–1140a,
        1154a–1155b
    of Quasimodo, 12:2406b
    see also Opera

Libro de las misiones, El. See Ortega y Gasset,
    José

Libro de Levante, El. See Azorín

Libro de poemas. See García Lorca, Federico

Libro del cortegiano, Il. See Castiglione,
    Baldesar, *The Book of the Courtier*

Libro delle trecentonovelle. See Sacchetti,
    Franco

Libro segreto. See D'Annunzio, Gabriele

Libussa. See Grillparzer, Franz

Lica. See Andrić, Ivo

Lice imagery, in Queneau's *The Skin of
    Dreams*, 12:2521a

"Licenciado, El." *See* Cervantes, Miguel de, "Master Glass"

Licenciado Vidriera, El. See Azorín, *Tomás Rueda*

License, The. See Pirandello, Luigi, *La patente*

Lidové noviny (People's Newspaper), 10:1566b, 1574a

Čapek and, 10:1578b, 1581b

Lie, Jonas

Hamsun and, 8:23a, 24a

Norwegian realism and, 9:1037a

Lie, The. See Moravia, Alberto; Sarraute, Nathalie, *Le mensonge*

Liebelei. See Schnitzler, Arthur, *Light-o-Love*

Liebestrank, Der. See Wedekind, Frank

Liebesverbot, Das. See Wagner, Richard

Liebknecht, Wilhelm, 8:154a

Liechtenstein, Alois Prinz, *The Man Without Qualities* and, 9:941b

Lied

of Heine, 5:493b, 494b

Storm and, 6:916b

"Lied, Das." *See* George, Stefan, *Das neue Reich*

"Lieder." *See* George, Stefan, *Der siebente Ring*

Lieder, Gedichte, Chöre. See Brecht, Bertolt

Lieder, Waclaw, George and, 8:455b

Liederbuch dreier Freunde. See Storm, Theodor

Liège (France), in Simenon's writing, 12:2480a-b

"Liens." *See* Apollinaire, Guillaume

"Lieutenant Schmidt." *See* Pasternak, Boris, *Deviat'sot piatyi god*

Life, A. See Maupassant, Guy de, *Une Vie*; Svevo, Italo

Life. *See Zhizn*

Life of the Bee, The. See Maeterlinck, Maurice, *La vie des abeilles*

Life of Beethoven. See Rolland, Romain

Life of the Brush. *See* Arp, Jean, "La vie de pinceau"

Life of Charlemagne. See Einhard

Life of the Cheerful Schoolmaster Maria Wutz, The. See Richter, Jean Paul, *Das Leben des vergnügten Schulmeisterlein Maria Wutz in Auenthal*

"Life and Death of Captain Renaud, The; or, The Malacca Cane." *See* Vigny, Alfred Victor de, *The Military Condition*

Life and Death of St. Genevieve, The. *See* Tieck, Ludwig, *Leben und Tod der heiligen Genoveva*

Life of Don Quixote and Sancho, The. See Ortega y Gasset, José, *Vida de Don Quijote y Sancho*; Unamuno, Miguel de, *La vida de Don Quijote y Sancho*

Life of Fibel, Author of the Bienrode ABC. See Richter, Jean Paul, *Das Leben Fibels, des Verfassers der Bienrodischen Fibel*

Life in the Fields. *See* Verga, Giovanni, *Vita dei campi*

Life of the Flea, The. *See* Zamyatin, Yevgeny Ivanovich, *Zhitie blokhi*

"Life flees and does not stop an hour." *See* Petrarch, *Canzoniere*, "La vita fugge et non s'arresta un'ora"

Life of Friedrich Schiller, The. See Carlyle, Thomas

Life of Galileo. See Brecht, Bertolt

Life of Goethe. See Lewes, George Henry

Life of Henri Brulard, The. See Stendhal, *La vie de Henri Brulard*

"Life of Homer." *See* Herodotus

Life Is a Dream. See Calderón de la Barca, Pedro

Life Is Elsewhere. See Kundera, Milan

Life Is a Game. *See* Moravia, Alberto, *La vita è gioco*

Life Is Not a Dream. See Quasimodo, Salvatore, *La vita non è sogno*

Life of Jesus. See Renan, Ernest, *Vie de Jésus*

Life of Jesus Critically Examined, The. See Strauss, David, *Das Leben Jesu kritisch bearbeitet*

Life of Klim Samgin, The. See Gorky, Maxim

Life of a Man. *See* Ungaretti, Giuseppe, *Vita d'un uomo*

Life of Matvei Kozhemyakin, The. See Gorky, Maxim

Life, Poetry, and Thoughts of Joseph Delorme, The. *See* Sainte-Beuve, Charles-Augustin, *Vie, poésies et pensées de Joseph Delorme*

Life of the Poets, The. *See* Tieck, Ludwig, *Dichterleben*

Life of Quintus Fixlein, Extracted from Fifteen Letterboxes, The. See Richter, Jean Paul, *Das Leben des Quintus Fixlein*

Life of Racine, The. *See* Mauriac, François, *Vie de Jean Racine*

Life of Rancé. *See* Chateaubriand, François René de, *Vie de Rancé*

Life of Saint Giles, A, on Charlemagne's sin, 1:100a

Life and Songs. *See* Rilke, Rainer Maria, *Leben und Lieder*

"Life Story Briefly Told." *See* Hesse, Hermann, "Kurzgefasster Lebenslauf"

Life and Times of Alexis Zorba. *See* Kazantzakis, Nikos, *Zorba the Greek*

Life and Work of Semmelweis, The. See Céline, Louis-Ferdinand, *La vie et l'oeuvre de Philippe-Ignace Semmelweis*

Life's Long Day. *See* Johnson, Eyvind, *Livsdagen lång*

Life's Superfluence. See Tieck, Ludwig, *Des Lebens Überfluss*

Ligazón. See Valle-Inclán, Ramón del

"Ligeia." *See* Poe, Edgar Allan

"Lighea." *See* Lampedusa, Giuseppe Tomasi di, *Two Stories and a Memory (Racconti),* "The Professor and the Siren"

Light of Day, The. *See* Milosz, Czeslaw, *Światło dzienne*

Light for Fools, A. See Ginzburg, Natalia

Light imagery
  in Butor, 13:3292b–3293a
  darkness and
    in Dante's *Paradiso,* 1:448b
    in Prudentius's works, 1:15b, 16a, 17a
  in Elytis' "I Genesis," 13:2968b
  in Ionesco's *The Killer,* 13:3000a

Light Tree and the Fourteenth Being, The. See Elytis, Odysseus, *To photodendro kai i dekati tetarti omorfia*

Light Under the Bushel, The. *See* D'Annunzio, Gabriele, *La fiaccola sotto il moggio*

Light of the World, The. *See* Laxness, Halldór, *Ljós heimsins*

Light-o-Love. See Schnitzler, Arthur

Lighthouses, The. *See* Baudelaire, Charles, "Les phares"

Lightness, Kundera and, 13:3407a–3409a

"Lightning's Pining, The." *See* Södergran, Edith, "Blixtens trångtan"

Lights of Bohemia. See Valle-Inclán, Ramón del, *Luces de bohemia*

Lights and Shadows. See Hugo, Victor, *Les rayons et les ombres*

Ligonier, Lord, Alfieri's duel with, 4:665b

Ligue, La. See Voltaire, *La henriade*

Likedeeler, Die. See Fontane, Theodor

Lilacs, in Proust's "A Girl's Confession," 8:562a

"Lilije" ("The Lilies"). *See* Mickiewicz, Adam

Lillo, George, *London Merchant,* Lessing and, 4:549b

Lily of the Valley, The. See Balzac, Honoré de, *Le lys dans la vallée*

"Limoni, I." *See* Montale, Eugenio, *Cuttlefish Bones (Ossi di seppia),* "The Lemon Trees"

Limping Sonnet. *See* Verlaine, Paul, "Sonnet boiteux"

Linaje, Poema de mio Cid and, 1:122b

Lindberger, Örjan, on Johnson, 12:2364a

Lindbergh, Anne Morrow, *Listen! the Wind,* Saint-Exupéry's preface to, 12:2317a

Lindegren, Erik, Ekelöf and, 12:2637a

"Lindenbaum, Der" ("The Linden Tree"). *See* Schubert, Franz

Lindsay, Anna, Benjamin Constant and, 4:410a-b, 411b–412a

"Line and Color." *See* Babel, Isaac, "Liniia i tsvet"

Lines of Life. See Mauriac, François

Linguistics
  Büchner and, 6:1178a–1182a
  Canetti and, 12:2616a–2617a, 2625a-b
  Diderot and, 4:486b–487b
  Erasmus and, 2:584b–585a
  of Khlebnikov, 10:1345b–1348a

Klopstock and, 4:515b, 532a-b
Kosztolányi and, 10:1240b–1244a
Luther and, 2:680b–681a
Machiavelli and, 2:599b
protomodermism of Mallarmé,
　　7:1578a–1579a, 1581a, 1588b–1589b
Sartre and, 12:2610a-b
Schlegel and, 5:193b–194b, 198a-b
Valéry and, 8:587b
see also Questione della lingua; Semiology
"Linguistics and Poetics." *See* Jakobson,
　　Roman, *Style in Language*
"Liniia i tsvet." *See* Babel, Isaac
Link, The. *See* George, Stefan, *Pilgerfahrten*
　　(Pilgrimages), "Die Spange"
Liolà. See Pirandello, Luigi
"Liompa." *See* Olesha, Yuri
"Lion, The." *See* Zamyatin, Yevgeny Ivanovich,
　　"Lev"
Lionne, abbé de, Lesage and, 3:320a
"Lion's Court, The." *See* La Fontaine, Jean de,
　　Fables, "La cour du lion"
Lion's Medulla, The. *See* Calvino, Italo, "Il
　　Midollo del leone"
Lipps, Theodor, Pirandello and, 8:391a
Lipsius, Justus, on Montaigne, 2:778b
Liren' group, Khlebnikov and, 10:1338a–1339b
Lirici greci. See Quasimodo, Salvatore
Lisbon
　　earthquake (1755), Goethe and, 5:2b
　　Pessoa in, 10:1483a-b
Lisbon Earthquake, Poem on the. See Voltaire,
　　Poème sur le désastre de Lisbonne
List of Assets, A. See Olesha, Yuri, *Spisok
　　blagodeyanii*
List of God's Gifts, A. See Laxness, Halldór,
　　Guðsgjafaþula
Listen! See Mayakovsky, Vladimir,
　　"Posluchaite!"
Listen! the Wind. See Lindbergh, Anne
　　Morrow
Listy do syna. See Witkiewicz, Stanisław
Liszt, Franz
　　Berlioz and, 6:783b, 789b, 790a
　　*Lettres d'un bachelier de musique (Letters
　　of a Bachelor of Music)*, 6:789b
　　Sand and, 6:826b

Litanie d'eau. See Butor, Michel
"Literal Literature." *See* Barthes, Roland
Literární listy (journal), Kundera and,
　　13:3393b–3394a
Literárni noviny (journal), Kundera and,
　　13:3391b, 3393a
Literary Conservative. *See Conservateur
　　littéraire, Le*
Literary criticism
　　of Andrić, 11:1770a-b
　　Benjamin on, 11:1708b–1709a, 1726b,
　　　1728b–1729a
　　determinism in, 10:1484b
　　La Bruyère on, 3:235b
　　New Criticism (Anglo-American school),
　　　11:1709b
　　Romantic, 11:1709a–1710a
　　　founder of, 5:200a-b
　　Schlegel and
　　　"creative criticism," 5:187a
　　　in *Dialogue on Poetry*, 5:186b–188a
　　　function of, 5:187b–188a
　　　in *Lucinde*, 5:191a, 192a-b
　　　paradox in, 5:177b–178a
　　　theory of, 5:186b–187b
　　　work on, 5:179b
　　Tasso's theory, 2:799b
　　Tsvetaeva on, 11:1742b
　　twentieth century, constructivism and,
　　　8:587a
　　see also Lukács, György
Literary Exhumations. See Gautier, Théophile,
　　Exhumations littéraires
Literary hoax, Mérimée's perpetration of,
　　6:747b, 750b
Literary Portraits. See Sainte-Beuve,
　　Charles-Augustin, *Portraits littéraires*
Literary Reminiscences. See Turgenev, Ivan
Literary South, The. *See* Andrić, Ivo, *Književni
　　jug*
Literary Values. *See* Azorín, *Los valores
　　literarios*
Literary Women. See Moers, Ellen
"Literatur." *See* Schnitzler, Arthur
*Literatur und Völkerkunde (Literature and
　　Ethnology)*, Richter and, 5:59a
Literature. *See* Schnitzler, Arthur, "Literatur"

Literature as the Spiritual Realm of the
Nation. *See* Hofmannsthal, Hugo von,
"Das Schrifttum als geistiger Raum der
Nation"
Literature of the World Revolution (journal),
11:2072b, 2073b
Lithography, Arp and, 10:1377a
Lithuania
in Mickiewicz's verse
Grazyna, 5:610a-b
Konrad Wallenrod, 5:616b–618a
Pan Tadeusz, 5:625a–629a
Litigants, The. *See* Racine, Jean, *Les plaideurs*
Littérature (French journal), 11:1939b
Breton and, 11:1939b–1940a
foundation of, 11:1939b
manifest of dadaism in, 11:2063a-b
see also Révolution surréaliste, La
"Littérature littérale." *See* Barthes, Roland,
"Literal Literature"
"Littérature objective." *See* Barthes, Roland,
"Objective Literature"
Littératures soviétiques. See Aragon, Louis
Little Bird in a Cage. *See* Khlebnikov, Velimir,
"Ptichka v kletke"
Little Black Cock, The. *See* Aymé, Marcel, *The
Wonderful Farm* (*Contes du chat
perché*), "Le petit coq noir"
*Little Book of Novellas. See Cento novelle
antich*
Little Boy I Know, A. *See* Ady, Endre, "Egy
ismerös kisfiú"
"Little Car, The." *See* Apollinaire, Guillaume,
Calligrammes, "La petite auto"
Little Castles in Bohemia. *See* Nerval, Gerard
de, *Petits châteaux de Bohème*
Little Devil, The. *See* Khlebnikov, Velimir,
"Chertik"
Little Eyolf. See Ibsen, Henrik
Little Fadette. See Sand, George
"Little Fish and the Fisherman, The." *See* La
Fontaine, Jean de, *Fables*, "Le petit
poisson et le pêcheur"
Little House in Kolomna, The. See Pushkin,
Alexander
"Little Ida's Flowers." *See* Andersen, Hans
Christian

Little Library of World Literature, A. See
Hesse, Hermann, *Eine Bibliothek der
Weltliteratur*
Little Man from Archangel, The. See Simenon,
Georges, *Le petit homme d'Arkangelsk*
Little Mariner, The. See Elytis, Odysseus, *O
mikros naftilos*
"Little Mermaid, The." *See* Andersen, Hans
Christian
Little Misery, The. See Mauriac, François, *Le
sagouin*
"Little Monologue." *See* Ungaretti, Giuseppe
Little Portable Cosmogony. *See* Queneau,
Raymond, *Petite cosmogonie portative*
Little Prince, The. See Saint-Exupéry, Antoine
de, *Le petit prince*
"Little Roque." *See* Maupassant, Guy de, "La
petite Roque"
Little Saint, The. See Simenon, Georges, *Le
petit saint*
"Little Shepherd, The." *See* John of the Cross,
St., *Cántico espiritual*
"Little Testament." *See* Montale, Eugenio, *The
Storm and Other Things* (*La bufera e
altro*), "Piccolo testamento"
Little Theater of the World, The. See
Hofmannsthal, Hugo von, *Das kleine
Welttheater oder die Glücklichen*
Little Town of Okurov, The. *See* Gorky, Maxim,
Gorodok Okurov
Little Town, The. See Mann, Heinrich, *Die
kleine Stadt*
Little Virtues, The. See Ginzburg, Natalia, *Le
piccole virtù*
Little Window, The. See Alfieri, Vittorio
Little Worlds and Ancient Civilizations. *See*
Ferreira de Castro, José Maria,
Pequenos mundos e velhas civilizações
"Liturgiia mne" (Liturgy to Me). *See* Sologub,
Vladimir Aleksandrovich
Liturgy, Greek Orthodox, Elytis' *The Axion Esti*
and, 13:2968a, 2970b
"Liubka Kozak" ("Liubka the Cossasck"). *See*
Babel, Isaac, *Odessa Tales*
"Liudi i polozheniia." *See* Pasternak, Boris
"Live Not By Lies." *See* Solzhenitsyn,
Aleksandr, "Zhit' ne po lzhi"

Lives of Haydn, Mozart, and Metastasio. *See* Stendhal, *Vies de Haydn, Mozart, et Métastase*

Lives of the Saints. *See* Butler, Alban

Livets Strand. See Gunnarsson, Gunnar

Living Hours. See Schnitzler, Arthur, *Lebendige Stunden*

Living Thoughts of Mazzini, The. See Silone, Ignazio, *Mazzini*

Living Thoughts of Nietzsche, The. See Mann, Heinrich

Living Together. See Huysmans, Joris Karl, *En ménage*

"Living Word About a Living Man, A." *See* Tsvetaeva, Marina, "Zhivoe o zhivom"

"Livre considéré comme objet, Le." *See* Butor, Michel

Livre d'amour. See Sainte-Beuve, Charles-Augustin

Livre de Christophe Colomb. See Claudel, Paul

Livre des hymnes. See Ronsard, Pierre de

Livre, Le. See Mallarmé, Stéphane

Livre populaire, Michelet and, 5:581b–582a, 595b

Livro de desassossego. See Pessoa, Fernando

Livsdagen lång. See Johnson, Eyvind

Livy (Titus Livius)
  as Alfieri's inspiration, 4:661a–b, 665a
  Dante and, 1:433b
  Histories, as source for Alfieri's *Virginia*, 4:680b
  history of Rome, Petrarch's adaptation, 2:503a
  Lessing and, 4:554b
  Sverris saga and, 1:383a
  Taine on, 7:1451a, 1454a

Liz, Diana de, Ferreira de Castro and, 11:2151b, 2152a

Lizárraga, Concepción, 8:286b

Ljós heimsins. See Laxness, Halldór

Ljósvetninga saga, 1:393b–394a

Llanto por Ignacio Sánches Mejías. See García Lorca, Federico

Löskekark, En. See Moberg, Vilhelm

"Lo ferm voler." *See* Arnaut Daniel

Lob der Dummheit, Das. See Richter, Jean Paul

Löberg (Icelandic children's periodical), 12:2475b

Local Anaesthetic. See Grass, Günter

Locandiera, La. See Goldoni, Carlo

Locarno agreement, Perse and, 10:1439a

L'Occasion. See Mérimée, Prosper, *The Opportunity*

Locke, John
  Diderot and, 4:483a
  Herder's politics compared to, 4:651a–652a
  Voltaire on, 4:372a, 385b
  Whitehead's critique of, 4:651a-b

L'Oeuvre. See Zola, Émile

Logbook. See Seferis, George, *Imerologio katastromatos*

Logic
  in plays of Feydeau, 7:1923b–1924a
  university teaching of, 1:409a

Logic as the Science of the Pure Concept. See Croce, Benedetto, *Logica come scienza del concetto puro*

Logic of Scientific Discovery, The. See Popper, Karl

"Logic of solids," in Bergson's thought, 8:60a-b

Logica come scienza del concetto puro. See Croce, Benedetto

Logical Investigations. See Husserl, Edmund, *Logische Untersuchungen*

Logical positivism, Broch and, 10:1388a-b

Logische Untersuchungen. See Husserl, Edmund

Lohengrin. See Wagner, Richard

Loin de Rueil. See Queneau, Raymond

Loisy, Nerval and, 6:963b, 964a

Loisy, Alfred, Bergson and, 8:64b

"Lokis." *See* Mérimée, Prosper

Lomax, John and Alan, *Folk Song U.S.A.*, Herder's influence on, 4:659a

Lombardo della Seta, Petrarch's *De viris illustribus*, compilation of, 2:480a-b

London, Fontane and, 6:1302b–1303a

London Bridge. *See* Céline, Louis-Ferdinand, *Pont de Londres*

London, Jack
  Böll and, 13:3167a
  Zamyatin and, 10:1188b
"London Lickpenny," 1:362a-b, 364a
London Merchant. See Lillo, George
Loneliness
  in Calvino, 13:3266a-b
  in Elytis, 13:2975b, 2976a
  in Pavese's works, 12:2765b
  in Schnitzler's works, 8:101a-b
Lonely Lives. See Hauptmann, Gerhart,
    Einsame Menschen
Lonely Way, The. See Schnitzler, Arthur, *Der*
    einsame Weg
Lonely Years, The. See Babel, Nathalie
Long Ago, You Were My Daughter. See Ady,
    Endre, "Valamikor lyányom voltál"
Long cours. See Simenon, Georges
Long Exile, The. See Simenon, Georges, *Long*
    cours
Longest Years, The. See Undset, Sigrid
Longfellow, Henry Wadsworth
  Baudelaire and, 7:1329b
  Hamsun and, 8:24a
"Longing for Nothingness, The." *See*
    Baudelaire, Charles
Longinus, Cassius
  On the Sublime, 3:199a
    translated by Boileau, 3:179b
Longueville, duchesse de. *See* Bourbon-Condé,
    Anne-Geneviève de
Longus, *Daphnis and Chloe*, influence on
    Renaissance pastoral literature, 2:903a,
    911b, 916a
Look Back on Happiness. See Hamsun, Knut,
    Den siste glede
Lope de Rueda
  Cervantes and, 2:2826a
  interludes and, 2:825b–826a
Lope de Vega, **2:845a–867b**
  Arcadia, 2:849a, 913b
  Azorín's literary criticism of, 9:645a
  Belardo el furioso (*Belardo the Madman*),
    2:848a-b
  Calderón and, 2:871a, 873b–874a, 878b,
    895a

  Cervantes and, 2:821b, 822b–823a,
    824b–825a
  El castigo sin venganza (*Justice Without*
    Revenge), 2:866b–867a
  El perro de hortelano (*The Dog in the*
    Manger), 2:863b–864a
  El remedio en la desdicha (*Misfortune's*
    Remedy), 2:845b
  "Extemporary Sonnet," 2:849b
  Fama póstuma (*Posthumous Fame*),
    2:845a-b
  Fuente Ovejuna, 2:855a, 864b, 865a-b
  Fuente Ovejuna (*The Village of Fuente*
    Ovejuna), adapted by Lorca,
    11:2199b–2200a
  influence on Grillparzer, 5:421b, 422b–423a
  Jiménez and, 9:1008a
  La corona trágica (*The Tragic Crown*),
    2:848a
  La Dorotea, 2:848a, 848b
  La Dragontea, 2:849a
  La gatomaquia (*The Battle of the Cats*),
    2:849a
  La hermosura de Angélica (*The Beauty of*
    Angelica), 2:849a
  La noche de San Juan (*Saint John's Night*),
    2:867b
  Las bizarrías de Belisa (*The Extravagances*
    of Belisa), 2:867a-b
  Las paces de los reyes, y la Judía de Toledo,
    as source for Grillparzer's *The Jewess of*
    Toledo, 5:442a
  Los pastores de Belén (*The Shepherds of*
    Bethlehem), 2:849a, 913b
  Machado and, 9:746b, 760a, 760b
  Partes, 2:855a
  pastoral poetry of, 2:913a-b
  Peribáñez y el comendador de Ocaña
    (*Peribáñez and the Knight Commander*
    of Ocaña), 2:864a–865b
  Steel in Madrid (*El acero de Madrid*),
    2:859a–860b
  The Best Magistrate, the King, 2:857b
  The Knight from Olmedo (*El caballero de*
    Olmedo), 2:855a, 865a–866b

"The New Art of Writing Comedies at This Time" ("El arte nuevo de hacer comedias en este tiempo"), 2:851a–852a, 854a

The Peasant in His Retreat (*El villano en su rincón*), 2:861a–863b

The Pilgrim in His Native Land (*El peregrino en su patria*), 2:845a, 849a, 855a-b

translated by Lesage, 3:320a

Lopes de Castanheda, Fernão. *See* Castanheda, Fernão Lopes de

López de Hoyos, Juan, Cervantes and, 2:819b

López de Villalobos, Francisco, 2:755b

López-Marrón, José, on Baroja's novels, 9:610b–611a

Lorca, Federico García. *See* García Lorca, Federico

Lord, Albert Bates, 1:67a, 67b

The Singer of Tales, oralist theories and, 1:126b

Lord Halewyn. See Ghelderode, Michel de

"Lord of the Island, The." *See* George, Stefan, *Die Bücher der Hirten- und Preisgedichte. . .* (*The Books of Eclogues and Eulogies*), *Hirtengedichte* poems

Lord Jim. See Conrad, Joseph

Lord of Labraz, The. See Baroja, Pío, *El mayorazgo de Labraz*

"Lord of Something Else." *See* Ekelöf, Gunnar

Lord's Prayer, Thélème and, 2:707a, 710a-b

"Loreley, La." *See* Apollinaire, Guillaume, *Alcools*

Lorenz, Max, Schnitzler and, 8:97b

Lorenzaccio. See Musset, Alfred de

Loris. *See* Hofmannsthal, Hugo von

Lorraine, Marguerite de, 3:76a

"Loss of Sons, The." *See* Egil Skallagrímsson, "Sonatorrek"

Lost Honor of Katharina Blum, The. See Böll, Heinrich, *Die verlorene Ehre der Katharina Blum*

Lost Horseman, The. *See* Ady, Endre, "Az eltévedt lovas"

Lost Illusions. See Balzac, Honoré de, *Illusions perdues*

Lost Mare, The. *See* Simenon, Georges, *La jument perdue*

Lost Smile, The. See Keller, Gottfried

Lost Way, The. *See* Čapek, Karel, "Ztracená cesta"

Lost Weekend, The (film), 13:3041a-b

Lotsen från Moluckas. See Martinson, Harry

Lotte in Weimar. See Mann, Thomas

"Lótusz" (Lotus). *See* Ady, Endre

Loubère, J. A. E., 13:3032b

Louis II de Bourbon, prince de Condé, 3:60a, 60b, 61b, 68a

Bossuet and, 3:152a, 154b

funeral oration, 3:166a

Louis IX of France, king, Aquinas and, 1:419b

Louis XIII of France, king, 3:264b

La Rochefoucauld and, 3:54b–55a

Louis XIV of France, king

Boileau and, 3:180a, 180b–181a

Bossuet and, 3:156a, 156b, 157a-b, 158a-b, 164b

celebrated and criticized, 3:280a-b

court of as reflected in Racine's plays, 3:226b

Fénelon and, 3:272a, 276b, 279b–281b

Télémaque, 3:284a-b

in La Bruyère's *Caractères*, 3:245a, 247a–248b

Lesage and, 3:321a, 325b, 327a-b

"L'État, c'est moi," Montesquieu and, 3:359b

Molière and, 3:101a, 102a, 103b, 105a, 109a

habit of flattery, 3:113a, 115a-b

quietism and, 3:268b

Racine and, 3:208a

regalia and, 3:167b–168a

revocation of the Edict of Nantes and, 3:264b

Richelieu and, 3:26a, 55b–56a, 56b

Voltaire and, 4:375b, 382a–383b

Louis XV of France, king

Alfieri's antagonism toward, 4:664a

and Beaumarchais, 4:563b–564a, 572a

Voltaire and, 4:374b–375a, 376b

Louis XVI of France, king

and Beaumarchais, 4:578b–579a

Chénier's defense of, 4:702b

in Dumas's works, 6:735a-b

Louis XVI of France, king (*cont.*)
  Schiller and, 5:37b
Louis de Bourbon, prince de Condé, La
      Bruyère and, 3:230b
Louis de France, duc de Bourgogne, Fénelon
      and, 3:269a, 272b–273a
Louis Lambert. See Balzac, Honoré de
Louis Philippe
  depicted by Michelet, 5:585b
  French romantic historiography and,
      5:572b–573a
  Heine's interest in, 5:500b
  Hugo and, 6:705a
  Vigny and, 5:463b, 483a
Louis, vicomte de Narbonne. *See* Narbonne,
      Louis de, vicomte
Louisiane. See Aymé, Marcel
"Loup et l'agneau, Le." *See* La Fontaine, Jean
      de, *Fables*
"Loup et les bergers, Le." *See* La Fontaine,
      Jean de, *Fables*
Loupežník. See Čapek, Karel
"Loupežný vrah před soudem." *See* Hašek,
      Jaroslav
Louppes, Antoinette de, 2:769b–770a
Lourdes. See Zola, Émile, *Les trois villes:
      Lourdes*
Lourie, Evgeniia Vladimirovna
  Pasternak's marriage to, 10:1594a, 1594b,
      1595a
  in Pasternak's *Second Birth*, 10:1605a
Louÿs, Pierre, Valéry and, 8:571b
Love
  in Ady's works, 9:866b–870b
  aging and, in Colette's works, 9:627b–631a,
      633a
  in Akhmatova's works, 10:1521b, 1528b
  Anouilh on, 13:2853a, 2853a-b
  in Ariosto, 2:629b
  art of, in medieval literature, 2:314b–315a
  Augustine on, 1:28a, 29b–30a
  in Balzac's works, 5:652b–653a
  in Baroja's works, 9:602a
  Bergson on, 8:63a
  Berlioz on, 6:773b, 778a-b, 794a
  Blok on, 9:968a–969b
  Breton's theory of convulsive love,
      11:1945a–1946a, 1954a
  in Butor's works, 13:3304a-b
  in Camoëns' works, 2:750b–751a
  in Čapek's *The Outlaw*, 10:1570b–1571a
  in Castiglione's works, 2:660a
  in Chekhov's *The Seagull*, 7:1876b
  Dante on, 1:438b, 441b
  Delacroix on, 5:539a
  in Dumas's works, 6:722a
  in English plot structure, 9:596a-b
  in French 18th-century novel, 4:393b–394a,
      405a-b, 415b–416a
  friendship and, Augustine on, 1:30a
  in Frisch's works, 13:2901a
  in George's *Hängende Gärten*, 8:459a
  God of, in Dante's *Vita nuova*, 1:437a, 437b
  in Goncharov's works, 6:1076a,
      1077b–1079a
  in Gottfried, 1:248a-b, 250a-b
    role of music and literature in,
      1:252b–253a
  in Hamsun's works, 8:22a, 30a–31b,
      32b–33a, 42a
  in Hugo's works, 6:702a, 703b–704a,
      713b–714a, 715b
  Jiménez on, 9:1010b
  Kierkegaard on, 6:1140a–1141b
  in La Bruyère's *Caractères*, 3:238b–239b
  in Leconte de Lisle's works, 6:1261a–1263a
  in Lermontov's works, 6:1203b, 1205b,
      1209b–1212a, 1216a
  as literary theme, acceptance of, 1:139b
  in Machado's "Galerías," 9:752a-b
  Marinetti on, 9:812a
  in Mérimée's works, 6:748b, 749b–750a,
      752b, 759a, 761b–762a, 763b
  in Mickiewicz's works, 5:614a–615a
  in Olesha's works, 11:2242a
  Ovid and, 1:139b
  in Pascoli's "The Weaver," 7:1846a
  in Perse's poetry, 10:1446a-b, 1451a
  in Proust's *Remembrance of Things Past*
    death and, 8:559a–561a
    psychology of, 8:555b–559a
  in *Romance of the Rose*, 1:309a–332a
    art of, 1:316a-b

psychology of, 1:327a–328a
rituals of, 1:318a
romantic, courtly poets and, 1:241b–243a
in Schnitzler's works, 8:93a–95b, 99b–100a,
    102b, 103b–104a, 104b, 112b
as sickness, in Gottfried, 1:252a-b
in Staël's *Corinne*, 5:100a, 101a, 102a
in Stendhal's works, 5:357b, 364a-b
in Tieck's works, 5:250b–251a
tragic, Maeterlinck on, 8:129b–130b
troubadour's theme of, 1:139b–140a
in Turgenev's works, 6:1277b, 1281b–1282b
in 12th-century lyric poetry, 1:315a-b
in Undset's works, 9:1032b–1033b
in Ungaretti's works, 10:1471a-b
unrequited, in *Kormáks saga*, 1:384b
in Verlaine's works, 7:1628b–1629a
in Walther's works, 292a–297a
in William of Saint Thierry's works, 1:170b
in Wolfram's works, 1:281b–282a
in Yourcenar's works, 12:2539a, 2542a-b,
    2543b–2544a, 2548b–2549a,
    2550b–2551a, 2552b, 2557b
in Zamyatin's writing
    prerevolutionary works, 10:1183b–1184b
    "The Fisher of Men," 10:1188a-b
    The Islanders, 10:1187b–1188a
    The North, 10:1188b
see also Adultery; Courtly love; Sexes,
    relations between; Sexuality
Love. *See* Michelet, Jules
"Love." *See* Olesha, Yuri; Södergran, Edith,
    "Kärlek"
Love. *See* Verlaine, Paul, *Amour*
*Love of Don Perlimplín for Belisa in His
    Garden, The. See* García Lorca,
    Federico, *El amor de Don Perlimplín
    con Belisa en su jardín*
"Love is a fire that burns invisibly." *See*
    Camoëns, Luís Vaz de, *Rimas* (*Lyrics*),
    "Amor é fogo que arde sem se ver"
"Love of Life." *See* Camus, Albert
Love of Ourselves. *See* Ady, Endre, "A magunk
    szerelme"
Love of Perdition, A. *See* Castelo Branco,
    Camilo, *Amor de Perdição*
Love poetry

Minnesang as, 1:290b–291a
Wolfram's attitude to, 1:266b–268a
Love Potion, The. *See* Wedekind, Frank, *Der
    Liebestrank*
"Love Song of J. Alfred Prufrock, The." *See*
    Eliot, T. S.
Love on St. Nicholas Tower. See Andersen,
    Hans Christian
Love-Girl and the Innocent, The. See
    Solzhenitsyn, Aleksandr, *Respublika
    truda*
Loved and the Unloved, The. See Mauriac,
    François
Loveless Love Affairs. *See* Pirandello, Luigi,
    Amori senza amore
Lovely. See Andersen, Hans Christian
"Lovely Morning, A." *See* Yourcenar,
    Marguerite, *Comme l'eau qui coule*
Lover of Venice, The. See Maurras, Charles,
    Les amants de Venise
Lover's Attempt, The. See Gide, André, *La
    tentative amoureuse*
Lovers of Avignon, The. See Triolet, Elsa, *Les
    amants d'Avignon*
Lover's Discourse, A: Fragments. See Barthes,
    Roland
Lover's Whim, The. *See* Goethe, Johann
    Wolfgang, *Laune des Verliebten*
Love's Comedy. See Ibsen, Henrik
Love's Guardian. *See* Jiménez, Juan Ramón,
    "Guardia de amor"
Love's Labor's Lost. See Shakespeare, William
Love's Remedy. See Ovid (Publius Ovidius
    Naso), *Remedia amoris*
"Lovets chelovekov." *See* Zamyatin, Yevgeny
    Ivanovich, "The Fisher of Men"
Lowe, Donald, *History of Bourgeois
    Perception*, 9:820a
Lowe-Porter, H. T., Thomas Mann and, 9:719a
Lower Depths, The. See Gorky, Maxim, *Na dne*
Lőwinger, György Bernát. *See* Lukács, György
Löwy, Yitzchak, Kafka and, 9:1153a, 1153b
Loyalty
    in the *Nibelungenlied*, 1:230a–231a, 232a,
        233b, 234a-b
    Walther and, 1:296b–297a, 305a-b

Loyola, Ignatius de, St.
  Spiritual Exercises
    Claudel's *The Satin Slipper* and, 8:492a
    Fénelon and, 3:274a
Lozinsky, Mikhail
  as acmeist mentor, 10:1632b
  in Akhmatova's *Poem Without a Hero*,
    10:1538a
  "To byl poslednii god" ("The Last Year"),
    foresight of, 10:1636a
Lucan, *Pharsalia*, Dante and, 1:447a
Lucas, bishop of Tuy, *Chronicon mundi*,
    1:130b
Lucas, Prosper, *Traité philosophique et
    physiologique de l'hérédité naturelle*
    (*Philosophical and Physiological
    Treatise on Natural Heredity*), 7:1522a
Luces de bohemia. See Valle-Inclán, Ramón
    del
Lucha de clases, La (Class Struggle) (journal),
    Unamuno's involvement with, 8:286b,
    287a
Lucha por la vida, La. See Baroja, Pío
Lucian
  Erasmus and, 2:577a
  German translation of, 4:610a
  Vera historia (*True History*), 9:657a
    Cervantes and, 2:827b–828a
Lucien Leuwen. See Stendhal
Lucienne et le boucher (*Lucienne and the
    Butcher*). *See* Aymé, Marcel
Lucifer
  in Vigny's "Eloa," 5:452b–453b
  see also Devil; Satan
Lucilius, *Saturae*, 1:337a
Lucinde. See Schlegel, Friedrich von
Lucky Per's Journey. See Strindberg, August
Lucky Peter. See Andersen, Hans Christian
Lucrèce. See Ponsard, François
Lucrèce Borgia. See Hugo, Victor
Lucretius
  De rerum natura (*On the Nature of Things*)
    Molière's *Misanthrope* and, 3:102a
    natural world as subject of, 4:707a
    Psychomachia and, 1:6a
    Rimbaud and, 7:1791b
    Strindberg and, 7:1753a

Ludwig II of Bavaria, king
  Algabal and, 8:453a
  in Apollinaire's "Song of the Unloved
    Lover," 9:890b
  Wagner and, 6:1158a, 1158b–1160a, 1162b,
    1163b
*Ludwig Feuerbach und der Ausgang der
    klassischen deutschen Philosophie*
    (*Ludwig Feuerbach and the Decline of
    Classical German Philosophy*). *See*
    Engels, Friedrich
Ludwig, Otto
  Hofmannsthal and, 9:694b
  poetic realism and, 6:913b–914a
Lug zelenyi. See Bely, Andrey
Lugné-Poë, Aurélien, Maeterlinck and,
    8:128b–129a, 130b, 133b, 137a
Lugo y Dávilla, Francisco, *Teatro popular*,
    defense of novella in, 2:951b
Lui et elle. See Musset, Paul de
"Lui?" *See* Maupassant, Guy de
Luis de León, Fray, pastoral poetry of, 2:913a
Luise Miller. See Schiller, Friedrich von,
    Kabale und Liebe
Luján, Micaela, Lope de Vega and, 2:847a
Lukács Circle, 10:1264a-b
Lukács, György, **10:1251a–1279b**
  "A lelki szegénységről" (On Poverty of
    Spirit), 10:1255a, 1263a
  A modern dráma fejlődésének története
    (History of the Development of the
    Modern Drama), 10:1253b, 1254b,
    1255a–1257b, 1271a
    on Hebbel, 10:1255b–1256b
    on Ibsen, 10:1256b–1257a
    on naturalism, 10:1256a
  on Ady, 9:860b
  Balázs Béla és akiknek nem kell (Béla
    Balázs and Those Who Have No Use for
    Him), 10:1264a
  Balzac und der französische Realismus
    (Balzac and French Realism), 10:1269b,
    1271a-b
  "Blum Theses," 10:1268b
  "Das Phänomen der Verdinglichung" ("The
    Phenomenon of Reification"),
    10:1267a-b

Der junge Hegel (*The Young Hegel*),
  10:1273a–1274a

Deutsche Realisten des 19. Jahrhunderts
  (German Realists of the Nineteenth
  Century), 10:1272a

"Die Antinomien des bürgerlichen Denkens"
  ("The Antinomies of Bourgeois
  Thought"), 10:1267b–1268a

Die Eigenart des Ästhetischen (The
  Characteristic Nature of the Aesthetic),
  10:1262b, 1273a, 1274a, 1275a–1276a

"Die Verdinglichung und das Bewusstsein
  des Proletariats" ("Reification and the
  Consciousness of the Proletariat"),
  10:1265b, 1266a, 1267a–1268a

Die Zerstörung der Vernunft (*The
  Destruction of Reason*), 10:1273a,
  1274b–1275a

Essays on Thomas Mann, 10:1272b

Esztétikai kultúra (Aesthetic Culture),
  10:1257b, 1276a

Goethe és kora (*Goethe and His Age*),
  10:1269b–1270b

Heidelberger Ästhetik, 10:1262b, 1275b

Heidelberger Philosophie der Kunst,
  10:1262b

History and Class Consciousness
  (*Geschichte und Klassenbewusstsein*),
  10:1265b, 1265b–1268b, 1274a,
  11:1716b

Mann's *Magic Mountain* and, 9:722b, 723a

"Mein Weg zur Marx" ("My Road to Marx"),
  10:1269a

*Moses Hess und die Probleme der
  idealistischen Dialektik* (Moses Hess
  and the Problems of Idealist Dialectics),
  10:1265b

Soul and Form (*A lélek és a formák*),
  10:1251b, 1253b, 1254b, 1257a-b,
  1258b, 1262b

Studies in European Realism, on Stendhal's
  The Charterhouse of Parma, 11:2023b

Tactics and Ethics, 10:1265b–1266a

The Theory of the Novel (*Die Theorie des
  Romans*), 9:1137b, 10:1252a, 1253a,
  1258b, 1259b–1262b, 1268b, 1271a,
  11:1705b–1706a

on historical dialectics, 10:1260b

on novelistic forms, 10:1261b–1262b

writing of, 10:1259b

Utam Marxhoz (My Road to Marx), 10:1266a

"Was ist orthodoxer Marxismus?" ("What Is
  Orthodox Marxism?"), 10:1265b,
  1266a–1267b

Zur Ontologie des gesellschaftlichen Seins
  (Toward an Ontology of Social Being),
  10:1273a, 1276a-b

Lukács, Jószef, 10:1252a-b

Lukasbund, in Richter's *The Comet*, 5:83a

Luke, Book of, in Villon's *Testament*, 2:563b,
  565b

Lulu plays. *See* Wedekind, Frank

Lumen. See Flammarion, Camille

Lumíe di Sicilia. See Pirandello, Luigi

Luminous Depths, The. *See* Čapek, Karel, and
  Josef Čapek, *Zářivé hlubiny*

Luna Benamor. See Blasco Ibáñez, Vicente

Luna e i falò, La. See Pavese, Cesare, *The
  Moon and the Bonfires*

Luna nueva, La. See Tagore, Rabindranath,
  The Crescent Moon

Luna-Park. See Triolet, Elsa

Lunacharskii, Anatoly
  Gorky and, 8:421a
  on surrealists, 11:2068b–2069a
  on women, 11:2240a

"Lundi rue Christine." *See* Apollinaire,
  Guillaume

Lundkvist, Artur, Ekelöf and, 12:2636b–2637a

"Lune de pluie, La." *See* Colette

Lune à la recherche d'elle-même, La. See
  Claudel, Paul

Lunes en papier. See Malraux, André

"Luoghi della mia prima infanzia, I." *See*
  Lampedusa, Giuseppe Tomasi di, *Two
  Stories and a Memory* (*Racconti*),
  "Places of My Infancy"

"Lupa, La." *See* Verga, Giovanni

Lusiads, The (*Os Lusíadas*). *See* Camoëns,
  Luís Vaz de

Lust. *See* Sexual passion

Lustige Witwe, Die. See Lehár, Franz

Lusus (god), 2:760a, 761a

Lusus pastorales
  defined, 2:909b
  influence of *Greek Anthology* on, 2:902b
  in Renaissance Venice, 2:909a-b
Lutèce
  Verlaine's works in, 7:1638b
  see also Nouvelle Rive Gauche, La
Lutetia. See Heine, Heinrich
Luther, Martin, **2:669a–691b**
  "A Mighty Fortress Is Our God," 2:680b
  A Sermon on the Mass, 2:676b
  A Treatise on the New Testament, 2:676b
  Acta Augustana (Proceedings at Augsburg),
    2:675b
  *Admonitions for Peace on the Twelve
    Articles*, 2:682a-b
  Against the Heavenly Prophets, 2:682a
  Against Latomus, 2:680a
  *Against the Papacy at Rome, Founded by
    the Devil*, 2:685a-b
  *Against the Thieving and Murderous Gangs
    of Peasants*, 2:682b
  in Bossuet's *History of the Variations in the
    Protestant Churches*, 3:170b–171a
  *Bull on the Last Banquet of Our Most Holy
    Lord the Pope*, 2:680a
  Carducci's poem on, 7:1504b–1505a
  Chateaubriand on, 5:137a
  Commentary on the Magnificat, 2:680a
  Confession Concerning the Lord's Supper,
    2:677b
  criteria of truth and, 3:8a-b
  *De servo arbitrio (On the Bondage of the
    Will)*, 2:685b
  Die Deutsche Messe (The German Mass),
    2:685a
  Erasmus and, 2:582b–583a, 585a–588b
  *Formula Missae et Communionis (Mass
    Service Book)*, 2:685a
  Fourteen Consolations, 2:676b
  Freedom of a Christian Man, 2:677b–678a
  Geistliche Lieder (Spiritual Songs), 2:685a
  Hamsun and, 8:34b
  Kirchenpostillen (Church Homilies), 2:685a
  Mann's *Doctor Faustus* and, 9:733b
  Ninety-five Theses, 2:674a–675a
  Of Councils and Churches, 2:688a
  Of the Jews and Their Lies, 2:685b
  *Open Letter Concerning the Hard Book
    Against the Peasants*, 2:682b
  *Open Letter to the Christian Nobility of the
    German Nation Concerning the Reform
    of the Christian Estate*, 2:676b–677a
  Papacy at Rome, 2:676b
  Postills: A Sermon on Good Works, 2:676b
  Resolution, 2:675a
  Sermon on Indulgence and Grace, 2:674b
  Strindberg's treatment of, 7:1739b, 1749b
  Table Talk, 2:684b
  The Great Catechism, 2:684b–685a
  The Short Catechism, 2:684b
  Theologica Germanica, 2:673a
  Threefold Righteousness, 2:672b–673a
  *To the Councillors of All the Towns in
    Germany, That They Should Establish
    Christian Schools*, 2:683b
  Von Ordnung Dienstes in der Gemeinde,
    2:685a
Lutheranism, Luther and, 2:683a-b, 689a
Lutrin, Le. See Boileau-Despréaux, Nicolas
"Lutta de classes." *See* Ferreira de Castro,
  José Maria
Lutte avec l'ange, La. See Malraux, André
Luzern *Passions*, 1:466a-b
Luzerne, M. de la (French ambassador to
  England), Chénier as private secretary
  to, 4:700a-b
Lycée Bonaparte (Condorcet), Vigny's
  schooling at, 5:449a
Lycidas. See Milton, John
Lycko-Pers resa. See Strindberg, August,
  Lucky Per's Journey
Lying, Augustine on, 1:48a–49a
Lying Woman. See Giraudoux, Jean, *La
  menteuse*
Lykkelige dager. See Undset, Sigrid, *Happy
  Times in Norway*
"Lykken gik J. J. snóksdal forbi, Da." *See*
  Gunnarsson, Gunnar
Lyly, John
  euphuism of, 9:1064a
  theatricality, 9:1068b
Lyons, massive workers' uprising in 1831,
  5:586a

Lyons, school of, Tyard and, 2:742a

Lyra. See Kalvos, Andreas; Pascoli, Giovanni

"Lyre, La." *See* Ronsard, Pierre de

"Lyric Caricatures." *See* Jiménez, Juan Ramón, *Españoles de tres mundos (caricatura lírica)*

Lyric Poetry. *See* Pascoli, Giovanni, *Lyra*; Poetry

Lyrical Ballads, The. See Wordsworth, William

Lyrical Intermezzo. See Heine, Heinrich, *Tragödien, nebst einem lyrischen Intermezzo*

Lyricism, "multilinear." *See* "Multilinear lyricism"

Lyricker im Zeitalter des Hochkapitalismus, Ein. See Benjamin, Walter

Lyrics. See Camoëns, Luís Vaz de, *Rimas*

Lyroon group. *See* Liren' group

Lys dans la vallée, Le. See Balzac, Honoré de

Lysistrata. See Aristophanes

"Lysty do poeta." *See* Tychyna, Pavlo, *Pluh*

"Lyubov'." *See* Olesha, Yuri, "Love"

M

M. See Lang, Fritz

"Ma grande lettre." *See* Sade, Donatien Alphonse François, marquis de

Ma non è una cosa seria. See Pirandello, Luigi

Mabille, Pierre, *Le miroir de merveilleux*, 11:1942b

Mabinogion: Gereint and Owein (The Lady of the Fountain), Arthurian legend and, 1:138a, 141a, 142b, 143b, 146a

MacArthur, Charles, and Hecht, Ben, *The Front Page*, Zamyatin's adaptation of, 10:1194a

Macaulay, Thomas, Taine on, 7:1452a

Macbeth. See Shakespeare, William

"*Macbeth*; or, Death-Infected." *See* Kott, Jan, *Shakespeare Our Contemporary*

Macbett. See Ionesco, Eugène

McCarthy, Joseph, 8:533a

McCarthy, Mary, on Ibsen, 7:1422a

McClintock, Robert, on Ortega y Gasset, 9:1124a

Mach, Ernst

   Beiträge zur Analyze der Empfindungen (Contributions to the Analysis of the Sensations), 9:939b

   Bergson and, 8:47b

   Musil and, 9:932b, 950a

Machado, Antonio, **9:743a–765b**

   Baroja and, 9:591a

   Campos de Castilla (Fields of Castile), 9:745b, 747b, 748a, 754a–758b

      "A José María Palacio" ("To José María Palacio"), 9:758a

      Nuevas canciones and, 9:759a, 760b

      "Proverbios y cantares" ("Proverbs and Songs"), 9:758a-b

   "Canciones a Guiomar" (Songs to Guiomar), 9:760b

   De un cancionero apócrifo (From an Apocryphal Songbook), 9:748a, 760b, 761a-b, 762a

      "El gran cero" ("The Great Zero"), 9:761a

      "El crimen fue en Granada" (The Crime Was in Granada), 9:760b, 761b

Machado, Antonio (*cont.*)
  gnostic-constructive erotism, 9:1128b
  Jiménez and, 9:996a, 1008a
  Juan de Mairena, 9:762a, 763a-b
  La guerra (The War), 9:761b
  Los complementarios (The
    Complementaries), 9:762a
  Nuevas canciones (New Songs),
    9:747b–748a, 758b–760b
    "Galerías" (Galleries), 9:759b
    "Glosando a Ronsard y otras rimas"
      (Glosses on Ronsard and Other
      Rhymes), 9:760a-b
    "Hacia la tierra baja" (Towards the Low
      Land), 9:759a-b
    "Olivo del camino" (Olive Tree on the
      Road), 9:758b–759a
    "Parergon," 9:760a
    "Proverbios y cantares" (Proverbs and
      Songs), 9:759b
  Páginas escogidas (Selected Pages), 9:746a,
    757a
    prologue, 9:761b–762a, 762b
  Poesía española (Spanish Poetry) and,
    9:763b
  Poesías completas (Complete Poems),
    9:746a, 747b–748a, 757a
  Soledades, galerías, y otros poemas
    (Solitudes, Galleries, and Other Poems),
    9:751b–753a, 753b–754a
    Campos de Castilla and, 9:757a
    "Canciones y coplas" (Songs and Verses),
      9:752b
    "El viajero" (The Traveler), 9:751b, 760a
    "Galerías" (Galleries), 9:751b–752b
  Soledades (Solitudes), 9:745b, 747b,
    748a–751b, 753a, 763b, 764a
    "Canciones" (Songs), 9:751b
    "Cenit" (Zenith), 9:748a-b
    "Crepúsculo" (Twilight), 9:749b–750a
    "Del camino" (Of the Way), 9:750a–751a
    "Humorismos, fantasías y apuntos"
      (Humorisms, Fantasies, and Sketches),
      9:751b, 753a-b
    "La fuente" (The Fountain), 9:749a-b
    "La saeta" (The Dart), 9:751a-b, 757b
    "Otoño" (Autumn), 9:749b

"Tarde" (Afternoon), 9:748b–749a
Valle-Inclán and, 8:331a
Machado de Assis, Joachim Maria, Eça and,
  7:1683b, 1691b, 1700a-b
Machado, Manuel, 9:747b, 760b
  Institución Libre de Enseñanza and, 9:1121a
  *Obras completas de Manuel y Antonio
    Machado* (Complete Works of Manuel
    and Antonio Machado), 9:746a-b
Machado y Álvarez, Antonio, 9:743b
Machar, J. S., Hašek and, 9:1096a
Machaut, Guillaume de, *Romance of the Rose*
  and, 1:332b
Machiavelli, Niccolò, **2:595a–618b**
  Alfieri and, 4:665b, 672a-b
  Baroja's inquiries about, 9:603a
  Bossuet and, 3:158a
  Corneille's *Cinna* and, 3:37b–38a
  Decennale primo (First Decade),
    2:597b–598a
  Decennale secondo (Second Decade), 2:598a
  *Del modo di trattare i popoli della
    Valdichiana ribellati* (On the Method of
    Dealing with the Rebellious Peoples of
    the Valdichiana), 2:597b
  *Descrizione del modo tenuto del duca
    Valentino nello ammazzare Vitellozi
    Vitelli . . .* (A Description of the Method
    Used by Duke Valentino in Killing
    Vitellozzo Vitelli . . .), 2:597a
  *Discorso o dialogo intorno alla nostra
    lingua* (A Dialogue on Language),
    2:599b
  *Discursus florentinarum rerum post mortem
    iunioris Laurentii Medices* (A Discourse
    on Remodeling the Government of
    Florence), 2:598b
  *Favola: Belfagor arcidiavolo che prese
    moglie* (A Fable: Belfagor, the Devil
    Who Took a Wife), 2:599a
  Frederick II's *Anti Machiavel* on, 4:374a
  French culture and, 2:694a
  Le maschere (The Masks), 2:599b
  *Parole da dirle sopra la provisione del
    danaio, facto un poco di proemio et di
    scusa* (Remarks on the Raising of
    Money), 2:597b

The Art of War (*Arte della guerra*), 2:598b, 603a

The Discourses on the First Decade of Titus Livius (*I Discorsi sopra la prima deca di Tito Livio*), 2:596a, 598a-b, 602a-b
    Alfieri and, 4:672a, 672b

The History of Florence (*Istorie fiorentine*), 2:598b–599a, 603a-b
    Alfieri and, 4:672a-b

The Life of Castruccio Castracani of Lucca (*La vita di Castruccio Castracane da Lucca*), 2:599a, 603a

The Mandrake Root (*La mandragola*), 2:599b, 613a–615a

The Prince (*Il principe*), 2:598a-b, 600a–608b
    "Exhortation to Liberate Italy from the Barbarians," 4:674a
    and Silone's hermit-pope, 12:2300a

Machiavellianism, 2:615a–617a

Machine, in Montesquieu's thought, 3:352a, 353a, 359a

Machine à écrire, La. See Cocteau, Jean

Machine infernale, La. See Cocteau, Jean, *The Infernal Machine*

Machinery imagery, in Olesha's *Envy*, 11:2238a-b

"Macht und Überleben." *See* Canetti, Elias, "Power and Survival"

MacLeish, Archibald
    "American Letter," Seferis' translation, 12:2259b
    "Men," 9:894a
    Seferis and, 12:2255a

McLuhan, Marshall, Marinetti and, 9:801a, 803b

MacNeice, Louis, Seferis and, 12:2261a

Macpherson, James
    "Ossianic" poetry of
        Chénier's aesthetics compared to, 4:707b
        Herder and, 4:641b, 648b

Macrobius, Ambrosius Theodosius, 1:325b

Macropulos Secret, The. See Čapek, Karel, *Věc Makropulos*

Mad Love. See Breton, André, *L'Amour fou*

"Mad Pomegranate Tree, The." *See* Elytis, Odysseus, *Prosanatolismi* (*Orientations*), "I treli rodia"

Madame Bovary. See Flaubert, Gustave

Madame Gervaisais. See Goncourt, Edmond Louis Antoine and Jules Alfred Huot de

Madame Legros. See Mann, Heinrich

"Madame Lucrezia Lane." *See* Mérimée, Prosper, "Il vicolo di Madama Lucrezia"

"Madame Tellier's Establishment." *See* Maupassant, Guy de, "La maison Tellier"

Madeleine Férat. See Zola, Émile

"Madeleine and tea" episode (Proust), 8:561b–562a, 562b–563a, 564a, 564b, 565a

Mademoiselle de Belle-Isle. See Dumas père, Alexandre

Mademoiselle de Maupin. See Gautier, Théophile

Mademoiselle Jaïre. See Ghelderode, Michel de, *Miss Jairus*

Madman and the Nun, The. See Witkiewicz, Stanisław Ignacy, *Wariat i zakonnica*

Madness. *See* Mental illness

Madness and Civilization: A History of Insanity in the Age of Reason. See Foucault, Michel

Madonna Dianora. See Hofmannsthal, Hugo von, *Die Frau im Fenster*

"Madonna of the Future, The." *See* James, Henry

Madonna-whore complex, Ady and, 9:869a

"Madre, La." *See* Ginzburg, Natalia

Madrid
    in Baroja's novels, 9:590a, 597a, 607a
    literary café society of, 9:592a
    Pérez Galdós and, 7:1598a–1600b, 1614b–1615b
    see also Free Institution of Teaching (Madrid)

Madrigals
    in Renaissance pastoral poetry, 2:909b–910a
    of Tasso, 2:815b–816a

Madwoman of Chaillot, The. See Giraudoux, Jean, *La folle de Chaillot*

Maestro-don Gesualdo. See Verga, Giovanni

Maeterlinck, Maurice, **8:119a–146b**
  Aglavaine and Sélysette (*Aglavaine et Sélysette*), 8:133b, 134b–135a
  Alladine and Palomides (*Alladine et Palomides*), 8:130b–131a, 134b
  Ariane et Barbe-Bleue, ou la délivrance inutile (*Ardiane and Barbe Blue*), 8:136a-b
  and Azorín, 9:641b, 648a
  in Bely's *Na rubezhe dvukh stoletii*, 9:911b
  Bulles bleues (Blue Bubbles), 8:120a-b, 121b, 143a
  Douze chansons (*Twelve Songs*), 8:135a
  Ghelderode and, 11:2113b, 2114b, 2115a
  Hesse's *Eine Stunde hinter Mitternacht* and, 9:835b
  Intérieur (*Interior* or *Home*), 8:130b, 131b–132a
  La mort de Tintagiles (*The Death of Tintagiles*), 8:130b, 132a-b
  La mort (*Death*), 8:140a-b
  La sagesse et la destinée (*Wisdom and Destiny*), 8:135a–136a
  La vie des abeilles (*The Life of the Bee*), 8:136a, 140a, 9:648a
  Le double jardin (*The Double Garden*), 8:137b–138a
  "Le Tragique quotidien" ("The Tragical in Daily Life"), 8:131b–132a
  Les aveugles (*The Blind*), 8:126b–127b, 9:651b
    Khlebnikov's "Gospozha Lenin" and, 10:1357a
  Les sept princesses (*The Seven Princesses*), 8:127b–128a
  L'Intelligence des fleurs (*The Intelligence of the Flowers*), 8:138a
  Monna Vanna, 8:136a, 137a-b
  Musil's *Young Törless* and, 9:951b
  Novalis and, 5:219a
  Olesha's *The Three Fat Men* and, 11:2248a
  "Onirologie" (Onirology), 8:123a-b
  "Pascalian Series," 8:142b
  Pelléas et Mélisande, 8:128b–130b, 136b–137a, 140a
    Anouilh's *Romeo and Jeannette* and, 13:2853b

  Apollinaire and, 9:886a, 889b
  post–World-War-I plays of, 8:141a–142a
  Princess Maleine (*La Princesse Maleine*), 8:124a–125b
  Serres chaudes (*Hot-Houses*), 8:122a, 123a-b
  Soeur Béatrice (*Sister Beatrice*), 8:136b
  spiritualism of, 9:592b
  Strindberg and, 7:1753b
  The Blue Bird (*L'Oiseau bleu*), 8:138b–140a, 141a-b
  The Intruder (*L'Intruse*), 8:125b–126b, 128b
  The Treasure of the Humble (*Le trésor des humbles*), 8:131b–132b, 133b–134a
  Villiers de l'Isle-Adam and, 8:121b–122a, 123a, 124b
  works on natural history, 8:136a, 138a, 142a-b
  Yourcenar and, 12:2537b
Maeztu, María de, on Ortega y Gasset, 9:1125b
Maeztu, Ramiro de
  in Generation of '98, 9:593a
  Ortega y Gasset and, 9:1122b
  political journalism, 9:1122a
  social criticism, 9:1121b
  Valle-Inclán and, 8:336b
"Magenta-Colored Clouds." *See* Montale, Eugenio, *The Storm and Other Things* (*La bufera e altro*), "Nubi color magenta"
Magic
  Ekelöf and, 12:2655a
  in Goethe's *Faust*, 5:19a, 22b
  in Gottfried, 1:253b
  in Olesha's *The Three Fat Men*, 11:2247b
  in Welsh legends, 1:142b
Magic Castle, The. *See* Tieck, Ludwig, *Das Zauberschloss*
Magic idealism, Novalis and, 5:210b
Magic Lantern, The. *See* Tsvetaeva, Marina, *Volshebnyi fonar'*
Magic Mountain, The. See Mann, Thomas
Magic play. *See* Zauberspiel (magic play)
Magic realism, in Azorín's works, 9:639b, 658a
"Magical Thinking" (Hesse), 9:844a, 852a
"Magician Dies, The." *See* Csáth, Géza, *A varászlo halála*

Magician, The. See Simenon, Georges, *Antoine et Julie*

Mágico prodigioso, El. See Calderón de la Barca, Pedro, *The Prodigious Magician*

Magie rouge. See Ghelderode, Michel de, *Red Magic*

"Magisches Denken." *See* "Magical Thinking" (Hesse)

Magister Ludi. See Hesse, Hermann

Magnasco, Alessandro, Butor and, 13:3306b

Magnet of Doom. See Simenon, Georges, *L'Aîné des Ferchaux*

Magnetic Fields, The. See Breton, André, and Soupault, Philippe

"Magnificat." *See* Claudel, Paul, *Cinq grandes odes*

Magnus, Olaus, *Carta marina et descriptio septentrionalium,* 12:2665b

Magoun, F. P., on Anglo-Saxon poetic techniques, 1:67a

Magpie on the Gallows, The. See Ghelderode, Michel de, *La pie sur le gibet*

"Magyar jakobinus dala." *See* Ady, Endre

Magyar közélet, 9:875a

Magyars, in Ady's "Flight from Worries," 9:862b

Mahé, Albert. *See* Camus, Albert

Mahé Family's Circle, The. See Simenon, Georges, *Le cercle des Mahé*

Mahler, Gustav
  Kindertotenlieder, 10:1234b
  Mann's *Doctor Faustus* and, 9:733b

Mahogany. See Pil'niak, Boris, *Krasnoe derevo*

Mahomet. See Voltaire

Mährisch-Weisskirchen Academy, 9:931b

"Mai." *See* Apollinaire, Guillaume, *Alcools*

Mai devi domandarmi. See Ginzburg, Natalia

Maia. See D'Annunzio, Gabriele

Maias, Os (The Maias). See Eça de Queiroz, José Maria

Maid, The. *See* Voltaire, *La pucelle*

Maid Maleen. See Brothers Grimm, *Jungfrau Maleen*

Maid of Orleans, The. See Schiller, Friedrich von

Maid to Marry. See Ionesco, Eugène, *Jeune fille à marier*

Maidens of the Rocks. See D'Annunzio, Gabriele, *Le vergini delle rocce*

Maid's Room, The. *See* Moberg, Vilhelm, *Jungfrukammare*

Maids, The. See Genet, Jean

Maigret and the Enigmatic Lett. See Simenon, Georges, *Petr-le-Letton*

Maigret et les témoins récalcitrants. See Simenon, Georges

Maigret et les vieillards. See Simenon, Georges

Maigret et son mort. See Simenon, Georges

Maigret and the Hundred Gibbets. See Simenon, Georges, *Le pendu de Saint-Pholien*

Maigret and the Reluctant Witnesses. See Simenon, Georges, *Maigret et les témoins récalcitrants*

Maigret in Society. See Simenon, Georges, *Maigret et les vieillards*

Maigret's First Case. See Simenon, Georges, *La première enquête de Maigret*

Maigret's Memoirs. See Simenon, Georges, *Les mémoires de Maigret*

Maigret's Special Murder. See Simenon, Georges, *Maigret et son mort*

Maikov, Apollon, Dostoevsky and, 7:1357a

Mailer, Norman, *The Naked and the Dead,* 13:3036a

Maillat, Henriette, Huysmans and, 7:1721a

Maimonides, Moses, Aquinas and, 1:422a

"Main d'écorché, La." *See* Maupassant, Guy de, "The Dead Hand"

Mainet, influence on *Gesta de las mocedades de Rodrigo,* 1:129a

"Mains de Jeanne Marie, Les." *See* Rimbaud, Arthur

Mains jointes, Les. See Mauriac, François

"Mainspring of Consumptive Disease, The." *See* Khlebnikov, Velimir, "Pruzhina chakhotki"

Maintenon, Madame de, Fénelon and, 3:269b–270b, 281b

Mairet, Jean
  Guarini's influence on, 2:919b
  Sophonisbe, 3:26b, 32b, 36a
  Sylvanire, 3:26b

Maison basse. See Aymé, Marcel, *The House of Men*

Maison de Claudine, Le. See Colette

Maison de France (Japan), Claudel and, 8:487a

Maison de rendez-vous, La. See Robbe-Grillet, Alain

"Maison du berger, La." *See* Vigny, Alfred Victor de, *Les destinées*

Maison Nucingen, La. See Balzac, Honoré de

"Maison Tellier, La." *See* Maupassant, Guy de

Maître de Santiago, Le. See Montherlant, Henry de, *The Master of Santiago*

Maître, Le. See Ionesco, Eugène

Maîtres sonneurs, Les. See Sand, George

Maja desnuda, La. See Blasco Ibáñez, Vicente

Majitelé klíčů. See Kundera, Milan

Majlath, Johann, Count, Grillparzer's letter to, 5:439b

Major Art Council of the Department of Theaters and Spectacles in Petrograd, The. *See* Otdela teatrov i zrelishch v Petrograde

Major Trends in Jewish Mysticism. See Scholem, Gershom

"Majorat, Das." *See* Hoffmann, E. T. A.

Majority rule, Tocqueville on, 6:896a-b

Májové výkřiky. See Hašek, Jaroslav

"Makar Chudra." *See* Gorky, Maxim

Makriyannis, Yannis, *Apomnimonevmata (Memoirs)*, 12:2257a-b, 2258a, 13:2969b

Makronisiotika. See Ritsos, Yannis

"Maksim Maksimych." *See* Lermontov, Mikhail Yurievich

"Mal, Le." *See* Rimbaud, Arthur

Mal aimés, Les. See Mauriac, François, *The Unfortunate Lovers*

Mal du siècle, in Vigny's "Moses," 5:457a

Mal, Le. See Mauriac, François, *The Enemy*

Mala hierba. See Baroja, Pío, *Weeds*

Malade imaginaire, Le. See Molière

"Malade, La." *See* Chénier, André

Maladie mentale et personnalité. See Foucault, Michel, *Mental Illness and Psychology*

"Malagueña." *See* García Lorca, Federico

Malamud, Bernard, Böll and, 13:3165b

Malanos, Timos, on Cavafy, 8:207b

Malaspina family, Dante and, 1:434b

Malaval, François, *Pratique facile*, Madame Guyon's quietism and, 3:268b

Malavoglia, I. See Verga, Giovanni

"Malé nedorozumęni." *See* Hašek, Jaroslav

Male/female relationships. *See* Love; Sexes, relations between; Sexual passion; Sexuality

Malebranche, Nicolas
Bossuet and, 3:171b–172a
Traité sur la nature et la grâce (Treatise on Nature and Grace), Fénelon and, 3:266b

Maleficio de la mariposa, El. See García Lorca, Federico

Malempin. See Simenon, Georges

Malentendu, Le. See Camus, Albert, *The Misunderstanding*

Malesherbes, Guillaume de, Chénier's help with king's defense by, 4:705a

Malherbe, François de
Chénier's marginalia on, 4:696b, 705b–706a
in "Epître à Huet," 3:79a
Queneau and, 12:2520b
Ronsard and, 2:741a

Malice, Schopenhauer's view of, 5:404b–405a, 405b

"Malinovaia shashka." *See* Khlebnikov, Velimir

Malinowski, Bronisław, Witkiewicz and, 10:1209a-b, 1212a-b

Malkoff, Karl, 13:2968a

Mallarmé, Stéphane, **7:1567a–1595b**
Ady and, 9:861b
"Angoisse" ("Anguish"), 7:1580a–1581a
Apollinaire and, 9:886b, 888b, 891b, 901b
"Autre éventail/de Mademoiselle Mallarmé" ("Another Fan/of Mademoiselle Mallarmé's"), 7:1581b
Breton and, 11:1939a, 1951a
Butor and, 13:3289b, 3300b
Claudel and, 8:472a, 485b, 490a
"Crayonné au théâtre" ("Theater Jottings"), Valéry and, 8:586a
"Crise de vers" ("Crisis of Verse"), 7:1577b
critical essays by, 7:1575b–1576a
decadence and, 7:1641a
Foucault and, 13:3353b–3354a

George and, 8:450a, 455b

Gide and, 8:495b

Hérodiade, 7:1581a–1583b

  "Salomé" and, 9:888b

  Valéry and, "Narcisse parle," 8:570b

hommages and *tombeaux* for fellow artists, 7:1573b–1574b

Huysmans and, 7:1586a–1587b, 1718b–1719a

Igitur, The Madness of Elbehnon (*Igitur ou la folie d'Elbehnon*), 7:1581a, 1588a–1589b

influence of, 7:1575b–1576a, 1586a, 1592a–1593b

Jarry and, 9:666a

Jiménez and, 9:993b

"L'Action restreinte" ("Action Restricted"), 7:1569a-b

L'Après-midi d'un faune, 7:1581a, 1583b–1587b

Le dernière mode (*The Latest Thing*) journal, 7:1576a-b, 1578a

Le livre (*The Book*), 8:472a, 571b

"Le nénuphur blanc" ("The White Water-Lily"), 7:1581b–1582a

"Le pitre châtié" ("The Clown Chastised"), 7:1572b–1573b

"Le tombeau d'Edgar Poe" ("The Tomb of Edgar Poe"), 7:1573b–1574b

"Le vierge, le vivace et le bel aujourd'hui," 7:1575a-b

in *Les délisquescences*, 7:1641a

"Les fenêtres" ("The Windows"), 7:1573b

Les mots anglais, 6:1036a

Maeterlinck and, 8:121a, 124a-b, 135a

Marinetti and, 9:805b

Pascoli and, 7:1826a, 1831b

popularity of, 8:297a

"Prose/*for des Esseintes*," 7:1586a–1587b

on public response to poetry, 9:1136a

Rilke and, 9:768a, 779b, 780a, 782b

Rimbaud and, 7:1785a, 1804b

"Sainte," 7:1578a–1579a

soirees of, 7:1620b

Sonnets to Orpheus and, 9:787a-b, 788a

theogony of, 7:1588a, 1589b

typographic innovations by, 7:1590a-b

Un coup de dés jamais n'abolira le hasard (*A Throw of the Dice Never Will Abolish Chance*), 7:1581a, 1589b–1592a, 13:3300b

"Une dentelle s'abolit . . ." ("A lace self-abolishes"), 7:1580b–1581a

Ungaretti and, 10:1458b–1459a

Valéry and, 8:569b, 571b, 572a

  "The Rower," 8:583b

Verlaine and, 7:1639b, 1640a

verse drama, 7:1426b

"Victorieusement fui le suicide beau," 7:1567b–1568b, 1569b–1570a, 1574b

Vittorini and, 12:2735b

Malmstad, John E., 9:925a

Malory, Sir Thomas, 1:470b

Arthurian legend and, 1:151a, 153b–154a

Morte Darthur, Arthurian legend and, decline after, 1:155a

Malraux, André, 12:2413a–2431b

Anti-Memoirs (*Antimémoires*), 12:2413b–2414a, 2416b, 2419a, 2427a-b, 2428a-b

Babel and, 11:1911b

Camus and, 13:3055b

Days of Wrath, 12:2415a, 2422a-b

on Dostoevsky, 7:1350a

Éternidade and, 11:2160a

La condition humaine, 12:2517b

La lutte avec l'ange (The Struggle with the Angel), 12:2427a

Le miroir des limbes (The Mirror of Limbo), 12:2427a

Le musée imaginaire de la sculpture mondiale (*The Imaginary Museum of World Sculpture*), 12:2415b

Le royaume farfelu (The Bizarre Kingdom), 12:2414a

Les puissances du désert (The Powers of the Wilderness), 12:2427a

L'Indochine, 12:2414b

Lunes en papier (Paper Moons), 12:2414a-b, 2416b

Man's Fate (*La condition humaine*), 12:2413a, 2413b, 2415a, 2419b–2422a, 13:3038a

Malraux, André (*cont.*)
   Man's Hope (*L'Espoir*), 12:2413a, 2413b,
     2422b–2424b, 2427b–2428a, 2429a-b
     Ekelöf and, 12:2649a
     Queneau and, 12:2511a
     Sarraute and, 12:2337a
   Saturne: Essai sur Goya (*Saturn: An Essay
     on Goya*), 12:2415b
     Silone and, 12:2273a, 2276b
     Simenon and, 12:2504a
   The Conquerors (*Les conquérants*),
     12:2413a, 2413b, 2415a, 2416b–2417b,
     2419a, 2429a
   The Metamorphosis of the Gods (*La
     métamorphose des dieux*), 12:2415b,
     2425b
   The Psychology of Art (*La psychologie de
     l'art*), 12:2415b, 2425b
   The Royal Way (*La voie royale*), 12:2413a,
     2413b, 2414a, 2415a, 2417b–2419a,
     2429a
   The Temptation of the West (*La tentation de
     l'Occident*), 12:2414b–2415a, 2416b
   The Voices of Silence (*Les voix du silence*),
     12:2415b, 2419a-b, 2425b, 2426b–2427a
   The Walnut Trees of Altenburg (*Les noyers
     de l'Altenburg*), 12:2413a, 2413b–2414a,
     2416b, 2424b–2425a, 2427a-b, 2428a-b
Malrik, Andrey, Khlebnikov's influence on,
   10:1332b
Maltaverne. *See* Mauriac, François
Malusha's Granddaughter. *See* Khlebnikov,
   Velimir, "Vnuchka Malushi"
Malvezzi, Teresa Carniani, Leopardi and,
   5:547a
"Mama, Rimma, i Alla." *See* Babel, Isaac
"Mamai." *See* Zamyatin, Yevgeny Ivanovich
Mamelles de Tirésias, Les. See Apollinaire,
   Guillaume
"Mammom szerzetes zsoltára." *See* Ady, Endre
Mammon, in poetry of Ady, 9:862b
Mamoulian, Rouben, Strindberg and, 7:1739a
Man
   final end of, Aquinas on, 1:424b–425a
   ideal, in Michelet's works, 5:578a
   nature of
     Aquinas' *Summa theologica* on, 1:423a-b

   Calderón's view of, 2:881a
   in Dante's *De monarchia*, 1:443b
   in Ferreira de Castro's *Jungle*, 11:2159b
   in La Bruyère's *Caractères*, 3:249a
   Leconte de Lisle's view of, 6:1259a–1269a
   in miracle plays, 1:464b–465a
   Montaigne on, 2:783b
   Prudentius on, 1:17b. 1.18a
   Sade's view of, 4:627b, 628b
   Schopenhauer's view of basic drives,
     5:404b–405b
Man. *See* Mayakovsky, Vladimir, *Chelovek*
"Man as an End." *See* Moravia, Alberto
Man with Bags. See Ionesco, Eugène,
   L'Homme aux valises
Man, Beast, and Virtue. See Pirandello, Luigi,
   L'Uomo, la bestia, e la virtù
Man with the Carnation, The. *See* Ritsos,
   Yannis, *O anthropos me to gharyfallo*
Man and Crisis. See Ortega y Gasset, José, *En
   torno a Galileo*
Man and Darwinian Theory. *See* Svevo, Italo,
   "L'Uomo e la teoria darvinia"
Man with Dropsy Lies in Wait for His Wife's
   Lover, A. *See* Witkiewicz, Stanisław
   Ignacy, *Człowiek z wodną puchliną
   zaczaja się na kochanka swej żony*
Man with the Flower in His Mouth, The. See
   Pirandello, Luigi, *L'Uomo dal fiore in
   bocca*
"Man hât hêr Gêrhart Atze ein pfert." *See*
   Walther von der Vogelweide
Man and His Desire. *See* Claudel, Paul,
   L'Homme et son désir
Man in the Holocene. See Frisch, Max
Man in the Iron Mask
   in Dumas's works, 6:733a
   in Hugo's works, 6:696b
Man in the Iron Mask, The. See Dumas père,
   Alexandre, *Le Vicomte de Bragelonne*
Man of La Mancha, 13:3033b
Man with the Little Dog, The. See Simenon,
   Georges, *L'Homme au petit chien*
Man and the Masses. See Toller, Ernst
Man and People. See Ortega y Gasset, José, *El
   hombre y la gente*

"Man seite mir ie von Tegersê." *See* Walther von der Vogelweide

"Man in a Shell, The." *See* Chekhov, Anton, "Chelovek v futlyare"

"Man and the Snake, The." *See* La Fontaine, Jean de, *Fables*, "L'Homme et la couleuvre"

Man of Straw. See Mann, Heinrich, *Der Untertan*

Man and Superman. See Shaw, George Bernard

Man, the Vast Garden. *See* Kundera, Milan, *Člověk zahrada širá*

Man Who Lived His Life Over, The. See Lagerkvist, Pär, *Han som fick leva om sitt liv*

"Man Who Loved the Néréids, The." *See* Yourcenar, Marguerite, *Nouvelles orientales*

Man Without Qualities, The. See Musil, Robert

Man Without a Soul, The. See Lagerkvist, Pär, *Mannen utan själ*

Man of the World, A. *See* Goldoni, Carlo, *Momolo cortesan*

Mana. See Ritsos, Yannis

"Mana tou Hristou, I." *See* Varnalis, Kostas

"Manchy, Le." *See* Leconte de Lisle, Charles Marie

Manciata di more, Una. See Silone, Ignazio

Mancini, Giuseppina, D'Annunzio and, 8:187b, 199b

Mandarin, The (O Mandarim). See Eça de Queiroz, José Maria

Mandarine. See Anouilh, Jean

Mandarins, The (Les Mandarins). See Beauvoir, Simone de

Mandelshtam, Emil Veniaminovich (father), cultural milieu of, 10:1621a

Mandelshtam, Flora Osipovna (mother)
cultural milieu of, 10:1621a
Mandelshtam's poem on her death, 10:1637a-b

Mandelshtam, Nadezhda, Pasternak's *My Sister, Life* and, 10:1599a-b

Mandelshtam, Osip, **10:1619a–1649b**
"A. Blok," cult and culture in, 10:1628a
acmeism and, 10:1523a, 1539b

in Akhmatova's *Poem Without a Hero*, 10:1535a, 1537b
"Akter i rabochii" ("The Actor and the Workman"), his arrest and, 10:1639a
"Barsuch'ia nora" ("The Badger's Den"), 9:986a
on Bely, 9:921b, 924b
Blok and, 9:985b, 986a
"Bloody Mystery Play of January Ninth" ("Krovavaia misteriia 9-go ianvaria"), Czarevich Alexis' death in, 10:1625b–1626a
Egipetskaia marka (The Egyptian Stamp), 10:1643a-b
Fourth Prose (Chetvertaia proza), 10:1643b–1644a
"Hagia Sophia," religious philosophy in, 10:1630b
"Ia budu skitat'sia . . ." (I shall roam . . .), 10:1642b
"Iazyk bulyzhnika," doomsday and, 10:1641b
"K nemetskoi rechi," 10:1645a
Khlebnikov's quarrel with, 10:1337a
"Konets romana" ("The End of the Novel"), censorship of, 10:1643a
"Kontsert na vokzale" ("Concert at the Railroad Station"), 10:1641a
literary celebrity, 11:1893b
on Mayakovsky, 11:1856a
"Nashedshii podkovu" ("He Who Finds a Horseshoe"), 10:1642a-b
"Ne iskushai chuzhikh narechii" ("Do not attempt foreign tongues . . ."), 10:1645a
"Notre Dame," aesthetic and ethical principle in, 10:1629b, 1630b
O poezii (On Poetry), censorship of, 10:1643a
"O prirode slova" ("On the Nature of the Word"), acmeist manifesto and, 10:1633a
"O sobesednike" ("About an Interlocutor"), Villon in, 10:1630a
Pasternak's defense of, 10:1595b
on Pasternak's *My Sister, Life*, 10:1599b–1600a

Mandelshtam, Osip (*cont.*)
"1 ianvarie 1924" ("January 1, 1924"),
doomsday and, 10:1641b
"Poems About Iron" ("Zhelezo"), 10:1646b
"Rakovina" ("Seashell")
acmeist announcement of,
10:1632b–1633a
Stone and, 10:1635a
Razgovor o Dante (*Conversation About Dante*), 10:1645a
"Segodnia nochiiu . . ." (Tonight . . .),
10:1642b
Siberian exile of, 10:1537b
"Solomiulea," Poe's influence on, 10:1637a
Stikhotvoreniia (*Poems*), censorship of,
10:1643a
Stone (*Kamen'*), 10:1634a–1635b
derivation of title for, 10:1624b,
1634b–1635b
third edition of, 10:1640b–1641a
"Sumerlei svobody" ("The Twilight of
Freedom"), Communist revolution and,
10:1638a-b
"Tender Assumption Church—Florence in
Moscow," Tsvetaeva's influence on,
10:1636b
The Egyptian Stamp, 11:1890a
The Journey to Armenia (*Puteshestvie v
Armeniiu*)
criticism for, 10:1645a-b
cult and culture in, 10:1628a-b
"The Morning of Acmeism" ("Utro
akmeizma")
poetics of, 10:1624b, 1633a
Tyutchev's stone in, 10:1634b
The Noise of Time (*Shum vremeni*),
11:1886b
on biography, 10:1621a
Georgii Blok's publication of, 10:1643a
Judaism in, 10:1623b
"The Slate Ode" ("Grifel'naia oda"),
10:1641b–1642a
"sermon of the plummet" in, 10:1629b
"The Word and Culture" ("Slovo i kul'tura")
acmeist manifesto and, 10:1633a
doomsday and, 10:1641a-b
on stone inscriptions, 10:1641b

"To Cassandra," Communist revolution and,
10:1638b
"Tristia," 10:1640b
Kuzmin's publication of, 10:1640a
Tsvetaeva and, 11:1735b, 1744b–1745a
"Verses on the Unknown Soldier" ("Stikhi o
neizvestnom soldate"), 10:1646b
Mandelshtam's birth in, 10:1621b
voice of the other, 11:1906a
Voronezhskie tetradi (Voronezh Notebooks),
10:1646b–1647a
Vtoraia kniga (*The Second Book*),
10:1640a-b
"Kontsert na vokzale" and, 10:1641a
sense of impending doomsday and,
10:1641a
"Za gremuchuiu doblest . . ." ("For the
resonant valor"), 10:1644b
"Zverinets" ("The Menagerie")
Plato's ether in, 10:1625b
Tsvetaeva's influence on, 10:1636b
"Mandoline." *See* Verlaine, Paul
Mandrake Root, The (*La Mandragola*). *See*
Machiavelli, Niccolò
"Månen." *See* Södergran, Edith, "The Moon"
"Månens hemlighet." *See* Södergran, Edith
Manet, Édouard, 7:1630b
Goncourts on, 7:1397a
Olympia, 6:1019b
social realism and, 7:1631a
Zola on, 7:1531a
Manette Salomon. See Goncourt, Edmond
Louis Antoine and Jules Alfred Huot de
Maneuverings. *See* Butor, Michel, *Travaux
d'approche*; Pirandello, Luigi,
"Armeggiamenti"
Mani, 1:28b
Mania. See Goldoni, Carlo
Manichaeanism
Apotheosis on, 1:8a
Augustine and, 1:28b
"Manifestations," as mode of futurist
expression, Marinetti, 9:802b–803a
"Manifeste des Cinq." *See* Zola, Émile, *La terre*
Manifeste du surréalisme. See Breton, André

Manifesto degli intellettuali antifascisti, Il (Manifesto of the Antifascist Intellectuals). *See* Croce, Benedetto

Manifesto dell'aereopoesia, Il. *See* Marinetti, Filippo Tommaso

"Manifesto futurista della lussuria." *See* Saint-Point, Valentine

"Manifesto of Integral Conformism, The." *See* Camus, Albert

"Manifesto tecnico della letteratura futurista." *See* Marinetti, Filippo Tommaso

Manifold Observations. *See* Södergran, Edith, *Brokiga iakttagelser*

Mann, Carla, 8:519b, 527b

Mann, Golo, 8:541a

Mann, Heinrich, **8:519a–543b**

  Das Bekenntnis zum Übernationalen ("Supernational Manifesto"), 8:536b, 541b

  Das Kaiserreich (The Era of the Kaiser), 8:535b

    Der Kopf (The Chief), 8:535b

    Die Armen (The Poor), 8:535b

  Der Atem (The Breath), 8:542a-b

  Der Hass: Deutsche Zeitgeschichte (Hatred: Essays in Modern German History), 8:537a

  Der Untertan (*Man of Straw*), 8:525a, 527a, 531a–533b, 535a, 537a

    in *Das Kaiserreich*, 8:535b

    in East Germany, 8:542a

  "Die Branzilla," 8:527b

  Die Göttinnen, oder die drei Romane der Herzogin von Assy (The Goddesses; or, Three Novels of the Duchess of Assy), 8:525a–526a

    Diana, 8:526a, 533a

  Die Jagd nach Liebe (The Hunt for Love), 8:527b

  Die Jugend des Königs Henri Quatre (*Young Henry of Navarre*), 8:537b–540b

  Die kleine Stadt (*The Little Town*), 8:530a–531a

  Die Unschuldige (*Not Guilty*), 8:534b–535a

  Die Vollendung des Königs Henri Quatre (*Henry, King of France*), 8:537b–540b

"Drei Minuten Roman" ("Three-Minute Novel"), 8:526b–527a, 528b

Ein ernstes Leben (*The Hill of Lies*), 8:536b

Ein Zeitalter wird besichtigt (*An Age Is Surveyed*), 8:542a

Empfang bei der Welt (Reception of the World), 8:542a

Es kommt der Tag (There Will Come a Day), 8:537a

Eugénie, oder Die Bürgerzeit (*The Royal Woman*), 8:536a

Geist und Tat (Spirit and Deed), 8:522b, 531a

Im Schlaraffenland (*Berlin*), 8:523a–525a, 535a, 536b

In einer Familie (Within a Family), 8:521b

Kobes, 8:535b

Madame Legros, 8:534b

Magic Mountain (by Thomas Mann) and, 9:723a

Mut, 8:537a

Mutter Marie (Mother Mary), 8:536a, 541b

Pippo Spano, 8:527a-b, 532a

Professor Unrat oder das Ende einer Tyrannen (translated as *Small-Town Tyrant* and *The Blue Angel*), 8:527a, 528a–529b

Reflections of a Nonpolitical Man (by Thomas Mann) and, 9:718b

The Living Thoughts of Nietzsche, 8:540b–541a

"The Violin," 8:520a

"Voltaire—Goethe," 8:531a

"Zola," 8:534a

Zwischen den Rassen (Between the Races), 8:529b–530a

Mann ist Mann. *See* Brecht, Bertolt, *A Man's a Man*

Mann, Katia, 8:525b

Mann, Klaus, 8:537a, 541a, 541b, 9:728a

Mann, Nellie Kröger, 8:536b, 541a-b, 542a

Mann ohne Eigenschaften, Der. *See* Musil, Robert, *The Man Without Qualities*

Mann, Thomas, **9:715a–742b**

  "A Weary Hour," 8:527a

  Altersstil of, 9:855a

Mann, Thomas (*cont.*)
   Bekenntnisse des Hochstaplers Felix Krull
      (*Confessions of Felix Krull*),
      9:736b–737b
   Buddenbrooks, 8:522a, 522b, 526a,
      9:716a–717b, 720a, 724b, 1017a
     characterization, 9:716b–717a
     history of family in novels and, 10:1500a
     Reflections of a Nonpolitical Man and,
      9:719a
     themes, 9:717a-b
   Cavafy and, 8:206a
   Death in Venice (*Der Tod in Venedig*),
      9:724a, 724b–725b, 738b
     "Drei Minuten Roman" (by Heinrich
      Mann) and, 8:526b
     Klein and Wagner and, 9:843a
     Lukács's *Soul and Form* and, 10:1257b
   Die Entstehung des "Doktor Faustus' (*The
     Story of a Novel*), 9:732b
   Doctor Faustus (*Doktor Faustus*), 9:728a,
     732a–736b, 737a, 738b, 1017a
     Ady's "Mihályi Rozália csókja" and,
      9:875a
     Carla Mann and, 8:527b
     Henry IV novels (by Heinrich Mann) and,
      8:539a
     Hesse's *Rosshalde* and, 9:838a
     sources, 9:733a-b
     themes, 9:733b–734b
   Fiorenza, The Little Town (by Heinrich
     Mann) and, 8:530b
   on Fontane, 6:1300a-b
   Freud and, 8:2a, 12a
   on Goethe, 5:3a
   Hamsun and, 8:21a, 36b
   Heinrich Mann and, 8:519b, 520a-b,
     522b–523a, 535a, 538a
     Berlin, 8:523a, 524b, 525a
     on *Der Atem*, 8:542b
     Man of Straw and, 8:533a
     1917 feud, 8:534a-b
     reconciliation, 8:535b
     under Nazism, 8:537a-b, 541b
   Hesse and, 9:847a, 855a
     Klein und Wagner, 9:842a
   on Hesse's *Steppenwolf*, 9:847b

   Johnson and, 12:2381b
   Joseph and His Brothers (*Joseph und seine
     Brüder*), 9:728a–732a, 737b
     Heinrich Mann and, 8:537b
     themes, 9:729a-b, 731b
   Königliche Hoheit (*Royal Highness*), 9:737b
   Lotte in Weimar, 9:737b–738a
   Lukács and, 10:1251b, 1252b, 1272b–1273a
   Mario und der Zauberer (*Mario and the
     Magician*), 9:725b–727b
   on monarchy, 5:214a
   Musil and, 9:933a, 937b, 957a
   Nobel Prize for literature, 9:1017a
   Pirandello and, 8:413b
   Reflections of a Nonpolitical Man
     (*Betrachtungen eines Unpolitischen*),
     8:534a, 9:718a–720a, 722a, 736a
   Rilke and, 9:771b
   Storm and, 6:917b–918a
   The Beloved Returns, 5:41b
   The Magic Mountain (*Der Zauberberg*),
     8:36b, 535b, 9:720a–723b
     Henry IV novels (by Heinrich Mann) and,
      8:539a
     Hesse's *At the Spa* and, 9:846a-b
     Lukács and, 10:1272b
     Reflections of a Nonpolitical Man and,
      9:719b
     Royal Highness and, 9:737b
     setting, 9:720a-b
     style, 9:722a
     themes, 9:723a
     Tristan and, 9:724a
     and Wieland, 4:594b
   Tonio Kröger, 8:526a, 9:724a, 724b
     Diana and, 8:526a
     Gertrude and, 9:837a
     Grillparzer compared to, 5:418b
     Lukács and, 10:1259a-b
     Professor Unrat and, 8:528a
   Tristan, 9:724a, 724b
   Völsunga saga and, 1:400b
   Yourcenar on, 12:2553a-b
Mannen utan själ. See Lagerkvist, Pär
Människor. See Lagerkvist, Pär
Manolescu, Georges, 9:736b

Manon Lescaut. See Prévost, Antoine-François, *Histoire du chevalier Des Grieux et de Manon Lescaut*

Manrique, Jorge, Machado and, 9:752a

Man's Fate. See Malraux, André

Man's Hope. See Malraux, André

Mans kvinna. See Moberg, Vilhelm, *Fulfillment*

Man's a Man, A. See Brecht, Bertolt

Mansfield, Katherine
Chekhov and, 7:1857b
Vittorini and, 12:2735b

Mantatofores. See Ritsos, Yannis

Mantovano (Mantuan; Mantuanus, Baptista), eclogues of, influence on Renaissance pastoral poetry, 2:907a-b

Manual labor. *See* Labor

Manual of Piety. See Brecht, Bertolt

Manuel, Don Juan, *El conde Lucanor (The Book of Count Lucanor and Patronio)*, Eastern influence on, 2:932a-b

Manuel II of Portugal, king, 11:2146a

"Manus ferens munera." *See Carmina Burana*

Manuscript illumination, Hiberno-Saxon style, 1:63b

Manutius, Aldus, Erasmus and, 2:577b–578a

Manzoni, Alessandro, **5:367a–394b**
A Vindication of Catholic Morality (Osservazioni sulla morale cattolica), 5:374a–375a
Adelchi, Goethe's interest in, 5:369a
Discorso su alcuni punti della storia longobardica in Italia (Treatise on Some Points of the History of the Longobards in Italy), 5:385b
Fermo e Lucia, 5:381b–382a, 385b
"Appendice storica su la colonna infame," 5:391b
on historical passages, 5:392a
in Ginzburg's *La famiglia Manzoni*, 13:3158a-b
Il cinque maggio (The Fifth of May)
autobiographical element of, 5:372a
Goethe's translation of, 5:369a
Il conte di Carmagnola
Goethe's review of, 5:369a
problem of morality in, 5:374a

Lettera sul romanticismo (Letter on Romanticism), rejection of mythology in, 5:373b–374a
Lettre à M. Chauvet sur l'unité de temps et de lieu dans la tragédie (Letter to M. Chauvet on the Unities of Time and Place in Tragedy)
Fauriel's publication of, 5:369a
significance of French language composition, 5:368a
manzoniani (followers of), Carducci's antagonism to, 7:1499b–1500a, 1513b
Pascoli and, 7:1829b, 1830b
The Betrothed: A Milanese Story of the Seventeenth Century Discovered and Retold by Alessandro Manzoni (I promessi sposi, storia milanese del secolo XVII scoperta e rifatta da Alessandro Manzoni), 5:75b–85b, 560b
A Vindication compared to, 5:375a
definitive version of, 5:390b–391a
Don Abbondio's character, 5:377b–380b
famine in, 5:385b–387a
Gertrude's character in, 5:384a–385a
Giuseppe Prina's murder transferred to, 5:370a
Goethe's *Hermann und Dorothea* and, 5:371a–372a
historical background of, 5:385b–392b
the Innominato's character in, 5:383b–384a
Lucia's character, 5:380b–383a
miraculous conversion of Innominato in, 5:372b
Pirandello's *Henry IV* and, 8:405a
the plague in, 5:385b–386a, 388b–390b
Scott's influence on, 5:370b, 371a
twentieth-century standards and, 5:367a
universal Italian of, 5:368a, 391a
unpopular realism of, 5:371a
Vittorini's *Women of Messina* and, 12:2751a
The Column of Infamy (Storia della colonna infame), 5:391a–392a
The Sacred Hymns (Inni sacri)
Goethe's reception of, 5:369a

Manzoni, Alessandro (*cont.*)
　The Sacred Hymns (*Inni sacri*) (*cont.*)
　　"The Resurrection" ("La rissurrezione"),
　　　5:373a-b
　　Urania
　　　his dissatisfaction with, 5:372b–373a
　　　"The Resurrection" compared to, 5:373a-b
Manzoni europeo. See Getto, Giovanni
Manzoni Family, The. See Ginzburg, Natalia,
　　La famiglia Manzoni
Maquet, Auguste
　Dumas and, 6:724b, 739a-b
　Le bonhomme Buvat (Bumbling Old Buvat),
　　6:724b
"Maradhatsz és szerethetsz." *See* Ady, Endre
Marais, Jean, and Cocteau, 10:1556a, 1558a,
　　1558b, 1559a
Marais Theater. *See* Troupe du Marais
Marañon, Gregorio, Group at the Service of the
　　Republic, 9:1146a
Marat, Jean-Paul, Chénier's outrage at
　　glorification of, 4:714b
Maravilhas artísticas do mundo, As. See
　　Ferreira de Castro, José Maria
Marbles, The. See Doni, Antonfrancesco, *I
　　marmi*
"Marburg." *See* Pasternak, Boris
Marburg school
　neo-Kantian philosophy, 9:1124a-b
　Ortega y Gasset's studies at, 9:1124a-b
　Sozialpedagogik, 9:1125b
Marcabru
　canson and, 1:372b
　carnal love in works of, 1:169b
　classical satire and, 1:339b–340a
　courtly love in works of, 1:166a, 169b–171b
　courtly values and, 1:167b
　figurative representation and, 1:369a
　importance of, 1:171a
　"L'Autrier jost' una sebissa" ("The other day
　　near a hedge"), 1:169b
　"Lo vers comenssa" ("The poem begins"),
　　1:360a-b
　morality in works of, 1:170b–171a
　naturalness in works of, 1:168a-b, 169a-b

　"Pois l'iverns d'ogan es anatz" ("Now that
　　this year's winter is gone"),
　　1:348a–349a, 369b
　prophet persona of, 1:359b–360a
　"Pus s'enfulleysson li verjan" ("Since the
　　branches leaf out"), 1:360a
　as troubadour, 1:166b–171a
　wordplay of, 1:372a
Marcel, Gabriel, Bergson and, 8:64a
Marcellinus, Ammianus, Prudentius and,
　　1:16b, 17a
March 1917. See Solzhenitsyn, Aleksandr, *The
　　Red Wheel*
March. See März
March Foundation Prize for Literature, Azorín
　　as winner of, 9:642b
Märchen, Das. See Schnitzler, Arthur
Märchen meines Lebens ohne Dichtung. See
　　Andersen, Hans Christian, *The True
　　Story of My Life*
Marchioness Rosalinda, The. See Valle-Inclán,
　　Ramón del, *La Marquesa Rosalinda*
Marcion, Prudentius and, 1:8a, 8b, 9a
Marcovaldi, Martha, 9:932b
Marcovaldo; ovvero, La stagioni in città. See
　　Calvino, Italo, *Marcovaldo; or, The
　　Seasons of the City*
Marcus Aurelius, Roman emperor
　in Chekhov's "The Duel," 7:1866b
　in Kosztolányi's poetry, 10:1246a
　Maeterlinck and, 8:135b
Marcuse, Herbert, Thomas Mann and, 9:722b,
　　723a
Marcuse, Ludwig, Heinrich Mann and, 8:519a
"Mardoche." *See* Musset, Alfred de
Mare au diable, La. See Sand, George, *The
　　Devil's Pool*
Mare nostrum. See Blasco Ibáñez, Vicente
Maréchale d'Ancre, La. See Vigny, Alfred
　　Victor de
Mare's Comments, The. See Aymé, Marcel,
　　"Propos de la jument"
Marfaka le futuriste (*Marfaka the Futurist*).
　　See Marinetti, Filippo Tommaso
Margen de los clásicos, Al. See Azorín
Marginalia on the Classics. See Azorín, *Al
　　margen de los clásicos*

"Margita élni akar" (Margita Wants to Live).
See Ady, Endre
Margot, consort of Henry IV of France, in
Heinrich Mann's novel, 8:538a, 538b,
539a
Marguerite de Valois. See Dumas père,
Alexandre, La reine Margot
Marguerite of Navarre
Heptaméron, 2:947b–948b
Boccaccio's influence on, 2:945b, 947a-b
pastoral poetry of, 2:911a
patronage of, 2:948b
"Mária és Veronika." See Ady, Endre
María Fontán. See Azorín
Maria Magdalena. See Hebbel, Friedrich
Maria Nephele. See Elytis, Odysseus
María Sabina. See Cela, Camilo José
Maria Theresa, wife of Louis XIV, funeral
oration on by Bossuet, 3:165b
Mariage d'argent, Le. See Scribe, Eugène
Mariage de Barillon, Le. See Feydeau, Georges
Mariage de Figaro, Le. See Beaumarchais,
Pierre-Augustin Caron de, The Marriage
of Figaro
Mariage de raison, Le. See Scribe, Eugène
Mariage d'inclination, Le. See Scribe, Eugène
Mariage d'Olympe, Le. See Augier, Émile
Mariamne. See Lagerkvist, Pär; L'Hermite,
Tristan
Marías, Julian, perspectivism, 9:1129a
Marie Antoinette of France, queen
defended by Staël, 5:91b–92a
in Dumas's works, 6:726b, 729a, 733a–734a
Marie de France, Brother Róbert and, 1:399b
Marie de Médicis, Counter-Reformation in
France and, 3:264b
Marie Tudor. See Hugo, Victor
Mariés de la Tour Eiffel, Les. See Cocteau,
Jean
Marigo, Aristide, 1:441b
Mariia. See Babel, Isaac
Marina. See Eliot, T. S.
"Marine." See Rimbaud, Arthur
Marinetti e il futurismo. See Marinetti, Filippo
Tommaso
Marinetti, Filippo Tommaso, **9:797a–832b**
"A l'automobile" (To the Car), 9:806b

Al di là del comunismo (Beyond
Communism), 9:826a
Apollinaire and, 9:884b, 894b
"Battaglia peso + odore" ("Battle Weight +
Smell"), 9:814b–815a
"Contro l'amore e il parlamentarismo"
("Against Amore and
Parliamentarism"), 9:811a
Destruction, 9:806a
"Distruzione della sintassi—Immaginazione
senza fili—Parole in libertà"
("Destruction of Syntax—Imagination
Without Strings—Words-in-freedom"),
9:815a
"Dune" ("Dunes"), 9:815a
Futurismo e fascismo (Futurism and
Fascism), 9:814a
Gli indomabili (The Untamables), 9:802a,
826a-b
Hylaean group and, 10:1335b
"Il Duce aviatore," 9:827a
Il manifesto dell'aereopoesia (The Manifesto
of Aero-Poetry), 9:827a
"Il teatro della sorpresa" ("The Theater of
Surprise"), 9:821b
"Il teatro di varietà" ("The Variety Theater"),
9:821b–822b
"Il teatro futurista sintetico" ("The Futurist
Synthetic Theater"), 9:821b, 822b
"Il teatro tattile" ("The Tactile Theater"),
9:821b
Khlebnikov's leaflet concerning, 10:1337a
La conquête des étoiles (The Conquest of
the Stars), 9:806a
La grande Milano tradizionale e futurista
(The Great Traditional and Futurist
Milan), 9:802a-b
L'Aereopoema del golfo dell Spezia (The
Aero-Poem on the Gulf of La Spezia),
9:827a
L'Alcova d'acciaio (The Steel Alcove),
9:825a-b
Le roi bombance (King Riot), 9:806a
"Les vieux marins" ("The Old Sailors"),
9:805b

Marinetti, Filippo Tommaso (*cont.*)

"Lo splendore geometrico e meccanico e la sensibilità numerica" ("Geometric and Mechanical Splendor and the Numerical Sensibility"), 9:815a

"Manifesto tecnico della letteratura futurista" ("Technical Manifesto of Futurist Literature"), 9:808b, 814b, 815a

Marfaka le futuriste (*Marfaka the Futurist*), 9:802a, 806b–807a, 826a

Marinetti e il futurismo, 9:825b

Olesha and, 11:2252a

8 anime in una bomba (*8 Souls in a Bomb*), 9:802a

Pascoli and, 7:1832a

Poesie a Beny, 9:827b

"Quarto d'ora di poesia della X Mas" ("Fifteen Minutes of Poetry on the X Mas"), 9:827b

Russian futurists and, 11:1840b–1841a, 2251a

Spagna veloce e toro futurista (*Speedy Spain and Futurist Bull*), 9:802a, 826b

"The Futurist Manifesto," 9:800b–801b, 803a, 807a-b

  interpretation of, 9:811b–812a, 814a

  points of, 9:809a–811a

  rebirth passage, 9:804a-b

  structure, 9:808a

  style, 9:808b–809a

"Uccidiamo il chiaro di luna!" ("Let's Murder the Moonshine!"), 9:812b–813a

Una sensibilità italiana nata in Egitto (*An Italian Sensibility Born in Egypt*), 9:802a-b, 805a

"Zang Tumb Tumb," 9:802a, 815a, 815b, 817b–819b

Marini, Giambattista

"Nera sì, ma se' bella" ("You Are Indeed Black, But You are Beautiful"), 2:753b

Petrarchan influence, 2:504a-b

Mario und der Zauberer (*Mario and the Magician*). *See* Mann, Thomas

Marion de Lorme. See Hugo, Victor

Marionette, che passione! See San Secondo, Rosso di

Marionetten (Marionettes). *See* Schnitzler, Arthur

Marionettes

  Dinesen and, 10:1297a

  Maeterlinck dramas for, 8:130b–131a

  see also Puppet stage

Marionettes de Ranson, Les, 8:131a

Marionettes, What Passions They Feel! *See* San Secondo, Rosso di, *Marionette, che passione!*

Maritain, Jacques

  Bergson and, 8:45a, 61a, 64a

  Gombrowicz and, 12:2567b

Marivaux, Pierre

  Anouilh and, 13:2855b, 2856a

  Giraudoux and, 9:1060a

  Télémaque travesti, 3:284b

Markens grøde. See Hamsun, Knut, *Growth of the Soil*

Market Eve. See Moberg, Vilhelm, *Marknadsafton*

Markish, Simon, on Isaac Babel, 11:1891a-b

"Markiza Dezes." *See* Khlebnikov, Velimir

Marknadsafton. See Moberg, Vilhelm

Markov, Vladimir, on Hylaea's poetics, 10:1345b

Marlowe, Christopher

  Grillparzer's *Hero and Leander* and, 5:436a-b

  Machiavelli and, 2:615b

  Mann's *Doctor Faustus* and, 9:735a

  "The Passionate Shepherd to His Love," 2:915a

Marmi, I. See Doni, Antonfrancesco

Marmion. See Scott, Sir Walter

Maronitis, D., 13:2969b, 2977b

Marot, Clément

  Art poétique français and, 2:725a

  François Villon and, 2:539a

  La Fontaine and, 3:79a

  pastoral poetry of, 2:911a

  Petrarch and, 2:504a, 729a

  Revolution of 1550 and, 2:721b

Marqués de Bradomín, El. See Valle-Inclán, Ramón del

Marquésa Rosalinda, La. See Valle-Inclán, Ramón del

Márquez, Gabriel García. *See* García Márquez, Gabriel

Marquis de Bradomín, The. *See* Valle-Inclán, Ramón del, *El Marqués de Bradomín*

Marquis Desaix, The. *See* Khlebnikov, Velimir, "Markiza Dezes"

Marquis of Keith, The (Der Marquis von Keith). See Wedekind, Frank

Marquise de Gange, La (The Marquise of Gange). See Sade, Donatien Alphonse François, marquis de

Marquise of O, The. See Kleist, Heinrich von

Marriage

  in Ariosto, 2:639b–640b

  Aymé's satire of, 12:2445b–2446a

  Boileau on, 3:183a-b

  Catholic view of, 2:883b

  in Chrétien's *Cligés*, 1:194b

  in Corneille's comedies, 3:46a

  Delacroix's views on, 5:27b, 519a

  in Feydeau's plays, 7:1922a

  in Ginzburg's works, 13:3148a-b

  Ibsen's *A Doll's House*, 7:1429b–1430a

  Kierkegaard and, 6:1140b–1141a

  in La Bruyère's *Caractères*, 3:238b

  in Laforgue's poetry, 7:1891a-b, 1905a

  Molière on, 3:103b–104b

  in Moravia's works, 12:2685a–2686a, 2689a-b

  in the *Nibelungenlied*, 1:221b–222a

  in Richter's *Siebenkäs*, 5:68a

  in Scribe's plays, 7:1912b–1913b

  in Tolstoy's works

    Anna Karenina, 7:1429b–1430a

    Family Happiness, 7:1487b–1488a

  in Vico's conception, 3:309b

  in Walther, 1:296b

  in Wolfram, 1:267b

Marriage: A Completely Improbable Event in Two Acts. See Gogol, Nikolay Vasilievich

Marriage of Figaro, The. See Beaumarchais, Pierre-Augustin Caron de, *La folle journée ou le mariage de Figaro*

Marriage from Inclination. *See* Scribe, Eugène, *Le mariage d'inclination*

Marriage of Heaven and Hell. See Blake, William

Marriage for Money. *See* Scribe, Eugène, *Le mariage d'argent*

Marriage of the Monk, The. See Meyer, Conrad Ferdinand, *Die Hochzeit des Mönchs*

Marriage of Mr. Mississippi, The. See Dürrenmatt, Friedrich

Marriage, The. See Gombrowicz, Witold

Marriage of Zobeide, The. See Hofmannsthal, Hugo von

"Marrons du feu, Les." *See* Musset, Alfred de

Mars (actress and mistress of comte de Mornay), Delacroix and, 5:520a

Marschalk, Margarete, Hauptmann and, 8:155b

Marsh, James, on Herder's *The Spirit of Hebrew Poetry*, 4:649b–650a

Marshlands. See Gide, André

Marsyas čili na okraj literatury. See Čapek, Karel

Mart semnadtsatogo. See Solzhenitsyn, Aleksandr, *The Red Wheel*

Martens, Adémar-Adolphe. *See* Ghelderode, Michel de

Martes de Carnaval. See Valle-Inclán, Ramón del

Martha and Her Clock. *See* Storm, Theodor, *Marthe und ihre Uhr*

Marthe, histoire d'une fille (Marthe, Story of a Prostitute). See Huysmans, Joris Karl

Marthe und ihre Uhr. See Storm, Theodor

Martin Salander. See Keller, Gottfried

Martino, Pierre, on Verlaine's stanza forms, 7:1637a

Martinson, Harry

  Ekelöf and, 12:2635a-b

  Lotsen från Moluckas (The Pilot from Moluccas), Ekelöf and, 12:2651a

  science and, 12:2635a

  symbolism and, 12:2635b

"Martirio de Santa Olalla." *See* García Lorca, Federico

Martoglio, Nino, Pirandello and, 8:393a

Márton Ajgó Set Off . . . *See* Hašek, Jaroslav, "Elindult az Ajgó Márton . . ."

Martyr of Many Christs. *See* Ady, Endre, "A krisztusok martirja"

Martyrdom
in Prudentius' works, 1:16a
Peristephanon, 1:11b, 12a
in Wolfram, 1:284a–285a

Martyries: Seira Dhefteri. See Ritsos, Yannis

Martyries: Sira Proti. See Ritsos, Yannis

Martyrs, Les (Martyrs). See Chateaubriand, François René de

Marvell, Andrew
pastoral poetry of, 2:915b
"The Garden"
Arcadia in, 2:899b–900a
complexity of, 2:915b

Marvelous, the, in Camoëns' *The Lusiads*, 2:762b

Marvels. *See Meraviglie*

"Marvels of War." *See* Apollinaire, Guillaume, "Merveille de la guerre"

Marx Brothers, Artaud and, 11:1967b, 1978a

Marx, Karl
Communist Manifesto
Marinetti and, 9:807b
Michelet and, 5:596b
Das Kapital
Lukács and, 10:1253b
Moravia and, 12:2679a
on exile, 9:727b
Gombrowicz and, 12:2567b
Gorky and, 8:419b
and Heine, 5:505b
Labriola and, 8:312b–313a
Marinetti and, 9:798b
Michelet's attitude to social problems and, 5:596b
property rights and, 4:651b
religion and, 5:213a-b
The Eighteenth Brumaire of Louis Bonaparte, Kosztolányi's *Bloody Poet* and, 10:1236a
Zur Kritik der Politische Ökonomie (The Critique of Political Economy), 11:1724a-b

Marx, Karl, and Friedrich Engels, *Herrn Eugen Dührings Umwältung der Wissenschaft (Herr Eugen Dühring's Revolution in Science)*, Lukács and, 10:1266a–1567a

Marxism
aesthetics and, 11:2104b, 2105a
Beauvoir and, 12:2725a, 2729a
Benjamin and, 11:1723a
Brecht and, 11:2089b, 2090b, 2092a, 2093b, 2094a, 2098b, 2101a, 2103b–2104a, 2104b
Camus and, 13:3067b
Croce and, 8:314b–316a
dialectics of, 10:1266a–1267a
drama and, 11:2098b
existentialism and, 12:2718a
of Hebbel, 6:1098b–1099a
and Heine, 5:501b–502a
Herder's stages of *Humanität* compared, 4:648a-b, 650a-b
Michelet and, 5:592a-b
Milosz and, 13:2930b
Moravia and, 12:2678b–2679a, 2681b–2682a
Ortega y Gasset on, 9:1142a
Pascoli and, 7:1849a
Quasimodo and, 12:2389a
Sartre and, 12:2603b–2606a
Unamuno and, 8:286b, 287a
of Valle-Inclán, 8:336b, 337a
Weil and, 12:2792a, 2807a, 2807b
Zola and, 7:1529b
see also Communism

Mary Stuart. See Alfieri, Vittorio

Mary and Veronica. *See* Ady, Endre, "Mária és Veronika"

Mary, Virgin. *See* Virgin Mary

März (journal), Hesse and, 9:837a

Mas . . .. See Ferreira de Castro, José Maria

Masaryk, Thomas G.
Čapek and, 10:1567a-b, 1587a
Spirit of Russia, Dostoevsky and, 7:1350a

Maschera e il volto, La. See Chiarelli, Luigi

Mascherata, La. See Moravia, Alberto, *The Fancy Dress Party*

Maschere, Le. See Machiavelli, Niccolò

Masculine principle, in Hugo's works, 6:703a-b

Mask and the Face, The. *See* Chiarelli, Luigi, *La maschera e il volto*

Maske, Die (The Mask). *See* Hoffmann, E. T. A.

Maskerad. See Lermontov, Mikhail Yurievich

Maski (Masks). *See* Bely, Andrey

Masks
in Ghelderode's plays, 11:2123a-b
in Hugo's works, 6:711a

Masks, The. See Machiavelli, Niccolò, *Le maschere*

Masochism, Rousseau and, 4:450a

Mason, Eudo, on Rilke, 9:770b

Masue for Some Tomorrow. See Céline, Louis-Ferdinand, *Féerie pour une autre fois I*

Masquerade, The. See Lermontov, Mikhail Yurievich, *Maskerad*

Masquerades, Camus and, 13:3057a-b, 3063a

Masques ostendais. See Ghelderode, Michel de

Mass culture, in fiction of Flaubert, 8:520b

Mass hysteria, Broch's fictional studies in, 10:1395b–1397b

Mass, Latin, Claudel's *La messe la-bàs* and, 8:485a–487a

Mass production methods
Céline on, 11:1872a-b
see also Industrialism

Mass There, The. *See* Claudel, Paul, *La messe là-bas*

Massacre at Chios. See Delacroix, Eugène

Masse und Macht. See Canetti, Elias, *Crowds and Power*

Massenwahntheorie. See Broch, Hermann

Masses, Canetti's view of, 12:2620a, 2623b–2628a

Massignon, Louis, Claudel and, 8:479b

Massillon, Jean Baptiste, 3:163a

Massine, Léonide, 9:899b

Masson, André
on Artaud, 11:1962b
Artaud and, 11:1966a
Breton on, 11:1949a, 1950a

Masson, Paul, and Colette, 9:620b

Master Bellringers, The. See Sand, George, *Les maîtres sonneurs*

Master Builder, The. See Ibsen, Henrik; Kazantzakis, Nikos, *O protomástoras*

Master Flea. See Hoffmann, E. T. A.

"Master Glass." *See* Cervantes, Miguel de

Master Heinrich Goes for a Ride. *See* Ady, Endre, "Heine úr lovagol"

Master of Hestviken. See Undset, Sigrid

Master of the Hunt legend, in Butor, 13:3296b

Master and Man. See Tolstoy, Leo

Master Olof. See Strindberg, August

Master of Santiago, The. See Montherlant, Henry de

Masterman, Neville, on Ady, 9:859b–860a

Masterpiece, The. See Zola, Émile, *L'Oeuvre*

Masterstvo Gogolia. See Bely, Andrey

Masuccio Salernitano, *Novellino*, 2:939a–940a

Masurovsky, Gregory, Butor and, 13:3305b–3306a

Mat'. See Gorky, Maxim, *Mother*

"Mat' i muzyka." *See* Tsvetaeva, Marina

Matador, The. See Montherlant, Henry de

Matches. *See* Böll, Heinrich, "Zundhölzer"

"Mateo Falcone." *See* Mérimée, Prosper

Material universe, in Descartes's *Meditations on First Philosophy*, 3:12b, 17a-b

Materialism
in Augier's plays, 7:1918a, 1920a
Diderot and, 4:490a–491b
Molière's *Don Juan* and, 3:114b
in Olesha's works
Envy, 11:2239b
"Liompa," 11:2242b–2243a
"The Cherry Stone," 11:2243b
Rimbaud's view of, 7:1818b–1819a
Staël's *De l'Allemagne* on, 5:108b
Unamuno's rejection of, 8:293b

"Materialism." *See* Södergran, Edith

Materialismo storico ed economia marxistica. See Croce, Benedetto

Mathematics
Descartes and, 3:10a-b, 11a, 8:573b
Diderot and, 4:480a
Pascal's works, 3:130a–132b
in Peletier's poetry, 2:742a
symbolism of, Valéry and, 8:587b
Valéry on, 8:575b, 576a

"Mathematics and the Idea of Necessity." *See* Butor, Michel

Mathilde Möhring. See Fontane, Theodor

Matière de rêves. See Butor, Michel

Matière et mémoire. See Bergson, Henri, *Matter and Memory*

Matin, Le (French periodical)
   Giraudoux and, 9:1043a
   Simenon's contributions to, 12:2484a

"Matinée d'ivresse." *See* Rimbaud, Arthur

Matisse, Henri
   Elytis and, 13:2961a-b
   Valle-Inclán and, 8:332b

Matiushin, Mikhail, Khlebnikov and, 10:1334a, 1336a

Matka. See Čapek, Karel; Witkiewicz, Stanisław Ignacy

"Matrenin dvor." *See* Solzhenitsyn, Aleksandr, "Matryona's Home"

Matriarchy, in Broch, 10:1396b–1397a

Matriliny. See Bachofen, Johann Jakob, *Das Mutterrecht*

"Matrone d'Ephèse, La" ("The Matron of Ephesus"). *See* La Fontaine, Jean de

"Matryona's Home." *See* Solzhenitsyn, Aleksandr

Matta, Roberto, automatism, 11:1949b

Matter, divinity of, in Yourcenar's works, 12:2536b–2537a

Matter of Britain
   Chrétien de Troyes and, 1:141a–142a, 148b, 187b
   lais and, 1:148b–149a

Matter and Memory. See Bergson, Henri

Matter of Rome, *Roman d'Eneas* and, 1:140a-b

Matthias' Demented Scholar. *See* Ady, Endre, "Mátyás bolond diákja"

"Mattino di un mezzadro, Il." *See* Lampedusa, Giuseppe Tomasi di, *Two Stories and a Memory*

Maturin, Charles
   Dostoevsky and, 7:1350b
   Lermontov and, 6:1205b
   Melmoth the Wanderer, 6:1205b

Maturity
   Gombrowicz and, 12:2566b, 2571a–2574a
   memory and, for Kundera, 13:3406a-b

Matute, Ana María, Baroja influences, 9:613a

Mątwa, czyli Hyrkaniczny światopoglæd. See Witkiewicz, Stanisław Ignacy

"Mátyás bolond diákja." *See* Ady, Endre

Maucroix, François, 3:75a

Maunoir, Camilla, Vigny's letters to, 5:480a

Maupassant, Guy de, **7:1759a–1784b**
   "À la Feuille de Rose, Maison Turque" ("At the Rose Leaf, Turkish Brothel"), 7:1763a
   "Au bord de l'eau" ("By the Edge of the Stream"), 7:1763b
   "Auprès d'un mort" ("Beside a Dead Man"), 7:1774b
   Babel and, 11:2250b
   Bel-ami, 7:1779b–1780a, 1781a, 1781b
   "Boule de Suif" (Roly-poly or Ball of Fat), 7:1760b, 1764a, 1764b–1766a
   characters, 12:2528a
   Chekhov and, 7:1857b, 1858b
   D'Annunzio and, 8:178a, 179b
   Des vers (*Some Poems*), 7:1763b, 1764a, 1766a
   "Deux amis" ("Two Friends"), 7:1770a-b
   "Duchoux," 7:1777a-b
   "En famille" ("A Family Affair"), 7:1767b–1768a
   "Essay on the Novel" ("Le roman"), 7:1762a
   Fort comme la mort (*Strong as Death*), 7:1781b–1782a
   "Garçon, un bock!" ("Waiter, a Beer!"), 7:1777a
   Goncourts and, 7:1416b
   Heinrich Mann and, 8:520b
   "Histoire du vieux temps" ("A Story of the Old Days"), 7:1763a
   "Histoire d'une fille de ferme" ("Story of a Farm Girl"), 7:1772b–1773a
   "La femme de Paul" ("Paul's Wife"), 7:1778b
   "La maison Tellier" ("Madame Tellier's Establishment"), 7:1767a-b, 1772b
   "La mère Sauvage" ("Mother Savage"), 7:1773b–1774a
   "La parure" ("The Necklace"), 7:1768b–1769a
   "La petite Roque" ("Little Roque"), 7:1776b–1777a

"La tombe" ("The Tomb"), 7:1775b

"La trahison de la comtesse de Rhune" ("The Treason of the Countess of Rhune"), 7:1763a

L'Angélus, 7:1782b

"Le Docteur Héraclius Gloss" ("Doctor Heraclius Gloss"), 7:1762b–1763a

"Le horla," 7:1776a-b

"Le père Milon" ("Old Milon"), 7:1774a

"Le père" ("The Father"), 7:1777a

"Les bijoux" ("The Jewels"), 7:1769a-b

Les dimanches d'un bourgeois de Paris (*A Parisian's Sundays*), 7:1766a

"L'Inutile beauté" ("Useless Beauty"), 7:1775a-b

"Lui?" ("He?"), 7:1775b–1776a

"Miss Harriet," 7:1770b–1771b

"Moiron," 7:1774b–1775a

"Monsieur Parent," 7:1777a

Mont-Oriol, 7:1780b, 1781a

Notre coeur (*A Woman's Heart*), 7:1781b

Pierre et Jean, 7:1760b, 1762a, 1780b–1781b

"Promenade" ("A Walk"), 7:1774b

Proust and, 8:551b

"Rosalie Prudent," 7:1773a-b

"Sauvée" ("Saved"), 7:1769b–1770a

"The Dead Hand" ("La main d'écorché"), 7:1760a, 1762b–1763a

"The Olive Grove" ("Le champ d'oliviers"), 7:1777a, 1777b–1778a, 1782b

"Un fils" ("A Son"), 7:1777b

"Un soir" ("One Evening"), 7:1771b–1772a

"Une répetition" (A Rehearsal"), 7:1763a

Une vie (*A Life*), 7:1779b, 1780a, 1781b

"Yvette," 7:1776b–1777a, 1778b–1779b

Zola and, 7:1527b, 1713a, 1761a, 1763a, 1763b–1764b

see also Soirées de Médan, Les

Maupertuis, Pierre Louis Moreau de, Voltaire and, 4:375b–376a

Mauprat. See Sand, George

Mauriac, Claude, Sarraute and, 12:2335a

Mauriac, François, **10:1307a–1330b**

A Kiss for the Leper (*Le baiser au lépreux*), 10:1320a–1321a

A Woman of the Pharisees (*La Pharisienne*), 10:1309b, 1312a, 1325a–1326a

Asmodée; or, The Intruder (*Asmodée*), 10:1326a

"Bordeaux ou l'adolescence" (Bordeaux or Adolescence), 10:1309a

Ce que je crois (*What I Believe*), 10:1309b–1310a

Claudel and, 8:488b

Commencements d'une vie (Beginnings), 10:1309a

conversion in work of, 7:1625b

D'Autres et moi (Other Writers and Myself), 10:1313a

Flesh and Blood (*Le chair et le sang*), 10:1318b–1319a

Génitrix, 10:1320a–1321b

God and Mammon, 10:1323a

on his characters, 12:2541a

La province (Province), 10:1315a

Le jeune homme (The Ardor of Youth), 10:1322a

Le sagouin (*The Little Misery*), 10:1312a

Les mains jointes (Joined Hands), 10:1308b

Lines of Life (*Destins*), 10:1323a-b

love theme, 12:2550b

Maltaverne (*Un adolescent d'autrefois*), 10:1308a, 1309b–1311a

Mes grands hommes (Men I Hold Great), 10:1313a

on Montherlant's *La relève du matin*, 11:1917b

placing the Infinite in man, 12:2552b

Questions of Precedence (*Préséances*), 10:1319a

on Simenon, 12:2479a, 2496b

Souffrances et bonheur du chrétien (*Anguish and Joy of the Christian Life*), 10:1323a

That Which Was Lost (*Ce qui était perdu*), 10:1323a-b

The Dark Angels (*Les anges noirs*), 10:1321a, 1323b–1324a

The Desert of Love (*Le désert de l'amour*), 10:1307b, 1321a

The End of the Night (*La fin de la nuit*), 10:1324b–1325b

The Enemy (*Le mal*), 10:1315b, 1321a

The Lamb (*L'Agneau*), 10:1326b

Mauriac, François (*cont.*)
    The Loved and the Unloved (*Galigaï*),
      10:1326b
    The River of Fire (*Le fleuve de feu*),
      10:1319a–1320a
    The Stuff of Youth (*La robe prétexte*),
      10:1317b–1318b
    The Unfortunate Lovers (*Les mal aimés*),
      10:1326a
    The Unknown Sea (*Les chemins de la mer*),
      10:1324b
    Thérèse Desqueyroux, 10:1321a–1322b
    Vie de Jean Racine (The Life of Racine),
      10:1322b–1323a
    Vipers' Tangle (*Le noeud de vipères*),
      10:1312a, 1323b–1324a
    Weil and, 12:2806a, 2808b, 2809a
    Young Man in Chains (*L'Enfant chargé de
      châines*), 10:1316a–1317b
Maurras, Charles
    Claudel and, 8:488b
    Les amants de Venise (*The Lovers of
      Venice*), 6:1000a
"Mauvais sang." *See* Rimbaud, Arthur
Mauvaises pensées et autres. See Valéry, Paul
Mavros Aghios, O. See Ritsos, Yannis
Max. See Grass, Günter
Maxibules, Les. See Aymé, Marcel
"Maxime et Zoé." *See* Mérimée, Prosper
Maximen und Reflexionen. See Goethe, Johann
    Wolfgang von
Maximes. See La Rochefoucauld, François VI,
    duc de, *Réflexions ou sentences et
    maximes morales*
Maximes et réflections sur la comédie. See
    Bossuet, Jacques Bénigne
Maximilian, Ferdinand, emperor of Mexico,
    Grillparzer's relations with, 5:418a
"Maximin experience" of Stefan George,
    8:462b–463b, 464a, 464b
Maxims, as literary genre, 3:64b–65a
Maxims and Reflections. See Goethe, Johann
    Wolfgang von, *Maximen und
    Reflexionen*
Maxims and Reflections on the Theater. See
    Bossuet, Jacques Bénigne

"May." *See* Apollinaire, Guillaume, *Alcools*,
    "Mai"
May Lamentation. *See* Ritsos, Yannis, *Ta
    Epikerika*
"May Night." *See* Musset, Alfred de, *Nights*
"May Song." *See* Goethe, Johann Wolfgang von
Mayakovsky, Vladimir, **11:1835a–1858b**
    Ady and, 9:874b
    Akhmatova's acmeism and, 10:1523a
    "Bez belykh flagov" (No White Flags),
      11:1842a
    Chelovek (Man), 11:1836a, 1843a–1844b
    "Domoi" (Homeward Bound), 11:1847b
    downfall of Petrine Russia and, 10:1620a-b
    Fleita-pozvonochnik (The Backbone Flute),
      11:1836a, 1843a, 1854b
    "How to Write Poetry," on Pasternak's
      achievement, 10:1602a
    Hylaea group and, 10:1335b
    "Iz ulitsy v ulitsu" (From Street to Street),
      11:1840a
    Khlebnikov aided by, 10:1341a
    on Khlebnikov's poetic creativity, 10:1349a
    Khorosho! Oktyabr'skaya poema (Good! A
      Poem of October), 11:1848b, 1853b
    "Koe-chto po povodu dirizhera" (The Case of
      the Bandleader), 11:1840b
    literary celebrity, 11:1893b
    *Misteriya-buff: Geroicheskoe, epicheskoe i
      satiricheskoe izobrazhenie nashei
      epokhi* (*Mystery-Bouffe: A Heroic, Epic,
      and Satirical Representation of Our
      Epoch*), 11:1836b, 1851a-b, 1855b
    Moe otkrytie Ameriky (My Discovery of
      America), 11:1837a
    *Moscow on Fire (1905): A Heroic Melomime/
      A Mass Spectacle with Songs and
      Words* (*Moskva gorit 1905*),
      11:1838b–1839a, 1852b–1853a
    "Neobychainoe priklyuchenie, byvshee s
      Vladimirom Mayakovskim letom na
      dache" (An Extraordinary Adventure,
      Which Happened to Vladimir
      Mayakovsky in the Summer, While on
      Vacation), 11:1845b, 1853b
    Oblako v shtanakh, 11:1841a, 1842b–1843a,
      1854b

Olesha and, 11:2236a, 2252a

150,000,000, 11:1836b, 1846a-b, 1855a-b

"Otvet na budushchie spletni" (An Answer to Future Gossip), 11:1837b

Pasternak and, 10:1593b, 1594b, 1598a, 1603a-b

in Pasternak's *A Safe-Conduct*, 10:1603a

in Pasternak's *Sketch for an Autobiography*, 10:1614a-b

Pasternak's *The Sublime Malady* valued by, 10:1601b

"Poet rabochii" (The Poet-Worker), 11:1845a-b

"Port" (Seaport), 11:1842a

"Posluchaite!" (Listen!), 11:1841a

Pro eto (About That), 11:1837b, 1847a, 1853b, 1854b

"Razgovor s fininspektorom o poezii" (Conversation with a Tax Collector, on Poetry), 11:1849b, 1850a, 1853a

"realization of metaphor" of, 10:1524b

Ritsos and, 12:2819a, 2837b, 2838a, 2838b

"Sebe lyubimomu, posvyashchaet eti stroki avtor" (To Himself, Beloved by Him, the Author Dedicates These Lines), 11:1842b

"Sergeyu Eseninu" (To Sergei Esenin), 11:1848a, 1849b–1850a

"Shtatskaya shrapnel" (A Civilian Shrapnel), 11:1841b

"Stikhi o sovetskom pasporte" (Verses on my Soviet Passport), 11:1837a

Stikhi ob Amerike (Verses about America), 11:1849a-b

suicide of, 11:2070b, 2071b

The Bathhouse: A Drama in Six Acts, with Circus and Fireworks, 11:1838b, 1852a-b

The Bedbug (*Klop*), 11:1838a, 1851b–1852a

Triolet and, 11:2070a

Vladimir Il'ich Lenin (*Vladimir Ilyich Lenin*), 11:1848b

Vladimir Mayakovskii: Tragediya (*Vladimir Mayakovsky: A Tragedy*), 11:1835b, 1850b–1851a

"Vo ves' golos" (At the Top of My Voice), 11:1838b, 1850a-b, 1853b, 1854b–1855a

voice of the other, 11:1906a

Voina i mir (War and the World), 11:1836a, 1843a-b

Zakovannyi fil'moi (Fettered by Film), 11:1836b

"Zastrel'shchiki" (Shock Workers), 11:1855b

"Zhivopis' segodnyashnego dnya" (The Painting of Today), 11:1841b

Maybe Yes, Maybe No. *See* D'Annunzio, Gabriele, *Forse che sì forse che no*

Mayer, Julius Robert von, Zamyatin's biography of, 10:1197b

Mayflower, The. See Blasco Ibáñez, Vicente

Maykov salon (St. Petersburg), Goncharov and, 6:1065a

Mayor of Zalamea. See Calderón de la Barca, Pedro

Mayorazgo de Labraz, El. See Baroja, Pío

Mazarin, Jules, La Rochefoucauld and, 3:58b, 59b, 60a, 61b, 63a

Maze, The. See Hervieu, Paul, *Le dédale*

Mazurca para dos muertos (Mazurka for Two Dead Men). *See* Cela, Camilo José

Mazzamuto, Pietro, on Quasimodo, 12:2398b–2399a

Mazzini. See Silone, Ignazio

Me to skountima. See Ritsos, Yannis

Me-ti, Buch der Wendungen (*Me-Ti, the Book of Twists and Turns*). *See* Brecht, Bertolt

Mea Culpa. See Céline, Louis-Ferdinand

Meaning

Barthes on, 13:3085b

Camus' view of, 13:3065a–3067a, 3076a

Measure for Measure. See Shakespeare, William

Meaux, Bossuet's stay at, 3:156a-b

Mecante fallito, Il. See Goldoni, Carlo

Mechanization

of human beings, in Dürrenmatt's works, 13:3229b–3330a, 3231a

in Pirandello's *Shoot!*, 8:400a-b

Medea, in Grillparzer's *The Golden Fleece*, 5:429b–430a

Medea. See Anouilh, Jean, *Médée*; Corneille, Pierre, *Médée*; Euripides; Grillparzer, Franz, *The Golden Fleece*; Seneca

Médecin volant, Le. See Molière

Médée. See Anouilh, Jean; Corneille, Pierre

Media, Marinetti and, 9:803b, 823a-b

Media noche, La. See Valle-Inclán, Ramón del

Medical literature
  Rabelais and, 2:695b
  Zola and, 7:1522a, 1528a

Medici, Catherine de'
  in Heinrich Mann's fiction, 8:538b, 540a
  Montaigne and, 2:779a

Medici family, Machiavelli and, 2:601a–602a

Medici, Giuliano de', in Castiglione,
  2:659a–660a

Medici, Lorenzo de'
  Altercazione, 2:906a-b
  Ambra, 2:906a
  Corinto, 2:906a
  Selve d'amore (Amatory Improvisations),
  2:906b

Medici, Marie de', Richelieu and, 3:55a, 56a

Médicin de campagne, Le. See Balzac, Honoré
  de

Medicinal Virtues of Ordinary Water, The. *See*
  Hecquet, Philippe, *Les vertus
  médicinales de l'eau commune*

Medicine
  Baroja's practice of, 9:590a, 591b, 592a
  Goldoni and, 4:423a-b
  knowledge of, Foucault and,
  13:3338b–3340a
  as portrayed in Lesage's *Gil Blas,* 3:333a-b
  profession of, Simenon and, 12:2482b

Médico de su honra, El. See Calderón de la
  Barca, Pedro, *The Physician of His
  Honor*

Medida velha poetry, 2:752b, 753b

Medieval poetry, Baudelaire and,
  7:1330b–1331a

Medievalism
  in Ghelderode's plays, 11:2129b, 2134a
  Schlegel and, 5:193b
  see also Middle Ages

Médiocrité. See Moderation, theme of

Meditaciones del Quijote. See Ortega y Gasset,
  José

"Meditation." *See* Lermontov, Mikhail
  Yurievich, "Duma"

Méditations esthétiques: Les peintres cubistes.
  See Apollinaire, Guillaume

Méditations poétiques. See Lamartine,
  Alphonse de

Meditations on Quixote. See Ortega y Gasset,
  José, *Meditaciones del Quijote*

Mediterranean culture, Ekelöf and, 12:2646a,
  2652b

"Mediterranean" ("Mediterranio"). *See*
  Montale, Eugenio, *Cuttlefish Bones*

Mednyi vsadnik. See Pushkin, Alexander, *The
  Bronze Horseman*

Meeres und der Liebe Wellen, Des. See
  Grillparzer, Franz, *Hero and Leander*

Meester, Johan de, Ghelderode and, 11:2115b

Meeting. *See* Butor, Michel, *Rencontre*

Meeting at Telgte, The. See Grass, Günter

"Megali eksodos, I." *See* Elytis, Odysseus, *To
  Axion Esti (The Axion Esti),* "Ta Pathi"

Megcsókolom Csók-kisasszonyt. See Ady,
  Endre

Meghali Elliniki Egkyklopedhia. See Ritsos,
  Yannis

Meghali ora. See Ritsos, Yannis, *Trakter*

"Megöltem egy pillangot." *See* Ady, Endre

Meier family, Hölderlin and, 5:164a, 167a

Meilhac, Henri, 7:1920b

Meillet, Antoine, *Les languages dans l'Europe
  nouvelle* (Languages in Contemporary
  Europe), Kosztolányi and, 10:1241a

"Mein Glaube." *See* Hesse, Hermann

"Mein Leben." *See* Nietzsche, Friedrich

Mein Name sei Gantenbein. See Frisch, Max

"Mein Vorsatz." *See* Hölderlin, Friedrich

"Mein Weg zur Marx." *See* Lukács, György

"Meine Erinnerungen au Beethoven." *See*
  Grillparzer, Franz

Meisling, Simon, Andersen and, 6:866b–867b

Meister Floh. See Hoffmann, E. T. A., *Master
  Flea*

Meistersinger von Nürnberg, Die. See Wagner,
  Richard

Měl jsem psa a kočku. See Čapek, Karel

Melancholy
  in Benjamin's works, 11:1717b–1718a
  in Camoëns' works, 2:750a-b, 759a
  in Jiménez' writings, 9:997a-b

poetic, Carducci, 7:1504a–1506a

see also Depression; Weltschmerz

Melancholy Watchman, The. See Apollinaire, Guillaume, *Le guetteur mélancolique*

Melanchthon, Philip, in Bossuet's *History of the Variations in the Protestant Churches*, 3:171a

Melancolia. See Jiménez, Juan Ramón

Mélange amusant de saillies d'esprit et de traits historiques des plus frappants. See Lesage, Alain-René

Mélanges posthumes. See Laforgue, Jules

Mêlées et démêlées. See Ionesco, Eugène

Meletimata. See Ritsos, Yannis

Meley, Gabrielle-Alexandrine, Zola and, 7:1519b

Mélingue, Gustave, Marie Dorval's affair with, 5:470b

Mélissa (Melissa). See Kazantzakis, Nikos

Melisseus. See Pontano, Giovanni

Mélite. See Corneille, Pierre

Melmoth the Wanderer. See Maturin, Charles

Melodrama
  of Berlioz, 6:782a–783a
  Dumas fils and, 7:1919b
  in Goncharov's works, 6:1084a
  Lessing and, 4:549a–551b
  in Maupassant's works, 7:1777b, 1778a
  in Mérimée's works, 6:748b, 749b, 752a
  Pixérécourt and, 7:1924b
  Sardou and, 7:1916b
  Scribe and, 7:1915b, 1916a

Melologue, Berlioz' innovation of musical drama, 6:781b–783a

Melusina. See Grillparzer, Franz

Melusine, Nerval's use of legend, 6:956a

Melville, Herman, 5:541a
  Camus and, 13:3055b
  Elytis and, 13:2957b
  Moby Dick, "decadence" of, 7:1896a

Memoir from the Time of Immaturity. *See* Gombrowicz, Witold, *Pamiętnik z okresu dojrzewania*

"Mémoire." *See* Rimbaud, Arthur, "Memory"

Mémoire sur l'état passif. See Fénelon, François de Salignac de la Mothe-

Mémoires. See Beaumarchais, Pierre-Augustin Caron de; Berlioz, Hector; Goldoni, Carlo; La Rochefoucauld, François VI, duc de; Retz, Cardinal de

Mémoires de Françoise de la Colline. See Cleland, John, *Fanny Hill*, French translation of

Mémoires de l'Estat de France, 2:771a

Mémoires de Maigret, Les. See Simenon, Georges

Mémoires d'Hadrien. See Yourcenar, Marguerite

Mémoires d'outre-tombe. See Chateaubriand, François René de

Mémoires d'un fou. See Flaubert, Gustave, *Memoirs of a Madman*

Mémoires d'une jeune fille rangée, See Beauvoir, Simone de, *Memoirs of a Dutiful Daughter*

Mémoires inédits: Fragments et projets. See Vigny, Alfred Victor de

Mémoires intimes. See Simenon, Georges

Memoires of a Man of Action. *See* Baroja, Pío, *Memorias de un hombre de acción*

Mémoires sur différents sujets du mathématiques. See Diderot, Denis

Memoirs. See Alfieri, Vittorio; Berlioz, Hector, *Mémoires*

Memoirs. *See* Makriyannis, Yannis, *Apomnimonevmata*

Memoirs of an Egotist. See Stendhal, *Souvenirs d'égotisme*

Memoirs of an Old Pupil. *See* Pascoli, Giovanni, "Ricordi di un vecchio scolaro"

"Memoirs of a Confidence Man." *See* Mann, Thomas, *Bekenntnisse des Hochstaplers Felix Krull*

Memoirs of a Dutiful Daughter. See Beauvoir, Simone de

Memoirs from Beyond the Grave. *See* Chateaubriand, François René de, *Mémoires d'outre-tombe*

Memoirs of a Good-for-Nothing. See Eichendorff, Joseph von

Memoirs of Hadrian. See Yourcenar, Marguerite, *Mémoires d'Hadrien*

Memoirs of Herr von Schnabelewopski, The. See Heine, Heinrich, *Aus den Memoiren des Herren von Schnabelewopski*

Memoirs of a Madman. See Flaubert, Gustave

Memoirs of a Man Without Memory. *See* Pérez Galdós, Benito, *Memorias de un desmemoriado*

Memorabilia. See Xenophon

Memorable Deeds and Words. *See* Valerius Maximus, *Facta et dicta memorabilia*

Memorial. *See* Ungaretti, Giuseppe, "In memoria"

Memorial Service at Poros. *See* Ritsos, Yannis, "Mnimosyno ston Poro"

Memorials. See Beaumarchais, Pierre-Augustin Caron de, *Mémoires*

Memorias de un desmemoriado. See Pérez Galdós, Benito

Memorias de un hombre de acción. See Baroja, Pío

Memories. *See* George, Stefan, *Algabal*, "Andenken"

"Memories." *See* Leopardi, Giacomo

"Memories of A. I. Odoevsky." *See* Lermontov, Mikhail Yurievich, "Pamyati A. I. Odoevskogo"

"Memories of Beethoven." *See* Grillparzer, Franz, "Meine Erinnerungen an Beethoven"

Memorization, in oral cultures, 1:56b–57a

Memory
    Augustine on, 1:40a-b, 45b, 46a
    Bergson's concept of, 8:52b–55a
    see also Time, Bergson's concept of
    involuntary, in Proust's *Remembrance of Things Past*, 8:562b, 564a–565a
    Kundera and, 13:3404b–3407a
    Proust on, 8:560a-b, 561b–565b
    in Richter's *Hesperus*, 5:64b
    Rimbaud's view of, 7:1802a–1804a
    in Stendhal, 5:355a-b

"Memory." *See* Rimbaud, Arthur

"Memory of Africa." *See* Ungaretti, Giuseppe, "Ricordo d'Africa"

Memory of Youth. See Moberg, Vilhelm

Men
    in Maupassant's fiction, 8:520b

    in Pirandello's works, 8:394a
    in Strindberg's works, 7:1749–1750a
    see also Homosexuality; Sexes, relations between

"Men." *See* MacLeish, Archibald

Men. *See* Verlaine, Paul, "Hombres"

Men I Hold Great. See Mauriac, François, *Mes grands hommes*

Men of Letters, The. See Goncourt, Edmond Louis Antoine and Jules Alfred Huot de, *Charles Demailly*

Men livet lever. See Hamsun, Knut, *The Road Leads On*

Men and Not Men. See Vittorini, Elio, *Uomini e no*

Men and Passions. *See* Lermontov, Mikhail Yurievich, *Menschen und Leidenschaften*

Men of Today. *See* Huysmans, Joris Karl, *Les hommes d'aujourd'hui*

"Men Who Turn Back." *See* Montale, Eugenio, *Satura*, "Gli uomini che si voltano"

"Menagerie, The." *See* Khlebnikov, Velimir, "Zverinets"; Mandelshtam, Osip, "Zverinets"

Mencken, H. L., on Ibsen, 7:1422a

Mendeleev, Dmitry Ivanovich, 9:66a

Mendeleeva, Lyubov' Dmitrievna, 9:916a
    Blok and, 9:967a, 975b
        affair of Lyubov', 9:978b–979a
        and Bely, 9:967b
        child born to Lyubov', 9:976b–977a
        courting of, 9:966a-b
        in later years, 9:983a-b

Mendelssohn, Felix
    Das Judentum in der Musik (Judaism in Music), 7:1651a
    on expressiveness of music, 5:413a
    Ortega y Gasset on, 9:1135b
    Strindberg and, 7:1748a
    Wagner and, 7:1651a

Mendelssohn, Moses
    Lessing and, 4:539a, 543b, 558a
    Pope ein Metaphysiker! (Pope a Metaphysician!), 4:543b

Mendès, Catulle
    Colette and, 9:620b

Verlaine and, 7:1620b
Mendicant orders
  in "Bataille des vices contre les vertus,"
    1:365a-b
  in medieval satire, 1:346a, 355b–356a
Menéndez Pidal, Ramón
  Chanson de Roland y el neotradicionalismo,
    on *chansons de geste* as news,
    1:101b–102a
  on *chansons de geste* as oral creations,
    1:106a
  Poema de mio Cid published by, 1:115a-b
  Primera crónica general published by,
    1:131b
Menéndez y Pelayo, Marcelino, lay schools,
  9:1124b
Meneur de loups, Le. See Dumas père,
  Alexandre
Menneskebonn. See Vesaas, Tarjei, *Children
  of Man*
Mensagem. See Pessoa, Fernando
Mensch erscheint im Holozän, Der. See Frisch,
  Max, *Man in the Holocene*
Menschen und Leidenschaften. See Lermontov,
  Mikhail Yurievich
Menschliches, Allzumenschliches. See
  Nietzsche, Friedrich, *Human, All
  Too-Human*
Mensonge, Le. See Sarraute, Nathalie
Mental illness
  among contemporary poets, 10:1411b
  Andersen and, 6:865a
  in Ariosto, 2:634b–635a
  of Artaud, 11:1975b–1978a, 1983b
  in Breton's *L'immaculée conception*,
    11:1943a
  in Büchner, 6:1182b–1186b, 1190a–1192a
  in Canetti's works, 12:2623a–2625b
  Foucault and, 13:3334a–3338b
  Gogol's *Notes of a Madman* and, 6:980a
  in Mann's *Doctor Faustus*, 9:735a
  in Maupassant's works, 7:1774a–1775a
  of Meyer, 6:937b–938a
  in Musil's *The Man Without Qualities*,
    9:936b
  of Nerval, 6:943a, 944b, 946a, 948b, 960b,
    963a, 966a–966b, 967b

  of Nietzsche, 7:1679b–1680a
  in Pirandello's *Henry IV*, 8:404a-b
  in Prudentius' works, 1:16b
  of Sade, 4:618b, 619b, 636b
  of Tasso, 2:792b–793b
  in Tieck, 5:246a
  of Trakl, 10:1411a-b, 1415b, 1421b–1422a
  see also Nervous breakdown
Mental Illness and Psychology. See Foucault,
  Michel
Mental phenomena. *See* Thought
Menteur, Le. See Corneille, Pierre
Menteuse, La. See Giraudoux, Jean
Mephistopheles. *See* Satan
"Mer au plus près, La." *See* Camus, Albert,
  "The Sea Close By"
Mérat, Albert
  Rimbaud and, 7:1796b
  "Tes mains," 7:1796b
  Verlaine and, 7:1620b
Meraviglie, Tasso and, 2:804b–805a, 816a
Merchant class. *See* Bourgeoisie
Merchant of Venice, The. See Shakespeare,
  William
"Merchant's Tale, The." *See* Chaucer, Geoffrey
Merck, Johann Heinrich, on Wieland,
  4:590b–591a
Mercure de France (journal), on Lesage,
  3:335a
Mercury (god)
  in Alfieri's *The Little Window*, 4:676b–677a
  in Camoëns' "The Two Amphitryons,"
    2:755b, 756a
"Mère Courage aveugle." *See* Barthes, Roland,
  "Mother Courage Blind"
Mère patrie, in Michelet's social thought,
  5:597a
"Mère Sauvage, La." *See* Maupassant, Guy de
"Meres tou 1896." *See* Cavafy, Constantine
Merezhkovsky, Dmitry
  affirmation of Petrine Russia by, 10:1620a
  Novyi put' (New Way), 9:962b
  Russian symbolism and, 9:962b, 967b
Meriano, Francesco
  fascism of, 11:1990a
  Montale and, 11:1987b

"Meriggiare pallido e assorto." *See* Montale,
    Eugenio, *Cuttlefish Bones*
Mérimée, Prosper, **6:745a–769b**
    African Love (L'Amour africain), 6:748a,
        748b, 749b
    "Arsène Guillot," 6:755a, 762b–763a
    Carmen, 6:755b, 756a, 756b, 759a, 761b,
        763a–764b
    *Chronicle of the Reign of Charles IX
        (Chronique du règne de Charles IX)*,
        6:724a, 745a-b, 751a, 752b–754a, 756a,
        758b, 759b, 761b
    Colomba, 6:755a, 759a, 761b–762b
    *Conjuration de Catalina (Cataline's
        Conspiracy)*, 6:765a
    Cromwell, 6:747a
    *Débuts d'un aventurier (An Adventurer's
        Beginnings)*, 6:755b
    "Djoumâne," 6:767a
    Dumas père and, 6:724a
    *Essai sur la guerre sociale (Essay on the
        Social Marsic War)*, 6:765a
    *Études sur l'histoire romaine (Studies in
        Roman History)*, 6:765a
    "Fédérigo," 6:758a, 758b, 759a
    Heaven and Hell (Le ciel et l'enfer), 6:748a,
        748b–749a, 750a
    Histoire de Don Pèdre Ier, roi de Castille,
        6:765b
    "Il vicolo di Madama Lucrezia" ("Madame
        Lucrezia Lane"), 6:764b
    *Inès Mendo, ou le préjugé vaincu (Inez
        Mendo, or Prejudice Overcome)*, 6:748a,
        748b
    *Inès Mendo, ou le triomphe du préjugé
        (Prejudice Triumphant)*, 6:748a
    "La chambre bleue" ("The Blue Room"),
        6:766b
    *La famille de Carvajal (The Carvajal
        Family)*, 6:752a-b
    La guzla, 6:747b, 750b–751a, 754a, 758b
    La Jaquerie, 6:751a–752b
    "L'Abbé Aubain" ("Abbot Aubain"), 6:764b
    "L'Enlèvement de la redoute" ("The
        Storming of the Redoubt"), 6:756b,
        757a, 757b

Les deux héritages (The Two Inheritances),
        6:755b
    *Les espagnols en Danemarck (The Spanish
        in Denmark)*, 6:748a, 749a, 750a
    "Lettres adressées d'Espagne" ("Letters from
        Spain"), 6:756b, 763a
    *Lettres à une inconnue (Letters to an
        Unknown Woman)*, 6:756a, 758a
    "Lokis," 6:766b–767a
    "Mateo Falcone," 6:756b, 757a, 757b, 758b,
        760a, 761b
    "Maxime et Zoé," 6:751a
    Mosaic (Mosaïque), 6:754a-b, 756a–759a
    *Notes d'un voyage en Corse (Notes on a
        Trip to Corsica)*, 6:761b
    Sand and, 6:820b
    "Souls in Purgatory" ("Les âmes du
        purgatoire"), 6:759a, 760a-b
    "Tamango," 6:757a, 757b–758a, 758b
    *The Carriage of the Holy Sacrament (Le
        carrosse du Saint-Sacrement)*, 6:748a,
        749b–750b
    *The Double Misunderstanding (La double
        méprise)*, 6:759a–760a
    "The Etruscan Vase" ("Le vase étrusque"),
        6:755a, 757b, 758b, 759b
    "The Game of Backgammon" ("La partie de
        tric-trac"), 6:758a-b, 759b
    The Opportunity (L'Occasion), 6:748a,
        749b–750a
    "The Venus of Ille" ("La Vénus d'Ille"),
        6:755a, 761a-b, 763a, 766b–767a
    *Théâtre de Clara Gazul (The Plays of Clara
        Gazul)*, 6:747a, 747b–750b, 752a, 754a,
        758b
    *Une femme est un diable, ou la tentation de
        Saint Antoine (A Woman Is a Devil; or,
        The Temptation of Saint Anthony)*,
        6:748a-b, 750a
    "Vision de Charles XI" ("Charles XI's
        Vision"), 6:756b, 757a, 757b, 759a
Merivale, H. C., on Leopardi, 5:541b
Merleau-Ponty, Maurice
    Bergson and, 8:52b, 64a
    Butor and, 13:3288a
    Foucault and, 13:3331a
    Sartre and, 12:2599b, 2602a–2603a

Simon and, 13:3021b

"Merlin et la vieille femme" ("Merlin and the Old Lady"). *See* Apollinaire, Guillaume, *Alcools*

Mérope. See Voltaire

Merry Widow, The. See Lehár, Franz, *Die lustige Witwe*

Mersenne, Marin
 Académie Mersenne and, 3:126a
 Descartes and, 3:2b, 6a-b, 20a

"Mert engem szeretsz." *See* Ady, Endre

"Merveille de la guerre." *See* Apollinaire, Guillaume

Merveilles de Rigomer, Les, Gawain in, 1:157b–158a

Merz movement, Arp and, 10:1365b, 1372b–1373a

Mes apprentissages. See Colette

Mes grands hommes. See Mauriac, François

Mes mémoires. See Dumas père, Alexandre

Mes souvenirs. See Adam, Juliette

Mese in U.R.S.S., Un. See Moravia, Alberto

Meshchane. See Gorky, Maxim, *The Petty Bourgeois*

"Mesimvrina parathyra." *See* Ritsos, Yannis

Mesmerism, of Schlegel, 5:198b

Message. See Pessoa, Fernando, *Mensagem*

Message of an Aged Faun. *See* Ady, Endre, "A vén faun üzenete"

Messaline: Roman de l'ancienne Rome. See Jarry, Alfred

Messe là-bas, La. See Claudel, Paul

Messes noires de La Bonne Auberge, Les. See Ionesco, Eugène, *La soif et la faim*

Messiah, The. See Klopstock, Friedrich Gottlieb

Messingkauf Dialogues, The. See Brecht, Bertolt, *Dialoge aus dem Messingkauf*

Mestiere di vivere, Il. See Pavese, Cesare, *Burning Brand: Diaries 1935–1950*

Metagraphes, 13:2981b
 of Seferis, 12:2269b

Métamorphose des dieux, La. See Malraux, André, *The Metamorphosis of the Gods*

Metamorphoses. See Ovid

Metamorphosis
 Canetti and, 12:2627a–2628a

in Elytis' *Sun the First*, 13:2962b–2963a

Metamorphosis of the Gods, The. See Malraux, André

Metamorphosis, The. See Kafka, Franz

Metaneira, in Mandelshtam's "Nashedshii podkovu," 10:1642a-b

Metaphilosophy, Schlegel and, 5:200a

Metaphor
 acmeist poetics and, 10:1633b–1634a
 in Kafka, 9:1157a, 1159a-b
 in Musil's works, 9:934a, 940b–941a, 941b–942b, 943b, 946a-b
 metonymy and, 9:948b, 949a, 951b–952a
 Ortega y Gasset and, 9:1136b–1137a
 philosophical, of Hebbel's "Welt und Ich," 6:1117b–1118a
 in symbolist poetry, 8:569b
 in Valéry's *The Graveyard by the Sea*, 8:578a, 578b–579a

Metaphysical poets, pastoral lyric and, 2:915b

Metaphysics
 Artaud's theater and, 11:1972b
 of Bely, 9:927a
 in Bergson's thought, 8:57b–59a
 of Elytis, 13:2965b
 in Goethe's *Urfaust*, 5:19b
 Mallarmé's protomodernist linguistic, 7:1578a–1579a, 1581a, 1588b–1589b
 Milosz and, 13:2944b–2948a
 Rousseau as, 4:449b
 of Schopenhauer
  death, 5:408b–409a
  music, 5:412a–414a
  sexual love, 5:409a-b
  the Will, 5:400b–401b
 Weil and, 12:2812b
 weltschmerz poets' despair of, 5:420a

Metaphysics. See Aristotle

Metastasio, Pietro, Alfieri's scorn for, 4:664a

"Metatheater," in Azorín's works, 9:642b

Meteor. See Čapek, Karel, *Povětroň*

Meteor, Der. See Dürrenmatt, Friedrich

Method of True Theology, The. See Erasmus, *Ratio verae theologiae*

"Metoden Bovary." *See* Johnson, Eyvind

Metonymy
 acmeist poetics and, 10:1633b–1634a

Metonymy (cont.)
Jakobson on, 9:944b
in Musil's *The Man Without Qualities*,
9:948b, 949a, 952a
Metrical Letters. *See* Petrarch, *Epistolae
metricae*
Metrics
Anglo-Saxon, 1:66b–67a, 68a
Augustine on, 1:46b, 47a
Greek, 1:68a, 8:176a
Lermontov's experiments with, 6:1199a-b
quantitative, 8:176a
see also particular meters
Metropolis. *See* Lang, Fritz
Metsys, Quentin, Erasmus and, 2:584a
Metz, Bossuet's stay at, 3:154a–156a
Meunier d'Angibault, Le. *See* Sand, George
Meuse River, Battle of the, 13:3023a-b
Mexía, Pero, *Silva de varia lección*, *King
Seleucus* and, 2:756b
Meyer, Conrad Ferdinand, **6:930a–938a**
Angela Borgia, 6:933b
Das Amulett (*The Amulet*), 6:935a
Das Leiden eines Knaben (*A Boy Suffers*),
6:933a
Der Heilige (*The Saint*), 6:935b
"Der römische Brunnen" ("The Roman
Fountain"), 6:931b–932a
Der Schuss von der Kanzel (*The Shot from
the Pulpit*), 6:934a-b
"Die Füsse im Feuer" ("The Feet in the
Fire"), 6:931a-b
Die Hochzeit des Mönchs (*The Marriage of
the Monk*), 6:936a
Die Richterin (*The Judge*), 6:933a-b
Die Versuchung des Pescara (*Pescara's
Temptation*), 6:933b
Frisch and, 13:2922b
George and, 8:449b–450a
Gustav Adolfs Page (*Gustav Adolf's Page*),
6:934a
Huttens letzte Tage (Hutten's Last Days),
6:932a–933a
Jürg Jenatsch, 6:933b–934a
Plautus im Nonnenkloster (*Plautus in the
Convent*), 6:934b–935a

Zwanzig Balladen von einem Schweizer
(Twenty Ballads by a Swiss), 6:931a-b
"Zwei Segel" ("Two Sails"), 6:931b–932a
Meyer, Karoline, 5:71a
Meyerbeer, Giacomo
Scribe and, 7:1910b–1911a
Wagner and, 6:1151b–1152a
Meyerhold, Vsevolod
Mayakovsky and, 11:1836b, 1838a, 1838b,
1851b
Olesha's "A List of Assets" and, 11:2245b
Meynert, Theodor
Freud and, 8:2b–3a
Schnitzler and, 8:90a
Mezhdu dvukh revoliutsii. *See* Bely, Andrey
Meztelenül. *See* Kosztolányi, Dezső
Mi religión y otros ensayos. *See* Unamuno,
Miguel de
Mia ghineka plai sti thalassa. *See* Ritsos,
Yannis
"Mia giornata paziente, La." *See* Quasimodo,
Salvatore
"Mia nichta stin akroyialia." *See* Seferis,
George, "Pantoum"
Mialaret, Athénaïs, Michelet and,
5:577a–578a, 601a
"Miasto bez imienia." *See* Milosz, Czeslaw
Miau. *See* Pérez Galdós, Benito
Michael Kohlhaas. *See* Kleist, Heinrich von
Michael Kramer. *See* Hauptmann, Gerhart
Michael Scot, 1:408b
Michaux, Henri, "Je vous écris d'un pays
lointain" ("I Write to You from a
Distant Place"), Seferis' translation,
12:2259b
Michel, Jean, *Passion*, 1:470a-b
Michelangelo
Alfieri and, 4:671b
Apollinaire and, 9:892b
Burckhardt on, 6:1232b–1233a
Delacroix on, 5:524b, 525a, 525b,
526b–527b
Petrarchan influence, 2:504a
Taine on, 7:1462b
Michelet, Jules, **5:571a–606b**
Barthes on, 13:3083b–3084a
Claudel and, 8:490b

Eça and, 7:1685a
on history, 8:288a
History of France (Histoire de France),
    3:170a, 5:585b, 588a, 588b, 589a
    criticized by contemporaries, 5:602b
*History of the French Revolution (Histoire
    de la révolution française*, 5:585b–586b,
    589a, 589b–590a, 597b–598a
    Jacobins and Girondins, 5:590a-b
*History of the Nineteenth Century (Histoire
    du XIXe siècle)*, 5:603a
*Introduction to Universal History
    (Introduction à l'histoire universelle)*,
    5:584b–585b, 588b–589a
Journal, 5:571a, 574a, 575b, 578a, 578b,
    587b–588a, 587b, 588b
    Athénaïs Mialaret in, 5:577b
    on fraternity, 5:593b–594a
    on history as a discipline, 5:579b
    liberal views, 5:575b
    on losing touch with the world, 5:598a
    on monarchy, 5:587b–588a
    Revolution of 1848 and, 5:595a, 601a
    on social problems, 5:596a-b
    on utopian socialists, 5:592a
L'Étudiant, 5:582a-b
Love (L'Amour), 5:601a
    Mickiewicz and, 5:630b
Our Sons (Nos fils), 5:596a
*Priests, Women, and Families (Du prêtre, de
    la femme et de la famille)*, 5:574a,
    590b–591a
Rimbaud and, 7:1790b, 1811a
Sainte-Beuve on, 6:845b
The Bird (L'Oiseau), 5:601a
The Jesuits (Des Jésuites), 5:589b
The Mountain (La montagne), 5:601a
The People (Le peuple), 5:591a, 602a
The Sea (La mer), 5:601a
    on social war, 5:597b
The Sorceress (La sorcière), 5:574b, 603b
translation of Vico's *Scienza nuova*,
    3:312a-b, 5:583a–584a
treatment of women, 7:1487b–1488a
Zola and, 7:1521a
Michelet par lui-même. See Barthes, Roland,
    Michelet

Mickiewicz, Adam, **5:607a–634b**
*Ad Napoleonem III, Caesarem Augustum,
    ode in Bomersundum captum*, 5:631b
*Books of the Polish Nation and Polish
    Pilgrimage (Księgi narodu polskiego i
    pielgrzymstva polskiego)*, 5:623a–624b
    international success of, 5:624a-b
"Do matki Polki" ("To a Polish Mother"),
    5:618b
Dziady (Forefathers), 5:610a–612b, 614a-b
    autobiographical elements in, 5:612a-b
    expelled from the Collège de France, 5:581a
"Farys. Kasyda" ("Faris. Quasida"), 5:616a
Forefathers' Eve, 5:632a
Forefathers' Eve, Part III (Dziady, część III),
    5:619a–623a
    "A Digression," 5:622a–623a
    as a drama of reportage, 5:619a-b
    national messianism in, 5:621a
    prologue, 5:619b
    "The Improvisation," 5:620a-b
    "The Senator," 5:621b
Gombrowicz and, 12:2582b
Grażyna, 5:610a-b
Kartofla (Potato), 5:608b
Konrad Wallenrod, 5:609a, 613b, 614a,
    616b–618a
    the "Polish hexameter" in, 5:617a-b
    prose foreword to, 5:617b
Les Slaves (The Slavs), 5:630b–631a
"Lilije" ("The Lilies"), 5:609b
Mérimée and, 6:750b
"Oda do młodości" ("Ode to Youth"), 5:608b
Pan Tadeusz, 5:619a, 625a–629a, 632a-b
    place of in Polish literary tradition, 5:628b
Poezye (Poetry), 5:6a-b, 610a–612b
"Romantyczność" ("Romanticism"), 5:609a-b
Sonety Krymskie (Crimean Sonnets), 5:613a,
    614a–616a
"Twardorski's Wife," 5:609b–610a
Micromégas. See Voltaire
Mid-Channel. See Pinero, Arthur Wing
Midas, king, in Ady's "The Descendant of
    King Midas," 9:878a
"Midász király sarja." *See* Ady, Endre
Midday Symphony. *See* Krleža, Miroslav,
    Podnevna simfonija

Middle Ages
   Generation of '98 and, 9:753a
   in Mérimée's works, 6:752a
   in Michelet's view, 5:588a
   in Mickiewicz's poetry, 5:623b
   in Novalis' works, 5:219b
   in Staël's works, 5:98a
   in Tieck's works, 5:250a-b
   in Undset's works, 9:1033b–1035a, 1037a
Middle class. *See* Bourgeoisie
Middle East. *See* Orient
Midnight. *See* Valle-Inclán, Ramón del, *La
      media noche*
"Midollo del leone, Il." *See* Calvino, Italo
Midsommardröm i fattighuset (*Midsummer
      Dream in the Workhouse*). *See*
      Lagerkvist, Pär
Midsummer Games. *See* Zamyatin, Yevgeny
      Ivanovich, "Kuny"
Midsummer Night's Dream, A. See
      Shakespeare, William
Mie prigioni, Le. See Pellico, Silvio
"Mie venture al venir son tarde et pigre." *See*
      Petrarch, *Canzoniere*
"Miért is tettem?" *See* Ady, Endre
"Mighty Fortress Is Our God, A." *See* Luther,
      Martin
Mignet, François Auguste, Büchner and,
      6:1172b–1173a
"Mihályi Rozália csókja." *See* Ady, Endre
Mihura, Miguel de, plays of, 9:642a
Mikhaylovskoe, Pushkin's stay at, 5:661b,
      662b–663a
Mikhoels, S., conspiracy charges, 11:1912a
Mikros naftilos, O. See Elytis, Odysseus
Milan
   Manzoni's identification with, 5:368a
   St. Martin's Day riots in, in Manzoni's *The
      Betrothed*, 5:386a-b, 388a-b
Mileposts I. *See* Tsvetaeva, Marina, *Versty I*
Milesian tale, Renaissance short fiction and,
      2:930b–931a
Milhaud, Darius, Claudel and, 8:485a, 488a
Milieu, of writer, Sainte-Beuve on, 6:848a-b
Military
   Aymé's satire of, 12:2441b
   in Feydeau's *Champignol in Spite of
      Himself*, 7:1924a
   Foscolo and, 5:315a, 318a
   Frisch on, 13:2899a-b
   Kleist and, 5:292a–293a
   Lermontov's career in, 6:1203b, 1204a-b,
      1207a–1208a, 1213a-b, 1221a-b, 1222b
   Machiavelli's view of, 2:608b–609b
   Maupassant's view of, 7:1763b
   Schnitzler's view of, 8:89a, 92a, 95b–96a,
      98b–99a
   Stendhal and, 5:345a–347a
Military Condition, The. See Vigny, Alfred
      Victor de
"Milk of Death, The." *See* Yourcenar,
      Marguerite, *Nouvelles orientales*
Mill on the Floss, The. See Eliot, George
Mill, John Stuart
   Bergson and, 8:51a
   on happiness, 7:1670b
   Jiménez and, 9:1007a
Mille et un plis. See Butor, Michel
Millennium, Herder's idea of *Humanität* and,
      4:650b
Miller, Arthur
   All My Sons, 7:1444a
   Ibsen's influence on, 7:1444a
   The Crucible, Aymé and, 12:2448a
   The Price, 7:1444a
Miller, Henry
   Céline and, 11:1859a, 1874a
   Hamsun and, 8:39a, 42a
   Queneau and, 12:2516a
Milosz, Aleksander, 13:2929b
Milosz, Czeslaw, **13:2929a–2952a**
   "Campo dei Fiori," 13:2942a-b, 2944b
   "Child of Europe" ("Dziecie Europy"),
      13:2943a-b
   Collected Poems, 1931–1987, 13:2932a
   "Gucio zaczarowany" ("Bobo's
      Metamorphosis"), 13:2949b
   Kontynenty (The Continents), 13:2938a
   "Miasto bez imienia" ("City Without a
      Name"), 13:2947a
   Native Realm (*Rodzinna Europa*),
      13:2931b–2932a
   Norton lectures, 13:2938a–2940a

"Notes on Exile," 13:2933a
Ocalenie (Salvation/Survival), 13:2931a,
    2932a, 2941b–2942b
Ogród nauk (The Garden of Learning),
    13:2938a
on Pasternak's *Second Birth*, 10:1605b
Pieśń niepodległa (The Invincible Song),
    13:2931a
Poemat o czasie zastygłym (Poem on Frozen
    Time), 13:2930b, 2940b–2941a
Prywatne obowiązki (Private Obligations),
    13:2938a
Selected Poems, 13:2932a
"Stan poetycki" ("A Poetic State"),
    13:2947b–2948a
"Świat" ("The World"), 13:2944b
Światło dzienne (The Light of Day),
    13:2931a, 2943a-b
The Captive Mind (*Zniewolony umysł*),
    13:2931b–2932a, 2932b, 2934b–2936a,
    2937b, 2943a
The Issa Valley (*Dolina Issy*), 13:2931b,
    2933a, 2934a-b, 2946b
The Land of Ulro (*Ziema Ulro*), 13:2935a,
    2936a–2938a
The Seizure of Power (*Zdobycie władzy*),
    13:2931b, 2932a, 2933b–2934b
The Witness of Poetry (*Świadectwo poezji*),
    13:2935a, 2938a, 2940a-b
"Traktat moralny" (Treatise on Morals),
    13:2931a, 2943b
Traktat poetycki (Treatise on Poetry),
    13:2931b, 2938a, 2943b–2944b
Trzy zimy (Three Winters), 13:2941a
Unattainable Earth (*Nieobjęta ziemia*),
    13:2945b, 2951a
Visions from San Francisco Bay (*Widzenia
    nad zatoką San Francisco*), 13:2935a
"Walc" (The Waltz), 13:2942b–2943a
"Zadanie" ("A Task"), 13:2951b–2952a
"Zaklęcie" ("Incantation"), 13:2947b
Milosz, Oscar V. de L., 13:2930a
Milton, John
Camoëns and, 2:765a, 765b–766a
Castiglione and, 2:650a
Chateaubriand on, 5:137a
Comus
    Lampedusa's "Lighea" and, 11:2032b
    theatricality of, 9:1068b
Epitaphium Damonis (*Lament for Damon*),
    Castiglione's influence on, 2:908b
Klopstock and, 4:513a-b, 520b–521a
Lycidas
    Castiglione's influence on, 2:908b
    classical influences on, 2:900b–901a
    complexity of, 2:915b
Paradise Lost
    Augustine's *Confessions* and, 1:31a
    Chateaubriand's translation of, 5:113b,
        138a
    language, 9:1081b
    as literary epic, 1:51a
    pastoral elements in Eden of, 2:916a
    in Vigny's works, 5:453a, 460b
Sade and Milton's Satan, 4:626a
Unamuno and, 8:297a
"Milyi drug, i v etom tikhom dome." *See* Blok,
    Alexander
Mime, Greek, 8:212b
Mimesis
    Boileau's discussion of tragedy and, 3:196b
    Croce on, 8:319b
    Marinetti and, 9:817b
"Mimische Partitur?" (Mimic Score?). *See*
    Frisch, Max
"Min barndoms träd." *See* Södergran, Edith,
    "My Childhood Trees"
Min svenska historia. Berättad för folket. See
    Moberg, Vilhelm
Mind
    body and, in Descartes's *Meditations on
        First Philosophy*, 3:17b–18a
    in Freud's metapsychology, 8:5a–6a
Mind-Energy. See Bergson, Henri, *L'Énergie
    spirituelle*
"Mine Field." *See* Calvino, Italo, *Difficult
    Loves*
*Mine-Haha, oder über die körperliche
    Erziehung der jungen Mädchen*
    (Mine-HaHa; or, On the Physical
    Education of Young Girls). *See*
    Wedekind, Frank
Mined Terrain. *See* Böll, Heinrich, *Vermintes
    Gelände*

Mines of Falun, The. See Hoffmann, E. T. A., *Die Bergwerke zu Falun*

Mining, as a literary theme, in Butor, 13:3308a-b

Minna von Barnhelm, oder das Soldatenglück (Minna von Barnhelm; or, The Soldier's Fortune). See Lessing, Gotthold Ephraim

Minnas. See Johnson, Eyvind

Minnelieder aus dem schwäbischen Zeitalter. See Tieck, Ludwig

Minnesang, 1:290b
   Tieck and, 5:250b
   Walther and, 1:292a–297a, 306a–307b

Minotaur, myth of, in Racine's *Phèdre*, 3:214b–216a

Minsky, Nikolay
   Mandelshtam and, 10:1629a
   religious philosophy of, 10:1628b–1629a

Minstrel
   troubadours and, 1:161a
   see also *Gleoman; Guslar*

Minutes de sable mémorial, Les (Minutes of Memorial Sand). *See* Jarry, Alfred

"Mio marito." *See* Ginzburg, Natalia

"Mio paese è l'Italia, Il." *See* Quasimodo, Salvatore

Mir iskusstva. See Diaghilev, Sergey

"Mirabeau Bridge, The." *See* Apollinaire, Guillaume, *Alcools*, "Le pont Mirabeau"

"Miracle of Ash Wednesday, The." *See* Zamyatin, Yevgeny Ivanovich, "O chude proisshedshem v Pepel'nuiu Sredu"

Miracle de St. Ignace, 1:464a-b

Miracle plays, 1:461b–465a
   Claudel's *The Tidings Brought to Mary* as, 8:483b
   German Easter plays and, 1:467a
   of the Virgin, 1:463a–465a

Miracle of the Roman Empress, 1:464b

Miracle, The, Reinhardt and, 8:487b

Miracles, in Aymé's works, 12:2438a-b

Miraculous Barber, The. See Aymé, Marcel

Miranda, Francisco de Sá de. *See* Sá de Miranda, Francisco de

Mirbeau, Octave

Le jardin des supplices (*The Garden of Torments*), 9:869b

Maeterlinck and, 8:124b, 125b, 128a, 129a, 135a

"Mire, The." *See* Ionesco, Eugène, "La vase"

Mirgorod. See Gogol, Nikolay Vasilievich

"Mirlo fiel, El." *See* Jiménez, Juan Ramón

Miró, Gabriel, Azorín's literary criticism of, 9:645a

Miró, Joan
   Breton on, 11:1950a
   Constellations, 11:1948b

Miroir de merveilleux, Le. See Mabille, Pierre

Miroir des limbes, Le. See Malraux, André

Miroir qui revient, Le. See Robbe-Grillet, Alain, *Ghosts in the Mirror*

Mirour de l'omme. See Gower, John

Mirror, the Cat. See Keller, Gottfried

Mirror of Fools. See Nigel de Longchamps, *Speculum stultorum*

Mirror of Limbo, The. See Malraux, André, *Le Miroir des limbes*

Mirror of Man. See Gower, John, *Mirour de l'omme*

"Mirroring Well, The." *See* Södergran, Edith, "Den speglande brunnen"

Mirrors, in Richter's *The Comet*, 5:83a

"Mirskontsa." *See* Khlebnikov, Velimir

Mirsky, Dmitri, on Zamyatin's "mother metaphor," 10:1191b

Mirth of Shipwrecks. See Ungaretti, Giuseppe, *Allegria di naufragi*

Mis páginas preferidas. See Cela, Camilo José

Misanthrope, Le. See Molière

Misanthropy, in Maupassant's works, 7:1768a

Miscellaneous Writings. See Heine, Heinrich, *Vermischte Schriften*

Miscellany, Being a Collection of Poems by Several Hands. See Behn, Aphra

Mise à mort, La. See Aragon, Louis

Miser, The. See Molière, *L'Avare*

Misérables, Les. See Hugo, Victor

"Miseria y esplendor de la traducción." *See* Ortega y Gasset, José

Misericordia. See Pérez Galdós, Benito

Miserliness, theme of. *See* Avarice

Misery and Splendor of Translation. *See* Ortega y Gasset, José, "Miseria y esplendor de la traducción"

Misfortune's Remedy. See Lope de Vega, *El remedio en la desdicha*

Mishima ou la vision du vide (Mishima: A Vision of the Void). See Yourcenar, Marguerite

Mishima, Yukio, Yourcenar on, 12:2556b–2557a

Misogyny
of Ady, 9:869b–870a
alleged, of La Fontaine, 3:97b
in Baroja's novels, 9:601b–602a
in Castiglione, 2:659a–660a
of the Goncourts, 7:1403b–1404a, 1406b–1407a
in Laforgue's *Pierrot the Dabbler*, 7:1891b
of Marinetti, 9:806b–807a
see also Sexes, relations between

"Miss Harriet." *See* Maupassant, Guy de

Miss Julie. See Strindberg, August

Miss Sara Sampson. See Lessing, Gotthold Ephraim

Missal of the Three, The. See Hylaea group, *Trebnik troikh*

"Missing Person." *See* Böll, Heinrich, "Suchanzeigen"

Missing Persons and Other Essays. See Böll, Heinrich

Mission, The. See Ferreira de Castro, José Maria

Missolonghi, Sally of (1826), 13:2971a

Mist. See Unamuno, Miguel de, *Niebla*

Mistaken Ambitions. See Moravia, Alberto

Mister, Mister. See Grass, Günter

Mister Price, czyli Bzik tropikalny (Mister Price; or, Tropical Madness). See Witkiewicz, Stanisław Ignacy

Misteriya-buff: Geroicheskoe, epicheskoe i satiricheskoe izobrazhenie nashei epokhi. See Mayakovsky, Vladimir

Mistress of the Inn, The. *See* Goldoni, Carlo, *La locandiera*

"Mistress into Maid." *See* Pushkin, Alexander

"Misunderstanding" (drama). *See Quiproquo*

Misunderstanding, The. See Camus, Albert

Mit Livs Eventyr. See Andersen, Hans Christian, *The Fairy Tale of My Life*

Mithridate. See Racine, Jean

Mitmacher, Der. See Dürrenmatt, Friedrich, *The Sell-out*

Mitsou, ou comment l'esprit vient aux filles (Mitsou, or How Girls Get Wise). See Colette

Mitteilung an meine Freunde, Eine. See Wagner, Richard

Mitterwurzer, Friedrich, 9:691b

Mixed Opinions and Maxims. See Nietzsche, Friedrich, *Anhang: Vermischte Meinungen und Sprüche*

Mixed-up Mix-ups. See Ionesco, Eugène, *Mêlées et démêlées*

"Mizhplanetni intervaly." *See* Tychyna, Pavlo, *Pluh*

"Mladočeské volby na Malé straně." *See* Hašek, Jaroslav

Mme. Caverlet. See Dumas fils, Alexandre

"Mnemosyne." *See* Hölderlin, Friedrich

"Mnimosyno ston Poro." *See* Ritsos, Yannis

Mob, The. See Blasco Ibáñez, Vicente, *La horda*

Moberg, Vilhelm, **11:2203a–2231b**
Änkeman Jarl (Widower Jarl), 11:2227a
A Time on Earth (Din stund på jorden), 11:2205b, 2226a–b, 2226b
A. P. Rosell, bankdirektör (A. P. Rosell, Bank Director), 11:2213b–2214a
Att övervaka överheten (On Being Vigilant of the Authorities), 11:2228b
Berättelser ur min levnad, 11:2208a
Brudarnas källa (The Bride's Spring), 11:2218b–2219a, 2227b
De Knutna händerna (The Clenched Hands), 11:2212a–11, 2213a, 2226b
Det Gamla riket (The Ancient Kingdom), 11:2228b
Domaren (The Judge), 11:2227b, 2228b
En löskekarl (A Vagabond), 11:2227a
Förrädarland (Land of Traitors), 11:2229a
Fulfillment (Mans kvinna), 11:2214a, 2215a, 2226b
Gudens hustru (Wife of the God), 11:2227b
Hustrun (The Wife), 11:2226b

Moberg, Vilhelm (*cont.*)
I vapenrock och linnebyxor (In Tunic and
Linen Trousers), 11:2209b
Jungfrukammare (The Maid's Room),
11:2227b
Komplotterna (The Conspiracies), 11:2228b
Kvinnas Man (Woman's Man), 11:2227a
Långt frå landsvägen (Far from the
Highway), 11:2212a–2213a
Lea och Rakel (Leah and Rachel), 11:2227b
Marknadsafton (Market Eve), 11:2227a
Memory of Youth (*Sänkt sedebetyg*),
11:2215a–2215b
Min svenska historia. Berättad för folket (*A
History of the Swedish People*),
11:2229a
Nattkyparen (The Night Waiter), 11:2227b
Prinsessan på Solklinten (The Princess at
Solklinten), 11:2209b
Raskens: En soldatfamiljs historia (The
Rasks: The Story of a Soldier's Family),
11:2205b, 2210b–2212a, 2226b
Ride This Night! (*Rid i natt!*),
11:2216b–2217a, 2218b, 2226b, 2228a
Sagoprinsen (The Fairytale Prince),
11:2227b, 2228b
Sanningen kryper fram (The Truth
Emerges), 11:2228b
Sömnlös (*Sleepless Nights*), 11:2215a,
2215b–2216a
Soldat med brutet gevär (Soldier with a
Broken Rifle), 11:2208a, 2209a, 2217a-b,
2218a, 2226b
Svensk strävan (The Swedish Struggle),
11:2228a
The Earth Is Ours! (*Giv oss jorden!*),
11:2206b, 2215a, 2216a, 2228a
The Emigrants (*Utvandrarna*), 10:1680a,
11:2219a
film version of, 11:2203a
The Last Letter Home (*Sista brevet till
Sverige*), 11:2219a
The Settlers (*Nybyggarna*), 11:2219a
Unto a Good Land (*Invandrarna*), 11:2219a
Våld (Violence), 11:2227a
Vår ofödde son (Our Unborn Son), 11:2227a

'*Vi är inte neutrala!*' (We Are Not Neutral!),
11:2228a
*Mobile: Study for a Representation of the
United States. See* Butor, Michel
Moby Dick. See Melville, Herman
Mocedades de Rodrigo, 1:129a–130b
Mocedades del Cid, Las. See Castro, Guillén
de
Mochulsky, Konstantin, on Bely, 9:921b, 926a
Model History, A. See Queneau, Raymond,
Une histoire modèle
Moderation, theme of
in Rabelais, 2:714a, 714b, 717a
in Walther, 1:296a–297a
Modern Architecture. See Tafuri, Manfredo
Modern Art. See Huysmans, Joris Karl, *L'Art
moderne*
Modern költők. See Kosztolányi, Dezső
Modern Odes. See Quental, Antero de, *Odes
modernas*
Modern Poets. See Kosztolányi, Dezső, *Modern
költők*
Modern teater. See Lagerkvist, Pär
Modern Theme, The. See Ortega y Gasset,
José, *El tema de nuestro tiempo*
"*Modern Virgin.*" *See* Södergran, Edith,
"*Vierge moderne*"
Moderner Bund (The Modern Association),
Arp and, 10:1367a
Modernism, 10:1484a, 1484b
anarchism and, 9:864b
Apollinaire and, 9:883b, 884b, 894b
in art, Ortega y Gasset on, 9:1135b–1136a
Baudelaire and, 7:1323a, 1340a
Benjamin and, 11:1703b, 1704b–1705a
Calvino and, 13:3259a
Croce's attack on, 11:1989b
German, Rilke and, 9:768a
Ghelderode and, 11:2113b, 2134a-b
Goncourt brothers, 7:1399a
Greek, *Mythistorema* and, 13:2956b
Hamsun and, 8:21a, 25a, 39b, 42a
Hesse and, 9:855a
Johnson and, 12:2368a-b, 2374b–2375b
Laforgue and, 7:1883a, 1889a, 1890a, 1907a
Lukács and, 10:1252a
Marinetti and, 9:799b

Montale's defense of, 11:1992a-b
parody in, 9:1097b–1098a
Pascoli and, 7:1826a, 1829b
of Pessoa, 10:1484b
in Robbe-Grillet's works, 13:3248a-b
Russian, Olesha and, 11:2251b
Sainte-Beuve and, 6:840b
Sartre and, 12:2591b
Spanish
 Darío and, 9:993b–994a
 Jiménez and, 9:991b, 992b, 993b–994a,
  1000a
 Machado and, 9:744b
 of Valle-Inclán, 8:336a-b
in Svevo's novels, 8:84a–86a
Trakl and, 10:1420a-b
in Yugoslavia, Krleža and, 11:1827a
see also Avant-gardism; Futurism
Modernismo. See Modernism, Spanish
Modernity
 Foucault and, 13:3325a-b
 Kundera and, 13:3396a
Moderskärlek (Motherlove). See Strindberg,
 August
Modersohn, Otto, 9:770a
Modification, La. See Butor, Michel, A Change
 of Heart
Modigliani, Amedeo, 9:898b
Modjeska, Helena, Witkiewicz and, 10:1208a
Mododaia gvardiia (Russian journal),
 Veshnev's contributions to, 11:1907b
Moðurminning. See Gunnarsson, Gunnar
"Modus vivendi." See Ekelöf, Gunnar
Moe otkrytie Ameriky. See Mayakovsky,
 Vladimir
Moers, Ellen, Literary Women, 5:90b, 100b
Möglichkeitssin. See "Sense of possibility"
 (Musil)
Mohicans of Paris, The. See Dumas père,
 Alexandre
Mohr, J. J., Hebbel and, 6:1091a-b
"Moi aussi je suis peintre." See Apollinaire,
 Guillaume
"Moi interv'iu." See Gorky, Maxim
"Moi listki: Odessa." See Babel, Isaac
"Moi pervyi gus." See Babel, Isaac
"Moi Pushkin." See Tsvetaeva, Marina

"Moi sputnik." See Gorky, Maxim
Moi universitety. See Gorky, Maxim, My
 Universities
Moira, 13:2980a
"Moiron." See Maupassant, Guy de
Moïse. See Chateaubriand, François René de
"Moïse." See Vigny, Alfred Victor de, Poèmes
 antiques et modernes
Moj obračun s njima. See Krleža, Miroslav
Moke, Camille. See Pleyel, Marie
Molé, Matthieu, Count, criticism of Vigny by,
 5:479b
Molière, **3:101a–123b**, 9:701a, 706b
 Amphitryon, 3:102a, 104a, 104b, 107a, 108b,
  109a
 Anouilh and, 13:2846a, 2854a-b, 2856b,
  2860a
 attacked by Bossuet, 3:173a
 Augier and, 7:1919b
 Beaumarchais and, 4:564a
 Bergson and, 8:56a
 Berlioz and, 6:805a
 Boileau's satire 2 addressed to, 3:183a
 Brieux and, 7:1921a
 Corneille and, 3:25b
 Don Juan, 3:102a, 108b–109a, 113a–117b,
  274a
  Anouilh's Ornifle and, 13:2858a
  on hypocrisy, 3:110a-b
  the last scene, 3:117b
  the protagonist's bearing and integrity,
   3:113b–114a
 George Dandin, 3:97a
 Giraudoux and, 9:1060a
 Goldoni and, 4:427b–428a
 Impromptu de Versailles, Ionesco's
  L'Impromptu de l'Alma and, 13:2999a
 La Fontaine and, 3:75a-b
 La jalousie du barbouillé (The Jealousy of
  Smut-Face), 3:102b
 Labiche and, 7:1921b
 L'Avare (The Miser), 3:102a, 106b, 107a-b,
  108a, 108b, 118a
  Camoëns' King Seleucus and, 3:757a

Molière (*cont.*)

Le bourgeois gentilhomme (*The Bourgeois Gentleman; or, The Would-be Gentleman*), 3:101a, 104a, 107b, 108b, 9:899a

Le dépit amoureux (*The Love Tiff*), 3:103a

Le docteur amoureux (*The Doctor in Love*), 3:103b

Le malade imaginaire (*The Imaginary Invalid*), 3:104b, 105a, 106a-b, 107a, 108a

Corneille's *Nicomède* and, 3:47a

Le médecin volant (*The Flying Physician*), 3:102b

Le misanthrope (*The Misanthrope*), 3:102a, 104a, 104b, 107b, 113b, 117b–122a, 274a

ambiguous positioning of between comedy and tragedy, 3:120a-b, 121a

L'École des femmes (*The School for Wives*), 3:104a, 9:1043a

L'École des maris (*The School for Husbands*), 9:1043a

Les fâcheux (*The Nuisances*), La Fontaine and, 3:75a

Les femmes savantes (*The Learned Ladies*), 3:102a, 106a, 106b, 107b, 108a-b

Le Cid and, 3:33a

materialist-rationalist debate in, 3:114b–115a

Les précieuses ridicules (*The Ridiculous Précieuses*), 3:64a, 103b

Lesage and, 3:321a, 322a, 326b–327a

Lessing and, 4:551a

L'Étourdi (*The Blunderer*), 3:103a

L'Impromptu de Versailles (*The Rehearsal at Versailles*), 9:1054b, 1063a

neoclassical tradition and, 9:1041a

praised by Boileau, 3:179a

Queneau and, 12:2527b

Racine and, 3:208a, 208b

Tartuffe, 3:103a, 104b, 107a, 107b–108a, 108b, 109b–113a

hypocrisy in, 3:110a-b

Proust's *Remembrance of Things Past* and, 8:552a

response to, 3:109b

Tartuffe compared with Don Juan, 3:117a

Weil and, 12:2809a

Molière. *See* Goldoni, Carlo

Molina

Jesuits and, 3:133a-b

Pascal's *Lettres provinciales* and, 3:136b

Molini, Giovan Claudio, publication of Alfieri's poetry by, 4:670a

Molinos, Michel, *Spiritual Guide*, 3:268b

Molinos, Miguel, Valle-Inclán and, 8:333a

Molinosism. *See* Quietism

"Molitva." *See* Lermontov, Mikhail Yurievich

Moll Flanders. *See* Defoe, Daniel

"Molle Luna, La." *See* Calvino, Italo, "The Soft Moon"

Molnen över Metapontion. *See* Johnson, Eyvind

Molodets. *See* Tsvetaeva, Marina

Molodoi kolkhoznik (Russian journal), Babel's stories in, 11:1910b

Moment of True Feeling, A. See Handke, Peter, *Die Stunde der wahren Empfindung*

Mommsen, Tycho, George and, 8:465a

Momolo cortesan. See Goldoni, Carlo

Momolo sulla brenta. See Goldoni, Carlo

"Mon cher Ludovic." *See* Apollinaire, Guillaume

Mon Faust. See Valéry, Paul

"Mon rêve familier." *See* Verlaine, Paul

Mona Lisa theft (1911), 9:881b, 883a

Monarchism, of Pessoa, 10:1480a, 1487a, 1494a

Monarchy

Alfieri's hatred of, 4:664a

Aquinas on, 1:425b

Baroja's ambivalence about, 9:594a

doctrine of divine right, 3:157a

in Fénelon's view, 3:280b–281a

French

Montaigne and, 2:779a

in satire of Deschamps, 1:362b–363b

Voltaire and the, 4:370b–372a, 374b–375b, 376b, 382a–383b, 391b

Icelandic, 1:382b

in La Bruyère's *Caractères*, 3:247b

Mann on, 5:214a

medieval satire and, 1:352a-b

Montesquieu on, 3:352b, 353b

Novalis on, 5:214a-b

principle of divine right, Bossuet's view on, 3:156b

Prussian, Voltaire and the, 4:373b–374a, 375a–376b, 377b, 390b

Spanish

under Carlists, 9:589a-b

weakening of, 9:612a-b

Swedish, Voltaire on the, 4:372b, 382a-b

Monarchy According to the Charter. See Chateaubriand, François René de, *De la monarchie selon la charte*

Monastery in Sendomir, The. *See* Grillparzer, Franz, *Das Kloster bei Sendomir*

Monasticism

Diderot and, 4:495b–497b

early, in Fénelon's works, 3:270b

in England

cultural and literary achievements, 1:63b, 64a

Germanic and Latin elements, 1:65a

Erasmus and, 2:572a-b

Huysmans and, 7:1726b, 1728a-b

Moncetti, G. B., 1:444a

Moncombie, Elisa, 7:1621b

Moncrieff, Scott, 8:562b

Mondain, Le. See Voltaire

Monday Chats. *See* Sainte-Beuve, Charles-Augustin, *Causeries du lundi*

"Monday rue Christine." *See* Apollinaire, Guillaume, "Lundi rue Christine"

Monday's Tales. See Daudet, Alphonse, *Contes du lundi*

Monde dramatique, Le (journal), 6:948a

Monde, Le. See Descartes, René

Monde où L'On s'ennuie. See Pailleron, Édouard

Monde réal, Le. See Aragon, Louis

"Mondnacht." *See* Eichendorff, Joseph von

Mondo creato. See Tasso, Torquato, *Le sette giornate del mondo creato*

Mondo è quello che è, Il. See Moravia, Alberto

Monemvasiotises. See Ritsos, Yannis

Monet, Claude, 7:1630b

Goncourts on, 7:1397a

Impression, Sunrise, 7:1631b

Japanese influence, 7:1398a

Money

in Anouilh's plays, 13:2848a

in Augier's plays, 7:1918a

in Balzac's works, 5:640b–641a

in Camoëns' *The Lusiads*, 2:764a

in La Bruyère's *Caractères*, 3:241b–242b

in Scribe's plays, 7:1912b

social change and, in nineteeenth century, 7:1323b

Money. See Zola, Émile, *L'Argent*

Money and Carnival. *See* Ady, Endre, "Pénz és karnevál"

Money, contempt for, in poetry of Ady, 9:862a-b

Money and Other Stories. See Čapek, Karel, *Trapné povídky*

Money Pool, The. See Labiche, Eugène, *La cagnotte*

"Mongo." *See* Lermontov, Mikhail Yurievich

Mongolism, in Bely's *Petersburg*, 9:921a, 923b

Monica (mother of Augustine), 1:27b, 29a, 30a-b, 31a-b, 38b–39a

Monism, Diderot and, 4:490a–491b

"Monkey, The." *See* Dinesen, Isak

"Monk's Tale." *See* Chaucer, Geoffrey, *Canterbury Tales*

Monna Vanna. See Maeterlinck, Maurice

Monogram, The (*To monogramma*). *See* Elytis, Odysseus

Monologue

dramatic, in modern long poems, 7:1906b

in Gunnarsson's works, 10:1498b

interior

in fiction of Simon, 13:3032a

in Johnson's works, 12:2364b–2365a, 2371a

"Monologue." *See* Novalis, *Sacred Songs*

Monology (Monologues). *See* Milan, Kundera

Monomania, Canetti and, 12:2618a–2619b

Monovasia. See Ritsos, Yannis

Monsieur Monde Vanishes. See Simenon, Georges, *La fuite de Monsieur Monde*

"Monsieur Parent." *See* Maupassant, Guy de

Monsieur Sylvestre. See Sand, George

Monsieur Teste. See Valéry, Paul

Monster image, in Hugo's works, 6:696a-b

Monstre (mystery play procession), 1:466a,
   468b
Monstres sacrés, Les. See Cocteau, Jean
"Mont des oliviers, Le." *See* Vigny, Alfred
   Victor de, *Les destinées*
Mont-Oriol. See Maupassant, Guy de
Montage technique, in fiction of Simon,
   13:3024b, 3025a-b, 3037a, 3041b
"Montagne des signes, La." *See* Artaud,
   Antonin, *D'un voyage au pays des
   Tarahumaras (Peyote Dance),* "The
   Mountain of Signs"
"Montagne qui accouche, La." *See* La
   Fontaine, Jean de, *Fables*
Montague, C. E., on Ibsen, 7:1427b–1428a
Montaigne, Michel de, **2:769a–790b**
   Azorín on, 9:645a
   Camoëns and, 2:759a
   Essays (*Essais*)
      "A Custom of the Island of Cea,"
         2:775b–776a
      "Apology for Raymond Sebond," 2:769a-b,
         772a, 776a–777a, 783a, 3:9a
      book 3, 2:779a–782a
      Cocteau and, 10:1559b
      Corneille and, 3:24a, 35b
      editions, 2:769a, 772b
      La Boétie and, 2:771a
      obscenity in, 2:783b
      "Of Cannibals," 2:753b
      "Of Drunkenness," 2:775a-b
      "Of Experience," 2:780b
      "Of Idleness," 2:774b
      "Of the Inequality That Is Between Us,"
         2:782b
      "Of Physiognomy," 2:782b
      "Of Repentance," 2:780a, 783b
      "Of the Resemblance of Children to
         Fathers," 2:777a
      "Of Three Kinds of Association," 2:780a
      "Of the Useful and the Honorable," 2:780a
      "Of Vanity," 2:774b
      "On Some Verses of Vergil," 2:780a
      in seventeenth century, 2:786a
      strata of, 2:772b, 779a, 782a
      style, 2:784a-b, 786b–787a
   Heinrich Mann and, 8:519b, 538a-b

   La Fontaine and, 3:79a
   Sainte-Beuve on, 6:858a–859a
   Sand and, 6:817b
   Travel Journal, 2:778a
   Valéry and, 8:572a
   "Various Outcomes of the Same Plan,"
      Cinna and, 3:38b, 44a
   Yourcenar and, 12:2538b, 2554a
Montaigne, Pierre de, 2:769b–770a, 771b, 772a
Montalbán, Juan Pérez de, *Sucesos y prodigios
   de amor en ocho novelas ejemplares
   (Amatory Happenings and Wonders in
   Eight Exemplary Novellas),* Inquisition
   and, 2:951b
Montale, Eugenio, **11:1987a–2008b**
   *Altri versi e poesie disperse (Otherwise:
      Last and First Poems of Eugenio
      Montale),* 11:2006a-b
      "Ah," 11:2006b
      "Ho tanta fede in te" ("I Have Such Faith
         in You"), 11:2006a-b
      "Nel '38" ("In '38"), 11:2006a
      "Quartetto" ("Foursome"), 11:2006a
   Cuttlefish Bones (Ossi di seppia),
      11:1993a–1997a, 12:2389b, 2391a
      as anti-D'Annunzian, 11:1988b
      "Arsenio," 11:1991a, 1996a-b
      "Chrysalis" ("Crisalide"), 11:1996b
      "Delta," 11:1996b
      "Forse un mattino, andando in un'aria di
         vetro" ("Perhaps Some Morning,
         Walking in a Vitreous, Clear Air"),
         11:1995a
      "Incontro" ("Encounter"), 11:1996b
      "Mediterranean" ("Mediterranio"),
         11:1993b–1994b
      "Meriggiare pallido e assorto" ("To Spend
         the Noontide, Pale and Absorbed"),
         11:1995a
      "Non chiederci la parola che squadri da
         ogni lato" ("Do Not Ask Us for the
         Word Which Can Give a Shape"),
         11:1995b–1996a
      "So l'ora in cui la faccia più impassibile"
         ("I Know the Hour When the Most
         Impassive Face"), 11:1995b

"Spesso il male di vivere ho incontrato" ("Ofttimes Have I Met the Grief of Living"), 11:1995a

"The Lemon Trees" ("I limoni"), 11:1993a-b

and Vittorini's *In Sicily*, 12:2742b

"Intenzioni (Intervista immaginaria)" ("Intentions [Imaginary Interview]")

on *Finisterre*, 11:2001a

on language of poetry, 11:2006b–2007a

sense of isolation in, 11:1997a

"La casa del doganiere" ("The Coast Guard's House"), 12:2391a

Le occasioni, 12:2755b

"L'Eroismo" ("Heroism"), Brandeis in, 11:1991b

Quasimodo and, 12:2387a, 2388b, 2391a, 2409a-b

Satura, 11:2004a–2006a

"After a Flight" ("Dopo una fuga"), 11:2005b–2006a

"Botta e risposta" (Thrust and Parry), 11:1991a, 2004a-b

"Cielo e terra" (Heaven and Earth), 11:2004b

"Dialogo" (Dialogue), 11:2004b

"Gli uomini che si voltano" ("Men Who Turn Back"), 11:1993a

"L'Angelo nero" ("The Black Angel"), 11:2005b

objects of satire in, 11:1992b–1993a

"Piove" (It's Raining), 11:2004b

title of, 11:1992b

"Xenia," 11:2004b–2005b

"Style and tradition" ("Stile e tradizione")

publication of, 11:1990b

twilight poets in, 11:1944a

Svevo and, 8:70b, 71a-b, 72a

The Butterfly of Dinard (*La farfalla di Dinard*)

on being fired from the Vieusseux, 11:1991a

publication of, 11:1992b

The Occasions (*Le occasioni*), 11:1997a–2000b

"Barche sulla Marna" ("Boats on the Marne"), 11:2000a

dedicated to Brandeis, 11:1991b

"Dora Markus," 11:1997b–1998a

"Eastbourne," 11:2000a

"Elegia di Pico Farnese" ("Elegy of Pico Farnese"), 11:1999b

"Gerti's Carnival" ("Carnevale di Gerti"), 11:1997b

"Mottetti" ("Motets"), 11:1998b–1999a

"New Stanzas" ("Nuove stanze"), 11:1998a-b, 1999a

"Notizie dall'Amiata" ("News from Amiata"), 11:2000b

"Palio," 11:1999b

"Stanzas" ("Stanze"), 11:1998a-b

The Storm and Other Things (*La bufera e altro*), 11:2000b–2003b

"Anniversary" ("Anniversario"), 11:2003a-b

"Dopo" ("Afterward"), 11:2001a

"Esiste un decadentismo in Italia?" ("Is There an Italian Decadence?"), 11:2003a

"For an 'Homage to Rimbaud'" ("Per un 'Omaggio a Rimbaud'"), 11:2002b–2003a

"From a Swiss Lake" ("Da un lago svizzero"), 11:2002b–2003a

"Gli orecchini" ("The Earrings"), 11:2001b

"Hitler Spring" ("La primavera hitleriana"), 11:2001b, 2002a

"Il fascismo e la letteratura" ("Fascism and Literature"), 11:2002b–2003a

"Intermezzo," 11:2001a

"La frangia dei capelli . . ." (The Strands of Hair . . .), 11:2001b

"L'Ombra della magnolia" ("The Shade of the Magnolia"), 11:2002a-b

"Nubi color magenta" ("Magenta-Colored Clouds"), 11:2002b

"Piccolo testamento" ("Little Testament"), 11:2003b

publication of, 11:1992b

"Rainbow" ("Iride"), 11:2001b–2002a

"The Prisoner's Dream" ("Il sogno del prigioniero"), 11:2003b

Vittorini and, 12:2735b

Montalembert, Charles de, Vigny and, 5:463b,
464a
Montalván, Juan Pérez de, Lope de Vega and,
2:845a-b
Montano, Ricco, 1:441a
Montauk. See Frisch, Max
Montdory, Guillaume, 3:25a, 25b, 27b
Monte Oliveto. See Tasso, Torquato
Montemayor, Jorge de
Los siete libros de la Diana (The Seven
Books of the Diana), 2:830a, 921b–922b
Abencerraje, 2:950a-b
influence on pastoral romance,
2:921b–922a, 922b–923b
Monterby, Yolande de, funeral oration on by
Bossuet, 3:163a-b
Montesquieu, Charles-Louis de Secondat,
baron de, **3:345a–366b**
*Considerations on the Causes of the
Greatness of the Romans and Their
Decline*, 3:346b, 347a, 352b–353a,
354a–355b, 356b, 358a
Diderot and, 4:483b
Discourse on the Function of the Kidneys,
3:352a
*Essay on Causes Affecting Minds and
Characters*, 3:350a, 350b–351a, 351b
on Montaigne, 2:786b
My Thoughts, 3:349b–350a, 351b, 354b,
358a, 361a-b
Observations on Natural History,
3:348a–349a
as political scientist, 3:348a
scientific memoirs of, 3:346a-b
The Persian Letters (*Lettres persanes*),
3:345a-b, 358a–363b, 4:401a
disintegration of the seraglio,
3:362b–363a
La Bruyère and, 3:229a, 257b–258a
The Spirit of the Laws (*De l'esprit des lois*),
3:345b, 347a-b, 352b, 353a
Alfieri and, 4:672b
Chénier and, 4:709a
on climatic influence on man, 3:357a-b
on despotic government, 3:363b–364a
Fénelon's *Télémaque* and, 3:289a
on government, 3:358b–359a

on island states, 3:355b–356a
metaphors in, 3:353a-b
on the necessity of opposition, 3:356b
principle of balance in, 3:357a
Staël's *De l'Allemagne* and, 5:106a
Vico and, 3:300b–301a
Montesquiou, Bertrand de, Proust and, 8:546b
Montez, Lola, influence of scandal on
Grillparzer's *The Jewess of Toledo*,
5:442a-b
Month in the Country, A. See Turgenev, Ivan
Month in the USSR, A. *See* Moravia, Alberto,
Un mese in U.R.S.S.
Montherlant, Henry de, **11:1915a–1938b**
Brocéliande, 11:1932b
Camus and, 13:3055b
Chaos and Night, 11:1919b, 1928a–1929a,
1932a
Celestino, 11:1928b–1929a
Demain il fera jour (*Tomorrow the Dawn*),
11:1932a
Don Juan, 11:1931a–1932a, 1934a
École Sainte-Croix de Neuilly experience,
11:1916a, 1923a
Fils de personne (No Man's Son), 11:1932a,
1932b–1933a
La reine morte (The Dead Queen), 11:1919a,
1931a, 1932a, 1933a
La relève du matin (The Changing of the
Guard), 11:1917a-b
La rose de sable (The Desert Rose),
11:1826a–1927b, 1918a, 1919b, 1934a
anticolonialist attitude, 11:1926a-b
Auligny, 11:1926b–1927b
Guiscart, 11:1927b, 1931a
La ville dont le prince est un enfant (The
Fire That Consumes), 11:1916a, 1916b,
1923a
Le cardinal d'Espagne (The Spanish
Cardinal), 11:1931a, 1932a
Le démon du bien (*The Hipogriff*), 11:1918b
Le solstice de juin (The Summer Solstice),
11:1918b–1919a, 1934a
L'Equinoxe de septembre (The September
Equinox), 11:1918b, 1934a

"Les après-midi de deux faunes" (correspondence with Peyrefitte), 11:1920a-b

"Les chevaleries" (The Knighthoods), 11:1924a

Les olympiques (The Olympians), 11:1917b, 1919b, 1924a-b, 1925a–1926a, 1934a

L'Exil (The Exile), 11:1916b

Pasiphaé, 11:1918a, 1931a, 1931b–1932a

Pitié pour les femmes (*Pity for Women*), 11:1918b

Port-Royal, 11:1919a, 1931a

Queneau and, 12:2511b

Service inutile (Useless Service), 11:1918b

"Syncrétisme et alternance," 11:1922b

The Bachelors (*Les célibataires*), 11:1917a, 1918a, 1927b–1928a

The Boys (*Les garçons*), 11:1916a, 1916b, 1919b, 1923a–1924a

"La Protection," 11:1923b–1924a

The Dream (*Le songe*), 11:1917b, 1924a-b, 1934a

Alban, 11:1935b–1936b

The Girls (*Les jeunes filles*), 11:1918b, 1919b, 1920a, 1924b–1925a, 1934a

Costals, 11:1921a–1922a, 1927b, 1931a, 1933a-b

The Lepers (*Les lépreuses*), 11:1918b, 1933b

The Master of Santiago (*Le maître de Santiago*), 11:1919a, 1931a, 1932a, 1933a

The Matador (*Les bestiaires*), 11:1916a, 1917b, 1919b, 1924a-b

Chaos and Night and, 11:1928a

Thrasylle (Thrasyllus), 11:1916b

Un assassin est mon maître (An Assassin Is My Master), 11:1919b, 1929a–1930a

Montherlant sans masque. See Sipriot, Pierre

Montménil, in Lesage's *Turcaret*, 3:322b

Montmorency, Henri, duc de, 3:56a

Montpensier, Duchesse de, in fiction of Heinrich Mann, 8:539b

Montreuil, Madame de, Sade and, 4:616a, 617b, 628a

Montreuil, Renée-Pélagie de marriage to Sade, 4:615b

Sade's letters to, 4:617a–618b

separation order obtained by, 4:626b–627a

Monts de piété. See Breton, André

Monument, Le. See Triolet, Elsa

Monument, The. See Khlebnikov, Velimir, "Pamiatnik"

Moon and the Bonfires, The. See Pavese, Cesare

Moon in Search of Herself, The. See Claudel, Paul, *La lune à la recherche d'elle-même*

"Moon Solo." See Laforgue, Jules

"Moon, The." See Södergran, Edith

Moonbirds. See Aymé, Marcel, *Les oiseaux de lune*

Mooney, Michael, *Vico in the Tradition of Rhetoric*, 8:325b

Moonlight, as futurist symbol, 9:812a-b

"Moonlight." See Apollinaire, Guillaume, "Clair de lune"

Moonlight. See Verlaine, Paul, "Clair de lune"

Moonlight Sonata, The. See Ritsos, Yannis, *I sonata tou selinofotos*

"Moonlit Night." See Eichendorff, Joseph von, "Mondnacht"

"Moon's Secret, The." See Södergran, Edith, "Månens hemlighet"

Moonstruck. See Simenon, Georges, *Le coup de lune*

Moore, George, Verlaine and, 7:1642a

Moore, Marianne, Seferis' translations, 12:2260a

Moore, Thomas, Berlioz and, 6:792b

"Moorish Vengeance." See Blasco Ibáñez, Vicente, "Venganza moruna"

Moors in Spain, in Machado's *Nuevas canciones*, 9:759a-b

Moral Letters to Sophie. See Rousseau, Jean Jacques

Moral Tales. See Laforgue, Jules, *Moralités légendaires*

Morale élémentaire. See Queneau, Raymond

Moralisme, Fénelon and, 3:265b

Moralistes (Moralists)

of seventeenth century, 3:273b

Yourcenar's association with, 12:2538a, 2538b

Moralités légendaires. See Laforgue, Jules

Morality
  in Andrić's works, 11:1755a
  art and, in Mann, 9:724a
  in art and religion, 8:269b
  Bergson's view of, 8:61b–62a
  Camus and, 13:3071b
  in Chrétien's works, 1:207b
    Cligés, 1:193a
  free love, 8:233b
  Frisch on, 13:2898b
  in Keller's novellas, 6:926b–929a
  in Marcabru's works, 1:170b–171a
  Milosz's views on, 13:2942a-b
  Nietzsche on
    Christianity and, 7:1672b–1673b
    creation of, 7:1676b
    eternal recurrence and, 7:1677b–1687a
    "master morality," 7:1671b–1672a
    Overman and, 7:1673b–1676a
    self-discipline and, 7:1677b
    value systems of, opposing,
      7:1671b–1672b
    will to power and, 7:1676b–1677b
  in *Romance of the Rose*, 1:313b
  in Schnitzler's works, 8:89b
  spirituality and, in Mann's *Joseph and His
    Brothers*, 9:729b
  in Svevo's novels, 8:74a-b
  Taine on, 7:1463a
  Tolstoy on literature and, 7:1487a-b
  Walther and, 1:290b
  Wedekind's definition, 8:237b
  Wolfram and, 1:280a
  see also Choice, moral; Ethics
Morality plays, 1:471a, 471b–472a
  Hofmannsthal and, 9:693b–694a, 701b–703
  Jesuit, influence on Austrian postromantic
    theatre, 5:421b
Moralized Ovid, 1:465a
Morasso, Mario
  Il nuovo aspetto mecanico del mondo (The
    New Mechanical Aspect of the World),
    9:806b
  La nuova arma (The New Weapon), 9:806b
Moratín. See Azorín
Moravia, Alberto, **12:2673a–2697a**

"A Fragment of Autobiography: About My
  Novels," 12:2677a-b
A Ghost at Noon (*Il disprezzo*),
  12:2685a–2686a
Agostino, 12:2680b–2681a, 2681b
Beatrice Cenci, 12:2690a
Boh (*The Voice of the Sea*), 12:2692b
Conjugal Love (*L'Amore coniugale*),
  12:2685a, 2689a, 2691a
Disobedience (*La disubbidienza*),
  12:2681a-b
Due cortigiane (Two Courtesans), 12:2680b
Erotic Tales (*La cosa e altri racconti*),
  12:2694b
I racconti, 12:2686a
I sogni del pigro (Lazy Man's Dreams),
  12:2679a
Il dio Kurt (Kurt, the God), 12:2690a
Il mondo è quello che è (*The World's the
  World*), 12:2690a
Il paradiso (*Bought and Sold*), 12:2688a,
  2692b
Il viaggio a Roma (The Trip to Rome),
  12:2696b
Impegno controvoglia (Commitment in Spite
  of Myself), 12:2692a-b
La bella vita (The Good Life), 12:2678a-b
La cintura (The Belt), 12:2696a
La speranza (Hope), 12:2681b–2682a
La vita è gioco (Life Is a Game), 12:2690a
L'Amante infelice (The Unfortunate Lover),
  12:2680b
*L'Angelo dell'informazione e altri testi
  teatrali* (The Angel of Information and
  Other Plays), 12:2696a
L'Automa (*The Fetish*), 12:2688a
L'Epidemia (The Epidemic), 12:2679a, 2690a
Lettere dal Sahara (Letters from the Sahara),
  12:2686a
L'Imbroglio (The Imbroglio), 12:2679a
L'Intervista (The Interview), 12:2690a
"Man as an End" ("L'Uomo come fine"),
  12:2274a, 2682a-b
Mistaken Ambitions (*Le ambizione
  sbagliate*), 12:2678b–2679a
More Roman Tales (*Nuovi racconti romani*),
  12:2683b

1934, 13:2693a–2694a

"Note sul romanzo" ("Notes on the Novel"), 12:2687a

Omaggio a James Joyce; ovvero, Il colpo di stato (Homage to James Joyce; or, The Coup d'État), 12:2696a

Passeggiate africane (African Walks), 12:2696b

"Racconto e romanzo" ("The Short Story and the Novel"), 12:2687b

"Ricordo de *Gli indifferenti*" ("Recalling *Time of Indifference*"), 12:2274a, 2675a

"Risposta a nove domande sul romanzo" ("Answers to Nine Questions on the Novel"), 12:2687b

Roman Tales (*Racconti romani*), 12:2683b

The Conformist (*Il conformista*), 12:2684b–2685a

The Empty Canvas (*La noia*), 12:2687a, 2687b, 2689a–2690b, 2691b

The Fancy Dress Party (*La mascherata*), 12:690a, 2679a–2680a

The Lie (*L'Attenzione*), 12:2689a–2690a, 2691b

The Red Book and the Great Wall (*La rivoluzione culturale in Cina*), 12:2686a, 2686b, 2692a

The Time of Indifference (*Gli indifferenti*), 12:2285a, 2675a–2677b, 2681b, 2682b, 2773a, 13:3137a

The Voyeur (*L'Uomo che guarda*), 12:2694b–2696a

The Woman of Rome (*La romana*), 12:2682b–2683a, 2688a

Time of Desecration (*La vita interiore*), 12:2692b–2693a, 2694a

Two: A Phallic Novel (*Io e lui*), 12:2691a–2692a

Two Women (*La ciociara*), 12:2683b–2684b

Un mese in U.R.S.S. (A Month in the USSR), 12:2686a

"Un uomo sfortunato" (An Unlucky Man), 12:2683a

Una cosa è una cosa (Command and I Will Obey You), 12:2688a

Un'altra vita (Lady Godiva), 12:2692b

Un'idea dell'India (An Idea of India), 12:2686a

Vittorini and, 12:2734b, 2739b, 2743a

Voltati parlami (Turn Over and Talk to Me), 12:2696a

Which Tribe Do You Belong To? (*A quale tribù appartieni?*), 12:2686a

Moravia, Carlo Pincherle, 12:2673b

Morbid Democracy. *See* Ortega y Gasset, José, "Democracia morbosa"

Morceau d'un drame. See Claudel, Paul

"Mörder, Der." *See* Schnitzler, Arthur

More de Venise, Le. See Vigny, Alfred Victor de

More Roman Tales. See Moravia, Alberto

More than Love. *See* D'Annunzio, Gabriele, *Più che l'amore*

More, Thomas
Erasmus and, 2:574a, 583b
Utopia, "Hymne de l'or" and, 2:732a

Moréas, Jean
Machado and, 9:744b, 750a
use of English and French, 8:210a

Moreau, Gustave
Breton and, 11:1939a
Huysmans and, 7:1720b

Moreau, Jean-Michel (the younger), in Goncourts' *L'Art du dix-huitième siècle*, 7:1397a

Moreno, Marguerite, and Colette, 9:620b

Morgan, Lewis Henry, property rights and, 4:651b

Morgenblatt (journal), Richter and, 5:79a, 83b

Morgenlandfahrt, Die. See Hesse, Hermann

Morgenröte. See Nietzsche, Friedrich

Morgenstern, Willi. *See* Rudinoff, W. W.

"Morgonen." *See* Lagerkvist, Pär

Morgonvinden. See Vesaas, Tarjei

Moriae encomium. See Erasmus, *The Praise of Folly*

Morice, Charles
Corbière and, 7:1640a
Verlaine and, 7:1638a-b, 1639a

Moritz, Karl Philipp, Richter's *The Invisible Lodge* and, 5:63a-b

Morkinskinna, 1:393a

Morley, Robert, on Sainte-Beuve, 6:839b

Morlini, Girolamo, *Novellae*, 2:940b

Mornay, comte de, Delacroix and, 5:519b–520a

Mornay, Madame de, in fiction of Heinrich Mann, 8:538b–539a

Mornay, Philippe de, Montaigne and, 2:779a

"Morning." *See* Seferis, George, "Proi"

"Morning of Acmeism, The." *See* Mandelshtam, Osip

"Morning Intoxication." *See* Rimbaud, Arthur, "Matinée d'ivresse"

Morning Star. *See* Ritsos, Yannis, *Proino astro*

Morning Stories. *See* Giraudoux, Jean, *Les contes d'un matin*

Morning Wind, The. See Vesaas, Tarjei, *Morgonvinden*

Morny, Mathilde de ("Missy"), 9:621b

Morocco, Delacroix in, 5:519b–520b

Morozov, Savva, Gorky and, 8:420a

Morris, William, *Völsunga saga* and, 1:400b

Morsa, La. See Pirandello, Luigi

Mort conduit l'attelage, La. See Yourcenar, Marguerite

Mort à credit. See Céline, Louis-Ferdinand, *Death on the Installment Plan*

Mort de Belle, La. See Simenon, Georges

Mort de Pompée, La. See Corneille, Pierre

Mort de Sénèque, La. See L'Hermite, Tristan

"Mort de Socrate, La." *See* Lamartine, Alphonse de

Mort de Tintagiles, La. See Maeterlinck, Maurice

"Mort de Valmiki, La." *See* Leconte de Lisle, Charles Marie

Mort du Docteur Faust, La. See Ghelderode, Michel de

"Mort du loup, La." *See* Vigny, Alfred Victor de, *Les destinées*

"Mort du moine, La." *See* Leconte de Lisle, Charles Marie

Mort heureuse, La. See Camus, Albert, *A Happy Death*

Mort, La. See Maeterlinck, Maurice

"Mort qui fait le trottoir, La." *See* Montherlant, Henry de, *Don Juan*

Mort regarde à la fenêtre, La. See Ghelderode, Michel de

Mort très douce, Une. See Beauvoir, Simone de, *A Very Easy Death*

Mortality
in Ionesco's plays
Exit the King, 13:3006b
Jacques, 13:2994a-b
see also Death

"Morte amoureuse, La." *See* Gautier, Théophile

Morte Darthur. See Malory, Sir Thomas

"Morte del ricco, La." *See* Pascoli, Giovanni

Mortification, in Fénelon's spirituality, 3:274b

"Morts de quatre-vingts-douze." *See* Rimbaud, Arthur

Morwitz, Ernst, 8:449a, 453b, 465a

Mosaic (Mosaïque). See Mérimée, Prosper

Mosca. *See* Tanzi, Drusilla

Mosca, Gaetano, on the masses, 9:1145b

"Moscas, Las." *See* Machado, Antonio, *Soledades* (Solitudes), "Humorismos, fantasías, y apuntos"

Moschus
Lament for Bion, Renaissance pastoral elegy and, 2:900b–901a
Renaissance pastoral poetry and, 2:900b–901a

Moscow
Benjamin in, 11:1721b
Lermontov's career in, 6:1197a–1199b, 1221a, 1222b
Lukács's stay in, 10:1269a–1273a
Mickiewicz's stay in, 5:613a
Tsvetaeva and, 11:1748a
early years, 11:1732a–1736b
Russian Revolution, 11:1736b–1739a

Moscow. See Bely, Andrey, *Moskva*

"Moscow." *See* Benjamin, Walter

Moscow Art Theater
Chekhov and, 7:1855a, 1857a, 1857b, 1877a
Gorky and, 8:419b, 435a
in *Na rubezhe dvukh stoletii*, 9:911b
Olesha and, 11:2244b
Witkiewicz and, 10:1218a

Moscow Eccentric, The. See Bely, Andrey, *Moskva*

*Moscow on Fire (1905): A Heroic Melomime /
Mass Spectacle with Songs and Words.*
See Mayakovsky, Vladimir

"Moscow Shoeshiners, The." *See* Böll,
Heinrich, "Die Moskauer Schuhputzer"

Moscow Under Siege. See Bely, Andrey,
Moskva

Moscow University, Goncharov at,
6:1063b–1064b

"Moscow-Petersburg." *See* Zamyatin, Yevgeny
Ivanovich, "Moskva-Peterburg"

"Moses." *See* Vigny, Alfred Victor de, *Poèmes
antiques et modernes*

*Moses Hess und die Probleme der
idealistischen Dialektik* (Moses Hess
and the Problems of Idealist Dialectics).
See Lukács, György

Moses (O.T. prophet), Strindberg's treatment
of, 7:1739a

Moses Saved. See Saint-Amant, Girard, *Moyse
sauvé*

"Moskauer Schuhputzer, Die." *See* Böll,
Heinrich

Moskovskii chudak. See Bely, Andrey, *Moskva*

Moskva. See Bely, Andrey

Moskva gorit (1905). See Mayakovsky,
Vladimir, *Moscow on Fire (1905)*

Moskva pod udarom. See Bely, Andrey,
Moskva

"Moskva-Peterburg." *See* Zamyatin, Yevgeny
Ivanovich

Most Ancient Wisdom of the Italians. See
Vico, Giovanni Battista, *De
antiquissima Italorum sapientia ex
linguae latinae originibus eruenda*

"Most na Žepa." *See* Andrić, Ivo

Mostoha. See Kosztolányi, Dezső

"Mot sur l'art moderne, Un." *See* Musset,
Alfred de

"Motets." *See* Montale, Eugenio, *The
Occasions (Le occasioni)*, "Mottetti"

Mothe-Fenélon, François. *See* Fénelon,
François de la Mothe-

Mothe-Guyon, Madame Jeanne Marie Bouvière
de la. *See* Guyon, Madame Jeanne Marie
Bouvière de la Mothe-

Mother

in Cela, 13:3107b–3108a

in Flaubert's writings, 7:1375b

Freud's concept of, 8:9b

in Michelet's works, 5:574a, 576b–577a

in *Narcissus and Goldmund*, 9:850b

in Nerval's works, 6:945a–946a

in Pascoli's "Thallusa," 7:1851b

relationship with son, in Camus,
13:3059a–3062a

Mother. *See* Ginzburg, Natalia, *La madre*;
Ritsos, Yannis, *Mana*

Mother. See Gorky, Maxim

Mother and Child. See Hebbel, Friedrich,
Mutter und Kind

"Mother Courage Blind." *See* Barthes, Roland

Mother Courage and Her Children. See Brecht,
Bertolt

Mother of God. *See* Varnalis, Kostas

Mother Mary. *See* Mann, Heinrich, *Mutter
Marie*

"Mother and Music." *See* Tsvetaeva, Marina,
"Mat' i muzyka"

Mother Right. See Bachofen, Johann Jakob,
Das Mutterrecht

"Mother Savage." *See* Maupassant, Guy de,
"La mère Sauvage"

Mother, The. See Brecht, Bertolt; Čapek, Karel,
Matka; Witkiewicz, Stanisław Ignacy

Motion

Aquinas' *Summa theologica* on, 1:420b

perpetual. *See* Perpetual motion

physics of, Descartes vs. Gassendi, 3:19a-b

Motion pictures. *See* Films

Motiv. See Lagerkvist, Pär

"Motiv der Kästchenwahl, Das." *See* Freud,
Sigmund

Motor Show, The. See Ionesco, Eugène, *Le
salon d'automobile*

Mots anglais, Les. See Mallarmé, Stéphane

Mots et les choses, Les. See Foucault, Michel,
The Order of Things

Mots, Les. See Sartre, Jean-Paul, *The Words*

"Mots sans rides, Les." *See* Breton, André, *Les
pas perdus*

"Motteti." *See* Montale, Eugenio, *The
Occasions*

Mouche bleue, La. See Aymé, Marcel

Mouches, Les. See Sartre, Jean-Paul, *The Flies*

Moulin de la sourdine, Le. See Aymé, Marcel, *The Secret Stream*

"Mount and the Grove, The." *See* Klopstock, Friedrich Gottlieb

"Mount of Olives, The." *See* Vigny, Alfred Victor de, *Les destinées*

Mountain, The. See Michelet, Jules

Mountain Folk. *See* Khlebnikov, Velimir, "Zhiteli gor"

Mountain Giants, The. See Pirandello, Luigi

"Mountain of Signs, The." *See* Artaud, Antonin, *D'un voyage au pays des Tarahumaras (Peyote Dance)*

"Mountain That Gives Birth, The." *See* La Fontaine, Jean de, *Fables*, "La montagne qui accouche"

Mountain, The. *See* Čapek, Karel, "Hora"

Mourgues, Odette de, *La Fontaine: "Fables,"* 3:91b

Mourning Becomes Electra. See O'Neill, Eugene

Mouseion, Greek literature influenced by, 8:211b–212a

Mousquetaire, Le. See Dumas père, Alexandre

Moussorgsky, Modest, *Boris Godunov*, 5:49b

"Mout jauzens." *See* William IX of Aquitaine, duke

"Mouvement." *See* Rimbaud, Arthur

Mouvement perpétuel, Le. See Aragon, Louis

"Movement." *See* Rimbaud, Arthur, "Mouvement"

"Mover d'olhos brando e piadoso, Um." *See* Camoëns, Luís Vaz de, *Rimas (Lyrics)*

Movie scripts. *See* Film scripts

Moving Away from Curse-City. *See* Ady, Endre, "Költözés Átok-városból"

"Moya zhizn." *See* Chekhov, Anton

Moyen court. See Guyon, Madame Jeanne Marie Bouvière de la Mothe-

Moyse sauvé. See Saint-Amant, Girard

Mozart and Salieri. See Pushkin, Alexander

Mozart, Wolfgang Amadeus, 9:707a
   Carnap's view of, 5:413b
   Don Giovanni, 3:117a, 5:71a-b, 74a
      in Akhmatova's *Poem Without a Hero*, 10:1535b, 1537a

Jean Genet and, 13:2884b
   in Hesse's *Steppenwolf*, 9:848a, 848b, 849a
   Hoffmann and, 5:274b–275a
   Mérimée and, 6:760b
   orginality and, 5:530a
   Richter and, 5:71a-b
   The Marriage of Figaro, see also Beaumarchais, Pierre-Augustin Caron de, *La folle journée ou le mariage de Figaro*

Mr. Florentin Versus Chocholka. *See* Hašek, Jaroslav, "Pan Florentin kontra Chocholka"

"Mr. Havlena's Verdict." *See* Čapek, Karel, "Soud pana Havleny"

Mr. Palomar. See Calvino, Italo

"Mr. Prokharchin." *See* Dostoevsky, Feodor

Mrs. Caldwell habla con su hijo. See Cela, Camilo José, *Mrs. Caldwell Speaks to Her Son*

Mrs. Dane's Defence. See Jones, Henry Arthur

"Mrs. Laneen." *See* Khlebnikov, Velimir, "Gospozha Lenin"

Mrs. Morli, One and Two. See Pirandello, Luigi, *La signora Morli, una e due*

Mrs. Warren's Profession. See Shaw, George Bernard

"Mstitel." *See* Chekhov, Anton

"Mtsyri." *See* Lermontov, Mikhail Yurievich

"Mucheniki nauki." *See* Zamyatin, Yevgeny Ivanovich

Mückenprinz, Der. See Wedekind, Frank

Muertos mandan, Los. See Blasco Ibáñez, Vicente

Muette de Portici, La. See Auber, Daniel François Esprit

"Mühle lass die arme still." *See* George, Stefan, *Pilgerfahrten*

Mulatto, The. See Andersen, Hans Christian

Mule sans frein, La
   Chrétien de Troyes and, 1:149b, 157a, 185b
   Gawain in, 1:157a

Müller, Adam, Musil's *The Man Without Qualities* and, 9:941b

Müller, Götz, on Musil's *The Man Without Qualities*, 9:941a-b, 942a

Müllner, Adolf

Grillparzer influenced by, 5:425a-b
Grillparzer's letter on *Sappho* to, 5:426b, 428a
"Multilinear lyricism," in "Zang Tumb Tumb," 9:819a-b
"Mum and the Sothsegger," 1:354b–355a
Mummy's Foot, The. *See* Gautier, Théophile, "Le pied de momie"
"Mumu." *See* Turgenev, Ivan
Munch, Edvard
   "Dance of Life," 8:33a
   Hamsun and, 8:28a, 33a
   Strindberg and, 7:1735b
   "The Sick Child," 8:33a
Mundo es ansí, El. See Baroja, Pío
Munich
   Wagner in, 6:1158a–1159a
   Wedekind in, 8:232a–233a, 236a–240b
Munich settlement of 1938, Čapek and, 10:1568a, 1585a
Munilla, José Ortega, editorship of *El imparcial*, 9:1122a
Muratori, Lodovico, influence on Manzoni, 5:368b
Muray, Philippe, on Céline, 11:1862a
Murder
   Camus and, 13:3070a–3071a
   child-murder, in Hauptmann, 8:159b–160b
   in D'Annunzio's works, 8:181b–183b
   Genet and, 13:2874a-b, 2875b, 2878b
   in Mérimée's works, 6:749a, 757b, 761b, 763b
   in Olesha's plays, 11:2248b
   in Schnitzler's works, 8:102a, 104a
   see also Death
Murder, The. *See* Schnitzler, Arthur, "Der Mörder"
Murderer and Robber in Court, A. See Hašek, Jaroslav, *Loupežný vrah před soudem*
Murderer, The. See Simenon, Georges, *L'Assassin*
Murders in the Rue Morgue, The. See Poe, Edgar Allan
Murger, Henri
   Scènes de la vie de bohème (Bohemians of the Latin Quarter), 7:1410b, 1712a, 1736b

Strindberg and, 7:1736b
Muri Easter play, 1:457a, 467b–468a
Muriel, Elena, 11:2153a
"Murke's Collected Silences." *See* Böll, Heinrich
Murner, Thomas, Luther and, 2:684a
Murray, John, 5:105a
Musarion, oder die Philosophie der Grazien (*Musarion: or, the Philosophy of the Graces*). *See* Wieland, Christoph Martin
Musäus, Johann, as source for Grillparzer's *Libussa*, 5:440b
Musco, Angelo, Pirandello and, 8:393a-b
Muse du département, La (*The Muse of the District*). *See* Balzac, Honoré de
Muse française, La. See Hugo, Victor
"Muse of the Twentieth Century, The." *See* Andersen, Hans Christian
Musée Grévin, Le. See Aragon, Louis
Musée imaginaire de la sculpture, Le. See Malraux, André
"Musenhof" (Court of the Muses), and Wieland, 4:589b
Muses galantes, Les. See Rousseau, Jean Jacques
Music: A Moral Portrait. *See* Wedekind, Frank, *Musik: Ein Sittengemälde*
Music
   as Alfieri's inspiration, 4:663a
   Augustine on, 1:46b–47b
   Bely on, 9:908b–909a, 911b, 927a
   Berlioz' view of, 6:773a, 774a, 779b, 786a, 787a, 795b–796a, 797b–798b, 805b–807b
   Broch and, 10:1400b–1401a
   Butor and, 13:3309a–3313b
   Castiglione on, 2:656b
   in Chekhov's works, 7:1870a-b, 1877a
   constructivism and, 8:573b
   in George's *Der Stern des Bundes*, 8:465a
   Gottfried and, 1:252b–253a
   Grillparzer's *Der arme Speilmann* (*The Poor Musician*), 5:439b–440a
   Hoffmann and, 5:263a-b, 268b–275a
   Kundera and, 13:3389b
   language and, 8:585b
   Luther and, 2:685a

Music (*cont.*)
in modern long poems, 7:1906b
national, Herder on, 4:644b
Ortega y Gasset on, 9:1135b
principles of, in Tieck, 5:248a–250a
in Rilke's works, 9:780a, 781a, 788a
Rousseau and, 4:450a–451b
Schopenhauer's metaphysics of,
   5:412a–414a
in Strindberg's works, 7:1742a, 1748a
symbolist poetry and, 8:571b
Tieck and, 5:238a-b, 249a-b
Trakl and, 10:1420a–1424b
in Valéry's poetry, 8:577a, 578a
in Verlaine's poetry, 7:1634a-b
Wagner and
   admiration for Italian, 6:1150b–1151a
   libretto, 6:1149b–1140a, 1154a–1155b
Walther and, 1:306a–307a
see also Counterpoint; *individual*
   composers; Opera
"Music for Brass." *See* Grass, Günter, *Die*
   Vorzüge der Windhühner (The
   Advantages of Windfowl), "Blechmusik"
Music criticism, of Berlioz, 6:774b, 779a–780a,
   784a–788a, 803b–805a, 809a, 810b
"Music of the Future." *See* Wagner, Richard,
   "Zukunftsmusik"
Music-Hall Sidelights. See Colette, *L'Envers*
   du music-hall
Musical Grotesques. *See* Berlioz, Hector, *Les*
   grotesques de la musique
Musical Travels in Germany and Italy. See
   Berlioz, Hector, *Voyage musical en*
   Allemagne et en Italie
"Musicalia." *See* Ortega y Gasset, José
Musik: Ein Sittengemälde. See Wedekind,
   Frank
Musil, Alfred, 9:931a-b
Musil, Hermine, 9:931a, 931b
Musil, Robert, 8:533a, 539a, **9:931a–958b**
Ady and, 9:859b, 860a
"Analyse und Synthese" ("Analysis and
   Synthesis"), 9:952b
Canetti and, 12:2615b
Die Schwärmer (The Visionaries), 9:934a

Die Verwirrungen des Zöglings Törless
   (*Young Törless*), 9:932a, 933a-b, 934a,
   951b
Drei Frauen (Three Women), 9:932b,
   933b–934a
Five Women, 9:932b
Hesse's *Beneath the Wheel* and, 9:836b
Pirandello and, 8:413b
on Rilke, 9:767a, 767b, 768b, 773a
Tagebücher (Notebooks), 9:934a
   criticism of Joyce's *Ulysses*, 10:1237b
The Man Without Qualities (*Der Mann ohne*
   Eigenschaften), 9:932b, 934a–952b
   "autism" in, 9:934a
   characterization, 9:944b, 953a
   conditions of authorship, 9:933a
   Frisch and, 13:2915b
   Nachlass, 9:952a
   plotlessness of, 9:939a
   themes, 9:935a, 936b
   uniqueness of, 9:931a
Vereinigungen (Unions), 9:932b, 933b, 956b
Vinzenz und die Freundin bedeutender
   Männer (Vincent and the Mistress of
   Important Men), 9:934a
see also Gedankenexperiment;
   Möglichkeitssin; Pastiche, principle of
   (Musil); "Sense of possibility" (Musil);
   Thought process, theme of
Musset, Alfred de, **6:999a–1032a**
À quoi rêvent les jeunes filles (*What Young*
   Girls Dream About), 6:1005b
André del Sarto, 6:1005b–1006a, 1027a-b
Armchair Theater (*Un spectacle dans un*
   fauteuil), 6:999b, 1005b, 1012a, 1018a
"Ballade à la lune" ("Ballad to the Moon"),
   6:1003a-b
Caprice (*Un caprice*), 6:1000a, 1012b, 1030b
Carmosine, 6:1012b, 1013a
Confessions of a Child of the Century (*La*
   confession d'un enfant du siècle),
   5:653a, 6:1013b–1017b, 1221a, 7:1519b,
   1602b
   apologetics of, 6:1012b
   autobiographical elements in, 6:1012b,
      1014a-b
   personal mythology in, 6:1001a

popularity of, 6:1000a, 1000b, 1013b, 1031b

purpose of, 6:999b

Sand's portrayal in, 6:1014b–1015a

Contes (*Tales*), 6:1000a, 1026b

"De la tragédie" (On Tragedy), 6:1030a

"Don Paez," 6:1003a

Fantasio, 6:1006b, 1007b–1008b

impression left by, 6:1008a-b

Giraudoux and, 9:1041b, 1060a

"Histoire d'un merle blanc" ("The History of a White Blackbird"), 6:1026b

Il faut qu'une porte soit ouverte ou fermée (*You Can't Have It Both Ways*), 6:1012b

Il ne faut jurer de rien (*Never Say Never*), 6:1012b

La coupe et les lèvres (*The Cup and the Lip*), 6:1005b

La nuit vénitienne, ou les noces de Laurette (*The Venetian Night; or, The Marriage of Lauretta*), 6:999b, 1005a-b

La quenouille de Barberine (*Barberine's Distaff*), 6:1012b

La quittance du diable (The Devil's Due), 6:1005a

Le chandelier (*The Candle-Bearer*), 6:1012b, 1013a

Lermontov and, 6:1221a

"Les deux maîtresses" ("The Two Mistresses"), 6:1026b

"Les marrons du feu" ("Irons from the Fire"), 6:1003a

"Les secrètes pensées de Rafael, gentilhomme français" ("The Secret Thoughts of Rafael, a French Gentleman"), 6:1004a-b

"Les voeux stériles" (Sterile Vows), 6:1004b–1005a

"Letters of Dupuis and Cotonet," 6:1029b

"Lettre à Lamartine" ("Letter to Lamartine"), 6:1025b

Lorenzaccio, 6:1006b, 1010b–1012a

after Nazi occupation, 6:1011b–1012a

production of, 6:1010a-b, 1012a

theme of, 6:1005a, 1011b

Vigny's *Chatterton* compared to, 5:471b

You Can't Trifle with Love and, 6:1008b

"Mardoche," 6:1003b

Nights (*Nuits*), 6:1017b, 1019b–1025b, 1031b

"August Night," 6:1022b–1023b

"December Night," 6:1021b–1022a

"May Night," 6:1020a–1021b, 1022b–1023a

"October Night," 6:1002b, 1023b–1025a

success of, 6:1000a, 1013b

"Remembrance," 6:1025b

"Reprise de *Bajazet* au Théâtre-Français" (Revival of Racine's *Bajazet* at the Comédie Française), 6:1030a

Rimbaud and, 7:1791a

"Rolla," 6:1017b–1019b

personal mythology in, 6:1001a

Sand's affair with, 6:820b–823a, 1006a-b, 1013a–1014b

Short Stories (*Nouvelles*), 6:1000a, 1026a-b

Taine on, 7:1460b–1461a

Tales of Spain and Italy (*Contes d'Espagne et d'Italie*)

address to critics of, 6:1004a

promise of Musset's future works, 6:1003a-b

scandal created by, 6:999b, 1003a

The Whims of Marianne (*Les caprices de Marianne*), 6:1006b–1007b

hero of, 6:1015a

"Titian's Son," 6:1026b–1028b

autobiographical material in, 6:1027a, 1027b–1028a

sonnets in, 6:1026a

"Tristesse" ("Sadness"), 6:1026a

"Un mot sur l'art moderne" ("A Word on Modern Art"), 6:1029a

"Une soirée perdue" ("A Wasted Evening"), 6:1025b–1026a

You Can't Trifle with Love (*On ne badine pas avec l'amour*), 6:1008b–1010a

Hugo's ideas on romanticism and, 6:1010a

Zola and, 7:1518b–1519b

Musset, Paul de

Alfred Musset and, 6:1002a

Lui et elle (*He and She*), 6:1000a

Mussolini, Benito
   Croce and, 8:311b, 326b, 327a
   D'Annunzio and, 8:196a, 11:1988b
   Ginzburg and, 13:3133b
   Machiavelli and, 2:616a
   Marinetti and, 9:824b, 825b, 826b
   in Moravia's works, 12:2679b
   Rilke and, 9:770b
   Schnitzler and, 8:111b
   Svevo and, 8:71a-b
   Valle-Inclán and, 8:337a
Must We Burn Sade? See Beauvoir, Simone de
"Mustapha Magyar" ("Mustafa Madžar"). *See* Andrić, Ivo
Mut. See Mann, Heinrich
"Mutability." *See* Shelley
Muteness, Diderot and, 4:486b–487a
Mutter Courage und ihre Kinder. See Brecht, Bertolt, *Mother Courage and Her Children*
Mutter, Die. See Brecht, Bertolt, *The Mother*
Mutter Marie. See Mann, Heinrich
Mutter und Kind. See Hebbel, Friedrich
Mutterrecht, Das. See Bachofen, Johann Jakob
"Muzhestvo." *See* Akhmatova, Anna
"Muzhiki." *See* Chekhov, Anton
Mužík, August Eugen, Hašek and, 9:1093a
My. See Zamyatin, Yevgeny Ivanovich; Zamyatin, Yevgeny Ivanovich, *We*
My Apprenticeship. See Gorky, Maxim
My Apprenticeships. See Colette, *Mes apprentissages*
"My Belief." *See* Hesse, Hermann, "Mein Glaube"
"My Childhood Trees." *See* Södergran, Edith
My Coffin-Stallion. See Ady, Endre, "Az én koporsó paripám"
"My Country Is Italy." *See* Quasimodo, Salvatore, "Il mio paese è l'Italia"
"My Cousin's Corner Window." *See* Hoffmann, E. T. A.
"My Dear Ludovic." *See* Apollinaire, Guillaume, "Mon cher Ludovic"
My Discovery of America. See Mayakovsky, Vladimir, *Moe otkrytie Ameriky*
My Dream-God. See Ady, Endre, "Álmom: Az Isten"

"My Familiar Dream." *See* Verlaine, Paul, "Mon rêve familier"
"My Father and His Museum." *See* Tsvetaeva, Marina, "Otets i ego muzei"
My Faust. See Valéry, Paul, *Mon Faust*
My Favorite Pages. *See* Cela, Camilo José, *Mis páginas preferidas*
"My First Goose." *See* Babel, Isaac, "Moi pervyi gus"
My Friend from Limousin. See Giraudoux, Jean, *Siegfried et le Limousin*
My Friend Manso. *See* Pérez Galdós, Benito, *El amigo Manso*
My Friends' Three Crimes. *See* Simenon, Georges, *Les trois crimes de mes amis*
"My good fortune is late and slow in coming." *See* Petrarch, *Canzoniere*, "Mie venture al venir son tarde et pigre"
"My Great Letter." *See* Sade, Donatien Alphonse François, marquis de
My Husband. *See* Ginzburg, Natalia, "Mio marito"
My Interviews. *See* Gorky, Maxim, "Moi interv'iu"
"My Italy." *See* Petrarch, *Canzoniere*, "Italia mia"
"My Life." *See* Chekhov, Anton, "Moya zhizn"; Nietzsche, Friedrich, "Mein Leben"
My Life. See Wagner, Richard
My Memoirs. See Dumas père, Alexandre, *Mes mémoires*
"My mistress' eyes are nothing like the sun." *See* Shakespeare, William
My Mother and I. *See* Ady, Endre, "Az anyám és én"
My Mother's House. See Colette, *Le maison de Claudine*
"My Notes: Odessa." *See* Babel, Isaac, "Moi listki: Odessa"
"My Patient Day." *See* Quasimodo, Salvatore, "La mia giornata paziente"
My Prisons. See Pellico, Silvio, *Le mie prigioni*
"My prophecy has come to pass." *See* Blok, Alexander, "Sbylos' prorochostvo moe"
"My Purpose." *See* Hölderlin, Friedrich, "Mein Vorsatz"

"My Pushkin." *See* Tsvetaeva, Marina, "Moi Pushkin"

"My Road to Marx." *See* Lukács, György, "Mein Weg zur Marx"; *Utam Marxhoz*

My Sister, Life. See Pasternak, Boris

My Thoughts. See Montesquieu, Charles-Louis de Secondat, baron de

"My Travelling Companion." *See* Gorky, Maxim, "Moi sputnik"

My Two Women. *See* Ady, Endre, "Az én két asszonyom"

My Universities. See Gorky, Maxim

"My v tsentre goroda." *See* Olesha, Yuri

My View on the Drama: A Reply to Professor Heilberg in Copenhagen. See Hebbel, Friedrich

"Mycenae." *See* Seferis, George, *Gymnopaidia*

Myricae. See Pascoli, Giovanni

Myrivilis, Stratis, Seferis and, 12:2255a

Myrmidon, Le (theatrical troupe), Ghelderode and, 11:2116b

Myrrha. See Alfieri, Vittorio

"Myrtho." *See* Nerval, Gérard de

Mystère d'Alceste, Le. See Yourcenar, Marguerite

"Mystère des trois cors, Le." *See* Laforgue, Jules

Mysteries (Mysterier). See Hamsun, Knut

Mystery of Alcestis, The. *See* Yourcenar, Marguerite, *Le mystère d'Alceste*

Mystery novel. *See* Detective novels

Mystery plays, 1:465b–470b
German, 1:466a–468b
Hofmannsthal and, 9:693b–694a
miracle plays and, 1:461b

Mystery of Sintra Road, The. *See* Eça de Queiroz, José Maria, and Ortigão, Ramalho, *O mistério da estrada de Sintra*

"Mystery of Three Horns, The." *See* Laforgue, Jules, "Le mystère des trois cors"

Mystery-Bouffe: A Heroic, Epic, and Satirical Representation of Our Epoch. See Mayakovsky, Vladimir, *Misteriya-buff: Geroicheskoe, epicheskoe i satiricheskoe izobrazhenie nashei epokhi*

Mysticism
Arp and, 10:1369b–1370a, 1377a–1378a
Baroja and, 9:593a
Bergson's view of, 8:62b–63a
Bossuet and, 3:172a
Christian
in Augustine's *On the Trinity*, 1:38b
Luther and, 2:673a-b
Cistercian, Gottfried and, 1:238a
common characteristics of, 9:1009a
Ekelöf and, 12:2662a-b
Fénelon and, 3:275a
Jewish, Lukács and, 10:1258a, 1258b
Jiménez, 9:1002b, 1008a–1009a
Madame Guyon and, 3:278b
in Novalis' works, 5:221b–222a
Persian, Elytis and, 13:2972b–2973a
Schlegel and, 5:198b–199a
Strindberg's view of, 7:1731a-b, 1736b–1737a, 1753a
Vesaas and, 11:2042a
Weil and, 12:2795a–2802a, 2810b, 2812a
in Yourcenar's *The Abyss*, 12:2555a
see also Fénelon, François de Salignac de la Mothe-

Myth
Bergson's view of, 8:62a-b
Broch and, 10:1394b
Canetti and, 12:2627b
in Foscolo's works, 5:327a–330b, 335b–338a
Hamsun's use of, 8:28b
history and, in Tsvetaeva's works, 11:1745a-b, 1747a
in Hoffmann's works, 5:272a-b
in Hölderlin's works, 5:158a-b
Johnson and, 12:2374b
Leconte de Lisle and, 6:1254b
in Mallarmé's works, 7:1579b
Manzoni's rejection of, 5:372b, 373a–374a
myth-making faculty, in Bergson's thought, 8:62b
in Pavese's works, 12:2772a-b
Romantics' rejection of, 5:372b
Schlegel and, 5:184b–185a
Staël's *De la littérature* on, 5:96a
in Strindberg's works, 7:1742, 1746a–1747a
Wagner and, 7:1651a-b

Myth of Sisyphus, The (Le mythe de Sisyphe).
  See Camus, Albert
Mythistorema. See Seferis, George
Mythologies. See Barthes, Roland
Mythology
  in Butor, 13:3293a–3294b, 3296a-b
  Christian
    in German Easter plays, 1:467b
    Jeu de Saint Nicolas and, 1:463b
    in miracle plays, 1:465a
  classical
    Anouilh's modernization of,
      13:2848b–2849a, 2850b
    Calderón and, 2:893a
    in Cavafy's poetry, 8:220b–222b
    in D'Annunzio, 8:190b–191a, 192b
    Elytis and, 13:2962b, 2977a
    French rejuvenation of, 9:1041a
    Giraudoux's use of, 9:1049b–1050a,
      1052b–1054b
    Hauptmann's *Atriden-Tetralogie* and,
      8:171a-b
    Prudentius and, 1:10a, 1:19b
    in Ritsos' poetry, 12:2831a–2833b,
      2834a-b
    in Seferis' writing, 12:2262a, 2267b–2268a
    in Ungaretti's poetry, 10:1465b–1466a
    in Yourcenar's plays, 12:2549a–2552b
    see also Paganism
  comparative, miracle plays and, 1:461b
  Hebrew
    Giraudoux's *Judith*, 9:1050b–1051a
    Mann's *Joseph and His Brothers* and,
      9:728a–732a
  in Klopstock, 4:529a-b
  in Middle Ages, 1:137a
  Norse
    in Laxness' writing, 12:2460a, 2461a,
      2466b–2467a, 2471b–2742a
    three-level hierarchy, 12:2461a–2462a
    see also Norse sagas
  Trakl and, 10:1418b
  Vittorini and, 12:2735a, 2740a
  in Yourcenar's works, 12:2544b
  see also Troy, legend of

N

Na dne. See Gorky, Maxim
Na kulichkakh. See Zamyatin, Yevgeny
  Ivanovich, *A God-Forsaken Hole*
"Na maidani kolo tserkvy." *See* Tychyna,
  Pavlo, *Pluh*
"Na meinei." *See* Cavafy, Constantine
Na opuštěné latríně. See Hašek, Jaroslav
"Na pole kulekovom." *See* Blok, Alexander
Na rannikh poyezdakh. See Pasternak, Boris,
  Early Trains
Na rubezhe dvukh stoletii. See Bely, Andrey
Na rubu pameti. See Krleža, Miroslav
"Na smert' mladentsa." *See* Blok, Alexander
"Na strimchastykh skeliakh." *See* Tychyna,
  Pavlo, *Soniachni klarnety*
"Na voinu." *See* Blok, Alexander
Nabis painting, 8:131a
Nabokov, Vladimir
  on Dostoevsky, 7:1349a
  on Mann, 9:715a
  Pnin, Akhmatova's imitators satirized in,
    10:1526b
  Podvig, on the end of Petrine Russia,
    10:1619a
  on Pushkin's *Eugene Onegin,* 5:673a
  on Tenishev School, 10:1624b
  on the value of Mandelshtam's poetry,
    10:1622b
  Zashchita Luzhina (The Defence), Tenishev
    School in, 10:1625a
Nachalo veka. See Bely, Andrey
Nachbarn. See Hesse, Hermann
Nachtstücke. See Hoffmann, E. T. A.
"Nad luchshim sozdaniem bozh'im." *See* Blok,
  Alexander
"Nada 'moderno' y 'muy siglo XX'." *See* Ortega
  y Gasset, José
Nadal, Octave, on Verlaine, 7:1633b–1634a
Nadeau, Maurice, on Flaubert, 7:1382b
Nadja. See Breton, André
"Något om material och symboler." *See*
  Johnson, Eyvind
Några steg mot tystnaden. See Johnson,
  Eyvind

Nail, The. *See* Pirandello, Luigi, "Il chiodo"

"Nain, Le." *See* Aymé, Marcel, *The Wonderful Farm*

Naipaul, V. S., on Silone's *The Fox and the Camellias*, 12:2297b

Naissance de la clinique. See Foucault, Michel, *The Birth of the Clinic*

Naissance du chevalier au cygne, La, lack of historical veracity of, 1:109b

Naissance du jour, La. See Colette

"Naissance d'une fée, La." *See* Céline, Louis-Ferdinand

Naked. *See* Kosztolányi, Dezső, *Meztelenül*

Naked and the Dead, The. See Mailer, Norman

Naked Maja, The. See Blasco Ibáñez, Vicente, *La maja desnuda*

Naked Streets, The. See Pratolini, Vasco, *Il quartiere*

Naming
    Barthes on, 13:3098b–3099a
    in Butor, 13:3294b

Nana. See Zola, Émile

Nanine. See Voltaire

Nantes, Michelet's stay at, 5:600b

Nantes, Edict of (1598), 3:264a, 264b
    revocation of, 3:158b–159a, 266a

Nantes, Edict of, in fiction of Heinrich Mann, 8:538b

Naples, Nerval and, 6:958b, 961a

Naples, University of, Vico and, 3:295b–296a, 298b

Napló (journal), 9:875a

Napoleon, Emperor of the French. *See* Bonaparte, Napoleon

Napoleon III (Louis Napoleon Bonaparte), emperor of the French
    capture of, 7:1656a
    Hugo and, 6:705b
    Mérimée and, 6:756a, 766a
    overthrow of Second Republic, Goncourts' *En 18 . . .* and, 7:1395a, 1396a
    Vigny's support for, 5:480a

Napoléon-le-Petit (Napoleon the Little). See Hugo, Victor

Napoleonic wars
    Hoffmann and, 5:275a-b
    in Mérimée's works, 6:748a, 757b

as reflected in Mickiewicz's *Pan Tadeusz*, 5:626b, 627b

Schnitzler's use of, 8:104b

Narbonne, Louis de, vicomte, 5:91a-b, 94a

Narbut, Vladimir, Mandelshtam's acmeist manifesto published by, 10:1633a

"Narcisse parle." *See* Valéry, Paul, *Amphion*

Narcissism, in prose of Chekhov, 7:1863a-b

Narcissus. See Gide, André, *Le traité du Narcisse*

Narcissus and Goldmund. See Hesse, Hermann, *Narziss und Goldmund*

"Narcissus Speaks." *See* Valéry, Paul, *Amphion*, "Narcisse parle"

Narcotics. *See* Drugs

"Narod i intelligentsiia." *See* Blok, Alexander

Národní listy (Czech periodical), Hašek's articles in, 9:1093a

Narr in Christo Emanuel Quint, Der. See Hauptmann, Gerhart

"Narration." *See* Seferis, George, "Aphigisi"

Narrative, story as mode of organizing experience, Barthes on, 13:3085a

Narrative poetry
    in Germanic society, 1:54a–55a
    Lermontov's work in, 6:1202b–1203b, 1214a–1216a
    Tasso and, 2:801a
    see also Epic

Narrative structure
    in Baroja's novels, 9:605b–608a
        history as, 9:610b–611a
    in Butor, 13:3292b
    Calvino and, 13:3263b, 3281a–3283a
    Calvino's innovations in *The Castle of Crossed Destinies*, 13:3279a-b
    in Camus, 13:3057a-b
    in Flaubert, 7:1391b–1393a
    in Grass, 13:3373b, 3380b
    in Hoffmann's prose, 5:287b
    of Johnson, 12:2375b, 2377b–2378a, 2378b, 2380a, 2380b, 2381a–2382a
    of Mérimée, 6:753b, 756b, 757a-b, 758b
    in Musil's *The Man Without Qualities*, 9:940b, 950b
    Proust and, 8:548a–549a
    of Richter, 5:54b, 57a, 66a-b

Narrative structure (*cont.*)
  of Sarraute, 12:2334b, 2339a, 2339b–2340a, 2342a
  shifting voice in modern literature, 9:601b
  Unamuno on the subjective basis of, 8:306a
  Verga's indirect discourse and, 7:1553a–1554a
Narrative viewpoint
  of Butor
      first-person, 13:3298a-b
      second-person, 13:3296b
  in Canetti's works, 12:2618b–2619a
  Gautier's innovations, 6:1038a-b
  of Gide, third-person, 8:502a, 503b, 508b
  in Gombrowicz's works, 12:2577a-b
  impersonal author, Mallarmé and, 7:1591b–1592a
  in Johnson's works, 12:2363b, 2372b, 2377a, 2379b, 2382b
  in Meyer, 6:935a
Narrenschiff, Das. See Brant, Sebastian
"Narrow Are the Vessels." *See* Perse, Saint-John
"Narrow Bridge of Art, The." *See* Woolf, Virginia, *Granite and Rainbow*
Narváez, Ramón María, in *¡Viva mi dueño!*, 8:339a
Narziss und Goldmund. See Hesse, Hermann
Nash put'. See Hašek, Jaroslav
"Nasha osnova." *See* Khlebnikov, Velimir
"Nashedshii podkovu." *See* Mandelshtam, Osip
Nasier, Alcofribas. *See* Rabelais, François
Nast, Immanuel and Louise, Hölderlin and, 5:144a
"Natal'ia Goncharova: zhizn'i tvorchestvo" ("Natalya Goncharova: Life and Work"). *See* Tsvetaeva, Marina
Natchez, Les. See Chateaubriand, François René de
Nathan der Weise (*Nathan the Wise*). *See* Lessing, Gotthold Ephraim
National Episodes. *See* Peréz Galdós, Benito, *Episodias nacionales*
National Office for Foreign Trade (France), Claudel and, 8:485a

National Problems and Youth. *See* Ortega y Gasset, José, "Los problemas nacionales y la juventud"
"National soul, Spanish." *See* "Spanish soul"
National temperament, Sainte-Beuve and, 6:849b
National Theater, German, Wagner and, 6:1163a
Nationalism
  aesthetic
      Goldoni and, 4:434b–435a
      Klopstock and, 4:515b–516a, 525a–526a
  Aymé's satire of, 12:2449a-b
  Camus and, 13:3056b–3057a
  Flemish, Ghelderode and, 11:2115b, 2116b
  French, of Michelet, 5:594a
  German
      Luther and, 2:670b–671a
      Nietzsche and, 7:1655b–1656a, 1659b–1660a
      Wagner on, 6:1147b, 1152a
      Walther von der Vogelweide and, 1:293a, 344b
  of Herder, 4:640a–641b, 644a, 646b, 654a
  Hungarian, Ady on, 9:860b, 863b–864a
  Italian
      Castiglione and, 2:645b–646a
      Machiavelli and, 2:601a-b
  Polish, Gombrowicz and, 12:2571a-b, 2573a–2574a
  Schiller and, 5:47b
  Staël and, 5:95b
  of Whitman, 4:657a
  see also Patriotism; Solidarity, national
Native Quarter. *See* Simenon, Georges, *Quartier négre*
Native Realm. See Milosz, Czeslaw
Natorp, Paul, Ortega y Gasset and, 9:1124a-b, 1125b
Natten og Drømmen. See Gunnarsson, Gunnar, *Kirken paa Bjerget*
Nattkyparen. See Moberg, Vilhelm
Nattövning. See Johnson, Eyvind
Natur der Dinge, Die. See Wieland, Christoph Martin
Natura corporis et animae, De. See William of Saint Thierry

Natural Daughter, The. See Goethe, Johann
    Wolfgang von, *Die natürliche Tochter*
Natural history
    Diderot and, 4:480a, 489a–492a
    Maeterlinck's works on, 8:136a, 138a,
        142a-b
    Michelet and, 5:601a-b, 602a
    Montesquieu's works on, 3:348a
Natural History. See Pliny
"Natural Obstacles." *See* Strindberg, August
Natural School (Russia), 6:996a, 7:1351b
    Goncharov and, 6:1065a-b, 1074a, 1078a
Natural signs, Augustine on, 1:26a-b, 42b
Natural Son, The. *See* Dumas fils, Alexandre,
    Le fils naturel
Natural Theology. See Sebond, Raymond,
    Theologia naturalis
Naturalism
    in Anouilh's plays, 13:2849b
    at Théâtre Libre, 7:1930b–1931a
    in Azorín's works, 9:639b
    Balzac and, 7:1711b
    Blasco Ibáñez and, 8:358b
        Reeds and Mud, 8:382b–383a
        The Cabin, 8:378a
        The Mayflower, 8:360a, 366b
    Camilo and, 7:1697a
    Camus and, 13:3074a
    Canetti and, 12:2626a
    Chekhov and, 7:1864a, 1868a
    compared to realism and *verismo*,
        7:1544b–1545a
    dramatic experimentations, 7:1443b
    Eça and, 7:1683a-b, 1796a-b
    Flaubert and, 7:1711b
    French
        Ady and, 9:861b
        Apollinaire and, 9:887a
    Friedrichshagen Circle, 8:235b
    Frisch and, 13:2916a
    George and, 8:448b
    Ghelderode and, 11:2119b–2120a
    Goncourts and, 7:1399a, 1416b
        in *Germinie Lacerteux*, 7:1406b
    Gorky and, 8:431a, 432a, 437b
    in Hamsun's works, 8:27b
    in Hašek's writing, 9:1097b

    Hauptmann and, 8:148a–149b, 152a
    Huysmans and, 7:1709a-b, 1711b, 1719b
    in Ibsen's plays, 7:1426b
    in Lukács's view, 10:1256a
    Maupassant's view of, 7:1764a
    Munich naturalist school, 8:232a
    naturalismo espiritual of Galdós,
        7:1610b–1611b
    Sainte-Beuve and, 6:844a–845b
    in Schnitzler's works, 8:110b–111a
    spiritual, Huysmans and, 7:1722a
    Storm and, 6:920b
    in Strindberg's works, 7:1741b–1742a
    in Svevo's novels, 8:72a
    in Wedekind's plays, 8:237a
    Zola and, 7:1407b, 1414a, 1523b–1524a,
        1526b–1527a, 1533a-b, 1607a, 1711b
    see also Gesellschaft für Modernes Leben
Naturalness
    in Bernart's works, 1:173b–174a
    in Marcabru's works, 1:168a-b, 169a-b
Naturaus. See Naturalness
Nature
    in Arp, 10:1374a–1377a
    in Baudelaire's poetry, 7:1340a
    Berlioz and, 6:780b–781a
    in Büchner, 6:1183b
    in Calvino, 13:3271b–3272a
    in Cela, 13:3110b
    in Freud's works, 8:9b
    in "Futurist Manifesto," 9:808b, 809a
    Goethe and, 5:2a, 15a
    Gogol and, 6:975a
    Goncharov's view of, 6:1072a-b
    in Gunnarsson's works, 10:1498a
    Hamsun's use of, 8:21b, 29b–30b, 34b, 39b
        8.42a
        see also Country, Hamsun's use of
    in Hölderlin's works, 5:148b–149b
    in Hugo's works, 6:703b, 708b, 711b–712a
    Khlebnikov's love of and knowledge about,
        10:1333a, 1350b–1351b
    in Klopstock, 4:521b–522a, 528a-b
    in Leconte de Lisle, 6:1246b, 1266b–1271a
    in Leopardi's works, 5:542b–543a, 558a-b,
        560a–561a
    in Lermontov's works, 6:1198a, 1213a

Nature (*cont.*)
  Maupassant's view of, 7:1775a
  Mauriac and, 10:1314b–1321b
  Milosz and, 13:2937a, 2946b
  in Novalis' works, 5:218a-b
  in Perse's poetry, 10:1432b, 1443b–1446a
  Prudentius on, 1:17b–18a
  Quasimodo and, 12:2396a-b
  in *Romance of the Rose*, 1:330a–331b
  Sade's libertine view of, 4:626a-b, 627b,
      629b–631a, 633a, 635b
  in Södergran's works, 11:1802b
  state of, Rousseau and, 4:453b–454a, 457a,
      461b–465b
  Vesaas and, 11:2055a
  in Vigny's "La maison du berger," 5:481b,
      483a
  weltschmerz poets' despair regarding,
      5:420a
  worship of, Stendhal and, 5:352a-b
  in Zamyatin's works, 10:1188b
  see also Earth, Mother; Natural history
Nature. *See* Emerson, Ralph Waldo
"Nature." *See* Turgenev, Ivan
Nature, human. *See* Human nature
Nature of Things, The. See Wieland,
      Christoph Martin, *Die Natur der Dinge*
Natürliche Tochter, Die. See Goethe, Johann
      Wolfgang von
Naturphilosophie
  Arp and, 10:1379b–1381a
  Novalis and, 5:210a
  Schelling and, 5:211b, 218b
Nausea (*La nausée*). *See* Sartre, Jean-Paul
Navagero, Andrea, *lusis pastorales* of,
      2:909a-b
Naval Odes. See D'Annunzio, Gabriele, *Odi
      navali*
Navarre, Collège de
  Bossuet and, 3:151a–152b
  Chénier's schooling at, 4:695a
Nave de los locos, La. See Baroja, Pío
Nave, La. See D'Annunzio, Gabriele
Navire d'argent, Le (French journal),
      Saint-Exupéry and, 12:2309a
"Navodnenie." *See* Zamyatin, Yevgeny
      Ivanovich, "The Flood"

"Nazaréen, La." *See* Leconte de Lisle, Charles
      Marie
Nazarene school, Tieck and, 5:252a
Nazarín. See Pérez Galdós, Benito
Nazione, La (Italian newspaper), Vittorini's
      writings in, 12:2736a
Nazism
  Benjamin and, 11:1722a
  Böll's opposition to, 13:3166b
  Brecht and, 11:2107a, 2109a
  Broch and, 10:1396a–1399a
  Čapek and, 10:1583b–1585a
      War with the Newts, 10:1574b
  Céline and, 11:1862a–1863a
  George and, 8:447b, 466a
  Ghelderode and, 11:2116a, 2116b
  Grass and, 13:3367a–3370a
  Gunarsson and, 10:1518a
  Hamsun and, 8:40a–41a
  Heinrich Mann and, 8:536b, 541a
  Hesse and, 9:852b, 853a
  intellectuals and, 9:718b
  Ionesco on, 13:2994a, 3001a-b
  Johnson and, 12:2370b
  Mann and, 9:727b
  Moberg and, 11:2203b, 2216a
  Musil and, 9:933a
  mythology of, 6:1166b
  Wagner's mythology and, 6:1166b
  see also Fascism; Totalitarianism; World
      War II
"Ne iskushai chuzhikh narechii." *See*
      Mandelshtam, Osip
"Ne lássatok meg!" *See* Ady, Endre
"Ne volnuisia, ne plach', ne trudi . . ." *See*
      Pasternak, Boris
Nea Estia, Seferis' articles in, 12:2258b
Nea Grammata (Greek journal), 12:2815b
  Elytis and, 13:2956b, 2959a
  Seferis' articles in, 12:2259a, 2259b
Nearly Doctrinal Prologue on the Novel, A. *See*
      Ortega y Gasset, José, "Prólogo casi
      doctrinal sobre la novela'
"Nebbia." *See* Pascoli, Giovanni
Necessity, doctrine of, Tocqueville on,
      6:898a-b
Nechaev, S. G., Dostoevsky and, 7:1354a-b

Necker, Anne Louise Germaine. *See* Staël, Madame de

Necker, Jacques, 5:89a, 91a, 93a
  Compte-rendu au roi (Report to the King), 5:94a

"Necklace, The." *See* Maupassant, Guy de, "La parure"

Nedda. See Verga, Giovanni

"Nedokrovna planeta kruh sontsia sokhla." *See* Tychyna, Pavlo, *V kosmichnomu orkestri*

Need for Roots, The. See Weil, Simone

Ne'er-Do-Well, The. *See* Zamyatin, Yevgeny Ivanovich, "Neputevyi"

"Negative path." *See Via negativa*

"Negra y la rosa, La." *See* Jiménez, Juan Ramón

Nègres, Les. See Genet, Jean, *The Blacks*

Negromante, Il. See Ariosto, Lodovico

Négy fal között. See Kosztolányi, Dezső

Neidhart von Reuental, "Kint, bereitet iuch der sliten ûf daz îs" ("Kids, get your sleds ready for the ice"), 1:367a-b

Neigauz, Zinaida Nikolaevna. *See* Nikolaevna, Zinaida

Neige était sale, La. See Simenon, Georges

Neiges. See Perse, Saint-John, *Snow*

Neighbors. See Hesse, Hermann, *Nachbarn*

Neither Vitalism Nor Rationalism. *See* Ortega y Gasset, José, "Ni vitalismo ni racionalismo"

Nekrasov, Nikolay, Turgenev and, 6:1281a

Nekro spiti, To. See Ritsos, Yannis

"Nekünk Mohács kell." *See* Ady, Endre

"Nel '38." *See* Montale, Eugenio, *Altri versi e poesie disperse*

"Nel dolce tempo de la prima etade." *See* Petrarch, *Canzoniere*

"Nel giusto tempo umano." *See* Quasimodo, Salvatore

Nemcová, Božena, *The Grandmother*, Kafka and, 9:1156a

Nemesianus, influence on Renaissance pastoral poetry, 2:902a-b

Nemiri. See Andrić, Ivo

Nemirovich-Danchenko, Vladimir, 7:1877b

Nemours, duc de, 3:61a-b

"Nénuphur blanc, Le." *See* Mallarmé, Stéphane

Neo-Aristotelian unities. *See* Unities, dramatic

Neo-Aristotelianism. *See* Aristotle

Neo-impressionism, Delacroix and, 5:538a-b

Neo-Stoicism, in plays of Corneille, 3:35b–36a

Neo-symbolism, Apollinaire and, 9:891b

"Neobychainoe priklyuchenie, byvshee s Vladimirom Mayakovskim letom na dache." *See* Mayakovsky, Vladimir

Neoclassicism
  David and, 5:523b
  establishment of, 5:523b
  Foscolo and, 5:327a–329a
  French, Lesage's *Turcaret*, 3:321b–322a
  in French theater, 6:719b
  German, and Lessing, 4:542b–543b, 544a-b
  Giraudoux and, 9:1041a
  Italian, Carducci and, 7:1500a-b
  launching of, in France, 9:1041a
  Schlegel and, 5:190b

Neohellenika Grammata (Greek journal), Seferis' articles in, 12:2259b

Neologisms
  in Ady's poetry, 9:874a
  in Khlebnikov's poetry, 10:1332b, 1334a, 1355a
    difficulty of translating, 10:1349b–1350a
    his theory of language and, 10:1346a–1348a
    sound painting with, 10:1350b
    typographical errors and, 10:1349a
  in Khlebnikov's prose, 10:1357b, 1362a

Neoplatonism
  Aristotelianism and, 1:407b
  Augustine and, 1:23a-b, 29a, 31b–32a, 42a
  in Castiglione, 2:662a-b
  Cavafy's poetry and, 8:216a
  Erasmus and, 2:574a
  Novalis and, 5:212b
  in Ronsard's "Amours de Cassandre," 2:744a
  see also Platonism

Neorealism, 12:2303b
  Calvino and, 13:3262a
  in Ginzburg's writing, 13:3137a-b
  Portuguese, 11:2149a, 2149b

Neorealism (*cont.*)
    Silone and, 12:2303b
    of Zamyatin, 10:1185b–1186a
    see also Synthetism
Neoromanticism, well-made play and, 7:1931a
NEP. *See* New Economic Policy
Nephele (Greek mythology), 13:2977a
Nepomuk, Johann, 9:706a
Neptune (god), in Camoëns' *The Lusiads*,
    2:761b, 763a
"Neputevyi." *See* Zamyatin, Yevgeny Ivanovich
"Nera sì, ma se' bella." *See* Marini,
    Giambattista
Nero
    in Kosztolányi's novel *The Bloody Poet*,
        10:1236a-b
    in Racine's *Britannicus*, 3:212b–213b
Nero. *See* Gutzkow, Karl
Neruda, Jan, 10:1578b
Neruda, Pablo
    "Batalla del Rio Jarama," 12:2649a
    Las alturas de Macchu Picchu (*The Heights
        of Macchu Picchu*), 9:1011b–1012a
Nerval, Gérard de, **6:943a–970b**, 7:1808b,
    8:562b, 9:881b
    Alchimiste (with Alexandre Dumas), 6:947b
    "Antéros," 6:951a–951b, 953a, 953b, 954a
    "Artémis," 6:955a, 957b, 958b, 959a, 959b
    Aurélia, 6:946a, 948a, 954b, 958b, 959a,
        960b, 966a–969b
    Baudelaire and, 7:1329a-b
    Berlioz and, 6:778b
    "Corilla," 6:960b
    on the creative process, 12:2348a
    Daughters of Fire (*Les filles du feu*), 6:943b,
        950a, 960b, 961a
    "Defica," 6:952a–953b, 954b, 956b
    "El Desdichado" (The Unfortunate), 6:950a,
        955a, 956b, 957a, 964b
      rhyme in, 6:959b, 961a
    "Fantaisie" ("Fantasy"), 6:947a
    French Romanticism and, 7:1685b
    Gautier on, 6:1047a-b
    Giraudoux and, 9:1060a
    "Golden Verses" ("Vers dorés"), 6:951b
    "Horus," 6:954a–954b
    "Isis," 6:961a
    Janin on, 6:943a
    "Le Christ aux oliviers," 6:950b
    Le monde dramatique and, 6:948a
    Le prince des sots (*The Prince of Fools*),
        6:947b
    Léo Burckart, 6:947b
    Les chimères (*Chimeras*), 6:944a,
        949a–960b, 964b, 968a, 969a
    Les illuminés (*The Enlightened*), 6:948b
    Les nuits d'octobre (October Nights),
        6:961b, 963a
    L'Imagier de Harlem (*The Image Maker of
        Harlem*), 6:958a
    "Myrtho," 6:952a–953b, 956b
    "Octavie," 6:960b–961a
    Petits châteaux de Bohème (Little Castles in
        Bohemia), 6:948
    Promenades et souvenirs, *The Chairs* and,
        13:2996a
    Sylvie, 6:946a, 949b, 960a–966a, 967b
    "The Speech of Christ" and, 5:59a
    Voyage en Orient (*Journey to the Orient*),
        6:948b
Nerval, Gérard de (joint author). *See* Dumas
    père, Alexandre, and Nerval, Gérard de,
    Piquillo
Nerve Meter, The. *See* Artaud, Antonin
Nervous breakdown
    Nerval and, 6:943a, 948b
    see also Insanity
"Nervous Breakdown, The." *See* Chekhov,
    Anton, "Pripadok"
"Neskol'ko polozhenii." *See* Pasternak, Boris
Nesnesitelná lehkost bytí. *See* Kundera, Milan,
    The Unbearable Lightness of Being
Nessi y Goñi, Doña Carmen, Baroja influenced
    by, 9:590a
Nest of Gentlefolk, A. *See* Turgenev, Ivan
"Nešťastná historie s kocourem." *See* Hašek,
    Jaroslav
Nestroy, Johann
    Der böse Geist Lumpazivagabundus (*The
        Evil Spirit Lumpazivagabundus*),
        weltschmerz and, 5:420b–421a
    theatrum mundi metaphor and, 5:422a
"Net, ya ne Bayron, ya drugoy." *See*
    Lermontov, Mikhail Yurievich

"Net, eto ne ia." *See* Akhmatova, Anna, *Requiem*

"Net, nikogda moei i ty nich' ei ne budesh." *See* Blok, Alexander

Net, The. *See* Ritsos, Yannis, "To dhihty"

Netochka Nezvanova. *See* Dostoevsky, Feodor

Neuchâtel Letters. *See* Charrière, Isabelle Agnès Élizabeth de, *Lettres neuchâteloises*

Neue Amadis, Der. *See* Wieland, Christoph Martin

Neue Christophorus, Der. *See* Hauptmann, Gerhart

Neue, das (the New), Klopstock and, 4:525a-b

Neue Folge der Vorlesungen zur Einführung in die Psychoanalyse. *See* Freud, Sigmund

Neue Gedichte. *See* Hebbel, Friedrich; Heine, Heinrich; Rilke, Rainer Maria

Neue Leben, Das. *See* Schöne Leben, Das

Neue Reich, Das. *See* George, Stefan

Neue Zürcher Zeitung, Wedekind's publications, 8:234a

Neuer Frühling. *See* Heine, Heinrich

Neuhuys, Paul, Ghelderode and, 11:2134b

Neumann, Karl Eugen, 8:166a

Neurophysiology, Bergson's view of, 8:52b, 54a

Neurosis, Freud's concept of, 8:3a-b, 6a-b, 16b–18b

Nevares, Marta de, Lope de Vega and, 2:847b–848a, 848b–849a

"Neve." *See* Pascoli, Giovanni, *Myricae* (Tamarisks), "L'Orfano"

Nevella da Polenta, Guido, Dante and, 1:435b

Never Must You Ask Me. *See* Ginzburg, Natalia, *Mai devi domandarmi*

Never Say Never. *See* Musset, Alfred de, *Il ne faut jurer de rien*

Nevertheless: A Humane Politics. *See* Broch, Hermann, "Trotzdem: Humane Politik"

"Nevesta." *See* Chekhov, Anton

Neveu de Rameau, Le. *See* Diderot, Denis

"Nevsky Avenue." *See* Gogol, Nikolay Vasilievich

New Amadis, The. *See* Wieland, Christoph Martin, *Der neue Amadis*

"New Art of Writing Comedies at This Time, The." *See* Lope de Vega

New Arts, The; or, The Role of Chance in Artistic Creation. *See* Strindberg, August, *Des arts nouveaux ou le hasard dans la production artistique*

New Christopher, The. *See* Hauptmann, Gerhart, *Der neue Christophorus*

New Colony, The. *See* Pirandello, Luigi, *La nuova colonia*

New Critical and Historical Essays. *See* Taine, Hippolyte, *Nouveaux essais de critique et d'histoire*

New Deliverance, The. *See* Witkiewicz, Stanisław Ignacy, *Nowe wyzwolenie*

New Eurydice, The. *See* Yourcenar, Marguerite, *La nouvelle Eurydice*

New Experiments Concerning the Vacuum. *See* Pascal, Blaise, *Expériences nouvelles touchant le vide*

New Fairy Tales. *See* Andersen, Hans Christian

New Forms in Painting and Misunderstandings Resulting Therefrom. *See* Witkiewicz, Stanisław Ignacy, *Nowe formy w malarstwie i wynikają stąd nieporozumienia*

New Generation, The. *See* Wedekind, Frank, *Die Junge Welt*

New Heartbreak. *See* Aragon, Louis, *Le nouveau crève-coeur*

New Introductory Lectures on Psycho-Analysis. *See* Freud, Sigmund, *Neue Folge der Vorlesungen zur Einführung in die Psychoanalyse*

New Justine; or, The Misfortunes of Virtue, Followed by the History of Juliette, Her Sister; or, The Prosperity of Vice, The. *See* Sade, Donatien Alphonse François, marquis de

"New Left" (politics), Simon's *Conducting Bodies* and, 13:3041a

New Life. *See* Dante Alighieri, *Vita nuova*; *Novaia zhizn'*

New Life (Russian newspaper). *See Novaia zhizn'*

New Lyrics. *See* Carducci, Giosue, *Rime nuove*

New Mechanical Aspect of the World, The. *See* Morasso, Mario, *Il nuovo aspetto mecanico del mondo*

New Novel. *See Nouveau roman*

New Plot Against the Industrialists, A. *See* Stendhal, *D'un nouveau complot contre les industriels*

New Poems. *See* Ungaretti, Giuseppe, *Nuove*

New Republic, Cowley's Silone critique, 12:2294a

New Revelations of Being, The. See Artaud, Antonin, *Les nouvelles révélations de l'être*

"New Russian Prose, The." *See* Zamyatin, Yevgeny Ivanovich, "Novaia russkaia proza"

New Science Concerning the Common Nature of Nations. See Vico, Giambattista, *Scienza nuova*

New Short Narrative Poems. *See* Pascoli, Giovanni, *Nuovi poemetti*

New Song. *See* D'Annunzio, Gabriele, *Canto novo*

New Songs. *See* Machado, Antonio, *Nuevas canciones*

"New Spirit and the Poets, The." *See* Apollinaire, Guillaume, "L'Esprit nouveau et les poètes"

"New spirit, the." *See* "Esprit nouveau, l'"

New Spring. See Heine, Heinrich, *Neuer Frühling*

"New Stanzas." *See* Montale, Eugenio, *The Occasions*

New Stories. *See* Andrić, Ivo, *Nove pripovetke*

New Tenant, The. See Ionesco, Eugène, *Le nouveau locataire*

New Testament. *See* Bible

New, the, Rimbaud's view of, 7:1786b–1787b, 1798a-b, 1821a

New Times. *See Novoe vremya*

New Topics (Roman review). *See Nuovi argomenti*

New Wanderings and Misadventures of Lazarillo de Tormes. *See* Cela, Camilo José, *Nuevas andanzas y desventuras de Lazarillo de Tormes*

New Wave, and Cocteau, 10:1560a-b

New Way. *See* Merezhkovsky, Dmitry, *Novyi put'*

New Weapon, The. *See* Morasso, Mario, *La nuova arma*

New Year Gift. *See* Hašek, Jaroslav, "Novoročni naděleni"

New York
  in Claudel's *Connaissance de l'Est*, 8:476a
  Jiménez and, 9:999b–1000b
  in Lorca's poetry, 11:2182a–2186a
  Schnitzler's work performed in, 8:98a-b

"New York, Oficina y denuncia" ("New York, Office and Denunciation"). *See* García Lorca, Federico

New York Times Magazine, Saint-Exupéry's articles in, 12:2322a

Newman, Ernest, Mann's *Doctor Faustus* and, 9:732a, 733b

"News from Amiata." *See* Montale, Eugenio, *The Occasions* (*Le occasioni*), "Notizie dall'Amiata"

News-Bearing Women. *See* Ritsos, Yannis, *Mantatofores*

Newspaper novels, realism of, 7:1601a

Newton, Isaac
  in Olesha's "Liompa," 11:2243a
  Principia, Descartes and, 3:1a
  reliance on faith by, 4:651b
  Voltaire on, 4:372a, 385b

Newtonian mechanics, Bergson and, 8:47b

"Neznakomka." *See* Blok, Alexander

Ni dnya bez strochki. See Olesha, Yuri

"Ni vitalismo ni racionalismo." *See* Ortega y Gasset, José

Niagara. See Butor, Michel

Nibbio, Il. See Pirandello, Luigi, *Se non cosí*

Nibelungen, Die. See Hebbel, Friedrich

"Nibelungen-Mythus als Entwurf zu einem Drama, Der" ("The Nibelungen Myth as Scheme for a Drama"). *See* Wagner, Richard

Nibelungenlied, The, **1:211a–236b**, 382b, 391a, 398a, 400a, 400b
  author of, 1:214a, 214b–216b
  Beowulf compared with, 1:75b
  character of the hero, 1:60b–61a
  composite plot of, 1:59a

Grillparzer's *The Golden Fleece* and,
5:429a-b
Hebbel's use as source, 6:1112b
interpretations of
Kriemhild, 1:221b–226a
"meaning" of poem, 1:226a–236a
manuscripts of, 1:214b–216b
metrical features, 1:216b–218a
Niflunga saga and, 1:401b
reaction to, 1:218a–220a
as source for Wagner's *Ring*, 7:1651a-b
sources of, 1:213a–214b
story outline of, 1:211a–213a
structure of, 1:220a–221b
Nibelungs, the *Nibelungenlied* and, 1:220a
Nibelungs. *See* Hebbel, Friedrich, *Die
Nibelungen*; Wagner, Richard, *Der Ring
des Nibelungen*
Nibelung's Ring, The. See Wagner, Richard,
Der Ring des Nibelungen
Nice Mess, A. *See* Céline, Louis-Ferdinand,
Les beaux draps
Nicholas I of Russia, czar
Lermontov and, 6:1197b, 1217b–1218a,
1221a, 1223b
Pushkin and, 5:662a
Nicholas of Durazzo, *Libellus de processione
Spiritus Sancti* (*Concerning the
Procession of the Holy Spirit*), 1:415a
Nicholas, St., in miracle plays, 1:461b,
462a–463b
Nichomachean Ethics. See Aristotle
"Nicht nur zur Weihnachtszeit." *See* Böll,
Heinrich
Nicolai, Friedrich
Richter's *The School for Aesthetics* and,
5:77b
Tieck and, 5:235a
Nicolas de Troyes, *Grand parangon des
nouvelles nouvelles*, 2:946b, 947a
Nicole, Pierre, 3:129a, 132b
Nicomachean Ethics. See Aristotle
Nicomède. See Corneille, Pierre
Nicotine, Alcohol, Cocaine, Peyote, Morphine,
and Ether. *See* Witkiewicz, Stanisław
Ignacy, *Nikotyna, alkohol, kokaina,
peyotl, morfina, eter*

Niebla. See Unamuno, Miguel de
Niebuhr, Barthold, Leopardi and, 5:546a
Nièce-épouse, La (*The Niece-Wife*). *See*
Ionesco, Eugène
Niedermayer, Franz, on Ortega y Gasset,
9:1148b
Niembsch Edler von Strehlenau, Nikolaus. *See*
Lenau, Nikolaus
Niemyte dusze. See Witkiewicz, Stanisław
Ignacy
Nienasycenie. See Witkiewicz, Stanisław
Ignacy
Nieobjĕta ziĕmia. See Milosz, Czeslaw,
Unattainable Earth
Niess, Robert, on the Goncourts, 7:1407b
Nietzsche contra Wagner. See Nietzsche,
Friedrich
Nietzsche, Elisabeth, 7:1646b–1647a, 1679a-b
Nietzsche, Friedrich, **7:1645a–1681b**
acmeism and, 10:1632b
on action, 9:813a
Ady and, 9:859b, 865b, 877b
Also sprach Zarathustra, Saint-Exupéry's
Wisdom of the Sands and, 12:2327a
Andreas-Salomé and, 9:769b
*Anhang: Vermischte Meinungen und
Sprüche* (*Mixed Opinions and Maxims*),
7:1666a
Apollinaire and, 9:901b
art and, 5:412a
Azorín's literary criticism of, 9:645a
Babel and, 11:1897b
Baroja influenced by, 9:591a-b
Beauvoir and, 12:2711a
Bergson and, 8:47b–48a
Beyond Good and Evil (*Jenseits von Gut
und Böse*)
aphorisms in, 7:1667a
on culture, 7:1660a
"good things" in, 7:1673b
philosophers in, 7:1671a-b
publication of, 7:1666a
Buddha and, 9:845a
Burckhardt and, 6:1229b
Canetti and, 12:2626a-b
in Claudel's *La nuit de Noël de 1914*, 8:485a

Nietzsche, Friedrich (*cont.*)
  D'Annunzio and, 8:183b, 184b–185b, 191b, 197b
  David Strauss, der Bekenner und der Schriftsteller (*David Strauss, the Confessor and Writer*), 7:1659a
  Der Fall Wagner (*The Case of Wagner*), 7:1666a
  Der Wanderer und sein Schatten (*The Wanderer and His Shadow*), 7:1666a
  Der Wille zur Macht (*The Will to Power*), 7:1666a
  dialectic, 7:1445a
  Die fröhliche Wissenschaft (*The Gay Science*), Musil and, 9:944a
  Die Gebürt der Tragödie (*The Birth of Tragedy*), Nerval's anticipation of, 6:961a
  Dionysian impulse, 9:1126b
  Dostoevsky and, 7:1349b–1350a
  dynamic revelry as cure for overcivilization, 7:1429b
  Ecce Homo, on philosophy, 7:1645a-b
  ego cult, 9:592b
  Foucault and, 13:3353b–3354a
  Generation of '98 and, 9:744b
  Gombrowicz and, 12:2567b–2568a
  Hamsun and, 8:23b, 25a, 29a, 31b, 32a
  Hauptmann and, 8:157a
  Heinrich Mann and, 8:519a, 521b, 536b, 540b–541a
  Hesse and, 9:836a, 841a
  Hofmannsthal and, 9:689b
  Human, All Too-Human (*Menschliches, Allzumenschliches*)
    on Goethe, 5:7b
    morals in, 7:1672b
    publication of, 7:1666a
    science and, Nietzsche's interest in, 7:1654b
  Ibsen and, 7:1429b, 1437a, 1442a
  intellect and, 6:1166a
  Kazantzakis and, 9:1071b–1072a-b
  Kosztolányi and, 10:1235a, 1239a
  Krleža and, 11:1811a, 1812a
  Kundera and, 13:3407a-b
  Lukács on, 10:1274b–1275a
  Mann and, 9:724a, 737b
  Mann's *Doctor Faustus* and, 9:733a-b
  Marinetti and, 9:798b, 799a, 800a, 801a
  on the masses, 9:1145b
  "Mein Leben" ("My Life"), 7:1646b
  Morgenröte (*Dawn*), 7:1666a
  Musil and, 9:938a, 939b, 956b
  Nietzsche contra Wagner, 7:1666a
  nihilism, 9:1072a-b
  On the Advantage and Disadvantage of History for Life (*Von Nützen und Nachtheil der Historie für das Leben*), 7:1661b, 1662a
    attack on historical fever in, 7:1660a-b
    questions raised by, 7:1663b–1664a
  On the Genealogy of Morals (*Zur Genealogie der Moral*)
    artist vs. work in, 6:1147a
    composition of, 7:1667a
    Heinrich Mann's *Die Göttinnen* and, 8:525a
    publication of, 7:1666a
    religion in, 7:1678b
    sickness as metaphor, 7:1668a
    value systems in, 7:1671b–1672a
    will in, 7:1670b
  on opera, 8:521a
  Ortega y Gasset and, 9:1122b
  perspectivism, 9:1129a
  on poetic inspiration, 11:2052b
  Richard Wagner in Bayreuth, 7:1665b
  on Richter, 5:53a
  Rilke and, 9:776b–777a
  Rimbaud and, 7:1809b, 1811b, 1812a
  Russian symbolists and, 11:1841b
  Sade compared to, 4:636a
  Saint-Exupéry and, 12:2327a, 2327b
  Schlegel and, 5:191b–192a, 197a
  Schopenhauer and, 5:397b, 398b–399a, 402b, 403b–404a, 411b–412a
  Schopenhauer as Educator (*Schopenhauer als Erzieher*), 7:1664a-b, 1664b, 1671a
  on search for truth, 5:408a
  seductiveness of power, 11:1900b, 1907a
  Strindberg and, 7:1736a, 1742b, 1753a
  superman model, 9:599a-b, 604a
  Svevo and, 8:68b–69a, 72a, 75b

The Anti-Christ (Der Antichrist), 7:1645a, 1676a

The Birth of Tragedy (Die Geburt der Tragödie), 7:1437a, 1656a–1659a, 1672a, 11:1812a
  Bely and, 9:912b
  Mann's Joseph and His Brothers and, 9:731b–732a
  meaning of life in, 7:1675a
  objectivity in, 7:1662a-b
  publication of, 7:1654b
  Schopenhauer's influence on, 5:411b–412a
  Sodergran and, 11:1800b
  on the study of history, 7:1660b–1661a
  style of, 7:1656a, 1666b
  Wagner and, 7:1656a-b

The Gay Science (Die fröhliche Wissenschaft)
  eternal recurrence in, 7:1677b–1678a
  God's death in, 7:1670a
  human meaning in, 7:1674b
  preface of, 7:1657b, 1669a
  publication of, 7:1666a
  on Socrates, 7:1668b
  types of decline in, 7:1669a

The Twilight of the Idols (Die Götterdämmerung), 7:1666a, 1668b, 1670b–1671a

Thus Spoke Zarathustra (Also sprach Zarathustra), 7:1736a
  affirmation of life in, 7:1670b–1671a
  Bely and, 9:912b
  inspiration for, 7:1667b
  Mandelshtam's critique of, 10:1635a-b
  publication of, 7:1666a
  Södergran and, 11:1792a

Trakl and, 10:1413a

Unzeitgemässe Betrachtungen (Untimely Meditations), 7:1654b

Versuch einer Selbstkritik (Attempt at Self-Criticism), George's Der Siebente Ring and, 8:463b

"Vom Nutzen und Nachteil der Historie für das Leben" ("The Use and Abuse of History"), Musil and, 9:949b

Wagner and, 6:1147a, 1148b, 7:1652b, 1653b, 1665a

  in Ecce Homo, 7:1665b
  friendship of, 6:1161b–1162a
  will in, 9:595b–596a, 608a
  will to power, 7:1676a, 1677a-b
  Witkiewicz and, 10:1208a, 1217b, 1223b–1224a

"Nietzsche, Marx, Freud." See Foucault, Michel

Nievo, Ippolito, on Manzoni as glory of Milan, 5:368a

Niflunga saga, 1:401b

Nigel de Longchamps, Speculum stultorum (Mirror of Fools), 1:372b–373a

"Night at Genoa" experience (Valéry), 8:572a, 573b

"Night at Vincennes, The." See Vigny, Alfred Victor de, The Military Condition

"Night on the Beach, A." See Seferis, George, "Pantoum"

"Night Before Christmas, The." See Gogol, Nikolay Vasilyevich, "Noch' pered Rozhdestvom"

"Night Birds' Refuge." See Quasimodo, Salvatore, "Rifugio d'uccelli notturni"

Night of the Black Moon, The. See Ady, Endre, "Fekete hold éjszakája"

Night and the Dream, The. See Gunnarsson, Gunnar, Kirken paa Bjerget (The Church on the Hill), Natten og Drømmen

"Night Driver, The." See Calvino, Italo, t zero

Night Flight. See Saint-Exupéry, Antoine de, Vol de nuit

"Night in Hell." See Rimbaud, Arthur, "Nuit de l'enfer"

Night imagery, in "Orion," 13:2959b–2960a

"Night Jasmine, The." See Pascoli, Giovanni, Canti di Castelvecchio (Songs of Castelvecchio), "Il gelsomino notturno"

Night Maneuvers. See Johnson, Eyvind, Nattövning

Night with the National Guard, A. See Scribe, Eugène, Une nuit de la Garde Nationale

Night in Otočac, A. See Ekelöf, Gunnar, En natti i Otočac

Night Pieces. See Hoffmann, E. T. A., Nachtstücke

"Night Search, The." See Khlebnikov, Velimir

"Night Song of a Wandering Shepherd of Asia." *See* Leopardi, Giacomo

Night Thoughts on Life, Death, and Immortality. See Young, Edward

Night in a Trench, A. *See* Khlebnikov, Velimir, "Noch' v okope"

Night Waiter, The. *See* Moberg, Vilhelm

Night-God, The. *See* Ady, Endre, "Éjszakai Isten"

Nightclub, The. See Simenon, Georges, *L'Âne rouge*

"Nightingale, The." *See* Andersen, Hans Christian

Nights. See Musset, Alfred de

Nighttime Headache. *See* Ritsos, Yannis, "Vradhinos ponokefalos"

Nightwalker. See Aragon, Louis, *Le paysan de Paris*

Nihilism
in Apollinaire's poetry, 9:901a
of Brecht, 11:2090b
Camus and, 13:3055a
of Ekelöf, 12:2638b–2639a
in Hebbel's works, 6:1098b
Jaspers and, 7:1670b
in Leconte de Lisle, 6:1264a-b
Nietzsche and, 7:1669b–1670b
Pisarev and, 7:1670a
in Richter's works, 5:59a, 73b
Russian, 7:1670a
of Schiller, 5:30a
in Turgenev, 6:1286a–1287a, 7:1669b

Nijinski, Waslaw, 7:1586a

"Nikdo se nebude smát." *See* Kundera, Milan, "Nobody Will Laugh"

Nikifóros Fokás. See Kazantzakis, Nikos

Nikitin, Afanasy, his travelogue and Khlebnikov's "Esir," 10:1359a

Nikolaeva, Nadezhda, Khlebnikov's romantic involvement with, 10:1336b

Nikolaevna, Zinaida, Pasternak and, 10:1594b, 1595a, 1605a, 1611a

"Nikolai." *See* Khlebnikov, Velimir

Nikolaus Marggraf. See Richter, Jean Paul, *Der Komet*

Nikotyna, alkohol, kokaina, peyotl, morfina, eter. See Witkiewicz, Stanisław Ignacy

Nikulás Bergthórsson, *Leiðarvísir ok borgaskipan* (*Itinerary and List of Cities*), 1:379a

Nilender, Vladimir, Tsvetaeva and, 11:1733b

Nils Holgerssons underbara resa. See Lagerlöf, Selma

Nilsson, Nils Åke, 7:1879a

Nin, Anaïs
Artaud's friendship with, 11:1972a, 1973a
Sarraute and, 12:2335a

Nineteen Eighty-Four. See Orwell, George

1914. See Johnson, Eyvind, *Romanen om Olof*

"Nineteen Thirteen." *See* Akhmatova, Anna, *Poem Without a Hero*

1934. See Moravia, Alberto

Nineteenth-Century French Philosophers, The. *See* Taine, Hippolyte, *Les philosophes français du XIXe siècle*

Ninety-five Theses. *See* Luther, Martin

Ninety-Three. See Hugo, Victor, *Quatrevingt-treize*

Ninfale d'Ameto. See Boccaccio, Giovanni

Ninfale fiesolano. See Boccaccio, Giovanni

Ninfeas. See Jiménez, Juan Ramón

"Niño loco, El." *See* García Lorca, Federico

"Niño mudo, El." *See* García Lorca, Federico

Niobe, in Ritsos' poetry, 12:2833a

"Niobé." *See* Leconte de Lisle, Charles Marie

"Niovi" (Niobe). *See* Ritsos, Yannis

Nirvana, Bely and, 9:912a

Nivola, Unamuno's concept of, 8:301a, 302a

Njáls saga (*Njal's Saga*), 1:390b–392a, 394a, 396b, 402a
Undset and, 9:1019b

No Day Without a Line. See Olesha, Yuri, *Ni dnya bez strochki*

No Exit. See Sartre, Jean-Paul

No hay cosa como callar. See Calderón de la Barca, Pedro, *There's Nothing Like Keeping Silent*

"No, I'm Not Byron, I'm Another." *See* Lermontov, Mikhail Yurievich, "Net, ya ne Bayron, ya drugoy"

No Man's Son. *See* Montherlant, Henry de, *Fils de personne*

"No, never mine, nor anyone's will you ever be." *See* Blok, Alexander, "Net, nikogda moei i ty nich' ei ne budesh"

"No, That Is Not I." *See* Akhmatova, Anna, *Requiem*

No Way. See Ginzburg, Natalia, *Vita immaginaria*

No White Flags. *See* Mayakovsky, Vladimir, "Bez belykh flagov"

Noailles, Anna de, Proust and, 8:546b

Noailles, Natalie de, Chateaubriand and, 5:127b

Nobel Prize for Literature
    Andrić, 11:1752b–1753a, 1769b, 1774a
    Bergson, 8:46a
    Böll, 13:3169a, 3182a
    Carducci's 1906, 7:1497b
    Elytis, 13:2981a-b
    Hamsun, 8:21a, 41b
    Hauptmann, 8:165a
    Jiménez, 9:991a
    Johnson, 12:2361a
    Lagerkvist, 10:1695b
    Laxness, 12:2457a, 2475a
    Maeterlinck, 8:139b
    Mann, 8:535b, 9:1017a
    Mauriac, 10:1311b
    Milosz, 13:2929a, 2932a-b
    Montale, 11:1993a
    Pasternak, 10:1597a-b
    Perse, 9:1448b
    Pirandello, 8:395a
    Quasimodo, 12:2387a, 2406b, 2464a-b
    Seferis, 12:2255a, 2256a–2257a, 2261b
    Simon, 13:3024a
    Solzhenitsyn, 13:3193a
    to Greek authors, 13:2955a
    Undset, 9:1017a

Nobility, theme of
    in Corneille's *Cinna*, 3:41b
    see also Duty, theme of; Honor, theme of

Noble class. *See* Aristocracy

Noble Glembays, The. *See* Krleža, Miroslav, *Gospoda Glembajevi*

"Noble savage" myth
    among Russian writers, 7:1478b–1479a
    Calvino and, 13:3266b–3267a

Ortega y Gasset's opposition to, 9:1145b

"Noble spirit." *See* Petrarch, *Canzoniere*, "Spirto gentil"

"Nobody Will Laugh." *See* Kundera, Milan

Noces. See Camus, Albert, *Nuptials at Tipasa*

"Noch' pered Rozhdestvom." *See* Gogol, Nikolay Vasilyevich

"Noch' v okope." *See* Khlebnikov, Velimir

Noch zehn Minuten bis Buffalo. See Grass, Günter, *Only Ten Minutes to Buffalo*

Noche de san Juan, La. See Lope de Vega

"Nochnoi obysk." *See* Khlebnikov, Velimir, "The Night Search"

Nocturne. See D'Annunzio, Gabriele, *Notturno*

"Nocturne." *See* Perse, Saint-John

"Nocturnos" (Nocturnes). *See* Jiménez, Juan Ramón

Nodier, Charles
    cénacle (salon) of, 7:1620b
    Vigny's participation in, 5:461a-b

Noeud de vipères, Le. See Mauriac, François, *Vipers' Tangle*

Noia, Leopardi and, 5:544b, 552b–553a

"Noia." *See* Ungaretti, Giuseppe

Noia, La. See Moravia, Alberto, *The Empty Canvas*

Noise of Time, The. See Mandelshtam, Osip

"Noisis." *See* Cavafy, Constantine

Nokkrar sögur. See Laxness, Halldór

Nomad persona, in Ungaretti's poetry, 10:1459a-b, 1461b

Nome e lacrime. See Vittorini, Elio, *Conversazione in Sicilia*

Nominalism
    Luther and, 2:669b–670a
    Ockham and, 1:427b

"Non chiederci la parola che squadri da ogni lato." *See* Montale, Eugenio, *Cuttlefish Bones*

Non serviam. See Ekelöf, Gunnar

Non si sa come. See Pirandello, Luigi

None But the Brave. See Schnitzler, Arthur

Nonexistent Knight, The. See Calvino, Italo

Nonresistance to evil
    Chekhov and, 7:1856b, 1862a, 1863a
    in "Ward No. 6," 7:1866a–1867a

Nonsense literature, Mallarmé and, 7:1574a,
1579a-b
Nordau, Max
Degeneration, 9:595a, 10:1487a
Pessoa and, 10:1487a
Nordiske Rige, Det (The Nordic Realm). *See*
Gunnarsson, Gunnar
Nordsee, Die. See Heine, Heinrich
Noregs konungatal (*Succession of the Kings of
Norway*), 1:379b
Normance: Féerie pour une autre fois II. See
Céline, Louis-Ferdinand
Normandy, Maupassant and, 7:1759b–1760a,
1765a, 1767a
Norn (Teutonic demigoddess), George and,
8:467a-b
Norse sagas, **1:377a–404b**
authorship of, 1:401b–402a
genres of, 1:377a
Icelandic-Norwegian relations and,
1:377b–378a, 381b
rímur and, 1:401b
Undset and, 9:1019b
see also individual sagas
Norsk kulturhistorie. See Undset, Sigrid
Norske helgener. See Undset, Sigrid
North. See Céline, Louis-Ferdinand, *Nord*
North Africa
Camus and, 13:3054b–3055a
Gide's visit to, 8:496a, 497a
North Sea, The. See Heine, Heinrich, *Die
Nordsee*
North and South, in Staël's *De l'Allemagne*,
5:107a-b
North, The. See Zamyatin, Yevgeny Ivanovich
Northam, John, on Ibsen, 7:1426b,
1440b–1441a
*Northern Messenger, The. See Severnye
vestnik*
Northern Symphony. See Bely, Andrey,
Symphonies
Norton lectures. *See* Milosz, Czeslaw
Norway
Hamsun and, 8:21b–22b, 27a-b, 28a,
29b–30b, 38b–39a
history and folklore

in Ibsen's plays, 7:1422b–1423a, 1424b,
1444b–1445a
sagas and, 1:377b–378a, 381b
resistance movement (World War II),
Johnson and, 12:2371a-b
Norwegian literature
Nordic god Othin in, 11:2052b
women in, 11:2039b
see also Nynorsk
"Nose, The." *See* Gogol, Nikolay Vasilievich
Nostalgia
in Baroja's novels, 9:593b, 605a
in Carducci's poetry, 7:1506a–1508a
in Goncharov's works, 6:1080b–1081a,
1085a-b
in Machado's *Soledades*, 9:748b
Mauriac and, 10:1314b–1321b
in Quasimodo's works, 12:2392b, 2394a
romanticism and, 10:1477a
saudade in Portuguese literature, 11:2148a
see also Reminiscence
"Nostaljia del mar." *See* Jiménez, Juan Ramón
Nostrand, H. L., on Ortega y Gasset, 9:1127a-b
Nostri antenati, I. See Calvino, Italo
Not Guilty. See Mann, Heinrich, *Die
Unschuldige*
Nota Emilianense, Chanson de Roland and,
1:102b
Note on Didymus the Cleric. *See* Foscolo, Ugo,
Notizia intorno a Didimo chierico
"Note sul romanzo." *See* Moravia, Alberto
"Note sur André Gide et son Journal." *See*
Barthes, Roland, "On Gide and His
Journal"
"Note sur le peyotl, Une" ("A Note on Peyote").
See Artaud, Antonin
Notebook of an Old Man. *See* Ungaretti,
Giuseppe, *Il taccuino del vecchio*
Notebooks. See Camus, Albert
Notebooks. *See* Musil, Robert, *Tagebücher*;
Valéry, Paul, *Cahiers*
Notebooks of Malte Laurids Brigge, The. See
Rilke, Rainer Maria, *Die
Aufzeichnungen des Malte Laurids
Brigge*
Notebooks on Morality. *See* Sartre, Jean-Paul,
Cahiers pour une morale

Notebooks of Serafino Gubbio, Cameraman.
See Pirandello, Luigi, *Si gira*
Notes of an Eccentric. *See* Bely, Andrey,
Zapiski chudaka; Ledianoi, Leonid,
Zapiski chudaka
Notes and Counternotes. See Ionesco, Eugène,
Notes et contre-notes
Notes of Dreamers. *See Zapiski mechtatelei*
Notes d'un voyage en Corse. See Mérimée,
Prosper
Notes et contre-notes. See Ionesco, Eugène
"Notes on Exile." *See* Milosz, Czeslaw
Notes from the Underground. See Dostoevsky,
Feodor
"Notes of a Madman." *See* Gogol, Nikolay
Vasilievich
Notes of a Madman. See Tolstoy, Leo
Notes on the Margins of Time. See Ritsos,
Yannis, *Piimata I*
"Notes on the Novel." *See* Moravia, Alberto,
"Note sul romanzo"
Notes on the Novel. See Ortega y Gasset, José,
Ideas sobre la novela
Notes on Renaissance Sculpture. See
Burckhardt, Jacob
Notes sur la poésie. See Breton, André, and
Éluard, Paul
Notes on a Trip to Corsica. See Mérimée,
Prosper, *Notes d'un voyage en Corse*
"Notes upon a Case of Obsessional Neurosis."
See Freud, Sigmund, "Bemerkungen
uber einen Fall von Zwangsneurose"
Notes on Various Mathematical Subjects. See
Diderot, Denis, *Mémoires sur différents
sujets de mathématiques*
"Nothing." *See* Södergran, Edith, "Ingenting"
Nothingness. *See Nulla*
Notizia intorno a Didimo chierico. See
Foscolo, Ugo
"Notizie dall'Amiata." *See* Montale, Eugenio,
The Occasions
Notre coeur. See Maupassant, Guy de
"Notre Dame." *See* Mandelshtam, Osip
Notre Dame Cathedral (Paris), Claudel and,
8:472a, 474a
Notre-Dame de Paris. See Hugo, Victor

"Notre-Dame-des Hirondelles." *See* Yourcenar,
Marguerite, *Nouvelles orientales*
Notre-Dame-des-Fleurs. See Genet, Jean, *Our
Lady of the Flowers*
Notte di festa. See Pavese, Cesare
"Notte di Natale, La." *See* Pascoli, Giovanni
"Notte dolorosa." *See* Pascoli, Giovanni,
Myricae
Notturno. See D'Annunzio, Gabriele
Noun-doubling of Marinetti, 9:817a
Nourritures Terrestres, Les. See Gide, André,
The Fruits of the Earth
Nouveau crève-coeur, Le. See Aragon, Louis
Nouveau dans la ville, Un. See Simenon,
Georges
Nouveau locataire, Le. See Ionesco, Eugène
Nouveau roman, 13:3249a
Aragon and, 11:2066a
Barthes and, 13:3240a
Chekhov and, 7:1857b
Johnson and, 12:2382a-b
origin of, 13:3237a-b
Robbe-Grillet and, 13:3237b, 3241a–3242a
"romanciers du regard" formed, 13:3237a-b
Sarraute's association with, 12:2333a–2334a
Simon and, 13:3021a, 3024a-b, 3035b, 3044a
theories of, 13:3241b–3242a
Nouveaux essais de critique et d'histoire. See
Taine, Hippolyte
Nouvele Héloïse, La. See Rousseau, Jean
Jacques
*Nouvelle aventures de Don Quichotte de la
Manche. See* Lesage, Alain-René
Nouvelle continuation des amours. See
Ronsard, Pierre de, *Les Amours*
Nouvelle critique (new criticism)
Barthes and, 13:3089b–3091a
representation of, 13:3249a
Nouvelle Eurydice, La. See Yourcenar,
Marguerite
Nouvelle Héloïse, La. See Rousseau, Jean
Jacques, *Julie, ou la nouvelle Héloïse*
*Nouvelle Justine, ou les malheurs de la vertu,
suivi de l'histoire de Juliette, sa soeur,
ou les prospérités du vice, La. See* Sade,
Donatien Alphonse François, marquis
de

Nouvelle revue française, La (journal)
Claudel and, 8:472b
Giraudoux published in, 9:1047a
Malraux and, 12:2415a
Perse's poetry in, 10:1434a, 1439a
Rivière's articles in, 11:1940a
Valéry and, 8:572b, 578a
Nouvelle Rive Gauche, La
Verlaine's works in, 7:1638a–1639a
see also Lutèce
Nouvelles. See Musset, Alfred de, *Short Stories*
Nouvelles Catholiques, Fénelon and,
3:265b–266a
Nouvelles en vers tirées de Boccace et de l'Arioste. See La Fontaine, Jean de
Nouvelles orientales. See Yourcenar,
Marguerite
Nouvelles récréations et joyeux devis. See Des
Périers, Bonaventure
Nouvelles révélations de l'être, Les. See
Artaud, Antonin
"Novaia russkaia proza." *See* Zamyatin,
Yevgeny Ivanovich
Novaia zhizn' (New Life) (journal)
Babel's articles in, 11:1904a
Gorky and, 8:421a, 421b
Novalis, **5:205a–231b**
Algabal and, 8:453b
Allgemeines Brouillon (General Outline),
5:215b–216a
Christendom or Europe (*Die Christenheit
oder Europa*), 5:219a–221a
New Jerusalem in, 5:220b–221a
Schleiermacher and, 5:219a
Encyclopaedisierungscalcul, 5:216a
Faith and Love (*Glauben und Liebe*),
5:213b–215b
publication of, 5:208b, 213b
Wilhelm III and, 5:213b–214a
Frisch and, 13:2922b
Heinrich von Ofterdingen, 5:225a–230a,
6:875b
blue flower in, 5:225a-b
duality resolved in, 5:208a
Klingsohr's tale, 5:228a–229b
Orphic myth tale, 5:226b
resolution of, 5:230a-b

Hesse and, 9:845b
in Hesse's *Steppenwolf*, 9:848a
Hymns to the Night, 5:221a–223b
autobiographical elements, 5:223b
duality resolved in, 5:208a
and *Sacred Songs*, 5:223b
Sophie in, 5:207b
"Klarisse," 5:206b–207a
Maeterlinck and, 8:123a, 132b, 134a
Pascoli and, 7:1834b
Pollen (*Blüthenstaub*), 5:213a-b
publication of, 5:208b, 212b–213a
Sacred Songs (*Geistliche Lieder*),
5:223b–225a
Christ in, reference to, 5:208a
and *Hymns*, 5:223b
Madonna song, 5:224a
"Monologue," 5:224b
"Wenn ich ihn nur habe" ("If only I have
him"), 5:223b–224a
"Wo bleibst du Trost der ganzen Welt"
("Where are you, solace of the whole
world"), 5:224a
Schiller's *The Gods of Greece* and, 5:39b
Schlegel and, 5:182a, 182b, 192b
The Novices of Sais, 5:216b–219a, 8:132b
"Hyazinth and Rosebloom," 5:217a–218a
quest for knowledge in, 5:216b–217a,
218b
on time and space, 9:783a
Nove pripovetke. See Andrić, Ivo
Novel
adventure, 6:992b
Baroja and, 9:608b
as *Bildungsroman*, 11:2217b
Cervantes and, 2:828a-b, 835b–836a,
841b–842a
Don Quixote, 2:828a-b, 835b–836a
"confessional," 6:1015a
development of, *see also* Lesage,
Alain-René; Wieland, Christoph Martin
as discussed by Lukács, 10:1261a-b
documentary, Manzoni's *Column of Infamy*
as, 5:391b
emigrant, 11:2219a–2226b
encyclopedic, Richter's *Walt and Vult* as,
5:76b

English, influence on Baroja, 9:593b–594b
epic, Moberg and, 11:2204a–2204b
epistemological, Broch and, 10:1388b
epistolary
    of Dostoevsky, 7:1351b
    of Ginzburg, 13:3155a–3160a
    in Laclos's *Les liaisons dangereuses*,
        4:402a–405a
as German *Novelle*, 11:2103a
Gide's concept of, 8:508a
Gogol's style in, 6:986b–990b
historical, 9:610a-b
Maupassant's use of form, 7:1780b
Ortega y Gasset and, 9:608b, 1137a-b
plot
    in Baroja, 9:594a
    Lope de Vega and, 2:854a-b
    in Pavese's works, 12:2768a-b
    Proust and, 8:549a-b, 550b–551a
    in Queneau's works, 12:2517b–2519b
    in Simenon's works, 12:2503b–2504a
    in traditional story, 1:58b
political, of Milosz, 13:2933b
Portuguese, 7:1696a–1697a
Proustian innovations, 8:548a–551a
Queneau's structural devices,
        12:2519b–2520b, 2521a-b, 2522b–2533a
realistic psychological, 6:995a
Rilke's *Notebooks of Malte Laurids Brigge*
    as, 790b
romantic, 2:828a, 9:596a-b
    Vittorini's contribution to, 12:2743a-b
romantic mystery, parodies of, 7:1687b
Russian, influence on Baroja, 9:593b–594b
Schnitzler's use of form, 8:102b–103b,
        108b–111a
of sensibility, Richter and, 5:69b
Strindberg's use of form, 7:1739b–1741a
structure, of Azorín, 9:645b, 660b–661b
structure of, Unamuno's innovations in,
        8:294b–295a, 301b–302a
Unamuno's theory of, 8:301a–302b
varied forms of, 6:986b
see also Autobiographical novel; Detective
    novels; Historical novel; *Künstlerroman*;
    Nouveau roman; Pastoral romance;
    Serial novel

Novel About Olof, The. *See* Johnson, Eyvind,
    Romanen om Olof
"Novel and Europe, The." *See* Kundera, Milan
Novel in France, The. See Turnell, Martin
Novel Pastimes and Merry Tales. *See* Des
    Périers, Bonaventure, *Nouvelles
    récréations et joyeux devis*
Novelas amorosas y exemplares. See Zayas y
    Sotomayor, María de
Novelas de santidad. See Pérez Galdós, Benito
Novelas ejemplares. See Cervantes, Miguel de,
    Exemplary Tales
Novella
    Ariosto and, 2:623a
    Boccaccio's contribution to, 2:510a
    Cervantes and, 2:831b, 832b
    Dumas's use of form, 6:740b–741a
    Fontane and, 6:1311b–1312b
    Goethe and, 5:16a, 9:725b
    Grass and, 13:3371b
    Lope de Vega and, 2:854a
    Machiavelli and, 2:599a
    Maupassant's use of form, 7:1764b–1765a,
        1767b–1768b, 1776b–1777b
    poetic realism and, 6:914b
    Schnitzler's use of form, 8:92b, 98b–99b,
        100a-b
    Tieck and, 5:252a-b
    see also Picaresque novel; Short fiction,
        Renaissance
Novellae. See Morlini, Girolamo
Novellas of Zurich. See Keller, Gottfried
Novelle. See Fortini, Pietro
Novelle per un anno. See Pirandello, Luigi
Novellino. See Masuccio Salernitano
Novellino, Il. See Cento novelle antich
Novels of Robbe-Grillet, The. See Morissette,
    Bruce
Novels of sanctity. *See* Pérez Galdós, Benito,
    novelas de santidad
Novels and Stories. *See* Böll, Heinrich,
    Romane und erzählungen
November. See Flaubert, Gustave
"Novice, The." *See* Lermontov, Mikhail
    Yurievich, "Mtsyri"
Novices of Sais, The. See Novalis
Novoe vremya (journal), Chekhov and, 7:1856a

"Novograde Cathedral, The." *See* Babel, Isaac, "Kostel v Novograde"

"Novoroční nadělení." *See* Hašek, Jaroslav

Novyi mir (Soviet journal), Solzhenitsyn's writings in, 13:3191a, 3191b, 3195a-b

Novyi put'. See Merezhkovsky, Dmitry

"Now that this year's winter is gone." *See* Marcabru, "Pois l'iverns d'ogan es anatz"

Now They Sing Again: Attempt at a Requiem. See Frisch, Max

Nowe formy w malarstwie i wynikające stąd nieporozumienia. See Witkiewicz, Stanisław Ignacy

Nowe wyzwolenie. See Witkiewicz, Stanisław Ignacy

Nowell codex, version of *Beowulf* in, 1:69b, 70b, 71a

Noyade des songes. See Ghelderode, Michel de, *Dreams Drowning*

Noyers de l'Altenburg, Les. See Malraux, André, *The Walnut Trees of Altenburg*

Nu var det 1914. See Johnson, Eyvind, *Romanen om Olof*

"Nubes, Las." *See* Azorín

"Nubi color magenta." *See* Montale, Eugenio, *The Storm and Other Things*

Nuclear age
    Dürrenmatt on, 13:3232a-b
    Ionesco's *The Bald Soprano* and, 13:2993a

Nuevas andanzas y desventuras de Lazarillo de Tormes. See Cela, Camilo José

Nuevas canciones. See Machado, Antonio

Nuisances, The. *See* Molière, *Les fâcheux*

"Nuit d'août." *See* Musset, Alfred de, *Nights (Nuits)*, "August Night"

"Nuit de Cléopâtre, Une." *See* Gautier, Théophile

"Nuit de décembre." *See* Musset, Alfred de, *Nights (Nuits)*, "December Night"

Nuit de la Garde Nationale, Une. See Scribe, Eugène

"Nuit de l'enfer." *See* Rimbaud, Arthur

"Nuit de mai." *See* Musset, Alfred de, *Nights (Nuits)*, "May Night"

Nuit de Noël de 1914, La. See Claudel, Paul

"Nuit d'octobre." *See* Musset, Alfred de, *Nights (Nuits)*, "October Night"

Nuit vénitienne, ou les noces de Laurette, La. See Musset, Alfred de

Nuits. See Musset, Alfred de, *Nights*

Nuits d'octobre, Les. See Nerval, Gérard de

Nulla, Leopardi and, 5:444b, 551b, 552b, 553a, 559a

Number perception, Bergson's view of, 8:49a–51a

Numbered, The. See Canetti, Elias

Numerology
    in Butor, 13:3304a-b
    in Calvino's *Mr. Palomar*, 13:3283b
    in Dante's *Vita nuova*, 1:437a, 438a
    of Elytis, 13:2960b–2961a
    Freud and the number seven, 8:15a
    see also Fourteen (numeral); Seven (numeral)

Nun singen sie wieder: Versuch eines Requiems. See Frisch, Max, *Now They Sing Again: Attempt at a Requiem*

Nun, The. See Diderot, Denis, *La religieuse*

Nuova arma, La. See Morasso, Mario

Nuova colonia, La. See Pirandello, Luigi

Nuove. See Ungaretti, Giuseppe

"Nuove stanze." *See* Montale, Eugenio, *The Occasions (Le occasioni)*, "New Stanzas"

Nuovi argomenti (New Topics [Roman review])
    Moravia and, 12:2686a, 2696a
    Vittorini's writings in, 12:2738b

Nuovi poemetti. See Pascoli, Giovanni

Nuovi racconti romani. See Moravia, Alberto, *More Roman Tales*

Nuovo aspetto mecanico del mondo, Il. See Morasso, Mario

Nuptials at Típasa. See Camus, Albert

Nürnberger Reise, Die. See Hesse, Hermann

Nutcracker and the Mouse King (Nussknacker und Mausekönig). See Hoffmann, E. T. A.

"Nuvola di smog, La." *See* Calvino, Italo, "Smog"

Nybyggarna. See Moberg, Vilhelm, *The Settlers*

Nye Eventyr. See Andersen, Hans Christian,
    New Fairy Tales
Nyelv és lélek. See Kosztolányi, Dezső
Nyhteridha (The Bat), Ritsos' role in, 12:2817a
Nymph of Admetus, The. See Boccaccio,
    Giovanni, *Ninfale d'Ameto*
Nymph of Fiesole, The. See Boccaccio,
    Giovanni, *Ninfale fiesolano*
"Nymph's Reply to the Shepherd, The." *See*
    Raleigh, Sir Walter
Nynorsk
    Rabindranath Tagore and, 11:2037a
    Vesaas and, 11:2036a–2036b
Nyugat, 9:866a, 872b, 873a, 875a
Nyugat (Occident), 10:1234a
    Lukács and, 10:1253b
Nyxis. See Ritsos, Yannis, *Piimata IV*

O

O. T. See Andersen, Hans Christian
"O artystucznym teatrze." *See* Witkiewicz,
    Stanisław Ignacy
"O chude proisshedshem v Pepel'nuiu Sredu."
    See Zamyatin, Yevgeny Ivanovich
O crime do Padre Amaro. See Eça de Queiroz,
    José Maria, *The Sin of Father Amaro*
"O da, liubov' vol'na, kak ptitsa." *See* Blok,
    Alexander
O Egipto. See Eça de Queiroz, José Maria
"O fajtám vére." *See* Ady, Endre
"O, how you laughed at us." *See* Blok,
    Alexander, "O, kak smeialis' vy nad
    nami"
O instinto supremo. See Ferreira de Castro,
    José Maria
O intervalo. See Ferreira de Castro, José Maria
"O, kak smeialis' vy nad nami." *See* Blok,
    Alexander
"O Khlebnikove: slavozhd'." *See* Kamensky,
    Vasily
"O literature, revoliutsii, entropii i o prochem."
    See Zamyatin, Yevgeny Ivanovich
"O lyubvi." *See* Chekhov, Anton
"O mina solbrandsfärgade toppar." *See*
    Södergran, Edith
O mistério de estrada de Sintra. See Eça de
    Queiroz, José Maria, and Ortigão,
    Ramalho
"O My Gentle Beasts." *See* Quasimodo,
    Salvatore
"O naznachenii poeta." *See* Blok, Alexander
O nejbližších věcech. See Čapek, Karel
"O, net, Ia ne khochu, chtob pali my s toboi"
    ("O, no! I do not wish for us to fall").
    See Blok, Alexander
"Opervoi liubvi." *See* Gorky, Maxim
O poezii. See Mandelshtam, Osip
O primo Basílio. See Eça de Queiroz, José
    Maria, *Cousin Bazilio*
"O prirode slova." *See* Mandelshtam, Osip
"O rasshirenii predelov russkoi slovesnosti."
    See Khlebnikov, Velimir

"O realismo como nova expressão da arte."
    See Eça de Queiroz, José Maria
"O segodniashnem i o sovremennom." See
    Zamyatin, Yevgeny Ivanovich
"O sintetizme." See Zamyatin, Yevgeny
    Ivanovich
"O sobesednike." See Mandelshtam, Osip
"O sovremennom sostoianii russkogo
    simvolizma." See Blok, Alexander
O Thou Pure Vine. See Laxness, Halldór,
    Salka Valka
O tom, kak istselen byl inok Erazm. See
    Zamyatin, Yevgeny Ivanovich
O věcech obedných čili Zóon politikon. See
    Čapek, Karel
"O vrede filosofii." See Gorky, Maxim
"O yes, love is free like a bird." See Blok,
    Alexander, "O da, liubov' vol'na, kak
    ptitsa"
"O, znal by ia, chto tak byvaet . . ." See
    Pasternak, Boris, Second Birth
Oaha. See Wedekind, Frank
Oak Beam in the Stone Bridge, The. See
    Džadžić, Petar, Hrastova greda u
    kamenoj kapiji
Oak and the Calf, The. See Solzhenitsyn,
    Aleksandr, Bodalsia telenok s dubom
Oak and Dog. See Queneau, Raymond, Chêne
    et chien
"Oak and the Reed, The." See La Fontaine,
    Jean de, Fables, "Le chêne et le roseau"
Oaten Flute, The. See Poggioli, Renato
"Obchod s rakvemi." See Hašek, Jaroslav
"Obecní býk v Jablečnu." See Hašek, Jaroslav
Oberlin, Johann, Büchner and, 6:1183a–1185a
Obermann. See Senancour, Étienne
Oberon. See Weber, Carl Maria von; Wieland,
    Christoph Martin
"Obět antimilitarismu." See Hašek, Jaroslav
Object, in Milosz's poetry, use of pars pro toto,
    13:2949b–2950a
Object language, Arp and, 10:1372a–1373b
Object-symbols
  in Grillparzer's drama
    Hero and Leander, 5:437a
    Sappho, 5:427a–428a
    The Ancestress, 5:426a-b

The Golden Fleece, 5:429a-b
  Tieck and, 5:254a
Objectification, Sartre and, 12:2598b–2599a
Objections and Exhortations. See Böll,
    Heinrich, Ein- und Zusprüche
"Objective correlative," in poetry of Pascoli,
    7:1831a
"Objective Literature." See Barthes, Roland
Objectivism, Broch and, 10:1391b–1392a
Objectivity, Nietzsche on, 7:1661b–1662b
Objet trouvé. See Trouvaille, la
Oblako v shtanakh. See Mayakovsky, Vladimir
Oblat, L' (The Oblate). See Huysmans, Joris
    Karl
"Obligatory scene." See Scène à faire
Oblomov. See Goncharov, Ivan
"Oblomov's Dream." See Goncharov, Ivan
Oboe sommerso. See Quasimodo, Salvatore,
    Sunken Oboe
Obra, la. See Jiménez, Juan Ramón
Obrázky z Holandska. See Čapek, Karel
Obryv. See Goncharov, Ivan, The Precipice
"Obscure Man, An." See Yourcenar,
    Marguerite, Comme l'eau qui coule
Observations on Natural History. See
    Montesquieu, Charles-Louis de
    Secondat, baron de
Observations sur le Nakaz. See Diderot, Denis
Observations on Torture. See Verri, Pietro,
    Osservazioni sulla tortura
Obsession
  in Calvino's "Argentine Ant," 13:3269a
  Freud's concept of, 8:16b–17a
"Obsession." See Baudelaire, Charles
Obshchestvo pochetnykh zvonarei. See
    Zamyatin, Yevgeny Ivanovich
Obshchestvo Predsedatelei Zemnogo Shara
    (Society of the Presidents of Planet
    Earth), Khlebnikov's founding of,
    10:1338b
Obšit. See Hašek, Jaroslav
Obstinacy and Whim. See Tieck, Ludwig,
    Eigensinn und Laune
Obyčejný život. See Čapek, Karel
Obyknovennaya istoriya. See Goncharov, Ivan
Ocalenie. See Milosz, Czeslaw

Occasions, The (*Le occasioni*). *See* Montale, Eugenio

Occident. See Nyugat

"Occident, The." *See* Trakl, Georg

Occult
Bely and, 9:916b, 919b
George and, 8:462b
in Hoffmann, 5:277a-b
Huysmans and, 7:1721b–1722a, 1725a-b
Strindberg's view of, 7:1731a-b, 1736b–1737a
see also Supernatural

Occupations, in Redentin Easter play, 1:468a

Ocean
in Hugo's works, 6:706b, 707b–708a, 713b–715a
as metaphor, in Johnson's works, 12:2362a

Ocean Litany. See Butor, Michel, *Litanie d'eau*

Ocean Voyage. See Simenon, Georges, *Long cours*

Ocean's Musical March, The. See Ritsos, Yannis, *To emvatirio tou ikeanou*

Ocherki i rasskazy. See Gorky, Maxim

Ocho comedias y ocho entremeses. See Cervantes, Miguel de, *Eight Plays and Eight Interludes*

Ockham, William of. *See* William of Ockham

O'Connor, Flannery, *The Violent Bear It Away*, Claudel's *La jeune fille Violaine* and, 8:481a

Octavia. See Alfieri, Vittorio

"Octavie." *See* Nerval, Gérard de

October 1916. See Solzhenitsyn, Aleksandr, *The Red Wheel*

"October Evening." *See* Pascoli, Giovanni, *Myricae* (Tamarisks), "Sera d'ottobre"

October Landscape. See Kosztolányi, Dezső, "Októberi táj"

"October on the Neva." *See* Khlebnikov, Velimir

"October Night." *See* Musset, Alfred de, *Nights*

October Nights. See Nerval, Gérard de, *Les nuits d'octobre*

October Revolution. See Russian Revolution (1917)

October Song. See Storm, Theodor, "Oktoberlied"

Octopus image, in Hugo's works, 6:714a-b

Octosyllabic verse, in La Fontaine's *Fables*, 3:81b, 82b

"Oda al rey de Harlem." *See* García Lorca, Federico

"Oda al Santísimo Sacramento del Altar." *See* García Lorca, Federico

"Oda do młodości." *See* Mickiewicz, Adam

"Odchyniaite dveri." *See* Tychyna, Pavlo, *Soniachni klarnety*

Odd Snorrason, *Óláfs saga Tryggvasonar*, 1:382a-b

Ode à Charles Fourier. See Breton, André

"Ode on a Grecian Urn." *See* Keats, John

Ode on the Taking of Namur. See Boileau-Despréaux, Nicolas

"Ode to Charlotte Corday." *See* Chénier, André

"Ode to Freedom." *See* Pushkin, Alexander, "Vol'nost"

Ode to the Most Holy Sacrament. *See* García Lorca, Federico, "Oda al Santísimo Sacramento del Altar"

"Ode to Versailles." *See* Chénier, André

"Ode to Youth." *See* Mickiewicz, Adam, "Oda do młodości"

Oderisi da Gubbio, Dante and, 1:432a

Odes, of Hölderlin, 5:155a-b, 161a-b

Odes. See George, Stefan, *Hymnen*

Odes. See Horace

Odes et ballades. See Hugo, Victor

Odes and Hymns. *See* Pascoli, Giovanni, *Odi e inni*

Odes modernas. See Quental, Antero de

Odessa
in Babel's writing, 11:1891a–1892a, 1900a-b
Mickiewicz's literary output in, 5:614a-b
Mickiewicz's stay in, 5:612b–613a
Pushkin's stay in, 5:661b

"Odessa." *See* Babel, Isaac

Odessa Tales. See Babel, Isaac

Odesskie rasskazy. See Babel, Isaac, *Odessa Tales*

Odets, Clifford, Ibsen's influence on, 7:1444a

Odi barbare. See Carducci, Giosue

Odi e inni. See Pascoli, Giovanni

Odi navali. See D'Annunzio, Gabriele

Odile. See Queneau, Raymond

"Odin." *See* Zamyatin, Yevgeny Ivanovich

Odin den' Ivana Denisovicha. See Solzhenitsyn, Aleksandr, *One Day in the Life of Ivan Denisovich*

Ödipus und die Sphinx. See Hofmannsthal, Hugo von

Odíssia. See Kazantzakis, Nikos

Odysseus, Canetti and, 12:2627b

Odyssey. See Homer

Odyssey, The: A Modern Sequel. See Kazantzakis, Nikos, *Odíssia*

Oedipe. See Voltaire

Oedipe-roi. See Cocteau, Jean

Oedipus
    Aristotle's doctrine of the tragedy and, 3:220a
    Brecht and, 11:2106a
    Cocteau and, 10:1554a–1555b, 1556a-b
    in Gide's *Theseus*, 8:515a-b
    in Robbe-Grillet's works, 13:3243b, 3244b, 3245a-b

Oedipus complex, Freud's concept of, 8:6b, 10a, 12b–13b, 16a

Oedipus Rex. See Cocteau, Jean, *Oedipe-roi*

Oedipus Rex. See Hofmannsthal, Hugo von, *König Ödipus*

Oedipus Rex. See Sophocles

Oedipus and the Sphinx. See Hofmannsthal, Hugo von, *Ödipus und die Sphinx*

Oehlenschläger, Adam, Hebbel and, 6:1095b

Oeil écoute, L'. See Claudel, Paul

Oerthel, Adam Lorenz, 5:55b–56a, 58a

Oeuvre au noir, L'. See Yourcenar, Marguerite

Oeuvre, L'. See Zola, Émile

Oeuvres complètes. See Chateaubriand, François René de

Oeuvres littéraires. See Faure, Elie

Oeuvres romanesques croisées d'Elsa Triolet et de Louis Aragon, Les. See Aragon, Louis

"Of Cannibals." *See* Montaigne, Michel de, *Essays*

Of Cats. See Storm, Theodor, "Von Katzen"

Of Councils and Churches. See Luther, Martin

Of a Devil Who Preached Wonders. See Ghelderode, Michel de, *D'un diable qui prêcha merveilles*

"Of Drunkenness." *See* Montaigne, Michel de, *Essays*

"Of Experience." *See* Montaigne, Michel de, *Essays*

"Of the Hoarder and the Monkey." *See* La Fontaine, Jean de, *Fables*, "Du thésauriseur et du singe"

"Of Idleness." *See* Montaigne, Michel de, *Essays*

"Of the Inequality That Is Between Us." *See* Montaigne, Michel de, *Essays*

"Of the Jews (A.D. 50)." *See* Cavafy, Constantine, "Ton Evraion (50 M.Ch.)"

Of the Jews and Their Lies. See Luther, Martin

Of Mice and Men. See Steinbeck, John

"Of Physiognomy." *See* Montaigne, Michel de, *Essays*

"Of Repentance." *See* Montaigne, Michel de, *Essays*

"Of the Resemblance of Children to Fathers." *See* Montaigne, Michel de, *Essays*

"Of Three Kinds of Association." *See* Montaigne, Michel de, *Essays*

Of True Religion. See Augustine, St., *De vera religione*

Of Tyranny. See Alfieri, Vittorio

"Of the Useful and the Honorable." *See* Montaigne, Michel de, *Essays*

"Of Vanity." *See* Montaigne, Michel de, *Essays*

Of the Way. See Machado, Antonio, *Soledades (So.'itudes)*, "Del camino"

Of Wisdom. See Charron, Pierre, *De la sagesse*

"Of . . ." *see also* "De . . ."

Offenbach, Jacques, 7:1917a, 1920b
    Hoffmann and, 5:261b–262a

"Offenbarung und Untergang." *See* Trakl, Georg, "Revelation and Downfall"

Oficio de tinieblas 5. See Cela, Camilo José

Ofis ke kríno. See Kazantzakis, Nikos

"Often a Coastland." *See* Quasimodo, Salvatore, "Sovente una riviera"

"Ofttimes Have I Met the Grief of Living." *See* Montale, Eugenio, *Cuttlefish Bones*

"Oggi ventuno marzo." *See* Quasimodo, Salvatore

Ogni sviatogo Dominika. See Zamyatin, Yevgeny Ivanovich

Ogonek, Babel's stories in, 11:1910a

Ogonyok (Soviet journal), Solzhenitsyn's writings in, 13:3195b

Ogród nauk. See Milosz, Czeslaw

"Oh, had I known that it happens so . . ." *See* Pasternak, Boris, *Second Birth*

"Oh My Sun-flame-colored Tops." *See* Södergran, Edith, "O mina solbrandsfärgade toppar"

"Oimè il bel viso." *See* Petrarch, *Canzoniere*

Oiseau bleu, L'. See Maeterlinck, Maurice, *The Blue Bird*

Oiseaux. See Perse, Saint-John, *Birds*

Oiseaux de lune, Les. See Aymé, Marcel

"Okhotnik Usa-Gali." *See* Khlebnikov, Velimir

Okhrannaia gramota. See Pasternak, Boris, *A Safe-Conduct*

"Oktiabr' na Neve." *See* Khlebnikov, Velimir, "October on the Neva"

Oktiabr' shestnadtsatogo. See Solzhenitsyn, Aleksandr, *The Red Wheel*

"Októberi táj." *See* Kosztolányi, Dezső

"Oktoberlied." *See* Storm, Theodor

Ólaf, St.
  in Norse saga, 1:382a
  in *Óláfs saga helga*, 1:387b–388a
  Undset and, 9:1023a-b, 1026a

Ólaf Tryggvason
  in *Hallfreðar saga*, 1:384b
  in *Heimskringla*, 1:388a

Óláfs saga. See Gunnlaug (monk)

Óláfs saga helga. See Snorri Sturluson

Óláfs saga Tryggvasonar. See Odd Snorrason

Olav Audunssøn og hans börn. See Undset, Sigrid, *Master of Hestviken*

Old age
  Montaigne on, 2:781b
  tragedy of, Alfieri's *Saul* as, 4:685a

Old Age. See Beauvoir, Simone de

Old Age. See Ginzburg, Natalia, "Vecchiaia"

Old English literature. *See* English literature, Anglo-Saxon

Old Faith and the New, The. See Strauss, David, *Der alte und der neue Glaube*

Old Goriot. See Balzac, Honoré de, *Le père Goriot*

"Old Izergil." *See* Gorky, Maxim, "Starukha Izergil'"

Old Jealous Husband, The. See Cervantes, Miguel de, *El viejo celoso*

Old Lizard, The. *See* García Lorca, Federico, "El lagarto viejo"

"Old Man on the River Bank, An." *See* Seferis, George, *Imerologio katastromatos B*, "Enas gerontas stin akropotamia"

Old Man, The. *See* Gorky, Maxim, *Starik*

Old Mazurka Set to the Rhythm of Rain, An. *See* Ritsos, Yannis, *Palia mazourka se rythmo vrohis*

"Old Milon." *See* Maupassant, Guy de, "Le père Milon"

"Old Park, The." *See* Pasternak, Boris, *Early Trains*

Old Régime and the French Revolution, The. See Tocqueville, Alexis de

Old Sailors, The. *See* Marinetti, Filippo Tommaso, "Les vieux marins"

"Old Shloime." *See* Babel, Isaac, "Staryi Shloime"

Old Testament. *See* Bible

Old Tramp, The. *See* Ady, Endre, "A vén csavargó"

Old Ukraine Must Change. *See* Tychyna, Pavlo, *Chernihiv*, "Stara Ukraina zminytys' musyt'"

"Old World Landowners." *See* Gogol, Nikolay Vasilievich

Old and the Young, The. See Pirandello, Luigi, *I vecchi ei giovani*

"Oleg and Kazimir. A Conversation." *See* Khlebnikov, Velimir, "Razgovor Olega i Kazimira"

Olen' i shalashovka. See Solzhenitsyn, Aleksandr, *Respublika truda*

Oles', Okleksandr, 10:1652b–1653a

Olesha, Yuri, **11:2233a–2253b**
  "Al'debaran" ("Aldebaran"), 11:2238a, 2242a-b
  "Angel" ("The Angel"), 11:2233b
  "Chelovecheski material" ("Human Material"), 11:2240b–2241a
  conspiracy charges, 11:1912a

Olesha, Yuri (*cont.*)
   Envy (*Zavist'*), 11:1904b, 2234a,
      2235b–2240b, 2242a, 2244b
     Mandelshtam's *Egipetskaia marka* and,
      10:1643a-b
     Pasternak's "Waves" and, 10:1605a
     The Three Fat Men and, 11:2246a, 2247b
     themes, 11:2239b–2240a, 2251b
   "Ivolga" ("The Oriole"), 11:2249a
   "Koe-chto iz sekretnykh zapisey poputchika
     Zanda" ("From the Secret Notebook of
     Fellow Traveler Zand"), 11:2235a
   "Liompa," 11:2242b–2243a, 2244a-b, 2252b
   "Love" ("Lyubov'"), 11:2242b, 2252b
   "My v tsentre goroda" ("We're in the Center
     of Town"), 11:2241b
   "Natasha," 11:2242b
   Ni dnya bez strochki (*No Day Without a
     Line*), 11:2235a-b, 2239a, 2240b,
     2249a–2250b, 2252b
   Spisok blagodeyanii (*A List of Assets*),
     11:2234a, 2245b–2246b, 2251a
   Strogi yunosha and, 11:2235a
   "The Chain" ("Cep'"), 11:2241a-b
   "The Cherry Stone" ("Vishnyovaya
     kostochka"), 11:2239b, 2243a–2244a,
     2249a, 2252b
   "The Death of Zand," 11:2248b
   The Three Fat Men (*Tri tolstyaka*), 11:2234a,
     2246b–2248a
   "Turkmen" ("The Turkoman"), 11:2249a
   "V mire" ("In the World"), 11:2241b
   "V tsirke" ("At the Circus"), 11:2240a,
     2241b–2242a
   "Vospominanie" ("A Recollection"),
     11:2249a
   "Ya smotryu v proshloe" ("I Look into the
     Past"), 11:2241a
   Zagovor chuvstv (*The Conspiracy of
     Feelings*), 11:2234a. 11.2244b–2245b
Oleszkiewicz, in Mickiewicz's poetry, 5:622b
Olier, Jean-Jacques, 3:265a, 265b
Oliva, Hernán Pérez de. *See* Pérez de Oliva,
   Hernán
"Olive Grove, The." *See* Maupassant, Guy de

Olive Tree on the Road. *See* Machado,
   Antonio, *Nuevas canciones* (New
   Songs), "Olivo del camino"
Oliveira Martins, Joaquim Pedro de
   Eça and, 7:1683a, 1693a, 1694a-b
   Portugal contemporáneo (Contemporary
     Portugal), 7:1687a
   Portugal e o socialismo (Portugal and
     Socialism), 7:1689b–1690a
Oliver Twist. See Dickens, Charles
"Olivo del camino." *See* Machado, Antonio,
   Nuevas canciones (New Songs)
Ölkofra þáttr, 1:395a
Ollier, Claude, Sarraute and, 12:2333a
Olof tetralogy. *See* Johnson, Eyvind, *Romanen
   om Olof*
Olsen, Regine, Kierkegaard and,
   6:1129a–1130b
Olsson, Hagar
   Kvinnan och nåden (The Woman and
     Grace), 11:1801a
   Södergran and, 11:1792a-b, 1800b, 1801a,
     1804b
Olympe's Marriage. See Augier, Émile, *Le
   mariage d'Olympe*
Olympia. See Manet, Édouard
Olympians, The. *See* Montherlant, Henry de,
   Les olympiques
Olympic Odes. See Pindar
"Olympio's Sorrow." *See* Hugo, Victor,
   "Tristesse d'Olympio"
Olympiques, Les. See Montherlant, Henry de
Om hösten. See Ekelöf, Gunnar
*Omaggio a James Joyce; ovvero, Il colpo di
   stato. See* Moravia, Alberto
Ombilic des limbes, Le. See Artaud, Antonin,
   The Umbilicus of Limbo
"Ombra della magnolia, L'2." *See* Montale,
   Eugenio, *The Storm and Other Things*
Ombre de mon amour. See Apollinaire,
   Guillaume
Omens, in Dumas's works, 6:735b–737a
Omerpaša Latas (Omerpasha Latas). *See*
   Andrić, Ivo
Omniscience, in Walther, 1:297b
"Omnyei." *See* Cavafy, Constantine
"Omphale." *See* Gautier, Théophile

"Omut." *See* Bely, Andrey, *Mezhdu dvukh revoliutsii*

On Abundance of Words and Ideas. *See* Erasmus, *De copia verborum ac rerum*

"On account of Zion I will not keep silent." *See* Walter of Châtillon, "Propter Sion non tacebo"

On the Advantage and Disadvantage of History for Life. See Nietzsche, Friedrich

On an Abandoned Latrine. *See* Hašek, Jaroslav, *Na opuštěné latríně*

On Angels. See Aquinas, Thomas, St., *De angelis*

On Antichrist and His Ministers. See William of Saint Amour, *Liber de Antichristo et eius ministris*

On Art and Antiquity. See Goethe, Johann Wolfgang von, *Über Kunst und Altertum*

"On Art Criticism." *See* Delacroix, Eugène

On Art and Literature. *See* Proust, Marcel, *Contre Sainte-Beuve*

On the Artistic Theater. *See* Witkiewicz, Stanisław Ignacy, "O artystucznym teatrze"

On Authority and Revelation. See Kierkegaard, Søren

On Axioms. See Aquinas, Thomas, St., *De hebdomadibus*

On the Basis of Morality. See Schopenhauer, Arthur

"On the Battlefield of Kulekovo." *See* Blok, Alexander, "Na pole kulekovom"

On Being and Essence. See Aquinas, Thomas, St., *De ente et essentia ad fratres et socios meos*

On Being Vigilant of the Authorities. *See* Moberg, Vilhelm, *Att övervaka överheten*

On Bonaparte and the Bourbons. See Chateaubriand, François René de, *De Buonaparte et des Bourbons*

On the Bondage of the Will. See Luther, Martin, *De servo arbitrio*

On the Border of Two Centuries. *See* Bely, Andrey, *Na rubezhe dvukh stoletii*

On the Calling of the Poet. *See* Blok, Alexander, "O naznachenii poeta"

"On the Causes of the Disorders Troubling France and Stopping the Establishment of Liberty." *See* Chénier, André

On the Centennial of a University. *See* Ortega y Gasset, José, "En el centenario de una universidad"

On Christian Doctrine. See Augustine, St.

On the Christian Teacher. See Augustine, St., *De magistro*

On contempt of the world. *See* Erasmus, *De contemptu mundi*

"On Cranial Nerves." *See* Büchner, Georg

On Crimes and Punishments. See Becarria, Cesare, *Dei delitti e delle pene*

On the Danger of Most Recent Times. See William of Saint Amour, *De periculis novissimorum temporum*

"On the Death of a Child." *See* Blok, Alexander, "Na smert' mladentsa"

On the Deeds of Caesar. *See* Petrarch, *De gestis Caesaris*

On Discourse. See Pontano, Giovanni, *De sermone*

On the Divine Names. See Aquinas, Thomas, St., *De divinis nominibus*

On Dramatic Poetry. See Diderot, Denis

"On Early Trains." *See* Pasternak, Boris, *Early Trains*

"On the Eastern Front." *See* Trakl, Georg, "Im Osten"

On the Edge of Reason. See Krleža, Miroslav, *Na rubu pameti*

On Eloquence in the Vernacular. See Dante Alighieri, *De vulgari eloquentia*

On England and Italy. See Archenholz, Johann von

On English Literature. *See* Chateaubriand, François René de, *Essai sur la littérature anglaise*

On Entry of Boys into Religious Life. See Aquinas, Thomas, St., *De ingressu puerorum in religione*

On Epic and Dramatic Poetry. See Goethe, Johann Wolfgang; Schiller, Friedrich von

On est toujours trop bon avec les femmes. See Queneau, Raymond

On Eternity Against the Critics. See Aquinas, Thomas, St., *De aeternitate contra murmurantes*

On the Eve. See Turgenev, Ivan

On Evil. See Aquinas, Thomas, St., *De malo*

On Fallacies. See Aristotle, *De fallaciis*

On Famous Women. See Boccaccio, Giovanni, *De mulieribus claris*

On Females. *See* Valle-Inclán, Ramón del, *Femeninas*

"On the Fetish-Character in Music and the Regression of Listening." *See* Adorno, Theodor, "Über den Fetischcharakter in der Musik und die Regression des Hörers"

On the Fourfold Root of the Principle of Sufficient Reason. See Schopenhauer, Arthur, *Über die vierfache Wurzel des Satzes vom zureichenden Grunde*

On Free Will. See Augustine, St., *De libero arbitrio*; Erasmus, *De libero arbitrio*

On the Freedom of the Will. See Schopenhauer, Arthur

On the French Stage. See Heine, Heinrich, *Über die französische Bühne*

On the Genealogy of Morals. See Nietzsche, Friedrich

"On German Music." *See* Wagner, Richard

On Germany. See Heine, Heinrich, *De l'Allemagne*; Staël, Madame de, *De l'Allemagne*

"On Gide and His Journal." *See* Barthes, Roland

On the Greek Style. See Seferis, George, *Dokimes*

On the Green by the Church. *See* Tychyna, Pavlo, *Pluh (The Plow)*, "Na maidani kolo tserkvy"

"On the Harm of Philosophy." *See* Gorky, Maxim, "O vrede filosofii"

"On the Heroic Mind." *See* Vico, Giovanni Battista, *De mente heroica*

On His Own Ignorance and That of Many Others. See Petrarch, *De sui ipsius et multorum ignorantia*

On the History of Religion and Philosophy in Germany. See Heine, Heinrich, *Zur Geschichte der Religion und Philosophie in Deutschland*

"On the Hook." *See* Böll, Heinrich, "An der Angel"

"On Hope." *See* Milosz, Czeslaw, Norton lectures

On Humor. See Pirandello, Luigi; Pirandello, Luigi, *L'Umorismo*

"On the Idea of History in *Agathon*." *See* Wieland, Christoph Martin

On Illustrious Men. *See* Petrarch, *De viris illustribus*

"On Khlebnikov: Gloryleader." *See* Kamensky, Vasily, "O Khlebnikove: slavozhd'"

On the Land of the Tribal Leader Bihar. *See* Ady, Endre, "Bihar vezér földjén"

"On Language as Such and on the Human Language." *See* Benjamin, Walter

On the Language and Wisdom of India. See Schlegel, Friedrich von

On the Last Day. See Andersen, Hans Christian

"On the Likeness of a Beautiful Woman." *See* Leopardi, Giacomo

On Literature. See Staël, Madame de, *De la littérature considérée dans ses rapports avec les institutions sociales*

"On Literature, Revolution, Entropy, and Other Matters." *See* Zamyatin, Yevgeny Ivanovich, "O literature, revoliutsii, entropii i o prochem"

On Love. See Stendhal

On Lying. See Augustine, St., *De mendacio*

On the Method of Dealing with the Rebellious Peoples of the Valdichiana. See Machiavelli, Niccolò, *Del modo di trattare i popoli della Valdichiana ribellati*

On the Method of Study. *See* Erasmus, *De ratione studii*

On Modal Propositions. See Aquinas, Thomas, St.

On Monarchy. See Dante Alighieri, *De monarchia*

"On the Monument of Dante." *See* Leopardi, Giacomo, "Sopra il monumento di Dante"

On Music. See Augustine, St., *De musica*

"On My Friends." *See* Klopstock, Friedrich Gottlieb

"On My Teacher Döblin." *See* Grass, Günter

On My Way. See Arp, Jean

On Naive and Sentimental Poetry. See Schiller, Friedrich

"On Nature." *See* Lebrun, "Pindare"

On the Nature of Things. See Lucretius, *De rerum natura*

"On the Nature of the Word." *See* Mandelshtam, Osip, "Oprirode slova"

On ne badine pas avec l'amour. See Musset, Alfred de, *You Can't Trifle with Love*

"On the Notions of 'Classic' and 'Romantic' in Music." *See* Berlioz, Hector

On Oratory. See Cicero, Marcus Tullius, *De oratore*

On Order. See Augustine, St., *De ordine*

On the Origin and Function of Literature. *See* Foscolo, Ugo, *Dell'origine e dell'ufficio della letteratura*

On Overgrown Paths. See Hamsun, Knut

On the Perfection of the Spiritual Life. See Aquinas, Thomas, St., *De perfectione spiritualis vitae*

On Poetry. See Mandelshtam, Osip, *O poèzii*

On Poland. See Heine, Heinrich, *Über Polen*

On Political Matters; or, Zoon Politikon. *See* Čapek, Karel, *O věcech obedných čili Zóon politikon*

On Poverty of Spirit. *See* Lukács, György, "A lelki szegénységről"

On the Power of God. See Aquinas, Thomas, St., *De potentia Dei*

"On prav—opiat'fonar', apteka." *See* Akhmatova, Anna

On the Predestination of Saints. See Augustine, St., *De praedestinatione sanctorum*

"On the Present State of Russian Symbolism." *See* Blok, Alexander, "O sovremennom sostoianii russkogo simvolizma"

On the Prince and Literature. See Alfieri, Vittorio, *The Prince and Letters*

On the Principles of Nature. See Aquinas, Thomas, St., *De principiis naturae ad Fratrem Sylvestrum*

On Racine. See Barthes, Roland

"On a Ray of Winter Sun." *See* Seferis, George, "Pano se mia himoniatiki ahtina"

On Realism in Painting. *See* Ortega y Gasset, José, "Del realismo en pintura"

On Religion. See Constant, Benjamin, *De la religion*; Schleiermacher, Friedrich, *Über die Religion*

On Religious Idleness. *See* Petrarch, *De otio religioso*

On Remedies for Both Kinds of Fortune. *See* Petrarch, *De remediis utriusque fortunae*

"On the Republic." *See* Elytis, Odysseus, *To photodendro kai i dekati tetarti omorfia* (*The Light Tree and the Fourteenth Being*), "Peri Politas"

"On Rereading the Poetic Selections 'The Wall in the Mirror' and 'Caretaker's Desk'." *See* Ritsos, Yannis, *Thyrorio*

On Restoring Concord in the Church. See Erasmus, *De sarcienda ecclesiae concordia*

On the Rule of Princes. See Aquinas, Thomas, St., *De regno*

On Separated Substances. See Aquinas, Thomas, St., *De substantiis separatis*

On the Solitary Life. See Petrarch, *De vita solitaria*

"On Some Omissions of Introspective Psychology." *See* James, William

"On Some Verses of Vergil." *See* Montaigne, Michel de, *Essays*

On the Soul. See Aquinas, Thomas, St., *De anima*; Aristotle, *De anima*

On the Spiritual Creatures. See Aquinas, Thomas, St., *De spiritualibus creaturis*

On the State of Religion. See Wagner, Richard

"On the State of the World." *See* Rutebeuf, "De l'estat du monde"

On Steep Cliffs. *See* Tychyna, Pavlo,
    Soniachni klarnety, "Na strimchastykh
    skeliakh"
"On the Study of Greek Poetry." *See* Schlegel,
    Friedrich von
On the Study Methods of Our Time. See Vico,
    Giovanni Battista
"On Synthetism." *See* Zamyatin, Yevgeny
    Ivanovich, "O sintetizme"
On the Third Day. *See* Pilinszky, János,
    Harmadnapon
On the Tisza River. *See* Ady, Endre, "A
    Tisza-parton"
On Tragedy. *See* Musset, Alfred de, "De la
    tragédie"
On the Trinity. See Augustine, St., *De trinitate;*
    Boethius, Anicius Manlius Severinus,
    De trinitate
On Union with the Incarnate Word. See
    Aquinas, Thomas, St., *De unione verbi
    incarnati*
On the Unity of the Intellect. See Aquinas,
    Thomas, St., *De unitate intellectus*
On the Virtues. See Aquinas, Thomas, St., *De
    virtutibus*
"On the Willow Boughs." *See* Quasimodo,
    Salvatore, "Sulle fronde dei salici"
On Writing Letters. *See* Erasmus, *De
    conscribendis epistolis*
"Once again I am in my room." *See* Blok,
    Alexander, "Vnov' u sebia . . . Unizhen,
    zol i rad"
Once I Was Rich and Beloved. *See* Hugh
    Primas, "Dives eram et dilectus"
Oncle Charles s'est enfermé. See Simenon,
    Georges
Onda sagor. See Lagerkvist, Pär
Ondine. See Giraudoux, Jean
"One of Cleopatra's Nights." *See* Gautier,
    Théophile, "Une nuit de Cléopâtre"
One Day in the Life of Ivan Denisovich. See
    Solzhenitsyn, Aleksandr
One Doesn't Know How. See Pirandello, Luigi,
    Non si sa come
One Fine Day. See Vesaas, Tarjei
150,000,000. See Mayakovsky, Vladimir

One Hundred Thousand Billion Poems. *See*
    Queneau, Raymond, *Cent mille
    milliards de poèmes*
One Hundred Years of Modern French Poetry.
    See Ekelöf, Gunnar, *Hundra år modern
    fransk dikt*
*One Principle and One End of Universal Law.
    See* Vico, Giovanni Battista, *Diritto
    universale*
One, The. See Alfieri, Vittorio, Political
    Tetralogy
*120 Days of Sodom; or, The School of
    Libertinism, The. See* Sade, Donatien
    Alphonse François, marquis de
One-Hundred-and-Four Misfortunes in a
    Night. *See* Goldoni, Carlo, *I cento e
    quattro accidenti in una notte*
One-Way Street. See Benjamin, Walter
O'Neill, Eugene
    Ibsen and, 7:1443b, 1754a
    Ile, 7:1443b
    Mourning Becomes Electra, 9:1053b,
        12:2549a
    Strindberg and, 7:1732a, 1754a
    The Iceman Cometh, Gorky's *The Lower
        Depths* and, 8:436a
Oneiric Cold, The. *See* Ionesco, Eugène, *La
    rhume onirique*
Ones and the Others, The. *See* Verlaine, Paul,
    Les uns et les autres
Oni. See Witkiewicz, Stanisław Ignacy
"Onirocritique." *See* Apollinaire, Guillaume
"Onirologie" (Onirology). *See* Maeterlinck,
    Maurice
Onís, Federico de, Unamuno and, 8:297a
Onkel, Onkel. See Grass, Günter, *Mister,
    Mister*
Only a Fiddler. See Andersen, Hans Christian
"Only If Love Should Pierce You." *See*
    Quasimodo, Salvatore, "Solo che amore
    ti colpisca"
"Only One, The." *See* Hölderlin, Friedrich,
    "Der Einzige"
Only Ten Minutes to Buffalo. See Grass,
    Günter
Only Way Out, The. *See* Witkiewicz, Stanisław
    Ignacy, *Jedyne wyjście*

Onomatopoeia
  in Chekhov's works
    "Rothschild's Fiddle," 7:1870b
    "The Steppe," 7:1861b
  in Pascoli's poetry, 7:1831b
Ontology
  in Lukács's works, 10:1276a-b
  Sartre and, 12:2594a-b
"Onuphrius." *See* Gautier, Théophile
Open Book. See Elytis, Odysseus, *Anihta hartia*
Open the Doors. *See* Tychyna, Pavlo, *Soniachni klarnety,* "Odchyniaite dveri"
"Open It, Write." *See* Ekelöf, Gunnar, "Tag och skriv"
Open Letter Concerning the Hard Book Against the Peasants. See Luther, Martin
Open Letter to the Christian Nobility of the German Nation Concerning the Reform of the Christian Estate. See Luther, Martin
Oper und Drama. See Wagner, Richard, *Opera and Drama*
Opéra: Oeuvre poetique. See Cocteau, Jean
Opera
  based on literature, "Cavalleria rusticana," 7:1548a-b
  Heine's influence on, 5:501a, 505a-b
  in Heinrich Mann's works, 8:530a-b
  Hofmannsthal's libretti for Richard Strauss, 9:705a–709a
  librettos
    by Maeterlinck, 8:136a–137a
    pastoral drama and, 2:919b
  Mann brothers and, 8:520b–521a
  Valéry's *The Young Fate* and, 8:577a
  Vittorini and, 12:2740b–2741a, 2755b
  see also Berlioz, Hector; Wagner, Richard
Opera and Drama. See Wagner, Richard
Operation Vega. *See* Dürrenmatt, Friedrich, *Das Unternehmen der Wega*
Operetta (Operetka). See Gombrowicz, Witold
Operette morali. See Leopardi, Giacomo
Opętani. See Gombrowicz, Witold, *Possessed; or, The Secrets of Myslotch*
Opitz, Martin

Grass and, 13:3382a–3383b
  Petrarchan influence, 2:504b
Opium. See Cocteau, Jean
Opium. *See* Drugs; Laudanum
"Opium Smoker, The." *See* Gautier, Théophile, "La pipe d'opium"
Opland, Jeff, 1:65a
  on styles of Germanic poetry, 1:54b
Opportunity, The. See Mérimée, Prosper
Opposites
  in Arp, 10:1377b–1378a
  reconciliation of
    Azorín's interest in, 9:651a
    Bely's interest in, 9:910b, 912a, 914a
    in Hesse's prose, 9:834a-b, 842b–843a, 843b, 845b
Oppression and Liberty (Oppression et liberté). See Weil, Simone
Oppressive Wind Blows Hot, The. *See* Akhmatova, Anna, "Zharko veet veter dushnyi"
Optical distortion, in Olesha's fiction, 11:2241b
Optimism
  of Elytis, 13:2957a-b
  of Leopardi, 5:561b–562a
  Voltaire on, 4:386a
    in *Candide,* 4:377b–378a, 379a, 386a–389b
Opus Oxoniense. See Duns Scotus, *Commentaries on the Sentences*
Opuscula sacra. See Boethius, Anicius Manlius Severinus
Ör (Dawn) (periodical), Hašek's editorship of, 9:1095a-b
Oracles, The. *See* Vigny, Alfred Victor de, *Les destinées (The Fates),* "Les oracles"
Oraisons funèbres et panégyriques. See Bossuet, Jacques Bénigne
Oral literature
  Anglo-Saxon poetry and, 1:67a-b
  Beowulf in context of, 1:57a–60a
  chansons de geste and, 1:106a
  Dinesen and, 10:1294a
  distinguished from written literature, 1:55b–56b
  German, 1:241b

Oral literature (*cont.*)
Lord's *The Singer of Tales* and, 1:126b
the *Nibelungenlied* and, 1:214a-b, 218a
novella and, 2:927b–928a, 928b–929a
poetic diction in, 1:67a
transmission of Norse sagas, 1:401b–402a
transmission of Villon's poetry, 2:539a-b
vocabulary of, in the *Nibelungenlied*, 1:217b–2188a
Yugoslavian poetry, 1:67a
see also Bardic tradition
Oratory
religious
discussed in La Bruyère's *Caractères*, 3:254a-b
see also Bossuet, Jacques Bénigne; Preaching; Sermons
see also Rhetoric
Orbecche. See Giraldi, Giambattista
Orbicianni, Bongiunta, Dante and, 1:432b
Orchestre, L'. See Anouilh, Jean
Orcibal, Jean, *Correspondance de Fénelon*, 3:266a, 267a
Orco, L'. See Sand, George
Ordeals, in Gottfried, 1:255a
"Orden." *See* Chekhov, Anton
Order of Things, The. See Foucault, Michel
Ordinary Life, An. See Čapek, Karel, *Obyčejný život*
Ordinationes, 1:413a
Ordkonst och bildkonst. See Lagerkvist, Pär
Ordre du discours, L'. See Foucault, Michel, *The Discourse on Language*
"Orecchini, Gli." *See* Montale, Eugenio, *The Storm and Other Things*
Oresteia. See Aeschylus
Orestes, Dumas's use of legend, 6:728a–731a
Orestes. See Alfieri, Vittorio
Orestis (Orestes). *See* Ritsos, Yannis
"Orfano, L'." *See* Pascoli, Giovanni, *Myricae*
Orfeo. See Poliziano, Angelo
"Organic originality" (Bely), 9:926b
Organon for the Theater. See Brecht, Bertolt, *Kleines Organon das Theater*
"Orgie parisienne, ou Paris se repeuple, L'." *See* Rimbaud, Arthur
Orient
Bely's fascination with East versus West, 9:916b–917a, 920b–921a
Flaubert and, 7:1378b–1380b, 1385a–1387a
George and, 8:457a
Goldoni and, 4:430a
in Hugo's works, 6:694b–695a, 699a-b
in Mickiewicz's poetry, 5:615a-b
religions, Maeterlinck and, 8:141b–142a
in Wolfram, 1:270a–271a
see also Montesquieu, Charles-Louis de Secondat, baron de, *The Persian Letters*
Oriental literature. *See* Eastern literature
Oriental philosophy. *See* Eastern philosophy
Oriental Tales. See Yourcenar, Marguerite, *Nouvelles orientales*
Orientales, Les. See Hugo, Victor
Orientations. See Elytis, Odysseus, *Prosanatolizmi*
"Oriflamme." *See* Ionesco, Eugène
"Origem de *O intervalo*." *See* Ferreira de Castro, José Maria, *Os fragmentos*
Origen y epílogo de la filosofía. See Ortega y Gasset, José
Origin of German Tragic Drama, The. See Benjamin, Walter
Origin of Philosophy, The. See Ortega y Gasset, José, *Origen y epílogo de la filosofía*
Origin of Sin, The. See Prudentius, *Hamartigenia*
Origin of Species, The. See Darwin, Charles
Original sin. *See* Sin, original
Originality
classicism and, 5:530a
Delacroix's view on, 5:530a
in romanticism, concept of, 5:530a
Origines de la France contemporaine, Les (*The Origins of Contemporary France*). *See* Taine, Hippolyte
Origins, Foucault's rejection of concept, 13:3325b–3326a, 3329a-b
Origins. *See* George, Stefan, "Ursprünge"
Origins of Contemporary France, The. See Taine, Hippolyte, *Les Origines de la France contemporaine*

"Origins of *Intermission*." *See* Ferreira de Castro, José Maria, *Os fragmentos*, "Origem de *O intervalo*"

"Oriole, The." *See* Olesha, Yuri, "Ivolga"

"Orion." *See* Elytis, Odysseus, *Prosanatolismi*

Orion aveugle. *See* Simon, Claude

Orion Blinded. *See* Birn, Randi

Orkneyinga saga, 1:380b–381a

Orlando furioso. *See* Ariosto, Lodovico

Orlando innamorato. *See* Boiardo, Matteo Maria

Orlando Mad. *See* Ariosto, Lodovico, *Orlando furioso*

Orléans, duc d', Hugo and, 6:705a

Orléans, duchesse de. *See* Lorraine, Marguerite de

Orléans, Gaston, duc d', 3:55b–56a

Orloff, Ida, Hauptmann and, 8:161a

Ormarr Ørlygsson. *See* Gunnarsson, Gunnar, *Borgslægtens Historie* (The History of the Family at Borg)

Ornifle ou le courant d'air (*Ornifle; or, The Draft*). *See* Anouilh, Jean

"Örök harc és nász." *See* Ady, Endre

Orosius, Paulus, 1:433b

Orphan Paul. *See* Gorky, Maxim, *Goremyka Pavel*

"Orphan, The." *See* Pascoli, Giovanni, *Myricae* (Tamarisks), "L'Orfano"

"Orphans' Gifts, The." *See* Rimbaud, Arthur, "Les étrennes des orphelins"

Orphée. *See* Cocteau, Jean

Orpheu (Orpheus) (journal)
  Pessoa's work in, 10:1485b, 1494a
  Verde's work in, 10:1485b

Orpheus
  in *Convivio*, 1:440a
  Nerval and, 6:959a, 966b

Orpheus. *See* Cocteau, Jean, *Orphée*

Orphism, Apollinaire and, 9:884a, 892a

Orta, Garcia da, *Colloquies of the Drugs and Simples of India*, 2:748b

Ortega y Gasset, José, **9:1119a–1150b**
  "Adán en el paraíso" (Adam in Paradise), 9:1133b, 1134a
    life vs. abstraction in, 9:606b
    neo-Kantian essay, 9:604a

  aesthetic writings, 9:1133b–1137a
    hermeneutic, 9:1138b–1141a
  on art, 9:762a, 1133b–1134a
  "Arte de este mundo y del otro" (Art of This World and of the Other World), 9:1134a
  "Azorín, o los primores de lo vulgar," 9:641a
  debate with Baroja, 9:608a-b
  "Del realismo en pintura" (On Realism in Painting), 9:1134b
  "Democracia morbosa" (Morbid Democracy), 9:1142b–1143a
  "El error Berenguer" (The Berenguer Error), 9:1146a
  El hombre y la gente (*Man and People*), 9:1138b, 1139b, 1147a–1148a
  "El intelectual y el otro" (The Intellectual and the Other), 9:1147a
  El libro de las misiones (The Book of Missions), 9:1139b
  El tema de nuestro tiempo (*The Modern Theme*), 9:1129a–1130a
    see also *Prólogo para alemanes*
  "En el centenario de una universidad" (On the Centennial of a University), 9:1132a
  En torno a Galileo (*Man and Crisis*), 9:1131a, 1132a, 1134a-b, 1138b, 1139a-b, 1147a
  "Ensayo de estética a manera de prólogo" (Essay in Aesthetics by Way of a Preface), 9:1134b
  "Ensimismamiento y alteración" ("The Self and the Other"), 9:1147a
  España invertebrada (*Invertebrate Spain*), 9:1143a–1144a, 1145b
  "Glosas" (Glosses), 9:1123a
  Goya, 9:1138b, 1140a, 1140b
  Group at the Service of the Republic, 9:1146a
  Guillermo Dilthey y la idea de la vida (Wilhelm Dilthey and the Idea of Life), 9:1140a
  Historia como sistema (*History as a System*), 9:1131a-b, 1132a
  historical works, 9:1132a–1133a
  Ideas sobre la novela (*Notes on the Novel*), 9:1137a, 1138a

Ortega y Gasset, José (*cont.*)
　Ideas y creencias (Ideas and Beliefs),
　　9:1131b
　Institute for the Humanities, 9:1147a
　Jiménez and, 9:1005b
　"La ciencia y la religión como problemas
　　políticos" (Science and Religion as
　　Political Problems), 9:1141b
　La deshumanización del arte (*The
　　Dehumanization of Art*), 9:608b, 1133b,
　　1135b–1136a, 1138b
　"La estética de 'Elenano Gregorio el Botero'"
　　(Gregorio el Botero the Dwarf), 9:1134a
　"La fiesta del trabajo" (The Workers' Feast
　　Day), 9:1142a-b
　*La idea de principio en Leibniz y la
　　evolución de la teoría deductiva* (*The
　　Idea of Principle in Leibniz and the
　　Evolution of Deductive Theory*),
　　9:1132b–1133b, 1138b, 1139b
　"Las dos grandes metáforas" (The Two
　　Great Metaphors), 9:1136b–1137a
　"Las ermitas de Córdoba" (The Hermitages
　　of Córdoba), 9:1123a
　League for Political Education,
　　9:1141b–1142a, 1142b
　literary criticism, 9:1137a–1138b
　Lorca and, 11:2181b
　"Los problemas nacionales y la juventud"
　　(National Problems and Youth), 9:1141b
　Meditaciones del Quijote (*Meditations on
　　Quixote*), 9:606b, 1128a-b, 1133b
　　"Breve tratado de la novela" ("Brief
　　　Treatise on the Novel"), 9:1137a-b,
　　　1140a
　"Miseria y esplendor de la traducción"
　　(Misery and Splendor of Translation),
　　9:1138b, 1139a
　on modernism, 8:336a
　"Musicalia," 9:1135a-b
　"Nada 'moderno' y 'muy siglo XX'," 9:1130a
　"Ni vitalismo ni racionalismo" (Neither
　　Vitalism Nor Rationalism), 9:1127a
　Obras completas (Collected Works), preface,
　　9:1126a
　Origen y epílogo de la filosofía (*The Origin
　　of Philosophy*), 9:1132a-b, 1138b

　perspectivism, 9:1128b–1129a
　phenomenology, 9:1127b
　political oratory, 9:1125b–1126a
　political and social thought, 9:1141a–1148b
　posthumous influence, 9:1148a-b
　"Prólogo casi doctrinal sobre la novela" (A
　　Nearly Doctrinal Prologue on the
　　Novel), 9:608b
　Prólogo para alemanes (*Preface for
　　Germans*), 9:1119a, 1120a, 1120b,
　　1126b
　　neo-Kantian thought, 9:1127b
　"Proverbios y cantares" and, 9:759b
　¿Qué es filosofía? (*What Is Philosophy?*),
　　9:1130a-b, 1145b
　"Qué es leer" (What Reading Is), 9:1138b,
　　1139a
　Rebelión de las masas (*The Revolt of the
　　Masses*), 9:1119a, 1131a, 1143b–1148a,
　　1143b–1145b
　"Rectificación de la República"
　　(Rectification of the Republic), 9:1146b
　"Reforma de la inteligencia" (Reform of
　　Intelligence), 9:1143a
　Revista de Occidente and, 9:1119b
　"Socialismo y aristocracia" (Socialism and
　　Aristocracy), 9:1141b
　on Spanish politics, 9:747a
　"Tiempo, distancia, y forma en el arte de
　　Proust" (Time, Distance, and Form in
　　the Art of Proust), 9:1138a
　"Tres cuadros del vino" (Wine in Three
　　Paintings), 9:1123b, 1134a
　"Vejamen de orador" (Vexation of the
　　Orator), 9:1127a
　Velázquez, 9:1138b, 1139b, 1140a, 1140b
　　"La reviviscencia de los cuadros"
　　　("Reviving the Paintings"), 9:1139a
　Vida de Don Quijote y Sancho (*The Life of
　　Don Quixote and Sancho*), 9:1128a
　vital reason, 9:1129b–1130a, 1132a
　"¡Viva la República!," 9:1146b
　Vives, 9:1148a
　"Yo soy yo y mis circunstancias," 9:1129a,
　　1131b
Ortigão, Ramalho
　Antero de Quental and, 7:1685b

Cennacle and, 7:1687b
Eça and, 7:1684b, 1687b, 1688a, 1692a-b
Ortigão, Ramalho (joint author). *See* Eça de Queiroz, José Maria, and Ortigão, Ramalho
örtlich betäubt. See Grass, Günter, *Local Anaesthetic*
Ortman, Peter, Ekelöf and, 12:2636b
Ortúzar, Elena, 8:356b
Örvar-Odds saga, 1:401a
Orwell, George
1984, 10:1188b
Silone's influence on, 12:2303a
Silone and, 12:2273a
in Simon's *The Georgics*, 13:3043b
"Such, Such Were the Joys," 9:932a
Zamyatin's influence on, 10:1181a, 1188b
Os enfatriões. See Camoëns, Luís Vaz de, *The Two Amphitryons*
"Oscar et Erick." *See* Aymé, Marcel
"Osenni vecher byl. Pod zvuk dozhdia stekliannvi." *See* Blok, Alexander
Oshibka smerti. See Khlebnikov, Velimir, *Death's Mistake*
Osiander, Andreas, Luther and, 2:686a
Oskolki (magazine), Chekhov and, 7:1858a
Osorio, Elena, Lope de Vega and, 2:846a, 848a
Osservazioni sulla morale cattolica. See Manzoni, Alessandro, *A Vindication of Catholic Morality*
Osservazioni sulla tortura. See Verri, Pietro
Ossi di seppia. See Montale, Eugenio, *Cuttlefish Bones*
"Ossianic" poetry. *See* Macpherson, James
Ostend Masks. See Ghelderode, Michel de, *Masques ostendais*
Ostenders, The. See Simenon, Georges, *Le clan des Ostandais*
"Ostern." *See* Storm, Theodor
Ostranenie. See Defamiliarization
Ostrich Feathers. See Tieck, Ludwig, *Straussfedern*
Ostrov Sakhalin. See Chekhov, Anton
Ostrovitiane. See Zamyatin, Yevgeny Ivanovich, *The Islanders*
Ostrovsky, Alexander
Groza (*The Storm*), 7:1868b

on mercantile class, 6:985a
Snegurochka (*The Snow Maiden*), Khlebnikov's "Snezhimochka" modeled after, 10:1355b
Osudy dobrého vojáka Švejka za světové války. See Hašek, Jaroslav
"Osudy medvěda od Hamagbúha." *See* Hašek, Jaroslav
Ószi koncert. See Kosztolányi, Dezső
Otage, L'. See Claudel, Paul
"Otan diegeirontai." *See* Cavafy, Constantine
Otdela teatrov i zrelishch v Petrograde (The Major Art Council of the Department of Theaters and Spectacles in Petrograd), Zamyatin's plays subsidized through, 10:1193a
"Otets." *See* Babel, Isaac, *Odessa Tales*
"Otets i ego muzei." *See* Tsvetaeva, Marina
Othello. See Shakespeare, William
"Other condition, the" (Musil), 9:937a, 952b, 953b, 955a, 955b
"Other day near a hedge, The." *See* Marcabru, "L'Autrier jost' una sebiss"
Other Man, The. *See* Schnitzler, Arthur, "Der Andere"
"Other Noah, The." *See* Elytis, Odysseus, *Exi kai mia tipsis yia ton ourano*
Other One, The. See Colette, *La seconde*
Other People's Heads. *See* Aymé, Marcel, *La tête des autres*
Other People's Reasons. See Pirandello, Luigi, *Se non cosí*
Other Tartuffe; or, The Guilty Mother, The. See Beaumarchais, Pierre-Augustin Caron de, *L'Autre tartuffe ou la mère coupable*
Other, the, Sartre and, 12:2598b–2599a
Other Woman, The. See Colette, *La femme cachée*
Other Writers and Myself. *See* Mauriac, François, *D'Autres et moi*
Other Writings on Art. *See* Claudel, Paul, *Autres textes sur l'art*
Otherwise: Last and First Poems of Eugenio Montale. See Montale, Eugenio, *Altri versi e poesie disperse*
Othon. See Corneille, Pierre
"Otkaz." *See* Khlebnikov, Velimir

"Otoño." *See* Machado, Antonio, *Soledades* (Solitudes)

Otro, El. See Unamuno, Miguel de

Otsup, Nikolai, on Pasternak's *Deviat'sot piatyi god*, 10:1602a

Otter's Children, The. *See* Khlebnikov, Velimir, "Deti Vydry"

8 anime in una bomba. See Marinetti, Filippo Tommaso

Otto of Bavaria, in Apollinaire's "Song of the Unloved Lover," 9:890b

Otto, Christian, 5:56a

"Otvet na budushchie spletni." *See* Mayakovsky, Vladimir

Otway, Thomas, *Venice Preserved*, Hofmannsthal's adaptation of, 9:698b

"Où." *See* Butor, Michel

Ouimette, Victor, on Ortega y Gasset, 9:1143a

"Oulipo." *See* Queneau, Raymond, *Ouvroir de littérature potentielle*

Oulipo group, Valéry and, 8:587a

Our Ancestors. *See* Calvino, Italo, *I nostri antenati*

"Our Attitude Towards Death." *See* Freud, Sigmund

Our Comrade. Nikos Zahariadhis. *See* Ritsos, Yannis, *O syntrofos mas. Nikos Zahariadhis*

Our Daily Dream. *See* Arp, Jean, *Unsern täglichen Traum*

"Our Fundamentals." *See* Khlebnikov, Velimir, "Nasha osnova"

Our Greed for Stories. *See* Frisch, Max, "Unsere Gier nach Geschichten"

Our Lady of the Flowers. See Genet, Jean

"Our Lady of the Swallows." *See* Yourcenar, Marguerite, *Nouvelles orientales*

"Our Language to Us." *See* Klopstock, Friedrich Gottlieb

Our Old House. *See* Ritsos, Yannis, *To palio mas spiti*

Our Own Things and People. *See* Ghelderode, Michel de, *Choses et gens de chez nous*

Our Sea. See Blasco Ibáñez, Vicente, *Mare nostrum*

Our Sons. See Michelet, Jules

"Our Sun." *See* Seferis, George, "O dhikos mas hellos"

Our Unborn Son. *See* Moberg, Vilhelm, *Vår ofödde son*

Our Way. *See* Hašek, Jaroslav, *Nash put'*

Ours et la lune, L'. See Claudel, Paul

Out of Africa. See Dinesen, Isak

Out of India. See Hesse, Hermann, *Aus Indien*

Outlaw, The. *See* Čapek, Karel, *Loupežník*

Outlines of a Philosophy of the History of Man. See Herder, Johann Gottfried von, *Ideen zur Philosophie der Geschichte der Menschheit*

Outpourings of an Art-loving Friar. *See* Tieck, Ludwig, *Herzensergiessungen eines Kunstliebenden Klosterbruders*

"Outsiders väg, En" (An Outsider's Way). *See* Ekelöf, Gunnar

Ouvroir de littérature potentielle. See Queneau, Raymond

Oväder (Storm Weather). See Strindberg, August

Overbeck, Franz, Nietzsche and, 7:1667b

"Overcoat, The." *See* Gogol, Nikolay Vasilievich

Overman
  Hamsun and, 8:23b
  Nietzsche's conception of, 7:1673b–1676a, 1677a-b, 1680a
  see also Superman

Ovid (Publius Ovidius Naso)
  alienation and, 9:863a
  allegory and, 1:323a-b
  Camoëns' *The Lusiads* and, 2:763a
  D'Annunzio and, 8:194a
  Dante on, 1:440a
    Inferno, 1:446b
  love and, 1:139b
  Medusa myth, in Petrarch's *Canzoniere*, 2:493b
  Metamorphoses
    Adonis and, 3:75a
    Cervantes and, 2:827b
    Chrétien de Troyes and, 1:185b
    Dante and, 1:447a
    Renaissance pastoral poetry and, 2:901b–902a

as source for Alfieri's *Myrrha*, 4:685a-b, 686b

Remedia amoris (*Love's Remedy*), "Quid luges, lirice?" and, 1:338b

Romance of the Rose and, 1:316a–317a

"Owe, hovelichez singen." *See* Walther von der Vogelweide

"Owê war sînt verswunden, alliu miniu jâr?" *See* Walther von der Vogelweide

Owen, Robert, Goncharov and, 6:1084b

Owen, Wilfred, "Strange Meeting," Trakl and, 10:1419b–1420a

Owners of the Keys, The. *See* Kundera, Milan, *Majitelé kličů*

Oxen, The. *See* Aymé, Marcel, *The Wonderful Farm* (*Contes du chat perché*), "Les boeufs"

Oxenhandler, Neal, *Scandal and Parade*, on Cocteau, 10:1548a

Oxford University, Grosseteste and, 1:409b

Oxymoron, in Undset's works, 9:1024b

"Oxymoron of form," in Musil's *The Man Without Qualities*, 9:940b

P

På gjenrodde stier. *See* Hamsun, Knut

Pa Ubu's Illustrated Almanac. *See* Jarry, Alfred, *Almanach illustré du Père Ubu*

Pabellón de reposo. *See* Cela, Camilo José; Cela, Camilo José, *Rest Home*

Pablo de Herlagnez. *See* Verlaine, Paul

"Pace non trovo et non ò da far guerra." *See* Petrarch, *Canzoniere*

Paces de los reyes, Las, y la Judía de Toledo. *See* Lope de Vega

Paciaudi, Paolo Maria, Alfieri inspired by, 4:664b

Pacific Society (Germany), Hauptmann and the, 8:151b, 157a

Pacifism
  Erasmus and, 2:583a
  Moberg's, 11:2216a, 2218a

Pacsirta. *See* Kosztolányi, Dezső

"Padre del Ciel, dopo i perduti giorni." *See* Petrarch, *Canzoniere*

Padre di famiglia. *See* Tasso, Torquato

Paean. *See* Ekelöf, Gunnar, "Samothrace," "Paian"

Paese di mare. *See* Ginzburg, Natalia

Paese Sera (Italian journal), on Silone's *Story of a Humble Christian*, 12:2300b

Paesi tuoi. *See* Pavese, Cesare, *The Harvesters*

Pagan School, Baudelaire and, 7:1329b

Paganini, Niccolò, 6:783b–784a

Paganism
  in Augustine's *City of God*, 1:34b
  neopaganism and German classicism, 5:39a
  Nerval and, 6:954a
  in Norse sagas, 1:389b
    Grettis saga, 1:392b
  Prudentius on, 1:9b, 13b
  Rimbaud's view of, 7:1818a-b

Page, Curtis, *Songs and Sonnets of Ronsard*, 6:1058a

Pages for Art. *See* Blätter für die Kunst

Pagès, Madeleine, 9:881a, 882a

Páginas escogidas. *See* Machado, Antonio

"Paian." *See* Ekelöf, Gunnar, "Samothrace"

Pailleron, Édouard, *Le monde où l'on s'ennuie*
(*The Art of Being Bored*), 7:1920b
Pain
in Leopardi's works, 5:563a-b
in Montaigne's *Essays*, 2:773b–774a, 775a
Schopenhauer's view of
critique of, 5:403a, 406b–407a
his pessimism and, 5:401a–403a
"Pain bénit, Le." *See* Claudel, Paul, *La messe
là-bas*
Pain dur, Le. See Claudel, Paul
Pain (Psycho-Physical Study). *See* Baroja, Pío,
El dolor (estudio de psico-física)
Paine, Thomas, in Büchner, 6:1181a-b
Painter
Ritsos as, 12:2819a
writer as, Hesse, 9:833a, 833b–834a, 841b,
854b
in Zola's *L'Oeuvre*, 7:1530b–1531b
Painter of His Dishonor, The. See Calderón de
la Barca, Pedro
"Painter of Modern Life." *See* Baudelaire,
Charles
Painter, William, *Palace of Pleasure*,
translations of Ser Giovanni's tales in,
2:936b
Painters of the *Fêtes galantes*, The. *See* Blanc,
Charles, *Les peintres des fêtes galantes*
Painter's Studio, The. See Courbet, Gustave
Painting
of Elytis, 13:2964b
futurist, Marinetti and, 9:815a, 817a
Lessing on, 4:545a, 546b
Prudentius' *Dittochaeon* on, 1:13a-b
of Simon, 13:3022a, 3022b, 3026a, 3037a
Painting as Challenge. *See* Aragon, Louis, *Le
peinture au défi*
Painting, The. See Ionesco, Eugène, *Le tableau*
Painting of Today, The. *See* Mayakovsky,
Vladimir, "Zhivopis' segodnyashnego
dnya"
Pál, bishop of Skálholt, 1:383b–384a
Palace, Le. See Simon, Claude
Palace of Pleasure. See Painter, William
Palace of the Summerland, The. *See* Laxness,
Halldór, *Höll sumarlandsins*
Palamas, Kostes, 13:2955b, 2956a

Seferis and, 12:2255b
on Seferis' *Turning Point*, 12:2258b, 2263a
Palamedes, William, in "Dives eram et
dilectus," 1:341b–342a, 356a
"Palata No. 6." *See* Chekhov, Anton
"Pale Horse." *See* Bryusov, Valery, "Kon' bled"
Paleography, invention of, 3:264b
Palestine Song. *See* Walther von der
Vogelweide, "Allerêrst lebe ich mir
werde"
Paley, Grace, Babel's influence on, 11:1890a,
1912b
Palia mazourka se rythmo vrohis. See Ritsos,
Yannis
Palindrome, Walther and, 1:300a
Palingenesien (Palingenesis). See Richter,
Jean Paul
"Palio." *See* Montale, Eugenio, *The Occasions*
Palio mas spiti, To. See Ritsos, Yannis
Palivoda's Death. *See* Khlebnikov, Velimir,
"Smert' Palivody"
Pallas, Gustav, *Slovníček literárni* (*Small
Dictionary of Literature*), 9:1116b
Pallavicino, Gaspare, in Castiglione,
2:659a–660a
"Palm Sunday." *See* Elytis, Odysseus, *To
photodendro kai i dekati tetarti omorfia*
(*The Light Tree and the Fourteenth
Being*), "Ton Vaion"
"Pálma a Hortobágyon" ("Palm Tree on the
Hungarian Plains"). *See* Reviczky, Gyula
Palomar. See Calvino, Italo, *Mr. Palomar*
Páls saga, 1:384a
Paludes. See Gide, André, *Marshlands*
Pamela, La. See Goldoni, Carlo
Pamela; or, Virtue Rewarded. See Richardson,
Samuel
"Pamiatnik." *See* Khlebnikov, Velimir
Pamiętnik teatralny. See Witkiewicz, Stanisław
Ignacy
Pamiętnik z okresu dojrzewania. See
Gombrowicz, Witold
"Pamyati A. I. Odoevskogo." *See* Lermontov,
Mikhail Yurievich
Pan, in Vergil's *Georgics*, 2:901b
Pan. See Hamsun, Knut; Krleža, Miroslav

"Pan Florentin kontra Chocholka." *See* Hašek, Jaroslav

Pan Tadeusz. See Mickiewicz, Adam

Pan-Scandinavian ideal, Gunnarsson and, 10:1517b–1518a

Pan-Slavism. *See* Slavic nationalism

Panchatantra
   Doni's translation of, 2:940b
   influence on Renaissance short fiction, 2:932a

Pancrazi, Pietro, "Eugenio Montale poeta fisico e metafisico" (Eugenio Montale as Physical and Metaphysical Poet), on Montale's *Cuttlefish Bones*, 11:1994b–1995a

Pandora's Box. See Wedekind, Frank

Pane e vino. See Silone, Ignazio

Panegyric to Trajan by Pliny. See Alfieri, Vittorio

"Panégyrique de Saint-Bernard." *See* Bossuet, Jacques Bénigne

Pange, François de, 5:92a
   Chénier's friendship with, 4:695b

"Pange, lingua, gloriosi proelium certaminis." *See* Venantius Fortunatus

"Pange lingua, necem Petri qui turbavit Angliam" ("Proclaim, tongue, the death of Peter who disrupted England"), 1:370a

"Panic theater," 12:2355a

Pankraz, the Sulker (Pankraz, der Schmoller). See Keller, Gottfried

Pannonius, Janus
   Ady's "Matthias' Demented Scholar" and, 9:863b
     "De amygdalo in Pannonia nata" ("An Almond Tree in Pannonia"), 9:863a

"Pano se mia himoniatiki ahtina." *See* Seferis, George

"Panorama." *See* Andrić, Ivo

Pansaers, Clément, Ghelderode and, 11:2134b, 2135a

Pantagleize. See Ghelderode, Michel de

Pantagruel. See Rabelais, François

Pantagrueline prognostication. See Rabelais, François

Pantheism
   Fénelon and, 3:275b
   Hölderlin and, 5:146b, 154b, 156a, 168a
   Lessing and, 4:560a, 561a
   and Romanticism, 5:211b
   Spinoza and, 5:211b

"Pantheon." *See* Boccaccio, Giovanni

Pantomime
   Hofmannsthal's view of, 9:692a
   Schnitzler's use of, 8:98a-b

"Pantomime." *See* Verlaine, Paul

"Pantoum." *See* Seferis, George

"Paolo Uccello." *See* Pascoli, Giovanni, *Poemi italici (Italian Poems)*

"Paon, Le." *See* Aymé, Marcel

Papacy
   Aquinas on, 1:425b–426a
   in Dante's *De monarchia*, 1:443a, 443b
   Luther on, 2:676b–677a
   satirized, in Walther's *Unmutston*, 1:365b
   Walther's dislike of, 1:291b, 301b–302b

Papacy at Rome. See Luther, Martin

Papadiamantopoulos, Yannis. *See* Moréas, Jean

Papal curia
   in "Gospel of the Silver Mark," 1:362a-b
   in medieval satire, 1:351a–352a

Papandreou, Nikos, preface to Ritsos' *Pera ap ton iskio ton kyparission*, 12:2825a

Papatsonis, T. K., Seferis and, 12:2260a

Papeles de Son Armadans (journal), Cela and, 13:3117b

Paper Moons. *See* Malraux, André, *Lunes en papier*

Paper Poems. See Ritsos, Yannis, *Hartina*

Paper Rose, The. *See* Valle-Inclán, Ramón del, *La rosa de papel*

"Papillons." *See* Schumann, Robert

Pár szó a nyelvújításhoz. See Kosztolányi, Dezső

Parable
   Brecht's use of, 11:2097b–2098a, 13:2916a
   Frisch's use of, 13:2910b–2911b, 2916a
   Rimbaud's use of, 7:1814b–1815a
   Schnitzler's use of, 8:92b–93a

Parabole du festin, La (The Parable of the Feast). *See* Claudel, Paul

Parabosco, Girolamo, *I diporti* (*The Diversions*), 2:944b

Paracelsus, Schnitzler's dramatic treatment of, 8:96b–97a

"Paracelsus." *See* Schnitzler, Arthur

Paraclesis. See Erasmus

Parade. See Cocteau, Jean

Parade (ballet), 9:898b, 899b

Parades (comic sketches), Beaumarchais and, 4:564b–565a

Paradísarheimt. See Laxness, Halldór

Paradise, allegory and, 1:324a–326b

"Paradise." *See* Zamyatin, Yevgeny Ivanovich, "Rai"

Paradise Lost. See Milton, John

Paradise Reclaimed. See Laxness, Halldór, *Paradísarheimt*

Paradisiacal Poem. *See* D'Annunzio, Gabriele, *Poema paradisiaco*

Paradiso, Il. See Moravia, Alberto

Paradox
    in Augustine's *On the Trinity*, 1:38a
    in Aymé's works, 12:2453b
    Barthes and, 13:3098b–3099a
    in Calderón's works, 2:878a
    in Kierkegaard, 6:1138b–1139b
    in La Rochefoucauld's maxims, 3:65a
    Lope de Vega and, 2:851b
    in Rilke, 9:781a, 781b
    in Schlegel's critical writings, 5:177b–178a
    in Schnitzler's works, 8:107a
    in Walther, 1:292a, 294a–295b

Paradox on Acting. See Diderot, Denis, *Paradoxe sur le comédien*

"Paradox on the Architect." *See* Valéry, Paul, "Paradoxe sur l'architecte"

Paradox, King (*Paradox, Rey*). *See* Baroja, Pío

Paradoxe sur la comédien. See Diderot, Denis

"Paradoxe sur l'architecte." *See* Valéry, Paul

"Paralayes pano se mian ahtida." *See* Elytis, Odysseus, *Ilios o protos*

Parallèlement. See Verlaine, Paul

Parallelism
    in *Hrafnkels saga*, 1:394b
    typology and, 1:3b
    in *Vápnfirðinga saga*, 1:395a
    in Wolfram, 1:276b–277b

"Paramones iliou." *See* Ritsos, Yannis, *Dhokimasia*

Paranoia
    Freud's concept of, 8:15a
    Rousseau and, 4:460a
    Strindberg afflicted with, 7:1736b–1737a

Paraprosodies. See Cocteau, Jean

"Parasha." *See* Turgenev, Ivan

Parataxis
    in Trakl, 10:1410b, 1417a
    in Ungaretti's poetry, 10:1462b

Paravents, Les. See Genet, Jean, *The Screens*

Parc, Marquise Du. *See* Gorla, Thérèse

Pardo Bazán, Emilia de
    Azorín's literary criticism of, 9:645a
    Blasco's *The Cabin* and, 8:375a
    La revolución y la novela en Rusia, 7:1614a
    Pérez Galdós and, 7:1613a–1614a

Parent-child conflict. *See* Family

Parentheses. See Ritsos, Yannis

Parents terribles, Les. See Cocteau, Jean, *Intimate Relations*

Parerga and Paralipomena. See Schopenhauer, Arthur

"Parergon." *See* Machado, Antonio, *Nuevas canciones*

Pareto, Vilfredo, on the masses, 9:1145b

Paria (*Pariah*). *See* Strindberg, August

Parini, Giuseppe, 5:369b

Paris
    in 1890's, 9:620b
    Ady and, 9:871b–872b
    Alfieri's stay in, 4:664a–b, 666b–667a
    in Balzac's works, 5:650b
    belle époque in, 9:744b
    Bergson in, 8:45b–46a
    Berlioz in, 6:774a–777a, 782b–784b, 790a–b, 793a, 799a–b
    in Flaubert's works, 5:650b
    Hamsun in, 8:29b
    Heine in, 5:498b, 499b
    in Hugo's works, 5:650b, 6:699b–703a, 710b–711a
    Jarry in, 9:668b–669a, 670b–671a
    in La Bruyère's *Caractères*, 3:242b–245b
    Lagerkvist and, 10:1682b

liberation after World War II, Camus and, 13:3069b

Mandelshtam's stay in, 10:1626a-b

Maupassant and, 7:1760a, 1760b–1761a, 1766a-b, 1778a–1779b

Mérimée's civil service career in, 6:754b

in Michelet's works, 5:573b, 574b, 577a

Parliament of, medieval drama and, 1:473a

Rilke in, 9:770a-b

Rimbaud's career in, 7:1788b–1789a, 1806a–1807a

Second Empire, Baudelaire and, 7:1330a-b

in Simenon's works, 12:2501b–2502a

Strindberg's career in, 7:1736a–1737a

in Sue's works, 5:650b

Svevo's reputation in, 8:69b, 71a

Ungaretti and, 10:1455b–1456a

Wagner and, 7:1656a

Wedekind in, 8:240a–257a

Witkiewicz's stay in, 10:1209a

Zamyatin's stay in, 10:1199b

Zola and, 5:650b, 7:1519a

see also Paris Commune

"Paris." See Vigny, Alfred Victor de

Paris. See Zola, Émile, Les trois villes: Paris

"Páris az én Bakonyom." See Ady, Endre

Paris Commune, 9:864a

Mallarmé and, 7:1568b–1569a

Mérimée and, 6:767a-b

Rimbaud and, 7:1785a, 1786b, 1789a, 1795b

Taine and, 7:1465a

Verlaine and, 7:1622b–1623a

"Paris Dream." See Baudelaire, Charles

Paris Impromptu. See Giraudoux, Jean

Paris Is My Bakony Mountain. See Ady, Endre, "Páris az én Bakonyom"

Paris Peasant. See Aragon, Louis, Le paysan de Paris

"Paris Rid of the Bastille." See Alfieri, Vittorio, Panegyric to Trajan by Pliny

Paris Spleen. See Baudelaire, Charles

Paris, University of. See University of Paris

Paris Wine. See Aymé, Marcel, Le vin de Paris

Paris-Midi (journal), and Cocteau, 10:1555b

Paris-moderne (journal), Verlaine's works in, 7:1638a

Paris-Soir (journal)

and Cocteau, 10:1555b–1556a

Saint-Exupéry's articles in, 12:2317a

"Párisba beszökött az ősz." See Ady, Endre

"Parish Priest and the Dead Man, The." See La Fontaine, Jean de, Fables, "Le curé et le mort"

Parisian Dawn, A. See Ady, Endre, "Egy párisi hajnalon"

Parisian Scenes. See Baudelaire, Charles, Tableaux Parisiens

Parisian Sketches. See Huysmans, Joris Karl, Croquis parisiens

Parisian's Sundays, A. See Maupassant, Guy de, Les dimanches d'un bourgeois de Paris

Parnasse contemporain, Verlaine's poetry in, 7:1621a-b

Parnassian poets

in Belgium, 8:121a

Leconte de Lisle and, 6:1251b

Rimbaud and, 7:1796a-b

Ronsard and, 2:741b

veneration of Chénier by, 4:693a

Verlaine and, 7:1621a

Parnok, Sofiia, Tsvetaeva and, 11:1735a-b

"Pároco da Aldeia, O." See Herculano, Alexandre

Parody

in Adam de la Halle's plays, 1:459b, 460a

in "Apocalypsis Goliae Episcopi," 1:354a

in Calvino, 13:3281a–3283a

in Camoëns' The Two Amphitryons, 2:755b

Cervantes' Don Quixote and, 2:828b

in Chekhov's prose, 7:1859b–1860a

in "Ego dixi," 1:347b

in Goncharov's works, 6:1067b–1068a, 1070b–1071b, 1072b, 1075a-b

of historical novel, 7:1705a

in Ionesco

Exit the King, 13:3006a-b

Macbett, 13:3013a

in Lermontov's works, 6:1222a-b

of literary decadence, 7:1641a

in Magic Mountain, 9:721a

in medieval satire, 1:369b–371a

in Arras, 1:459a

Olesha's Envy as, 11:2240b

Parody (*cont.*)
 in "Pange lingua, necem Petri qui turbavit
  Angliam," 1:370a-b
 of Portuguese romanticism, 7:1687b
 of religious literature, 1:369b
 of romantic mystery novels, 7:1687b
 in "Utar contra vitia carmine rebelli," 1:352a
 in William IX's works, 1:163a
*Parole da dirle sopra la pravisione del danaio,
 facto un poco di proemio et di scusa.*
 See Machiavelli, Niccolò
Parole in libertà. See Free-word style
Parole sceniche, 6:1160b
Paronomasia, in Villon's writing, 2:538b
Parricide
 in Bely's *Petersburg,* 9:920b, 921a-b
 Schiller and, 5:32a, 49a
Parrott, Cecil, on Hašek, 9:1093a
Parrucca, La. See Ginzburg, Natalia
Parry, Milman, 1:67a, 67b
Parsifal. See Wagner, Richard
Parson in Jubilee, The. *See* Richter, Jean Paul,
 Der Jubelsenior
Partage de midi, Le. See Claudel, Paul
Partes. See Lope de Vega
Parthenais. See Baggensen, Jens Immanuel
"Parthenias." *See* Petrarch
Partie carrée. See Gautier, Théophile
"Partie de tric-trac, La." *See* Mérimée, Prosper,
 "The Game of Backgammon"
Partiia vede. See Tychyna, Pavlo
Partito Politico Futurista, 9:825b
"Party at Therese's, The." *See* Hugo, Victor,
 "La fête chez Thérèse"
Party in the Country, The. *See* Tieck, Ludwig,
 Die Gesellschaft auf dem Lande
Party Leads, The. *See* Tychyna, Pavlo, *Partiia
 vede*
"Parure, La." *See* Maupassant, Guy de
"Parus." *See* Lermontov, Mikhail Yurievich
"Parusia, I." *See* Elytis, Odysseus, *Maria
 Nephele*
Parzival. See Wolfram von Eschenbach
Pas perdus, Les. See Breton, André
Pascal, Blaise, **3:125a–150b**
 Apollinaire and, 9:898b, 901b
 Chateaubriand and, 5:121b

 Claudel and, 8:472a, 486a
 Copies, 3:148b
 De l'esprit géométrique (The Spirit of
  Geometry), 3:130b–131a, 131b–132a,
  134a
 Descartes and, 3:21b
 Diderot and, 4:483b
 Essay pour les coniques (Essay on Conic
  Sections), 3:126a
 Expériences nouvelles touchant le vide (New
  Experiments Concerning the Vacuum),
  3:126b, 127b
 Fénelon and, 3:262b
 Kosztolányi and, 10:1232a
 Lettres provinciales (*The Provincial Letters*),
  3:129a, 132b–138b
  on books of casuistry, 3:134b–135a
  diversity of forms, 3:137b
  effect of, 3:132b–133a
  geometrical principles in, 3:134a
  on grade, 3:136a
  on intention, 3:135b
  presentation of, 3:137a
  on probable opinions, 3:135a-b
  Voltaire's view on, 3:125a
 Maeterlinck and, 8:142b
 Marya Volkonsky and, 7:1474b
 Mauriac and, 10:1313b–1314a
 Mémorial, 3:145b
 Montaigne and, 2:783a, 786a
 Pensées (Thoughts), 2:785b, 3:129a, 137a,
  138a, 138b–146a
  argument of the wager, 3:141a–143b, 256b
  Chateaubriand's *Génie* and, 5:121b
  dialectical mode of thinking in, 3:144a
  on the dynamics of religious conversion,
   3:143a-b
  editions of, 3:148b
  on Epicureans, 3:140b
  French classicism and, 3:273b
  on human nature, 3:144a-b
  on justice, 3:140a
  La Bruyère and, 3:229a, 255a
  on the Old Testament, 3:144b–145a
  "Ordre," 3:139b, 141a
  on the original sin, 3:144a

on Pascal's ecstatic experience,
3:145b–146a
polar ideas of, 3:139a
response to, 3:147b
on Stoics, 3:140b
on three main classes of people, 3:146b
on three orders of reality, 3:146a
on three powers of knowing, 3:146b–147a
on the three ways leading to faith, 3:143b
title of, 3:138b–139a
"Vanité" and "Misère," 3:139b
Voltaire's *Lettre philosophique* on, 4:373a,
385b–386a
Recueil original, 3:148b
Saint-Exupéry and, 12:2327a
Weil and, 12:2803a, 2803b, 2804a
Yourcenar and, 12:2538b
Zola and, 7:1523a
Pascal, Étienne, 3:125a–126a, 138a
Pascal, Jacqueline, 3:125b, 127a, 128a, 128b,
130a
Pascoaes, Teixeira de. *See* Teixeira de
Pascoaes
Pascoli, Giovanni, **7:1825a–1854b**
Canti di Castelvecchio (Songs of
Castelvecchio), 7:1828a-b, 1843b–1846a
"Il gelsomino notturno" ("The Night
Jasmine"), 7:1844a-b
Latin poetry and, 7:1850b, 1852b
"Castanea" ("The Chestnut"), 7:1828b
Epos (Epic Poetry), 7:1828b
"Fanum vacunae" (The Temple of Vacuna),
7:1851a
Il fanciullino, 7:1833a–1836a, 1841a, 1841b
"Le rane" and, 7:1845b
Poemi conviviali and, 7:1846b
"Il ritorno a San Mauro," 7:1845a–1846a
"La tessitrice" ("The Weaver"), 7:1846a
"Le rane" ("The Frogs"), 7:1845a–1846a
"La grande proletaria si è mossa" (The
Great Proletariat Has Stirred), 7:1829a,
1849b–1850a
"La morte del ricco" (The Death of the Rich
Man), 7:1827b
"La notte di Natale" (Christmas Night),
7:1829a
"La poesia" (Poetry), 7:1835b–1836a

"La voce" (The Voice), 7:1827b
"L'Avvento" (The Accession), 7:1849a
Lyra (Lyric Poetry), 7:1828b
Myricae (Tamarisks), 7:1828b, 1836a–1841a
"Arano" ("Plowing"), 7:1839b–1840a,
1845a
Canti di Castelvecchio and, 7:1843b,
1845a
form, 7:1840b
"Il giorno dei morti" (The Day of the
Dead), 7:1836b
"L'Assiuolo" ("The Horn Owl"),
8:1837b–1838a
Latin poetry and, 7:1850b, 1852b
"L'Orfano" ("The Orphan"),
7:1836b–1837a
"L'Ultima passeggiata" (The Last
Promenade), 7:1838b–1841a, 1845a
"Notte dolorosa" (Sorrowful Night),
7:1838a-b
"Sera d'ottobre" ("October Evening"),
7:1837a
themes of, 7:1836a–1837a
Vergil and, 7:1828a
"Nebbia" ("Fog"), 7:1829b–1830b
Nuovi poemetti (New Short Narrative
Poems), 7:1828b, 1841b
"Pietole," 7:1842a
Odi e inni (Odes and Hymns), 7:1829a,
1847b, 1850b
Poemetti (Short Narrative Poems),
7:1841b–1843b
Canti di Castelvecchio and, 7:1843b
"Digitale purpurea" ("The Purple
Foxglove"), 7:1842b–1843a
editions of, 7:1828b
Gnoli on, 7:1825b
"Le rane" and, 7:1845b
Poemi conviviali (Convivial Poems),
7:1828b, 1846a–1847a
"Gog e Magog" ("Gog and Magog"),
7:1847a
Latin poetry and, 7:1850b
"L'Ultimo viaggio" ("The Last Voyage"),
7:1846b–1847a
"Solon," 7:1846b

Pascoli, Giovanni (*cont.*)
  Poemi del Risorgimento (Poems of the
    Risorgimento), 7:1829a, 1847b
  Poemi italici (Italian Poems), 7:1829a,
    1847b–1848a
    "Paolo Uccello," 7:1847b–1848a
  Primi poemetti (First Short Narrative
    Poems), 7:1828b, 1841b
    "Italy," 7:1842a
    "La canzone del bucato" (The Washing
      Song), 7:1842a
    "Ricordi di un vecchio scolaro" (Memoirs of
      an Old Pupil), 7:1827a
  Scritti vari inediti, 7:1834b
    "Temporale" ("Thunderstorm"), 7:1832b
    "Thallusa" (Tallusa), 7:1829a, 1851a–1852b
    "Veianius," 7:1828a
  Vittorini and, 12:2735b
Pasenow oder die Romantik (*Pasenow; or,
    Romanticism*). *See* Broch, Hermann
Paseo de Buster Keaton, El. See García Lorca,
    Federico
Pasiphaé. See Montherlant, Henry de
Påsk. See Strindberg, August, *Easter*
"Paskhal'nyi krestnyi khod." *See* Solzhenitsyn,
    Aleksandr
Pasqua di Gea. See Pirandello, Luigi
Pasquier, Étienne
  on Montaigne, 2:784b
  on Ronsard, 2:740b
Passage de Milan. See Butor, Michel
"Passagenarbeit." *See* Benjamin, Walter,
    Arcades Project
Passager clandestin, Le. See Simenon,
    Georges
Passengers of Destiny. See Aragon, Louis
"Passant de Prague, Le." *See* Apollinaire,
    Guillaume, *Le flâneur des deux rives*
Passatismo
  in "Futurist Manifesto," 9:809a, 809b, 810b
  manifestations of, 9:799a
  Marinetti and, 9:797b
"Passé." *See* Hugo, Victor
Passé défini, Le. See Cocteau, Jean
Passeggiate africane. See Moravia, Alberto
Passing By. *See* Queneau, Raymond, *En
    passant*

Passing Time. See Butor, Michel, *L'Emploi du
    temps*
Passion
  in Mann's *Magic Mountain*, 9:721a
  in Rousseau, 4:456a-b
  sin and, Augustine on, 1:44a–45a
  Staël's *Essai sur les fictions* on, 5:99b
  see also Love; Sexual passion
Passion. See Greban, Arnoul; Michel, Jean
Passion dans le désert, Une (*The Passion in
    the Desert*). *See* Balzac, Honoré de
Passion of Jesus Christ, Elytis' *The Axion Esti*
    and, 13:2968a
Passion plays, 1:466a–467a, 469a, 469b
"Passion, The." *See* Elytis, Odysseus, *To Axion
    Esti* (*The Axion Esti*), "Ta Pathi"
Passion, Valenciennes. *See* Valenciennes
    Passion
Passion-reason dichotomy, in Foscolo, 5:320b
"Passionate Shepherd to His Love, The." *See*
    Marlowe, Christopher
Passions de l'âme. See Descartes, René
Passions of Psyche and Cupid, The. See La
    Fontaine, Jean de, *Les amours de
    Psyché et de Cupidon*
Passions of the Soul, The. See Descartes,
    René, *Passions de l'âme*
Passivity, in Camus' *The Stranger*,
    13:3060b–3061a
Past Tense. See Cocteau, Jean, *Le passé défini*
Past, the. *See* History
"Past, The." *See* Hugo, Victor, "Passé"
Pasternak, Boris, **10:1591a–1617b**
  A Safe-Conduct (*Okhrannaia gramota*),
    10:1602a–1604a
    Mayakovsky's death and, 10:1594b
    Sketch for an Autobiography and,
      10:1613b
  Above the Barriers (*Poverkh bar'erov*),
    10:1598a
  "Bezliub'e" ("Without Love"), as precursor to
    Doctor Zhivago, 10:1600a
  Bliznets v tuchakh (Twin in the Clouds),
    10:1598a
  composition of, 10:1593a
  Blok and, 9:985b, 986b

Deviat'sot piatyi god (The Year 1905), 10:1601b–1602a

"Deviat'sot piatyi god" (The Year 1905), 10:1592b, 1601b–1602a

"Lieutenant Schmidt," 10:1602a

Doctor Zhivago, 6:986b, 10:1609b–1613a

  Blok and, 9:986b

  model for Lara in, 10:1593b

  Nobel Prize for, 10:1597a–b

  Second Birth and, 10:1604b

  Stalinist Terror denounced in, 10:1595b

  The Last Summer and, 10:1606a

  women in, 10:1592a

  writing and publication of, 10:1596a–1597a

Early Trains (*Na rannikh poyezdakh*), 10:1608a–1609a

  "On Early Trains," 10:1608a–b

  "The Old Park," 10:1608b

  "The War Months," 10:1608b

  "To the Memory of Marina Tsvetaeva," 10:1608b

Hamlet, 10:1607a–b

I Remember: Sketch for an Autobiography (*Avtobiograficheskii ocherk*), 10:1613a–1615a

  Tsvetaeva promoted by, 10:1596a

last years of, 10:1521a

literary celebrity, 11:1893b

"Liudi i polozheniia" ("People and Situations"), 9:985b

on Mandelshtam's doomsday poetry, 10:1641a

"Marburg," rejected love in, 10:1593a

Mayakovsky and, 11:1835a, 1856a

My Sister, Life (*Sestra moia-zhizn'*), 10:1598b–1600a

  "Summer," 10:1599a

  When the Skies Clear and, 10:1615a

"Neskol'ko polozhenii" ("Some Tenets"), poetics of, 10:1604a

Rasskazy (Stories), 10:1600b–1601a

  "Apellesova cherta" ("The Apelles Mark"), 10:1600b

  "Pis'ma iz Tuly" ("Letters from Tula"), 10:1600b

"Vozdushnye puti" ("Aerial Ways"), 10:1600b

"Zhenia's Childhood" ("Detstvo Liuvers"), 10:1593b, 1600b–1601a

Rilke and, 9:768a

Second Birth (*Vtoroe rozhdenie*), 10:1604a–1605b

  "Death of a Poet," 10:1594b, 1605a

  "Ne volnuisia, ne plach', ne trudi . . ." ("Don't fret, don't cry, don't pine . . ."), 10:1605a

  "O, znal by ia, chto tak byvaet . . ." ("Oh, had I known that it happens so . . ."), 10:1605a

  "Waves," 10:1605a

Spektorskii

  The Last Summer and, 10:1606a–b

  Tsvetaeva's influence on, 10:1594a

Stalin's questions about Mandelshtam to, 10:1646a

The Blind Beauty (*Slepaia krasavitsa*), 10:1615b–1616b

The Childhood of Luvers, 11:1886b

The Last Summer (*Povest'*), 10:1605b–1606b

  women in, 10:1592a

The Sublime Malady (*Vysokaia bolezn'*), 10:1601a–b

The Vast Earth (*Zemnoi prostor*), 10:1609a–b

Themes and Variations (*Temy i variatsii*), 10:1598a–b

  "Illness," 10:1598b

  "The Break," 10:1598b

  "Themes and Variations," 10:1598a–b

translations by, 10:1606b–1608a

Tsvetaeva and, 11:1739b, 1740b, 1742a, 1743a, 1747b

"Uezd v tylu" ("A District Behind the Lines"), model for Zhenia in, 10:1593b

"Veter (Chetyre otryvka o Bloke)" ("The Wind [Four Fragments About Blok]"), 9:986b

the West and, 10:1620b

When the Skies Clear (*Kogda razguliaetsia*), 10:1615a–b

  publication of, 10:1613a–b

"Zhenshchiny v detstve" ("Women in [My] Childhood"), women in, 10:1592a

Pasternak, Leonid Osipovich
  Boris Pasternak's letter on *Doctor Zhivago* to, 10:1610a
  disagreements with Scriabin, 10:1592a-b
  social standing of, 10:1591b
"Pasteurs et troupeaux." *See* Hugo, Victor
Pastiche, principle of (Musil), 9:941a-b
Pastor fido. See Guarini, Giambattista
Pastoral
  Dinesen and, 10:1297b
  Jiménez's *Platero and I* as, 9:997a
  Manzoni's disenchantment with, 5:371b
  Trakl and, 10:1418b
"Pastoral." *See* Ronsard, Pierre de, "Bergerie"
Pastoral novel, Cela and, 13:3110b–3111a
Pastoral poetry
  Camoëns on, 2:759b
  Christianization of, 2:903b
  medieval, 2:903a–905b
  Renaissance, **2:899a–926b**
    classical sources and predecessors of, 2:900a–903a
    culture and, 2:899a–900a
    in England, 2:914b–916a, 920a, 923a-b
    in France, 2:911a–912b, 923b–924b
    in Italy, 2:906a–910b, 916a–919b, 920b–921b
    lyric, 2:905b–916a
    medieval sources and predecessors of, 2:903a–905b
    in northern Europe, 2:914b
    Petrarch on, 2:484a
    romance, 2:920b–924b
    in Spain, 2:912b–914a, 921b–923a
    themes, 2:485b
  of Tasso, 2:797a–798a
  Trakl's "To the Boy Elis" and, 10:1418b
  Walther and, 1:294a-b
Pastoral romance
  Cervantes and, 2:820b, 822a, 828b–829a, 830a
  in France, 9:923b–924a
  Lope de Vega and, 2:849a
  in Spain, 2:921b–923a
Pastoral Symphony, The. See Gide, André

Pastoral Tragedy in Three Acts. See Valle-Inclán, Ramón del, *Tragedia pastoril en tres actos*
"Pastorale." *See* Tasso, Torquato, *Aminta*
Pastorales. See Jiménez, Juan Ramón
"Pastorcico, El." *See* Juan de la Cruz, San, *Cántico espiritual*
Pastorela
  Colin and, 1:181a
  as genre in troubadour poetry, 1:167a
Pastores de Belén, Los. See Lope de Vega
Pastourelle
  influence on Renaissance pastoral, 2:903b
  Jeu de Robin et Marion and, 1:460b–461a
'Pataphysics
  College of 'Pataphysics and, 9:685b–686a
  in Jarry
    Doctor Faustroll, 9:676a–677a
    "Guignol," 9:671a
    Heb cycle, 9:670a
  Queneau and, 12:2532a-b
Pátečníci. See Friday Circle
Patente, La. See Pirandello, Luigi
Paternity, dubious, in Maupassant's works, 7:1775a, 1777a–1778a
Path of the Conquistadors, The. See Gumilev, Nikolai, *Put' konkvistadorov*
Path to the Nest of Spiders, The. See Calvino, Italo
Path to Paradise, The. *See* Krleža, Miroslav, *Put u raj*
Pathelin, 1:472a-b
Pathetic fallacy, in Klopstock, 4:520a, 521b–522a
"Pathi, Ta." *See* Elytis, Odysseus, *To Axion Esti*
Patmore, Coventry, translated by Claudel, 8:489a
"Patmos." *See* Elytis, Odysseus, *Maria Nephele*; Hölderlin, Friedrich
Patrañuelo, El. See Juan de Timoneda
Patricius (father of Augustine), 1:29a, 38b, 39a
Patrie en danger, La (The Fatherland in Danger). See Goncourt, Edmond Louis Antoine and Jules Alfred Huot de
Patriotism
  in Blok's poetry, 9:979a–985b

in Carducci's poetry, 7:1510b–1511a, 1513b
in Corneille's *Cinna*, 3:42b, 43a
in D'Annunzio's writings, 8:191b–192a
in Foscolo, 5:320b–321b
in Gombrowicz, 12:2581b–2582b
Kleist and, 5:306a-b
in Klopstock's plays, 4:523a–524b
of Marinetti, 9:805a, 824a, 825a
in Olesha's "A List of Assets," 11:2246a-b
in Pascoli, 7:1847a-b
    "La grande proletaria si è mossa,"
        7:1849b–1850a
Schnitzler's view of, 8:106a-b
see also Nationalism
Patronage
    in 17th-century France, 3:319b
    Alfieri's opposition to, 4:673a-b
    medieval satire and, 1:351a
    Walther and, 1:288a-b, 304b–306a
    Wolfram and, 1:263a-b
Pattes de mouche, Les. See Sardou, Victorien
Pauken und Trompeten. See Brecht, Bertolt,
    Trumpets and Drums
Paul et Virginie. See Saint Pierre, Bernardin
    de
Paul, Jean, Hesse and, 9:845b, 846a, 849b
"Paul les Oiseaux ou la place de l'amour"
    ("Paul the Birds; or, The Place of
    Love"). *See* Artaud, Antonin, *The
    Umbilicus of Limbo* (*L'Ombilic des
    limbes*)
Paul, St.
    Augustine and, 1:38b, 43b
    Cavafy and, 8:206a
    Luther and, 2:672a-b
"Paul Verlaine et les poètes symbolistes et
    decadents" ("Paul Verlaine and the
    Symbolist and Decadent Poets"). *See*
    Lemaître, Jules
"Paula." *See* Södergran, Edith
Pauli, Johannes, *Schimpf und Ernst* (Wit and
    Solemnity), 2:952b
Paulinus of Nola, on Prudentius, 1:18b
Paulus, Sophie, 5:84a
Paumgartten, Charlotte von, Grillparzer's *Das
    Kloster bei Sendomir* and, 5:435b
Paustovsky, Konstantin, Babel and, 11:1892a

Pautasso, Sergio, on Vittorini, 12:2739a,
    2741b, 2746a
Pauvre Bitos. See Anouilh, Jean, *Poor Bitos*
"Pauvres gens, Les." *See* Hugo, Victor
"Pauvres à l'église, Les." *See* Rimbaud, Arthur
Pavarotti, Luciano, 8:530b
Pavese, Cesare, **12:2759a–2784b**
    Among Women Only (*Tra donne sole*),
        12:2780b–2781b
    Burning Brand: Diaries 1935-1950 (*Il
        mestiere di vivere*), 12:2759a, 2765a-b,
        2767b
    Calvino and, 13:3261b–3262a
    Dialogues with Leucò (*Dialoghi con Leucò*),
        12:2759b, 2761b
    Ginzburg and, 13:3137a, 3141a, 3152a
    Lavorare stanca (*Hard Labor: Poems*),
        12:2760b, 2764a, 2764b
    Notte di festa, "Terra d'esilio" ("Land of
        Exile"), 12:2766b, 2768a
    Prima che il gallo canti (Before the Cock
        Crows), 12:2759a, 2776b
    Silone and, 12:2303b
    The Beach (*La spiaggia*), 12:2767b,
        2774a–2775a
    The Beautiful Summer (*La bella estate*),
        12:2759a, 2772a–2774a
    The Comrade (*Il compagno*),
        12:2775b–2776b
    The Devil in the Hills (*Il diavolo sulle
        colline*), 12:2767b, 2777a–2780b
    The Harvesters (*Paesi tuoi*), 12:2767b,
        2770a–2772b
    The House on the Hill (*La casa in collina*),
        12:2776b–2779a
    The Moon and the Bonfires (*La luna e i
        falò*), 12:2759a, 2759b, 2764b, 2776b,
        2781b–2784a
    The Political Prisoner (*Il carcere*), 12:2766b,
        2767b, 2768b–2770a, 2776b, 2777b
    Vittorini and, 12:2743a, 2755a
Pavura de los condes de Carrión. See
    Quevedo, Francisco de
"Pays de Cocagne." *See* Baudelaire, Charles
Paysage de répons. See Butor, Michel
Paysan de Paris, Le. See Aragon, Louis
Paysans, Les. See Balzac, Honoré de

Paz en la guerra. See Unamuno, Miguel de

Paz, Octavio

    Jiménez and, 9:1011b–1012a

    on Ortega y Gasset, 9:1120a

Pazzi Conspiracy, The. See Alfieri, Vittorio

"Peace I do not find, and I have no wish to
make war." *See* Petrarch, *Canzoniere*,
"Pace non trovo et non ò da far guerra"

Peace, theme of, in works of Prudentius, 1:11a

Peace in War. See Unamuno, Miguel de, *Paz
en la guerra*

Peaceful Departure. *See* Ady, Endre, "A békés
eltávozás"

Peacock, The. *See* Aymé, Marcel, "Le paon"

Pearl image, in Arp, 10:1380a–1381a

Pearls and Gold. See Andersen, Hans
Christian

"Pearls, The." *See* Dinesen, Isak

Peasant and the Farm Laborer, The. See
Krylov, Ivan Andreyevich

Peasant in His Retreat, The. See Lope de Vega

Peasant literature

    downfall of Petrine Russia and peasant
poets, 10:1620a-b

    German tradition of, 6:929a

"Peasant Marei, The." *See* Dostoevsky, Feodor

"Peasant Wives." *See* Chekhov, Anton, "Baby"

Peasants

    Aymé's satire of, 12:2438b–2440b

    in Balzac's *Les paysans*, 7:1532a-b

    in Chekhov's works, 7:1868b–1869a

    in Deschamps' satire, 1:362b–364a

    in Ferreira de Castro's *A lã e a neve*,
11:2153b–2154a

    in Maupassant's works, 7:1772b–1774a

    revolts

        Hauptmann's plays about, 8:152b,
156a–157a

        Luther and, 2:682a-b

        Portugal, 1846-1848, 11:2145b

    Sand's interest in customs of, 6:829a-b

    in Tolstoy's works, 7:1488b–1489a

    Verga and, 7:1543a, 1547a

    in Zola's works

        Germinal, 7:1529a–1530b

        La terre, 7:1531b–1533a

    see also Folk song and folklore

Peasants, The. See Balzac, Honoré de, *Les
paysans*

"Peasants, The." *See* Chekhov, Anton,
"Muzhiki"

Peau de chagrin, La. See Balzac, Honoré de

Peau-Asie. See Vitrac, Roger

Pečat (The Stamp), Krleža and, 11:1821a-b,
1828b

Pecham, John, vs. Aquinas, 1:418a, 418b,
423b, 426b

Pechat' i revolutsiia (Russian journal), Babel's
articles in, 11:1889b

Pecorone, Il. See Ser Giovanni Fiorentino

"Peculiarities of a Fair-Haired Girl." *See* Eça
de Queiroz, José Maria, "Singularidades
duma rapariega loura"

Pederasty

    of Montherlant, 11:1920a–1921a, 1922a-b

    of Peyrefitte, 11:1920a, 1920b

    see also Homosexuality

Pedigree. See Simenon, Georges

Pedro I of Castile, king, in Mérimée's works,
6:765a, 765b

Pedro de Souza e Holstein, Dom, 5:93a

Pedro de Urdemalas. See Cervantes, Miguel de

Peer Gynt. See Ibsen, Henrik

Péguy, Charles

    Bergson and, 8:45a, 61a, 64b

    Claudel and, 8:484b

    Proust and, 8:547a

*Peintres des fêtes galantes: Watteau, Lancret,
Pater, Boucher, Les. See* Blanc, Charles

Peinture au défi, Le. See Aragon, Louis

Peire Cardenal, 1:178a

    "Aquesta gens, cant son en lur gaieza"
("These people, when they are in good
spirits"), 1:371b–372a

Pelagius, Jesuits and, 3:133b

Pelant, Karel, in Hašek's *Politické a sociální
dějiny*, 9:1104a

Pelayo, Marcelino Menéndez, Lope de Vega's
plays and, 2:856a-b, 859b

Peletier, Jacques, 2:726a, 742a

Pelikanen (The Pelican). *See* Strindberg,
August

Pelléas et Mélisande. See Maeterlinck, Maurice

"Pellegrinaggio." *See* Ungaretti, Giuseppe, *Allegria di naufragi*

Pellegrini, Isabella, 5:101b

Pellico, Silvio, *Le mie prigioni* (*My Prisons*), compared to *Uncle Tom's Cabin*, 5:370a

PEN Club, Heinrich Mann and, 8:537b

"Penal Colony, The." *See* Kafka, Franz

Pendu de Saint-Pholien, Le. See Simenon, Georges

Penitential Psalms. *See* Petrarch, *Psalmi poenitentiales*

Pensaci, Giacomino! See Pirandello, Luigi

Pensando en España. See Azorín

Pensée et le mouvant, la. See Bergson, Henri, *The Creative Mind*

Pensées. See Pascal, Blaise

Pensées d'août. See Sainte-Beuve, Charles-Augustin

Pensées philosophiques. See Diderot, Denis

Pensées sur l'interprétation de la nature. See Diderot, Denis

Pensieri. See Leopardi, Giacomo

"Pensiero dominante, Il." *See* Leopardi, Giacomo, "The Dominant Thought"

Pentamerone, Il. See Basile, Giambattista, *Lo cunto de li cunti*

"Pente de la rêverie, La." *See* Hugo, Victor

Penthesilea. See Kleist, Heinrich von

"Pénz és karnevál." *See* Ady, Endre

People of Hemsö, The. See Strindberg, August, *Hemsöborna*

"People and the Intelligentsia, The." *See* Blok, Alexander, "Narod i intelligentsiia"

People and Life. See Ehrenburg, Ilya

People of Seldwyla, The. See Keller, Gottfried

"People and Situations." *See* Pasternak, Boris, "Liudi i polozheniia"

People, The. *See* Azorín, *Pueblo*

People, The. See Michelet, Jules

Pepel. See Bely, Andrey

Pequenos mundos e velhas civilizações. See Ferreira de Castro, José Maria

Per Abbat, *Poema de mio Cid* authorship and, 1:127b

Per Amica Silentia Lunae. See Yeats, William Butler

"Per un 'Omaggio a Rimbaud'." *See* Montale, Eugenio, *The Storm and Other Things* (*La bufera e altro*), "For an 'Homage to Rimbaud'"

Pera ap ton iskio ton kyparission. See Ritsos, Yannis

Perception
    Augustine on, 1:40a
    Bergson's view of, 8:49a–51a, 52b–53a, 54b
    Sartre and, 12:2589b–2590a

Perception, sensual, in Simenon's works, 12:2500b–2501a, 2502a

Perceptions of a Christian. See Wieland, Christoph Martin, *Empfindungen eines Christen*

Percy, Thomas
    Fontane and, 6:1304a
    Reliques of Ancient English Poetry
        Chénier's aesthetics compared to, 4:707b
        Herder and, 4:641b–642a

"Père, Le." *See* Maupassant, Guy de

Père de famille, Le. See Diderot, Denis

Père Goriot, Le. See Balzac, Honoré de

Père humilié, Le. See Claudel, Paul

"Père Milon, Le." *See* Maupassant, Guy de

Père prodigue, Un. See Dumas fils, Alexandre

Pereda, José María, Blasco Ibáñez and, 8:357b, 359a

Peredur, 1:143b

Peregrino en su patria, El. See Lope de Vega, *The Pilgrim in His Native Land*

Peregrinus Proteus. See Wieland, Christoph Martin, *Die geheime Geschichte des Philosophen Peregrinus Proteus*

"Perekhod cherez Zbruch." *See* Babel, Isaac

Péret, Benjamin, Breton and, 11:1954b

Pérez, Alonso, *Segunda parte de la Diana* (The Second Part of the Diana), influence on pastoral romance, 2:922a, 922b–923b

Pérez de Ayala, Ramón
    Group at the Service of the Republic, 9:1146a
    social criticism, 9:1121b

Pérez de Oliva, Hernán, 2:755b

Pérez Galdós, Benito, **7:1597a–1618b**
    Angel Guerra, 7:1613a, 1615b, 1616b
    Azorín and, 9:644b, 645a

Pérez Galdós, Benito (*cont.*)
on Baroja, 9:592b
Blasco Ibáñez and, 8:357b, 375a
Doña Perfecta, 7:1605a–1606b, 1614a
El amigo Manso (My Friend Manso),
    7:1609a-b
El caballero encantado (The Enchanted
    Knight), 7:1615b
Electra (play), 7:1616b
Episodios nacionales (National Episodes),
    7:1602a–1604a, 1604a–1605a, 1613a,
    1615b, 9:610b
  La guerra carlista and, 8:338a-b
Fortunata y Jacinta, 7:1598a, 1610b–1613a,
    1614a
Gloria, 7:1605a, 1608b
Halma, 7:1614b
La de Bringas (The Bringas Woman),
    7:1609b–1610a, 1614a
La desheredada (*The Disinherited Lady*),
    7:1607a–1609a, 1615b
La fontana de oro (The Fountain of Gold),
    7:1600b–1601b
La incognita (The Unknown One),
    7:1612b–1613a
La segunda casaca (The Turncoat),
    7:1604b–1605a
Lo prohibido (That Which Is Prohibited),
    7:1610a-b
Memorias de un desmemoriado (Memoirs of
    a Man Without Memory), 7:1597a-b
Miau, 7:1612b
Misericordia (Charity), 7:1614b–1615b
naturalistic novels of, 7:1606b–1607b,
    1609b–1610b
Nazarín, 7:1614a-b
  Luis Buñuel film of, 7:1617a
  Nazarín as Christlike figure, 8:296b
novelas de santidad (novels of sanctity),
    7:1614a–1615a
novelas españolas contemporáneas,
    7:1608b–1609a
Ortega y Gasset and, 9:1122b
Realidad (Reality) (novel), 7:1612b–1613a
Realidad (*Reality*) (play), 7:1615b, 1616b
Tormento, 7:1609b, 1615b

Torquemada series novels, 7:1613b–1614a
Tristana, 7:1613a-b, 1616a
"Perezoriuiut zori." *See* Tychyna, Pavlo, *Pluh*
Perfectibility, historical, Staël on, 5:96a, 96b,
    105a, 108a
Perfecting of a Love, The. See Musil, Robert,
    Vereinigungen
Perfume, as motif in Symbolist poetry, 9:749b
"Perhaps Some Morning, Walking in a
    Vitreous, Clear Air." *See* Montale,
    Eugenio, *Cuttlefish Bones* (*Ossi di
    seppia*), "Forse un mattino, andando in
    un'aria di vetro"
"Peri Politas." *See* Elytis, Odysseus, *To
    photodendro kai i dekati tetarti omorfia*
Peribáñez y el comendador de Ocaña
    (*Peribáñez and the Knight Commander
    of Ocaña*). *See* Lope de Vega
Périgord, idealized in Fénelon's works, 3:263a
"Perimenontas tous varvarous." *See* Cavafy,
    Constantine
Peripezie. See Reversals
Periphrasis, in Laforgue's *The Imitation of Our
    Lady of the Moon*, 7:1897b
Peristephanon. See Prudentius, *Liber
    Peristephanon*
Perjury, Augustine on, 1:49a
Perlesvaus, Gawain in, 1:158a
Perloff, Marjorie
    on Marinetti, 9:815b, 820b
    The Futurist Moment, 9:803b
Perpetual motion, Croce on, 8:317b
Perpetual Motion. *See* Aragon, Louis, *Le
    mouvement perpétuel*
Perrault, Charles, 8:139a
    Boileau and, 3:184a
    Le siècle de Louis XIV, Boileau and, 3:180b
Perrichon's Journey. See Labiche, Eugène, *Le
    voyage de M. Perrichon*
Perrin, Reine Sainte-Marie, 8:479b
Perro de hortelano, El. See Lope de Vega
Perros, George, Butor and, 13:3307a
Perruchot, Henri, on Montherlant, 11:1934a
Perse, Saint-John, **10:1429a–1452b**
    Anabasis, publication of, 10:1436a-b,
        1438a–1439b

Birds (*Oiseaux*), 10:1448b–1449a

"Celebration of a Childhood" ("Pour fêter une enfance") group of poems, 10:1431b–1432a

Chant pour un équinoxe (*Song for an Equinox*), 10:1449a–1451b

"Chant par celle qui fut là" ("Sung by One Who Was There"), 10:1449a-b

"Chant pour un équinoxe," 10:1449b–1450b

Chronique, 10:1432a, 1447b–1448b

Éloges (*Éloges and Other Poems*)
  interest in, 10:1437a-b
  new edition of, 10:1439a
  poetry after, 10:1433a
  publication of, 10:1431b, 1433b, 1434a
  recognition from, 10:1438b

Exile (*Exil*), 10:1442b–1443a, 1443b

"Friendship of the Prince" ("Amité du Prince"), 10:1433a-b

La gloire des rois (The Glory of Kings), 10:1433a-b

"Narrow Are the Vessels" ("Étroits sont les vaisseaux"), 10:1446b

"Nocturne," 10:1450a-b

"Pictures for Crusoe" ("Images à Crusoé"), 10:1431a, 1438b

"Poem to a Foreign Lady" ("Poème à l'étrangère"), 10:1442b, 1443a-b

Rains (*Pluies*), 10:1432b, 1442b, 1443b–1444a

"Recitation to the Glory of a Queen" ("Récitation à la gloire d'une Reine"), 10:1433a-b

Seamarks (*Amers*), 10:1436b, 1446a–1447a, 1450b

"Sécheresse" ("Drought"), 10:1450b–1451a

Snows (*Neiges*), 10:1432b, 1444a-b

Winds (*Vents*), 10:1432b, 1444b–1446a

Persécuté persécuteur (The Persecuted and the Persecutor). *See* Aragon, Louis

Persefoni (Persephone). *See* Ritsos, Yannis, *Tetarti dhiastasi*

Perseus, in Lampedusa's *The Leopard*, 11:2012a

Persian Bride, The. *See* Goldoni, Carlo, *La sposa persiana*

Persian Letters, The. See Montesquieu, Charles-Louis de Secondat, baron de

Persians, The. See Seferis, George

Persiles y Sigismunda. See Cervantes, Miguel de, *The Trials of Persiles and Sigismunda*

Persius
  on Horace, 1:351a
  Marcabru and, 1:369a

Personification
  allegory and, 1:322a–324a
  in classical literature, 1:5b–6a, 366b–367a
  in Dante's *Vita nuova*, 1:441a
  in medieval satire, 1:369b
  in Prudentius' *Symmachus*, 1:11b
  see also Allegory; Animal characters

Perspectivism, in Ortega y Gasset's writing, 9:1128b–1129a

Pertharite, roi des Lombards. See Corneille, Pierre

"Pervaia liubov." *See* Babel, Isaac

Perverted Sensuality. *See* Baroja, Pío, *La sensualidad pervertida*

Pervoe svidanie. See Bely, Andrey

"1 ianvarie 1924." *See* Mandelshtam, Osip

Pesanteur et la grâce, La. See Weil, Simone, *Gravity and Grace*

Pescara's Temptation. See Meyer, Conrad Ferdinand, *Die Versuchung des Pescara*

Pèsenerfs, Le. See Artaud, Antonin, *The Nerve Meter*

"Pesenka." *See* Akhmatova, Anna, "Folk Song"

Peshchera. See Zamyatin, Yevgeny Ivanovich

Peshkov, Aleksey Maksimovich. *See* Gorky, Maxim

"Pesn' Ada." *See* Blok, Alexander

"Pesn' miriazia." *See* Khlebnikov, Velimir

"Pesnia poslednei vstrechi." *See* Akhmatova, Anna, "Song of the Last Meeting"

Pesnia sud'by. See Blok, Alexander

"Pesnya pro tsarya Ivana Vasilevicha." *See* Lermontov, Mikhail Yurievich

"Peso." *See* Ungaretti, Giuseppe

Pessanha, Camilo
  Baudelaire and, 10:1483b, 1485a
  Pessoa and, 10:1483b, 1484a, 1484b–1485a

Pessimism
    of Beckett, 13:3034b
    in Blasco Ibáñez' *The Cabin*, 8:376a, 376b
    of Grillparzer, 5:422b
    "heroic," of Kazantzakis, 9:1071a-b
    "historical," 5:551b, 559a
    in Laforgue's "Nostalgia for the Prehistoric,"
        7:1893a
    of Leopardi, 5:541a, 546b, 551b, 559a-b
    in Maupassant's works, 7:1774b
    in Mérimée's works, 6:752a, 758b
    of Schopenhauer, 5:398a, 402a–403a,
        414b–415a
    of Simon, 13:3025b–3026a, 3026b–3027a,
        3032b, 3033b
    in Svevo's novels, 8:84a–86a
    of Vigny, 5:447a
    Voltaire on, 4:386a
    see also Ecstatic pessimism
Pessoa, Fernando, **10:1475a–1495b**
    A invasão dos judeus (The Invasion of the
        Jews), 10:1481a
    heteronyms of, 11:2148
    importance of, 7:1683a
    Livro do desassossego (Book of Disquiet),
        10:1476b, 1492a–1493b
    Mensagem (Message), 10:1477b–1478a,
        1480a-b, 1488b
    "Saudação a Walt Whitman" ("Salute to
        Walt Whitman"), 10:1491a-b
    35 Sonnets, 10:1489a-b
Peste, Le. See Camus, Albert, *The Plague*
Pestilence in literature. *See* Plague in
    literature
Pétain, Henri Philippe, Valéry and, 8:584a
Peter I the Great, czar of Russia
    Akhmatova's view of, 10:1532b
    in Mickiewicz's poetry, 5:622a-b
    in Pushkin's works, 5:669a–670b, 675b
Peter Camenzind. See Hesse, Hermann
Peter of Gaveston, 1:370a
Peter of Hibernia, 1:410b
Peter Lombard
    Dante and, 1:433b
    Sententiae in IV libris distinctae (The Four
        Books of the Sentences), 1:407a-b,
        412a-b

"Peter and Rosa." *See* Dinesen, Isak
Peter Schlemihl. See Chamisso, Adelbert von
Peterburg. See Bely, Andrey
"Peterburg" Belogo. See Ivanov-Razumnik,
    V. R., *Belyjs "Peterburg"*
Petersburg. See Bely, Andrey, *Peterburg*
"Petersburg Tale." *See* Akhmatova, Anna
"Petit Cénacle, Le," Gautier in, 6:1034b
"Petit coq noir, Le." *See* Aymé, Marcel, *The
    Wonderful Farm*
Petit de Julleville, L., 1:464b
Petit homme d'Arkangelsk, Le. See Simenon,
    Georges
"Petit poisson et le pêcheur, Le." *See* La
    Fontaine, Jean de, *Fables*
Petit prince, Le. See Saint-Exupéry, Antoine de
Petit saint, Le. See Simenon, Georges
"Petite auto, La." *See* Apollinaire, Guillaume,
    Calligrammes
Petite Bourgeoisie. *See* Vittorini, Elio, *Piccola
    borghesia*
Petite Fadette, La. See Sand, George, *Little
    Fadette*
Petite Molière, La. See Anouilh, Jean, and
    Barrault, Jean-Louis
"Petite Roque, La." *See* Maupassant, Guy de
Petite sirène, La. See Yourcenar, Marguerite
"Pétition." *See* Laforgue, Jules
Petits châteaux de Bohème. See Nerval, Gérard
    de
Petits maîtres, Les. See Lesage, Alain-René
Petnikov, Grigorii, Khlebnikov and, 10:1336b,
    1338a-b
Petőfi, Sándor
    Ady and, 9:860a, 864b, 874b
    Az apostol (The Apostle), Ady's *Margita élni
        akar* and, 9:873b
Petr-le-Letton. See Simenon, Georges
Petrarch, **2:475a–507b**
    "Ad se ipsum" ("To Himself"), 2:478b
    Africa, 2:479b, 480a, 480b–482b, 496a
    Alfieri and, 4:663b, 670b, 671b
    "Amor pastorius" ("The Amorous
        Shepherd"), 2:484b
    "Argus," 2:484b
    Ariosto and, 2:620b
    on Aristotle, 2:488a

Blok and, 9:969b

Boccaccio and, 2:509b–510a, 527b–528b, 529a-b

on the Griselda story, 2:526b, 528a

Bucolicum carmen (Bucolic Song), 2:484a–485b

Camoëns and, 2:747a, 750a, 750b, 751a. 2.752b, 758a

cancioneiros and, 2:753a

canzone form of, 5:555b

Canzoniere, 2:475a-b, 479b, 483b, 492b–502b

"A qualunque animale alberga in terra" ("For whatever animals dwell on earth"), 2:496a

"Anima che diverse cose tante" ("Soul, who see so many different things"), 2:497a

ballads, sonnets, and madrigals, 2:500b

"Benedetto sia 'l giorno" ("Blessed be the day"), 2:502a-b

canzoni and sestinas, 2:500b–501a

"Chi vuol veder quantunque po Natura" ("Whoever wishes to see"), 2:496b

"Chiare fresche et dolci acque" ("Clear, fresh, sweet waters"), 2:498a

classical sources, 2:493a-b

"Erano i capei d'oro a l'aura sparsi" ("Her golden hair was loosed to the breeze"), 2:495a, 496a-b

"Giovane donna sotto un verde lauro" ("A youthful lady under a green laurel"), 2:499b

habitus, modification of, 2:498a-b

"I' vo piangendo i miei passati tempi" ("I go weeping for my past time"), 2:495b–496a

"In qual parte del Ciel" ("In what part of Heaven"), 2:496b

influence, 2:504a-b

"Io son sì stanco" ("I am so weary"), 2:502a

"Italia mia" ("My Italy"), 2:494b–495a

"La vita fugge et non s'arresta un'ora" ("Life flees and does not stop an hour"), 2:495b, 499b–500a

"L'Aura celeste che 'n quel verde lauro" ("The heavenly breeze that breathes in that green laurel," 2:497a

laurel imagery, 2:496b–497a

"Li angeli eletti et l'anime beate" ("The elect angels and blessed souls"), 2:495b

"Mie venture al venir son tarde et pigre" ("My good fortune is late and slow in coming"), 2:502a

"Nel dolce tempo de la prima etade" ("In the sweet time of my first age"), 2:498b

"Oimè il bel viso" ("Alas the lovely face"), 2:495b

"Pace non trovo e non ò da far guerra" ("Peace I do not find, and I have no wish to make war"), as prototype, 2:751a

"Pace non trovo et non ò da far guerra" ("Peace I do not find, and I have no wish to make war"), 2:501b

"Padre del Ciel, dopo i perduti giorni" ("Father of Heaven, after the lost days"), 2:497a-b

"Quando il soave mio fido conforto" ("When my gentle, faithful comforter"), 2:497a

"Rotta è l'alta colonna e'l verde lauro" ("Broken are the high column and the green laurel"), 2:495b

"S'amor non è" ("If it is not love"), 2:502a, 504a

"Se 'l pensier che mi strugge" ("If the care that torments me"), 2:498a

"Solo et pensoso i più deserti campi" ("Alone and filled with care"), 2:498b–499a

as source for Mickiewicz, 5:614b

"Spirito gentil" ("Noble spirit"), 2:494b

"Standomi un giorno solo a la fenestra" ("Being one day alone at the window"), 2:500a, 501b

structural devices, 2:493b–494a, 500a–501b

thematic axes, 2:495a

translations, 2:503b

"Tutto 'l dì piango" ("All the day I weep"), 2:498b

Petrarch (*cont.*)
  Canzoniere (*cont.*)
    use of *adynata*, 2:502a
    "Voglia mi sprona" ("Desire spurs me"),
      2:498a
    "Voi ch'ascoltate" ("You who hear"),
      2:494a-b
    "Zefiro torna" ("Zephyrus returns"), 2:499a
  "Conflictatio" ("The Conflict"), 2:485b
  De gestis Caesaris (On the Deeds of
    Caesar), 2:480a
  "De obedentia ac fide uxoria mythologia"
    ("Story About Wifely Obedience and
    Fidelity"), 2:528a
  De otio religioso (On Religious Idleness),
    2:483b
  De remediis utriusque fortunae (On
    Remedies for Both Kinds of Fortune),
    2:484a, 485b, 486b–487a
  De sui ipsius et multorum ignorantia (*On
    His Own Ignorance and That of Many
    Others*), 2:479a-b, 484a, 487b–488a
  De viris illustribus (On Illustrious Men),
    2:480a-b
  De vita solitaria (*On The Solitary Life*),
    2:484a, 485b–486b
  "Di pensier in pensier, di monte in monte"
    ("From thought to thought, from
    mountain to mountain"), 2:483b
  "Divortium" ("Separation"), 2:484b–485a
  Epistolae metricae (Metrical Letters), 2:484a,
    490a
  Epistolae seniles (Letters of Old Age),
    2:484a, 489a, 489b–490a
    on Boccaccio's *Decameron*, 2:527b–528a
  Epistolae variae (Various Letters), 2:478b,
    490a
  Foscolo and, 5:319b
  French culture and, 2:694a
  French poetry and, 2:729a
  "Galatea," 2:485b
  in George's *Der Teppich*, 8:462a
  "Grazie ch'a pochi il Ciel largo destina"
    ("Graces that generous Heaven allots to
    few"), as prototype, 2:752a
  I trionfi (*The Triumphs*), 2:491a–492b, 503a,
    515b

  King Seleucus and, 2:756b
  translations, 2:503b
influence, 2:502b–505a
  on Renaissance pastoral poetry, 2:904a-b
Invectiva contra eum qui maledixit Italiae
  (Invective Against Him Who Slandered
  Italy), 2:484a, 487b
Invectiva contra medicum (Invective Against
  a Doctor), 2:484a, 487a
*Invectiva contra quendam magni status
  hominem sed nullius scientiae aut
  virtutis* (Invective Against a Certain
  Man of High Status But of No
  Knowledge or Excellence), 2:484a, 487b
Italian works, 2:490a–502b
Itinerarium Syriacum (Voyage to the Holy
  Land), 2:484a, 485b–486a, 488b
Latin works, 2:479b–490b
"Laurea Occidens" ("The Fallen Laurel"),
  2:485a-b
laurel crown, oration on reception of, 2:477b
Les Amours and, 2:728b
letters to the ancients, 2:489b
Liber sine nomine (*Petrarch's Book Without
  a Name*), 2:484a, 484b, 490a
"Parthenias," 2:484b
on pastoral poetry, 2:484a
Physicke Against Fortune, 2:487a
on Pier Celestine, 12:2299b
"Pietas pastoralis" ("The Shepherd's Filial
  Piety"), 2:484b
Posteritati (*Letter to Posterity*), 2:476a, 479b
Psalmi poenitentiales (Penitential Psalms),
  2:483b
Quasimodo and, 12:2390b, 2407b
"Querulus" ("Lamentation"), 2:485a
Rerum familiarium libri (Books on Personal
  Matters), 2:478b, 484a, 489a, 503a
Rerum memorandarum libri (Books on
  Matters to Be Remembered), 2:483b
on Robert of Naples, 2:480b, 484b
Ronsard and, 2:729a, 731b
Secretum (*Petrarch's Secret*), 2:482b–483b,
  494a
Tasso and, 2:815b–816a
Tyard's *Erreurs amoureuses* and, 2:742b
see also Laura (Petrarchan character)

Petrarchism, 2:475b, 503b, 504b
    in Ungaretti's poetry, 10:1461a-b, 1469a-b
Petrarch's Book Without a Name. See Petrarch,
    Liber sine nomine
Petrarch's Secret. See Petrarch, *Secretum*
Petrashevsky, Mikhail, Dostoevsky and,
    7:1354a
Petres Epanalipsis Kigklidhoma. See Ritsos,
    Yannis
Petrocchi, Giorgio, *Storia della poesia di
    Giovanni Pascoli*, 7:1844b
Petronius, Gaius
    Céline and, 11:1873a
    Satyricon
        influence on Renaissance short fiction,
        2:931a-b
        La Fontaine and, 3:95b, 96b
Petrov, Stepan. *See* "Skitalets"
Petrus Alfonsi
    Disciplina clericalis (Instruction for Living)
        Eastern influence on, 2:932a
        "Ingólfs þáttr" and, 1:393b
Pettegolezzi delle donne, I. See Goldoni, Carlo
Petty Bourgeois, The. See Gorky, Maxim
Petty bourgeoisie. *See* Bourgeoisie
Peyote, Artaud's experience with,
    11:1974a–1975a, 1976a-b, 1981b
Peyote Dance. See Artaud, Antonin, *D'un
    voyage au pays des Tarahumaras*
Peyre, Henri
    on French 19th-century writers, 7:1400a
    Qu'est-ce que le classicisme?, 3:80a-b
Peyrefitte, Roger
    Les amitiés particulières (Special
        Friendships), 11:1923b
    "Les après-midi de deux faunes"
        (correspondence with Montherlant),
        11:1920a-b
    on Montherlant, 11:1933b
    Montherlant and, 11:1920a-b
    Propos secrets (Secret Remarks), 11:1920a
Phaedo. See Plato
Phaedra, D'Annunzio's *Fedra* play on, 8:197b
Phaedra. See Ritsos, Yannis, *Tetarti dhiastasi*
    (*The Fourth Dimension*), "Fedhra"
Phalange group, Apollinaire and, 9:891b
Phalange, La (journal), 9:894a

Breton's articles in, 11:1939a
    Leconte de Lisle and, 6:1249a-b
Phallicism, in Rabelais's *Pantagruel*, 2:702b
"Phänomen der Verdinglichung, Das." *See*
    Lukács, György
*Phantasien über die Kunst für Freunde der
    Kunst. See* Tieck, Ludwig
Phantasier og Skizzer. See Andersen, Hans
    Christian, *Fantasies and Sketches*
Phantasus. See Tieck, Ludwig
Phantom Baron, The. *See* Cocteau, Jean, *Le
    baron fantôme*
Phantom Lady, The. See Calderón de la Barca,
    Pedro
"Phantoms." *See* Turgenev, Ivan
"Phares, Les." *See* Baudelaire, Charles
Pharisee and the publican (N.T. parable), in
    medieval satire, 1:358a–359a
Pharisienne, La. See Mauriac, François, *A
    Woman of the Pharisees*
Pharos and Pharillon. See Forster, E. M.
Pharsalia. See Lucan
Phèdre. See Racine, Jean
Phenomenology
    Bergson and, 8:52a-b
    Foucault and, 13:3331a–3333b
    Kierkegaard and, 6:1141b–1142a
    in Ortega y Gasset's writing, 9:1127b–1128b
    Sartre and, 12:2592a-b
Phenomenology of Spirit. See Hegel, Georg
    Wilhelm Friedrich
"Phenomenon of Reification, The." *See* Lukács,
    György, "Das Phänomen der
    Verdinglichung"
Philanthropy, in 19th century, 6:995b
Philhellenes, Elizabeth Chénier and, 4:695a
Philip. See Alfieri, Vittorio
Philip II of Spain, king, in Alfieri's *Philip*,
    4:678b–680b
Philip IV of Spain, king, Anne of France and,
    3:57a
Philippe, Charles-Louis, Laforgue and,
    7:1883a
Philippe, duc d'Orléans
    Fénelon and, 3:273a
    Lesage and, 3:334a-b

Philistinism
  Nietzsche on, 7:1659b–1660a, 1664b–1665a
  in Zamyatin's writing
      prerevolutionary works, 10:1182b–1183b,
      1185a
    The Islanders, 10:1187b–1188a
Phillips, William, on Silone, 12:2294a
Philoctetes. *See* Ritsos, Yannis, *Filoktitis*
Philology
  according to Vico, 3:303b–304a
  founding of, 7:1649a
  Leopardi and, 5:544a, 548b
  Michelet's definition of, 5:579b
  Nietzsche and, 7:1649a
  Schlegel and, 5:177a, 1935–194b
  see also Vico, Giovanni Battista
Philomaths, 5:608a-b
  arrest and trial of, 5:612b
"Philomel." *See* Ritsos, Yannis, *Epanalipsis*
Philomena. See Chrétien de Troyes
Philosopher, Rousseau as, 4:449b
Philosopher king, Augustus as, in Corneille's
      Cinna, 3:43b–44a
Philosopher's Stone; or, Lute, Crossbow, and
      Whip, The. *See* Wedekind, Frank, *Der*
      Stein der Weisen, oder Laute, Armbrust,
      und Peitsche
Philosophes
  Diderot, 4:475a, 483a–489a
  La Bruyère and, 3:257b
Philosophes français du XIXe siècle, Les. See
      Taine, Hippolyte
Philosophic Thoughts. See Diderot, Denis,
      Pensées philosophiques
Philosophical dialogue, in Sade's *The 120*
      Days of Sodom, 4:625a–626b
Philosophical Dictionary. See Voltaire,
      Dictionnaire philosophique
Philosophical Fragments. See Kierkegaard,
      Søren
Philosophical Investigations. See
      Wittgenstein, Ludwig
Philosophical Letters. See Voltaire, *Lettres*
      philosophiques
Philosophical and Physiological Treatise on
      Natural Heredity. See Lucas, Prosper

Philosophical Studies. *See* Balzac, Honoré de,
      Études philosophiques
Philosophie dans le boudoir, La. See Sade,
      Donatien Alphonse François, marquis
      de
Philosophie de l'art. See Taine, Hippolyte
Philosophie de l'art dans les Pays-Bas. See
      Taine, Hippolyte
Philosophie de l'art en Grèce. See Taine,
      Hippolyte
Philosophie de l'art en Italie. See Taine,
      Hippolyte
Philosophische Arbeiten, 9:1124b
Philosophy
  in Alexandria, influence on literature,
      8:215b
  Baroja and, 9:591a-b, 594a, 607b–608a
    conflicts in
      in *Tree of Knowledge*, 9:605b–606a
      in *Zalacaín the Adventurer*, 9:602a
  Broch and, 10:1393a
  of Burckhardt, 6:1241b–1244a
  Butor and, 13:3287b–3288a
  Camus and, 13:3055a
  Chekhov's interest in, 7:1864b–1867b
  of Croce, 8:312a, 316a–326a
  in *De un cancionero apócrifo*, 9:761a
  Descartes on, 3:21a
  Eastern. *See* Eastern philosophy
  Foucault and, 13:3329b–3330b,
      3348b–3349a
  Gombrowicz and, 12:2586b
  of Hebbel, 6:1098b–1099a
  of Hegel, 8:323a–325a
  of Leopardi, 5:550a–553a
  linguistic. *See* Linguistic philosophy
  in Machado's *Nuevas canciones*, 9:759b
  of Nietzsche, 7:1664a, 1667b–1669a
  pagan, Augustine on, 1:35b, 44a
  personified, in Dante's *Convivio*, 1:439b,
      440b
  Queneau and, 12:2517a-b
  of Schiller, 5:37a–40a
  of Schopenhauer, 7:1649b–1651a

see also Existentialism; Idealism;
Kierkegaard, Søren; Libertinism;
Lukács, György; Philosophy of religion;
Schopenhauer, Arthur

Philosophy of Art. See Taine, Hippolyte,
Philosophie de l'art

Philosophy in the Bedroom. See Sade,
Donatien Alphonse François, marquis
de

"Philosophy of Composition, The." *See* Poe,
Edgar Allan

Philosophy of Giambattista Vico, The. See
Croce, Benedetto, *La filosofia di
Giambattista Vico*

Philosophy of History, The. See Schlegel,
Friedrich von

Philosophy of Language, The. See Schlegel,
Friedrich von

Philosophy of Life, The. See Schlegel,
Friedrich von

Philosophy, Poetry, History. See Croce,
Benedetto, *Filosofia, poesia, storia*

*Philosophy of the Practical: Economic and
Ethic. See* Croce, Benedetto, *Filosofia
della pratica: Economica ed etica*

Philosophy of religion
of Artaud, 11:1976b–1977b, 1981b–1982a
Eastern, influence on Schopenhauer, 5:403a,
405b, 410a
Herder's contribution to, 4:649b–650a
in Mandelshtam's writing, 10:1627b–1631b
in Vigny's works, 5:466a, 481a, 486a-b

Philosophy of the Unconscious. See
Hartmann, Eduard von

Philotas. See Lessing, Gotthold Ephraim

Phobia, Freud's concept of, 8:16a

Phöbus (journal), Kleist and, 5:301b–302a

"Phoenix, The." *See* Strindberg, August

Phoenix Too Frequent, A. See Fry, Christopher

Phokimasia. See Ritsos, Yannis

Photo du colonel, La. See Ionesco, Eugène

*Photodendro kai i dekati tetarti omorfia, Ta.
See* Elytis, Odysseus

"Photographer's Missus, The." *See* Colette, "La
dame du photographe"

Photography
Barthes on, 13:3101b–3102b

Witkiewicz and, 10:1209a

"Phrases." *See* Rimbaud, Arthur

"Phyllis and Flora," 1:454b

Physicality. *See* Body, human; Carnality;
Sensory impressions

Physician of His Honor, The. See Calderón de
la Barca, Pedro

Physicians
Aymé's satire of, 12:2443b
in Chekhov's works, 7:1865a

Physicists, The. See Dürrenmatt, Friedrich

Physicke Against Fortune. See Petrarch

Physics
in Descartes's *Principles of Philosophy*,
3:21b
Pascal's works, 3:126b, 127b, 130a–132b,
132a-b
Zamyatin's philosophy and, 10:1197b–1198a
see also Motion, physics of

Physiker, Die. See Dürrenmatt, Friedrich, *The
Physicists*

Physiognomy. See Lavater, Johann Kaspar

Physiologie du mariage, La. See Balzac,
Honoré de

Physiology, in Montesquieu's works, 3:350b

Piacere dell'onestà, Il. See Pirandello, Luigi

Piacere, Il. See D'Annunzio, Gabriele, *The
Child of Pleasure*

Piacevoli notti. See Straparola, Gianfrancesco

Piaf, Edith, and Cocteau, 10:1554a, 1561a

"Pianto antico." *See* Carducci, Giosue

"Piazza di San Petronio, Nella." *See* Carducci,
Giosue

Piazza Mercanti, Battle of (1919), 9:825b

Picabia, Francis, 9:896b

Picard, Raymond, Barthes and, 13:3090a-b

Picaresque novel
birth of, 2:950b
Cela and, 13:3111b–3112a
Cervantes and, 2:829b–830a
Confessions of Felix Krull as, 9:736b
in Diderot, 4:499b–501a
and Lesage's *Gil Blas*, 3:329a-b, 330a-b
Sade's inversion of, 4:629a-b

Picaresque Saint, The. See Lewis, R. W. B.

Picasso, Pablo
  Apollinaire and, 9:881a, 881b, 889b, 891b,
    898b
  Cela and, 13:3119a
  "classico-expressionist" style of, 9:898b
  Cocteau and, 10:1545b–1546a
  on cubism, 9:896b
  Demoiselles d'Avignon, 9:891b
  Elytis and, 13:2965b–2966a
  French language and, 9:882a
  Kafka and, 9:1170b
  Laforgue and, 7:1897a
  Les saltimbanques, Rilke and, 9:773a
  Marinetti and, 9:800a
  Parade and, 9:899b
  planned Apollinaire memorial of, 9:901a
  poetic modernism and, 9:768a
  portrait of Stalin, 11:2082b–2083a
  surrealism and, 11:2071a
  in *The Cubist Painters*, 9:892b
  Valle-Inclán and, 8:332b
  Witkiewicz and, 10:1213b, 1216a
Piccola borghesia. See Vittorini, Elio
Piccole virtù, Le. See Ginzburg, Natalia
"Piccolo testamento." *See* Montale, Eugenio,
    The Storm and Other Things
Piccolomini, Enea Silvio (Aeneas Sylvius),
    Historia de duobus amantibus (The
    History of Two Lovers), 2:937a-b
Piccolominis, The. See under Schiller,
    Friedrich von, *Wallenstein*
Pickwick Papers, The. See Dickens, Charles
Pico della Mirandola, Giovanni
  French culture and, 2:694a
  Valle-Inclán and, 8:333a
Picó, López, Ortega y Gasset on, 9:1135a
Picon, Gaëtan, on Malraux, 12:2430a
Picot, Claude, 3:20b
Picture of Dorian Gray, The. See Wilde, Oscar
Picture, The. See Houwald, Ernst
"Pictures for Crusoe." *See* Perse, Saint-John
Pie sur le gibet, La. See Ghelderode, Michel de
Pièce bien faite. See Well-made play
Pièce à clef, German, 20th century,
    8:269b–270a
Pièce à thèse. See Thesis plays
"Pied de momie, Le." *See* Gautier, Théophile

Pied Piper, The. *See* Tsvetaeva, Marina,
    Krysolov
Piedmont
  Alfieri's voluntary exile from, 4:666a
  veneration of Alfieri by intellectuals in,
    4:687a
Piedra y cielo. See Jiménez, Juan Ramón
Pierre et Jean. See Maupassant, Guy de
Pierret, T.-B., Delacroix and, 5:518b–519a,
    520a
Pierrot. See Queneau, Raymond, *Pierrot mon
    ami*
Pierrot fumiste (*Pierrot the Dabbler*). *See*
    Laforgue, Jules
Pierrot, Jean, on Edmond Goncourt,
    7:1416b–1417a
Pierrot le Fou. See Godard, Jean-Luc
Pierrot lunaire. See Schoenberg, Arnold
Pierrot mon ami. See Queneau, Raymond
Pieśń niepodległa. See Milosz, Czeslaw
"Pietà, La." *See* Ungaretti, Giuseppe
"Pietas pastoralis." *See* Petrarch
"Pietole." *See* Pascoli, Giovanni, *Nuovi
    poemetti*
Piéton de l'air, Le. See Ionesco, Eugène
Piimata I, II, III, or *IV. See* Ritsos, Yannis
Pikovaya dama. See Pushkin, Alexander, *The
    Queen of Spades*
"Piktors Verwandlungen" ("Piktor's
    Metamorphoses"). *See* Hesse, Hermann,
    Märchen
Pilate, Pontius
  in German Easter plays, 1:467b
  in Muri Easter play, 1:468a
Pilgerfahrten. See George, Stefan
Pilgrim in His Native Land, The. See Lope de
    Vega
Pilgrim på havet (*Pilgrim at Sea*). *See*
    Lagerkvist, Pär
"Pilgrimage." *See* Ungaretti, Giuseppe,
    Allegria di naufragi (Mirth of
    Shipwrecks), "Pellegrinaggio"
Pilgrimage theme, in Strindberg's works,
    7:1746a-b
"Pilgrimage to Beethoven." *See* Wagner,
    Richard
Pilgrimages. *See* George, Stefan, *Pilgerfahrten*

Pilgrims in the Snow. *See* George, Stefan, *Das Jahr der Seele* (The Year of the Soul), "Waller im Schnee"

Pilinszky, János, *Harmadnapon* (On the Third Day), modeled on Kosztolányi, 10:1247b–1248a

Pillar and Ground of Truth. *See* Florenskii, Pavel, *Stolp i utverzhdenie istiny*

Pillars of Society. See Ibsen, Henrik

Pil'niak, Boris
    Babel and, 11:1900b
    Krasnoe derevo (*Mahogany*), persecution for, 10:1199a

Pilot from Moluccas, The. *See* Martinson, Harry

Pilote de guerre. See Saint-Exupéry, Antoine de

Pincherle, Alberto, *Diciotto liriche* (Eighteen Lyrics), 12:2674b–2675a

Pinchon, Robert, Maupassant and, 7:1763b

Pindar
    Klopstock and, 4:533b–534a
    Machado and, 9:751a
    Mandelshtam and, 10:1642a
    Odes, translated by Hölderlin, 8:460b–461a
    Olympic Odes, George's *Der Stern des Bundes* and, 8:465a
    Ronsard and, 2:726a, 726b

Pindare (Pindar). *See* Yourcenar, Marguerite

Pindaric hymns, of Hölderlin, 5:158b–159a, 164a

Pinero, Arthur Wing, 7:1927a–1928a
    Mid-Channel, 7:1927b–1928a

Pinget, Robert, Sarraute and, 12:2333a

Pinheiro Chagas, Manuel Joaquim
    Antero de Quental and, 7:1685a
    Eça and, 7:1689b, 1692b, 1693b, 1694a
    romanticism and, 7:1692b

Pinter, Harold, Ibsen and, 7:1754a

Pintor de su deshonra, El. See Calderón de la Barca, Pedro, *The Painter of His Dishonor*

Pious Memories. *See* Yourcenar, Marguerite, *Souvenirs pieux*

"Piove." *See* Montale, Eugenio, *Satura*

Piovene, Guido, on Silone's *Story of a Humble Christian*, 12:2300a-b

Pipa de kif, La. See Valle-Inclán, Ramón del

"Pipe d'opium, La." *See* Gautier, Théophile

Pipe of Kif, The. *See* Valle-Inclán, Ramón del, *La pipa de kif*

Pippo Spano. See Mann, Heinrich

Piquillo. See Dumas père, Alexander, and Nerval, Gérard de

Pir pobeditelei. See Solzhenitsyn, Aleksandr, *Victory Celebration*

"Pir vo vremia chumy." *See* Pushkin, Alexander

Pirandello, Luigi, **8:389a–416b**
    All'uscita (*At the Exit*), 8:391a, 412a, 413a
    Amori senza amorc (*Loveless Love Affairs*), 8:391b
    Anouilh and, 13:2862b
    "Armeggiamenti" (Maneuverings), 8:392b
    Arte e scienza (*Art and Science*), 8:395b
    Beffe della vita e della morte (*Tricks of Life and Death*), 8:391b
    "Certi obblighi" ("A Wronged Husband"), 8:401a
    "Cinci," 8:413a
    "Colloquii coi personaggi" (Dialogues with the Characters), 8:397a
    Come prima, meglio di prima (*Florian's Wife*), 8:394a
    Come tu mi vuoi (*As You Desire Me*), 8:394b, 395a
    Così è (se vi pare) (*Right You Are If You Think So*), 8:393b, 394a, 401b, 402b–403a
    "Di sera, un geranio" (In the Evening, a Geranium), 8:413a
    Diana e la Tuda (*Diana and Tuda*), 8:394b
    Each in His Own Way (*Ciascuno a suo modo*), 8:395a, 405a, 409a–410b
    Elegie renane (*Rhenish Elegies*), 8:391a
    Epistolario familiare giovanile, 8:392b
    "Fatti che or son parole" (Deeds That Have Now Become Words), 8:392b
    "Gli uccelli dell'alto" (The Birds on High), 8:392b
    Henry IV (*Enrico IV*), 8:394a, 398a, 400b, 403a–405a, 408b
    I vecchi ei giovani (*The Old and the Young*), 8:389b–390a, 390b

Pirandello, Luigi (*cont.*)
Ibsen and, 7:1754a
Il berretto a sonagli (*Cap and Bells*), 8:393b, 401a, 402a
Il carnevale dei morti (Dead Men's Carnival), 8:390b
"Il chiodo" (The Nail), 8:413a
Il dovere del medico (*The Doctor's Duty*), 8:393a
"Il fumo" ("Fumes"), 8:400a
Il giuoco delle parti (*The Rules of the Game*), 8:394a, 401b, 402b
Il piacere dell'onestà (*The Pleasure of Honesty*), 8:394a, 401b, 402a-b
Joseph and His Brothers and, 9:731a
"La balia" ("The Wet-Nurse"), 8:400a
"La casa del Granella" ("The Haunted House"), 8:396b, 397a-b
La favola del figlio cambiato (The Story of the Changeling), 8:391a, 394b, 412b
La giara (*The Jar*), 8:394a
La morsa (*The Vise*), 8:393a
La nuova colonia (*The New Colony*), 8:393a, 394b, 412b
La patente (*The License*), 8:394a, 402a
La signora Morli, una e due (*Mrs. Morli, One and Two*), 8:394a
"La tragedia di un personaggio" ("The Tragedy of a Character"), 8:396b
"La verità" ("Sicilian Honor"), 8:401a
L'Amica delle mogli (*The Wives' Friend*), 8:394b
L'Aria del continente (The Air of the Continent), 8:393b
"L'Azione parlata" ("Spoken Action"), 8:392a-b
Lazzaro (*Lazarus*), 8:394b, 412b
"Leonora, addio!," 8:410b
Liolà, 8:393b, 399a, 401a
Lumíe di Sicilia (*Sicilian Limes*) [play], 8:393a
"Lumíe di Sicilia" ("Sicilian Limes") [short story], 8:400a
L'Umorismo (*On Humor*), 8:395b
L'Uomo dal fiore in bocca (*The Man with the Flower in His Mouth*), 8:412a
L'Uomo, la bestia, e la virtù (*Man, Beast, and Virtue*), 8:394a
Ma non è una cosa seria (*It's Only a Joke*), 8:394a
Non si sa come (*One Doesn't Know How*), 8:394b
Novelle per un anno (Stories for a Year), 8:391b
On Humor, Manzoni's Don Abbondio compared with Don Quixote, 5:380b
Pasqua di Gea (Gaea's Easter), 8:391a
Pensaci, Giacomino! (*Think it Over, Giacomino!*), 8:393b, 401a
"Provando la commedia" ("Rehearsing the Play"), 8:392b
Quand'ero matto (When I Was Crazy), 8:391b
Quando si è qualcuno (*When Someone Is Somebody*), 8:394b
Questa sera si recita a soggetto (*Tonight We Improvise*), 8:394b, 395a, 405b, 407b
analysis, 8:410b–412a
Sagra del signore della nave (*The Festival of Our Lord of the Ship*), 8:391a
Se non cosí . . . (*If Not Thus . . .*), 8:393a
Si gira (*Shoot!*), 8:393a, 399b–401a
themes, 8:400a-b
Six Characters in Search of an Author (*Sei personaggi in cerca d'autore*), 8:393a, 393b, 394a, 395a, 396b
1933 edition, 8:405b
analysis, 8:406b–409a
Each in His Own Way and, 8:410b
Frisch and, 13:2919b
Henry IV and, 8:405a
preface, 8:397a, 397b, 407b–408a
premiere, 8:406a
staging, 8:409a
The Mountain Giants and, 8:412a
Unamuno's *Mist* and, 8:303a
"Soffio" (A Breath), 8:413a
Sogno (ma forse no) (*I'm Dreaming, But Am I?*), 8:394b
Sortie de l'acteur and, 11:2119a
Spanish translations, 9:1119b
Strindberg and, 7:1754a
Suo marito (Her Husband), 8:393a

The Late Mattia Pascal (*Il fu Mattia Pascal*), 8:396b, 397b–399b, 400b, 401a, 413a

The Mountain Giants (*I giganti della montagna*), 8:391a, 395a, 412a–413a

theater-in-the-theater and, 9:1063a

Trovarsi (*To Find Oneself*), 8:394b

Tutto per bene (translated as *All as It Should Be* and *All for the Best*), 8:394a, 401b, 402b

Un cavallo nella luna (*Horse in the Moon*), 8:391b

"Un critico fantastico" (A Whimsical Critic), 8:396a

"Un preteso poeta umorista del secolo XIII" (A So-Called Humorist Poet of the Thirteenth Century), 8:391a

"Una giornata" ("A Day Goes By"), 8:413a

Vestire gli ignudi (*To Clothe the Naked*), 8:402b

Piranesi, Giovanni, Gautier and, 6:1044a

Pisan Cantos. See Pound, Ezra

Pisando la dudosa luz del dia. See Cela, Camilo José

Pisarev, Dmitry
    nihilism and, 7:1670a
    on Turgenev, 6:1287b, 1290a

Piscator, Erwin, on Hauptmann, 8:171a-b

"Pis'ma iz Tuly." *See* Pasternak, Boris, *Rasskazy* (Stories)

"Pis'menno." *See* Zamyatin, Yevgeny Ivanovich

"Pismo is 1920 godine." *See* Andrić, Ivo

Pissarro, Camille, 7:1630b
    Huysmans and, 7:1714a

Pitcher. *See* Ritsos, Yannis, *Ydhria*

Pitoëff, Georges
    Anouilh and, 13:2844b
    Pirandello's *Six Characters* and, 8:407b

Pitollet, Camille, Blasco Ibáñez and, 8:374a, 378a

"Pitre châtié, Le." *See* Mallarmé, Stéphane

Pitt, Penelope, Alfieri's affair with, 4:665b

Pitt, William, 5:90a

Pity for Women. See Montherlant, Henry de, *Pitié pour les femmes*

Più che l'amore. See D'Annunzio, Gabriele

Pius V, pope, Aquinas and, 1:419b

Pius IX, pope, Mickiewicz's audience with, 5:631a-b

Pius XI, pope, *Studiorem ducem*, 1:427b–428a

Piva, Carolina Cristofori (Lidia), Giosue Carducci and, 7:1497b, 1498b–1499a, 1505a, 1506a, 1512b–1513a

Pixérécourt, Guilbert de, 7:1909b, 1924b

"Pixy at the Grocer's, The." *See* Andersen, Hans Christian

Place royale, La. See Corneille, Pierre

"Places of My Infancy." *See* Lampedusa, Giuseppe Tomasi di, *Two Stories and a Memory*

Plagiarism, by Eça, 7:1700a

Plague in literature
    in Artaud's "Le théâtre et la peste," 11:1971b–1972a
    in Boccaccio's *Decameron*, 2:518b–519a, 523b, 524b, 527a
    in Manzoni's works
        The Betrothed, 5:385b–386a, 388b–390b, 392a-b
        The Column of Infamy, 5:391a–392a
    in Pushkin's *Feast in Time of the Plague*, 5:682a-b

Plague, The. See Camus, Albert

Plaidoyer d'un fou, Le (*A Madman's Defense*). *See* Strindberg, August

"Plain, The." *See* Arp, Jean, "Die Ebene"

Plain-chant. See Cocteau, Jean

Plaisir du texte, Le. See Barthes, Roland, *The Pleasure of the Text*

Plaisirs et les jours, Les. See Proust, Marcel

Plamen (The Flame), Krleža and, 11:1813a-b

Plan d'une université pour le gouvernement de Russie. See Diderot, Denis

Planétarium, Le. See Sarraute, Nathalie

Planète sans visa, La (Planet Without a Visa), 11:2071a

"Planeterna" ("The Planets"). *See* Södergran, Edith

"Plank-over-the-abyss" analogy (Valéry), 8:574b

Plant imagery, in Arp, 10:1380a-b

Plant propagation and physiology, in Montesquieu's *Observations on Natural History*, 3:348a–349a

Platen, August von
  Die verhängnisvolle Gabel (The Fateful
    Fork), fate tragedies parodied in, 5:425a
  Heine on, 5:497b
*Platero y yo: Elegia andaluza (Platero and I:
  An Andalusian Elegy).* See Jiménez,
    Juan Ramón
Plath, Sylvia, Sarraute and, 12:2335a
Platner, Ernst, 5:56b
Plato
  Castiglione and, 2:652a-b, 662a-b
  Croce and, 8:318b, 320b
  Elytis and, 13:2964b, 2965b, 2981a
  Freud and, 8:14a
  fundamental ethical question of, 5:405a-b
  Hofmannsthal and, 9:689b
  Hölderlin and, 5:145b–147a, 145a-b
  hostility to art of, 5:412a
  Jiménez and, 9:1012a
  Kafka and, 9:1168b
  Leopardi and, 5:546a, 559a
  Marinetti and, 9:826a
  Phaedo, Elytis' "To amygdalo tou kosmou"
    and, 13:2982b
  Republic, 6:1109b
    Rousseau and, 4:455b
    Ungaretti and, 10:1470b
  the sage vs. the artist in, 5:412a
  Schopenhauer and, 5:395b, 398b, 411a-b
  Symposium, 2:782a
    Freud and, 8:14a
    Hölderlin and, 5:146a, 147a, 150a, 152a
    Valéry's *Socrates and His Physician* and,
      8:584b
    The Banquet, as source for Vigny's *Daphné*,
      5:477a
  Vico and, 3:295b, 298a, 300b
  in Vigny's *Stello*, 5:469a-b
  Weil and, 12:2805b, 2806a, 2809b
  the will distrusted by, 5:400b
Platonic Academy, George and, 8:448b
Platonism
  Augustine's *City of God* and, 1:36a
  Hauptmann and, 8:155b
  Hölderlin and, 5:146a–147a
  Jiménez and, 9:1008a-b
  Khlebnikov and, 10:1338b, 1348b
  Lagerkvist and, 10:1679a-b, 1689b–1690a
  in Mallarmé, 7:1572b, 1573b, 1577b, 1587b
  Romance of the Rose and, 1:330a-b
  scholastic dialectic and, 1:406b
  in Vigny's works
    Daphné, 5:477a–478a
    "La flûte," 5:484b
  William of Auvergne and, 1:409a
  see also Neoplatonism
"Platzangst." *See* Grass, Günter,
  "Claustrophobia"
*Plautus im Nonnenkloster (Plautus in the
  Convent). See* Meyer, Conrad Ferdinand
Plautus, Titus Maccius
  adapted by Molière, 3:102a
  Amphitryon, The Two Amphitryons and,
    2:755a-b, 755b, 756a
  Machiavelli and, 2:613a-b
  Renaissance drama and, 1:473a
*Play About the Arms of the City of Coimbra.
  See* Vicente, Gil, *Comédia sobre a
  divisa da cidade de Coimbra*
Play of Adam. See Representacio Adae
Play at Patience. *See* Ekelöf, Gunnar, *Lägga
  patience*
Play of Filodemo, The. See Camoëns, Luís Vaz
  de, *Auto de Filodemo*
Play of Frau Jutta, 1:471a
Play of India. See Vicente, Gil, *Auto da Índia*
Play of the Magi. See Auto de los reyes magos
Play of Robin and Marion. *See* Adam de la
  Halle
Play of Rubena. See Vicente, Gil, *Comédia de
  Rubena*
Play of the Sacrament, 1:471a
Play of the Wise and Foolish Virgins, 1:462a,
  470a
Play-making. See Archer, William
Playden, Annie, 9:881b, 887b, 891a
Playing with Straw. *See* Gunnarsson, Gunnar,
  Kirken paa Bjerget (The Church on the
  Hill), *Leg med Straa*
Plays of Clara Gazul, The. See Mérimée,
  Prosper, *Théatre de Clara Gazul*
*Pleasant Memoirs of the Marquis de
  Bradomín, The. See* Valle-Inclán,
  Ramón del, *Sonatas*

Pleasant Nights. See Straparola,
    Gianfrancesco, *Piacevoli notti*
Pleasure
    Schopenhauer's view of
        boredom and, 5:407a-b
        critique of, 5:403a, 406b–407a
        his ethics and, 5:405a
        medieval view vs., 5:402b–403a
Pleasure of Honesty, The. See Pirandello,
    Luigi, *Il piacere dell'onestà*
Pleasure principle, Freud's concept of, 8:5b
Pleasure of the Text, The. See Barthes, Roland
Pleasures and Days. See Proust, Marcel, *Les
    plaisirs et les jours*
Plebejer proben den Aufstand, Die. See Grass,
    Günter, *The Plebeians Rehearse the
    Uprising*
Pledge, The. See Dürrenmatt, Friedrich
*Pléiade, La: Revue littéraire, artistique,
    musicale et dramatique* (literary review),
    8:122a, 124a
Pléiade Oeuvres poétiques complètes. See
    Verlaine, Paul
Pléiade, the, 2:723b–724a, 742a–743b, 743a-b
    du Bellay's *Défense et illustration de la
        langue française* and, 2:911b
    language, 11:1859b
    pastoral poetry of, 2:911b–912a
Plenniki. See Solzhenitsyn, Aleksandr,
    Prisoners
"Plennyi dukh." *See* Tsvetaeva, Marina
Plessis, Armand-Jean du. *See* Richelieu,
    Cardinal de
Pleyel, Marie (Camille Moke), Berlioz and,
    6:780a-b
"Pliaski smerti." *See* Blok, Alexander
Pliny the Elder
    Montaigne and, 2:775a
    Natural History, Calderón and, 2:892a
Pliny the Younger, in Alfieri's *Panegyric to
    Trajan by Pliny*, 4:675b
Ploetz, Alfred, Hauptmann and, 8:151b, 155b
Plot. *See* Novel
Plotinus
    Augustine and, 1:29a
    Enneads, Aristotelianism and, 1:407b
Plow, The. *See* Tychyna, Pavlo, *Pluh*

"Plowing." *See* Pascoli, Giovanni, *Myricae*
    (Tamarisks), "Arano"
Pluh. See Tychyna, Pavlo
Pluies. See Perse, Saint-John, *Rains*
Plutarch
    Alfieri and, 4:661a-b, 672a, 676a
    Corneille and, 3:35b
    King Seleucus and, 2:756a
    Machiavelli and, 2:596b
"Pluviose," allegorical concept in Baudelaire's
    poems, 7:1337a
Pnin. See Nabokov, Vladimir
Pobeda nad solntsem. See Kruchenykh,
    Aleksei, and Velemir Khlebnikov
Pobeda smerti. See Sologub, Vladimir
    Aleksandrovich
Pochemu ia stal simvolistom. See Bely, Andrey
Podnevna simfonija. See Krleža, Miroslav
Podvig. See Nabokov, Vladimir
Poë, Aurélien Lugné. *See* Lugné-Poë, Aurélien
Poe, Edgar Allan
    Ady and, 9:876a
    Baudelaire and, 7:1324b, 1326a
    Blok and, 9:979a
    Eça and, 7:1685b
    French translations of, 8:572a
    Gogol and, 6:979b
    Hoffmann and, 5:266b
    Jiménez and, 9:993b, 1000a
    Laforgue and, 7:1906a
    "Ligeia," Lampedusa's "Lighea" and,
        11:2032b–2033a
    Maeterlinck and, 8:123a
    Mallarmé's homage to, 7:1573b–1574b
    Mandelshtam and, 10:1637a, 1646b
    Marinetti and, 9:805b
    Maupassant and, 7:1762b, 1763a
    Pascoli and, 7:1826a
    poetic theory of, 7:1906a-b
    "Power of Words," Mandelshtam's "Verses
        On the Unknown Soldier" and, 10:1646b
    Rimbaud and, 7:1797b
    Strindberg and, 7:1732b
    supernatural in works of, 5:551a-b
    "The Fall of the House of Usher," Baroja
        compared to, 9:593b
    "The Gold Bug," Olesha and, 11:2241b

Poe, Edgar Allan (*cont.*)
    The Murders in the Rue Morgue, 12:2485b
    "The Philosophy of Composition," Valéry
      and, 8:572a
    "The Raven," composition of, 8:572a
Poedinok. *See* Kuprin, Aleksandr
"Poem begins, The." *See* Marcabru, "Lo vers
    comenssa"
"Poem of the End, The." *See* Tsvetaeva,
    Marina
Poem on Frozen Time. *See* Milosz, Czeslaw,
    Poemat o czasie zastgyłm
Poem on the Lisbon Earthquake. *See* Voltaire,
    Poème sur le désastre de Lisbonne
"Poem of the Mountain, The." *See* Tsvetaeva,
    Marina
"Poem Read at the Marriage of André
    Salmon." *See* Apollinaire, Guillaume,
    "Poème lu au mariage d'André Salmon"
"Poem for a Russian Doll." *See* Yourcenar,
    Marguerite, *Les charités d'Alcippe et
    autres poèmes*
"Poem of the Staircase, The." *See* Tsvetaeva,
    Marina, "Poema lestnitsy"
"Poem to a Foreign Lady." *See* Perse,
    Saint-John
Poem Without a Hero. *See* Akhmatova, Anna
Poema, Gogol's conception of, 6:992b
"Poema bez geroia." *See* Akhmatova, Anna
Poema bez geroia. *See* Akhmatova, Anna,
    Poem Without a Hero
Poema de Fernán González, as source of
    Mocedades de Rodrigo, 1:130b
Poema de mio Cid, 1:113a–129a
    authorship of, 1:126a–129a, 128a
    ballads derived from, 1:132a
    form and metrics of, 1:115b–117b, 120b
    historical and factual basis of, 1:120b–122b
    influence on *Sancho II y cerco de Zamora*,
      1:132b
    literary qualities of, 1:124a–126a
    manuscript and text of, 1:113a–115b
    sources of, 1:122b–124a
    themes of, 1:119a–120b
    traditionalist view of, 1:126a-b
Poema del cante jondo. *See* García Lorca,
    Federico, *Deep Song*

"Poema, El." *See* Jiménez, Juan Ramón
Poema genre, Tsvetaeva and, 11:1738a-b,
    1739b, 1741a, 1743a
"Poema gory." *See* Tsvetaeva, Marina, "The
    Poem of the Mountain"
"Poema kontza." *See* Tsvetaeva, Marina, "The
    Poem of the End"
"Poema lestnitsy." *See* Tsvetaeva, Marina
Poema paradisiaco. *See* D'Annunzio, Gabriele
Poema (Russian poetic genre), Khlebnikov
    and, 10:1352a
Poemas mágicos y dolientes. *See* Jiménez,
    Juan Ramón
Poemat o czasie zastgyłym. *See* Milosz,
    Czeslaw
Poème du Quinquina. *See* La Fontaine, Jean
    de
Poème héroique. *See* Epic
"Poème à l'étrangère." *See* Perse, Saint-John,
    "Poem to a Foreign Lady"
"Poème lu au mariage d'André Salmon." *See*
    Apollinaire, Guillaume
"Poème pour une poupée russe." *See*
    Yourcenar, Marguerite, *Les charités
    d'Alcippe et autres poèmes*
Poème sur le Désastre de Lisbonne. *See*
    Voltaire
Poèmes. *See* Vigny, Alfred Victor de
Poèmes antiques. *See* Leconte de Lisle,
    Charles Marie
Poèmes barbares. *See* Leconte de Lisle,
    Charles Marie
Poèmes et poèsies. *See* Leconte de Lisle,
    Charles Marie
"Poèmes retrouvés." *See* Apollinaire,
    Guillaume
Poèmes sans prénoms. *See* Arp, Jean
Poèmes saturniens. *See* Verlaine, Paul
Poèmes tragiques. *See* Leconte de Lisle,
    Charles Marie
Poemetti. *See* Pascoli, Giovanni
Poemi conviviali. *See* Pascoli, Giovanni
Poemi del Risorgimento. *See* Pascoli, Giovanni
Poemi italici. *See* Pascoli, Giovanni
Poems, 1853 and 1854. *See* Heine, Heinrich,
    Gedichte 1853 und 1854

Poems. *See* Gunnarsson, Gunnar, *Digte*; Södergran, Edith, *Dikter*

Poems. *See* Heine, Heinrich, *Gedichte*; Ibsen, Henrik; Mandelshtam, Osip, *Stikhotvoreniia*; Vigny, Alfred Victor de

"Poems About Iron." *See* Mandelshtam, Osip

Poems About the Most Beautiful Lady. *See* Blok, Alexander, *Stikhi o Prekrasnoi Dame*

Poems about poetry
 by Carducci, 7:1503b–1504b, 1509a
 by Mallarmé, 7:1567a, 1568a, 1579b–1580a

Poems About Russia. *See* Blok, Alexander, "Stikhi o Rossii"

Poems Addressed to Our Age. *See* George, Stefan, *Der siebente Ring* (The Seventh Ring), "Zeitgedichte"

Poems of the Orient. *See* Hugo, Victor, *Les orientales*

Poems in Prose. See Turgenev, Ivan

Poems of the Risorgimento. *See* Pascoli, Giovanni, *Poemi del Risorgimento*

"Poems to Blok." *See* Tsvetaeva, Marina, "Stikhi k Bloky"

Poems Without First Names. *See* Arp, Jean, *Poèmes sans prénoms*

Poesia, Marinetti and, 9:806a

Poesia. See Jiménez, Juan Ramón

Poesía española, Machado and, 9:763b

"Poesia, La." *See* Pascoli, Giovanni

"Poesia y literatura." *See* Jiménez, Juan Ramón

Poesías. See Unamuno, Miguel de

Poesías completas. See Machado, Antonio

Poesie. See Foscolo, Ugo

Poesie a Beny. See Marinetti, Filippo Tommaso

Poesie disperse. See Ungaretti, Giuseppe

Poésies. See Gautier, Théophile

Poet
 Hugo's view of role, 6:710a
 Nerval and, 6:963b, 964a, 965a
 persona of
  in "Complainte de sainte Eglise," 1:361b
  in Ghelderode's plays, 11:2123a
  of Keats, 10:1487a-b
  of Pessoa, 10:1487b–1488a
  of Whitman, 10:1487b, 1491b

 as prophet, Hölderlin's view, 5:155a
 responsibility of, Ritsos on, 12:2829a

Poet Assassinated, The. See Apollinaire, Guillaume, *Le poète assassiné*

"Poet on Criticism, A." *See* Tsvetaeva, Marina, "Poet o kritike"

Poet of the Hortobágy, The. *See* Ady, Endre, "A Hortobágy poétája"

Poet in New York. See García Lorca, Federico, *Poeta en Nueva York*

"Poet o kritike." *See* Tsvetaeva, Marina

"Poet and the Politican, The." *See* Quasimodo, Salvatore

Poet and the Politician and Other Essays, The. See Quasimodo, Salvatore

"Poet rabochii." *See* Mayakovsky, Vladimir

"Poet, The." *See* Dinesen, Isak

"Poet" ("The Poet"). *See* Khlebnikov, Velimir

Poet in Times of Confusion, The. *See* George, Stefan, *Das neue Reich* (The Kingdom Come), "Der Dichter in Zeiten der Wirren"

Poet-Worker, The. *See* Mayakovsky, Vladimir, "Poet rabochii"

Poeta e il politico, e altri saggi, Il. See Quasimodo, Salvatore, *The Poet and the Politician and Other Essays*

Poeta en Nueva York. See García Lorca, Federico

Poète assassiné, Le. See Apollinaire, Guillaume

Poète-maudit (accursed poet)
 Baudelaire and, 7:1572a-b
 Mallarmé and, 7:1572a-b, 1580a–1581a
 Trakl and, 10:1411b

"Poètes de sept ans, Les." *See* Rimbaud, Arthur

"Poètes maudits, Les." *See* Verlaine, Paul

Poètes maudits, Les. See Mallarmé, Stéphane

Poeti dello specchio, I. See Quasimodo, Salvatore

Poetic Art. See Claudel, Paul, *Art poétique*

Poetic Edda, *Prose Edda* and, 1:386b

Poetic Image of Luis de Góngora, The. *See* García Lorca, Federico, "La imágen poética de don Luis de Góngora"

Poetic inspiration. *See* Inspiration, poetic

Poetic realism, **6:913a–942b**
"Poetic State, A." *See* Milosz, Czeslaw, "Stan poetycki"
Poetical Politics. *See* Jiménez, Juan Ramón, "Política poética"
Poetics
  of Akhmatova, 10:1523b–1525b
    the "Akhmatova line," 10:1523b
  of Alfieri, 4:674a
  of Canetti, 12:2617b
  of Cela, 13:3106b
  of Chénier, 4:705a–711a
  Dinesen's, 10:1301b–1302a
  of Elytis, 13:2965a-b, 2976a-b
  of Foscolo, 5:328a-b
  futurist
    of Hylaea group, 10:1344b–1345b
    of Khlebnikov, 10:1335b, 1345a–1348a
  of George, 8:451a
  in Italy, 2:799b
  of Jiménez, 9:1000b–1001a
  of Klopstock, 4:525a–527a
  of Laforgue, 7:1907a
  of Leopardi, 5:553a–554b
  of Machado, 9:761b–764a
    in *Soledades, galerías, y otros poemas*, 9:752a
  of Mallarmé, 7:1577b–1578a, 1578b–1579b
    typographical innovations, 7:1590a-b
  of Mandelshtam, 10:1626b–1627a, 1633a-b
  of Milosz, 13:2938a–2940a
  of Montale, 11:1990b
  of Pasternak, 10:1603a–1604a
  of Pléiade poets, 2:911b
  of Rilke, 9:778b–782a
  Rimbaud's experiments, 7:1794a, 1796b–1797a, 1797b, 1805a–1806a, 1805b–1806a, 1808b, 1813b, 1816a
  of Ritsos, 12:2835b–2836a
  in sixteenth century, 2:749b–750a, 763b
  Verlaine's innovations in stanza form, 7:1637a-b
  of Vigny, 5:481b–482a
  see also Acmeism; Aesthetics; Futurists; Symbolists
Poetics. See Aristotle
Poetics of Space, The. See Richter, Jean Paul

Poetry
  Augustine on, 1:27a, 35a-b, 46a-b, 47a–48a
  Brecht's view of, 11:2101b
  epic. *See* Epic poetry
  folk poetry vs. "civilized" poetry, 4:641b–642b
  form, Schnitzler's use of, 8:93b
  Hamann on, 5:3b
  Hamsun's view of, 8:33a
  Leconte de Lisle on, 6:1269b
  lyric, Leopardi's views on, 5:554a-b
  Mallarmé on, "pure poetry," 7:1567a, 1568a, 1579b–1580a
  narrative, of Ritsos, 12:2820a–2821a
  Nerval's view of, as *chimères*, 6:949b
  Pascoli on, 7:1835a-b
  Poe on, 7:1906a-b
  popular, Blok's use of, 9:961b–962a
  Prudentius on, 1:13b–14a
  Rimbaud's view of, 7:1787a-b, 1792a–1793b, 1799a, 1810a-b, 1820a
  Ronsard on, 2:735a, 739a
  rustic, etymology of term, 2:902a
  Schlegel's formula for ideal, 5:183a–184a
  Valéry on, 8:575b–576a, 585a
  vernacular, Augustine's *On Christian Doctrine* and, 1:43b
  Vesaas and, 11:2054a–2057a
  see also Aesthetics; Epic poetry; Free verse; Pastoral poetry; Poet; Poetics; Prose poem
Poetry. See Mickiewicz, Adam, *Poezye*
Poetry. See Pascoli, Giovanni, "La poesia"
"Poetry and Abstract Thought." *See* Valéry, Paul
Poetry of Banditry, The. *See* Veshnev, V., "Poeziia banditizma"
Poetry and Literature. *See* Jiménez, Juan Ramón, "Poesia y literatura"
Poetry and Truth. See Goethe, Johann Wolfgang von, *Dichtung und Wahrheit*
Poets, Pascoli on, 7:1833b–1834a, 1849a
Poet's Bazaar, A. See Andersen, Hans Christian
"Poet's brotherhood." *See* Dichterbund
Poet's Guild. *See* Acmeism

Poet's House, The. *See* Laxness, Halldór, *Hús skáldsins*

Poets of the Mirror. *See* Quasimodo, Salvatore, *I poeti dello specchio*

Poets, The. *See* Alfieri, Vittorio

"Poeziia banditizma." *See* Veshnev, V.

Poezye. See Mickiewicz, Adam

Poggenpuhls, Die. See Fontane, Theodor

Poggio Bracciolini, Gian Francesco, *Liber facetiarum* (Book of Jokes), 2:937b–938a

Poggioli, Renato
  on Chekhov's "The Darling," 7:1873b–1874a
  The Oaten Flute, on pastoral poetics, 2:916a

Pogrom, in Babel's writing, 11:1894b, 1897a, 1897b, 1899b

Poiein (the word), 8:585a, 587a

Poiemata. See Seferis, George

Poincaré, Henri, Bergson and, 8:47b

Poincaré, Raymond, 8:471b

Point Counter Point. See Huxley, Aldous

Point du jour. See Breton, André

Point final. See Artaud, Antonin

"Point sur Robbe-Grillet, Le?" *See* Barthes, Roland, "The Last Word on Robbe-Grillet?"

Point of view. *See* Authorial viewpoint

Point of View for My Work as an Author, The. See Kierkegaard, Søren

"Pois l'iverns d'ogan es anatz." *See* Marcabru

Poissenot, Bénigne, *L'Esté*, 2:949b

Poissons rouges ou mon père ce héros, Les. See Anouilh, Jean

Poitiers, court of, troubadours and, 1:162a, 162b

Pojęcia i twierdzenia implikowane przez pojęcie istnienia. See Witkiewicz, Stanisław Ignacy

Pokhoron druha. See Tychyna, Pavlo

Polak, Ernst, Kafka and, 9:1155a

Poland
  cultural life in after 1919, 10:1214a-b
  émigrés from, Mickiewicz and, 5:624a
  Gombrowicz and, 12:2571a-b
  national messianism, Mickiewicz and, 5:621a, 623a
  partitions of, *see also* Mickiewicz, Adam
  russianization of, 5:607b

Polarities
  Arp and, 10:1369b–1370a
  in Baudelaire, 7:1331b, 1333a–1335b
  in Storm, 6:922b

Pole Poppenspäler. See Storm, Theodor

Polemical satire. *See* Satire

Polemicism
  in *Beowulf*, 1:57b
  of Chateaubriand, 5:113a-b, 127b–129a
  in oral cultures, 1:56b

"Polemos." *See* Ritsos, Yannis

Polgar, Alfred, on Wedekind's *Lulu* plays, 8:253b

Police, Aymé's satire of, 12:2442a

Polikushka. See Tolstoy, Leo

"Polis, I." *See* Cavafy, Constantine

Polish Flag. *See* Grass, Günter, *Die Vorzüge der Windhühner* (The Advantages of Windfowl), "Polnische Fahne"

Politecnico, Il (Italian journal), Vittorini's editorship of, 12:2733b, 2749a

Politeness, in La Bruyère's *Caractères*, 3:240b

"Política poética." *See* Jiménez, Juan Ramón

Political Council of Intellectual Workers (Germany), Heinrich Mann and, 8:535a

Political liberalism. *See* Liberalism

Political Prisoner, The. See Pavese, Cesare

Political Reflections Concerning Several Writings of the Day and the Interests of All the French. *See* Chateaubriand, François René de, *Réflexions politiques sur quelques écrits du jour et sur les intérêts de tous les français*

Political science, Montesquieu and, 3:348a

Political and Social History of the Party of Moderate Progress Within the Limits of the Law. *See* Hašek, Jaroslav, *Politické a sociální dějiny Strany mírného pokroku v mezích zákona*

Political systems
  in La Bruyère's *Caractères*, 3:247a–248b
  Rimbaud's view of, 7:1790b, 1795a

Political theory
  Broch and, 10:1395b–1398b, 1403a–1404a
  of Büchner, 6:1169a–1192a
  Staël on, 5:97a-b

Political theory (*cont.*)
  of Tocqueville, 6:893b–894a, 895a–899b,
      910b
  see also Communism; Democracy; Fascism
Politicians, Aymé's satire of, 12:2442b–2443a
*Politické a sociální dějiny Strany mírného
      pokroku v mezích zákona. See* Hašek,
      Jaroslav
Politics
  of Ady, 9:865a–866b
  Anouilh's literary response to,
      13:2858b–2859a
  of Aquinas, 1:425b–426a
  artist and, Robbe-Grillet's views,
      13:3239b–3240a
  Augustine's *City of God* and, 1:37a
  of Aymé, 12:2433b
  in Baroja's novels, 9:590a–591a, 597b–598a,
      600b–601a, 603a-b
  of Blok, 9:974a-b
  Calvino and, 13:3262a–3263b, 3273a–3274b
  Camus and, 13:3067b
  of Carducci, 7:1497a-b, 1499a, 1500a,
      1501b–1502b, 1513b
  in Castiglione, 2:660a–661b
  in Corneille's *Le Cid*, 3:28a
  Flaubert on, 7:1373a-b, 1390a
  force in, in Gombrowicz's works, 12:2565b
  Foucault and, 13:3356b–3359a
  French
      Delacroix's views on, 5:535b–536a
      Hugo's career in, 6:704b–705b
      Leconte de Lisle and, 6:1250b–1251b
      Sainte-Beuve and, 6:838b–839a
      Sand and, 6:831b
      Tocqueville and, 6:897a
      see also Dreyfus Affair
  in Galdos's novels, 7:1601b
  German
      after Congress of Vienna (1815), 5:491a-b
      Böll and, 13:3165b–3166a, 3170a-b
      Burckhardt and, 6:1228b
      Grass and, 13:3376a–3380a
      Heine and, 502b–505b
      Keller and, 6:923b–924a
      Luther and, 2:669a–689b
      Wagner and, 6:1153a, 1158a–1160a

  in Goncharov's works, 6:1083b, 1084a-b
  of Hesse, 9:852a
  Ibsen on, 7:1423b
  idealism vs., Musset's view, 6:1004b–1005a
  Laxness and, 12:2475b
  Machiavelli's view of, 2:595a–617a
      factions, 2:610b–611a
  of Marinetti, 9:825a–826b
  Moberg on, 11:2218a
  of Pascoli, 7:1849a–1850a
  repression, in Canetti's *Die Blendung*,
      12:2623b–2624a
  repression in, in Gorky's fiction, 8:427a
  of Richter, 5:79b–80a, 84a-b
  Sainte-Beuve on, 6:853a–855b
  Sartre and, 12:2590b, 2597b, 2600a–2604a
  in Schiller's works
      Mary Stuart, 5:45a, 45b–46a
      The Maid of Orleans, 5:47b
  Silone and, 12:2274a, 2275a, 2277b–2278a,
      2285a, 2292b
  Simon and, 13:3029a
  of Staël, 5:96b–97a
  Walther and, 1:297b, 301b–302b
  Yourcenar and, 12:2553a
  Zola on, 7:1520a-b
  see also Conservatism; Fascism; Nazism;
      and other political movements
*Politique tirée des propres paroles de l'écriture
      sainte. See* Bossuet, Jacques Bénigne
Politis, Linos, on Seferis, 12:2263b–2264a,
      2266a
Polivanov, Lev Ivanovich, 9:911a
Poliziano, Angelo
  anecdotes by, 2:938b
  Orfeo, Renaissance pastoral drama and,
      2:916b
  pastoral scholarship of, 2:910b
  Sylvae, contribution to Renaissance pastoral
      poetry, 2:906b
Pollen. See Novalis
"Polnische Fahne." *See* Grass, Günter, *Die
      Vorzüge der Windhühner*
Polonskii, V., on Babel's *Red Cavalry*,
      11:1908b
Poltava. See Pushkin, Alexander
"Poly spanios." *See* Cavafy, Constantine

Polyhistorical novel, Broch and, 10:1394a-b

Polynices. See Alfieri, Vittorio

Polyphonic technique, of Milosz, 13:2950b–2951a

Polytechnic University of Athens, 13:2980b–2981a

Pombal, Marquis de, 11:2144b

Pomegranate tree imagery, in Elytis' "I treli rodia," 13:2960b

"Pomoc!" *See* Čapek, Karel

Pompey's Death. See Corneille, Pierre, *La mort de Pompée*

Ponsard, François, *Lucrèce*, 6:1030a

"Pont Mirabeau, Le." *See* Apollinaire, Guillaume, *Alcools*

Pontano, Giovanni
   De sermone (*On Discourse*), anecdotes in, 2:938b
   Lepidina, Renaissance pastoral poetry and, 2:907a, 908b
   Melisseus, innovation of, 2:906b–907a

Ponte, Il (Florentine review), Vittorini's writings in, 12:2753b

Ponti, Vitaliano, Marinetti and, 9:806a

Pontmartin, Armand, on Edmond Goncourt, 7:1414a

Ponty, Maurice Merleau-. *See* Merleau-Ponty, Maurice

Poor Bitos. See Anouilh, Jean

"Poor in Church, The." *See* Rimbaud, Arthur, "Les pauvres à l'église"

Poor Folk. See Dostoevsky, Feodor

"Poor Folks." *See* Hugo, Victor, "Les pauvres gens"

Poor laborer persona, in medieval satire, 1:362a

Poor Musician, The. See Grillparzer, Franz, *Der arme Spielmann*

Poor, The. *See* Mann, Heinrich, *Das Kaiserreich* (The Era of the Kaiser), *Die Armen*

"Poor" writing. *See* Verga, Giovanni, *scrittura povera*

Pope, role of as a universal lawgiver, 3:156b

Pope, Alexander
   Boileau's *Art poétique* and, 3:181a
   Chénier and, 4:707a, 710a

Dunciad, 5:57a
   Chénier's "The Republic of Letters" compared to, 4:710a
   "Essay on Man," 5:57a
   Lessing and, 4:543b
   Mendelssohn and, 4:543b
   The Rape of the Lock, source for Mickiewicz's *Dziady*, 5:611a

Pope ein Metaphysiker! (*Pope a Metaphysician!*). *See* Lessing, Gotthold Ephraim

Popper, Karl
   positivism and, 5:209a
   The Logic of Scientific Discovery, 5:209a-b

Popper, Léo, Lukács and, 10:1254b–1255a, 1262b

"Poprygunya." *See* Chekhov, Anton

Popular Theater of Macedonia, Ritsos' plays, 12:2817a

Populists, Russian, in Gorky's *Children of the Sun*, 8:436b

Poquelin, Jean-Baptiste. *See* Molière

Por Guadalquivir arriba, Poema de mio Cid as source for, 1:132a

Porcupine Company, The. *See* Compagnia del Porcospino

Pornografia. See Gombrowicz, Witold

Pornography
   in Robbe-Grillet's works, 13:3240b, 3253a–3254a
   Sade's writings and, 4:622b, 631b–632a, 637a
   in Verlaine's works, 7:1626b

Porphyry, *Isagoge*, 1:405a

Porretane, Le. See Sabadino, Giovanni

"Port." *See* Mayakovsky, Vladimir

Port-Royal
   compared with Cahors, 3:263a-b
   Jansenism and, 3:172b
   Racine and, 3:208a, 208b, 210a
   see also Jansenists

Port-Royal. See Montherlant, Henry de; Sainte-Beuve, Charles-Augustin

Porte étroite, La. See Gide, André

"Porter's Lodge." *See* Ritsos, Yannis, *Thyrorio*

Portinari, Bice. *See* Beatrice

Porto Empedocle, Sicily, Pirandello and, 8:390b
Porto, Luigi da
Romeo and Juliet
Masuccio's influence on, 2:940a
structure of, 2:928b
Porto sepolto, Il. See Ungaretti, Giuseppe
Portrait of the Artist as a Young Man, A. See Joyce, James
Portrait de La Rochefoucauld par lui-même. See La Rochefoucauld, François VI, duc de
Portrait de l'artiste en jeune singe. See Butor, Michel
Portrait du Cardinal de Retz. See La Rochefoucauld, François VI, duc de
Portrait d'un inconnu. See Sarraute, Nathalie
"Portrait of a Friend." See Ginzburg, Natalia, "Ritratto d'un amico"
"Portrait of a Lady." See Eliot, T. S.
Portrait of a Man Unknown. See Sarraute, Nathalie, Portrait d'un inconnu
"Portrait, The." See Gogol, Nikolay Vasilievich
Portraits. See Albrizzi, Isabella Teotochi
Portraits contemporains. See Sainte-Beuve, Charles-Augustin
Portraits de femmes. See Sainte-Beuve, Charles-Augustin
Portraits littéraires. See Sainte-Beuve, Charles-Augustin
Portraits, The. See Tieck, Ludwig, Die Gemálde
Portraits of Women. See Sainte-Beuve, Charles-Augustin, Portraits de femmes
Portraits-souvenirs. See Cocteau, Jean
Portugal
constitution of, 1822, 11:2145a
history, 11:2143b–2146b
Camoëns and, 10:1476b
in Camoëns' The Lusiads, 2:761a-b
Pessoa and, 10:1476a–1480b
revolution (1974), 11:2146a-b
Ferreira de Castro and, 11:2143a, 2155a
Salazar government, Ferreira de Castro and, 11:2148b, 2154a-b
Portugal contemporáneo. See Oliveira Martins, Joaquim Pedro de

Portugal e o socialismo. See Oliveira Martins, Joaquim Pedro de
Portugal Face to Face with the Spanish Revolution. See Quental, Antero de, Portugal perante a revolução da Espanha
Portugal (magazine), Ferreira de Castro and, 11:2151a
Portugal perante a revolução da Espanha. See Quental, Antero de
Portugal and Socialism. See Oliveira Martins, Joaquim Pedro de, Portugal e o socialismo
"Portugiesin, Die." See Musil, Robert, Drei Frauen
Portuguese language
Camoëns and, 10:1476b
Pessoa and, 10:1476b
Portuguese literature
Darwinism and, 10:1484b
Eça on, 7:1689a
imitation in, 10:1484a
Martins on, 7:1702a
Pessoa and, 10:1483b–1484a
philosophical perpsectives in, 10:1484a-b
politics and, 10:1484a-b
romanticism and, 10:1487a
satire in, Eça, 7:1687b, 1688a
Sormenho on, 7:1689a
Verde and, 10:1485a
Portuguese Renaissance, 11:2148a
Poshchechina obshchestvennomu vkusu (A Slap in the Face of Public Taste), 11:1835b, 1839a
see also Hylaea group
Poshlost, 7:1861b
Position politique du surréalisme. See Breton, André
Positivism
Bergson and, 8:47a–48a, 63b
Blok and, 9:961b
criticized in Kosztolányi's Golden Kite, 10:1239b
in French historiography, 5:573a, 583a
Michelet and, 5:580a
Ginzburg and, 13:3133a
Novalis and, 5:209a

Poema de mio Cid scholarship and, 1:127a-b
poetic realism and, 6:914a
Popper and, 5:209a
Portuguese literature and, 10:1484a-b
Sainte-Beuve and, 6:844a–845b
and Symbolist aesthetics, 7:1577a, 1587a-b
Taine's support for, 7:1451b–1452a
Unamuno's early interest in, 8:285a-b
Posle Rossii. See Tsvetaeva, Marina
Poslední máj. See Kundera, Milan
"Posledniaia roza." *See* Akhmatova, Anna
Poslednie dni imperatorskoi vlasti. See Blok, Alexander
Posledny syn volnosti. See Lermontov, Mikhail Yurievich
Poslednye. See Gorky, Maxim
"Posluchaite!" *See* Mayakovsky, Vladimir
Possédés, Les. See Camus, Albert, *The Possessed*
Possessed; or, The Secrets of Myslotch. See Gombrowicz, Witold
Possessed, The. See Dostoevsky, Feodor
"Possessions, Les." *See* Breton, André, *L'Immaculée conception*
"Possibilité, Un." *See* Butor, Michel
Post-Romantic movement
Grillparzer's link to, 5:422b
see also weltschmerz poets
Postclassical literature
Arnold and, 5:182a
Eliot and, 5:182a
Schlegel and, 5:182a-b
Postcript to Praise. *See* Ritsos, Yannis, *To isteroghrafo tis dhoxas*
Posteritati. See Petrarch
Posthumous Fame. See Lope de Vega, *Fama póstuma*
Posthumous Writings and Poems of Hermann Lauscher, The. *See* Hesse, Hermann, *Hinterlassene Schriften und Gedichte von Hermann Lauscher*
Postills: A Sermon on Good Works. See Luther, Martin
Postmodernism
Canetti and, 12:2618b
Cela and, 13:3122a
Gombrowicz and, 12:2577a, 2586b
of Robbe-Grillet, 13:3256a
Poststructuralism
Bergson and, 8:64a
Foucault and, 13:3334a
Postsymbolism
Boileau's aesthetic attitudes and, 3:194b
in Czech literature, 10:1568b–1569b
Milosz and, 13:2951b
"Postwar Poetry." *See* Quasimodo, Salvatore
"Pot de terre et le pot de fer, Le." *See* La Fontaine, Jean de, *Fables*
Pot-Bouille. See Zola, Émile
Potato. *See* Mickiewicz, Adam, *Kartofla*
Potebnia, Aleksandr
on the language of poetry, 10:1524a-b
Mandelshtam and, 10:1524a
Potiphar (O.T. character), in Mann's *Joseph and His Brothers*, 9:728b–729a
Potomak, Le. See Cocteau, Jean
"Potselui." *See* Babel, Isaac
Potwory (Witkiewicz's charcoal drawings), 10:1209a
Pound, Ezra
acmeism and, 10:1522b
Apollinaire and, 9:882b
Cantos, Laforgue and, 7:1906a
Ekelöf and, 12:2645b–2646a
Elytis' *Maria Nephele* and, 13:2977a
on futurism, 9:820a
Gautier and, 6:1058a-b
Hugh Selwyn Mauberley, 6:1058b
on Ibsen, 7:1443b
Laforgue and, 7:1883b, 1896a
Marinetti and, 9:800a
Pisan Cantos, Ungaretti and, 10:1470a
Rilke and, 9:768a
Schlegel and, 5:197a
Seferis' translations of, 12:2260a, 2261a, 2269b
Poupeye, Camille, 11:2134b
Pour en finir avec le jugement de dieu. See Artaud, Antonin, *To Have Done with the Judgment of God*
Pour encre, poète. See Claudel, Paul

"Pour fêter une enfance." *See* Perse, Saint-John, "Celebration of a Childhood"

Pour Lucrèce. See Giraudoux, Jean

Pour préparer un oeuf dur. See Ionesco, Eugène

Pour un art révolutionnaire indépendant. See Breton, André, and Trotsky, Leon

Pour un nouveau roman. See Robbe-Grillet, Alain

Pour un oui ou pour un non. See Sarraute, Nathalie

"Pour un papillon." *See* Sartre, Jean-Paul

Pour un réalisme socialiste. See Aragon, Louis

Pour une morale de l'ambiguité, See Beauvoir, Simone de, *The Ethics of Ambiguity*

"Pourquoi est-ce que j'écris?" *See* Ionesco, Eugène

"Pousses." *See* Arp, Jean

Pousseur, Henri, Butor and, 13:3309b–3312b

Poussin, Nicolas
   Delacroix and, 5:525b–526a, 527b, 528b–529a, 531a
   Ortega y Gasset on, 9:1134a
   The Blind Orion Searching for the Dawn, 13:3026a-b, 3043b

Poussinists, Rubensists and, 5:538b

Poverkh bar'erov. See Pasternak, Boris, *Above the Barriers*

Poverty
   in La Bruyère's *Caractères*, 3:240b–242b
   in Vittorini's works, 12:2738b, 2744b

Povest'. See Pasternak, Boris, *The Last Summer*

Povesti Belkina. See Pushkin, Alexander

Povětroň. See Čapek, Karel

Povídky z druhé kapsy. See Čapek, Karel

Povratak Filipa Latinovicza. See Krleža, Miroslav

Power
   Foucault and, 13:3325b–3361b, 3355b–3359a
   Marinetti and, 9:800a
   political, in Corneille's plays, 3:47b
   political, vs. literature, Alfieri on, 4:673a–674a

Staël's *De l'Allemagne* on German respect for, 5:108b–109a

Power of Darkness, The. See Tolstoy, Leo

Power and Glory. See Čapek, Karel, *Bílá nemoc*

"Power and Survival." *See* Canetti, Elias

"Power of Words." *See* Poe, Edgar Allan

Powers of the Wilderness, The. *See* Malraux, André, *Les puissances du désert*

Pożegnanie jesieni. See Witkiewicz, Stanisław Ignacy

Pragmatism
   Czech postsymbolist writers and, 10:1568b
   in Goethe's *Urfaust*, 5:19a-b

Pragmatism; or, The Philosophy of Practical Life. *See* Čapek, Karel, *Pragmatismus čili Filosofie practického života*

Pragmatismus čili Filosofie practického života. See Čapek, Karel

Pragmatyści (The Pragmatists). See Witkiewicz, Stanisław Ignacy

Prague, literary culture, 9:1092a

Prague Film and Music School, Kundera and, 13:3391a-b

Prague Spring, Kundera and, 13:3393b

Praise of Folly, The. See Erasmus

Praise poem
   in *Beowulf*, 1:55a
   Caedmon's *Hymn* as, 1:65b

Praise of Stupidity, The. *See* Richter, Jean Paul, *Das Lob der Dummheit*

Praises of the Sky, of the Sea, of the Earth, and of the Heroes. *See* D'Annunzio, Gabriele, *Laudi del cielo del mare della terra e degli eroi*

Pratolini, Vasco
   Ginzburg and, 13:3137a
   Il quartiere (The Naked Streets), epigraph from Montale in, 11:1996a
   Silone and, 12:2303b
   Vittorini and, 12:2734b, 2743a

"Pravaia kist." *See* Solzhenitsyn, Aleksandr

"Pravda istinnaia." *See* Zamyatin, Yevgeny Ivanovich, "The Real Truth"

Prayer. *See* Hebbel, Friedrich, "Gebet"

"Prayer, A." *See* Lermontov, Mikhail Yurievich, "Molitva"

"Prayer to the Rain." *See* Quasimodo,
Salvatore, "Preghiera alla pioggia"
Prayer of the Universe, The. See Teilhard de
Chardin, Pierre, *Hymne de l'univers*
Praying to God Baal. *See* Ady, Endre, "Ima
Baál Istenhez"
Pre-Raphaelite movement
Arthurian legend and, 1:159a
Machado and, 9:753a
Maeterlinck and, 8:123a, 130b
Preaching, 1:43a
Erasmus on, 2:591b
see also Oratory
Precepts. *See* Maxims
Precepts for the Young Charles IX. *See*
Ronsard, Pierre de, "Institution pour
l'adolescence du roi Charles IX"
Précieuses ridicules, Les. See Molière
Preciosa and the Wind. *See* García Lorca,
Federico, "Preciosa y el aire"
"Preciosa y el aire." *See* García Lorca,
Federico
Préciosité, La Rochefoucauld and, 3:63b, 64a,
66b
Precipice, The. See Goncharov, Ivan
Preconscious, Freud's concept of, 8:5b
"Predchuvstvuiu Tebia." *See* Blok, Alexander
"Predskazanie." *See* Lermontov, Mikhail
Yurievich
Preface for Germans. See Ortega y Gasset,
José, *Prólogo para alemanes*
Prefaces, Gautier on, 6:1038a
*Préfaces et manifestes littéraires (Prefaces and
Literary Manifestos). See* Goncourt,
Edmond Louis Antoine and Jules Alfred
Huot de
"Preghiera alla pioggia." *See* Quasimodo,
Salvatore
Preisgedichte poems. *See* George, Stefan, *Die
Bücher der Hirten- und Preisgedichte
. . .*
Prejudice, as portrayed in La Bruyère's
Caractères, 3:250b
Prejudice Triumphant. See Mérimée, Prosper,
Inès Mendo, ou le triomphe du préjugé

"Prélude au temps de cerises" (Prelude to
Cherry Blossom Time). *See* Aragon,
Louis
*Premier accroc coûte deux cents francs, Le.
See* Triolet, Elsa
Premier homme, Le. See Camus, Albert
Premier, The. See Simenon, Georges, *Le
président*
Première enquête de Maigret, La. See Simenon,
Georges
"Première soirée." *See* Rimbaud, Arthur
Préséances. See Mauriac, François, *Questions
of Precedence*
"Presence, The." *See* Elytis, Odysseus, *Maria
Nephele*, "I Parusia"
*Présent passé, passé présent (Present Past,
Past Present). See* Ionesco, Eugène
"Present State of Symbolism in Russia, The."
See Blok, Alexander
Président, Le. See Simenon, Georges
President Masaryk Tells His Story. See Čapek,
Karel, *Hovory s T. G. Masarykem*
Press and Revolution (Russian journal). *See
Pechat' i revolutsiia*
Presse, La, Gautier and, 7:1913b, 1915a
Préstamo de la difunta, El. See Blasco Ibáñez,
Vicente
Prestuplenie i nakazanie. See Dostoevsky,
Feodor, *Crime and Punishment*
"Presveis ap' tin Alexandreia." *See* Cavafy,
Constantine
Pretenders, The. See Ibsen, Henrik
"Preteso poeta umorista del secolo XIII, Un."
See Pirandello, Luigi
"Pretty Redhead, The." *See* Apollinaire,
Guillaume, "La jolie rousse"
Prévost, Antoine-François, **4:393a–400a,
416a–417a**
*Histoire de M. Cleveland, fils naturel de
Cromwell, écrite par lui-même, et
traduite de l'anglais (The Story of Mr.
Cleveland, Natural Son of Cromwell,
Written by Himself . . .)*, 4:395a
*Histoire du chevalier Des Grieux et de
Manon Lescaut (The Story of the
Chevalier Des Grieux and Manon
Lescaut)*, 4:393a–394a, 395b–400a, 415b

Prévost, Antoine-François (*cont.*)
  *Histoire du chevalier Des Grieux et de
    Manon Lescaut* (*cont.*)
    Sand and, 6:822b–823a
  *Mémoires et aventures d'un homme de
    qualité qui s'est retiré du monde*
    (*Memoirs and Adventures of a Retired
    Man of the World*), 4:394b
Prévost, Jean, 12:2309a
Prezzolini, Giuseppe, *La Voce* and, 10:1456a
Price of Intellect, The. *See* Aragon, Louis, "Le
    prix de l'esprit"
Price, The. See Miller, Arthur
Pride
  in Calderón's works, 2:990a
  in Rabelais's works, 2:714b
"Pridu tuda, i otletit tomlen'e." *See*
    Akhmatova, Anna
"Priest of the Serapeum." *See* Cavafy,
    Constantine, "Iefers tou Serapiou"
Priesthood, Walther and, 1:291b, 302a-b
Priests, Women and Families. See Michelet,
    Jules
Priests. *See* Clergy
Priest's Wards, The. *See* Dinis, Júlio, *As
    Pupilas do Senhor Reitor*
"Prigovor." *See* Akhmatova, Anna, *Requiem*
Prima che il gallo canti. See Pavese, Cesare
Primal horde, Freud's concept of, 8:12b–13a
Primal scene, Freud's concept of, 8:17b–18a
"Primal Words. Orphic." *See* Goethe, Johann
    Wolfgang von, "Urworte. Orpheus"
"Primavera hitleriana, La." *See* Montale,
    Eugenio, *The Storm and Other Things*
    (*La bufera e altro*), "Hitler Spring"
Prime of Life, The, See Beauvoir, Simone de
Primer, The. See George, Stefan, *Die Fibel*
Primera crónica general, epics of the Cid in,
    1:114b, 131a
  see also *Estoria de España*
Primera parte. See Calderón de la Barca,
    Pedro
Primi poemetti. See Pascoli, Giovanni
Primitivism
  foundations of, 11:1965b
  of Hylaea group, 10:1353a
  of Khlebnikov, 10:1353a-b

Primo de Rivera, Miguel, 9:746a, 746b, 747a
  dictatorship of, 9:612b
  exile of Unamuno by, 8:304b
  in Valle-Inclán's *Martes de Carnaval*, 8:350a
Primo vere. See D'Annunzio, Gabriele
"Prin apo to xekinama." *See* Tsatsos,
    Constantine
Prince
  duties of, in La Bruyère's *Caractères*,
    3:248a-b
  government by, Machiavelli and,
    2:600a–604a
Prince of Darkness. *See* Satan
Prince of Darkness Tempts Saint Theresa with
    the Aid of a Waiter from Budapest, The.
    See Witkiewicz, Stanisław Ignacy,
    *Książę ciemności kusi Św. Teresę przy
    pomocy kelnera z Budapesztu*
Prince des sots, Le (*The Prince of Fools*). *See*
    Nerval, Gérard de
Prince frivole, Le. See Cocteau, Jean
Prince of Gnats, The. *See* Wedekind, Frank,
    Der Mückenprinz
Prince and Letters, The. See Alfieri, Vittorio
Prince, The. See Machiavelli, Niccolò
Prince Zerbino; or, The Journey to Good Taste.
    See Tieck, Ludwig, *Prinz Zerbino; oder,
    Die Reise nach dem guten Geschmacke*
Princess at Solklinten, The. *See* Moberg,
    Vilhelm, *Prinsessan på Solklinten*
Princess Ligovskaya. See Lermontov, Mikhail
    Yurievich
Princess Maleine (*La Princesse Maleine*). *See*
    Maeterlinck, Maurice
"Princess Mary." *See* Lermontov, Mikhail
    Yurievich
"Princess and the Pea, The." *See* Andersen,
    Hans Christian
Princess Russalka. See Wedekind, Frank,
    Fürstin Russalka
"Princess, The." *See* Chekhov, Anton,
    "Knyaginya"
Princesse de Clèves, La. See La Fayette,
    Marie-Madeleine de
Príncipe constante, El. See Calderón de la
    Barca, Pedro, *The Constant Prince*

Principe, Il. See Machiavelli, Niccolò, *The Prince*

Principia. See Newton, Isaac

Principia philosophiae. See Descartes, René

Principle of Hope, The. See Bloch, Ernst, *Das Prinzip Hoffnung*

Principles of Philosophy, The. See Descartes, René, *Principia philosophiae*

Prinsessan på Solklinten. See Moberg, Vilhelm

Printemps, Le. See Yver, Jacques

Printing press
    Luther and, 2:683b–684a
    medieval drama and, 1:466a

Prinz Friedrich von Homburg. See Kleist, Heinrich von

Prinz Zerbino; oder, Die Reise nach dem guten Geschmacke. See Tieck, Ludwig

Prinzip Hoffnung, Das. See Bloch, Ernst

"Pripadok." *See* Chekhov, Anton

"Priscella." *See* Calvino, Italo

Prise de Neuville, 1:459a

Prison
    Diderot and, 4:486a
    Dostoevsky in, 7:1354a–1355a
    in Dumas's works, 6:731a–733b
    Ritsos and, 12:2817b–2818a
    Sade in, 4:617a, 618b–619b, 620a-b
    Turgenev and, 6:1280b
    Verlaine in, 7:1624b–1625a, 1638b
    see also Soviet Union, labor camps

"Prison, La" (The Prison). *See* Vigny, Alfred Victor de, *Poèmes antiques et modernes*

Prison Notebooks. See Gramsci, Antonio, *Quaderni dal carcere*

Prison, The. *See* Pavese, Cesare, *The Political Prisoner*

Prison Tree and the Women, The. See Ritsos, Yannis, *To dhentro tis fylakis kai ghinekes*

Prisoner of the Caucasus, The. See Lermontov, Mikhail Yurievich, *Kavkazky plennik*; Pushkin, Alexander

"Prisoner of the Khan." *See* Tsvetaeva, Marina, "Khanskii Polon"

Prisoner-of-war camps, Simon and, 13:3023b

Prisoners. See Solzhenitsyn, Aleksandr

"Prisoner's Dream, The." *See* Montale, Eugenio, *The Storm and Other Things*

Prisonnière, La. See Proust, Marcel, *Remembrance of Things Past (À la recherche du temps perdu), The Captive*

Privacy, in Rousseau, 4:467b–468b

Private Life of the Master Race, The. See Brecht, Bertolt, *Furcht und Elend des Dritten Reiches*

Private Obligations. *See* Milosz, Czeslaw, *Prywatne obowiązki*

Private Self Is Dead, The. *See* Ekelöf, Gunnar, "Den enskilde är död"

"Prix de l'esprit, Le." *See* Aragon, Louis

Prix de Rome, Berlioz and, 6:777a, 780a-b, 783a

Prix Sainte-Beuve, Artaud's reception of, 11:1980b

Pro eto. See Mayakovsky, Vladimir

"Proba." *See* Andrić, Ivo

Probability, Pyrrhonian skeptics and, 3:9a

"Problema, El" ("The Problem"). *See* Azorín

"Problemas nacionales y la juventud, Los." *See* Ortega y Gasset, José

"Problème." *See* Tyutchev, Fedor

"Problems of the Chinese Revolution." *See* Trotsky, Leon

"Probuzhdenie." *See* Babel, Isaac

Proceedings at Augsburg. See Luther, Martin, *Acta Augustana*

Processional pour saluer le siècle nouveau (Processional with Which to Greet the New Century). *See* Claudel, Paul

Processions
    in English cycle plays, 1:469a
    in medieval drama, 1:465b–466a
    see also Prophets, procession of

"Proclaim, tongue, the death of Peter who disrupted England." *See* "Pange lingua, necem Petri qui turbavit Angliam"

Proclus, *Elements of Theology,* 1:407b

Procreation. *See* Reproduction, sexual

Prodicus of Cos, 1:6a

Prodigal Father, A. See Dumas fils, Alexandre, *Un père prodigue*

Prodigal Son, Parable of the, Schiller's "The Robbers" and, 5:31a

"Prodigal Son, The." *See* Gumilev, Nikolai, "Bludnyi syu"

Prodigal, The. *See* Goldoni, Carlo, *Momolo sulla brenta*

Prodigious Magician, The. See Calderón de la Barca, Pedro

Profanity, Cela on, 13:3125b

Professional Secrets. See Cocteau, Jean, *Le secret professionnel*

Professional Zeal of Mr. Štěpán Brych, Tollman on a Prague Bridge. *See* Hašek, Jaroslav, "Úřední horlivost pana Štěpána Brycha, výběrčího na pražském mostě"

Professor Bernhardi. See Schnitzler, Arthur

"Professor and the Siren, The." *See* Lampedusa, Giuseppe Tomasi di, *Two Stories and a Memory*

Professor Unrat oder das Ende einer Tyrannen. See Mann, Heinrich

Progress, idea of
  Herder's criticism of, 4:640a-b, 644a-b
  Herder's *Fortgang* (advance) compared to, 4:646a, 648a–649b
  Machiavelli's view of, 2:606b–607a
  Renaissance and, 3:168b

Prohibido, Lo. See Pérez Galdós, Benito

"Proi." *See* Seferis, George

Proino astro. See Ritsos, Yannis

"Project for the Constitution of Corsica." *See* Rousseau, Jean Jacques

Project for a Revolution in New York. See Robbe-Grillet, Alain

Project of a Universal Science. See Descartes, René, *Discours de la méthode*

Projet pour une revolution à New York. See Robbe-Grillet, Alain, *Project for a Revolution in New York*

Prokleta avlija. See Andrić, Ivo, *Devil's Yard*

"Prolégomènes à un troisième manifeste du surréalisme ou non" (*Prolegomena to a Third Manifesto of Surrealism or Else*). *See* Breton, André

Proletariat
  in Johnson's works, 12:2364b–2365a, 2366b
  Weil and, 12:2788b, 2790b–2791b

  see also Class structure; Masses; Working class

"Prólogo casi doctrinal sobre la novela." *See* Ortega y Gasset, José

Prólogo para alemanes. See Ortega y Gasset, José

"Promenade" ("A Walk"). *See* Maupassant, Guy de

Promenade du sceptique, La. See Diderot, Denis

Promenader (Promenades). *See* Ekelöf, Gunnar

Promenades et souvenirs. See Nerval, Gérard de

"Promeneur dans Paris insurgé, Un." *See* Sartre, Jean-Paul

Promessi sposi, storia milanese del secolo XVII scoperta e rifatta da Alessandro Manzoni, I. See Manzoni, Alessandro, *The Betrothed: A Milanese Story of the Seventeenth Century Discovered and Retold by Alessandro Manzoni*

Prométhée mal enchaîné, Le. See Gide, André, *Prometheus Misbound*

Prometheus, Rimbaud and, 7:1805a

Prometheus Bound. See Aeschylus

Prometheus Misbound. See Gide, André

Promised Land, in Ungaretti's works, 10:1453b–1454a, 1459b–1460b, 1461a-b

Promised Land, The. *See* Ungaretti, Giuseppe, *La terra promessa*

Promontorium somnii. See Hugo, Victor

Propaganda
  Fascist, Marinetti and, 9:827a
  Nazi, German intellectuals and, 9:736a
  of Voltaire, 4:367a–368b, 390a–391a
  of Walther, 1:304b–306a

Propertius, Petrarch's *Canzoniere* influenced by, 2:493b

Property, in Rousseau, 4:470a

Prophecy, in Camoëns' *The Lusiads*, 2:761a-b

"Prophecy, A." *See* Lermontov, Mikhail Yurievich, "Predskazanie"

Prophet, Burckhardt as, 6:1238b–1240b

Prophet persona, in medieval satire, 1:359b–360a

Prophets, procession of, in medieval drama, 1:458b

Propos de la jument. See Aymé, Marcel

Propos rustiques. See Du Fail, Noël

Propos secrets. See Peyrefitte, Roger

Propp, Vladimir, on plot in the traditional story, 1:58b

"Propter Sion non tacebo." *See* Walter of Châtillon

Prosanatolismi. See Elytis, Odysseus

Prosas bárbaras. See Eça de Queiroz, José Maria

Prose Edda. See Snorri Sturluson, *Edda*

Prose poem
 of Marinetti, 9:802a, 808a
 Mérimée's use of form, 6:747b, 750b–751a, 754a
 Rimbaud's use of, 7:1808b

"Pros e/*for des Esseintes." See* Mallarmé, Stéphane

"Proshchay, nemytaya Rossiya." *See* Lermontov, Mikhail Yurievich

Prostitution
 in Baudelaire, 7:1332a-b, 1333b
 in Galdós' works, 7:1610a-b, 1611b, 1614b
 in Goncourts' *La fille Elisa*, 7:1396b, 1712a
 in Huysmans' works, 7:1711–1713a, 1725a
 in Laforgue, 7:1902a
 in Maupassant's works, 7:1765a–1766b, 1767a-b
 in Wedekind's plays, 8:250a–252a, 265a

"Prota poiemata." *See* Elytis, Odysseus, *Prosanatolismi*

"Prota-Prota." *See* Elytis, Odysseus, *Anihta hartia (Open Book)*

"Protectress of Sinners, The." *See* Zamyatin, Yevgeny Ivanovich, "Spodruchnitsa greshnykh"

Protée. See Claudel, Paul

"Proterty si kovrik pod ikonoi." *See* Akhmatova, Anna

Protestant Reformation
 Büchner and, 6:1170b–1171a
 criteria of truth and, 3:8a-b
 Erasmus and, 2:585a–588b
 Luther and, 2:669a–689b

Protestantism

Bossuet's attitude to, 3:154b–155b 120
 History of the Variations in the Protestant Churches, 3:170b–171a
 Dürrenmatt and, 13:3215a
 French, 3:264a, 264b
  Fénelon and, 3:266a-b
 and Heine, 5:492b–493a
 medieval drama and, 1:473a
 Montaigne on, 2:783a, 785a
 Ronsard's attack on, 2:737b–738a

Proteus. *See* Claudel, Paul, *Protée*

Protomástoras, O. See Kazantzakis, Nikos

"Protsessy." *See* Vaksberg, Arkady

Proudhon, Pierre-Joseph
 Eça and, 7:1685a
 Herder's individualism compared to, 4:652a
 Leconte de Lisle and, 6:1267b
 Michelet's *History of the French Revolution* and, 5:586b
 Rimbaud and, 7:1811a
 treatment of women, 7:1487b

Proust, Adrien, 8:545a-b

Proust, Marcel, **8:545a–568b**
 Ady and, 9:859b
 Apollinaire and, 9:890b
 on art, 8:471a
 Baudelaire and, 7:1340a-b
 Bergson and, 8:45b, 64b
 Cavafy and, 8:206a
 Céline and, 11:1859a, 1883b
 Chateaubriand and, 5:140a
 Colette and, 9:636b
 Contre Sainte-Beuve (On Art and Literature), 6:840b–841a, 842a-b
 experience and, 11:1727b
 fragmentation of culture and, 8:471b
 Ginzburg and, 13:3133a, 3151a
 on the Goncourts, 7:1417b
 Heinrich Mann and, 8:529a, 539a
 Hesse and, 9:855a
 Jean Santeuil, 8:547a-b, 548b, 562a
 Johnson and, 12:2364b
 Lampedusa and, 11:2018a, 2026b
 Les plaisirs et les jours (Pleasures and Days), 8:547a
  "A Girl's Confession," 8:562a

Proust, Marcel (*cont.*)

Musil's *The Man Without Qualities* and,
9:946b, 950b, 957a

Olesha and, 11:2250a

Ortega y Gasset on, 9:1137a, 1138a

Pirandello and, 8:413b

psychological development in, 9:608b

on "raturer à l'avance" technique, 5:382b

*Remembrance of Things Past (À la
recherche du temps perdu)*, 6:1045a,
7:1417b, 11:1874a

Benjamin's translation of, 11:1722a

Cities of the Plain (Sodome et Gomorrhe),
8:547b, 549b–550a, 550a, 552b, 554a,
554b

cyclical structure, 8:551a

genre of, 5:645b, 653b

Heinrich Mann's "Drei Minuten Roman"
and, 8:526b

Jean Santeuil and, 8:547b

Mauriac and, 10:1313a

narration, 8:548b–549a

Nerval and, 6:969a

Perse and, 10:1437b

Pléiade edition, 8:548a

plot, 8:549a–551a

Sarraute on, 12:2338a

style, 8:566b–567a

Swann's Way (Du côté de chez Swann),
8:547b, 548b, 549b, 550a, 554a,
556b–558a, 560a-b, 561b, 562a

The Captive (La prisonnière), 8:547b,
550a

The Fugitive (La fugitive), 8:547b, 550a

*The Guermantes Way (Le côté de
Guermantes)*, 8:547b, 549b, 552b

Time Regained (Le temps retrouvé),
8:547b, 550a, 551b, 555a, 566a-b

*Within a Budding Grove (À l'ombre des
jeunes filles en fleurs)*, 8:547b, 549b,
555b, 556a, 561b, 563a

"Zone" and, 9:896a

Sand and, 6:813a

Sarraute and, 12:2333a, 2334a-b, 2337b,
2351b

Sartre on, 12:2707a

Schopenhauer's *The World as Will and Idea*
and, 13:3025b

sexual liaisons of, 9:671a

Simon and, 13:3024b, 3029b

Vittorini and, 12:2735b

Weil and, 12:2706a

Proust, Robert, 8:546a-b

"Provando la commedia." *See* Pirandello, Luigi

Provençal language, of troubadours, 1:162a

"Proverbios y cantares." *See* Machado,
Antonio, *Campos de Castilla* (Fields of
Castile); Machado, Antonio, *Nuevas
canciones* (New Songs)

Proverbs

Italian, Verga's use of, 7:1554a-b, 1556a-b

Solzhenitsyn's use of, 13:3208b–3209a

Proverbs and Songs. *See* Machado, Antonio,
Campos de Castilla (Fields of Castile),
"Proverbios y cantares"; Machado,
Antonio, *Nuevas canciones* (New
Songs), "Proverbios y cantares"

Providence

in Camoëns' *The Lusiads*, 2:764b

in Dumas's works, 6:733b–739a

Province, La. See Mauriac, François

Provincial Celebrity in Paris, A. See Balzac,
Honoré de, *Un grand homme de
province à Paris*

Provincial Letters, The. See Pascal, Blaise,
Lettres provinciales

Provincial Tale, A. See Zamyatin, Yevgeny
Ivanovich

Provinciales. See Giraudoux, Jean

Prozess, Der. See Kafka, Franz, *The Trial*

Prozess der Jeanne d'Arc zu Rouen, Der. See
Brecht, Bertolt, *The Trial of Joan of Arc
at Rouen*

Prudentius, **1:1a–22b**

Apotheosis (The Divinity of Christ), 1:7b–8b

Dittochaeon (Twofold Nourishment),
1:13a-b

Hamartigenia (The Origin of Sin), 1:8a,
8b–9b

*Liber Cathemerinon (The Book of Daily
Hymns)*, 1:6b–7b, 12a, 12b, 19a, 19b

Liber Peristephanon (*The Book of the Crowns of Martyrdom*), 1:11b–12b, 14b, 16a, 16b–17a
Psychomachia (*The Battle for Man's Soul*), 1:322a–323a
  allegory in, 1:5a-b
  "Bataille des vices contre les vertus" and, 1:365a
  Cassian's *Institutiones* and, 1:15a
  Cathemerinon and, 1:7a
  Church Fathers and, 1:20a
  Hamartigenia and, 1:9a
  influence of, 1:20b
  Macklin Smith on, 1:2b
  Peristephanon and, 1:12b
  Symmachus and, 1:11a
  themes, 1:9b
Two Books Against the Address of Symmachus, 1:9b–11b, 14b, 20a
Prud'hon, Pierre-Paul
  Delacroix and, 5:527b, 528a-b
  in Goncourts' *L'Art du dix-huitième siècle*, 7:1397a
"Prudoterie," 3:97a
Prussian Academy of Arts, Heinrich Mann and, 8:536b
Prussian Nights (*Prusskie nichi*). *See* Solzhenitsyn, Aleksandr
"Pruzhina chakhotki." *See* Khlebnikov, Velimir
První parta. See Čapek, Karel
Prywatne obowiązki. See Milosz, Czeslaw
Przhetslavskii, Vl. *See* Veshnev, V.
Psalm of the Monk of Mammon, The. *See* Ady, Endre, "Mammom szerzetes zsoltára"
Psalmi poenitentiales. See Petrarch
Psalms
  Augustine on, 1:48a
  Erasmus and, 2:591a-b
  Luther and, 2:672a
Psalms, Book of, Psalm 109, in Villon's *Testament*, 2:561a–563a
Pseudo-concept, Croce on, 8:317b
Pseudo-Dionysius
  Aquinas and, 1:415b–416a
  Fénelon and, 3:270b
Pseudo-Turpin Chronicle. *See Historia Karoli Magni et Rotholandi*

Pseudonyms
  Camus and, 13:3057a
  Dinesen and, 10:1281b
  Kierkegaard and, 6:1123a–1124a
  of Leger, 10:438b, 1429a
  Stendhal and, 5:343a
Psikheia. See Tsvetaeva, Marina
Psyche (Greek mythology), Chekhov's "The Darling" and, 7:1873b–1874a
Psyche, human
  in Balzac's works, 5:643b
  Bergson on states of, 8:48b–52b, 54b
  harmonizing forces of, in Hölderlin's works, 5:150b–151a
  Leopardi on dilemma of, 5:552a
  see also Self
"Psyches ton geronton, I." *See* Cavafy, Constantine
"Psychiatrická záhada (A Psychiatric Enigma). *See* Hašek, Jaroslav
Psychiatry, Foucault and, 13:3330b
Psychoanalysis
  art and, in Mallarmé, 7:1584a
  Croce on, 8:326a
  Freud and, 8:5a–8b, 16a–18b
  in Ginzburg's *I Married You for Fun*, 13:3154a
  Hamsun and, 8:37a, 38a
  of Hesse, 9:838b–839a, 839b, 846b
  Nietzsche and, 7:1678a
  Racine and, 3:220b
  Rimbaud and, 7:1787a-b
  Sartre and, 12:2595a-b
  in Svevo's novels, 8:80a-b, 83a–84b
  Witkiewicz and, 10:1211b
  see also Freud, Sigmund
Psychologia Balnearia. See Hesse, Hermann, *Kurgast*
Psychological literature, Russian, 11:2252a
Psychological novel, German, and Wieland, 4:594b, 596b
Psychological realism, in Lermontov's works, 6:1209a, 1218a-b, 1220a-b
"Psychological theatre," of Racine, 3:224a–225b
Psychologie de l'art, La. See Malraux, André, *The Psychology of Art*

Psychology
    allegory and, 1:323a–324a
    Bergson's view of, 8:48b–52b
    Berlioz and, 6:791b–792a
    in Goncharov's works, 6:1061b, 1081a
    Hamsun's use of, 8:25b
    Kierkegaard and, 6:1139a–1140a
    in Mérimée's works, 6:758a, 759a-b, 763a,
        763b, 767a
    psycho-physical, Bergson's view of,
        8:48b–51a
    in Schnitzler's works, 8:89a-b, 108a-b,
        109a-b, 112a
    Simenon and, 12:2488b–2489a
    in Svevo's novels, 8:72a-b, 76b
Psychology of Art, The. See Malraux, André
Psychology of the Imagination, The. See
        Sartre, Jean-Paul
Psychomachia. See Prudentius
Psychopathia Sexualis. See Krafft-Ebing,
        Richard von
Psychopathology
    in Schnitzler's works, 8:99a, 100b, 111a
    see also Madness
Psychopathology of Everyday Life, The. See
        Freud, Sigmund, *Zur Psychopathologie
        des Alltagslebens*
"Psyhosavvato." *See* Ritsos, Yannis, *Ydhria*
Ptákovina, čili Dvoje uši—dvoje svadba. See
        Kundera, Milan
"Ptichka v kletke." *See* Khlebnikov, Velimir
Public Diary. *See* Vittorini, Elio, *Diario in
        pubblico*
Public life
    Montaigne on, 2:781a
    Prudentius on
        Cathemerinon, 1:19b
        Peristephanon, 1:12b
Public opinion, discussed in La Bruyère's
        Caractères, 3:251a
Public rituals, in La Bruyère's *Caractères*,
        3:243a–244b
Público, El. See García Lorca, Federico
Publishing industry
    Iberian peninsula, 2:748b–749a
    see also Aldine Press

Puccini, Giacomo, Heinrich Mann and, 8:521a,
        530b
Pucelle, La. See Chapelain, Jean; Voltaire
Puddles. *See* García Lorca, Federico,
        "Remansos"
Pueblecito, Un. See Azorín
Pueblo. See Azorín; Social classes, Spanish
Pueblo, El (newspaper), Blasco Ibáñez and,
        8:356a, 363b, 369a, 370a
*Pueblos, La Andalucia tragica, y ostros
        articulos, Los.* See Azorín
Pugachev, Emilian, revolt of
        Lermontov and, 6:1205a-b
        Pushkin and, 5:663a, 688a–689a
Puget, Pierre, Delacroix and, 5:526a, 527b,
        528a
Pugliatti, Salvatore, Quasimodo and,
        12:2392a-b
Puissances du désert, Les. Malraux, André
Pullini, Giorgio, on Silone, 12:2294a
Punctuation
    of Apollinaire's *Alcools*, 9:882a-b
    in Elytis' *Orientations*, 13:2960b
Punin, Nikolai, Pasternak's intercession for,
        10:1595b
Punished Son, The. See Greuze, Jean Baptiste
Punishment, Foucault and, 13:3357a–3359a
Punishments. See Hugo, Victor, *Châtiments*
Punitive fantasies, of Kafka, 9:1161b–1162a,
        1163a-b, 1167b–1168a, 1169b, 1173a-b
Puns
    in Ekelöf's works, 12:2644b
    in medieval satire, 1:371a-b
    in Queneau's works, 12:2515b–2516a, 2524a
Puntila and Matti, His Hired Man. See Brecht,
        Bertolt
Pupilas do Senhor Reitor, As. See Dinis, Júlio
Pupilla, La. See Goldoni, Carlo
"Puppenspieler, Der." *See* Schnitzler, Arthur
Puppet, man as (Pirandello), 8:400b
Puppet Show, The. See Blok, Alexander,
        Balaganchik
Puppet theater
    Gogol and, 6:975a
    Schnitzler's work for, 8:101a
    see also Marionettes

"Puppeteer, The." *See* Andersen, Hans Christian

Puppeteer, The. *See* Schnitzler, Arthur, "Der Puppenspieler"

Pur et l'impur, Le. See Colette

Purdie, Edna, on Hebbel, 6:1104b

Pure concept, Croce on, 8:317b

Pure Form
   aesthetic theory of, 10:1215a–1218b
   in painting, 10:1225a-b
   see also Witkiewicz, Stanisław Ignacy

Pure and the Impure, The. See Colette, *Le pur et l'impur*

"Pure Spirit, The." *See* Vigny, Alfred Victor de, *Les destinées*

Purgatorio. See Dante Alighieri

Purgatory, in Dante's *Divine Comedy*, 1:447a-b

Purge, The. *See* Anouilh, Jean, *Épuration*

Purity, Mauriac and, 10:1309b–1310a

Purity of Heart Is to Will One Thing. See Kierkegaard, Søren

Purple Foxglove, The. *See* Pascoli, Giovanni, *Poemetti* (Short Narrative Poems), "Digitale purpurea"

Purple Thunderclap. *See* Hašek, Jaroslav, "Fialový hrom"

"Pus de chantar." *See* William IX of Aquitaine, duke

"Pus s'enfulleysson li verjan." *See* Marcabru

"Pus vezem." *See* William IX of Aquitaine, duke

Pushkin, Alexander, **5:659a–691b**
   A Journey to Erzurum, 5:663b
   Ady and, 9:860a
   Akhmatova and, 10:1522a, 1534a, 1535b, 1537a, 1538b
   Angelo, 5:663a
   Blok and, 9:985a-b
   Boris Godunov, 5:662a, 678a–679b, 6:765b
      Khlebnikov's "Sestry-molnii" and, 10:1361a
      permission to publish, 5:662b
   "Conversation Between a Bookseller and a Poet" ("Razgovor knigoprodavtsa a Poetom"), Akhmatova's *Poem Without a Hero* and, 10:1534a, 1538b
   Count Nulin, 5:668a-b

Demetrius and, 5:49b

Dostoevsky and, 7:1350b

Eugene Onegin, 5:661b, 662a, 662b, 663a, 670b–673b, 6:986b, 1211b
   Ady's *Margita élni akar* and, 9:873b
   literary realism and, 6:1065b–1066a
   Mandelshtam's birth and, 10:1621b

Feast in Time of the Plague, 5:663a, 682a-b
   Khlebnikov's *Death's Mistake* and, 10:1357b

Gogol and, 6:972a

Goncharov and, 6:1064b, 1065b–1066a

"I Have Raised to Myself a Monument," 5:676a-b

"I Remember a Wondrous Moment," 5:674b–675a, 677a

"In the Country," 5:675b

Khlebnikov and, 10:1352b, 1353b, 1356b, 1357b, 1358b

"Kirdzhali," Khlebnikov and, 10:1358b

Lermontov and, 6:1195a, 1199a, 1202b, 1205a, 1209a, 1212b–1213a, 1214a, 1215a, 1217b, 1222b, 1224a

lyrics, 5:673b–678a

Mandelshtam and, 10:1621b, 1624a-b, 1630a, 1645a
   Egipetskaia marka, 10:1643a-b

Mayakovsky and, 11:1854a

Mérimée's translations of, 6:750b, 765a-b

Mickiewicz and, 5:613a-b

"Mistress into Maid," 5:687a

Mozart and Salieri, 5:663a, 680b–681b

"Nereida," 5:674b

"No, I Do Not Value," 5:675a

"Pir vo vremia chumy" ("A Feast During the Plague"), Khlebnikov's "Markiza Dezes" and, 10:1356b

Poltava, 5:669a–670a

Ruslan and Lyudmila, 5:661a, 664b–665a

"Ruslan and Lyudmila," Khlebnikov's "Vnuchka Malushi" and, 10:1352b

The Blackamoor of Peter the Great, 5:662b

The Bronze Horseman (*Mednyi vsadnik*), 5:663a, 669b, 670a-b
   Akhmatova's "Petersburg Tale" and, 10:1537a
   Bely's *Petersburg* and, 9:922b, 923b

Pushkin, Alexander (*cont.*)
 The Bronze Horseman (*Mednyi
  vsadnik*) (*cont.*)
  Khlebnikov's "Gibel' Atlantidy" and,
   10:1353b
  Mickiewicz's "Digression" and, 5:623a
  moral dilemma of, 10:1619a
 The Captain's Daughter (*Kapitanskaya
  dochka*), 5:663b, 688a–689a, 6:1205a
 The Covetous Knight, 5:663a, 678b,
  679b–680a
 The Fountain of Bakhchisaray, 5:661b,
  666b–667a
  religious motives in, 5:676b
 The Gabrieliad, 5:661b, 662a, 665a-b
  supernatural creatures in, 5:677a
 The Gypsies, 5:661b, 667a-b, 6:662a
 The History of Pugachev, 5:663a
 The Little House in Kolomna, 5:662b,
  668b–669a
 The Prisoner of the Caucasus, 5:661b,
  666a-b
  compared to *Count Nulin*, 5:668a
 The Queen of Spades (*Pikovaya dama*),
  5:663a, 687a–688a, 6:1209a, 1222b
  Merimée's translation of, 6:765a
 "The Shot," 5:685b–686a
  Merimée's translation of, 6:765b
 "The Snowstorm," 5:686a
 "The Stationmaster," 5:686a-b
 The Stone Guest, 5:663a, 681b–682a
  Akhmatova's *Poem Without a Hero* and,
   10:1537a
 *The Tale of the Dead Princess and the
  Seven Bogatyrs*, 5:684a-b
 The Tale of the Fisherman and the Fish,
  5:683a-b
 The Tale of the Golden Cockerel, 5:663b,
  684b–685a
 *The Tale of the Priest and His Workman
  Balda*, 5:663a
 The Tale of the Tsar Saltan, 5:663a,
  683b–684a
 *The Tale of the Village Priest and His
  Workman Balda*, 5:683a
 The Tales of Belkin (*Povesti Belkina*),
  5:662b, 685a–687a

  Khlebnikov's "Markiza Dezes" and,
   10:1356b
 "The Undertaker," 5:686b–687a
 Tsvetaeva's work about, 11:1746b–1747a
 "Tsygany" ("Gypsies"), Mandelshtam's
  allusion to, 10:1634a
 Turgenev and, 6:1281b
 "Vol'nost" ("Ode to Freedom"), Communist
  revolution and, 10:1638a
Puss-in-Boots. See Tieck, Ludwig, *Der
 gestiefelte Kater*
"Pust' na mogil'noi plite prochtut . . ." *See*
 Khlebnikov, Velimir
Put Away the Sun. *See* Johnson, Eyvind, *Lägg
 undan solen*
Put' konkvistadorov. See Gumilev, Nikolai
Put to Death. *See* Aragon, Louis, *La mise à
 mort*
Put u raj. See Krleža, Miroslav
Puteshestvie v Armeniiu. See Mandelshtam,
 Osip, *The Journey to Armenia*
Putevye zametki. See Bely, Andrey
Putta onoratta, La. See Goldoni, Carlo
Pygmalion. See Rousseau, Jean Jacques
Pylades, Dumas's use of legend, 6:728a–731a
Pyra, Jakob Immanuel, Klopstock and,
 4:532b–533a
Pyramid Skirt, The. *See* Arp, Jean, *Der
 Pyramidenrock*
Pyramidenrock, Der. See Arp, Jean
Pyrrhonism, Montaigne's "Apology for
 Raymond Sebond" on, 2:776b
Pyrrhus et Cinéas. See Beauvoir, Simone de
Pythagoras, Nerval and, 6:951b
"Pythie, La" ("The Pythia"). *See* Valéry, Paul,
 Charmes
Pytlík, Radko, on Jaroslav Hašek, 9:1092b,
 1093a, 1102b, 1115b

Q

"Qaïn." *See* Leconte de Lisle, Charles Marie

"Qant je voi lou tans refroidier." *See* Colin Muset

Quaderni dal carcere. See Gramsci, Antonio

Quaderni della critica (journal), Croce and, 8:327b

Quaderni di Serafino Gubbio operatore. See Pirandello, Luigi, *Si gira*

Quadruple fond. See Butor, Michel

Quaestiones disputate de veritate. See Aquinas, Thomas, St.

Quakers
Bossuet on, 3:171b
Voltaire's letter about, 4:384b–385a

Quand j'étais vieux. See Simenon, Georges

Quand prime le spirituel. See Beauvoir, Simone de, *When Things of the Spirit Come First*

Quand'ero matto. See Pirandello, Luigi

"Quando il soave mio fido conforto." *See* Petrarch, *Canzoniere*

Quando si è qualcuno. See Pirandello, Luigi

"Quanto scommettiamo." *See* Calvino, Italo, *Cosmicomics*

Quarante-cinq, Les. See Dumas père, Alexandre

45 degrés à l'ombre. See Simenon, Georges

Quarrel of the ancients and moderns, 3:230b–231a
La Bruyère and, 3:235b

Quarrel of the Dogs and the Cats, and the One Between the Cats and the Mice. *See* La Fontaine, Jean de, *Fables*, "La querelle des chiens et des chats, et celle des chats et des souris"

Quarry, The. See Dürrenmatt, Friedrich

Quartette. See Gautier, Théophile, *Partie carrée*

"Quartetto." *See* Montale, Eugenio, *Altri versi e poesie disperse*

Quartier négre. See Simenon, Georges

Quartiere, Il. See Pratolini, Vasco

"Quarto d'ora di poesia della X Mas." *See* Marinetti, Filippo Tommaso

Quasimodo, Salvatore, **12:2387a–2410a**
A Sibilla, 12:2388b
"Airone morto" ("Dead Heron"), 12:2397b–2398a
"Al padre" ("To My Father"), 12:2405a-b
"Alla nuova luna" ("To the New Moon"), 12:2405b
"Ànapo" ("The Ànapo"), 12:2397b
"Anno Domini MCMXLVII," 12:2403a-b
"Autunno" ("Autumn"), 12:2396b
"D'alberi sofferte forme" ("Suffered Forms of Trees"), 12:2396a-b
Dare e avere (*Debit and Credit*), 12:2408a
Day After Day (*Giorno dopo giorno*), 12:2399a, 2400a–2402b
"Discourse on Poetry," 12:2404b–2405a
"Dolore di cose che ignoro" ("Sorrow of Things I Do Not Know"), 12:2394b
"Epitaffio per Bice Donetti" ("Epitaph for Bice Donetti"), 12:2402b
Erato and Apollyon (*Erato e Apòllion*), 12:2387b, 2397a–2398b
"Già la pioggia è con noi" ("The Rain Is Already with Us"), 12:2400a
"Homecomings" ("I ritorni"), 12:2393b–2394a
I poeti dello specchio (Poets of the Mirror), 12:2400a
"Il mio paese è l'Italia" ("My Country Is Italy"), 12:2403a
"La mia giornata paziente" ("My Patient Day"), 12:2396b
La vita non è sogno (*Life Is Not a Dream*), 12:2402b–2404a
"Lamento per il Sud" ("Lament for the South"), 12:2403b–2404a
"Lettera alla madre" ("Letter to My Mother"), 12:2402b–2403a
Lirici greci (Greek Lyric Poets), 12:2387b–2388a, 2398b–2399a
"Nel giusto tempo umano" ("In the Right Human Time"), 12:2397b
New Poems, 12:2397a, 2399a–2400a
"O My Gentle Beasts," 12:2402a-b
"Oggi ventuno marzo" ("Today, the Twenty-first of March"), 12:2405b–2406a

Quasimodo, Salvatore (*cont.*)
  "Postwar Poetry," 12:2407a
  "Preghiera alla pioggia" ("Prayer to the
      Rain"), 12:2396b
  "Rifugio d'uccelli notturni" ("Night Birds'
      Refuge"), 12:2394b
  "Sardegna" ("Sardinia"), 12:2398a
  "Senza memoria di morte" ("Without
      Memory of Death"), 12:2396b
  "Solo che amore ti colpisca" ("Only If Love
      Should Pierce You"), 12:2408b–2409a
  "Sovente una riviera" ("Often a Coastland"),
      12:2398a
  "Strada di Agrigentum" ("Street in
      Agrigentum"), 12:2399b–2400a
  Suddenly It's Evening (*Ed è subito sera*),
      12:2388a, 2400a-b
  "Sulle fronde dei salici" ("On the Willow
      Boughs"), 12:2401a-b
  Sunken Oboe (*Oboe sommerso*), 12:2387b,
      2395a–2397a, 2401a
  "Terra" ("Earth"), 12:2394a-b
  The False and True Green (*Il falso e vero
      verde*), 12:2404b–2405a
  "The Ferry," 12:2401b
  "The Gentle Hill" ("Dolce collina"),
      12:2399a-b
  The Incomparable Earth (*La terra
      impareggiabile*), 12:404b, 2405a–2406a
  "The Poet and the Politician," 12:2389a-b
  *The Poet and the Politician and Other
      Essays* (*Il poeta e il politico, e altri
      saggi*), 12:2389a-b, 2406b–2407b
  "Varvàra Alexandrovna," 12:2408a-b
  Waters and Lands (*Acque e terre*), 12:2387b,
      2390b–2395a
  "Wind at Tindari" ("Vento a Tindari"),
      12:2391a–2393b
"Quatre cavaliers, Les." *See* Jouve, Pierre Jean
Quatre premiers livres des odes, Les. See
      Ronsard, Pierre de
Quatre vérités, Les. See Aymé, Marcel
Quatrevingt-treize. See Hugo, Victor
¿Qué es filosofía? (*What Is Philosophy?*). *See*
      Ortega y Gasset, José
"Qué es leer." *See* Ortega y Gasset, José

"Que vlo-ve?" *See* Apollinaire, Guillaume,
      L'Hérésiarque et cie
Queen Calafia. *See* Blasco Ibáñez, Vicente, *La
      reina Calafia*
Queen Christina. See Strindberg, August
Queen of Spades, The. See Pushkin, Alexander
Queen's Necklace, The. See Dumas père,
      Alexandre, *Le collier de la reine*
Queer People. See Gorky, Maxim, *Chudaki*
Queiroz e Almeida, Joaquim José de,
      7:1683b–1684a
Queneau, Raymond, **12:2511a–2534b**
  autobiographical elements, 12:2513a, 2514a
  Bâtons, chiffres et lettres (Sticks, Numbers
      and Letters), 12:2511b, 2516b, 2517b,
      2519b
    "Écrit en 1937," 12:2516b
  Bouvard et Pécuchet, 12:2516a
  Céline's influence on, 11:1859a
  Cent mille milliards de poèmes (One
      Hundred Thousand Billion Poems),
      12:2521b
  Chêne et chien (Oak and Dog), 12:2513a,
      2514b, 2515b, 2517b, 2518a
  cinema and, 12:2517b
  En passant (Passing By), 12:2521b
  Gueule de pierre (Stone Mug), 12:2515b
  Jarry's *Ubu Roi* and, 12:2532b
  Le chien à la mandoline (Dog with
      Mandolin), 12:2515b
    "La chair chaude des mots," 12:2525b
  Le chiendent (*The Bark Tree*), 12:2512a,
      2514a, 2515a-b, 2515b, 2517b, 2522a,
      2526a, 2528b, 2531a, 2531b, 2533a
    pataphysical point of view, 12:2532b
    plot, 12:2519a
    structure, 12:2520a-b
  Le dimanche de la vie (*The Sunday of Life*),
      12:2512b, 2516b, 2517b, 2528b–2529a
    crowd symbolism, 2526b–2527b
    epigraph, 12:2532a
    language, 12:2523a, 2524a
    plot, 12:2518b–2519a
  Le vol d'Icare (*The Flight of Icarus*),
      12:2517b
  Les derniers jours (The Last Days),
      12:2515a

Les enfants du limon (Children of the Slime), 12:2514a, 2515a, 2524b, 2527b, 2531a-b

Les exercices de style (*Exercises in Style*), 12:2521a, 2524b–2525b

Les fleurs bleues (*The Blue Flowers*), 12:2514b, 2517b, 2519a-b, 2527b, 2532b

Les Ziaux, 12:2522a

L'Instant fatal
"Adieu ma terre ronde" (Good-bye, My Round Earth), 12:2533a
"Si tu t'imagines" (If You Imagine), 12:2515a

Loin de Rueil (*The Skin of Dreams*), 12:2512b, 2515a, 2517b, 2528b, 2529b–2530b
cyclical form, 12:2520b–2521a
lyric poetry, 12:2515a

Morale élémentaire (Elementary Ethics), 12:2521b

Odile, 12:2513b–2514a, 2517b, 2518a, 2522b, 2528a, 2530b

On est toujours trop bon avec les femmes (*We Always Treat Women Too Well*), 12:2516b

Ouvroir de littérature potentielle, 12:2521a

Petite cosmogonie portative (Little Portable Cosmogony), 12:2517a, 2523a, 2532b

Pierrot mon ami (*Pierrot*), 12:2512b, 2515a, 2518a-b, 2529a
characters, 12:2528a
cyclical form, 12:2520b

Saint Glinglin, 12:2514b, 2520b, 2524b, 2532b

Sally Mara, 12:2516b
stylistic exercises, 12:2524b

Un rude hiver (*A Hard Winter*), 12:2518a-b, 2530a, 2531a

Une histoire modèle (A Model History), 12:2514b

Zazie dans le métro (*Zazie*), 12:2514b, 2516b, 2517a, 2523b
characters, 12:2528a
cyclical form, 12:2520b
film adaptation, 12:2517b
Gabriel, 12:2530a
plot, 12:2519a

Trouscaillon, 12:2531a, 2531b

Quenouille de Barberine, La. See Musset, Alfred de

Quental, Antero de, 11:2147b
at Democratic Conferences of 1871, 7:1688b–1689a
"Casino Lectures," 10:1484a
Castilho and, 7:1685a-b
Cennacle and, 7:1686a, 1688b
Eça and, 7:1685a, 1686b, 1694a-b
Odes modernas (Modern Odes), 7:1685a
Portugal perante a revolução da Espanha (Portugal Face to Face with the Spanish Revolution), 7:1686a-b
Ramalho and, 7:1685b
socialism and, 7:1685a

Quentin Durward. See Scott, Sir Walter

Querela. See Complaint

Querela pacis. See Erasmus

"Querelle des chiens et des chats, et celle des chats et des souris, La." See La Fontaine, Jean de, *Fables*

"Querulus." See Petrarch

Quesnel, Pasquier, *Moral Reflections on the New Testament*, Bossuet and, 3:172b

Quesnet, Marie-Constance, as Sade's lover, 4:627a

Quest of the Absolute, The. See Balzac, Honoré de, *La recherche de l'absolu*

Qu'est ce que le surréalisme? See Breton, André

Quest, The. See Baroja, Pío, *La busca*

Quest theme
advantages of, 1:150a-b
in Butor, 13:3292b–3293a
Chrétien's and, 1:150a
in *Romance of the Rose*, 1:317b
in Wolfram, 1:274a–275a

"Qu'est-ce pour nous?" See Rimbaud, Arthur

"Qu'est-ce que la critique?" See Barthes, Roland, "What Is Criticism?"

Qu'est-ce que la littérature? See Sartre, Jean-Paul, *What Is Literature?*

Qu'est-ce que le classicisme? See Peyre, Henri

Qu'est-ce que le surréalisme? See Breton, André

"Qu'est-ce qu'un auteur?" *See* Foucault, Michel, "What Is an Author?"

"Qu'est-ce qu'un classique?" *See* Sainte-Beuve, Charles-Augustin

Questa sera si recita a soggetto. See Pirandello, Luigi

Queste del Saint Graal, 1:152a, 158a-b
see also Grail legend

Quester, The. See Quevedo, Francisco de, *El buscón*

Questio de aqua et terra (Discourse on the Nature of Water and Earth), Dante and, 1:444a

Questione della lingua (language controversy)
Ariosto and, 2:620b, 624a-b
Castiglione and, 2:651b–652a
Machiavelli and, 2:599b

"Questions on Beauty." *See* Delacroix, Eugène

"Questions de méthode." *See* Sartre, Jean-Paul, *Search for a Method*

"Questions de théâtre" (Questions of the Theater). *See* Jarry, Alfred

Questions of Precedence. See Mauriac, François

Quête intermittente, La. See Ionesco, Eugène

Quevedo, Francisco de
Camoëns and, 2:752a
Cela and, 13:3116a
El buscón (The Sharper), 9:596b
realism of, 2:914a
Machado and, 9:752a
pastoral poetry and, 2:913a–914a
Pavura de los condes de Carrión, 1:133b
Petrarchan influence, 2:504b
Valle-Inclán and, 8:346a

Qui n'a pas son Minotaure? See Yourcenar, Marguerite

"Quid luges, lirice?" *See* Hugh Primas

Quiet Musician, A. *See* Storm, Theodor, *Ein stiller Musikant*

"Quiet Spot, A." *See* Turgenev, Ivan

Quietism
Bossuet and, 3:172a, 173a
Fénelon and, 3:268a-b
La Bruyère and, 3:258b–259a
Madam Guyon and, 3:268a-b

Quinault, judged by Boileau, 3:195b

Quinet, Edgar, 5:581b–582a
on July 1830 revolution, 5:587a
Michelet and, 5:574b–575a, 577a
Mickiewicz and, 5:630b
The Jesuits (Des Jésuites), 5:589b
translation of Herder, 5:583b

Quintessence of Ibsenism, The. See Shaw, George Bernard

Quintilian
Institutio oratoria (The Education of an Orator), anecdotes in, 2:930a
Pascal's *Lettres provinciales* and, 3:138b

Quintus Fixlein. See Richter, Jean Paul, *Das Leben des Quintus Fixlein*

Quiproquo
in plays
An Italian Straw Hat, 7:1922b
of Augier, 7:1918b
of Bauernfeld, 7:1925b
of Dumas, 7:1918b
of Feydeau, 7:1923b
of Hervieu, 7:1921a
of Ibsen, 7:1929a, 1930a
of Pinero, 7:1927b
of Scribe, 7:1911b

Quitt. See Fontane, Theodor

Quittance du diable, La. See Musset, Alfred de

Quitte pour la peur. See Vigny, Alfred Victor de

Quo Vadis? See Sienkiewicz, Henryk

Quodlibeta. See Duns Scotus

R

Rabbi Esra. See Wedekind, Frank, *Fürstin Russalka*

Rabelais. See Barrault, Jean-Louis

Rabelais, François, **2:693a–720b**
  Apollinaire and, 9:892b
  Babel and, 11:1900b
  Céline and, 11:1859a, 1873a
  Flaubert and, 7:1380a
  Fourth Book, 2:697a-b, 699a, 711b–712b, 714a
  Gargantua, 2:704b–708a
    Baldus and, 2:698b
    Camoëns' *The Play of Filodemo* and, 2:758a
    clown, 11:1877a
    Fifth Book and, 2:713a, 718a
    Pantagruel and, 2:704b–705a
    publication of, 2:696b
    Sorbonne and, 2:697a
    Third Book and, 2:710a
  Gargantua et Pantagruel, 9:674a
  Gautier and, 6:1035b
  influence on du Fail, 2:947a
  Jarry and, 9:673b
  La Fontaine and, 3:79a
  Le Cinquiesme et dernier livre des faicts et dicts héroïques du bon Pantagruel (The Fifth and Last Book of the Heroic Deeds and Sayings of the Good Pantagruel), 2:698a, 711b, 712b–717b
  L'Isle sonante (Ringing Island), 2:697b, 698a
  Pantagruel, 2:699a, 701b–704b
    Baldus and, 2:698b
    chapter eight, 2:703a
    chapter one, 2:702a-b, 704b
    Fifth Book and, 2:713a, 718a
    publication of, 2:696a, 696b
    Sorbonne and, 2:697a
    sources of, 2:701b–702a
    Third Book and, 2:708a
  Pantagrueline prognostication, 2:696a
  Pathelin and, 1:472a, 472b
  Queneau and, 12:2512a, 2523b, 2524a
  Richter and, 5:61a, 81b
  Third Book, 2:697a, 698b–699a, 708a–711b
    Gargantua and, 2:710a
    Pantagruel and, 2:704a, 708a
    prologue, 2:701b, 715b
  Vittorini and, 12:2734a

Raber, Vigil, 1:466b, 469a, 470a

Rabutin-Chantal, Marie de. *See* Sévigné, marquise de

Racan, Honorat de
  Bergeries, 3:25b
  Guarini's influence on, 2:919b

Racconti. See Lampedusa, Giuseppe Tomasi di, *Two Stories and a Memory*

Racconti, I. See Calvino, Italo; Moravia, Alberto

Racconti romani. See Moravia, Alberto, *Roman Tales*

"Racconto e romanzo." *See* Moravia, Alberto

Race: A Study in Modern Superstition. See Barzun, Jacques

Race, Taine's concept of, 7:1454a–1456a

Races. See Bruckner, Ferdinand, *Die Rassen*

Rachel (actress in Musset's plays), 6:1030a-b

Racine et Shakespeare. See Stendhal

Racine, Jean, **3:207a–228b**, 263b
  Alexandre le grand (Alexander the Great), 3:208a
    preface to, 3:209a-b, 218b
  alexandrine meter and, 6:1033b
  Andromaque, 3:207a, 208b, 210b–212b, 220b, 221a-b, 222a-b, 224b
    compared with Racine's other plays, 3:212a
    military metaphors in, 3:211b
    plot of, 3:210b–211a
  Athalie, 3:207b, 209a, 210b, 216a–217b, 222b–223a
    compared to other plays, 3:216a-b
    depiction of court in, 3:226b
    preface to, 3:216a, 219a
  attacked by Bossuet, 3:173a
  Bajazet, 3:207b, 224a-b
    depiction of court in, 3:226a, 226b
    preface to, 3:226a
    unity of action and, 3:218a
  Barthes on, 13:3090a–3091a

Racine, Jean (*cont.*)
  Baudelaire and, 7:1327b, 1340b–1341b
  Bérénice, 3:207a, 207b, 213b–214a, 222a,
      224b
    depiction of court in, 3:226a
    preface to, 3:218b–219a, 219a-b
    unity of action and, 3:217b
  Boileau on, 3:179a, 199a
  Britannicus, 3:207a, 212b—213b, 220b,
      224b
    compared to *Andromaque*, 3:212a
    depiction of court life in, 3:226a
    unity of action and, 3:217b–218a
  Corneille and, 3:23a, 25b, 48a
    Cinna, 3:39a, 41a
  Dostoevsky and, 7:1350b
  Esther, 3:209a
    preface to, 3:210a
  French language and, 6:1033b
  Giraudoux and, 9:1060a
  Hebbel and, 6:1109b
  La Bruyère and, 3:34a, 230b
  La thébaïde, ou les frères ennemis (*The
      Thebaid*), 3:208a, 220a, 220b
  Le Cid and, 3:33a
  Les plaideurs (The Litigants), 3:208b
  letters from Boileau, 3:182a, 183a
  Mairet and, 3:36a
  Mauriac and, 10:1313b, 1322b–1323a
  Mithridate, 3:217a
    depiction of court in, 3:236b
    as source of Alfieri's *Philip*, 4:678b
  neoclassical tradition and, 9:1041a
  as one of French *classiques*, 3:273b
  Phèdre, 3:183b, 207a, 214a–216a, 223b,
      225a-b, 227a, 7:1583a
    compared to *Andromaque*, 3:212a-b
    monsters in, 3:215a-b
    preface to, 3:208b–209a, 215a
    role of gods in, 3:215a
    unity of action and, 3:217b
  Sainte-Beuve on, 6:847a, 857b
  Taine on, 7:1460a
Racine, Louis
  on Jean Racine, 3:209a-b, 214a
  Reflections on Poetry, Chénier and, 4:707a
Racism

  in Aymé's works, 12:2448b
  in Ghelderode's plays, 11:2135b–2136a
  in Ionesco's *Rhinocéros*, 13:3002a-b
  Portuguese, 11:2147a
  Tocqueville on, 6:896b
  see also Barzun, Jacques, *Race: A Study in
      Modern Superstition*
Radcliffe, Ann, Dostoevsky and, 7:1350b
"Raderberg, Raderthal." *See* Böll, Heinrich
Radicalism in politics
  Greece, Elytis' *Maria Nephele* and,
      13:2976b–2977a
  Russian, Turgenev and, 6:1287b–1288b,
      1292b, 1293a
Radiguet, Raymond
  and Cocteau, 10:1544b, 1545b, 1547a-b,
      1551a
  Le bal du Comte Orgel (*Count Orgel*),
      10:1547b
  Le diable au corps (*Devil in the Flesh*),
      10:1547b
Radio, Butor's *6 810 000 litres d'eau par
      seconde* written for, 13:3304a-b
Radio, Butor's *6 810 000 litres d'eau par
      seconde*
Raft of the Medusa, The. See Géricault,
      Théodore
Ragazza di Bube, La. See Cassola, Carlo
Raggio, Carmen Baroja y, 9:590b
Raggio, Rafael Caro, 9:590b
"Raging inside with violent anger." *See*
      Archpoet, "Estuans instrinsicus ira
      vehementi"
Ragionamenti. See Firenzuola, Angelo
Ragione degli altri, La. See Pirandello, Luigi,
      Se non così
Ragnars saga Loðbrókar, 1:400b
"Rags, The." *See* Andersen, Hans Christian
Rags-to-riches theme, Andersen and,
      6:881a–882a
"Rai." *See* Zamyatin, Yevgeny Ivanovich
Railway. *See* Trains
Raimon de Miraval
  courtly love in works of, 1:166a
  as troubadour, 1:175a-b
Raimon Vidal, as troubadour, 1:161b
Raimund, Ferdinand

Der Diamant des Geisterkönigs (The Diamond of the King of Spirits), adapted by Andersen, 6:875a

Hofmannsthal and, 9:706a

theatrum mundi metaphor and, 5:422a

weltschmerz and, 5:420b

Rain, in Cela, 13:3124a-b

"Rain." *See* Tychyna, Pavlo, *Soniachni klarnety*

Rain at Dawn. *See* Johnson, Eyvind, *Regn i gryningen*

"Rain Is Already with Us, The." *See* Quasimodo, Salvatore, "Già la pioggia è con noi"

"Rainbow." *See* Montale, Eugenio, *The Storm and Other Things*

Rains. See Perse, Saint-John

"Rainy Moon, The." *See* Colette, "La lune de pluie"

Rait, A. W., on the Goncourts, 7:1405a-b

Raizis, Byron, 13:2980b

Rákosi, Jenö, 9:865b

Rákosi, Mátyás, Lukács and, 10:1273a

"Rakovina." *See* Mandelshtam, Osip

Rakovyi korpus. See Solzhenitsyn, Aleksandr, *Cancer Ward*

Ralentir travaux. See Breton, André

Rambouillet, marquise de. *See* Vivonne, Catherine de

Rameau's Nephew. See Diderot, Denis, *Le neveu de Rameau*

"Rameur, Le." *See* Valéry, Paul, *Charmes*

Ramsay, André Michel, *Voyages de Cyrus*, Wieland and, 4:596b

Ramt. See Gunnarsson, Gunnar

Randomness, theme of

in Calvino, 13:3279a-b

in Richter, 5:55b, 69b

"Rane, Le." *See* Pascoli, Giovanni, "Il ritorno a San Mauro"

Ranieri, Antonio, Leopardi and, 5:547b, 548b–549a

Ranieri, Paolina, Leopardi and, 5:544b–550a, 562a

Rank, Otto, Freud and, 8:4a-b

Ranke, Leopold von, in Johan Droysen's view, 5:579b

Raoul de Cambrai, 1:108a-b

Raoul de Houdenc, *Songe d'Enfer* (*Dream of Hell*), 1:325b

Rape, in Ionesco's *The Lesson*, 13:2993b–2994a

Raphael, 9:768b

Delacroix on, 5:524b, 526b–527b

Disputà, 5:525a, 529b

frescoes of, 5:525a

Gottfried and, 1:249a-b

RAPP (Russian Association of Proletarian Writers), 11:2072b

Mayakovsky and, 11:1837b, 1838b

Pil'niak's persecution by, 10:1199a

Zamyatin's persecution by, 10:1199a

"Rapsodhia toy gymoy fotos, I." *See* Ritsos, Yannis, *Phokimasia*

Rarefaction, Foucault's theory of, 13:3346b

Raskens: En soldatfamiljs historia (The Rasks: The Story of a Soldier's Family). *See* Moberg, Vilhelm

Rasputin, Bely's *The Silver Dove* and, 9:918a

Rassegna d'Italia, La (Italian review), Vittorini's writings in, 12:2734a

Rassen, Die. See Bruckner, Ferdinand

Rassenfosse, Edmond, George and, 8:455b

"Rasskaz o samom glavnom." *See* Zamyatin, Yevgeny Ivanovich, "A Story About the Most Important Thing"

Rasskazy. See Pasternak, Boris

"Rat et l'huître, Le." *See* La Fontaine, Jean de, *Fables*

Rat Man, Freud and, 8:16b–17b

"Rat and the Oyster, The." *See* La Fontaine, Jean de, *Fables*, "Le rat et l'huître"

Rat, The. See Grass, Günter

Rathenau, Walther, Musil's *The Man Without Qualities* and, 9:937b

Ratio verae theologiae. See Erasmus

Rationalism

Bergson and, 8:46b–46a

in fiction of Simon, 13:3027b

German, Baroja questions, 9:594b

Goethe and, 5:1a

Gombrowicz and, 12:2567b

Ortega y Gasset and, 9:1127a–1129b

Ratten: Berliner Tragikomödie, Die (*The Rats*).
   See Hauptmann, Gerhart
Rättin, Die. See Grass, Günter, *The Rat*
Räuber, Die. See Schiller, Friedrich von
Rauða Kverið. See Laxness, Halldór
Ravaisson, Felix, Bergson and, 8:46b
Ravel, Maurice, 8:546b
  and Jarry, 9:670b
"Raven, The." *See* Poe, Edgar Allan
Rævepelsene. See Gunnarsson, Gunnar
Ravissement de Scapin, Le. See Claudel, Paul
Raw Youth, A. See Dostoevsky, Feodor
Raymond de Penaforte, Aquinas' *Summa
   contra Gentiles* and, 1:414a
Raymond, Marcel, *L'Influence de Ronsard sur
   la poésie française (1550–1585)*,
   2:740a-b
Raymond of Toledo, Archbishop, 1:408a
Rayons et les ombres, Les. See Hugo, Victor
"Rayons jaunes, Les." *See* Sainte-Beuve,
   Charles-Augustin
"Razgovor knigoprodavtsa s Poetom." *See*
   Pushkin, Alexander, "Conversation
   Between a Bookseller and a Poet"
Razgovor o Dante. See Mandelshtam, Osip
"Razgovor Olega i Kazimira." *See* Khlebnikov,
   Velimir
"Razgovor s fininspektorom o poezii." *See*
   Mayakovsky, Vladimir
"Razgovor s Gojom." *See* Andrić, Ivo
Razin, Sten'ka, Gorky and, 8:422a
Razluka. See Tsvetaeva, Marina
Re Torrismondo, Il. See Tasso, Torquato
Reader participation
  in Hoffmann, 5:281b, 287b
  Yourcenar and, 12:2541a
  see also Audience participation
Reader-response criticism, Unamuno's
   anticipation of, 8:296b
Reading, act of, in Beauvoir's *Memoirs of a
   Dutiful Daughter*, 12:2706b–2707a
Reading, as process
  Barthes on, 13:3096a–3097b
  Unamuno's views on, 8:305a-b
Readings for a Shadow. *See* Giraudoux, Jean,
   Lectures pour une ombre

Real duration, in Bergson's thought, 8:50a-b,
   56a-b, 58a-b, 59a-b
*Real History of the Philosopher Peregrinus
   Proteus, The. See* Wieland, Christoph
   Martin, *Die geheime Geschichte des
   Philosophen Peregrinus Proteus*
"Real Truth, The." *See* Zamyatin, Yevgeny
   Ivanovich
Real World, The. *See* Aragon, Louis, *Le monde
   réel* cycle
Realidad. See Pérez Galdós, Benito
Realism
  in 19th-century French literature, 7:1410a
  in Augier's plays, 7:1919b, 1920b
  in Austrian drama, Grillparzer's influence
   on, 5:423a-b, 444a
  in Azorín's works, 9:639b
  Baroja's scorn for, 9:590b
  Baudelaire and, 7:1329b–1330a
  Bergson's view of, 8:54b
  in Böll's writing, 13:3172b–3173a
  Broch and, 10:1390a
  Camus and, 13:3067a
  compared to naturalism and *verismo*,
   7:1544b–1545a
  Dostoevsky and, 7:1362a-b
  Eça and, 7:1683a-b, 1689a, 1696a-b,
   1700b–1701a
  in English literature, Sade's admiration for,
   4:627a-b
  Flaubert and, 7:1382a-b
  in the French theater, 7:1415b
  generations of, in Denmark, 9:1037a
  Genet and, 13:2885b
  in German drama, 11:2098a
  in Goethe's works
   Urfaust, 5:18b
   Wilhelm Meister, 5:16a
  Gogol and, 6:995b, 996a
  in Goncharov's works, 6:1061a,
   1065b–1067b, 1068a
  in the Goncourts' works, 7:1399a-b, 1403a-b,
   1405a-b, 1414a
  in Hamsun's works, 8:27b
  of Hesse, 9:833b–834a
  in Ibsen's plays, 7:1444a

in Lermontov's works, 6:1195a,
1206b–1207a, 1209a, 1218a-b
literary devices of, 9:1037a-b
Maupassant's view of, 7:1764a
Milosz and, 13:2939a-b
Moberg's, 11:2204a, 2208a
Moravia and, 12:2676a, 2695b
Nerval and, 6:962a, 962b
poetic, **6:913a–942b**
Schlegel and, 5:183b
Portuguese literature and, 10:1484b
Proust and, 8:565b–566a
in Richter's *Siebenkäs*, 5:69b–70a
in Robbe-Grillet's works, 13:3241a-b
Russian, Bely and, 9:927b
in Scribe's plays, 7:1915b–1916a
Stendhal and, 5:353a-b
supernatural, Huysmans and,
7:1720b–1721b
Undset and, 9:1019a, 1037a-b
Verde and, 10:1484b
and Wieland, 4:596a
see also Naturalism; Social realism
Realism as a New Expression of Art. *See* Eça
de Queiroz, José Maria, "O realismo
como nova expressão da arte"
Reality
in Ariosto, 2:635a
art and
Johnson on, 12:2372b–2373a
Milosz on, 13:2938b–2939a
in Balzac's works, 5:639a-b, 641a–642a
in Butor, 13:3307a
Céline's truth-to-impression and,
11:1860b–1861a
eternity and, in Calderón's *Life Is a Dream*,
889b–890a
fantasy and, for Hoffmann, 5:281a-b
Frisch and, 13:2900a, 2914a-b
Gautier's filtering of, 6:1045b–1046a
illusion and, in Anouilh's works, 13:2843a
Kierkegaard and, 6:1131b–1132a
language and, Mallarmé's theories of,
7:1576a–1578a, 1587a-b, 1588b–1589b
Moravia and, 12:2686b, 2688a–2689a, 2688b
objective vs. subjective, in Breton's thought,
11:1944a, 1945b–1946a, 1955a-b

Rimbaud's view of, 7:1791a, 1792a,
1792b–1793b, 1797a, 1799a, 1805a-b,
1809b
in Rousseau, 4:462a–463a
Sartre and, 12:2594b–2595b
theater and, Maeterlinck on, 8:130b–131b,
137b
in Wolfram's romances, 1:265b, 281b–282b
geographical, 1:271b–272a
historical, 1:272a-b, 282b–285b
Reality. See Pérez Galdós, Benito, *Realidad*
(play and novel)
Reality (Dreamed), A. *See* Ekelöf, Gunnar, "En
verklighet (drömd)"
Reason
Augustine on, 1:44b, 46b
faith and, Aquinas on, 1:424b
Foucault and, 13:3334a–3338b
Gombrowicz and, 12:2570a-b
Kant's critiques of, 5:399a-b
Novalis on, 5:211a-b
Ortega y Gasset's theory of, 9:1128a-b,
1129a–1132a
in *Romance of the Rose*, 1:328a–329b
Reasonable Marriage, The. See Scribe, Eugène,
Le mariage de raison
"Reawakening, The." *See* Leopardi, Giacomo
Rebecque, Henri-Benjamin Constant de. *See*
Constant, Benjamin
Rebel, artist as, Ady, 9:876b
Rebel, The. See Camus, Albert
Rebelión de las masas. See Ortega y Gasset,
José
Rebellion in the Cevennes, The. See Tieck,
Ludwig, *Der Aufruhr in den Cevennen*
Rebelliousness, Hamsun's use of, 8:38b–39a
Rebirth, in Hugo's works, 6:711b
Rebours, À. See Huysmans, Joris Karl
"Recalling *Time of Indifference." See* Moravia,
Alberto, "Ricordo de *Gli indifferenti*"
Récamier, Julie, Benjamin Constant and,
4:410b, 413a-b
Recently and Formerly. *See* Verlaine, Paul,
Jadis et naguère
Reception of the World. *See* Mann, Heinrich,
Empfang bei der Welt

"Recherche de Dieu, La." *See* Leconte de Lisle, Charles Marie

Recherche de l'absolu, La. See Balzac, Honoré de

Reciprocity
    in Montesquieu's thought, 3:347b–364a
    in Walther, 1:293b–297a

Recircled Sun, The. *See* Arp, Jean, *Le soleil recerclé*

Récit form, in Yourcenar's works, 12:2538a, 2539a, 2544a

Recitation, Marinetti and, 9:818a-b

"Recitation to the Glory of a Queen" ("Récitation à la gloire d'une Reine"). *See* Perse, Saint-John

Récits, of Gide, 8:503b–516a

Récits fantastiques. See Gautier, Théophile

"Recollection, A." *See* Olesha, Yuri, "Vospominanie"

Recollections of Alexis de Tocqueville, The. See Tocqueville, Alexis de, *Souvenirs*

Recollections of the Golden Triangle. See Robbe-Grillet, Alain

Recollections of My Youth. See Renan, Joseph Ernest, *Souvenirs de jeunesse*

Recollections of Rubens. See Burckhardt, Jacob

Reconciliation, Sartre and, 12:2595b–2596a

Reconciliation, The. See Hauptmann, Gerhart, *Das Friedensfest*

"Rectificación de la República" (Rectification of the Republic). *See* Ortega y Gasset, José

Red and the Black, The. See Stendhal

Red Book and the Great Wall, The. See Moravia, Alberto

Red Booklet, The. *See* Laxness, Halldór, *Rauða Kverið*

Red Carnation, The. See Vittorini, Elio, *Il garofano rosso*

Red Cavalry. See Babel, Isaac

Red Chariot on the Sea. *See* Ady, Endre, "Vörös szekér a tengeren"

Red Dawn. See Baroja, Pío

Red Donkey, The. *See* Simenon, Georges, *L'Âne rouge*

"Red Front." *See* Aragon, Louis, "Front rouge"

Red Hen, The. See Hauptmann, Gerhart, *Der rote Hahn*

Red Magic. See Ghelderode, Michel de

Red Notebook, The. See Constant, Benjamin, *Le cahier rouge*

Red Robe, The. See Brieux, Eugène, *La robe rouge*

Red Room, The. *See* Strindberg, August, *Röda rummet*

"Red Shoes, The." *See* Andersen, Hans Christian

Red Virgin Soil (Russian journal). *See Krasnaia nov'*

Red Warrior. *See Krasnyi voin*

Red Wheel, The. See Solzhenitsyn, Aleksandr

Red Withering. *See* Kosztolányi, Dezső, "Vörös hervadás"

"Rede des toten Christus vom Weltgebäude herab, dass kein Gott sei." *See* Richter, Jean Paul

Redegonda's Diary. *See* Schnitzler, Arthur, "Das Tagebuch der Redegonda"

Redemption
    in Klopstock, 4:516b–521a
    in Milosz's works, 13:2941b
    see also Salvation

Redentin Easter play, 1:468a

Redgauntlet. See Scott, Sir Walter

Rediscovered Poems. *See* Apollinaire, Guillaume, "Poèmes retrouvés"

Rediscovered Satchel, A. *See* Lesage, Alain-René, *La valise trouvé*

"Reed, The." *See* Akhmatova, Anna, "Trostnik"

Reeds and Mud. See Blasco Ibáñez, Vicente

Reeve, F. D., on Blok, 9:961b, 977b–978a

Reflection, idea of, in Benjamin's works, 11:1724b–1725a

Reflections. *See* Leopardi, Giacomo, *Pensieri*

Reflections of an Unpolitical Man. See Mann, Thomas

"Reflections on the Composition of *Memoirs of Hadrian*." *See* Yourcenar, Marguerite, "Carnet de notes de *Mémoires d'Hadrien*"

Reflections on the French Revolution. See Burke, Edmund

Reflections on History. See Burckhardt, Jacob

"Reflections on the Ideals of the Ancients."
See Wieland, Christoph Martin,
"Gedanken über die Ideale der Alten"
Reflections of a Nonpolitical Man. See Mann,
Thomas
Reflections on Poetry. See Racine, Louis
"Reflections on the Spirit of the Party." *See*
Chénier, André, "Réflexions sur l'esprit
de parti"
"Reflections on Truth in Art." *See* Vigny,
Alfred Victor de, *Cinq-Mars ou une
conjuration sous Louis XIII (Cinq-Mars;
or, A Conspiracy under Louis XIII),*
"Réflexions sur la vérité dans l'art"
Reflections on the World Today. See Valéry,
Paul, *Regards sur le monde actuel*
Réflexion sur la question juive. See Sartre,
Jean-Paul, *Anti-Semite and Jew*
Réflexions critiques sur Longin. See
Boileau-Despréaux, Nicolas
Réflexions diverses. See La Rochefoucauld,
François VI, duc de
Réflexions ou sentences et maximes morales.
See La Rochefoucauld, François VI, duc
de
*Réflexions politiques sur quelques écrits du
jour et sur les intérêts de tous les
français. See* Chateaubriand, François
René de
"Réflexions sur la vérité dans l'art." *See* Vigny,
Alfred Victor de, *Cinq-Mars ou une
conjuration sous Louis XIII*
"Réflexions sur l'esprit de parti." *See* Chénier,
André
Reflexiveness, in Richter's *Walt and Vult,*
5:76a-b
Reform of Intelligence. See Ortega y Gasset,
José, "Reforma de la inteligencia"
"Reforma de la inteligencia." *See* Ortega y
Gasset, José
Reformation, Protestant. *See* Protestant
Reformation
Refugee Conversations. See Brecht, Bertolt,
Flüchtlingsgespräche
Refus, theme of, of Mallarmé, 7:1581b–1582a,
1583b, 1585b, 1588b–1589a
"Refusal." *See* Khlebnikov, Velimir, "Otkaz"

Refutation of the Catechism of Paul Ferry. See
Bossuet, Jacques Bénigne
*Réfutation de l'ouvrage d'Helvétius intitulé
"L'Homme" (Refutation of Helvetius'
Work Entitled "Man"). See* Diderot,
Denis
Regalia, Gallican church and, 3:167b–168a
Regarding the Authority of Cassianus. See
Fénelon, François de Salignac de la
Mothe-
Regards sur le monde actuel. See Valéry, Paul
Regenerationism, Ortega y Gasset and,
9:1121b, 1123b
"Régi énekek ekhója." *See* Ady, Endre
Régicide, Un. See Robbe-Grillet, Alain
Reginald of Piperno, 1:416a, 417b, 418a, 418b,
419a
Regionalism, in Mauriac, 10:1315a–1316a
Regn i gryningen. See Johnson, Eyvind
Regoli, Teresa Mocenni, Alfieri's letters to,
4:669a-b
"Regrets, Les." *See* Bellay, Joachim du
Regula Amrain and Her Youngest Son. See
Keller, Gottfried
Regularis concordia. See Ethelwold of
Winchester, bishop
Rehabilitation, literary, of Akhmatova,
10:1529b, 1530b, 1531a, 1541a
Rehearsal at Versailles, The. See Molière,
L'Impromptu de Versailles
Rehearsal, The. *See* Andrić, Ivo, "Proba"
Rehearsal, The. See Anouilh, Jean, *La
répétition ou l'amour puni*
Rehearsing the Play. *See* Pirandello, Luigi,
"Provando la commedia"
Rei Seleuco, El-. See Camoëns, Luís Vaz de
Reichssprüche. See Walther von der
Vogelweide
"Reification and the Consciousness of the
Proletariat." *See* Lukács, György, "Die
Verdinglichung und das Bewusstsein
des Proletariats"
Reigen. See Schnitzler, Arthur, *Hands Around*
Reign of Terror
Chénier's death during, 4:691a-b, 692a
Law of Suspects, Chénier's arrest under,
4:713b–714a

Reign of Terror (*cont.*)
    Sade's revulsion toward, 4:628a
    see also French Revolution of 1789
Reina Calafia, La. See Blasco Ibáñez, Vicente
Reina castiza, La. See Valle-Inclán, Ramón del
Reinald von Dassel, in "Fama tuba dante
    sonum," 1:342b–343a
Reinar después de morir. See Guevara, Luis
    Vélez de
Reincarnation, Schopenhauer's doctrine of,
    5:410a
Reine Margot, La. See Dumas père, Alexandre
Reine morte, La. See Montherlant, Henry de
Reinhardt, Max
    Gorky's *Enemies* and, 8:420b
    Hofmannsthal and, 9:691a, 694a, 697b, 700a
    Pirandello's *Six Characters* and, 8:407b
    Strindberg and, 7:1748a
    The Miracle and, 8:487b
    Viennese theater and, 9:693a-b
Reinitz, Béla, 9:861b
Reinmar von Hagenau
    Walther and, 1:293a-b
    Wolfram and, 1:264a
Reis, Ricardo, 10:1487b–1488a, 1491b–1492a
"Reise durch die deutsche Inflation." *See*
    Benjamin, Walter
Reise von München nach Genva. See Heine,
    Heinrich
Reisebilder. See Heine, Heinrich
Reiter, Heinrich, 9:931b
Reiteration. *See* Repetition
"Reka vremen." *See* Derzhavin, Gavrül
Rekviem. See Akhmatova, Anna, *Requiem*
Relation d'un voyage de Paris en Limousin.
    See La Fontaine, Jean de
Relation sur le quiétisme. See Bossuet,
    Jacques Bénigne
Relativism
    in Broch, 10:1397b, 1405a
    in Čapek's works, 10:1571a–1582b
    of Herder, 5:1b
    of Hesse, 9:843b, 846b
    Leconte de Lisle and, 6:1256b
    Leopardi and, 5:542a
    of Richter, 5:56a-b

Relativity, special theory of, Mann's *Magic
    Mountain* and, 9:722b
Relativity themes, in Mallarmé, 7:1591b–1592a
Relève du matin, La. See Montherlant, Henry
    de
Relic, The. See Eça de Queiroz, José Maria
Religieuse, La. See Diderot, Denis
Religion
    Andersen on, 6:878a
    in Aymé's works, 12:2439b
    Bergson on, 8:46b–47a, 61b–64b
    Berlioz on, 6:773a
    Broch and, 10:1398a
    customs and practices, discussed in La
        Bruyère's *Caractères*, 3:253b
    Diderot and, 4:477a–479a
    in Dürrenmatt's works, 13:3217b,
        3219b–3220b
    Eça and, 7:1693b
    Freud's concept of totemism, 8:12a–13a
    Goethe on, 5:19b
    Goncharov on, 6:1083b
    in Grass, 13:3369a
    in Hebbel's works, 6:1102a
    Heine's opposition to, 5:499a
    Huysmans and, 7:1709b, 1719a–1720a,
        1726a
    in Ionesco's works, 13:3017a
    Kazantzakis on god and man,
        9:1074b–1075a
    in Klopstock, 4:532a–533b
    in La Bruyère's *Caractères*, 3:255b–257b
    La Rochefoucauld and, 3:62a
    Leconte de Lisle and, 6:1250a-b
        critique of, 6:1252b–1255b
    Lessing on, 4:545a
    Lope de Vega and, 2:847a-b
    Machiavelli on, 2:610a
    Mandelshtam and, 10:1627b–1630b
    Manzoni's defense of, 5:374a–375a
    Marx and, 5:213a-b
    Mérimée on, 6:746b, 748b–749a, 752b,
        753b–754a, 762b
    Milosz and, 13:2937b–2938a
    Moberg on, 11:2221a, 2223a, 2225a
    Nerval on, 6:960a, 968b
    Nietzsche and, 7:1645a-b, 1648a-b, 1678b

Novalis on, 5:213a-b

in Pascoli's poetry, 7:1830b

philosophy of. *See* Philosophy of religion

in Portugal during Pessoa's time, 10:1477a

in Proust's *Remembrance of Things Past*, 8:551b

Richter on, 5:79b

in Rilke's poetry, 9:768b, 776a, 776b, 777a
  Das Stundenbuch, 9:769b–770a

in Rousseau, 4:468b–469a

Sand and, 6:824b–825b

in Sartre's works, 13:3220b

Schlegel and, 5:182b–183a, 194b

Schleiermacher and, 5:219a

Södergran and, 11:1803a

in Strindberg's works, 7:1745b

in Ungaretti's poetry, 10:1466a-b

Voltaire on
  anti-clericalism themes, 4:367a–368a, 378a–379b, 383b–384a, 390b–391a
  Protestant sects, 4:384a–385a

vs. science. *See* Science, vs. religion

Wagner and, 7:1665b

Walther and, 1:302b–304b

Weil and, 12:2788b, 2792b, 2802a, 2804a-b, 2805a-b, 2806b

see also Christianity; Faith; Protestantism; Roman Catholic Church

Religious drama. *See Autos sacramentales*; Drama, religious; Miracle plays; Mystery plays

Religious literature, parodied, in medieval satire, 1:369b–370a

Religious orders
  boys in, Aquinas on, 1:417b
  in *Speculum stultorum*, 1:373a
  see also Dominicans; Franciscans; Jesuits; Mendicant orders

Religious symbolism. *See* Symbolism, religious

Reliques of Ancient English Poetry. See Percy, Thomas

Relíquia, A. See Eça de Queiroz, José Maria, *The Relic*

"Remansos." *See* García Lorca, Federico

Remarks on the Raising of Money. See Machiavelli, Niccolò, *Parole da dirle sopra la provisione del danaio, facto un poco di proemio et di scusa*

Rembrandt van Rijn, Taine on, 7:1462a

Remedia amoris. See Ovid

Remedio en la desdicha, El. See Lope de Vega

Remembering. *See* Johnson, Eyvind, *Minnas*

Remembering Mother. *See* Gunnarsson, Gunnar, *Moðurminning*

Remembrance, theme of, in Foscolo, 5:332a-b

"Remembrance." *See* Hölderlin, Friedrich, "Andenken"; Musset, Alfred de

Remembrance of Things Past. See Proust, Marcel

Reményi, József, 9:864a

Remeslo. See Tsvetaeva, Marina

Reminiscence, in Olesha's fiction, 11:2240b, 2241b, 2252b

Reminiscences of A. A. Blok. *See* Bely, Andrey, *Vospominaniia o A. A. Bloke*

Reminiscences of Steiner. *See* Bely, Andrey, *Vospominaniia o Shteinere*

Remontage (remounting), in Rousseau, 4:463a-b

Remorses. See Elytis, Odysseus, *Exi kai mia tipsis yia ton ourano*

Renaissance
  autobiography and, 12:2703b
  Burckhardt on, 6:1232a, 1235a–1236b
  Croce on, 8:319a
  Delacroix's description of, 5:525a
  idea of progress and, 3:168b
  interpenetration of life and literature, Petrarch as exemplar, 2:502b–503a
  Schnitzler's treatment of, 8:97b–98a
  see also Portuguese Renaissance

Renaissance de l'Occident (literary group), Ghelderode and, 11:2115a

Renaissance man, Herder as one of the last, 4:639b–640a

Renaissance poetry. *See particular poets*; Pastoral poetry, Renaissance

Renaissance Storybook, A. See Bishop, Morris

Renan, Ernest, 3:318a
  Bergson and, 8:46b, 47a
  Claudel and, 8:472a, 490b

Renan, Ernest (*cont.*)
  compared with Michelet, 5:599a, 599b–600a
  divine revelation, 7:1456b
  Leconte de Lisle and, 6:1256a
  Mathilde Bonaparte and, 7:1416a
  Ortega y Gasset and, 9:1122b
  portrayal of French culture, 7:1400a-b
  Souvenirs de jeunesse (*Recollections of My Youth*), 3:318a-b
  Taine and, 7:1449a, 1452a, 1464a
  Vie de Jésus (*Life of Jesus*), 7:1464b–1465a, 1546a, 8:471a
Renascença Portuguêsa. See Portuguese Renaissance
Renaud et Armide. See Cocteau, Jean
Renaud, Madeleine, Giraudoux and, 9:1058b
Renaut de Beaujeu, *Le Bel Inconnu*, 1:149a-b
Rencontre. See Butor, Michel
Render unto Caesar. See Yourcenar, Marguerite, *Rendre à César*
Rendez-vous de Senlis, Le. See Anouilh, Jean
Rendez-vous, Le. See Ionesco, Eugène, *La soif et la faim*
Rendezvous at Senlis, The; Dinner with the Family. See Anouilh, Jean, *Le rendez-vous de Senlis*
Rendre à César. See Yourcenar, Marguerite
René. See Chateaubriand, François René de
Renée Mauperin. See Goncourt, Edmond Louis Antoine and Jules Alfred Huot de
"*Renégat, Le.*" *See* Camus, Albert, *The Renegade*
Reneri, Heinrich, 3:19b
Reneville, Roland de, *L'expérience poetique*, Seferis' translation, 12:2259b
Renoir, Auguste, 7:1630b
Renoir, Jean, Mérimée and, 6:750b
"*Reparties de Nina, Les.*" *See* Rimbaud, Arthur
Répertoire. See Butor, Michel
Repetition
  Freud's concept of, 8:14a–16a
  historical
    in Johnson's works, 12:2376a-b
    in *Macbeth*, 13:3012b
  as literary device
    in Baudelaire, 7:1338a–1339b
    in Cela, 13:3111a

  in Ekelöf's works, 12:2654b
  in Ritsos, 12:2837a-b
  in Robbe-Grillet's works, 13:3246b–3247a, 3249a-b
"*Répetition, Une*" ("*A Rehearsal*"). *See* Maupassant, Guy de
Repetition. See Kierkegaard, Søren
Repetitions. See Ritsos, Yannis, *Epanalipsis*
"Réponse aux injures et calomnies de je ne sçay quels Predicantereaux et Ministreaux de Genéve." *See* Ronsard, Pierre de
Report to Greco. See Kazantzakis, Nikos, *Anaforá ston Gréko*
Report to His Majesty Ludwig II, King of Bavaria, Concerning a German Music School to Be Erected in Munich." *See* Wagner, Richard, "Bericht an Seine Majestät der König Ludwig II von Bayern Über eine in München zu erichtende deutsche Musikschule"
Report to the King. *See* Necker, Jacques, *Compte-rendu au roi*
Reportata Parisiensia. See Duns Scotus, *Commentaries on the Sentences*
Reportationes, 1:412b–413a
Representacio Adae (*Play of Adam*), 1:456a, 457a, 457b–458b
Representation
  allegorical, 1:5b
  figurative. *See* Figurative representation
  Foucault and, 13:3324a–3326b
Repression, Freud's concept of, 8:6a
Repression, political. *See* Political repression
Reprieve, The. See Sartre, Jean-Paul
"Reprise de *Bajazet* au Théâtre-Français." *See* Musset, Alfred de
Reproduction, sexual
  Aquinas' *Summa theologica* on, 1:423b
  Schopenhauer's metaphysics and, 5:409a-b
Reproductions of Banality. See Kaplan, Alice
Republic. See Plato
Republic of Labor. *See* Solzhenitsyn, Aleksandr, *Respublika truda*
Republic of Letters, The (*La république des lettres*). *See* Chénier, André
Republican Party (U.S.), 8:533a

Republicanism
    Machiavelli and, 2:600a–604a
    in Novalis' *Faith and Love*, 5:214b–215a
    in Portugal, 11:2146a-b
    during Pessoa's time, 10:1487a
Republika (The Republic), Krleža and,
        11:1823a
Requiem. See Akhmatova, Anna; Berlioz,
        Hector
Requiem. *See* Gunnarsson, Gunnar,
        Sálumessa
"Requiem für eine Freundin" ("Requiem for a
        Friend"). *See* Rilke, Rainer Maria
Requiem, Lc. See Cocteau, Jean
Rerum familiarium libri. See Petrarch
Rerum memorandarum libri. See Petrarch
Rerum vulgarium fragmenta. See Petrarch,
        Canzoniere
Rescuing Horace. See Lessing, Gotthold
        Ephraim, *Rettungen des Horaz*
Resende, Emilia, 7:1693a
Resende, Garcia de, *Cancioneiro geral*, 2:749a,
        753a
Residencia de los Estudiantes (Madrid), Lorca
        and, 11:2169a-b
Residential Quarter. See Aragon, Louis, *Les
        beaux quartiers*
Resignation, in Goethe's *Wilhelm Meister's
        Travels*, 5:23b
"Resistances to Psychoanalysis." *See* Freud,
        Sigmund, "Die Widerstände gegen die
        Psychoanalyse"
Resistible Rise of Arturo Ui, The. See Brecht,
        Bertolt
Resolution. See Luther, Martin
Resplandor de la hoguera, El. See
        Valle-Inclán, Ramón del, *La guerra
        carlista*
Responsibility
    Butor on, 13:3311a
    of the individual, in Büchner,
        6:1180a–1182a
    Sartre and, 12:2595b
Respublica play, 1:471b
Respublika truda. See Solzhenitsyn, Aleksandr
Rest Home. See Cela, Camilo José
Restless Heart. See Anouilh, Jean

Restlessness of Shanti Andía, The. See Baroja,
        Pío, *Las inquietudes de Shanti Andía*
Resurrection, 1:456a
Resurrection
    of Christ, in German Easter plays, 1:467a
    in Dürrenmatt's works, 13:3220a-b
    in Ekelöf's works, 12:2641a
    in Elytis' poetry, 13:2967b
    Proust on, 8:561a
    Prudentius on, 1:17a, 18a
    in Rabelais's *Pantagruel*, 2:703b–704a
Resurrection. See Tolstoy, Leo
"Resurrection, The." *See* Manzoni, Alessandro,
        The Sacred Hymns
Résurrection, Ghelderode and, 11:2134b
Retablillo de don Cristóbal. See García Lorca,
        Federico
Retablo de las maravillas, El. See Cervantes,
        Miguel de, *The Wonder Show*
"Retorno fugaz." *See* Jiménez, Juan Ramón
"Retour d'Artaud le mômo, Le." *See* Artaud,
        Antonin
Retour de l'U.R.S.S.. See Gide, André
Retractationes. See Augustine, St.
Retraite sentimentale, La. See Colette
Retreat from Love, The. See Colette, *La retraite
        sentimentale*
Retribution. See Blok, Alexander
Rettungen des Horaz. See Lessing, Gotthold
        Ephraim
Return. See Goldoni, Carlo
"Return of Artaud, le Mômo, The." *See* Artaud,
        Antonin, "Le retour d'Artaud le mômo"
Return from the U.S.S.R.. See Gide, André,
        Retour de l'U.R.S.S.
Return of Iphigenia, The. *See* Ritsos, Yannis, *I
        epistrofi tis Ifighenias*
Return of Philip Latinovicz, The. See Krleža,
        Miroslav, *Povratak Filipa Latinovicza*
Return of the Soldier, The. *See* Johnson,
        Eyvind, *Soldatens återkomst*
Return to the Future. See Undset, Sigrid
Return to Ithaca. See Johnson, Eyvind
Returning Home. *See* Bely, Andrey,
        Vozvrashchenie na rodinu
Retz, Cardinal de, 3:59a, 68a
    Mémoires, 3:60a

Reunification, in Broch's *Death of Vergil*, 10:1400b–1402a

Révai, József, on Ady, 9:860b

"Revanche." *See* Södergran, Edith

Rêve de d'Alembert. See Diderot, Denis

"Rêve de l'huitre, Le." *See* Butor, Michel

Rêve, Le. See Zola, Émile

"Rêve parisien." *See* Baudelaire, Charles, "Paris Dream"

Réveil municipal de Clichy, Claudel and, 8:484b

Réveille-Matin des François, 2:771a

"Revelation and Downfall." *See* Trakl, Georg

"Revelation and Downfall." *See*

"Revelation of Golias the Bishop." *See* "Apocalypsis Goliae Episcopi"

Revelation of St. John. *See* Apocalypse

"Revenge." *See* Södergran, Edith, "Revanche"

Revenge, theme of. *See* Vengeance, theme of

Reverdie, Colin and, 1:181a

"Reverendo, Il." *See* Verga, Giovanni

"Rêverie." *See* Dali, Salvador

Rêveries du promeneur solitaire (Reveries of a Solitary Stroller). See Rousseau, Jean Jacques

Reversal, principle of, Foucault and, 13:3349a–3350b

Reversals, Tasso's use as plot mechanism, 2:795a

Reviczky, Gyula, "Pálma a Hortobágyon" ("Palm Tree on the Hungarian Plains"), 9:863a

Revista de Occidente, 9:1119a

Revista de Portugal. See Eça de Queiroz, José Maria

Revival of Racine's *Bajazet* at the Comédie Française. *See* Musset, Alfred de, "Reprise de *Bajazet* au Théâtre-Français"

Revolt of the masses, Ortega y Gasset's views, 9:1142a-b, 1143b–1145a

Revolt of the Masses, The. See Ortega y Gasset, José, *Rebelión de las masas*

Révolte dans les Asturies (Revolt in the Asturias). *See* Camus, Albert

Revolución y la novela en Rusia, La. See Pardo Bazán, Emila de

Revolution of 1550, France, in literature, 2:721a, 739a-b, 742a

Revolution of 1848
  Germany
    Fontane and, 6:1306b–1307a
    Heine and, 5:507a
    Wagner and, 6:1153a
  Leconte de Lisle and, 6:1250b–1251b
  Michelet and, 5:595a, 598a, 600a, 601a
  Sainte-Beuve and, 6:838b–839a
  Sand and, 6:829a–832a
  Storm and, 6:915a–916a
  Tocqueville and, 6:900a–905a

Revolution of July 1830. *See* France, Revolution of July 1830

Revolution and the novel in Russia, The. See Pardo Bazán, Emila de, *La revolución y la novela en Rusia*

Revolution, political
  Ady and, 9:864a-b, 866a-b
  in Bely's *Petersburg*, 9:921a
  Blasco Ibáñez' *The Cabin* and, 8:376a
  Büchner and, 6:1176b–1182a
  in Ghelderode's plays
    La transfiguration dans le cirque, 11:2129a
    Pantagleize, 11:2127a–2129a
  mentality
    in Grass's *Local Anaesthetic*, 13:3378a–3379a
    in Kundera's *Life Is Elsewhere*, 13:3402b–3403a
  in Richter's *Hesperus*, 5:66b
  in Schiller's works
    The Robbers, 5:31b–32a
    William Tell, 5:49a
  Tocqueville on, 6:904a-b
  in Valle-Inclán's *Tirano Banderas*, 8:339b–341a
  Zamyatin's philosophy of, 10:1187a, 1198a
  see also French Revolution of 1789; Russian Revolution (1917); *under names of countries*

Révolution surréaliste, La (journal), 11:2066b–2067a
  Arp and, 10:1371b
  Artaud's contributions to, 11:1966a-b

Breton's articles in, 11:1941a

illustrations in, 11:2071a

Revolutionaries. *See* Ritsos, Yannis, "Epanastates"

Revolver à cheveux blancs. See Breton, André

Revue de l'instruction publique (journal), Taine's articles for, 7:1451b

Revue de Paris (journal), Delacroix's essays in, 5:524a, 524b–525a

Revue des deux mondes (journal), Musset's works in, 6:1006b

Revue indépendante (journal), Sand and, 6:826a

Rexroth, Kenneth, 9:883b

Reybaz, André, 11:2116b

"Reyerta." *See* García Lorca, Federico

Reykdœla saga, 1:395b–396a

Reysner, Larisa, Mandelshtam protected by, 10:1638b–1639a

Rhapsody of Naked Light. See Ritsos, Yannis, *Phokimasia*

"Rhein, Der." *See* Hölderlin, Friedrich

"Rhénanes." *See* Apollinaire, Guillaume, *Alcools*

Rhenish Elegies. See Pirandello, Luigi, *Elegie renane*

"Rhenish Night." *See* Apollinaire, Guillaume, *Alcools*, "Nuit rhénane"

Rhetoric

Augustine on, 1:43a-b

Büchner and, 6:1178a–1182a

Christian, Augustine's *On Christian Doctrine* and, 1:27b, 43a

Ciceronian, Augustine and, 1:38a-b, 42a, 43a

Gottfried's use of, 1:246a–250a

pagan, Prudentius and, 1:18b–19a

vs. action, in Büchner's *Danton's Death*, 6:1177a–1182a, 1191a–1192a

see also Bossuet, Jacques Bénigne; Oratory

Rhetoric. See Aristotle

Rhin, Le. See Hugo, Victor

Rhine, The. See Hugo, Victor, *Le Rhin*

Rhinegold, The. See Wagner, Richard, *Der Ring des Nibelungen*

Rhinocéros. See Ionesco, Eugène

Rhume onirique, La. See Ionesco, Eugène

Rhyme

in Berlioz' works, 6:793a

in *canso*, 1:176a-b

in Gautier's poetry, 6:1056a, 1058a

in La Fontaine's *Fables*, 3:83b–86b

Leopardi's use of, 5:555b

Nerval and, 6:959b–960a

in the *Nibelungenlied*, 1:216a-b

in Pascoli's poetry, 7:1832b–1833a

Queneau's use of, 12:2520a-b

in troubadour poetry, 1:161b, 176a-b

unrhymed verse, Carducci and, 7:1508b–1509b

in Verlaine's poetry, 7:1635b–1636b, 1637b

Rhymes and Rhythms. *See* Carducci, Giosue, *Rime e ritmi*

Rhythm

Augustine on, 1:47b

in Gombrowicz's *Trans-Atlantyk*, 12:2581a-b

Ribbing, Adolf, Count, 5:91b, 92a

"Ribeira." *See* Gautier, Théophile

Ribeiro, Aquilino, Ferreira de Castro, 11:2149a

Ribemont-Dessaignes, Georges, *Un cadavre*, 12:2513b

Ribera, Jusepe, Gautier and, 6:1042a

Ribot, Théodule-Armand, Strindberg and, 7:1753b

Ricard, Louis Xavier de, Verlaine and, 7:1620b

Ricci Gramitto family, 8:390a

Ricciarda. See Foscolo, Ugo

Rich Man, The. See Simenon, Georges, *Le riche homme*

Richard Darlington. See Dumas père, Alexandre

Richard, Jean-Pierre, on Verlaine, 7:1633a, 1633b–1634a

Richard the Pilgrim, *chansons de geste* of, 1:109b

"Richard the Redeles." *See* "Mum and the Sothsegger"

Richard of St. Victor, Dante and, 1:433b

Richard Wagner in Bayreuth. See Nietzsche, Friedrich

Richards, J. D., on Zamyatin, 10:1185a

Richardson, Samuel

Antoine-François Prévost's translations of, 4:394b

Richardson, Samuel (*cont.*)
  Beaumarchais and, 4:565a
  Clarissa Harlowe, 2:516a, 4:394b
    compared to Sade's *Aline and Valcour,*
     4:628b–629a
  Diderot and, 4:495a-b
  Dostoevsky and, 7:1351b
  Goethe's *The Sorrows of Young Werther*
    and, 5:5b, 6b
  Laclos's *Liaisons dangereuses* and, 6:401b
  Pamela; or, Virtue Rewarded, 4:401a-b
    Lessing and, 4:549b
  Richter's *The School for Aesthetics* and,
    5:78a
  Sade's admiration for, 4:627a-b
  Sir Charles Grandison, 4:394b
  Staël and, 5:89b, 99b
  Taine on, 7:1463a
Riche homme, Le. See Simenon, Georges
Richelet, Pierre, on Boileau's *Art poétique,*
  3:181a-b
Richelieu, Cardinal de
  Académie Française and, 3:68a
  Corneille and, 3:26a–28a
  La Rochefoucauld and, 3:54a, 54b, 57b, 58a
  Louis XIII and, 3:55b–56a, 56b
  Marie de' Medici and, 3:55a-b
  Mazarin and, 3:58b
  Vigny's view of, 5:458b–459a
  vs. Queen Anne, 3:57a, 57b
Richter, Jean Paul, **5:53a–88b**
  "Abelard und Heloise," 5:56a
  Andersen and, 6:877a-b
  Auswahl aus des Teufels Papieren
    (Selection of the Devil's Papers),
    5:57b–58a, 72a
  Blumen-, Frucht- und Dornenstücke (*Flower,*
    Fruit, and Thorn Pieces), 5:68a–70b,
    79a
  Briefe und bevorstehender Lebenslauf (Jean
    Paul's Letters and Conjectural
    Biography), 5:72a
  Das Kampanerthal (*The Campan Thal*),
    5:71b, 79b

  Das Leben des Quintus Fixlein, aus
    fünfzehn Zettelkästen gezogen (*The Life*
    of Quintus Fixlein, Extracted from
    Fifteen Letterboxes), 5:55a, 66a, 67a-b
  Das Leben des vergnügten Schulmeisterlein
    Maria Wutz in Auenthal (*The Life of the*
    Cheerful Schoolmaster Maria Wutz),
    5:59b–60b, 63b, 67a, 67b, 80b
  Das Leben Fibels, des Verfassers der
    Bienrodischen Fibel (*The Life of Fibel,*
    Author of the Bienrode ABC), 5:66a-b,
    81a-b
  Das Lob der Dummheit (The Praise of
    Stupidity), 5:57a-b
  Der Jubelsenior (The Parson in Jubilee),
    5:71b
  Der Komet, oder Nikolaus Marggraf, eine
    komische Geschichte (The Comet; or,
    Nicholas Marggrave, a Comic Story),
    5:81b–83b
  Des Amts-Vogts Josuah Freudel Klaglibell
    gegen seinen verfluchten Dämon (Bailiff
    Joshua Freudel's Complaint Against His
    Accursed Demon), 5:60b
  Des Feldpredigers Schmelzle Reise nach
    Flätz (*Army Chaplain Schmelzle's Trip*
    to Flätz), 5:80b–81a
  Des Rektors Florian Fälbels und seiner
    Primaner Reise nach dem Fichtelberg
    (The Journey of Headmaster Fälbel and
    His Seniors to Fichtelberg), 5:60b
  "Des toten Shakespear's Klage unter den
    toten Zuhörern in der Kirche, das kein
    Gott sei" (Lament of the Dead
    Shakespeare Among the Dead
    Congregation in Church Because There
    Is No God), 5:58b
  "Die Rede des toten Christus vom
    Weltgebäude herab, dass kein Gott sei"
    ("The Speech of Christ"), 5:59a
  "Die Schönheit des Sterbens in der Blüte
    des Lebens" (The Beauty of Dying in
    the Prime of Youth), 5:80a
  Die unsichtbare Loge (*The Invisible Lodge*),
    5:60b–63b, 66b, 207b
  characterization, 5:63a
  Hesperus and, 5:64a

plot, 5:61b
themes, 5:62a-b
Doktor Katzenbergers Badereise (Dr. Katzenberger's Trip to a Spa), 5:80b
"Ein Traum von einem Schlachtfeld" (A Dream of a Battlefield), 5:80a
"Etwas über den Menschen" (Some Thoughts About Humanity), 5:57a
Flegeljahre (*Walt and Vult*), 5:74b–77a
Freiheitsbüchlein (Freedom Booklet), 5:80a
George and, 8:460b
Grönländische Prozesse (*The Greenland Lawsuits*), 5:57b, 61a
Hesperus: Oder 45 Hundesposttagen (*Hesperus; oder, 45 Dog-Post-Days*), 5:63b–67a, 72a, 80a
Goethe on, 5:70b
plot, 5:63b–64a
themes, 5:65b–66a
"Jean Pauls biographische Belustigungen unter der Gehirnschale einer Riesin" (Jean Paul's Biographical Amusements Under the Cranium of a Giantess), 5:67b
Keller and, 6:923b
Levana, 5:79b
Palingenesien (*Palingenesis*), 5:72a
Selberlebensbeschreibung (*Autobiography*), 5:54b–55a
Selina, 5:79b
Titan, 5:66a, 71b–74b
as source for Vigny's *Daphné*, 5:477a
"Übungen im Denken" (Exercises in Thinking), 5:56a
Vorschule der Aesthetik (*School for Aesthetics*), 5:59b, 68a, 77b–78b, 79a, 80a
self and, 5:84b
on style, 5:84a
Richter und sein Henker, Der. See Dürrenmatt, Friedrich, *The Judge and His Hangman*
Richterin, Die. See Meyer, Conrad Ferdinand
"Ricordanze, Le." *See* Leopardi, Giacomo, "Memories"
"Ricordi di un vecchio scolaro." *See* Pascoli, Giovanni
"Ricordo d'Africa." *See* Ungaretti, Giuseppe

"Ricordo de *Gli Indifferenti*." *See* Moravia, Alberto
Rictus, Jehan
Queneau and, 12:2523a
translated by Ady, 9:862a
Rid i natt! See Moberg, Vilhelm, *Ride This Night!*
Riddara saga, 1:397a, 399b, 401b
Ride This Night! See Moberg, Vilhelm
Rider on the White Horse, The. See Storm, Theodor
Riders to the Sea. See Synge, John Millington
Ridiculous Précieuses, The. See Molière, *Les précieuses ridicules*
Riegl, Alois, *Spätrömische Kunstindustrie* (The Late Roman Art Industry), 11:1715b–1716a
Rienzi. See Wagner, Richard
Riesbeck, Johann Kaspar, on Wieland, 4:587a-b
Riesebilder. See Heine, Heinrich
Riesener, Henri, Delacroix and, 5:514b
"Rifugio d'uccelli notturni." *See* Quasimodo, Salvatore
Rigadoon. See Céline, Louis-Ferdinand, *Rigodon*
"Right Hand, The." *See* Solzhenitsyn, Aleksandr, "Pravaia kist"
Right You Are (If You Think So). See Pirandello, Luigi, *Così è (se vi pare)*
Rihaku, "Letter of an Exile," 12:2259a
Rilke, Rainer Maria, **9:767a–795b**
Ady and, 9:859b
"An die Musik" ("To Music"), 9:779a-b, 780a
on artifice, 9:732a
"Ausgesetzt auf den Bergen des Herzens" ("Exposed on the Mountains of the Heart"), 9:782a-b
on belief, 9:730b
Das Buch der Bilder (*The Book of Pictures*), 9:770b
"Eingang" ("Entering"), 9:783b–784b, 785b
Das Stundenbuch (*The Book of Hours*), 9:769b, 770a, 777a, 784a

Rilke, Rainer Maria (*cont.*)
  *Die Aufzeichnungen des Malte Laurids
    Brigge* (*The Notebooks of Malte Laurids
    Brigge*), 9:641b, 770a, 773a, 790a–792a
  Die Göttinnen and, 8:525a
  Die Letzten (*The Last Ones*), 11:1796a
  *Die Weise von Liebe und Tod des Cornets
    Christoph Rilke* (*The Lay of the Love
    and Death of the Cornet Christoph
    Rilke*), 9:769a-b
  Duineser Elegien (*Duino Elegies*), 9:771a,
    772b, 773a, 773b, 774b, 782a
    First, 9:781b
    Fourth, 9:772a
    Hölderlin and, 9:771b
    Ninth, 9:775b, 776a, 788b
  "Ein Frülingswind" ("A Springtime Wind"),
    9:775a-b
  "Elegie an Marina Zwetajewa-Efron,"
    11:1743a
  epitaph, 9:774a
  "Es winkt zu Fühlung" ("A Summons to
    Feeling"), 9:782a
  Eupalinos and, 8:584b
  "Fünf Gesänge" ("Five Songs"), 9:771b
  Heinrich Mann and, 8:519a
  Hesse and, 9:847b, 855b
  Hesse's *Beneath the Wheel* and, 9:836b
  Hölderlin and, 5:143a, 173b
  "Improvisationen aus dem Capreser Winter"
    ("Improvisations from Winter on
    Capri"), 9:774b–775a
  Kleist and, 5:310b–311a
  Kosztolányi and, 10:1234a-b
  Leben und Lieder (Life and Songs), 9:769b
  Mährisch-Weisskirchen Academy and,
    9:931b
  Musil and, 9:933a
  Neue Gedichte (*New Poems*), 9:770a, 773a,
    790a-b, 791a
    "Archaïscher Torso Apollos" ("Archaic
     Torso of Apollo"), 9:784b–786b, 787b,
     789a, 790a
  Pasternak and, 10:1592a, 1602b
    A Safe-Conduct, 10:1602b
    Sketch for an Autobiography, 10:1614a

  "Requiem für eine Freundin" ("Requiem for
    a Friend"), 9:770a
  Sonette an Orpheus (*Sonnets to Orpheus*),
    9:773a-b, 782a, 786b–789a
  "Sonnen-Untergang" ("Sunset"),
    9:777b–778a, 778b
  Tsvetaeva and, 11:1742b–1743a, 1744b
  "Wendung" ("Turning-Point"), 9:771a
  Yourcenar and, 12:2538a
Rim estramp, 1:176b–177a
Rimas. See Bécquer; Camoëns, Luís Vaz de;
  Jiménez, Juan Ramón
Rimbaud, Arthur, **7:1785a–1824b**
  "À la musique" ("To Music"), 7:1788b,
    1789b–1790a
  A Season in Hell (*Une saison en enfer*),
    7:1785a-b, 1793a, 1796a, 1804b, 1806a,
    1807b, 1808a, 1810a, 1811a,
    1812b–1813a, 1817a–1821a
  "Adieu," 7:1820b–1821a
  Ady and, 9:861b
  "After the Deluge" ("Après le deluge"),
    7:1808a, 1815b–1816a
  Apollinaire and, 9:881b, 882a
  Beauvoir and, 12:2710a, 2716a
  Brecht and, 11:2101
  Breton and, 11:1939a, 1950b
  "Ce qu'on dit au poète à propos des fleurs"
    ("What Is Said to the Poet Concerning
    Flowers"), 7:1796a–1797b
  Céline and, 11:1859b
  Claudel and, 8:472a
  in Claudel's *Break of Noon*, 8:478a
  "Coeur de pitre" ("Heart of a Clown"),
    7:1794a
  "Conte" ("Story"), 7:1813b, 1814b–1815a
  on the creative process, 12:2348a
  "Délires I: Vierge folle/L'Époux infernal"
    ("Delirium I: The Foolish Virgin/The
    Infernal Bridegroom"), 7:1820a-b
  "Délires II: Alchimie du verbe" (Delirium II:
    Alchemy of the Word"), 7:1084b,
    1820a-b
  Ekelöf and, 12:2657a, 2658b, 2666a-b
  "Enfance" ("Childhood"), 7:1810a,
    1813b–1814a

"Fêtes de la patience" ("Festivals of Patience"), 7:1808b

"Génie" ("Genius"), 7:1808a, 1816a–1817a

"Jeunesse" ("Youth"), 7:1811b

Laforgue's "Simple Death Throes" and, 7:1901b

"Le dormeur du val" ("The Sleeper in the Valley"), 7:1795a

"Les étrennes des orphelins" ("The Orphans"), 7:1788a-b

Les illuminations (*Illuminations*), 7:1640a, 1785a, 1793b, 1801b, 1806a, 1807b, 1808a–1817a, 1818b

  Ady and, 9:865b

  Khlebnikov's "Ka" and, 10:1358b

  "Onirocritique" and, 9:891b

"Les mains de Jeanne Marie" ("The Hands of Jeanne Marie"), 7:1796b

"Les pauvres à l'église" ("The Poor in Church"), 7:1791a

"Les poètes de sept ans" ("Seven-Year-Old Poets"), 7:1787b–1788a, 1795a

"Les reparties de Nina" ("The Customs Men"), 7:1790a

"Les soeurs de charité" ("Sisters of Charity"), 7:1793b

"L'Éternité" ("Eternity"), 7:1792b

Lettres du voyant, 7:1787a, 1789a, 1797b, 1805b, 1808b, 1809b, 1810a, 1811a-b, 1813a, 1818b, 1820b, 1880b

"L'Impossible" ("The Impossible"), 7:1820b

"L'Orgie parisienne, ou Paris se repeuple" ("Parisian Orgy or Paris Repopulated"), 7:1795b–1796a

Mallarmé and, 7:1785a, 1804b

"Marine," 7:1808b

"Matinée d'ivresse" ("Morning Intoxication"), 7:1811b–1812a

"Mauvais sang" ("Bad Blood"), 7:1819b, 1821a

"Memory" ("Mémoire"), 7:1802a–1804a

Montale's defense of, 11:2002b–2003b

"Morts de quatre-vingts-douze" ("Dead of '92"), 7:1790b

"Mouvement" ("Movement"), 7:1808b, 1813b

Nerval and, 6:964a

"Nuit de l'enfer" ("Night in Hell"), 7:1819b–1820a

"Phrases," 7:1813b, 1815a-b

"Première soirée" ("First Evening"), 7:1788a-b

"Qu'est-ce pour nous?" ("What Does It Matter?"), 7:1816a

"Sensation," 7:1788b

"Sun and Flesh" ("Soleil et chair," "Credo in unam"), 7:1788b, 1791a–1792b

"The Blacksmith" ("Le forgeron"), 7:1788b, 1790b, 1792b

"The Drunken Boat" ("Le bateau ivre"), 7:1797b–1802b, 1806a, 1813b, 1818b

  "Crépusculo" and, 9:750a

  Valéry's "The Rower" and, 8:583b

"The Tortured Heart" ("Le coeur volé"), 7:1789a, 1794a–1795a, 1794a-b

Trakl and, 10:1420b

Verlaine and, 7:1623a–1624b, 1625b, 1639b, 1786b, 1789a, 1806a–1807b, 1808b

Vers nouveaux et chansons, 7:1807a

"Voyelles" ("Vowels"), 7:1802a, 1804a–1805a

Rime. See Tasso, Torquato

Rime e ritmi. See Carducci, Giosue

Rime nuove. See Carducci, Giosue

Rímur, 1:399b, 401b

Rinaldo. See Tasso, Torquato

Rinascita, La (Italian Communist review), Vittorini's contributions to, 12:2749a

"Rinconete and Cortadillo." *See* Cervantes, Miguel de

Ring composition

  in *Beowulf*, 1:75a

  in Homer's *Iliad*, 1:75a

Ring des Nibelungen, Der. See Wagner, Richard

Ring Is Closed, The. See Hamsun, Knut, *Ringen sluttet*

Ring Round the Moon. See Anouilh, Jean, *L'Invitation au château*

Ringen sluttet. See Hamsun, Knut

Ringen (The Ring). *See* Gunnarsson, Gunnar

Ringing Island. See Rabelais, François, *L'Isle sonante*

Ríos, Francisco Giner de los, Jiménez and,
9:1006a

Ripamonti, Giuseppe, as source for Manzoni's
The Betrothed, 5:383a

Ripening Seed, The. See Colette, *Le blé en
herbe*

Ripley, George, "Life of Herder," 4:653b

Ripoll, *Carmen Campidoctoris*, *Poema de mio
Cid* and, 1:122b

Riquer, Martín de, on French influence in
Poema de mio Cid, 1:126b

Rire, Le. See Bergson, Henri, *Laughter*

*Rise and Fall of the State of Mahagonny, The.
See* Brecht, Bertolt

Risorgimento. *See* Italy

"Risorgimento, Il." *See* Leopardi, Giacomo,
"The Reawakening"

"Risposta a nove domande sul romanzo." *See*
Moravia, Alberto

"Rissurrezione, La." *See* Manzoni, Alessandro,
The Sacred Hymns

Ristori, Adelaide, comparing Ovid's and
Alfieri's treatment of Myrrha,
4:685b–686a

"Rite of the Peyote Among the Tarahumara,
The." *See* Artaud, Antonin

Rite of Spring, The. *See* Simon, Carl

Rite of Spring, The. See Stravinsky, Igor

"Ritorni, I." *See* Quasimodo, Salvatore,
"Homecomings"

"Ritratto d'un amico." *See* Ginzburg, Natalia

Ritschl, Friedrich, Nietzsche and, 7:1649b

Ritsos, Yannis, **12:2815a–2842b**

  Aghrypnia (Vigilance), 12:2817b

    "Irini" (Peace), 12:2834b–2835a

  Anipotahti politia (Unsubdued City),
12:2920b

  *Ariostos o prosehtikos afighite stighmes tou
viou tou kai tou ipnou tou* (Aristos the
Mindful Narrates Moments from His
Life and Sleep), 12:2839a

  "Athina sta opla" (Athens in Arms),
12:2817a, 2821b

  "Atomikistis" (The Individualist), 12:2829b

  choral poems, 12:2821a–2822a

    lyricism, 12:2821b–2822a

*Dhekaohto lianotraghoudha tis pikris
patridhas* (Eighteen Short Songs of the
Bitter Motherland), 12:2837b

Dhiadhromos kai skala (Corridor and
Stairs), 12:2819a, 2826a, 2827b, 2830a

  "Sto keno" (In the Void), 12:2827b

Dhiaplasi ton pedhon (Bringing Up
Children), 12:2815b

Dhokimasia (Trial), 12:2820a

  "Mesimvrina parathyra" (Southerly
Windows), 12:2835a

dramatic monologues, 12:2822a–2825b

Earini symfonia (Spring Symphony),
12:2837b

Epanalipsis (Repetitions), 12:2820a,
2832a-b, 2834b

  "Filomila" ("Philomel"), 12:2834b

"Epanastates" (Revolutionaries), 12:2829b

Epitafios, 12:2816b–2817a, 2820b, 2830a

  repetition, 12:2837b

  Varnalis' "I mana tou Hristou" and,
12:2829b

essays on poetry, 12:2838a-b

"ESSD" (To the Soviet Union), 12:89b

Fedhra (Phaedra), 12:2823a–2825b

  characters, 12:2824a

  prologue and epilogue, 12:2823a–2824a,
2825b

Filoktitis (Philoctetes), 12:2822b, 2830a,
2831b, 2836b

Ghignesthe (Becoming), *Imerologhio mias
vdhomadhas* (A Week's Diary),
12:2830a

Ghrafi tiflou (Scripture of the Blind),
12:2819b, 2826a, 2826b, 2827b–2828b,
2829b–2830a, 2839a-b

  "Kina thaymata" (Common Miracles),
12:2831a

Gkragkanta, 12:2821a

Hartina (Paper Poems), 12:2833b

Hironomies (Gestures), 12:2826a, 2826b,
2827a, 2827b

Hrysothemis (Chrysothemis), 12:2822b

I arhitektoniki ton dhentron (The
Architecture of Trees), 12:2818a-b,
2833b

I Eleni (Helen), 12:2820a, 2822b, 2830a, 2831b–2832a, 2834a, 2836b

I epistrofi tis Ifighenias (The Return of Iphigenia), 12:2822b

I ghefira (The Bridge), 12:2822b

I ghitonies tou kosmou (The World's Neighborhoods), 12:2819b, 2820b, 2829b

"I rapsodhia toy gymoy fotos" (Rhapsody of Naked Light), 12:2837b

I sonata tou selinofotos (*The Moonlight Sonata*), 12:2818a, 2822a-b, 2837b

I teleftea pro Anthropou ekatontaetia (The Last One Hundred Years Before Man), 12:2830a, 2835a

"Imitelis kai ypotypodhis triloghia" (The Unfinished and Undeveloped Trilogy), 12:2839a

Ismini (*Ismene*), 12:2822b, 2834a, 2836a

Italiko triptyho (Italian Triptych), 12:2833b

Kato ap ton iskio tou vounou (*Beneath the Shadow of the Mountain*), 12:2818b

Kodhonostasio (Belfry), 12:2821a, 2830a, 2831a, 2837a

laic, 12:2838a

literary prizes, 12:2819a

Makronisiotika (From Makronisos), 12:2833b

Mana (Mother), 12:2821b

Mantatofores (News-Bearing Women), 12:2830b, 2831a, 2836a, 2837a

Martyries, 12:2826a, 2836a, 2838b
introduction, 12:2838a

Martyries: Seira Dhefteri, 12:2820a

Martyries: Sira Proti, 12:2820a
"Arheo theatro" (Ancient Theater), 12:2833a

Me to skountima (With a Nudge of the Elbow), 12:2839a

Meghali Elliniki egkyklopedhia (The Large Greek Encyclopedia), 12:2816a

Meletimata (Studies), 12:2826a, 2838a-b
essay on Ilya Ehrenburg, 12:2829a
essay on Paul Éluard, 12:2829a-b

Mia ghineka plai sti thalassa (A Woman Beside the Sea), 12:2822a

"Mnimosyno ston Poro" (Memorial Service at Poros), 12:2832b

Monemvasiotises (Women of Monemvasia), 12:2829b

Monovasia, 12:2833b

mythic monologue, 12:2323a-b

"Niovi" (Niobe), 12:2833a

O afanismos tis Milos (The Annihilation of Milos), 12:2830b, 2832a

O anthropos me to gharyfallo (The Man with the Carnation), 12:2830a

O mavros Aghios (The Black Saint), 12:2830a

O syntrofos mas. Nikos Zahariadhis (Our Comrade, Nikos Zahariadhis), 12:2830a

"O Talos" (Talos), 12:2832b–2833a

O tihos mesa ston kathrefti (*The Wall in the Mirror*), 12:2818b, 2827b, 2830a, 2838a

"On Rereading the Poetic Selections 'The Wall in the Mirror' and 'Caretaker's Desk'," 12:2824b–2825a

Orestis (Orestes), 12:2822b, 2830a

Palia mazourka se rythmo vrohis (An Old Mazurka Set to the Rhythm of Rain), 12:2837b

Parentheses, 12:2819b, 2826a

Pera ap ton iskio ton kyparission (Beyond the Shadow of the Cypress Trees), 12:2817a, 2821b, 2825a

Petres Epanalipsis Kigklidhoma (*Stones, Repetitions, Barriers*), 12:2820a, 2827a, 2827b
"Elladha" (Greece), 12:2827a

Piimata I (Poems I), *Simiosis sta perithoria tou hronou* (*Notes on the Margins of Time*), 12:2826b

Piimata II (Poems II), 12:2821a

Piimata III (Poems III)
Askisis (*Exercises*), 12:2826a
"Ghramma sto Zolio Kioyri" (Letter to Joliot-Curie), 12:2820b, 2829b

Piimata IV (Poems IV), 12:2819b
Nyxis (Allusions), 12:2819b

"Polemos" (War), 12:2820a

Proino astro (Morning Star), 12:2818a

prose works, 12:2838b–2839a

Romiosini, 12:2817b, 2820b, 2830a, 2833a

Ritsos, Yannis (*cont.*)
  Septiria kai dhafniforia (Laureled Septeria),
    12:2820a
  short poems, 12:2825b–2828b
  "Sto Marx" (To Marx), 12:2829b
  "Stous propodhes tis siopis" (At the Base of
    Silence), 12:2817b
  Ta Epikerika (The Timely)
    Anthropi kai topia (People and Places),
      12:2830a
    Thrinos tou mai (May Lamentation),
      12:2830a, 2837b
  Tanaghries (*Tanagra Women*), 12:2819b
  Tetarti dhiastasi (*The Fourth Dimension*),
    12:2820a, 2822b, 2830b
    Aghamemnon (Agamemnon), 12:2822b,
      2830a, 2831b, 2836b
    Aias (Ajax), 12:2822b, 2834a
    Fedhra (Phaedra), 12:2822b
    Persefoni (Persephone), 12:2822b
  Thyrorio ("Caretaker's Desk" or "Porter's
    Lodge"), 12:2824b, 2825a, 2826b, 2827b,
    2830a, 2834b
    introduction, 12:22838a
  Ti paraxena pramata (What Strange
    Things), 12:2839a
  Tiresias, 12:2834, 2837a
  To dhentro tis fylakis kai i ghinekes (*The
    Prison Tree and the Women*),
    12:2821a-b
  "To dhihty" (The Net), 12:2830b, 2836a
  To emvaritio tou ikeanou (The Ocean's
    Musical March), 12:2837b
  To horiko ton sfouggaradhon (Sponge
    Diver's Chorale), 12:2830b–2831a,
    2834b, 2836a
  To isteroghrafo tis dhoxas (Postcript to
    Praise), 12:2830a
    "Ston Ari" (To Ari), 12:2835b
  To nekro spiti (*The Dead House*), 12:2818b,
    2822b, 2832a, 2834a-b
  To palio mas spiti (Our Old House),
    12:2816a
  To roptro (Doorbell), 12:2819b, 2834b
  To soma kai to ema (Body and Blood),
    12:2821a, 2830a
  To traghoudi tis adhelfis mou (Song of My
    Sister), 12:2837b
  Trakter (Tractor), 12:2815b, 2820a, 2829b
    "Ghermania" (Germany), 12:2830b
    Maghali ora (Great Hour), 12:2830a
  translations, 12:2819a, 2837b–2838a
    introductions to, 12:2838a
  Tria horika (Three Chorals), 12:2821a,
    2821b, 2830b
  voices, 12:2836a-b
  Volidhoskopos (The Sounder), 12:2821a,
    2829b, 2835a
  "Vradhinos ponokefalos" (Nighttime
    Headache), 12:2835b
  Ydhria (Pitcher), "Psyhosavvato" (All Soul's
    Day), 12:2819a
  Ymnos kai thrinos ghia tin Kypro (A Hymn
    and Lament for Cyprus), 12:2819b,
    2837b
"Ritter Gluck." *See* Hoffmann, E. T. A.
Rittner, Tadeusz, *W małym domku*, Witkiewicz
  and, 10:1221a
Ritual, in Butor, 13:3291b–3292a
Rivals, The. See Sheridan, Richard
Rivas y Larra. See Azorín
River of Fire, The. See Mauriac, François
"River of Time, The." *See* Derzhavin, Gavrïl,
  "Reka vremen"
Rivera, Diego, 8:332b
"Rivers, The." *See* Ungaretti, Giuseppe
Rivet, Charles, Delacroix's letter to, 5:527a
Rivière, Jacques
  Artaud's correspondence published by,
    11:1964b
  Artaud's letters to, 11:1964a-b
  Claudel and, 8:479b, 480a, 487b
  on Dada, 11:1940a
  influence on Artaud, 11:1963b–1964b
  Perse and, 10:1433b
  Valéry's *The Graveyard by the Sea* and,
    8:578a
Rivoluzione culturale in Cina, La. See
  Moravia, Alberto, *The Red Book and the
  Great Wall*
Rizospastis (Greek Communist newspaper),
  Ritsos' poetry in, 12:2816b
Röda rummet. See Strindberg, August

Ro tou Erota, Ta. See Elytis, Odysseus
Road imagery, in works of Prudentius, 1:18b
Road Leads On, The. See Hamsun, Knut
Road to the City, The. See Ginzburg, Natalia
Road to the Open, The. See Schnitzler, Arthur
"Roads Round Pisa, The." *See* Dinesen, Isak
Roads to Freedom, The. *See* Sartre, Jean-Paul,
    Les chemins de la liberté
Roannez, duc de, Pascal and, 3:128a, 129a,
    129b
Roar! The Gauntlets: 1908–1914. *See*
    Khlebnikov, Velimir, *Ryav! Perchatki:*
    1908–1914
Robbe-Grillet, Alain, **13:3237a–3256a**
    Angélique ou L'Enchantement (Angélique;
        or, Being Enchanted), 13:3241a,
        3247b–3248a, 3252b, 3256a
    Barthes on, 13:3084b–3086a
    Butor and, 13:3288b
    fictional characters of, 8:304a
    Ghosts in the Mirror (*Le miroir qui revient*),
        13:3238b, 3241a, 3245b, 3247a, 3251a-b,
        3252b, 3256a
    "Histoire de rats ou La vertu c'est ce qui
        mène au crime" (A Story of Rats; or,
        Virtue Leads to Crime), 13:3253a-b
    In the Labyrinth (*Dans le labyrinthe*),
        13:240a-b, 3239b, 3251b–3253a
    Jealousy (*La jalousie*), 13:3240a-b,
        3248a–3251b
    La belle captive (The Beautiful Captive),
        13:3240b
    La maison de rendez-vous (*The House of
        Assignation*), 13:3240b, 3253a,
        3254a–3255b
    Last Year at Marienbad (*L'Année dernière à
        Marienbad*), 13:3240b
    Le jeu avec le feu (Fire Games), 13:3240b
    L'Eden et après (Eden and Afterward),
        13:3240b
    L'Homme qui ment (The Liar), 13:3240b
    on plot, 13:3044a
    Pour un nouveau roman (For a New Novel),
        13:3024a, 3240a, 3241a, 3248b
    Project for a Revolution in New York (*Projet
        pour une revolution à New York*),
        13:3240b, 3253a, 3255b
    Recollections of the Golden Triangle
        (*Souvenirs du triangle d'or*), 13:3241a,
        3253a, 3255b
    Sarraute and, 12:2333a
    Slow Slide into Pleasure (*Glissements
        progressifs du plaisir*), 13:3240b
    Snapshots (*Instantanés*), 13:3240b, 3253a
    The Erasers (*Les gommes*), 13:3240a,
        3242a–3245b, 3252a, 3255a
    The Immortal One (*L'Immortelle*), 13:3240b
    The Voyeur (*Le voyeur*), 13:3240a,
        3245b–3247b
    Topology of a Phantom City (*Topologie
        d'une cité fantôme*), 13:3241a, 3253a,
        3255b
    Trans-Europ-Express, 13:3240b
    Un régicide, 13:3240a
Robbe-Grillet, Catherine, *L'Image*, 13:3240b
Robbe-Grillet, Gaston, 13:3238a-b
Robbers, The. See Schiller, Friedrich von, *Die
    Räuber*
Robe prétexte, La. See Mauriac, François, *The
    Stuff of Youth*
Robe rouge, La. See Brieux, Eugène
*Róbert, Brother, 1:399b
Robert Guiskard. See Kleist, Heinrich von
Robert, Marthe, Artaud aided by,
    11:1978b–1979a
Robert Mayer. See Zamyatin, Yevgeny
    Ivanovich
Robert of Naples, king, Petrarch on, 2:480b,
    484b
Robertis, Giuseppe de, on Silone's *Fontamara*,
    12:2294a
Robertson, Tom, 7:1926a-b
    Caste, 7:1926b
Robespierre, Maximilien
    Büchner and, 6:1174a, 1176b–1182a
    in Dumas's works, 6:733b
    in Vigny's *Stello*, 5:468b–469a
Robin et Marion, Jeu de. See Adam de la
    Halle, *Jeu de Robin et Marion*
Robin Hood, Schiller's "The Robbers" and,
    5:31a
"Robin and Marion," 1:457a
"Robinja." *See* Andrić, Ivo
Robinson Crusoe. See Defoe, Daniel

Robinson, Fred C., on *Beowulf*, 1:74a

"Robot," derivation of, 10:1571b

Rocca, John de, 5:93b

Rocking Back and Forth. See Grass, Günter

Röda rummet. See Strindberg, August, *The Red Room*

Rodchenko, Aleksandr, Mayakovsky and, 11:1837b, 1838a

Rodenbach, Georges, 8:121a, 122b

Roderick Random. See Smollett, Tobias

Rodez Notebooks, The. *See* Artaud, Antonin, *Cahiers de Rodez*

Rodin, Auguste, 8:471b
  "Archaic Torso of Apollo" and, 9:785a
  Balzac sculpture by, 5:636a
  poetic modernism and, 9:768a
  Rilke and, 9:770a, 771a, 771b, 777a

"Rodinná tragédie." *See* Hašek, Jaroslav

Roditi, Édouard, on Cavafy, 8:226a

Rodogune. See Corneille, Pierre

Rodrigo. See Mocedades de Rodrigo

Rodzinna Europa. See Milosz, Czeslaw, *Native Realm*

Roham/Sturm (Charge) (Hungarian-German periodical), Hašek's articles in, 9:1095a

Rohan-Montbazon, Marie de, 3:54b, 55b, 57a, 61a

Roi bombance, Le. See Marinetti, Filippo Tommaso

Roi s'amuse, Le. See Hugo, Victor

Roi se meurt, Le. See Ionesco, Eugène

Rojas, Fernando de
  La Celestina, 9:644b–645a
    Brecht and, 13:2905b
    Camoëns and *The Play of Filodemo*, 2:758a
    Camoëns and *The Two Amphitryons*, 2:755b–756a
    Frisch and, 13:2905b
    Lope de Vega and, 2:848b
    Pérez Galdós and, 7:1613a

Rojas, Francisco de, translated by Lesage, 3:320a, 320b

Roland Barthes par Roland Barthes. See Barthes, Roland, *Roland Barthes by Roland Barthes*

Role playing, in Machiavelli, 2:605b–606a

Role reversal, in Andersen's tales, 6:881b–882b

"Rolla." *See* Musset, Alfred de

Rolland, Romain
  Claudel and, 8:472a
  Life of Beethoven, 9:1004a

Rollwagenbüchlein. See Wickram, Jörg

Rölvaag, O. E., Hamsun and, 8:38a

Roly-Poly or Ball of Fat. *See* Maupassant, Guy de, "Boule de Suif"

Romains, Jules
  acmeism and, 10:1522b, 1523a
  Claudel and, 8:488b

"Roman, Le." *See* Maupassant, Guy de, "Essay on the Novel"

Roman Catholic Church
  Action Française and, 13:3238a
  Alfieri's opposition to, 4:672b
  Aristotelianism and, 1:408b–409a
  Artaud and, 11:1962b–1963a, 1976a–1977a
  Aymé and, 12:2441a-b
  in Balzac's *Le curé de village*, 5:652a
  Beauvoir and, 12:2707b, 2711a, 2712a, 2713a, 2713b, 2724a
  Bergson and, 8:46a-b, 61a, 64a-b
  Bloy and, 7:1709b
  Böll and, 13:3165a-b, 3167a
  Claudel and, 7:1709b, 10:1431a-b
    The Tidings Brought to Mary, 8:484b
  Cocteau and, 10:1551a
  councils, Aquinas and, 1:415b
  Eliot and, 5:195a
  in George's "Windmill Cease to Move Your Arms," 8:452a
  Germany, Böll's criticism of role, 13:3180a
  Gombrowicz and, 12:2570a
  Hugo's view of, 6:699b–700a
  Huysmans and, 7:1625a, 1724b–1726a
  in Lampedusa's *The Leopard*, 11:2012b
  liturgy of, Claudel's *La messe là-bas* and, 8:485a–487a
  Luther and, 2:670a–684a
  Manzoni and
    apologetics, 5:374a–375a
    influence of conversion on his writing, 5:372a–375a
    lack of popularity due to, 5:370b

the "miracle of Saint Roch," 5:372b
rejection of mythology and, 5:373b–374a
in *The Betrothed*, 5:375b
marriage and, 2:883b
Mauriac and, 10:1312a, 1316a–1317b, 1320a
Michelet and, 5:582b
Montale's antagonism toward,
 11:1999b–2000a
in Novalis' works, 5:220a-b
reform of, Erasmus and, 2:581b–583a,
 585a–588b
Robbe-Grillet and, 13:3238a
in Schiller's *Mary Stuart*, 5:46a
Schlegel and, 5:193a, 194b–195a
Sismondi's attack on, 5:374a–375a
Tasso and, 2:816b
Tocqueville's attitude to, 6:909a-b
Undset and, 9:1023a-b, 1025b–1026a
Veit and, 5:195b
Verlaine and, 7:1625a-b
Walther and, 1:301a–303b
Weil and, 12:2792b, 2794a, 2797a, 2800a,
 2801b, 2802a, 2808b
see also Church fathers; *Index of Prohibited
 Books*
Roman de Brut. See Wace
Roman de la momie, Le. See Gautier,
 Théophile, *The Romance of a Mummy*
Roman de Rou. See Wace
Roman de Troie. See Sainte-Maure, Benoît de
Roman d'Eneas, Matter of Rome and, 1:140a-b
Roman Elegies. *See* D'Annunzio, Gabriele,
 Elegie romane
Roman Elegies. *See* Goethe, Johann Wolfgang
 von
Roman Empire, *see also* Classical world
Roman expérimental, Le. See Zola, Émile
"Roman Fountain, The." *See* Meyer, Conrad
 Ferdinand, "Der römische Brunnen"
Roman law, Vico and, 3:296b, 298b–304b
Roman Matron, The. See Tieck, Ludwig,
 Vittoria Accorombona
Roman Profiles. *See* Kosztolányi, Dezső, *Latin
 arcélek*
Roman Tales. See Moravia, Alberto
Roman-feuilleton. See Serial novel

Romana, La. See Moravia, Alberto, *The
 Woman of Rome*
Romance
 chivalric
  Gottfried and, 1:237a–260b
  Wolfram and, 1:268a–281a
 epic
  of Ariosto, 2:624b–643b
  Gawain in, 1:158b
  of Tasso, 2:792b
 French
  Arthurian legend and, 1:143b–148a
  Chrétien de Troyes and, 1:185a
  Welsh legends and, 1:143b
 genre of, 1:154a-b
 novel and, 2:828a
 see also Pastoral romance
"Romance de la Guardia Civil española." *See*
 García Lorca, Federico
Romance de lobos. See Valle-Inclán, Ramón
 del, *Las comedias bárbaras*
Romance of a Mummy, The. See Gautier,
 Théophile
*Romance of Roncevaux. See Chanson de
 Roland*
Romance of the Rose (*Roman de la rose*),
 1:309a–335b
 allegorical portraits, 1:310b–311b
 as allegory, 1:318b–319a, 321a-b, 322a–323a
 differences in authors' approaches,
  1:328a-b, 331b
 Il Fiore and, 1:444b
 language, 2:548a-b, 556b–557a
 love as innovative theme in, 314a-b
 narrator of, 2:311a
 Ovidian influences, 1:316b–317a, 323a-b
 Psychomachia and, 1:20b
 and Villon's *Legacy*, 2:544b
"Romance sonámbulo." *See* García Lorca,
 Federico
Romance of the Spanish Civil Guard. *See*
 García Lorca, Federico, "Romance de la
 Guardia Civil española"
Romance of Troy. See Benoît de Sainte-Maure,
 Roman de Troie
Romancero general, the Cid ballads in, 1:133a
Romancero gitano. See García Lorca, Federico

Romances sans paroles. See Verlaine, Paul
Romanciero de destierro. See Unamuno,
    Miguel de
"Romanciers du regard." *See Nouveau roman*
Romane und Erzählungen. See Böll, Heinrich
Romanen om Olof. See Johnson, Eyvind
"Romanfunderingar." *See* Johnson, Eyvind
Romanitas, according to Vico, 3:302b
Romanos the Melodist, 13:2969, 2984a
Romantic School, The. See Heine, Heinrich,
    Die Romantische Schule
Romantic Songs. See Hesse, Hermann,
    Romantische Lieder
Romantic Tale. *See* Johnson, Eyvind,
    Romantisk berättelse
Romanticism
    of Ady, 9:859b–860a, 861b, 862a, 873b–874a
    Augustine's *On Christian Doctrine* and,
        1:43b–44a
    Baudelaire and, 7:1330a, 1339b–1340b
    Berlioz and, 6:771a-b, 777b, 778a-b, 779b,
        780b, 782a-b, 793a-b, 800b–801a
    Brecht and, 11:2108b
    Büchner and, 6:1170b, 1183b–1186b,
        13:2923b
    Calvino and, 13:3266b
    Chénier as link to, 4:693a-b
    critical journal of, 11:1713a-b
    critical theory of, 11:1709a–1710a
    Danish, Andersen and, 6:872a-b
    Dinesen and, 10:1296a–1297b
    Dumas and, 6:721b, 722b–723b, 731a,
        737a-b
    Dürrenmatt and, 13:3217a
    Eça and, 7:1685b, 1687b, 1689a-b, 1697a
    Eliot and, 10:1455a
    Foucault and, 13:3328a
    French
        fall of, 6:1030a
        Heine and, 5:501a-b
        linguistic reform and, 6:1035a
    Gautier and, 6:1034b
    German, 5:572a, 9:846b
        Andersen and, 6:878b–879a
        Arp and, 10:1366b, 1376a-b
        blue flower and, 5:225a-b
        Gogol and, 6:975a

        Heine on, 5:107a
        Herder's influence on, 4:645b, 650a
    Giraudoux and, 9:1042b
    of Goethe, 5:5a, 18b
    Gombrowicz and, 12:2579b–2580a,
        2582b–2853a
    Goncharov and, 6:1064a-b, 1065a
    Grabbe and, 13:2923b
    Grillparzer's departure from, 5:422b, 423b,
        425b
    in Hamsun's works, 8:27b–28a
    Heine and, 5:501b–502a
    Hesperus and, 5:65a
    in Hugo's works, 6:694a–695b, 699b,
        700b–701a, 703b, 707b–708a
    "immanent criticism" and, 11:1709b
    Italian
        Foscolo and, 5:313a
        Manzoni's manifesto, 5:373b–374a
    Khlebnikov's *Zangezi* and German Romantic
        drama, 10:1362a
    language and, 10:1477a
    Leopardi and, 5:553a-b, 558a
    in Lermontov's works, 6:1195a, 1206b,
        1215a–1216a, 1215a-b
    Mallarmé and, 7:1571b–1573a, 1577a
    Mandelshtam and, 10:1627a
    Maupassant's view of, 7:1764a
    in Mérimée's works, 6:745a-b, 746b, 749a-b,
        753b, 756b, 760a
    Montaigne and, 2:786b–787a
    Musset and, 6:999b, 1010a
    Nerval and, 6:946b
    new appreciation of Pascal and, 3:148a
    Nodier's *cénacle* and, 5:461a-b
    nostalgia and, 10:1477a
    Novalis and, 5:225a-b
    originality concept in, 5:530a
    and pantheism, 5:211b
    Pinheiro Chagas and, 7:1692b
    in poetry
        Heine's approach to, 5:494a-b
        Visconti's manifesto, 5:371b
    in Poland, *see also* Mickiewicz, Adam
    Portuguese, parody of, 7:1687b
    Portuguese literature and, 10:1487a
    Rabelais and, 2:700b

rationalistic, Leopardi and, 5:542a
Richter and, 5:84b–85a
  in *Siebenkäs*, 5:70b
  The Invisible Lodge, 5:63a
Russian, 6:1064a-b
Sainte-Beuve and, 6:838b
Sand and, 6:813b
Schlegel and
  concept of, 5:190a–191a
  in *Dialogue on Poetry*, 5:181a-b,
    183b–184a
  founding of, 5:177a
  in *Lucinde*, 5:191a, 192b
  neoclassism and, 5:190b–191a
"sick," Goncourt brothers, 7:1399a-b
Simon and, 13:3028a
Spanish, of Valle-Inclán, 8:333b
Spinoza and, 5:211b
of Staël, 5:99a, 105b
Stendhal and, 5:351b–353b
in Strindberg's works, 7:1754a
symbolism and, 9:963b
Tieck and, 5:234b–251b
Trakl and, 10:1413a
Vesaas and, 11:2039a–2039b
Vigny and, 5:447a
  "new" drama, 5:462a-b
see also Sturm und Drang
Romantische Lieder. See Hesse, Hermann
Romantische Schule, Die. See Heine, Heinrich
Romantisk berättelse. See Johnson, Eyvind
Romantisme d'Alfred de Musset, Le. See
    Gastinel, Pierre
*Romantisme et le goût esthétique du XVIIIe
    siècle, Le. See* Simches, Seymour
"Romantyczność." *See* Mickiewicz, Adam
Romanzero. See Heine, Heinrich
Romas, Mikhail, 8:442a
Rome. See Zola, Émile, *Les trois villes: Rome*
Rome, ancient
  as Alfieri's inspiration, 4:661a-b, 664b–665a
  in Corneille
    Cinna, 3:43a
    Horace, 3:34b, 35a
  empire
    in Augustine's *City of God*, 1:33a-b
  in Kosztolányi's *Bloody Poet*, 10:1236a,
    1237a
  in Prudentius' works, 1:2b, 9b, 10b, 11b,
    14b
  as seen by Montesquieu, 3:354a–355b
  Weil and, 12:2799b, 2800a
  republic, Machiavelli and, 2:606b–607a
Rome (city)
  Ady and, 9:872b
  in Carducci's poetry, 7:1509b–1510b
  history, 14th century, 2:478a-b
Rome, Naples, and Florence. See Stendhal
Roméo et Juliet. See Berlioz, Hector
Roméo et Juliette. See Cocteau, Jean
Romeo and Jeannette (Roméo et Jeannette).
    See Anouilh, Jean
Romeo and Juliet. See Berlioz, Hector, *Roméo
    et Juliet*; Porto, Luigi da; Shakespeare,
    William
Romeo und Julia auf dem Dorfe. See Keller,
    Gottfried, *A Village Romeo and Juliet*
Romiosini. See Ritsos, Yannis
"Römische Brunnen, Der." *See* Meyer, Conrad
    Ferdinand
Romulus the Great (Romulus der Grosse). See
    Dürrenmatt, Friedrich
Rondeau, in Greban's *Passion*, 1:469b
Rondisti (literary school), 12:2389b
Rondon, Cândido, 11:2155a
Ronsard, Louis de, 2:722a
Ronsard, Pierre de, **2:721a–746b**
  "À sa maîtresse" (To His Mistress),
    2:727b–728a
  *Abrégé de l'art poétique françois (Summary
    of the Art of French Poetry)*, 2:726a
  "Amours de Cassandre," 2:729a-b, 731a,
    743b–744a
  "Amours de Marie," 2:729b–730b
  Apollinaire and, 9:885a
  Baudelaire and, 7:1327b
  "Bergerie" ("Pastoral"), 2:727a
  *Cinquiéme livre des odes (The Fifth Book of
    the Odes)*, 2:726b–727a
  death imagery, 12:2533a
  Discours, 2:737b–738a
  "Elégie XVII," 2:721b–722a

Ronsard, Pierre de (*cont.*)
   Elégies, mascarades et bergeries,
      2:740b–741a
   "Epitaphe de Marie," 2:730b
   "Exhortation au camp du Roy Henry II,"
      2:736a-b, 737a-b
   "Exhortation pour la paix," 2:736b–737b
   Franciade, 2:734b–735b
   "Hercule chrestien," 2:744a-b
   "Hymne de Henry Deuxiesme," 2:732a
   "Hymne de l'or," 2:733a–734a
   "Hymne à la philosophie," 2:732b
   "Institution pour l'adolescence du roi
      Charles IX" (Precepts for the Young
      Charles IX), 2:727a
   "La Lyre," 2:735b
   "Le Voyage d'Hercueil" (The Journey to
      Hercueil), 2:723a-b
   Les Amours, 2:727a–731b
   "Les Daimons," 2:733a
   Les Derniers vers de Pierre Ronsard,
      2:739b–740a
   Les Quatre premiers livres des odes (The
      First Four Books of the Odes), 2:726a
   "L'Hylas," 2:744a
   Livre des hymnes, 2:731b
   Machado and, 9:760a-b
   pastoral poetry of, 2:911b–912a
   Petrarchan influence, 2:504b
   "Réponse aux injures et calomnies de je ne
      sçay quels Predicantereaux et
      Ministreaux de Genéve," 2:738a–739b,
      740b
   Sainte-Beuve's study of, 6:837b
   Second livre des hymnes, 2:731b
   "Sonnets pour Hélène," 2:730b–731b
   "Sur la Mort de Marie," 2:730b
Ronsasvals, Charlemagne's sin in, 1:100a-b
Roofing Feast, The. See Strindberg, August,
   Taklagsöl
Roosevelt, Franklin Delano, Heinrich Mann
   and, 8:542a
Rootlessness, in Johnson's works, 12:2362a,
   2364a
Roots of American Culture, The. See Rourke,
   Constance M.
Rops, Felicien, Ghelderode and, 11:2133a

Roptro, To. See Ritsos, Yannis
Rosa. See Hamsun, Knut
Rosa de papel, La. See Valle-Inclán, Ramón
   del
"Rosalie Prudent." *See* Maupassant, Guy de
Rosary. See Akhmatova, Anna, *Chetki*
Rose Altar, The. *See* Södergran, Edith,
   Rosenaltaret
Rose Bernd. See Hauptmann, Gerhart
Rose and the Cross, The. See Blok, Alexander,
   Roza i krest
Rose de sable, La. See Montherlant, Henry de
Rose et Blanche. See Sand, George
Rose Garden in the Desert. *See* Ady, Endre,
   "Rózsaliget a pusztán"
Rose imagery
   in Ronsard's verse, 2:728a-b, 731a
   see also Romance of the Rose
Rosenaltaret. See Södergran, Edith
Rosenkavalier, Der. See Hofmannsthal, Hugo
   von
Rosenzweig, Franz
   Benjamin and, 11:1716b
   Der Stern der Erlösung (*Star of
      Redemption*), 11:1716b
Rosmersholm. See Ibsen, Henrik
Rosmonda. See Goldoni, Carlo
Rosmunda. See Alfieri, Vittorio
Rossetti, Dante Gabriel, Bely and, 9:912a
Rossini, Gioacchino, 6:776a-b
   The Barber of Seville, see also
      Beaumarchais, Pierre-Augustin Caron
      de, *Le barbier de Séville*
"Rosso Malpelo." *See* Verga, Giovanni
Rossum's Universal Robots. *See* Čapek, Karel,
   R.U.R.
Rostand, Edmond, Giraudoux and, 9:1041b
Rotativismo, 11:2145b
Rote Hahn, Der. See Hauptmann, Gerhart
Roth, Joseph, Heinrich Mann and, 8:537a
Roth, Philip
   Babel's influence on, 11:1890a, 1912a,
      1912b
   The Ghost Writer, 11:1912a
"Rothschild's Fiddle." *See* Chekhov, Anton,
   "Skripka Rotshilda"

Rotrou, Jean de, *Hercule mourant* (*Dying Hercules*), 3:26b

"Rotta è l'alta colonna e'l verde lauro." *See* Petrarch, *Canzoniere*

Rotting Magician, The. See Apollinaire, Guillaume, *L'Enchanteur pourrissant*

Roucher, Antoine, guillotined with Chénier, 4:691a, 716b

Rouge et le noir, Le. See Stendhal, *The Red and the Black*

Rougon-Macquart, Les: Histoire naturelle et sociale d'une famille sous le Second Empire. See Zola, Émile

Round Trip. *See* Aymé, Marcel, *Aller retour*

Roundheads and the Peakheads, The. See Brecht, Bertolt, *Die Rundköpfe und die Spitzköpfe*

Rourke, Constance M.
  American Humor: A Study of the National Character, Herder's influence on, 4:658a
  The Roots of American Culture, Herder's influence on, 4:658a-b

"Rousseau." *See* Hölderlin, Friedrich

Rousseau, Emil, Hebbel and, 6:1094a-b

Rousseau, Henri, 9:969b
  and Jarry, 9:672b

Rousseau, Jean Jacques, **4:449a–474b**
  Alfieri and, 664a, 4:662a
  Anouilh and, 13:2846b
  Apollinaire and, 9:882a
  Blasco Ibáñez and, in *Reeds and Mud*, 8:382a
  character of, 4:664a
  Chénier contrasted with, 4:709b
  Confessions, 4:460b–461a, 469a–470a, 7:1429b
    Fénelon's *Télémaque* and, 3:289a
    Montaigne and, 2:786b
    Nerval style and, 6:949b
    painful confessions in, 5:129b
  Considerations on the Government of Poland, 4:461a
  Dialogues: Rousseau juge de Jean-Jacques, 4:461a-b
  Diderot and, 4:480a-b, 504b–505b

Discours sur les sciences et les arts (*Discourse on the Sciences and the Arts*)), 4:453a

Discours sur l'origine de l'inégalité parmi les hommes (*Discourse on the Origins of Inequality*), 4:453b–454a, 6:727b

Dissertation on Modern Music, 4:451b

Dostoevsky and, 7:1350b, 1351b

in Dumas's works, 6:727a-b

Émile, 4:457a–459a, 7:1475a
  Richter and, 5:56b, 79b
  Staël and, 5:89b

expanding plenitude, 7:1477b

on Fénelon, 3:273a

Foscolo and, 5:319b–320a

Goethe's *The Sorrows of Young Werther* and, 5:5b, 6b

Goldoni and, 4:432b

Hamsun and, 8:29b, 32a, 34b

Herder's antagonistic viewpoint toward, 4:643b–644a

Hölderlin and, 5:145a-b, 166b

Julie, ou la nouvelle Héloïse (*Julie; or, The New Heloise*), 4:456a–457a, 6:1015a, 7:1486a
  Balzac and, 5:651a
  Beaumarchais and, 4:565a
  popularity of, 4:378a
  Richter and, 5:56b

La Bruyère's *Caractères* and, 3:257b

on La Rochefoucauld's *Maximes*, 3:53a

Le devin du village (The Village Soothsayer), 4:453a

Les muses galantes (*The Gallant Muses*), 4:451b

on Lesage's *Gil Blas*, 3:339b

Letter on Providence (*Lettre sur la providence*), 4:454b–455a

Letter to the Archbishop of Paris, 4:459a

Letters Written from the Mountain, 4:459a

Lettre à M. d'Alembert sur les spectacles (*Letter to M. d'Alembert on Theater*), 4:377a, 455b

Machiavelli and, 2:615b

Marya Volkonsky and, 7:1474b

Michelet and, 5:573b

Rousseau, Jean Jacques (*cont.*)
  on Molière's *Le misanthrope*, 3:119b, 120b,
    121b
  Montaigne and, 2:784b
  Moral Letters to Sophie, 4:455a
  Narcissus, 4:453a
  in Nerval's *Sylvie*, 6:965b–966a
  noble savage myth, 9:1145b
    in Tolstoy's writing, 7:1478b
  "Project for the Constitution of Corsica,"
    4:459a
  Pygmalion, 4:460b
  Rêveries du promeneur solitaire (*The
    Reveries of a Solitary Stroller*), 4:461b
    Chénier and, 4:698a
  Richter and, 5:53a-b, 56a
  Sainte-Beuve on, 6:858a-b, 7:1411a
  Sand and, 6:815b–816a, 825a
  Schlegel and, 5:197b
  Simon and, 13:3027b
  Staël and, 5:97b
  Storm and Stress and, 5:4b
  The Social Contract, 4:457b–458a, 6:727b
    Chénier and, 4:709a
  Voltaire and, 4:369a
  Wieland and, 4:599b
Rousseau, Pauline, Michelet and, 5:576a-b,
  577a-b
Roussel, Raymond
  Butor and, 13:3301a
  sound association, 11:1954a
Roussie, Jeanne, 9:997a
Route des Flandres, La. *See* Simon, Claude
Routine. *See* Zola, Émile, *Pot-Bouille*
Rouvroy, Claude-Henri de. *See* Saint-Simon,
  Comte de
Roux, Saint-Pol (Paul), 8:121b
"Rower, The." *See* Valéry, Paul, *Charmes*, "Le
  rameur"
Rowohlt, Ernst
  Kafka and, 9:1152b
  Musil and, 9:933a
Royal Academy of Amsterdam, 7:1828a,
  1850b, 1851a
Royal Highness. *See* Mann, Thomas,
  Königliche Hoheit
Royal Italian Academy, Pirandello and, 8:395a

Royal Shakespeare Company, Gorky and,
  8:417b, 434b
Royal Spanish Academy for the Language,
  Baroja elected to, 9:612b
Royal Way, The. *See* Malraux, André
Royal Woman, The. *See* Mann, Heinrich,
  Eugénie
Royalty, in Dumas's works, 6:725b–726b,
  733b, 735a–736a
Royaume farfelu, Le. *See* Malraux, André
Royère, Jean, Breton and, 11:1939a
Roza i krest. *See* Blok, Alexander
Rozanov, Vasilii
  on Gogol, 6:996b
  Temnyilik (*The Dark Visage*), Mandelshtam
    and, 10:1637b
Rozerot, Jeanne, Zola and, 7:1528a-b, 1533b
"Rozmluvas cenzorem." *See* Hašek, Jaroslav
"Rózsaliget a pusztán." *See* Ady, Endre
R's of Eros, The. *See* Elytis, Odysseus, *Ta Ro
  tou Erota*
Rubble Woman. *See* Grass, Günter,
  Gleisdreieck (Triangle Junction),
  "Trümmerfrau"
Rubens, Peter Paul
  Burckhardt on, 6:1233a–1234a
  Christ in the Tomb, Claudel and, 8:487b
  Delacroix and, 5:528a
  Gautier and, 6:1042b–1043a
  Taine on, 7:1462b
  The Descent from the Cross, Vigny on,
    5:459a
Rubensists, Poussinists and, 5:538b
Rubinstein, Arthur, on Zakopane, 10:1209b
Rubinstein, Ida, 8:488a
Rude hiver, Un. *See* Queneau, Raymond
Ruden, Bella, 9:911a
Rudin. *See* Turgenev, Ivan
Rudinoff, W. W., Wedekind and, 8:236a, 241a
Rueda de los ocios, La. *See* Cela, Camilo José
Ruedo ibérico, El. *See* Valle-Inclán, Ramón del
Rueil, Peace of (1649), 3:60a
Ruf des Lebens, Der. *See* Schnitzler, Arthur
Rufián viudo, El. *See* Cervantes, Miguel de
Ruggeri, Ruggero, Pirandello and,
  8:393b–394a, 395a
Rühmen (the word), 9:773b

"Ruins and Poetry." *See* Milosz, Czeslaw,
Norton lectures
Ruiz, José Martínez. *See* Azorín
Rulers, in medieval satire, 1:356a
Rules of the Game, The. See Pirandello, Luigi,
Il giuoco delle parti; Simenon, Georges,
La boule noire
Rumble. *See* García Lorca, Federico
Rundköpfe und die Spitzköpfe, Die. See
Brecht, Bertolt
Runenberg, Der. See Tieck, Ludwig
Runólf Dálksson, 1:385a
Ruolantes Liet, 1:91a
R.U.R.. See Čapek, Karel
"Rus." *See* Zamyatin, Yevgeny Ivanovich
Ruskin, John
influence of, 9:591a
Taine and, 7:1449a
Ruslan and Lyudmila. See Pushkin, Alexander
"Ruslan and Lyudmila." *See* Pushkin,
Alexander
Russell, Bertrand, *A History of Western
Philosophy*, Croce and, 8:327b
Russia
Berlioz in, 6:793b, 810a-b
Decembrist uprising, Pushkin and, 5:662a
Diderot and, 4:503a-b
emancipation of the serfs, in Turgenev,
6:1278a–1279a
Hamsun's works in, 8:33b
Hašek in, 9:1094a–1095b
history, Blok and, 9:959a-b
in Mickiewicz's *Forefathers' Eve, Part III*,
5:622a–623a
Mickiewicz's stay in, 5:612b–614a
political refugees, Zola and, 7:1529b
politics, Dostoevsky and, 7:1354a-b
Rilke's trips to, 9:769b
serfdom in, in Turgenev's stories,
6:1278a–1279a
Södergran in, 11:1782b
Staël on, 5:93b–94a
Westernization of, 7:1349b
Russian Academy of Sciences
Chekhov and, 7:1856a
see also Soviet Academy of Sciences

Russian Association of Proletarian Writers.
See RAPP
"Russian Language, The." *See* Turgenev, Ivan
Russian literature
Age of Pushkin, 13:3210b
civil servant in, 6:980b, 981b–982b, 983a
French translations, influence in Spain,
7:1614a
glorification of Caucasus, 7:1478b
Gogol's characters in, 6:990b
Golden Age, Chekhov and, 7:1857a-b
Jewish, Babel's contribution to, 11:1890a
Lermontov's contribution to modern prose,
6:1206a-b
"Letter to Gogol" in, 6:974a
literary celebrity, 11:1893b–1894b
literary tradition, Solzhenitsyn's place in,
13:3196b
lyric poetry, Blok, 9:959b–961b, 986b
mercantile class in, 6:985a
Mérimée's translations of, 6:765a–766a
post-Stalinist, ideology in, 11:2251b–2252a
postrevolutionary prose fiction, 11:1885b,
1893a
proverbs, 13:3208b–3209a
Pushkin's importance in, 5:659a
relation of art to fiction, 13:3202a
resurgence of, in 1900s, 11:1731b
Saint Petersburg writers, 7:1471b–1472a
serfs in, 6:985b
Silver Age of, 10:1619a–1620b, 11:1732a
Chekhov and, 7:1857b
poetry in, 11:1732a
skaz, 11:1906a
"social purpose" in, 6:996a
symbolism and, 11:1731b
varied novels in, 6:986b
Russian opera, Pushkin and, 5:659a-b
Russian Orthodox Church
Akhmatova's religious imagery and,
10:1527a–1528a
Gogol and, 6:973b
Mandelshtam and, 10:1637b–1638a
Russian Revolution (1905), 11:1891a-b
Gorky and, 8:420a
Enemies, 8:436b
Mother, 8:418a, 433a

Russian Revolution (1905) (*cont.*)
  Gorky and (*cont.*)
    The Life of Matvei Kozhemyakin, 8:433a
  spirituality and, 8:434a
Russian Revolution (1917)
  Bely and, 9:924a, 925a
  Blok and, 9:979a-b, 979a–985b
  Finnish civil war and, 11:1790b–1791a
  Gorky and, 8:421a-b
    in *Dostigaev*, 8:439a
  inevitability theme, 13:3210a
  Khlebnikov and, 10:1331b
  Lukács and, 10:1264b1265a
  Mayakovsky and, 11:1844b–1846b
  Olesha and, 11:2233b, 2234a-b
    in *The Three Fat Men*, 11:2247a
  Pasternak's *Doctor Zhivago* as spiritual
    history of, 10:1609b–1612b
  in Solzhenitsyn's *The Red Wheel*, 13:3207a,
    3210a
  Tychyna and, 10:1654a-b, 1665b–1666a
  Witkiewicz on, 10:1213b
  Zamyatin's response to, 10:1187a-b
  see also Bolsheviks
Russian Thought. See Russkaya mysl
Russian Word. *See Russkoe Slovo*
Russian-Polish War (1830–1831), 5:613a-b
  Mickiewicz and, 5:618b–619a
Russian-Polish War (1920), in Babel's *Red
  Cavalry*, 11:1885b
Russkaya mysl (*Russian Thought*) (journal),
  7:1868b, 1871b
Russkoe bogatstvo (Wealth of Russia)
  (magazine), Gorky and, 8:419a
Russkoe Slovo (Russian Word) (magazine),
  Gorky's *Childhood* in, 8:440a
Russo, Luigi, on Silone, 12:2294a
Russo-Japanese War, Khlebnikov's reaction to,
  10:1336b
Rusteghi, I. See Goldoni, Carlo, *The Boors*
Rustic Commune, The. *See* Carducci, Giosue,
  "Il comune rustico"
Rustic poetry. *See* Pastoral poetry
Rustic Talk. See Du Fail, Noël, *Propos
  rustiques*
Ruta de don Quijote, La. See Azorín
Ruta del aventurero, La. See Baroja, Pío

Rutebeuf
  "Bataille des vices contre les vertus" ("Battle
    of the Vices Against the Virtues"),
    1:364b–365b
  "Complainte de sainte Eglise," 1:361b
  "De l'estat du monde" ("On the State of the
    World"), 1:355b–356a
  "De Sainte Eglise" ("About Holy Church"),
    1:361a-b
  "Des Jacobins," 1:346a–347a
  Miracle de Théophile, 1:464a
  Speculum stultorum and, 1:373a
  wordplay of, 1:371b
Ruy Blas. See Cocteau, Jean; Hugo, Victor
Ruysbroeck, Jan van
  Maeterlinck and, 8:122b–123a, 124a
  The Adornment of Spiritual Marriage,
    Maeterlinck translation of, 8:123a, 124a
Ryav! Perchatki: 1908–1914. See Khlebnikov,
  Velimi

S

Sá de Miranda, Francisco de, Camoëns and, 2:755a

Sabadino, Giovanni, *Le Porretane* (Tales from the Baths at Porretta), 2:940a-b

Sabatier, Pierre, on the Goncourts, 7:1406a

Sabbath, Augustine on, 1:33a

Sablé, marquise de, 3:62b, 64a

Sablonnière, Anna, as procuress for Sade, 4:616b

Sac au dos. See Huysmans, Joris Karl

Sacchetti, Franco
    Libro delle trecentonovelle (Book of Three Hundred Novellas), 2:934b–935a
    vernacular composition of, 2:906a

Sachot, Jacques, as model for La Bruyère's Théotime, 3:252a

Sachs, Hans, 6:1151b, 1159b
    Schwänke in works of, 2:953a

Sack on Back. *See* Huysmans, Joris Karl, *Sac au dos*

Sacramental plays. *See Autos sacramentales*

Sacraments
    Luther and, 2:677a-b
    medieval drama and, 1:471a
    terminology of, in Hugh Primas' "Ego dixi," 1:347b–348a
    see also Roman Catholic Church

Sacre du printemps, Le. See Simon, Claude; Stravinsky, Igor, *The Rite of Spring*

Sacred Hymns, The. See Manzoni, Alessandro

Sacred Songs. See Novalis

Sacred Studies. See Boethius, Anicius Manlius Severinus, *Opuscula sacra*

Sacrifice
    in Kierkegaard, 6:1138a
    in Mann's *Doctor Faustus*, 9:736a
    in Schnitzler's works, 8:99b, 100b

Sacrificio, Il. See Beccari

Sacrilegio (Sacrilege). *See* Valle-Inclán, Ramón del

Sad Dances. *See* George, Stefan, *Das Jahr der Seele (The Year of the Soul)*, "Traurige Tänze"

Sad Fate of the Railway Mission, The. *See* Hašek, Jaroslav, "Smutný osud nádražní misie"

Sad Shepherd, The. See Jonson, Ben

Sad Songs. *See* Jiménez, Juan Ramón, *Arias tristes*

Sade, Donatien Alphonse François, marquis de, **4:615a–638b**
    Aline et Valcour
        compared to Richardson's *Clarissa*, 4:628b–629a
        depiction of vice defended, 4:627b
        publication of, 4:627a
        Sade's childhood mirrored in, 4:615a
    Céline and, 11:1880b
    Contes et fabliaux du dix-huitième siècle (Tales and Stories of the Eighteenth Century), *Justine* and, 4:629a
    Histoire secrète d'Isabelle de Bavière, reine de France (The Secret History of Isabella of Bavaria, Queen of France), 4:637a
    Les journées de Florbelle, ou la nature dévoilée (Florbelle's Days; or, Nature Unveiled), 4:636b
    Justine; or, The Misfortunes of Virtue (Justine, ou les malheurs de la vertu), 4:628a–632a, 13:3253a
        denial of authorship of, 4:627b–628a
        publication of, 4:627a
    La nouvelle Justine, ou les malheurs de la vertu . . . (The New Justine; or, The Misfortunes of Virtue . . .), 4:632a–634a
        publication of, 4:627a
    letters of, 4:617a–618b, 637a
    literary lewdness and, 13:3253a
    "Ma grande lettre" ("My Great Letter"), 4:617a-b
    La marquise de Gange (The Marquise of Gange), 4:636b
    The 120 Days of Sodom; or, The School of Libertinism (Les 120 journées de Sodom, ou l'école du libertinage), 4:620a–626b
        influence of, 4:629a
        Justine and, 4:629b–630a

Sade, Donatien Alphonse François, marquis
     de (*cont.*)
     Philosophy in the Bedroom (*La philosophie
          dans le boudoir*), 4:634a–636a,
          13:3253a
          publication of, 4:627a
          "Yet Another Effort, Frenchmen, If You
               Would Become Republicans,"
               4:635a–636a
          "The Author of *The Crimes of Love* to
               Villeterque, Hack Writer," 4:628a-b
          The Crimes of Love (*Les crimes de l'amour*),
               4:627a–628b
               "Essay on the Novel" ("Idée sur les
                    romans"), 4:627a-b
               "Florville and Courval," 4:628b
Sade, Fourier, Loyola. See Barthes, Roland
Sadism
     in Bely's *Moskva*, 9:925b
     in Flaubert, 7:1386b–1387a
     Grass and, 13:3371a
     origin of the term, 6:637a
"Sadness." *See* Musset, Alfred de, "Tristesse"
"Sadness of Cornelius Berg, The." *See*
     Yourcenar, Marguerite, *Nouvelles
     orientales*
Sadok sudei. See Hylaea group
Sadok sudei, II. See Hylaea group
Sadomasochism
     in Ady's verse, 9:869b
     in Gombrowicz, 12:2574a–2577a,
          2583a–2584b
Sadovskaia, Kseniia Mikhailovna, 9:965b
"Saeta, La." *See* Machado, Antonio, *Soledades*
     (Solitudes)
Safe Conduct, A. See Pasternak, Boris
Safety Net, The. See Böll, Heinrich
Saga of Saints. See Undset, Sigrid, *Norske
     helgener*
Sagan om Fatumeh. See Ekelöf, Gunnar
Sagas, Norse. *See* Norse sagas
Sage, the, Schopenhauer's denial of will and,
     5:411a–412a, 414a
Sagen und Sänge. See George, Stefan, *Die
     Bücher der Hirten- und Preisgedichte*
     . . .

"Sager mir ieman waz ist minne?" *See*
     Walther von der Vogelweide
Sagesse. See Verlaine, Paul
Sagesse et la destinée, La. See Maeterlinck,
     Maurice
Sagesse, ou la parabole du festin, La. See
     Claudel, Paul
Saggio sullo Hegel. See Croce, Benedetto
Sagittario (Sagittarius). See Ginzburg, Natalia
Sagoprinsen. See Moberg, Vilhelm
Sagouin, Le. See Mauriac, François
Sagra del Signore della nave. See Pirandello,
     Luigi
"Sagt an, her Stoc." *See* Walther von der
     Vogelweide
Saianov, Vissarion, Khlebnikov negated by,
     10:1331b
"Sail, The." *See* Lermontov, Mikhail Yurievich,
     "Parus"
"Sailor-boy's Tale, The." *See* Dinesen, Isak
St. Bartholomew's Day massacre, in Mérimée's
     works, 6:752b–753b
"Saint Cecelia; or, The Power of Music." *See*
     Kleist, Heinrich von
St. Denis-du-Saint-Sacrement, Delacroix's
     painting, 5:520b, 532a
Saint Emmanuel the Good, Martyr. See
     Unamuno, Miguel de, *San Manuel
     Bueno, mártir*
Saint Francis. See Kazantzakis, Nikos, *O
     ftohúlis tu Theú*
Saint Genet: Actor and Martyr (*Saint Genet,
     comédien et martyr*). *See* Sartre,
     Jean-Paul
St. Germain fair, theatrical productions at,
     3:326a-b
Saint Glinglin. See Queneau, Raymond
St. Jacques (Dominican priory: Paris), 1:413b
Saint Joan. See Shaw, George Bernard
Saint Joan of the Stockyards. See Brecht,
     Bertolt, *Die Heilige Johanna der
     Schlachthöfe*
Saint John's Night. See Lope de Vega, *La
     noche de san Juan*
"Saint Julian the Hospitaller." *See* Flaubert,
     Gustave

Saint June Is Calling. *See* Ady, Endre, "Szent Junius hivása

St. Lebuin school, Erasmus and, 2:571b–572a

St. Mark, Cathedral of (Venice), in Proust's *Remembrance of Things Past*, 8:564b

St. Martin's Day. *See* Carducci, Giosue, "San Martino"

St. Petersburg, 6:971b, 972b, 973a, 980b
  Akhmatova's association with, 11:1748a
  Lermontov's career in, 6:1203b–1204a, 1207b–1208a, 1209a, 1211a, 1212b, 1216a-b, 1217a-b, 1221b–1222a
  in Mickiewicz's *Forefathers' Eve, Part III*, 5:622a–623a
  Mickiewicz's stay in, 5:613b
  in Pushkin's *The Bronze Horseman*, 5:670a-b

St. Petersburg Polytechnic Institute, Zamyatin's years at, 10:1181b–1182b

St. Petersburg University
  Khlebnikov's attendance at, 10:1333a
  Mandelshtam's education at, 10:1632a

Saint Pierre, Bernardin de
  Berlioz and, 6:775a
  Paul et Virginie, 6:775a
    Balzac and, 5:651a
    Sainte-Beuve on, 7:1411a

Saint, the, Schopenhauer's denial of will and, 5:410b–411a

Saint, The. See Meyer, Conrad Ferdinand, *Der Heilige*

Saint-Aignan, Madame de, in Vigny's *Stello*, 5:468b

Saint-Amant, Girard
  Moyse sauvé (*Moses Saved*), as biblical pastoral, 2:912b
  pastoral poetry of, 2:912b

Saint-Aubin, Charles de, in Goncourts' *L'Art du dix-huitième siècle*, 7:1397a

Saint-Cyr (school for girls), 3:269b

Saint-Exupéry, Antoine de, **12:2307a–2331b**
  "An Open Letter to Frenchmen Everywhere," 12:2321b–2322a
  Citadelle (*The Wisdom of the Sands*), 12:2325a, 2326b–2328b, 2329a
  Courrier sud (*Southern Mail*), 12:2310a, 2316b, 2328b

"L'Aviateur" ("The Aviator"), 12:2309a, 2310a

Le petit prince (*The Little Prince*), 12:2308b, 2322b–2325a, 2323a, 2329a, 2329b

letter to Léon Werth, 12:2322a-b

"Lettre au Général X," 12:2325a-b

Lettre à un otage (*Letter to a Hostage*), 12:2322a-b, 2328b

Lettres de jeunesse (Letters of His Youth), 12:2310a

Lettres à l'amie inventée (Letters to His Invented Friend), 12:2310a

Lettres à sa mère (Letters to His Mother), 12:2310a

"L'évasion de Jacques Bernis" (The Escape of Jacques Bernis), 12:2310a–2312a

"Message to Young Americans," 12:2321b

Pilote de guerre (*Flight to Arras*), 12:2319b, 2320a–2321b, 2328b
  Böll's *Pilote de guerre*, 13:3178b

"Seigneur berbère," 12:2326a

Terre des hommes (*Wind, Sand, and Stars*), 12:2312b, 2316b–2317a, 2317b–2319a
  "Au centre du désert" ("In the Center of Desert"), 12:2318a-b
  critical reception, 12:2319a
  "Dans le désert" ("Men of the Desert"), 12:2318a
  desert fox, 12:2324a
  "Les Hommes" ("The Men"), 12:2318b–2319a
  "Oasis," 12:2318a

Un sens à la vie (*A Sense of Life*), 12:2317a

Vol de nuit (*Night Flight*), 12:2309b, 2312b–2316a, 2320a, 2328b, 2329b
  Rivière, 12:2314b–2316a, 2327b

Saint-Georges, Vernoy de, 7:1911a

Saint-Paul, Albert, George and, 8:455b

Saint-Point, Valentine de, "Manifesto futurista della lussuria" ("Futurist Manifesto of Lust"), 9:811a

Saint-Simon, marquis de
  Fénelon and, 3:281b
  on La Bruyère, 3:230b

Saint-Simonianism
  Heine and, 5:498b–499a
  Rimbaud and, 7:1811a

Saint-Simonianism (*cont.*)
  Sainte-Beuve and, 6:853b
  Sand and, 6:824a-b
  Vigny and, 5:463b–464b
Saint-Sulpice, parish of, Fénelon and, 3:265b
Saint-Sulpice, Church of, Delacroix's painting,
  5:520b, 537a, 539a
Saint-Victor, Paul de
  Goncourts and, 7:1408b
  Sainte-Beuve on, 7:1411a
"Sainte." *See* Mallarmé, Stéphane
Sainte Lydwine de Schiedam. See Huysmans,
  Joris Karl
Sainte-Beuve, Charles-Augustin, **6:837a–861b**
  Balzac and, 5:652b
  on Baudelaire, 7:1335a-b
  on Bossuet, 3:174b
  Cahier vert (*Green Notebook*), 6:844a
  Causeries du lundi (*Monday Chats*), 6:839a
  Chateaubriand et son group littéraire
    (Chateaubriand and His Literary
    Group), 6:839a
  Chénier promoted by, 4:693a, 715b
  on Chénier's love for Fanny Lecoulteux,
    4:712a
  Critiques et portraits littéraires (Critical and
    Literary Portraits), 6:838a
  "Dix ans après en littérature" (Ten Years
    After in Literature), 6:838b
  Étude sur Virgile (*Studies of Vergil*), 6:839a
  on the Goncourts, 7:1401a, 1411a
  Hugo and, 6:694a, 697b
  "La Rochefoucauld," 6:838b
  on Leopardi, 5:557a
  Les consolations (*Consolations*), 6:838a
  "Les rayons jaunes" (Yellow Sunbeams),
    6:841b–842a
  Livre d'amour (*The Book of Love*), 6:838a
  Mathilde Bonaparte and, 7:1416a
  Mérimée and, 6:746b, 757a
  on Montaigne, 2:784a, 785b
  on Pascal, 3:148a
  Pensées d'août (*Thoughts of August*), 6:838a
  Port-Royal, 6:838b, 846a
    on Montaigne, 2:787a
  Portraits contemporains (Contemporary
    Portraits), 6:838b

Portraits de femmes (Portraits of Women),
  6:838b
Portraits littéraires (Literary Portraits),
  6:838b
"Qu'est-ce qu'un classique?" ("What Is a
  Classic?"), 6:854b–859b
Sand and, 6:820a
on Staël and Napoleon, 5:92b
on Staël's *Considerations on the Principal
  Events of the French Revolution*, 5:94a
*Tableau historique et critique de la poésie
  française et du théâtre français au
  XVIème siècle* (Historic Tableau of
  French Poetry and the French Theater in
  the Sixteenth Century), 6:837a-b
  on Ronsard, 2:741b
Taine and, 7:1449a, 1464a
Vie, poésies et pensées de Joseph Delorme
  (The Life, Poetry, and Thoughts of
  Joseph Delorme), 6:837b–838a
Vigny and, 5:478b, 479a
  Cinq-Mars reviewed by, 5:460b
  The Military Condition reviewed by,
    5:476b
Volupté, 5:653a, 6:838a, 1015a
Saints and Animals. *See* Hašek, Jaroslav,
  "Světci a zvířata"
Saints' lives, in Gottfried, 1:250b–251b
Saison en enfer, Une. See Rimbaud, Arthur, *A
  Season in Hell*
Sakkas, Ammonios, in Cavafy's poetry, 8:216a
Salamanca, University of, Unamuno's career
  at, 8:286b
"Salamina tis Kypros." *See* Seferis, George
"Salamis in Cyprus." *See* Seferis, George,
  "Salamina tis Kypros"
Salammbô. See Flaubert, Gustave
Salas Barbadillo, Alonso Jerónimo de, *Casa
  del placer honesto* (House of Virtuous
  Pleasure), Boccaccio's influence on,
  2:951a
Salazar, Antonio de Oliveira, 11:2146b
  Pessoa and, 10:1479b–1480a
Salazar-Caetano dictatorship
  Ferreira de Castro and, 11:2143a, 2148b,
    2149a, 2154a-b, 2161b, 2164a
    Emigrants, 11:2156a

Salel, Hughes, *eglogue marine* of, 2:911b
Salices. See Sannazaro, Jacopo
Salieri, Antonio
   in Pushkin's *Mozart and Salieri*,
     5:680b–681b
   Tarare, 4:583a-b
Salige er de Enfoldige. See Gunnarsson,
   Gunnar
Salinas, Pedro, Jiménez and, 9:992a, 1005b
Salinger, J. D., Böll's translations, 13:3167b
Salisbury, Lord, Pessoa and, 10:1478b–1479a
Salka Valka. See Laxness, Halldór
Sally Mara. See Queneau, Raymond
Saloma. See Krleža, Miroslav
"Salomé." *See* Apollinaire, Guillaume
Salomé. *See* Krleža, Miroslav, *Saloma*
Salomon, Elisabeth, 8:464b
Salomon and Marculf, 1:471b
Salon of 1846. See Baudelaire, Charles
"Salon of 1859." *See* Baudelaire, Charles
Salon d'automobile, Le. See Ionesco, Eugène
Salon, Der. See Heine, Heinrich
Salon II-IV. See Heine, Heinrich
Salon, The. See Heine, Heinrich, *Der Salon*
Salons. See Diderot, Denis
Salons, literary
   French, of Madame Jean-Baptiste Suard,
     4:407b
   Sainte-Beuve on, 6:850b–851a
Salten, Felix
   Hofmannsthal and, 9:690b
   Schnitzler and, 8:92a
Saltimbanques, Les. See Picasso, Pablo
Sálumessa. See Gunnarsson, Gunnar
Salutati, Coluccio, on Petrarch, 2:475a
"Salute to Walt Whitman." *See* Pessoa,
     Fernando, "Saudação a Walt Whitman"
Salvadora de Olbena. See Azorín
Salvation
   in Ekelöf's works, 12:2641a
   in Goethe's *Faust*, 5:21b, 22b
   in Mann's *Doctor Faustus*, 9:736a
   in Milosz's works, 13:2941a, 2943b
   pagan rhetoric and, 1:19a-b
   paternal, in Simenon's works, 12:2483a-b,
     2491b–2492a
   Prudentius and, 1:14a, 15a-b

   in Schlegel's works, 5:191b
   see also Redemption
Salvation history
   in Prudentius' works, 1:2b, 10b
     Hamartigenia, 1:9b
Salvation/Survival. *See* Milosz, Czeslaw,
   Ocalenie
Salvatores Dei: Askitikí. See Kazantzakis,
   Nikos
"Salve mundi domine, Cesar noster ave." *See*
   Archpoet
Salviati, Cassandra, 2:727b
Salzburg Everyman, The. See Hofmannsthal,
   Hugo von
Salzburg Festival, Hofmannsthal and, 9:690b,
   693b–694b
Salzburg Great Theater of the World, The (Das
   Salzburger grosse Welttheater). See
   Hofmannsthal, Hugo von
Samarskaia gazeta, Gorky and, 8:419a
Samfundets støtter. See Ibsen, Henrik
Sammlung, Die, Heinrich Mann and, 8:537a
"S'amor no è." *See* Petrarch, *Canzoniere*
"Samothrace." *See* Ekelöf, Gunnar
Samson; or, Shame and Jealousy. *See*
   Wedekind, Frank, *Simson, oder Scham*
   und Eifersuch
Samuel, Emanuel (Osmund), 5:70b
Samuel Henzi. See Lessing, Gotthold Ephraim
Samum. See Strindberg, August
Sæmund Sigfússon the Learned, 1:379b
"San i java." *See* Dream and reality
San Manuel Bueno, mártir. See Unamuno,
   Miguel de
"San Martino." *See* Carducci, Giosue
San Secondo, Rosso di, *Marionette, che*
   passione! (Marionettes, What Passions
   They Feel!), 8:393b
Sánchez de las Brozas, Francisco, 2:751b
Sánchez Ferlosio, Rafael, *El Jarama*, 12:2649a
Sánchez, Tomás Antonio, *Colección de*
   poesías castellanas anteriores al siglo
   XV, Poema de mio Cid in, 1:113a-b,
   115a
Sancho II y cerco de Zamora
   ballads of the Cid and, 1:132a-b
   Poema de mio Cid and, 1:132b

Sancta Clara, Abraham a, 5:41a

Sanctification, Elytis' *To Axion Esti* and, 13:2968a

Sand, George, **6:813a–836b**, 7:1532a

  Aimée, 6:819b

  Berlioz and, 6:789b

  Consuelo, 6:825b–826a

  Countess Rudolstadt, 6:825b–826a

  Delacroix and, 5:516b, 521b–523a

  "Dialogues familiers sur la poésie des prolétaires" ("Familiar Dialogues on the Poetry of the Proletarians"), 6:829a

  diary of, 6:1013b

  Dostoevsky and, 7:1351a-b

  Elle et lui (*She and He*), 6:821b, 999b–1000a

  François the Waif, 6:813a, 829b

  on the French Revolution, 5:589a

  Horace, 6:826a-b

  Indiana, 6:819a-b

  Jacques, 6:822b

  Jeanne, 6:829b

  Journal intime (*Intimate Journal*), 6:821b

  La cause du peuple and, 6:831b

  La dernière Aldini (*The Last Aldini*), 6:823a

  Le compagnon du tour de France (*Journeyman Joiner*), 6:825b

  Le dernier amour (*The Last Love*), 6:832a

  Le meunier d'Angibault, 6:829b

  Le voyage en Auvergne (Travels in Auvergne), 6:818b

  Le voyage en Espagne (Travels in Spain), 6:818b

  Lélia, 6:820a

  Leone Leoni, 6:822b–823a

  Les maîtres sonneurs (*The Master Bellringers*), 6:829b

  Lettres d'un voyageur (*Letters of a Traveler*), 6:789b, 821b, 822b

  Lettres à Marcie (Letters to Marcy), 6:824a

  Little Fadette, 6:813a, 829b

  L'Orco, 6:823a

  L'Uscoque, 6:823a

  Mathilde Bonaparte and, 7:1416a

  Mauprat, 6:826b–827b

  Mérimée and, 6:755a

  Monsieur Sylvestre, 6:832a

  Musset and, 6:820b–823a

    impact on, 6:1001b, 1006a-b

    love affair between, 6:1001b, 1006a, 1014a

    portrayal of, in *Confessions*, 6:999b–1000a, 1014b–1015a

    in Venice, 6:999b, 1001b, 1006a-b, 1014a-b

  philanthropism of, 6:995b

  Revue indépendante founded by, 6:826a

  Rose et Blanche, 6:819a

  Spiridion, 6:825b

  The Devil's Pool, 6:829b–830a

  The Seven Strings of the Lyre (*Les sept cordes de la lyre*), 6:825b

  The Story of My Life, 6:815a–816a

    religion in, 6:824b–825a

  treatment of the lower classes, 7:1478a

  "Une conspiration en 1537" ("A Conspiracy in 1537"), 6:1006b

  Valentine, 6:820a

"Sandales d'Empédocle, Les" (The Sandals of Empedocles). *See* Leconte de Lisle, Charles Marie

Sandalwood Tree, The. *See* Vesaas, Tarjei, *Sandeltreet*

Sandburg, Carl

  Good Morning, America, 9:1012a

  Jiménez and, 9:1012a

Sandeau, Jules, Sand and, 6:818b–820a

Sandeltreet. *See* Vesaas, Tarjei

Sandor, Andras, on Benjamin and Rilke, 9:777a-b

Sang des autres, Le. *See* Beauvoir, Simone de, *The Blood of Others*

Sang du pauvre, Le. *See* Böll, Heinrich

Sang d'un poète, Le. *See* Cocteau, Jean

Sang och strid. *See* Lagerkvist, Pär

"Sanglot de la terre, Le." *See* Laforgue, Jules

Sangre y arena. *See* Blasco Ibáñez, Vicente

Sänkt sedebetyg. *See* Moberg, Vilhelm, *Memory of Youth*

Sannazaro, Jacopo

  Arcadia, 2:920b–921b

    French pastoral poetry and, 2:911b

    pastoral romance and, 2:921b

  piscatorial poetry of, 2:908b–909a

  Salices (*Willows*), Ovidian myth in, 2:909a

Sanningen kryper fram. See Moberg, Vilhelm

"Sans âge." *See* Éluard, Paul

Sanskrit, Schlegel and, 5:177a, 194a

Santa Cruz: Eine Romanze (Santa Cruz: A Romance). *See* Frisch, Max

Santarosa, Santorre, inspired by Alfieri, 4:687b

Sant'Elia, Antonio, 9:825a

Santillana, Marquès de, Petrarchan sonnets, 2:504a

"Santorini." *See* Seferis, George, *Gymnopaidia*

Santos, Luis Martín
    Baroja influences, 9:613a
    Spain's "time of silence," 9:1147a
    Tiempo de silencio (Time of Silence), 9:596b

Sanz del Río, Julián, Krausism inspired by, 9:591b

"Sapienza poetica," 8:325b

Sappho
    Elytis and, 13:2981b, 2984a
    Leopardi and, 5:565a-b
    in Pascoli's "Solon," 7:1846b

Sappho. See Grillparzer, Franz

Sarcey, Françisque, 7:1912a-b, 1924b, 1927a

"Sardegna" ("Sardinia"). *See* Quasimodo, Salvatore

Sardou, Victorien, 7:1916a-b
    Les pattes de mouche (The Scrap of Paper), 7:1916a, 1922b
    verse drama, 7:1426b

Saroyan, William, Vittorini and, 12:2740b

Sarragá, Salamão, 7:1689b

Sarrasine. See Balzac, Honoré de

Sarraute, Nathalie, **12:2333a–2359b**
    Butor and, 13:3288b
    C'est beau (It's Beautiful), 12:2354b–2355a, 2356b–2357a
    "disent les imbéciles" ("fools say"), 12:2353b–2354a
    Elle est là (It Is There), 12:2355a, 2357a-b
    Enfance (Childhood), 12:2335a
    Entre la vie et la mort (Between Life and Death), 12:2343b, 2347b–2352b
    fictional characters of, 8:304a
    Isma (Izzum), 12:2354b, 2356a-b

    Le mensonge (The Lie), 12:2354b, 2355b–2356a
    Le planétarium (The Planetarium), 12:2340b–2343b
    Le silence (The Silence), 12:2354b, 2355b
    L'Ère du soupçon (The Age of Suspicion), 12:2334a, 2334b–2335a, 2351b
        "From Dostoevsky to Kafka," 12:2337b
    Les fruits d'or (The Golden Fruits), 12:2343b–2347b
    L'Usage de la parole (The Use of Speech), 12:2354a
        "À très bientôt" ("See You Soon"), 12:2354a
    Martereau, 12:2339b–2340b, 2341b, 2342a
    Portrait d'un inconnu (Portrait of a Man Unknown), 12:2333a, 2337a, 2338a–2339b
    Pour un oui ou pour un non (At the Drop of a Hat), 12:2355a, 2357b
    technique, 12:2337a, 2349a
    Tropismes (Tropisms), 12:2336b–2337b, 2342a, 2354a
    Vous les entendez? (Do You Hear Them?), 12:2352b–2353b

Sárszeg, in Kosztolányi's novels, 10:1237a–1238b

Sartor Resartus. See Carlyle, Thomas

Sartorelli, Gabriele, on Silone's *Story of a Humble Christian*, 12:2300b

Sartre, Jean-Paul, **12:2589a–2614b 2788a**
    Anti-Semite and Jew (Réflexion sur la question juive), 12:2601a
    Baudelaire, 12:2597a, 2607a
    Beauvoir and, 12:2702a, 2711b, 2717b, 2720a, 2728b
    Being and Nothingness: An Essay on Phenomenological Ontology (L'Être et le néant: Essai d'ontologie phénoménologique), 12:2594b–2597a, 2600a-b, 2717b, 2722a, 2723b
    interrelatedness in, 12:2598b
    as philosophy, 12:2590b
    unity and, 12:2610b
    Bergson and, 8:52b, 64a
    bourgeois intelligentsia, 9:1120b
    Butor and, 13:3288a

Sartre, Jean-Paul (*cont.*)

Cahiers pour une morale (Notebooks on Morality), 12:2607b

Camus and, 13:3050b, 3074a

on Céline, 11:1862a

Céline's influence on, 11:1859a

Chénier compared to, 4:715b

Critique of Dialectical Reason (*Critique de la raison dialectique*), 12:2603a–2606a, 2611b

on Dostoevsky, 7:1350a

epiphany of the absurd, 9:1126b

existentialism, 11:1948a

Existentialism and Humanism, Unamuno as precursor of, 8:299b

Foucault and, 13:3331a-b

Genet and, 13:2866b, 2867a

Giraudoux and, 9:1041b

Hesse and, 9:844a

Imagination: A Psychological Critique (*L'Imagination*), 12:2590a

Kierkegaard and, 6:1140a

Krleža and, 11:1828a-b

Les chemins de la liberté (The Roads to Freedom), 12:2594a

L'Être et le néant (*Being and Nothingness*), Barthes and, 13:3083b

Mauriac and, 10:1324b–1326a

Nausea (*La nausée*), 9:607b, 12:2512b, 2591a–2593a, 2611a-b, 2715a

No Exit (*Huis clos*), 12:2598b–2599a

and Anouilh's *Jézebel*, 13:2850a

Ortega y Gasset and, 9:1131a

"Pour un papillon" (For a Butterfly), 12:2598a

on pre–World War II authors, 12:2707a

preface to Sarraute's *Portrait of a Man Unknown*, 12:2333a

Queneau and, 12:2511b, 2512b

Saint Genet: Actor and Martyr (*Saint Genet, comédien et martyr*), 12:2597a, 2606a–2608a, 13:2867a, 2890a, 2891a

on Sarraute, 12:2337a

Search for a Method, 12:2603a–2604a

Silone and, 12:2276b

Simenon and, 12:2504a

The Age of Reason (*L'Âge de raison*), 12:2594a

The Communists and Peace ("Les communistes et la paix"), 12:2602a-b

The Devil and the Good Lord (*Le Diable et le bon Dieu*), 12:2601b–2602a

The Emotions: Outline of a Theory (*Esquisse d'une théorie des émotions*), 12:2593a-b

The Family Idiot (*L'Idiot de la famille: Gustave Flaubert de 1821 à 1857*), 12:2590a, 2597a, 2606b–2611a

The Flies (*Les mouches*), 9:753b, 12:2549a, 2601a

Moral Tales and, 7:1907a

religion in, 13:3220b

spiritual despair in, 13:3217a

The Ghost of Stalin ("Le fantôme de Staline"), 12:2603a

The Psychology of the Imagination (*L'Imaginaire*), 12:2590a, 2593a

The Reprieve (*Le sursis*), 12:2594a

The War Diaries (*Les carnets de la drôle de guerre: November 1939–Mars 1940*), 12:2598a, 2600a

The Words (*Les mots*), 12:2597a-b, 2611a

"Un promeneur dans Paris insurgé" (A Stroller in the Paris Insurrection), 12:2601b

What Is Literature? (*Qu'est-ce que la littérature?*), 12:2525b, 2597b–2598a, 2611a-b, 2708a

Barthes and, 13:3082a

Yourcenar and, 12:2539a

Sashka. See Lermontov, Mikhail Yurievich

Satan

in Akhmatova's *Poem Without a Hero*, 10:1536b, 1537a, 1539a

Hugo's view of, 6:713a-b

the Sadean hero and Milton's Satan, 4:626a

see also Devil

"Satan racheté" (Satan Redeemed). *See* Vigny, Alfred Victor de

Satan Redeemed. See Hugo, Victor, *La fin de Satan*

"Satan sauvé" (Satan Redeemed). *See* Vigny, Alfred Victor de

Satanism, Huysmans and, 7:1722a, 1724b
Satie, Erik, 8:546b, 9:899b
Satin Slipper, The. See Claudel, Paul
Satire
  Ariosto and, 2:620b–622a
  of Aymé, 12:2438b–2449b
  in Berlioz' works, 6:785a, 787b–788a
  in Boileau's literary criticism, 3:178a
  Calvino and, 13:3271a-b
  classical. *See* Classical literature, satire
  didactic, 1:341a-b, 348a, 354a
  Diderot and, 4:499a-b
  Erasmus and, 2:578b–579b
  of Foscolo, 5:325a
  in Giraudoux's works, 9:1043b
  Goldoni and, 4:428b
  Heinrich Mann on, 8:521b
  in Jarry's works, 9:672b, 674a
  of Jiménez, 9:1005b
  of Leopardi, 5:547b
  in Lermontov's works, 6:1202b,
    1210b–1211a
  in Mann's *Confessions of Felix Krull*, 9:737a
  in Maupassant's works, 7:1765a-b, 1768a,
    1769b, 1775b–1776a, 1780b
  medieval, **1:337a–375b**
    of Arras, 1:459a
    audience participation in, 1:364b, 365b
    Christianity and, 1:337b–338a, 338b,
      339a, 340a, 356a
    on estates, 1:348a, 354a–356a, 372b
    figurative representation in, 1:367a-b
    on foreigners, 1:344b, 350a-b
    forms of, 1:372a–373a
    personae of, 1:358b–361b
    self-criticism in, 1:356b
    technique of, 1:364b, 365b–372a
    themes of, 1:350a
  in Molière's *Le misanthrope*, 3:121a
  of Moravia, 12:2679a–2680a, 2692a
  in Musil's *The Man Without Qualities*,
    9:937b, 938b, 939a, 940b, 943b
    characterization and, 9:953a
    Müller on, 9:942a
  polemical, 1:340b–341a, 341b, 343a-b
  in Portuguese literature, Eça, 7:1687b, 1688a

pseudo-Homeric, in Leopardi's works,
  5:565a
purpose of, 1:337a-b, 340a-b
in Rabelais's *Fifth Book*, 2:715a
in Richter's works, 5:57a-b, 66b
Staël on, 5:109b
as term, 1:337b
Voltaire's use of, 4:367b, 385a-b
in William IX's works, 1:162b–163a
see also Boileau-Despréaux, Nicolas;
  Lesage, Alain-René; Wieland, Christoph
  Martin
Satires. See Alfieri, Vittorio;
  Boileau-Despréaux, Nicolas; Horace;
  Juvenal
Satura. See Montale, Eugenio
Saturae. See Lucilius
Saturne: Essai sur Goya (*Saturn: An Essay on
  Goya*). *See* Malraux, André
Saturnian Poems. *See* Verlaine, Paul, *Poèmes
  saturniens*
"Satyr and the Passerby, The." *See* La
  Fontaine, Jean de, *Fables*, "Le satyre et
  le passant"
"Satyre, Le." *See* Hugo, Victor
"Satyre et le passant, Le." *See* La Fontaine,
  Jean de, *Fables*
Satyricon. See Petronius, Gaius
"Saudação a Walt Whitman." *See* Pessoa,
  Fernando
Saugrenu. See Humor, Gide's use of
Saul. See Alfieri, Vittorio
Saulsaye, La: Eglogue de la vie solitaire. See
  Scève, Maurice
Saussure, Ferdinand de
  Barthes and, 13:3087a
  Ortega y Gasset and, 9:1138b
  semiotics of, 11:1965b
Sauvage, La. See Anouilh, Jean, *Restless Heart*
"Sauvage, La." *See* Vigny, Alfred Victor de,
  Les destinées
"Sauvée." *See* Maupassant, Guy de
Sauzet, Jean Pierre, Tocqueville on, 6:902a-b
Savage Paris. See Zola, Émile, *Le ventre de
  Paris*
Savage Woman, The. *See* Vigny, Alfred Victor
  de, *Les destinées*, "La sauvage"

Savary, Anne, 5:93a-b, 105a

"Saved." *See* Maupassant, Guy de, "Sauvée"

Savidis, George, 13:2968a-b

Savinkov, Boris, Mandelshtam and, 10:1626a

Saviors of God, The: Spiritual Exercises. See Kazantzakis, Nikos, *Salvatores Dei: Askitikí*

Sawa, Alejandro, in Valle-Inclán's *Luces de bohemia*, 8:347a

Saxo Grammaticus, *Gesta Danorum* (*History of the Danes*), 1:400a, 401a

"Sayings of the Four Philosophers, The," 1:369a

"Sbylos' prorochostvo moe." *See* Blok, Alexander

Scala, Bartolommeo della, Dante and, 1:434b

Scala, Can Grande della, Dante and, 1:435a, 435b, 444b–445a, 445b

Scaliger, J. C., pastoral scholarship of, 2:910b

Scalvini, Giovita, Manzoni's *The Betrothed* criticized by, 5:375b

Scamp, The. *See* Goldoni, Carlo, *La birba*

Scandal and Parade. See Oxenhandler, Neal

Scandals, sexual, *see also* Libertines

Scapegoat
    Camus and, 13:3074a-b
    Kafka and, 9:1167a

Scarron, Paul, characters, 12:2528a

Scène à faire, 7:1911b, 1921a, 1929a, 1929b

Scènes de la vie de bohème (Scenes of Bohemian Life). *See* Murger, Henri

Scènes de la vie privée. See Balzac, Honoré de

Scenes from the Desert: The Almeh (*Scènes du désert: L'Almeh*). *See* Vigny, Alfred Victor de

Scenes from Private Life. *See* Balzac, Honoré de, *Scènes de la vie privée*

"Scenes of Portuguese Life." *See* Eça de Queiroz, José Maria

Scève, Maurice
    La Saulsaye: Eglogue de la vie solitaire (The Willow Grove: An Eclogue of the Solitary Life), Renaissance pastoral poetry and, 2:911a-b
    Petrarchan influence, 2:504a

Schach Lolo. See Wieland, Christoph Martin

Schach von Wuthenow. See Fontane, Theodor

Schapp, Wilhelm, *Geschichten verstrickt: Zum Sein von Mensch und Ding* (Entangled in Stories: On the Existence of Man and Thing), Frisch and, 13:2915b

"Schatten des Esels, Der." *See* Wieland, Christoph Martin

Schauertragödie (Horror Tragedy), by Wedekind, 8:252b

Schauspielkunst: Ein Glossarium. See Wedekind, Frank

Scheherazade, Butor and, 13:3307b–3308a

Scheinglueck. See Fortune, false

Scheinpflugová, Olga
    Čapek and, 10:1566a-b
    Čský román (A Czech Novel), 10:1566b

Scheler, Max
    Machado and, 9:761b
    phenomenology, 9:1127b

"Scheli v Sadu vyryty." *See* Akhmatova, Anna

Schelling, Friedrich Wilhelm von
    Dogmatism and Criticism, 5:211b
    Goncharov and, 6:1064a
    Hölderlin and, 5:145a
    Lukács on, 10:1274b
    Naturphilosophie and, 5:211b, 218b
    Novalis and, 5:10a, 206a
    System of Transcendental Idealism, Hegel and, 10:1273b

Schenk, Claus, George and, 8:468a

Scherer, Wilhelm, Taine and, 7:1452a

Schildt, Runar, Södergran and, 11:1785a, 1789a, 1791a-b

Schiller, Friedrich von, **5:27a–52b**
    Aesthetic Letters, 5:37a, 37b, 38a, 39a
    Brecht and, 11:2093b–2095b, 2101a, 2105a
    compared to Alfieri, 4:661b
    "Das verschleierte Bild zu Sais" ("The Veiled Image of Sais"), 5:216b–217a
    Demetrius, 5:49b, 50a
    on Diderot's art criticism, 11:2028a
    Die Räuber (*The Robbers*), 5:28b, 31a–32b, 37b, 40a, 50b, 6:1209a, 7:1428a
    Frisch and, 13:2897a
    Don Carlos, 5:34b–36a, 36b, 40b, 47b, 50b, 6:1201a
    influence on Grillparzer's *Blanca von Kastilien*, 5:424a-b

Dostoevsky and, 7:1350b

Geschichte des Abfalls der vereinigten Niederlande (*History of the Revolt of the United Netherlands from the Spanish Government*), 5:36b

Geschichte des dreissigjährigen Krieges (*History of the Thirty Years War*), 5:36b

Goethe and, 5:1a, 38b–39a, 40a–42a, 50a

Goncharov and, 6:1064a

Grillparzer and, 5:417b, 423b, 424a, 443b

   Hero and Leander, 5:436a-b

in Heinrich Mann's works

   "A Weary Hour," 8:527a

   Man of Straw, 8:532a

   Professor Unrat, 8:528a

Hofmannsthal and, 9:689b, 690a

Hölderlin and

   letters to, 5:147b, 164a

   professorships of, 5:148a

   publication of Hölderlin's work by, 5:150b

   support of, 5:155a, 164a

Kabale und Liebe (*Intrigue and Love*), 5:33a–34b, 50b

Kallias, 5:37a, 38a

Klopstock and, 4:512b

Lermontov and, 6:1199a, 1201a, 1201b, 1209a

Lessing's influence on, 4:558a

Letters on Don Carlos, 5:35a

Lukács on, 10:1256b–1256a

Mary Stuart, 5:45a–46b

On Epic and Dramatic Poetry, 11:2093b

Richter and, 5:54a, 71a, 72a

The Artists, 5:39b

The Bride of Messina, 5:47b–48a

"The Conqueror," 5:29b

The Conspiracy of Fiesco at Genoa, 5:32b–33a

The Gods of Greece, 5:39b, 222b

The Maid of Orleans, 5:46b–47b, 50b

The Walk, 5:40a

Thomas Mann on, 9:737b

"To Joy," 5:36a

Über Anmut und Würde (*On Grace and Dignity*), 5:38b, 39a, 44a

Über naive und sentimentalisch Dichtung (*On Naive and Sentimentive Poesy*), 5:38b

   Chénier's aesthetics and, 4:709b–710a

Wallenstein, 5:36b, 11:2095a

   Grillparzer on, 5:431b, 432a-b

   The Piccoliminis, 5:44a-b

   Wallenstein's Camp, 5:41a, 43a, 43b, 71b

   Wallenstein's Death, 5:43b

and Wieland, 4:589a-b, 606b

William Tell, 5:48a–49b

   Goethe and, 5:41a

Xenia, 5:41b–42a

Schiller, Johann Kaspar, 5:27a

Schiller Museum (Marbach), 8:447a

Schiller Prize, to Hebbel, 6:1098a

"Schillerpreis-Rede." See Frisch, Max

Schimmelreiter, Der. See Storm, Theodor, *The Rider on the White Horse*

Schimpf und Ernst. See Pauli, Johannes

Schizophrenia, in Calvino, 13:3267b–3268b

Schlacht bei Hemmingstedt, Die. See Hebbel, Friedrich

Schlafwandler, Die. See Broch, Hermann, *The Sleepwalkers*

Schlegel, August Wilhelm

on Alfieri

   Myrrha, 4:685b

   Virginia, 4:682b

Friedrich von Schlegel and, 5:177a, 194a

and Heine, 5:491b–492a

Lectures on Dramatic Art, Alfieri praised by, 4:661b

Novalis and, 5:206a

Richter and, 5:75b, 77b

Staël and, 5:92b

Schlegel, Caroline, on Novalis, 5:208a

Schlegel, Friedrich von, **5:177a–203b**

A Course of Lectures on Modern History, 5:196a

Alarcos, 5:193a

Benjamin's work on, 11:1704a-b

Dialogue on Poetry

   Andrea's lecture in, 5:188a–189b

   Antonio's reading in, 5:189b–190a, 195a

   classicism in, 5:181a-b

   literary criticism in, 5:186a–188a

Schlegel, Friedrich von (*cont.*)
   Dialogue on Poetry (*cont.*)
     Ludovico's lecture in, 5:184b–185a
     Marcus's essay in, 5:190b
   Dostoevsky and, 7:1350b
   Goethe and, 5:190a, 11:1710a
   on Goethe's *Wilhelm Meister*, 5:16b
   Herder misinterpreted by, 4:658b
   *History of the Poetry of the Greeks and
     Romans*, 5:179a-b
   Ideas, 5:182b–183a, 190a, 205b
   *Lectures on the History of Ancient and
     Modern Literature*, 5:196b, 198b
   Lucinde, 5:68a, 191a-b
     Nietzsche and, 5:191b–192a
     popularity of, 5:193a
   Lukasbund and, 5:83a
   Novalis and, 5:205a–206a, 208b
   *On the Language and Wisdom of India
     (Über die Sprache und Weisheit der
     Indier)*, 5:194a-b
     Michelet and, 5:579a
   "On the Study of Greek Poetry," 5:179b
   Richter and, 5:54b, 71b, 75b, 78a-b
     Siebenkäs, 5:70b
     The School for Aesthetics, 5:77b
     Walt and Vult, 5:76a
   Staël and, 5:92b, 106a, 108a
   "Talk on Mythology," 5:184b–185a
   The Philosophy of History, 5:184b, 199a
   The Philosophy of Language, 5:199a, 200a
   The Philosophy of Life, 5:199a-b
Schleier der Beatrice, Der. *See* Schnitzler,
   Arthur
"Schleier der Pierrette, Der." *See* Schnitzler,
   Arthur
Schleiermacher, Friedrich
   elaboration of Kant's views by, 5:395b–396a
   Novalis and, 5:206a
   religion and, 5:219a
   Schlegel and, 5:182a, 182b
   Über die Religion (*On Religion*), 5:219a
Schlemiel, in Svevo's novels, 8:86b
Schlenther, Paul, Schnitzler and, 8:98a
Schlésinger, Élise, Flaubert and, 7:1374l
"Schlesischen Weber, Die." *See* Heine,
   Heinrich

Schleswig
   Fontane and, 6:1314b–1315a
   Storm and, 6:918b–919a
Schlolem, Gershom, Benjamin and,
     11:1703b–1704a, 1720b
Schlöndorff, Volker, adaptation of Yourcenar's
     Coup de Grâce, 12:2544a
Schloss, Das. See Kafka, Franz, *The Castle*
Schloss Wetterstein: Drama in Drei Akten. See
     Wedekind, Frank, *Castle Wetterstein:
     Drama in Three Acts*
Schmidt, Julian, poetic realism and, 6:913b
Schmitz, Paul, influence on Baroja, 9:595b,
     609a
*Schnellmaler, oder Kunst und Mammon, Der.
     See* Wedekind, Frank
Schnier, Hans, in Böll's *Ansichten eines
     Clowns*, 13:3180b
Schnitzler, Arthur, **8:89a–117b**
   "Alkandis Lied" (Alkandi's Song), 8:93b
   Anatol, 8:90a, 93b–94b, 113b
   Aphorismen und Betrachtungen (Aphorisms
     and Observations), 8:103b, 106a
   Casanovas Heimfahrt (*Casanova's
     Homecoming*), 8:108b–109a
   "Das Bacchusfest" (The Festival of
     Bacchus), 8:106b
   Das Märchen (The Fairy Tale), 8:89a, 94b
   "Das Tagebuch der Redegonda"
     ("Redegonda's Diary"), 8:103b–104a
   Das Vermächtnis (*The Legacy*), 8:96b
   Das weite Land (*Undiscovered Country*),
     8:104b–105a
   "Der Andere" (The Other Man), 8:92b
   "Der blinde Geronimo und sein Bruder"
     (Blind Geronimo and His Brother),
     8:99b
   Der einsame Weg (*The Lonely Way*),
     8:101a-b
   Der Gand zum Weiher (The Walk to the
     Pond), 8:107a-b
   Der junge Medardus (Young Medardus),
     8:104b
   "Der Mörder" (The Murder), 8:104a
   "Der Puppenspieler" (The Puppeteer),
     8:101a

Der Ruf des Lebens (The Call of Life), 8:102a

Der Schleier der Beatrice (The Veil of Beatrice), 8:97b–98a

"Der Schleier der Pierrette" (The Veil of Pierrette), 8:98a-b

"Der tapfere Cassian" (Gallant Cassian), 8:101a

"Der Tod des Junggesellen" ("The Death of a Bachelor"), 8:103b–104a

Der Witwer (The Widower), 8:97a

"Die Drei Elixire" (The Three Elixirs), 8:92b–93a

"Die Egoisten" (The Egoists), 8:101a-b

"Die Frau mit dem Dolche" (The Lady with the Dagger), 8:100b

"Die Fremde" ("The Stranger"), 8:100a-b

"Die Gefährtin" (His Helpmate), 8:96b–97a

"Die Hirtenflöte" (The Shepherd's Pipe), 8:104a

"Die letzten Masken" (Last Masks), 8:100b

Die Schwestern oder Casanova in Spa (The Sisters or Casanova in the Spa), 8:107a

Doktor Gräsler, Badearzt (Dr. Graesler, Resort Physician), 8:108b

"Er wartet auf den vazierenden Gott" (He Is Waiting for the Itinerant God), 8:92b

Fink und Fliederbusch (Fink and Fliederbusch), 8:107a

Flucht in die Finsternis (Flight into Darkness), 8:111a

Frau Beate und ihr Sohn (Beatrice), 8:100a

Frau Berta Garlan (Bertha Garlen), 8:99b–100a

Fräulein Else, 8:109a

Free Game (Freiwild), 8:89a, 90a, 95b–96a

"Grosse Szene" (The Great Scene), 8:106b

Hands Around (Reigen), 8:96a, 111b–112a, 113b

Hofmannsthal and, 9:690b

Ibsen's influence on, 7:1443b

Im Spiel der Sommerlüfte (In the Play of the Summer Breezes), 8:103a

Komödie der Verführung (Comedy of Seduction), 8:107b–108a

Komödie der Worte (Comedies of Words), 8:106b

Komtesse Mizzi oder der Familientag (Countess Mizzi; or, The Family Reunion), 8:102a

Lebendige Stunden (Living Hours), 8:100b–101a

Light-o-Love (Liebelei), 8:95a-b, 113b

"Literatur" (Literature), 8:100b–101a

Marionetten (Marionettes), 8:101a

None But the Brave (Leutnant Gustl), 8:89a, 92b, 98b–99b, 109a

"Paracelsus," 8:90a, 96b–97a

Professor Bernhardi, 8:89a, 90a, 105b–106a

Spiel im Morgengrauen (Daybreak), 8:91a, 110a-b

Sterben (Dying), 8:93a

"Stunde des Erkennens" (Hour of Recognition), 8:106b

"The Green Cockatoo" ("Der grüne Kakadu"), 8:96b–97a, 98a, 101a

The Road to the Open (Der Weg ins Freie), 8:102b–103b

Therese: Chronik eines Frauenlebens (Theresa: The Chronicle of a Woman's Life), 8:110b–111a

Traumnovelle (Rhapsody), 8:109b–110a

"Um eine Stund" (For One Hour), 8:93a

"Und einmal wird der Friede wieder kommen" (Someday Peace Will Return), 8:106a

"Zum grossen Wurstel" (The Big Wurstel Puppet Theater), 8:95b, 101a

Zwischenspiel (Intermezzo), 8:101b–102a

Scholar personae, in medieval satire, 1:362a

Scholasticism

in Castiglione, 2:659a-b

dialectic and, 1:405a-b

Erasmus and, 2:573a-b, 579a

Luther and, 2:674b–675a, 686b

Scholem, Gershom, *Major Trends in Jewish Mysticism*, 12:2349a

Schomberg, duchesse de. *See* Hautefort, Marie de

Schönberg, Arnold

George's *Hängende Gärten* and, 8:465a

Mann's *Doctor Faustus* and, 9:733b

Pierrot lunaire, 9:734b

Schöne Leben, das, 8:463a

Schöne Leben, das (cont.)
  in George's Der Teppich, 8:461a-b
"Schönheit des Sterbens in der Blüte des
      Lebens, Die." See Richter, Jean Paul
School for Aesthetics. See Richter, Jean Paul,
      Vorschule der Aesthetik
School for Buffoons, The. See Ghelderode,
      Michel de
School of Dictators, The. See Silone, Ignazio,
      La scuola dei dittatori
"School of good sense." See "École du bon
      sens"
School for Husbands, The. See Molière,
      L'École des maris
School for Indifference, The. See Giraudoux,
      Jean, L'École des indifférents
School for Wives, The. See Molière, L'École
      des femmes
Schopenhauer als Erzieher. See Nietzsche,
      Friedrich, Schopenhauer as Educator
Schopenhauer, Arthur, **5:395a–415b**
  on artists, 7:1657b, 1675a-b
  Baroja influenced by, 9.591ab, 9:595b–596a,
      606a-b
  Beauvoir and, 12:2711a
  Beckett and, 13:3026a
  Bely and, 9:911a, 912a
  Generation of '98 and, 9:744b
  Hebbel and, 6:1097b
  Kafka and, 9:1154b
  Kazantzakis and, 9:1076b
  Klein and Wagner and, 9:842b
  Laforgue and, 7:1884b, 1889a, 1890a, 1904b
  in Laforgue's poetry
      Pierrot the Dabbler, 7:1891b
      "The Lament of the Pianos You Hear in
          Rich Neighborhoods" and, 7:1886b,
          1887a
  Machado and, 9:761b
  Mann and
      Buddenbrooks, 9:717a
      Doctor Faustus, 9:733a
  Maupassant and, 7:1774b
  Moberg and, 11:2208b, 2209a, 2224b
  Nietzsche and, 7:1649b, 1650b–1651a
  On the Basis of Morality, 5:404a–406b
      submission for academic prize, 5:396b

On the Freedom of the Will
  Kant's influence on, 5:414b
  submission for academic prize, 5:396b
Ortega y Gasset and, 9:1130b
Parerga and Paralipomena, 6:1161b
  publication of, 5:397a
Rimbaud and, 7:1797b
Strindberg and, 7:1753a
Svevo and, 8:72a, 74b–75a
The World as Will and Idea,
    11:2208b–2209a
  Proust and, 13:3025b
The World as Will and Representation (Die
    Welt als Wille und Vorstellung),
    5:399b–401b
  Hauptmann and, 8:165b–166a
  initial reception of, 5:396a
  Lukács on, 10:1274–1275a
  music in, 5:412b–413b
  On the Basis of Morality vs., 5:405b–406b
  sexual love in, 5:409a-b
  treatment of death in, 5:408b–409a
Über die vierfache Wurzel des Satzes vom
    zureichenden Grunde (On the Fourfold
    Root of the Principle of Sufficient
    Reason), 5:396a
Wagner and, 6:1161a, 7:1651b–1652a
Schopenhauer as Educator. See Nietzsche,
    Friedrich
Schoppe, Amalia, Hebbel and, 6:1192a,
    1193b–1194a
Schramme, Cécile, Artaud's engagement to,
    11:1974b
Schreber, Daniel, Freud and, 8:16a
"Schreiben eines Klostergeistlichen an seinen
    Freund in der Hauptstadt." See
    Hoffmann, E. T. A.
Schreyvogel, Joseph, Grillparzer and, 5:424b,
    425a-b, 437a
Schriften. See Benjamin, Walter; Lessing,
    Gotthold Ephraim
"Schrifttum als geistiger Raum der Nation,
    Das." See Hofmannsthal, Hugo von
Schröder, Emma, Hebbel and, 6:1095a
Schröder, Rudolf Alexander, 9:691a
  George and, 8:463a

Schubart, Christian Daniel, Schiller's "The Robbers" and, 5:31a

Schubert, Franz
"Der Lindenbaum" ("The Linden Tree"), in Mann's *Magic Mountain*, 9:723b
Jiménez and, 9:994b

Schuchardt, Hugo, Machado y Álvarez and, 9:743b

Schuldlosen, Die. See Broch, Hermann, *The Guiltless*

Schuler, Alfred, George and, 8:462b

Schumann, Robert, "Papillons," 5:77a

Schurf, Hieronymus, Luther and, 2:686a

Schuss von der Kanzel, Der. See Meyer, Conrad Ferdinand

Schuster, Jean, attack on Aragon, 11:2085a

Schwab, Gustav, Hölderlin and, 5:173b

Schwank. See Farce

Schwänk. See Short fiction, Renaissance

Schwärmer, Die. See Musil, Robert

Schwarz, Josepha (Beppi), 6:1094b

"Schwarzen Schafe, Die." *See* Böll, Heinrich

Schwestern oder Casanova in Spa, Die. See Schnitzler, Arthur

Schweyk im zweiten Weltkrieg (*Schweyk in the Second World War*). *See* Brecht, Bertolt

Schwierige, Der. See Hofmannsthal, Hugo von, *The Difficult Man*

Schwob, Marcel, and Colette, 9:620b

Sciascia, Leonardo, on Pirandello, 8:401b

Science
Augustine on, 1:40b, 42a, 42b
Broch and, 10:1388b–1389a, 1393a
Calvino and, 13:3275a, 3277a–3278b
Chekhov and, 7:1862b, 1865a, 1866a
in Chénier's aesthetics, 4:706b–707a
development of, *see also* Montesquieu, Charles-Louis de Secondat, baron de
Frisch's views of, 13:2902a
in Khlebnikov's writings, 10:1341a-b
Leconte de Lisle and, 6:1254a
Martinson and, 12:2635a
in Musil's *The Man Without Qualities*, 9:948b–949a
of nature vs. history, Burckhardt on, 6:1238b
Nietzsche and, 7:1653b–1654b, 1658a-b
Novalis and, 5:208a, 209a-b

Ortega y Gasset on, 9:1133b
philosophy of, in Croce's *Il concetto della storia nelle sue relazione col concetto dell'arte*, 8:313b–314a
Sainte-Beuve and, 6:844a-b
Schlegel and, 5:184b, 185b
unity of, in Descartes's *Discourse on the Method*, 3:3b–4a
vs. religion, in Musil's *The Man Without Qualities*, 9:935a, 935b, 953a-b
see also Technology

Science fiction
in Czech literature. *See* Čapek, Karel
influence of Zamyatin's *We* on, 10:1188b
of Khlebnikov, 10:1359b
Voltaire's *Micromégas* as, 4:375b, 389b–390a

Science of Knowledge. See Fichte, Johann Gottlieb, *Wissenschaftslehre*

Science and the Modern World. See Whitehead, Alfred North

Science and Religion as Political Problems. *See* Ortega y Gasset, José, "La ciencia y la religión como problemas políticos"

Scientific abstractionism, in Baroja, 9:594b, 603b–604a, 606b–608a

Scientific determinism, Unamuno's rejection of, 8:293b

Scientific humanism, Bergson and, 8:46b–48a

Scientific method
Bergson and, 8:47a–48a
Burckhardt and, 6:1227b
in Descartes's *Discourse on the Method*, 3:3b–4a, 5a, 7a
of Gassendi, 3:19a-b
of Montesquieu's *Observations on Natural History*, 3:348b–349a
in Taine's writing, 7:1453a-b

Scientific style, Flaubert and, 7:1380b–1383b

Scienza nuova. See Vico, Giambattista; Vico, Giovanni Battista

Scipio Africanus the Elder
Petrarch's biography of, 2:480b–482b
siege of Carthage, 2:481a-b

"Scommetta di Prometeo, La." *See* Leopardi, Giacomo, "The Wager of Prometheus"

Scotland, Fontane and, 6:1303b–1304b

Scott, Robert Falcon, Dürrenmatt and, 13:3218b–3219b
Scott, Sir Walter
  Andersen and, 6:866b, 877a
  Berlioz and, 6:777a
  Dostoevsky and, 7:1351a
  Fontane and, 6:1304a
  Garrett and, 7:1696b
  influence in Germany of, 5:431b
  Lermontov and, 6:1199a, 1203a
  on Lesage, 3:339a-b
  Lukács on, 10:1271a-b
  Manzoni's *The Betrothed* and, 5:370b, 371a
  Marmion, 6:1203a
  Mérimée and, 6:751a-b, 752a
  Pérez Galdós and, 7:1597b, 1602a-b
  Quentin Durward, Hugo's review of, 5:458b
  Redgauntlet, 6:1005a
  Talisman, 6:777a
Scourge of God, The. *See* Zamyatin, Yevgeny Ivanovich, *Bich Bozhii*
Scrap of Paper, The. *See* Sardou, Victorien, *Les pattes de mouche*
Scratch Across the Sky, A. *See* Khlebnikov, Velimir, "Tsarapina po nebu"
Screens, The. See Genet, Jean
Scriabin, Alexander
  Mandelshtam's essay on, 10:1621b, 1630a
  Pasternak and, 10:1592a-b, 1614a
Scribe, Eugène, 7:1910a–1916a, 1917a, 1918a-b
  Adrienne Lecouvreur, 7:1914b–1915a, 1925a
  Bataille des dames (*The Ladies' Battle*), 7:1926b
  Berlioz and, 6:793a-b
  Bertrand et Raton (Bertrand and Raton), 7:1914b, 1925b
  Dix ans de la vie d'une femme (Ten Years in the Life of a Woman), 7:1913a-b
  Dumas fils and, 7:1919b
  farceurs and, 7:1922a, 1922b, 1923a
  German drama and, 7:1925a
  Ibsen and, 7:1928a-b, 1930b
  influence of, 7:1924b–1925b
  La calomnie (Slander), 7:1914b
  Le mariage d'argent (Marriage for Money), 7:1910b, 1913a

Le mariage de raison (The Reasonable Marriage), 7:1913a
Le mariage d'inclination (Marriage from Inclination), 7:1913a
Le verre d'eau (*The Glass of Water*), 7:1914b
twentieth-century drama and, 7:1931b–1932a
Une nuit de la Garde Nationale (A Night with the National Guard), 7:1910b
Scriptum super Sententias. See Aquinas, Thomas, St.
Scripture of the Blind. See Ritsos, Yannis, *Ghrafi tiflou*
Scritti vari inediti. See Pascoli, Giovanni
Scrittura povera. See Verga, Giovanni
Scrutiny of a Conscience. *See* Fénelon, François de Salignac de la Mothe-, *Examen de conscience*
Scudéry, Madeleine de
  Carte de tendre, in Vigny's *Cinq-Mars*, 5:460b
  La Rochefoucauld and, 3:63a
Sculpture
  Arp and, 10:1374a–1375a
  Lessing on, 4:545b–546b
Scuola dei dittatori, La. See Silone, Ignazio
Scurani, Alessandro, on Silone's *Story of a Humble Christian*, 12:2300b
Scythians (Skify), Zamyatin's involvement with, 10:1187a
Scythians, The. See Blok, Alexander, *Skify*
"Scythians, The." *See* Blok, Alexander, "Skify"
"Scythians?" *See* Zamyatin, Yevgeny Ivanovich
Se dig inte om! See Johnson, Eyvind, *Romanen om Olof*
"Se 'l pensier che mi strugge." *See* Petrarch, *Canzoniere*
Se non cosí. See Pirandello, Luigi
Se una notte d'inverno un viaggiatore. See Calvino, Italo, *If on a winter's night a traveler*
Sea, The. See Michelet, Jules
"Sea Close By, The." *See* Camus, Albert
Sea Nostalgia. *See* Jiménez, Juan Ramón, "Nostaljia del mar"
Sea symbolism, in poetry of Machado, 9:757b–758a

Seafarer (Anglo-Saxon poem), 1:65b
Seagull, The. See Chekhov, Anton
Seamarks. See Perse, Saint-John
Seaport. *See* Mayakovsky, Vladimir, "Port"
Search, Alexander, 10:1482b, 1488a
Search for God, The. *See* Leconte de Lisle,
    Charles Marie, "La recherche de Dieu"
Search for a Method. See Sartre, Jean-Paul
"Seashell." *See* Mandelshtam, Osip,
    "Rakovina"
Seashell and the Clergyman, The. See Artaud,
    Antonin, *La coquille et le clergyman*
Seaside Resort. See Ginzburg, Natalia, *Paese*
    di mare
Season in Hell, A. See Rimbaud, Arthur
Seat of Air, The. *See* Arp, Jean, *Le siège de*
    l'air
Sebastian im Traum (Sebastian Dreaming).
    See Trakl, Georg
Sebastian of Portugal, king, 10:1477a-b,
    11:2144a
Sebastianism
    as anti-republican doctrine, 10:1477b
    origin of, 10:1477b
    Pessoa and, 10:1477b–1478a, 1494a
Sebastianismo. See Sebastianism
"Sebe lyubimomu, posvyashchaet eti stroki
    avtor." *See* Mayakovsky, Vladimir
Sebillet, Thomas, *Art poétique français*,
    2:725a
Sebond, Raymond, *Theologia naturalis*
    (*Natural Theology*), 2:769b
"Sécheresse." *See* Perse, Saint-John
Second Avant-Garde, Milosz and,
    13:2940b–2941a
Second Birth. See Pasternak, Boris
Second Book of Laughable Loves, The. See
    Kundera, Milan
Second Book, The. *See* Mandelshtam, Osip,
    Vtoraia kniga
Second Coming of Christ
    Prudentius on, 1:2b, 11a-b
    in *Psychomachia*, 1:6b
    in *Symmachus*, 1:10b
Second Decade. See Machiavelli, Niccolò,
    Decennale secondo

"Second Dedication." *See* Akhmatova, Anna,
    Poem Without a Hero
"Second Dialogue on Poetry." *See* Seferis,
    George, "Defteros dialogos i monologos
    pano stin poiesi"
Second Face, The. See Aymé, Marcel
Second livre des hymnes. See Ronsard, Pierre
    de
"Second manifest du surréalisme" ("Second
    Manifest of Surrealism, The"). *See*
    Breton, André
"Second Meeting." *See* Dinesen, Isak
Second Part of the Diana, The. See Pérez,
    Alonso, *Segunda parte de la Diana*
Second Poetic Anthology. *See* Jiménez, Juan
    Ramón, *Segunda antolojía poética*
Second Sex, The. See Beauvoir, Simone de
Second sous-sol. See Butor, Michel
Second Symphony. See Bely, Andrey,
    Symphonies
Seconde, La. See Colette
Secret Book. *See* D'Annunzio, Gabriele, *Libro*
    segreto
Secret Dictionary. *See* Cela, Camilo José,
    Diccionario segreto
Secret Doctrine, The. See Besant, Annie
Secret History of Isabella of Bavaria, Queen of
    France, The. See Sade, Donatien
    Alphonse François, marquis de
Secret of Luca, The. See Silone, Ignazio, *Il*
    segreto di Luca
Secret Remarks. *See* Peyrefitte, Roger, *Propos*
    secrets
Secret Stream, The. See Aymé, Marcel
"Secret Thoughts of Rafael, a French
    Gentleman, The." *See* Musset, Alfred de,
    "Les secrètes pensées de Rafael,
    gentilhomme français"
Secretary, The. *See* Ginzburg, Natalia, *La*
    segretaria
"Secrètes pensées de Rafael, gentilhomme
    français, Les." *See* Musset, Alfred de
"Secrets of Handwriting, The." *See* Čapek,
    Karel, "Tajemstuí písma"
Secretum. See Petrarch

Secularism
European philosophical tradition of, 9:591a-b
Keller and, 6:924a-b
Security, psychological, Gombrowicz and, 12:2564a
Sedaine, Michel, Vigny's championing of literary ownership and, 5:479a-b
Seduction, theme of
in Ionesco's *Jacques*, 13:2994a
Kierkegaard and, 6:1131a–1132a
in Kundera, 13:3398a–3399b
"See You Soon." *See* Sarraute, Nathalie, *L'Usage de la parole*
Seed Beneath the Snow, The. See Silone, Ignazio, *Il seme sotto la neve*
Seed, The. See Vesaas, Tarjei
Seekers, Bossuet on, 3:171b
Sefer Yetsirah (*The Book of Creation*), literary technique, 12:2349a
Seferis, George, **12:2255a–2271b**, 13:2955a, 2964b
Aeschylean notion of justice, 12:2257a-b
"Agianapa I," 12:2261a
"Agianapa II," 12:2261a
"Aiolia," 12:2258b
"Aphigisi" ("Narration"), 12:2260a
"Apo to imerologio tou '46" ("' From the Diary of '46"), 12:2261a
Apocalypse and, 13:2981b
"Defteros dialogos i monologos pano stin poiesi" ("Second Dialogue on Poetry"), 12:2259b
demotic language, 12:2260a
"Dialogos pano stin poiesi" ("Dialogue on Poetry"), 12:2259b
Dokimes (Essays), 12:2269b
"Enas logos gia to kalokairi" ("A Word for Summer"), 12:2265b
"Epikaleo toi ten theon" ("I Surely Call upon God"), 12:2261a
"Fog," 12:2258a
free verse, 12:2263b
"Gramma tou Mathiou Paskali" ("Letter of Mathios Paskalis"), 12:2258b
Gymnopaidia, 12:2260a
"Mycenae," 12:2259a, 2264b–2265a

"Santorini," 12:2259a, 2264b
Hajimihail and, 12:2259a
"I apophasi tis lysmonias" ("The Decision to Forget"), 12:2260a
I sterna (*The Cistern*), 12:2258b, 2259b, 2260a, 2263b, 2269a
Imerologio katastromatos (*Logbook I*)
"I teleftaia mera" ("The Last Day"), 12:2266a
"O vasilias tis asinis" ("The King of Asir e"), 12:2260b, 2266a–2267b
Imerologio katastromatos B (*Logbook II*), 12:2260a-b, 2267b
"Enas gerontas stin akropotamia" ("An Old Man on the River Bank"), 12:2267b
"Teleftaios stathmos" ("The Last Stop"), 12:2267b
Imerologio katastromatos C (*Logbook III*), 12:2261a-b, 2268b
"Eleni" ("Helen"), 12:2261a, 2268b–2269a
Imerologio katastromatos (*Logbook I*), 12:2260a, 2265b–2267b
Kazantzakis and, 9:1068b–1069a
Kichle (*Thrush*), 12:2257b, 2260b, 2262b, 2267b–2268a, 2269a
Kypron, ou m'ethespisen (*To Cyprus, Where Apollo Foretold Me*), 12:2261b, 2268b
"Leophoros Syngrou, 1930" ("Syngrou Avenue, 1930"), 12:2258b
"Leptomereies stin Kypro" ("Details on Cyprus"), 12:2261a
"Letter on the *Thrush*," 12:2257b
on Makriyannis, 12:2257a-b
Mythistorema, 12:2258b–2259a, 2260a, 2263b–2264a, 13:2956b
"O dhikos mas hellos" ("Our Sun"), 12:2259b–2260a
"Pano se mia himoniatiki ahtina" ("On a Ray of Winter Sun"), 12:2269a
"Pantoum," 12:2258b
Poiemata (Poems I), 12:2260a
"Proi" ("Morning"), 12:2260a
"Salamina tis Kypros" ("Salamis in Cyprus"), 12:2261a
Strophe (*Turning Point*), 12:2258b, 2260a, 2261b, 2815a-b, 13:2956b

"Erotikos logos" (Song of Love), 12:2258b, 2263a, 2263a-b
style, 12:2263b–2264a
T. S. Eliot, 12:2259a
Tetradio gymnasmaton (*Book of Exercises*), 12:2265b
The Persians, 12:2257a-b
"To fillo tis lefkas" ("The Leaf of the Poplar"), 12:2259b
"To telos enos dialogou" (End of a Dialogue), 12:2259b
"Treis moules" ("Three Mules"), 12:2261a
Tria krypha poiemata (*Three Secret Poems*), 12:2262a, 2269a
Segelfoss by (*Scgelfoss Town*). See Hamsun, Knut
Seger i mörker. See Lagerkvist, Pär
"Segno nello spazio, Un." See Calvino, Italo, *Cosmicomics*
"Segodnia nochiiu . . ." See Mandelshtam, Osip
Segretaria, La. See Ginzburg, Natalia
Segreto di Luca, Il. See Silone, Ignazio
Segunda antologjía poética. See Jiménez, Juan Ramón
Segunda casaca, La. See Pérez Galdós, Benito
Segunda parte de la Diana. See Pérez, Alonso
Sei personaggi in cerca d'autore. See Pirandello, Luigi, *Six Characters in Search of an Author*
Seidler, Irma, Lukács and, 10:1254b–1255a, 1257a-b, 1262b
Seifullina, Lydia, conspiracy charges, 11:1912a
Seige of Corinth. See Byron, George Gordon, Lord
"Seigneur berbère." See Saint-Exupéry, Antoine de
Sein und Zeit. See Heidegger, Martin
Seismograph image, of Frisch, 13:2922b, 2924a
Seize et une variations. See Butor, Michel
Seizure of Power, The. See Milosz, Czeslaw
Selberlebensbeschreibung. See Richter, Jean Paul
Selbstbiographie. See Grillparzer, Franz
Selden, Camille

Les derniers jours de H. Heine, 5:509b
Taine and, 7:1463a
Selected Pages. See Machado, Antonio, *Páginas escogidas*
Selection of the Devil's Papers. See Richter, Jean Paul, *Auswahl aus des Teufels Papieren*
Selections. See Elytis, Odysseus, *Ekloyi*
Self
in Apollinaire's poetry, 9:883a, 889a, 891b
in Canetti's autobiography, 12:2631b–2632a
cult of, in Nietzsche, 9:592b
in Descartes's *Meditations on First Philosophy*, 3:11a–12b, 18b
in Ionesco's plays, 13:3007a, 3018b
Marinetti and, 9:817a, 818b, 819a, 820b
in Musil's *The Man Without Qualities*, 9:954a
in Pascoli's poetry, 7:1831a, 1832a-b
Proust on, 8:560a
in Richter's works, 5:84b
Hesperus, 5:64b–65a
Siebenkäs, 5:68b, 69a
in romantic autobiography, 1:25a-b
Sartre and, 12:2591a–2597a, 2610a-b
Valéry on, 8:571b–572a, 5171a
The Young Fate, 8:576b–577a
see also Psyche
"Self and the Other, The." See Ortega y Gasset, José, "Ensimismamiento y alteración"
Self-consciousness in art, Unamuno and, 8:303b–304a
Self-contradiction, in Calvino, 13:3265b
Self-criticism
in "Estuans instrinsicus ira vehementi," 1:358a
in Grass, 13:3383a-b
of Horace, 1:356a
in medieval satire, 1:356a–359a
in Villon's *Testament*, 1:359a
Self-deception
in Canetti's *Die Blendung*, 12:2619a, 2622a-b
in Kafka, 9:1161a, 1165a
in Svevo's novels, 8:72b, 76b–77a, 79a-b
see also Dreams
Self-denial, in Andersen, 6:883b

Self-destruction
  in Camus, 13:3063a, 3073b
  in Canetti's *Die Blendung*, 12:2622b–2624b
Self-determination, Kierkegaard and, 6:1139b
Self-interest. *See* Self-love
Self-knowledge
  in Augustine's works
    Confessions, 1:25b–26a, 32a
    On the Trinity, 1:41a-b
  in Cela, 13:3116b–3117a
  La Rochefoucauld and, 3:53b, 64a, 67a
  in Maupassant's works, 7:1777a, 1779a,
    1779b–1780a, 1781a
  in Montaigne's *Essays*, 2:780b–781a,
    783b–784a
  Sartre and, 12:2598b–2599a
  in Walther, 1:300b–301a, 304a
Self-love
  in Augustine's *On the Trinity*, 1:40b
  in Camoëns' *The Lusiads*, 2:764a-b
  in La Rochefoucauld's *Maximes*, 3:65b–66a,
    66b–67a
Self-Portrait. *See* Böcklin, Arnold
Self-positioning, in Stendhal, 5:356a
Self-realization, in Andersen, 6:883b
Self-referentiality
  allegory and, 1:324a
  in Calvino, 13:3283a
Self-reliance
  Hesse on, 9:841a
    in *Siddhartha*, 9:845a
  in Montaigne's *Essays*, 2:782a
"Self-Reliance." *See* Hesse, Hermann,
    "Eigensinn"
"Self-Statement." *See* Khlebnikov, Velimir
Selfishness, in La Bruyère's *Caractères*,
    3:249b–250a
Selina. *See* Richter, Jean Paul
Sell-out, The. *See* Dürrenmatt, Friedrich
"Selpwahsen kind, dû bist zu krump." *See*
    Walther von der Vogelweide
Selva, A. *See* Ferreira de Castro, José Maria,
    Jungle
Selva oscura, La. *See* Baroja, Pío
Selve d'amore. *See* Medici, Lorenzo de'
Semaine sainte, La. *See* Aragon, Louis
Seme sotto la neve, Il. *See* Silone, Ignazio

Semenov, Vasili, 8:441b
Semi-heteronym, of Pessoa, 10:1492b–1493b
Semiology
  Barthes and, 13:3087a–3103b
  in Sarraute's works, 12:2338a
Sémiramis. *See* Voltaire
"Semiramis-Lieder" of George. *See* Coblenz,
    Ida
Sempere, Francisco, Blasco Ibáñez' *The Cabin*
    and, 8:370a
Sempione strizza l'occhio al Fréjus, Il. *See*
    Vittorini, Elio
Señora Carrar's Rifles. *See* Brecht, Bertolt
Senancour, Étienne, *Obermann*, 6:1015a
Sendemann Huskuld. *See* Vesaas, Tarjei
Seneca, Lucius Annaeus
  Diderot and, 4:504a-b
  in Kosztolányi's *Bloody Poet*, 10:1236a-b
  Medea, Corneille and, 3:26b
  Montaigne and, 2:775a, 775b, 783a
Seniles. *See* Petrarch, *Epistolae seniles*
Senilità. *See* Svevo, Italo, *As a Man Grows
    Older*
Senos. *See* Gómez de la Serna, Ramón
Sens à la vie. *See* Saint-Exupéry, Antoine de
Sensation, Mach on, 9:939b
"Sensation." *See* Rimbaud, Arthur
Sensationalism, Stendhal and, 5:351a
Sensatsiia (A Sensation). *See* Zamyatin,
    Yevgeny Ivanovich
Sense of Life, A. *See* Saint-Exupéry, Antoine
    de, *Un sens à la vie*
"Sense of possibility" (Musil), 9:936a,
    936b–937a, 943b–947a, 950b–952b,
    956a-b
Senses, derangement of, in Rimbaud's works,
    7:1794b–1795a, 1806a–1807b,
    1811a–1813a
Sensibilità italiana nata in Egitto, Una. *See*
    Marinetti, Filippo Tommaso
Sensual perception. *See* Perception, sensual
Sensualidad pervertida, La. *See* Baroja, Pío
Sensuality
  Circe as emblem of, 2:751b–752a
  in Flaubert's work, 7:1374a–1375b, 1377a,
    1380a
  and Heine, 5:499a

Italian, Wagner and, 6:1150b
   in Rimbaud's works, 7:1791a–1792a, 1802a
Sent på jorden. See Ekelöf, Gunnar
"Sentence, The." *See* Akhmatova, Anna,
      Requiem
Sentences of Laon, 1:406b
Sentences (maxims). *See* Maxims
Sententiae in IV libris distinctae. See Peter
      Lombard
Sentiero dei nidi di ragno, Il. See Calvino,
      Italo, *The Path to the Nest of Spiders*
Sentiment of Time. *See* Ungaretti, Giuseppe,
      Sentimento del tempo
"Sentimental Conversation." *See* Verlaine,
      Paul, "Colloque sentimental"
Sentimental Education. See Flaubert, Gustave
Sentimental France. *See* Giraudoux, Jean, *La
      France sentimentale*
Sentimental Journey. See Sterne, Laurence
Sentimentality
   Gogol and, 6:975a, 991b
   in Maupassant's works, 7:1780b
   in Ungaretti's poetry, 10:1462a-b
   Vesaas and, 11:2041b
Sentimento del tempo. See Ungaretti,
      Giuseppe
"Senza memoria di morte." *See* Quasimodo,
      Salvatore
Separation. *See* Tsvetaeva, Marina, *Razluka*
Sepmaine où création du monde, La. See Du
      Bartas
Sept cordes de la lyre, Les. See Sand, George,
      The Seven Strings of the Lyre
"Sept epées, Les." *See* Apollinaire, Guillaume,
      "La chanson du mal-aimé"
Sept péchés capitaux, Les (motion picture),
      13:3005b
Sept petit sketches. See Ionesco, Eugène
Sept princesses, Les. See Maeterlinck, Maurice
September Ecstasy. *See* Kosztolányi, Dezső,
      "Szeptemberi áhítat"
September Equinox, The. *See* Montherlant,
      Henry de, *L'Equinoxe de septembre*
Septemberlyran (The September Lyre). *See*
      Södergran, Edith
Septiria kai dhafniforia. See Ritsos, Yannis
Sepulchral genre. *See* Graveyard meditations

Ser Giovanni Fiorentino, *Il pecorone*, 2:936a-b
"Sera del dì di festa, La." *See* Leopardi,
      Giacomo, "The Evening of the Feast
      Day"
"Sera d'ottobre." *See* Pascoli, Giovanni,
      Myricae
"Sera fiesolana, La." *See* D'Annunzio, Gabriele
Serafimovich, Aleksandr, Gorky and, 8:419b
Seraglio, in Montesquieu's *Persian Letters*,
      3:358a–363b
Serao, Matilde, 8:183a
Serapion Brotherhood
   Shklovski and, 11:2251a
   Zamyatin's involvement with,
      10:1192b–1193a
Serapions-Brüder, Die. See Hoffmann, E. T. A.,
      The Serapion Brethren
Sercambi, Giovanni, of Lucca, novellas of,
      2:935a–936a
Serdarda, Pasternak's participation in,
      10:1592b
"Serdityi vzor bestsvetnykh glaz." *See* Blok,
      Alexander
Serebrianyi golub'. See Bely, Andrey
Seret professionnel, Le. See Cocteau, Jean
Sergeev family, 8:441a
"Sergeyu Eseninu." *See* Mayakovsky, Vladimir
Sérgio, António, *Eternidade* and, 11:2152a
Serial novel
   Dumas's use of form, 6:724b–725a
   Zola's use of form, 7:1520a
   see also Feuilleton
Serial technique, in Ariosto, 2:626a-b
Sérizay, Jacques de, 3:68a
Sermini, Gentile
   Boccacio's influence on, 2:936b–937a
   novellas of, 2:936b–937a
"Sermon Concerning God's Law." *See* Bossuet,
      Jacques Bénigne, "Le sermon sur la loi
      de Dieu"
"Sermon Concerning the Good Will and
      Severity of the Lord." *See* Bossuet,
      Jacques Bénigne
"Sermon Concerning Preparation for Death."
      See Bossuet, Jacques Bénigne, "Le
      sermon pour la préparation à la mort"

"Sermon on Death." *See* Bossuet, Jacques
Bénigne, "Sermon sur la mort

Sermon on Indulgence and Grace. See Luther,
Martin

Sermon on the Mass, A. See Luther, Martin

*Sermon on the Occasion of the Coronation of
the Elector of Cologne. See* Fénelon,
François de Salignac de la Mothe-,
*Discours pour le sacre de l'électeur de
Cologne*

"Sermon pour la préparation à la mort, Le."
See Bossuet, Jacques Bénigne

"Sermon sur la loi de Dieu, Le." *See* Bossuet,
Jacques Bénigne

"Sermon sur la mort." *See* Bossuet, Jacques
Bénigne

Sermones. See Horace (Quintus Horatius
Flaccus), *Satires*

Sermons
discussed in La Bruyère's *Caractères*,
3:254a-b
in France, 3:159b
Kierkegaard and, 6:1123b
see also Bossuet, Jacques Bénigne;
Religious oratory

Serna, Ramón Gomez de la. *See* La Serna,
Ramón Gomez de

Serooskerken, Isabelle Agnes Elizabeth van
Tuyll van. *See* Charrière, Isabelle Agnès
Élizabeth de

Serpent
edenic, in Valéry's "Sketch of a Serpent,"
8:582a–583a
self-devouring
Proust's *Remembrance of Things Past*
and, 8:551a
Valéry and, 8:583a, 587b

Serra, Renato, on Pascoli, 7:1826a

Serres chaudes. See Maeterlinck, Maurice

Servant of Two Masters, The. See Goldoni,
Carlo

Servants
Goldoni's treatment of, 4:436a
in Gombrowicz's works, 12:2568b
in Proust's *Remembrance of Things Past*,
8:551b–552b

Service Booklet. *See* Frisch, Max,
Dienstbüchlein

Service de travail obligatoire (Service of
Required Work, or STO), Robbe-Grillet
and, 13:3239a-b

Service inutile. See Montherlant, Henry de

Service, theme of, in Hesse's works, 9:851a,
853b

Servitore de due patrone, Il. See Goldoni,
Carlo, *The Servant of Two Masters*

Servitude et grandeur des français. See
Aragon, Louis

Servitude et grandeur militaires. See Vigny,
Alfred Victor de, *The Military Condition*

Sessa, Duke of, Lope de Vega and, 2:847a,
860a

Sestina, structure, 2:501a

Sestra moia-zihzn'. See Pasternak, Boris, *My
Sister, Life*

"Sestry-molnii." *See* Khlebnikov, Velimir

"Sete anos de pastor Jacob servia." *See*
Camoëns, Luïs Vaz de, *Rimas (Lyrics)*

Sette giornate del mondo creato, Le. See
Tasso, Torquato

Setterwall, Monica, "The Unwritten Story,"
Johnson and, 12:2367a

Setting, in Pavese's works, 12:2767a

"Setting of the Moon, The." *See* Leopardi,
Giacomo

Settlers, The. See Moberg, Vilhelm

Settling Accounts. *See* Krleža, Miroslav, *Moj
obračun s njima*

Seuil, La. See Colette, *Le blé en herbe*

Sevastopol Sketches. See Tolstoy, Leo

Seven Books of the Diana, The. *See*
Montemayor, Jorge de, *Los siete libros
de la Diana*

Seven Days of the Created World. See Tasso,
Torquato, *Le sette giornate del mondo
creato*

Seven Days' Darkness. See Gunnarsson,
Gunnar, *Salige er de Enfoldige*

Seven Deadly Sins, The. See Brecht, Bertolt,
Die sieben Todsünden Kleinbürger

Seven Deadly Sins, The (motion picture). *See
Sept péchés capitaux, Les*

Seven Gothic Tales. See Dinesen, Isak

Seven Legends. See Keller, Gottfried
Seven (numeral), Elytis and, 13:2960b, 2975b
Seven Princesses, The. See Maeterlinck,
   Maurice, *Les sept princesses*
Seven Short Sketches. *See* Ionesco, Eugène,
   Sept petit sketches
Seven Strings of the Lyre, The. See Sand,
   George
"Seven Swords, The." *See* Apollinaire,
   Guillaume, "La chanson du mal-aimé"
   ("The Song of the Unloved Lover"), "Les
   sept epées"
"Seven years a shepherd Jacob served." *See*
   Camoëns, Luís Vaz de, *Rimas (Lyrics)*,
   "Sete anos de pastor Jacob servia"
Seven Years War, Voltaire and, 4:377b
"Seven-Year-Old Poets." *See* Rimbaud, Arthur,
   "Les poètes de sept ans"
Seventh Ring, The. *See* George, Stefan, *Der
   siebente Ring*
Sever. See Zamyatin, Yevgeny Ivanovich, *The
   North*
Severina. See Silone, Ignazio
Severnaia simfoniia. See Bely, Andrey,
   Symphonies
Severnye vestnik (The Northern Messenger),
   7:1860b
Sévigné, marquise de
   on Boileau's *Art poétique*, 3:181b
   La Rochefoucauld and, 3:62b, 68b
Sexes, relations between
   amorous stroll (*passeggiata*), in
      D'Annunzio's poetry, 8:178a-b, 190a
   in Blasco Ibáñez' *The Mayflower*, 8:367b
   in Colette's *The Vagabond*, 9:625b–626a
   in D'Annunzio's works, 8:183b–184b,
      199a–200a
   in George's *Hängende Gärten*, 8:459a-b
   in Ghelderode's plays, 11:2125b–2126b
   in Hebbel's works, 6:114b–1115a, 1106a-b,
      1110a-b
      Herod and Mariamne, 6:1106a-b
      Lay of the Nibelungs, 6:1114b–1115a
   in Musset's *Whims of Mariamne*, 6:1007a-b
   in Simenon's works, 12:2493a–2494a
   Wedekind on, 249a–250a, 8:241a-b
Sextus Empiricus, 3:9a, 18b

Sexual passion
   in Augustine
      Confessions, 1:29a-b
      On the Trinity, 1:39b
   Barthes on, 13:3099a–3101b
   Calderón and, 2:874b–875a
   in Calvino, 13:3275a-b
   in Kundera, 13:3392a
   in Laforgue, 7:1892b–1893a, 1901a-b, 1905a
   in Marcabru, 1:169b
   in *Romance of the Rose*, 1:316b–317b,
      326b–332a
   social evil equated with sexual misconduct,
      7:1610a-b
   in Strindberg, 7:1744a
   in Walther, 1:294a–295b
   in Witkiewicz *622 Downfalls of Bungo*,
      10:1210a-b
   see also Desire; Love
Sexuality
   in Beauvoir, 12:2714b, 2715a, 2715b,
      2723a-b, 2725b
   bourgeoisie and, 7, 1891a-b
   in Broch, 10:1391b, 1405a
   in Cela, 13:3120a-b
   in Chrétien, 1:147a
   Diderot on, 4:491b, 496b–497a
   in Dumas fils' plays, 7:1920a
   in Elytis' "Peri Politas," 13:2974a
   in Ferreira de Castro
      Eternidade, 11:2160a
      Jungle, 11:2159a-b
   in Flaubert, 7:1374a–1375b, 1379b, 1389a
   Foucault and, 13:3359a–3361b
   Freud's concept of, 8:3a-b, 4a, 6a-b, 16a–18b
   Genet and, 13:2877a
   in Ghelderode's *Don Juan*, 11:2125b–2126b
   in Gombrowicz, 12:2568a-b, 2583a–2584b
   in Goncharov, 6:1085a
   in Heinrich Mann, 8:537b–538a
   in Hugo, 6:701a–702a, 714a-b, 715a-b
   Jarry and, 9:671a-b
   in Laforgue's "Legend," 7:1903a-b
   in Maupassant, 7:1775a-b
   Moberg on, 11:2214a–2214b
   Montesquieu on, 3:351b
   in Moravia, 12:2691a-b, 2693a

Sexuality (*cont.*)
  of Novalis, 5:206b
  in Olesha, *Envy*, 11:2237a, 2239a-b
  repressed, Andersen and, 6:868a–869b
  in Rimbaud, 7:1789a, 1794b–1795a,
    1802b–1803a
  Sade's contribution to knowledge of,
    4:621a–622b
  in Schnitzler, 8:89b, 96a, 100a, 108a,
    108b–109b, 113a
  Schopenhauer's metaphysics and, 5:409a-b
  sexual innuendo, in Chrétien's *Lancelot*,
    1:198a-b, 199a
  in Simon, 13:3026b, 3036b
  in Wedekind, 8:241a-b, 243b–245a, 245a,
    249b, 251b–252a
  Weil and, 12:2789a-b, 2806a
  see also Carnality; Eroticism; Libertinism;
    Reproduction, sexual; Sensuality
Sezima, Karel, on Hašek's *Good Soldier Švejk*,
  9:116b
Sfortunato. See Argenti
Shablia Kotovs'koho. See Tychyna, Pavlo
Shackle, The. See Colette, *L'Entrave*
"Shade of the Magnolia, The." *See* Montale,
  Eugenio, *The Storm and Other Things*
  (*La bufera e altro*), "L'Ombra della
  magnolia"
Shadow of the Cathedral, The. See Blasco
  Ibáñez, Vicente, *La catedral*
Shadow Falls, The. See Simenon, Georges, *Le
  testament Donadieu*
Shadow of the Future, The. *See* Södergran,
  Edith, *Framtidens skugga*
Shadow of My Love. See Apollinaire,
  Guillaume, *Ombre de mon amour*
"Shadow, The." *See* Andersen, Hans Christian
"Shadowgraphs." *See* Kierkegaard, Søren
Shadows on the Grass. See Dinesen, Isak
Shadwell, Thomas, *Squire of Alsatia*, Lessing
  and, 4:549b
Shaftesbury, Earl of, Diderot and, 4:481b
Shakespeare Our Contemporary. See Kott, Jan
Shakespeare, William
  A Midsummer Night's Dream, Wieland and,
    4:605b
  Andersen and, 6:866b

Anouilh and, 13:2862b
Antony and Cleopatra, 6:808b
  Grillparzer's *The Golden Fleece* compared
    to, 5:430a
Ariosto and, 2:629a
As You Like It
  in Gautier's *Mademoiselle de Maupin*,
    6:1039b–1040a, 1054a–1055a
  pastoral romances and, 2:920a
  Proust and, 8:559a
Bandello as source for, 2:943a-b
Berlioz and, 6:777b–778b, 782a, 790b, 791a,
  791b, 792b, 802a-b, 807b–808b
Camus and, 13:3055b
Castiglione and, 2:664b
Chateaubriand on, 5:137a-b
Croce on, 8:319a
Delacroix and, 5:518b, 519a, 519b
Dinesen and, 10:1281a-b, 1294b
Dostoevsky and, 7:1350b
Eça and, 7:1691a
French Romantic movement and,
  5:461b–462a
Freud and, 8:15b
in George's *Der Teppich*, 8:462a
German translations of, 4:609b–610a
Goethe and
  Egmont, 5:9a-b
  Götz von Berlichingen, 5:4a
Hamlet, 7:1733b, 1749a
  Cocteau and, 10:1554b–1555a
  "decadence" of, 7:1896a
  Electra myth and, 12:2549a
  Laforgue and, 7:1904b
  in Olesha's "A List of Assets," 11:2246a,
    2246b
  Pasternak's *Doctor Zhivago* and,
    10:1610a-b
  Pasternak's translation of, 10:1607a-b
  Svarfdœla saga and, 1:398b
  Turgenev on, 6:1283a
Henry IV, Grillparzer on historical accuracy
  of, 5:432b
Henry VI, Schiller's *The Maid of Orleans*
  and, 5:46b
Hofmannsthal and, 9:689b
Ibsen and, 7:1436a-b, 1439a

Julius Caesar, German translation of, 4:543a

King John, Grillparzer on historical accuracy of, 5:432b

King Lear

Alfieri's *Saul* compared to, 4:685a

Freud and, 8:15b

Schopenhauer's pessimism and, 5:402a

Kosztolányi's translation of, 10:1234a

Lermontov and, 6:1201b

Lessing on, 4:544b, 548a

Love's Labor's Lost, Mantovano's (Mantuan's) poetry in, 2:907a-b

Macbeth

Grillparzer's *The Ancestress* compared to, 5:426a

Macbett and, 13:3012a, 3013a

translations of, 8:139b–140a

Machado and, 9:760a

Machiavelli and, 2:615b

Maeterlinck and, 8:124b, 125b, 137b, 139b–140a

Marinetti and, 9:801b, 822a

Measure for Measure

Giraldi as source for, 2:944b

Giraudoux and, 9:1058b

Wagner and, 6:1155a

Mérimée and, 6:751a

Milosz's translations of, 13:2931a

Much Ado About Nothing, 6:807b–808b

"My mistress' eyes are nothing like the sun," 2:751b

Othello, 6:808b

Giraldi's *Gli ecatommiti* as source for, 2:943b

Lessing on, 4:547a

Vigny's translation of, 5:462a–463a

Petrarchan influence, 2:504b

Pushkin and, 5:678b, 680a

Racine compared with, 3:227a

reconciliation plays, 7:1436a-b, 1440b

Richard II, Schiller's *Wallenstein* and, 5:43a

Richard III, Schiller's *The Robbers* and, 5:31b

Richter and, 5:66b

Romeo and Juliet

Grillparzer's *Hero and Leander* compared to, 5:436a

Lessing on, 4:547a

Soulié's adaptation of, 5:462a

Vigny's and Deschamps' translation of, 5:462a

see also Cocteau, Jean

Schiller and, 5:44b, 51a

Sonnets

Proust's *Remembrance of Things Past* and, 8:562b

Rilke's *Sonnets to Orpheus* and, 9:773a

translated by George, 8:447a

Strindberg and, 7:1742b, 1745b, 1749a

Taine on, 7:1458b–1459a, 1460a

Taming of the Shrew, *Svarfdœla saga* and, 1:398b

The Merchant of Venice

Masuccio's *Novellino* as source for, 2:940a

Ser Giovanni's *Il pecorone* as source for, 2:936b

Vigny's translation of, 5:463a

The Tempest, 6:782a

Ekelöf and, 12:2651a

Platner and, 5:56b

The Winter's Tale, pastoral romances and, 2:920a

Tieck and, 5:243a-b

tragedies of, 3:219a, 219b

translated by Gundolf, 8:464b

Two Gentlemen of Verona, Montemayor's *Diana* as source of, 2:923a

Undset and, 9:1021b

Valle-Inclán and, 8:339a, 350a

Vigny's promotion of, 5:462a

Voltaire on, 4:372a, 385b

Wagner and, 6:1155a

Shakespeare's Mädchen und Frauen (*Shakespeare's Maidens and Ladies*). See Heine, Heinrich

Shakespeare's Preparatory School. See Tieck, Ludwig, *Shakespeares Vorschule*

Shakespeares Vorschule. See Tieck, Ludwig

Shakuntala, in Apollinaire's "The Song of the Unloved Lover," 9:889b

"Shaman i Venera" (The Shaman and Venus). See Khlebnikov, Velimir

Shame, in Kafka's works, 9:1169b–1170a

Shameless Ones, The. *See* Augier, Émile, *Les effrontés*

"Shamelessly, endlessly sinning." *See* Blok, Alexander, "Greshit' besstydno, neprobudno"

Sharers, The. *See* Fontane, Theodor, *Die Likedeeler*

Sharper, The. See Quevedo, Francisco de, *El buscón*

Shattuck, Roger, 8:546b, 9:900a

Shaw, George Bernard
  Alfieri's *The Divorce* compared to plays of, 4:677a
  Anouilh and, 13:2860a
  Back to Methuselah, Čapek and, 10:1576b
  Böll's translations, 13:3167b
  on Brieux, 7:1921a
  Candida, 7:1747a
  on Ibsen, 13:3215b
  Ibsen and, 7:1754a
  Man and Superman, Frisch and, 13:2906a
  Mrs. Warren's Profession, 7:1743b
    morality and economics in, 13:3232a
  Queneau and, 12:2523b
  Saint Joan, 5:47a, 8:488a
  Strindberg and, 7:1731b, 1742a, 1743b, 1747a, 1749a, 1754a
  The Quintessence of Ibsenism, 7:1436b
  The Simpleton of the Unexpected Isles, Dürrenmatt and, 13:3221b
  well-made play and, 7:1931a

Shchedrin, N., *Istoriia odnogo goroda* (*The History of a Town*), Zamyatin's stage adaptation of, 10:1194a

She Came to Stay. See Beauvoir, Simone de

She and He. See Sand, George, *Elle et lui*

"She-Wolf, The." *See* Verga, Giovanni, "La Lupa"

Sheaf of Fables Without Love. *See* Cela, Camilo José, *Gavilla de fábulas sin amor*

Sheldon, Edward, Ibsen's influence on, 7:1443b

Shelley, Mary, *Frankenstein*, Čapek and, 10:1572a

Shelley, Percy Bysshe
  "Hymn to Intellectual Beauty," 9:1004a
  Jiménez and, 9:998b, 1004a
  Mérimée and, 6:752a
  "Mutability," 9:998b
  supernatural in works of, 5:551a-b
  The Cenci, production of in Czechoslovakia, 10:1566b
  Undset and, 9:1021b

Shephearde's Calendar. See Spenser, Edmund

Shepherds of Bethlehem, The. See Lope de Vega, *Los pastores de Belén*

Shepherd's Chameleon, The. See Ionesco, Eugène, *L'Impromptu de l'Alma*

"Shepherd's Filial Piety, The." *See* Petrarch, "Pietas pastoralis"

"Shepherds and Flocks." *See* Hugo, Victor, "Pasteurs et troupeaux"

Shepherd's Hut, The. *See* Vigny, Alfred Victor de, *Les destinées*

Shepherd's Pipe, The. *See* Schnitzler, Arthur, "Die Hirtenflöte"

Sheridan, Richard, *The Rivals*, Vigny's wife compared to Mrs. Malaprop, 5:454b

Shevchenko, Taras, 10:1665a
  Tychyna and, 10:1651b, 1652b, 1667a

Shikibu, Murasaki, *Genghi-Monogotari*, Yourcenar's adaptation, 12:2545a-b

"Shinel'." *See* Gogol, Nikolay Vasilyevich, "The Overcoat"

"Ship of Death, The." *See* Lawrence, D. H.

Ship of Fools, The. *See* Baroja, Pío, *La nave de los locos*

Ship of Fools. See Brant, Sebastian, *Das Narrenschiff*

Ship imagery
  in Ady's verse, 9:875a-b
  in Klopstock, 4:532a-b

Ship, The. *See* D'Annunzio, Gabriele, *La nave*

Ships in the Sky. See Gunnarsson, Gunnar, *Kirken paa Bjerget*

"Shipwreck, The." *See* Erasmus

Shiragi, Jun, 12:2543a

Shklovski, Viktor
  on Babel, 11:1905a, 1910a
  Babel's influence on, 11:1912a
  on Chekhov, 7:1858b
  formalist criticism, 11:2250b–2251b
  Olesha and, 11:2235b, 2249a, 2249b

on Zamyatin's "actional images," 10:1191b

Shock therapy. *See* Electroshock therapy

Shock Workers. *See* Mayakovsky, Vladimir,
"Zastrel'shchiki"

Shoemakers, The. See Witkiewicz, Stanisław
Ignacy, *Szewcy*

Shoot! See Pirandello, Luigi, *Si gira*

"Shooting Party, The." *See* Chekhov, Anton,
"Drama na okhote"

Shore of Life, The. *See* Gunnarsson, Gunnar,
Livets Strand

Short Catechism, The. See Luther, Martin

Short fiction
Renaissance, **2:927a–956b**
classical and medieval antecedents of,
2:929b–933b
in France, 2:945b–949b
in Italy, 2:933b–945b
in northern Europe, 2:952a–953a
novella defined, 2:927a–929b
in Spain, 2:949b–952a
Schnitzler's use of, 8:93a-b, 99b, 103b–104a

Short Method. See Guyon, Madame Jeanne
Marie Bouvière de la Mothe-, *Moyen
court*

Short Narrative Poems. *See* Pascoli, Giovanni,
Poemetti

Short Plays. *See* Gunnarsson, Gunnar, *Smaa
Skuespil*

Short stories
Brecht and, 11:2102a
Diderot and, 4:501a–502a
Maupassant's use of form, 7:1762b–1763a,
1764a, 1766a, 1769b
of Pavese, 12:2766a-b, 2776b–2777a
Strindberg's use of form, 7:1732a,
1739b–1741a
Vesaas and, 11:2051a–2053a
Vittorini and, 12:2766b

"Short Story and the Novel, The." *See* Moravia,
Alberto, "Racconto e romanzo"

Shot from the Pulpit, The. See Meyer, Conrad
Ferdinand, *Der Schuss von der Kanzel*

"Shot, The." *See* Pushkin, Alexander

Shrieks of May. See Hašek, Jaroslav, *Májové
výkřiky*

Shrove Tuesday. See Valle-Inclán, Ramón del,
Martes de Carnaval

"Shtatskaya shrapnel." *See* Mayakovsky,
Vladimir

"Shtoss." *See* Lermontov, Mikhail Yurievich

Shuffled Cards. *See* Ekelöf, Gunnar, *Blandade
kort*

Shum vremeni. See Mandelshtam, Osip, *The
Noise of Time*

Shylock; or, The Merchant of Venice. See
Vigny, Alfred Victor de

Si gira. See Pirandello, Luigi

Si, soy Guiomar. See Valderrama, Pilar de

"Si tu t'imagines." *See* Queneau, Raymond,
L'Instant fatal

Siblings, The. See Elytis, Odysseus, *Ta
eterothale*

Sibyllan (*The Sibyl*). *See* Lagerkvist, Pär

Sic et non. See Abélard, Peter

Sicilian dialect theater. *See* Drama, Sicilian

"Sicilian Honor." *See* Pirandello, Luigi, "La
verità"

Sicilian Limes. See Pirandello, Luigi, *Lumíe di
Sicilia*

Sicilian Tragedy. *See* Hebbel, Friedrich, *Ein
Trauerspiel in Sizilien*

Sicily
history, *see also* Risorgimento
in Lampedusa's *The Leopard*, 11:2016a,
2019a-b
Pirandello and, 8:390b–391a, 401b–402a
Verga and, 7:1544a–1545a

"Sick Autumn." *See* Apollinaire, Guillaume,
Alcools, "Automne malade"

"Sick Child, The." *See* Munch, Edvard

Sick Man, The. *See* Azorín, *El enfermo*

Sickness
in Azorín's *El enfermo*, 9:655a-b
Hesse's *At the Spa* and, 9:846a-b
of Leopardi, 5:544a-b
Mann's *Magic Mountain* and, 9:720a, 722b,
846a-b
"spleen" as romantic malady, 6:780b
Trakl and, 10:1411a-b
see also Syphilis; Tuberculosis

Sickness unto Death, The. See Kierkegaard,
Søren

Sidaner, Henri Le, Jiménez and, 9:994a

Siddhartha. See Hesse, Hermann

Side Effects. See Aymé, Marcel

Sidney, Sir Philip, Petrarchan influence, 2:504b

Sido. See Colette

Sidónio Pais, Major, Pessoa and, 10:1479b

Sidonius, on Burgundians, 1:350a-b

Sidste Fortaellinger. See Dinesen, Isak, *Last Tales*

Sieben Legenden. See Keller, Gottfried, *Seven Legends*

Sieben Todsünden Kleinbürger, Die. See Brecht, Bertolt

Siebenkäs. See Richter, Jean Paul, *Blumen-, Frucht- und Dornenstücke*

Siebente Ring, Der. See George, Stefan

Siècle de Louis XIV, Le. See Perrault, Charles; Voltaire

"Sieg des Sommers." *See* George, Stefan, *Das Jahr der Seele* (*The Year of the Soul*)

Siège de l'air, Le. See Arp, Jean

Siège d'Ostende, Le. See Ghelderode, Michel de

Siege of Numantia, The. See Cervantes, Miguel de, *El cerco de Numancia*

Siegfried
Kriemhild and, in the *Nibelungenlied*, 1:213a, 213b
the *Nibelungenlied* and, 1:211a–213a, 220b–225a

Siegfried. See Giraudoux, Jean

Siegfried et le Limousin. See Giraudoux, Jean

Siegfried's Death (*Siegfried's Tod*). *See* Hebbel, Friedrich, *Die Nibelungen*

Sienkiewicz, Henryk
Gombrowicz and, 12:2582b–2583a
Quo Vadis?, influence on Montherlant, 11:1915a

Sierra, Gregorio Martínez, Valle-Inclán and, 8:332b

622 upadki Bunga, czyli Demoniczna kobieta. See Witkiewicz, Stanisław Ignacy

Siete infantes de Lara, vengeance motif in, 1:125a

Siete libros de la Diana, Los. See Montemayor, Jorge de

Siger of Brabant, 1:410a, 418a-b

Sight
Barthes on, 13:3088b
see also Blindness

"Sign of Jesus, The." *See* Babel, Isaac, "Iisusov grekh"

"Sign in Space, A." *See* Calvino, Italo, *Cosmicomics*, "Un segno nello spazio"

Signal, The. See Vesaas, Tarjei, *Signalet*

Signalet. See Vesaas, Tarjei

Signaux de fumée. See Butor, Michel

"Signe de Musset," 6:1030b

Signifiers
in Calvino, 13:3277b–3278a, 3279b–3280b
Foucault and, 13:3348b–3349a

Signora Morli, una e due, La. See Pirandello, Luigi

Signs, Augustine on, 1:26a-b, 42a-b, 45b–46a

Signs by the Roadside. *See* Andrić, Ivo, *Znakovi pored puta*

Sigrid Stallbrokk. See Vesaas, Tarjei

"Siite." *See* Tychyna, Pavlo, *Pluh*

Sikelianos, Angelos, 13:2955b, 2956a
Seferis and, 12:2255b

Silence de la mer, Le (*Silence of the Sea*). *See* Vercors

Silence, Le. See Sarraute, Nathalie

Silence, use of, by Maeterlinck, 8:131b–132a, 142b

Sileni Alcibiadis ("The Sileni of Alcibiades"). *See* Erasmus

Silesia, Hauptmann's plays about, 8:152b–153b, 157b–158a, 163b

"Silesian Weavers, The." *See* Heine, Heinrich, "Die Schlesischen Weber"

Silhouette du scandale. See Aymé, Marcel

Silone, Ignazio, **12:2274a–2305b**
Ed egli si nascose (*And He Did Himself*), 12:2302a
Europa Socialista and, 12:2302a
Fontamara, 12:2279a–2285a, 2293a-b
cafoni, 12:2274b–2275a, 2280a-b, 2281a, 2288b
character names, 12:2284b
critical reception, 12:2283b–2284a, 2293b–2294b
narrator, 12:2282a

political themes, 12:2278b–2279a

"Solitary Stranger," 12:2283b

title's symbolism, 12:2280a

Il segreto di Luca (*The Secret of Luca*), 12:2296b, 2297b

Il seme sotto la neve (*The Seed Beneath the Snow*), 12:2290a–2295b

Aunt Eufemia story, 12:2291b

critical reception, 12:2293b–2294b

Pietro Spina, 12:2290a–2291b, 2293a-b

pluralistic interpretation, 12:2293a

Information and, 12:2302a

La scuola dei dittatori (*The School of Dictators*), 12:2301b–2302a

La volpe e le camelie (*The Fox and the Camellias*), 12:2296b–2297b

critical reception, 12:2297b

language, 12:2279b–2280a

L'Avventura d'un povero cristiano (*Story of a Humble Christian*), 12:2298a, 2298b–2301a

Mazzini (*The Living Thought of Mazzini*), 12:2302a

Pane e vino (*Bread and Wine*), 12:2275a, 2285a–2290a, 2293b

cafoni, 12:2286a, 2288b

critical reception, 12:2293b–2295b

state vs. individual, 12:2290a

Severina, 12:2301a-b

Tempo presente and, 12:2302a

Un dialogo difficile: Sono liberi gli scrittori russi? (*An Impossible Dialogue Between Ivan Anissimov and Silone*), 12:2302a

Una manciata di more (*A Handful of Blackberries*), 12:2275a–2296b

Uscita di sicurezza (*Emergency Exit*), 12:2275b, 2279a, 2298b

Silva de varia lección. See Mexía, Pero

Silver Dove, The. See Bely, Andrey, *Serebrianyi golub'*

Silver Face. *See* Valle-Inclán, Ramon del, *Las comedias bárbaras* (Barbaric Plays), *Cara de Plata*

"Silver Gift Poem." *See* Elytis, Odysseus, *To photodendro kai i dekati tetarti omorfia* (*The Light Tree and the Fourteenth Being*), "Doro asimenio poiema"

Šimánek, Josef, Hašek and, 9:1096a

Simatologion. See Elytis, Odysseus

Simches, Seymour, *Le romantisme et le goût esthétique du XVIIIe siècle*, 9:1397a

Simenon, Georges, **12:2479a–2510b**

absence of will theme, 12:2498b

Antoine et Julie, 12:2492b–2493a

Au pont des Arches (*At the Arches Bridge*), 12:2479a

Betty, 12:2481a

Ceux de la soif (*Those Who Thirst*), 12:2484b

"difficulty of being a man" leitmotiv, 12:2483b, 2489b–2490a, 2491b, 2504a

Dimanche (*Sunday*), 12:2493a-b

Faubourg (*Home Town*), 12:2482a

Je me souviens, 12:2480a

La boule noire (*The Blackball*), 12:2490a

La fuite de Monsieur Monde (*Monsieur Monde Vanishes*), 12:2495b–2496b

La jument perdue (*The Lost Mare*), 12:2501b

La mort de Belle (*Belle*), 12:2490a-b

La neige était sale (*The Snow Was Black*), 12:2483a, 2491a-b

La première enquête de Maigret (*Maigret's First Case*), 12:2486a-b

La vieille, 12:2481a

L'Aîné des Ferchaux (*The Elder of Ferchaux*), 12:2484b

L'Âne rouge (*The Red Donkey*), 12:2483b

L'Assassin (*The Murderer*), 12:2495b

Le bourgemestre de Furnes (*The Burgomaster of Furnes*), 12:2482a, 2500b, 2501a

Le cercle des Mahé (*The Mahé Family's Circle*), 12:2501a

Le chat (*The Cat*), 12:2493a

Le clan des Ostandais (*The Ostenders*), 12:2489a-b, 2493b–2494a

Le coup de lune (*Moonstruck*), 12:2484a-b, 2498b–2499a

Le destin des Malou (*The Fate of the Malous*), 12:2483a

Simenon, Georges (*cont.*)
  Le fils (*The Son*), 12:2483a, 2492a
  Le fond de la bouteille (*The Bottom of the Bottle*), 12:2501b
  Le grand Bob (*Big Bob*), 12:2481b, 2494a–2495a
  Le passager clandestin (*The Stowaway*), 12:2484b
  Le pendu de Saint-Pholien (*Maigret and the Hundred Gibbets*), 12:2483b
  Le petit homme d'Arkangelsk (*The Little Man from Archangel*), 12:2490b–2491a
  Le petit saint (*The Little Saint*), 12:2497b–2498b
  Le président (*The Premier*), 12:2502a–2503a
  Le riche homme (*The Rich Man*), 12:2482a
  Le temps d'Anaïs (*The Girl in His Past*), 12:2503b
  Le testament Donadieu (Donadieu's Will), 12:2499b
  L'Enterrement de Monsieur Bouvet (*The Burial of Monsieur Bouvet*), 12:2497a
  Les anneaux de Bicêtre (*The Bells of Bicêtre*), 12:2496b–2497a
  Les clients d'Avrenos (*Avrenos's Clients*), 12:2484a
  Les fiançailles de M. Hire (*M. Hire's Engagement*), 12:2490b
  Les frères Rico (*The Brothers Rico*), 12:2501b
  Les mémoires de Maigret (*Maigret's Memoirs*), 12:2488a
  Les trois crimes de mes amis (My Friends' Three Crimes), 12:2483b
  Les volets verts (The Green Shutters), 12:2496b
  L'Escalier de fer (*The Iron Staircase*), 12:2493a
  Lettre à mon juge (Letter to My Judge), 12:2492b
  L'Homme au petit chien (*The Man with the Little Dog*), 12:2503b
  L'Horloger d'Everton (*The Watchmaker of Everton*), 12:2490a
  Long cours (Ocean Voyage), 12:2484b
  Maigret et les témoins récalcitrants (*Maigret and the Reluctant Witnesses*), 12:2501b
  Maigret et les vieillards (*Maigret et les vieillards*), 12:2487b
  Maigret et son mort (*Maigret's Special Murder*), 12:2500b–2501a
  Malempin (*The Family Lie*), 12:2482a
  Mémoires intimes (*Intimate Memoirs*), 12:2485a
  Oncle Charles s'est enfermé (*Uncle Charles Has Locked Himself In*), 12:2482a
  Pedigree, 12:2480a–2483b
  Petr-le-Letton (*Maigret and the Enigmatic Lett*), 12:2488a
  Quand j'étais vieux (*When I Was Old*), 12:2482a, 2489a
  45 degrés a l'ombre, 12:2484b
  Quartier négre (Native Quarter), 12:2484a, 2499a-b
  Touriste de bananes (*Banana Tourist*), 12:2484b, 2499b–2500a
  Un homme comme un autre, 12:2504b–2505a
  Un nouveau dans la ville (A Stranger in Town), 12:24909a
Simfoniia. See Bely, Andrey, *Symphonies*
Simile, in "Futurist Manifesto," 9:808b
Simiosis sta perithoria tou hronou. See Ritsos, Yannis, *Piimata I*
Simmel, Georg, Lukács and, 10:1253b
Simon, Claude, **13:3021a–3048b**
  Gulliver, 13:3031b, 3035b
  Histoire, 13:3022a, 3024a, 3030a, 3038b–3040b
    Collège Stanislas and, 13:3022b, 3031a
    montage technique in, 13:3025a-b
  La bataille de Pharsale (*The Battle of Pharsalus*), 13:3040b, 3042a-b
  La corde raide (The Taut Rope), 13:3031a, 3031b
  La route des Flandres (The Flanders Road), 13:3022a, 3024a, 3026b, 3028b, 3036a–3037a
    Histoire and, 13:3038b
    Triptyque and, 13:3043a
    verisimilitude of, 13:3023a
  Le palace (*The Palace*), 13:3030b, 3037a–3038b

Le sacre du printemps (The Rite of Spring), 13:3032a-b

Le tricheur (The Cheat), 13:3031a, 3031b, 3032a

Le vent (*The Wind*), 13:3031a, 3032b–3034a

Leçon de choses (*The World About Us*), 13:3043a

Les corps conducteurs (*Conducting Bodies*), 13:3022a, 3022b, 3040b–3042b

Les géorgiques (*The Georgics*), 13:3028b, 3043a-b

L'Herbe (*The Grass*), 13:3030a, 3034a–3036a

Orion aveugle (The Blind Orion), 13:3042b

Sarraute and, 12:2333a

Triptyque (*Triptych*), 13:3043a

Simon le pathétique (Simon the Susceptible). *See* Giraudoux, Jean

Simonnet, Claude, on Queneau, 12:2517b

Simony, in Dante's *Inferno*, 1:446a

Simoom. See Strindberg, August, *Samum*

"Simple agonie." *See* Laforgue, Jules

"Simple Death Throes." *See* Laforgue, Jules, "Simple agonie"

"Simple Heart, A." *See* Flaubert, Gustave

Simpleton of the Unexpected Isles, The. See Shaw, George Bernard

Simplicissimus. See Grimmelshausen, Hans von

Simplicissimus (journal)
Hesse and, 9:837a
Wedekind's contributions, 8:257b

Simplon Winks at the Fréjus. See Vittorini, Elio, *Il Sempione strizza l'occhio al Fréjus*

Simson, oder Scham und Eifersucht. See Wedekind, Frank

Simultaneity
in Broch, 10:1385a
Johnson and, 12:2376a

Simultanism, Apollinaire and, 9:892a, 897a, 897b, 899a

Simvolizm. See Bely, Andrey

Sin
Aquinas on, 1:422b
Kierkegaard and, 6:1139b

"occupational," in Redentin Easter play, 1:468a, 468b

original
Augustine on, 1:26a, 26b, 45a
in Ionesco's *Le piéton de l'air*, 13:2998a
Schopenhauer's view vs. Christian view, 5:403b

passion and, Augustine on, 1:44a–45a

in Undset's works, 9:1031b

Sin of Father Amaro, The. See Eça de Queiroz, José Maria

Sin of Father Mouret, The. See Zola, Émile, *La faute de l'abbé Mouret*

"Sin of Jesus, The." *See* Babel, Isaac, "Iisusov grekh"

"Since the branches leaf out." *See* Marcabru, "Pus s'enfulleysson li verjan"

"Since we see." *See* William IX of Aquitaine, duke, "Pus vezem"

Sinclair, Emil. *See* Hesse, Hermann

Sinclair, Isaac von
Hölderlin and
meeting of, 5:149a
support of, 5:150a, 155a, 167a-b

Singer, Isaac Bashevis, Hamsun and, 8:21a

Singer of Tales, The. See Lord, Albert Bates

Singer, The. *See* Goldoni, Carlo, *La cantatrice*

"Singers, The." *See* Turgenev, Ivan

Singspiel, Hoffmann and, 5:276b

"Singularidades duma rapariega loura." *See* Eça de Queiroz, José Maria

Sinner, persona of, in medieval satire, 1:358a–359a, 361b–362a

Sinner's Temptation, A. See Khlebnikov, Velimir, "Iskushenie greshnika"

Sintesi, of Marinetti, 9:802b, 821b

Sipriot, Pierre
as editor, "Les après-midi de deux faunes," 11:1920b
on Montherlant, 11:1933b
Montherlant sans masque (Montherlant Unmasked), 11:1925b

Sir Charles Grandison. See Richardson, Samuel

Sir Gawain and the Green Knight
Chrétien de Troyes and, 1:149b
Gawain in, 1:158b

Sir Gawain and the Green Knight (*cont.*)
  superiority of, over other Arthurian
    romances, 1:154a
Sireine. See D'Urfé, Honoré
Sirin, 9:920b
"Sirni, sirni, sirni." *See* Ady, Endre
"Sirventes on motz no falh." *See* Bertran de
  Born
Sirventes (poetic genre), 1:167a, 340a
Sirventes in which not a word fails of its
    mark, A. *See* Bertran de Born, "Un
    sirventes on motz no falh"
Sisam, Kenneth, on *Beowulf*, 1:73b–74a
Sisley, Alfred, 7:1630b
Sismondi, Simonde de, 5:92a, 93a
  *Histoire des républiques italiennes du
    Moyen Âge*
    Manzoni's confutation of, 5:374a–375a
    as source for Manzoni's *Il conte di
      Carmagnola*, 5:374a
Sista brevet till Sverige. See Moberg, Vilhelm,
  The Last Letter Home
Sista mänskan. See Lagerkvist, Pär
Siste kapitel. See Hamsun, Knut
Sister Beatrice. See Maeterlinck, Maurice,
  Soeur Béatrice
Sisters or Casanova in the Spa, The. *See*
    Schnitzler, Arthur, *Die Schwestern oder
    Casanova in Spa*
Sisters-Lightning Flashes. *See* Khlebnikov,
  Velimir, "Sestry-molnii"
Sisyphus
  in Camus's *Myth of Sisyphus*,
    13:3065a–3067a
  in Vigny's "La flûte," 5:484a
"Situation du surréalisme entre les deux
    guerres." *See* Breton, André
Sivori, Ernesto, Montale's musical education
    by, 11:1987a
Six Characters in Search of an Author. See
  Pirandello, Luigi
Six, Les, and Cocteau, 10:1546a, 1550b
6 810 000 litres d'eau par seconde. See Butor,
  Michel, *Niagara*
Six and One Remorses for the Sky. See Elytis,
  Odysseus, *Exi kai mia tipsis yia ton
  ourano*

Sixteen and One Variations. *See* Butor, Michel,
  Seize et une variations
622 Downfalls of Bungo, The; or, The
    Demonic Woman. *See* Witkiewicz,
    Stanisław Ignacy, *622 upadki Bunga,
    czyli Demoniczna kobieta*
Sjælemesse. See Gunnarsson, Gunnar
Sjálfstætt fólk. See Laxness, Halldór
Sjöberg, Alf, Strindberg and, 7:1750b
Skaebne Anekdoter. See Dinesen, Isak,
    Anecdotes of Destiny
Skald, 1:66a
Skaldic verse, 1:378a–379a, 384a-b, 386b
"Skáldskaparmál." *See* Snorri Sturluson, *Edda*
"Skaparegestalter." *See* Södergran, Edith
Skapti Þóroddsson, 1:378a
Skaz technique
  Gogol and, 6:983a, 988a
  in Zamyatin's writing, 10:1186a, 1186b
"Skazka o Gospodine Koroshem i o miloi
    baryshne." *See* Zamyatin, Yevgeny
    Ivanovich
Skazki Mel'pomene. See Chekhov, Anton
"Skeleton of the Day, The." *See* Arp, Jean
Skepticism
  Burckhardt on, 6:1243a
  Corneille's *Cinna* and, 3:44a
  Diderot and, 4:483a–484a
  Kundera and, 13:3397a-b
  of Montaigne, 2:786b
  Sainte-Beuve and, 6:843b–844a
  of Sextus Empiricus, 3:9a
  Voetius on, 3:20a
  see also Doubt; Pyrrhonism
Skeptic's Walk, The. See Diderot, Denis, *La
    promenade du sceptique*
Sketch for an Autobiography. See Pasternak,
    Boris, *I Remember: Sketch for an
    Autobiography*
Sketch Artist, The; or, Art and Mammon. *See*
    Wedekind, Frank, *Der Schnellmaler,
    oder Kunst und Mammon*
"Sketch of a Serpent." *See* Valéry, Paul,
    Charmes, "Ebauche d'un serpent"
Sketch of the Universal Judgment. See Alfieri,
    Vittorio
Sketchbook 1946–1949. See Frisch, Max

Sketchbook 1966–1971. See Frisch, Max

Sketches. *See* Kosztolányi, Dezső, *Tollrajzok*

Skibe paa Himlen. See Gunnarsson, Gunnar, *Kirken paa Bjerget* (The Church on the Hill), *Ships in the Sky*

Skify. See Blok, Alexander

"Skify." *See* Blok, Alexander

"Skify li?" *See* Zamyatin, Yevgeny Ivanovich, "Scythians?"

Skin of Dreams, The. See Queneau, Raymond, *Loin de Rueil*

"Skitalets," Gorky and, 8:419b

"Skjærgaardső." *See* Hamsun, Knut

Skjöldunga, 1:381a

"Skorbna Maty." *See* Tychyna, Pavlo, *Soniachni klarnety*

Skorovoda, in Tychyna's poetry, 10:1672b

Skothending, 1:378b

"Skripka Rotshilda." *See* Chekhov, Anton

Skrypnyk, Mykola, 10:1657a

"Skuchnaya istoriya." *See* Chekhov, Anton

Skylark. *See* Kosztolányi, Dezső, *Pacsirta*

Slander, in Croce's *Filosofia della pratica,* 8:322a

Slander. *See* Scribe, Eugène, *La calomnie*

Slang

Pérez Galdós' use of, 7:1598b, 1608b–1609a, 1612b–1613a

in Zola's *L'Assommoir,* 7:1525b–1526b

see also Argot; Idiomatic language

Slap in the Face of Public Taste, A. *See* Hylaea group, *Poshchechina obshchestvennomu vkusu*

"Slate Ode, The." *See* Mandelshtam, Osip

Slave, The. *See* Andrić, Ivo, "Robinja"

"Slave, The." *See* Khlebnikov, Velimir, "Esir"

Slaves, Les. See Mickiewicz, Adam

Slavic nationalism, of Khlebnikov, 10:1336b–1337a, 1352b

Slavishness and Greatness of the French People, The. *See* Aragon, Louis, *Servitude et grandeur des français*

Slavs, The. *See* Mickiewicz, Adam, *Les Slaves*

Sleep, Proust on, 8:561a

"Sleep of the Brave, The." *See* Elytis, Odysseus, *Exi kai mia tipsis yia ton ourano* (*Six and One Remorses for the Sky*), "O Ipnos ton Yeneon"

"Sleeper in the Valley, The." *See* Rimbaud, Arthur, "Le dormeur du val"

Sleeping Woman, The. *See* Claudel, Paul, *L'Endormie*

Sleepless Nights. See Moberg, Vilhelm, *Sömnlös*

Sleepwalkers, The. See Broch, Hermann

"Sleepy." *See* Chekhov, Anton, "Spat khochetsya"

"Slepac." *See* Andrić, Ivo

"Šlépěj." *See* Čapek, Karel

Slight Misunderstanding, A. *See* Hašek, Jaroslav, "Malé nedorozuměni"

Sloop, The. *See* Zamyatin, Yevgeny Ivanovich, "Ela"

"Slough, The." *See* Bely, Andrey, *Mezhdu dvukh revoliutsii*

Slovníček literárni. See Pallas, Gustav

"Slovo i kul'tura." *See* Mandelshtam, Osip, "The Word and Culture"

Slovo kak takovoe. See Khlebnikov, Velimir; Kruchenykh, Aleksei, and Khlebnikov, Velimir

"Slovo o El'." *See* Khlebnikov, Velimir

"Slovo predostavliaetsia tovarishchu Churyginu." *See* Zamyatin, Yevgeny Ivanovich

Slow Slide into Pleasure. See Robbe-Grillet, Alain

Słowacki, Juliusz, Gombrowicz and, 12:2585a

Slub. See Gombrowicz, Witold, *The Marriage*

"Sluchai na stantsii Kochetovka." *See* Solzhenitsyn, Aleksandr

"Sluchay iz praktiki." *See* Chekhov, Anton

"Slugi starogo veka." *See* Goncharov, Ivan

Slutspel i ungdomen. See Johnson, Eyvind, *Romanen om Olof*

Sly Foxes, The. *See* Gunnarsson, Gunnar, *Rævepelsene*

Smaa Historier. See Gunnarsson, Gunnar

Smaa Historier, Ny Samling. See Gunnarsson, Gunnar

Smaa Skuespil. See Gunnarsson, Gunnar

"Smaabyliv" (Small-Town Life). *See* Hamsun, Knut

Small Dictionary of Literature. See Pallas, Gustav, *Slovníček literárni*

Small Town, A. *See* Azorín, *Un pueblecito*

Small-Town Tyrant. See Mann, Heinrich, *Professor Unrat, oder das Ende einer Tyrannen*

Smell, sense of
in Proust's *Remembrance of Things Past*, 8:562a, 563a-b
in Simon's *The Palace*, 13:3037a-b

"Smert' Dolgusheva." *See* Babel, Isaac

"Smert' Palivody." *See* Khlebnikov, Velimir

"Smert poeta." *See* Lermontov, Mikhail Yurievich

Smert' Vazir-Mukhtara. See Tynianov, Yurii

Směšné lásky. See Kundera, Milan, *Laughable Loves*

Smith, C., *Poema de mio Cid* and, 1:127a-b

Smith, Macklin, on Prudentius' *Psychomachia*, 1:2b

"Smog." *See* Calvino, Italo

Smoke. See Turgenev, Ivan

Smoke, smoke, smoke. See Tsvetaeva, Anastasiia, *Dym, dym, dym*

Smolentz, Marie von, Grillparzer and, 5:435b, 436a, 442b

Smollett, Tobias
his translation of Lesage's *Gil Blas*, 3:339a
Roderick Random, influenced by Lesage's *Gil Blas*, 3:339a

"Smrt u Sinanovoj tekjii." *See* Andrić, Ivo

"Smutný osud nádražní misie." *See* Hašek, Jaroslav

"Snail and the Rosebush, The." *See* Andersen, Hans Christian

Snake image, in Hoffmann's "Golden Pot," 5:283b–284a

Snake and Lily. See Kazantzakis, Nikos, *Ofis ke kríno*

Snapshots. See Robbe-Grillet, Alain

Snegurochka. See Ostrovsky, Alexander

"Snezhimochka." *See* Khlebnikov, Velimir

Snezhnaia maska. See Blok, Alexander

Snorra Edda, 12:2471b–2472a

Snorri Sturluson

Edda, 1:381a, 386a-b, 401a

Egils saga, 1:386b–387b, 390a, 392a

Heimskringla (*History of the Norwegian Kings*), 1:380a, 388a-b, 389b
Gunnarsson and, 10:1505b

Ólafs saga helga, 1:380b, 383a, 385a, 387b–388a, 402a

on skaldic verse, 1:378b, 379a

Ynglinga saga, 1:381a, 388a

Snow Maiden, The. See Ostrovsky, Alexander, *Snegurochka*

Snow Mask, The. *See* Blok, Alexander, *Snezhnaia maska*

Snow Was Black, The. See Simenon, Georges, *La neige était sale*

Snow White story, in Pushkin's fairy tale, 5:684a-b

Snowchild Baby. *See* Khlebnikov, Velimir, "Snezhimochka"

Snows. See Perse, Saint-John

"Snowstorm, The." *See* Pushkin, Alexander

"So dnia Kupal'nitsy-Agrafeny." *See* Akhmatova, Anna

"So gentle and so full of dignity my lady appears." *See* Dante Alighieri, *Vita nuova* (*New Life*), "Tanto gentile e tanto honesta pare"

"So l'ora in cui la faccia più impassibile." *See* Montale, Eugenio, *Cuttlefish Bones*

So-Called Humanity Gone Mad. *See* Witkiewicz, Stanisław Ignacy, *Tak zwana ludzkość w obłedzie*

"So-called Humorist Poet of the Thirteenth Century, A." *See* Pirandello, Luigi, "Un preteso poeta umorista del secolo XIII"

Soares, Bernardo, 10:1492b–1493b

Sobańska, Countess Karolina, Mickiewicz and, 5:613a

"Sôbolos rios." *See* Camoëns, Luís Vaz de, *Rimas*

Sobranie sochinenii. See Solzhenitsyn, Aleksandr

Sobranie stikhotvorenii v trekh knigakh. See Blok, Alexander

"Sobre la lectura y interpretación del 'Quijote'." *See* Unamuno, Miguel de

Soccer, in Olesha's *Envy*, 11:2239a, 2239b

Social activism, Johnson and,
    12:2362b–2363a, 2365a
Social change
    Baudelaire and, 7:1323a-b
    Büchner and, 6:1169a–1170a
    in Ferreira de Castro's *Eternidade*, 11:2160b
    medieval satire and, 1:340a, 351a
    Portugal, 11:2147a-b
    Walther and, 1:289b, 297a–301a
Social class. *See* Aristocracy; Bourgeoisie;
    Class, social; Masses; Peasants;
    Proletariat
Social concerns, of Pessoa, 10:1475b–1476a
Social conflict, Machiavelli's view of,
    2:607b–608b, 610b–611a
Social Contract, The. See Rousseau, Jean
    Jacques
Social criticism
    Hoffmann and, 5:264a
    Hugo's efforts at, 6:710a-b
    Keller and, 6:927b–928a
    Leconte de Lisle and, 6:1249a-b
Social Democratic Party (Russian), Gorky and,
    8:420a, 421a
Social Democrats
    Ady and, 9:866a
    Johnson and, 12:2366b
Social injustice
    Blasco Ibáñez on, 8:357a, 370b
    in Ferreira de Castro's *Jungle*, 11:2158b,
      2159a
    Gorky on, 8:426b, 427a
      in *The Three of Them*, 8:432b
    Moberg and, 11:2204b
    in Pascoli's "Thallusa," 7:1851b
    see also Exploitation
Social order, discussed in La Bruyère's
    Caractères, 3:257a-b
Social realism
    Andersen and, 6:870a
    Degas and, 7:1631a
    Manet and, 7:1631a
    poetic realism and, 6:913a–914b
    see also Realism
Social reform
    Sand and, 6:823a–827b, 829a–832a
    Storm and, 6:918a

Social revolution, futurism and, 9:797b,
    798a-b
Social structure
    Benjamin on, 11:1723a–1724a
    Marx on, 11:1723a-b
Socialism
    Antero de Quental and, 7:1685a
    Baroja and, 9:590b–591a, 594a
    Croce and, 8:315b
    in Ferreira de Castro's works
      A curva da estrada, 11:2162a-b
      Eternidade, 11:2152a
    French, Mickiewicz and, 5:631b
    in Germany, 8:147b–148a, 154a
    Heine and, 5:498b–499a
    Italian, Ginzburg and, 13:3133a-b
    Johnson and, 12:2361b, 2366b
    Moberg and, 11:2207a
    in Musil's *The Man Without Qualities*,
      9:940b
    Oliveira Martins and, 7:1689b–1690a
    Pascoli and, 7:1849a–1850a
    Portugal, Quental and, 11:2147b
    Sartre and, 12:2603a–2606a
    Svevo's view of, 8:85a
    Tocqueville on, 6:900b
    of Unamuno, 8:286b–287b
    utopian, 5:586b
      in Michelet's view, 5:592a
    Zola and, 7:1529b
    see also Marx, Karl; Marxism
"Socialismo y aristocracia" (Socialism and
    Aristocracy). *See* Ortega y Gasset, José
Socialist Party
    in France, 8:546b
    in Italy, Silone's involvement with, 12:2294b
    in Spain, Unamuno's membership of,
      8:286b–287a
Socialist realism
    Aragon and, 11:2075a, 2076a, 2077b
    Kundera and, 13:3390b–3391b
    in Yugoslavia
      Andrić and, 11:1766a-b
      Krleža and, 11:1809a
Socialist Workers Party (Germany, 1869),
    8:154a
Société des Amis de Montaigne, 2:787b

Society of 1789, Chénier as spokesman of, 4:701a

Society of the 317. *See* Obshchestvo Predsedatelei Zemnogo Shara

Society

Bergson's view of, 8:61b–63a

Berlioz' view of, 6:795a-b, 797b

Büchner's view of, 6:1183b–1186a

disintegration of, Broch and, 10:1389a–1393b

Goncharov's view of, 6:1072a-b, 1079b

in Hamsun's work, 8:28b–30a, 30b

Leconte de Lisle's view of, 6:1269a–1271b

Lermontov's view of, 6:1202a-b, 1208a-b, 1210a–1211a, 1216b–1217a

Mérimée's view of, 6:747a-b, 748a, 751b, 762a, 766a

relationship to individual, 9:598b–599a

Rimbaud's view of, 7:1785b–1787a, 1789a–1790b

Sainte-Beuve on, 6:848b–855b

Schnitzler's view of, 8:94a-b, 102a, 105a-b, 112b, 114a

Society of Honorable Bell Ringers, The. *See* Zamyatin, Yevgeny Ivanovich, *Obshchestvo pochetnykh zvonarei*

Society of Jesus. *See* Jesuits

Society for Modern Life. *See* Gesellschaft für Modernes Leben

Society of Philomaths, 5:608a

Society of the Presidents of Planet Earth. *See* Obshchestvo Predsedatelei Zemnogo Shara

Society for the Propagation of the Faith (Metz), 3:155b

Society tale, in Lermontov's works, 6:1220a

Sociologia criminal, La. See Azorín

Sociology, implications of Herder's emphasis on folk subculture, 4:643b

Socrate et son médecin. See Valéry, Paul

Socrates

Leopardi and, 5:559a

Montaigne on, 2:782a, 783a

Nietzsche and, 7:1658a-b, 1663b, 1668b–1669a

Strindberg's treatment of, 7:1739a

Valéry and, 8:584b–586b

Socrates Gone Mad; or, Diogenes of Sinope's Discourses. See Wieland, Christoph Martin, *Sokrates Mainomenos, oder die Dialogen des Diogenes von Sinope*

Socrates and His Physician. See Valéry, Paul, *Socrate et son médecin*

Socratic method, Kierkegaard and, 6:1138b–1139a

Södergran, Edith, **11:1781a–1806b**

"Aftonvandring" ("Evening Promenade"), 11:1793a-b

"Alvdrottningens spira" ("The Elf-Queen's Wand"), 11:1800a

"Arrival in Hades" ("Ankomst i Hades"), 11:1803b, 1804a

"Beslut" ("Decision"), 11:1801a-b

"Blixtens trångtan" ("The Lightning's Pining"), 11:1801b

Brokiga iakttagelser (Manifold Observations), 11:1798b

"Claudia," 11:1783a, 1784a

"Dagen svalnar" ("The Day Is Cooling"), 11:1787b–1788a

"Den speglande brunnen" ("The Mirroring Well"), 11:1787a-b

"Den stora trädgården" ("The Great Garden"), 11:1801b

"Det fasansfulla tåget" ("The Terrible Procession"), 11:1796b

Die fröhliche Wissenschaft (*The Joyful Wisdom*), 11:1791a

"Die Zukunft" ("The Future"), 11:1783a

Dikter (Poems), 11:1785a–1786a, 1787b, 1790a-b

"Du store Eros" ("Thou Great Eros"), 11:1799b

Edith Södergran's dikter 1907-1909 (Edith Södergran's Poems 1907-1909), 11:1782b–1783a

Ekelöf and, 12:2668a

"Förhoppning" ("Hope"), 11:1794a-b

"Fragment" ("Fragment"), 11:1795b–1796a

"Framtidens skugga," 11:1799b

Framtidens skugga (The Shadow of the Future), 11:1798b–1802a

"Gryningen" ("The Dawn"), 11:1795a

"Hamlet," 11:1800b–1801a

"Ingenting" ("Nothing"), 11:1789b–1790a

"Jag" ("I"), 11:1786a

"Kärlek" ("Love"), 11:1788b–1789a

"Kyrkogårdsfantasi" ("Churchyard Phantasy"), 11:1803b

Landet som icke är (The Land That Is Not), 11:1781a, 1802a, 1803b–1804a, 12:2663b

"Landskap i solnedgång" ("Landscape in Sunset"), 11:1794a

"Månens hemlighet" ("The Moon's Secret"), 11:1793b

"Materialism," 11:1800b, 1801a

"My Childhood Trees" ("Min barndoms träd"), 11:1802a, 1802b, 1803a-b

"O mina solbrandsfärgade toppar" ("Oh My Sun-flame-colored Tops"), 11:1792b–1793a

"Paula," 11:1783a, 1784a

"Planeterna" ("The Planets"), 11:1799a

"Revanche" ("Revenge"), 11:1795a-b

Rosenaltaret (The Rose Altar), 11:1789a, 1791a, 1796a–1798b

Septemberlyran (The September Lyre), 11:1791a, 1792a, 1794b–1796a

"Skaparegestalter" ("Figures of Creation"), 11:1798b–1799a

"Sommarminnen" ("Summer Memories"), 11:1783b

"Stjärnan" ("The Star"), 11:1801b

"The Gypsy Woman" ("Zigenerskan"), 11:1802a-b

"The Moon" ("Månen"), 11:1802a, 1803b–1804a

"Till Eros" ("To Eros"), 11:1786a-b

"Tjuren" ("The Bull"), 11:1792b

"Tolerans" ("Tolerance"), 11:1799a

"Triumf att finnas till" ("Triumph of Existing"), 11:1792b

"Två vägar" ("Two Paths"), 11:1788a-b

"Upptäckt" ("Discovery"), 11:1792b

"Verktygets klagan" ("The Tool's Lament"), 11:1797a-b

Vesaas and, 11:2054a

"Vierge moderne" ("Modern Virgin"), 11:1787a

"Violetta skymningar" ("Violet Twilights"), 11:1786b–1787a

"Visan från molnet" ("The Song from the Cloud"), 11:1793b

Sodome et Gemorrha (*Sodom and Gomorrah*). *See* Giraudoux, Jean

Sodome et Gomorrhe. See Proust, Marcel, *Remembrance of Things Past* (*À la recherche du temps perdu*), *Cities of the Plain*

Soeur Béatrice. See Maeterlinck, Maurice

Soeur Philomène. See Goncourt, Edmond Louis Antoine and Jules Alfred Huot de

"Soeurs de charité, Les" ("Sisters of Charity"). *See* Rimbaud, Arthur

Soeurs Vatard, Les. See Huysmans, Joris Karl

"Soffio." *See* Pirandello, Luigi

Sofoniia of Riazan, "Zadonshchina" (Beyond the Don), 9:974b

"Soft Moon, The." *See* Calvino, Italo

Sogni del pigro, I. See Moravia, Alberto

"Sogno del prigioniero, Il." *See* Montale, Eugenio, *The Storm and Other Things* (*La bufera e altro*), "The Prisoner's Dream"

Sogno, ma forse no? See Pirandello, Luigi

Soif et la faim, La. See Ionesco, Eugène

"Soir, Un" ("One Evening"). *See* Maupassant, Guy de

"Soirée avec Monsieur Teste, Une." *See* Valéry, Paul

"Soirée perdue, Une." *See* Musset, Alfred de

Soirées de l'orchestre, Les. See Berlioz, Hector, *Evenings with the Orchestra*

Soirées de Médan, Les (Evenings at Médan), 7:1713b, 1763b–1764a

Soirées de Paris, Les, 9:894b, 896b

Sokel, Walter, on Böll, 13:3178b

Sokrates Mainomenos, oder die Dialogen des Diogenes von Sinope. See Wieland, Christoph Martin

Sol, El (Spanish periodical), Ortega y Gasset's articles in, 9:1145b, 1146a

Solana, José Gutiérrez, Valle-Inclán and, 8:332b

Solar Spectrum, The. See Wedekind, Frank

Solaria (Florentine review)

Solaria (Florentine review) (*cont.*)
  Ginzburg's stories in, 13:3136b
  Svevo and, 8:71a-b
  Vittorini's writings in, 12:2736a, 2736b
Soldat med brutet gevär. See Moberg, Vilhelm
Soldatens återkomst. See Johnson, Eyvind
"Soldati." *See* Ungaretti, Giuseppe, *Allegria di
    naufragi*
Soldier with a Broken Rifle. *See* Moberg,
    Vilhelm, *Soldat med brutet gevär*
"Soldiers." *See* Ungaretti, Giuseppe, *Allegria
    di naufragi* (Mirth of Shipwrecks),
    "Soldati"
Soldier's Legacy, A. See Böll, Heinrich, *Das
    Vermächtnis*
Soledad sonora, La. See Jiménez, Juan Ramón
Soledades. See Góngora, Luis de; Machado,
    Antonio
Soledades, galerías, y otros poemas. See
    Machado, Antonio
Soleil recerclé, Le. See Arp, Jean
Soleil se couche, Le. See Ghelderode, Michel
    de
"Soleils couchants." *See* Hugo, Victor
Solger, K. W., on Richter's *The School for
    Aesthetics*, 5:78b
Solidarity
  in Cela, 13:3115a-b
  national, in Ekelöf's works, 12:2652a-b
Solifidianism, Luther and, 2:672b–673a
Solipsism, in Richter's *Clavis*, 5:74a
Solitaire, Le. See Ionesco, Eugène
Solitary Hours, The. *See* Baroja, Pío, *Las
    horas solitarias*
Solitude
  in Apollinaire's "The Traveler," 9:893a, 893b
  in Delacroix's works, 5:533a–535a
  Genet and, 13:2889b
  in Mann's *Doctor Faustus*, 9:733b–734b
  in pastoral poetry, 2:904a-b, 911a-b, 914a
  in Pavese's works, 12:2765a-b, 2769a-b,
    2788a-b
"Solitude." *See* Lenau, Nikolaus, "Einsamkeit"
Solitudes. See Góngora, Luis de, *Soledades*
Solitudes, Galleries, and Other Poems. *See*
    Machado, Antonio, *Soledades, galerías,
    y otros poemas*

Sollers, Philippe, Céline's influence on,
    11:1859a
Solmi, Sergio, Quasimodo and, 12:2398a
"Solo che amore ti colpisca." *See* Quasimodo,
    Salvatore
"Solo et pensoso più deserti campi." *See*
    Petrarch, *Canzoniere*
Sologub, Vladimir Aleksandrovich
  "Liturgiia mne" (Liturgy to Me), Khlebnikov
    and, 10:1356a
  Pobeda smerti (The Triumph of Death),
    Khlebnikov and, 10:1357a
"Solomiulea." *See* Mandelshtam, Osip
Solomon. See Klopstock, Friedrich Gottlieb
Solomon, Song of. *See* Bible
Solomos, Dionysios, 13:2955b, 2956a
  "Imnos is tin Eleftheria" ("Hymn to
    Liberty"), 13:2970b
"Solon." *See* Pascoli, Giovanni, *Poemi
    conviviali*
Solov'ev, Vladimir Sergeevich
  Blok and, 9:963b
  downfall of Petrine Russia, 10:1619a-b
  Mandelshtam and, 10:1630b
  "Panmongolism," 10:1619b
  Russian symbolism and, 9:963b
Solovyov family, Bely and, 9:911a, 911b,
    912b–913a, 914b–915a, 917a, 919b,
    922b
Solska, Irena, affair with Witkiewicz, 10:1210a
Solstad, Dag, Vesaas and, 11:2035a
Solstice de juin, Le. See Montherlant, Henry
    de
Solus ad solam. See D'Annunzio, Gabriele
"Solvet seclum." *See* Leconte de Lisle, Charles
    Marie
Solzhenitsyn, Aleksandr, **13:3187a–3213b**
  Bodalsia telenok s dubom (*The Oak and the
    Calf*), 13:3191a, 3194a, 3207a
  Cancer Ward (*Rakovyi korpus*), 13:3190a,
    3192a, 3195b, 3203b–3205a
    foreign publication, 13:3192b
  chronology of works, 13:3196b
  "Dlia pol'zy dela" ("For the Good of the
    Cause"), 13:3203b
  "Dorozhenka" (The way), 13:3189b–3190a
  essays and interviews, 13:3194b–3195a

genre conventions, 13:3196b–3197a
  dramatic, 13:3197b–3198a
  short prose works, 13:3201a–3203b
"Matryona's Home" ("Matrenin dvor"),
    13:3190b, 3191a, 3191b, 3202a-b
  different versions of, 13:3196a
"Nobel Lecture," 13:3195b
One Day in the Life of Ivan Denisovich
    (*Odin den' Ivana Denisovicha*),
    13:3189b, 3190b, 3191a-b, 3193a,
    3201a–3202a
  different versions of, 13:3196a
  Richter's *Wutz* and, 5:60b
  third-person narrative, 13:3201a
"Paskhal'nyi krestnyi khod" ("The Easter
    Procession"), 13:3203b
polyphonic mode, 13:3200b–3201a, 3208b
"Pravaia kist" ("The Right Hand"), 13:3191a,
    3203b
Prisoners (*Plenniki*), 13:3190a, 3197b,
    3198a, 3198b
Prussian Nights (*Prusskie nochi*), 13:3190b,
    3197a-b
recurring characters, 13:3198a-b
Respublika truda (Republic of Labor),
    13:3190a-b, 3197b, 3198a-b
  title, 13:3198a
"Sluchai na stantsii Kochetovka" ("Incident
    at Krechetovka Station"),
    13:3202b–3203a
Sobranie sochinenii (Collected works),
    13:3196a, 3198b
Svecha na vetru (*A Candle in the Wind*),
    13:3190b
The First Circle (*V kruge pervom*), 13:3189a,
    3190b, 3195b, 3203b, 3207a
  "Buddha's Smile," 13:3198a–3201a
  different versions of, 13:3196a,
    3198b–3199a, 3199b–3200a
  foreign publication, 13:3192b
  inescapable physicality theme, 13:3204b
  style, 13:3208b
  title's significance, 13:3199a, 3205b
The Gulag Archipelago (*Arkhipelag GULag*),
    13:3188b–3189a, 3189b, 3190b, 3191b,
    3192a, 3195b, 3205a–3207b, 3211a

Manzoni's *The Column of Infamy* and,
    5:391b
  Soviet reaction to, 13:3194a
  Western impact, 13:3193b–3194a
The Red Wheel (*Krasnoe koleso*), 13:3192b,
    3207a–3210b, 3211a
  Aprel' semnadtsatogo (April 1917),
    13:3208a
  August 1914 (*Avgust chetyrnadtsatogo*),
    13:3188a, 3192b, 3195a, 3196a, 3198b,
    3207b–3208a
  Mart semnadtsatogo (March 1917),
    13:3207b
  Oktiabr' shestnadtsatogo (October 1916),
    13:3207b
  organizational method, 13:3207b
  red wheel imagery, 13:3209b–3210a
  revisions, 13:3207b–3208a
  stylistic innovations, 13:3208b–3209a
  themes, 13:3209a-b
Victory Celebration (*Pir pobeditelei*),
    13:3190a, 3191b, 3197b, 3198a
"Zakhar-Kalita" ("Zakhar-the-Pouch"),
    13:3203b
"Zhit' ne po izhi" ("Live Not By Lies"),
    13:3195b
Znaiut istinu tanki (Tanks Know the Truth),
    13:3190b
Soma kai to ema, To. See Ritsos, Yannis
"Soma tou kalokeriou." *See* Elytis, Odysseus,
    Ilios o protos
Somber Lives. *See* Baroja, Pío, *Vidas sombrías*
Some Poems. See Maupassant, Guy de, *Des
    vers*
Some Steps Toward Silence. *See* Johnson,
    Eyvind, *Några steg mot tystnaden*
"Some Tenets." *See* Pasternak, Boris,
    "Neskol'ko polozhenii"
Some Thoughts About Humanity. *See* Richter,
    Jean Paul, "Etwas über den Menschen"
Someday Peace Will Return. *See* Schnitzler,
    Arthur, "Und einmal wird der Friede
    wieder kommen"
"Something on Material and Symbols." *See*
    Johnson, Eyvind, "Något om material
    och symboler"
"Somewhere Beyond." *See* Kundera, Milan

Somewhere Spring Was Approaching. *See* Tychyna, Pavlo, *Soniachni klarnety,* "Des' nadkhodyla vesna"

"Sommarminnen." *See* Södergran, Edith

"Sommer." *See* Trakl, Georg

Somnambulist Ballad. *See* García Lorca, Federico, "Romance sonámbulo"

Sömnlös. See Moberg, Vilhelm

Somov i drugie (Somov and Others). *See* Gorky, Maxim

"Son." *See* Lermontov, Mikhail Yurievich

"Son, A." *See* Maupassant, Guy de, "Un fils"

Son Avenger, the. See Undset, Sigrid, *Master of Hestviken*

Son of Gog and Magog. *See* Ady, Endre, "Góg és Magóg"

Son of a Servant, The. See Strindberg, August

Son, The. See Simenon, Georges, *Le fils*

Sonata Belzebuba, czyli Prawdziwe zdarzenie w Mordowarze. See Witkiewicz, Stanisław Ignacy

Sonata by the Sea. *See* Gunnarsson, Gunnar, *Sonate-ved Havet*

Sonata de estio. See Valle-Inclán, Ramón del, *Sonatas*

Sonata de invierno. See Valle-Inclán, Ramón del, *Sonatas*

Sonata de otoño. See Valle-Inclán, Ramón del, *Sonatas*

Sonata de primavera. See Valle-Inclán, Ramón del, *Sonatas*

Sonata form, Hesse's *Steppenwolf* and, 9:849a

Sonata tou selinofotos, I. See Ritsos, Yannis

"Sonataform, Methylated Prose." *See* Ekelöf, Gunnar

Sonatas. See Valle-Inclán, Ramón del

Sonate-ved Havet. See Gunnarsson, Gunnar

"Sonatorrek." *See* Egil Skallagrímsson

Sonetos espirituales. See Jiménez, Juan Ramón

Sonette an Orpheus. See Rilke, Rainer Maria

Sonety Krymskie. See Mickiewicz, Adam

Song for an Equinox. See Perse, Saint-John, *Chant pour un équinoxe*

"Song of Czar Ivan Vasilevich, the Young Oprichnik [Bodyguard], and the Bold Merchant Kalashnikov, The." *See* Lermontov, Mikhail Yurievich, "Pesnya pro tsarya Ivana Vasilevicha"

Song of Fate, The. See Blok, Alexander, *Pesnia sud'by*

"Song from the Cloud, The." *See* Södergran, Edith, "Visan från molnet"

"Song of Hell, The." *See* Blok, Alexander, "Pesn' Ada"

"Song of the Horseman." *See* García Lorca, Federico, "Canción de jinete"

Song of a Hungarian Jacobine. *See* Ady, Endre, "Magyar jakobinus dala"

"Song of the Husbandman, The," 1:366a, 369b

Song of L, The. *See* Khlebnikov, Velimir, "Slovo o El'"

"Song of the Last Meeting." *See* Akhmatova, Anna

Song of Love. *See* Seferis, George, *Strophe*

Song of Love (motion picture). *See Canzone dell'amore, La*

Song of My Sister. *See* Ritsos, Yannis, *To traghoudi tis adhelfis mou*

"Song of Myself." *See* Whitman, Walt

Song of Roland. See Chanson de Roland

Song of Songs. See Bible, Song of Solomon

Song, The. *See* George, Stefan, *Das neue Reich* (The Kingdom Come), "Das Lied"

"Song of Triumphant Love, The." *See* Turgenev, Ivan

"Song of the Unloved Lover." *See* Apollinaire, Guillaume, "La chanson du mal-aimé"

Song upon Nothing, A. *See* Kosztolányi, Dezső, "Ének a semmiről"

"Song upon the Tailors." *See* "Ego dixi, dii estis"

Songbook of Three Friends. *See* Storm, Theodor, *Liederbuch dreier Freunde*

Songe de Vaux, Le. See La Fontaine, Jean de

Songe d'Enfer. See Raoul de Houdenc

Songe, Le. See Montherlant, Henry de, *The Dream*

Songes et les sorts, Les. See Yourcenar, Marguerite

Songs. See García Lorca, Federico, *Canciones*

Songs. *See* Machado, Antonio, *Soledades* (Solitudes), "Canciones"

Songs of Castelvecchio. *See* Pascoli, Giovanni, *Canti di Castelvecchio*

Songs of the Heart. See Lagerkvist, Pär, *Hjärtats sånger*

Songs of Innocence. See Blake, William

Songs of Maldoror. See Lautréamont, Comte de, *Chants de Maldoror*

Songs and Sonnets of Ronsard. See Page, Curtis

Songs of the Suburb. *See* Baroja, Pío, *Canciones del suburbio*

Songs to Guiomar. *See* Machado, Antonio, "Canciones a Guiomar"

Songs and Verses. *See* Machado, Antonio, *Soledades, galerías, y otros poemas* (Solitudes, Galleries, and Other Poems), "Canciones y coplas"

Songs of a Wandering Minstrel. *See* George, Stefan, *Die Bücher der Hirten- und Preisgedichte . . .* (The Books of Eclogues and Eulogies), *Sagen und Sänge* poems

Soniachni klarnety. See Tychyna, Pavlo

"Sonnen-Untergang." *See* Rilke, Rainer Maria

Sonnenspektrum, Das. See Wedekind, Frank, *The Solar Spectrum*

Sonnet
    of Alfieri, 4:670a–671b
    Baudelaire and, 7:1333a
    of Cervantes, 2:819a, 823b–824b
    Foscolo and, 5:326a–328b
    Hebbel and, 6:1117b–1118a
    in Italian literature, self-portrait tradition, 4:671a
    Jiménez, 9:997b–998b
    Machado and, 9:760a
    Musset and, 6:1026a
    origin, 2:500b
    of Pessoa, 10:1489a-b
    Petrarchan, 2:500b, 504a, 6:959b
    Renaissance, 2:751a
    of Ronsard, 2:727a–731b, 739b–740a
    see also Mickiewicz, Adam

"Sonnet boiteux." *See* Verlaine, Paul

Sonnets. See Shakespeare, William

"Sonnets pour Hélène." *See* Ronsard, Pierre de

Sonnets of the Spirit. *See* Jiménez, Juan Ramón, *Sonetos espirituales*

Sonnets to Orpheus. See Rilke, Rainer Maria, *Sonette an Orpheus*

Sonnleithner, Anna Franziska. *See* Grillparzer, Anna Franziska

Sontag, Susan, on Artaud, 11:1967b

Sophie. See Staël, Madame de

Sophiological doctrine, of Mandelshtam, 10:1630b

Sophocles
    Antigone
        Hölderlin's translation of, 5:172a
        Marinetti and, 9:813a
        Corneille and, 3:34b
            Cinna, 3:39a, 41a, 43b
            Le Cid, 3:33a, 33b
    Electra, Pirandello's *The Late Mattia Pascal* and, 8:400b
    Freud and, 8:9a
    Hofmannsthal and, 9:697a, 697b
    Oedipus Rex, 5:48a
        Freud and, 8:9a
        Guarini's *Pastor fido* and, 2:919b
        Moravia and, 12:2690a
    Svevo and, 8:84b
    see also Cocteau, Jean

Sophocles' Dance. See Cocteau, Jean, *La danse de Sophocle*

Sophonisbe. See Mairet, Jean

"Sopra il monumento di Dante." *See* Leopardi, Giacomo

"Sopra il ritratto di una bella donna." *See* Leopardi, Giacomo, "On the Likeness of a Beautiful Woman"

Sorbonne
    ban on Greek language study, 2:695b
    Beauvoir and, 12:2710b
    Bossuet and, 3:152a-b, 155b–156a
    French Evangelicals and, 2:694b
    on the Gallican church, 3:167b
    Rabelais and, 2:697a, 697b

"Sorcerer's Apprentice, The." *See* Goethe, Johann Wolfgang von, "Der Zauberlehrling"

Sorcery
in Dumas's works, 6:735b–737a
in Welsh legends, 1:142b
see also Witchcraft
Sorel, Charles, *Le berger extravagant*, 3:51b
Sorel, Georges, Labriola and, 8:314b
Sorgen och stjrnan. See Ekelöf, Gunnar
"Sorochinsky Fair" *See* Gogol, Nikolay
Vasilievich
Sorolla, Joaquín, Blasco Ibáñez' *The
Mayflower* and, 8:361b
Soromenho, Augusto, on Portuguese literature,
7:1689a
"Sorpresa." *See* García Lorca, Federico
Sorrow on the Hearth. *See* Gunnarsson,
Gunnar, *Brandur paa Bjarg*
Sorrow and the Star, The. *See* Ekelöf, Gunnar,
Sorgen och stjrnan
"Sorrow of Things I Do Not Know." *See*
Quasimodo, Salvatore, "Dolore di cose
che ignoro"
"Sorrow-Acre." *See* Dinesen, Isak
Sorrowful Night. *See* Pascoli, Giovanni,
Myricae (Tamarisks), "Notte dolorosa"
Sorrowing Man, in Villon's *Testament*, 2:558a,
558b–559a, 565b
Sorrowing Mother. *See* Tychyna, Pavlo,
Soniachni klarnety, "Skorbna Maty"
Sorrows of Young Werther, The. See Goethe,
Johann Wolfgang von
Sortie de l'acteur. See Ghelderode, Michel de
Sosa, Rafael, on Blasco Ibáñez' *The
Mayflower*, 8:359a
Soties, of Gide, 8:498b–503b
Sottie, 1:471a, 471b, 472a, 473a
*Sottie of the Triumphant Fools Who Trick
Everyman*, 1:472b
Souchère, Eléna de La, professorial republic,
9:1146a-b
"Soud pana Havleny." *See* Čapek, Karel
Souffrances et bonheur de chrétien. See
Mauriac, François
Soul
beauty of the, Maeterlinck on, 8:134a–135a
Foucault and, 13:3358a-b
nature of
Aquinas' *Summa theologica* on, 1:423a-b

Augustine on, 1:41a
discussed in La Bruyère's *Caractères*,
3:256b–257a
Prudentius' *Apotheosis* on, 1:8a
Soul of Castile (1600–1800), The. *See* Azorín,
El alma castellana (1600–1800)
Soul and Form. See Lukács, György
"Soul, who see so many different things." *See*
Petrarch, *Canzoniere*, "Anima che
diverse cose tante"
"Soul of the Wine, The." *See* Baudelaire,
Charles
Soulage, Pierre, Butor and, 13:3306b
Soulié, Fréderic, adapted Shakespeare's
Romeo and Juliet, 5:462a
Soulier de satin, Le. See Claudel, Paul
"Souls of Old Men, The." *See* Cavafy,
Constantine, "I psyches ton geronton"
"Souls in Purgatory." *See* Mérimée, Prosper
Sound, in Verlaine's poetry, 7:1635a-b
Sound and the Fury, The. See Faulkner,
William
Sound symbolism
in Chekhov's "The Steppe," 7:1861b
Tieck and, 5:249b–250a
Sounder, The. *See* Ritsos, Yannis,
Volidhoskopos
Soupault, Philippe, 11:2067b
dadaism and, 11:2063a-b, 2064a
Littérature (French journal), 11:1939b–1940a
Soupault, Philippe (joint author). *See* Breton,
André
Source grecque, La. See Weil, Simone, *The
Greek Source*
*Sources et l'évolution des "Essais" de
Montaigne, Les. See* Villey, Pierre
Sous bénéfice d'inventaire. See Yourcenar,
Marguerite
Sous le signe du dragon. See Claudel, Paul
Sousa, Manuel de Faria e. *See* Faria e Sousa,
Manuel de
South Africa, Pessoa in, 10:1481b–1483a
Southerly Windows. *See* Ritsos, Yannis,
"Mesimvrina parathyra"
Southern Mail. See Saint-Exupéry, Antoine de,
Courrier sud

Souvenirs: My Life with Maeterlinck. See
Leblanc, Georgette, *Souvenirs*
1895–1918
Souvenirs. See Tocqueville, Alexis de
Souvenirs de jeunesse. See Renan, Joseph
Ernest
Souvenirs d'égotisme. See Stendhal
Souvenirs dramatiques. See Dumas père,
Alexandre
Souvenirs du triangle d'or. See Robbe-Grillet,
Alain, *Recollections of the Golden*
Triangle
Souvenirs pieux. See Yourcenar, Marguerite
"Sovente una riviera." *See* Quasimodo,
Salvatore
Soviet Academy of Sciences
Chekhov and, 7:1857b
see also Russian Academy of Sciences
Soviet Literature. *See* Aragon, Louis,
Littératures soviétiques
Soviet Union
Beauvoir and, 12:2728a
Dostoevsky's critical standing, 7:1349a-b
labor camps, Solzhenitsyn on, 13:3188b,
3201a-b, 3205b–3206a, 3207a
New Economic Policy (NEP)(1921–1928),
11:1887a, 1892a
Mayakovsky and, 11:1836b
Zamyatin and, 10:1198b
political journalism, 9:1095a
see also Cheka; Russia; Stalinism
Sovietish Heimland (Yiddish language
journal), Babel's writings in, 11:1888a
Sovietskaya Tatariya (Soviet Tartary) (Soviet
journal), 9:1109a-b
Sovremennik (The Contemporary) (Russian
periodical)
Gorky's "Khoziain" in, 8:440a
Tolstoy's contributions to, 7:1471a, 1477b
Sow. *See* Tychyna, Pavlo, *Pluh* (*The Plow*),
"Siite"
Space, in Calvino, 13:3277b–3279a
Space. *See* Jiménez, Juan Ramón, "Espacio"
Space and time relationship. *See* Time and
space relationship
"Space without quantity," in Bergson's
thought, 8:49b

Spagna veloce e toro futurista. See Marinetti,
Filippo Tommaso
Spagnolo, Giovanni Battista. *See* Mantovano
Spain
Bourbon Restoration of 1874,
7:1607a–1609a, 1610b–1611a
Civil War (1936–1939), 9:612b–613a, 761b
Cela and, 13:3105a-b, 3119a–3121a
Ekelöf and, 12:2648a
Jiménez during, 9:992a-b
Machado and, 9:747a-b, 761b
Ortega y Gasset and, 9:1146b–1147a
Pérez Galdós and, 7:1616b
in Simon's works, 13:3022b, 3032b,
3037a–3038b, 3043b
Unamuno's involvement in, 8:307b
see also García Lorca, Federico
domination of Portugal, 11:2144a
effect of Spanish-American War, 9:745a
Generation of '98, 9:744b, 1121b
Baroja and, 9:613a
ideas of, 9:589b, 591a, 593a
Machado and, 9:744b, 745b
Middle Ages and, 9:753a
Unamuno and, 9:592b
history
Unamuno's view of, 8:284a
see also Carlist Wars
la gloriosa (liberal revolution), 7:1600a,
1603a
Mérimée's travels in, 6:754b, 755b, 763a
national character
Unamuno's view of, 8:288b
see also Casticismo
politics and government
in early 20th century, 9:600b–601a
in Valle-Inclán's fiction, 8:336b–341a
"regenerationism," 9:1121b, 1125a
Baroja experiences, 9:589a
"Los Tres" in, 9:593a
Republic (1873), 9:1121a
Republic (1931), 9:747a, 1145b–1146a
in Ferreira de Castro's *A curva da estrada*,
11:2161b–2162a
Revolution of 1868, 9:743a
in Valle-Inclán's fiction, *El ruedo ibérico*,
8:338b–339a

591

Spain (*cont.*)
  social classes. *See* Class, social
  "the problem of," 8:331a-b
    Blasco Ibáñez and, 8:357b
    trienio liberal period (1820–1823),
      7:1600b–1601b, 1604a-b
"Spange, Die." *See* George, Stefan,
  Pilgerfahrten (Pilgrimages)
Spaniards in Paris. *See* Azorín, *Españoles en
  Paris*
Spaniards, The. *See* Lermontov, Mikhail
  Yurievich, *Ispantsy*
Spaniards of Three Worlds (Lyrical
  Caricatures). *See* Jiménez, Juan Ramón,
  *Españoles de tres mundos (caricatura
  lírica)*
Spanish Cardinal, The. *See* Montherlant,
  Henry de, *Le cardinal d'Espagne*
Spanish in Denmark, The. See Mérimée,
  Prosper, *Les espagnols en Danemarck*
Spanish language, Camoëns and, 2:747a-b
Spanish literature
  Grillparzer influenced by, 5:421b
  poetry, popular
    Generation of '98 and, 9:753a
    Machado and, 9:763b, 764a
    Renaissance, Calderón and, 2:894b–895a
    traditions of, 7:1607a-b
Spanish Poetry. *See* Machado, Antonio, *Poesía
  española*
Spanish Readings. *See* Azorín, *Lecturas
  españolas*
"Spanish soul," modernist writers and,
  9:745a-b, 753a
Spanish-American War
  Blasco Ibáñez' *The Cabin* and, 8:375b
  Eça during, 7:1695a-b
  Valle-Inclán and, 8:331b
Sparks from the Forge. *See* D'Annunzio,
  Gabriele, *Le faville del maglio*
"Sparrow, The." *See* Turgenev, Ivan
"Spartaks Helden." *See* Hašek, Jaroslav
Spasmènes psihés. See Kazantzakis, Nikos
"Spat khochetsya." *See* Chekhov, Anton
Späte Rosen. See Storm, Theodor
Spätrömische Kunstindustrie. See Riegl, Alois

Spaziani, Maria Luisa, as Montale's
  fox-woman, 11:1992a
Spazier, R. O., 5:79a
Speak Out! See Grass, Günter, *Über das
  Selbstverständliche*
Special Friendships. *See* Peyrefitte, Roger, *Les
  amitiés particulières*
species, 56
Specificity, principle of, Foucault and,
  13:3349b–3350b
Spectacle dans un fauteuil, Un. See Musset,
  Alfred de, *Armchair Theater*
"Spectre de la rose, Le." *See* Gautier,
  Théophile
Spectrum imagery. *See* Color imagery
Speculazione edilizia, La. See Calvino, Italo
Speculum stultorum. See Nigel de
  Longchamps
Speech act theory, Augustine and, 1:48b
"Speech of Christ, The." *See* Richter, Jean
  Paul, "Die Rede des toten Christus vom
  Weltgebäude herab, dass kein Gott sei"
Speed
  in "Futurist Manifesto," 9:810a
  in "Technical Manifesto of Futurist
    Literature," 9:814b
Speedy Spain and Futurist Bull. See Marinetti,
  Filippo Tommaso, *Spagna veloce e toro
  futurista*
"Speglande brunnen, Den." *See* Södergran,
  Edith
Spektorskii. See Pasternak, Boris
Spence, Joseph, *Observations, Anecdotes, and
  Characters of Books and Men*, on
  Lesage, 3:327b–328a
Spencer, Bernard, *The King of Asine and
  Other Poems*, 12:2260b
Spencer, Herbert
  Bergson and, 8:47a, 64b
  influence of, 9:591a
  Maupassant and, 7:1774b
  Unamuno influenced by, 8:285a-b
Spender, Stephen, Silone and, 12:2273a,
  2297b
Spengler, Oswald
  *Der Untergang des Abendlandes (Decline of
    the West)*, 9:1142a

on the masses, 9:1145b

Ortega y Gasset and, 9:1130a, 1142b

second religiousness, 9:1076b

"Spenglerian" question, Malraux and, 12:2424a-b

Spenser, Edmund

Ariosto and, 2:642a

Castiglione and, 2:664b–665a

pastoral poems of, 2:914b–915a

Petrarchan influence, 504b

Ronsard and, 2:741a

Shephearde's Calendar, influence on English eclogues, 2:914b–915a

The Faerie Queene

as literary epic, 1:51a

pastoral interlude in, 2:910b, 915b–916a

Speranza, La. See Moravia, Alberto

Speroni, Charles, *Wit and Wisdom of the Italian Renaissance*, anecdotes in, 2:938b

"Spesso il male di vivere ho incontrato." *See* Montale, Eugenio, *Cuttlefish Bones*

Spezialetti, Amelia, 12:2388a-b

Spiaggia, La. See Pavese, Cesare, *The Beach*

Spice Dish, The. See Huysmans, Joris Karl, *Le drageoir à épices*

Spider image

in Hugo's works, 6:701a–702a

in Montesquieu's thought, 3:350b–364a

Spiegel, das Kätzchen. See Keller, Gottfried, *Mirror, the Cat*

Spiegel, Der (German newspaper), Böll's articles in, 13:3170a-b

Spiel im Morgengrauen. See Schnitzler, Arthur

Spies, Johann, *Faustbuch*, 4:549a

Spinoza, Baruch

amor intellectualis, 9:1128b

Lessing and, 4:560a, 561a

Novalis and, 5:210a

reason as abstraction, 9:1126b

romanticism and, 5:211b

Schlegel and, 5:185a-b

Taine and, 7:1464a

Spiridion. See Sand, George

Spirit and Deed. *See* Mann, Heinrich, *Geist und Tat*

Spirit of Geometry, The. *See* Pascal, Blaise, *De l'esprit géometrique*

Spirit of Hebrew Poetry, The. See Herder, Johann Gottfried von

Spirit of the Laws, The. See Montesquieu, Charles-Louis de Secondat, baron de

Spirit of Mediterranean Places, The. See Butor, Michel

Spirit of Utopia. See Bloch, Ernst, *Geist der Utopie*

Spirite. See Gautier, Théophile

Spiritism, Pirandello and, 8:396b

Spiritual being, Kierkegaard and, 6:1139b–1140a

Spiritual Body and Celestial Earth. See Corbin, Henri

Spiritual Canticle. See John of the Cross, St., *Cántico espiritual*

Spiritual despair

in Dürrenmatt's works, 13:3216b–3217a

in Sartre's works, 13:3217a

Spiritual Exercises. See Loyola, Ignatius

Spiritual Franciscans. *See* Franciscans, Spiritual

Spiritual naturalism, Huysmans and, 7:1722a

Spiritual Songs. See Luther, Martin, *Geistliche Lieder*

Spiritualism

and Heine, 5:499a

Hugo and, 6:706b–707b

of Maeterlinck, 9:592b

of Pessoa, 10:1494a

Spirituality

Heinrich Mann on, 8:521b, 536a

in Mann's fiction, 9:730b

Buddenbrooks, 9:717b

Joseph and His Brothers, 9:729b

manual labor and, Aquinas on, 1:413a-b

see also Religion

"Spiritualization," in Baudelaire's *Flowers of Evil*, 8:451a

Spirituals (music), Yourcenar's translations, 12:2543a

"Spirto gentil." *See* Petrarch, *Canzoniere*

Spisok blagodeyanii. See Olesha, Yuri

Spitzer, Leo, *Stilstudien*, on Boileau, 3:184b

"Spleen." *See* Baudelaire, Charles; *Noia*

Splendeurs et misères des courtisanes. See Balzac, Honoré de

Splendor of the Bonfire, The. *See* Valle-Inclán, Ramón del, *La guerra carlista* (The Carlist War), *El resplandor de la hoguera*

"Splendore geometrico e meccanico e la sensibilità numerica, Lo." *See* Marinetti, Filippo Tommaso

Splendors and Miseries of Courtesans. See Balzac, Honoré de, *Splendeurs et misères des courtesans*

"Spodruchnitsa greshnykh." *See* Zamyatin, Yevgeny Ivanovich

"Spoken Action." *See* Pirandello, Luigi, "L'Azione parlata"

Spöksonaten. See Strindberg, August, *The Ghost Sonata*

Sponge Diver's Chorale. *See* Ritsos, Yannis, *To horiko ton sfouggaradhon*

Sponsus, 1:455a-b, 458a

"Sporenwache." *See* George, Stefan, *Die Bücher der Hirten- und Preisgedichte . . . (The Books of Eclogues and Eulogies), Sagen und Sänge* poems

"Sportovní fejeton" (Sports Column). *See* Hašek, Jaroslav

Sports, in Olesha's works, 11:2237a-b, 2250a

Sportsman's Sketches. See Turgenev, Ivan

Sposa persiana, La. See Goldoni, Carlo

"Sprache als Hort der Freiheit, Die." *See* Böll, Heinrich

Sprachkrise, 9:768a-b
Rilke and, 9:767b

"Spring 1939." *See* Ionesco, Eugène, *La photo du colonel*

Spring, in Elytis' *To imerologio enos atheatou Apriliou*, 13:2983a

Spring. *See* Undset, Sigrid, *Vaaren*

Spring. See Yver, Jacques, *Le printemps*

Spring Ballads. *See* Jiménez, Juan Ramón, *Baladas de primavera*

Spring Night. See Vesaas, Tarjei

Spring Poems. *See* Gunnarsson, Gunnar, *Vorljóð*

Spring Sonata. *See* Valle-Inclán, Ramón del, *Sonatas: Memorias del Marqués de Bradomín (The Pleasant Memoirs of the Marquis de Bradomín), Sonata de primavera*

Spring Symphony. *See* Ritsos, Yannis, *Earini symfonia*

Spring's Awakening. See Wedekind, Frank

"Springtime Wind, A." *See* Rilke, Rainer Maria, "Ein Frülingswind"

"Sprouts." *See* Arp, Jean, "Pousses"

"Spurt of Blood, The." *See* Artaud, Antonin, "Le jet de sang"

Squabbles of Chioggia, The. See Goldoni, Carlo

Squire of Alsatia. See Shadwell, Thomas

"Sredi intelligentsii." *See* Gorky, Maxim, *My Universities*

"Sredi poklonnikov Karmen." *See* Blok, Alexander

Sri Aurobindo, Jiménez and, 9:1002b

Šta sanjam i šta mi se dogadja. See Andrić, Ivo

Staat (the word), *George-Kreis* and, 8:457b

Stabreim (alliterative meter), Wagner and, 6:1155b

Stad i ljus. See Johnson, Eyvind

Stad i mörker. See Johnson, Eyvind

Stadt Lucca, Die. See Heine, Heinrich

Staël, Anne-Louise-Germaine de, Benjamin Constant and, 4:410a–412b

Staël, Eric de, 5:89b, 90a-b, 91b, 92b

Staël, Madame de, **5:89a–111b**
Chénier compared to, 4:709a
Considérations sur la Révolution française (Considerations on the Principal Events of the French Revolution), 5:94a, 96a, 96b
in Constant's *Cécile*, 4:411a
Corinne, 5:90a, 90b, 93a, 94b, 100a–105a
on enthusiasm, 5:109b–110a
setting, 5:101a-b, 107a
De la littérature considérée dans ses rapports avec les institutions sociales (On Literature), 5:92a, 92b, 94b–99a, 100a, 107a
on satire, 5:109b

De l'Allemagne (*On Germany*), 4:411b, 544b, 5:93a-b, 94b, 96a, 105a–110a
  Heine on, 5:501a-b
  Vigny's *Stello* compared to, 5:468a
De l'influence des passions (*Influence of the Passions on the Happiness of Individuals and Nations*), 5:91b
Delphine, 5:90b, 91a, 92b, 104b
Dix années d'exil (*Ten Years of Exile*), 5:92a, 93a-b, 94a, 97a
Essai sur les fictions (*Essay on Fictions*), 5:92b, 99a–100a
Germania, 7:1454b
"Reflections on the Trial of the Queen, by a Woman," 5:91b
Sophie, 5:90b
Wieland and, 4:600b, 605a
"Stag fährt Gondel, Ein." *See* Arp, Jean
Stages on Life's Way. See Kierkegaard, Søren
Stagg, Geoffrey, Cervantes' *Don Quixote* and, 2:837a-b
Staging (theatrics)
  in medieval drama, 1:456a, 465b–466a
  Strindberg's use of, 7:1747a–1748a
  see also Theater
Stain on the Snow, The. See Simenon, Georges, *La neige était sale*
Stal' i nizhnist'. See Tychyna, Pavlo
"Stalin." *See* Elytis, Odysseus, *Maria Nephele*
Stalin, Joseph
  break with Tito, 11:1823b, 1824a
  Gorky and, 8:422a, 423b
  Heinrich Mann and, 8:536a, 542a
  Mandelshtam's satire of, 10:1645b–1646a
  Mayakovsky and, 11:1837a, 1837b, 1856b
  portrait of by Picasso, 11:2082b–2083a
  in Solzhenitsyn's works, 13:3200a, 3203b, 3206b
  Zamyatin's appeal to, 10:1199a
Stalinism
  aesthetics of, 11:2090a
  Akhmatova and, 10:1521a–1522a, 1529b, 1530a–1531a, 1531a
  Babel on, 11:1889a
  Brecht and, 11:2107
  Camus and, 13:3070a-b
  fate of poets under, 10:1521a

Khlebnikov's disfavor under, 10:1331b
Krleža on, 11:1809b, 1824a-b
Milosz and, 13:2935b
Olesha and, 11:2234b–2235a
Sartre and, 12:2601b–2603b
Terror under, 10:1529b
  in Akhmatova's poetry, 10:1521b, 1531a–1533b, 1534b, 1539a
  authors arrested, 11:1911a–1912a
  Babel's arrest, 11:1887b, 1911a-b
  Mandelshtam and, 10:1646a–1647a
  Pasternak's denunciation of, 10:1595b
  in the Ukraine, 10:1656b–1657a
Zamyatin's persecution under, 10:1198b–1199a
Zoshchenko's persecution under, 10:1530a-b
see also Communism; Soviet Union; Totalitarianism
Stamm, Therese Dolan, on the Goncourts, 7:1408b
"Stan poetycki." *See* Milosz, Czeslaw
"Standomi un giorno solo a la fenestra." *See* Petrarch, *Canzoniere*
Stanislavsky, Konstantin
  Chekhov and, 7:1855a, 1857a, 1877a, 1877b
  Maeterlinck and, 8:138b–139a
  Witkiewicz and, 10:1218a
Stankevich, Nikolay
  Goncharov and, 6:1064a
  Turgenev and, 6:1276b
"Stanzas" ("Stanze"). *See* Montale, Eugenio, *The Occasions*
Star of the Covenant, The. *See* George, Stefan, *Der Stern des Bundes*
Star imagery
  in Elytis' "Orion," 13:2959b–2960a
  of Rilke, 9:778b
Star of Redemption. See Rosenzweig, Franz, *Der Stern der Erlösung*
"Star, The." *See* Södergran, Edith, "Stjärnan"
"Stara Ukraina zminytys' musyt'." *See* Tychyna, Pavlo, *Chernihiv*
Starik. See Gorky, Maxim
Staritsky, Ania, Butor and, 13:3306a, 3312a
Starkie, Walter, Blasco Ibáñez and, 8:355a
"Star's Sadness, A." *See* Apollinaire, Guillaume, "Tristesse d'une étoile"

"Starshina." *See* Zamyatin, Yevgeny Ivanovich
"Starting from My Europe." *See* Milosz,
    Czeslaw, Norton lectures
"Starukha Izergil'." *See* Gorky, Maxim
"Staryi Shloime." *See* Babel, Isaac
State and church. *See* Church and state
State of Siege. See Camus, Albert
State, the
    Aquinas on, 1:425a–426a
    art and, Staël on, 5:97a
    in satire of Deschamps, 1:363b
"Stationmaster, The." *See* Pushkin, Alexander
Stations of the Cross, in Claudel's *Coronal*,
    8:491a-b
Statue, The. See Triolet, Elsa, *Le monument*
Stauffenberg family, George and, 8:468a
Stavisky, Serge, 9:736b
"Št'avnická Idyla." *See* Hašek, Jaroslav
Steaming Cauldron. See Zola, Émile,
    Pot-bouille
Stechlin, Der. See Fontane, Theodor
Steegmuller, Francis, on Apollinaire, 9:886a-b
Steel Alcove, The. See Marinetti, Filippo
    Tommaso, *L'Alcova d'acciaio*
Steel in Madrid. See Lope de Vega
Steel and Tenderness. *See* Tychyna, Pavlo,
    Stal' i nizhnist'
Stefan George. See Brodersen, Arvid
Stefan George und die Blätter für die Kunst
    (Stefan George and Pages for Art). *See*
    Wolters, Friedrich
Stein, Charlotte von, 5:11a, 11b–12a
Stein der Weisen, oder Laute, armbrust, und
    Peitsche, Der. See Wedekind, Frank
Stein, Gertrude
  on Paris, 9:871b
  Vittorini and, 12:2746b
Steinbach, Bruno, Lukács and, 10:1259b
Steinbeck, John
  Of Mice and Men, Vittorini's *Men and Not*
    Men and, 12:2745b
  The Grapes of Wrath, Vittorini's *Women of*
    Messina and, 12:2750a
Steiner, George, on Simenon, 12:2502a
Steiner, Jacob, on Rilke, 9:784b
Steiner, Rudolf
  Bely and, 9:919b, 920a, 922b

"Johannesbau" and, 9:908a, 923b
  Södergran and, 11:1798b
Stekel, Wilhelm, Freud and, 8:13a
Stella. See Goethe, Johann Wolfgang von
Stello. See Vigny, Alfred Victor de
Stendhal, **5:343a–366b**
  Apollinaire and, 9:882a
  Armance, 5:348a-b
  art criticism by, 5:523b
  Baudelaire and, 7:1332b
  Charterhouse of Parma, Simon and,
    13:3036a
  D'un nouveau complot contre les industriels
    (A New Plot Against the Industrialists),
    5:350b
  Goncourts and, 7:1410a
  Heinrich Mann and, 8:520b, 536a
  Histoire de la peinture en Italie (History of
    Painting in Italy), 5:347a
  La vie de Henri Brulard (The Life of Henri
    Brulard), 5:343a–344b
  on Laclos's *Les liaisons dangereuses*,
    4:400b
  Lampedusa's "Lezioni su Stendhal" on,
    11:2011b, 2020b–2021a
  Lucien Leuwen, 5:349b–350a, 358b–361b
  Mérimée and, 6:747b, 749a, 760b
  On Love, 5:347a-b
  Ortega y Gasset on, 9:1138a
  Racine et Shakespeare, 5:348a, 6:747a
    Vigny and, 5:461b
  Rome, Naples, and Florence, 5:347a
  Sainte-Beuve and, 6:841a
  Sand and, 6:821a
  Sarraute and, 12:2333b
  Souvenirs d'égotisme (Memoirs of an
    Egotist), 5:345b
  Taine and, 7:1449a, 1461a, 1464a
  The Charterhouse of Parma (*La chartreuse*
    de Parme), 5:361b–364b, 7:1461a,
    9:599a
    astronomy in, 11:2021b–2022a
    Cocteau and, 10:1547b, 1549b
    Lampedusa and, 11:2020b–2026b
    in Proust's *Remembrance of Things Past*,
    8:553b

The Red and the Black (*Le rouge et le noir*),
5:353b–358b
Remembrance of Things Past and, 8:550b
Vies de Haydn, Mozart, et Métastase (Lives
of Haydn, Mozart, and Metastasio),
5:347a
Vittorini and, 12:2735b
Zola on, 10:1271b
"Step." *See* Chekhov, Anton
"Stepan Razin." *See* Gorky, Maxim
Stepmother. *See* Kosztolányi, Dezső, *Mostoha*
"Steppe, The." *See* Chekhov, Anton, "Step"
Steppenwolf, Der. See Hesse, Hermann
Sterben. See Schnitzler, Arthur
Sterile Vows. *See* Musset, Alfred de, "Les
voeux stériles"
Stern der Erlösung, Der. See Rosenzweig,
Franz
Stern des Bundes, Der. See George, Stefan
Sterna, I. See Seferis, George
Sterne, Laurence
Foscolo and, 5:315a-b
Hoffmann and, 5:286a-b
Kundera and, 13:3397b
Marya Volkonsky and, 7:1474b
Richter's *The Invisible Lodge* and, 5:61a,
62b
Sentimental Journey, Hesperus and, 5:65a
Tristram Shandy, 6:986a
Richter and, 5:56b
Sternheim, Carl, Kafka and, 9:1156b
Stevens, Wallace
"Anecdote of the Jar," 13:3089a
Barthes and, 3103b
Jiménez and, 9:1013b
Laforgue and, 7:1883b, 1889b, 1897a
"major men," 7:1457b
Rilke and, 9:768a
Rimbaud and, 7:1787a
"Thirteen Ways of Looking at a Blackbird,"
13:2963a
on Valéry's *Eupalinos*, 8:587a
Stevenson, Robert Louis
Jekyll and Hyde story, 11:1922b–1923a
Vittorini and, 12:2735b
"Waif Woman," 1:389b

Štiavnica Idyll. *See* Hašek, Jaroslav,
"Šťavnická Idyla"
"Stichworte." *See* Böll, Heinrich
Sticks, Numbers and Letters. *See* Queneau,
Raymond, *Bâtons, chiffres et lettres*
Stift, Hölderlin and, 5:144b–145a
Stifter, Adalbert, Hofmannsthal and, 9:690a
"Stigma, To" ("The Stigma"). *See* Elytis,
Odysseus, *Maria Nephele*
"Stikhi k Bloku." *See* Tsvetaeva, Marina
"Stikhi o neizvestnom soldate." *See*
Mandelshtam, Osip, "Verses on the
Unknown Soldier"
Stikhi o Prekrasnoi Dame. See Blok, Alexander
"Stikhi o Rossii." *See* Blok, Alexander
"Stikhi o sovetskom pasporte." *See*
Mayakovsky, Vladimir
"Stikhiia i kul'tura." *See* Blok, Alexander
Stikhotvoreniia. See Mandelshtam, Osip
"Stile e tradizione." *See* Montale, Eugenio,
"Style and Tradition"
Stiller. See Frisch, Max
Stiller Musikant, Ein. See Storm, Theodor
Stimmen der Völker in Liedern. See Herder,
Johann Gottfried von
Stine. See Fontane, Theodor
Stirb und werde
Goethe and, 11:1801a
Steiner and, 11:1798b
"Stjärnan." *See* Södergran, Edith
STO. *See* Service de travail obligatoire
"Sto keno." *See* Ritsos, Yannis, *Dhiadhromos
kai skala*
"Sto Marx." *See* Ritsos, Yannis
Stock market in literature, Zola's *L'Argent*,
7:1534a–1535a
Stoicism
Augustine and, 1:23a-b
in Croce's *Filosofia della pratica*, 8:322a,
322b
Kosztolányi and, 10:1236a-b, 1246b–1247a
Montaigne and, 2:775a
in Pascal's view, 3:140b
of Vigny's "La mort du loup," 5:483b–484a
Weil and, 12:2787b, 2792b
see also Neo-Stoicism

"Stoker, The." *See* Kafka, Franz, *Amerika*, "Der Heizer"

Stolberg, Louise, countess of Albany, Alfieri and, 4:665b–666a, 670b

Stolp i utverzhdenie istiny. *See* Florenskii, Pavel

"Ston Ari." *See* Ritsos, Yannis, *To isteroghrafo tis dhoxas*

Stone. *See* Mandelshtam, Osip

Stone Guest, The. *See* Pushkin, Alexander

Stone Mug. *See* Queneau, Raymond, *Gueule de pierre*

Stone and Sky. *See* Jiménez, Juan Ramón, *Piedra y cielo*

Stone symbolism, of Seferis, 12:2264b–2265a

Stones, Repetitions, Barriers. *See* Ritsos, Yannis, *Petres Epanalipsis Kigklidhoma*

Stoppard, Tom, *Rosencranz and Guildenstern*, possible inspiration of, 10:1586b

Stora landsvägen. *See* Strindberg, August

"Stora trädgårdem, Den." *See* Södergran, Edith

Store spelet, Det. *See* Vesaas, Tarjei, *The Great Cycle*

"Storia del genere umano." *See* Leopardi, Giacomo, "The Story of the Human Race"

Storia della colonna infame. *See* Manzoni, Alessandro, *The Column of Infamy*

Storia della poesia di Giovanni Pascoli. *See* Petrocchi, Giorgio

Storia d'Europa nel secolo XIX. *See* Croce, Benedetto

Storia d'Italia dal 1871 al 1915. *See* Croce, Benedetto

"Storia ridotta sotto il concetto generale dell'arte." *See* Croce, Benedetto

Stories. *See* Calvino, Italo, *I racconti*

Stories. *See* Pasternak, Boris, *Rasskazy*

Stories and Sketches. *See* Gorky, Maxim, *Ocherki i rasskazy*

Stories for a Year. *See* Pirandello, Luigi, *Novelle per un anno*

Storm and Other Things, The. *See* Montale, Eugenio

Storm and Stress. *See* Klinger, Friedrich Maximilian von, *Sturm und Drang*

Storm and Stress movement. *See* Sturm und Drang

Storm, The. *See* Ferreira de Castro, José Maria, *A tempestade*

Storm, The. *See* Ostrovsky, Alexander, *Groza*

Storm, Theodor, **6:915a–922b**
  Aquis submersus, 6:921a-b
  Curator Carsten (*Carsten Curator*), 6:919b–920a
  Ein Doppelgänger (A Double), 6:920b
  Ein stiller Musikant (A Quiet Musician), 6:919b 920a
  "Gräber an der Küste" (Graves on the Coast), 6:916a-b
  Hans und Heinz Kirch (Hans and Heinz Kirch), 6:920a-b
  Im Saal (*In the Great Hall*), 6:917a
  Im Sonnenschein (*In the Sunlight*), 6:918a
  Immensee, 6:917a–918b
  Liederbuch dreier Freunde (Songbook of Three Friends), 6:915b
  Marthe und ihre Uhr (Marthe and Her Clock), 6:916b–917a
  on novella, 5:16a
  "Oktoberlied" (October Song), 6:916a
  "Ostern" (Easter), 6:916a
  Pole Poppenspäler, 6:918a
  Späte Rosen (Late Roses), 6:917a
  The Rider on the White Horse (*Der Schimmelreiter*), 6:922a-b
  "Von Katzen" (Of Cats), 6:916b

"Storming of the Redoubt, The." *See* Mérimée, Prosper, "L'Enlìvement de la redoute"

"Storozh." *See* Gorky, Maxim

"Story." *See* Rimbaud, Arthur, "Conte"

"Story About the Most Important Thing, A." *See* Zamyatin, Yevgeny Ivanovich

Story of Björn the Hítadal Champion, The. *See* *Bjarnar saga Hítdælakappa*

Story of the Changeling, The. *See* Pirandello, Luigi, *La favola del figlio cambiato*

Story of the Chevalier Des Grieux and Manon Lescaut, The. *See* Prévost, Antoine-François, *Histoire du chevalier Des Grieux et de Manon Lescaut*

Story of the Confederates, The. *See* *Bandamanna saga*

Story of Droplaug's Sons, The. See Droplaugarsona saga

"Story of a Farm Girl." *See* Mapuassant, Guy de, "Histoire d'une fille de ferme"

Story of Gunnlaug Serpent-Tongue, The. See Gunnlaugs saga ormstungu

Story of the Honorable Caspar and Fair Annie, The. See Brentano, Clemens, *Geschichte vom Braven Kasperl und dem schönen Annerl*

"Story of the Human Race, The." *See* Leopardi, Giacomo

Story of a Humble Christian. See Silone, Ignazio, *L'Avventura d'un povero cristiano*

Story of Killer-Glúm, The. See Víga-Glúms saga

Story of the Moor-killings, The. See Heiðarvíga saga

"Story of a Mother, The." *See* Andersen, Hans Christian

Story of Mr. Cleveland, Natural Son of Cromwell, Written by Himself and Translated from the English. *See* Prévost, Antoine-François, *Histoire de M. Cleveland, fils naturel de Cromwell* . . .

Story of My Dovecote, The. See Babel, Isaac

Story of My Life, The. See Sand, George

Story of My Pet Animals, The. See Dumas père, Alexandre, *Histoire de mes bêtes*

Story of Njál of the Burning, The. See Njáls saga

Story of a Novel, The. See Mann, Thomas, *Die Entstehung des "Doktor Faustus"*

"Story of the Old Days, A." *See* Maupassant, Guy de, "Histoire du vieux temps"

"Story of Poor Relations." *See* Balzac, Honoré de, "Histoire des parents pauvres"

"Story of the Quarrel of Ivan Ivanovich with Ivan Nikivorovich, The." *See* Gogol, Nikolay Vasilievich

Story of Rats; or, Virtue Leads to Crime, A. *See* Robbe-Grillet, Alain, "Histoire de rats ou La Vertu c'est ce qui mène au crime"

Story of Thórd Tumult, The. See Þórðar saga hreðu

Story of Thorstein Staff-struck, The. See Þorsteins þattr stangarhöggs

Story of Tobit and Sara, The. *See* Claudel, Paul, *L'Histoire de Tobie et de Sara*

"Story of a White Blackbird, The." *See* Musset, Alfred de, "Histoire d'un merle blanc"

Story of William Lovell, The. *See* Tieck, Ludwig, *Geschichte des Herrn William Lovell*

"Storyteller, The." *See* Benjamin, Walter, "Der Erzähler"

Storytelling

   Andrić and, 11:1774b, 1775b–1777b

   Benjamin on, 11:1728a

"Stous propodhes tis siopis." *See* Ritsos, Yannis

Stowaway, The. See Simenon, Georges, *Le passager clandestin*

Stowe, Calvin E., on Herder's understanding of Hebrew poetry, 4:653b–654a

Stowe, Harriet Beecher, *Uncle Tom's Cabin*, compared to Pellico's *Le mie prigioni* (*My Prisons*), 5:370a

Strada che va in città, La. See Ginzburg, Natalia, *The Road to the City*

"Strada di Agrigentum." *See* Quasimodo, Salvatore

Strait Is the Gate. See Gide, André, *La porte étroite*

Strakhov, N. N., Dostoevsky and, 7:1357a

Strändernas svall. See Johnson, Eyvind, *Return to Ithaca*

Strands of Hair, The. *See* Montale, Eugenio, *The Storm and Other Things* (*La bufera e altro*), "La frangia dei capelli"

Strange and Exemplary Histories. *See* Céspedes y Meneses, Gonzales, *Historias peregrinas y ejemplares*

Strange Fellow. See Lermontov, Mikhail Yurievich, *Stranny chelovek*

Strange Rider, The. See Ghelderode, Michel de, *Le cavalier bizarre*

"Strange Story, A." *See* Turgenev, Ivan

Stranger, Bear Word to the Spartans We . . .
　　See Böll, Heinrich, *Wanderer kommst
　　du nach Spa . . .*
Stranger, The. See Blok, Alexander,
　　Neznakomka; Camus, Albert
Stranger, The. See Schnitzler, Arthur, "Die
　　Fremde"
Stranger in Town, A. See Simenon, Georges,
　　Un nouveau dans la ville
Stranny chelovek. See Lermontov, Mikhail
　　Yurievich
Stransky, Christine von, Schlegel and, 5:198b
Straparola, Gianfrancesco, *Piacevoli notti
　　(Pleasant Nights)*, 2:941a-b
"Strashnaia mest'." *See* Gogol, Nikolay
　　Vasilyevich
Strauss, David
　　*Das Leben Jesu kritisch bearbeitet (The Life
　　　of Jesus Critically Examined*, 7:1659a-b
　　*Der alte und der neue Glaube (The Old
　　　Faith and the New)*, 7:1659b
　　Nietzsche and, 7:1659a-b
Strauss, Richard
　　Hofmannsthal and, 9:690a, 691a, 699b,
　　　705a–709a
　　Mann's *Doctor Faustus* and, 9:733b
Straussfedern. See Tieck, Ludwig
Stravinsky, Igor, 9:800a
　　and Cocteau, 10:1554a-b
　　The Rite of Spring (Le sacre du printemps),
　　　13:3032a
　　　acmeism and, 10:1632b
　　　and Cocteau, 10:1545b
Strawberry Ice Cream Cone. See Ginzburg,
　　Natalia, *Fragola e panna*
Stream-of-consciousness technique
　　Bergson and, 8:56b, 64b
　　Kafka and, 9:1160b–1161a
　　in Laforgue's poems, 7:1887b, 1906a
　　Schnitzler's use of, 8:98b–99a, 109a
"Street in Agrigentum." *See* Quasimodo,
　　Salvatore, "Strada di Agrigentum"
Street Ballads. See Laforgue, Jules, *Les
　　complaintes*
Strega Prize, awarded to Lampedusa's *The
　　Leopard*, 11:2011a
Streicher, Andreas, 5:32b

Streltsy, the, in Akhmatova's *Requiem*,
　　10:1532b
Strength to Wait, The. *See* Breton, André, "La
　　force d'attendre"
Strict Youth, The (motion picture). *See Strogi
　　yunosha*
Strife. See Galsworthy, John
Strindberg, August, **7:1731a–1757b**, 11:2203a
　　"A Doll House," 7:1753b
　　A Dream Play (Drömspelet), 7:1732a, 1739a,
　　　1741b, 1746b, 1748a, 1748b, 1752a-b,
　　　12:2663b
　　　Ionesco and, 13:3016b
　　　Lagerkvist and, 10:1687a
　　Advent, 7:1739a
　　Anouilh and, 13:2860a
　　Antibarbus, 7:1738a
　　"Autumn," 7:1740a
　　Bandet (The Bond), 7:1744b–1745a
　　Blok and, 9:978b
　　Blomstermålningar (Flower Paintings),
　　　8:29b
　　Brända tomten (The Burned House),
　　　7:1741b, 1744b
　　Charles XII, 7:1745b
　　Chekhov and, 7:1855a
　　Creditors (Fordringsägare), 7:1732b, 1735a,
　　　1736a, 1741b, 1742a, 1744a
　　Crimes and Crimes (Brott och brott),
　　　7:1739a, 1744a, 1748b
　　Debit och Kredit (Debit and Credit), 7:1744b
　　Den Fredlöse (The Freethinker), 7:1741a
　　Den starkare (The Stronger), 7:1744a, 1745a
　　*Des arts nouveaux, ou Le hasard dans la
　　　production artistique* (The New Arts; or,
　　　The Role of Chance in Artistic
　　　Creation), 7:1738a-b
　　Dikter på vers och prosa, 12:2657a
　　Easter (Påsk), 7:1739a, 1742a, 1745b,
　　　1751b–1752a
　　Ekelöf and, 12:2657a–2658a, 2663b
　　En häxa (A Witch), 7:1741a
　　Ensame (Alone), 7:1738b, 1739a
　　Erik XIV, 7:1745b, 1749b
　　Études funèbres (Graveyard Reveries),
　　　7:1738a

Första varningen (*The First Warning*), 7:1743b

Getting Married (*Giftas*), 7:1732a-b, 1739b–1740a

Ghelderode and, 11:2113b

Gustav Vasa, 7:1745b

Hamsun and, 8:23a, 24a, 25a, 26a, 29b–30a

Hemsöborna (*The People of Hemsö*), 7:1740a–1741b, 11:2208a

Herr Bengts Husfru (*Herr Bengt's Wife*), 7:1735a, 1753b

Himmelrikets nycklar (*The Keys to the Kingdom of Heaven*), 7:1746a

I havsbandet (*By the Open Sea*), 7:1741a

Ibsen and, 8:29a

"Indiansommar" (Indian Summer), 12:2657a-b

Inferno, 7:1736a, 1736b, 1738a

Inför döden (*In the Face of Death*), 7:1743b

Jarry and, 9:666a

Kafka and, 9:1156a

Kamraterna (*Comrades*), 7:1753b, 1754a

Klostret (*The Cloister*), 7:1736a

Kronbruden (*The Bridal Crown*), 7:1739

Le plaidoyer d'un fou (*A Madman's Defense*), 7:1734b

Légendes (*Legends*), 7:1738b

Lucky Per's Journey (*Lycko-Pers resa*), 7:1735a, 1746a

Master Olof, 7:1745b, 1749b, 1754a

Miss Julie (*Fröken Julie*), 7:1732b, 1735a-b, 1736a, 1741b–1742a, 1745a, 1749b, 1750a-b

Moberg and, 11:2208a

Moderskärlek (*Motherlove*), 7:1743b

"Natural Obstacles," 7:1740a

O'Neill and, 7:1443b

Oväder (*Storm Weather*), 7:1741b, 1747b

Paria (*Pariah*), 7:1744b, 1745a

Pelikanen (*The Pelican*), 7:1741b, 1744a, 1745a

Queen Christina (*Kristina*), 7:1739a, 1745b, 1750b

Röda rummet (The Red Room), 11:2213b

Samum (*Simoom*), 7:1745a

Stora landsvägen (*The Great Highway*), 7:1741a, 1746a

Svanevit (*Swanwhite*), 7:1739a, 1747b

Svarta fanor (Black Banners), 7:1741a

Sylva sylvanum, 7:1738a

Syndaboken (*The Scapegoat*), 7:1741a

Taklagsöl (*The Roofing Feast*), 7:1741a

The Blue Book, 7:1739a

The Dance of Death (*Dödsdansen*), 7:1739a, 1742a, 1743b, 1749a-b

The Father (*Fadren*), 7:1732b, 1735a, 1736a, 1741b, 1742a, 1743a, 1745a-b, 1749a-b, 1750b–1751a

The Ghost Sonata (*Spöksonaten*), 7:1739, 1741b, 1744b, 1746b–1747a

Lagerkvist and, 10:1679b

"The Phoenix," 7:1740a

The Red Room (*Röda rummet*), 7:1739b–1740a, 1740b–1741a

The Son of a Servant (*Tjänstekvinnans son*), 7:1732a, 1732b–1733a, 1739b, 1743a-b, 1754a-b, 8:26a

To Damascus (*Till Damaskus*), 7:1737b, 1739a, 1741b, 1746a, 1747b, 1751a-b, 1753a, 1753b

Ionesco and, 13:3015a, 3016b

Tschandala, 7:1741a

well-made play and, 7:1931a

Strogi yunosha (The Strict Youth) (motion picture), Olesha and, 11:2235a, 2248b

Stroll in the Air, A. See Ionesco, Eugène, *Le piéton de l'air*

Stroller in the Paris Insurrection, A. *See* Sartre, Jean-Paul, "Un promeneur dans Paris insurgé"

Strömberg, Ragnar, Ekelöf and, 12:2636a

Strong as Death. See Maupassant, Guy de, *Fort comme la mort*

Stronger than Death. See Gautier, Théophile, *Spirite*

Stronger, The. See Strindberg, August, *Den starkare*

Strophe. See Seferis, George

Strophic form

Deschamps and, 1:372b

in Hebbel's "Welt und Ich," 6:1117b–1118a

Strountes. See Ekelöf, Gunnar

Struck. *See* Gunnarsson, Gunnar, *Ramt*

Structuralism, 13:3079a–3080b

Structuralism (*cont.*)
Barthes and, 13:3079a, 3087a–3089a, 3092b–3094a, 3095b
Foucault and, 13:3334a-b
Gombrowicz and, 12:2568a, 2569a–2570a
origins of, 13:3092a-b
Rabelais and, 2:701a
Valéry and, 8:587a
vs. academic criticism, 13:3089b–3091a
Structure, in Strindberg's works, 7:1745a–1747a
Structures, Foucault and, 13:3331a–3333b
Struggle with the Angel, The. *See* Malraux, André, *La lutte avec l'ange*
Struggle for Life, The. *See* Baroja, Pío, *La lucha por la vida*
Stuarts, Les. *See* Dumas père, Alexandre
"Stückchen Theologie, Ein." *See* Hesse, Hermann
Studien über Hysterie (*Studies in Hysteria*). *See* Freud, Sigmund (with Joseph Breuer)
Studien über Shakespeare und das alt-englische Theater. See Tieck, Ludwig
Studies. *See* Ritsos, Yannis, *Meletimata*
Studies in European Realism. See Lukács, György
Studies of Manners in the Nineteenth Century. *See* Balzac, Honoré de, *Études de moeurs au XIXme siècle*
Studies in Roman History. *See* Mérimée, Prosper, *Études sur l'histoire romaine*
Studies of Shakespeare and the Old English Theater. *See* Tieck, Ludwig, *Studien über Shakespeare und das alt-englische Theater*
Studies of Vergil. See Sainte-Beuve, Charles-Augustin, *Étude sur Virgile*
Studiiya impressionistov (Impressionists' Studio) (miscellany), Khlebnikov's participation in, 10:1334a
Studiorem ducem. See Pius XI, Pope
Study, A. *See* Hašek, Jaroslav, "Etuda"
Stuff of Dreams, The. *See* Butor, Michel, *Matière de rêves*
Stuff of Youth, The. See Mauriac, François
Stumpf, Carl, Musil and, 9:932a

Stund på jorden, Din. See Moberg, Vilhelm, *A Time on Earth*
Stunde der wahren Empfindung, Die. See Handke, Peter
"Stunde des Erkennens" (Hour of Recognition). *See* Schnitzler, Arthur
Stunde hinter Mitternacht. See Hesse, Hermann
Stunden im Garten. See Hesse, Hermann
Stundenbuch, Das. See Rilke, Rainer Maria
Sturla Thórðarson
Hákonar saga gamla, 1:399a-b
Íslendinga saga (*History of the Icelanders*), 1:399a
Kristni saga, 1:399a
Sturlubók, 1:393a, 396b, 397a, 397b
Sturlu saga, 1:399a
Sturlubók. See Sturla Thórðarson
Sturlunga saga, 1:377a, 390b, 396a, 398b, 399a
Gunnarsson and, 10:1515a
Sturm und Drang
Burckhardt and, 6:1226b
Goethe and, 5:4b, 5a, 16b, 18b, 20a
Goethe's *Götz von Berlichingen* and, 5:431b
Herder's influence on, 4:645b
Klopstock and, 4:523a
Lessing's influence on, 4:546b
Lukács on, 10:1270a
Schiller and, 5:31a, 33b
Wieland and, 4:609b–610a
Sturm und Drang. See Klinger, Friedrich Maximilian von
Sturzenegger, Hans, Hesse and, 9:837a
Style, Musil on, 9:954a-b
Style Goncourt, 7:1397b, 1399a-b, 1400b–1401a, 1402b–1403a
in Verlaine's works, 7:1630b, 1632a
Style of La Fontaine's "Fables," The. See Biard, Jean Dominique
Style in Language. See Jakobson, Roman
"Style and Tradition." *See* Montale, Eugenio
Styrmir the Learned, 1:388a, 399a
"Su sitio fiel." *See* Jiménez, Juan Ramón
Suard, Madame Jean-Baptiste, the salon of, 4:407b
Suarès, André, Claudel and, 8:487b

Subjective, allegory and, 1:321b–322a
Subjectivism
    Foscolo and, 5:328b
    Proust on, 8:565b–566a
Subjectivity, Foucault and, 13:3324a–3326a
Subjugation, Foucault and, 13:3326a
Sublime Malady, The. See Pasternak, Boris
Sublime moment, Klopstock and, 4:511b
Submerged Seaport, The. *See* Ungaretti,
    Giuseppe, *Il porto sepolto*
Substance, Aquinas on, 1:424a
Succession of the Kings of Norway. See
    Noregs konungatal
"Succession without distinction," in Bergson's
    thought, 8:50a
Sucesos y prodigios de amor en ocho novelas
    ejemplares. See Montalbán, Juan Pérez
    de
"Such, Such Were the Joys." *See* Orwell,
    George
"Suchanzeigen." *See* Böll, Heinrich
"Sud." *See* Babel, Isaac
Suddenly It's Evening. See Quasimodo,
    Salvatore
Sudermann, Hermann, Ibsen's influence on,
    7:1443b
Sue, Eugène
    Dostoevsky and, 7:1351a-b
    Maupassant and, 7:1776a
Sueur, Eustache, Delacroix and, 5:531a
"Suffered Forms of Trees." *See* Quasimodo,
    Salvatore, "D'alberi sofferte forme"
Suffering, theme of
    in Apollinaire's "The Hills," 9:900b
    in Kundera, 13:3398b
    in Leconte de Lisle, 6:1265a–1266a
    in Mauriac, 10:1323b
    Schopenhauer on, 11:2224b
Sufferings of an Inventor, The. See Balzac,
    Honoré de, *David Séchard ou les*
    souffrances d'un inventeur
Suffrage, universal, Tocqueville on, 6:896a
Suhrkamp, Peter, Frisch and, 13:2902a,
    2907a-b
Suicide
    Alfieri's view of, 5:321b
    of Antero de Quental, 7:1694b
    in Apollinaire's "The Song of the Unloved
        Lover," 9:890b
    Artaud on, 11:1967a
    of Benjamin, 11:1729a
    Blok and, 9:965b, 979a
    Camus and, 13:3066a
    in Chateaubriand's works, 5:121a
    in Corneille's *Le Cid*, 3:29a-b, 30a
    in Elytis' "Light Tree," 13:2973a
    in Frisch's works, 13:2918b
    in Galdós' *Miau*, 7:1612b
    in Goethe's works
        Faust, 5:20a-b
        The Sorrows of Young Werther, 5:5b, 6a,
            6b, 7a-b
    Gorky and, 8:418a
    in Hölderlin's works, 5:157a-b, 158a
    in Ibsen's *Rosmersholm*, 7:1930a
    Kierkegaard and, 6:1128b–1129a
    of Kleist, 5:309a–310a
    in Leopardi's works, 5:544b, 557b
    in Lukács' "On Poverty of Spirit,"
        10:1254b–1255a
    in Mallarmé's "Victorieusement fui le
        suicide beau," 7:1567b–1568b,
        1569b–1570a, 1574b
    in Maupassant, 7:1774b
    of Mayakovsky, 11:1839a
    of Moberg, 11:2229b
    Montaigne's "A Custom of the Island of
        Cea" on, 2:775b–776a
    of Montherlant, 11:1934b–1935a
    in Musset's works, 6:1001a
    Nerval and, 6:943b, 957b, 968a
    Novalis and, 5:207a
    Pavese and, 12:2759a-b, 2763a, 2781b
    in Richter's works
        Hesperus, 5:65b
        "The Speech of Christ," 5:59a
        Titan, 5:74a
    Schopenhauer's view of, 5:409b–410a
    Staël on, 5:92b
    Trakl and, 10:1416a
    of Tsvetaeva, 11:1748a
    Vesaas and, 11:2041b, 2052a
    Witkiewicz and, 10:1211b–1212b

"Suicide from Enthusiasm." *See* Berlioz, Hector

Suite de l'entretien. See Diderot, Denis

Suite du menteur, La. See Corneille, Pierre

"Sulak." *See* Babel, Isaac

Sulfur mining, Pirandello and, 8:390b, 391b

"Sulla forma scientifica del materialismo storico." *See* Croce, Benedetto, *Materialismo storico ed economia marxistica*

"Sulle fronde dei salici." *See* Quasimodo, Salvatore

Sult. See Hamsun, Knut

"Sumerlei svobody." *See* Mandelshtam, Osip

Sumichrast, Frederick-Caesar de, translations of Gautier by, 6:1035b–1036a, 1054a

Summa. See Albertus Magnus

Summa contra Gentiles. See Aquinas, Thomas, St.

Summa (journal), Broch and, 10:1386b

Summa theologica. See Aquinas, Thomas, St.

Summary Against the Gentiles, A. See Aquinas, Thomas, St., *Summa contra Gentiles*

Summary of the Art of French Poetry. See Ronsard, Pierre de, *Abrégé de l'art poétique*

Summary of Theology, A. See Aquinas, Thomas, St., *Summa theologica*

Summer. See Camus, Albert

Summer. See Jiménez, Juan Ramón, *Estío*

"Summer." *See* Pasternak, Boris, *My Sister, Life*; Trakl, Georg, "Sommer"

Summer Folk. See Gorky, Maxim, *Dachniki*

"Summer Memories." *See* Södergran, Edith, "Sommarminnen"

Summer Rages. See D'Annunzio, Gabriele, "Furit aestus"

Summer Solstice, The. See Montherlant, Henry de, *Le solstice de juin*

Summer Sonata. See Valle-Inclán, Ramón del, *Sonatas: Memorias del Marqués de Bradomín* (*The Pleasant Memoirs of the Marquis de Bradomín*), *Sonata de estío*

"Summer in the South, A." *See* Andrić, Ivo

Summer's Victory. See George, Stefan, *Das Jahr der Seele* (The Year of the Soul), "Sieg des Sommers"

Summing Up, A. See Kosztolányi, Dezső, *Számadás*

"Summons to Feeling, A." *See* Rilke, Rainer Maria, "Es winkt zu Fühlung"

Sun the First. See Elytis, Odysseus, *Ilios o protos*

"Sun and Flesh" ("Soleil et chair," "Credo in unam"). *See* Rimbaud, Arthur

Sun imagery
   in Elytis's poetry, 13:2974a
      "I Genesis," 13:2968b
      Ilios o protos, 13:2961a
      "Lakonikon," 13:2967a
   in Laforgue's poetry
      "The Ballad of the King of Thule," 7:1889b–1890a
      in "The Mystery of Three Horns," 7:1899b

Sun King. *See* Louis XIV of France, king

Sun Sets, The. See Ghelderode, Michel de, *Le soleil se couche*

Sunday. See Simenon, Georges, *Dimanche*

Sunday Circle. *See* Lukács Circle

Sunday of Life, The. See Queneau, Raymond, *Le dimanche de la vie*

"Sundays." *See* Laforgue, Jules, "Dimanches"

"Sung by One Who Was There." *See* Perse, Saint-John, *Chant pour un équinoxe* (*Song for an Equinox*), "Chant par celle qui fut là"

Sunken Bell, The. See Hauptmann, Gerhart

Sunken Oboe. See Quasimodo, Salvatore

Sun's Eve. See Ritsos, Yannis, *Dhokimasia*

Sunset. See Babel, Isaac, *Zakat*

"Sunset." *See* Rilke, Rainer Maria, "Sonnen-Untergang"

Sunset Boulevard, Heinrich Mann and, 8:527b, 528b

"Sunsets." *See* Hugo, Victor, "Soleils couchants"

Suo marito. See Pirandello, Luigi

Superego, Freud's concept of, 8:4b, 6a

Superfluous man, Turgenev and, 6:1279a-b

Supermale, The. See Jarry, Alfred, *Le surmâle*

Superman

Babel's version of, 11:1900b–1901a, 1907a
Baroja's protagonists and, 9:599a-b, 604a
in Chekhov's "The Black Monk," 7:1867a-b
in D'Annunzio's writings, 8:68b, 180a,
    184b–186b, 188b, 191a-b, 202a
in Nietzsche's thought, 8:184b–185b
in Svevo's novels, 8:74b, 75b, 85b
see also Overman
"Supernational Manifesto." *See* Mann,
    Heinrich, *Das Bekenntnis zum
    Übernationalen*
Supernatural
in Ariosto, 2:639b–640a
Baroja and, 9:593a
in Chrétien's works, 1:145a
in Emerson's works, 5:551a-b
in Hoffmann, 5:280a-b, 281b–286a,
    283a–285b
Huysmans and, 7:1720b–1722a
in Mérimée's works, 6:746b, 760b–761b,
    764b
in Mickiewicz's *Forefathers*, 5:611a-b
in Poe's works, 5:551a-b
in Shelley's works, 5:551a-b
in Tieck, 5:243a, 252b
in Turgenev, 6:1281a-b, 1289a
in Welsh legends, 1:142b–143a
see also Ghosts; Occult
Supernatural order, Aquinas on, 1:424b
Supernatural realism, Huysmans and,
    7:1720b–1721b
Superrealismo. See Azorín, *El libro de Levante*
Superstition
Strindberg and, 7:1731a, 1736b
in Valle-Inclán's *Flor de santidad*, 8:336a-b
Supertales (*sverkhpovesti*), of Khlebnikov,
    10:1359b–1362b
Superwoman themes, in D'Annunzio, 8:196a,
    197a-b
Suppers, The. See Grazzini, Antonfrancesco,
    Le cene
Supplément au voyage de Bougainville. See
    Diderot, Denis
Supplément au voyage de Cook. See
    Giraudoux, Jean
Suppositi, I. See Ariosto, Lodovico
Suppôts et supplications. See Artaud, Antonin

Supreme Instinct, The. *See* Ferreira de Castro,
    José Maria, *O instinto supremo*
"Sur la Mort de Marie." *See* Ronsard, Pierre de
"Sur la route de San Romano." *See* Breton,
    André
Sur Racine. See Barthes, Roland, *On Racine*
Suréna. See Corneille, Pierre
Surf Heath. *See* Gunnarsson, Gunnar,
    Brimheiði
Surgères, Hélène de, 2:730b
Surmâle, Le. See Jarry, Alfred
Surprise. *See* García Lorca, Federico,
    "Sorpresa"
Surrealism
in Anouilh's writing, 13:2862b
Apollinaire and, 9:895a, 896a, 899b
in Apollinaire's "The Hills," 9:901a
Aragon and, 11:2066b
Arp and, 10:1365b, 1371a–1372a
Artaud and, 11:1964b–1965a, 1966b–1967a
automatism, 11:1949b, 1951b–1952a, 1954a,
    1957a-b
in Azorín's works, 9:639b, 652a-b
Benjamin's essays on, 11:1722a-b
Breton's contribution to, 11:1940a–1941a,
    1943b, 1944b–1945a, 1946b–1947a,
    1958a-b, 2064a-b, 2066b
Cela and, 13:3116a–3117b
Cocteau and, 10:1546b–1547a
communism and, 11:2072a–2073b
Dadaism and, 11:2062b, 2064a
"daily magic," 11:1942a
definition, 11:1951b
Ekelöf and, 12:2635a, 2639b
Elytis and, 13:2957b–2958b, 2960b, 2962b
in France, *see also* Aragon, Louis
French communists and, 11:2069a-b
Greek poetry and, 12:2815b
Kafka and, 9:1157a-b
Kundera and, 13:3389b
Moravia and, 12:2679a
painting, Breton on, 11:1949b–1950a
period of activity, 11:1948a
politicization of, 11:2067a–2068b
post–World War II, 11:1948a-b
Queneau and, 12:2513b–2514a
Rimbaud and, 7:1787a-b

Surrealism (*cont.*)
  theory of immanence, 11:1943a
  Valéry and, 8:569a, 581a, 583b–584a
  see also Azorín, *El libro de Levante* (The
    Book of the Levante); Breton, André
Surrealism and Painting. See Breton, André,
  Le surréalisme et la peinture
Surréalisme au service de la révolution, Le
  (Surrealism at the Service of the
  Revolution), 11:2071a-b, 2073b–2074b
Surréalisme et la peinture, Le. See Breton,
  André
Surrealist Manifesto. See Breton, André,
  Manifeste du surréalisme
Sursis, Le. See Sartre, Jean-Paul, *The Reprieve*
Surveiller et punir. See Foucault, Michel,
  Discipline and Punish
Suspicion, The. *See* Dürrenmatt, Friedrich,
  The Quarry
Sutton Hoo ship burial, *Beowulf* and, 1:64b,
  69b
Suvorin, Aleksey S., Chekhov and, 7:1856a
Suzanne et le Pacifique (*Suzanne and the
  Pacific*). *See* Giraudoux, Jean
Svanevit (*Swanwhite*). *See* Strindberg, August
Svarfdœla saga, 1:398b
Sværmere. See Hamsun, Knut
Svarstad, Anders Castus, 9:1022a-b
Svarstad, Christiane Undset, 9:1018a
Svarstad, Hans Benedict Undset, 9:1018b
Svarta fanor (Black Banners). *See* Strindberg,
  August
Svarte hestane, Dei. See Vesaas, Tarjei
Svartfugl. See Gunnarsson, Gunnar
Svecha na vetru. See Solzhenitsyn, Aleksandr
"*Svedskaya spichka.*" *See* Chekhov, Anton
Svensk strävan. See Moberg, Vilhelm
Sverris saga. See Karl Jónsson
Svĕt zvířat (Animal World), Hašek's editorship
  of, 9:1093b
"*Svĕtci a zvířata.*" *See* Hašek, Jaroslav
Svevo, Italo, **8:67a–87b**
  A Life (*Una vita*), 8:68a-b, 72a–76b, 82b,
    85b
  As a Man Grows Older (*Senilità*), 8:68a-b,
    69a, 74b, 76b–79b, 82b, 84b
  Ginzburg and, 13:3133a

"*L'Uomo e la teoria darvinia*" (Man and
  Darwinian Theory), 8:85b
The Confessions of Zeno (*La coscienza di
  Zeno*), 8:69b, 73b, 80a–84a, 84b, 85a,
  85b
  Vittorini and, 12:2735b
Sviatogor's Mound. *See* Khlebnikov, Velimir,
  "*Kurgan Sviatogora*"
"*Svoiasi.*" *See* Khlebnikov, Velimir,
  "Self-Statement"
Svyatopolk-Mirsky, Dmitri, Prince
  on Mandelshtam's *The Noise of Time*,
    10:1623b, 1624a
  on Pasternak, 10:1598b, 1600a
"Swallow and the Little Birds, The." *See* La
  Fontaine, Jean de, *Fables*, "L'Hirondelle
  et les petits oiseaux"
"Swan, The." *See* Baudelaire, Charles
"Swanland in the Future." *See* Khlebnikov,
  Velimir, "*Lebediia budushchego*"
Swann's Way. See Proust, Marcel,
  Remembrance of Things Past (*À la
  recherche du temps perdu*)
Swastika, in Ionesco's *The Lesson*,
  13:2993b–2994a
Sweden, Strindberg in, 7:1733b, 1737b–1738a,
  1739a-b
Swedenborg, Emanuel
  Arcana coelestia, 7.1737.b
  De coelo et ejus mirabilibus et de inferno,
    7:1737b
  Ekelöf and, 12:2668a-b
  Richter and, 5:58b
  Strindberg and, 7:1737b, 1753a
Swedish Academy
  Ekelöf in, 12:2637b
  Moberg's criticism of, 11:2203b
Swedish literature, translations of Chrétien's
  works, 1:153a
"Swedish Match, The." *See* Chekhov, Anton,
  "*Svedskaya spichka*"
Swedish Struggle, The. *See* Moberg, Vilhelm,
  Svensk strävan
Sweeney Agonistes. See Eliot, T. S.
"Sweet Memories of Past Glory." *See* Camoëns,
  Luís Vaz de, *Rimas* (*Lyrics*), "Doces
  lembranças da passada glória"

Świadectwo poezji. See Milosz, Czeslaw, *The Witness of Poetry*

"*Świat.*" *See* Milosz, Czeslaw

Światło dzienne. See Milosz, Czeslaw

Swift, Jonathan
  A Tale of a Tub, 9:674a-b
  Čapek and, 10:1574a, 1574b, 1575b
  Céline and, 11:1872a
  Dinesen and, 10:1294b
  Discourse Concerning the Mechanical Operation of the Spirit, 9:674b
  and Jarry, 9:674a-b
  La Rochefoucauld's *Maximes* and, 3:53a

Swinburne, Algernon Charles
  Maupassant and, 7:1760a
  Sade praised by, 4:637a

Switzerland, Södergran in, 11:1784b

Sword of Kotovs'kyi. *See* Tychyna, Pavlo, *Shablia Kotovs'koho*

Sworn Borthers, The. See Gunnarsson, Gunnar

Sybil of Cumae, 6:952b

Sydney, Philip
  Arcadia, 2:923b
    Gil Polo's sequel to *Diana* and, 2:923a

Syllogism, in Ionesco's *Rhinocéros,* 13:3001b–3002a

"Sylphe, Le" ("The Sylph"). *See* Valéry, Paul, *Charmes*

Sylva sylvanum. See Strindberg, August

Sylvae. See Poliziano, Angelo

Sylvanire. See Mairet, Jean

Sylvester I, pope, 1:443a-b

Sylvester II, pope, scholasticism and, 1:406a

Sylvie. See Nerval, Gérard de

Symbolism
  allegory and, 1:6b, 320a–321b
  art and, 7:1709b
  Baudelaire and, 7:1333a-b
  biblical, Augustine's *On Christian Doctrine* and, 1:43b
  in Blasco Ibáñez' *The Mayflower,* 8:363b–364a
  in Broch's writings, 10:1404b–1405a
  Camus and, 13:3074a
  Canetti and, 12:2627b–2628a
  in Colette's works, 9:629b–630a, 634b
  Ekelöf and, 12:2635a-b

Gombrowicz and, 12:2569b
in Hesse's works, 9:844a-b
  Narcissus and Goldmund, 9:850a
in Ibsen's works, 7:1431a, 1431a-b, 1434a, 1434b, 1439b–1440a, 1445b
  Rosmersholm, 7:1930a-b
in Lampedusa's *The Leopard,* 11:2011b–2020b
in Machado's "El viajero," 9:751b
in Mann's *Magic Mountain,* 9:722b
Martinson and, 12:2635b
mathematical. *See* Mathematical symbolism
in Pavese's works, 12:2772a
in Prudentius' works, 1:15b
  Cathemerinon, 1:6b, 7a-b
in Rabelais's *Gargantua,* 2:706a, 707b
religious
  in Akhmatova's poetry, 10:1526b–1527b
  in Hesse's *Demian,* 9:840a-b
  in Ionesco's *Hunger and Thirst,* 13:3010a
  in Musil's *The Man Without Qualities,* 9:942a
  in Sarraute's works, 12:2353a-b
in Sarraute's works, 12:2343a, 2352a
in Strindberg's works, 7:1742a
Trakl and, 10:1413a, 1418b–1419a
in Vesaas' works, 11:2049a–2049b, 2050b
in Vittorini's works, 12:2739a
see also Bely, Andrey, *Simvolizm;* Blok, Alexander, "On the Present State of Russian Symbolism'; Criminal symbolism; Object-symbols; Religious symbolism

Symbolist movement
  Ady and, 9:859b, 863a
  Apollinaire and, 9:885b, 887a, 890b
    Alcools, 9:886a
  Arp and, 10:1366b
  Azorín and, 9:639b
  in Belgium, Maeterlinck and, 8.121ab, 8:123b, 124b–125b
  dramas, by Maeterlinck, 8:124b–125b
  Dreyfus Affair and, 9:886b
  French
    Dinesen and, 10:1298a
    in drama, 7:1931a
    literary devices of, 10:1484a

Symbolist movement (*cont.*)
   French (*cont.*)
      Pascoli and, 7:1831b
      Pessoa and, 10:1484a, 1485b
      positivism and, 7:1577a
      Seferis and, 13:2956b
      in Spain, 9:744b–745a, 753a
      Tsvetaeva and, 11:1734a
      Verlaine and, 7:1641b, 1709b
    George and, 8:450a, 450b
    Gide and, 8:495a, 495b
    influence on Greek poetry, 12:2815b
    Jarry and, 9:674b–675a
    Juliette Adam and, 8:572b
    Machado and, 9:750a, 753b
    Mallarmé and, 7:1567a, 1572a-b, 1577a,
      1592b, 1641b, 1709b
    Marinetti and, 9:798b, 799a, 805b, 812a
    Mauriac and, 10:1308b
    Novalis as precursor of, 5:224b
    Rimbaud and, 7:1623a
    Russian, 9:963a-b, 974b–975a, 11:1731b,
      1839a-b
      acmeism and, 10:1522b–1523a
      Akhmatova's objections to, 10:1522b
      Akhmatova's *Poem Without a Hero* and,
        10:1534a
      Bely and, 9:913b–914a, 919b, 926b–927a
      Blok and, 9:961a-b, 962b–964a, 967b
      Blok's essay on, 9:972b, 974a, 976a-b
      crisis in, 9:976a-b
      downfall of Petrine Russia and, 10:1619a,
        1620a-b
      Khlebnikov and, 10:1333b–1334a, 1348b
      Lermontov and, 6:1200b
      Mandelshtam and, 10:1626b–1627b
      Merezhkovsky and, 9:962b, 967b
      Pasternak and, 10:1592a, 1598a
      romanticism and, 9:963b
      in St. Petersburg, 9:967b
      Tsvetaeva and, 11:1731b–1732a
    Seferis and, 12:2260b–2261a, 2269a
    Spanish, Jiménez and, 9:994a, 995b, 1009b,
      1010b–1011b
    Tychyna and, 10:1662b–1663b
    Valéry and, 8:569b, 571b
    Yourcenar and, 12:2537b

    see also Neo-symbolism
Symbolist Movement in Literature, The. See
    Symons, Arthur
Symbols of Transformation. See Jung, Carl
"Symetha." *See* Vigny, Alfred Victor de,
    Poèmes antiques et modernes
Symmachus. See Prudentius, *Two Books*
    Against the Address of Symmachus
Symmachus, Quintus Aurelius, 1:9b–10a, 14b,
    17a
Symons, Arthur
   on the Goncourts, 7:1401b, 1406a
   Ibsen and, 7:1436b
   The Symbolist Movement in Literature,
     7:1642a
   Verlaine and, 7:1642a
Sympathien. See Wieland, Christoph Martin
Symphilosophy, Schlegel and, 5:200a
"Symphonie en blanc majeur." *See* Gautier,
    Théophile
Symphonie fantastique. See Berlioz, Hector
Symphonie funèbre et triomphale. See Berlioz,
    Hector
Symphonie pastorale, La. See Gide, André,
    The Pastoral Symphony
Symphonies. See Bely, Andrey
"Symposion." *See* Kundera, Milan
Symposium. See Plato
Synaesthesia, Trakl and, 10:1418b–1419a
Syncretism, in Camoëns' "Sôbolos rios,"
    2:754a
"Syncrétisme et alternance." *See* Montherlant,
    Henry de
Syndaboken (The Scapegoat). See Strindberg,
    August
Synecdoche, in Rabelais's *Fourth Book*, 2:712b
Synesthesia, in poetry of Apollinaire, 9:886b,
    887b
Synge, John Millington
   on Ibsen, 7:1436b
   Jiménez and, 9:992a
   Riders to the Sea, 9:1004a
"Syngrou Avenue, 1930." *See* Seferis, George,
    "Leophoros Syngrou, 1930"
Syntax
   in Butor's *Degrees*, 13:3298a

deconstruction of, by Marinetti, 9:814b,
816a-b, 817a

Trakl's, 10:1420a-b

see also Language

Syntheim, John, Erasmus and, 2:572a

"Syntheses," futurist. *See Sintesi*

Synthesis, *see also* Dualism

Synthesis, Hegelian. *See* Dialectics, Hegelian

Synthetism

of Zamyatin, 10:1198a-b

see also Neorealism

Syphilis

Ady's account of, 9:875a

Baudelaire and, 7:1325a

Dinesen and, 10:1286b, 1287b, 1290b–1291a

in Mann's *Doctor Faustus*, 9:733a-b, 735a,
875a

Maupassant and, 7:1761b, 1782b

Nietzsche and, 7:1679b

Systematic theology. *See* Theology, systematic

Système de la mode. See Barthes, Roland, *The
Fashion System*

Systole and Diastole. *See* Montherlant, Henry
de, "Syncrétisme et alternance"

Számadás. See Kosztolányi, Dezső

Szekfü, Gyula, 9:865b

"Szent Junius hivása." *See* Ady, Endre

"Szeptemberi áhítat." *See* Kosztolányi, Dezső

Szerda (journal), 9:875a

"Szeretném, ha szeretnének." *See* Ady, Endre

Szewcy. See Witkiewicz, Stanisław Ignacy

Szymanowski, Karol, Witkiewicz and,
10:1209a-b, 1211b–1212a

T

T. S. Eliot. See Seferis, George

t zero. See Calvino, Italo

Tabidze, Titsian, Pasternak and, 10:1595b,
1614b

Table ronde, La (journal), Mauriac and,
10:1307b

Table Talk. See Luther, Martin

Table-aux-crevés, La. See Aymé, Marcel, *The
Hollow Field*

*Tableau historique et critique de la poésie
française et du théâtre française au
XVIième siècle. See* Sainte-Beuve,
Charles-Augustin

Tableau, Le. See Ionesco, Eugène

Tableaux, Strindberg's use of, 7:1747a–1748b

Tableaux Parisiens. See Baudelaire, Charles

Taccuino del vecchio, Il. See Ungaretti,
Giuseppe

Tacitus, Cornelius

Alfieri's *Philip* compared to trial accounts
of, 4.680a

De Germania

Hölderlin and, 5:165a

Staël's *De l'Allemagne* and, 5:105a

Machiavelli and, 2:597a

Vico and, 3:298a

Tactics and Ethics. See Lukács, György

"Tactile art," 9:899a

"Tactile Theater, The." *See* Marinetti, Filippo
Tommaso, "Il teatro tattile"

Tactilism, Marinetti and, 9:826b

"Taedium vitae." *See Noia*

Tafuri, Manfredo

on artists, 9:823a

on futurist theater, 9:821a

Modern Architecture, 9:803b

"Tag des Hirten." *See* George, Stefan, *Die
Bücher der Hirten- und Preisgedichte
. . .* (The Books of Eclogues and
Eulogies), *Hirtengedichte*

"Tag och skriv." *See* Ekelöf, Gunnar

"Tage." *See* George, Stefan, *Algabal*

Tage der Kommune, Die. See Brecht, Bertolt

Tagebuch 1946–1949. See Frisch, Max,
  Sketchbook 1946–1949
Tagebuch 1966–1971. See Frisch, Max,
  Sketchbook 1966–1971
"Tagebuch der Redegonda, Das." *See*
  Schnitzler, Arthur
Tagebuch mit Marion. See Frisch, Max
Tagebücher. See Musil, Robert
Tageliet. See Dawn songs
Tagore, Rabindranath
  Gitanjali, 9:1003b
    Perse and, 10:1434b
  Jiménez and, 9:992a, 1003b
  Lagerkvist and, 10:1687a
  The Crescent Moon, 9:1003b
Taine, Hippolyte, **7:1449a–1469b**, 8:471a
  art histories, 7:1461b–1464a
  Bergson and, 8:46b, 47a
  causality, 7:1453a-b
  De L'Intelligence (*On Intelligence*), 7:1449a,
    1464a-b
  determinism and, 10:1484b
  Eça and, 7:1685a
  Goncourts and, 7:1400a
  Histoire de la littérature anglaise (*History of
    English Literature*), 7:1449b,
    1452a–1461a
    French vs. English literature, 7:1460a
    race, moment, and milieu, 7:1454a–1456b
    Sainte-Beuve on, 6:849b–850a
  influence of, 9:591a
  L'Ancien Régime (*The Ancient Regime*),
    7:1465b–1466b
  Les origines de la France contemporaine
    (*The Origins of Contemporary France*),
    7:1449a-b, 1465a–1467b
  Les philosophes français du XIXe siècle
    (*The Nineteenth-Century French
    Philosophers*), 7:1452a, 1464b–1465a
  master faculty, 7:1451a, 1452b,
    1453b–1454a
    Shakespeare's, 7:1459a
  Mathilde Bonaparte and, 7:1416a
  Nouveaux essais de critique et d'histoire
    (New Critical and Historical Essays),
    7:1451b
  Ortega y Gasset on, 9:1123a

Philosophie de l'art dans les Pays-Bas (*Art
  in the Netherlands*), 7:1461b
Philosophie de l'art en Grèce (*Art in
  Greece*), 7:1461b
Philosophie de l'art en Italie (*Art in Italy*),
  7:1461b
Philosophie de l'art (*Philosophy of Art*),
  7:1461b
Voyage aux eaux des Pyrénées (*A Tour
  Through the Pyrenees*), 7:1451b
Voyage en Italie (Trip to Italy), 7:1461b
Zola and, 7:1520b–1521b
Tak zwana ludzkość w obłędzie. See
  Witkiewicz, Stanisław Ignacy
"Take and Write." *See* Ekelöf, Gunnar, "Tag
  och skriv"
Taklagsöl. See Strindberg, August
*Tale of the Dead Princess and the Seven
  Bogatyrs, The. See* Pushkin, Alexander
Tale of Fatumeh, The. *See* Ekelöf, Gunnar,
  Sagan om Fatumeh
Tale of the Fisherman and the Fish, The. See
  Pushkin, Alexander
Tale of the Golden Cockerel, The. See
  Pushkin, Alexander
Tale of Love, A. *See* Valle-Inclán, Ramón del,
  Epitalamio
Tale of the Merchant's Son and His Four
  Servants, The. *See* Hofmannsthal, Hugo
  von, *Das Märchen der 672. Nacht*
*Tale of the Priest and His Workman Balda,
  The. See* Pushkin, Alexander
Tale of Tales, The. *See* Basile, Giambattista,
  Lo cunto de li cunti
Tale of a Tub, A. See Swift, Jonathan
"Tale of the Woods." *See* Tasso, Torquato,
  Aminta
Tales. See Musset, Alfred de, *Contes*
Tales of Belkin, The. See Pushkin, Alexander
Tales of the Fantastic. *See* Gautier, Théophile,
  Récits fantastiques
Tales of the Fantastic. *See* Hoffmann, E. T. A.,
  Contes fantastiques
Tales from the Adventurous World. *See*
  Comptes du monde adventureux, Les
Tales from the Baths at Porretta. *See*
  Sabadino, Giovanni, *Le Porretane*

Tales from the Calendar. See Brecht, Bertolt

Tales from Hollywood. See Hampton, Christopher

Tales from London. *See* Eça de Queiroz, José Maria, *Crónicas de Londres*

Tales from One Pocket. *See* Čapek, Karel, *Povídky z jedné kapsy*

Tales from the Other Pocket. *See* Čapek, Karel, *Povídky z druhé kapsy*

Tales from the Phantasus. See Tieck, Ludwig, *Phantasus*

Tales from the Ražice Water-Bailiff's Cottage. *See* Hašek, Jaroslav, "Historky z ražické bašty"

Tales from Two Pockets. See Čapek, Karel

Tales for Grown-Up Children. *See* Zamyatin, Yevgeny Ivanovich, *Bol'shim detiam skazki*

Tales of King Arthur and the Knights of the Round Table. *See* Undset, Sigrid, *Fortællinger om Kong Artur og ridderne av det runde bord*

Tales of the Late Ivan Petrovich Belkin. See Pushkin, Alexander, *Tales of Belkin*

Tales of Melpomene. See Chekhov, Anton, *Skazki Mel'pomene*

Tales for Ninon. See Zola, Émile, *Contes à Ninon*

Tales of Spain. See Musset, Alfred de

Tales and Stories of the Eighteenth Century. See Sade, Donatien Alphonse François, marquis de

Tales of Student Life. See Hesse, Hermann, *Bertold*

Tales in Verse Drawn from Boccaccio and Ariosto. *See* La Fontaine, Jean de, *Nouvelles en vers tirées de Boccace et de l'Arioste*

Talisman. See Scott, Sir Walter

"Talk on Mythology." *See* Schlegel, Friedrich von

Talk on Receiving the Schiller-Prize. *See* Frisch, Max, "Schillerpreis-Rede"

Talleyrand, Charles de, 5:91a, 91b
    Delacroix and, 5:514b–515a

Tallusa. *See* Pascoli, Giovanni, "Thallusa"

Talos. *See* Ritsos, Yannis, "O Talos"

"Talos, O." *See* Ritsos, Yannis

"Taman." *See* Lermontov, Mikhail Yurievich

"Tamango." *See* Mérimée, Prosper

Tamarisks. *See* Pascoli, Giovanni, *Myricae*

Tamayo, Rufino, Breton on, 11:1950a

"Tambovskaya kaznacheysha" ("The Tambov Cashier's Wife"). *See* Lermontov, Mikhail Yurievich

Taming of the Shrew. See Shakespeare, William

Tanaghries (Tanagra Women). See Ritsos, Yannis

"Tancerz mecanasa Kraykowskiego." *See* Gombrowicz, Witold

Tanguy, Yves, Breton on, 11:1949b, 1950a

Tanks Know the Truth. *See* Solzhenitsyn, Aleksandr, *Znaiut istinu tanki*

"Tannhäuser." *See* Heine, Heinrich

Tannhäuser. See Wagner, Richard

"Tanto gentile e tanto honesta pare." *See* Dante Alighieri, *Vita nuova*

"Tanto viro locuturi." *See* Walter of Châtillon

Tanzi, Drusilla, Montale's marriage to, 11:1991b

Tao-te Ching. See Lao-tzu

Tapestry of Life and the Songs of Dream and Death, with a Prelude, The. *See* George, Stefan, *Der Teppich des Lebens und die Lieder von Traum und Tod, mit einem Vorspiel*

Tapestry in Love, The. *See* Gautier, Théophile, "Omphale," "La tapisserie amoureuse"

"Tapfere Cassian, Der." *See* Schnitzler, Arthur

"Tapisserie amoureuse, La." *See* Gautier, Théophile, "Omphale"

Taprobana, in Camoëns' *The Lusiads*, 2:766a

Tarare. See Beaumarchais, Pierre-Augustin Caron de; Salieri, Antonio

"Taras Bulba." *See* Gogol, Nikolay Vasilievich

"Tarde." *See* Machado, Antonio, *Soledades* (Solitudes)

Tare. *See* Tychyna, Pavlo, *Zamist' sonetiv i oktav*, "Kukil"

Tarjumā al-ashwāq. See Ibn al-'Arabī

Tarn. *See* Kosztolányi, Dezső, *Tengerszem*

Tårnet. See Vesaas, Tarjei

Tartuffe. See Molière

"Task, A." *See* Milosz, Czeslaw, "Zadanie"

"Task of the Translator, The." *See* Benjamin, Walter

Tasso, Bernardo, 2:792a-b, 798b

  Amadigi, 2:792a, 798b

Tasso, Torquato, **2:791a–818b**

  Aminta, 2:792b, 793a, 794a–798a, 917b–918a

    impact on Renaissance pastoral drama, 2:916b

  Ariosto and, 2:643a-b

  Dialogues, 2:793b, 814b

  Discorsi del poema eroico (*Discourses on the Heroic Poem*), 2:794a, 813b

  Discorsi dell'arte poetica, 2:799b–800b, 814a

  Gerusalemme conquistada (*Jerusalem Conquered*), 2:793b–794a, 813a–814a

    Lope de Vega and, 2:849a

  Gerusalemme liberata (*Jerusalem Delivered*), 2:800b–813a

    Ariosto's *Orlando furioso* and, 2:791a

    composition method of, 2:803a

    concern for coherence and gravity in, 2:799a

    drafts of, 2:792a, 792b, 798b

    Lampedusa's *The Leopard* and, 11:2013b–2014a

    Mickiewicz and, 5:610b

    pastoral interlude in, 2:910a

    pirated editions of, 2:793a, 793b

    revision of, 2:800b–801a

    style of, 2:801b–802a

    subject of, 2:801a-b

  Giudizio sulla G.C. (*Judgment on the G.C.*), 2:794a

  Goethe and, 5:12b–13b

  Il Re Torrismondo, 2:792b, 814a-b

  Le sette giornate del mondo creato (*The Seven Days of the Created World*), 2:794a, 816a–817a

  Monte Oliveto, 2:794a

  Padre di famiglia (*Father of the Family*), 2:814b

  pastoral poetry of, 2:910a

  Rime, 2:815a

  Rinaldo, 2:792a, 798a–799b, 801b

Taste, sense of, in Proust's *Remembrance of Things Past*, 8:562a

Tata. See Borel, Jacques

Tattet, Alfred, Musset and, 6:1002b

Taueber, Sophie

  Arp and

    literary collaborations, 10:1370a, 1371b–1372a

    marriage, 10:1369a

  death of, 10:1378b–1379a

Tausk, Victor, Freud and, 8:13a

Taut Rope, The. *See* Simon, Claude, *La corde raide*

Tavola Ritonda, 1:153a

Taxation, in La Bruyère's *Caractères*, 3:241b–242a

Taylor, Baron Isidore, Berlioz and, 6:772a

Taylor, John Russell, 7:1927b

Tchaikovsky, Peter Ilyich, *Doctor Faustus* and, 9:733b

Tcherniak, Nathalie. *See* Sarraute, Nathalie

Te Deum. See Berlioz, Hector

Teacher

  Butor as, 13:3288a-b

  Erasmus as, 2:573b

  Luther as, 2:671a–672b

"Teacher of Literature." *See* Chekhov, Anton, "Uchitel slovesnosti"

Teacher and Student. See Khlebnikov, Velimir

Teaching profession, Aymé's satire of, 12:2443b–2444b

Teater. Den svåra stunden. See Lagerkvist, Pär

Teatr. See Witkiewicz, Stanisław Ignacy

Teatro comico, Il. See Goldoni, Carlo

Teatro d'Arte di Roma, 8:394b–395a

Teatro de los teatros de los pasados y presentes siglos. See Candamo, Francisco Bances

"Teatro della sorpresa, Il." *See* Marinetti, Filippo Tommaso

"Teatro di varietà, Il." *See* Marinetti, Filippo Tommaso

"Teatro futurista sintetico, Il." *See* Marinetti, Filippo Tommaso

Teatro nel teatro (theater-in-the-theater), 9:1063a

Teatro popular. See Lugo y Dávilla, Francisco

Teatro San Luca, Goldoni and, 4:429b–431b

Teatro Sant'Angelo, Goldoni and, 4:426b–426b

"Teatro tattile, Il." *See* Marinetti, Filippo Tommaso

"Technical Manifesto of Futurist Literature." *See* Marinetti, Filippo Tommaso, "Manifesto tecnico della letteratura futurista"

Technik des Dramas, Die. See Freytag, Gustav

Technique of the Drama, The. See Freytag, Gustav, *Die Technik des Dramas*

Technology

    Apollinaire and, 9:884a-b, 894b

    Čapek's view of. *See* Dystopia

    in D'Annunzio's poetry, 8:187b–188a

    Delacroix's views of, 5:536a-b

    Frisch's views of, 13:2909a

    Hesse on, 9:847a-b

    idea of progress and, in late 19th-century thought, 10:1484b

    language of, Marinetti and, 9:803b

    in Olesha's *The Three Fat Men*, 11:2247b

    social role, in Böll's "Der Wegwerfer," 13:3177a-b

    Unamuno's opposition to, 8:296a

    see also Industrialization; Mass production; Science

Tegernsee *Antichrist*, 1:455b, 456b, 468a

Tegnér, Esaias, *Friðþjófs saga* and, 1:401a

Teilhard de Chardin, Pierre

    Bergson and, 8:64b

    Hymne de l'univers (*The Prayer of the Universe*), creative process, 12:2348a

Teit (son of Bishop Ísleif), school of, 1:379b

Tel quel. See Valéry, Paul

Tel quel (periodical), 8:570a

"Teleftaia mera, I." *See* Seferis, George, *Imerologio katastromatos*

Teleftaíos pirasmós, O. See Kazantzakis, Nikos

"Teleftaios stathmos." *See* Seferis, George, *Imerologio katastromatos B*

Teleftea pro Anthropou ekatontaetia, I. See Ritsos, Yannis

"Teleiomena." *See* Cavafy, Constantine

Telémaque. See Fénelon, Francois de Selignac de la Mothe-

Téllez, Gabriel. *See* Tirso de Molina

"Telos enos dialogou, To." *See* Tsatsos, Constantine

Tema de nuestro tiempo, El. See Ortega y Gasset, José

Temnyilik. See Rozanov, Vasilii

Tempered Heart, The. From Montenegrin Life. *See* Khlebnikov, Velimir, "Zakalennoe serdtse. Ia chernogorskoi zhizni"

Tempest, The. See Shakespeare, William

Tempestade, A. See Ferreira de Castro, José Maria

"Tempests." *See* Dinesen, Isak

Tempier, Étienne, bishop of Paris, 1:418b, 426a, 426b

    Romance of the Rose and, 1:332a

Temple du goût, Le (*Temple of Taste*). *See* Voltaire

Temple of Taste. *See* Voltaire, *Le temple du goût*

Temple of Vacuna, The. *See* Pascoli, Giovanni, "Fanum vacunae"

Tempo presente (Roman Socialist journal), 12:2302a

"Temporale." *See* Pascoli, Giovanni

Temps, ce grand sculpteur, Le. See Yourcenar, Marguerite

Temps d'Anaïs, Le. See Simenon, Georges

Temps modernes, Les (journal)

    Beauvoir and, 12:2727a

    Sartre and, 12:2590b, 2601a–2603a

Temps retrouvé, Le. See Proust, Marcel, *Remembrance of Things Past* (*À la recherche du temps perdu*), *Time Regained*

Temptation of Quiet Veronica, The. See Musil, Robert, *Vereinigungen*

Temptation of Saint Anthony, The. See Flaubert, Gustave

Temptation, theme of, in *Representacio Adae*, 1:457b

Temptation of the West, The. See Malraux, André

Temptress, The. See Blasco Ibáñez, Vicente, *La tierra de todos*

Temy i variatsii. See Pasternak, Boris, *Themes and Variations*

Ten Most Beautiful Words, The. *See* Kosztolányi, Dezső, *A tíz legszebb*

Ten Years After in Literature. *See* Sainte-Beuve, Charles-Augustin, "Dix ans après en littérature"

Ten Years of Blood. *See* Krleža, Miroslav, *Deset krvavih godina*

Ten Years of Exile. See Staël, Madame de, *Dix années d'exil*

Ten Years in the Life of a Woman. *See* Scribe, Eugène, *Dix ans de la vie d'une femme*

Ten-Minute Drama, A. *See* Zamyatin, Yevgeny Ivanovich, "Desiatiminutnaia drama"

"Tenda, La." *See* Pavese, Cesare, *The Beautiful Summer*

"Tender Assumption Church—Florence in Moscow." *See* Mandelshtam, Osip

Tender as a Memory. See Apollinaire, Guillaume, *Tendre comme le souvenir*

Tendre comme le souvenir. See Apollinaire, Guillaume

Tenebrae Service 5. See Cela, Camilo José, *Oficio de tinieblas 5*

Tengerszem. See Kosztolányi, Dezső

Tenishev School
    in Mandelshtam's poetry, 10:1625a-b
    in Nabokov's *Zazhchita Luzhina* (*The Defence*), 10:1625a
    spirited alumni of, 10:1624b–1625a

"Tennis Court, The." *See* Chénier, André

Tennyson, Alfred, 7:1426b
    "Godiva," Mandelshtam's reference to, 10:1644b
    In Memoriam, Nerval's "El Desdichado" and, 6:950b
    Taine on, 7:1460b–1461a
    Unamuno and, 8:297a

Tenor, The. See Wedekind, Frank, *Der Kammersänger*

Tenso (*tenson, tenzon*)(poetic genre), 1:167a
    Boccacio's *Ninfale d'Ameto* and, 2:905b
    jeu parti and, 1:459a

Tentation de l'Occident, La. See Malraux, André, *The Temptation of the West*

Tentation de Saint Antoine, Le. See Flaubert, Gustave, *The Temptation of Saint Anthony*

Tentative amoureuse, La. See Gide, André

Teoria da vontade. See Eça de Queiroz, Jose Maria

Teoria e storia della storiografia. See Croce, Benedetto

Teppich des Lebens und die Lieder von Traum und Tod, mit einem Vorspiel, Der. See George, Stefan

Terboven, Joseph, Hamsun and, 8:40a

Tercera antologjía poética. See Jiménez, Juan Ramón

Tercets, 1:445b

Terence
    Hrosvitha and, 1:451a-b
    La Fontaine's play *L'Eunuque* and, 3:74a
    quoted by Boileau, 3:183b
    Renaissance drama and, 1:473a

Teresa, Santa, Machado and, 9:763b

Teriade, E., 13:2965b, 2972a

"Terra." *See* Quasimodo, Salvatore

"Terra d'esilio." *See* Pavese, Cesare, *Notte di festa*

Terra fria. See Ferreira de Castro, José Maria

Terra impareggiabile, La. See Quasimodo, Salvatore, *The Incomparable Earth*

Terra promessa, La. See Ungaretti, Giuseppe

Terra trema, La (film). *See* Verga, Giovanni, *I Malavoglia*

Terre des hommes. See Saint-Exupéry, Antoine de

Terre, La. See Zola, Émile

"Terrible Procession, The." *See* Södergran, Edith, "Det fasansfulla tåget"

"Terrible Vengeance, A." *See* Gogol, Nikolay Vasilyevich, "Strashnaia mest'"

"Terror." *See* Tychyna, Pavlo, *Zamist' sonetiv i oktav*

Terror, Stalinist. *See* Stalinism

Terrorism, in Bely's *Petersburg*, 9:921b

Tertullian
    Apotheosis and, 1:8a
    De Spectaculis, personification in, 1:6a

Terza rima, 2:491a, 503b, 511b
    Dante and, 1:445b

"Tes mains." *See* Mérat, Albert

Teseida. See Boccaccio, Giovanni

"Teseida delle nozze d'Emilia." *See* Boccaccio, Giovanni

Tessa. *See* Giraudoux, Jean

"Tessitrice, La." *See* Pascoli, Giovanni, "Il ritorno a San Mauro"

Testament, literary, as Renaissance poetic form, 2:538a-b, 545a-b

Testament Donadieu, Le. *See* Simenon, Georges

Testament of Orpheus, The (*Le testament d'Orphée*). *See* Cocteau, Jean

Testament, The. *See* Villon, François

Testus, Jean, *Traité d'anatomie humaine* (*Treatise on Human Anatomy*), Simenon and, 12:2482b

Tetarti dhiastasi. *See* Ritsos, Yannis

Tête d'Or. *See* Claudel, Paul

Têtes de bois. *See* Ghelderode, Michel de, *Blockheads*

Têtes des autres, La. *See* Aymé, Marcel

Tethered Souls. *See* Ady, Endre, "Lelkek a pányván"

Tethys (goddess), 2:763b

Tetradhio, Elytis and, 13:2962a

Tetradio gymnasmaton. *See* Seferis, George

Teufels General, Des. *See* Zuckmayer, Carl

Teutonic Knights, in Mickiewicz's poetry, 5:613b, 616b–618a

Teutsche Merkur, Der. *See* Wieland, Christoph Martin

Texeira de Pascoaes (Joaquim Pereira Texeira de Vasconcelos), 11:2148a

Text, Butor's manipulations of, 13:3306a–3307a

Tezei: Ariadna. *See* Tsvetaeva, Marina

Thackeray, William Makepeace, Eça and, 7:1691a

Thaïs. *See* France, Anatole

Thália Company, Lukács and, 10:1254a-b

Thalia (journal), Schiller and, 5:34b, 35a

"Thallusa." *See* Pascoli, Giovanni

That Mighty Sculptor, Time. *See* Yourcenar, Marguerite, *Le temps, ce grand sculpteur*

That Which Is Prohibited. *See* Pérez Galdós, Benito, *Lo prohibido*

That Which Was Lost. *See* Mauriac, François

Þættir, 1:377a-b, 381b, 384a

Theater

amateur

18th century, 4:377a

Jean Jacques Rousseau on the, 4:377a

Voltaire and, 4:377a, 380a

Andersen and, 6:865a–866a, 872b–875a

Ariosto and, 2:622a–624b

Artaud's theories regarding, 11:1969b–1970a, 1971b, 1972a–1973a

Barthes on, 13:3086a–3087a

Brecht's influence in, 11:2089a–2090a

Büchner's view of, 6:1175a–1176a

Camus and, 13:3053a

Castiglione and, 2:647b

Eastern, Artaud influenced by, 11:1972b

English, Delacroix's interest in, 5:519b

French

during First Empire, 6:719b

Jarry's *Ubu Roi* and, 9:665a–666a, 671b–672a

German, Frisch and, 13:2897a-b

Gogol and, 6:982b–985b

Hofmannsthal's view of, 9:692a-b

in Hungary, Lukács and, 10:1254a

Italian

Alfieri's commentary on, 4:677b–678a

Moravia and, 12:2690a-b

Kierkegaard and, 6:1134a

Machiavelli and, 2:599b, 613a–615a

Musset's work in, 6:1010b

Polish, *see also* Witkiewicz, Stanisław Ignacy

Portuguese, Eça and, 7:1684b

in post-1919 Poland, 10:1215a

reform of, Goldoni and, 4:425b, 427a–436b

Russian, Blok and, 9:966a

Spanish, Lorca and, 11:2199a–2200b

Tieck and, 5:257a

variety theater of Marinetti, 9:821b–822b

Witkiewicz's theory of Pure Form and, 10:1215a–1218b

see also Witkiewicz, Stanisław Ignacy, *Teatr*; *Zauberspiel* (magic play)

Theater of the absurd. *See* Absurd, theater of the

Theater of cruelty, 12:2355a

"Theater of the grotesque," Pirandello and, 8:393b

Theater of imitation, Frisch and, 13:2910b

Theater and Its Double, The. See Artaud, Antonin, *Le théâtre et son double*

"Theater Jottings." *See* Mallarmé, Stéphane, "Crayonné au théâtre"

"Theater and the Plague, The." *See* Artaud, Antonin, "Le théâtre et la peste"

"Theater of Surprise, The." *See* Marinetti, Filippo Tommaso, "Il teatro della sorpresa"

Theater of the Theaters of Past and Present Centuries. See Candamo, Francisco Bances, *Teatro de los teatros de los pasados y presentes siglos*

Theater-in-the-theater (*teatro nel teatro*), 9:1063a
Pirandello and, 8:395b, 405b, 408a, 412a

Theater-Novel. *See* Aragon, Louis, *Théâtre-roman*

Theatralische Bibliothek. See Lessing, Gotthold Ephraim

Théâtre Alfred Jarry, Artaud's involvement with, 11:1971a-b

Théâtre de Clara Gazul. See Mérimée, Prosper

Théâtre de la foire, Lesage and, 3:326a-b, 327a

Théâtre de l'Equipe, Le, 13:3053a

Théâtre des Nouveautés, Musset's works at, 6:1005a

"Théâtre et la peste, Le." *See* Artaud, Antonin

Théâtre et son double, Le. See Artaud, Antonin

Théâtre Français (Paris), Scribe and, 7:1914a

Théâtre II. See Yourcenar, Marguerite

Théâtre Libre-Antoine (Paris), 7:1415a-b, 1930b–1931a
naturalist plays, 7:1443b

Théâtre National Populaire, Musset's works at, 6:1007b, 1009b

Théâtre-roman. See Aragon, Louis

Theatrical Library. See Lessing, Gotthold Ephraim, *Theatralische Bibliothek*

Theatricalism, in Giraudoux's works, 9:1063a-b

"Theatron tis Sidonos" ("Theater of Sidon"). *See* Cavafy, Constantine

Theatrum mundi (theatre of the world) metaphor
in baroque literature, 5:422a
influence on Grillparzer, 5:421b–422a, 429b

Thébaïde, La, ou les frères ennemis (The Thebaid). See Racine, Jean

"Their Beginning." *See* Cavafy, Constantine, "I archi ton"

Their Morning Is the Darkness. *See* Frisch, Max, *When the War Was Over*

"Theme of Three Caskets, The." *See* Freud, Sigmund, "Das Motiv der Kästchenwahl"

Themes and Variations. See Pasternak, Boris

Theocritus
Chénier compared to, 4:717a
Idylls, 2:900a
Chénier and, 4:699b
Lament for Daphnis, Renaissance pastoral elegy and, 2:900b–901a
Renaissance pastoral poetry and, 2:900a, 901a–902a

Theodorakis, Mikis, 13:2971b

Theodoricus (Norwegian cleric), *Historia de antiquitate regum Norwagiensium (History of Norwegian Kings from Ancient Times)*, 1:380b

Theodosius, Roman emperor, Prudentius and, 1:1a, 10a, 10b

Theologia naturalis. See Sebond, Raymond

Theologica Germanica. See Luther, Martin

Theological symbolism. *See* Symbolism, religious

Theology
Aristotelianism and, 1:408a
of Augustine's *On the Trinity*, 1:37b
of Augustinians, 1:409b
Benjamin and, 11:1075b
Diderot and, 4:478a–479a
in Greban's *Passion*, 1:469b–470a
of Huysmans, 7:1726a-b
Kierkegaard and, 6:1128a-b
Luther and, 2:669a–689a
pagan. *See* Gods, pagan
systematic

in Aquinas' *Summa theologica*,
1:416b–417a
in Peter Lombard's *Sententiae*, 1:407a
see also Christianity; Religion
Theophrastus, *Characters*, La Bruyère and,
3:231b–232a
Theorie des Romans, Die. See Lukács, György
Theory of Color. See Goethe, Johann Wolfgang
von
Theory of Mass Psychology. *See* Broch,
Hermann, *Massenwahntheorie*
Theory of the Novel, The. See Lukács, György
Theory of the Will. *See* Eça de Queiroz, Jose
Maria, *Teoria da vontade*
Theosophy
Bely and, 9:916b, 919b
Pirandello and, 8:396b
Theotokas, George, Seferis and, 12:2255a
"There Is a Difference." *See* Andersen, Hans
Christian
There Is Something. *See* Ekelöf, Gunnar, "Det
finns någonting"
There Is/Are. See Apollinaire, Guillaume, *Il y
a*
"There Was a Child Went Forth." *See*
Whitman, Walt
There Was a Prisoner. See Anouilh, Jean,
Y'avait un prisonnier
There Will Come a Day. *See* Mann, Heinrich,
Es kommt der Tag
There's Nothing Like Keeping Silent. See
Calderón de la Barca, Pedro
Therese: Chronik eines Frauenlebens
(*Theresa: The Chronicle of a Woman's
Life*). *See* Schnitzler, Arthur
Thérèse Desqueyroux. See Mauriac, François
Thérèse Raquin. See Zola, Émile
"These people, when they are in good spirits."
See Peire Cardenal, "Aquesta gens, cant
son en lur gaieza"
These Pleasures. *See* Colette, *Le pur et l'impur*
Theseid of the Nuptials of Emilia. *See*
Boccaccio, Giovanni, "Teseida delle
nozze d'Emilia"
Theses on Atheism. See Voetius, Gysbertus
Theseus. See Gide, André
Theseus legend, 12:2551b–2552a

Theseus-Ariadne. *See* Tsvetaeva, Marina,
Tezei: Ariadna
Thesis, Hegelian. *See* Dialectics, Hegelian
Thesis plays
of Augier, 7:1919a
of Brieux, 7:1921a
of Dumas fils, 7:1918b–1919a
of Henry Arthur Jones, 7:1926b–1927a
of Pinero, 7:1928a
They. See Witkiewicz, Stanisław Ignacy, *Oni*
They Led You Away at Dawn. *See* Akhmatova,
Anna, *Requiem (Rekviem)*
"They Should Have Taken Care." *See* Cavafy,
Constantine, "As frontizan"
They Will Outshine the Stars. *See* Tychyna,
Pavlo, *Pluh (The Plow)*, "Perezoriuiut
zori"
Thibaudet, Albert
on the Goncourts, 7:1400a
Montaigne and, 2:787b
Thibault d'Aussigny, bishop, in Villon's
Testament, 2:557b, 559a-b
Thibault, Julie, Huysmans and, 7:1722a,
1724a-b
Thibaut IV de Champagne, as trouvère, 1:181a
Piðreks saga, 1:401b
"Thief, The." *See* Apollinaire, Guillaume,
Alcools, "Le larron"
Thief's Journal, The. See Genet, Jean
Thienemann, Marie, Hauptmann and, 8:150b,
151b–152a
Thierry, Augustin, 5:572b
Thiers, Adolphe
art criticism by, 5:523b
Büchner and, 6:1172b–1173a
Delacroix and, 5:514b, 520b
"Thieves." *See* Chekhov, Anton, "Vory"
Thieves' Carnival. See Anouilh, Jean
"Thing-symbol"
in Keller, 6:928a
poetic realism and, 6:914b
Storm and, 6:920b–921a
"Things That Are Dangerous." *See* Cavafy,
Constantine, "Ta epikindyna"
Think It Over, Giacomino! See Pirandello,
Luigi, *Pensaci, Giacomino!*
Thinker (the word), Valéry on, 8:586b–587a

Thinking. *See* Thought

Thinking of Spain. *See* Azorín, *Pensando en España*

Third Book. See Rabelais, François

Third Book of Laughable Loves, The. See Kundera, Milan

Third Floor Below Ground. *See* Butor, Michel, *Troisième dessous*

"Third and Last Dedication." *See* Akhmatova, Anna, *Poem Without a Hero*

Third Poetic Anthology. *See* Jiménez, Juan Ramón, *Tercera antolojía poética*

Third Reich. *See* Germany; Nazism

"Thirst." *See* Andrić, Ivo

Thirteen, The. See Balzac, Honoré de, *L'Histoire des treize*

"Thirteen Ways of Looking at a Blackbird." *See* Stevens, Wallace

Thirty Years' War
  in Manzoni's *The Betrothed*, 5:385b–386a, 387a–388b, 392a-b
  Meyer and, 6:933b–934a
  in Schiller's *Wallenstein*, 5:42a–44b

Thirty-three Poems. See Heine, Heinrich, *Drei und dreissig Gedichte*

35 Sonnets. See Pessoa, Fernando

"31 B.C. in Alexandria." *See* Cavafy, Constantine, "To 31 P.Ch. stin Alexandreia"

"Thitia tou kalokeriou, I." *See* Elytis, Odysseus, *Prosanatolismi*

Thjódólf of Hvin, "Ynglingatal" ("Enumeration of the Ynglings"), 1:388a

Thoma, Ludwig, in Wedekind's *Oaha*, 8:270b

Thomas Aquinas, St. *See* Aquinas, Thomas, St.

Thomas, Augustus, Ibsen's influence on, 7:1443b

Thomas of Brittany
  Gottfried and, 1:240a–241b, 257b
  Tristan
    Chrétien's *Cligés* and, 1:192b
    Tristrams saga and, 1:399b
    Tristan story and, 1:148b, 153a

Thomas à Kempis
  The Imitation of Christ (Imitatio Christi), 9:991a

Corneille and, 3:24b–25a
  French Evangelicals and, 2:694b
  Goncourts on, 7:1411a-b
  Vigny and, 5:449b

Thomas, Lewis, on Montaigne, 788a-b

Thomas l'imposteur (Thomas the Impostor). See Cocteau, Jean

Thomas, Signy, 9:1017b

Thomism, Gombrowicz and, 12:2570a-b

Thomson, James, Chateaubriand on, 5:137a

Þórðar saga hreðu (The Story of Thórd Tumult), 1:397a-b

Thoré-Burger, Théophile, on Delacroix, 5:521a

Thoreau, Henry David, Herder's individualism compared to, 4:652a

Thorez, Maurice, Aragon and, 11:2082a

Þorgeirs drápa. See Thormód

Þorgils saga ok Haflioða, 1:399a, 400a

Thorlák Runólfsson, 1:381b

Thorlák Thórhallsson, 1:381b, 383b

Þorláks saga helga, 1:383b

Thormód, *Þorgeirs drápa*, 1:385a

Þormóðar þáttr, 1:384a, 385a

Þorsteins þáttr stangarhöggs (The Story of Thorstein Staff-struck), 1:395a-b

Thorvaldsen, Albert Bertel, Hebbel and, 6:1095b

Those Pleasures. See Colette, *Ces plaisirs*

Those Who Thirst. *See* Simenon, Georges, *Ceux de la soif*

Those Whom I Kiss. *See* Ady, Endre, "Akit én csókolok"

Those Whose Wet Nurse I Am. *See* Ady, Endre, "Akiknek dajkája vagyok"

"Thou Great Eros." *See* Södergran, Edith, "Du store Eros"

Thou Shalt Not Lie. See Grillparzer, Franz

Thought
  action and
    in Croce's *Filosofia della pratica*, 8:321b–322b
    in Valéry's *Dance and the Soul*, 8:586b
  Augustine on, 1:40b
  existence and, in Descartes's *Meditations on First Philosophy*, 3:11b, 12a-b, 17b
  in Musil's *The Man Without Qualities*, 9:931a, 935b, 947a-b, 952b–957b

nature of, Croce on, 8:317a–318a, 324a

source of, in Descartes's *Meditations on First Philosophy*, 3:13a-b, 14a

Valéry on, 8:572a, 572b, 575a, 575b

"The Introduction to the Method of Leonardo da Vinci," 8:572b–573b

Thought-Forms. See Leadbeater, C. W.

Thoughts. See Pascal, Blaise, *Pensées*

Thoughts of August. See Sainte-Beuve, Charles-Augustin, *Pensées d'août*

"Thoughts on Dostoevsky's *Idiot.*" *See* Hesse, Hermann, *Blick ins Chaos (In Sight of Chaos)*, "Gedanken zu Dostojewsky's Idiot"

Thoughts on the Interpretation of Nature. See Diderot, Denis, *Pensées sur l'interprétation de la nature*

Thoughts on the Novel. *See* Johnson, Eyvind, "Romanfunderingar"

Thousand and One Folds, A. *See* Butor, Michel, *Mille et un plis*

Thousand and One Nights

French translation of, 3:325b

influence on Renaissance short fiction, 2:932a

Vittorini and, 12:2736a

Wieland and, 4:605b

Thrasylle. See Montherlant, Henry de

Three Cantos. *See* George, Stefan, *Drei Gesänge*

Three Chorals. *See* Ritsos, Yannis, *Tria horika*

Three clerics legend, 1:462b

Three Days. *See* Zamyatin, Yevgeny Ivanovich, "Tri dnia"

Three Elixirs, The. *See* Schnitzler, Arthur, "Die Drei Elixire"

Three Essays on the Theory of Sexuality. See Freud, Sigmund, *Drei Abhandlungen zur Sexualtheorie*

Three Fat Men, The. See Olesha, Yuri

Three Intellectuals in Politics. See Joll, James

"Three Mules." *See* Seferis, George, "Treis moules"

Three Musketeers, The. See Dumas père, Alexandre, *Les trois mousquetaires*

Three Poems Under a Flag of Convenience. *See* Elytis, Odysseus, *Tria poiemata me simea efkerias*

Three Righteous Combmakers, The. See Keller, Gottfried

Three Roses, The. See Blasco Ibáñez, Vicente, *Arroz y tartana*

Three Secret Poems. See Seferis, George, *Tria krypha poiemata*

Three Sisters, The. See Chekhov, Anton

Three Symphonies. *See* Krleža, Miroslav, *Tri simfonije*

Three, The. See Hylaea group, *Troe*

Three of Them, The. See Gorky, Maxim, *Troe*

Three Truths. See Charron, Pierre, *Trois Veritez*

Three Winters. *See* Milosz, Czeslaw, *Trzy zimy*

Three Women. *See* Musil, Robert, *Drei Frauen*

"Three Years." *See* Chekhov, Anton, "Tri goda"

"Three-Minute Novel." *See* Mann, Heinrich, "Drei Minuten Roman"

Threefold Righteousness. See Luther, Martin

Threepenny Opera, The. See Brecht, Bertolt

Threshold, The. See Colette, *Le blé en herbe*

"Threshold, The." *See* Turgenev, Ivan

Thresholdism, Tieck and, 5:235b, 239a–242b

Thrinos tou mai. See Ritsos, Yannis, *Ta Epikerika*

"Through the Crack." *See* Babel, Isaac

Through the Looking Glass. See Carroll, Lewis

"Through the Mirror." *See* Elytis, Odysseus, *Maria Nephele*

"Thrower-Away, The." *See* Böll, Heinrich

Thrush. See Seferis, George, *Kichle*

Thrust and Parry. *See* Montale, Eugenio, *Satura*, "Botta e risposta"

Þú vínviður hreini. See Laxness, Halldór, *Salka Valka*

Thucydides

Cavafy and, 8:206a

Corneille and, 3:34b

Peloponnesian War, Athenian massacre of Milos, 12:2832a

"Thuiskon." *See* Klopstock, Friedrich Gottlieb

"Thumbelina." *See* Andersen, Hans Christian

"Thunderstorm." *See* Pascoli, Giovanni, "Temporale"

"Thunderstorm, The." *See* Trakl, Georg

Thurn und Taxis, Marie von, Rilke and, 9:771a

Thus Spoke Zarathustra. See Nietzsche, Friedrich

Thyestes. *See* Foscolo, Ugo, *Tieste*

Thyrorio. See Ritsos, Yannis

Ti con zero. See Calvino, Italo, *t zero*

Ti ho sposato per allegria. See Ginzburg, Natalia, *I Married You for Fun*

Ti paraxena pramata. See Ritsos, Yannis

Tidens gäng. See Johnson, Eyvind

Tidings Brought to Mary, The. See Claudel, Paul, *L'Annonce faite à Marie*

Tidström, Skoglar, Ekelöf and, 12:2648a-b, 2649b

Tieck, Ludwig, **5:233a–260b**

Andersen and, 6:867b, 877a-b

Das Zauberschloss (The Magic Castle), 5:252a

Der Aufruhr in den Cevennen (*The Rebellion in the Cevennes*), 5:252a

Der blonde Eckbert (*Blond Eckbert*), 5:245b–248b

Der gestiefelte Kater (*Puss-in-Boots*), 5:243a, 244a–245b

Der junge Tischlermeister (The Young Master Carpenter), 5:242b

Der Runenberg, 6:887b

Des Lebens Überfluss (*Life's Superfluence*), 5:252b–255a

Dichterleben (The Life of the Poets), 5:243b–244a

Die Gemälde (The Portraits), 5:252a

Die Gesellschaft auf dem Lande (The Party in the Country), 5:252a

Die verkehrte Welt (*The Land of Upside Down*), 5:244a

Eigensinn und Laune (Obstinacy and Whim), 5:252a

Fortunat (Fortunatus), 5:244a

Franz Sternbalds Wanderungen (Franz Sternbald's Travels), 5:237a–242b, 6:875b

Geschichte des Herrn William Lovell (The Story of William Lovell), 5:235a-b

Gogol and, 6:975a

Herzensergiessungen eines Kunstliebenden Klosterbruders (Outpourings of an Art-loving Friar), 5:236a–237a

historical tragedy and, 5:432a

Kaiser Octavianus (Emperor Octavian), 5:244a

Khlebnikov's *Zangezi* and, 10:1362a

Leben und Tod der heiligen Genoveva (The Life and Death of St. Genevieve), 5:244a

Minnelieder aus dem schwäbischen Zeitalter (Courtly Love Songs from the Swabian Epoch), 5:250b

Novalis and, 5:206a, 208b

Phantasien über die Kunst für Freunde der Kunst (Fantasies on Art for Friends of Art), 5:236a–237a

Phantasus (Tales from the Phantasus), 5:251b

Prinz Zerbino; oder, Die Reise nach dem guten Geschmacke (Prince Zerbino; or, The Journey to Good Taste), 5:244a

on Richter's works

The School for Aesthetics, 5:78b

Walt and Vult, 5:77a

romanticism and fate tragedies, 5:425b

Schlegel and, 5:182a

Shakespeares Vorschule (Shakespeare's Preparatory School), 5:243b

Straussfedern (Ostrich Feathers), 5:245b

Studien über Shakespeare und das alt-englische Theater (Studies of Shakespeare and the Old English Theater), 5:243b

"The Entrance of Romance," 5:250a

Über Shakespeares Behandlung des Wunderbaren (Concerning Shakespeare's Handling of the Marvelous), 5:243a

Vittoria Accorombona (*The Roman Matron*), 5:255a-b

Waldeinsamkeit (Forest Solitude), 5:247a–250a, 255b–256b

Tiedge Prize, Hebbel's award of, 6:1115b–1116a

Tiempo de silencio. See Santos, Luis Martín

"Tiempo, distancia, y forma en el arte de Proust." *See* Ortega y Gasset, José

Tierra de todos, La. See Blasco Ibáñez, Vicente

Tieste. See Foscolo, Ugo

Tiger at the Gates. See Giraudoux, Jean

Tihos mesa ston kathrefti, O. See Ritsos, Yannis

Tilbake til fremtiden. See Undset, Sigrid, *Return to the Future*

Till Damaskus. See Strindberg, August, *To Damascus*

"*Till Eros.*" *See* Södergran, Edith

Till Eulenspiegel. See Wedekind, Frank, *Oaha*

Timans och rättfärdigheten (Timans and Justice). *See* Johnson, Eyvind

Time
   art and, Proust on, 8:566a-b
   in Baudelaire, 7:1338b–1339a
   Bergson's concept of, 8:48a, 49b–51a, 52a
       see also Memory, Bergson's concept of
   in Butor, 13:3293a-b, 3304a-b
   in Calvino, 13:3277b–3279a
   in Camoëns' poetry, 2:752a-b
   in Chekhov, 7:1874b–1875a
   chronological, Breton's dismissal of, 11:1955b
   in Dinesen, 10:1295b
   in Ekelöf's works, 12:2660a–2661a, 2664b–2665a, 2665b–2666a, 2667a-b
   in Goncharov's works, 6:1078a-b, 1081b–1082a
   Grillparzer's drama, 5:422a-b, 432b–433a
   imagery of, in Elytis' "Dionysus," 13:2960a
   Khlebnikov's theory of history, 10:1341b–1344a
   Kierkegaard and, 6:1135a–1136b
   in Klopstock, 4:522a, 527a-b
   in Rabelais's *Third Book*, 2:709b
   relative, in Mann's *Magic Mountain*, 9:722b
   relativity of, as discussed in La Bruyère's *Caractères*, 3:251b
   in Robbe-Grillet's works, 13:3241b, 3245b–3246b
   space and
       in Marinetti, 9:800b
       in Rilke, 9:783a-b, 787a
   in Tolstoy's works, as the medium of growth, 7:1481b–1482a

weltschmerz poets' obsession with, 5:420a-b

Time of Desecration. See Moravia, Alberto

Time, Distance, and Form in the Art of Proust. *See* Ortega y Gasset, José, "Tiempo, distancia, y forma en el arte de Proust"

Time and Free Will: An Essay on the Immediate Data of Consciousness. See Bergson, Henri

Time of Indifference, The. See Moravia, Alberto

Time (magazine). *See* Dostoevsky, Feodor

Time Regained. See Proust, Marcel, *Remembrance of Things Past* (À la recherche du temps perdu)

Time Remembered. See Anouilh, Jean

Time of Silence. *See* Santos, Luis Martín, *Tiempo de silencio*

Time—The Measure of the World. *See* Khlebnikov, Velimir, *Vremia mera mira*

Timeless Gentleman, The. *See* Azorín, *El caballero inactual*

Timely, The. *See* Ritsos, Yannis, *Ta Epikerika*

Times Literary Supplement, on Silone, 12:2294a

Timoleon. See Alfieri, Vittorio

Tin Drum, The. See Grass, Günter

"*Tinderbox, The.*" *See* Andersen, Hans Christian

Tinker, Tailor, Soldier, Spy. See Le Carré, John

Tirano Banderas. See Valle-Inclán, Ramón del, *The Tyrant*

Tiresias. See Ritsos, Yannis

Tiroirs de l'inconnu, Les. See Aymé, Marcel, *The Conscience of Love*

Tirol Passion plays, 1:466b–467a, 469a

Tirsi. See Castiglione, Baldesar

Tirso de Molina
   Cigarrales de Toledo (Country-Houses of Toledo), 2:951b–952a
   Deleitar aprovechando (To Enjoy Profitably), 2:951b

Tischbein, Johann Heinrich, 5:14a

Tisza, István, 9:865a

Titan. See Richter, Jean Paul

Tite et Bérénice. See Corneille, Pierre

Titian
  Bachanal, Ortega y Gasset's commentary on, 9:1123b
  Burckhardt on, 6:1233a
  Ortega y Gasset on, 9:1134a
Titian's Death. *See* Hofmannsthal, Hugo von, *Der Tod des Tizian*
"Titian's Son." *See* Musset, Alfred de
Tito, Josip Broz
  break with Stalin, 11:1823b, 1824a
  Krleža and, 11:1809b, 1821a
Titurel. See Wolfram von Eschenbach
Tiutchev, Fedor, Pasternak and, 10:1598a
Tjänstekvinnans son. See Strindberg, August, *The Son of a Servant*
"Tjuren." *See* Södergran, Edith
"To 31 P.Ch. stin Alexandreia." *See* Cavafy, Constantine
"To the Age of Enlightenment." *See* Lesage, Alain-René, "Au siècle des lumières"
"To Anna Akhmatova." *See* Blok, Alexander, "Anne Akhmatovoi"
To Ari. *See* Ritsos, Yannis, *To isteroghrafo tis dhoxas*
To Be Consumed by Embraces. *See* Ady, Endre, "Elfogyni az ölelésben"
To Be or Not to Be? See Andersen, Hans Christian
"To the Boy Elis." *See* Trakl, Georg, "An den Knaben Elis"
"To byl poslednii god." *See* Lozinsky, Mikhail
To the Car. *See* Marinetti, Filippo Tommaso, "A l'automobile"
"To Cassandra." *See* Mandelshtam, Osip
"To the Catafalque of Philip II in Seville." *See* Cervantes, Miguel de
To Clothe the Naked. See Pirandello, Luigi, *Vestire gli ignudi*
To the Councillors of All the Towns in Germany, That They Should Establish Christian Schools. See Luther, Martin
To Cyprus, Where Apollo Foretold Me. See Seferis, George, *Kypron, ou m'ethespisen*
To Damascus. See Strindberg, August
To Each His Minotaur. *See* Yourcenar, Marguerite, *Qui n'a pas son Minotaure?*

"To Ebert." *See* Klopstock, Friedrich Gottlieb
To Enjoy Profitably. *See* Tirso de Molina, *Deleitar aprovechando*
"To Ennui." *See* Ungaretti, Giuseppe
"To Eros." *See* Södergran, Edith, "Till Eros"
"To Fanny." *See* Klopstock, Friedrich Gottlieb
To the Fatherland. *See* Keller, Gottfried, "An das Vaterland"
To Find Oneself. See Pirandello, Luigi, *Trovarsi*
"To the Fly." *See* Heine, Heinrich, "Für die Mouche"
"To Friend and Foe." *See* Klopstock, Friedrich Gottlieb
"To the Germans." *See* Hölderlin, Friedrich, "An die Deutschen"
To the Giant Whale. *See* Ady, Endre, "A nagy cethalhoz"
To Have Done with the Judgment of God. See Artaud, Antonin
"To Himself." *See* Leopardi, Giacomo; Petrarch, "Ad se ipsum"
To Himself, Beloved by Him, the Author Dedicates These Lines. *See* Mayakovsky, Vladimir, "Sebe lyubimomu, posvyashchaet eti stroki avtor"
"To His Lady." *See* Leopardi, Giacomo
To His Mistress. *See* Ronsard, Pierre de, "A sa maîtresse"
"To the Infinite One." *See* Klopstock, Friedrich Gottlieb
"To Italy." *See* Apollinaire, Guillaume, "A l'Italie"; Leopardi, Giacomo, "All'Italia"
To José María Palacio. *See* Machado, Antonio, *Campos de Castilla* (Fields of Castile), "A José María Palacio"
"To Joy." *See* Schiller, Friedrich von
To the Lighthouse. See Woolf, Virginia
To Marx. *See* Ritsos, Yannis, "Sto Marx"
"To the Memory of Marina Tsvetaeva." *See* Pasternak, Boris, *Early Trains*
"To the Moon." *See* Leopardi, Giacomo
"To Music." *See* Rilke, Rainer Maria, "An die Musik"
"To My Double." *See* Blok, Alexander, "Dvoiniku"

"To My Father." *See* Quasimodo, Salvatore, "Al padre"

"To My Muse." *See* Blok, Alexander, "K Muze"

"To the New Moon." *See* Quasimodo, Salvatore, "Alla nuova luna"

"To a Polish Mother." *See* Mickiewicz, Adam, "Do matki Polki"

"To the Proletariat." *See* Apollinaire, Guillaume, "Au prolétaire"

"To the Reader." *See* Baudelaire, Charles

To Reign After Death. *See* Guevara, Luis Vélez de, *Reinar después de morir*

"To Remain." *See* Cavafy, Constantine, "Na meinei"

To Revolutionary Intellectuals. *See* Aragon, Louis, *Aux intellectuels révolutionnaires*

"To S." *See* Lermontov, Mikhail Yurievich, "K S."

"To Sensual Pleasure." *See* Cavafy, Constantine, "Idoni"

To Sergei Esenin. *See* Mayakovsky, Vladimir, "Sergeyu Eseninu"

To the Soviet Union. *See* Ritsos, Yannis, "ESSD"

"To Spend the Noontide, Pale and Absorbed." *See* Montale, Eugenio, *Cuttlefish Bones*

"To Spring." *See* Leopardi, Giacomo

"To Sylvia." *See* Leopardi, Giacomo

"To this gracious and joyful tune." *See* Arnaut Daniel, "En cest sonet coind'e leri"

To the Tragedian. *See* Hebbel, Friedrich, "An den Tragiker"

"To Two Cousins." *See* Grillparzer, Franz, "Auf zwei Vettern"

"To War." *See* Blok, Alexander, "Na voinu"

To Weep, to Weep, to Weep. *See* Ady, Endre, "Sirni, sirni, sirni"

To a Young Leader in the First World War. *See* George, Stefan, *Drei Gesänge* (*Three Cantos*), "Einem jungen Führer im ersten Weltkrieg"

Tobogán de hambientos. See Cela, Camilo José

Tocqueville, Alexis de, **6:893a–911b**
   Democracy in America (*De la démocratie en Amérique*), 5:105b, 6:895a–899b
   Souvenirs, 6:901a–905a

The Old Régime and the French Revolution (*L'Ancien régime et la révolution*), 6:905b–909a

Tod des Empedokles, Der. See Hölderlin, Friedrich

"Tod des Junggesellen, Der." *See* Schnitzler, Arthur

Tod des Tizian, Der. See Hofmannsthal, Hugo von

Tod des Vergil, Der. See Broch, Hermann, *The Death of Vergil*

Tod und Teufel. See Wedekind, Frank, *Death and the Devil*

Tod in Venedig, Der. See Mann, Thomas, *Death in Venice*

"Today, the Twenty-first of March." *See* Quasimodo, Salvatore, "Oggi ventuno marzo"

Togliatti, Palmiro, Italian Communist Party and, 12:2273b

Toilers of the Sea, The. See Hugo, Victor, *Les travailleurs de la mer*

Toison d'or, La. See Corneille, Pierre

Tolerance, Voltaire on, 4:380a

"Tolerance." *See* Södergran, Edith, "Tolerans"

"Tolerans." *See* Södergran, Edith

Tolkien, J. R. R., on *Beowulf*, 1:71b–72a

"Tolle, Scribe." *See* Ekelöf, Gunnar, "Tag och skriv"

Toller, Ernst
   Hoppla, 7:1748a
   Man and the Masses, 7:1748a
   Strindberg and, 7:1748a
   We're Alive!, 7:1748a

Tollrajzok. See Kosztolányi, Dezső

Tolomeo of Lucca, 1:416a

Tolstoy, Alexey, slapped by Mandelshtam, 10:1645b

Tolstoy, Leo, **7:1471a–1493b**
   A Confession, 7:1472b, 1485a-b
   "After the Ball," 7:1490a
   Anna Karenina, 7:1429b–1430a, 1472a, 1482b, 1483a–1484b
      Chekhov's "The Lady with a Dog" and, 7:1874a-b
      compared to Pushkin's *Eugene Onegin*, 5:671b

Tolstoy, Leo (*cont.*)
  Anna Karenina (*cont.*)
    death theme, 7:1486a
    family in, 11:2240a
    Proust's *Remembrance of Things Past*
      and, 8:550b, 556a
    treatment of marriage, 7:1488a
  Babel and, 11:1886b
  Chekhov and, 7:1862b
    "In the Ravine," 7:1869a, 1869b
  on Chekhov's "The Darling," 7:1873b
  Childhood, 7:1471a, 1472b, 1476b,
    1477b–1478b, 1479b, 1480a, 1488b,
    1490a, 1860a
    death theme, 7:1485b
  diaries, 7:1475b–1477b
  Family Happiness, 7:1472b, 1480a,
    1487b–1488a
  Father Sergius, 7:1472b, 1485b,
    1489b–1490a
  Four Epochs of Growth, 7:1477b
  Ginzburg and, 13:3161a
  Goncharov and, 6:1067a, 1082a
  Gorky and, 8:418a, 418b, 419b, 422a, 442a
    in the Crimea, 8:442b, 443a-b
    The Lower Depths, 8:435b
  Hadji-Murad, 7:1472b, 1490a, 1490b
  "How Much Land Does a Man Need?,"
    Chekhov's "Gooseberries" and, 7:1871b
  Kafka and, 9:1154b
  Lermontov and, 6:1196b, 1220a, 1224a
  letter to Alexandra Tolstoy, 7:1480a
  letter to Aunt Toinette, 7:1473b–1474a
  literary celebrity, 11:1893b
  Lukács on, 10:1272a-b
  Master and Man, 7:1472b, 1489b
  Moberg and, 11:2208a
  Notes of a Madman, 7:1485a
  Pasternak and, 10:1593a, 1613b–1614a
  peasantry in works of, 7:1488b–1489a
  Polikushka, 7:1489a
  Resurrection, 7:1472b, 1488b
  Rilke and, 9:769b
  Ritsos' translations of, 12:2838a
  Schopenhauer's influence on, 5:397a
  Sevastopol Sketches, 7:1471a-b, 1479b,
    1480a

    death theme, 7:1485b
  Solzhenitsyn and, 13:3187a, 3196b
  The Cossacks, 7:1472b, 1478b–1480a
    narrator's voice, 11:1906b–1907a
  The Death of Ivan Ilich, 7:1472b, 1485b,
    1486b–1487a, 1489a
  "The Deathbed Notes of the Elder Fyodor
    Kuzmich," 7:1490a
  The Kreutzer Sonata, 7:1472b, 1488a
  The Power of Darkness, 7:1489a-b
  "Three Years" and, 7:1869b
  War and Peace (*Voina i mir*), 6:986b, 1067a,
    1082a, 1196b, 7:1472a, 1474b, 1479b,
    1480a–1483a, 1488b–1489a
    death theme, 7:1485b–1486a, 1486b
    epilogue, 7:1482b–1483a, 1486a
    family in, 11:2240a
    form, 13:3196b
    Kotik Letaev and, 9:905b
    Lampedusa's *The Leopard* and, 11:2012b,
      2030a
    Lukács on, 10:1261b–1262a
    Proust's *Remembrance of Things Past*
      and, 8:550b
    treatment of marriage, 7:1488a
  What Is Art?, 7:1472b, 1487a-b
    Chekhov on, 7:1862b–1863a
  Zola compared with, 7:1536b–1537a
Tolstoyanism
  Chekhov and, 7:1856b, 1861b–1863a, 1864a,
    1864b, 1869b
  in "Gusev," 7:1865b
  in "My Life," 7:1868b
Tom Jones. See Fielding, Henry
Tomás Rueda. See Azorín
Tomashevskii, Boris, on Mayakovsky,
  11:1894a
Tomaso di Caluso, Alfieri and, 4:664b, 669b
"Tomb of Edgar Poe, The." See Mallarmé,
  Stéphane, "Le tombeau d'Edgar Poe"
"Tomb of Iasis." See Cavafy, Constantine,
  "Iasi tofos"
Tomb image, in Foscolo, 5:332a–335b
"Tombe, La" ("The Tomb"). See Maupassant,
  Guy de
"Tombeau d'Edgar Poe, Le." See Mallarmé,
  Stéphane

Tommaso de'Guardati. *See* Masuccio Salernitano

Tommaso, Piero de, on Vittorini, 12:2748b

"Tomorrow." *See* Zamyatin, Yevgeny Ivanovich, "Zavtra"

Tomorrow the Dawn. See Montherlant, Henry de, *Demain il fera jour*

Tomorrow's Eve. See Villiers de l'Isle-Adam, *L'Eve future*

"Ton Vaion." *See* Elytis, Odysseus, *To photodendro kai i dekati tetarti omorfia*

Tonal progression, in Trakl, 10:1416b

Tongue Set Free, The. See Canetti, Elias

Tonight . . . *See* Mandelshtam, Osip, "Segodnia nochivu . . ."

Tonight We Improvise. See Pirandello, Luigi, *Questa sera si recita a soggetto*

Tonio Kröger. See Mann, Thomas

"Tonka." *See* Musil, Robert, *Drei Frauen*

Tontine, La. See Lesage, Alain-René

Too Many. See Alfieri, Vittorio, Political Tetralogy

"Too Many Trips to Heidelberg." *See* Böll, Heinrich, *Du fährst zu oft nach Heidelberg und andere Erzählungen*

"Tool's Lament, The." *See* Södergran, Edith, "Verktygets klaga"

Topology of a Phantom City (Topologie d'un cité fantôme). See Robbe-Grillet, Alain

Tor und der Tod, Der. See Hofmannsthal, Hugo von, *Death and the Fool*

Tormento. See Pérez Galdós, Benito

Tornada, 1:176a

Tornimparte, Alessandra. *See* Ginzburg, Natalia

Torquato Tasso. See Goethe, Johann Wolfgang von

Torquemada en la cruz (Torquemada at the Cross). See Pérez Galdós, Benito, Torquemada series novels

Torquemada en la hoguera (Torquemada at the Stake). See Pérez Galdós, Benito, Torquemada series novels

Torquemada y San Pedro. See Pérez Galdós, Benito, Torquemada series novels

Torrent, The. See Blasco Ibáñez, Vicente, *Entre naranjos*

"Torrents of Spring." *See* Turgenev, Ivan

Torso, The. *See* Andrić, Ivo, "Trup"

"Tortured Heart, The." *See* Rimbaud, Arthur, "Coeur volé"

Total Season with the Songs of the New Light, The. *See* Jiménez, Juan Ramón, *La estación total con las canciones de la nueva luz*

Totalitarianism
  Broch's opposition to, 10:1405a-b
  forecast in Witkiewicz's *Mątwa*, 10:1223a
  Ionesco's *Rhinocéros* and, 13:3001b
  Kafka and, 9:1167a
  Kundera and, 13:3389a–3411b
  Lagerkvist's response to, 10:1690a–1691b
  Milosz and, 13:2936a
  in Witkiewicz's plays, 10:1227a-b
  see also Fascism; Nazism; Stalinism

Totality, concept of
  in Broch, 10:1385a
  in Greek culture, 10:1260b–1261a
  in Lukács's philosophy, 10:1253a, 1256a, 1258b

Totem and Taboo (Totem und Tabu). See Freud, Sigmund

Totemism, Freud's concept of, 8:12a–13a

Totentag. See Trakl, Georg

Totentanz. See Wedekind, Frank, *Death and the Devil*

Toth, Catherine, 11:2116a

Toulouse, Edouard, influence on Artaud, 11:1963b

Toulouse-Lautrec, Henri de, and Jarry, 9:665a

Tour de Nesle, La. See Dumas père, Alexandre

"Tour Eiffel, La." *See* Barthes, Roland, "The Eiffel Tower"

"Tour Through the German Inflation, A." *See* Benjamin, Walter, "Reise durch die deutsche Inflation"

Tour Through the Pyrenees, A. See Taine, Hippolyte, *Voyage aux eaux des Pyrénées*

Touriste de bananes. See Simenon, Georges

"Tournesol." *See* Breton, André

Tourneur, Cyril, on Ibsen, 7:1445b

Tous les hommes sont mortels. See Beauvoir, Simone de, *All Men Are Mortal*

Toute compte fait. See Beauvoir, Simone de, *All Said and Done*

Toutounier, Le. See Colette

Továrna na absolutno. See Čapek, Karel

Toward an Ontology of Social Being. *See* Lukács, György, *Zur Ontologie des gesellschaftlichen Seins*

Toward Socialist Realism. *See* Aragon, Louis, *Pour un réalisme socialiste*

Towards the Low Land. *See* Machado, Antonio, *Nuevas canciones* (New Songs), "Hacia la tierra baja"

Towards a New Novel. See Robbe-Grillet, Alain, *Pour un nouveau roman*

Towards White Infinity. *See* Arp, Jean, *Vers le blanc infini*

Tower, The. See Hofmannsthal, Hugo von

Tower, The. *See* Vesaas, Tarjei, *Tårnet*

"Tower, The." *See* Yeats, W. B.

"Tower, The

Towiański, Andrzej, Mickiewicz and, 5:630a–631a

Towneley cycle plays, 1:469a

Tozzetti, Fanny Targioni, 5:548b, 549a-b, 564b–565a

Tra donne sole. See Pavese, Cesare, *Among Women Only*

"Trabajo gustoso, El." *See* Jiménez, Juan Ramón

Trabajo gustoso, El. See Jiménez, Juan Ramón

Trabajos de Persiles y Sigismunda, Los. See Cervantes, Miguel de, *The Trials of Persiles and Sigismunda*

Tractatus Logico-Philosophicus. See Wittgenstein, Ludwig

Tractor. *See* Ritsos, Yannis, *Trakter*

Tradition
in Blasco Ibáñez' *The Dead Command*, 8:385a-b
religious, in Novalis' works, 5:223b

Tradition des nouveaux mystiques, La (*Tradition of the New Mystics*). *See* Bossuet, Jacques Bénigne

Tradition, Western. *See* Civilization, Western

Traditional story
Beowulf as, 1:58a–60a, 71, 72b
characteristics of, 1:58a-b

Grettis saga as, 1:59a-b

Traditionalism
in *Beowulf*, 1:57b–58a
Gombrowicz and, 12:2578b–2579a
in oral cultures, 1:56b–57a

Traducianism, Prudentius' *Apotheosis* on, 1:8a

Traffic jams, in plays of Ionesco, 13:2998b, 3015b

Tragédia da Rua das Flores, A. See Eça de Queiroz, José Maria

Tragedia de ensueño. See Valle-Inclán, Ramón del

"Tragedia di un personaggio, La." *See* Pirandello, Luigi

Tragedia pastoril en tres actos. See Valle-Inclán, Ramón del

Tragedias grotescas, Las. See Baroja, Pío

Tragedies with a Lyrical Intermezzo. See Heine, Heinrich, *Tragödien, nebst einem lyrischen Intermezzo*

Tragedy
Apollonian versus Dionysian, 7:1656b–1657b
Calderón and, 2:883a-b
comedy and, Lope de Vega and, 2:851b, 865b
Croce on, 8:317b–318a
Dürrenmatt and, 13:3218a–3219b
in French literature
Alfieri's critique of, 4:664a
Boileau on, 3:196b
Camus and, 13:3064a-b
Corneille and, 3:34b
Ionesco's *Exit the King* and, 13:3006a-b
Lessing on German theater and, 4:544a-b, 547b–548a
see also Corneille, Pierre; Racine, Jean
Greek
Corneille and, 3:34b
Kleist and, 5:300b–301a
Schiller's *The Bride of Messina* as, 5:47b
Staël's *De la littérature* on, 5:96b
in Italian literature, Alfieri and, 4:661a, 665a-b
in Kundera, 13:3400b–3401a
Lessing on, 4:547a–548a

Lukács on, 10:1255b–1256a, 1258b
middle-class, of Hebbel, 6:1102b–1105b
pan-tragedy in Hebbel's works, 6:1098b, 1111a
in Svevo's novels, 8:77b–78a, 84a–86a
see also Drama; *Schauertragödie*; Tragicomedy
"Tragedy of Central Europe, The." *See* Kundera, Milan
"Tragedy of Central Europe, The
"Tragedy of a Character, The." *See* Pirandello, Luigi, "La tragedia di un personaggio"
Tragedy of Flores Street, The. *See* Eça de Queiroz, José Maria, *A tragédia da Rua das Flores*
Traghoudi tis adhelfis mou, To. See Ritsos, Yannis
Tragic Andalusia. *See* Azorín, *La Andalucia trágica*
Tragic Crown, The. See Lope de Vega, *La corona trágica*
Tragic Sense of Life in Men and Nations, The. See Unamuno, Miguel de, *Del sentimiento trágico de la vida en los hombres y los pueblos*
Tragic Sense of Life, The. See Ortega y Gasset, José, *Del sentimento trágico de la vida*
Tragic, the, Sartre and, 12:2589b
"Tragical in Daily Life, The." *See* Maeterlinck, Maurice, "Le Tragique quotidien"
Tragicomedy
  audience response to, 8:268a
  Camoëns' *The Two Amphitryons* as, 2:755b
  Corneille and, 3:34b
    Le Cid as, 3:31b, 33b
  Goldoni and, 4:425a
  Guarini's defense of, 2:917a-b, 919a
  origins of, 2:917a-b
  Wedekind's definition, 8:235a
"Tragique quotidien, Le." *See* Maeterlinck, Maurice
Tragiques, Les. See Aubigné, Théodore Agrippa d'
Tragödien, nebst einem lyrischen Intermezzo. See Heine, Heinrich
"Trahison de la comtesse de Rhune, La." *See* Maupassant, Guy de

Train bleu, Le. See Cocteau, Jean
Train Was on Time, The. See Böll, Heinrich
Training in Christianity. See Kierkegaard, Søren
Trains
  Carducci on
    "Alla stazione in una mattina d'autunno," 7:1512b–1513a
    "Davanti San Guido," 7:1507a-b
  in Zola's *La bête humaine*, 7:1534a-b
Traité d'anatomie humaine. See Testus, Jean
Traité de la connaisance de Dieu et de soi-même, La. See Bossuet, Jacques Bénigne
Traité de l'éducation des filles. See Fénelon, François de Salignac de la Mothe-
Traité de l'existence de Dieu. See Fénelon, François de Salignac de la Mothe-
Traité d'instrumentation et d'orchestration moderne. See Berlioz, Hector
Traité du Narcisse, Le. See Gide, Andre
Traité du style, Le. See Aragon, Louis
Traité du vain combat, Le. See Yourcenar, Marguerite, *Alexis ou le traité du vain combat*
Traité philosophique et physiologique de l'hérédité naturelle. See Lucas, Prosper
Traité sur la nature et la grâce. See Malebranche, Nicolas
Traité sur la tolérance. See Voltaire
Trajan, Roman emperor, in Alfieri's *Panegyric to Trajan by Pliny*, 4:675b
Trakl, Georg, **10:1409a–1427b**
  "An den Knaben Elis" ("To the Boy Elis"), 10:1417b–1418b
  Böll and, 13:3167a
  "Dream and Madness" ("Traum und Umnachtung"), 10:1420b, 1421b–1422b
  "Ein Winterabend" ("A Winter Evening"), 10:1417a-b
  Fata Morgana, 10:1413b
  Gedichte (Poems), 10:1414a
  "Grodek," 10:1419a–1420b
  "Helian," 10:1420b–1421a
  Hölderlin and, 5:143a, 173b
  "Im Osten" ("On the Eastern Front"), 10:1425a-b

Trakl, Georg (*cont.*)
  "Revelation and Downfall" ("Offenbarung
    und Untergang"), 10:1420b
  Sebastian im Traum (Sebastian Dreaming),
    10:1414b
  "Sommer" ("Summer"), 10:1416a–1417a
  "The Occident" ("Abendland"),
    10:1410a–1411a, 1423b–1424a
  "The Thunderstorm" ("Das Gewitter"),
    10:1422b–1423b
  Totentag (All Souls Day), 10:1413b
"Traktat moralny." *See* Milosz, Czeslaw
Traktat poetycki. See Milosz, Czeslaw
Trakter. See Ritsos, Yannis
"Tramonto della luna, Il." *See* Leopardi,
    Giacomo, "The Setting of the Moon"
"Tranchée, La." *See* Apollinaire, Guillaume,
    Tendre comme le souvenir
Tranquilli, Secondo. *See* Silone, Ignazio
Trans-Atlantyk. See Gombrowicz, Witold
Trans-Europ-Express. See Robbe-Grillet, Alain
Transcendence
  Broch and, 10:1387b
  Kierkegaard and, 6:1137b–1140a
  in Klopstock, 4:521a
Transcendentalism, Herder's influence on,
    4:654a
Transference, Freud's concept of, 8:6a-b,
    7b–8a, 16a
Transfiguration of Christ, in Dante's *Convivio*,
    1:440a
Transfiguration dans le cirque, La
    (Transfiguration in the Circus). *See*
    Ghelderode, Michel de
"Transfigurazione" ("Transfiguration"). *See*
    Ungaretti, Giuseppe
Transformation
  metaphysical, Rilke on, 9:776b, 777a
  personal, in Corneille's plays, 3:23b, 28a,
    29b–30a, 31a, 33b
  in Rabelais's works, 2:715a
  Sartre and, 12:2604a–2611a
  see also Metamorphosis
Transience, Sartre and, 12:2591b–2592a
Transient Hour, The. See Aymé, Marcel
transition (review), Arp and, 10:1371b
Translations

of *Aeneid*, by Leopardi, 5:545b
Benjamin's view of, 11:1707b–1708b
by Chateaubriand, 5:113b, 137b–138a
by Dinesen, 10:1291b–1292b
by Hölderlin, 5:172a
by Jiménez, 9:992a, 1003b–1004a
by Kosztolányi, 10:1234a
by Musset, 6:1002b
by Pasternak, 10:1606a–1608a
French, of Cleland's *Fanny Hill*, 6:1033a
of Gunnarsson's works, 10:1504b, 1512a,
    1518a-b
of Leopardi, 5:541a
Russian, of Perse, 10:1439a
of Trakl, 10:1425a-b
Translator
  Baudelaire as, 7:1326a
  Büchner as, 6:1182b
  Butor as, 13:3288a
  Diderot as, 4:481b–482a
  Erasmus as, 2:577a
  Foscolo as, 5:315a
  Luther as, 2:680a-b
  Mérimée as, 6:765a–766a
Transmutation, in Arp, 10:1378a
Transparency, in Rousseau, 4:468b–470a
"Transpositions d'art"
  in Baudelaire's works, 6:1043a
  in Gautier's works, 6:1041a–1043b, 1045a
Transrational language
  futurism and, 10:1345b
  of Khlebnikov, 10:1347b–1348a, 1524b
Transtales. *See* Supertales
Transubstantiation, Luther and, 2:677a
Transvestism, in Ghelderode's *Escurial*,
    11:2118a
Trap for Judges. *See* Hylaea group, *Sadok
    sudei*
Trap for Judges, A, II. See Hylaea group,
    Sadok sudei, II
Trapné povídky. See Čapek, Karel
Trapobanian-Isle. *See* Taprobana
"Trappiste, Le" (The Trappist). *See* Vigny,
    Alfred Victor de, *Poèmes antiques et
    modernes*
Trarieux, Gabriel, tribute to Zola, 7:1539b
Trato de Argel, El. See Cervantes, Miguel de

Trattatello in laude di Dante. See Boccaccio, Giovanni

Trauerspiel (dramatic genre), Benjamin's study of, 11:1714a–1721a

Trauerspiel in Sizilien, Ein. See Hebbel, Friedrich

Traum ein Leben, Der. See Grillparzer, Franz, *A Dream Is Life*

"Traum und Umnachtung." *See* Trakl, Georg, "Dream and Madness"

"Traum von einem Schlachtfeld, Ein." *See* Richter, Jean Paul

"Traum von einem Schlachtfeld, Ein Madness"

Traumdeutung, Die. See Freud, Sigmund, *The Interpretation of Dreams*

"Träume vom Tod und Leben." *See* Arp, Jean

Traumnovelle (Dream Novella), Schnitzler's use of form, 8:109b–110a

Traumnovelle (Rhapsody). *See* Schnitzler, Arthur

"Traurige Tänze." *See* George, Stefan, *Das Jahr der Seele*

Travailleurs de la mer, Les. See Hugo, Victor

Travaux d'approche. See Butor, Michel

Travel
  Alfieri's satire of, 4:675a
  Andersen and, 6:867b–868a
  in Ionesco's plays, 13:3015a
  symbolism of
    in Broch, 10:1392a
    of Seferis, 12:2263a

Travel Journal. See Montaigne, Michel de

Travel notes, in Lermontov's works, 6:1218a-b, 1219b

Travel Notes. See Bely, Andrey, *Putevye zametki*

Travel Pictures. See Heine, Heinrich, *Reisebilder*

Travel writing
  Andersen and, 6:871a-b, 877a-b
  of Berlioz, 6:789a–790a
  Butor's approach to, 13:3303a-b
  Cela and, 13:3112a–3113a
  of Chateaubriand, 5:113a, 115b
  of Gautier, 6:1048a–1049b
  Goncharov's work in, 6:1071a–1073a
  of Heine, 5:495b–497b

  Mérimée's work in, 6:756b, 761b
  of Moravia, 12:2686a, 2696b
  Sand and, 6:822b
  of Unamuno, 8:284b
  of Ungaretti, 10:1453a

"Traveler, The." *See* Apollinaire, Guillaume, *Alcools*, "Le voyageur"; Machado, Antonio, *Soledades, galerías, y otros poemas* (Solitudes, Galleries, and Other Poems), "El viajero"

Traveler Without Luggage. See Anouilh, Jean

"Traveling Companion, The." *See* Andersen, Hans Christian

Travelingue. See Aymé, Marcel, *The Miraculous Barber*

Traveller, If You Come to Spa . . . . See Böll, Heinrich, *Wanderer kommst du nach Spa . . .*

Travels in America. See Chateaubriand, François René de, *Voyage en Amérique*

Travels in Auvergne. See Sand, George, *Le voyage en Auvergne*

Travels in Russia. See Gautier, Théophile

Travels in Spain. See Gautier, Théophile

Travels in Spain. See Sand, George, *Le voyage en Espagne*

Travels in Switzerland. See Dumas père, Alexandre, *Impressions de voyage en Suisse*

Travels Through the March of Brandenburg. See Fontane, Theodor, *Wanderungen durch die Mark Brandenburg*

Travels Through My Land. See Garrett, Almeida, *Viagens na minha terra*

Travnića hronika. See Andrić, Ivo, *Bosnian Chronicle*

"Treason of the Countess of Rhune, The." *See* Maupassant, Guy de, "La trahison de la comtesse de Rhune"

Treason of the Illiterate, The. See Kosztolányi, Dezső, *Az irástudatlanok árulása*

Treasure of the Humble, The. See Maeterlinck, Maurice

"Treasure and the Two Men, The." *See* La Fontaine, Jean de, *Fables*, "Le trésor et les deux hommes"

Treatise on Eden, A. *See* Wedekind, Frank, "Abhandlung Eden"

Treatise on the Education of Girls. See Fénelon, François de Salignac de la Mothe-, *Traité de l'éducation des filles*

Treatise on the Existence of God. See Fénelon, François de Salignac de la Mothe-, *Traité de l'existence de Dieu*

Treatise on Human Anatomy. See Testus, Jean, *Traité d'anatomie humaine*

Treatise of Human Nature, A. See Hume, David

Treatise on Instrumentation and Orchestration. See Berlioz, Hector, *Traité d'instrumentation et d'orchestration moderne*

Treatise on the Knowledge of God and of Oneself. See Bossuet, Jacques Bénigne, *La traité de la connaissance de Dieu et de soi-même*

Treatise on Morals. *See* Milosz, Czeslaw, "Traktat moralny"

Treatise on Nature and Grace. See Malebranche, Nicolas, *Traité sur la nature et la grâce*

Treatise on the New Testament, A. See Luther, Martin

Treatise on Poetry. *See* Milosz, Czeslaw, *Traktat poetrycki*

Treatise in Praise of Dante. See Boccaccio, Giovanni, *Trattatello in laude di Dante*

Treatise on Some Points of the History of the Longobards in Italy. *See* Manzoni, Alessandro, *Discorso su alcuni punti della storia longobardica in Italia*

Treatise on Tolerance. *See* Voltaire, *Traité sur la tolérance*

Trebnik troikh. See Hylaea group

"Tree." *See* Apollinaire, Guillaume, "Arbre"

Tree, H. D. Beerbohm, 9:889a

Tree of Knowledge, The. See Baroja, Pío

Treffen in Telgte, Das. See Grass, Günter, *The Meeting at Telgte*

"Treis moules." *See* Seferis, George

Treitschke, Heinrich von, on French loyalty in Alsace-Lorraine, 7:1655a

"Treli rodia, I." *See* Elytis, Odysseus, *Prosanatolismi*

"Trench, The." *See* Apollinaire, Guillaume, *Tendre comme le souvenir (Tender as a Memory)*, "La tranchée"

Trent, Council of, 3:264a

Tres cortes armara el rey, Poema de mio Cid as source for, 1:132a

"Tres cuadros del vino." *See* Ortega y Gasset, José

"Tres, Los"
  Baroja's contact with, 9:597a
  in Spanish regeneration, 9:593a

Tresor des humbles, Le. See Maeterlinck, Maurice, *The Treasure of the Humble*

"Trésor et les deux hommes, Le." *See* La Fontaine, Jean de, *Fables*

Třetí sešit směšných lásek. See Kundera, Milan, *The Third Book of Laughable Loves*

Treuer Diener seines Herrn, Ein. See Grillparzer, Franz, *A Faithful Servant of His Master*

Trézenik, Charles, 7:1640a

"Tri dnia." *See* Zamyatin, Yevgeny Ivanovich

"Tri goda." *See* Chekhov, Anton

Tri sestry. See Chekhov, Anton, *The Three Sisters*

Tri simfonije. See Krleža, Miroslav

Tri tolstyaka. See Olesha, Yuri, *The Three Fat Men*

Tria horika. See Ritsos, Yannis

Tria krypha poiemata. See Seferis, George

Tria poiemata me simea ekerias. See Elytis, Odysseus

Trial. *See* Ritsos, Yannis, *Dhokimasia*

Trial of Joan of Arc at Rouen, The. See Brecht, Bertolt

"Trial, The." *See* Babel, Isaac, "Sud"

Trial, The. See Kafka, Franz

Trials of Persiles and Sigismunda, The. See Cervantes, Miguel

Trials, The. *See* Vaksberg, Arkady, "Protsessy"

Triangle, in Descartes's *Meditations on First Philosophy*, 3:16a

Triangle Junction. *See* Grass, Günter, *Gleisdreieck*

Trianon, Treaty of, Kosztolányi and, 10:1235a
Tribune des peoples, La (journal), 5:631b
Tricheur, Le. See Simon, Claude
Tricks of Life and Death. *See* Pirandello,
    Luigi, *Beffe della vita e della morte*
Trier Easter play, 1:465b
Trieste
    art and culture, 13:3132b–3133a
    Svevo in, 8:67a–68a
Trifling Tales. See Juan de Timoneda, *El
    patrañuelo*
Trilling, Lionel
    Babel and, 11:1889a, 1894b
    distrust of culture, 9:1136a
Trilogia della villeggiatura, La. See Goldoni,
    Carlo
Trinitarianism, in Augustine's *On the Trinity*,
    1:37b–38a
Trinity, Walther and, 1:302b–303a
Triolet, Elsa
    Aragon and, 11:2061b, 2070a–2071a, 2076b
    Aragon's poems for, 11:2061a
    during French Resistance, 11:2078a–2081a
    Le cheval blanc (*The White Horse* and *The
        White Charger*), 11:2081a
    Le monument (The Statue), 11:2083a
    Le premier accroc coûte deux cents francs
        (*A Fine of Two Hundred Francs*),
        11:2070a
    Les amants d'Avignon (*The Lovers of
        Avignon*), 11:2078b, 2079a
    Luna-Park, 11:2083b
    Mayakovsky and, 11:1837a, 2070a
Triolet, Elsa, and Aragon, Louis, translation of
    Céline's *Journey to the End of the Night*,
    11:1861b–1862a
Trionfi, I. See Petrarch
Trionfo della morte, Il. See D'Annunzio,
    Gabriele
Trip to Dauphiné. *See* Berlioz, Hector, "Voyage
    en Dauphiné"
Trip to Italy. See Taine, Hippolyte, *Voyage en
    Italie*
Trip to Rome, The. *See* Moravia, Alberto, *Il
    viaggio a Roma*
Triptych: Three Scenic Panels. See Frisch,
    Max

Triptych. See Simon, Claude, *Triptyque*
Triptychon: Drei szenische Bilder. See Frisch,
    Max, *Triptych: Three Scenic Panels*
Triptyque. See Simon, Claude
Trissino, Gian Giorgio, *Italia liberata dai goti*
    (*Italy Freed from the Goths*), 2:798b,
    801a
Tristan. See Mann, Thomas; Thomas of
    Brittany
Tristan and Isolde. See Gottfried von
    Strassburg; Wagner, Richard
Tristan story
    Arthurian legend and, 1:148b
    Béroul and, 1:148b
    Chrétien de Troyes and, 1:148b
        Cligés, 1:192b
        Conte du Graal, 1:207b–208a
    Eilhart von Oberge and, 1:148b
    Gottfried von Strassburg and, 1:148b
    Thomas of Brittany and, 1:148b
    in Wagner's works, 6:1156b, 1157a-b
Tristan und Isold. See Gottfried von
    Strassburg
Tristan und Isolde. See Wagner, Richard,
    Tristan and Isolde
"Tristesse." *See* Musset, Alfred de
"Tristesse de Cornélius Berg, La." *See*
    Yourcenar, Marguerite, *Nouvelles
    orientales*
"Tristesse d'Olympio." *See* Hugo, Victor
"Tristesse d'une étoile." *See* Apollinaire,
    Guillaume
Tristia. See Berlioz, Hector
"Tristia." *See* Mandelshtam, Osip
Tristram Shandy. See Sterne, Laurence
Tristrams saga, 1:393a, 398a, 399b
Triton (god), in Camoëns' *The Lusiads*, 2:763a
"Triumf att finnas till." *See* Södergran, Edith
Triumph of Death. See D'Annunzio, Gabriele
Triumph of Death, The. See Beaumont,
    Francis, and Fletcher, John
Triumph of Death, The. *See* Sologub, Vladimir
    Aleksandrovich, *Pobeda smerti*
"Triumph of Existing." *See* Södergran, Edith,
    "Triumf att finnas till"
Triumphlied. See Brahms, Johannes
Triumphs, The. See Petrarch, *I trionfi*

Trobar clus, in satire of Marcabru, 1:360a

Troe. See Gorky, Maxim; Hylaea group

"Troes." *See* Cavafy, Constantine

Trois crimes de mes amis, Les. See Simenon, Georges

Trois Glorieuses. See France, Revolution of July 1830

Trois mousquetaires, Les. See Dumas père, Alexandre

Trois Veritez. See Charron, Pierre

Trois villes. See Zola, Émile

Troisième dessous. See Butor, Michel

"Trojans." *See* Cavafy, Constantine, "Troes"

Trojans, The. See Berlioz, Hector, *Les Troyens*

Trommeln in der Nacht. See Brecht, Bertolt, *Drums in the Night*

Tronchin, Théodore, 5:90a

Tronson, Louis
  Fénelon and, 3:265a
  Madame Guyon and, 3:270b

Trope allegory
  in the Bible, 1:5b
  in Prudentius' *Cathemerinon*, 1:7b

Trope, musical, medieval drama and, 1:451b, 453b–454a

Tropic Moon. See Simenon, Georges, *Le coup de lune*

Tropical Madness. See Witkiewicz, Stanisław Ignacy

Tropism, in Sarraute's works, 12:2334b–2335a, 2336a-b, 2337a-b, 2354b, 2355a

Tropismes (*Tropisms*). *See* Sarraute, Nathalie

Tropology, Cassian on, 1:4b

"Trostnik." *See* Akhmatova, Anna

Trotsky, Leon
  on fellow travelers, 11:2248b
  Malraux and, 12:2417b
  "Problems of the Chinese Revolution," 12:2278a
  surrealists and, 11:2071a

Trotsky, Leon (joint author). *See* Breton, André

"Trotzdem: Humane Politik." *See* Broch, Hermann

Trotzig, Birgitta, Ekelöf and, 12:2636a-b

Troubadour poetry, **1:161a–177b**
  Arthurian legend and, 1:153a
  Chrétien de Troyes and, 1:179a, 185b

conventionalization of, 1:178a-b

Dante and, 1:433b, 438b

effects of, 1:178b–179a

genres of, 1:167a

love as theme of, 1:139b–140a

parodied by Marcabru, 1:372a

rhyme in, 1:176a-b

tradition de refus, Mallarmé's themes of, 7:1581b–1582a, 1583b, 1585b, 1588b–1589a

trouvères and, 1:178b–179a

Troupe du Marais, 3:25b, 27b

Trouvaille, la, in Breton's thought, 11:1945b–1946a, 1952b–1953a, 1954b

Trouvères, **1:177b–182b**

Trouvères, *see also* Troubadours

Trovarsi. See Pirandello, Luigi

Troy, legend of
  in Baudelaire, 7:1340b–1341a
  in Foscolo, 5:333b–334a
  Giraudoux's *Tiger at the Gates*, 9:1052b–1053b
  in Racine's *Andromaque*, 3:210b–212b
  see also Berlioz, Hector, *Les Troyens*

Troyens, Les. See Berlioz, Hector

"Truba Gul'-Mully." *See* Khlebnikov, Velimir

Truba marsian. See Khlebnikov, Velimir

Truck symbolism, in Vittorini's *The Women of Messina*, 12:2750a-b, 2751b

Trudaine, Louis and Michel, Chénier's friendship with, 4:695a, 698a-b, 699a

True History (*True Story*). *See* Lucian, *Vera historia*

True Story of My Life, The. See Andersen, Hans Christian

"Trümmerfrau." *See* Grass, Günter, *Gleisdreieck*

Trumpet of the Martians, The. See Khlebnikov, Velimir, *Truba marsian*

Trumpet symbolism, in Silone's *A Handful of Blackberries*, 12:2296a

Trumpets and Drums. See Brecht, Bertolt

"Trup." *See* Andrić, Ivo

Truth
  Foucault and, 13:3347a–3348b
  Johnson and, 12:2372b
  Kafka on, 9:1160b

in Kundera, 13:3398b

Rimbaud's view of, 7:1820b

17th-century struggle with criteria of, 3:8a–9a

in Stendhal, 5:354a, 362a-b

in Vico's epistemology, 3:297b–298a

in Wolfram, 1:268b–269a

Truth Emerges, The. *See* Moberg, Vilhelm, *Sanningen kryper fram*

Truth on the March. See Zola, Émile, *La vérité en marche*

Tryflings. *See* Ekelöf, Gunnar, *Strountes*

Trypanis, Constantine, on Greek poetry, 13:2955a

Trzy zimy. See Milosz, Czeslaw

Tsar Maiden, The. *See* Tsvetaeva, Marina, "Tsar'-devitsa"

Tsar Saltan. See Pushkin, Alexander

"Tsar'-devitsa." *See* Tsvetaeva, Marina

"Tsarapina po nebu." *See* Khlebnikov, Velimir

Tsatsos, Constantine, "To telos enos dialogou" (End of a Dialogue), 12:2259b

Tschandala. See Strindberg, August

Tsirkas, Stratis, Alexandrian history, 8:209b–210a

"Tstvit v moemu sertsi." *See* Tychyna, Pavlo, *Soniachni klarnety*

Tsvetaev, Ivan Vladimirovich, 11:1732a–1733a

Tsvetaeva, Anastasiia, *Dym, dym, dym* (*Smoke, smoke, smoke*), Mandelshtam and, 10:1637a

Tsvetaeva, Marina, 9:920a, **11:1731a–1750b**

  on Akhmatova's name, 10:1522a

  Blok and, 9.985B, 9:986a-b

  "Chert" ("The Devil"), 11:1746b

  "Dom u Starogo Pimena" ("The House at Old Pimen's"), 11:1746a

  "Istoriia odnogo posviashcheniia" ("The History of a Dedication,") 11:1744b–1745a

  Iunosheskie stikhi (Youthful Verses), 11:1734b

  Iz dvukh knig (From Two Books), 11:1734b

  "Khanskii Polon" ("Prisoner of the Khan"), 11:1739a

  Kovcheg (The Ark), 11:1741a

  Krysolov (The Pied Piper), 11:1741b–1742a

  Lebedinyi stan (*The Demesne of the Swans*), 11:1738a

  literary celebrity, 11:1893b

  Mandelshtam's love for, 10:1636b–1637a

  "Mat' i muzyka" ("Mother and Music"), 11:1746a-b

  "Moi Pushkin" ("My Pushkin"), 11:1746b–1747a

  Molodets, 11:1741a-b

  "Natal'ia Goncharova: zhizn'i tvorchestvo" ("Natalya Goncharova: Life and Work"), 11:1744b

  "Otets i ego muzei" ("My Father and His Museum"), 11:1746a-b

  Pasternak and, 10:1593b–1594a, 1596a, 1598b, 1599b, 1608b, 1614b

  "Plennyi dukh" ("A Captive Spirit"), 11:1745b–1746a

  "Poema lestnitsy" ("The Poem of the Staircase"), 11:1743a-b

  "Poet o kritike" (A Poet on Criticism), 11:1742b

  Posle Rossii (After Russia), 11:1741a, 1743b, 1744a

  Psikheia, 11:1739b

  Razluka (Separation), 11:1739b

  Remeslo (Craft), 11:1738b–1739a, 1739b

  Stikhi k Bloku (Poems to Blok), 9:986a, 11:1736b, 1739b

  Tezei: Ariadna (Theseus-Ariadne), 11:1741b

  "The Poem of the End" ("Poema Kontsa"), 11:1741a

  "The Poem of the Mountain" ("Poema gory"), 11:1741a

  "Tsar'-devitsa" (The Tsar Maiden), 11:1738a-b, 1739b

  Vechernii al'bom (Evening Album), 11:1733b–1734a

  Versty I (Mileposts I), 11:1734b, 1736a-b, 1737b

  Versty II (Mileposts II), 11:1738b

  Volshebnyi fonar' (The Magic Lantern), 11:1733b, 1734b

  "Vot on—gliadi—ustavshii ot chuzhbin" ("Here he is—look—exhausted from foreign lands"), 9:986a-b

Tsvetaeva, Marina (*cont.*)
 Zemnye primety (Earthbound Omens),
  11:1737b
 "Zhivoe o zhivom" ("A Living Word About a
  Living Man"), 11:1745a-b
"Tsvety zapozdalye." *See* Chekhov, Anton
"Tsygany." *See* Pushkin, Alexander
Tuberculosis, in Mann's *Magic Mountain*,
 9:720b
Tübingen Seminary, Schiller and, 5:28a-b
Tueur sans gages. See Ionesco, Eugène
Tui-Novel. See Brecht, Bertolt
Tukhachevskii, Marshal Mikhail, Pasternak's
 refusal to condemn, 10:1595b
Tulip noire, La. See Dumas père, Alexandre
Túlvilági séták. See Kosztolányi, Dezső
Tumor Mózgowicz (*Tumor Brainiowicz*). *See*
 Witkiewicz, Stanisław Ignacy
"Tunnel, Der." *See* Dürrenmatt, Friedrich
Tunnel über der Spree (Tunnel over the Spree)
 (club), Fontane and, 6:1304b–1305b
Turandot; or, The Congress of Whitewashers
 (*Turandot oder Der Kongress der
 Weisswäscher*). See* Brecht, Bertolt
Turanism, 9:864a
Turati, Filippo, Ginzburg and,
 13:3134b–3135a
Turcaret. See Lesage, Alain-René
Turgenev, Ivan, **6:1275a–1297b**
 "A Desperate Character," 6:1293b
 A Hunter's Notes, 6:1277b–1278b
 "A King Lear of the Steppes," 6:1291b
 A Month in the Country, 6:1280a
  Gorky's *Dachniki* and, 8:436a
 A Nest of Gentlefolk, 6:1284a–1285a
 "A Quiet Spot," 6:1281b
 "A Strange Story," 6:1291b
 "Andrey Kolosov," 6:1277b
 "Asya," 6:1281b–1282a
 "Bezhin Meadow," 6:1278a
 Chekhov and, 7:1857b, 1858b, 1859b
 "Christ," 6:1294b
 "Conversation," 6:1294b
 "Diary of a Superfluous Man," 6:1279a-b
 "Enough," 6:1288b–1289a
 "Excursion to the Woodlands," 6:1294b
 Fathers and Sons, 6:1286a–1287a

 nihilism and, 7:1669b
 "Faust," 6:1281a-b
 "First Love," 6:1282a
  whipping scene, 11:1896b
 genre and, 6:986b
 Gogol and, 6:972b
 Goncharov and, 6:1063a, 1065a,
  1077b–1078a, 1082b–1083a
 "Hamlet and Don Quixote," 6:1282b–1283a
 "Kasyan of Krasivaya Mecha," 6:1278a-b
 "Khor and Kalinych," 6:1277b–1278a
 "Klara Milich," 6:1294a
 "Knock . . . Knock . . . Knock," 6:1289a-b
 Lermontov and, 6:1217b, 1224a
 Mathilde Bonaparte and, 7:1416a
 Maupassant and, 7:1763a-b, 1764a
 Mérimée and, 6:755b, 765b–766a
 "Mumu," 6:1278b–1279a
 "Nature," 6:1294b
 On the Eve, 6:1285a–1286a
 Ortega y Gasset on, 9:1124a
 "Parasha," 6:1277b
 "Phantoms," 6:1288b
 Poems in Prose, 6:1294a–1295b
 Rudin, 6:1283a–1284a
 serfs of, 6:985b
 Smoke, 6:1289b–1290a
 Solzhenitsyn and, 13:3196b
 Sportsman's Sketches, class structure,
  7:1478a
 "The Dog," 6:1289a
 "The Huntsman" and, 7:1860b
 "The Insect," 6:1295a
 "The Russian Language," 6:1294b–1295a
 "The Singers," 6:1278b
 "The Song of Triumphant Love," 6:1294a
 "The Sparrow," 6:1295a
 "The Threshold," 6:1294b
 Tolstoy and, 7:1472a
 "Torrents of Spring," 6:1291b–1292a
 Turgeneva and, 9:920a
 "Two Landowners," 6:1278b
 Virgin Soil, 6:1292a–1293a
 "We Will Still Put Up a Fight," 6:1295a
 Zamyatin's "Neputevyi" compared to,
  10:1184b
Turgeneva, Asya, 9:917a, 919b, 920a, 923b

leaves Bely, 9:924a, 924b

Turin, Alfieri's education at, 4:663a

"Turkmen." *See* Olesha, Yuri

"Turkoman, The." *See* Olesha, Yuri, "Turkmen"

Turm, Der. See Hofmannsthal, Hugo von, *The Tower*

Turn Over and Talk to Me. *See* Moravia, Alberto, *Voltati parlami*

Turncoat, The. *See* Pérez Galdós, Benito, *La segunda casaca*

Turnell, Martin

    The Art of French Fiction, on the Goncourts, 7:1401a, 1402a

    The Novel in France, Stendhal's Fabrice and, 11:2021a

Turning Point. See Seferis, George, *Strophe*

"Turning-Point." *See* Rilke, Rainer Maria, "Wendung"

Turoldus, authorship of *Chanson de Roland* and, 1:98a-b

Tuscany

    Carducci on Maremma in, 7:1496a, 1506a–1507b

    in D'Annunzio's poetry, 8:192b, 193b–194a

Tutor, The. See Brecht, Bertolt

Tutti i nostri ieri. See Ginzburg, Natalia, *A Light for Fools*

"Tutto 'l dì piango." *See* Petrarch, *Canzoniere*

Tutto per bene. See Pirandello, Luigi

"Tutuguri, The Rite of the Black Sun." *See* Artaud, Antonin

"Tüzes seb vagyok." *See* Ady, Endre

Två sagor om livet. See Lagerkvist, Pär

"Två vägar." *See* Södergran, Edith

Tvoreniia 1906–1908. See Khlebnikov, Velimir

Twain, Mark

    Gorky and, 8:420b

    Hamsun and, 8:24a, 25a, 28a

    Joan of Arc and, 8:488a

    What Is Man?, public apathy toward, 5:541a

"Twardorski's Wife." *See* Mickiewicz, Adam

Twelve, The. See Blok, Alexander

Twelve Songs. See Maeterlinck, Maurice, *Douze chansons*

Twelve Tables, law of, Vico on, 3:302b, 303a, 304a-b, 306a, 308a, 309b, 310b

Twentieth Century, The. See Zwanzigste Jahrhundert, Das

Twenty Ballads by a Swiss. *See* Meyer, Conrad Ferdinand, *Zwanzig Balladen von einem Schweizer*

Twenty Years After. See Dumas père, Alexandre, *Vingt ans après*

"Twenty-Six Men and a Girl." *See* Gorky, Maxim, "Dvadtsat' shest' i odna"

"Twickenham Garden." *See* Donne, John

Twilight. See Machado, Antonio, *Soledades* (Solitudes), "Crepúsculo"

Twilight of the Elephant, The. See Vittorini, Elio, *Il sempione strizza l'occhio al Fréjus*

"Twilight of Freedom, The." *See* Mandelshtam, Osip, "Sumerlei svobody"

Twilight of the Idols, The. See Nietzsche, Friedrich

Twilight poets, 7:1514a, 12:2389b

    antagonism to D'Annunzio of, 11:1988b–1989a

    in Croce's *Storia d'Italia*, 11:1997a

    Montale and, 11:1989a

    Svevo and, 8:70b–71a

Twilight Songs. See Hugo, Victor, *Les chants du crépuscule*

Twin in the Clouds. *See* Pasternak, Boris, *Bliznets v tuchakh*

"Twin Knight, The." *See* Gautier, Théophile, "Le chevalier double"

Twins, The. See Hugo, Victor, *Les jumeaux*

Twins, The. See Richter, Jean Paul, *Flegeljahre*

Two: A Phallic Novel. See Moravia, Alberto

Two Ages: The Age of Revolution and the Present Age. See Kierkegaard, Søren

Two Amphitryons, The. See Camoëns, Luís Vaz de

"Two Archers, The." *See* Hugo, Victor, "Les deux archers"

"Two Aspects of the World, The." *See* Elytis, Odysseus, *To photodendro kai i dekati tetarti omorfia* (*The Light Tree and the Fourteenth Being*), "Ta dio kou kosmou"

Two Baronesses, The. See Andersen, Hans Christian

Two Books Against the Address of Symmachus. See Prudentius

Two Brothers. See Lermontov, Mikhail Yurievich, *Dva brata*

Two Cheers for Democracy. See Forster, E. M.

Two Courtesans. See Moravia, Alberto, *Due cortigiane*

"Two Criticisms, The." *See* Barthes, Roland

"Two Friends." *See* Maupassant, Guy de, "Deux amis"

Two Friends or the Merchant of Lyon, The. See Beaumarchais, Pierre-Augustin Caron de, *Les deux amis ou le négociant de Lyon*

Two Gentlemen of Verona. See Shakespeare, William

Two Great Metaphors, The. See Ortega y Gasset, José, "Las dos grandes metáforas"

Two Inheritances, The. See Mérimée, Prosper, *Les deux héritages*

"Two Landowners." *See* Turgenev, Ivan

Two Lives and a Dream. See Yourcenar, Marguerite, *Comme l'eau qui coule*

Two Luises and Other Essays, The. See Azorín, *Los dos Luises y otros ensayos*

Two Maidens, The. See Andersen, Hans Christian

"Two Mistresses, The." *See* Musset, Alfred de, "Les deux maîtresses"

"Two Paths." *See* Södergran, Edith, "Två vägar"

Two Poets, The. See Balzac, Honoré de, *Les deux poètes*

"Two Sails." *See* Meyer, Conrad Ferdinand, "Zwei Segel"

Two Sources of Morality and Religion, The. See Bergson, Henri

Two Stories and a Memory. See Lampedusa, Giuseppe Tomasi di

2001: A Space Odyssey, 13:3017a

Two Women. See Moravia, Alberto

Twofold Nourishment. See Prudentius, *Dittochaeon*

Tyard, Pontus de, 2:742a-b
  Erreurs amoureuses, 2:742b

Tychyna, Pavlo, **10:1651a–1676b**

Chernihiv, 10:1656b, 1671b–1672b, 1673b
  "A chy ne iest' tse sami nakhvalky abo zh zapomorochennia vid uspikhov" ("But This Is Not Simply Bragging or Dizziness from Success"), 10:1672a
  "Stara Ukraina zminytyś' musyt'" (Old Ukraine Must Change), 10:1672a-b

Chuttia iedynnoi rodyny (A Feeling of One Family), 10:1657b

Iz shchodennykovykh zapysiv (Excerpts from Diaries), 10:1662b

Partiia vede (The Party Leads), 10:1657a-b, 1658a-b, 1673a

Pluh (The Plow), 10:1654b, 1665b–1668a, 1670a
  "I Bileyi i Blok i Iesenin i Kliuiev" (And Bely and Blok and Esenin and Kluiev), 10:1667b
  "Lysty do poeta" (Letters to the Poet), 10:1667a-b
  "Mizhplanetni intervaly" (Interplanetary Intervals), 10:1668a
  "Na maidani kolo tserkvy" (On the Green by the Church), 10:1667b–1668a
  "Perezoriuiut zori" (They Will Outshine the Stars), 10:1666b–1667a
  "Pluh," 10:1665b–1666a
  poems on Shevchenko, 10:1667a
  "Siite" (Sow), 10:1666b
  "Zrazuzh za selom" (Directly Beyond the Village), 10:1668a

Pokhoron druha (A Friend's Funeral), 10:1658a, 1674a

Shablia Kotovs'koho (Sword of Kotovs'kyi), 10:1674a

Skorovoda. Symfonia, 10:1656a, 1658b, 1671b, 1672b

Soniachni klarnety (Clarinets of the Sun), 10:1651b, 1654a, 1659a, 1659b–1662b, 1663a, 1663b–1665b
  "Des' nadkhodyla vesna" (Somewhere Spring Was Approaching), 10:1661a-b
  impressionism in, 10:1661b–1662b
  "Ishche ptashky . . ." (The Birds Are Still . . .), 10:1661b–1662a
  "Na strimchastykh skeliakh" (On Steep Cliffs), 10:1664b

"Odchyniaite dveri" (Open the Doors),
    10:1664b

"Rain," 10:1662b

"Skorbna Maty" (The Sorrowing Mother),
    10:1664b–1665a

"Tstvit v moemu sertsi" (A Blossom in My
    Heart), 10:1661a

untitled opening poem, 10:1660a-b

"Zolotyi homin" (The Golden Resonance),
    10:1665a-b

Stal' i nizhnist' (Steel and Tenderness),
    10:1657b

V kosmichnomu orkestri (In the Cosmic
    Orchestra), 10:1655b–1656a, 1670a-b

"Ia dukh, dukh vichnosti," 10:1670b

"Nedokrovna planeta kruh sontsia
    sokhla," 10:1670b

V sertsi u moim (In My Heart), 10:1658b,
    1661a

Viter z Ukrainy (Wind from the Ukraine),
    10:1656a, 1657a, 1658a, 1670b–1671b

Zamist' sonetiv i oktav (Instead of Sonnets
    and Octaves), 10:1654b, 1662b,
    1668a–1669b, 1670a

"Kukil" (Tare), 10:1669a-b

opening poem, 10:1668b

"Terror," 10:1663b, 1668b–1669a

Zibrannia tvoriv v dvanadtsiaty tomakh
    (Collected Works in Twelve Volumes),
    10:1659a

Zolotyi homin. Poezii, 10:1669a-b

Tyl Eulenspiegel, Renaissance short fiction
    and, 2:953a

Tynan, Kenneth, Ionesco and, 13:2991b, 2998b

Tynianov, Yurii
    on Blok and Khlebnikov, 11:1894a
    on Khlebnikov, 10:1349b, 1362a
    Smert' Vazir-Mukhtara (*Death of the
        Minister Plenipotentiary*),
        Mandelshtam's *Egipetskaia marka* and,
        10:1643a-b

Typewriter, The. See Cocteau, Jean, *La
    machine à écrire*

Typography
    Butor and, 13:3301a, 3303b–3306a
    Marinetti and, 9:815a, 816a, 817b–819b

Typology, biblical, 1:3b

Cassian on, 1:4b
in Christian art, 1:13a
in Prudentius' *Apotheosis*, 1:8b

Tyranny
    Alfieri on, 4:661b, 671b–673a, 675a,
        678b–680b, 684a-b
    see also Totalitarianism

Tyrant, The. See Valle-Inclán, Ramón del

Tyrtaeus, George and, 8:466a

"1830. Maya, 16 chisla" ("1830. May 16"). *See*
    Lermontov, Mikhail Yurievich

Tyutchev, Fedor
    Mandelshtam and, 10:1627a, 1627b, 1634a-b
    "Problème," Mandelshtam's *Stone* and,
        10:1634b

Tzara, Tristan
    Dadaism and, 11:1940a, 2062b–2063a
    Parisian Dadaists' veneration of, 11:1965a
    Sept manifestes dada: Lampisteries,
        11:2063a-b

"Tzigane, La." *See* Apollinaire, Guillaume,
    Alcools

U

U agoniji. *See* Krleža, Miroslav

"U babushki." *See* Babel, Isaac

"U holîe." *See* Hašek, Jaroslav

"U musafirhani." *See* Andrić, Ivo

"Über das Marionettentheater." *See* Kleist, Heinrich von

Über das Selbstverständliche. *See* Grass, Günter

"Über den Fetischcharakter in der Musik und die Regression des Hörers." *See* Adorno, Theodor

Über die französische Bühne. *See* Heine, Heinrich

Über die Religion. *See* Schleiermacher, Friedrich

Über die vierfache Wurzel des Satzes vom zureichenden Grunde. *See* Schopenhauer, Arthur

Über Kunst und Altertum. *See* Goethe, Johann Wolfgang von

"Über meinen Lehrer Döblin." *See* Grass, Günter, "On My Teacher Döblin"

"Über mich selbst." *See* Böll, Heinrich

Über naive und sentimentalisch Dichtung. *See* Schiller, Friedrich von

Über Polen. *See* Heine, Heinrich

Über Shakespeares Behandlung des Wunderbaren. *See* Tieck, Ludwig

"Über Sprache über-haput and über die Sprache des Menschen." *See* Benjamin, Walter, "On Language as Such and on the Human Language"

"Über Staat und Religion." *See* Wagner, Richard, "On the State of Religion"

Übermensch. *See* Overman

"Überschriften und Widmungen." *See* George, Stefan, *Das Jahr der Seele*

Ubu cocu (*Ubu Cuckolded*). *See* Jarry, Alfred

Ubu enchaîné (*Ubu Enchained*). *See* Jarry, Alfred

Ubu the King. *See* Jarry, Alfred, *Ubu Roi*

Ubu on the Mound. *See* Jarry, Alfred, *Ubu sur la butte*

Ubu Roi. *See* Jarry, Alfred

Ubu sur la butte. *See* Jarry, Alfred

"Übungen im Denken." *See* Richter, Jean Paul

"Uccelli dell'alto, Gli." *See* Pirandello, Luigi

"Uccello le poil" ("Uccello the Hair"). *See* Artaud, Antonin

Uccello, Paolo, Artaud on, 11:1968b–1969b, 1970a-b

"Uccidiamo il chiaro di luna!" *See* Marinetti, Filippo Tommaso

Uchitel' i uchenik. *See* Khlebnikov, Velimir, *Teacher and Student*

"Uchitel slovesnosti." *See* Chekhov, Anton

"Üdvözlet a győzőnek." *See* Ady, Endre

"Uezd v tylu." *See* Pasternak, Boris

Uezdnoe. *See* Zamyatin, Yevgeny Ivanovich, *A Provincial Tale*

"Ugly Duckling, The." *See* Andersen, Hans Christian

Uhland, Ludwig
  Hebbel and, 6:1091b–1092a, 1094a
  Hölderlin and, 5:173b

Új versek. *See* Ady, Endre

"Új vizeken jarok." *See* Ady, Endre

Ukjende mennene, Dei. *See* Vesaas, Tarjei

Ukraine
  in the 1930s, Tychyna and, 10:1656b–1657b
  cultural policies in the 1920s, 10:1654b–1655b
  in Pushkin's *Poltava,* 5:669a–670a
  see also Tychyna, Pavlo

"Ülök az asztal-trónon." *See* Ady, Endre

Ulrich von Zatzikhoven, *Lanzelet,* Arthurian legend and, 1:152b

"Ultima passeggiata, L'." *See* Pascoli, Giovanni, *Myricae*

Ultimate Commandment. *See* Hebbel, Friedrich, "Höchstes Gebot"

Ultimatum. *See* Vesaas, Tarjei

Ultime lettere di Jacopo Ortis. *See* Foscolo, Ugo

"Ultimo canto di Saffo." *See* Leopardi, Giacomo, "The Last Song of Sappho"

"Ultimo viaggio, L'." *See* Pascoli, Giovanni, *Poemi conviviali*

Ultimo viene il corvo. *See* Calvino, Italo, *Adam, One Afternoon, and Other Stories*

"Ultimo viene il corvo." *See* Calvino, Italo, "The Crow Comes Last"

Últimos románticos, Los. See Baroja, Pío

"Ultra coelos." *See* Leconte de Lisle, Charles Marie

Ulysses
  in Apollinaire's "The Song of the Unloved Lover," 9:889b, 890b
  in Pascoli's "L'Ultimo viaggio," 7:1846b–1847a

Ulysses. See Joyce, James

"Ulysses' Companions." *See* La Fontaine, Jean de, *Fables*

"Um eine Stund." *See* Schnitzler, Arthur

Umbilicus of Limbo, The. See Artaud, Antonin

Uměni románu. See Kundera, Milan

Umorismo. See Humorism

Umorismo, L'. See Pirandello, Luigi

Umwege. See Hesse, Hermann

Unamuno, Miguel de, **8:283a–310b**
  Abel Sanchez, 8:304a-b
  "¡Adentro!," 8:292a–293a
  amor intellectualis, 9:1128b
  Amor y pedagogia (Love and Education), 8:294b–295a
  Azorín's approval of, 9:644b
  Baroja and, 9:591a, 592b
  Blasco Ibáñez' *The Mayflower* and, 8:365b
  Cancionero (Songbook), 8:291b, 298a-b
  "Civilización y cultura," 8:290a
  Cómo se hace una novela (*How to Make a Novel*), 8:304b–306a
  De mi país (Of My Land), 8:204b
  Del sentimiento trágico de la vida en los hombres y en los pueblos (*The Tragic Sense of Life*), 8:293a, 299a–301a, 9:1127b–1128a
    Machado and, 9:757b
  Diario íntimo (Intimate Diary), 8:290b–291a
  Eça and, 7:1683b
  El Cristo de Velázquez (*The Christ of Velázquez*), 8:284b
  El hermano Juan (Brother Juan), 8:301a
  El otro (The Other), 8:301a
  En torno al casticismo (In Search of the National Identity), 8:287b–289a, 9:745a
  exiled, 9:746b–747a

inescapable death, 9:1126b
Institución Libre de Enseñanza and, 9:1121a
Jiménez and, 9:1005b, 1008
La esfinge (The Sphinx), 8:301a
"La fe" (Faith), 8:293a-b
La venda (The Blindfold), 8:301a
La vida de Don Quijote y Sancho (*The Life of Don Quixote and Sancho*), 8:295b–297a
"La vida es sueño" (Life Is a Dream), 8:291b
Machado and, 9:745b, 753a
on the masses, 9:1145b
Mi religión y otros ensayos (My Religion and Other Essays), 8:298b
nativism, 9:1124a
Niebla (*Mist*), 8:302a, 302b–303b
Ortega y Gasset and, 9:1122a-b, 1123b–1124a, 1124b–1125b
on Pascal, 3:148a
Paz en la Guerra (*Peace in War*), 8:289b–290a
Poesías, 8:297a–298a
political journalism, 9:1122a
regenerationism, 9:1121b
Romancero del destierro (Ballads of Exile), 8:298a
San Manuel Bueno, mártir (*Saint Emmanuel the Good, Martyr*), 8:306a–307b, 9:612a
skepticism of, 9:597a
"Sobre la lectura y interpretación del 'Quijote'" ("On the Reading and Interpretation of 'Don Quixote'"), 8:295b
symbolism and, 9:745a
Valle-Inclán and, 8:331a, 338a

Unanticipated Reencounter, The. See Hebel, Johann Peter, *Unverhofftes Wiedersehen*

Unattainable Earth. See Milosz, Czeslaw

Unbearable Lightness of Being, The. See Kundera, Milan

Unbekannte Grösse, Die. See Broch, Hermann, *The Unknown Quantity*

Uncertainty, in Calvino, 13:3272b

Uncle Agrippa Goes by in a Train. See Vittorini, Elio, *Le donne di Messina*

Uncle Charles Has Locked Himself In. See Simenon, Georges, *Oncle Charles s'est enfermé*

Uncle Tom's Cabin. See Stowe, Harriet
    Beecher
Uncle Vanya. See Chekhov, Anton
"Uncle's Dream." *See* Dostoevsky, Feodor
Uncollected Poems. *See* Ungaretti, Giuseppe,
    Poesie disperse
Uncommon Story, An. See Goncharov, Ivan
Unconscious
    Freud's concept of, 8:5b, 11a
    in Hugo's works, 6:696a, 697a–698a, 702a-b,
        704a-b, 707b–708a, 711a-b
    Laforgue and, 7:1889a, 1890b
    in Pirandello, 8:413a
    Schnitzler's use of, 8:109a–110a
    surrealism and, 8:581a
    see also Consciousness
"Und einmal wird der Friede wieder kommen."
    See Schnitzler, Arthur
Und Pippa tanzt! See Hauptmann, Gerhart
Und sagte kein einziges Wort. See Böll,
    Heinrich, *And Never Said a Word*
"Under der linden an der heide." *See* Walther
    von der Vogelweide
Under høststjernen (*Under the Autumn Star*).
    See Hamsun, Knut
Under the Northern Sky. See Balmont,
    Constantine
Under the Pear Tree. *See* Fontane, Theodor,
    Unterm Birnbaum
Under the Sign of the Dragon. *See* Claudel,
    Paul, *Sous le signe du dragon*
"Understanding." *See* Cavafy, Constantine,
    "Noisis"
Understatement, Gombrowicz and, 12:2566a
"Undertaker, The." *See* Pushkin, Alexander
Undine. See Hoffmann, E. T. A.
Undir helgahnúuk. See Laxness, Halldór
Undiscovered Country. See Schnitzler, Arthur,
    Das weite Land
Undset, Anna Charlotte, 9:1019a, 1020a–1021a
Undset, Ingvald, 9:1019a-b
    Fra Norges ældre jernalder (The Beginnings
        of the Iron Age in Northern Europe),
        9:1019b
Undset, Sigrid, **9:1017a–1040b**
    Caterina av Siena (*Catherine of Siena*),
        9:1024a, 1025b–1026a

Den Brændende busk (*The Burning Bush*),
    9:1023b
Den trofaste hustru (*The Faithful Wife*),
    9:1023b
Fortællingen om Viga-Ljot og Vigdis
    (*Gunnar's Daughter*), 9:1022b
*Fortællinger om Kong Artur og ridderne av
    det runde bord* (Tales of King Arthur
    and the Knights of the Round Table),
    9:1022b
Fru Marta Oulie (Mrs. Marta Oulie), 9:1022a
Gymnadenia (*The Wild Orchid*), 9:1023b
Hamsun and, 8:42a
Happy Times in Norway, 9:1018b,
    1024–1025a
Ida-Elisabeth, 9:1023b–1024a
Jenny, 9:1022b
*Kirke ag klosterliv: Tre essays fra norsk
    middelalder* (Church and Monastic Life:
    Three Essays On the Norwegian Middle
    Ages), 9:1023a
Kristin Lavransdatter, 9:1026a–1035a
    and Catholic doctrine, 9:1023b
    control in, 9:1037b
    home in, 9:1030b–1031a
    Husfru (*The Mistress of Husaby*),
        9:1027b, 1029a
    importance of, 9:1023a, 1026a-b
    independence in, 9:1020a, 1032a-b
    Korset (*The Cross*), 9:1027b–1028a,
        1029a–1030b
    Kransen (*The Bridal Veil*), 9:1027a-b,
        1028a–1029a
    love in, 9:1032b–1033b
    sin and guilt in, 9:1030b–1031b
    uncertainty in, 9:1031b–1032a
    women's position in, 9:1026b–1027a
Madame Dorthea, 9:1021a, 1024a
Master of Hestviken, 9:1035b–1037a
    criticism of, 9:1035a
    importance of, 9:1023a
    and *Kristin Lavransdatter*, 9:1035a-b,
        1037a
Moberg and, 11:2208b
Norsk kulturhistorie, 9:1023a
Norske helgener (*Saga of Saints*), 9:1023a

Olav Audunssøn og hans börn (*The Son Avenger*), 9:1035a, 11:2208b
Return to the Future, 9:1019a, 1024a-b
The Longest Years, 9: 1021b, 1018b, 1020a-b
Vaaren (Spring), 9:1022b
Unfaithful Wife, The. *See* García Lorca, Federico, "La casada infiel"
Unfinished and Undeveloped Trilogy, The. *See* Ritsos, Yannis, "Imitelis kai ypotypodhis triloghia"
Unfortunate Business with a Tomcat, An. *See* Hašek, Jaroslav, "Nešt'astná historie s kocourem"
Unfortunate Lover, The. *See* Moravia, Alberto, *L'Amante infelice*
Unfortunate Lovers, The. See Mauriac, François
Unfortunate One, The. See Argenti, *Sfortunato*
Unfortunate One, The. *See* Nerval, Gérard de, "El Desdichado"
Ungaretti, Giuseppe, **10:1453a–1473b**
  Allegria di naufragi (Mirth of Shipwrecks), 10:1456b, 1458a
    "Distacco" ("Detachment"), 10:1457a
    "Fratelli" ("Brothers"), 10:1457a
    "In dormiveglia" ("Half Awake"), 10:1457a
    "Pellegrinaggio" ("Pilgrimage"), 10:1457b
    "Peso" ("Weight"), 10:1457a
    "Soldati" ("Soldiers"), 10:1457a
  "Damnation" ("Dannazione"), 10:1466b–1467a
  Dialogo (Dialogue), 10:1471a-b
  "Fine di Crono" ("End of Cronos"), 10:1465b
  "Girovage" ("Wanderer"), 10:1454b
  Il deserto e dopo (The Desert and After), 10:1453a, 1455a, 1459a
  Il dolore (Grief), 10:1459a-b, 1460b–1461a
  Il porto sepolto (The Submerged Seaport), 10:1454a, 1455a, 1456b
  Il taccuino del vecchio (The Notebook of an Old Man), 10:1455a, 1469b–1471a
  "In memoria" (Memorial), 10:1454b, 1463a
  "La guerre" (The War), 10:1458b
  "La pietà," 10:1466a-b, 1468b
  La terra promessa (The Promised Land), 10:1453b–1454a, 1461a-b, 1468b–1469a
  L'Allegria (The Joy)
    cosmic elements in, 10:1467b
    hendecasyllable in, 10:1463a
    immediacy of, 10:1461a
    promised land in, 10:1460b
    sensualism in, 10:1463b
    Ungaretti on, 10:1454b–1455a
    verse in, 10:1463a, 1465a-b
  "Little Monologue," 10:1469b
  Montale contrasted with, 11:1988a
  "Noia" ("Ennui"), 10:1462a
  Nuove (New Poems), 10:1471a-b
  Poesie disperse (Uncollected Poems), 10:1461b–1462a
  "Ricordo d'Africa" ("Memory of Africa"), 10:1454a-b
  Sentimento del tempo (Sentiment of Time), 10:1454a, 1460b–1461a, 1465a, 1466a
  "The Rivers," 10:1464b–1465a, 1469b–1470a
  "To Ennui" ("Alla noia"), 10:1465b–1466a
  "Transfigurazione" ("Transfiguration"), 10:1463b–1464a
  Un grido e paesaggi (A Cry and Landscapes), 1469b–1470a, 10:1461a
  Vita d'un uomo (Life of a Man), 10:1455a
  Vittorini and, 12:2755a
  "You Shattered," 10:1467b, 1468b
Ungdoms-Forsøg. See Andersen, Hans Christian, *Youthful Attempts*
Unge Ørn, Den. See Gunnarsson, Gunnar
Unger, C. R., *Heilagra manna sögur*, 9:1023b
Unglück (ill chance), in Kleist, 5:303a-b
Unglücklichen Liebhaber, Die. See Grillparzer, Franz
Unguarded House, The. See Böll, Heinrich
Unhappy Lovers, The. *See* Grillparzer, Franz, *Die unglücklichen Liebhaber*
"Union libre, L'." *See* Breton, André
Union of Practitioners of Imaginative Literature, Zamyatin's membership in, 10:1192b
Union of Soviet Writers
  expulsion of Solzhenitsyn, 13:3192b
  Gorky and, 8:423a
Unions. *See* Musil, Robert, *Vereinigungen*
United States
  Beauvoir and, 12:2728a

United States (*cont.*)
  Brecht's influence in, 11:2089b
  Breton in, 11:1946b
  Butor and, 13:3300b–3303a
  Claudel in, 8:475b–476b
  culture
    Aymé's satire of, 12:2447b–2449a
    Pavese and, 12:2762b–2763a, 2784a-b
  Giraudoux in, 9:1042b, 1043b
  Gorky's trip to, 8:420a-b
  Heinrich Mann in, 8:541a–542a
  Herder's influence in, 4:653a–658b
  Maeterlinck in, 8:141b, 142b
  Moberg on, 11:2205a, 2228b
  Pavese and, 12:2784a-b
  Perse in, 10:1441b–1447a
  Schiller's reputation in, 5:50b
  Tocqueville on, 6:895a–897a
  Wedekind's problematic citizenship,
    8:230a-b
  see also America
Unities, dramatic
  in Corneille's works, 3:34a
    Horace, 3:36b
    Le Cid, 3:27a
  introduction into French drama, 3:26b–27a
  in Ionesco's *Exit the King*, 13:3006a-b
  Racine and, 3:217a, 217b–218a
  Richelieu and, 3:26a-b
  Scribe and, 7:1915b
  in Yourcenar's *Coup de Grâce*, 12:2544a
Unity, personal, Sartre and, 12:2610b–2612a
Unity, theme of, in Montaigne's *Essays*,
    2:777a, 779b
Universal Law. See Vico, Giovanni Battista,
    Diritto universale
Universality, regionalism and, 4:647b–648a
Universe, material. *See* Material universe
University
  medieval, Aristotelianism and, 1:408b–409a
  mission of in Michelet's view, 5:582b
University of Paris
  vs. Aubriot, 1:345b
  vs. mendicant orders, 1:346a, 413b–414a
"Unizhenie." *See* Blok, Alexander
Unklare (Musil), in *The Man Without
    Qualities*, 9:942b, 943a

Unkle, Kurt, 11:2163b
Unknown Lady, The. See Blok, Alexander,
    Neznakomka
Unknown Masterpiece, The. See Balzac,
    Honoré de, *Le chef d'oeuvre inconnu*
Unknown Men, The. *See* Vesaas, Tarjei, *Die
    ukjende mennene*
Unknown One, The. *See* Pérez Galdós, Benito,
    La incognita
Unknown Quantity, The. See Broch, Hermann
Unknown Sea, The. See Mauriac, François
"Unluck." *See* Baudelaire, Charles
Unlucky Man, An. *See* Moravia, Alberto, "Un
    uomo sfortunato"
Unmutston. See Walther von der Vogelweide
Unrug, Jadwiga, Witkiewicz and, 10:1225b
Uns et les autres, Les. See Verlaine, Paul
Unschuldige, Die. See Mann, Heinrich
"Unsere Gier nach Geschichten." *See* Frisch,
    Max
Unsern täglichen Traum. See Arp, Jean
Unsichtbare Loge, Die. See Richter, Jean Paul
Unsubdued City. *See* Ritsos, Yannis,
    Anipotahti politia
Untamables, The. See Marinetti, Filippo
    Tommaso, *Gli indomabili*
Untergang des Abendlandes, Der. See
    Spengler, Oswald
Unterm Birnbaum. See Fontane, Theodor
Unterm Rad. See Hesse, Hermann
Unternehmen der Wega, Das. See Dürrenmatt,
    Friedrich
Untertan, Der. See Mann, Heinrich
Untimely Meditations. See Nietzsche,
    Friedrich, *Unzeitgemässe Betrachtungen*
Unto a Good Land. See Moberg, Vilhelm
Unverhofftes Wiedersehen. See Hebel, Johann
    Peter
Unwashed Souls. *See* Witkiewicz, Stanisław
    Ignacy, *Niemyte dusze*
Unwiederbringlich. See Fontane, Theodor
"Unwritten Story, The." *See* Setterwall, Monica
Unzeitgemässe Betrachtungen. See Nietzsche,
    Friedrich
"Uomini che si voltano, Gli." *See* Montale,
    Eugenio, *Satura*
Uomini e no. See Vittorini, Elio

Uomo che garda, L'. See Moravia, Alberto, *The Voyeur*
"Uomo come fine, L'." *See* Moravia, Alberto, "Man as an End"
Uomo dal fiore in bocca, L'. See Pirandello, Luigi
"Uomo e la teoria darvinia, L'." *See* Svevo, Italo
Uomo, la bestia, e la virtù, L'. See Pirandello, Luigi
"Uomo sfortunato, Un." *See* Moravia, Alberto
Up There. *See* Huysmans, Joris Karl, *Là-haut*
Upanishads
   Freud and, 8:14a
   mysticism in, 9:1009a
Upbuilding Discourses in Various Spirits. See Kierkegaard, Søren
"Upbuilding" literature, of Kierkegaard, 6:1123b–1124a
Updike, John, 13:3022a, 3022b
Upper classes. *See* Aristocracy; Class, social
"Upptåckt." *See* Södergran, Edith
"Uram, ostorozz meg." *See* Ady, Endre
Urania. See Manzoni, Alessandro
Uranus. See Aymé, Marcel, *The Barkeep of Blémont*
Urban IV, pope
   Aquinas and, 1:415a, 416a
   Aristotelianism and, 1:409a
Urban society
   in Calvino, 13:3269a–3272a, 3280a–3281a
   Ionesco's *The New Tenant* and, 13:2998b
   in La Bruyère's *Caractères*, 3:242b–245b
Urbina, Isabel de, Lope de Vega and, 2:846b–847a
Urbino, Court of, Castiglione and, 2:650a–665a
"Úřední horlivost pana Štěpána Brycha, výběrčího na pražském mostě." *See* Hašek, Jaroslav
Urfaust. See Goethe, Johann Wolfgang von
Urfé, Honoré d'
   in La Fontaine's "Epître à Huet," 3:79a
   L'Astrée, La Rochefoucauld and, 3:51a-b, 64a
Urien's Voyage. See Gide, André, *Le voyage d'Urien*

Urpflanze, Arp's poetry and, 10:1376a-b
Ursprung des deutschen Trauerspiels. See Benjamin, Walter, *The Origin of German Tragic Drama*
"Ursprünge." *See* George, Stefan
"Urteil, Das." *See* Kafka, Franz
"Urworte. Orpheus." *See* Goethe, Johann Wolfgang von
"Usa-Gali." *See* Khlebnikov, Velimir, "Okhotnik Usa-Gali"
Usage de la parole, L'. See Sarraute, Nathalie
Uscita di sicurezza. See Silone, Ignazio
Uscoque, L'. See Sand, George
"Use and Abuse of History, The." *See* Nietzsche, Friedrich, "Vom Nutzen und Nachteil der Historie für das leben"
Use of Poetry and the Use of Criticism, The. See Eliot, T. S.
Use of Speech, The. See Sarraute, Nathalie, *L'Usage de la parole*
Useless Mouths. See Beauvoir, Simone de, *Les bouches inutiles*
Useless Service. *See* Montherlant, Henry de, *Service inutile*
Usova, Nikolaevna, Zamyatin's marriage to, 10:1182a
Utam Marxhoz. See Lukács, György
"Utar contra vitia carmine rebelli" (I will use against vices rebellious song), 1:351a–352a
Utesov, L., conspiracy charges, 11:1912a
Utflykter. See Ekelöf, Gunnar
Utopia
   Canetti and, 12:2628a–2630b
   in fiction of Olesha, 11:2251b
   in Khlebnikov's works, 10:1359b
   in Klopstock, 4:525a-b
   Machiavelli and, 2:606a
   in Rousseau, 4:467b–468b
   Thélème as, 2:706b–707a
   totalitarian, Kundera and, 13:3406a, 3411a-b
   Zamyatin's *We* and, 10:1188b
Utopia. See More, Thomas
Utopianism, Icarian colonies (United States), Hauptmann and, 8:151b
"Utro akmeizma." *See* Mandelshtam, Osip, "The Morning of Acmeism"

Utvandrarna. See Moberg, Vilhelm, *The Emigrants*

"Uvodili tebia na rassvete." *See* Akhmatova, Anna, *Requiem* (*Rekviem*)

"Uz vizeken járok." *See* Ady, Endre

V

"V. G. Korolenko." *See* Gorky, Maxim

"V Amerike." *See* Gorky, Maxim

V kosmichnomu orkestri. See Tychyna, Pavlo

V kruge pervom. See Solzhenitsyn, Aleksandr, *The First Circle*

V liudiakh. See Gorky, Maxim, *My Apprenticeship*

"V mire." *See* Olesha, Yuri

"V ovrage." *See* Chekhov, Anton

"V podvale." *See* Babel, Isaac

"V shchelochku." *See* Babel, Isaac

"V ssylke." *See* Chekhov, Anton

"V tsirke." *See* Olesha, Yuri

Våld. See Moberg, Vilhelm

Vår ofödde son. See Moberg, Vilhelm

Vårnatt. See Vesaas, Tarjei, *Spring Night*

Vacation themes, in D'Annunzio, 8:192a–194b

Vaché, Jacques
     Dada and, 11:2062a-b, 2064a
     umour, influence on Breton, 11:1939a-b

Vacheret, Étienne, on Taine, 7:1450a-b

Vacquerie, August, Musset and, 6:1031a

Vademecum for Mr. Sam Gotth. Lange, A. See Lessing, Gotthold Ephraim

Vadim. See Lermontov, Mikhail Yurievich

Vagabond, A. *See* Moberg, Vilhelm, *En löskekarl*

Vagabonde, La (*The Vagabond*). *See* Colette

"Vague des passions," in Chateaubriand's works, 5:119b–120a

Vagues, Les. See Woolf, Virginia, *The Waves*

"Vajjon milyennek láttál." *See* Ady, Endre

Vakhtangov Theater, Olesha and, 11:2234a, 2235b, 2244b, 2245a

Vakhtangov's Third Studio, Tsvetaeva and, 11:1738a

Vaksberg, Arkady, "Protsessy" (The Trials), 11:1911b

Vaksel, Olga, Mandelshtam's poems for, 10:1642b

Valade, Léon, Verlaine and, 7:1620b

"Valamikor lyányom voltál." *See* Ady, Endre

Valaoritis, Nanos, 12:2260b

Valčík na rozloučenou. See Kundera, Milan,
  The Farewell Party
Valderrama, Pilar de, 9:760b–761a
  Si, soy Guiomar (Yes, I Am Guiomar),
  9:746b
Valdès Léal, Juan de, Gautier and, 6:1042a-b
Valdés, Palacio, *José*, 8:359a
Valencia, Baroja's medical training in, 9:590a
Valencian Tales. *See* Blasco Ibáñez, Vicente,
  Cuentos valencianos
Valenciennes *Passion*, 1:456a
Valentine. See Sand, George
Valentino. See Ginzburg, Natalia
Valentino, Rudolph, in *The Four Horsemen of
  the Apocalypse*, 8:386a
Valerius Maximus, *Facta et dicta memorabilia*
  (Memorable Deeds and Words),
  anecdotes in, 2:930a-b
Valéry, Paul, **8:569a–588b**
  Album des vers anciens, 1890-1920 (*Album
    of Old Verses*), 8:576a
  Amphion, 8:570b
    "Narcisse parle" ("Narcissus Speaks"),
    8:570b–571b, 576a
  Apollinaire and, 9:888b
  Breton and, 11:1939a, 1951b
  Cahiers (Notebooks), 8:569a, 569b, 570a,
    579b, 583a, 587b
    extracts published, 8:584a
    "Gladiator," 8:574b–575b
    on language, 8:574b
  Charmes, 8:570a, 580a–583b
    "Ebauche d'un serpent" ("Sketch of a
      Serpent"), 8:582a–583a
    "La Pythie" ("The Pythia"), 8:580b–581b,
      582a
    "Le Rameur" ("The Rower"), 8:583a-b
    "Le Sylphe" ("The Sylph"), 8:580a-b
  Degas danse dessin (*Degas, Dance,
    Drawing*), 8:586a-b
  Eupalinos, 8:570b, 584b, 585a-b, 587a
  "Fragments du Narcisse" ("Fragments of
    Narcissus"), 8:571a
  Hesse and, 9:855b
  Huysmans and, 7:1710a
  "Introduction à la méthode de Léonard de
    Vinci" ("Introduction to the Method of
    Leonardo da Vinci"), 8:569b,
    572b–573b, 584b
  Jarry and, 9:670b
  Jiménez and, 9:1001a, 1006a
  La jeune parque (*The Young Fate*), 8:569a,
    576a–577a, 577b, 580a
    Laforgue and, 7:1906a
  L'Âme et la danse (*Dance and the Soul*),
    8:584b, 586a-b
  Le cimetière marin (*The Graveyard by the
    Sea*), 8:577a–579b, 580a, 586b
  Mallarmé's influence on, 7:1586a, 1590b,
    1592a-b
  Mauvaises pensées et autres (*Bad Thoughts
    and Others*), 8:584a
  Mon Faust (*My Faust*), 8:584a, 584b
  Monsieur Teste, 8:574a-b
  Montale and, 11:2006b
  on Montesquieu's *Persian Letters*, 3:360b
  "Paradoxe sur l'architecte" ("Paradox on the
    Architect"), 8:585a
  on Pascal, 3:148a
  "Poetry and Abstract Thought," Pascoli and,
    7:1832a
  Queneau and, 12:2520b
  Regards sur le monde actuel (*Reflections on
    the World Today*), 8:584a
  Rilke and, 9:768a, 787b
  Socrate et son médecin (*Socrates and His
    Physician*), 8:584b–585a
  Tel quel (Just as They Are), 8:584a-b
  translated by Rilke, 9:772b
  "Une soirée avec Monsieur Teste" ("An
    Evening with Mr. Teste"), 8:569b,
    573b–574a
    Greek translation, 12:2258a-b
Valfrndskaper. See Ekelöf, Gunnar
Valise trouvé, La. See Lesage, Alain-René
Valkyrie, The. See Wagner, Richard, *Der Ring
  des Nibelungen*
Valla, Lorenzo, Erasmus and, 2:576b–577a
Valla-Ljóts saga, 1:393b, 395a
Valle y Peña, Ramón José Simón. *See*
  Valle-Inclán, Ramón

Valle-Inclán, Ramón del, **8:331a–353b,**
    11:2169a, 2169b
    Comedia de ensueño (*Dream Comedy*),
        8:342a, 343b, 349a
    Cuento de abril (April Tale), 8:345a
    Divinas palabras (*Divine Words*),
        8:347b–348b
    El Marqués de Bradomín (The Marquis de
        Bradomín), 8:342a-b
    El ruedo ibérico (The Iberian Cycle),
        8:338b–339a
        Baza de espadas (Intervention of Swords),
            8:339a
        La corte de los milagros (The Court of
            Miracles), 8:339a, 345b
        ¡Viva mi dueño! (Hurrah to the Hilt!),
            8:339a
    El yermo de las almas (The Barrenness of
        Souls), 8:341b–342a
    Epitalamio (A Tale of Love), 8:333b
    Farsa de la enamorada del rey (The Farce of
        the Girl Who Loved the King), 8:345b
    Farsa y licencia de la reina castiza (The
        Farce of the Noble Queen), 8:338b
    Femeninas (On Females), 8:333b
    Flor de santidad (Flower of Sanctity),
        8:336a-b
    La guerra carlista (The Carlist War),
        8:337a–338b
        El resplandor de la hoguera (The
            Splendor of the Bonfire), 8:337b
        Gerifaltes de antaño (The Ancient
            Gyrfalcons), 8:338a
        Los cruzados de la causa (The Crusaders
            of the Cause), 8:337a-b
    La lámpara maravillosa (*The Lamp of
        Marvels*), 8:333a-b
    La Marquesa Rosalinda (The Marchioness
        Rosalinda), 8:345a, 348b
    La media noche (Midnight), 8:337b–338a
    La pipa de kif (The Pipe of Kif), 8:346a
    La reina castiza, 8:345b
    La rosa de papel (The Paper Rose),
        8:348b–349a, 350a
    Las comedias bárbaras (Barbaric Plays),
        8:342b–344b, 344b, 348b
        Aguila de blasón (The Emblazoned
            Eagle), 8:342b, 343b–344a
        Cara de Plata (Silver Face), 8:342b–343b
        Romance de lobos (Wolf Song), 8:342b,
            344a-b
    Ligazón (Blood Pact), 8:349b–350a, 350a
    Luces de bohemia (*Lights of Bohemia*),
        8:346a–347a
    Machado and, 9:745b
    Martes de Carnaval (Shrove Tuesday),
        8:350a–351a
        La hija del capitán (The Captain's
            Daughter), 8:350a
        Las galas del difunto (The Corpse's
            Regalia), 8:350a
        Los cuernos de Don Friolera (Don
            Friolera's Horns), 8:350a–351a
    Ortega y Gasset on, 9:1133b
    Sacrilegio (Sacrilege), 8:349a-b, 350a
    *Sonatas: Memorias del Marqués de
        Bradomín* (*The Pleasant Memoirs of the
        Marquis de Bradomín*), 8:333b–336a,
        336b, 342a-b
        Sonata de estío (Summer Sonata),
            8:334b–335a
        Sonata de invierno (Winter Sonata),
            8:335b–336a
        Sonata de otoño (Autumn Sonata),
            8:335a-b
        Sonata de primavera (Spring Sonata),
            8:334a-b
    The Tyrant (*Tirano Banderas*), 8:339b–341a
    Tragedia de ensueño (Dream Tragedy),
        8:342a-b
    Tragedia pastoril en tres actos (Pastoral
        Tragedy in Three Acts), 8:344b–345a
    Voces de gesta (Epic Voices), 8:337a
Valles, Jules
    Céline and, 11:1860a, 1864a, 1873a
    L'Étudiant, 11:1860a
Valois, Nerval and, 6:960b, 963b
Valois dynasty
    end of, 3:264a
    Hapsburg rivalry with, 2:736a
Valores literarios, Los. See Azorín
Valse aux adieu, La. See Kundera, Milan, *The
    Farewell Party*

Valse des toréadors, La. See Anouilh, Jean,
The Waltz of the Toreadors
Valtolla, Vico's stay at, 3:294b, 295b
"Van Bagaden." *See* Céline, Louis-Ferdinand
Van der Noot, Jan, Petrarchan influence,
2:504b
*Van Gogh, le suicidé de la societé (Van Gogh,
the Man Suicided by Society). See*
Artaud, Antonin
Van Gogh, Vincent, Artaud on, 11:1980a-b
Van Lerberghe, Charles, Maeterlinck and,
8:121a–122b, 130b, 140a
Vanguardists in Menton, The. *See* Calvino,
Italo, "Gli avangardisti a Mentone"
Vanier, Léon, Verlaine and, 7:1638a-b
Vanity, theme of, Canetti and, 12:2628b
"Vanloo" school of painting, Delacroix on,
5:531b
VAPLITE (literary group), 10:1675a
Tychyna and, 10:1655b, 1656b
Vápnfirðinga saga, 1:395a
Vararen. See Undset, Sigrid
Varg i veum. See Gunnarsson, Gunnar
Variae. See Heine, Heinrich; Petrarch,
Epistolae variae
Variation
in Anglo-Saxon poetic technique, 1:68a-b
theory of, Frisch and, 13:2913a, 2917b
Variation on a theme
Kundera and, 13:3404b–3405a
in Robbe-Grillet's works, 13:3250a
"Variations of Beauty." *See* Delacroix, Eugène
"Variations on a Sunbeam." *See* Elytis,
Odysseus, *Ilios o protos (Sun the First)*,
"Paralayes pano se mian ahtida"
Variété, La (journal), Leconte de Lisle and,
6:1248a
Varieties of Religious Experience. See James,
William
"Variety Theater, The." *See* Marinetti, Filippo
Tommaso, "Il teatro di varietà"
Various Letters. *See* Petrarch, *Epistolae variae*
"Various Observations About Marriage in
Reply to Objections." *See* Kierkegaard,
Søren
"Various Outcomes of the Same Plan." *See*
Montaigne, Michel de

Varnalis, Kostas
"I mana tou Hristou" (Mother of God),
Ritsos' *Epitafios* and, 12:2829b
Ritsos and, 12:2816b, 2829b
"Várom a másikat." *See* Ady, Endre
Varro, Augustine's *City of God* on, 1:35a
"Varvàra Alexandrovna." *See* Quasimodo,
Salvatore
Varvary. See Gorky, Maxim
Vasconcelos, Joaquim Pereira Teixeira de. *See*
Teixeira de Pascoaes
"Vase étrusque, Le." *See* Mérimée, Prosper,
"The Etruscan Vase"
"Vase, La." *See* Ionesco, Eugène
Vases communicants, Les. See Breton, André
Vasileyeva, Klavdiya, *Vospominaniia o Belom*,
9:924b–925a
"Vasilias tis asinis, O." *See* Seferis, George,
Imerologio katastromatos
Vasos comunicantes, Los (Communicating
Vessels). *See* Cela, Camilo José
Vassa Zheleznova. See Gorky, Maxim
Vast Earth, The. See Pasternak, Boris
Vatard Sisters, The. See Huysmans, Joris Karl,
Les soeurs Vatard
"Vaterländische Gesänge," 5:167b
Vatican Swindle, The. See Gide, André
Vatnsdœla saga, 1:389b–390a, 397b
Vaudevilles. *See Comédie-vaudevilles*
Vaurien, Le. See Aymé, Marcel
Vauthier, Jean, symbolistic drama, 12:2355a
Växjö, Lagerkvist and, 10:1680a-b
Věc Makropulos. See Čapek, Karel
Vecchi ei giovani, I. See Pirandello, Luigi
"Vecchiaia." *See* Ginzburg, Natalia
Vecchio bizzaro, Il. See Goldoni, Carlo
Vecher. See Akhmatova, Anna
Vechernii al'bom. See Tsvetaeva, Marina
Vedova scaltra, La. See Goldoni, Carlo
Vega, Garcilaso de la
Azorín's approval of, 9:644b
Camoëns and, 2:750a, 750b, 752b
cancioneiros and, 2:753a
Cervantes and, 2:823b
Jiménez and, 9:998a
Machado and, 9:752a
pastoral poetry of, 2:912b–913a

Vega, Garcilaso de la (*cont.*)
  Petrarchan influence, 2:504b
Vegetarianism, in Michelet's historiography,
    5:603a
Vegetius (Flavius Vegetius Renatus), *De re
    militari*, 2:546b
Végzet és veszély. *See* Kosztolányi, Dezső
"Veianius." *See* Pascoli, Giovanni
Veil of Beatrice, The. *See* Schnitzler, Arthur,
    Der Schleier der Beatrice
Veil of Isis, The. *See* Leconte de Lisle, Charles
    Marie, "Le voile d'Isis"
Veil of Pierrette, The. *See* Schnitzler, Arthur,
    "Der Schleier der Pierrette"
"Veiled Image of Sais, The." *See* Schiller,
    Friedrich von, "Das verschleierte Bild zu
    Sais"
"Veillée de Vincennes, La." *See* Vigny, Alfred
    Victor de, *The Military Condition*
Veit, Dorothea, Schlegel and, 5:191a-b, 195b
"Vejamen de orador." *See* Ortega y Gasset,
    José
Veláquez. *See* Ortega y Gasset, José
Velázquez, Diego Rodríguez de Silva
  Los borrachos (*The Drunkards* or *Homage
    to Bacchus* or *Bacchus and His
    Companions*), 9:1134a
    mythology and contemporaneity in, 2:913b
  Ortega y Gasset on, 9:1134a, 1140b–1141a,
    1148a
  Unamuno's poem about, 8:284b
Veleidades de la fortuna, Las. *See* Baroja, Pío
"Velik-Den." *See* Khlebnikov, Velimir
Velikaia Krinitsa. *See* Babel, Isaac
Velikaia Staritsa. *See* Babel, Isaac
"Velitelem města Bugulmy." *See* Hašek,
    Jaroslav
Venality. *See* Greed
Venantius Fortunatus, "Pange, lingua, gloriosi
    proelium certaminis," parodied,
    1:370a-b
Venda, La. *See* Unamuno, Miguel de
"Vendémiaire." *See* Apollinaire, Guillaume
Vendryès, Joseph
  Grammaire du vieil irlandais, 12:216b
  Le langage, 12:2516b
Venereal disease

Heine and, 5:506b
  see also Syphilis
Venetian Epigrams. *See* Goethe, Johann
    Wolfgang von
Venetian Lawyer, The. *See* Goldoni, Carlo,
    L'Avvocato veneziano
Venetian Night; or, The Marriage of Lauretta,
    The. *See* Musset, Alfred de, *La nuit
    vénitienne, ou les noces de Laurette*
Venetian Twins, The. *See* Goldoni, Carlo, *I
    due gemelli veneziani*
Venezis, Elias, Seferis and, 12:2255a
"Venganza moruna." *See* Blasco Ibáñez,
    Vicente
Vengeance, theme of
  in *Bjarnar saga Hítdœlakappa*, 1:385a
  in *Cinna*, 3:42a, 42b
  in Dumas's works, 6:739a
  in *Heiðarvíga saga*, 1:385b
  in Kundera, 13:3400a-b
  in *Njála*, 1:391a
  in Yourcenar's *Electre*, 12:2549b
Venice
  Goldoni and, 4:421a–422b
  Marinetti and, 9:813b–814a
  as symbol, 9:725a
Venice Preserved. *See* Hofmannsthal, Hugo
    von, *Das Gerettete Venedig*
Venice Preserved. *See* Otway, Thomas; Weil,
    Simone
Venise sauvée. *See* Weil, Simone, *Venice
    Preserved*
Vent, Le. *See* Simon, Claude
"Vento a Tindari." *See* Quasimodo, Salvatore,
    "Wind at Tindari"
Ventre de Paris, Le. *See* Zola, Émile
Vents. *See* Perse, Saint-John, *Winds*
Venus
  in Baudelaire's works, 7:1327b–1329a
  in Camoëns' *The Lusiads*, 2:761b, 763a
  in Fénelon's *Télémaque*, 3:286a, 287a, 288a
  in Rimbaud's works, 7:1791b
Vénus. *See* Ghelderode, Michel de
"Venus of Ille, The" ("La Vénus d'Ille"). *See*
    Mérimée, Prosper
Vér és arany. *See* Ady, Endre
Vera historia. *See* Lucian

Veraldar saga (*History of the World*), 1:383a

Verardi, *Historia Baetica*, 1:471a

Verblovsky, Flora Osipovna. *See* Mandelshtam, Flora Osipovna

Vercelli Book, 1:64b

Vercors, *Le silence de la mer* (*Silence of the Sea*), 11:2078b

Verdacht, Der. See Dürrenmatt, Friedrich, *The Quarry*

Verde, Cesário
  Baudelaire and, 10:1483b, 1485a
  Orpheu and, 10:1485b
  Pessoa and, 10:1483b, 1484a, 1484b–1485b
  Portuguese literature and, 10:1485a
  realism and, 10:1485a

"Verde verderol." *See* Jiménez, Juan Ramón

Verdi, Giuseppe
  in Heinrich Mann's *The Little Town*, 8:530b
  Hugo and, 6:703b
  La forza del destino, 8:410b
  Requiem dedicated to Manzoni, 5:367a
  Schiller and, 5:50b
  Un ballo in maschera, 5:91b
  Verdi, influence on Vittorini's writing, 12:2740b–2741a
  verse drama, 7:1426b

"Verdinglichung und das Bewusstsein des Proletariats, Die." *See* Lukács, György

Vereinigungen. See Musil, Robert

Verga, Giovanni, **7:1543a–1565b**
  Cavalleria rusticana, 7:1548a-b, 8:183a-b
  D'Annunzio and, 8:179b, 183a-b
  Darwinism in, 7:1552b, 1554a, 1561b
  "I galantuomini" ("The Gentry"), 7:1558a-b
  I Malavoglia (*The House by the Medlar Tree*), 7:1551b–1557a, 1562b, 8:76a, 12:2280b
    Blasco Ibáñez' *The Mayflower* and, 8:359a
    Mena compared to Manzoni's Lucia, 5:382b
  "Il come, il quando, ed il perché" ("How, When, and Why"), 7:1543b–1544a
  "Il reverendo" ("His Reverence"), 7:1557b–1558a
  "Jeli il pastore" (Jeli the Shepherd), 7:1549b–1550a

"La Lupa" ("The She-Wolf"), 7:1548b–1549a, 1563a

"Libertà" ("Liberty"), 7:1558b–1559a

Maestro-don Gesualdo, 7:1559a–1562b

Nedda, 7:1550b–1551b

Novelle rusticane (Brief Novels of the Country), 7:1557a–1559a, 1560b

Pascoli and, 7:1829b

plays by, 7:1563a–1564a

"Rosso Malpelo," 7:1550a-b

scrittura povera ("poor" writing), 7:1557a

Svevo and, 8:76b

Vita dei campi (Life in the Fields), 7:1543b–1544a, 1547b–1550b

Vittorini and, 12:2750b

Vergil (Publius Vergilius Maro)
  Aeneid, 6:696a
  Ariosto and, 2:630b–631a
  Augustine and, 1:27a, 34b–35a, 47a
  Baudelaire and, 7:1340b–1342b
  Beowulf and, 1:70a
  Berlioz and, 6:773b, 775b, 781a, 801a, 802a-b
  Boccaccio's use of, 2:513b
  Boileau on, 3:182b
  Broch's *Death of Vergil*, 10:1398b–1402b
  Camoëns' *The Lusiads* and, 2:747a, 761a, 761b, 762a, 765a
  Cela and, 13:3107a
  Chénier's tribute to, 4:706a-b
  Corneille and, 3:34a, 34b, 37a, 37b
  Dante and, 1:432b
    in *Divine Comedy*, 1:446b, 448a
  Eclogues
    influence on Renaissance pastoral poetry, 2:901a
    Petrarch's *Canzoniere*, influence on, 2:493b
  Fourth Eclogue
    Pascoli and, 7:1828a, 1841a
    Prudentius' *Cathemerinon* and, 1:7b, 19b
  Georgics
    influence on Renaissance pastoral poetry, 2:901a-b
    natural world as subject of, 4:707a
    Petrarch's adaptation of, 2:477b–478a
    Simon and, 13:3043b

Vergil (Publius Vergilius Maro) (*cont.*)
Hugo and, 6:696a
Italian translation of, Tasso and, 2:799b
La Fontaine and, 3:79b
Leopardi and, 5:545b, 554b
Nerval and, 6:953b, 967a
Prudentius and, 1:6a, 11b, 16b
Renaissance pastoral poetry and, 2:900a,
901a–902a
Sainte-Beuve on, 6:856b
Tasso and, 2:801b
on universal law, cited by Vico, 3:299b
Vergini delle rocce, Le. See D'Annunzio,
Gabriele
Verhaeren, Émile
Apollinaire and, 9:886b–887a
Marinetti and, 9:805b
Verhängnisvolle Gabel, Die. See Platen,
August von
Verheyen, Renaat, 11:2119b
Verismo style, Verga and the, 7:1544b–1545b,
1548b, 1560a, 1561b
"Verità, La." *See* Pirandello, Luigi
Vérité en marche, La. See Zola, Émile
Verkehrte Welt, Die. See Tieck, Ludwig
"Verklighet (drömd), En." *See* Ekelöf Gunnar
Verklighetsflykt. See Ekelöf, Gunnar
"Verktygets klaga." *See* Södergran, Edith
Verlaine, Paul, **7:1619a–1643b**, 8:297a
Ady and, 9:859b, 860a, 861b
Amour (Love), 7:1626a
Apollinaire and, 9:881b, 882b, 885a, 886b
"Ariettes oubliées," 7:1624a, 1633a–1634a,
1634b–1635b
art and, 7:1709b
"Art poétique" ("The Art of Poetry"),
7:1630a, 1635b–1636a, 1638a, 1639a
"Cellulairement" (Cellularly), 7:1625a,
1626a
"Chanson d'automne" (Autumn Song),
7:1621b, 1637a
"Charleroi," 7:1632b
Choix de poésies (Choice of Poetry), 7:1626b
"Clair de lune" (Moonlight), 7:1628a,
1629a-b
Claudel and, 8:487b

"Colloque sentimental" ("Sentimental
Conversation"), 7:1629b–1630a
"En patinant" (While Skating), 7:1629a,
1629b
Femmes (Women), 7:1626b
Fêtes galantes (Gallant Festival),
7:1621b–1622a, 1626a-b, 1627a–1630a
personal situation in, 7:1621b
stanza forms in, 7:1637a
Ginzburg and, 13:3133a, 3151a
Hombres (Men), 7:1626b
"hunting horn" motif and, 9:894b
Jadis et naguère (Recently and Formerly),
7:1626a–1627a
Jiménez and, 9:993b, 994b–995a
La bonne chanson (The Good Song)
collection of, 7:1626a-b
description of Verlaine in, 7:1620a
poems in, 7:1622a
Les amies (Friends), 7:1626b
in *Les délisquescences*, 7:1641a
"Les ingénus" (The Youths), 7:1629b
Les poètes maudits (The Damned or
Maligned Poets), 7:1640a-b, 1804a
Les poètes maudits (*The Damned or
Maligned Poets*), 7:1639b
Les uns et les autres (The Ones and the
Others), 7:1626b
Machado and, 9:763a
Mandelshtam and, 10:1626b–1627a, 1634a
"Mandoline," 7:1628b, 1630a
Marinetti and, 9:805b
"Mon rêve familier" ("My Familiar Dream"),
7:1621a-b, 1636b
Ortega y Gasset on, 9:1135b
"Pantomime," 7:1628b, 1629a
Parallèlement (In a Parallel Manner),
7:1626b
Pascoli and, 7:1826a
Pléiade Oeuvres poétiques complètes,
7:1627a
Poèmes saturniens (Saturnian Poems),
7:1626a-b, 1627a-b
Baudelaire's influence on, 7:1640b
description of Verlaine in, 7:1620a
publication of, 7:1621a, 1621b
"Puppets" ("Fantoches"), 7:1628b

Rimbaud and, 7:1785b, 1786b, 1789a, 1804a, 1806a–1807b, 1808b, 1820a

Romances sans paroles, 7:1625b, 1626a-b

Sagesse, 7:1625a, 1637a-b, 1639b

"Sonnet boiteux" (Limping Sonnet), 7:1636b

symbolism and, 9:744b–745a

Valéry and, 8:569b

"Verlöbung in St. Domingo, Die." *See* Kleist, Heinrich von, "The Betrothal in Santo Domingo"

Verlorene Ehre der Katharina Blum, Die. See Böll, Heinrich

Verlorne Lachen, Das. See Keller, Gottfried, *The Lost Smile*

Vermächtnis, Das. See Böll, Heinrich; Schnitzler, Arthur

Vermeer, Jan, Claudel and, 8:487b

Vermenoux, Madame de, 5:89a

Vermintes Gelände. See Böll, Heinrich

Vermischte Schriften. See Heine, Heinrich

Vernacular
Ariosto and, 2:620b, 624a-b
Castiglione and, 2:651b–652a
Dante on, 1:440a, 441a
Luther and, 2:669a
Machiavelli and, 2:599b
in medieval drama. *See* Drama, medieval, vernacular; Mystery plays

Verne, Jules
Baroja reads, 9:589b
Rimbaud and, 7:1979b

Verre d'eau, Le. See Scribe, Eugène

Verri, Pietro, *Osservazioni sulla tortura* (*Observations on Torture*), Manzoni's *The Column of Infamy* and, 5:391b

Vers, as genre in troubadour poetry, 1:167a

"Vers comenssa, Lo." *See* Marcabru

"Vers dorés." *See* Nerval, Gérard de, "Golden Verses"

Vers le blanc infini. See Arp, Jean

Vers nouveaux et chansons. See Rimbaud, Arthur

Vers-libre poetry. *See* Free verse

"Versa est in luctum." *See* Walter of Châtillon

Versailles
Chénier's stay at, 4:711a–713b
Goldoni and, 4:432a–433a

Versailles, Treaty of (1919), 13:3023a

"Verschleierte Bild zu Sais, Das." *See* Schiller, Friedrich von

Verschollene, Der. See Kafka, Franz, *Amerika*

Verses about America. *See* Mayakovsky, Vladimir, *Stikhi ob Amerike*

Verses on my Soviet Passport. *See* Mayakovsky, Vladimir, "Stikhi o sovetskom pasporte"

"Verses on the Unknown Soldier." *See* Mandelshtam, Osip

Versprechen, Das. See Dürrenmatt, Friedrich, *The Pledge*

Versty I. See Tsvetaeva, Marina

Versty II. See Tsvetaeva, Marina

Versuch einer Selbstkritik. See Nietzsche, Friedrich

Versuchung des Pescara, Die. See Meyer, Conrad Ferdinand

Versudung der stillen Veronika, Die. See Musil, Robert, *Vereinigungen*

Versunkene Glocke, Die. See Hauptmann, Gerhart, *The Sunken Bell*

"Vertigo." *See* Čapek, Karel

Vertus médicinales de l'eau commune, Les. See Hecquet, Philippe

Veruda, Umberto, Svevo and, 8:68a, 72a

Verum-factum principle, formulated by Vico, 3:297a-b

Verve, 13:2965b, 2966a

Verwandlung, Die. See Kafka, Franz, *The Metamorphosis*

Verwey, Albert, George and, 8:463a

Verwirrungen des Zöglings Törless. See Musil, Robert

Verwundung und andere frühe Erzählungen, Die. See Böll, Heinrich

Very Easy Death, A. See Beauvoir, Simone de

"Very Seldom." *See* Cavafy, Constantine, "Poly spanios"

Verzauberung, Die. See Broch, Hermann

Vesaas, Tarjei, **11:2035a–2059b**
Bok um finn (The Book About Finn), 11:2037b
Brannen (The Fire), 11:2039, 2047b–2048a
Dei Svarte hestane (The Black Horses), 11:2040a

Vesaas, Tarjei (*cont.*)

Die ukjende mennene (The Unknown Men), 11:2040b, 2041b

Fars reise (Father's Journey), 11:2040b

Grinde-kveld eller den gode engelen (Evening at Grinde; or, The Good Angel), 11:2040a

Grindegard. Morgonen (The Farm at Grinde. The Morning), 11:2036b, 2040a

Guds bustader (The Dwelling Places of God), 11:2053a

Hjarte høyrer sine heimlandstonar (The Heart Hears Its Native Music), 11:2040b, 2041b

Kjeldene (The Wellsprings), 11:2054a–2054b

Kvinnor ropar heim (Women Call: Come Home), 11:2043a

Leiret og hjulet (The Clay and the Wheel), 11:2051b

Menneskebonn (Children of Man), 11:2036b, 2038a, 2039a

Morgonvinden (The Morning Wind), 11:2053a

One Fine Day (En vakker dag), 11:2052b

Sandeltreet (The Sandalwood Tree), 11:2042a

Sendemann Huskuld (Huskuld the Herald), 11:2038a, 2039b, 2042a

Signalet (The Signal), 11:2045b–2046a

Sigrid Stallbrokk, 11:2040b

Spring Night (Vårnatt), 11:2046a–2046b

Tagore and, 11:2037a

Tårnet (The Tower), 11:2039, 2045b

The Bell in the Knoll (Klokka i haugen), 11:2051a

The Birds (Fuglane), 11:2046b–2047b, 2052a, 2053b, 2055b

The Bleaching Yard (Bleikeplassen), 11:2045a–2045b, 2053b

The Boat in the Evening (Båten om kvelden), 11:2049b–2051a

The Bridges (Bruene), 11:2049a–2049b

The Great Cycle (Det store spelet), 11:2041b, 2042a–2042b

The House in the Dark (Huset i mørkret), 11:2044b–2045b

The Ice Palace (Is-slotter), 11:2035a, 2048b

The Seed (Kimen), 11:2043b–2044b, 2053b, 2054a

Ultimatum, 11:2053a

Vindane (The Winds), 11:2051b–2052a

Veshnev, V., "Poeziia banditizma" (The Poetry of Banditry), 11:1907b–1908a

Vestire gli ignudi. See Pirandello, Luigi

Vesuvius, Mount, Goethe at, 5:13b–14a

Vesy (journal), 9:962b

Bely's The Silver Dove and, 9:919a

Vészi, Margit, 9:872a-b, 873b

"Veter (Chetyre otryvka o Bloke)." See Pasternak

"Vetters Eckfenster, Des." See Hoffmann, E. T. A., "My Cousin's Corner Window"

Vexation of the Orator. See Ortega y Gasset, José, "Vejamen de orador"

Vgvisare till underjorden. See Ekelöf, Gunnar, Guide to the Underworld

"Vi är inte neutrala!" See Moberg, Vilhelm

Via negativa, in Augustine's Confessions, 1:31a-b

Viagens na minha terra. See Garrett, Almeida

Viaggio a Roma, Il. See Moravia, Alberto

Viaggio in Sardegna. See Vittorini, Elio

Viaje del Parnaso. See Cervantes, Miguel de, Journey to Parnassus

Viaje a la Alcarria. See Cela, Camilo José, Journey to Alcarria

"Viajero, El." See Machado, Antonio, Soledades, galerías, y otros poemas (Solitudes, Galleries, and Other Poems)

Vian, Boris

Giraudoux and, 9:1041b

Strindberg and, 7:1754a

Viardot, Pauline, Turgenev and, 6:1277a

Viau, Théophile de

Amours tragiques de Pyrame et Thisbé, 3:36a

pastoral poetry of, 2:912b

Vicar of Tours, The. See Balzac, Honoré de, Le curé de Tours

Vicar of Wakefield, The. See Goldsmith, Oliver

Vice

allegory and, 1:322b–323a

portrayed in La Bruyère's Caractères, 3:249b–250a

Vicente, Gil
  Auto da Índia (*Play of India*), 2:756a
  Camoëns and, 2:755a, 756b
  Comédia de Rubena (*Play of Rubena*),
    Camoëns' *The Play of Filodemo* and,
    2:757b
  *Comédia sobre a divisa da cidade de
    Coimbra* (*Play About the Arms of the
    City of Coimbra*), Camoëns' *The Play of
    Filodemo* and, 2:757b
  Jiménez and, 9:1008a
Vices. *See* Virtues and vices
Vico, Giovanni Battista, **3:293a–316b**
  Affetti di un disperato ("Feelings of a
    Desperate Man"), 3:295b
  Autobiografia, Croce and, 8:311a-b, 314a,
    319b–320a
  Autobiography (*Autobiografia*), 3:293a,
    293b, 294b–295a, 305a
  Cartesianism and, 3:279b
  Croce and, 8:323a
    La filosofia di Giambattista Vico,
      8:325a–326a
  *De antiquissima Italorum sapientia ex
    linguae latinae originibus eruenda*
    (*Most Ancient Wisdom of the Italians*),
    3:297a, 298a
  De constantia jurisprudentia liber alter. *See*
    Vico, Giovanni Battista, *Diritto
    universale*
  De mente heroica ("On the Heroic Mind"),
    3:312a
  *De universi juris uno principio et fine uno
    liber unum.* *See* Vico, Giovanni Battista,
    Diritto universale
  Diritto universale (*Universal Law*), 3:295b,
    299a, 299a–304b, 303b–304a
    compared with *Scienza nuova*, 3:305b
    on natural law of nations, 3:308a-b
    reception of, 3:304b
  "Discovertà del vero Dante" ("Discovery of
    the True Dante"), 3:312a
  Manzoni and, 5:368b
  On the Study Methods of Our Time (*De
    nostri temporis studiorum ratione*),
    3:295b, 296a–297a, 299b
  Rimbaud and, 7:1811a

  Scienza nuova (*New Science*), 3:293a-b,
    305a–311b, 7:1811a
    axioms of, 3:306a-b
    as a comprehensive theory of culture,
      3:313a-b
    Croce and, 8:313a, 319b–320a
    on history of human ideas, 3:307b–308a
    impact of, 3:313a-b
    on natural law of nations, 3:308a-b
    on "philosophical criticism," 3:308a
    on "philosophy of authority," 3:307b
    on philosophy of history, 3:308a, 311a-b,
      313b
    on poetry, 3:308b–309a, 310a-b
    possible interpretations of, 3:312b–313a
    principles of history, 3:313b
    principles of, 3:306b
    principles of universal history, 3:308b
    on the process of naming, 3:309a
    seven principal aspects of, 3:307a-b
    translated by Michelet, 5:583a–584a
    versions of, 3:305a
    on wisdom, 3:307a-b
  Unamuno and, 8:291b
  *Vita di Giambiattista Vico scritta da se
    medesimo.* *See* Vico, Giovanni Battista,
    Autobiography
Vico in the Tradition of Rhetoric. *See* Mooney,
  Michael
"Vicolo di Madama Lucrezia, Il." *See* Mérimée,
  Prosper
Vicomte de Bragelonne, Le. *See* Dumas père,
  Alexandre
Victim of Antimilitarism, A. *See* Hašek,
  Jaroslav, "Obět antimilitarismu"
Victim characters, in Gombrowicz's works,
  12:2577b
Victimes du devoir (*Victims of Duty*). *See*
  Ionesco, Eugène
"Victoire, La." *See* Apollinaire, Guillaume
Victor. *See* Vitrac, Roger
Victor ou les enfants au pouvoir (*Victor; or,
  The Children in Power*). *See* Vitrac,
  Roger
Victoria. *See* Hamsun, Knut
"Victorieusement fui le suicide beau." *See*
  Mallarmé, Stéphane

Victory. *See* Hašek, Jaroslav, "Vítězství!"

Victory Celebration. See Solzhenitsyn, Aleksandr

Victory of Samothrace, 9:810a

"Victory, The." *See* Apollinaire, Guillaume, "La Victoire"

Vid lägereld. See Lagerkvist, Pär

Vida de Don Quijote y Sancho. See Ortega y Gasset, José

Vida de Don Quijote y Sancho, La. See Unamuno, Miguel de

Vida es sueño, La. See Calderòn de la Barca, Pedro, *Life Is a Dream*

"Vida es sueño, La." *See* Unamuno, Miguel de

Vida, Marco Girolamo, pastoral scholarship of, 2:910b

Vida nueva (Spanish periodical), Ortega y Gasset's articles in, 9:1121b, 1123a

Vidal, Gaston, *Figures et anecdotes de la grand guerre*, Babel adaptations, 11:1905a-b, 1907a

Vidas sombrías. See Baroja, Pío

"Videnie." *See* Zamyatin, Yevgeny Ivanovich

Vidriera the Licentiate. *See* Azorín, *Tomás Rueda*

Vie, Une (A Life). See Maupassant, Guy de

Vie de bohème, La. See Murger, Henri

Vie de Henri Brulard, La. See Stendhal

Vie de Jean Racine. See Mauriac, François

Vie de Jésus. See Renan, Ernest

"Vie de pinceau, La." *See* Arp, Jean

Vie de Rancé. See Chateaubriand, François René de

Vie des abeilles, La. See Maeterlinck, Maurice

Vie est ailleurs, La. See Kundera, Milan, *Life Is Elsewhere*

"Vie et la mort du capitaine Renaud, La, ou la canne de jonc." *See* Vigny, Alfred Victor de, *The Military Condition*

Vie et l'oeuvre de Philippe Semmelweis, La. See Céline, Louis-Ferdinand

Vie heureuse, La. See Camus, Albert, *A Happy Death*

Vie, poésies et pensées de Joseph Delorme. See Sainte-Beuve, Charles-Augustin

Vie publique de Pantagleize, La. See Ghelderode, Michel de

Vieille, La. See Simenon, Georges

Vieillesse, La. See Beauvoir, Simone de, *Old Age*

Viejo celoso, El. See Cervantes, Miguel de

Viéle-Griffin, Francis, Breton and, 11:1939a

Vienna
   fin-de-siècle
      decadence in, 8:113a-b
      theater in, 9:692b–693b
   Freud in, 8:2b, 4b, 13a-b
   Hebbel in, 6:1096b–1097b
   literary culture, 9:1092a
   Schnitzler in, 8:89a, 92a, 112a

Vienna Opera House, The. See Wagner, Richard, *Das Wiener Hof-Operntheater*

"Vier Knöpfe zwei Löcher vier Besen." *See* Arp, Jean

"Vierge moderne." *See* Södergran, Edith

Viertel, Salka, Heinrich Mann and, 8:541a

Vies de Haydn, Mozart, et Métastase. See Stendhal

Vietnam War, Simon's *Conducting Bodies* and, 13:3041a

Vieusseux, Giampietro, Leopardi and, 5:547a-b

"Vieux marins, Les." *See* Marinetti, Filippo Tommaso

Víga-Glúms saga (The Story of Killer-Glúm), 1:393a-b

"Vigilance." *See* Breton, André

Vigilance. *See* Ritsos, Yannis, *Aghrypnia*

Víglundar saga, 1:398a-b

Vigne, Céleste Buisson de la, Chateaubriand and, 5:116a, 127b

Vigneulles, Phillip de, *Les cent nouvelles nouvelles de Phillipe de Vigneulles*, sources of, 2:946b

Vigny, Alfred Victor de, **5:447a–488b**
   Chatterton, 5:470b–472b
      motivation for, 5:467b
   Cinq-Mars ou une conjuration sous Louis XIII (Cinq-Mars; or, A Conspiracy Under Louis XIII), 5:458a–461a
      artistic license in *Stello* and, 5:469a
      historical anachronisms in, 5:460b
      planning of, 5:452a-b

"Réflexions sur la vérité dans l'art" ("Reflections on Truth in Art"), 5:458b–459a

Daphné, 5:476b–478b

"Eloa ou la soeur des anges" (Eloa; or, The Sister of Angels), 5:452b–454a, 6:1216a
  as fable, 5:455b
  first work on, 5:452a
  as short epic, 5:455a

Giraudoux and, 9:1041b, 1060a

"Hunting Horn" and, 9:894b

Journal d'un poète, on his vocation as a writer, 5:447a-b

La maréchale d'Ancre (*The Wife of the Marshall d'Ancre*), 5:466a–467a

"L'Anté-Christ" (The Anti-Christ), 5:452a

Le more de Venise (Shakespeare's *Othello*), 5:462a–463a
  La maréchale d'Ancre and, 5:466b
  "Lettre à Lord ***" (Letter to Lord ***) as preface of, 5:462a-b

Lermontov and, 6:1216a, 1220b

Les destinées (*The Fates*), 5:480b–486b
  "La colère de Samson" ("The Wrath of Samson"), 5:483b
  "La flûte" (The Flute), 5:479b, 484a-b
  "La maison du berger" (The Shepherd's Hut), 5:465a, 481a–483a
  "La mort du loup" (The Death of the Wolf), 5:479a, 479b, 483b–484a
  "La sauvage" (The Savage Woman), 5:479b, 483a
  "Les destinées," 5:481a
  "Les oracles" (The Oracles), 5:483a
  "The Bottle in the Sea" ("La bouteille à la mer"), 5:465a, 485b–486a
  "The Mount of Olives" ("Le mont des oliviers"), 5:456a, 484b–485b
  "The Pure Spirit" ("L'Esprit pur"), 5:447b, 479b, 486a-b

Mémoires inédits: Fragments et projets, his schooling in, 5:448b

"Mont des Oliviers," Nerval style and, 6:950b

"Paris," 5:464a–465a

Poèmes antiques et modernes, 5:454b–458a
  "Dolorida," 5:450b, 455b

"La dryade" (The Dryad), 5:455a

"La femme adultère" (The Adulterous Woman), 5:450b, 455b, 456a

"La fille de Jephté," 5:455b–456a, 457a

"La prison" (The Prison), 5:455b

"Le bain d'une dame romaine" (The Bath of a Roman Lady), 5:455a

"Le bal" ("The Ball"), 5:451a, 455a

"Le déluge," 5:455a, 455b, 457a-b, 458a

"Le trappiste" (The Trappist), 5:455b

"Moses" ("Moïse"), 5:455a, 455b, 456a–457a, 458a

"Symetha," 5:455a

"The Horn," 5:457b–458a

Poèmes (*Poems*), 5:451b
  "Helena," 5:451b

Quitte pour la peur (Getting Off with a Fright), 5:470a-b

Richter's "The Speech of Christ" and, 5:59a

"Satan racheté" (Satan Redeemed), 5:452a

"Satan sauvé" (Satan Redeemed), 5:454a

Scenes from the Desert: The Almeh (*Scènes du désert: L'Almeh*), 5:465a–466a
  Daphné compared to, 5:477b

Shylock; or, The Merchant of Venice translated by, 5:463a

Stello, 5:467a–469b
  Chénier's affair with de Coigny in, 4:693a
  Daphné as continuation of, 5:476b

The Military Condition (*Servitude et grandeur militaires*), 5:472b–476b, 6:1220b
  "Laurette; or, The Red Seal" ("Laurette ou le cachet rouge"), 5:473a, 473b
  motivation for, 5:467b
  "The Life and Death of Captain Renaud; or, The Malacca Cane" ("La vie et la mort du capitaine Renaud ou la canne de jonc"), 5:473b, 474b–476a
  "The Night at Vincennes" ("La veillée de Vincennes"), 5:473a, 474a-b
  work begun on, 5:470b

translated Shakespeare's *Romeo and Juliet* (with Deschamps), 5:462a

Vikings of Helgeland, The. *See* Ibsen, Henrik

Vikivaki. *See* Gunnarsson, Gunnar

"Vil wol gelopter got." *See* Walther von der Vogelweide

"Vila i leshii" (The Vila and the Wood-Goblin). *See* Khlebnikov, Velimir

Vildanden. See Ibsen, Henrik, *The Wild Duck*

Vil'iam-Vil'mont, Nikolai, on Pasternak's *Hamlet*, 10:1607b

Vilkiṅa saga, 1:401b

"Villa Natacha." *See* Elytis, Odysseus, *Ta eterothale*

Villaespesa, Francisco, Jiménez and, 9:993b

Village of Fuente Ovejuna, The. See Lope de Vega, *Fuente Ovejuna*

Village Parson, The. See Balzac, Honoré de, *Le curé de village*

Village Priest, The. *See* Herculano, Alexandre, "O Pároco da aldeia"

Village Romeo and Juliet, A. See Keller, Gottfried

Village Soothsayer, The. *See* Rousseau, Jean Jacques, *Le devin du village*

Village of Vučjak, The. *See* Krleža, Miroslav, *Vučjak*

Villalobos, Francisco López de. *See* López de Villalobos, Francisco

Villani, Filippo, Boccaccio biography, 2:510b–511a

Villani, Giovanni, *Chronicle*, as source of Ser Giovanni's *Il pecorone*, 2:936b

Villano, Lope de Vega and, 2:853a-b

Villano en su rincón, El. See Lope de Vega, *The Peasant and His Retreat*

Villard, Nina de, 7:1620b

Ville dont le prince est un enfant, La. See Montherlant, Henry de

Ville, La. See Claudel, Paul

Villegas, Esteban Manual de, Cervantes and, 2:823a

Villegas, Francisco Gomez de Quevedo y, Azorín's literary criticism of, 9:645a

Villeterque (journalist), Sade and, 4:627b–628a, 628a-b

Villey, Pierre, *Les sources et l'évolution des "Essais" de Montaigne*, 2:774b

Villiers de l'Isle-Adam, Auguste de, 8:121b–122a, 123a, 124b

Axel, Apollinaire and, 9:886a, 889b

Contes cruels (*Cruel Tales*), 8:121b

L'Eve future (*Tomorrow's Eve*), 8:121b

Verlaine and, 7:1620b

Villon, François, **2:535a–570b**

Apollinaire and, 9:882b, 885a

"Ballad of the Women of Paris," 2:566b

Céline and, 11:1859a

concept of commemoration, 2:543b–544a

death imagery, 12:2533a

"Debate Between the Poet and His Heart," 2:543a

funerary monuments, 2:536a, 541b–542a

literary monuments and, 2:542a, 550b

Gautier and, 6:1046a-b

identity in death, 2:536a-b, 542a-b

imprisonment, 2:537b, 544a, 556b

individual versus society, 2:543a

Mandelshtam's essays on, 10:1629b–1630a

"Pour prier Nostre Dame," 2:560a

"The Ballad of the Fried Tongues," 2:566b

"The Contradiction of Franc Gonthier," 2:566b

The Legacy, 2:536b, 537b, 538a, 538b

bequests, 2:548b–549b

decomposition and recomposition imagery, 2:540b–541a, 552b

discourse on death, 2:539b–540b

dual ending, 2:554a–555b

"Finablement, en escripvant," 2:554b–555a

"*Item*, a celle que j'ai dit," 2:551a-b

"*Item* a maistre Ythier Marchant," 2:552a-b

Je, Françozs Villon, 2:556a

"La tres amoureuse prison," 2:544a

language, literal vs. figurative, 2:547b–548a, 552b–553a, 554a

language, of reflection, 2:548b

language, of the self, 2:553b–554a

love bond, 2:544a–545a

motivation for, 2:544a

"my tents and my pavilions," 2:549b–550a, 555b

"Near Christmas, the dead season," 2:547a-b, 553b

poetic devices, 2:541a, 548b–549a, 550b, 553b, 567a

poetic form, 2:539b

"Puisque mon sens fut a repos," 2:555a-b

shift in speaker's voice, 2:546a–547a

testamentary form, 2:555b, 567b

testamentary rhetoric, 2:551b

and *The Testament*, distinguishing features, 2:543a–544a

two afterlives, 2:545b–546a

winter love, 2:547a-b

The Testament, 1:358b–359a, 2:536b, 537b, 538a, 538b, 555b–569a

"anguish-pears," 2:558b

arma Christi, 2:559a, 559b

"Ballad of the Women of Olden Times," 2:564a, 564b

"Belle Heaulmière," 2:564a, 564b

bergeronnette, 2:567b

biblical quotations, 2:561a, 563b

carpe diem theme, 2:563a

collective "I," 2:566a-b, 568a-b

congé and, 1:460a

historical precedents, 2:564a-b

humiliation and suffering themes, 2:558a-b, 567b

imminence of death, 2:565a-b

"Je crie a toutes gens mercis" (I cry everyone's pardon), 2:568b

language, of libertinage, 2:559b

on the Latin poet Horace, 2:541a-b

motivation for, 544a

multiple endings, 2:567a-b

narrative voices, 2:556a, 557a, 557b, 559a, 559b–560a, 560b–561a, 563b–564a, 567a, 568a

number symbolism, 2:562b

palinode, 2:557a, 563a

poet/hero, 2:557b–558a

poetic form, 2:539b

Psalm 109, 2:561a–563a

religious conversion, 2:560a, 563b

resurrection imagery, 2:556b, 568b–569a

Sorrowing Man, 2:558a, 558b–559a, 565b

thirst metaphor, 2:565a-b

ubi sunt lamentation, 2:564a-b, 567a

victimization narrative, 2:561b

of youth, 2:563a–564b

use of paronomasia, 2:538b, 550b, 559a-b, 566b

"Villon's Epitaph," 2:539b–540a, 542a, 545b, 552b

Weil and, 12:2809a

"Villon's Epitaph." *See* Villon, François

Villot, Frédéric, Delacroix's letter to, 5:538b

Vilmorin, Louise de, Malraux and, 12:2415b–2416a

Vin de Paris, Le. See Aymé, Marcel

Vincennes, Sade's imprisonment at, 4:617a–618b

Vincent de Paul, St., Bossuet and, 3:153b–154a

Vincent and the Mistress of Important Men. *See* Musil, Robert, *Vinzenz und die Freundin bedeutender Männer*

Vindane. See Vesaas, Tarjei

Vindication of Catholic Morality, A. See Manzoni, Alessandro

Vineyard imagery, in Rabelais's *Fifth Book*, 2:715a

Vingt ans après. See Dumas père, Alexandre

Vinland, 1:380a, 381b

Vinzenz und die Freundin bedeutender Männer. See Musil, Robert

Violence

in Baroja's novels, 9:593b

in Cela's fiction, 13:3109a-b

in Chrétien's *Philomena*, 1:186b–187b

in Dürrenmatt's works, 13:3233a-b

futurist, Marinetti and, 9:809a–814a, 828a

in Pavese's works, 12:2770a, 2783b–2784a

in Welsh legends, 1:143a

Violence. *See* Moberg, Vilhelm, *Våld*

Violent Bear It Away, The. See O'Connor, Flannery

Violet Souls. *See* Jiménez, Juan Ramón, *Almas de violeta*

"Violetta skymningar" ("Violet Twilights"). *See* Södergran, Edith

"Violin, The." *See* Mann, Heinrich

Viollet-le-Duc, Eugène, Taine and, 7:1461a

Víos ke politía tu Aléksi Zorbá. See Kazantzakis, Nikos, *Zorba the Greek*

"Vipère, La." *See* Leconte de Lisle, Charles Marie

Vipers' Tangle. *See* Mauriac, François
Virdia, Ferdinando, on Silone, 12:2294b
Virgilio, Giovanni del, Dante and, 1:444a
Virgin Mary
  in *Divine Comedy*, 1:448a
  Elytis and, 13:2977a, 2983b
  in German Easter plays, 1:467b
  in Greban's *Passion*, 1:470a
  in miracle plays, 1:463b–465a
  in Play of the Wise and Foolish Virgins,
    1:462a
  Walther and, 1:295b, 302b–303a
Virgin persona, in Ekelöf's works,
    12:2642a–2643a, 2647a, 2653a-b
Virgin Soil. See Turgenev, Ivan
Virginia. See Alfieri, Vittorio
Virgins' God, The. *See* Khlebnikov, Velimir,
    "Devii bog"
Virtue
  allegory and, 1:322b–323a
  in Dante's *De vulgari eloquentia*, 1:441b
  and genius, in Staël's *De la littérature*,
    5:95a
  in Machiavelli, 2:602b
  Robbe-Grillet on, 13:3253a-b
  in Rousseau, 4:456a-b
  vs. self-love, in La Rochefoucauld's
    Maximes, 3:66b
"Virtue Unknown." *See* Alfieri, Vittorio
Virtues and vices
  personified
    in *Castle of Perseverance*, 1:471b
    in classical literature, 1:6a
    in classical satire, 1:366b–367a
    in medieval satire, 1:369b
    in *Speculum stultorum*, 1:373a
Virtuous Island, The. See Giraudoux, Jean,
    Supplément au voyage de Cook
"Visan från molnet." *See* Södergran, Edith
Vischard, César, abbot of Saint-Réal, *Don
    Carlos*, as source of Alfieri's *Philip*,
    4:678b
Vischer, Friedrich Theodor, Meyer and, 6:930b
Visconte dimezzato, Il. See Calvino, Italo, *The
    Cloven Viscount*

Visconti, Ermes, *Idee elementari sulla poesia
    romantica*, as fundamental manifesto,
    5:371b
Visconti, Luchino, 7:1556b
Vise, The. See Pirandello, Luigi, *La morsa*
Vises sten, De. See Lagerkvist, Pär
Vishney sad. See Chekhov, Anton, *The Cherry
    Orchard*
Vishnupurana, mysticism in, 9:1009a
"Vishnyovaya kostochka." *See* Olesha, Yuri,
    "The Cherry Stone"
Vision, in Rimbaud's works, 7:1792b,
    1811a–1812b, 1816b–1817a,
    1819b–1820a, 1820b–1821a
"Vision." *See* Musset, Alfred de, *Nights*
Vision, A. See Yeats, William Butler
"Vision de Charles XI." *See* Mérimée, Prosper
Vision on the Marsh. *See* Ady, Endre, "Vizió a
    lápon"
Vision of the Seeress, The. See Völuspá
Visionaries, The. *See* Baroja, Pío, *Los
    visionarios*; Musil, Robert, *Die
    Schwärmer*
Visions, Vesaas and, 11:2056b
"Visions actuelles et futures." *See* Jarry, Alfred
Visions from San Francisco Bay. See Milosz,
    Czeslaw
Visions of Present and Future. *See* Jarry,
    Alfred, "Visions actuelles et futures"
Visions of Simone Machard, The. See Brecht,
    Bertolt
Visit of the Old Lady, The. See Dürrenmatt,
    Friedrich, *The Visit*
Visit, The. See Dürrenmatt, Friedrich
Visit to Portugal, A. See Andersen, Hans
    Christian
Visitatio sepulchri, 1:453b, 471a
Viso Wettini, on Charlemagne's sins, 1:100a
*Vísperas, festividad y octava de San Camilo
    del año 1936 en Madrid* (Eve, Festivity,
    and Octave of Saint Camillus in the
    Year 1936 in Madrid). *See* Cela, Camilo
    José
Visual arts. *See* Art
Visual metaphors, Sartre and, 12:2598b–2599b
Visual poetry. *See* Concrete poetry
Vita, una. See Svevo, Italo, *A Life*

Vita dei campi. See Verga, Giovanni

Vita di Castruccio Castracani da Lucca, La.
    See Machiavelli, Niccolò, *The Life of*
    Castruccio Castracani of Lucca

Vita d'un uomo. See Ungaretti, Giuseppe

Vita è gioco, La. See Moravia, Alberto

"*Vita fugge et non s'arresta un'ora, La.*" *See*
    Petrarch, *Canzoniere*

Vita immaginaria. See Ginzburg, Natalia

Vita interiore, La. See Moravia, Alberto, *Time*
    of Desecration

Vita non è sogno, La. See Quasimodo,
    Salvatore

Vita nuova. See Dante Alighieri

Vita, Una. See Svevo, Italo, *A Life*

Vitalism
    in Olesha's works
        "Aldebaran," 11:2242a-b
        Envy, 11:2239b
        "The Cherry Stone," 11:2243b
    in Wedekind's plays, 8:240a–257a
        Lulu dramas, 8:253b

Vitam impendere amori. See Apollinaire,
    Guillaume

Viter z Ukrainy. See Tychyna, Pavlo

"*Vítězství!*" *See* Hašek, Jaroslav

Vitrac, Roger
    Peau-Asie, 11:1953a
    Victor ou les enfants au pouvoir (Victor; or,
        The Children in Power), 13:2862b
        Anouilh's production of, 13:2849b, 2861b
        Sarraute's *C'est beau* and, 12:2356b

Vitrier, Jean, Erasmus and, 2:576b

Vittoria Accorombona. See Tieck, Ludwig

Vittorini, Elio, **12:2733a–2757b**
    Calvino and, 13:3261b, 3264a
    Conversazione in Sicilia (*In Sicily*),
        12:2289b, 2735a, 2740a–2745b, 2749b,
        2754a, 2766b
        epilogue, 12:2742a
        the Great Lombard, 12:2744b,
            2754b–2755a
        language, 12:2755b
        Quasimodo and, 12:2389a
        as romance, 12:2743a-b
        structure, 12:2741b

Diario in pubblico (Public Diary), 12:2734a,
    2736a
    "Maestri cercando" (Looking for Masters),
        12:2735b

Erica e i suoi fratelli (Erica and Her
    Siblings), 12:2734b, 2738a–2740a,
    2753b

Ginzburg and, 13:3137a

ideology of, 12:2743a, 2749b–2750a, 2750b,
    2751b

Il garofano rosso (*The Red Carnation*),
    12:2734a, 2735a, 2736b–2738a, 2740a
    language, 12:2738a, 2739a
    political themes, 12:2737a-b
    preface, 12:2737b

Il sempione strizza l'occhio al Fréjus (*The
    Twilight of the Elephant*), 12:2735a,
    2740a, 2747b–2749b

La Garibaldina, 12:2753b–2755a

Lampedusa's *The Leopard* rejected by,
    11:2010b

language, 12:2740b, 2742b, 2746a-b,
    2755a-b

Le donne di Messina (*The Women of
    Messina*), 12:2285a-b, 2734a-b, 2735a,
    2736b, 2747a, 2749b–2753b, 2754a
    second version, 12:2751a, 2752a-b
    symbolism of truck, 12:2750a-b, 2751b

Pavese and, 12:2762b

Piccola borghesia (Petite Bourgoisie),
    12:2736a, 2738b

Quasimodo and, 12:2389a

Silone and, 12:2303b

Uomini e no (*Men and Not Men*), 12:2735a,
    2745b–2749b, 2749b, 2754a
    revisions, 12:2746b

Viaggio in Sardegna (Voyage in Sardinia),
    12:2736a, 2736b, 2738b

"¡Viva la República!" *See* Ortega y Gasset,
    José

¡Viva mi dueño! See Valle-Inclán, Ramón del,
    El ruedo ibérico

Vivaldi, Antonio, Goldoni and, 4:425a

Vivas, Eliseo, on Céline, 11:1872b

Vives. See Ortega y Gasset, José

Vives, Juan Luis, Azorín's approval of, 9:644b

Vivonne, Andrée de. *See* La Rochefoucauld, Andrée, duchesse de

Vivonne, Catherine de, 3:24b, 26b, 62b, 63b, 66b

Vivos Voco, Hesse and, 9:845b

"Viy, The" *See* Gogol, Nikolay Vasilievich

"Vizier's Elephant, The." *See* Andrić, Ivo

"Vizió lápon." *See* Ady, Endre

"Vkhozhu ia v temnye khramy." *See* Blok, Alexander

Vlaamsche Volkstoneel, Het. *See* Flemish Peoples' Theater

Vladimir Il'ich Lenin. See Mayakovsky, Vladimir

Vladimir Mayakovskii: Tragediya (Vladimir Mayakovsky: A Tragedy). See Mayakovsky, Vladimir

"Vlas." *See* Dostoevsky, Feodor

"Vnov' u sebia . . . Unizhen, zol i rad." *See* Blok, Alexander

"Vnuchka Malushi." *See* Khlebnikov, Velimir

"Vo ves' golos." *See* Mayakovsky, Vladimir

"Voce, La." *See* Pascoli, Giovanni

Voce, La (literary journal)
   Prezzolini and, 10:1456a
   Ungaretti's poetry in, 10:1456a

Voces de gesta. See Valle-Inclán, Ramón del

Voci della sera, Le. See Ginzburg, Natalia, *Voices in the Evening*

Voetius, Gysbertus, 3:19b–20b
   Theses on Atheism, 3:19b–20a

"Voeux stériles, Les." *See* Musset, Alfred de

vogel selbdritt, der. See Arp, Jean

"Vogelschau." *See* George, Stefan, *Algabal*

"Voglia mi sprona." *See* Petrarch, *Canzoniere*

Vogue, La, 7:1896b, 1897a, 1897b

Vogue la galère. See Aymé, Marcel

"Voi ch'ascoltate." *See* Petrarch, *Canzoniere*

"Voice from the Chorus, A." *See* Blok, Alexander, "Golos iz khora"

Voice of the Sea, The. See Moravia, Alberto, *Boh*

Voice, The. *See* Pascoli, Giovanni, "La voce"; *Voce, La*

Voices in the Evening. See Ginzburg, Natalia

Voices of the People in Song. See Herder, Johann Gottfried von, *Stimmen der Völker in Liedern*

Voices of Silence, The. See Malraux, André

Voie de Paradis (Road to Paradise), 1:325b

Voie royale, La. See Malraux, André, *The Royal Way*

"Voile d'Isis, Le." *See* Leconte de Lisle, Charles Marie

Voina i mir. See Mayakovsky, Vladimir; Tolstoy, Leo, *War and Peace*

"Voina v myshelovke." *See* Khlebnikov, Velimir, "War in a Mousetrap"

Voiture, Vincent, La Fontaine and, 3:79a

Voix du silence, Les. See Malraux, André, *The Voices of Silence*

Voix humaine, La. See Cocteau, Jean

Voix intérieures, Les. See Hugo, Victor

Vokrug sveta (Round the World) (Soviet journal), 9:1109a

Vol de nuit. See Saint-Exupéry, Antoine de

Vol d'Icare, Le. See Queneau, Raymond

Volets verts, Les. See Simenon, Georges

Volgar' (journal), Gorky's *Orphan Paul* in, 8:427a

Volidhoskopos. See Ritsos, Yannis

Volkonsky, Prince Nicholas, Tolstoy and, 7:1474a

Volkonsky, Princess Marya, Tolstoy and, 7:1474a–1475a

Volkslieder. See Folk song, German

Volksstücke (folk play), of Austria, influences on, 5:421b

Vollendung der Liebe, Die. See Musil, Robert, *Vereinigungen*

Vollendung des Königs Henri Quatre, Die. See Mann, Heinrich

"Vol'nost." *See* Pushkin, Alexander

"Vol'nye mysli." *See* Blok, Alexander

Volokhova, Natal'ya Nikolaevna, 9:970b

Voloshin, Maksimilian, Tsvetaeva and, 11:1734a, 1738a, 1745a-b

Volpe e le camelie, La. See Silone, Ignazio

Volshebnyi fornar'. See Tsvetaeva, Marina

Völsunga saga, 1:400a-b, 401b

Volta, 1:176a

Volta ao mundo, A. See Ferreira de Castro,
José Maria
Voltaire, **4:367a–392b**
  Alfieri's relationship to, 4:667b, 688a
  Alzire, 4:373b
  antireligious works, 4:390b–391a
  Beaumarchais and, 4:569b, 570a, 573a, 578a
  Berlioz and, 6:771b
  Candide, 4:377b–378a, 379a, 386a–389b,
    391b
    Staël on, 5:99b
    Titan and, 5:73a
    Vigny's "The Mount of Olives" compared
      to, 5:485a
  Céline and, 11:1859b, 1872a
  Chénier and, 4:709a
  Claudel and, 8:490b
  correspondence, 4:391a-b
  Dictionnaire philosophique, 4:368b, 380a
  Diderot and, 4:483a-b
  Discours en vers sur l'homme (*Discourse in
    Verse on Man*), 4:373b
  Essai sur les moeurs et l'esprit des nations
    (*An Essay on the Manners and Spirit of
    Nations*), 4:376b, 383b–384a
  Essay on Epic Poetry, Chénier and, 4:707a,
    709a
  on Fénelon, 3:273a
  Goldoni and, 4:431b–432a
  Histoire de Charles XII, roi de Suède
    (*History of Charles XII*), 4:372b, 382a-b
  Histoire de Jenni, 4:387b
  histories, 4:371a–372b, 375b, 382a–384a
  Hofmannsthal and, 9:689b
  Irène, 4:380b
  on La Bruyère's *Caractères*, 3:259a
  La henriade, 4:371a–372a
  La pucelle (The Maid), 4:373b
    Schiller's *The Maid of Orleans* and, 5:46b
  Le blanc et le noir (*The White and the
    Black*), as source for Grillparzer's *A
    Dream Is Life*, 5:437b
  Le diatribe du docteur Akakia (The Diatribe
    of Doctor Akakia), 4:375b–376b
  Le mondain, 4:386a

  Le siècle de Louis XIV (The Age of Louis
    XIV), 3:328b–329a, 4:375b, 382a–383b,
    538b
    on Bossuet, 3:164b
    on La Rochefoucauld's *Maximes*, 3:53a,
      63a
  Le temple du goût (Temple of Taste),
    4:372b–373a
  on Lesage's *Gil Blas*, 3:328b–329a, 339b
  Lessing and, 4:538b
  Letters on England, De l'Allemagne and,
    5:105a
  Lettres philosophiques (*Philosophical
    Letters*), 4:372b–373b, 384b–386a
    on Montaigne, 2:786a
  life of, 4:368b–381a
  L'Ingénu, 4:390a
  literary diversity of, 4:367a–368b, 381a-b,
    391b
  Mahomet, 4:373b
  Marya Volkonsky and, 7:1474b
  memoirs, 4:390a-b
  Mérope, 4:373b, 381b
  Micromégas, 4:375b, 389b–390a
    Fénelon's *Télémaque* and, 3:289a
  on Molière, 3:101a
  Montaigne and, 2:786b
  Nanine, Lessing on, 4:548b
  Oedipe, 4:370b–371a
  on Pascal, 3:125a
    Pensées, 3:143a, 147b
  philosophical letters, 4:372b–373b,
    384b–386a
  philosophical tales, 4:386a–387a
  Poème sur le désastre de Lisbonne (Poem
    on the Lisbon Earthquake), 4:377a-b
  Rousseau and, 4:454b–455a
  Sémiramis, Lessing on, 4:548a
  tragedies, 4:381b–382a
  Traité sur la tolérance (Treatise on
    Tolerance), 4:379a–380a
  Yourcenar and, 12:2538b
  Zadig, 4:375a, 378a
    Staël on, 5:99b
  Zaïre, Lessing on, 4:544b
"Voltaire—Goethe." *See* Mann, Heinrich
Voltati parlami. See Moravia, Alberto

Voluntad de vivir, La. See Blasco Ibáñez, Vicente

Voluntad, La. See Azorín

Volupté. See Sainte-Beuve, Charles-Augustin

Völuspá (*The Vision of the Seeress*), 1:386a, 391b–392a

Volzhina, Ekaterina Pavlovna, 8:419a

Vom Geist der ebräischen Poesie. See Herder, Johann Gottfried von, *The Spirit of Hebrew Poetry*

"Vom Nutzen und Nachteil der Historie für das Leben." *See* Nietzsche, Friedrich

"Vom Ritter der sich verliegt." *See* George, Stefan, *Die Bücher der Hirten- und Preisgedichte* . . . (The Books of Eclogues and Eulogies), *Sagen und Sänge* poems

"Vom Steppenwolf." *See* Hesse, Hermann

"Vom Umgang mit dem Einfall." *See* Frisch, Max

"Von Katzen." *See* Storm, Theodor

Von Nützen und Nachtheil der Historie für das Leben. See Nietzsche, Friedrich, *On the Advantage and Disadvantage of History for Life*

Von Ordnung Dienstes in der Gemeinde. See Luther, Martin

Vonnegut, Kurt, Céline's influence on, 11:1859a

Vor dem Sturm. See Fontane, Theodor

Vor Sonnenaufgang, Soziales Drama. See Hauptmann, Gerhart

Vorljóð. See Gunnarsson, Gunnar

Vormärz (political poetry), poetic realism and, 6:913b

Voronezh, Mandelshtam's exile to, 10:1646a–1647a

"Voronezh." *See* Akhmatova, Anna

Voronezhskie tetradi (Voronezh Notebooks). *See* Mandelshtam, Osip

Voronskii, Alexander, on Babel, 11:1908b–1909a

Voronyi, Mykola, 10:1652b–1653a

"Vörös hervadás." *See* Kosztolányi, Dezső

"Vörös szekér a tengeren." *See* Ady, Endre

Vörösmarty, Mihály, Ady and, 9:860a, 864b

"Vorrede eines Dichters zu seinen ausgewählten Werken." *See* Hesse, Hermann

Vorschule der Aesthetik. See Richter, Jean Paul

"Vory." *See* Chekhov, Anton

Vorzüge der Windhühner, Die. See Grass, Günter

"Vospominanie." *See* Olesha, Yuri

Vospominaniia o A. A. Bloke. See Bely, Andrey

Vospominaniia o Belom. See Vasileyeva, Klavdiya

Vospominaniia o Shteinere. See Bely, Andrey

Vossische Zeitung (newspaper), Fontane and, 6:1309b–1310b

"Vot on—gliadi—ustavshii ot chuzhbin." *See* Tsvetaeva, Marina

Votre Faust: Fantaisie variable genre opéra. See Butor, Michel

Vouivre, La. See Aymé, Marcel, *The Fable and the Flesh*

Vous les entendez? See Sarraute, Nathalie

"Vowels." *See* Rimbaud, Arthur, "Voyelles"

Voyage, Le. See Baudelaire, Charles

Voyage au bout de la nuit. See Céline, Louis-Ferdinand, *Journey to the End of Night*

Voyage aux eaux des Pyrénées. See Taine, Hippolyte

"Voyage à Cythère, Un." *See* Baudelaire, Charles

Voyage de M. Perrichon, Le. See Labiche, Eugène

"Voyage d'Hercueil, Le." *See* Ronsard, Pierre de

Voyage d'Urien, Le. See Gide, André

Voyage en Amérique. See Chateaubriand, François René de

Voyage en Auvergne, Le. See Sand, George

"Voyage en Dauphiné." *See* Berlioz, Hector

Voyage en Espagne. See Gautier, Théophile, *Travels in Spain*

Voyage en Espagne, Le. See Sand, George

Voyage en Italie. See Taine, Hippolyte

Voyage en Orient. See Nerval, Gérard de

Voyage en Russie. See Gautier, Théophile, *Travels to Russia*

"Voyage, Le." *See* Baudelaire, Charles

Voyage musical en Allemagne et en Italie. See Berlioz, Hector

Voyage in Sardinia. See Vittorini, Elio, *Viaggio in Sardegna*

"Voyage to Cythera, A." *See* Baudelaire, Charles, "Un voyage à Cythère"

Voyage to the Holy Land. See Petrarch, *Itinerarium Syriacum*

Voyages
   in Rabelais's works, 2:711b, 714a
   symbolic, in Valéry's "The Rower," 8:583b

Voyages chez les morts. See Ionesco, Eugène

Voyages de Cyrus. See Ramsay, André Michel

"Voyageur, Le." *See* Apollinaire, Guillaume, *Alcools*

Voyageur sans bagage, Le. See Anouilh, Jean, *Traveler Without Luggage*

Voyageurs de l'impériale, Les. See Aragon, Louis

"Voyelles." *See* Rimbaud, Arthur

Voyeur, The. See Moravia, Alberto

Voyeur, The (Le voyeur). See Robbe-Grillet, Alain

"Voyou Paul, brave Virginie." *See* Céline, Louis-Ferdinand

Voysey Inheritance, The. See Granville-Barker, Harley

"Vozdushnye puti." *See* Pasternak, Boris, *Rasskazy (Stories)*

Vozmezdie. See Blok, Alexander, *Retribution*

Voznesensky, Andrey, Khlebnikov's influence on, 10:1332a-b

Vozvrashchenie na rodinu. See Bely, Andrey

Vozvrat. See Bely, Andrey, *Symphonies*

"Vozzvanie predsedatelei zemnogo shara." *See* Khlebnikov, Velimir

"Vradhinos ponokefalos." *See* Ritsos, Yannis

"Vragi." *See* Chekhov, Anton

Vragi. See Gorky, Maxim

"Vremia Korolenko." *See* Gorky, Maxim

Vremia mera mira. See Khlebnikov, Velimir

Vrettakos, Nikephoros, Seferis and, 12:2255a-b

Vserossiiskii soiuz pisatelei (All-Russian Union of Writers)

   expulsion of Pasternak from, 10:1597a
   Stalinist persecution of, 10:1198b–1199a
   Zamyatin's involvement with, 10:1193a

VSP. *See* Vserossiiskii soiuz pisatelei

"Vstrecha." *See* Zamyatin, Yevgeny Ivanovich

Vtoraia kniga. See Mandelshtam, Osip

Vtoroe rozhdenie. See Pasternak, Boris, *Second Birth*

Vučjak. See Krleža, Miroslav

Vuillard, Édouard, and Jarry, 9:665a

Vulgarity, Gogol and, 6:976a, 980b, 991b

Vulgate cycle, works in, 1:150b

"Vykhozhu odin ia na dorogu." *See* Lermontov, Mikhail

"Výprava zloděje Šejby." *See* Hašek, Jaroslav

Vyskočil, Quido Maria, Hašek's satire of, 9:1104b

Vysokaia bolezn'. See Pasternak, Boris, *The Sublime Malady*

Vysotskaia, Ida, Pasternak's love for, 10:1593a

W

W małym dworku. See Witkiewicz, Stanisław
  Ignacy

Wace
  Roman de Brut, Chrétien's *Cligés* and,
    1:192b
  Roman de Rou, Chanson de Roland
    mentioned in, 1:103a
  on Saint Nicholas' "miracles," 1:462a

Wackenroder, Wilhelm, Schlegel and, 5:182a

Wager, in Pascal's *Pensées*, 3:141a–143b

"Wager of Prometheus, The." *See* Leopardi,
  Giacomo

Wagner, Richard, **6:1147a–1167b**
  "An End in Paris," 6:1151b
  Andersen and, 6:871a
  on art, 7:1651a-b
  *Art and Revolution (Die Kunst und die
    Revolution)*, 6:1153b
  *Artwork of the Future (Das Kunstwerk der
    Zukunft)*, 6:1153b, 1154b, 7:1651a
  Baudelaire and, 7:1343a
  Beethoven, 6:1161b–1162a
  in Bely's *Na rubezhe dvukh stoletii*, 9:911b
  "Bericht an Seine Majestät der König
    Ludwig II von Bayern Über eine in
    München zu erichtende deutsche
    Musikschule" ("Report to His Majesty
    Ludwig II, King of Bavaria, Concerning
    a German Music School to Be Erected in
    Munich"), 6:1158a
  Berlioz and, 6:805b–807a
  Brahms and, 7:1665a-b
  D'Annunzio and, 8:184b, 186b
  Das Liebesverbot (The Ban on Love),
    6:1150b, 1155a
  *Das Wiener Hof-Operntheater (The Vienna
    Opera House)*, 6:1158a-b
  Der Ring des Nibelungen, 6:1155a–1156b,
    1158a, 1158b, 7:1651b, 1652a
    Götterdämmerung, Céline's *Nord* and,
      11:1882a
    Mandelshtam's poem on, 10:1635b–1636a
    Siegfried, 6:1155b, 1156b, 1160b

  The Rhinegold, 6:1155b, 1156b, 1157a,
    1160a
  The Valkyrie, 6:1155b, 1156b, 1157a,
    1160a
  Völsunga saga and, 1:400b
  Die Feen (The Fairies), 6:1150b, 1155a
  Die Meistersinger von Nürnberg
    final act of, 6:1161b
    German Folk in, address to, 6:1159b
    orthodoxy of Wagner and, 6:1160b
    premiere of, 6:1160a
    success of, 6:1157b–1158a
  Eine Kapitulation (*A Capitulation*), 6:1163a
  Eine Mitteilung an meine Freunde (*A
    Communication to My Friends*), 6:1156a
  "German Art and German Politics,"
    6:1159b–1160a
  Gesamtkunstwerk, 7:1651a-b
  Ginzburg and, 13:3133a, 3151a
  in Heinrich Mann's writings
    Man of Straw, 8:532b
    The Living Thoughts of Nietzsche, 8:540b
  Herder and, 7:1651b
  Jewry in Music (*Das Judentum in der
    Musik*), 6:1153b–1154a
  Leubald, 6:1149a-b
  Lohengrin, 6:1152b, 1155a
  Mallarmé's homage to, 7:1573b, 1576a
  Mann and
    Death in Venice, 9:725a
    Doctor Faustus, 9:733b
  Mann on, 8:520b, 9:737b
  Mendelssohn and, 7:1651a
  in Musil's *The Man Without Qualities*,
    9:938a
  My Life, 6:1165a-b
    youthful enthusiasm, remembrance of,
      6:1150b
  "Nibelungen-Mythus als Entwurf zu einem
    Drama, Der" ("The Nibelungen Myth as
    Scheme for a Drama"), 6:1153a
  Nibelungenlied and, 7:1651a, 1651b
  Nietzsche and
    at Tribschen, 7:1652a–1653a
    Bayreuth project, 7:1659a
    differences between, 7:1655b–1656a,
      1657b

664

influence on, 7:1649b
last meeting of, 7:1665b
meeting of, 7:1651a, 1652a
relationship between, 7:1653a-b
"On German Music," 6:1151b–1152a
On the State of Religion (Über Staat und Religion), 6:1158b, 1161b
Opera and Drama (Oper und Drama), 6:1154a-b, 1155a, 7:1651a
language of national drama in, 6:1155a
and music flowing from verse, theory of, 6:1154b, 1161a-b
and solution to text difficulties, 6:1155b
The Destiny of Opera and, 6:1162a
Tristan and Isolde and, 6:1160a-b
operas of, 7:1651a, 1651b–1652a
Parsifal, 6:1164a–1165a, 7:1665b
basis for, 6:1164b
as final opera, 6:1163b
Marinetti and, 9:801b, 812a
"Pilgrimage to Beethoven," 6:1151b
Rienzi, 6:1151a, 1152a, 1152b, 1155a
Schopenhauer and, 5:397a, 415a, 7:1651b–1652a
Tannhäuser, 6:1152b, 1155a
Heine's influence on, 5:505a-b
Parisian premiere of, 7:1656a
The Flying Dutchman (Der Fliegende Holländer), 6:1152a-b, 1155a
Heine's influence on, 5:501a
The Huguenots, 6:1151b, 1152b
The Wibelungs, 6:1153a
Tristan und Isolde (Tristan and Isolde), 7:1651b–1652a
completion of, 6:1156b–1157b
premiere of, 6:1159a
Schopenhauer's influence on, 5:415b
Valéry's *The Young Fate* and, 8:577a
verse drama, 7:1426b
"Zukunftsmusik" ("Music of the Future"), 6:1161a
see also Wagnerism
Wagnerism, 6:1147a-b
Anti-Semitism of, 6:1152a
downfall of, 6:1148b
Hanslick and, 6:1148b
ideas behind, 6:1159a

intellect and, 6:1166a
mythology of, 6:1166b
official journal of, 6:1163b, 1164a, 1166b
societies of, 6:1148a, 1163b
Wolf and, 6:1148a
works at heart of, 6:1153b
Wahl, Jean, Butor and, 13:3288a
Wahlverwandtschaften, Die. See Goethe, Johann Wolfgang von, *Elective Affinities*
Waiblingen. *See* Guelfs and Ghibellines
Waiblinger, Wilhelm
Friedrich Hölderlins Leben, Dichtung und Wahnsinn, 5:172b–173a
Hölderlin and, 5:172b
"Waif Woman." *See* Stevenson, Robert Louis
"Waiter, a Beer!" *See* Maupassant, Guy de, "Garçon, un bock!"
"Waiting for the Barbarians." *See* Cavafy, Constantine, "Perimenontas tous varvarous"
Waiting for God. See Weil, Simone
Waiting for Godot. See Beckett, Samuel
"Wakefield Master," 1:469a
"Walc." *See* Milosz, Czeslaw
Waldeinsamkeit. See Tieck, Ludwig
Walk, The. See Schiller, Friedrich von
Walk to the Pond, The. *See* Schnitzler, Arthur, *Der Gand zum Weiher*
Walking on the Hesitant Light of Day. *See* Cela, Camilo José, *Pisando la dudosa luz del dia*
Wall in the Mirror, The. See Ritsos, Yannis, *O tihos mesa ston kathrefti*
Wallace, Henry A., Jiménez and, 9:992b
Wallenrod. See Mickiewicz, Adam, *Konrad Wallenrod*
Wallenstein. See Schiller, Friedrich von
Wallenstein's Camp. See Schiller, Friedrich von, *Wallenstein*
Wallenstein's Death. See Schiller, Friedrich von, *Wallenstein*
"Waller im Schnee." *See* George, Stefan, *Das Jahr der Seele*
Wallonie, La (literary review), 8:121a-b, 124a
Walls Taken in the New World. *See* Kosztolányi, Dezső, *Túlvilági séták*

Walnut Trees of Altenburg, The. See Malraux,
    André
Walpole, Horace
  on Beaumarchais, 4:569b
  Schopenhauer and, 5:412b
Walser, Martin, *wirklich* and *realistisch*,
    13:3172b
Walt and Vult. See Richter, Jean Paul,
    Flegeljahre
Walter of Châtillon
  "Propter Sion non tacebo" ("On account of
    Zion I will not keep silent"), 1:352a,
    367b–368b
  satires of, 1:339a
  "Tanto viro locuturi" ("Before such a
    renowned man"), 1:352b
  "Versa est in luctum" ("It has turned into
    mourning"), 1:367b
Waltharius legend, Anglo-Saxon poetic
    fragments, 1:66a
Walther von der Vogelweide, **1:287a–308b**
  "Ahî wie kristenlîche nû der bâbest lachet"
    (Ho, ho, in how Christian a manner the
    Pope is now laughing), 1:302a
  "Allerêrst lebe ich mir werde" (For the first
    time I live worthily), 1:303b
  "Dêswar Reimar, dû rinwest mich," 1:307b
  "Frô Welt" ("Dame World"), 1:298a-b
  "Frouwe Mâze" ("Lady Moderation"), 1:296a
  "Got, dîner trinitâte," 1:302b–303a
  "Herzeliebez frowelîn," 1:296a–297a
  "Ich hân mî lehen al die werlt, ich hâ mîn
    lêhen," 1:300b
  "Ich horte ein wazzer diezen," 1:291b
  "Ich innoz verdienen swachen haz,"
    1:304a-b
  "Ich sach mit mînen ongen," 1:291b
  "Ich saz ûf eime steine," 1:291a
  "Ir sult sprechen willekomen," 1:293a
  "Man hât hêr Gêrhart Atze ein pfert,"
    1:299b–300a
  "Man seite mir ie von Tegersê," 1:299b
  "Owe, hovelichez singen" ("Alas, courtly
    singing"), 1:367a
  "Owê war sint verswunden, alliu miniu jâr?"
    ("Alas, where have all my years
    vanished?"), 1:174a, 297a–298a

  Reichssprüche, 1:289a, 291a-b
  "Sager mir ieman waz ist minne?," 1:292b
  "Sagt an, her Stoc" (Explain, Mr. Offering
    Box), 1:344b
  satire of, 1:356a
  "Selpwahsen kint, dû bist zu krump,"
    1:300b
  "Under der linden an der heide,"
    1:294a–295b
  Unmutston (Bad-Humor Poem), 1:344a-b,
    365b
  "Vil wol gelopter got," 1:304a
  "Wîp muoz iemer sîn der wîbe hohste
    name," 1:292b
Waltz, The. *See* Milosz, Czeslaw
Waltz of the Toreadors, The. See Anouilh, Jean
Wanderer, The. See Hamsun, Knut
"Wanderer." *See* Ungaretti, Giuseppe,
    "Girovage"
Wanderer and His Shadow, The. See
    Nietzsche, Friedrich, *Der Wanderer und
    sein Schatten*
Wanderer kommst du nach Spa . . . . See Böll,
    Heinrich
"Wanderer of Prague, The." *See* Apollinaire,
    Guillaume, *Le flâneur des deux rives*
    (*The Left- and Right-Bank Stroller*), "Le
    passant de Prague"
Wanderer, The. See Alain-Fournier, *Le Grand
    Meaulnes*
Wanderer und sein Schatten, Der. See
    Nietzsche, Friedrich
Wandering Jew. *See* Ahasuerus (the
    Wandering Jew)
Wandering Lady, The. *See* Baroja, Pío, *La
    dama errante*
"Wanderung, Die." *See* Hölderlin, Friedrich
Wanderungen durch die Mark Brandenburg.
    See Fontane, Theodor
War
  Apollinaire and, 9:897a–898b
  Ariosto on, 2:633a-b, 638b–639a
  Aymé's satire of, 12:2449a
  Christian
    in Prudentius' *Hamartigenia*, 1:8b–9a
    in Prudentius' *Psychomachia*, 1:6a
    in Prudentius' works, 1:15b–16a

in Dante's *De vulgari eloquentia*, 1:441b
in Fénelon's view, 3:282a, 282b
fiction dealing with, 13:3036a-b
in "Futurist Manifesto," 9:810a-b
Giraudoux and, 9:1043a-b
in La Bruyère's *Caractères*, 3:248a
Marinetti and, 9:798b, 823a, 825a, 827b
   in "Zang Tumb Tumb," 9:819b–820a
in Ungaretti's poetry, 10:1456b–1458a,
   1463b, 1465a
Wolfram on, 1:284a–285b
War of the Brothers (Portugal: 1826–1834),
   11:2145a-b
War correspondent, Fontane as,
   6:1307a–1308b
War Diaries, The. See Sartre, Jean-Paul
"War Months, The." *See* Pasternak, Boris,
   Early Trains
"War in a Mousetrap." *See* Khlebnikov,
   Velimir
War with the Newts, The. See Čapek, Karel,
   Válka s mloky
War and Peace. See Tolstoy, Leo
War of the Spanish Succession, in Scribe's
   The Glass of Water, 7:1914b
War, The. See Machado, Antonio, *La guerra*;
   Ungaretti, Giuseppe, "La guerre"
War and the World. See Mayakovsky,
   Vladimir, *Voina i mir*
War of the Worlds. See Wells, H. G.
"Ward No. 6." *See* Chekhov, Anton, "Palata
   No. 6"
Ward, The. See Goldoni, Carlo, *La pupilla*
Wariat i zakonnica. See Witkiewicz, Stanisław
   Ignacy
Warner, Rex, 12:2255b, 2261a
"Warning to the People of France About Their
   True Enemies, A." *See* Chénier, André
Wartenegg, Wilhelm von, conversation with
   Grillparzer, 5:426a
"Was ist orthodoxer Marxismus?" *See* Lukács,
   György
Was soll aus dem Jungen bloss werden? See
   Böll, Heinrich
Washing Song, The. *See* Pascoli, Giovanni,
   Primi poemetti (First Short Narrative
   Poems), "La canzone del bucato"

Washington, George, 5:98b
Wasserman, Jakob, Schnitzler and, 8:114a
Waste Land, The. See Eliot, T. S.
"Wasted Evening, A." *See* Musset, Alfred de,
   "Une soirée perdue"
"Watch, The." *See* Zamyatin, Yevgeny
   Ivanovich, "Chasy"
Watcher, The. See Calvino, Italo
Watchmaker of Everton, The. See Simenon,
   Georges, *L'Horloger d'Everton*
"Watchman, The." *See* Gorky, Maxim,
   "Storozh"
Water Hen, The. See Witkiewicz, Stanisław
   Ignacy, *Kurka wodna*
Water Lilies. *See* Jiménez, Juan Ramón,
   Ninfeas
"Water and the Spirit." *See* Claudel, Paul,
   Cinq grandes odes (*Five Great Odes*),
   "L'Esprit et l'eau"
Water symbolism
   in Hesse's prose, 9:843a, 844b
   Leonardo and, 8:573a
   in Musil's *The Man Without Qualities*,
      9:947b–948b, 949b–950a, 950b–951b
Waterloo, Battle of, in Chateaubriand's
   autobiography, 5:136b
Waters and Lands. See Quasimodo, Salvatore
Watson, Thomas, Petrarchan influence, 2:504b
Watteau, Jean Antoine
   commedia dell'arte and, 7:1628a-b
   Delacroix and, 5:531b
   in Goncourts' *L'Art du dix-huitième siècle*,
      7:1397a
   L'embarquement pour l'île de Cythère (*The
      Embarkation for Cythera*), 7:1628b
     Delacroix and, 5:523b
     Gautier on, 6:1042a
     Nerval and, 6:963b
     Verlaine and, 7:1627b–1630b
Waugh, Evelyn, Böll and, 13:3167a
"Waves." *See* Pasternak, Boris, *Second Birth*
Waves, The. See Woolf, Virginia
Wax Museum, The. *See* Aragon, Louis, *Le
   museé Grévin*
"Way It Used to Be Done in Odessa, The." *See*
   Babel, Isaac, *Odessa Tales*

Way, The. *See* Solzhenitsyn, Aleksandr, "Dorozhenka"

Way to Perfection. *See* Baroja, Pío, *Camino de perfección*

Way of the World, The. *See* Baroja, Pío, *El mundo es ansi*

Wayfarers. See Hamsun, Knut, *Landstrykere*

Wayside Crosses. See Čapek, Karel, *Boží muka*

We. See Zamyatin, Yevgeny Ivanovich

We Always Treat Women Too Well. See Queneau, Raymond, *On est toujours trop bon avec les femmes*

"We are not long given to admire." *See* Blok, Alexander, "I nam ne dolgo liubovat'sia"

We Are Not Neutral! *See* Moberg, Vilhelm, "*Vi är inte neutrala!*"

We Fought Our Fight. *See* Ady, Endre, "A harcunkat megharcoltuk"

We Need Mohács. *See* Ady, Endre, "Nekünk Mohács kell"

"We Will Still Put Up a Fight." *See* Turgenev, Ivan

Wealth
    in La Bruyère's *Caractères*, 3:240b–242b
    Machiavelli's view of, 2:610a-b
    in Walther, 1:304a-b

Wealth of Russia. *See Russkoe bogatstvo*

"Weary Hour, The." *See* Mann, Thomas

"Weaver, The." *See* Pascoli, Giovanni, "Il ritorno a San Mauro," "La tessitrice"

Weavers, The. See Hauptmann, Gerhart, *Die Weber*

Weber, Carl Maria von, *Oberon*, Wieland's influence on, 4:605b

Weber, Die. See Hauptmann, Gerhart

Weber, Ernst von, Wagner and, 6:1164b

Weber, Max, Lukács and, 10:1258b–1259a

Webster, John, *The White Devil*, Tieck and, 5:255b

Wechsel (exchange), Walther and, 1:294a

Weckherlin, Georg Rudolph, Petrarchan influence, 2:504b

Wedding. See Canetti, Elias

"Wedding Preparations in the Country." *See* Kafka, Franz, "Hochzeitsvorbereitungen auf dem Lande"

Wedekind, Frank, **8:229a–281b**
    Abhandlung Eden (A Treatise on Eden), 8:241b
    acting career, 8:258a, 259b–260a
        Die Elf Scharfrichter, 8:260a-b
    anti-bourgeois sentiment, 8:240b, 243b, 250a
        change in, 8:277b–278a
    Bethel, 8:245b–246b
        Stupid Augustus, 8:245b
    Bismarck, 8:278b–279a
    Brecht and, 11:2101
    Castle Wetterstein: Drama in Three Acts (*Schloss Wetterstein: Drama in Drei Akten*), 8:271a–274a
        Lustmord, 8:273b
        Part 1: *In allen Sätteln gerecht* (Ready for Anything), 8:271b–272a
        Part 2: *Mit allen Hunden gehetzt* (Beset Upon on All Sides), 8:272a-b
        Part 3: *Mitt allen Wassern gewaschen* (Too Clever by Half), 8:272b–273b
        theme, 8:273b
    De scriptore (Concerning the Writer), 8:231a-b
    Death and the Devil (*Tod und teufel*), 8:264b–266a
    Der Kammersänger (The Tenor), 8:258a
    Der Liebestrank (The Love Potion), 8:241b, 242b–250b
        attack on family life, 8:249a
        attack on German education, 8:247a-b
        juxtaposition of dramatic figures, 8:248a-b
    Der Mückenprinz (The Prince of Gnats), 8:244a
    Der Schnellmaler, oder Kunst und Mammon (The Sketch Artist; or, Art and Mammon), 8:232a-b
    Der Stein der Weisen, oder Laute, Armbrust, und Peitsche (The Philosopher's Stone; or, Lute, Crossbow, and Whip), 8:274a–276a
        theme, 8:274b–275a
    Der Witz und seine Sippe (Wit and Its Kindred), 8:234a-b

Die Flöhe, oder der Schmerzenstanz (The Fleas; or, The Dance of Pain), 8:242b–243b

Die junge Welt (The New Generation), 8:236a-b, 237a

Die Kaiserin von Neufundland (The Empress of Newfoundland), 8:244a–245b

  stage production, 8:260b

Die Zensur: Eine Theodizee in einem Akt (Censorship: a Theodicy in One Act), 8:268b–269b

dramatic technique, 8:239b, 259a-b, 278b

  theme and variation, 8:253a, 256a-b

Earth Spirit (*Erdgeist*), 8:252b–255a

  Gewaltmensch image, 8:253b–254a

  Lulu's self-awareness, 8:255b

  Schigolch, 8:254b–255a

  theme and variation technique, 8:253a

  Wedekind's acting role, 8:258a

elasticity principle, 8:234a-b, 241a, 248a

Elins Erweckung (Elin's Awakening), 8:233a–234a

  Schigolch, 8:254b

Felix und Galathea, 8:231b

Franziska: Ein Modernes Mysterium in fünf Akten (Franziska: A Modern Mystery Play in Five Acts), 8:276a–278a

Fürstin Russalka (*Princess Russalka*), 8:242a-b, 257b

Hauptmann and, 8:150a-b

Herakles, 8:278b–279a

on Ibsen's *The Master Builder*, 7:1440b

image of women, 8:249a–250a, 251b–252a, 267a

Karl Hetmann, der Zwergriese (Karl Hetmann, the Pygmy-Giant), 8:262b–264b

  soliloquy, 8:264a

König Nicolo, oder So ist das Leben (*King Nicolo; or, Such Is Life*), 8:260b–262b

  theme, 8:261b–262a

life-art relationship, 8:250b, 257a, 278a

Lulu plays, 8:252b–257a

  Lulu's identity, 8:252b–253a, 255a-b, 256a

  Lulu's names, 8:254a-b

  Lustmord, 8:256b

  portrait of Lulu, 8:256b–257a

Mine-Haha, oder über die körperliche Erziehung der jungen Mädchen (Mine-HaHa; or, On the Physical Education of Young Girls), 8:241b–242a

  revision, 8:258a

Musik: Ein Sittengemälde (Music: A Moral Portrait), 8:266a–267a, 268a-b

Oaha, 8:269b–271a

Pandora's Box (*Die Büchse der Pandora*), 8:240a, 241b, 252a, 255a–257a

pantomimes, 8:242b–246b

Schauspielkunst: Ein Glossarium (A Commentary on the Art of Acting), 8:259b–260b

Simson, oder Scham und Eifersuch (Samson; or, Shame and Jealousy), 8:278a–279a

Spring's Awakening, 8:237a–240a, 248b

  attack on German education, 8:238a-b, 247a-b

  image of women, 8:249a-b

  indictment of family life in, 8:237b–238a

  language and humanity, 8:238b

  Masked Gentleman, 8:237b, 239a-b

  parody of in *Franziska*, 8:276b

  Stupid Augustus, 8:264a

  theme of puberty, 8:237a-b

Strindberg and, 7:1737b

The Marquis of Keith (*Der Marquis von Keith*), 8:258b–259b

  language and structure, 8:259a-b

The Solar Spectrum (*Das Sonnenspektrum*), 8:241b, 250a–252a

  theme, 8:257a

Zirkusgedanken (Circus Thoughts), 8:234a-b, 241a

Weeds. *See* Baroja, Pío

Week of the Creation of the World, The. *See* Du Bartas, *La Sepmaine où création du monde*

Week's Diary, A. *See* Ritsos, Yannis, *Ghignesthe*

Weg ins Freie, Der. *See* Schnitzler, Arthur, *The Road to the Open*

"Wegwerfer, Der." *See* Böll, Heinrich, "The Thrower-Away"

Weh dem, der lügt! See Grillparzer, Franz,
  Thou Shalt Not Lie
Weidig, Ludwig, Büchner and, 6:1173b–1174b
Weigand, Hermann J., 5:48a
  on Mann brothers, 8:536b
Weight, Kundera and, 13:3407a–3409a
"Weight." *See* Ungaretti, Giuseppe, "Peso"
"Weihe." *See* George, Stefan, *Hymnen* (*Odes*)
Weil, Simone, **12:2787a–2812b**
  Beauvoir and, 12:2789a
  First and Last Notebooks, 12:2799a
  Gravity and Grace (*La pesanteur et la
      grâce*), 12:2787b, 2803a
  Historical and Political Writings (*Écrits
      historiques et politiques*), 12:2799b
  *Intimations of Christianity Among the
      Ancient Greeks*, 12:2796a, 2799a, 2803a
  Intuitions préchrétiennes, 12:2799a
  La connaissance surnaturelle, 12:2799a
  Oppression and Liberty (*Oppression et
      liberté*), 12:2792a
  Selected Essays, 12:2796b, 2799b
  Silone and, 12:2301b
  The Greek Source (*La source grecque*),
      12:2799a
  The "Iliad," or, The Poem of Force
      (*"L'Iliade"; ou Le poème de la force*),
      12:2794a, 2807b–2808a
  The Need for Roots (*L'Enracinement*),
      12:2787b, 2796b, 2798b, 2800b, 2807b,
      2810b
  Venice Preserved (*Venise sauvée*), 12:2794a
  Waiting for God (*Attente de Dieu*), 12:2788a,
      2796a, 2810a, 2811b
  Writings from London and Last Letters
      (*Écrits de Londres et dernières lettres*),
      12:2796b
Weimar Republic
  Heinrich Mann and, 8:535a
  Thomas Mann and, 8:535b
  see also Germany
Weinberg, Bernard, *French Realism: The
      Critical Reaction 1830–1870*, 7:1403a-b
Weiner Hof-Operntheater, Das. See Wagner,
      Richard
"Weingott, Dem." *See* Hölderlin, Friedrich,
      "Brot und Wein"

Weinstein, Leo, on Taine, 7:1449b
*Weise von Liebe und Tod des Cornets
      Christoph Rilke, Die. See* Rilke, Rainer
      Maria
Weisse Fächer, Der. See Hofmannsthal, Hugo
      von, *The White Fan*
weisst du schwarzt du. See Arp, Jean
Weite Land, Das. See Schnitzler, Arthur
"Weitere Bemerkungen über die
      Abwehrneuropsychosen." *See* Freud,
      Sigmund
Welf. *See* Guelfs and Ghibellines
We'll to the Woods No More. See Dujardin,
      Édouard, *Les lauriers sont coupés*
Well-made play, **7:1909a–1934b**
  Ghelderode's *Sortie de l'acteur* as, 11:2119a
  Ionesco's *The Bald Soprano* as, 13:2992a
Well-meaning Grouch, The. *See* Goldoni,
      Carlo, *Le bourru bienfaisant*
Wellek, René, Schlegel and, 5:177a
Wells, H. G.
  Čapek and, 10:1572a, 1574a
  Food of the Gods, Čapek and, 10:1576b
  Hamsun and, 8:21a, 36b
  Marinetti and, 9:826a
  Olesha's *Envy* and, 11:2238a
  War of the Worlds, Khlebnikov's *Truba
      marsian* and, 10:1338b
Wellsprings, The. *See* Vesaas, Tarjei, *Kjeldene*
Welsh legends
  Arthurian legend and, 1:137a–138a
  bards and, 1:141a
  Chrétien de Troyes and, 1:143b
  French romance and, 1:143b
  magic and sorcery in, 1:142b
  supernatural in, 1:142b–143a
  violence in, 1:143a
  women in, 1:143a-b
Welt als Wille und Vorstellung, Die. See
      Schopenhauer, Arthur, *The World as
      Will and Representation*
"Welt und Ich." *See* Hebbel, Friedrich
Weltgeschichtliche Betrachtungen, Die. See
      Burckhardt, Jacob, *Reflections on
      History*
Weltinnenraum, in Rilke's poetry, 9:782a

Weltliteratur (world literature), Sainte-Beuve and, 6:855b

Weltrevolution (World Revolution) (German periodical), Hašek's articles in, 9:1095a

Weltsch, Felix, 9:1152b

Weltschmerz poets, 5:419b–420b
unheroic characters of, 5:434a-b
see also Melancholy, poetic

"Wendung." *See* Rilke, Rainer Maria

Wenger, Ruth, Hesse and, 9:845b

"Wenn ich ihn nur habe." *See* Novalis, *Sacred Songs*

We're Alive! See Toller, Ernst

"We're in the Center of Town." *See* Olesha, Yuri, "My v tsentre goroda"

Werfel, Alma Mahler, Heinrich Mann and, 8:541a

Werfel, Franz
Heinrich Mann and, 8:541a
on Mann's *Buddenbrooks*, 9:716a

Werke, Grosse kommentierte Berliner und Frankfurter Ausgabe. See Brecht, Bertolt

Werner, Heinz, on metaphor, 9:1136b–1137a

Werner, Zacharias, 5:93a
Grillparzer and, 5:425a-b
Hoffmann and, 5:265a

Werther. See Goethe, Johann Wolfgang von, *Die Leiden des jungen Werthers*

West-östlicher Divan (*West-Eastern Divan*). *See* Goethe, Johann Wolfgang von

Westhoff, Clara, 9:770a

"Wet-Nurse, The." *See* Pirandello, Luigi, "La balia"

"What Do You Want?" *See* Apollinaire, Guillaume, *L'Hérésiarque et cie* (*The Heresiarch and Co.*), "Que vlo-ve?"

"What Does It Matter?" *See* Rimbaud, Arthur, "Qu'est-ce pour nous?"

What I Believe. See Mauriac, François, *Ce que je crois*

What I Dream and What Happens to Me. *See* Andrić, Ivo, *Šta sanjam i šta mi se dogadja*

"What Is an Author?" *See* Foucault, Michel

What Is Art? See Tolstoy, Leo

"What Is a Classic?" *See* Sainte-Beuve, Charles-Augustin, "Qu'est-ce qu'un classique?"

"What Is Criticism?" *See* Barthes, Roland

What Is Literature? See Sartre, Jean-Paul

What Is Living and What Is Dead of the Philosophy of Hegel. See Croce, Benedetto, *Ciò che è vivo e ciò che è morto nella filosofia di Hegel*

What Is Man? See Twain, Mark

"What Is Orthodox Marxism?" *See* Lukács, György, "Was ist orthodoxer Marxismus?"

"What Is Said to the Poet Concerning Flowers." *See* Rimbaud, Arthur, "Ce qu'on dit au poète à propos des fleurs"

What Is Surrealism? See Breton, André, *Qu'est ce que le surréalisme?*

What Is to Be Done? See Chernyshevski, Nikolay, *Chto delat'?*

What Maisie Knew. See James, Henry

"What the Mouth of Darkness Says." *See* Hugo, Victor, "Ce que dit la bouche d'ombre"

What Reading Is. *See* Ortega y Gasset, José, "Qué es leer"

What Strange Things. *See* Ritsos, Yannis, *Ti paraxena pramata*

What Will Become of the Czechoslovak Bourgeois Republic? *See* Hašek, Jaroslav, "Chto budet c chekhoslovatskoy burzhuaznoy respublikoy"

What Women Are Like. *See* Hašek, Jaroslav, "Jak vypadají ženy"

What Young Girls Dream About. See Musset, Alfred de, *À quoi rêvent les jeunes filles*

What? Eternity. *See* Yourcenar, Marguerite, *Quoi? L'Éternité*

What's to Become of the Boy? See Böll, Heinrich, *Was soll aus dem Jungen bloss werden?*

Wheel of Idle Moments, The. *See* Cela, Camilo José, *La rueda de los ocios*

When Dead, We Meet. *See* Ady, Endre, "Ha holtan találkozunk"

"When I see the weather grow cold." *See* Colin Muset, "Qant je voi lou tans refroidier"

When I Was Crazy. See Pirandello, Luigi, *Quand'ero matto*

When I Was Old. See Simenon, Georges, *Quand j'étais vieux*

"When my gentle, faithful comforter." *See* Petrarch, *Canzoniere*, "Quando il soave mio fido conforto"

When My Head I Rest. *See* Ady, Endre, "Ha fejem lehajtom"

When the Skies Clear. See Pasternak, Boris

When Someone Is Somebody. See Pirandello, Luigi, *Quando si è qualcuno*

"When They Are Roused." *See* Cavafy, Constantine, "Otan diegeirontai"

"When They Slip Out." *See* Ekelöf, Gunnar

When Things of the Spirit Come First. See Beauvoir, Simone de

When the War Was Over. See Frisch, Max

When We Dead Awaken. See Ibsen, Henrik

"When the woods." *See* Bernart de Ventadorn, "Can lo boschatges"

"Where are you, solace of the whole world." *See* Novalis, *Sacred Songs* (*Geistliche Lieder*), "Wo bleibst du Trost der ganzen Welt"

Which Tribe Do You Belong To? See Moravia, Alberto

"Whii werre and wrake in londe and manslauht is i-come" (Why war and vengeance and manslaughter have come into the land), 1:349a-b, 354a-b

While Skating. *See* Verlaine, Paul, "En patinant"

Whims of Marianne, The. See Musset, Alfred de

Whimsical Critic, A. *See* Pirandello, Luigi, "Un critico fantastico"

Whistle, The. *See Gudok*

Whistler, James Abbott McNeill, Japanese influence, 7:1398a

White and the Black, The. See Voltaire, *Le blanc et le noir*

White Charger, The. See Triolet, Elsa, *Le cheval blanc*

White Christ. *See* Gunnarsson, Gunnar, *Hvide-Krist*

White, E. B., *Essays*, on Montaigne, 2:788a

White Fan, The. See Hofmannsthal, Hugo von

White Goddess, The. See Graves, Robert

White, Hayden, on Strauss, 7:1659b

White Horse, The. See Triolet, Elsa, *Le cheval blanc*

White Notebook, The. See Gide, André

White Sea-Baltic Canal in the Name of Stalin, The. See Belomorsko-Baltyskii Kanal imeni Stalina

"White Water-Lily, The." *See* Mallarmé, Stéphane, "Le nénuphur blanc"

White Woman of the Fort, The. *See* Ady, Endre, "A vár fehér asszonya"

White-Collar Workers. *See* Kracauer, Siegfried, *Die Angestellten*

White-Haired Revolver, The. *See* Breton, André, *Le revolver à cheveux blancs*

Whitehead, Alfred North
  Bergson and, 8:64a
  Science and the Modern World, critique of Locke's ideas of natural rights and property rights, 4:651a-b

Whitelock, Dorothy, on the composition of *Beowulf*, 1:70a

Whites and the Blues, The. See Dumas père, Alexandre, *Les blancs et les bleus*

Whites (Florentine political faction). *See* Blacks and Whites (political factions)

Whitfield, J. H., on Leopardi, 5:561a, 565a

Whitman, Walt
  A Backward Glance O'er Travel'd Roads, on Herder's legacy, 4:655b
  Apollinaire and, 9:884b
  Ekelöf and, 12:2651a
  folk influences on, 4:656b
  Hamsun and, 8:24a, 26a
  Henri and, 4:658a
  Herder's influence on, 4:655b–657b
  Jiménez and, 9:1000a
  Laforgue and, 7:1897b–1898a, 1899a
  Maeterlinck and, 8:123b
  Marinetti and, 9:805b
  Mayakovsky and, 11:1841a
  Pessoa and, 10:1491a-b

poetic personalities of, 10:1487b, 1491b

"Song of Myself," 7:1898a

"There Was a Child Went Forth," 13:2962b

"Who is this lady who comes, and every man looks at her?" See Cavalcanti, Guido, "Chi è questa che vèn, ch'ogn'om la mira?"

"Whoever wishes to see." See Petrarch, Canzoniere, "Chi vuol veder quantunque po Natura"

Wholeness, personal, Montaigne on, 2:781b

Why Do I Write? See Ionesco, Eugène, "Pourquoi est-ce que j'écris"

Why Have I Done It? See Ady, Endre, "Miért is tettem?"

Why I Became a Symbolist. See Bely, Andrey, Pochemu ia stal simvolistom

"Why the lament, poet?" See Hugh Primas, "Quid luges, lirice?"

Why war and vengeance and manslaughter have come into the land. See "Whii werre and wrake in londe and manslauht is i-come"

Wibelungs, The. See Wagner, Richard

Wicked Cooks, The. See Grass, Günter

Wickram, Jörg, Rollwagenbüchlein (Coach-Traveler's Companion), 2:952b

Widening Gyre, The. See Frank, Joseph

"Widerstände gegen die Psychoanalyse, Die." See Freud, Sigmund

Widowed Pimp, The. See Cervantes, Miguel de, El rufián viudo

Widower Jarl. See Moberg, Vilhelm, Änkeman Jarl

Widower, The. See Schnitzler, Arthur, Der Witwer

Widows, in La Fontaine's Fables, 3:95a–99a

Widsith (Anglo-Saxon poem), 1:66a, 401a

Widzenia nad zatoką San Francisco. See Milosz, Czeslaw, Visions from San Francisco Bay

"Wie wenn am Feiertage." See Hölderlin, Friedrich

Wieland, Christoph Martin, **4:587a–614b**

Agathodämon, 4:589b, 607a, 608b–609a

Alceste, 4:611a

Araspes und Panthea, 4:592b

Aristipp und einige seiner Zeitgenossen (Aristipp and Some of His Contemporaries), 4:589b, 607a, 609a-b

Attisches Museum (Attic Museum), 4:610a

"Briefe an einen jungen Dichter" ("Advice to a Young Author"), 4:596a

Clementina von Porretta, 4:592b

Comische Erzählungen (Comic Tales), 4:588b, 591b

Cyrus, 4:592b

Danischmend, 4:589b, 602a, 602b

Das Hexameron von Rosenhain, 4:607b

Der goldene Spiegel (The Golden Mirror), 4:589a, 599a–601a, 602b

    reviewed by Merck, 4:590b

Der neue Amadis (The New Amadis), 4:588b

"Der Schatten des Esels" ("The Ass's Shadow"), 4:603a-b

Der Teutsche Merkur (The German Mercury), 4:589b, 601a–602b, 610a-b

Die Abenteuer des Don Sylvio von Rosalva (The Adventures of Don Sylvio of Rosalva), 4:588b, 592b–594b

Die geheime Geschichte des Philosophen Peregrinus Proteus (The Real History of the Philosopher Peregrinus Proteus), 4:589b, 602a, 607a–608b

Die Geschichte der Abderiten (The History of the Abderites), 4:589b, 602a, 602b–605a

Die Geschichte des Agathon (The History of Agathon), 4:588b, 592b–593a, 594a–597b, 609b

Die Natur der Dinge (The Nature of Things), 4:588a, 591a, 591b

Dschinnistan, 4:607b

Empfindungen eines Christen (Perceptions of a Christian), 4:590b

Gandalin, 4:605b

"Gedanken über die Ideale der Alten" ("Reflections on the Ideals of the Ancients"), 4: 596a

Idris und Zenide, 4:587b, 588b, 602a

Lady Johanna Gray, 4:592b

    Lessing on, 4:545a

Wieland, Christoph Martin (*cont.*)
  Musarion, oder die Philosophie der Grazien (*Musarion; or, The Philosophy of the Graces*), 4:597b–599a
  Oberon, 4:589b, 602a, 605a–607b, 609b
    George and, 8:457a
  "On the Idea of History in *Agathon*," 4:595b
  on Richter's *Hesperus*, 5:66b
  Schach Lolo, 4:604b
  Sokrates Mainomenos, oder die Dialogen des Diogenes von Sinope (*Socrates Gone Mad; or, Diogenes of Sinope's Discourses*), 4:589a
  Sympathien, 4:590b
  The Dialogues of Diogenes of Sinope, 4:604a
Wieland; or, The Transformation. *See* Brown, Charles Brockden
Wiener, Norbert, *Cybernetics; or, Control and Communication in the Animal and the Machine*, 13:2909a
Wife of the God. *See* Moberg, Vilhelm, *Gudens hustru*
Wife of the Marshall d'Ancre, The. *See* Vigny, Alfred Victor de, *La maréchale d'Ancre*
"Wife, The." *See* Chekhov, Anton, "Zhena"
Wife, The. *See* Moberg, Vilhelm, *Hustrun*
Wife-murder plays, of Calderón, 2:884a–887b
Wig, The. *See* Ginzburg, Natalia, *La parrucca*
Wigalois. *See* Wirnt von Gravenberg
Wild Ass's Skin, The. *See* Balzac, Honoré de, *La peau de chagrin*
Wild Duck, The. *See* Ibsen, Henrik
Wild Orchid, The. *See* Undset, Sigrid, *Gymnadenia*
Wilde, Oscar, 8:135a
  Céline and, 11:1860a
  credo on art, 9:592b, 595b
  Gide and, 8:495b, 496a
  Jarry and, 9:666a
  Jiménez and, 9:993b
  Lady Windermere's Fan, Lorca and, 11:2191a
  literary art and, 11:1705a
  Machado and, 9:744b
  The Picture of Dorian Gray, 7:1716b
    and Wedekind's Lulu portrait, 8:257a

Wilder, Billy, *Sunset Boulevard*, Heinrich Mann and, 8:527b
Wilder, Thornton, Sarraute and, 12:2335a
Wilderness of Mirrors, A. *See* Frisch, Max
Wilhelm Dilthey and the Idea of Life. *See* Ortega y Gasset, José, *Guillermo Dilthey y la idea de la vida*
Wilhelm Meisters Lehr- und Wander-jahre. *See* Goethe, Johann Wolfgang von
Wilhelm Tell: A School Text (*Wilhelm Tell für die Schule*). *See* Frisch, Max
Wilkins, Eithne, 9:936b
Wilkinson, Elizabeth, 5:38b
Will
  in Corneille's plays, 3:31a
  French *classiques* and, 3:273b–274a
  general, in Rousseau, 4:457b–458a, 466b–467a
  Gombrowicz and, 12:2568a
  as philosophical concept, 9:591a-b, 595b–596a, 608a
    influence on Baroja, 9:593a
  Plato's view of, 5:400b
  Schopenhauer's view of, 5:399b–401a
    death and, 5:408b–409a
    denial of will and, 5:409b, 410a–412a, 413b
    music and, 5:412b, 413a, 413b
    Platonic Forms and, 5:411a-b
    sexual love and, 5:409b
    suicide and, 5:410a
  to power, Canetti and, 12:2626b–2627a
Will, free. *See* Free will
Will to Bondage, The. *See* La Boétie, Étienne de, *Discours de la servitude volontaire*
Will to Live, The. *See* Blasco Ibáñez, Vicente, *La voluntad de vivir*
Will to Power, The. *See* Nietzsche, Friedrich, *Der Wille zur Macht*
"Will Ulrike Meinhof Gnade oder freies Geleit?" *See* Böll, Heinrich
Wille zur Macht, Der. *See* Nietzsche, Friedrich
Willehalm. *See* Wolfram von Eschenbach
William IX of Aquitaine, duke
  "Ab la dolchor," 1:165a
  "Ben vuelh" ("I would like"), 1:163a-b

"Compaigno, no puosc mudar" ("Friends, I cannot change"), 1:163b–164a

"Companho faray un vers" ("I shall make a song"), 1:163b

"Companho" poems of, 1:163b–164a

"Companho, taint ai agutz d'avols contres," 1:163b

courtly love in works of, 1:165a–166a

courtly values and, 1:167b

"Farai un vers de dreyt nien," 1:164b

"Mout jauzens," 1:165a–166b

parody in works of, 1:163a

"Pus de chantar," 1:166b

"Pus vezem" ("Since we see"), 1:164a

satire in works of, 1:162b–163a

as troubadour, 1:162a–166b

William of Auvergne, 1:409a

William de la Mare, 1:423b, 426b

William of Malmesbury, *Chronicle of the Kings of England*, song of Roland mentioned in, 1:103a, 155a

William of Moerbeke, 1:408b, 415a, 417a

William of Ockham, Aquinas and, 1:427a-b

William Ratcliff. See Heine, Heinrich

William of Saint Amour

    Collationes Catholicae et canonicae scripturae (*Collations of Catholic and Canonical Scripture*), 1:417a-b

    De periculis novissimorum temporum (*On the Danger of Most Recent Times*), 1:414a

    Liber de Antichristo et eius ministris (*On Antichrist and His Ministers*), 1:413b

William of Saint Thierry, *De natura corporis et animae*, 1:170b

William Tell. See Schiller, Friedrich von

William of Tocco, 1:411b, 419a

Williams, Tennessee, Ibsen's influence on, 7:1444a

Willow Grove, The: An Eclogue of the Solitary Life. *See* Scève, Maurice, *La Saulsaye: Eglogue de la vie solitaire*

"Willow, The." *See* Akhmatova, Anna, "Iva"

Willows. See Sannazaro, Jacopo, *Salices*

Willy. See Gauthier-Villars, Henry

Wilmot, John, earl of Rochester, *Satyr Against Reason and Mankind*, 3:114b, 115a

Wilno Catastrophists. *See* Żagary

Wilno (Vilna), Milosz in, 13:2929b–2930a

Wilno (Vilna) University, 5:608a

Wilson, Edmund

    on Apollinaire, 9:886a

    on Chekhov, 7:1868a

    on Taine's *Les origines de la France contemporaine*, 7:1467a

Wilson, Robert, 13:3017a

Winckelmann, Johann

    Goethe and, 5:14b

    Goncharov and, 6:1064b

    History of the Art of Antiquity, and Lessing, 4:546a

    Schlegel, and, 5:179a-b

"Wind at Tindari." *See* Quasimodo, Salvatore

Wind from the Ukraine. *See* Tychyna, Pavlo, *Viter z Ukrainy*

Wind imagery, in Rilke's "Ein Frülingswind," 9:775a-b

Wind, Sand, and Stars. See Saint-Exupéry, Antoine de, *Terre des hommes*

Wind, The. See Simon, Claude, *Le vent*

"Wind, The (Four Fragments About Blok)." *See* Pasternak, Boris, "Veter (Chetyre otryvka o Bloke)"

Windelband, Wilhelm, Bergson and, 8:47b

Windmill cease to move your arms. *See* George, Stefan, *Pilgerfahrten* (*Pilgrimages*), "Mühle lass die arme still"

"Windows, The." *See* Apollinaire, Guillaume, *Calligrammes*, "Les fenêtres"

Winds. See Perse, Saint-John

Winds, The. *See* Vesaas, Tarjei, *Vindane*

"Wine God, The." *See* Hölderlin, Friedrich, "Brot und Wein"

Wine imagery

    in Rabelais's works, 2:716a–717a

        Gargantua, 2:705a, 707b, 715b, 7:705b–706a

        Third Book, 2:701b

Wine in Three Paintings. *See* Ortega y Gasset, José, "Tres cuadros del vino"

"Wingolf." *See* Klopstock, Friedrich Gottlieb

Winsnes, A. H., 9:1017b–1018a

Winter, in Klopstock, 4:529b–530b

"Winter Evening, A." *See* Trakl, Georg, "Ein Winterabend"

"Winter Notes on Summer Impressions." *See* Dostoevsky, Feodor

Winter Scene. *See* Gozzano, Guido, "Invernale"

Winter Sonata. *See* Valle-Inclán, Ramón del, *Sonatas: Memorias del Marqués de Bradomín* (*The Pleasant Memoirs of the Marquis de Bradomín*), *Sonata de invierno*

"Winterabend, Ein." *See* Trakl, Georg

Winter's Tale. See Heine, Heinrich, *Deutschland: Ein Wintermärchen*

Winter's Tale, The. See Shakespeare, William

Winter's Tales. See Dinesen, Isak

"Wîp muoz iemer sîn der wîbe hohste name." *See* Walther von der Vogelweide

Wirnt von Gravenberg
  Wigalois, Arthurian legend and, 1:152b
  Wolfram and, 1:264b

Wisdom, Augustine on, 1:40b, 44b

Wisdom of the Ancients, The. See Bacon, Francis

Wisdom and Destiny. See Maeterlinck, Maurice, *La sagesse et la destinée*

Wisdom of the Sands, The. See Saint-Exupéry, Antoine de, *Citadelle*

Wisdom; or, The Parable of the Feast. *See* Claudel, Paul, *La sagesse, ou la parabole du festin*

Wissenschaftslehre. See Fichte, Johann Gottlieb

Wit
  in Castiglione, 2:653a
  of Donne, 2:874b
  Renaissance forms of, 2:874b

Wit and Its Kindred. *See* Wedekind, Frank, *Der Witz und seine Sippe*

Wit and Solemnity. *See* Pauli, Johannes, *Schimpf und Ernst*

Wit and Wisdom of the Italian Renaissance. See Speroni, Charles

Witchcraft
  in *Eyrbyggja*, 1:389b
  in *Grettis saga*, 1:392b
  see also Sorcery

"With Fear I Gaze upon the Future." *See* Lermontov, Mikhail Yurievich, "Glyazhu na budushchnost s boyaznyu"

With Leda in the Spring. *See* Ady, Endre, "Lédával a Tavaszban"

With Muted Strings. See Hamsun, Knut, *En vandrer spiller med sordin*

With a Nudge of the Elbow. *See* Ritsos, Yannis, *Me to skountima*

With Open Eyes. See Yourcenar, Marguerite, *Les yeux ouverts*

Withdrawal, theme of, in Musil's *The Man Without Qualities*, 9:935a

Within a Budding Grove. See Proust, Marcel, *Remembrance of Things Past* (*À la recherche du temps perdu*)

Within a Family. *See* Mann, Heinrich, *In einer Familie*

"Without Age." *See* Éluard, Paul, "Sans âge"

"Without Love." *See* Pasternak, Boris, "Bezliub'e"

"Without Memory of Death." *See* Quasimodo, Salvatore, "Senza memoria di morte"

Witkacy. *See* Witkiewicz, Stanisław Ignacy

Witkiewicz, Stanisław Ignacy, **10:1205a–1230b**, 1206b–1207b, 1210b–1211a
  Człowiek z wodną puchliną zaczaja się na kochanka swej żony (A Man with Dropsy Lies in Wait for His Wife's Lover), 10:1209a
  Demonizm Zakopanego (Zakopane Demonism), 10:1209b–1210a
  Gyubal Wahazar, czyli na przełęczach bezsensu (Guybal Wahazar; or, Along the Cliffs of the Absurd), 10:1223a
  Jedyne wyjście (The Only Way Out), 10:1226b
  Karaluchy (Cockroaches), 10:1207b–1208a
  Książę ciemności kusi Św. Teresę przy pomocy kelnera z Budapesztu (The Prince of Darkness Tempts Saint Theresa with the Aid of a Waiter from Budapest), 10:1209a
  Kurka wodna (The Water Hen), 10:1221b–1222b

Listy do syna (Letters to His Son), 10:1208a, 1208b, 1213a

Matka (*The Mother*), 10:1224a-b

Mątwa czyli Hyrkaniczny światopogląd (*The Cuttlefish; or, The Hyrcanian World View*), 10:1223a-b

Mister Price, czyli Bzik tropikalny (*Mister Price; or, Tropical Madness*), 10:1219b–1220a

Niemyte dusze (Unwashed Souls), 10:1211b, 1227a

Nienasycenie (*Insatiability*), 10:1226a-b

Nikotyna, alkohol, kokaina, peyotl, morfina, eter (Nicotine, Alcohol, Cocaine, Peyote, Morphine, and Ether), 10:1226b

Nowc formy w malarstwie i wynikające stąd nieporozumienia (New Forms in Painting and Misunderstandings Resulting Therefrom), 10:1213b, 1215a-b

Nowe wyzwolenie (*The New Deliverance*), 10:1220b–1221a

"O artystucznym teatrze" (On the Artistic Theater), 10:1228a

Oni (*They*), 10:1222b–1223a

Pamiętnik teatralny, 10:1212b, 1214b

Pojęcia i twierdzenia implikowane przez pojęcie istnienia (The Concepts and Principles Implied by the Concept of Existence), 10:1213b, 1227b

Pożęgnanie jesieni (Farewell to Autumn), 10:1225b–1226a

Pragmatyści (*The Pragmatists*), 10:1218b–1219b

622 upadki Bunga, czyli Demoniczna kobieta (The 622 Downfalls of Bungo; or, The Demonic Woman), 10:1210a–1211a

Sonata Belzebuba, czyli Prawdziwe zdarzenie w Mordowarze (The Beelzebub Sonata; or, What Really Happened in Mordovar), 10:1224b–1225a

Szewcy (*The Shoemakers*), 10:1227a-b

Tak zwana ludzkość w obłędzie (So-Called Humanity Gone Mad), 10:1228a

Teatr (Theater), 10:1216b–1218a, 1216b–1224a

Tumor Mózgowicz (*Tumor Brainiowicz*), 10:1220a-b

W małym dworku (In a Small Country House), 10:1221a-b

Wariat i zakonnica (*The Madman and the Nun*), 10:1223b–1224a

Witness of Poetry, The. See Milosz, Czeslaw

Wittgenstein, Ludwig
Bergson and, 8:65a
Croce and, 8:312a-b
Nietzsche and, 7:1678a
Philosophical Investigations, 8:65a
on the self and others, 5:406b
Tractatus Logico-Philosophicus, Moravia and, 12:2688a-b
Trakl and, 10:1415a
Valéry and, 8:575a

Witwer, Der. See Schnitzler, Arthur

Witz und seine Beziehung zum Unbewussten, Der. See Freud, Sigmund

Witz und seine Sippe, Der. See Wedekind, Frank

Wives' Friend, The. See Pirandello, Luigi, *L'Amica delle mogli*

"Wo bleibst du Trost der ganzen Welt." *See* Novalis, *Sacred Songs*

Wo warst du, Adam. See Böll, Heinrich

Woe from Wit. See Griboedov, Alexander, *Gore ot uma*

Wohl, Robert, *The Generation of 1914 and Modernism*, 9:800a

Wohryzek, Julie, 9:1154b

Wolf, Hugo
in Hesse's *The Journey to the East*, 9:852a
Mann's *Doctor Faustus* and, 9:733a, 733b
Wagnerism and, 6:1148a

"Wolf and the Lamp, The." *See* La Fontaine, Jean de, *Fables*, "Le loup et l'agneau"

Wolf Man, Freud and, 8:17b–18b

Wolf Man, The. See Dumas père, Alexandre, *Le meneur de loups*

Wolf in Sacred Places. *See* Gunnarsson, Gunnar, *Varg i veum*

"Wolf and the Shepherds, The." *See* La Fontaine, Jean de, *Fables*, "Le loup et les bergers"

Wolf Song. *See* Valle-Inclán, Ramón del, *Las comedias bárbaras* (Barbaric Plays), *Romance de lobos*

Wolf-Stormersee, Alexandria, marriage to Lampedusa, 11:2010a

Wolfe, Thomas, Hesse and, 9:846b

Wolfe, Tom, *The Bonfire of the Vanities*, 13:3044a

Wolff, Kurt
  Heinrich Mann and, 8:535a
  Kafka and, 9:1152b, 1155b–1156a

Wolfram von Eschenbach, **1:263a–286b**
  Der helden minne ir klage, 1:267a-b
  Ez ist nu tac, 1:267b–268a
  Gottfried and, 1:243a–244b
  Parzival, 1:268a–281a
    Arthurian legend and, 1:152b
    Grass and, 13:3372b
    verse form of, 1:216b
  Titurel, 1:281a–282b
  Walther and, 1:287a-b
  Willehalm, 1:282b–285b

Wolfskehl, Karl, George and, 8:460b, 462b

wolkenpumpe, die. See Arp, Jean

Wolters, Friedrich
  on George, 8:448a
  Stefan George und die Blätter für die Kunst (Stefan George and Pages for Art), 8:457b

"Woman, A." *See* Blok, Alexander, "Zhenshchina"

Woman Beside the Sea, A. *See* Ritsos, Yannis, *Mia ghineka plai sti thalassa*

Woman of Charm, A. *See* Goldoni, Carlo, *La donna de garbo*

Woman Destroyed, The. See Beauvoir, Simone de

Woman in the Eighteenth Century. *See* Goncourt, Edmond Louis Antoine and Jules Alfred Huot de, *La femme au dix-huitième siècle*

Woman from Sarajevo, The. See Andrić, Ivo

Woman and Grace, The. *See* Olsson, Hagar, *Kvinnan och nåden*

Woman and Her Shadow. *See* Claudel, Paul, *La femme et son ombre*

Woman Is a Devil, A; or, The Temptation of Saint Anthony. See Mérimée, Prosper, *Une femme est un diable, ou la tentation de Saint Antoine*

Woman Is Talking, A. *See* Kosztolányi, Dezső, *Egy asszony beszál*

Woman of the Pharisees, A. See Mauriac, François

"Woman on the Rock." *See* Andrić, Ivo

Woman of Rome, The. See Moravia, Alberto

"Woman of Tears, The." *See* Ady, Endre, "A könnyek asszonya"

Woman Triumphant. See Blasco Ibáñez, Vicente, *La maja desnuda*

Woman Without a Shadow, The, Hofmannsthal, Hugo von, *Die Frau ohne Schatten*

Woman's Heart, A. See Maupassant, Guy de, *Notre Coeur*

"Woman's Kingdom, A." *See* Chekhov, Anton, "Babe tsarstvo"

Woman's Man. *See* Moberg, Vilhelm, *Kvinnas Man*

Womb, The. *See* Zamyatin, Yevgeny Ivanovich, "Chrevo"

Women
  in Andrić's works, 11:1757a–1758a, 1768a-b, 1773b–1774a
  in Arthurian legend, 1:228a
  as artists, in Staël's *Corinne*, 5:100a, 101a
  athletic female of Montherlant, 11:1924a-b
  Augustine on, 1:39b
  autobiography and, 12:2704a
  Beauvoir and, 12:2702a–2703a, 2721a–2726b
  Berlioz' view of, 6:780b, 801a-b
  in Boccaccio's *Decameron*, 2:518b–519a, 523a-b
  in Calvino's works, 13:3275b
  in Castiglione, 2:658b–660a
  in Chekhov's prose, 7:1864b
  Christianity and, in Staël's *De l'Allemagne*, 5:107b
  in Claudel's plays, 8:484a
  in Corneille's plays, 3:45b
  in Dumas's works, 6:722b, 723a-b
  in Eça's works, 7:1691b
  in Elytis' poetry, 13:2967b, 2975b, 2976a-b

The Light Tree and the Fourteenth Being, 13:2973b–2974a

To Axion Esti, 13:2968b, 2971a-b

extraordinary, in Staël's works, 5:92b, 100a-b

feminine beauty in Gautier's works, 6:1040a-b

futurism and, 9:811a

in Galdós' novels, 7:1612a-b

George and, 8:464b–465a

in Ghelderode's plays, 11:2136a-b

in Giraudoux's works, 9:1059b, 1061b–1062a

Gogol and, 6:976a, 980b, 985a, 992b–993a

Goldoni's treatment of, 4:437a–445b

in Goncharov's works, 6:1062b, 1073b, 1078a, 1082a-b

Goncourts' misogynistic portrayal of, 7:1403b–1404a

in Grass's *The Flounder*, 13:3380a–3381a

Hašek's attitude towards female sexuality, 9:113b–1114a

in Hebbel's works, 6:1096a, 1101a

in Heinrich Mann's fiction, 8:520b, 521a-b, 525a-b, 538a, 538b–539a

in Hölderlin's works, 5:150a

Hugo's view of, 6:696b–697a, 711b–712a, 713a-b, 714b, 715a-b

Ibsen on, 11:2039b

ideal of, in Vigny's "La maison du berger," 5:481a, 482a-b

inconstancy of, in La Fontaine's "The Widow of Ephesus," 3:97b

Kazantzakis's metabiological view, 9:1074a

Kierkegaard and, 6:1140a–1141b

in La Bruyère's *Caractères*, 3:237a–238b

in La Rochefoucauld's *Mémoires*, 3:63b–64a

Laforgue on, 7:1891a–1892a, 1900b–1901a

literary

  Ginzburg on, 13:3137b

  La Rochefoucauld and, 3:62b

in Lope de Vega's works, 2:853b–254a

María de Zayas y Sotomayor's feminism, 2:952a

in Maupassant's works, 7:1765a–1766b, 1767a-b, 1769a, 1770b–1771b, 1772a, 1772b–1774a, 1775a, 1778b–1779b

Mérimée and, 6:754b–755b

Michelet's views, 5:574a, 576b, 577b, 578a, 590a

  Barthes on, 13:3083b–3084a

in Montherlant's novels, 11:1921a–1922a, 1933a-b

Moravia's view of, 12:2692a-b

Moslem, Montherlant on, 11:1927a-b

Nerval on, 6:961b

in the *Nibelungenlied*, 1:228a-b

Nietzsche's depiction of, 7:1647a

in Norwegian literature, 11:2039b

in Olesha's *Envy*, 11:2239a-b, 2240a

Pavese's view of, 12:2761a, 2773a-b

in Perse's poetry, 10:1433a

Prudentius on, 1:18a

in Richter's *The Invisible Lodge*, 5:62a

Rimbaud's view of, 7:1811a

Sand's *Indiana* on, 6:819a

Schnitzler's portrayal of, 8:92a, 92b–93a, 100a, 107a, 107b, 108a, 110b–111a, 112a

Simenon and, 12:2483a

Staël's *De l'Allemagne* on, 5:107b–108a

in Strindberg's works, 7:1734a–1735a, 1740a, 1750a–1752b

in Svevo's novels, 8:77a

in Undset's works, 9:1026b–1027a

in Valéry's *Charmes*, 8:580b

in Walther, 1:292a–293b

Wedekind's image of, 236b, 8:241a-b, 249a-b, 251b–252a, 276b

Weil and, 12:2789b

in Welsh legends, 1:143a-b

in Wolfram, 1:276b

see also Eroticism; Libertinism; Misogyny; Sexes, relationship between; Sexuality; Verlaine, Paul, *Femmes*

Women at the Pump, The. See Hamsun, Knut, *Konerne ved vandposten*

Women Call: Come Home. *See* Vesaas, Tarjei, *Kvinnor ropar heim*

Women of Messina, The. See Vittorini, Elio, *Le donne di Messina*

Women of Monemvasia. *See* Ritsos, Yannis, *Monemvasiotises*

"Women in [My] Childhood." *See* Pasternak, Boris, "Zhenshchiny v detstve"
Women in a River Landscape. See Böll, Heinrich
Women's Gossip. See Goldoni, Carlo, *I pettegolezzi delle donne*
Wonder. See Meraviglie
Wonder Maid. See Kosztolányi, Dezső, *Édes Anna*
Wonder Show, The. See Cervantes, Miguel de
Wonderful Adventures of Nils, The. See Lagerlöf, Selma, *Nils Holgerssons underbara resa*
Wonderful Farm, The. See Aymé, Marcel
Wood Demon, The. See Chekhov, Anton, *Uncle Vanya*
Wool and Snow. *See* Ferreira de Castro, José Maria, *A lã e a neve*
Woolf, Leonard, Svevo and, 8:71b
Woolf, Virginia
    Bergson and, 8:64b
    Cavafy and, 8:206a
    on the creative process, 12:2348a
    Granite and Rainbow, "The Narrow Bridge of Art," 9:953b–954a, 955b
    Hesse and, 9:855b
    Laforgue and, 7:1887b
    on Montaigne, 2:788a
    Musil's *The Man Without Qualities* and, 9:953b–954a, 955a, 955b, 957a
    Rilke and, 9:790a
    Sarraute and, 12:2334b
    Spanish translations, 9:1119b
    The Waves, 7:1906a
        Yourcenar's translation, 12:2543a
    To the Lighthouse, Musil and, 9:956a
    on Tolstoy, 7:1472a
"Word and Culture, The." *See* Mandelshtam, Osip
"Word on Modern Art, A." *See* Musset, Alfred de, "Un mot sur l'art moderne"
Word as Such, The. See Khlebnikov, Velimir, and Kruchenykh, Aleksei
"Word for Summer, A." *See* Seferis, George, "Enas logos gia to kalokairi"
Word-Dreams and Black Stars. *See* Arp, Jean, *wortträume und schwarze sterne*

Wordplay
    in Elytis' *Tria poiemata me simea efkerias*, 13:2982b–2983a
    in "Manus ferens munera," 1:364b
    in medieval satire, 1:371a–372a
    in "Utar contra vitia carmine rebelli," 1:352a
Words. *See* Arp, Jean, "Worte"
Words, The. See Sartre, Jean-Paul
Words Without Wrinkles. *See* Breton, André, *Les pas perdus*
Words-in-freedom. *See* Free-word style
Wordsworth, William
    classical forms and mythology discarded by, 5:372b
    "Intimations of Immortality," 13:2982b
    Jiménez and, 9:1013a
    Richter and, 5:65a, 81b
    The Lyrical Ballads, on science as subject matter of poetry, 4:706b–707a
Work. *See* Johnson, Eyvind, *Arbetet*; Labor
Work in Black, The. *See* Yourcenar, Marguerite, *L'Oeuvre au noir*
Work Is Tiring. *See* Pavese, Cesare, *Lavorare stanca*
Workers' Feast Day, The. *See* Ortega y Gasset, José, "La fiesta del trabajo"
"Workers' Song." *See* Buchez, Philippe, "Chant d'ouvrier"
Working class
    in Büchner's works, 6:1189a–1192a
    Camus and, 13:3056b
    Goncourts on, 7:1407a
    Ortega y Gasset's on, 9:1142a-b, 1143b—1145a
    in Pascoli, 7:1849a-b
    in Russian novel, 7:1478a
    Verga's *Dal tuo al mio*, 7:1563b–1564a
    Zola's novels about, 7:1525b–1526b
    see also Artisan class; Class structure; Masses; Proletariat
Working Diary. See Brecht, Bertolt, *Arbeitsjournal*
Works. See Lessing, Gotthold Ephraim, *Schriften*
Works of Fiction. *See* Yourcenar, Marguerite, *Oeuvres romanesques*
Works of Love. See Kierkegaard, Søren

World About Us, The. See Simon, Claude, *Leçon de choses*

World of Art. *See* Diaghilev, Sergey, *Mir iskusstva*

World and I, The. *See* Hebbel, Friedrich, "Welt und Ich"

World Light. See Laxness, Halldór, *Heimsljós*

World Literature Publishing House, Zamyatin's involvement with, 10:1192b

"World in Reverse, The." *See* Khlebnikov, Velimir, "Mirskontsa"

"World, The." *See* Milosz, Czeslaw, "Świat"

World War I
  Ady and, 9:860a, 879a
  Akhmatova and, 10:1529a
  Apollinaire and, 9:897a–898a
  Baroja's disgust with, 9:609a
  Bergson and, 8:61a
  Blasco Ibáñez and, 8:356b, 357b
  Claudel and, 8:484b–485a
  Cocteau and, 10:1545a
  D'Annunzio in, 8:198a-b, 200a
  Demian and, 9:839a
  futurism and, 9:825a
  George and, 8:466a
  Giraudoux during, 9:1043a-b
  Heinrich Mann and, 8:533b
  Hesse and, 9:838b
  Khlebnikov and, 10:1337a–1338b
  Krleža and, 11:1812b–1813a
  Lagerkvist and, 10:1684b
  Maeterlinck's propaganda work for Allies, 8:140b–141a
  Mandelshtam's response to, 10:1636a-b
  Mann and, 8:533b, 9:718a
    in *Magic Mountain*, 9:723b
  Montale and, 11:1987b–1988a
  in Montale's *The Occasions*, 11:1998b–1999a, 2000a
  Pirandello and, 8:392a
  Portugal and, 11:2146a-b
  Rilke and, 9:771b–772a
  Schnitzler and, 8:106a–107a
  Trakl and, 10:1415b
  Ungaretti and, 10:1456b–1458a, 1460b–1461a, 1463b, 1465a
  in Valle-Inclán's plays, 8:345b–346a
  La media noche, 8:337b–338a
  Witkiewicz and, 10:1212b–1213b, 1228a
  see also Young Bosnia movement

World War II
  Akhmatova's poetry and, 10:1529b–1530a
  Aragon and, 11:2078a–2079b
  Breton and, 11:1946b–1947a
  Calvino and, 13:3259a–3263b
  Camus and, 13:3053b–3054b
  Cocteau and, 10:1558a
  Croce's role in Italian liberation, 8:327b
  Dürrenmatt and, 13:3215a
  Elytis and, 13:2961a-b, 2966a
  France and, 13:3023a-b
  French resistance, 12:2320b–2321a
  in Ginzburg's writing, 13:3136a-b, 3148b
  Giraudoux during, 9:1044a
  in Gombrowicz's works, 12:2583b–2584b
  Grass and, 13:3367a–3370a
  Greece and, 13:2961a
  Hamsun and, 8:21a-b, 40a–41a
  Hauptmann's *Atriden-Tetralogie* and, 8:171a
  Italian resistance, in Vittorini's novels, 12:2745b, 2749a
  Johnson in, 12:2370b–2371b
  Krleža and, 11:1821b
  Lagerkvist and, 10:1692b–1693a
  Malraux in, 12:2415a-b
  Mann and, 9:1017a-b
  Milosz during, 13:2930b–2931a
  Montherlant on German defeat of France, 11:1918b–1919a
  Moravia and, 12:2680a, 2684b
  Pasternak's poetry concerning, 10:1608b–1609a
  Perse during, 10:1441a
  Ritsos and, 12:2817a-b
  Robbe-Grillet during, 13:3239a-b
  in Saint-Exupéry's works, 12:2319a–2320a, 2320b–2321a, 2325a, 2325b–2326a
  Sartre and, 12:2600a–2601a
  Svevo's widow and, 8:71b
  Undset and, 9:1017a-b, 1024a–1025a
  Vesaas and, 11:2043b–2045a

World We Live In, The. See Čapek, Karel, *R.U.R.*

World as Will and Idea, The. See
Schopenhauer, Arthur
World as Will and Representation, The. See
Schopenhauer, Arthur
Worldliness, Walther and, 1:297a–301a
World's Neighborhoods, The. *See* Ritsos,
Yannis, *I ghitonies tou kosmou*
"Worlds, The." *See* Klopstock, Friedrich
Gottlieb
World's the World, The. See Moravia, Alberto,
Il mondo è quello che è
Worringer, Wilhelm
Abstraction and Empathy, 10:1216a-b
Form probleme der Gotik (*Form Problems of
the Gothic*), Ortega y Gasset's review,
9:1134a
Kunstwollen, 9:1140a
Ortega y Gasset on, 9:1140a
"Worte." *See* Arp, Jean
wortträume und schwarze sterne. See Arp,
Jean
Woyzeck. See Büchner, Georg
Wozzeck. See Berg, Alban
"Wrath of Samson, The." *See* Vigny, Alfred
Victor de, *Les destinées*
"Write It Down." *See* Ekelöf, Gunnar, "Tag och
skriv"
Writer
Aymé's satire of, 12:2444b
social responsibility of
in Ronsard's "Hymne de l'or," 2:733b
Solzhenitsyn on, 13:3196b
types of, 13:3215b
Writer, The. *See* Azorín, *El escritor*
Writer-reader-character relationship, in Butor,
13:3296b, 3298a-b
Writer's Preface to His Selected Works, A. *See*
Hesse, Hermann, "Vorrede eines
Dichters zu seinen ausgewählten
Werken"
"Writer's Profession, The." *See* Canetti, Elias
Writer's Union (Soviet). *See* Vserossiiskii
soiuz pisatelei
Writing
Barthes on, 13:3096a–3097b
Castiglione on courtier's practice of, 2:656a
Cela on, 13:3126a-b

Frisch on, 13:2903b–2904a, 2907b, 2922b
Writing, automatic. *See* Automatic writing
Writing Degree Zero. See Barthes, Roland
Writings. *See* Benjamin, Walter, *Schriften*
Writings from London and Last Letters. See
Weil, Simone
Wrong Side and the Right Side, The. See
Camus, Albert
"Wronged Husband, A." *See* Pirandello, Luigi,
"Certi obblighi"
Wu-Tao-Tse, legend of, Vesaas and, 11:2035b
Wulf and Eadwacer (Anglo-Saxon poem),
1:66a
Wuthering Heights. See Brontë, Emily
Wutz. See Richter, Jean Paul, *Das Leben des
vergnügten Schulmeisterlein Maria Wutz
in Auenthal*
Wyatt, Thomas, Petrarchan influence, 2:504a
Wyspiański, Stanisław, 10:1221b

X

"X." *See* Zamyatin, Yevgeny Ivanovich, "Iks"

"Xenia." *See* Montale, Eugenio, *Satura*

Xenia. See Schiller, Friedrich von

Xenophobia, in Heinrich Mann's fiction, 8:524b–525a

Xenophon

    Anabasis, Johnson and, 12:2378a

    Memorabilia, on Prodicus of Cos, 1:6a

Y

"Ya k vam pishu." *See* Lermontov, Mikhail Yurievich

"Ya smotryu v proshloe." *See* Olesha, Yuri

Yang and yin, Ekelöf and, 12:2642a-b

Yasnaya Polyana, Tolstoy at, 7:1473a–1475b, 1480b

Y'avait un prisonnier. See Anouilh, Jean

Year 1905, The. *See* Pasternak, Boris, *Deviat'sot piatyi god*

Year of the Soul, The. *See* George, Stefan, *Das Jahr der Seele*

Yearning, in Frisch's works, 13:2899b

Yeats, William Butler

    A Vision, 13:2973b

    Autobiography, 9:666a-b

    Castiglione and, 2:665a

    Crazy Jane Talks to the Bishop, 2:552a

    on Ibsen, 7:1436b

    Ibsen's influence on, 7:1444a

    and Jarry, 9:666a-b

    Jiménez and, 9:992a, 1004a

    Nerval's style and, 6:944b

    Per Amica Silentia Lunae, 9:1011b

    Seferis' translations, 12:2269b

    The Countess Cathleen, 9:1004a

    "The Tower," 7:1578a

Yegor Bulychov and Others. See Gorky, Maxim, *Egor Bulychov i drugie*

Yellow Flame, The. *See* Ady, Endre, "A sárga láng"

Yellow Loves. *See* Corbière, Tristan, *Les amours jaunes*

Yellow Sunbeams. *See* Sainte-Beuve, Charles-Augustin, "Les rayons jaunes"

Yermo de las almas, El. See Valle-Inclán, Ramón del

Yes, I Am Guiomar. *See* Valderrama, Pilar de, *Sí, soy Guiomar*

Yes and No. See Abélard, Peter, *Sic et non*

"Yes, thus does inspiration dictate." *See* Blok, Alexander, "Da, tak diktuet vdokhnovenie"

Yesterday. *See* Hofmannsthal, Hugo von, *Gestern*

"Yet Another Effort, Frenchmen, If You Would
Become Republicans." *See* Sade,
Donatien Alphonse François, marquis
de, *Philosophy in the Bedroom*
Yeux d'Elsa, Les. See Aragon, Louis
Yeux ouverts, Les. See Yourcenar, Marguerite
Yiddish theater, Kafka and, 9:1153a
Ymnos kai thrinos ghia tin Kypro. See Ritsos,
Yannis
Ynglinga saga. See Snorri Sturluson
"Ynglingatal." *See* Thjódólf of Hvin
Yong, Bartholomew, Montemayor's *Diana*
translated by, 2:923a
York cycle plays, 1:469a
"York Realist," 1:469a
"You are indeed black, but you are beautiful."
See Marini, Giambattista, "Nera sì, ma
se' bella"
You Are a Young Lady From a Better-Class
Family. *See* Hašek, Jaroslav, "Jste
dcerou z lepší rodiny"
You Can't Have It Both Ways. See Musset,
Alfred de, *Il faut qu'une porte soit
ouverte ou fermée*
You Can't Trifle with Love. See Musset, Alfred
de
You Go to Heidelberg Too Often and Other
Stories. *See* Böll, Heinrich, *Du fährst zu
oft nach Heidelberg und andere
Erzählungen*
You May Remain and Love Me. *See* Ady,
Endre, "Maradhatsz és szerethetsz"
"You Scream to Life." *See* Ekelöf, Gunnar, "Du
skriker till livet"
"You Shattered." *See* Ungaretti, Giuseppe
"You who hear." *See* Petrarch, *Canzoniere*,
"Voi ch'ascoltate"
Young Bosnia movement, Andrić in,
11:1752a-b
"Young Captive, The." *See* Chénier, André
Young Collective Farmer. *See Molodoi
kolkhoznik*
Young Czech Party's Election in the Lesser
Town, The. *See* Hašek, Jaroslav,
"Mladočeské volby na Malé straně"
Young Eagle, The. *See* Gunnarsson, Gunnar,
Den unge Ørn

Young, Edward
Chateaubriand on, 5:137a
Conjectures on Original Composition,
Chénier and, 4:707a
Klopstock and, 4:528b–529a, 534a
*Night Thoughts on Life, Death, and
Immortality*, 5:6b, 58b
Young Fate, The. See Valéry, Paul, *La jeune
parque*
Young German literary movement, 8:235a-b
Büchner and, 6:1175a
Burckhardt and, 6:1226b
Grillparzer's unpopularity due to, 5:430b
Hebbel in, 6:1094b
Heine and, 5:502b–503a
Tieck and, 5:233b
Young Hegel, The. See Lukács, György, *Der
junge Hegel*
Young Henry of Navarre. See Mann, Heinrich,
Die Jugend des Königs Henri Quatre
"Young Man with the Carnation, The." *See*
Dinesen, Isak
Young Man in Chains. See Mauriac, François
Young Master Carpenter, The. *See* Tieck,
Ludwig, *Der junge Tischlermeister*
Young Medardus. *See* Schnitzler, Arthur, *Der
Junge Medardus*
Young Scholar, The. See Lessing, Gotthold
Ephraim, *Der junge Gelehrte*
Young Siegfried, The. See Wagner, Richard,
Der Ring des Nibelungen, Siegfried
Young Socialists (organization), Johnson and,
12:2361b
"Young Tarentine, The." *See* Chénier, André
Young Törless. See Musil, Robert, *Die
Verwirrungen des Zöglings Törless*
"Young Vienna," Schnitzler and, 8:92a
"Young Widow, The." *See* La Fontaine, Jean
de, *Fables*, "La jeune veuve"
Your Faust: Variable Fantasy in the Operatic
Mode. *See* Butor, Michel, *Votre Faust:
Fantaisie variable genre opéra*
Yourcenar, Marguerite, **12:2535a–2561b**
Alexis ou le traité du vain combat (Alexis),
12:2537b–2538a, 2544b
Archives du nord (Archives of the North),
12:2536a

Blues et gospels, 12:2543a

"Carnet de notes de *Mémoires d'Hadrien*," 12:2541a

Cinq nô modernes (Five Modern Nō), 12:2543a

Comme l'eau qui coule (*Two Lives and a Dream*)
  "Anna, soror" ("Anna, Sister"), 12:2539b–2540a, 2557b–2558a
  "D'après Rembrandt" (According to Rembrandt), 12:2540a
  "Un homme obscur" ("An Obscure Man"), 12:2540a, 2557a-b
  "Une belle matinée" ("A Lovely Morning"), 12:2540a, 2557b

Denier du rêve (*A Coin in Nine Hands*), 12:2540a-b, 2541a-b

Electre ou la chute des masques (Electra; or, the Fall of the Masks), 12:2549a–2550a

Feux (*Fires*), 12:2541b–2542b, 2544b, 2557b

Fleuve profond, sombre rivière (Deep, Dark, Troubled River), 12:2543a

La couronne et la lyre (The Crown and the Lyre), 12:2543a

La mort conduit l'attelage (Death Drives the Team), 12:2539b–2540a
  "D'après Dürer" (According to Dürer), 12:2539b
  "D'après Greco" (According to Greco), 12:2539b

La nouvelle Eurydice (The New Eurydice), 12:2539a

La petite sirène (*The Little Mermaid*), 12:2546a

Le coup de grâce (*Coup de Grâce*), 12:2538b, 2543b–2544b, 2557b

Le dialogue dans le marécage (The Dialogue in the Marsh), 12:2539b

Le jardin des chimères (The Garden of the Chimeras), 12:2537a-b

Le labyrinthe du monde (The Labyrinth of the World), 12:2536a

Le mystère d'Alceste (The Mystery of Alcestis), 12:2550a–2551b, 2552b

Le temps, ce grand sculpteur (*That Mighty Sculptor, Time*), 12:2558b

Les Charités d'Alcippe et autres poèmes (*The Alms of Alcippe*), 12:2553a
  "Poème pour une poupée russe" ("Poem for a Russian Doll"), 12:2553a

Les dieux ne sont pas morts (Gods Are Not Dead), 12:2537b

Les songes et les sorts (Dreams and Destinies), 12:2545b–2546a

Les yeux ouverts (*With Open Eyes*), 12:2535b, 2537a, 2556b

L'Oeuvre au noir (*The Abyss*), 12:2538b, 2539b, 2541b, 2553b–2556b
  "L'Abîme" ("The Abyss"), 12:2555b
  research for, 12:2553b–2554a
  rewriting of, 12:2540b–2541a

Mémoires d'Hadrien (*Memoirs of Hadrian*), 12:2537b, 2538b, 2539a-b, 2544b, 2546b–2549a
  epilogue, 12:2548a

Mishima ou la vision du vide (*Mishima: A Vision of the Void*), 12:2557a

Nouvelles orientales (*Oriental Tales*), 12:2544b–2545b
  "Comment Wang-Fô fut sauvé" ("How Wang-Fo Was Saved"), 12:2545b
  "La tristesse de Cornélius Berg" ("The Sadness of Cornelius Berg"), 12:2545a
  "Le dernier amour du Prince Genghi" ("The Last Love of Prince Genghi"), 12:2545a-b
  "Le lait de la mort" ("The Milk of Death"), 12:2545a
  "L'Homme qui a aimé les Néréides" ("The Man Who Loved the Néréids"), 12:2545a
  "Notre-Dame-des-Hirondelles" ("Our Lady of the Swallows"), 12:2545a

Oeuvres romanesques (Works of Fiction), 12:2541b, 2542a

Pindare (Pindar), 12:2539a

Présentation critique de Constantin Cavafy, 12:2543a-b

Qui n'a pas son Minotaure? (To Each His Minotaur), 12:2551b–2552b

Quoi? L'Éternité (What? Eternity), 12:2536a

Rendre à César (Render unto Caesar), 12:2541a-b

Yourcenar, Marguerite (*cont.*)
Sous bénéfice d'inventaire (*The Dark Brain of Piranesi and Other Essays*), 12:2553a
Souvenirs pieux (Pious Memories), 12:2536a
Théâtre II, 12:2546a
as translator, 12:2543a-b
Weil and, 12:2806a
Youth, in Leconte de Lisle's works, 6:1259a–1261a
Youth. See Ifjúság
"Youth." *See* Rimbaud, Arthur, "Jeunesse"
Youth and Egolatry. See Baroja, Pío, *Juventud, egolatria*
Youthful Attempts. See Andersen, Hans Christian
"Youthful lady under a green laurel, A." *See* Petrarch, *Canzoniere*, "Giovane donna sotto un verde lauro"
Youthful Verses. *See* Tsvetaeva, Marina, *Iunosheskie stixi*
Youths, The. *See* Verlaine, Paul, "Les ingénus"
Yugoslav Lexicographic Institute, Krleža and, 11:1810a, 1823b
Yugoslavia, Fiume, D'Annunzio as Comandante of, 8:198b–199a
Yuriy Miloslavsky, ili Russkie v 1612 godu (*Yuri Miloslavsky; or, The Russians in 1612*). *See* Zagoskin, Mikhail
Yvain. See Chrétien de Troyes
Yver, Jacques, *Le printemps* (*Spring*), 2:949b
"Yvette." *See* Maupassant, Guy de

Z

Z vln života. See Hašek, Jaroslav
"Za gremuchuiu doblest . . ." *See* Mandelshtam, Osip
"Za logorovanja." *See* Andrić, Ivo, "In the Camp"
"Zadanie." *See* Milosz, Czeslaw
Zadig. See Voltaire
"Zadonshchina." *See* Sofoniia of Riazan
Zagarrio, Giuseppe, Quasimodo and, 12:2392a
Żagary, Milosz and, 13:2930a
Zagoskin, Mikhail
Lermontov and, 6:1205a, 1206b
Yuriy Miloslavsky, ili Russkie v 1612 godu (*Yuri Miloslavsky; or, The Russians in 1612*), 6:1205a
Zagovor chuvstv. See Olesha, Yuri
Zagreb, Krleža and, 11:1808a, 1810b, 1813b
Zaïre. See Voltaire
"Zakalennoe serdtse. Ia chernogorskoi zhizni." *See* Khlebnikov, Velimir
Zakat. See Babel, Isaac
"Zakhar-Kalita" ("Zakhar-the-Pouch"). *See* Solzhenitsyn, Aleksandr
"Zaklěcie." *See* Milosz, Czeslaw
"Zakliatie smekhom." *See* Khlebnikov, Velimir
Zakopane
as a cultural center, 10:1207a
Witkiewicz's life in, 10:1209a–1210a
Zakopane Demonism. *See* Witkiewicz, Stanisław Ignacy, *Demonizm Zakopanego*
Zakovannyi fil'moi. See Mayakovsky, Vladimir
Zaks. *See* Camus, Albert
"Zakulisy." *See* Zamyatin, Yevgeny Ivanovich
Zalacaín the Adventurer. *See* Baroja, Pío, *Zalacaín el aventurero*
Zalai, Béla, 10:1235a
Allgemeine Theorie der System (General System Theory), Kosztolányi and, 10:1233a
Zamist' sonetiv i oktav. See Tychyna, Pavlo
Zamyatin, Yevgeny Ivanovich, **10:1181a–1203b**
A God-Forsaken Hole (*Na kulichkakh*)
Alatyr' compared to, 10:1184a

love in, 10:1183b
primitivism in, 10:1183a-b
A Provincial Tale (Uezdnoe)
 A God-Forsaken Hole compared to, 10:1183b
 Alatyr' compared to, 10:1184a
 grotesque exaggeration in, 10:1186a
 love in, 10:1183b, 1184a
 primitivism in, 10:1182b–1183a
 "Rus" compared to, 10:1194b
 success of, 10:1182b
"A Story About the Most Important Thing" ("Rasskaz o samom glavnom"), 10:1194b–1195a
"Afrika" (Africa), 10:1185b
 The North and, 10:1188b
Afrikanskii gost' (The African Guest), 10:1193b
Alatyr', 10:1184a-b
 "Afrika" compared to, 10:1185b
"Aprel'" ("April"), 10:1184b
Atilla, 10:1193b
"Avtobiografiia" ("Autobiography"), on his first story, 10:1182b
Babel and, 11:1893a
Bich Bozhii (The Scourge of God), 10:1200a-b
Blokha (The Flea), 10:1194a
 foreign staging of, 10:1199a-b
 Zhitie Blokhi and, 10:1195b
Bol'shim detiam skazki (Tales for Grown-Up Children), publication of, 10:1187b
"Chasy" ("The Watch"), 10:1200a
"Chrevo" (The Womb), 10:1185a
 "The Flood" and, 10:1196b
"Desiatiminutnaia drama" (A Ten-Minute Drama), 10:1199b
"Devushka" (The Girl), 10:1182a-b
"Drakon" ("The Dragon"), 10:1191a
"Ela" (The Sloop), 10:1196a-b
"Glaza" (Eyes), 10:1191a
"Ia boius'" ("I Am Afraid"), 10:1197a-b
"Iks" ("X"), 10:1195a
Istoriia goroda Glupova (The History of Sillytown), 10:1194a
"Kriazhi" (The Diehards), 10:1185b
"Kuny" (Midsummer Games), 10:1194b

"Lev" ("The Lion"), 10:1200a
"Mamai," 10:1191a
 imagery in, 10:1191b
"Moskva-Peterburg" ("Moscow-Petersburg"), 10:1198b
"Mucheniki nauki" ("Another Turning of the Worm"), 10:1199b–1200a
"Neputevyi" (The Ne'er-Do-Well), 10:1184b
"Novaia russkaia proza" ("The New Russian Prose"), 10:1198a-b
"O chude proisshedshem v Pepel'nuiu Sredu" ("The Miracle of Ash Wednesday"), 10:1195b
"O literature, revoliutsii, entropii i o prochem" ("On Literature, Revolution, Entropy, and Other Matters"), 10:1197b–1198a
"O segodniashnem i o sovremennom" ("The Day and the Age"), 10:1197b
"O sintetizme" ("On synthetism"), 10:1198a
O tom, kak istselen byl inok Erazm (The Healing of the Novice Erasmus), 10:1196a
Obshchestvo pochetnykh zvonarei (The Society of Honorable Bell Ringers), 10:1194a
"Odin" (Alone), 10:1182a
Ogni sviatogo Dominika (The Fires of St. Dominic), 10:1193a-b, 1194a
Peshchera (The Cave), 10:1194a
"Pis'menno" (By Letter), 10:1185a-b
"Rai" ("Paradise"), 10:1197b
Robert Mayer, 10:1197b
"Rus" ("In Old Russia"), 10:1194b
"Scythians?" ("Skify li?"), 10:1187a
 as philosophic nucleus for future writing, 10:1197a
 We and, 10:1188b, 1190a
Sensatsiia (A Sensation), 10:1194a
"Skazka o Gospodine Khoroshem i o miloi baryshne" (A Fable About Mr. Good and a Sweet Girl), 10:1182a
"Slovo predostavliaetsia tovarishchu Churyginu" ("Comrade Churygin Has the Floor"), 10:1195a-b
"Spodruchnitsa greshnykh" ("The Protectress of Sinners"), 10:1191a-b

Zamyatin, Yevgeny Ivanovich (*cont.*)
  "Starshina" (The Elder), 10:1185a
  "The Cave" ("Peshchera"), 10:1190b
    film based on, 10:1194a
    imagery in, 10:1191b
    stage adaptation of, 10:1194a
  "The Fisher of Men" ("Lovets chelovekov"),
    10:1188a-b
    "Rus" and, 10:1194b
  "The Flood" ("Navodnenie"),
    10:1196b–1197a
  The Islanders (*Ostrovitiane*),
    10:1187b–1188a
    entropy as theme in, 10:1197b
    stage adaptations of, 10:1194a
    "The Fisher of Men" and, 10:1188a-b
    We and, 10:1190a
  The North (*Sever*), 10:1188b
    entropy as theme in, 10:1197b
    film based on, 10:1194a
    "Rus" and, 10:1194b
  "The Real Truth" ("Pravda istinnaia"),
    10:1187b
  "Tri dnia" (Three Days), 10:1184b
  "Videnie" (The Apparition), 10:1200a
  "Vstrecha" (The Encounter), 10:1200a
  We (*My*), 10:1188b–1190b
    color symbolism in, 10:1192a
    entropy as theme in, 10:1197b
    his critical essays and, 10:1197a
    his persecution for, 10:1199a
    Silone's influence on, 12:2303a
    Western writers and, 10:1181a
  "Zakulisy" ("Backstage"), denunciation of,
    10:1199a
  "Zavtra" ("Tomorrow"), 10:1191a
  Zhitie blokhi (The Life of the Flea),
    10:1195b–1196a
Zañartu, Enrique, Butor and, 13:3305a
Zandonai, Riccardo, *Francesca da Rimini*
  opera, 8:196a
"Zang Tumb Tumb." *See* Marinetti, Filippo
  Tommaso
Zangezi. See Khlebnikov, Velimir
"Zápas o duše." *See* Hašek, Jaroslav
Zapiski chudaka. See Bely, Andrey

Zapiski iz podpol'ia. See Dostoevsky, Feodor,
  Notes from Underground
Zapiski mechtatelei (Notes of Dreamers)
  (journal), Bely and, 9:924a
Zarathustra. *See* Zoroaster
Zarathustra and the Youth. *See* Krleža,
  Miroslav, *Zaratustra i mladić*
"Zarathustras Wiederkehr" ("Zarathustra's
  Return"). *See* Hesse, Hermann
Zaratustra i mladić. See Krleža, Miroslav
Zashchita Luzhina. See Nabokov, Vladimir
Zastave. See Krleža, Miroslav
"Zastrel'shchiki." *See* Mayakovsky, Vladimir
Zauberberg, Der. See Mann, Thomas, *The*
  Magic Mountain
"Zauberlehrling, Der." *See* Goethe, Johann
  Wolfgang von
Zaubermärchen (magic folk tales), Andersen
  and, 6:880b–881a
Zauberschloss, Das. See Tieck, Ludwig
Zauberspiel (magic play) of Austria
  influences on, 5:421b–422a
  Raimund's contribution to, 5:420b
Zavety group, Zamyatin's involvement with,
  10:1185b
Zavist'. See Olesha, Yury, *Envy*
"Závrať." *See* Čapek, Karel
"Zavtra." *See* Zamyatin, Yevgeny Ivanovich
Zayas y Sotomayor, María de
  Desengaños amorosos (Amatory
    Disillusions), 2:952a
  Novelas amorosas y exemplares (Amatory
    and Exemplary Tales), 2:952a
Zazie. See Queneau, Raymond, *Zazie dans le*
  métro
Zazie dans le métro. See Queneau, Raymond
Żdobycie władzy. See Milosz, Czeslaw, *The*
  Seizure of Power
"Žedj." *See* Andrić, Ivo, "Thirst"
"Zefiro torna." *See* Petrarch, *Canzoniere*
Zeit Konstantins des Grossen, Die. See
  Burckhardt, Jacob, *The Age of*
  Constantine the Great
Zeitalter wird besichtigt, Ein. See Mann,
  Heinrich
"Zeitgedichte." *See* George, Stefan, *Der*
  siebente Ring

"Zeitgenosse und die Wirklichkeit, Der." *See* Böll, Heinrich

"Zeko." *See* Andrić, Ivo

Zelinskii, on Pasternak's *Second Birth*, 10:1604b–1605a, 1605b

Zeller, Pauline, Edmond Goncourt and, 7:1413b–1414a

Země mnoha jmen. See Čapek, Karel

Zemnoi prostor. See Pasternak, Boris, *The Vast Earth*

Zemnye primety. See Tsvetaeva, Marina

"*Žena na kamenu.*" *See* Andrić, Ivo, "Woman on the Rock"

Zenith. *See* Jiménez, Juan Ramón, "Cenit"; Machado, Antonio, *Soledades* (Solitudes), "Cenit"

Zensur, Die: Eine Theodizee in einem Akt. See Wedekind, Frank

"Zephyrus returns." *See* Petrarch, *Canzoniere*, "Zefiro torna"

Zerbrochene Krug, Der. See Kleist, Heinrich von, *The Broken Jug*

"Zero ending," 7:1858b, 1859a, 1870b, 1877b, 1879a

Zerstörung der Vernunft, Die. See Lukács, György

Žert. See Kundera, Milan, *The Joke*

Zest for Life. See Zola, Émile, *La joie de vivre*

Zeune, August, the *Nibelungenlied* and, 1:219a

Zeus, Ady as, 9:867b

Zhakovi pored puta. See Andrić, Ivo

"Zharko veet veter dushnyi." *See* Akhmatova, Anna

Zhdanov, Andrei
    attack on Akhmatova and Zoshchenko by, 10:1530a
    Pasternak persecuted by, 10:1596b

"Zhelezo." *See* Mandelshtam, Osip, "Poems About Iron"

"Zhena." *See* Chekhov, Anton

"Zhenia's Childhood." *See* Pasternak, Boris, *Rasskazy* (Stories)

"Zhenshchina." *See* Blok, Alexander

"Zhenshchiny v detstve." *See* Pasternak, Boris

Zhirmunsky, Victor, on Tenishev School, 10:1624b

"Zhit' ne po Izhi." *See* Solzhenitsyn, Aleksandr

"Zhiteli gor." *See* Khlebnikov, Velimir

Zhitie Blokhi. See Zamyatin, Yevgeny Ivanovich

"Zhivoe o zhivom." *See* Tsvetaeva, Marina

"Zhivopis' segodnyashnego dnya." *See* Mayakovsky, Vladimir

Zhizn' iskusstva (Russian journal), Babel's articles in, 11:1904a

Zhizn' Klima Samgina. See Gorky, Maxim, *The Life of Klim Samgin*

Zhizn (Life) (journal), 7:1869a

Zhizn' Matveia Kozhemiakina. See Gorky, Maxim, *The Life of Matvei Kozhemyakin*

Zholkovsky, Alexander, on the eternal and temporal in Mandelshtam's poetry, 10:1627b

Zhukovskii, Vasilii, Pasternak's method of translation compared to, 10:1607b

"Zhuravl'." *See* Khlebnikov, Velimir, "The Crane"

Zhurnal dlya vsekh (*Journal for All*), 7:1874b

"Zhurnal Pechorina predlisovie." *See* Lermontov, Mikhail Yurievich

Zhurnal zhurnalov (Russian journal), Babel's stories in, 11:1903b

Ziaux, Les. See Queneau, Raymond

Zibaldone. See Leopardi, Giacomo

Zibrannia tvoriv v dvanadtsiaty tomakh. See Tychyna, Pavlo

"Zigenerskan." *See* Södergran, Edith, "The Gypsy Woman"

Zimea Ulro. See Milosz, Czeslaw, *The Land of Ulro*

Zimmer, Ernst, Hölderlin and, 5:172b, 173a

"Zimmern, An." *See* Hölderlin, Friedrich

Zinn, Ernst, Rilke and, 9:771a, 773b

Zinoviev, Grigori, Gorky and, 8:421b

"Zio Agrippo passa in treno, Lo." *See* Vittorini, Elio, *Le donne di Messina*

Zirkusgedanken. See Wedekind, Frank

Zitats, Prinzip des. See Pastiche, principle of (Musil)

Život a dílo skladatele Foltýna. See Čapek, Karel

Život je jinde. See Kundera, Milan, *Life Is Elsewhere*

"Zlaté jablko věčné touhy." *See* Kundera, Milan, "The Golden Apple of Desire"

Znaiut istinu tanki. See Solzhenitsyn, Aleksandr

Znanie (organization), Gorky and, 8:419b–420a, 440a

Zniewolony umysł. See Milosz, Czeslaw, *The Captive Mind*

Zodiac, signs of, Broch's story cycle and, 10:1395a

"Zola." *See* Mann, Heinrich

Zola, Émile, **7:1517a–1541b**

Ady and, 9:861b

Au bonheur des dames (*Ladies' Delight*), 7:1528b–1529a

Berlioz and, 6:787a, 805b

Blasco Ibáñez and, 8:358b, 359a, 374a, 374b, 380b, 382b

changing evaluations of, 7:1517a-b, 1538b–1539b

Chekhov and, 7:1856a, 1864a, 1868a

Contes à Ninon (*Tales for Ninon*), 7:1518b, 1519b

Eça and, 7:1693a

on Flaubert, 7:1392b–1393a

Germinal, 7:1529a–1530b

Ginzburg and, 13:3151b

Goncourts and, 7:1398b, 1400a, 1407b, 1413a-b, 1414a, 1416b, 1712a

Hamsun and, 8:23a

Heinrich Mann and, 8:534a

Professor Unrat, 8:528a

Hugo and, 7:1764b

Huysmans and, 7:1709a-b, 1711b–1712a, 1713a, 1719b

Ibsen and, 7:1443b

J'Accuse (*I Accuse*), 7:1520a, 1538b–1539a

La bête humaine (*The Human Beast*), 7:1534a-b

"The Peasants" and, 7:1869a

La confession de Claude (*Claude's Confession*), 7:1519b–1520a

La curée (*The Kill*), 7:1524a-b

La débâcle, 7:1534a, 1535a–1535a

La faute de l'abbé Mouret (*The Sin of Father Mouret*), 7:1518b–1519a, 1524b–1525b, 1534b, 1764b

La fortune des Rougon (*The Fortune of the Rougons*), 7:1523b–1524a

La joie de vivre (*Zest for Life*), 7:1528b

La république et la littérature, 7:1764b

La terre (*Earth*), 7:1526b, 1531b–1533a, 1534b

"The Peasants" and, 7:1869a

La vérité en marche (*Truth on the March*), 7:1538b–1539a

Laforgue and, 7:1885a

L'Argent (*Money*), 7:1534a–1535a

L'Assommoir (*The Drunkard*), 7:1413a, 1525b–1526b

Laforgue and, 7:1899b

Le docteur Pascal (*Doctor Pascal*), 7:1522b–1522b, 1534a, 1536a-b

Le rêve (*The Dream*), 7:1533a–1534a

Le roman expérimental (*The Experimental Novel*), 7:1414a, 1528a-b

Chekhov and, 7:1865a

Le ventre de Paris (*Savage Paris*), 7:1524a-b

Les Rougon-Macquart, histoire naturelle et sociale d'une famille sous le Second Empire, 7:1398b, 1407b, 1522a-b, 1523b–1536a, 1528b–1529a, 1607a

Les trois villes: Lourdes, 7:1536b–1537a

Les trois villes: Paris, 7:1519a, 1536b–1537a

Les trois villes: Rome, 7:1536b–1537a

L'Oeuvre (*The Masterpiece*), 6:787a, 7:1530b–1531b

Lukács on, 10:1271b

Madeleine Férat, 7:1521a–1522a

Marinetti and, 9:805a, 805b

Maupassant and, 7:1713a, 1761a, 1763a, 1763b–1764b, 1766b, 1769a, 1782b

Musil's *The Man Without Qualities* and, 9:952a

Nana, 7:1527a-b

Proust's *Remembrance of Things Past* and, 8:550b

naturalism, 7:1407b, 1414a, 1526a–1527a, 1711b

Taine's contribution to, 7:1449a

Pérez Galdós and, 7:1606b–1607a, 1608a-b

on poetry, and politics, 7:1569b–1570a

Pot-bouille (*Steaming Cauldron*), 7:1528b–1529a

Laforgue's verse and, 7:1885b

Proust and, 8:545b, 551b

Quatre évangiles (*Four Gospels*), 7:1536b–1537a

Sarraute and, 12:2333b

Scribe and, 7:1915b

Strindberg and, 7:1732b, 1753b

Svevo and, 8:76b

on Taine, 7:1457a

Thérèse Raquin, 7:1521a–1522a

Turgenev and, 6:1291a

Une campagne (*A Campaign*), 7:1888a

Verga influenced by, 7:1554a, 1558b, 1562a-b

on working classes, 7:1407a

see also *Soirées de Médan, Les*

"Zolotyi homin." *See* Tychyna, Pavlo, *Soniachni klarnety*

"Zone." *See* Apollinaire, Guillaume, *Alcools*

Zorba the Greek. See Kazantzakis, Nikos

Zorilla y Moral, José

Don Juan Tenorio, 9:650b

Frisch and, 13:2906a

Valle-Inclán and, 8:333b

Zoroaster, Prudentius and, 1:15b

Zoshchenko, Mikhail

Mandelshtam's *Egipetskaia marka* and, 10:1643a-b

Zhdanov's attack on, 10:1530a

"Zrazuzh za selom." *See* Tychyna, Pavlo, *Pluh*

"Ztracená cesta." *See* Čapek, Karel

Zubilo. *See* Olesha, Yuri

Zuckmayer, Carl, *Des Teufels General* (*The Devil's General*), Frisch and, 13:2902a

Zug war pünktlich, Der. See Böll, Heinrich, *The Train Was on Time*

"Zúg-Zeng a jégcimbalom." *See* Ady, Endre

"Zukunft, Die." *See* Södergran, Edith

"Zukünftigen Chancen der psychoanalytischen Therapie, Die." *See* Freud, Sigmund

"Zukunftsmusik." *See* Wagner, Richard

Zuloaga, Ignacio

Ortega y Gasset on, 9:1134a

Valle-Inclán and, 8:332b

"Zum grossen Wurstel." *See* Schnitzler, Arthur

"Zundhölzer." *See* Böll, Heinrich

"Zur Dynamik der Übertragung." *See* Freud, Sigmund

Zur Genealogie der Moral. See Nietzsche, Friedrich, *On the Genealogy of Morals*

Zur Geschichte der Religion und Philosophie in Deutschland. See Heine, Heinrich

Zur Kritik der Politische Ökonomie. See Marx, Karl

Zur Ontologie des gesellschaftlichen Seins. See Lukács, György

Zur Psychopathologie des Alltagslebens. See Freud, Sigmund

Zurbarán, Francisco de, Gautier and, 6:1042a

Zurich

literary society, 19th century, 8:235a

Wedekind in, 8:233a–235b

Zürich-Transit: Skizze eines Films. See Frisch, Max

Züricher Novellen. See Keller, Gottfried, *Novellas of Zurich*

Zuylen, Isabelle Agnes Elizabeth van Tuyll van. *See* Charrière, Isabelle Agnès Élizabeth de

"Zverinets." *See* Khlebnikov, Velimir; Mandelshtam, Osip

Zwanzig Balladen von einem Schweizer. See Meyer, Conrad Ferdinand

Zwanzigste Jahrhundert, Das, Heinrich Mann and, 8:521b

"Zwei Segel." *See* Meyer, Conrad Ferdinand

Zweig, Stefan, 9:689a, 691a

Freud and, 8:2a

on Montaigne, 2:787b–788a

Zwischen den Rassen. See Mann, Heinrich

Zwischenspiel. See Schnitzler, Arthur

Zykovy (*The Zykovs*). *See* Gorky, Maxim

LIST OF CONTRIBUTORS

CHARLES AFFRON
New York University
HONORÉ DE BALZAC

ARTHUR TILO ALT
Duke University
FRIEDRICH HEBBEL

JAROSLAW ANDERS
MILAN KUNDERA

JONATHAN ARAC
Columbia University
CHARLES BAUDELAIRE

MARGUERITE ARCHER†
Lehman College,
City University of New York
JEAN ANOUILH

JOSEPHINE V. ARNOLD
HENRY DE MONTHERLANT

CIRIACO MORÓN ARROYO
Cornell University
ANTONIO MACHADO

HUBERT F. BABINSKI
ANDRÉ CHÉNIER

HENRYK BARAN
State University of New York
at Albany
VELIMIR KHLEBNIKOV

STANISLAW BARANCZAK
Harvard University
CZESLAW MILOSZ

TEODOLINDA BAROLINI
University of California,
Berkeley
GIOVANNI BOCCACCIO

MICHAEL S. BATTS
University of British
Columbia
The Nibelungenlied

JARED M. BECKER
Columbia University
EUGENIO MONTALE
ITALO SVEVO

LUCILLE F. BECKER
Drew University
GEORGES SIMENON

JEAN BÉDÉ
ÉMILE ZOLA

ANN M. BEGLEY
Westmont College
SIMONE WEIL
MARGUERITE YOURCENAR

THOMAS G. BERGIN†
Yale University
SALVATORE QUASIMODO

SANDRA BERMANN
Princeton University
GIOVANNI PASCOLI

ALBERT BERMEL
City University of New York
JEAN GIRAUDOUX
AUGUST STRINDBERG

CLIFFORD ALBRECHT BERND
University of California,
Davis
THEODOR FONTANE

HARALDUR BESSASON
University of Akureyri,
Iceland
HALLDÓR LAXNESS

PETER BIEN
Dartmouth College
CONSTANTIN CAVAFY
NIKOS KAZANTZAKIS

MARIANNA D. BIRNBAUM
University of California,
Los Angeles
ENDRE ADY

MARILYN JOHNS BLACKWELL
Ohio State University
EYVIND JOHNSON

GENE BLUESTEIN
California State University,
Fresno
JOHANN GOTTFRIED VON HERDER

RALPH BOGERT
Harvard University
MIROSLAV KRLEŽA

JULIA CONWAY BONDANELLA
Indiana University
PETRARCH

PETER BONDANELLA
Indiana University
BALDESAR CASTIGLIONE
NICCOLÒ MACHIAVELLI

C. P. BRAND
University of Edinburgh
LODOVICO ARIOSTO
TORQUATO TASSO

693

LIST OF CONTRIBUTORS

GERMAINE BRÉE
Vilas Professor Emerita,
University of Wisconsin
ALBERT CAMUS

LEROY C. BREUNIG
Barnard College
GUILLAUME APOLLINAIRE
THÉOPHILE GAUTIER

DOROTHY BRODIN
Emerita of Lehman College,
City University of New York
MARCEL AYMÉ

JULES BRODY
Harvard University
NICOLAS BOILEAU-DESPRÉAUX

ERIC BURNS
MICHEL FOUCAULT
ARTHUR RIMBAUD

JUDITH BUTLER
Johns Hopkins University
JEAN-PAUL SARTRE

GIUSEPPE CAMBON
University of Connecticut
GIUSEPPE UNGARETTI

CARLA CAPPETTI
City College of New York
NATALIA GINZBURG

PATRICIA CARDEN
Cornell University
LEO TOLSTOY

OTTAVIO M. CASALE
Kent State University
GIACOMO LEOPARDI

MARLENE CIKLAMINI
Rutgers University
SIGRID UNDSET

FURIO COLOMBO
Columbia University
GIOVANNI VERGA

ROBERT CONARD
University of Dayton
HENRICH BÖLL

MASON COOLEY
Columbia University
ROLAND BARTHES
HIPPOLYTE TAINE

ROY C. COWEN
University of Michigan
MAX FRISCH
FRANZ GRILLPARZER

STEPHEN CRITES
Wesleyan University
SØREN KIERKEGAARD

GORDON CUNLIFFE
University of Wisconsin
GÜNTER GRASS

PELLEGRINO D'ACIERNO
Hofstra University
FILIPPO TOMMASO MARINETTI

DAVID DAMROSCH
Columbia University
HEINRICH VON KLEIST

JOSEPH P. DANE
University of Southern
California
MEDIEVAL DRAMA

RICHARD DANNER
Ohio University
JEAN DE LA FONTAINE

HUGH M. DAVIDSON
University of Virginia
BLAISE PASCAL

LENNARD J. DAVIS
Brandeis University
GUSTAVE FLAUBERT

ROBERT T. DENOMMÉ
University of Virginia
ALFRED VICTOR DE VIGNY

MARIA DIBATTISTA
Princeton University
MADAME DE STAËL

DANIEL B. DODSON
Columbia University
GOTTHOLD EPHRAIM LESSING

HERMAN K. DOSWALD
Virginia Polytechnic Institute
and State University
HUGO VON HOFMANNSTHAL

SAM DRIVER
Brown University
ANNA AKHMATOVA

JOHN J. DUGGAN
University of California,
Berkeley
THE *CHANSON DE ROLAND* AND THE
CHANSONS DE GESTE

DORIS L. EDER
JEAN COCTEAU
ANDRÉ MALRAUX

MILTON EHRE
University of Chicago
IVAN GONCHAROV

MARTIN ESSLIN
Stanford University
BERTOLT BRECHT

INGA-STINA EWBANK
University of Leeds
ISAK DINESEN

SARAH FAUNCE
Brooklyn Museum
EUGÈNE DELACROIX

OTIS FELLOWS
Columbia University
ALAIN-RENÉ LESAGE

ALBERT BADES FERNANDEZ
Cornell University
JOSÉ ORTEGA Y GASSET

JOHN FRANCES FETZER
University of California,
Davis
LUDWIG TIECK

GAIL FINNEY
Harvard University
POETIC REALISM: GOTTFRIED
KELLER, CONRAD FERDINAND
MEYER, AND THEODOR STORM

694

LIST OF CONTRIBUTORS

ROBERT J. FRAIL
Centenary College, New Jersey
JACQUES BÉNIGNE BOSSUET
FRANÇOIS MAURIAC

DONALD M. FRAME†
National Humanities Center
MICHEL DE MONTAIGNE

GREGORY FREIDIN
Stanford University
ISAAC BABEL

W. M. FROHOCK†
Hunter College
ANDRÉ MALRAUX

PAUL H. FRY
Yale University
JEAN JACQUES ROUSSEAU

JOHN GEAREY
*Graduate School of the
City University of New York*
JOHANN WOLFGANG VON GOETHE

EMERY E. GEORGE
University of Michigan
GYÖRGY LUKÁCS

DANIEL GEROULD
City University of New York
STANISŁAW IGNACY WITKIEWICZ

STEPHEN GILMAN
Harvard University
BENITO PÉREZ GALDÓS

T. H. GOETZ
*Fredonia State University
College*
EDMOND LOUIS ANTOINE DE
GONCOURT AND JULES ALFRED
HUOT DE GONCOURT

ULRICH K. GOLDSMITH
University of Colorado
STEFAN GEORGE

LIONEL GOSSMAN
Princeton University
JULES MICHELET

GEORGE G. GRABOWICZ
Harvard University
PAVEL TYCHYNA

RICHARD B. GRANT
University of Texas
VICTOR HUGO

RONALD GRAY
*Emmanuel College,
Cambridge*
HENRIK IBSEN

DENNIS H. GREEN
Trinity College, Cambridge
WOLFRAM VON ESCHENBACH

V. H. H. GREEN
Lincoln College, Oxford
SAINT THOMAS AQUINAS AND
SCHOLASTICISM
MARTIN LUTHER

DOROTHY M-T GREGORY
Rutgers University
ODYSSEUS ELYTIS

HARVEY GROSS
*State University of New York
at Stony Brook*
GEORG TRAKL

NATHAN GROSS
PIERRE CORNEILLE

JACQUES GUICHARNAUD
Yale University
RAYMOND QUENEAU

ROBERT W. GUTMAN
RICHARD WAGNER

DAVID T. HABERLEY
University of Virginia
JOSÉ MARIA FERREIRA DE CASTRO

ROBERT W. HANNING
Columbia University
BEOWULF AND ANGLO-SAXON
POETRY

JOSUÉ HARARI
Johns Hopkins University
MONTESQUIEU

WILLIAM E. HARKINS
Columbia University
KAREL ČAPEK
YURI OLESHA

THOMAS R. HART
University of Oregon
LUÍS VAZ DE CAMOËNS

DAVID HAYMAN
*University of Wisconsin–
Madison*
LOUIS FERDINAND CÉLINE

MICHAEL HAYS
Cornell University
GEORG BÜCHNER
CARLO GOLDONI

ANTHONY HEILBUT
HEINRICH MANN

F. W. J. HEMMINGS
University of Leicester
ALEXANDRE DUMAS PÈRE
MARCEL PROUST

MARGARET R. HIGONNET
University of Connecticut
JEAN PAUL RICHTER

MICHAEL HOOKER
Bennington College
RENÉ DESCARTES

JOHN PORTER HOUSTON
Indiana University
JULES LAFORGUE

C. STEPHEN JAEGER
Bryn Mawr College
GOTTFRIED VON STRASSBURG

ROBERTA JOHNSON
Scripps College
PÍO BAROJA

VIDA T. JOHNSON
Tufts University
IVO ANDRIĆ

695

LIST OF CONTRIBUTORS

DONALD R. KELLEY
University of Rochester
GIOVANNI BATTISTA VICO

LAURA KENDRICK
Dalhousie University
MEDIEVAL SATIRE

LOUIS KIBLER
Wayne State University
ALBERTO MORAVIA

J. MARIN KING
Boston University
MARINA TSVETAEVA

ALEX KLIMOFF
Vassar College
ALEXANDER SOLZHENITSYN

CHARLES KLOPP
Ohio State University
GIOSUE CARDUCCI
GABRIELE D'ANNUNZIO

BETTINA KNAPP
Hunter College
NATHALIE SARRAUTE

PAULINE KRA
Yeshiva University
JEAN DE LA BRUYÈRE

GEORGE J. LEONARD
San Francisco State University
CLAUDE SIMON

HELENA LEWIS
Center for European Studies,
Harvard University
LOUIS ARAGON

ROBERT LIMA
Pennsylvania State University
RAMÓN DEL VALLE-INCLÁN

JOHN LINDON
University College, London
UGO FOSCOLO

MARIE-ROSE LOGAN
Columbia University
THE PLÉIADE
PIERRE DE RONSARD

SYLVÈRE LOTRINGER
Columbia University
ANTONIN ARTAUD

ROBERT E. LOTT
University of Illinois
AZORÍN

JOHN LUKACS
Chestnut Hill College
JACOB BURCKHARDT
ALEXIS DE TOCQUEVILLE

ALFRED MacADAM
Barnard College
FERNANDO PESSOA

JOHN A. McCARTHY
University of Pennsylvania
CHRISTOPH MARTIN WIELAND

ANNE McCLINTOCK
Columbia University
SIMONE DE BEAUVOIR

JANE McLELLAND
University of Iowa
MONTESQUIEU

JAMES R. McWILLIAMS
University of Oregon
ARTHUR SCHNITZLER

PATRICK J. MAHONY
Université de Montréal
SIGMUND FREUD

GUY DE MALLAC
University of California,
Irvine
BORIS PASTERNAK

ROBERT E. MATLAW
University of Chicago
NIKOLAY VASILIEVICH GOGOL

J. H. MATTHEWS
Syracuse University
ANDRÉ BRETON

GITA MAY
Columbia University
DENIS DIDEROT
GEORGE SAND

JEREMY T. MEDINA
Hamilton College
VICENTE BLASCO IBÁÑEZ

PHILIP MELLEN
Virginia Polytechnic Institute
and State University
GERHART HAUPTMANN

EDWARD MENDELSON
Columbia University
JORIS KARL HUYSMANS

JOHN MERSEREAU, JR.
University of Michigan
MIKHAIL YURIEVICH LERMONTOV

JEFFREY MEYERS
University of Colorado
at Boulder
GIUSEPPE TOMASI DE LAMPEDUSA

JAMES V. MIROLLO
Columbia University
RENAISSANCE PASTORAL POETRY
RENAISSANCE SHORT FICTION

P. M. MITCHELL
Cornell University
GUNNAR GUNNARSSON

JULIUS A. MOLINARO
University of Toronto
VITTORIO ALFIERI

CHARLES A. MOSER
George Washington University
IVAN TURGENEV

HELEN MUCHNIC
Smith College
ANDREY BELY

MARK MUSA
Indiana University
DANTE ALIGHIERI
PETRARCH

KOSTAS MYRSIADES
University of Pennsylvania
YANNIS RITSOS

696

LIST OF CONTRIBUTORS

HARALD S. NAESS
University of Wisconsin
KNUT HAMSUN

JOHN NEUBAUER
University of Pittsburgh
NOVALIS

MARTIN J. NEWHOUSE
FRIEDRICH NIETZSCHE

STEPHEN G. NICHOLS, JR.
Dartmouth College
FRANÇOIS VILLON

KENNETH J. NORTHCOTT
University of Chicago
WALTHER VON DER VOGELWEIDE

JOHN OLIN
Fordham University
ERASMUS

ERIKA OSTROVSKY
New York University
SAINT-JOHN PERSE

D. D. R. OWEN
University of St. Andrew
ARTHURIAN LEGEND
CHRÉTIEN DE TROYES

SERGIO PACIFICI
Queens College,
City University of New York
CESARE PAVESE
IGNAZIO SILONE
ELIO VITTORINI

HAROLD E. PAGLIARO
Swarthmore College
FRANÇOIS VI, DUC DE
LA ROUCHEFOUCAULD

JEFFREY M. PERL
University of Texas at Austin
STÉPHANE MALLARMÉ
FRIEDRICH VON SCHLEGEL

BRIGITTE PEUCKER
Yale University
FRIEDRICH GOTTLIEB KLOPSTOCK

MANFREDI PICCOLOMINI
Lehman College,
City University of New York
BENEDETTO CROCE

GERALD PIROG
Rutgers University
ALEXANDER BLOK

JEANINE P. PLOTTEL
Hunter College,
City University of New York
ALAIN ROBBE-GRILLET
THREE FRENCH NOVELISTS:
CHODERLOS DE LACLOS,
BENJAMIN CONSTANT,
ANTOINE-FRANÇOIS PRÉVOST

SHARLENE POLINER
Princeton University
FRANÇOIS RABELAIS

RANDOLPH D. POPE
Washington University
CAMILO JOSÉ CELA

CHARLES A. PORTER
Yale University
FRANÇOIS RENÉ DE CHATEAUBRIAND

IRVING PUTTER
University of California,
Berkeley
CHARLES MARIE LECONTE DE LISLE

ROBERT PYNSENT
University of London
JAROSLAV HAŠEK

AUSTIN QUIGLEY
Columbia University
JEAN GENET

OLGA RAGUSA
Columbia University
ALESSANDRO MANZONI
LUIGI PIRANDELLO

KATHERINE KOLB REEVE
University of Minnesota
HECTOR BERLIOZ

JOHN REXINE
Colgate University
GEORGE SEFERIS

JOHN RICHETTI
Rutgers University
PIERRE-AUGUSTIN CARON
DE BEAUMARCHAIS
THE MARQUIS DE SADE AND THE
FRENCH LIBERTINE TRADITION
GUY DE MAUPASSANT

PETER S. ROGERS
Texas A & M University
PAUL CLAUDEL

JAMES ROLLESTON
Duke University
RAINER MARIA RILKE

OMRY RONEN
University of Michigan
OSIP MANDELSHTAM

VINIO ROSSI
Oberlin College
ANDRÉ GIDE

LAWRENCE ROTHFIELD
Columbia University
CHARLES-AUGUSTIN SAINTE-BEUVE

LEON ROUDIEZ
Columbia University
MICHEL BUTOR

JEFFREY L. SAMMONS
Yale University
HEINRICH HEINE
FRIEDRICH VON SCHILLER

JEAN SAREIL
Columbia University
VOLTAIRE

PAUL SCHACH
University of Nebraska
NORSE SAGAS

STEVEN PAUL SCHER
Dartmouth College
E. T. A. HOFFMANN

LIST OF CONTRIBUTORS

GEORGE C. SCHOOLFIELD
Yale University
EDITH SÖDERGRAN

SANFORD R. SCHWARTZ
Pennsylvania State University
HENRI BERGSON

BERTRAM EUGENE
SCHWARZBACK
FRANÇOIS DE SALIGNAC DE LA
MOTHE-FÉNELON

HAROLD B. SEGEL
Columbia University
MAXIM GORKY

HENNING K. SEHMSDORF
*University of Washington
at Seattle*
TARJEI VESAAS

MICHAEL SEIDEL
Columbia University
ALFRED JARRY
MOLIÈRE
STENDHAL

ALEX M. SHANE
*State University of New York
at Albany*
YEVGENY IVANOVICH ZAMYATIN

J. THOMAS SHAW
*University of Wisconsin–
Madison*
ALEXANDER PUSHKIN

LEROY R. SHAW
*University of Illinois
at Chicago*
FRANK WEDEKIND

DAVID SICES
Dartmouth College
ALFRED DE MUSSET

ERNEST J. SIMMONS†
FEODOR DOSTOEVSKY

LEIF SJOBERG
*State University of New York
at Stony Brook*
GUNNAR EKELÖF

COLIN C. SMITH
*Saint Catharine's College,
Cambridge*
THE CID IN EPIC AND BALLAD

WALTER H. SOKEL
University of Virginia
ELIAS CANETTI
FRANZ KAFKA

ROBERT M. STEIN
*State University of New York
at Purchase*
WALTER BENJAMIN

PHILIP STEPHAN
Northeastern University
PAUL VERLAINE

IRWIN STERN
Columbia University
JOSÉ MARIA EÇA DE QUEIROZ

J. P. STERN
University College, London
THOMAS MANN

JOAN HINDE STEWART
*North Carolina State
University*
COLETTE

RICHARD S. STOWE
Lawrence University
MAURICE MAETERLINCK
PROSPER MÉRIMÉE

MIHÁLY SZEGEDY-MASZÁK
Indiana University
DEZSŐ KOSZTOLÁNYI

SAM TANENHAUS
ITALO CALVINO

MICHAEL TANNER
*Corpus Christi College,
Cambridge*
ARTHUR SCHOPENHAUER

RALPH TARICA
University of Maryland
ANTOINE DE SAINT-EXUPÉRY

VICTOR TERRAS
Brown University
VLADIMIR MAYAKOVSKY

EWA M. THOMPSON
Rice University
WITOLD GOMBROWICZ

LESLIE TOPSFIELD
*Saint Catharine's College,
Cambridge*
TROUBADOURS AND TROUVÈRES

ALBERTO TRALDI
University of Puerto Rico
IGNAZIO SILONE

RICHARD UNGER
University of Georgia
FRIEDRICH HÖLDERLIN

EUGENE VANCE
University of Montreal
SAINT AUGUSTINE

BRUCE WARDROPPER
Duke University
PEDRO CALDERÓN DE LA BARCA
MIGUEL DE CERVANTES
LOPE DE VEGA

LARS G. WARME
*University of Washington
at Seattle*
PÄR LAGERKVIST
VILHELM MOBERG

HARRIETT WATTS
*Herzog August Bibliothek,
Wölfenbüttel*
JEAN ARP

ARNOLD WEINSTEIN
Columbia University
FEDERICO GARCÍA LORCA
GIOVANNI VERGA

WIKTOR WEINTRAUB
Harvard University
ADAM MICKIEWICZ

698

LIST OF CONTRIBUTORS

GEORGE WELLWARTH
*State University of New York
at Binghamton*
FRIEDRICH DÜRRENMATT

H. J. WESTRA
University of Calgary
PRUDENTIUS

WINTHROP WETHERBEE
University of Chicago
THE *ROMANCE OF THE ROSE* AND
MEDIEVAL ALLEGORY

MATTHEW H. WIKANDER
Columbia University
EUGÈNE IONESCO

SIMON WILLIAMS
*University of California,
Santa Barbara*
THE WELL-MADE PLAY

DAVID WILLINGER
*The City College and the
Graduate Center, City
University of New York*
MICHEL DE GHELDERODE

THOMAS G. WINNER
Boston University
ANTON CHEKHOV

STEVEN WINSPUR
Columbia University
PAUL VALÉRY

MICHAEL WOOD
University of Exeter
GÉRARD DE NERVAL
JEAN RACINE

VICTORIA YABLONSKY†
ROBERT MUSIL

HOWARD T. YOUNG
Pomona College
JUAN RAMÓN JIMÉNEZ
MIGUEL DE UNAMUNO

THEODORE ZIOLKOWSKI
Princeton University
HERMANN BROCH
HERMANN HESSE

JACK ZIPES
*University of Wisconsin–
Milwaukee*
HANS CHRISTIAN ANDERSEN

ACKNOWLEDGMENTS

The following pamphlets in the Columbia University Press Series *Columbia Essays on Modern Writers* have been revised by their authors for *European Writers* and have been reprinted here by special arrangement with Columbia University Press, the publisher.

VOLUME 6

Moser, Charles: *Ivan Turgenev*
Copyright © 1972 Columbia University Press

VOLUME 7

Bédé, Jean-Albert: *Émile Zola*
Copyright © 1974 Columbia University Press

Simmons, Ernest J.: *Feodor Dostoevsky*
Copyright © 1969 Columbia University Press

VOLUME 8

Bien, Peter: *Constantine Cavafy*
Copyright © 1964 Columbia University Press

Lima, Robert: *Ramón del Valle-Inclán*
Copyright © 1972 Columbia University Press

Ragusa, Olga: *Luigi Pirandello*
Copyright © 1968 Columbia University Press

Goldsmith, Ulrich K.: *Stefan George*
Copyright © 1970 Columbia University Press

Rossi, Vinio: *André Gide*
Copyright © 1968 Columbia University Press

VOLUME 9

Stern, J. P.: *Thomas Mann*
Copyright © 1967 Columbia University Press

ACKNOWLEDGMENTS

Ziolkowski, Theodore: *Hermann Hesse*
Copyright © 1966 Columbia University Press

Breunig, LeRoy C.: *Guillaume Apollinaire*
Copyright © 1970 Columbia University Press

Young, Howard T.: *Juan Ramón Jiménez*
Copyright © 1967 Columbia University Press

Bien, Peter: *Nikos Kazantzakis*
Copyright © 1972 Columbia University Press

Sokel, Walter H.: *Franz Kafka*
Copyright © 1966 Columbia University Press

VOLUME 10

Cambon, Glauco: *Giuseppe Ungaretti*
Copyright © 1967 Columbia University Press

Ziolkowski, Theodore: *Hermann Broch*
Copyright © 1964 Columbia University Press

VOLUME 11

Esslin, Martin: *Bertolt Brecht*
Copyright © 1969 Columbia University Press

Hayman, David: *Louis-Ferdinand Céline*
Copyright © 1965 Columbia University Press

Matthews, J. H.: *André Breton*
Copyright © 1967 Columbia University Press

VOLUME 12

Brodin, Dorothy: *Marcel Aymé*
Copyright © 1968 Columbia University Press

Frohock, W. M.: *André Malraux*
Copyright © 1974 Columbia University Press

Guicharnaud, Jacques: *Raymond Queneau*
Copyright © 1965 Columbia University Press

VOLUME 13

Archer, Marguerite: *Jean Anouilh*
Copyright © 1971 Columbia University Press

Brée, Germaine: *Albert Camus*
Copyright © 1964 Columbia University Press

Roudiez, Leon S: *Michel Butor*
Copyright © 1965 Columbia University Press

ACKNOWLEDGMENTS

The essays "Cesare Pavese" and "Elio Vittorini" in volume 12 were originally published in *The Modern Italian Novel from Pea to Moravia* by Sergio Pacifici. Copyright © 1979 by Southern Illinois University Press. Revised by the author and reprinted by permission of the publisher.

The essay "Georges Simenon" in volume 12 is based on the author's Twayne's World Authors volume (Boston, 1977) and is revised here by the author, Lucille F. Becker.

The publishers additionally wish to thank
the following for permission to quote from
published editions and translations.

VOLUME 2

"François Villon": Quotations from *The Poems of François Villon* translated by Galway Kinnell. Copyright © 1965, 1977 by Galway Kinnell. Reprinted by permission of Houghton Mifflin Company.

"Michel de Montaigne": Quotations reprinted from *The Complete Essays of Montaigne,* translated by Donald M. Frame, with the permission of the publishers, Stanford University Press. © 1958 by the Board of Trustees of the Leland Stanford Junior University.

VOLUME 5

"Friedrich von Schlegel": Quotations from *Friedrich Schlegel's "Lucinde" and the Fragments,* translated by Peter Firchow. Copyright © 1983 by the University of Minnesota Press. All rights reserved. Original edition published by the University of Minnesota Press. Quotations from *Dialogue on Poetry and Literary Aphorisms by Friedrich Schlegel,* translated by Ernst Behler and Roman Struc. Copyright © 1968 Pennsylvania State University Press. Reprinted by kind permission of the publisher.

"Ludwig Tieck": Quotations from *Der blonde Eckert,* translated by Helene Scher. Originally published in *Four Romantic Tales from Nineteenth-Century Germany.* Copyright © 1975 by Helene Scher. Reprinted by permission of Helene Scher.

"Giacomo Leopardi": Quotations from the works of Giacomo Leopardi, translated by Ottavio M. Casale. Originally published in *A Leopardi Reader* by the University of Illinois Press © 1981 by The Board of Trustees of the University of Illinois. The author gratefully acknowledges the permission granted by the University of Illinois Press.

"Alexander Pushkin": Quotations from *The Letters of Alexander Pushkin* © 1963 by J. Thomas Shaw. Originally published by Indiana University Press and University of Pennsylvania Press. Reprinted in paperback, copyright © 1967 by the Regents of the University of Wisconsin. The author gratefully acknowledges the permission granted by the University of Wisconsin Press.

ACKNOWLEDGMENTS

VOLUME 8

"Pierre-Augustin Caron de Beaumarchais": Quotations from
Beaumarchais: "The Barber of Seville" and *"The Marriage of Figaro"*
translated by John Wood. Copyright © 1964 by John Wood. Reprinted
by permission of Penguin Books Ltd.

VOLUME 9

"Rainer Maria Rilke": Excerpts of poetry from *Samtliche Werke.*
Reprinted by permission of Insel Verlag, Frankfurt. Excerpt from
"Burnt Norton" in *Collected Poems 1909–1962,* copyright 1936 by
Harcourt Brace Jovanovich, Inc., copyright © 1964, 1963 by T. S. Eliot,
reprinted by permission of Harcourt Brace Jovanovich, Inc.,
and Faber and Faber Ltd.

VOLUME 10

"Jean Arp": Excerpts of poetry from *Gesammelte Gedichte.* © by Limes
Verlag in F. A. Herbig Verlagsbuchhandlung GmgH, Munich.

"Georg Trakl": Excerpts of poetry from *Dichtungen und Briefe,* 2. Aufl.
Otto Muller Verlag Salzburg; 1987.

"Saint-John Perse": Excerpts of poetry from *Oeuvres complètes.* Copyright
Marcel Dormoy and Andre Rousseau by will of Mrs. Leger,
Saint-John Perse's widow.

"Guiseppe Ungaretti": Excerpts of poetry from *Vita d'un uomo. Tutte
le poesie.* 1990, Arnoldo Mondadori Editore S.p.A., Milano.

"Fernando Pessoa": Excerpts of poetry from *Obras Completas,* Edicoes
Atica, Pontinha, Portugal.

"Par Lagerkvist": Excerpts of poetry from *Dikter.* © The estate of
Par Lagerkvist 1990. Published in agreement with Albert Bonniers Forlag
AB, Stockholm.

VOLUME 11

"Edith Södergran": Excerpts of poetry from *Edith Södergrans dikter 1907–1909.*
Reprinted by permission of Holger Schildts Forlagsaktiebolag, Helsingfors.

"Tarjei Vesaas": Excerpts of poetry from *Dikt i sampling,* Olaf Norlis
Bokhandel, AS, Oslo, Norway.

"Louis Aragon": "Front rouge" and "Complainte des chomeurs" from
Les ouevres romanesques croisées d'Elsa Triolet et de Louis Aragon, Editions
Gallimard, Paris, 1946. "Prelude au temps de cerises" from *Les critiques de
notre temps et Aragon,* Editions Garnier, Paris, 1976. "Plus belle
que les larmes" from *Les yeux d'Elsa,* Les Editions Seghers SA, Paris, 1942.

ACKNOWLEDGMENTS

VOLUME 12

"George Seferis": Excerpts of poetry from *George Seferis: Collected Poems, 1924–1955,* translated by Edmund Keeley and Philip Sherrard. Copyright © 1967 Princeton University Press. Reprinted by permission of Princeton University Press. Excerpt from *The Charioteer,* 27, pp. 25–27. Copyright © 1985 by Pella Publishing Co. Reprinted by permission. Excerpt from *The Odyssey of Homer,* translated by Robert Fitzgerald. Copyright © 1961, 1963 by Robert Fitzgerald. Copyright renewed © 1989 by Benedict R. C. Fitzgerald, on behalf of the Fitzgerald children. Reprinted by permission of Vintage Books, a Division of Random House Inc.

"Salvatore Quasimodo": Excerpts of poetry from *Tutte le poesie.* 1990, Arnoldo Mondadori Editore S.p.A., Milano.

"Gunnar Ekelof": Excerpts of poetry from *Dikter, 1965–1968* and from *Ord och bild* 65, no. 9, 1956. © Ingrid Ekelof, 1990. Published in agreement with Albert Bonniers Forlag AB, Stockholm. Excerpt from *Diwan over the Prince of Emgion.* Copyright © 1971 Ingrid Ekelof, translation copyright © 1971 W. H. Auden and Leif Sjoberg. Reprinted by permission of Curtis Brown Ltd. Excerpt reprinted from *Guide to the Underworld,* Gunnar Ekelof, rendered from the Swedish by Rika Lesser (Amherst: University of Massachusetts Press, 1980), copyright © 1980 by Rika Lesser. Excerpts from *Selected Poems* by Gunnar Ekelof, translated by Muriel Rukeyser and Leif Sjoberg, Irvington Publishers, New York.

VOLUME 13

"Yannis Ritsos": Excerpt from "Common Miracles," © copyright 1989 by Kimon Friar and Kostas Myrsiades and reproduced from *Yannis Ritsos: Selected Poems 1938–1988* with the permission of BOA Editions, Ltd., 92 Park Ave., Brockport, NY 14420. Excerpt from "Helen" translated by Nikos Tsingos and Gwendolyn McEwen. © copyright 1989 by Nikos Tsingos and Gwendolyn McEwen. Excerpts from "Memorial Service at Poros" and "O Talos" translated by N. C. Germanacos. © copyright by N. C. Germanacos. Reprinted by permission.

"Czeslaw Milosz": "Hope" excerpted from "The World," copyright © 1984 by Czeslaw Milosz. From *The Separate Notebooks,* first published by The Ecco Press in 1984. Reprinted by permission. Excerpts from "Child of Europe," "Slow River," "A Song on the End of the World," "Campo Dei Fiori," "Preparation," "Dedication," "Esse," "An Hour," "Account," "Temptation," "Incantation," "From the Rising of the Sun," "With Trumpets and Zithers," "Throughout Our Lands," "Outskirts," "Bobo's Metamorphosis," "Elegy for N.N.," "Counsels," "Sentences," "Ars Poetica?" and "A Task," copyright © 1988 Czeslaw Milosz Royalties, Inc. From *The Collected Poems, 1931–1987,* first published by The Ecco Press in 1988. Reprinted by permission.

"Odysseus Elytis": Excerpts of poetry reprinted from *The Axion Esti* by Odysseus Elytis, translated by Edmund Keeley and George Savidis, by permission of the University of Pittsburgh Press. © 1974 by Edmund Keeley and George Savidis. "Poem III" from *Odysseus Elytis; The Sovereign Sun,* translated by Kimon Friar © 1974 by Temple University. Reprinted by permission of Temple University Press. "Anniversary" from *Odysseus Elytis: Selected Poems,* translated by Edmund Keeley and Philip Sherrard. Copyright © 1981 by Edmund Keeley and Philip Sherrard. Reprinted by permission of Viking Penguin, a division of Penguin Books USA, Inc.

ACKNOWLEDGMENTS

"The Silver Gift" from *Odysseus Elytis: Selected Poems,* translated by
John Stathatos. Copyright © 1981 by John Stathatos. Reprinted
by permission of Viking Penguin, a division of Penguin Books USA, Inc.

"Roland Barthes": Excerpt from "Anecdote of the Jar" by Wallace Stevens. Copyright
1923 and renewed 1951 by Wallace Stevens. Reprinted from *The Collected Poems
of Wallace Stevens,* by permission of Alfred A. Knopf, Inc.

"Aleksandr Solzhenitsyn": Excerpt from "The Wheel" from *Sobranie Sochinenii,*
vol. 11, Editions YMCA Press, Paris.